HANDBOOK OF RESEARCH METHODS AND APPLICATIONS IN EMPIRICAL MICROECONOMICS

HANDBOOKS OF RESEARCH METHODS AND APPLICATIONS

Series Editor: Mark Casson, *University of Reading, UK*

The objective of this series is to provide definitive overviews of research methods in important fields of social science, including economics, business, finance and policy studies. The aim is to produce prestigious high-quality works of lasting significance. Each *Handbook* consists of original contributions by leading authorities, selected by an editor who is a recognised leader in the field. The emphasis is on the practical application of research methods to both quantitative and qualitative evidence. The *Handbooks* will assist practising researchers in generating robust research findings that policy-makers can use with confidence.

While the *Handbooks* will engage with general issues of research methodology, their primary focus will be on the practical issues concerned with identifying and using suitable sources of data or evidence, and interpreting source material using best-practice techniques. They will review the main theories that have been used in applied research, or could be used for such research. While reference may be made to conceptual issues and to abstract theories in the course of such reviews, the emphasis will be firmly on real-world applications.

Titles in the series include:

Handbook of Research Methods and Applications in Social Capital
Edited by Yaojun Li

Handbook of Research Methods and Applications in Transport Economics and Policy
Edited by Chris Nash

Handbook of Research Methods and Applications in Heterodox Economics
Edited by Frederic S. Lee and Bruce Cronin

Handbook of Research Methods and Applications in Happiness and Quality of Life
Edited by Luigino Bruni and Pier Luigi Porta

Handbook of Research Methods and Applications in Political Science
Edited by Hans Keman and Jaap J. Woldendorp

Handbook of Research Methods and Applications in Experimental Economics
Edited by Arthur Schram and Aljaž Ule

Handbook of Research Methods and Applications in Comparative Policy Analysis
Edited by B. Guy Peters and Guillaume Fontaine

Handbook of Research Methods and Applications for Mobilities
Edited by Monika Büscher, Malene Freudendal-Pedersen, Sven Kesselring and Nikolaj Grauslund Kristensen

Handbook of Research Methods and Applications in Empirical Microeconomics
Edited by Nigar Hashimzade and Michael A. Thornton

Handbook of Research Methods and Applications in Empirical Microeconomics

Edited by

Nigar Hashimzade

Professor, Department of Economics and Finance, Brunel University London, UK

Michael A. Thornton

Senior Lecturer, Department of Economics and Related Studies, University of York, UK

HANDBOOKS OF RESEARCH METHODS AND APPLICATIONS

Edward Elgar
PUBLISHING

Cheltenham, UK • Northampton, MA, USA

Published by
Edward Elgar Publishing Limited
The Lypiatts
15 Lansdown Road
Cheltenham
Glos GL50 2JA
UK

Edward Elgar Publishing, Inc.
William Pratt House
9 Dewey Court
Northampton
Massachusetts 01060
USA

Paperback edition 2023

A catalogue record for this book
is available from the British Library

Library of Congress Control Number: 2021946091

This book is available electronically in the **Elgar**online
Economics subject collection
http://dx.doi.org/10.4337/9781788976480

ISBN 978 1 78897 647 3 (cased)
ISBN 978 1 78897 648 0 (eBook)
ISBN 978 1 0353 1889 6 (paperback)

Typeset by Westchester Publishing Services
Printed and bound by CPI Group (UK) Ltd, Croydon, CR0 4YY

Contents

Contributors

Oleg Badunenko, Brunel University London, UK.

Giovanni Baiocchi, University of Maryland, USA.

Otávio Bartalotti, Iowa State University, USA.

Christopher F. Baum, Boston College, USA.

Marinho Bertanha, University of Notre Dame, USA.

Anna Gloria Billé, University of Verona, Italy.

Sebastian Calonico, Columbia University, USA.

Khai X. Chiong, University of Texas at Dallas, USA.

Ugo Colombino, University of Turin, Italy.

Emmanuel Duguet, Université Paris-Est, France.

Denis Fougère, CNRS and Sciences Po, Paris, France.

Nigar Hashimzade, Brunel University London, UK.

Arne Henningsen, University of Copenhagen, Denmark.

Géraldine Henningsen, Technical University of Denmark, Denmark.

Yu-Wei Hsieh, University of South Carolina, USA.

Martin Huber, University of Fribourg, Switzerland.

Nicolas Jacquemet, Université Paris 1 Panthéon-Sorbonne and Ecole d'Economie de Paris, France.

Andrew M. Jones, University of York, UK.

Noemi Kreif, University of York, UK.

Tong Li, Vanderbilt University, USA.

Gergő Literáti, Centrica plc, UK.

Giovanni Millo, Generali Investments, Italy.

Alfonso Miranda, Centre for Economic Research and Teaching (CIDE), Mexico.

Ryo Okui, Seoul National University, Korea.

Tho Pham, University of Reading, UK.

Vishalie Shah, University of York, UK.

Matthew Shum, California Institute of Technology, USA.

Pedro C.L. Souza, Queen Mary University London, UK.

Piotr Śpiewanowski, Institute of Economics, Polish Academy of Sciences, Poland.

Oleksandr Talavera, University of Birmingham.

Michael A. Thornton, University of York, UK.

Pravin K. Trivedi, University of Queensland, Australia.

Natalya Zelenyuk, University of Queensland, Australia.

Valentin Zelenyuk, University of Queensland, Australia.

Xiaoyong Zheng, North Carolina State University.

Introduction to the *Handbook of Research Methods and Applications in Empirical Microeconomics*
Nigar Hashimzade and Michael A. Thornton

Few areas in economics have seen the growth in interest and influence over the last two decades experienced by empirical microeconomics. The development of modern research methods in microeconomics has been driven, on the one hand, by the accumulation of numerous data sets at the level of individuals, households and firms, and, on the other hand, by an increase in the capacity and speed of computers. While the more traditional empirical methods were largely limited to establishing correlation among economic variables, the new methods aim to uncover causality. At the same time, progress in computing has enabled researchers to estimate complex relationships among variables suggested by economic theory, without resorting to crude approximation, or to use entirely data-driven estimation. These advances have opened new possibilities for applied research in microeconomics and many other fields in economics and social sciences, most notably, in the estimation of sophisticated structural models and in the evaluation of policy interventions.

This volume introduces a range of modern empirical methods with applications in microeconomics and some illustrations of the use of software packages. The first section, "Econometric Methods in Microeconomics", presents a selection of linear, non-linear and semiparametric methods, with examples from political economy, labour economics and the analysis of auctions.

The focus of the opening chapter, by Ryo Okui, is on the estimation of linear dynamic panel models, common in applied microeconomics (Chapter 1). The chapter gives an overview of the difficulties arising in application of the standard generalised method of moments estimator and presents potential solutions. The empirical example demonstrates the use of this more advanced methodology in estimation of a relationship between economic environment and democracy. The next chapter, by Anna Gloria Billé, presents spatial autoregressive non-linear models (Chapter 2). These models are a natural extension of non-linear models to the empirical context where cross-sectional dependence can be related to relative proximity of cross-sectional units. The empirical example illustrates how the geographical coordinates of regions in Europe can be exploited in the analysis of the employment patterns across European countries. This is followed by a chapter by Tong Li and Xiaoyong Zheng that investigates semiparametric methods and partial identification approaches in the empirical analysis of the auction data (Chapter 3). Particular attention is paid to the role of the informational assumptions in the models. The concluding chapter in this part, by Martin Huber, introduces the reader to several flexible methods of policy evaluation, including randomised and quasi-random treatment, instrumental variables, difference-in-differences, regression discontinuities and data-driven approaches based on machine learning (Chapter 4). These methods are presented in more detail with examples in subsequent parts of this volume.

Each chapter in the second section, "Households, Businesses and Societies", presents key empirical methodologies used in the analysis of contemporary economic, social and policy issues. The wide variety of applications illustrated in this section includes econometric analysis of fertility, measurement of discrimination in the labour market, design and evaluation of tax-transfer systems, pricing strategies, performance analysis of banking and social epidemiology. The main focus of the chapters in this section is on a selection of statistical, structural, semi- and nonparametric methods.

The section opens with a chapter by Alfonso Miranda and Pravin K. Trivedi presenting several methods of estimation of a structural microeconomic model from cross-section and panel data, including the standard ordinary least squares, count models, hazard models and a discrete-time multi-spell duration model (Chapter 5). The advantages and shortcomings of each method are discussed in the context of their application to estimation of the socioeconomic and demographic determinants of fertility. This is followed by a chapter by Emmanuel Duguet reviewing several methods of empirical investigation of discrimination in the labour market, with a focus on discrimination in hiring and on wage discrimination (Chapter 6). The range of methods includes statistical and structural evaluation, such as the comparison tests, stacked regressions, component models and extended Blinder–Oaxaca decomposition. The focus of the next chapter, by Ugo Colombino, is on the structural empirical methods of policy evaluation with application to the evaluation and design of tax and transfer systems (Chapter 7). This chapter presents a range of structural approaches to the empirical analysis, such as the random utility maximisation, and labour supply responses to taxes and transfer at the extensive and the intensive margins. It concludes with an illustration of how structural microeconometric modelling can be combined with microsimulation and numerical optimisation. The next chapter, by Khai X. Chiong, Yu-Wei Hsieh and Matthew Shum, considers methods to construct bounds on counterfactual choice probabilities useful for counterfactual exercises in aggregate discrete-choice demand models, motivated by an empirical application using scanner data (Chapter 8). By taking a semiparametric approach, the analysis accommodates a wide variety of substitution patterns among alternatives while remaining a tractable linear programming problem. The next chapter, by Natalya Zelenyuk and Valentin Zelenyuk, expounds the current state of the art methodologies for the analysis of the performance of banks (Chapter 9). Beginning with the popular productivity and efficiency methods, data envelopment analysis and stochastic frontier analysis, the chapter reviews other methods whose popularity comes from the finance literature before changing focus to the issues of casual inference, such as differences-in-differences and regression discontinuity design, among others, that are the subject of the next section. This section concludes with a discussion by Christopher F. Baum of how the research methods commonly used in empirical microeconomics, for example to study disparities in income, wealth and human capital within and between societies, are becoming increasingly relevant to research in social epidemiology, particularly in understanding the origins of health disparities and analysing the policies used to address them (Chapter 10). As part of the discussion, this chapter highlights various techniques, including fixed-effects models, instrumental variables methods, difference-in-difference models, binary and ordered response models, count data models and conditional mixed-process models.

A detailed exposition of the modern methods of causal inference for policy evaluation and the statistical models underlying these methods is presented in the third section, "Policy Evaluation and Causality". The approaches covered in this section include experimental and quasi-experimental methods, regression discontinuity designs, matching and difference-in-differences. The section begins with an overview chapter, by Denis Fougère and Nicolas Jacquemet, describing the main impact evaluation methods, both experimental and quasi-experimental, and their underlying statistical models (Chapter 11). Regression discontinuity designs, which enable researchers to identify parameters of interest using discontinuities in the implementation of the policy across the population, have gained great popularity in policy evaluation in the recent years. This approach is the subject of the next chapter, by Otávio Bartalotti, Marinho Bertanha and Sebastian Calonico (Chapter 12). The chapter discusses key matters to consider for estimation, inference and overall implementation, such as local polynomial estimation, bandwidth choice and robust inference alongside recent extensions addressing common challenges, such as running variable manipulation, multiple cut-offs, measurement error and sample selection. The section concludes with a chapter by Emmanuel Duguet covering one of the most widely explored areas for policy evaluation,—the labour market (Chapter 13). The author uses evaluation of the impact of health events, for example, illness or accident, on labour market outcomes, such as labour market participation, to motivate a detailed exposition of the most common methods of estimation of the treatment effect in cross-sectional and panel data.

The fourth section, "Networks and Big Data in Microeconomics", presents computationally intensive empirical methods. The applications illustrated in this section include the analysis of data generated by social media, econometric analysis of network and the machine-learning methods in causal inference.

The collection, visualisation and empirical analysis of the new flows of data that can be harvested from social media and web searching is the topic of the first chapter in this section, by Tho Pham, Piotr Śpiewanowski and Oleksandr Talavera (Chapter 14). This chapter presents a comprehensive overview of the tools and methods used in the economic literature, including discussion of the Stata and Python codes. These methods are illustrated in practical examples of the analysis of exchange rate responses to political uncertainty and labour market responses to the COVID-19 pandemic. Taking this topic further, the next chapter, by Pedro C.L. Souza, surveys the growing literature on the econometrics of networks when the network itself is either not observed or only partially so, this is to say when the meta-data concerning connections between nodes, or who is following or talking to whom, is not available (Chapter 15). It highlights recent research on the use of aggregate relational data and how connections might be inferred from observable (endogenous and exogenous) covariates. Next, Vishalie Shah, Noemi Kreif and Andrew M. Jones discuss the estimation of heterogeneous treatment effects across population subgroups based on their observed characteristics using three machine learning algorithms, the X-learner, the R-learner and causal forests (Chapter 16). These techniques are then illustrated in a policy impact evaluation of a national health insurance programme in Indonesia.

The concluding section showcases the use in empirical microeconomics of the two most popular software packages, Stata and R, with examples both of how to use existing routines and of how to write bespoke code. Applications include stochastic frontier analysis and estimation of the traditional and nested constant-elasticity-of-substitution (CES) function.

The first chapter in this section, by Oleg Badunenko, looks at stochastic frontier analysis using Stata (Chapter 17). As well as covering existing routines and packages, it includes a guide on coding new, bespoke commands using Stata's own matrix programming language, Mata, with a particular focus on the analysis of panel data. The remaining chapters in the section discuss the use of the open-source statistical package, R. The topic of the first of these, by Giovanni Baiocchi, is the "ecosystem" of existing data processing R packages known as the *tidyverse*, that can facilitate econometric research workflows (Chapter 18). This wide-ranging chapter discusses the deployment of these existing resources for a wide array of popular models, including generalised linear models, binary, count, multinomial, ordered, censored and truncated responses, fraction and proportion responses and applications in several fields of empirical microeconomics, including instrumental variables, panel data and quantile regression. The next chapter, by Giovanni Millo, concentrates on one of the most widely explored of those fields, introducing the mechanics of panel data econometrics with R before expanding upon the various robust estimators, which relax the restrictive hypothesis of error homoskedasticity, available in the *plm* package, and how to employ them in a microeconomic context (Chapter 19). The final chapter, by Arne Henningsen, Géraldine Henningsen and Gergő Literáti, explores the estimation of the CES function, which, despite being widely used across economics, is rarely estimated as it is not amenable to linear regression (Chapter 20). The authors show how to estimate CES functions, first with the traditional two arguments and then with three or more arguments, in R using the package micEconCES.

The intended readership is graduate students in economics and other social sciences as well as researchers looking for the most advanced methods of micro-level data analysis and policy evaluation. It is assumed that the readers are familiar with the core methods in econometrics and statistics for data analysis in economics, business and social sciences, at least at an intermediate level. For background reading on the core and advanced methods, along with the basics of Stata and R software, we recommend the excellent texts listed below, among others.

Lastly, we would like to express our gratitude to Professor Mark Casson for encouraging us to edit this volume, as well as our previous edited volume in this series, on research methods and application in empirical macroeconomics.

RECOMMENDED BACKGROUND READING

Baum, Christopher F. (2016). *An Introduction to Stata Programming*. 2nd edition, Stata Press.
Baltagi, Badi H. (2021). *Econometric Analysis of Panel Data*. 6th edition, Springer.
Cameron, A. Colin and Pravin Trivedi (2021). *Microeconometrics Using Stata*. 3rd edition, Stata Press.
Croissant, Yves and Giovanni Millo (2018). *Panel Data Econometrics with R*. Wiley.
Wooldridge, Jeffrey M. (2010). *Econometric Analysis of Cross Section and Panel Data*. 2nd edition, MIT Press.

PART I

ECONOMETRIC METHODS IN MICROECONOMICS

1. Linear dynamic panel data models[*]
Ryo Okui

1. INTRODUCTION

Dynamic panel data models have been widely applied in many empirical studies across various fields of economics. Leading examples include labor economics (for example, Meghir and Pistaferri, 2004), economic growth (for example, Levine et al., 2000; Acemoglu et al., 2008), industrial organization (for example, Nickell 1996; Blundell and Bond, 2000) and international economics (for example, Clerides et al., 1998). This chapter provides a review of the estimation of linear dynamic panel data models, which in the past 30 years has become a very active research area in theoretical econometrics. As such, we now have a good understanding of the mathematical structure of this class of models and the statistical properties of the estimators. It is then sensible to provide an account of current best practice for analyzing these models.

The first half of this chapter reviews the generalized method of moments (GMM) estimation of linear dynamic panel data models. In this, we focus on a first-order autoregressive (AR) model with individual effects, called a panel AR(1) model as the most representative and simplest of the dynamic panel data models. We then consider the GMM estimator proposed by Arellano and Bond (1991) and Holtz-Eakin et al. (1988). While the GMM estimator is the most popular method to estimate dynamic panel data models, in certain circumstances it may not behave well. In particular, GMM may suffer from the problems of weak (Staiger and Stock, 1997; Stock and Wright, 2000) and many (Kunitomo, 1980; Morimune, 1983; Bekker, 1994; Donald and Newey, 2001; Newey and Windmeijer, 2009) instruments. Fortunately, a number of methods are available to alleviate these problems, for which we discuss solutions in situations specific to the GMM estimation of dynamic panel data models.

In the second half of the chapter, we consider the fixed effects estimator. While well known even in introductory econometrics textbooks as the representative estimation method for panel data analysis, it may not be possible to apply the fixed effects estimator to dynamic panel data analysis as often as the GMM estimator. In particular, the fixed effects estimator is not consistent when the length of the time series is fixed (Nickell, 1981), and even with moderately long time series, it is biased and this bias makes statistical inference problematic (Hahn and Kuersteiner, 2002). In this chapter, we discuss the source of this bias and the bias-correction methods provided by Hahn and Kuersteiner (2002) and Dhaene and Jochmans (2015), the outcome being that bias-corrected fixed effects estimators tend to have small variance and are useful when the length of the time series is moderately large.

Ultimately, the chapter identifies the best practices available for the estimation of dynamic panel data analysis based on the existing literature. As useful background, many graduate-level econometrics texts, research monographs and review articles discuss the estimation of dynamic panel data models at length. Wooldridge (2010) is an excellent and popular textbook on graduate-level microeconometrics, while Arellano (2003) is an outstanding monograph on panel data analysis. Elsewhere, Bun and Sarafidis (2015) provide a recent summary focusing on GMM estimation, with a comprehensive but rather less detailed review available in Sarafidis and Wansbeek (2021). Further, the interested reader may easily implement many, although not all, of the methods discussed in this chapter using readily available econometrics software, including STATA, EViews, R and gretl. These all have built-in commands/functions to analyze dynamic panel data models, and readers can implement the GMM estimator and its variations with these pieces of software very easily. We provide a short empirical illustration at the end of this chapter using a dataset from Acemoglu et al. (2008).

2. SETTINGS AND MODELS

Panel data are data for multiple entities where we observe each at multiple times. A panel has the form

$$y_{it}, \quad i = 1, \ldots, N, \quad t = 1, \ldots, T,$$

where i denotes an observation unit such as individual, firm, country, and so on and t denotes a time period, such as a year. For example, y_{it} is the income of individual i at time t, and we have a random sample of many individuals over several time periods. Dynamic panel data models describe the dynamics of y_{it}.

In most parts of this chapter, we consider the following panel AR(1) model:

$$y_{it} = \mu_i + \alpha y_{i,t-1} + \varepsilon_{it},$$

where α is the autoregressive coefficient parameter, μ_i is the unobserved individual (fixed) effect for i and ε_{it} is an unobserved idiosyncratic error. The fixed effects, μ_is, do not depend on t. The error term is assumed to have mean zero, $E(\varepsilon_{it}) = 0$ and to be serially uncorrelated. This panel AR(1) model is the simplest dynamic panel data model. In practice, more complex models could also be estimated. For example, dynamic panel data models often include regressors:

$$y_{it} = \mu_i + \alpha y_{i,t-1} + \beta' X_{it} + \varepsilon_{it},$$

where X_{it} is the vector of regressors and β is a vector of coefficients. Nonetheless, most of the theoretical issues in dynamic panel data models can be discussed under the simple panel AR(1) model. We thus consider the panel AR(1) model for most of the chapter.

3. GMM ESTIMATION

In this section we discuss the GMM estimation of panel AR(1) models. GMM is the most popular estimation method for dynamic panel data models. However, it may not behave well in certain practically relevant situations. In particular, it may face the problems of weak and many instruments. A large number of studies have considered these problems, including proposals to improve the performance of the GMM estimator.

3.1   Endogeneity Issue

We first discuss the motivation for GMM estimation. Why do we use GMM instead of least squares estimators? The answer is that least squares methods face an endogeneity problem and cannot provide a consistent estimator when T is fixed.

Recall that the model is

$$y_{it} = \mu_i + \alpha y_{i,t-1} + \varepsilon_{it}.$$

The parameter of interest is α. This model may not be estimated directly because of the presence of fixed effects. Note that μ_i and $y_{i,t-1}$ are corrected by the structure of the model and OLS does not yield a consistent estimate if we regard μ_i as part of the error term. If μ_is are regarded as parameters, then the number of parameters tends to infinity as $N \rightarrow \infty$.

A solution is to eliminate the fixed effects by, for example, taking the first difference:

$$y_{it} - y_{i,t-1} = \alpha(y_{i,t-1} - y_{i,t-2}) + (\varepsilon_{it} - \varepsilon_{i,t-1}). \tag{1.1}$$

The OLS estimator applied to this transformed model is known as the first difference (FD) estimator:

$$\hat{\alpha}_{FD} = \frac{\sum_{i=1}^{N} \sum_{t=3}^{T} (y_{i,t-1} - y_{i,t-2})(y_{it} - y_{i,t-1})}{\sum_{i=1}^{N} \sum_{t=3}^{T} (y_{i,t-1} - y_{i,t-2})^2}.$$

Unfortunately, the FD estimator is not consistent as $N \rightarrow \infty$ when T is fixed. The regressor, $y_{i,t-1} - y_{i,t-2}$, and the error term, $\varepsilon_{it} - \varepsilon_{i,t-1}$, are correlated because $y_{i,t-1}$ and $\varepsilon_{i,t-1}$ are correlated. Note that while there are other ways to eliminate individual effects, this endogeneity problem arises for any transformation.

A solution to the endogeneity problem is to use instruments. Recall that an instrumental variable is correlated with the regression and orthogonal to the error term. Anderson and Hsiao (1981), the seminal paper on dynamic panel data models, observe that lagged dependent variables satisfy the requirement for instrumental variable. See also Anderson and Hsiao (1982). The Anderson–Hsiao estimator, denoted as $\hat{\alpha}_{AH}$, estimates (1) using $y_{i,t-2}$ as an instrument:

$$\hat{\alpha}_{AH} = \frac{\sum_{i=1}^{N} \sum_{t=3}^{T} y_{i,t-2}(y_{it} - y_{i,t-1})}{\sum_{i=1}^{N} \sum_{t=3}^{T} y_{i,t-2}(y_{i,t-1} - y_{i,t-2})}.$$

Note that $y_{i,t-2}$ and $\varepsilon_{it} - \varepsilon_{i,t-1}$ are uncorrelated under the assumption that ε_{it} is serially uncorrelated. Moreover, we expect that $y_{i,t-2}$ and $(y_{i,t-1} - y_{i,t-2})$ are correlated because both involve $y_{i,t-2}$.

3.2   The Arellano–Bond Estimator

In this section, we introduce the Arellano–Bond estimator, which is arguably the most popular estimator for dynamic panel data models, being an extension of the earlier Anderson–Hsiao estimator. The key observation is that lags other than $y_{i,t-2}$ can be used as instruments. If we use all the available lags as instruments, we obtain the Arellano–Bond estimator.

To define the Arellano–Bond estimator, we introduce some notations. Let Δ be the first difference operator. Define

$$\Delta\varepsilon_i = \begin{pmatrix} \varepsilon_{i3} - \varepsilon_{i2} \\ \cdots \\ \varepsilon_{iT} - \varepsilon_{i,T-1} \end{pmatrix}, \quad \Delta y_i = \begin{pmatrix} y_{i3} - y_{i2} \\ \cdots \\ y_{iT} - y_{i,T-1} \end{pmatrix}, \quad \text{and } \Delta y_{i,-1} = \begin{pmatrix} y_{i2} - y_{i1} \\ \cdots \\ y_{i,T-1} - y_{i,T-2} \end{pmatrix}.$$

Note that $\Delta y_i = \alpha \Delta y_{i,1} + \Delta\varepsilon_i$. Also, define

$$\mathbf{Z}_i = \begin{pmatrix} [y_{i1}] & 0 & \cdots & 0 \\ 0 & [y_{i1}, y_{i2}] & \cdots & 0 \\ \cdots & & & 0 \\ 0 & \cdots & 0 & [y_{i1}, \ldots, y_{i,T-2}] \end{pmatrix}.$$

This is a matrix of instruments. The j-th row of $\mathbf{Z}_i$ is a vector of instruments for $y_{i,j+1} - y_{i,j}$. Arellano and Bond (1991) and Holtz-Eakin et al. (1988) propose to estimate α using GMM based on the following moment conditions:

$$E(\mathbf{Z}_i'\Delta\varepsilon_i) = 0.$$

We obtain the Arellano–Bond estimator by minimizing the following objective function:

$$\min_a \left(\frac{1}{N} \sum_{i=1}^n \mathbf{Z}_i'(\Delta y_i - a\Delta y_{i,-1}) \right)' W \left(\frac{1}{N} \sum_{i=1}^n \mathbf{Z}_i'(\Delta y_i - a\Delta y_{i,-1}) \right)',$$

where W is a weighting matrix. The following matrix yields an efficient GMM estimator (Hansen, 1982):

$$\hat{W}^{opt} = \left(\frac{1}{n} \sum_{i=1}^n \mathbf{Z}_i \Delta\hat{\varepsilon}_i \Delta\hat{\varepsilon}_i' \mathbf{Z}_i' \right)^{-1},$$

where $\Delta\varepsilon_i = \Delta y_i - \hat{\alpha}\Delta y_{i,-1}$ and $\hat{\alpha}$ is a preliminary consistent estimator of α. The explicit form of the Arellano–Bond estimator is

$$\hat{\alpha}_{AB} = \left\{ \left(\sum_{i=1}^n \Delta y_{i,-1}' \mathbf{Z}_i \right) W \left(\sum_{i=1}^n \mathbf{Z}_i' \Delta y_{i,-1} \right) \right\}^{-1} \left(\sum_{i=1}^n \Delta y_{i,-1}' \mathbf{Z}_i \right) W \left(\sum_{i=1}^n \mathbf{Z}_i' \Delta y_i \right).$$

We may iterate the estimation of α and the computation of $\hat{W}^{opt}$. This iteration converges and the resulting GMM estimator avoids the arbitrariness of the choice of preliminary estimator for $\hat{W}^{opt}$ (Hansen and Lee, 2021).

The Arellano–Bond estimator is arguably the most popular estimator for dynamic panel data models. One reason is that it is consistent and asymptotically normal as $N \to \infty$ and can be computed easily with commonly available econometric software (for example, STATA, EViews). As a result, many know it simply as the GMM estimator. However, we do not recommend this because GMM is a generic estimation method and other estimators for dynamic panel data models build on GMM principles. Thus, calling it the GMM estimator can be confusing.

Nevertheless, the Arellano–Bond estimator may suffer from bias in certain situations. We now consider two situations in which the Arellano–Bond estimator does not behave well, namely, the weak instruments problem and the many moments problem. These two problems arise in ways specific to dynamic panel data models. We also review the possible solutions in the literature.

3.3   Weak Instruments Problem

The Arellano–Bond estimator suffers from a weak instruments problem when the data are persistent. We first discuss the source of the weak instruments problem and then discuss the System-GMM estimator that may help attenuate the problem.

An instrument is called "weak" if it is only weakly correlated with the regressor. An instrumental variables estimator based on weak instruments suffers from bias and its distribution is not well approximated by a normal distribution (Staiger and Stock, 1997; Stock and Wright, 2000). In our context, $y_{i,t-1}$ is an instrument and the regressor is $y_{it} - y_{i,t-1}$. When the process is close to a unit root (that is, α is close to 1), the correlation between $y_{i,t-1}$ and $y_{it} - y_{i,t-1}$ is small.

Here, we show that the correlation between $y_{i,t-1}$ and $y_{it} - y_{i,t-1}$ tends to zero as $\alpha \uparrow 1$. Note that it is difficult to compute the correlation when $\alpha = 1$ because the variance of $y_{i,t-1}$ may not be well defined under a unit root unless we specify the initial condition. We thus assume stationarity and take α to be one. The discussion here follows that of Blundell and Bond (1998). We assume that μ_i and ε_{it} are independent, the sample is independently and identically distributed (i.i.d.) across i and $Var(\varepsilon_{it}) = \sigma_\varepsilon^2$ (homoscedasticity). Let $E(\mu_i^2) = \sigma_\mu^2$. Observe that

$$E(y_{i,t-1}(y_{it} - y_{i,t-1})) = E(y_{i,t-1}((\alpha - 1)y_{i,t-1} + \mu_i + \varepsilon_{it}))$$
$$= -(1-\alpha)E(y_{i,t-1}^2) + E(y_{i,t-1}\mu_i).$$

If y_{it} is stationary, then we have

$$y_{it} = \frac{\mu_i}{1-\alpha} + \sum_{j=0}^{\infty} \alpha^j \varepsilon_{i,t-j}.$$

It follows that

$$-(1-\alpha)E(y_{i,t-1}^2) + E(y_{i,t-1}\mu_i)$$

$$= -\frac{(1-\alpha)}{(1-\alpha)^2}E(\mu^2) + \frac{1}{1-\alpha}E(\mu^2) - (1-\alpha)E\left(\left(\sum_{j=0}^{\infty}\alpha^j\varepsilon_{i,t-j}\right)^2\right)$$

$$= -\frac{\sigma_\varepsilon^2}{1+\alpha}.$$

Thus, the variance of $y_{i,t-1}$ is

$$\frac{\sigma_\mu^2}{(1-\alpha)^2} + \frac{\sigma_\varepsilon^2}{1-\alpha^2},$$

and the variance of $(y_{it} - y_{i,t-1})$ is

$$2\sigma_\varepsilon^2 + \frac{2}{1+\alpha}\sigma_\mu^2.$$

Hence, the correlation coefficient is

$$-\frac{\sqrt{(1-\alpha)^2}}{1+\alpha} \frac{\sigma_\varepsilon^2}{\sqrt{2\sigma_\varepsilon^2 + \frac{2}{1+\alpha}\sigma_\mu^2}\sqrt{\sigma_\varepsilon^2 + \frac{1-\alpha}{1+\alpha}\sigma_\mu^2}},$$

which tends to 0 as $\alpha \uparrow 1$. We note that the weak instruments problem arises not because the covariance becomes zero (note that $-\sigma_\varepsilon^2 / 2$ is nonzero). It occurs because the variance of the instruments diverges. This is in contrast to standard theoretical analysis of the weak instruments problem, although in the end we encounter the same problem and the Arellano–Bond estimator does not behave well.

We now discuss solutions to the weak instruments problem. The most commonly used solution is to employ an additional set of moment conditions that are relatively robust to persistent data. The System-GMM estimator proposed by Arellano and Bover (1995) and Blundell and Bond (1998) uses this set of moment conditions in addition to those used in the Arellano–Bond estimator. Note that we still assume stationarity and we do not offer a solution to cases with $\alpha = 1$.

The additional moment condition used in the System-GMM estimator is

$$E((\mu_i + \varepsilon_{it})(y_{i,t-1} - y_{i,t-2})) = 0.$$

This moment condition holds for $t = 4, \ldots, T$. For $t = 3$, it holds if the initial observations (y_{i0}) are generated from the stationary distribution. Proposed by Arellano and Bover (1995) and Blundell and Bond (1998), these are called "level moment conditions."

We now show that the level moment conditions hold. First, we observe that $E(\varepsilon_{it}(y_{i,t-1} - y_{i,t-2})) = 0$. Thus, we need to show

$$E(\mu_i(y_{i,t-1} - y_{i,t-2})) = 0.$$

This holds because $E(\mu_i y_{it})$ is constant for any $t \geq 4$. If the initial observations are generated from the stationary distribution, then it holds with $t = 3$.

The System-GMM estimator solves the sample analog of the level moment conditions:

$$E((y_{it} - \alpha y_{i,t-1})(y_{i,t-1} - y_{i,t-2})) = 0,$$

for $t = 3, \ldots, T$, in addition to those used for the Arellano–Bond estimator ($E(\mathbf{Z}_i'(\Delta y_i - \alpha \Delta y_{i,-1}) = 0$ Blundell and Bond (1998) demonstrate in their simulations that the System-GMM estimator exhibits a small bias.

While the System-GMM estimator is frequently used in empirical research, its good proper-ties may not be guaranteed. Bun and Kiviet (2006) analytically derive an approximation to the bias, which indicates that the results of Blundell and Bond (1998) may be an artifact of their simulation designs. In general, they show that the System-GMM estimator suffers from bias. Hayakawa (2007) shows that the difference moment conditions and the level moment conditions yield biases with opposite directions. This finding implies that we may expect a small bias when we use both types of moment conditions. Alternatively, Bun and Windmeijer (2010) argue that the level moment conditions are weak when the variance of the fixed effects is large. Kruiniger (2009) demonstrates situations in which both types of moment conditions become weak.

The other criticism of the System-GMM estimator is that the System-GMM estimator heavily depends on the assumption of stationarity. If violated, the System-GMM estima-tor may not behave well. However, note that there are two kinds of possible violations of stationarity relevant in this context. The first is the unit root case ($\alpha = 1$). Bun and Kleibergen (2013) argue that in the Arellano–Bond and System-GMM estimations the identification of the parameter is irregular when α is close to one. The other type of nonstationarity concerns the initial condition. That is, the distribution of the initial observations y_{i0} is not a stationary distribution. Bun and Sarafidis (2015) provide an excellent survey about dynamic panel data models and include a good discussion of the initial condition problem. Hayakawa (2009b) and Hayakawa and Nagata (2016) show that the Arellano–Bond estimator works well when the initial conditions are not generated from the stationary distribution, even when α is close to one.

There is an additional type of moment conditions implied by the model. Ahn and Schmidt (1995) provide the complete list of moment conditions for the panel AR(1) model to achieve efficiency. This additional type of moment conditions is nonlinear and may not frequently apply in applied research. However, Bun and Sarafidis (2015) advocate its use and provide simulation evidence of its good properties.

3.4   Many Instruments Problem

The second problem with the Arellano–Bond estimator is that the number of moment condi-tions is large when T is large. It is also known that the GMM estimator suffers from bias when the number of instruments is large (Kunitomo, 1980; Morimune, 1983; Bekker, 1994; Donald and Newey, 2001; Newey and Windmeijer, 2009). However, its variance decreases with the number of instruments. The number of instruments (or moment conditions) can be large in the GMM estimation of dynamic panel data models. For example, y_{i1} is an instrument for $y_{i2} - y_{i1}$. But for $y_{i10} - y_{i9}$, there are nine instruments ($y_{i1}, \ldots, y_{i9}$). In total, the number of moment conditions is of order $O(T^2)$. Even if T is only moderately large, the number of moment conditions is still large.

Alvarez and Arellano (2003) demonstrate that the Arellano–Bond estimator suffers from bias when both N and T tend to infinity. Bun and Kiviet (2006) and Okui (2009) provide a closer investigation of the problem of many moments bias in the moment-based estimation of dynamic panel data models. In sum, the bias depends on the number of instruments for each regressor, not the total number of moment conditions, such that the variance becomes small as the number of moment conditions increases. Okui (2009) also proposes a method to choose the number of moment conditions. Relatedly, Carrasco and Nayihouba (2020) propose a regularization method to alleviate the many moments bias.

A simple solution is proposed by Hayakawa (2009a), which is an estimator that is consistent even when T is small. This does not suffer from the many instruments bias yet achieves asymptotic efficiency when T is large and is referred to as the double filter instrumental variable (DFIV) estimator.

The DFIV estimator employs "forward orthogonal deviation" to eliminate the individual effects. Let

$$y_{it}^* = \sqrt{\frac{T-t}{T-t+1}}\left(y_{it} - \frac{y_{i,t+1}+\ldots+y_{iT}}{T-t}\right)$$

$$x_{it}^* = \sqrt{\frac{T-t}{T-t+1}}\left(y_{i,t-1} - \frac{y_{i,t}+\ldots+y_{i,T-1}}{T-t}\right).$$

This transformation subtracts the average of future values. The term $\sqrt{(T-t)/(T-t+1)}$ equalizes the variances of the variables across t under homoscedasticity. When applied to a time-invariant variable, we obtain zero, thus eliminating the fixed effects.

The model for the transformed variables is

$$y_{it}^* = \alpha x_{it}^* + \varepsilon_{it}^*.$$

The DFIV estimator is an instrumental variable estimator for this transformed model, in which x_{it}^* is instrumented by the lagged dependent variable transformed by "backward orthogonal deviation":

$$z_{it} = \sqrt{\frac{T-t}{T-t+1}}\left(y_{i,t-1} - \frac{y_{i,t-1}+\ldots+y_{i1}}{t-1}\right).$$

Note that this estimator uses only one instrument for each regressor. The closed form of the DFIV estimator is

$$\hat{\alpha}_H = \left(\sum_{i=1}^{N}\sum_{t=2}^{T-1}z_{it}x_{it}^*\right)^{-1}\sum_{i=1}^{N}\sum_{t=2}^{T-1}z_{it}y_{it}^*.$$

This estimator is consistent as long as N and/or T tend to infinity. Moreover, when $T \to \infty$ and ε_{it} is i.i.d. normal, it achieves the efficiency bound derived by Hahn and Kuersteiner (2002) and Iwakura and Okui (2012).

The DFIV estimator is extended to more general dynamic panel data models by Hayakawa, et al. (2019). They consider general panel data models with predetermined regressors with fixed effects including panel AR models and show that the estimator is asymptotically equivalent to a biased corrected version of the fixed effects estimator. Relatedly, Roodman (2009) suggests using the sum of predetermined variables as an instrument to reduce the number of instruments.

3.5   With Regressors

We can also estimate dynamic panel data models with regressors following the same argument. Let X_{it} be a vector of regressors for i at t. Note that all elements of X_{it} need to be time varying. A time-invariant regressor is eliminated from the model in the process of eliminating the individual effects. We consider the following panel AR(1) model with regressors:

$$y_{it} = \mu_i + \alpha y_{i,t-1} + \beta' X_{it} + \varepsilon_{it}.$$

This model can be estimated by GMM with additional moment conditions regarding the relationship between X_{it} and ε_{it}. There are two kinds of exogeneity assumptions regarding X_{it}. The first is strict exogeneity. This means that $E(X_{it}\varepsilon_{is}) = 0$ for any t and s. In this case, we use moment conditions $E(X_{it}(\varepsilon_{is} - \varepsilon_{i,s-1})) = 0$ for any t and s. The second assumption is predeterminedness, where $E(X_{it}\varepsilon_{is}) = 0$ for $t \le s$. In this case, we use $E(X_{it}(\varepsilon_{is} - \varepsilon_{i,s-1})) = 0$ for $t < s$. Which assumption is more appropriate depends on the application. Let z_{it} be the row vector of instruments for the equation at time $t+1$. When X_{it} is strictly exogenous $z_{it} = (y_{i1}, \ldots y_{it}, X'_{i1}, \ldots, X'_{iT})$, and when X_{it} is predetermined then $z_{it} = (y_{i1}, \ldots y_{it}, X'_{i1}, \ldots, X'_{i,t+1})$. The GMM estimator has the same formula as that of the Arellano–Bond estimator except that $\mathbf{Z}_i$ is replaced by

$$\mathbf{Z}_i = \begin{pmatrix} z_{i1} & 0 & \cdots & 0 \\ 0 & z_{i2} & \cdots & 0 \\ \cdots & & \cdots & 0 \\ 0 & \cdots & 0 & z_{i,T-2} \end{pmatrix}.$$

Note that we may also add the level moment conditions. The bias of the GMM estimator in models with regressors is examined by Bun and Kiviet (2006).

3.6   Inferences and Specification Tests

The Arellano–Bond estimator is a GMM estimator and asymptotically normal, so statistical inferences can use the usual standard errors for the GMM estimator. However, the empirical size of a test or the coverage probability of a confidence interval based on the usual standard errors may not be close to the nominal size or coverage (see, for example, simulation studies in Okui, 2009). Moreover, if the weighting matrix depends on an initial consistent estimate, the problem becomes more severe. To solve the problem, Windmeijer (2005) proposes an alternative standard error formula called the standard error with the Windmeijer correction. This generates better coverage and is frequently used. Hwang et al. (2021) extend this to provide valid standard errors even in the presence of misspecification.

Another important inference for dynamic panel data models is specification testing. That is, it is important to examine the validity of moment conditions. Because the Arellano–Bond estimator is a GMM estimator, the *J*-test for overidentifying restrictions by Hansen (1982) can be used. However, the presence of many moment restrictions may cause size distortion. To address this issue, specification tests tailored to dynamic panel data models have been duly proposed.

The key assumption for the estimation of dynamic panel data models is the serial uncorre-latedness of ε_{it}. Given first-order serial correlation is used for the estimation and is not testable, Arellano and Bond (1991) propose a test for the second-order serial correlation in ε_{it}. Yamagata (2008) extends this to construct a joint test for second- and higher-order serial correlations.

4. BIAS-CORRECTED FIXED EFFECTS ESTIMATOR

This section discusses the fixed effects estimator. Although it is the most representative estima-tion method in the panel data literature, it does not provide a consistent estimator in dynamic panel data models when T is fixed. When T tends to infinity, it is consistent but suffers from bias. Several bias-corrected estimators have been proposed to alleviate the bias when T is moderately large.

4.1 Fixed Effects Estimation

The fixed effects estimator is an ordinary least squares (OLS) estimator applied to panel data using a fixed effects transformation. The fixed effects transformation subtracts the mean of the variables and thus eliminates the fixed effects from the model. However, the fixed effects estimator is biased and is inconsistent when T is fixed.

The fixed effects estimator is computed as follows. We first eliminate the individual effects by subtracting the individual averages:

$$y_{it} - \bar{y}_i = \alpha(y_{i,t-1} - \bar{y}_{-1,i}) + \varepsilon_{it} - \bar{\varepsilon}_i,$$

where $\bar{y}_i = \sum_{t=2}^{T} y_{it} / T$, $\bar{y}_{-1,i} = \sum_{t=2}^{T} y_{i,t-1} / T = \sum_{t=1}^{T-1} y_{it} / T$ and $\bar{\varepsilon}_i = \sum_{t=2}^{T} \varepsilon_{it}$. We then apply OLS to this transformed model. The resulting estimator is the fixed effects estimator, denoted as $\hat{\alpha}_{FE}$, namely

$$\hat{\alpha}_{FE} = \left(\sum_{i=1}^{N} \sum_{t=2}^{T} (y_{i,t-1} - \bar{y}_{-1,i})^2 \right)^{-1} \left(\sum_{i=1}^{N} \sum_{t=2}^{T} (y_{i,t-1} - \bar{y}_{-1,i})(y_{it} - \bar{y}_i) \right).$$

However, the fixed effects estimator is not consistent when $N \to \infty$ but T is fixed. The source of inconsistency is the correlation between the regressor and the error term. Note that in the transformed model, the regressor is $y_{i,t-1} - \bar{y}_{-1,i}$ and the error term is $\varepsilon_{it} - \bar{\varepsilon}_i$. The problem is that $\bar{y}_{-1,i}$ includes the dependent variables from $t = 1$ to $t = T-1$ and $\bar{\varepsilon}_i$ includes the error terms from $t = 2$ to T. By the nature of the model, y_{is} and ε_{it} are correlated if $s \geq t$. We thus have

$$E((y_{i,t-1} - \bar{y}_i)(\varepsilon_{it} - \bar{\varepsilon}_i)) \neq 0.$$

This observation implies that

$$\hat{\alpha}_{FE} = \alpha + \left(\sum_{i=1}^{N} \sum_{t=1}^{T} (y_{i,t-1} - \bar{y}_{-1,i})^2 \right)^{-1} \left(\sum_{i=1}^{N} \sum_{t=1}^{T} (y_{i,t-1} - \bar{y}_{-1,i})(\varepsilon_{it} - \bar{\varepsilon}_i) \right)$$

$$\rightarrow_p \alpha + \left(E\left[\sum_{t=1}^{T} (y_{i,t-1} - \bar{y}_{-1,i})^2 \right] \right)^{-1} \left(E\left[\sum_{t=1}^{T} (y_{i,t-1} - \bar{y}_{-1,i})(\varepsilon_{it} - \bar{\varepsilon}_i) \right] \right) \neq \alpha.$$

Thus, $\hat{\alpha}_{FE}$ is not consistent.

Of course, $\hat{\alpha}_{FE}$ is consistent when $T \rightarrow \infty$. The correlation between $y_{i,t-1} - \bar{y}_{-1,i}$ and $\varepsilon_{it} - \bar{\varepsilon}_i$ becomes negligible as T increases. In particular, when N is fixed and $T \rightarrow \infty$, it is a time series problem and the consistency of the OLS estimator has been established in the time series literature.

Nonetheless, the bias may not be negligible in finite samples, even when T is moderately large (Hahn and Kuersteiner, 2002; Alvarez and Arellano, 2003). Moreover, even when T is large, if the ratio between N and T is also large, the asymptotic distribution becomes biased and standard inference procedures may not be valid.

4.2   Bias Correction

We now discuss bias-correction methods for the fixed effects estimator. There have been several attempts to alleviate the bias of the fixed effects estimator. They still require $T \rightarrow \infty$ but the finite sample properties of bias-corrected fixed effects estimators are promising even with moderate T. Moreover, they tend to have a smaller variance than those of the GMM-type estimators.

We first discuss analytical bias correction. Hahn and Kuersteiner (2002) propose a simple bias-corrected estimator:

$$\hat{\alpha}_{HK} = \frac{T+1}{T} \hat{\alpha}_{FE} + \frac{1}{T} = \hat{\alpha}_{FE} + \frac{1}{T}\left(1 + \hat{\alpha}_{FE}\right).$$

This estimator is motivated by the following observation. When $N, T \rightarrow \infty$ and $N/T \rightarrow \kappa$, where $0 < \kappa < \infty$, Hahn and Kuersteiner (2002) show that

$$\sqrt{NT}(\hat{\alpha}_{FE} - \alpha) \rightarrow_d N(-\sqrt{\kappa}(1+\alpha), 1-\alpha^2),$$

under homoscedasticity (that is, $Var(\varepsilon_{it}) = \sigma_\varepsilon^2$, where σ_ε^2 does not depend on i or on t). Thus, the asymptotic distribution of the fixed effects estimator is not centered around zero even when $T \rightarrow \infty$. Alternatively, we may write that

$$\sqrt{NT}\left(\hat{\alpha}_{FE} - \alpha + \frac{1}{T}(1+\alpha)\right) \rightarrow_d N(0, 1-\alpha^2).$$

Thus, we have

$$\sqrt{NT}(\hat{\alpha}_{HK} - \alpha) = \sqrt{NT}\left(\hat{\alpha}_{FE} - \alpha + \frac{1}{T}(1+\alpha)\right) + \sqrt{\frac{N}{T}}(1+\hat{\alpha}_{FE} - (1+\alpha))$$

$$\rightarrow_d N(0, 1-\alpha^2).$$

Note that, when T is fixed, $\hat{\alpha}_{HK}$ is still inconsistent.

Several studies discuss the bias properties of the fixed effects estimator and bias correction methods for models with regressors. Kiviet (1995) examines the bias problem in panel AR(1) models with regressors and proposes a bias-corrected estimator. The bias is also examined in Bun and Kiviet (2006). Bun and Carree (2005) propose a bias-corrected estimator that is consistent, even when T is fixed. However, the bias-correction methods proposed in these papers may appear more complex than that by Hahn and Kuersteiner (2002). Gouriéroux et al. (2010) propose a bias correction through indirect inference.

The discussion here focuses on panel AR(1) models, but similar arguments hold for the other dynamic panel data models. For example, Lee (2012) considers the fixed effects estimation of panel AR(p) models. Lee et al. (2018) examine the bias of the fixed effects estimator and propose a simple analytical bias correction in panel AR(∞) models. Arellano (2016) considers dynamic panel data models with predetermined regressors. Okui (2010) considers bias-corrected estimations of autocovariances and autocorrelations for panel data with fixed effects.

4.3 Jackknife Bias Correction

An alternative bias correction method draws on jackknife. Here, we consider the half-panel jackknife (HPJ) bias correction proposed by Dhaene and Jochmans (2015) and available for general dynamic panel data models, including nonlinear models.

The HPJ procedure is as follows. Let $\hat{\alpha}$ be an estimator. Let $\hat{\alpha}^{(1)}$ and $\hat{\alpha}^{(2)}$ be the estimators of α computed using $\{\{y_{it}\}_{t=1}^{T/2}\}_{i=1}^{N}$ and $\{\{y_{it}\}_{t=T/2+1}^{T}\}_{i=1}^{N}$, respectively, with even T. Let $\bar{\alpha} = (\hat{\alpha}^{(1)} + \hat{\alpha}^{(2)})/2$. The HPJ bias-corrected estimator of H is defined by

$$\hat{\alpha}^{H} = \hat{\alpha} - (\bar{\alpha} - \hat{\alpha}) = 2\hat{\alpha} - \bar{\alpha}.$$

The main idea for the HPJ bias correction is the following. Consider the fixed effects estimator, $\hat{\alpha}_{FE}$, which exhibits a bias of order T^{-1}. We thus have

$$\hat{\alpha}_{FE} = \alpha + \frac{B}{T} + mean\,zero\,term\,and\,small\,terms,$$

where B is a constant. Each $\hat{\alpha}^{(i)}$ for $i = 1, 2$ is based on panel data whose length is $T/2$. Thus, we have

$$\bar{\alpha} = \alpha + \frac{2B}{T} + mean\,zero\,term\,and\,small\,terms.$$

Thus, the bias of order $1/T$ of $\hat{\alpha}_{FE}$ is estimated by $\bar{\alpha} - \hat{\alpha}_{FE}$. Therefore, the HPJ estimator $\hat{\alpha}^{H} = \hat{\alpha}_{FE} - (\bar{\alpha} - \hat{\alpha}_{FE})$ reduces the bias of order $1/T$ of $\hat{\alpha}_{FE}$.

4.4 Inferences

We suggest bootstrap methods to conduct statistical inferences based on (bias-corrected) fixed effects estimators. Although standard inference procedures, for example t-statistics with usual standard errors, are asymptotically valid, their finite sample properties may not be encouraging because bias correction may not be able to eliminate the bias completely in finite samples, and this affects the variability of the estimator. Galvao and Kato (2014) propose a cross-sectional bootstrap method. This is a nonparametric bootstrap procedure treating each time series as the unit of observation. Let $y_i = (y_{i1}, \ldots, y_{iT})$. The algorithm is as follows:

1. Randomly draw $y_1^*, \ldots y_N^*$ from $\{y_i\}_{i=1}^N$ with replacement.
2. Compute the statistics of interest, say $\hat{S}^*$, from $\{y_i^*\}_{i=1}^N$.
3. Repeat 1 and 2 B times. Let $\hat{S}^*(b)$ be the estimate computed in the bth bootstrap sample.
4. Compute the quantities of interest from the empirical distribution of $\{\hat{S}^*(b)\}_{b=1}^B$.

For example, a 95 per cent confidence interval for α is $[\hat{\alpha} - q_{0.975}^*, \hat{\alpha} - q_{0.025}^*]$ where $\hat{\alpha}$ is an estimate of α, and $q_{0.975}^*$ and $q_{0.025}^*$ are the 97.5 and 2.5 percentiles of the empirical distribution of $\{\hat{\alpha}^*(b) - \hat{\alpha}\}_{b=1}^B$. This bootstrap procedure can be used in any panel data model as long as the panel is cross-sectionally independent. Okui and Yanagi (2019) apply it for statistical inferences for parameters characterizing heterogeneity in dynamics. Gonçalves and Kaffo (2015) propose different bootstrap methods that exploit the features of dynamic panel data models.

5.   MOTIVATIONS

In this section, we discuss motivations behind the use of dynamic panel data models. We give the definitions of unobserved heterogeneity and state dependence and discuss their importance in analyzing economic problems. They are important not only in the analysis of dynamics, but also in cases in which the research interest is on the effect of some regressor because of the need to be controlled to obtain an unbiased estimate of the coefficient of the regressor.

5.1   Unobserved Heterogeneity and State Dependence

We consider the importance of distinguishing between unobserved heterogeneity and state dependence. As an example, we consider income dynamics, although analysis of many other economic variables would face similar problems. The income process is typically serially correlated. For example, individuals receiving high incomes in previous years tend to earn a high income this year. This phenomenon can be explained by unobserved heterogeneity and/or state dependence.

Unobserved heterogeneity may explain serial correlation in income dynamics. Those who have high incomes are productive workers (heterogeneity in productivity or ability). Therefore, they tend to receive high incomes throughout their life. For this reason, we may consider it spurious serial correlation because it does not cause serial correlation in the individual dynamics. In other words, we observe serial correlation only in the cross-sectional dimension if caused purely by unobserved heterogeneity.

Conversely, state dependence means that serial correlation in income arises because of a temporal dependence in the income process. That is, those who earned high incomes by chance may subsequently receive high incomes. However, this time dependency in income does not reflect the difference in ability and may result from some market imperfection (such as wage rigidity).

We want to distinguish between unobserved heterogeneity and state dependence for several reasons. First, it helps us to build a better model for income dynamics, which in turn is used as a key part of, for example, large macro models. Second, unobserved heterogeneity and state dependence provide very different policy implications. If serial correlation is caused by unobserved heterogeneity, the observed persistent income inequality is an outcome of the difference in ability. As such, a redistribution policy cannot be justified from any concern with efficiency; instead, it should draw on some normative criteria (for example, we think income inequality is bad). Alternatively, if caused only by state dependence, then persistent income inequality simply reflects that some people are lucky and others are not. As such, a redistribution policy can be justified from an efficiency perspective and thus considered as a risk-sharing mechanism.

Of course, unobserved heterogeneity and state dependence are not mutually exclusive. It would be more reasonable to assume that both play roles in determining the serial correlation structure of income dynamics. Thus, it would be desirable to have statistical methods with which we can evaluate the contribution of each factor while controlling for the other.

The panel AR(1) model is useful to investigate to what extent each interpretation of the persistency in income is relevant. Recall that the panel AR(1) model is

$$y_{it} = \mu_i + \alpha y_{i,t-1} + \varepsilon_{it}.$$

In this model, μ_i (individual (fixed) effect) represents the unobserved heterogeneity, and α (AR(1) parameter) represents the degree of state dependence. This chapter focuses on the estimation of α. That is, we discuss how we can estimate the degree of state dependence while controlling for unobserved heterogeneity.

Distinguishing between state dependence and unobserved heterogeneity becomes important even when we are not interested in the dynamics itself, but rather in the effect of a regressor. Note that controlling for unobserved heterogeneity is standard in panel data analysis. Dynamic panel data models allow us to control both unobserved heterogeneity and state dependence simultaneously.

For example, Asiedu and Lien (2011) consider the effect of democracy on foreign direct investment (FDI) and investigate whether it depends on the availability of natural resources. Their model is

$$fdi_{it} = \mu_i + \alpha\, fdi_{i,t-1} + \beta dem_{it} + \gamma dem_{it} \times nat_{it}$$
$$+\text{other regressors} + \varepsilon_{it},$$

where fdi_{it} is the amount of FDI, dem_{it} is an index of the degree of democracy and nat_{it} indicates the availability of natural resources. The parameters of interest are β and γ. In this application, α may not be the parameter of primary interest but $fdi_{i,t-1}$ still needs to be added to estimate β and γ unbiasedly.

It would be natural to think that the degree of democracy correlates with unobserved time-invariant characteristics of countries, such as culture, and that these characteristics would affect the amount of FDI. Moreover, past FDI may affect the current level of democracy through international politics, and we would expect that FDI would possess state dependence. Thus, to estimate the effect of democracy on FDI, we should control for unobserved heterogeneity across countries and the state dependence of FDI. Otherwise, the regression suffers from omitted variable bias. The dynamic panel data model provides a simple way to achieve this goal. However, the estimation of that model faces several statistical challenges as already discussed in this chapter.

Economic theory may also imply dynamic panel data models. An important example is the estimation of production functions. Suppose that the production is of a Cobb–Douglas type so that the log output y_{it} is determined by

$$y_{it} = a_{it} + \beta k_{it} + \gamma l_{it},$$

where a_{it} is the log productivity level of firm i at period t, k_{it} is log capital and l_{it} is log labor. Suppose that a_{it} follows $a_{it} = \mu_i + \alpha a_{i,t-1} + \xi_{it}$, where μ_i is the time-invariant part of productivity and ξ_{it} is an idiosyncratic productivity shock. By subtracting αy_{it} from both sides and rearranging terms, we obtain

$$y_{it} = \mu_i + \alpha y_{i,t-1} + \beta k_{it} - \beta \alpha k_{i,t-1} + \gamma l_{it} - \gamma \alpha l_{i,t-1} + \xi_{it}.$$

This transformed model is a dynamic panel data model and the techniques discussed in this chapter may be applied. For details on the estimation of production functions from the perspective of dynamic panel data models, see Blundell and Bond (2000). Ackerberg et al. (2015) discuss its relation to other approaches for production function estimation.

6.   EMPIRICAL ILLUSTRATION

In this section, we illustrate procedures for the estimation and inference of dynamic panel models through an empirical example. We revisit the study by Acemoglu et al. (2008) on the effect of economic situation on democracy. The statistical computation is conducted with STATA MP15.1 on macOS Big Sur 11.1.

We use the 5 year panel data originally used in Acemoglu et al. (2008).[1] The data consist of observations from 90 countries from 1970 to 2000 (the length of time series is 7) and is balanced.[2] We investigate the effect of economic situation measured by GDP per capita on a measure of democracy. The Freedom House democracy index is used as the measure of democracy. See Acemoglu et al. (2008) for the details of the data.

We subtract cross-sectional averages from variables to eliminate time effects. Let dem_{it} be the democracy index for country i at year t and gdp_{it} the GDP per capita for county i at year t. Define $\log(\widetilde{dem}_{it}) = \log(dem_{it}) - \sum_{j=1}^{N} \log(dem_{jt})/N$ and $\log(\widetilde{gdp}_{it}) = \log(gdp_{it}) - \sum_{j=1}^{N} \log(gdp_{jt})/N$. We estimate the following dynamic panel data models.

$$\log(\widetilde{dem}_{it}) = \beta \log(\widetilde{dem}_{i,t-1}) + \theta \log(\widetilde{gdp}_{i,t-1}) + \alpha_i + \varepsilon_{it}, \tag{1.2}$$

where α_i is the country effect. Note that time effects are eliminated by cross-sectional demeaning and are not included in the model. We assume that $\log(\widetilde{gdp}_{i,t-1})$ is predetermined. The main parameter of interest is θ. It measures the effect of economic growth on democracy, controlling for the state dependency of democracy and unobserved heterogeneity among countries.

Various packages are available for the estimation of dynamic panel data models with STATA; xtdpdgmm by Kripfganz (2017) implements all GMM estimators discussed in this chapter; xtspj by Sun and Dhaene (2019) implements the half-panel jackknife bias correction for the fixed effects estimator. The estimation results discussed are obtained with these packages. Unfortunately, at the time of writing, it is still burdensome to implement cross-sectional bootstrap for panel data methods using STATA.

Table 1.1 presents the estimation results from various estimation procedures. The estimated values of the coefficients vary across estimation methods. This result indicates the importance of understanding different properties of various estimation methods. The OLS estimate of θ is positive and statistically significant. It suggests an economically important and statistically significant effect of income on democracy. However, this result is overturned once we take into account unobserved heterogeneity. The Anderson–Hsiao estimate is negative and large, but its standard error is large too. The Arellano–Bond estimator also yields negative estimates which are statistically insignificant. The system-GMM estimates of θ are positive. However, the estimate from the iterative GMM is not statistically significant and its magnitude is not large either. The fixed effects estimator of θ is negative and the bias correction inflates the size of the effect. On the other hand, the panel data used in this empirical exercise are short and these fixed effects methods may not be particularly reliable compared with the GMM procedures in the current case.

Our results are consistent with those of Acemoglu et al. (2008). Once we take into account unobserved heterogeneity and state dependence, we tend to find either negative or small and statistically insignificant effect of income on democracy. The system-GMM estimator yields statistically significant positive results, but the results are not robust and the iterative version is small and statistically insignificant. It is thus sensible to conclude that there is no solid statistical evidence that good economic situation promotes democracy.

7.   CONCLUSION

This chapter provides a review of the estimation of linear dynamic panel data models. We consider a panel AR(1) model and its extensions. We consider two estimation methods: GMM and the bias-corrected fixed effects estimator. Lastly, we consider the economic motivation to analyze dynamic panel data models.

We suggest the following as best practice depending on the length of time series of the data. When the panel is short (say, $T < 7$), then the Arellano–Bond approach may be used. We would iterate the estimation of the parameter and computation of the weighting matrix as suggested by Hansen and Lee (2020). Statistical inferences are conducted with standard errors based on the Windmeijer (2005) correction. In contrast, when the panel is moderately long (say, $T \geq 7$), bias-corrected fixed estimators such as those suggested by Hahn and Kuersteiner (2002) and Dhaene and Jochmans (2015) are suggested. Statistical inferences may be conducted with cross-sectional bootstraps as in Galvao and Kato (2014). Regardless of the length of time series, the DFIV estimator by Hayakawa (2009a) does not suffer from bias, and inferences based on it have correct coverage and size but may have a large variance in finite samples. Note that the previously-mentioned cutoff at $T = 7$ is suggested

Table 1.1 Estimation results of model (2)

Estimator weights	OLS	FD	AH	AB one	AB two	AB ite	Sys one	Sys two	Sys ite	FE	HPJ
$\hat{\beta}$	0.675	−0.248	0.348	0.376	0.362	0.346	0.534	0.605	0.912	0.29	0.541
	(0.050)	(0.062)	(0.126)	(0.107)	(0.107)	(0.110)	(0.066)	(0.074)	(0.063)	(0.064)	(0.064)
$\hat{\theta}$	0.070	−0.056	−0.362	−0.228	−0.158	−0.13	0.072	0.080	0.031	−0.064	−0.114
	(0.015)	(0.056)	(0.162)	(0.123)	(0.098)	(0.101)	(0.022)	(0.026)	(0.032)	(0.052)	(0.052)
Country effects	No	Yes	Yes	Yes	Yes	Yes	Yes	Yes	Yes	Yes	Yes
Standard errors	CR	CR	CR	CR	WC	WC	CR	WC	WC	CR	CR

Note: FD: first difference estimator. AH: Anderson–Hsiao estimator. AB: Arellano–Bond estimator. Sys: system-GMM estimator. FE: fixed effects estimator. HPJ: fixed effects estimator with half-panel jackknife bias correction. one: weighting matrix optimal under homoskedasticity. two: heteroskedasticity optimal weighting matrix based on the one-step procedure. ite: iterative GMM. CR: cluster robust standard errors. WC: cluster robust standard errors with Windmeijer's correction.

by the simulation results in, for example, Hahn and Kuersteiner (2002) and Okui (2009), but is not definite.

This chapter considers panel AR(1) models with fixed effects, and because of space constraints we do not discuss more complex models also used in the literature. These include models with time effects, individual specific time trends, and interactive effects. Hahn and Moon (2006) show that the bias-correction method by Hahn and Kuersteiner (2002) can be applied even when the model includes time effects. Okui (2014) argues that time effects create bias for the estimation of autocovariances, but because they affect the estimator in a multiplicative way, it is not present for autocorrelation estimators because we take a ratio between autocovariances. Phillips and Sul (2007) examine the role of individual specific time trends in the bias of the fixed effects estimator, and Okui (2011) does so for the estimation of autocovariances and autocorrelations. Models with interactive effects (models with factor structure) are examined by Phillips and Sul (2007) and Moon and Weidner (2015, 2017). The GMM estimation of models with interactive effects is considered by Robertson and Sarafidis (2015). Pesaran (2015) provides an excellent summary of these advanced topics, particularly for panel data with long time series.

Lastly, we suggest some possible future research topics. In particular, we argue that heterogeneity and misspecification are two important topics in the literature on dynamic panel data models. Pesaran and Smith (1995), Hsiao et al. (1999), Phillips and Moon (1999) and Pesaran (2006) consider panel AR(1) models with heterogeneous coefficients, that is, models in which α depends on i, and consider the estimation of the cross-sectional mean of the heterogeneous coefficients. How to estimate the entire distribution of heterogeneous coefficients is examined by Okui and Yanagi (2019, 2020). See also Jochmans and Weidner (2018), Arellano and Bonhomme (2012) and Barras et al. (2018). The other important issue is model misspecification. Okui (2008) shows that popularly used panel AR(1) estimators, such as the Arellano–Bond and fixed effects estimators, converge in probability to first-order autocorrelation when $T \to \infty$ followed by $N \to \infty$ even if the panel AR(1) model is misspecified. Okui (2017) demonstrates their probability limits when the model is misspecified and the panel exhibits heterogeneous dynamics. Torgovitsky (2019) uses a potential outcome framework to examine the identification of state dependence and unobserved heterogeneity when y_{it} is binary. It is important to examine what we can learn from the techniques for dynamic panel data models when they exhibit model misspecification and heterogeneity is not totally accounted for in the model. We fully expect research to concentrate on these issues in the future.

NOTES

* The author gratefully acknowledges the financial support of the School of Social Sciences and a New Faculty Startup Grant at Seoul National University and the Housing and Commercial Bank Economic Research Fund in the Institute of Economic Research at Seoul National University. Junho Choi provided excellent research assistance. The usual disclaimer applies.

1. The authors made this dataset available to the research community via openICPSR, a repository of the Inter-university Consortium for Political and Social Research (ICPSR). The URL address is https://www.openicpsr.org/openicpsr/project/113251/version/V1/view.
2. The dataset is taken from "5 Year Panel" sheet in "Income and Democracy AER adjustment-1" available as a supplemental material of Acemoglu et al. (2008). We use a subset which satisfies *samplebalancegmm* = 1 so that the subset constitutes a balanced panel.

REFERENCES

Acemoglu, Daron, Simon Johnson, James A. Robinson, and Pierre Yared (2008). "Income and democracy". In: *American Economic Review* 98.3, pp. 808–42.

Ackerberg, Daniel, Kevin Caves, and Garth Frazer (2015). "Identification properties of recent production function estimators". In: *Econometrica* 83.6, pp. 2411–51.

Ahn, Seung C. and Peter Schmidt (1995). "Efficient estimation of models for dynamic panel data". In: *Journal of Econometrics* 68, pp. 5–27.

Alvarez, Javier and Manuel Arellano (2003). "The time series and cross-section asymptotics of dynamic panel data estimators". In: *Econometrica* 71.4, pp. 1121–59.

Anderson, Theodore Wilbur and Cheng Hsiao (1981). "Estimation of dynamics models with error components". In: *Journal of the American Statistical Association* 76.375, pp. 598–606.

Anderson, Theodore Wilbur and Cheng Hsiao (1982). "Formulation and estimation of dynamic models using panel data". In: *Journal of econometrics* 18.1, pp. 47–82.

Arellano, Manuel (2003). *Panel Data Econometrics*. Oxford University Press.

Arellano, Manuel (2016). "Modelling optimal instrumental variables for dynamic panel data models". In: *Research in Economics* 70, pp. 238–61.

Arellano, Manuel and Stephen Bond (1991). "Some tests of specification for panel data: Monte Carlo evidence and an application to employment equations". In: *Review of Economics Studies* 58, pp. 277–97.

Arellano, Manuel and Stéphane Bonhomme (2012). "Identifying distributional characteristics in random coefficients panel data models". In: *Review of Economic Studies* 79, pp. 987–1020.

Arellano, Manuel and Olympia Bover (1995). "Another look at the instrumental variable estimation of error-component models". In: *Journal of Econometrics* 68, pp. 29–51.

Asiedu, Elizabeth and Donald Lien (2011). "Democracy, foreign direct investment and natural resources". In: *Journal of International Economics* 84, pp. 99–111.

Barras, Laurent, Patrick Gagliardini, and Olivier Scaillet (2018). "The cross-sectional distribution of fund skill measures". mimeo.

Bekker, Paul A (1994). "Alternative approximations to the distributions of instrumental variable estimators". In: *Econometrica* 62.3, pp. 657–81.

Blundell, Richard and Stephen Bond (1998). "Initial conditions and moment restrictions in dynamic panel data models". In: *Journal of Econometrics* 87, pp. 115–43.

Blundell, Richard and Stephen Bond (2000). "GMM estimation with persistent panel data: an application to production functions". In: *Econometric reviews* 19.3, pp. 321–40.

Bun, Maurice J. G. and Martin A. Carree (2005). "Bias-corrected estimation in dynamic panel data models". In: *Journal of Business & Economic Statistics* 23.2, pp. 200–210.

Bun, Maurice J. G. and Jan F. Kiviet (2006). "The effects of dynamic feedbacks on LS and MM Estimator accuracy in panel data models". In: *Journal of Econometrics* 132, pp. 409–44.

Bun, Maurice J. G. and Frank Kleibergen (2013). "Identification and inference in moments based analysis of linear dynamic panel data models". mimeo.

Bun, Maurice J. G. and Vasilis Sarafidis (2015). "Dynamic Panel Data Models". In: *The Oxford Handbook of Panel Data*, ed. by Badi H. Baltagi. Oxford University Press, pp. 76–110.

Bun, Maurice J. G. and Frank Windmeijer (2010). "The weak instrument problem of the system GMM estimator in dynamic panel data models". In: *The Econometrics Journal* 13.1, pp. 95–126.

Carrasco, Marine and Ada Nayihouba (2020). "A regularization approach to the dynamic panel data model estimation". Mimeo.

Clerides, Sofronis K., Saul Lach, and James R. Tybout (1998). "Is learning by exporting important? micro-dynamic evidence from Colombia, Mexico, and Morocco". In: *Quarterly Journal of Economics* 113.3, pp. 903–47.

Dhaene, Geert and Koen Jochmans (2015). "Split-panel jackknife estimation of fixed-effect models". In: *The Review of Economic Studies* 82.3, pp. 991–1030.

Donald, Stephen G. and Whitney K. Newey (2001). "Choosing the number of instruments". In: *Econometrica* 69.5, pp. 1161–91.

Galvao, Antonio F. and Kengo Kato (2014). "Estimation and inference for linear panel data models under misspecification when both n and T are large". In: *Journal of Business & Economic Statistics* 32.2, pp. 285–309.

Gonçalves, Sílvia and Maximilien Kaffo (2015). "Bootstrap inference for linear dynamic panel data models with individual fixed effects". In: *Journal of Econometrics* 186.2, pp. 407–26.

Gouriéroux, Christian, Peter C. B. Phillips, and Jun Yu (2010). "Indirect inference for dynamic panel models". In: *Journal of Econometrics* 157.1, pp. 68–77.

Hahn, Jinyong and Guido Kuersteiner (2002). "Asymptotically unbiased inference for a dynamic panel model with fixed effects when both n and T are large". In: *Econometrica* 70.4, pp. 1639–57.

Hahn, Jinyong and Hyungsik Roger Moon (2006). "Reducing Bias of MLE in a dynamic panel model". In: *Econometric Theory* 22, pp. 499–512.

Hansen, Bruce E. and Seojeong Lee (2021). "Inference for iterated GMM under misspecification". In: *Econometrica* 89.4, pp. 1419–47.

Hansen, Lars Peter (1982). "Large sample properties of generalized method of moments estimators". In: *Econometrica* 50.4, pp. 1029–53.

Hayakawa, Kazuhiko (2007). "Small sample properties of the system GMM estimator in dynamic panel data models". In: *Economics Letters* 95, pp. 32–8.

Hayakawa, Kazuhiko (2009a). "A simple efficient instrumental variable estimator for panel AR(p) models when both N and T are large". In: *Econometric Theory* 25, pp. 873–90.

Hayakawa, Kazuhiko (2009b). "On the effect of mean-nonstationarity in dynamic panel data models". In: *Journal of Econometrics* 153, pp. 133–5.

Hayakawa, Kazuhiko and Shuichi Nagata (2016). "On the behavior of the GMM estimator in persistent dynamic panel data models with unrestricted initial conditions". In: *Computational Statistics and Data Analysis* 100, pp. 265–303.

Hayakawa, Kazuhiko, Meng Qi, and Jörg Breitung (2019). "Double filter instrumental variable estimation of panel data models with weakly exogenous variables". In: *Econometric Reviews* 38.9, pp. 1055–88.

Holtz-Eakin, Douglas, Whitney Newey, and Harvey S. Rosen (1988). "Estimating vector autoregressions with panel data". In: *Econometrica* 56.6, pp. 1371–95.

Hsiao, Cheng, M. Hashem Pesaran, and A. K. Tahmiscioglu (1999). "Bayes estimation of short-run coefficients in dynamic panel data models". In: *Analysis of Panels and Limited Dependent Variables Models*, ed. by K. Lahiri, C. Hsiao, L.F. Lee, and M.H. Pesaran. Cambridge University Press, pp. 268–96.

Hwang, Jungbin, Byunghoon Kang, and Seojeong Lee (2021). "A doubly corrected robust variance estimator for linear GMM". Forthcoming in the *Journal of Econometrics*.

Iwakura, Haruo and Ryo Okui (2012). "Asymptotic efficiency in dynamic panel data models with factor structure". mimeo.

Jochmans, Koen and Martin Weidner (2018). "Inference on a distribution from noisy draws". In: *arXiv preprint arXiv:1803.04991*.

Kiviet, Jan F. (1995). "On bias, inconsistency, and efficiency of various estimators in dynamic panel data models". In: *Journal of Econometrics* 68, pp. 53–78.

Kripfganz, Sebastian (Aug. 2017). *XTDPDGMM: Stata module to perform generalized method of moments estimation of linear dynamic panel data models*. Statistical Software Components, Boston College Department of Economics. https://ideas.repec.org/c/boc/bocode/s458395.html.

Kruiniger, Hugo (2009). "GMM estimation and inference in dynamic panel data models with persistent data". In: *Econometric Theory*, pp. 1348–91.

Kunitomo, Naoto (1980). "Asymptotic expansions of the distributions of estimators in a linear functional relationship and simultaneous equations". In: *Journal of the American Statistical Association* 75, pp. 693–700.

Lee, Yoon-Jin, Ryo Okui, and Mototsugu Shintani (2018). "Asymptotic inference for dynamic panel estimators of infinite order autoregressive processes". In: *Journal of Econometrics* 204.2, pp. 147–58.

Lee, Yoonseok (2012). "Bias in dynamic panel models under time series misspecification". In: *Journal of Econometrics* 169, pp. 54–60.

Levine, Ross, Norman Loayza, and Thorsten Beck (2000). "Financial intermediation and growth: Causality and causes". In: *Journal of Monetary Economics* 46, pp. 31–77.

Meghir, Costas and Luigi Pistaferri (2004). "Income variance dynamics and heterogeneity". In: *Econometrica* 72.1, pp. 1–32.

Moon, Hyungsik Roger and Martin Weidner (2015). "Linear regression for panel with unknown number of factors as interactive fixed effects". In: *Econometrica* 83.4, pp. 1543–79.

Moon, Hyungsik Roger and Martin Weidner (2017). "Dynamic linear panel regression models with interactive fixed effects". In: *Econometric Theory* 33, pp. 158–95.

Morimune, Kimio (1983). "Approximate distribution of the k-class estimators when the degree of overidentifiability is large compared with the sample size". In: *Econometrica* 51.3, pp. 821–41.

Newey, Whitney K. and Frank Windmeijer (2009). "Generalized method of moments with many weak moment conditions". In: *Econometrica* 77.3, pp. 687–719.

Nickell, Stephen (1981). "Biases in dynamic models with fixed effects". In: *Econometrica* 49.6, pp. 1417–26.

Nickell, Stephen J. (1996). "Competition and corporate performance". In: *Journal of Political Economy* 104.4, pp. 724–46.

Okui, Ryo (2008). "Panel AR(1) estimators under misspecification". In: *Economics Letters* 101, pp. 210–13.

Okui, Ryo (2009). "The optimal choice of moments in dynamic panel data models". In: *Journal of Econometrics* 151, pp. 1–16.

Okui, Ryo (2010). "Asymptotically unbiased estimation of autocovariances and autocorrelations with long panel data". In: *Econometric Theory* 26, pp. 1263–304.

Okui, Ryo (2011). "Asymptotically unbiased estimation of autocovariances and autocorrelations for panel data with incidental trends". In: *Economics Letters* 112, pp. 49–52.

Okui, Ryo (2014). "Asymptotically unbiased estimation of autocovariances and autocorrelations with panel data in the presence of individual and time effects". In: *Journal of Time Series Econometrics* 6.2, pp. 129–81.

Okui, Ryo (2017). "Misspecification in dynamic panel data models and model-free inferences". In: *Japanese Economic Review* 68.3, pp. 283–304.

Okui, Ryo and Takahide Yanagi (2019). "Panel data analysis with heterogeneous dynamics". In: *Journal of Econometrics* 212.2, pp. 451–75.

Okui, Ryo and Takahide Yanagi (2020). "Kernel estimation for panel data with heterogeneous dynamics". In: *The Econometrics Journal* 23.1, pp. 156–75.

Pesaran, M. Hashem (2006). "Estimation and inference in large heterogeneous panels with a multifactor error structure". In: *Econometrica* 74.4, pp. 967–1002.

Pesaran, M. Hashem (2015). *Time Series and Panel Data Econometrics*. Oxford University Press.

Pesaran, M. Hashem and Ron Smith (1995). "Estimating long-run relationships from dynamic heterogeneous panels". In: *Journal of Econometrics* 68.1, pp. 79–113.

Phillips, Peter C. B. and Hyungsik Roger Moon (1999). "Linear regression limit theory for nonstationary panel data". In: *Econometrica* 67.5, pp. 1057–111.

Phillips, Peter C. B. and Donggyu Sul (2007). "Bias in dynamic panel estimation with fixed effects, incidental trends and cross section dependence". In: *Journal of Econometrics* 137, pp. 162–88.

Robertson, Donald and Vasilis Sarafidis (2015). "IV estimation of panels with factor residuals". In: *Journal of Econometrics* 185.2, pp. 526–41.

Roodman, David (2009). "A note on the theme of too many instruments". In: *Oxford Bulletin of Economics and Statistics* 71.1, pp. 135–58.

Sarafidis, Vasilis and Tom Wansbeek (2021). "Celebrating 40 years of panel data analysis: Past, present and future". In: *Journal of Econometrics* 220, pp. 215–226.

Staiger, D. and James H. Stock (1997). "Instrumental variables regression with weak instruments". In: *Econometrica* 65.3, pp. 557–86.

Stock, James H. and Jonathan H. Wright (2000). "GMM with weak identification". In: *Econometrica* 68, pp. 1097–126.

Sun, Yutao and Geert Dhaene (May 2019). *XTSPJ: Stata module for split-panel jack-knife estimation*. Statistical Software Components, Boston College Department of Economics. https://ideas.repec.org/c/boc/bocode/s458651.html.

Torgovitsky, Alexander (2019). "Nonparametric inference on state dependence in unemployment". In: *Econometrica* 87.5, pp. 1475–505.

Windmeijer, Frank (2005). "A finite sample correction for the variance of linear efficient two-step GMM estimators". In: *Journal of Econometrics* 126, pp. 25–51.

Wooldridge, Jeffrey M. (2010). *Econometric Analysis of Cross Section and Panel Data*. Second edition. The MIT Press.

Yamagata, Takshi (2008). "A joint serial correlation test for linear panel data models". In: *Journal of Econometrics* 146, pp. 135–45.

2. Spatial autoregressive nonlinear models in R with an empirical application in labour economics
Anna Gloria Billé

1. INTRODUCTION TO SPATIAL MICROECONOMETRICS

Microeconomic data usually refer to individual-level data on the economic behaviour of individuals, firms or groups of them (for example households, industrial districts, and so on), and they are typically collected using cross-section or panel data surveys. The analysis of microeconomic data has a long history, both from a theoretical and an empirical point of view. There are several peculiarities that mark microeconomic data. First of all, data at a low disaggregated level are often discrete or censored/truncated by nature, leading to the use of *nonlinear models* such as probit/logit, Tobit, count data regressions, where the type of nonlinearity in the model specification refers to the *nonlinearity in parameters*, and for which iterative estimation procedure are necessary (McFadden, 1984; Amemiya, 1985; Maddala, 1986). Secondly, disaggregation is often a source of *heterogeneity* that should be accounted for to obtain valid inferences in regression analyses. In addition, the growing availability of this type of data has brought out a number of additional problems including, for example, *sample selection*, *measurement errors*, *missing data* (see the book by Cameron and Trivedi (2005) for an overview of methods in microeconometrics). Differently from macroeconomic data, microeconomic data are more affected by these issues, but at the same time they provide a greater flexibility in specifying econometric models and a larger amount of information.

Adding spatial autoregressive processes to nonlinear models has increased the theoretical, methodological and computational problems in estimating the parameters and interpreting the results. Indeed, in a recent review, Billé and Arbia (2019) pointed out the main difficulties and the proposed solutions as well as the lack of a continuous development of this specific field in the econometric literature. Although spatial econometrics is now a consolidated discipline, most of the literature in spatial microeconometrics has only seen a growth of empirical applications with the use of micro data and spatial linear models, see for example Conley (2010), Arbia et al. (2021). In addition, to the best of my knowledge, methods, for example to deal with *measurement error* problems, have been developed only for spatial linear models. For instance, Conley and Molinari (2007) investigated the impact of location/distance measurement errors on the accuracy of both some parametric and nonparametric estimators through MC simulations, whereas Le Gallo and Fingleton (2012) evaluated the consequences of measurement errors in an independent variable on the Ordinary Least Squares (OLS) estimates. The argumentation and explanation of the different estimation procedures and their statistical properties according to different types of spatial limited dependent variable models is vast and somehow complicated. For a recent "state of the art" of the theoretical and methodological issues of spatial nonlinear models the reader is referred to Billé and Arbia (2019), Billé and Leorato (2020) and references therein.

This chapter is devoted to the analysis of spatial autoregressive nonlinear probit models, with a detailed illustration of how to use available packages in R through an empirical application in Labour Economics. The rest of the chapter is organized as follows. Section 2 lays the foundation for spatial econometric models by defining the weighting matrices. Section 3 specifies a spatial autoregressive nonlinear probit model and explains the marginal effects (subsection 3.1). Finally, section 4 describes how to fit and interpret these types of models in R. An empirical illustration on the employments rates in Europe is also included (subsection 4.1).

2.   DEFINITION OF SPATIAL WEIGHTING MATRICES

There are several different ways in which the spatial weights can be defined. Actually, their definition is somehow arbitrary, leading to potential problems of model misspecification due to wrongly assumed weighting matrices. This has led to an interesting debate in the literature. Many researchers began to evaluate the sensitivity of the estimated parameters on the use of different types of spatial weighting matrices through Monte Carlo simulations, see for example Billé (2013) in a spatial probit context, among many others. Some others criticized the exogeneity assumption behind its construction, highlighting the importance of including information coming from the economic theory, see for example Fingleton and Arbia (2008) and Corrado and Fingleton (2012), or estimating the elements of this matrix through an appropriate procedure, see for example Pinkse et al. (2002), Bhattacharjee and Jensen-Butler (2013), and Ahrens and Bhattacharjee (2015). Finally, LeSage (2014) argued that *a Bayesian approach provides one way to introduce subjective prior information in choosing the weighting matrix*, while LeSage and Pace (2014) stressed that, if the partial derivatives defining the spatial marginal effects are correctly specified and the goal is to have approximately correct scalar summary measures (see subsection 3.1), then the weighting matrices have approximately no impact on estimates and inferences.

Discussions on the definition of different spatial weighting matrices as well as model specifications can now be found in several spatial book references, see for example Anselin (1988), LeSage and Pace (2009), Elhorst (2014), Arbia (2014), Kelejian and Piras (2017). A first definition comes from the use of geographical information, as the spatial data are typically associated with georeferenced data, for example firms, provinces, and so on. Depending on the type of spatial units, that is points, lines or areas, distance-based definition or contiguity-based criteria to build the spatial weight matrix (*geometric W*) can be used, see for example Getis and Aldstadt (2004). Contiguity-based criteria typically define a *sparse* weighting matrix, see also Pace and Barry (1997). The starting point is to define a Boolean matrix as in the following. Let $W = \{w_{ij}\}$ be the spatial weighting matrix with elements equal to the weights among pairs of random variables y_i, y_j for $i, j = 1, \ldots, n$, with n the sample size, then

$$
\begin{cases}
w_{ij} = 1 & \textit{iff } y_j \textit{ is close to } y_i, \ j \neq i \\
w_{ij} = 0 & \textit{otherwise}
\end{cases}
$$

where the term "is close to" is justified by the adopted criterion. Several contiguity-based criteria, for example queen and rook, fall within the above definition, as well as a distance-based approach called *k*-nearest neighbours that will be explained in the section devoted to the empirical application. The peculiarity of contiguity-based criteria is the use of borders or angles to select the neighbourhood of each spatial unit, and therefore they are particularly suitable for areal/polygon data. Distance-based weights define, instead, *dense* weighting matrices. In this case, the geographical information comes from the numerical value of the distance (measured in km, miles, and so on) between pairs of spatial units. A general distance-based weight matrix can be defined in the following way

$$w_{ij} = f(d_{ij}), \quad j \neq i$$

where $f(\cdot)$ can be any continuous monotonically decreasing function that ensures decreasing weights as distances d_{ij} increase. Examples of such functions are, for instance, the negative exponential or the inverse-distance. Figure 2.1 graphically shows the difference between *sparse* and *dense* matrices, with the non-zero elements in black.

The cut-off approach is a particular type of distance-based definition that leads to *sparse* weighting matrices. The aim is to put at zero all the weights referred to as distances greater than a pre-specified distance (*radius, r*),

$$\begin{cases} w_{ij} = f(d_{ij}) \, if\!f \quad d_{ij} < r, \quad j \neq i \\ \quad w_{ij} = 0 \quad otherwise. \end{cases}$$

Regardless the way of defining the spatial weights, all the spatial weighting matrices must be such that (i) all the diagonal elements are zero, $w_{ii} = 0 \ \forall i$ and (ii) their row and column sums are uniformly bounded in absolute value. Assumption (i) is a simple normalization rule and means that each spatial unit is not viewed as its own neighbour, while (ii) limits the spatial correlation to a manageable degree and ensures that the spatial process is not explosive. Moreover, nonnegative weighting matrices are typically used, $w_{ij} \geq \forall i \neq j$, as follows from the definition of *distance* (metric). For theoretical details, see for example Kelejian and Prucha (1998), Lee (2004), Kelejian and Prucha (2010).

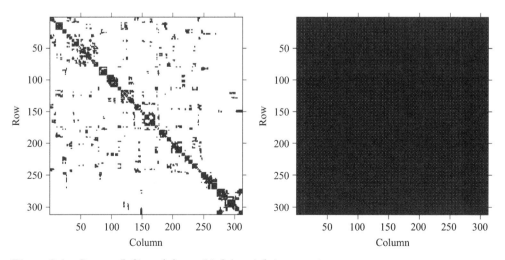

Figure 2.1   Sparse (left) and dense (right) weighting matrices

W is typically row-normalized such that $\Sigma_j w_{ij} = 1, \forall i$. This ensures that the autoregressive term of the model lies in the interval $(-1, 1)$. Indeed, the parameter space of the autoregressive term depends in general on the eigenvalues of W. Although the row-normalization rule provides an easy interpretation of the spatial model, that is each geo-located dependent variable depends on a weighted average of neighbouring dependent variables, it does not ensure the equivalence of the model specifications before and after normalizations of the weights, with the exception of the use of the k-nearest neighbour approach. To ensure this equivalence, an alternative normalization rule based on the spectral radius of W has been proposed by Kelejian and Prucha (2010). Finally, although the definition of *distance* requires the symmetric property, the weighting matrix can be in some cases an asymmetric matrix, whose definition can be particularly useful in the following cases.

Spatial econometric methods can also be used for modelling, for instance, economic agents' behaviours or financial data, see Catania and Billé (2017), since the aim is to easily capture cross-sectional dependence through an appropriate parametrization. However, individual data of this type are not georeferenced, making difficult the connection between them. Economic definitions of distance can be useful in this case, see for example Case et al. (1993) and Anselin and Bera (1998). Moreover, the inclusion of spatially lagged dependent variables Wy, both in the linear and in the nonlinear model specification, adds an endogeneity problem due to the simultaneity of n equations. Therefore, the exogeneity assumption behind the geographical definition of the spatial weights has been criticized by Pinkse and Slade (2010), and proper estimation methods have been developed, see for example Kelejian and Piras (2014) and Qu and Lee (2015). For instance, Qu and Lee (2015) proposed the use of additional exogenous regressors, say X_2, to control for potential endogeneity of the spatial weight matrix in a cross-sectional setting. The weights are defined as

$$w_{ij} = h(Z_{ij}, d_{ij}), \ j \neq i$$

where $h(\cdot)$ is a proper bounded function, Z is a matrix of variables and d_{ij} is the distance between two units. Within a two-stage IV estimation, they first regress the endogenous matrix Z on X_2 through the OLS estimator applied to the following equation

$$Z = X_2 \Gamma + \varepsilon$$

where Γ is the matrix of coefficients and ε is a column vector of innovations. Then, they used $(Z - X_2 \Gamma)$ as control variables in the linear spatial model to control for the potential endogeneity of W in the second stage. Furthermore, the authors argued that the spatial weight matrix W can be exogenous/predetermined, but the term Wy remains endogenous due to the potential correlation among the error terms of the two equations.

Still within the IV approach, Kelejian and Piras (2014) directly proposed estimating the elements of W through a linear approximation with a finite set of parameters in a panel data setting. Otto and Steinert (2018) proposed the use of the least absolute shrinkage and selection operator (LASSO) approach to estimate the weighting matrix with potential structural breaks in a spatio-temporal model. Finally, a recent alternative way to estimate the elements of the weighting matrix is based on exploiting more the time information in a spatio-temporal model, see Billé et al. (2019). This spatio-temporal model specification, combined with the generalized autoregressive score (GAS) procedure, is able to estimate via Maximum

Likelihood Estimation (MLE) the elements of the spatial weighting matrix $W = \{w_{ij}\}$ through a proper parametrization of the weights over time and a nonlinear function of the past information. In this way, the estimation procedure is able to identify the *radius* within which the spatial effects have their highest impacts. For detailed discussion on different estimation procedures with endogenous weighting matrices the reader is referred to section 2 of Billé et al. (2019). However, none of the above approaches for endogenous W matrices have been yet developed for spatial model with limited dependent variables.

3. MODEL SPECIFICATION AND INTERPRETATION

In this section we define one of the possible general specifications of the spatial probit model and its nested-model specifications. For details on different spatial binary probit specifications see Billé and Arbia (2019). Then, we provide the model interpretation and in subsection 3.1 the definition of the marginal effects.

Let y be a n-dimensional vector of binary dependent variables. A spatial (first-order) autoregressive probit model with (first-order) autoregressive disturbances (SARAR(1,1)-probit) (Billé and Leorato, 2020; Martinetti and Geniaux, 2017) can be defined in the following way

$$\begin{cases} y^* = \rho W_1 y^* + X\beta + u \quad u = \lambda W_2 u + \varepsilon \quad \varepsilon \sim \mathcal{N}\left(0, I\right) \\ y = \mathbb{1}\left(y^* > 0\right) \end{cases}$$

where y^* is a n-dimensional vector of continuous latent dependent variables, typically associated with individual unobserved utility functions, W_1 and W_2 are (possibly) two different n-dimensional spatial weighting matrices to govern different spatial processes, X is the n by k matrix of regressors, u is the n-dimensional vector of autoregressive error terms, ε is a vector of homoscedastic innovations of the same dimension with $\sigma_\varepsilon^2 = 1$ for identification and $\mathbb{1}(\cdot)$ is the indicator function such that $y_i = 1 \Leftrightarrow y^* > 0 \; \forall i$. The terms $\rho W_1 y^*$ and $\lambda W_2 u$ capture the global *spatial spillover effects* in the latent dependent variables and among the shocks, respectively. The term *spillover effects* refers to the indirect effects due to the neighbouring random variables. This concept will be clarified below. Two nested-model specifications can be easily obtained by setting $\lambda = 0$ or $\rho = 0$. The two models are called spatial (first-order) autoregressive probit (SAR(1)-probit) model and spatial (first-order) autoregressive error probit (SAE(1)-probit) model, respectively.

When we consider nonlinear binary models, we are generally interested in evaluating the changes in the probability of being equal to 1 by the binary dependent variables given the set of regressors of the model specification, that is, $E(y|X) = P(y=1|X)$. If we assume that the error terms are normally distributed, then a probit model can be considered and the probabilities can be evaluated by using the normal cumulative density function, that is, $P(y = 1|X) = \Phi(\cdot)$, where the cdf $\Phi(\cdot)$ is a function of the unknown parameters $\theta = (\rho, \lambda, \beta')$ and the exogenous regressors X. Therefore, the estimated β coefficients cannot be interpreted as the marginal effects anymore, due to both the nonlinearity in parameters and the presence of spatial dependence. In subsection 3.1 we explain in detail how to calculate proper marginal effects for these types of models.

Due to the simultaneity of the model specification, reduced forms of the spatial models are typically derived. Under some regularity conditions, see for example Billé and Leorato (2020), the model can be written in reduced form as

$$
\begin{cases}
y^* = A_\rho^{-1} X\beta + v \quad v \sim \mathcal{N}\left(0, \Sigma_v\right) \\
y = \mathbb{1}\left(y^* > 0\right)
\end{cases}
$$

where $v = A_\rho^{-1} B_\lambda^{-1}\varepsilon$, $A_\rho^{-1} = \left(I - \rho W_1\right)^{-1}$, $B_\lambda^{-1} = \left(I - \lambda W_2\right)^{-1}$ and $\Sigma_v = A_\rho^{-1} B_\lambda^{-1} B_\lambda^{-1'} A_\rho^{-1'}$. Now, the inverse matrices, A_ρ^{-1} and B_λ^{-1}, can be written in terms of the infinite series expansion as

$$
\begin{cases}
A_\rho^{-1} = \displaystyle\sum_{i=0}^{\infty}\rho^i W_1^i = I + \rho W_1 + \rho^2 W_1^2 + \rho^3 W_1^3 + \ldots + \rho^\infty W_1^\infty \\
B_\lambda^{-1} = \displaystyle\sum_{i=0}^{\infty}\lambda^i W_2^i = I + \lambda W_2 + \lambda^2 W_2^2 + \lambda^3 W_2^3 + \ldots + \lambda^\infty W_2^\infty
\end{cases}
$$

where, focusing on the first expansion, the first right-hand term (the identity matrix I) represents a direct effect on y^* of a change in X due to the fact that its diagonal elements are ones and its off-diagonal elements are zero. On the contrary, the second right-hand term (ρW_1) represents an indirect effect on y^* of a change in X, also called *spillover effects*. The other terms are referred to the indirect effects of higher orders, that is, the spatial effects due to the neighbours of the neighbours, and so on. The term *spillover effects* also refers to the autoregressive process in the error terms, focusing on the second finite series expansion, although the difference in the interpretation is that A_ρ^{-1} enters both in the mean and in the variance-covariance matrix of the conditional distribution of $y|X$, whereas B_λ^{-1} only in the variance–covariance matrix.

Higher-order effects also have another meaning in spatial econometrics. Indeed, the higher-order effects can be also defined through the orders of the autoregressive processes, as is typically done in time-series econometrics (consider for example an ARMA(1,1) vs. an ARMA(2,2)). Nevertheless, the specification and interpretation for these types of spatial linear models is not obvious as in time, and none of these specifications have been found with limited dependent variables. For details the reader is referred to Badinger and Egger (2011), Elhorst et al. (2012), Arbia et al. (2013), Debarsy and LeSage (2018) and Han et al. (2017).

3.1   Marginal Effects

Marginal effects of nonlinear models differ substantially from the linear ones. Indeed, in nonlinear specifications, these effects depend both on the estimated parameters and the level of the explanatory variable of interest x_h. In addition, when considering *spatial dependence*, total marginal effects have inside two distinct sources of information: (i) *direct effects* due to the direct impact of the regressor x_{ih} in a specific region i on the dependent variable y_i and (ii) *indirect effects* due to the presence of the spatial spillover effects, that is, the impact from other regions x_{jh} $\forall j \neq i$, see LeSage et al. (2011). Note that the term *region* is a general definition of spatial data, and the observations $i = 1, \ldots, n$ can also be referred to individuals, for example economic agents.

In this way, the usual interpretation "a unit variation of a specific regressor determines a specific and constant variation in the dependent variable" is no longer valid. To preserve the link between econometric models and economic theory, proper marginal effects should always be defined. In the following, we discuss the definition of the marginal effects for spatial probit models.

Let $x_h = (x_{1h}, x_{2h}, \ldots, x_{ih}, \ldots, x_{nh})'$ be an n-dimensional vector of units referred to the h-th regressor, $h = 1, \ldots, k$ and $x_{i.} = (x_{i1}, x_{i2}, \ldots, x_{ih}, \ldots, x_{ik})$ be a k-dimensional vector of regressors referred to unit i. Billé and Leorato (2020), among others, propose the following specifications of the marginal effects:

$$\frac{\partial P\left(y_i = 1 \mid X_n\right)}{\partial x'_{.h}}\bigg|_{\bar{x}} = \phi\left(\{\Sigma\}_{ii}^{-1/2}\left\{A_\rho^{-1}\bar{X}\right\}_{i.}\beta\right)\{\Sigma\}_{ii}^{-1/2}\{A_\rho^{-1}\}_{i.}\beta_h,$$

$$\frac{\partial P\left(y_i = 1 \mid X_n\right)}{\partial x'_{.h}}\bigg|_{x} = \phi\left(\{\Sigma\}_{ii}^{-1/2}\left\{A_\rho^{-1}X\right\}_{i.}\beta\right)\{\Sigma\}_{ii}^{-1/2}\{A_\rho^{-1}\}_{i.}\beta_h,$$

where Σ is the variance–covariance matrix implied by the reduced form of the spatial probit model, $\bar{X}$ is an n by k matrix of regressor means, $\{\cdot\}_{i.}$ is the i-th row of the matrix inside and $\{\cdot\}_{ii}$ is the i-th diagonal element of a square matrix. Note that Σ depends on ρ or λ if a SAR(1)-probit model or a SAE(1)-probit model is considered, respectively.

The first specification of the above equations explains the impact of a marginal change in the mean of the h-th regressor, that is, $\bar{x}_{.h}$, on the conditional probability of $\{y_i = 1\}$, that is, $P(y_i = 1 \mid X_n)$, setting $\bar{x}_{.h'}$ for all the remaining regressors, $h' = 1, \ldots, k - 1$. The second specification of the above equations considers instead the marginal impact evaluated at each single value of $x_{.h}$. This is particularly informative in space in terms of *spatial heterogeneity* due to the possibility of evaluating a marginal impact with respect to a particular region value x_{ih}. The results are two n-dimensional square matrices for $\{y_1, y_2, \ldots, y_n\}$. Finally, the average of the main diagonals provides a synthetic measure of the *direct impact*, while the average of the off-diagonal elements provides a synthetic measure of the *indirect impact*. Note that, since the above matrices of marginal effects are functions of the autocorrelation parameters that enter in the main diagonal, the direct effects are also slightly affected by the presence of spatial dependence.

4. FITTING SPATIAL ECONOMETRIC NONLINEAR MODELS IN R

In this section we explain how to fit spatial nonlinear (probit) models in R. There are at least three packages that one can use to estimate a SAR(1)-probit or a SAE(1)-probit model: (i) `McSpatial`, (ii) `ProbitSpatial`, (iii) `spatialprobit`. The first one has inside different functions to estimate a SAR(1)-probit model, the linearized GMM proposed by Klier and McMillen (2008) and an MLE-based function. However, the linearized GMM approach is accurate as long as the true autocorrelation coefficient is relatively small. In addition, there is no discussion about the asymptotic behaviour of this estimator and no other forms of model specifications are allowed for. A recent variant of this GMM-based estimator is the one proposed by Santos and Proença (2019). The second package has the `SpatialProbitFit` function that fits both the SAR(1)-probit and the SAE(1)-probit model through an approximate MLE approach, see Martinetti and Geniaux (2017). Although it is computationally very fast for large datasets, see also Mozharovskyi and Vogler (2016) for a similar approach, this estimation procedure does not account for more general model specifications and the possible use of *dense* weighting matrices. In addition, there is no discussion about its asymptotic behaviour. Finally, the third one is based on the Bayesian approach; see for example LeSage et al. (2011). Alternative Maximum Likelihood (ML)–based estimation approaches have been recently proposed by Wang et al. (2013) and Billé and Leorato (2020). Here, we focus the attention on the use of the `SpatialProbitFit` function in the `ProbitSpatial` package.

A brief description of the approximate MLE is as follows. First of all, one of the main problems in estimating both linear and nonlinear spatial models, especially with a large dataset as is typically the case in microeconometrics, is related to the repeated calculations of the determinants of n-dimensional matrices; see for example Smirnov and Anselin (2001) and Pace and LeSage (2004). In addition, within spatial nonlinear probit models, an n-dimensional integral problem for the estimation of the parameters arises. In view of these features, there are two different approaches that have been proposed by Martinetti and Geniaux (2017): (i) maximization of the full log likelihood function by means of a multi-dimensional optimization algorithm and (ii) maximization of the log likelihood conditional to ρ. They propose to approximate the multi-dimensional integral by the product of the univariate conditional probabilities $\Phi_n(x_1 \in A_1,\ldots,x_n \in A_n) = \mathcal{P}(x_1 \in A_1)\Pi_{i=2}^{n}\mathcal{P}(x_i \in A_i \{x_1 \in A_1,\ldots,x_{i-1} \in A_{i-1}\})$. Then, by considering the Cholesky decomposition of the variance–covariance matrix $\Sigma_{v(\rho,\lambda)} = CC'$, the interval limits are transformed $S_i = (a_i',b_i')$ by taking advantage of the lower triangular matrix C. The algorithm iteratively substitutes the univariate conditional probabilities with the quantities $\tilde{z}_i = \frac{\phi(a_i')-\phi(b_i')}{\Phi(b_i')-\Phi(a_i')}$ and it ends when the probability of the last random variable is computed and the approximation $\Phi_n(x_1 \in A_1,\ldots,x_n \in A_n) \approx \Pi_{i=1}^{n}(\Phi(b_i')-\Phi(a_i'))$ is reached.

The algorithm starts with the computation of $X^* = \frac{(I-\rho W_n)^{-1}X}{\sqrt{\left(\sum_{i=1}^{n}\Sigma_{ii}\right)}}$ where the matrix $(I - \rho W_n)^{-1}$ is computed by a truncation of its Taylor approximation and a starting value of ρ. Then, the interval limits (a_i, b_i) and $\left(\Phi\left(\frac{b_i}{\sqrt{(\Sigma_{ii})}}\right) - \Phi\left(\frac{a_i}{\sqrt{(\Sigma_{ii})}}\right)\right)$ are computed for each conditional probabilities starting from a random variable. By using the lower triangular matrix of Σ they compute the transformed interval limits $(\hat{b}_i,\hat{a}_i)$ and the quantities $U_i = \Phi(\hat{b}_i) - \Phi(\hat{a}_i)$. Finally, the log likelihood function is simply the sum of each contribution $\log(U_i)$.

In the following subsection we implement the above estimation procedure in R to fit spatial probit models and to empirically explain their spatial marginal effects.

4.1   Empirical Application in Labour Economics

The analysis of employment/unemployment rates at a more disaggregated geographical level began at least 20 years ago; see for example Pischke and Velling (1997). Not too long after, several researchers started to introduce in labour economics the concept of *socio-economic distance* and to use spatial and spatio-temporal econometric techniques to deal with interdependences between countries/regions of the employment/unemployment rates; see Conley and Topa (2002), Patacchini and Zenou (2007), Schanne et al. (2010), Cueto et al. (2015),

Halleck Vega and Elhorst (2016), Watson and Deller (2017) and Kosfeld and Dreger (2019), among others.

In this section we analyse a dataset that contains information freely available at the Eurostat website: https://ec.europa.eu/eurostat/data/database. After some data manipulation, the dataset consists of 312 observations (European regions at NUTS2 level) in 2016, with information on employment rates (*employment*, in %), GDP at current market price (*gdp*, measured in Euro per inhabitant), education level of population aged 25–64 (in %) for three different levels: (i) secondary school or lower (*isced_02*), (ii) high school or lower (*isced_34*) and (iii) degree, post degree, Ph.D. (*isced_58*). The involved countries are the following: Austria (AT), Belgium (BE), Bulgaria (BG), Cyprus (CY), Czech Republic (CZ), Germany (DE), Denmark (DK), Estonia (EE), Greece (EL), Spain (ES), Finland (FI), France (FR), Croatia (HR), Hungary (HU), Ireland (IE), Italy (IT), Lithuania (LT), Luxembourg (LU), Latvia (LV), Montenegro (ME), Macedonia (MK), Malta (MT), Netherlands (NL), Norway (NO), Poland (PL), Portugal (PT), Romania (RO), Serbia (RS), Sweden (SE), Slovenia (SI), Slovakia (SK), Turkey (TR) and the United Kingdom (UK). The aim of this section is to study the impact of the explanatory variables on a new binary variable, that is, the employment status (*bin.emp*), at a regional level in 2016. In a recent study (Gazzola and Mazzacani, 2019), the impact of language skills on the individual employment status within some European countries has been analysed through a probit model. In their paper there are also details on the use of the *isced* levels for education.

Once the data from the Eurostat website were read in R and after some data manipulation, we saved a `dataframe` with extension `.RData`. The function `load` is able to load the dataset called "`Dataset.RData`" specifying the right directory (path), while the function `nrow` calculates the number of rows of the dataframe that corresponds to the sample size *n*. The output can be seen by using the function head, which shows the first six rows.

```
load("C:/Users/Anna Gloria/Dropbox/Handbook/Data/Dataset.RData")
n <- nrow(data)
n
## [1] 312
head(data)
##   nuts_id  country_id  employment    gdp  isced_02  isced_34
## 1   AT11          AT        74.1  28600      16.5      55.7
## 2   AT12          AT        77.4  33300      14.7      55.1
## 3   AT13          AT        69.7  49200      16.9      43.2
## 4   AT21          AT        73.6  34200      10.6      60.0
## 5   AT22          AT        75.3  36500      14.0      58.6
## 6   AT31          AT        79.3  41600      15.7      55.3

##   isced_58   long    lat
## 1     27.9  16.52  47.53
## 2     30.2  15.75  48.24
## 3     39.9  16.39  48.19
## 4     29.4  13.88  46.77
## 5     27.4  14.98  47.26
## 6      .1  13.95  48.15
```

The dataset data already contain the spatial coordinates, that is, longitude (*long*) and latitude (*lat*), of the spatial polygons (European regions). Since the spatial observations are polygons/areas, then the spatial coordinates correspond here to their *centroids*. After having installed a package through the code install.packages("name of the package"), we can easily upload it through the use of the function library. The function readOGR in the package rgdal is particularly useful to read and transform different types of OGR vector maps (shapefiles) into spatial objects. Then, the function coordinates into the package sp is able to calculate the centroids from a spatial (polygon) object as in the following:

```
library(rgdal)
eu                       <- readOGR("C:/Users/Anna
   Gloria/Dropbox/Handbook/Data/Shapefile/EU_reg.shp")
## OGR data source with driver: ESRI Shapefile
## Source: "C:\Users\Anna
   Gloria\Dropbox\Handbook\Data\Shapefile\EU_reg.shp", layer:
   "EU_reg"
## with 312 features
## It has 5 fields
coords                   <- coordinates(eu)
colnames(coords) <- c("long", "lat")
head(coords)
##           long        lat
## 0    4.583496    50.66619
## 1    4.028426    50.44180
## 2    5.744833    50.51087
## 3    5.529503    49.95737
## 4   16.523298    47.53059
## 5   15.747114    48.24467
```

Finally, the function colnames provides column names. Figure 2.2 shows the employment rates (per cent) in 2016 for all the considered European regions. As we can observe, the majority of the highest values of the employment rates are associated with Northern and Central Europe, especially Germany, UK, Scandinavia.

Let us now move to the estimation procedure. To estimate a SAR(1)-probit model and a SAE(1)-probit model from section 3, we consider the function SpatialProbitFit in the ProbitSpatial package. The dependent variable *employment* is a continuous variable, so we need to create a dichotomous dependent variable before estimating the spatial models. To this purpose, we use the mean of the European area employment rate (EA19) as a threshold, which was equal to 70 per cent in 2016. So, if the employment rate in one European region is greater or equal than the EA19 mean value, then its binary dependent variable takes the value 1, otherwise 0. The definition of the binary variable (*bin.emp*) can be easily obtained by using the function ifelse in R.

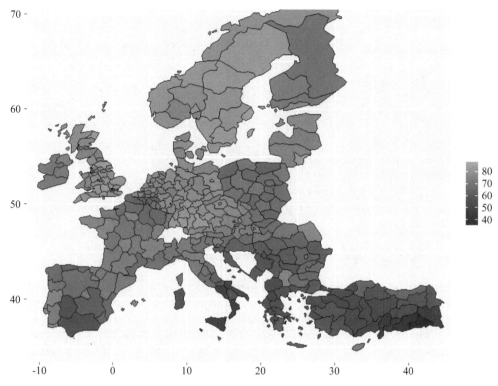

Figure 2.2   Employment rates (per cent) in 2016

```
bin.emp <- ifelse(data$employment >= 70, 1, 0)
data     <- data.frame(data,bin.emp)
```

We first regress a standard probit model without the intercept by using the glm function and see the output through the function summary.

```
fit            <- glm(bin.emp ~ gdp + isced_02 + isced_34 + isced_58 + 0,
                   family = binomial(link="probit"),data=data)
summary(fit)
##
## Call:
## glm(formula = bin.emp ~ gdp + isced_02 + isced_34 + isced_58 +
##     0, family = binomial(link = "probit"), data = data)
##
## Deviance Residuals:
##     Min        1Q    Median        3Q       Max
## -3.7458   -0.1808    0.2046    0.5790    2.4590
##
```

```
## Coefficients:
##                Estimate Std. Error z value Pr(>|z|)
## gdp           6.697e-05  1.110e-05   6.036  1.58e-09 ***
## isced_02     -4.707e-02  6.361e-03  -7.401  1.36e-13 ***
## isced_34      2.503e-03  4.219e-03   0.593     0.553
## isced_58      2.832e-03  1.069e-02   0.265     0.791
## -
## Signif. codes:  0 `***' 0.001 `**' 0.01 `*' 0.05 `.' 0.1 ` ` 1
##
## (Dispersion parameter for binomial family taken to be 1)
##
##          Null deviance: 432.52 on 312 degrees of freedom
## Residual deviance: 203.84 on 308 degrees of freedom
## AIC: 211.84
##
## Number of Fisher Scoring iterations: 7
```

Now consider the spatial probit model specifications. In order to fit a spatial model, we need to build our spatial weighting matrix. In this case we exploit the information of the geographical coordinates (centroids) of the spatial polygons, that is, of the European regions. For this application we use the *k*-nearest neighbour criterion defined as follows. Let $W = \{w_{ij}\}$ be the spatial weighting matrix with elements equal to the weights among pairs of random variables y_i, y_j for $i, j = 1, \ldots, n$, with n the sample size, then

$$\begin{cases} w_{ij} = 1 \ \textit{iff} \ y_j \in \mathcal{N}_k \\ w_{ij} = 0 \ \textit{otherwise} \end{cases}$$

where $\mathcal{N}_k$ is the set of nearest random variables y_j to y_i defined by k. Finally, W is row-normalized such that $\sum_j w_{ij} = 1, \forall i$.

To build our weighting matrix W we first load the package spdep; see Bivand and Piras (2015). The function knearneigh provides a list of class *knn* with the information into the first member of the region number IDs to define the nearest neighbours for each random variable (in this case $k = 11$). The knn2nb function transforms the object of class *knn* into an object of class *nb* (neighbour list). The argument sym=T forces the weighting matrix to be symmetric. The nb2mat function transforms, instead, an object of class *nb* into an *n*-dimensional weighting matrix. The argument style = "W" directly row-normalizes the weights, while the function as(, "CsparseMatrix") defines the weighting matrix to be sparse. Finally, the function dim provides information about the dimension of the spatial weighting matrix.

```
library(spdep)
knn11 <- knn2nb(knearneigh(cbind(data$long,data$lat), k=11),sym=T)
Wknn_sparse <- as(nb2mat(knn11,style="W"),"CsparseMatrix")
dim(Wknn_sparse)

## [1] 312 312
```

We can now load the package `ProbitSpatial` and use the function `SpatialProbitFit` inside. This function is able to fit the SAR(1)-probit model or the SAE(1)-probit (also SEM-probit) model defined in section 3. The argument `DGP=` specifies the type of model, while `W=` and `method=` provide information on the weighting matrix and the estimation method, respectively. For details use the help function in R as `?SpatialProbitFit`.

```
library(ProbitSpatial)
fit.sp1 <- SpatialProbitFit(bin.emp ~ gdp + isced_02 + isced_34 +
     isced_58 + 0,
                             data=data, W=Wknn_sparse, DGP='SAR',
                             method="full-lik")
## St. dev. of beta conditional on rho and Lik-ratio of rho
##                  Estimate      Std. Error    z-value     Pr(>|z|)
## gdp           3.754825e-05   6.839877e-06   5.4896086  4.028254e-08
## isced_02     -3.114469e-02   4.231689e-03  -7.3598718  1.840750e-13
## isced_34     -1.523355e-03   2.993939e-03  -0.5088129  6.108834e-01
## isced_58      9.102693e-03   7.938271e-03   1.1466846  2.515120e-01
## lambda        5.084473e-01             NA  19.6485634  9.307326e-06


fit.sp2 <- SpatialProbitFit(bin.emp ~ gdp + isced_02 + isced_34 +
     isced_58 + 0,
                             data=data, W=Wknn_sparse, DGP='SEM',
                             method="full-lik")
## St. dev. of beta conditional on rho and Lik-ratio of rho
##                  Estimate      Std. Error    z-value     Pr(>|z|)
## gdp           7.476664e-05   1.414341e-05   5.2863230  1.247994e-07
## isced_02     -5.220912e-02   7.059491e-03  -7.3955937  1.407763e-13
## isced_34      1.445296e-02   4.171657e-03   3.4645615  5.310968e-04
## isced_58     -9.685959e-03   1.192018e-02  -0.8125681  4.164657e-01
## rho           6.372373e-01             NA  13.5257220  2.353158e-04
```

Table 2.1 shows the estimation results of the standard probit model, the SAR(1)-probit model and the SAE(1)-probit model, respectively. Regardless of the specific European region, the variables *gdp* and *isced_02* are statistically significant at $\alpha = 0.001$ for all the three model specifications. This reflects on a higher probability of being employed for higher values of *gdp* due to the positive sign of its coefficient and a lower probability of being employed for higher percentage values of people with a secondary school education level at most due to its negative coefficient.

Specifically for the spatial models, both the estimated autoregressive coefficients ($\hat{\rho}, \hat{\lambda}$) are significant. Their estimates are quite high with respect to the upper bound 1, highlighting an important role played by spatial dependence. Moreover, due to their positive signs, both the autoregressive processes in the dependent variables and in the error terms are not inhibitory, leading to a positive interconnection (clustering process) between units over space. From

Table 2.1   Estimation results

	Standard probit	SAR(1)-probit	SAE(1)-probit
gdp	0.00007	0.00004	0.00007
s.e.	0.00001	0.00001	0.00001
isced_02	−0.04707	−0.03114	−0.05221
s.e.	0.00636	0.00423	0.00704
isced_34	0.00250	−0.00152	0.01445
s.e.	0.00422	0.00299	0.00415
isced_58	0.00283	0.00910	−0.00969
s.e.	0.01069	0.00794	0.01186
rho	NA	0.50845	NA
s.e.	NA	NA	NA
lambda	NA	NA	0.63724
s.e.	NA	NA	NA
Loglik	−101.92212	92.09784	95.15926

an economic point of view, the higher the probability of being employed in one region the higher the probability of being employed in its neighbourhood, and vice versa. These effects propagate with a decreasing magnitude through all the other regions.

Let us now consider the marginal effects. As explained in subsection 3.1, one way to calculate the marginal effects in probit models consists in evaluating the average of the individual (local) marginal effects with respect to each regressor of interest. In a spatial context, these local effects depend on the estimated coefficients $(\hat{\beta}, \hat{\rho}, \hat{\lambda})$, according to the type of model specification. The result with respect to each regressor is a square matrix of impacts, where the diagonal elements are the *direct effects* whereas the off-diagonal elements are the *indirect effects*. The average of these elements provides a summary measure of the impact due directly to the regressor and a summary measure due to the neighbouring dependent variables, respectively. In the following we can observe these average effects for the SAR(1)-probit model with respect to each regressor:

```
m.effects.sar <- rbind(av.dir.eff,av.ind.eff,av.tot.eff)
rownames(m.effects.sar) <- c("direct","indirect","total")
colnames(m.effects.sar) <- c("gdp","isced_02","isced_34",
  "isced_58")
m.effects.sar
##                   gdp      isced_02       isced_34     isced_58
## direct    5.836276e-06 -0.004840945 -0.0002367812 0.001414868
## indirect  5.699937e-06 -0.004727858 -0.0002312499 0.001381816
## total     1.153621e-05 -0.009568804 -0.0004680311 0.002796685
```

There is a clear balance between average direct and average indirect effects for all the considered regressors, while the greatest total impact in absolute value is due to *isced_02*. Note that although some regressor coefficients are not significant, like *isced_34* and *isced_58*, in this case the average direct, indirect and total impacts should be considered since the autoregressive coefficient ρ is instead significant and directly affects all the marginal effects.

The same occurs for the SAE(1)-probit specification, where in this case the impacts due to the spillover effects seem to be more pronounced.

```
m.effects.sae <- rbind(av.dir.eff,av.ind.eff,av.tot.eff)
rownames(m.effects.sae) <- c("direct","indirect","total")
colnames(m.effects.sae) <- c("gdp","isced_02","isced_34",
   "isced_58")
m.effects.sae
##                    gdp      isced_02      ced_34       isced_58
## direct    3.985610e-06 -0.002783129 0.0007704489 -0.0005163326
## indirect  6.395970e-06 -0.004466270 0.0012363899 -0.0008285928
## total     1.038158e-05 -0.007249399 0.0020068387 -0.0013449255
```

Figures 2.3 and 2.4 show the local (total) marginal effects from a SAR(1)-probit model and a SAE(1)-probit model, respectively, sorted from low to high values. In this way, we

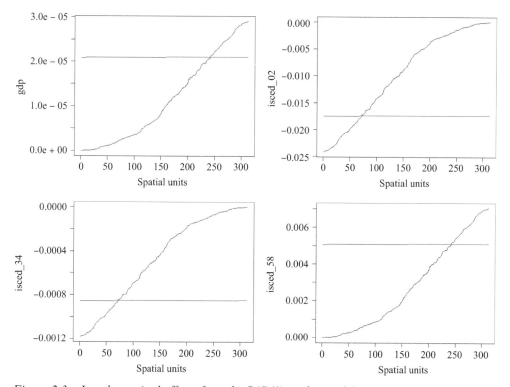

Figure 2.3   Local marginal effects from the SAR(1)-probit model

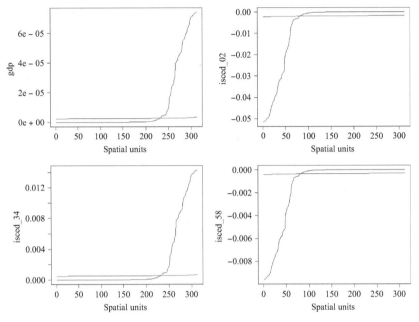

Figure 2.4   Local marginal effects from the SAE(1)-probit model

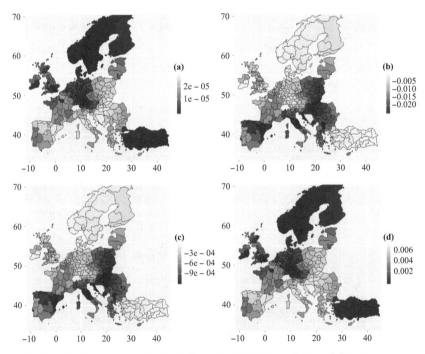

Figure 2.5   Local total marginal effects from the SAR(1)-probit model in Europe:
(a) gdp, (b) isced_02, (c) isced_34, (d) isced_58

are able to evaluate the range of variation of the total marginal effects for different regions and compare these values with the average one. For instance, it is interesting to note that, in Figure 2.4, the distributions of the marginal effects are more asymmetric than the ones in Figure 2.3.

Figures 2.5 and 2.6 show instead the local marginal effects from a SAR(1)-probit model and a SAE(1)-probit model, respectively, on the different European regions. The point in this case is to geographically identify regions with greater or lower marginal impacts. As we can observe from Figure 2.5, the positive total impact of the *gdp* on employment rates reaches its lowest values in Scandinavia, UK, Germany and Turkey. Although the magnitude is different according to different regressors, the same occurs for the variable *isced_58*. On the contrary, quite the opposite can be found for the variable *isced_02* and *isced_34*, because of the negative sign in these cases. A plausible conclusion might be that both the direct effects from the regressors and the indirect effects due to neighbouring regions generally have a lower impact in Scandinavia, UK, Germany and Turkey, with respect to the other European countries. It is finally worth noting that one can be interested in evaluating only the direct or the indirect effects, although both of them depend on the spatial dependence coefficient. Careful attention should be paid to the proper interpretation of the marginal effects, since they are the link between estimation results and policy interventions.

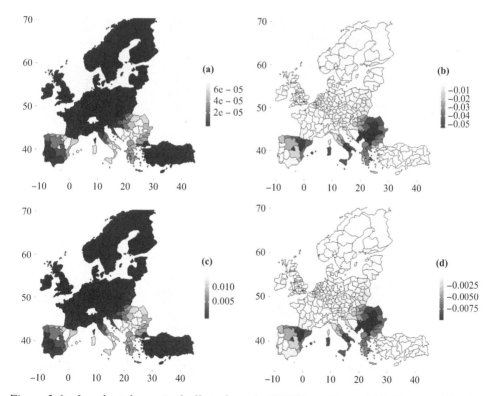

Figure 2.6   Local total marginal effects from the SAE(1)-probit model in Europe: (a) gdp, (b) isced_02, (c) isced_34, (d) isced_58

REFERENCES

Ahrens, Achim, and Arnab Bhattacharjee. 2015. "Two-Step Lasso Estimation of the Spatial Weights Matrix." *Econometrics* 3 (1): 128–55.

Amemiya, Takeshi. 1985. *Advanced Econometrics*. Harvard University Press.

Anselin, Luc. 1988. *Spatial Econometrics: Methods and Models*. Vol. 4. Springer Science & Business Media.

Anselin, Luc, and Anil K Bera. 1998. "Spatial Dependence in Linear Regression Models with an Introduction to Spatial Econometrics", in: Ullah, A. and Giles, D. (eds.), *Handbook of Applied Economic Statistics*, Marcel Dekker, 237−89.

Arbia, Giuseppe. 2014. *A Primer for Spatial Econometrics: With Applications in R*. Springer.

Arbia, Giuseppe, Marco Bee, and Giuseppe Espa. 2013. "Testing Isotropy in Spatial Econometric Models." *Spatial Economic Analysis* 8 (3): 228–40.

Arbia, Giuseppe, Giuseppe Espa, and Diego Giuliani. 2021. *Spatial Microeconometrics*. Routledge, Taylor & Francis Group.

Badinger, Harald and Peter Egger. 2011. "Estimation of Higher-Order Spatial Autoregressive Cross-Section Models with Heteroscedastic Disturbances." *Papers in Regional Science* 90 (1): 213–35.

Bhattacharjee, Arnab, and Chris Jensen-Butler. 2013. "Estimation of the Spatial Weights Matrix Under Structural Constraints." *Regional Science and Urban Economics* 43 (4): 617–34.

Billé, Anna Gloria. 2013. "Computational Issues in the Estimation of the Spatial Probit Model: A Comparison of Various Estimators." *Review of Regional Studies* 43 (2, 3): 131–54.

Billé, Anna Gloria, and Giuseppe Arbia. 2019. "Spatial Limited Dependent Variable Models: A Review Focused on Specification, Estimation and Health Economics Applications." *Journal of Economic Surveys* 33 (5): 1531–54.

Billé, Anna Gloria, Francisco Blasques, and Leopoldo Catania. 2019. "Dynamic Spatial Autoregressive Models with Time-Varying Spatial Weighting Matrices." Available at SSRN 3241470.

Billé, Anna Gloria, and Samantha Leorato. 2020. "Partial ML Estimation for Spatial Autoregressive Nonlinear Probit Models with Autoregressive Disturbances." *Econometric Reviews* 39 (5): 437–75.

Bivand, Roger, and Gianfranco Piras. 2015. "Comparing Implementations of Estimation Methods for Spatial Econometrics." *Journal of Statistical Software*, https://doi.org/10.18637/jss.v063.i18.

Cameron, A Colin, and Pravin K Trivedi. 2005. *Microeconometrics: Methods and Applications*. Cambridge University Press.

Case, Anne C, Harvey S Rosen, and James R Hines Jr. 1993. "Budget Spillovers and Fiscal Policy Interdependence: Evidence from the States." *Journal of Public Economics* 52 (3): 285–307.

Catania, Leopoldo, and Anna Gloria Billé. 2017. "Dynamic Spatial Autoregressive Models with Autoregressive and Heteroskedastic Disturbances." *Journal of Applied Econometrics* 32 (6): 1178–96.

Conley, Timothy G. 2010. "Spatial Econometrics." In *Microeconometrics*, 303–13. Springer.

Conley, Timothy G, and Francesca Molinari. 2007. "Spatial Correlation Robust Inference with Errors in Location or Distance." *Journal of Econometrics* 140 (1): 76–96.

Conley, Timothy G, and Giorgio Topa. 2002. "Socio-Economic Distance and Spatial Patterns in Unemployment." *Journal of Applied Econometrics* 17 (4): 303–27.

Corrado, Luisa, and Bernard Fingleton. 2012. "Where Is the Economics in Spatial Econometrics?" *Journal of Regional Science* 52 (2): 210–39.

Cueto, Begoña, Matías Mayor, and Patricia Suárez. 2015. "Entrepreneurship and Unemployment in Spain: A Regional Analysis." *Applied Economics Letters* 22 (15): 1230–35.

Debarsy, Nicolas, and James LeSage. 2018. "Flexible Dependence Modeling Using Convex Combinations of Different Types of Connectivity Structures." *Regional Science and Urban Economics* 69: 48–68.

Elhorst, J Paul. 2014. *Spatial Econometrics: From Cross-Sectional Data to Spatial Panels*. Vol. 479. Springer.

Elhorst, J Paul, Donald J Lacombe, and Gianfranco Piras. 2012. "On Model Specification and Parameter Space Definitions in Higher Order Spatial Econometric Models." *Regional Science and Urban Economics* 42 (1–2): 211–20.

Fingleton, Bernard, and Guiseppe Arbia. 2008. "New Spatial Econometric Techniques and Applications in Regional Science." *Papers in Regional Science* 87 (3): 311–17.

Gazzola, Michele, and Daniele Mazzacani. 2019. "Foreign Language Skills and Employment Status of European Natives: Evidence from Germany, Italy and Spain." *Empirica* 46 (4): 713–40.

Getis, Arthur, and Jared Aldstadt. 2004. "Constructing the Spatial Weights Matrix Using a Local Statistic." *Geographical Analysis* 36 (2): 90–104.

Halleck Vega, Solmaria, and J Paul Elhorst. 2016. "A Regional Unemployment Model Simultaneously Accounting for Serial Dynamics, Spatial Dependence and Common Factors." *Regional Science and Urban Economics* 60: 85–95.

Han, Xiaoyi, Chih-Sheng Hsieh, Lung-fei Lee. 2017. "Estimation and Model Selection of Higher-Order Spatial Autoregressive Model: An Efficient Bayesian Approach." *Regional Science and Urban Economics* 63: 97–120.

Kelejian, Harry H, and Gianfranco Piras. 2014. "Estimation of Spatial Models with Endogenous Weighting Matrices, and an Application to a Demand Model for Cigarettes." *Regional Science and Urban Economics* 46: 140–49.

Kelejian, Harry H, and Gianfranco Piras. 2017. *Spatial Econometrics*. Academic Press.

Kelejian, Harry H, and Ingmar R Prucha. 1998. "A Generalized Spatial Two-Stage Least Squares Procedure for Estimating a Spatial Autoregressive Model with Autoregressive Disturbances." *The Journal of Real Estate Finance and Economics* 17 (1): 99–121.

Kelejian, Harry H, and Ingmar R Prucha. 2010. "Specification and Estimation of Spatial Autoregressive Models with Autoregressive and Heteroskedastic Disturbances." *Journal of Econometrics* 157 (1): 53–67.

Klier, Thomas, and Daniel P McMillen. 2008. "Clustering of Auto Supplier Plants in the United States: Generalized Method of Moments Spatial Logit for Large Samples." *Journal of Business & Economic Statistics* 26 (4): 460–71.

Kosfeld, Reinhold, and Christian Dreger. 2019. "Towards an East German Wage Curve-Nuts Boundaries, Labour Market Regions and Unemployment Spillovers." *Regional Science and Urban Economics* 76: 115–24.

Le Gallo, Julie, and Bernard Fingleton. 2012. "Measurement Errors in a Spatial Context." *Regional Science and Urban Economics* 42 (1–2): 114–25.

Lee, Lung-Fei. 2004. "Asymptotic Distributions of Quasi-Maximum Likelihood Estimators for Spatial Autoregressive Models." *Econometrica* 72 (6): 1899–1925.

LeSage, James P. 2014. "What Regional Scientists Need to Know About Spatial Econometrics." *The Review of Regional Studies* 44 (1): 13.

LeSage, James, and R Kelly Pace. 2014. "The Biggest Myth in Spatial Econometrics." *Econometrics* 2 (4): 217–49.

LeSage, James P, R Kelley Pace, Nina Lam, Richard Campanella, and Xingjian Liu. 2011. "New Orleans Business Recovery in the Aftermath of Hurricane Katrina." *Journal of the Royal Statistical Society: Series A (Statistics in Society)* 174 (4): 1007–27.

LeSage, James P, and R Kelley Pace. 2009. *Introduction to Spatial Econometrics*. Chapman & Hall/CRC.

Maddala, Gangadharrao S. 1986. *Limited-Dependent and Qualitative Variables in Econometrics*. Cambridge University Press.

Martinetti, Davide, and Ghislain Geniaux. 2017. "Approximate Likelihood Estimation of Spatial Probit Models." *Regional Science and Urban Economics* 64: 30–45.

McFadden, Daniel L. 1984. "Econometric Analysis of Qualitative Response Models." In *Handbook of Econometrics* 2: 1395–1457.

Mozharovskyi, Pavlo, and Jan Vogler. 2016. "Composite Marginal Likelihood Estimation of Spatial Autoregressive Probit Models Feasible in Very Large Samples." *Economics Letters* 148: 87–90.

Otto, Philipp, and Rick Steinert. 2018. "Estimation of the Spatial Weighting Matrix for Spatiotemporal Data Under the Presence of Structural Breaks." *arXiv Preprint arXiv:1810.06940*.

Pace, R Kelley, and Ronald Barry. 1997. "Sparse Spatial Autoregressions." *Statistics & Probability Letters* 33 (3): 291–97.

Pace, R Kelley, and James P LeSage. 2004. "Chebyshev Approximation of Log-Determinants of Spatial Weight Matrices." *Computational Statistics & Data Analysis* 45 (2): 179–96.

Patacchini, Eleonora, and Yves Zenou. 2007. "Spatial Dependence in Local Unemployment Rates." *Journal of Economic Geography* 7 (2): 169–91.

Pinkse, Joris, and Margaret E Slade. 2010. "The Future of Spatial Econometrics." *Journal of Regional Science* 50 (1): 103–17.

Pinkse, Joris, Margaret E Slade, and Craig Brett. 2002. "Spatial Price Competition: A Semiparametric Approach." *Econometrica* 70 (3): 1111–53.

Pischke, Jörn-Steffen, and Johannes Velling. 1997. "Employment Effects of Immigration to Germany: An Analysis Based on Local Labor Markets." *Review of Economics and Statistics* 79 (4): 594–604.

Qu, Xi, and Lung-fei Lee. 2015. "Estimating a Spatial Autoregressive Model with an Endogenous Spatial Weight Matrix." *Journal of Econometrics* 184 (2): 209–32.

Santos, Luís Silveira, and Isabel Proença. 2019. "The Inversion of the Spatial Lag Operator in Binary Choice Models: Fast Computation and a Closed Formula Approximation." *Regional Science and Urban Economics* 76: 74–102.

Schanne, Norbert, Rüdiger Wapler, and Antje Weyh. 2010. "Regional Unemployment Forecasts with Spatial Interdependencies." *International Journal of Forecasting* 26 (4): 908–26.

Smirnov, Oleg, and Luc Anselin. 2001. "Fast Maximum Likelihood Estimation of Very Large Spatial Autoregressive Models: A Characteristic Polynomial Approach." *Computational Statistics & Data Analysis* 35 (3): 301–19.

Wang, Honglin, Emma M Iglesias, and Jeffrey M Wooldridge. 2013. "Partial Maximum Likelihood Estimation of Spatial Probit Models." *Journal of Econometrics* 172 (1): 77–89.

Watson, Philip, and Steven Deller. 2017. "Economic Diversity, Unemployment and the Great Recession." *The Quarterly Review of Economics and Finance* 64: 1–11.

3. Econometric analyses of auctions: a selective review[*]
Tong Li and Xiaoyong Zheng

1. INTRODUCTION

Auctions have been used as an important trading mechanism when there is asymmetric information among bidders and also between the seller and bidders, in which case other mechanisms such as posting prices, contracting or bargaining may not be as effective for determining prices or allocating goods. Over the past half century, beginning with the seminal work of Vickrey (1961), theoretical studies of auctions based on game theory with incomplete and asymmetric information have been conducted extensively, and auction theory has been very successful in providing insight into players' strategic behavior and in addressing mechanism design questions. For surveys of the theoretical literature on auctions, see Krishna (2010), Klemperer (2004) and Milgrom (2004).

Auctions have also provided opportunities for researchers to analyze field data, which are widely available due to the widespread use of auctions; for instance, Outer Continental Shelf (OCS) drilling rights auctions, timber auctions organized by both federal and state governments, state government-run procurement auctions, among others, have been extensively studied in the empirical literature. Empirical analysis of auction data has become a very active and fruitful area since the work of Kenneth Hendricks and Robert Porter (for example Hendricks and Porter, 1988); their work has pioneered testing predictions from the theory under the incomplete information environment. The structural analysis, developed later since Paarsch (1992), has demonstrated its ability to integrate economic theory, econometric methods and data analysis into a unified framework to uncover the underlying model fundamentals and thereby conduct counterfactual analyses offering insight into the players' strategic behavior, to address mechanism design questions and to provide guidance in public policy debates. The fast-growing literature on the structural approach has been helped by the advances in econometric theory and methods; the structural analysis of auctions that consists of identification, estimation and inference, on the other hand, has raised many challenging issues and pushed the frontier of econometric research.

There have been a number of surveys that review the methods developed in the empirical analysis of auction data; see for example Perrigne and Vuong (1999), Paarsch and Hong (2006), Athey and Haile (2007), Hendricks and Porter (2007), Hickman et al. (2012), and Gentry et al. (2018). These surveys have different focuses and, given that nonparametric identification and estimation have made significant advances in the structural analysis of auction data and seen wide applications, considerable attention has been paid to the nonparametric approaches in auctions, with Athey and Haile (2007) fully devoted to this topic and most other surveys also discussing the topic at length. In our survey, we will review the work on the following topics: testing, semiparametric methods and partial identification approaches. These topics are important in their own right, yet they have either received less attention or some of the most recent work has not been discussed in the existing surveys.

We also view these three approaches as vital for future research in the empirical analysis of auctions.

Testing model implications or informational assumptions has been one of the most important goals for empirical researchers studying auction data since the seminal work of Hendricks and Porter (1988). The semiparametric approach provides a useful middle ground between a fully parametric approach that makes strong distributional assumptions for the model primitives and a fully nonparametric approach that often requires a large data set and may also suffer from the curse of dimensionality problem. The partial identification approach since the seminal work by Haile and Tamer (2003) offers promising alternatives to cases where weaker assumptions are made in order to render point identification and/or more general or realistic information structures are considered.

This survey is organized as follows. In section 2, we survey the work on testing model implications or informational assumptions. In section 3, we survey the work on the semiparametric approaches. In section 4, we survey the work on the partial identification approaches. Section 5 concludes.

2.   TESTING

This section discusses the empirical auction literature on testing either predictions or implications from game-theoretic models or on testing the informational assumptions. While most of the related work uses the reduced-form approach, it is closely related to theory as predictions/ implications are derived from the theoretical model and the informational assumptions are made to derive testable implications.

2.1   Testing Predictions/Implications from Game-Theoretic Auction Models

Kenneth Hendricks and Robert Porter pioneered the field of testing predictions from game-theoretic auction models by using OCS data to test predictions from symmetric or asymmetric common value models. In Hendricks et al. (1987), the authors test whether the bidding behavior observed in the OCS auctions (both wildcats and drainage tracts) is consistent with implications from the common value auction model using data on ex post values of the auctioned object (π) and the oil production and drilling costs. Their first test is to compare the average $\pi - B$ (where B is the bid) for each firm on the tracts the firm won and the tracts the firm did not win. Results show that, for each firm, the average profit $\pi - B$ is substantially lower on tracts the firm won than on the tracts the firm did not win. This is consistent with the winner's curse, a key prediction from the common value auction model.

Their second exercise calculates the revenues a firm would have earned had it rescaled all its bids by a factor of θ, holding constant the bids of all other firms. Specifically, θ^* is the solution to the following maximization problem:

$$R_i(\theta) = \sum_{k \in K_i} \left(\pi_k - \theta b_{ik} \right) I\left\{ \theta b_{ik} - \bar{B}_{ik} \right\},$$

where K_i is the set of tracts firm i had bid on, π_k is the ex post value of tract k, b_{ik} is firm i's bid for tract k and $\bar{B}_{ik}$ represents the highest bid other than firm i's bid on tract k; $I\{\theta b_{ik} - \bar{B}_{ik}\} = 1$

if $\theta b_{ik} - \bar{B}_{ik} \geq 0$. If firms choose their bids according to the risk-neutral Nash equilibrium, then the optimal θ^* should be close to 1 as, by the definition of the Nash equilibrium, firms have no incentives to deviate from the actual bids and they bid according to the equilibrium. Results show that, for most firms, θ^* is less than 1. This means firms actually over-bid. This again indicates the presence of the winner's curse.

Hendricks and Porter (1988) test the implications from a common-value, first-price, sealed bid auction with asymmetric bidders. One informed bidder (neighbor firm) and n uninformed bidders (non-neighbor firms) participate in the auction. The uninformed bidders only observe a public signal of the unknown common value, while the informed bidder observes both the public signal as well as a private signal. Furthermore, the private signal is a sufficient statistic for the public signal. The authors solve the model and derive the following model implications: (1) The event that no neighbor firm bids occurs less frequently than the event that no non-neighbor firm bids. (2) The neighbor firm wins at least one half of the tracts. (3) Expected profits to non-neighbor firms are zero. They are negative on the set of tracts where no neighbor firm bids and positive on the set of tracts where the neighbor firm bids. (4) Expected profits to the neighbor firm contain an information premium, which makes its earnings above "average". (5) If the value of the tract for the informed bidder is the same as that of the uninformed bidders, the ex ante bid distributions (that is, prior to the realization of the private signal X) are approximately the same. (6) The bidding strategy of the neighbor firm is independent of the number of non-neighbor firms. (7) The bidding strategy of the neighbor firm is an increasing function of the public signal, when a larger signal is "good news".

The authors have the following data for each tract auctioned: the date of the auction; the location and acreage of the auction; which firms bid and the value of their bids; and the ex post value of the auctioned tract. Using this set of information, the authors tested the first four model implications using summary statistics of the data. For example, to test model implication 1, they counted the number of tracts that received no neighbor bids and the number of tracts that received no non-neighbor bids. To test for model implications 5–7, the authors estimate the following bivariate equation system:

$$Y_{it} = \log(B_{it} / R_t) = W_{it}'\theta_i + \varepsilon_{it} \text{ if } Y_{it} \geq 0$$

$$= 0 \text{ otherwise,}$$

where $i = I, U$ and I and U stand for informed and uninformed, respectively; R_t is the reserve price for auction t, B_{it}s are the highest bids among informed/uninformed bidders, W_{it} is a vector of regressors and θ_is are the parameters to be estimated. The errors $\{\varepsilon_{It}, \varepsilon_{Ut}\}$ are bivariate normal with zero mean, variances σ_I^2 and σ_U^2 and covariance σ_{IU}. The variable W_{it} includes the acreage of the tract, the ex post value of this tract and its square (to test 6), the number of non-neighbor bids (to test 7), the number of nearby tracts and the ex post values of adjacent tracts and their squares. The tracts in the data can be partitioned into three mutually exclusive sets: Ω_{++} is the set of tracts with at least one neighbor bid and at least one non-neighbor bid, Ω_{+0} is the set of tracts with at least one neighbor bid and no non-neighbor bids and Ω_{0+} is the set of tracts with no neighbor bids and at least one non-neighbor bid. The log likelihood function for the entire sample can then be written as

$$\log L = \sum_{t \in \Omega_{++}} l_{1t} + \sum_{t \in \Omega_{+0}} l_{2t} + \sum_{t \in \Omega_{0+}} l_{3t},$$

where

$$l_{1t} = -\left[\log(2\pi) + (1/2)\log|\Sigma|\right]$$
$$-(1/2)\left(\varepsilon_{It}, \varepsilon_{Ut}\right)\Sigma^{-1}\left(\varepsilon_{It}, \varepsilon_{Ut}\right)'$$
$$-\log\left(1 - Z(-W'_{Ut}\theta_U / \sigma_U, -W'_{It}\theta_I / \sigma_I; \rho_{IU})\right),$$

$$l_{2t} = \log\left(\Phi\left\{\left[-W'_{Ut}\theta_U - \sigma_{IU}\sigma_I^{-2}\varepsilon_{It}\right] / \left[\sigma_U^2 - \sigma_{IU}^2\sigma_I^{-2}\right]^{1/2}\right\}\right)$$
$$-\log(\sigma_I) + \log(\phi(\varepsilon_{It} / \sigma_I))$$
$$-\log\left(1 - Z(-W'_{Ut}\theta_U / \sigma_U, -W'_{It}\theta_I / \sigma_I; \rho_{IU})\right),$$

$$l_{3t} = \log\left(\Phi\left\{\left[-W'_{It}\theta_I - \sigma_{IU}\sigma_U^{-2}\varepsilon_{Ut}\right] / \left[\sigma_I^2 - \sigma_{IU}^2\sigma_U^{-2}\right]^{1/2}\right\}\right)$$
$$-\log(\sigma_U) + \log(\phi(\varepsilon_{Ut} / \sigma_U))$$
$$-\log\left(1 - Z(-W'_{Ut}\theta_U / \sigma_U, -W'_{It}\theta_I / \sigma_I; \rho_{IU})\right),$$

where Σ is the covariance matrix, ρ_{IU} is the correlation coefficient and $Z(.,.)$ is the function for the probability of an event for which no bid is observed on a tract.[1]

Hendricks et al. (2003) test implications from a symmetric, affiliated value (AV) model with entry. They also test the implications of a special case of this model, that is, the symmetric common value (CV) model with entry. They define potential bidders as those who have commissioned a survey of the area containing tract t, active bidders as those who invest in tract-specific survey and actual bidders as those who actually bid. They use l to denote the number of potential bidders and n to denote the number of active bidders. Bidder i's utility is $U_i = u(V, S_i)$, where V is the common value and S_i is bidder i's signal; $(V, S_1, \ldots, S_I)$ are affiliated.

Definition (Milgrom and Weber, 1982): Let z and z' be vectors, $z \vee z'$ denote the component-wise maximum of z and z' and $z \wedge z'$ denote the component-wise minimum of z and z'. We say that the variables are affiliated if, for all z and z', we have

$$f(z \vee z')f(z \wedge z') \geq f(z)f(z'), \tag{3.1}$$

where $f(z)$ is the joint probability density of z.

Denote Y_1 as the maximal signal among bidder 1's rivals. Define

$$w(s, y) = E[u(V, s) | S_1 = s, Y_1 = y, N \geq 2]$$

and

$$w(s) = E[u(V, s) | S_1 = s, N = 1].$$

The authors proved in Lemma 2 that both $w(s,s)$ and $w(s)$ are increasing in s.

Suppose each bidder adopts the monotone increasing bidding strategy $b = \beta(s)$ and the inverse bidding function as $\eta(b)$. Under the assumption of risk neutrality, bidder 1's optimization problem can be written as

$$\Pi(b,s) = (1 - p_0(s))\int_{\underline{s}}^{\eta(b)}(w(s,y) - b)h_{Y_1|S_1}(y|s)dy + p_0(s)(w(s) - b),$$

where $p_0(s) = \Pr(N = 1|S_1 = s, N \geq 1)$ is the probability that bidder 1 is the only active bidder, $h_{Y_1|S_1}(y|s)$ is the conditional probability density function (pdf) for $Y_1 = y$ conditional on $S_1 = s$ and $H_{Y_1|S_1}(\cdot|\cdot)$ is the corresponding cumulative density function (cdf). Note here that, when active bidders bid, they observe the number of potential bidders but not the number of active bidders. The first-order condition (FOC) to this maximization problem can be written as

$$(1 - p_0(s))\left[(w(s,s) - \beta(s))\frac{h_{Y_1|S_1}(s|s)}{\beta'(s)} - H_{Y_1|S_1}(s|s)\right] - p_0(s) = 0. \tag{3.2}$$

Denote B_1 the bid of bidder 1 and M_1 the highest bid of his rivals if there is at least one rival and r (the reserve price) if there is no other rival, then the conditional cdf of M_1 given B_1 can be written as

$$G_{M_1|B_1}(m|b) = \Pr(M_1 \leq m|B_1 = b) \tag{3.3}$$

$$= \left[1 - p_0(s)\right]\Pr(M_1 \leq m|B_1 = b) + p_0(s)\Pr(r \leq m|B_1 = b)$$

$$= \left[1 - p_0(\eta(b))\right]\Pr(Y_1 \leq \eta(m)|S_1 = \eta(b)) + p_0(\eta(b))$$

$$= \left[1 - p_0(\eta(b))\right]H_{Y_1|S_1}(\eta(m)|\eta(b)) + p_0(\eta(b)),$$

where the third equality follows from the fact that we only consider $m \geq r$ with the observed bids. As a result,

$$g_{M_1|B_1}(m|b) = \frac{\left[1 - p_0(\eta(b))\right]h_{Y_1|S_1}(\eta(m)|\eta(b))}{\beta'(\eta(m))}. \tag{3.4}$$

Substituting (3.3) and (3.4) into (3.2), we get

$$w(\eta(b),\eta(b)) = b + \frac{G_{M_1|B_1}(m|b)}{g_{M_1|B_1}(m|b)} = \xi(b,G). \tag{3.5}$$

One model implication is that $w(s, s)$ and $w(s)$ are increasing in s. To test this, equivalently, we can test whether $\xi(b, G)$ is increasing in b.

When the model is the special case of CV, that is, $u(V, S) = V$, we have

$$w(s,s) = E[V|S_1 = s, Y_1 = y, N \geq 2] \tag{3.6}$$

$$= E[V|B_1 = b, M_1 = b, N \geq 2]$$

$$= \zeta(b).$$

Therefore, from (3.5) and (3.6), we also have

$$\zeta(b) = \xi(b,G)$$

for $N \geq 2$. Therefore, to test the CV model, we can test whether $\zeta(b) = \xi(b, G)$.

To test whether $\xi(b, G)$ is increasing, they estimate $\xi(b, G)$ using the nonparametric kernel method,

$$\hat{\xi}(b,G) = b + \frac{h_m \sum_{t=1}^{T} \frac{1}{n_t^*} \sum_{i=1}^{n_t^*} k\left(\frac{b-B_{it}}{h_b}\right) I(M_{it} < b)}{\sum_{t=1}^{T} \frac{1}{n_t^*} \sum_{i=1}^{n_t^*} k\left(\frac{b-B_{it}}{h_b}\right) k\left(\frac{b-M_{it}}{h_m}\right)},$$

where k is the kernel function, h_m and h_b are the tuning parameters and $I(\cdot)$ is the indicator function. Here, T is the number of auctions and n_t^* is the number actual bidders in auction t. The authors then plot $\xi(b, G)$ against b and examine whether it is increasing.

Second, to test whether $\zeta(b) = \xi(b, G)$, they also need to estimate $\zeta(b) = E[V|B_1 = b, M_1 = b, N \geq 2]$. This is only feasible if data on V, the common value, are available. In the particular application of OCS wildcat auctions, the authors have good estimates of the common value, so this is feasible. The authors estimate $\zeta(b) = E[V|B_1 = b, M_1 = b, N \geq 2]$ using the following local linear regression:

$$\min_{v, r_1, r_2} \sum_{t=1}^{T} \frac{1}{n_t^*} \sum_{i=1}^{n_t^*} [v_t - v - r_1(b - B_{it}) - r_2(b - M_{it})]^2 \, k\left(\frac{b-B_{it}}{h_b}\right) k\left(\frac{b-M_{it}}{h_m}\right).$$

Here, $\hat{v}$ is then an estimate for $\zeta(b)$. Then the authors examine whether $\hat{\xi}(b,G) - \hat{\zeta}(b)$ is statistically significantly from 0 using a bootstrap procedure.

2.2   Testing the Underlying Information Structure

Since a game-theoretic auction model is used to model bidders' strategic behavior under asymmetric and incomplete information, the assumptions made on the underlying information structure are crucial for the validity of the model's predictions and implications, and for when the model is used to analyze the data using the structural approach. For instance, Wilson (1977) shows that rational bidders will anticipate the winner's curse problem in a common value equilibrium and adjust their bids accordingly. In particular, he establishes that, when the number of bidders goes to infinity, the winning bid converges to the true (yet unknown) value of the auctioned object, a striking result that does not hold in a private value model. Moreover, whether bidders' valuations are independent or affiliated can also have different implications. For instance, when bidders' valuations are independent, they become more competitive as the number of bidders increases. However, this may not be true if their valuations are affiliated as, in addition to the usual competition effect, as the number of bidders rises, there is an effect termed the "affiliation effect" by Pinkse and Tan (2005), which is opposite to the competition effect. Therefore, it is important to develop econometric procedures to test the underlying information structure.

2.2.1 Testing for common values

Haile et al. (2003) propose a nonparametric procedure to test between all private value and all common value first-price sealed-bid auction models within the AV framework of Milgrom and Weber (1982). Suppose each bidder i has a value of U_i and each has a signal of X_i. All values and signals are affiliated. Denote s_n as the strictly increasing bidding strategy when there are n bidders in the auction. Bidder i's maximization problem can be written as

$$E\left[(U_i - b)1\left\{s_n(x_j) \le b \forall j \neq i\right\} \mid X_i = x_i\right].$$

The FOC is

$$v(x,x,n) = s_n(x) + \frac{s_n'(x)F_n(x \mid x)}{f_n(x \mid x)},\tag{3.7}$$

where $F_n(\cdot \mid x)$ is the cdf of $\max_{j \neq i} X_j$ conditional on $X_i = x$, $f_n(\cdot \mid x)$ is the corresponding pdf and $v(x, x', n) = E[U_i \mid X_i = x_i, \max_{j \neq i} X_j = x']$. When values are private, $v(x, x', n) = E[U_i \mid X_i = x, \max_{j \neq i} X_j = x'] = x$ is independent of n. When values are common, $v(x, x', n) = E[U_i \mid X_i = x, \max_{j \neq i} X_j = x']$ strictly increases in X_j for all j and it can be easily proven that $v(x, x,n)$ decreases in n.

Similar to Hendricks, Pinkse and Porter (2003), the FOC (3.7) can be written as

$$v(x,x,n) = b + \frac{G_n(b \mid b)}{g_n(b \mid b)},$$

where $G_n(\cdot \mid b)$ is the cdf of $\max_{j \neq i} b_j$ conditional on $b_i = b$ and $g_n(\cdot \mid b)$ is the corresponding pdf. As a result, the pseudo-values can be computed using

$$\hat{v}_{it.} = b_{it} + \frac{\hat{G}_n(b_{it}, b_{it})}{\hat{g}_n(b_{it}, b_{it})},\tag{3.8}$$

where

$$\hat{G}_n(b,b) = \frac{1}{T_n \times h_G \times n} \sum_{t=1}^{T_n}\sum_{i=1}^{n} k\left(\frac{b - b_{it}}{h_G}\right)1\left(\max_{j \neq i} b_{jt} < b, n_t = n\right)$$

$$\hat{g}_n(b,b) = \frac{1}{T_n \times h_g \times n} \sum_{t=1}^{T_n}\sum_{i=1}^{n} 1(n_t = n)k\left(\frac{b - b_{it}}{h_g}\right)k\left(\frac{b - \max_{j \neq i} b_{jt}}{h_g}\right).$$

Here, h_g and h_G are bandwidths, T_n is the number of auctions with n bidders and $k(\cdot)$ is a kernel function.

The fact that $v(x, x, n)$ is independent of n in private value models while it is decreasing in n in common value models implies the following hypothesis:

$$H_0 : \mu_{\underline{n},\tau} = ... = \mu_{\overline{n},\tau}$$

$$H_1 : \mu_{\underline{n},\tau} > ... > \mu_{\overline{n},\tau},$$

where $\underline{n}$ and $\bar{n}$ are the lower and upper bounds of number of bidders and $\mu_{n,\tau}$ is the quantile-trimmed mean pseudo-value from auctions with n bidders. The trimming is needed for nonparametric estimation of $\hat{g}_n$ in (3.8). More specifically, $\mu_{n,\tau}$ is estimated using

$$\hat{\mu}_{n,\tau} = \frac{1}{T_n \times n} \sum_{t=1}^{T_n} \sum_{i=1}^{n} \hat{v}_{it} 1\left(\hat{b}_{\tau,n} \le b_{it} \le \hat{b}_{1-\tau,n}, n_t = n \right),$$

where $\hat{b}_{\tau,n}$ is the τ-th quantile of marginal bid distribution for bids from n-bidder auctions.

The proposed test is a likelihood ratio test and the test statistic takes the form of

$$\bar{\chi}^2 = \sum_{n=\underline{n}}^{\bar{n}} a_n (\mu^*_{n,\tau} - \bar{\mu})^2,$$

where

$$\bar{\mu} = \frac{\sum_{n=\underline{n}}^{\bar{n}} a_n \hat{\mu}_{n,\tau}}{\sum_{n=\underline{n}}^{\bar{n}} a_n},$$

where $a_n = \frac{T_n h}{\sigma_n}$. $h = h_G = h_g$ is the bandwidth and σ_n is the asymptotic variance for $\hat{\mu}_{n,\tau}$. $\mu^*_{n,\tau}$s are the solution to the following minimization problem,

$$\min_{\mu_{\underline{n},\tau} \cdots, \mu_{\bar{n},\tau}} \sum_{n=\underline{n}}^{\bar{n}} a_n (\hat{\mu}_{n,\tau} - \mu_n)^2 \tag{3.9}$$

$$s.t. \mu_{\underline{n}} \ge \ldots \ge \mu_{\bar{n}}.$$

Under the null private value hypothesis, $\bar{\chi}^2$ follows a mixture of chi-square distribution, that is,

$$\Pr(\bar{\chi}^2 \ge c) = \sum_{k=2}^{\bar{n}-\underline{n}+1} \Pr(\chi^2_{k-1} \ge c) w(k, \Sigma),$$

where $w(k, \Sigma)$ is the probability that the solution to (3.9) has exactly k distinct values and Σ is the variance–covariance matrix for $\hat{\mu}_{n,\tau}$s.

The authors also propose two other tests, one based on the quantiles of the pseudo-values and the other based on a Kolmogorov–Smirnov-type statistic for equality of the distributions. Both are omitted for brevity purposes.

Hill and Shneyerov (2013) propose a nonparametric test of common values in first-price auctions. It is well known that, in the Milgrom and Weber (1982) model, where the common value and bidders' signals are affiliated, the bidding strategy $B(s)$ in the first-price auction satisfies the following first-order condition

$$\left[v(s) - B(s) \right] f_{Y_1|S_1}(s|s) - B'(s) F_{Y_1|S_1}(s|s) = 0 \tag{3.10}$$

subject to the boundary condition $B(s*) = r$, where $v(s) = E[U_i|S_i = s, Y_1 = s]$ and r is the binding reserve price. Here, U_i is bidder i's value, S_i is bidder i's signal and $Y_i = max_{j\neq i} S_j$. $B(s)$ is the bidding strategy; $s*$ is the screening level such that only bidders with signals higher than $s*$ will enter and submit a bid.

For a bidder with signal s, his value conditional on winning is

$$w(s) = E\left[U_i \mid S_i = s, Y_i < s\right].$$

Therefore, we must have $w(s*) = r$ as the marginal bidder should have zero expected profit. Therefore, when values are private where $E[U_i|S_i, Y_i]$ only depends on S_i, we have $w(s*) = v(s*) = r$. Evaluating (3.10) at $s*$ implies that $B'(s*) = 0$. On the other hand, when there is common value and hence $E[U_i|S_i, Y_i]$ depends on Y_i, we have $w(s*) = r < v(s*)$. Evaluating (3.10) at $s*$ implies that $B'(s*) > 0$. As $B(s*) = r$, these results imply that the slopes of the bidding functions around the reserve price are different for private value and common value models and this difference can be exploited to test the presence of common value.

Normalize the bids by the reserve price, that is, $B^* = \frac{B}{r} - 1$, and define $G*(b) = Pr[B*(S_i) \le b|S_i \ge s*]$. Then, under regularity conditions, it is proved that

$$G^*(b) = cb^\kappa(1 + O(b^\kappa)),$$

as $b \to 0$ for some $c > 0$, where $\kappa = 1$ under the common value (CV) framework and $\kappa = \frac{1}{2}$ under the private value (PV) framework. This essentially shows that, under CV, $G*(b)$ approaches a positive constant when $b \to 0$. But, under PV, it approaches 0 when $b \to 0$. Therefore, testing PV versus CV is equivalent to testing whether $\kappa = \frac{1}{2}$.

To test this, the authors propose the following test statistic:

$$\tau_{m_n} = m_n^{1/2}\left(\hat{\kappa}_{m_n}^{-1} - 2\right)/\hat{\kappa}_{m_n}^{-1},$$

where

$$\hat{\kappa}_{m_n}^{-1} = \frac{1}{m_n}\sum_{i=1}^{m_n}\left(\log b^*_{(m_n+1)} - \log b^*_{(i)}\right).$$

Here, m_n is the number of bids near the reserve price and $b^*_{(i)}$ is the i-th order statistic of the observed normalized bids. Under the null $\kappa = \frac{1}{2}$, τ_{m_n} follows a standard normal distribution. The authors then discussed how to choose m_n in practice.

2.2.2   Testing for affiliation

Jun et al. (2010) propose a nonparametric test of affiliation in auction models. Milgrom and Weber (1982) have shown that a monotone pure strategy equilibrium exists in a symmetric environment if the private signals and the common value of the object being auctioned are affiliated. In this case, the affiliation of the signals implies the affiliation of the bids and, therefore, one can test for the affiliation of the signals or the model by testing the affiliation of the bids.

The test statistics are based on the following quantity:

$$T(Q) = \int \max(Q,0)w(a,b,\delta)dadbd\delta$$
$$= \int \max(Q,0)dW,$$

where $Q(a, b; \delta) = p_\delta(a)p_\delta(b) - p_\delta(a \vee b)p_\delta(a \wedge b)$ a, b and δ are vectors of the same dimension, $p_\delta(a) = \Pr[\xi \in B(a, \delta)]$, $B(a, \delta)$ is a cube with volume δ and centroid a, $a \vee b$ denotes the element-wise maximum of a and b and $a \wedge b$ the element-wise minimum of a and b. With affiliation, $Q \leq 0$ for any a, b, δ. As a result, $T(Q) = 0$ if elements of ξ are affiliated and $T(Q) > 0$ implies rejection of the model. To achieve a pivotal limiting distribution under the null, the authors propose the following slightly different test statistic with a sample size–dependent input parameter,

$$\hat{\tau}_n = \sqrt{n}\frac{T_n(\hat{Q})}{2\hat{v}},$$

where $T_n(Q) = \int_{Q>-\beta_n} QdW$ and β_n is the sample size–dependent input parameter that converges to 0 when n goes to infinity. Furthermore, they have

$$\hat{Q}(a,b,\delta) = \frac{1}{n(n-1)}\sum_{i=1}^{n}\sum_{j\neq i}h_{ij}^*,$$

where $h_{ij}^* = I(\xi_i \in B(a,\delta))I(\xi_j \in B(b,\delta)) - I(\xi_i \in B(a \vee b,\delta))I(\xi_i \in B(a \wedge b,\delta))$,

$$\hat{v}^2 = \frac{\sum_{i=1}^{n}\sum_{j\neq i}\sum_{t\neq i,j}h_{nij}h_{nit}}{n(n-1)(n-2)} - \left(\frac{\sum_{i=1}^{n}\sum_{j\neq i}h_{nij}}{n(n-1)}\right)^2$$

and

$$h_{nij} = \int_{Q>-\beta_n}(h_{ij}^* + h_{ji}^*)dW/2.$$

The authors then prove their test is consistent in the sense that it rejects all alternatives with probability 1 when the sample size is large enough. Also, with an additional assumption, the test statistic has a standard normal limiting distribution. The assumption is satisfied as long as one element of ξ is continuous. Finally, the authors provide some guidance on how to choose the input parameter β_n in practice.[2]

Li and Zhang (2010) propose a test for affiliation among potential bidders' private information (either private signals or entry costs) based on the implication of affiliation on the entry behavior. The authors first prove that, in two first-price auction models with entry, when the potential bidders' entry costs or their private signals are affiliated, their entry behaviors are also affiliated. Therefore, testing whether the entry decisions are affiliated is equivalent to testing the affiliation of potential bidders' private information.

The "reduced form" entry decision for a potential bidder can be written as follows:

$$D_{li} = 1(x_l\beta + z_{li}\gamma + \eta_l + \varepsilon_{li} > 0),$$

where x_l and η_l are observed and unobserved auction heterogeneity, z_{li} is auction and bidder specific heterogeneity and ε_{li} is the error term. With this specification, if $\varepsilon_{l1},...,\varepsilon_{IN_l}$ are affiliated, then $D_{l1},...,D_{IN_l}$ are affiliated, where N_l is the number of potential bidders for auction l. The authors further assume that $\eta_l,\varepsilon_{l1},...,\varepsilon_{IN_l}$ follow a joint normal distribution with zero means and covariance matrix

$$\Sigma = \begin{bmatrix} \sigma^2 & 0 & ... & 0 \\ 0 & 1 & & \rho \\ ... & & ... & \\ 0 & \rho & & 1 \end{bmatrix}.$$

In this setting, $\varepsilon_{l1},...,\varepsilon_{IN_l}$ are affiliated if $\rho \geq 0$. Therefore, testing whether $D_{l1},...,D_{IN_l}$ are affiliated is equivalent to estimating ρ and testing whether $\rho \geq 0$.

To estimate the model parameters, one can maximize the joint likelihood function for observations from all auctions. The likelihood function for l can be written as follows if all potential bidders participate in that auction:

$$p_l(\theta) = \Pr(D_{li} = 1, i = 1,...,N_l)$$
$$= \int_{-\infty}^{+\infty}\int_{-\infty}^{+\infty}...\int_{-\infty}^{+\infty}1(\varepsilon_l \in A_l)f(\eta_l,\varepsilon_{l1},...,\varepsilon_{IN_l})d\varepsilon_{l1}...d\varepsilon_{IN_l}d\eta_l,$$

where A_l denotes the set $\{\varepsilon_l | \varepsilon_{il} > - (x_l\beta + z_{li}\gamma + \eta_l), i = 1,. . .,N_l\}$ and θ collects all the model parameters. Due to the presence of multiple integrals, the authors use the Geweke–Hajivassiliou–Keane (GHK) simulator to estimate the model using the simulated maximum likelihood estimation method and then test whether $\rho \geq 0$.

2.3   Testing Collusion

Bid rigging or collusion among bidders has been a serious problem in procurement auctions. Developing tools to detect collusive behavior is of paramount importance for policy makers and regulators. However, it is often difficult to distinguish between competitive and collusive behaviors without a deep institutional knowledge and detailed data, as detecting the collusive behavior is usually based on finding distinctions between market conducts and outcomes with and without collusion.[3]

2.3.1   Testing for collusive behavior
Porter and Zona (1993) provide empirical strategies to examine whether bid rigging has occurred in auctions. The setting is New York State Department of Transportation's construction contracts auctions. In 1984, five firms were identified as participants in bid-rigging schemes when one firm was convicted in a federal court. The authors designate these firms as "cartel" firms and other firms as "competitive" firms. They examine whether there are

systematic differences in the bid levels as well as the rank distributions of bids by the cartel versus noncartel firms and take systematic differences as evidence for bidding rigging by the cartel firms.

Their empirical analysis starts with the following regression:

$$\log(b_{it}) = \alpha_t + \beta X_{it} + \varepsilon_{it}, \tag{3.11}$$

where b_{it} is the bid by firm i in auction t, α_t is the auction specific fixed effects, X_{it} is a vector of observed firm and auction-specific characteristics that determine the bids and ε_{it} is the error term. The error term has mean 0 and variance σ_t^2. Then, (3.11) can be estimated using generalized least squares (GLS) as this is a linear regression model with heteroskedasticity. We can estimate (3.11) twice, once with data from the cartel firms only and once with data from the noncartel firms only. This will give us two sets of estimates for β. If the two sets of estimates for β are significantly different from each other, then this is preliminary evidence for bid rigging by the cartel firms, as this means they behaved differently than the noncartel firms when forming their bids. One potential explanation is that they colluded. But of course there could be other non-collusive explanations.

The authors then further examine the rank of the bids. Multiplying both sides of (3.11) by $\sqrt{\pi/6}/\sigma_t$, we have

$$\sqrt{\frac{\pi}{6}}/\sigma_t \log(b_{it}) = \theta_t + \beta X_{it}\sqrt{\frac{\pi}{6}}/\sigma_t + \varepsilon_{it}\sqrt{\frac{\pi}{6}}/\sigma_t. \tag{3.12}$$

In this case, the new error term $\varepsilon_{it}\sqrt{\pi/6}/\sigma_t$ now has a variance of $\frac{\pi}{6}$, the variance of the type I extreme value error. Assuming the new error term indeed follows the type I extreme value distribution, (3.12) implies that

$$\Pr(b_{it} < b_{jt} \,\forall j \neq i) = \frac{\exp(\beta Z_{it})}{\sum_j \exp(\beta Z_{jt})},$$

where $Z_{it} = X_{it}\sqrt{\frac{\pi}{6}}/\sigma_t$. In this case, if we denote the index of the firm with bid ranked m in order from the smallest to the largest by r_m, the likelihood of the observed ranking for auction t can be written as

$$\Pr(b_{r_1 t} < b_{r_1 t} < \ldots < b_{r_{n_t} t}) = \prod_{i=1}^{n_t} \frac{\exp(\beta Z_{r_i t})}{\sum_{j=i}^{n_t} \exp(\beta Z_{r_j t})},$$

where n_t is the number of bids in auction t. This result is from Beggs et al. (1981). The likelihood for the entire sample is then

$$L(\beta) = \prod_{t=1}^{T} \prod_{i=1}^{n_t} \frac{\exp(\beta Z_{r_i t})}{\sum_{j=i}^{n_t} \exp(\beta Z_{r_j t})}, \tag{3.13}$$

where T is the total number of auctions. The likelihood (3.13) can be further factored into two independent parts: the likelihood of the lowest bids from each auction and the likelihood of the rankings of all other bids observed. The two parts can be estimated separately, yielding two sets of estimates for β. If we estimate the two parts separately using data from the noncartel firms only and these two sets of estimates are not statistically significantly different, then model misspecification is not suggested. We can also estimate the two parts separately using data from the cartel firms only. If the two sets of estimates are found to be statistically significantly different here but not in the case when only data from noncartel firms are used, then this is evidence for phantom bidding by the nonwinning cartel firms. Phantom bidding refers to the practice where, each time the cartel firms submit multiple bids with only one competitive bid from the chosen winner, other cartel members submit noncompetitive bids.

Baldwin et al. (1997) test for evidence of bidder collusion in US Forest Service timber sales. They focus on the second-price or oral ascending (English) auction within the Independent Private Value (IPV) framework. They estimate a total of five empirical auction models: the noncooperative model with unit supply; the collusion model with unit supply; the noncooperative multiunit supply model; and two nesting models that allow both collusion and multiunit supply. They estimate the models using the maximum likelihood approach and select the model that fits the data the best by comparing the values of the log likelihood function at convergence. Their results show that the collusive model with unit supply is the preferred model, lending support to the collusion hypothesis.

Let V_{in} denote bidder n's valuation in auction i. It is assumed that $\ln\frac{V_{in}}{v_i}$ follows a normal distribution with mean $\beta'z_i$ and variance σ^2, where z_i is a vector of observed auction characteristics and v_i is the volume of timber in auction i. For some auctions in the data set, we only observe whether the winning bid is within 5.5 per cent of the reserve price r_i, not the exact winning bid. We denote this set of auctions as I_b. For the rest of the auctions, we observe the exact amounts of winning bids, and these auctions are collected in I_a. Let $f_\alpha(u|r, n)$ and $F_\alpha(u|r, n)$ denote the density and distribution functions of the α-th highest order statistic of n independent draws from a standardized normal distribution that is truncated below by r, that is,

$$f_\alpha(u\,|\,r,n) = n\binom{n-1}{\alpha-1}\phi(u)\left[1-\Phi(u)\right]^{\alpha-1}\left[\Phi(u)-\Phi(s)\right]^{n-\alpha}\left[1-\Phi(s)\right]^{-n},$$

$$F_\alpha(u\,|\,r,n) = \sum_{j=1}^{\alpha-1}\binom{n}{j}\left[1-\Phi(u)\right]^{j}\left[\Phi(u)-\Phi(s)\right]^{n-j}\left[1-\Phi(s)\right]^{-n},$$

where $u = \frac{\ln(b/v)-\beta'z}{\sigma}$ and $s = \frac{\ln(r/v)-\beta'z}{\sigma}$. Here, u and s are the standardized log of the bid and the log of the reserve price, respectively.

The first model considered is the noncooperative model with unit supply. In this model, it is well known that the observed winning bid equals the second highest value. Therefore, in this case, the likelihood function can be written as

$$L(\beta,\sigma) = \left[\prod_{i\in I_a}\frac{v_i}{\sigma b_i}f_2(u_i\,|\,r_i,n_i)\right]\left[\prod_{i\in I_b}F_2(y_i\,|\,r_i,n_i)\right],$$

where $y = \frac{\ln(1.055r/v)-\beta'z}{\sigma}$ is the upper bound of the standardized log of bids for auctions in set I_b.

The second model considered is the collusive model with unit supply. It is assumed that each bidder in auction i joins the ring C_i with probability

$$p_i = \frac{\exp(\gamma' w_i)}{1+\exp(\gamma' w_i)},$$

where w_i is a set of observed auction characteristics. In this model, the observed winning price depends on who joins the ring. For example, if K_i bidders join the ring for auction i and these bidders are the ones with the highest values, then the observed winning price will equal the $K_i + 1$-th highest value. Let us order the values in auction i from the largest to the smallest as $V_{i1} \geq V_{i2} \geq \dots \geq V_{in_i}$. Then, with $q^c_{i(n_i+1)} = p_i^{n_i}$ probability, all bidders collude and the observed winning price equals r_i, the reserve price. With $q^c_{i2} = 1 - p_i^2$ probability, either the highest value bidder or the second highest value bidder is not in the ring. In this case, the observed winning price will be V_{i2}. Finally, with $q^c_{i\alpha} = p_i^{\alpha-1}(1 - p_i)$ probability, the $\alpha - 1$ bidders with the highest values are in the ring while the bidder with the α-th highest value is not in the ring. In this case, the observed winning price is $V_{i\alpha}$. Therefore, the density for the standardized winning price is

$$h_c(u_i) = \sum_{\alpha=2}^{n_i} q^c_{i\alpha} f_\alpha(u_i \mid r_i, n_i)$$

for $u_i > s_i$ and its distribution is

$$H_c(u_i) = p_i^{n_i} + \sum_{\alpha=2}^{n_i} q^c_{i\alpha} F_\alpha(u_i \mid r_i, n_i)$$

for $u_i \geq s_i$. And the likelihood function in this case is

$$L(\beta, \sigma, \gamma) = \left[\prod_{i \in I_a} \frac{v_i}{\sigma b_i} h_c(u_i) \right] \left[\prod_{i \in I_b} H_c(y_i) \right].$$

The third model considered is the noncooperative model with multiunit supply. It is assumed that bidders in auction i face M_i items and each one only demands at most one. It is assumed that M_i follows the standard Poisson process with mean μ_i, which in turn is assumed to follow the exponential distribution,

$$g_i(\mu) = \frac{1}{a_i} \exp(-\frac{1}{a_i}\mu).$$

With these assumptions, we can derive

$$\Pr(M_i = 0) = \int_0^\infty \exp(-\mu_i) \frac{1}{a_i} \exp(-\frac{1}{a_i}\mu_i) d\mu_i$$

$$= \frac{1}{1+a_i}.$$

Similarly, we can derive

$$\Pr(M_i = 1) = \frac{a_i}{\left(1 + a_i\right)^2}$$

and therefore,

$$\Pr(M_i = 1 \mid M_i > 0) = \frac{1}{1 + a_i}.$$

Using the same method, we can derive

$$\Pr(M_i = \alpha - 1 \mid M_i > 0) = \theta_i^{\alpha-2}(1 - \theta_i)\,\text{for}\,\alpha = 2,\ldots,n_i,$$

where $\theta_i = \frac{a_i}{1 + a_i}$. The value of θ_i is then specified to be $\theta_i = \frac{\exp(\delta' x_i)}{1 + \exp(\delta' x_i)}$. In this model, the observed winning price depends on the number of units M_i. If there are M_i units, then the winning price should equal the $M_i + 1$-th highest value as long as $M_i < n_i$. With $q_{ia}^s = 1 - \theta_i$ probability, $M_i = 1$ and the observed winning price equals the second highest value V_{i2}. With $q_{ia}^s = \theta_i^{\alpha-2}(1 - \theta_i)$ probability, $M_i = \alpha - 1$ and the observed winning price equals V_{ia}. Finally, with $q_{ia}^s = \theta_i^{n_i-1}$ probability, $M_i \geq n_i$ and the winning price equals the reserve price. The likelihood function for this model is the same as that of the second model with the only difference that q_{ia}^c is replaced with q_{ia}^s.

The authors also estimate two other models that allow both collusion and multiunit supply, both of which are mixtures of the second and third models. Estimation results show that the second model, that is, the collusion model with unit supply, fits the data the best, lending support for the hypothesis of collusion.

In a lawsuit filed in Ohio, thirteen dairies were charged with collusion in school milk auctions for the years 1980 through 1990 inclusive. Porter and Zona (1999) use reduced form methods to test whether the behavior of some of the indicted firms was more consistent with competition or collusion compared with a control group of firms, that is, firms that were not indicted.

First, the authors examine the bid submission behavior using probit models. They test for differences between the slope coefficients estimated using data from the control group and those estimated using data from the defendant firms using the following procedure. The procedure is applied to one defendant firm at a time: (1) append the bid submission data for a given defendant to the control group data; (2) estimate a model under the null hypothesis that the slope coefficients are the same for the firm and the control group firms (the intercept is allowed to differ); (3) estimate a model under the alternative hypothesis of separate slope coefficients for the defendant; (4) conduct the likelihood ratio test using results from steps (2) and (3). A result in favor of the model estimated in (3) means rejection of the null hypothesis that the slope coefficients for the control group data and the data from the defendant firm are identical.

Next, the authors examine the level of bids using the following procedure, again one defendant firm at a time: (1) compute the predicted bid for the defendant firm based on the control group bid equation estimates; (2) compute the residuals, that is, the difference between the actual bids and the predicted bids, for the defendant firm; (3) regress the residuals on the independent variables in the control group bid equation and do the F test to test whether all the slope coefficients are jointly zero. Rejection of this F test means rejection of the null hypothesis that the slope coefficients for the control group data and the data from the defendant firm are identical.

Simply finding the behavioral differences from the two tests is not necessarily the result of anticompetitive behavior. One needs to further examine the nature of the differences in the behavior of the defendants from the control group. To do so, the authors first examine whether the defendant and control group firms differ when they adjust their bid submission and bid-level decisions with respect to distance, a key cost variable. They find that the defendant firms bid more frequently than what the control group model predicts for several distance bands. Also, they find that the bid levels decrease with distance for defendant firms, while they increase with distance as expected for the control group firms. Next, they examine whether the defendant firms behave in a parallel fashion. They test for statistical independence of the bid submission decisions by a pair of defendant firms by computing the Spearman correlation coefficients of the residuals based on the control group probit models applied to data from the two defendant firms. They also perform a similar analysis for the residuals based on the levels of bids submitted.

2.3.2   Testing whether collusion is efficient

Pesendorfer (2000) studies collusion in multiunit first-price auctions for school milk contracts in Florida and Texas during the 1980s. Different from other collusion papers, which focus on testing the presence of collusion, this paper takes collusion as given. Instead, it tests whether the cartel is efficient. A cartel mechanism is efficient if it designates the member with the lowest cost to submit the lowest cartel bid. The author considers two collusion mechanisms. The first one is the weak cartel mechanism, which does not allow side payments, while the second is the strong cartel that allows side payments. The author shows that, when the number of units being auctioned approaches infinity, both collusion mechanisms are efficient. As a result, if the bidders in the ring and bidders outside of the ring are symmetric, meaning they draw their private costs from the same distribution, then the bidder that represents the cartel on average has a higher probability of having a lower cost than other bidders. This results in an auction with asymmetric bidders. Two implications emerge. First, the non-collusive bidders bid more aggressively than the bidder from the cartel. Second, the ex ante bid distribution of any noncartel bidders dominates that of the cartel bidder.

To test for the first implication, that is, difference in bidding behavior by the cartel bidder and the non-collusive bidders, the following log linear regressions are estimated:

$$\ln(b_{ij}^c) = X_{ij}\beta^c + \varepsilon_{ij}^c$$

$$\ln(b_{ij}^{nc}) = X_{ij}\beta^{nc} + \varepsilon_{ji}^{nc},$$

where X_{ij} is a vector of firm and contract-specific variables, c denotes a bid from the cartel bidder and nc denotes a bid from the non-collusive bidders. Testing for a difference in bidding behavior is equivalent to testing for $\beta^c = \beta^{nc}$. Three subsets of the data are considered: low cartel bids plus all noncartel bids; low cartel bids; and all noncartel bids. A Chow test for equality of the coefficients can be constructed using two sets of estimates. First, the coefficients are estimated using low cartel bids in addition to all noncartel bids. Second, the coefficients are estimated using noncartel bids and cartel bids separately. Under the null hypothesis of no differences, the estimates from the two sub-samples are identical to those from the full sample. To test the second implication, that is, whether the bid distribution of the noncartel bidders dominates that of the cartel bidder, this is equivalent to testing whether the residuals from the log linear regressions for the noncartel bids dominate those of the cartel bids. The empirical cdfs of the distributions are plotted to show that one distribution stochastically dominates the other. Furthermore, a rank test is used to test this. Cartel and noncartel residuals are ordered and each residual is assigned a rank corresponding to its position in the total ordering. Under the null hypothesis of identical distributions, the sum of noncartel ranks equals the expected sum of randomly drawn ranks.

Hendricks, Porter and Tan (2008) study legal collusion in common value auction models with affiliated private signals. Two models are studied. In the first model, it is assumed that bidders do not learn anything about each other's information regarding the object being auctioned from each other's decision on whether to join the collusion ring. In the second model, it is assumed that bidders update their beliefs about each other's information of the object being auctioned from observing other bidders' decisions on whether to join the collusion ring. The authors show that, in the first model, efficient collusion may not be possible as buyers with higher signals may not have incentives to join the ring. Here, collusion is efficient if the buyer with the highest signal is given the exclusive right to purchase the asset and they do so if and only if the expected value of the asset, conditional on the signals of all buyers, exceeds the reserve price. In the second model, on the other hand, efficient collusion is always possible.

In OCS wildcat auctions, the setting is closer to the first model. Therefore, the theoretical analysis predicts that joint ventures are unlikely to occur, especially on marginal tracts with a small number of competitors. The authors show this is indeed the case using summary statistics on the frequency of joint bids by the 12 major bidders in this market.

2.4   Testing for Risk Aversion

Because of uncertainty faced by bidders in auctions, bidders can exhibit a risk-aversion attitude when making their decisions. Also, auction models assuming risk neutrality and risk aversion generate different results. For example, the revenue equivalence result derived under the risk neutrality assumption no longer holds for risk-averse bidders; in particular, ascending auctions generate less revenue for the seller than first-price auctions when bidders are risk averse. As a result, it is useful to test bidders' risk attitude in applications.

Fang and Tang (2014) propose nonparametric tests for bidders' risk attitudes in ascending auctions with endogenous entry. There are N potential bidders. They have symmetric IPV values and make endogenous entry decisions. In the entry stage, each potential bidder decides whether to incur an entry cost K to become an active bidder. Upon entry, each active bidder draws a private value V and then competes in an ascending auction at the bidding stage. There is a binding reserve price r. All bidders have the same utility function u with $u' > 0$ and the sign of u'' does not change over R_+.

Assumption 1: K is randomly drawn from F_K on $[\underline{k}, \bar{k}]$. Conditional on K, private values are drawn independently from the same distribution $F_{V|K}$.

Let A denote the number of active bidders or entrants and A_{-i} the set and number of entrants that i competes with if he enters. Define $P_i = \max\{r, \max_{j \in A_{-i}}\{V_j\}\}$ as i's payment if he enters and wins while all competitors in A_{-i} follow their weakly dominant bidding strategies of bidding their own values. Let $w(k; \lambda_{-i})$ denote the expected utility for bidder i conditional on paying an entry cost k and potential competitors entering with probabilities $\lambda_{-i} = (\lambda_1, \ldots, \lambda_{i-1}, \lambda_{i+1}, \ldots, \lambda_N)$, then $w(k; \lambda_{-i})$ can be written as

$$w(k; \lambda_{-i}) = u(-k)F_{V|K}(r) + \int_r^{\bar{v}} h(v, k; \lambda_{-i}) dF_{V|K}(v)$$

where,

$$h(v, k; \lambda_{-i}) = u(v - r - k)F_{P_i}(r \mid k, \lambda_{-i})$$
$$+ \int_r^v u(v - p - k) dF_{P_i}(p \mid k, \lambda_{-i})$$
$$+ u(-k)[1 - F_{P_i}(v \mid k, \lambda_{-i})]$$

with F_{P_i} being the distribution for P_i.

Then the authors prove that, when assumption 1 holds, for any entry cost k with $w(k; (1, \ldots, 1)) < u(0) < w(k; (0, \ldots, 0))$, there exists a unique symmetric mixed-strategy equilibrium in which all bidders enter with the same probability λ_k^* such that

$$w(k; (\lambda_k^*, \ldots, \lambda_k^*)) = u(0). \tag{3.14}$$

The authors then propose two nonparametric tests for bidders' risk attitudes under this model. The first test assumes that data or estimates of entry costs are available while the second test does not need such data. Here, we focus on their second test as the data requirement there is less.

Assumption 2: For all i, $V_i = h(Z) + \eta_i$ where Z is a vector of observed auction heterogeneity and η_i are independent and identically (iid) draws from F_η that is independent of Z and N.

Let $\lambda_{z,n}$ denote bidders' equilibrium entry probabilities in auctions with $Z = z$ and $N = n$. For $0 \le a \le n - 1$, define

$$\rho_{a,z,n} = \Pr(A_{-i} = a \mid Z = z, N = n)$$
$$= \binom{n-1}{a} \lambda_{z,n}^a (1 - \lambda_{z,n})^{n-a-1}.$$

From (3.14), one has that, in equilibrium,

$$u(0) = \sum_{a=0}^{n-1} \psi_a(z) \rho_{a,z,n}, \tag{3.15}$$

where

$$\psi_a(z) = E[u((V_i - P_i)_+ - k) \mid A_{-i} = a, Z = z]$$
$$= E[u((\eta_i - \eta^{a:a})_+ - k)],$$

where $\eta^{a:a}$ is the largest among a independent draws from F_η, $(V_i - P_i)_+ = V_i - P_i$ if $(V_i - P_i) > 0$ and $= 0$ otherwise. The second equality follows from the assumption that η is independent of Z and N. Clearly, for $a \geq 1$, $\psi_a(z)$ is independent of z and can be denoted as ψ_a^*. For $a = 0$,

$$\psi_0(z) = E[u((V_i - 0)_+ - k) \,|\, A_{-i} = 0, Z = z]$$
$$= E[u(h(z) + \eta_i - k)].$$

Here, the reserve price is implicitly assumed to be 0 for simplicity.

Assumption 3: There exist z, z', z'' and some n such that $0 < \lambda_{z,s} < 1$ for all $2 \leq s \leq n$ and $\lambda_{z',n}$, $\lambda_{z'',n} \in (0, 1)$

With assumption 3, we have the following from (3.15):

$$
\begin{pmatrix}
\rho_{0,z'',n} & 0 & 0 & \rho_{2,z'',n} & \cdots & \rho_{n-1,z'',n} \\
0 & \rho_{0,z',n} & 0 & \rho_{2,z',n} & \cdots & \rho_{n-1,z',n} \\
0 & 0 & \rho_{0,z,2} & 0 & \cdots & 0 \\
0 & 0 & \rho_{0,z,3} & \rho_{2,z,3} & \cdots & 0 \\
\cdots & \cdots & \cdots & \cdots & \cdots & \cdots \\
0 & 0 & \rho_{0,z,n} & \rho_{2,z,n} & \cdots & \rho_{n-1,z,n}
\end{pmatrix}
\times
\begin{pmatrix}
\psi_0(z'') \\
\psi_0(z') \\
\psi_0(z) \\
\psi_2^* \\
\cdots \\
\psi_{n-1}^*
\end{pmatrix}
$$

$$
=
\begin{pmatrix}
u(0) \\
\cdots \\
\cdots \\
\cdots \\
\cdots \\
u(0)
\end{pmatrix}
-
\begin{pmatrix}
\rho_{1,z'',n} \\
\rho_{1,z',n} \\
\rho_{1,z,2} \\
\cdots \\
\cdots \\
\rho_{1,z,n}
\end{pmatrix}
\psi_1^*.
$$

The linear system has $n + 2$ unknowns $(\psi_0(z''), \psi_0(z'), \psi_0(z), \psi_1^*, \ldots, \psi_{n-1}^*)$ and $n + 1$ equations. Set $u(0) = 0$ and ψ_1^* as an arbitrary nonzero constant. Assumption 3 guarantees that the coefficient matrix on the left-hand side has full rank. As a result, one can solve the system of linear equations and obtain the unique solutions, $\tilde{\psi}_0(z''), \tilde{\psi}_0(z'), \tilde{\psi}_0(z), \tilde{\psi}_2^*, \ldots, \tilde{\psi}_{n-1}^*$. Note that the authors assume that A and N are observed and hence the equilibrium entry probabilities and ρs can be computed.

Then, the authors prove that

$$\frac{\tilde{\psi}_0(z') - \tilde{\psi}_0(z)}{\tilde{\psi}_0(z'') - \tilde{\psi}_0(z')} \begin{array}{c} > \\ = \\ < \end{array} \frac{h(z') - h(z)}{h(z'') - h(z')} \text{ iff } u'' \begin{Bmatrix} < \\ = \\ > \end{Bmatrix} 0$$

where $h(z'') > h(z') > h(z)$ and

$$h(z_1) - h(z_2) = E(W \,|\, Z = z_1, A = a) - E(W \,|\, Z = z_2, A = a)$$

and W is the transaction price of the auction. Based on this key result, the authors then propose the following test statistic to test for bidders' risk attitudes:

$$\tilde{\tau} = \frac{\tilde{\psi}_0(z') - \tilde{\psi}_0(z)}{\tilde{\psi}_0(z'') - \tilde{\psi}_0(z')} - \hat{R}$$

where

$$\hat{R} = \sum_{a=2}^{n-1} \hat{q}_a \left(\frac{\hat{E}(W \mid Z = z', A = a) - \hat{E}(W \mid Z = z, A = a)}{\hat{E}(W \mid Z = z'', A = a) - \hat{E}(W \mid Z = z', A = a)} \right).$$

Here, $\hat{E}(W \mid Z = z, A = a)$ is a kernel estimator for the expected transaction price given $Z = z$ and $A = a$. $\hat{q}_a = \frac{\hat{\sigma}_a^{-2}}{\sum_{s=2}^{n-1} \hat{\sigma}_s^{-2}}$ and $\hat{\sigma}_a$ is the standard error for $\frac{\hat{E}(W|Z=z',A=a)-\hat{E}(W|Z=z,A=a)}{\hat{E}(W|Z=z'',A=a)-\hat{E}(W|Z=z',A=a)}$. The critical values for the test statistics are obtained using bootstrap resampling.

Li et al. (2015) study auctions with selective entry and risk-averse bidders. There are two stages. In the first stage, bidders draw private signals and then decide whether to enter the auction based on these signals. In the second stage, the entrants then draw private values of the object being auctioned and decide how to bid. The authors study both the first-price auctions and ascending auctions. The key implication from their theoretical study is that, when bidders' utility function exhibits decreasing absolute risk aversion, the ascending auction has a higher participation rate than the first-price auction; when bidders' utility function exhibits constant absolute risk aversion, the two formats of auctions have the same participation rate; when bidders' utility function exhibits increasing absolute risk aversion, the ascending auction has a lower participation rate than the first-price auction.

To empirically test this model implication, the authors specify the following conditional expectation function for the participation rate:

$$E(p \mid X, N, FPA) = G(\alpha + X\beta + \gamma FPA + \delta N),$$

where p is the participation rate, X is the auction heterogeneity, FPA is the dummy variable indicating this is a first-price rather than an ascending auction, N is the number of potential bidders and $G(\cdot)$ is a cdf such as a standard normal distribution or a logistic function. This model can be estimated using the quasi-maximum likelihood methods proposed by Papke and Wooldridge (1996) by maximizing the following likelihood function:

$$\max_\theta \sum_{i=1}^{L} \left\{ p_i \log G(X_i, N_i, FPA_i) + (1 - p_i) \log(1 - G(X_i, N_i, FPA_i)) \right\},$$

where θ collects all the parameters.

3. SEMIPARAMETRIC APPROACHES

As is well known, the semiparametric approach often provides a useful middle ground between the nonparametric and parametric approaches, and it is adopted usually for circumventing the curse of dimensionality problem arising from the nonparametric approach when covariates are needed to be controlled for, or in cases where a parametric specification of one part of the model can be more easily justified than the other part of the model. One of the first papers in using the semiparametric approaches in structural auctions is Li et al. (2003), which proposes a semiparametric method to estimate the optimal reserve price in first-price auctions within the symmetric affiliated private value framework. As it turns out, the problem that the authors consider does not fall into the two categories mentioned for use of a semiparametric approach. The semiparametric approach is natural in this case because the authors derive from the theory the optimal reserve price as a solution to a maximization problem in terms of the distribution of the bids, which can be nonparametrically estimated as in Li et al. (2002). Specifically, the authors first show that in the symmetric Affiliated Private Value (APV) model, the optimal reserve price p_0^* satisfies the following equation:

$$p_0^* = v_0 + \frac{\int_{p_0^*}^{\bar{v}} L(p_0^* \mid u) F_{y_1 \mid v_1}(u \mid u) f_{v_1}(u) du}{F_{y_1 \mid v_1}(p_0^* \mid p_0^*) f_{v_1}(p_0^*)},$$

where $f_{v_1}(\cdot)$ is the marginal density for the private value of the first bidder, $F_{y_1 \mid v_1}(\cdot \mid \cdot)$ denotes the conditional distribution of $y_1 = \max_{j \neq i} v_j$ conditional on v_1, $f_{y_1 \mid v_1}(\cdot \mid \cdot)$ denotes the corresponding density and $L(p_0^* \mid u) = \exp[-\int_{p_0^*}^{u} f_{y_1 \mid v_1}(x \mid x) / F_{y_1 \mid v_1}(x \mid x) dx]$. Equivalently, the optimal reserve price can be written as $p_0^* = \xi(x_0)$, where $\xi(b) = b + \frac{G_{B_1 \mid b_1}(b \mid b)}{g_{B_1 \mid b_1}(b \mid b)}$ is the inverse bidding function, $G_{B_1 \mid b_1}(\cdot \mid \cdot)$ is the distribution of $B_1 = \max_{j \neq 1} b_j$ conditional on bidder 1's bid b_1, $g_{B_1 \mid b_1}(\cdot \mid \cdot)$ is its corresponding density and x_0 maximizes the following expected profit function:

$$\Pi(x) = E\left[v_0 1(B_1 \leq x) 1(b_1 \leq x) + n[b_1 + (\xi(x) - x) \Lambda(x \mid b_1)] 1(B_1 \leq b_1) 1(b_1 \geq x) \right],$$

where v_0 is the seller's value of the auctioned object, $\Lambda(x \mid b_1) = \exp[-\int_x^{b_1} g_{B_1, b_1}(u, u) / G_{B_1 \times b_1}(u, u) du]$, $G_{B_1 \times b_1}(u, u) = G_{B_1 \mid b_1}(u \mid u) g_{b_1}(u)$ and $g_{B_1, b_1}(u, u)$ is the joint density of B_1 and b_1.

As for estimation, the authors first use kernel estimators similar to those used in Li et al. (2002) and Guerre et al. (2000) to obtain nonparametric estimates for $\hat{G}_{B_1 \times b_1}$ and $\hat{g}_{B_1, b_1}$ and hence $\hat{\Lambda}$. Then they estimate $\hat{x}_{0n}$ as the maximizer to the following equation:

$$\frac{1}{L_n} \sum_{l=1}^{L_n} \frac{1}{n} \sum_{i=1}^{n} \left[v_0 1(B_{il} \leq x) 1(b_{il} \leq x) + n[b_{il} + \frac{\hat{G}_{B_1 \times b_1}(x, x)}{\hat{g}_{B_1, b_1}(x, x)} \hat{\Lambda}(x \mid b_{il})] 1(B_{il} \leq b_{il}) 1(x \leq b_{il} \leq b_{\max} - \delta) \right],$$

where L_n is the number of auctions with n bidders and $b_{il} \leq b_{\max} - \delta$ is due to trimming in kernel estimation. Finally, the optimal reserve price can be estimated using

$$p_{0n}^* = \hat{\xi}(\hat{x}_{0n}) = \hat{x}_{0n} + \frac{\hat{G}_{B_1 \times b_1}(\hat{x}_{0n}, \hat{x}_{0n})}{\hat{g}_{B_1, b_1}(\hat{x}_{0n}, \hat{x}_{0n})}.$$

Hubbard et al. (2012) propose a semiparametric estimator for the first-price auctions within the symmetric affiliated private value framework. Li et al. (2002) have studied the nonparametric identification and estimation of the same model. However, their estimator suffers from the curse of dimensionality when the number of bidders or of covariates becomes large. In addition, Li et al. (2002) do not impose affiliation in their estimation strategy and hence the first-order condition used in their estimation need not constitute an equilibrium.

Consider a model with $n \geq 2$ bidders. Bidders' private values $\mathbf{V}$ follow the joint distribution $F_{\mathbf{V}}(\mathbf{V})$ and $F_i(v_i)$ is the marginal cdf for one private value. The latter is symmetric so that $F_i(v_i) = F_0(v_i)$ for all i. Then, by Sklar's theorem, there exists a unique copula function C such that

$$F_{\mathbf{V}}(\mathbf{v}) = C\left[F_1(v_1),....,F_n(v_n)\right]$$
$$= C\left[F_0(v_1),....,F_0(v_n)\right].$$

In the auction model, the equilibrium bidding strategy $\sigma(\cdot)$ is monotone increasing, in which case we have the relationship $G_0(s_i) = F_0(v_i)$, where $s_i = \sigma(v_i)$ is the bid and G_0 is its distribution. Therefore, the joint distribution for all the bids $\mathbf{S}$ can be written as

$$G_{\mathbf{S}}(\mathbf{s}) = C\left[G_0(s_1),....,G_0(s_n)\right].$$

The proposed semiparametric estimator has two steps. In the first step, using the observed bids, $G_0(s)$ and $g_0(s)$ are estimated nonparametrically using the method similar to that of Guerre et al. (2000). In the second step, the copula function C is parametrically specified and let θ denote its parameters. Then, θ is estimated using maximum likelihood estimation method based on the joint density of the observed bids, that is,

$$g_{\mathbf{S}}(\mathbf{s}) = C_{12...n}\left[\tilde{G}_0(s_1),....,\tilde{G}_0(s_n);\theta\right]\prod_{i=1}^{n}\tilde{g}_0(s_i),$$

where $\tilde{G}_0$ and $\tilde{g}_0$ are estimates from the first step. One advantage of this approach is that, in the second step, the $\prod_{i=1}^{n}\tilde{g}_0(s_i)$ part of the likelihood function does not depend on the parameters to be estimated and hence this approach does not suffer from the parameter-dependent support problem that often renders Maximum Likelihood Estimation (MLE) inappropriate for structural auction models. The authors then prove that this semiparametric estimator is consistent and asymptotically normal. Furthermore, they show that the joint density of private values can be estimated at the same rate as the marginal density of private values, thus faster than the nonparametric estimator considered in Li et al. (2002).

Lu and Perrigne (2008) mainly study the nonparametric identification and estimation of bidders' private value distribution and utility function (and hence risk aversion) when data from both the ascending auctions and the first-price sealed-bid auctions are available. Part of the paper also proposes a semiparametric estimation method for estimating the risk aversion parameter where the private value distribution is estimated nonparametrically while a parametric specification is used for the utility function. Our review focuses on this part of the paper.

This is an IPV auction model with I bidders. Bidders are assumed to have the same utility function $U(\cdot)$ such that $U'(\cdot) > 0$, $U''(\cdot) \leq 0$ and $U(0) = 0$. In the ascending auctions, in equilibrium, bidders bid their own values, that is, $b_{il} = v_{il}$, where i denotes a bidder and l denotes an auction. In ascending auctions, the observed winning bid equals to the second highest private value; hence we have

$$G(w) = I(I-1)\int_0^{F(v)} t^{I-2}(1-t)dt.$$

With the observed winning bids, $G(w)$, the distribution for the winning bids can be estimated nonparametrically, which in turn leads to a nonparametric estimate of $F(v)$ as there is a one-to-one mapping between $G(w)$ and $F(v)$.

In the first-price sealed bid auction, the equilibrium is characterized by the following first-order condition:

$$v_{il} = b_{il} + \lambda^{-1}\left(\frac{1}{I-1}\frac{G(b_{il})}{g(b_{il})}\right), \tag{3.16}$$

where $\lambda = \frac{U(\cdot)}{U'(\cdot)}$ and $G(\cdot)$ and $g(\cdot)$ are the cdf and pdf of the observed bids. When the utility function is specified to be constant relative risk aversion (CRRA), that is, $U(x) = x^{1-c}$ with $c \geq 0$ measuring the constant relative risk aversion, we have $\lambda(x; c) = x/(1-c)$ and hence $\lambda^{-1}(y; c) = (1-c)y$. As a result, (3.16) becomes

$$v_{il} = b_{il} + (1-c)\left(\frac{1}{I-1}\frac{G(b_{il})}{g(b_{il})}\right),$$

or

$$c = 1 - (v_{il} - b_{il})(I-1)\frac{g(b_{il})}{G(b_{il})}$$

$$= 1 - \left(F^{-1}(G(b_{il})) - b_{il}\right)(I-1)\frac{g(b_{il})}{G(b_{il})},$$

where the second equality follows from the fact that $G(b_{il}) = F(v_{il})$ as the equilibrium bidding strategy is monotone increasing. Therefore, the risk aversion parameter can be estimated as

$$c = 1 - \frac{1}{N}\sum_{il}\left[\left(\hat{F}^{-1}(\hat{G}(b_{il})) - b_{il}\right)(I-1)\frac{\hat{g}(b_{il})}{\hat{G}(b_{il})}\right],$$

where $\hat{g}$ and $\hat{G}$ are nonparametric estimates of the pdf and cdf of the observed bids and $\hat{F}$ is the nonparametric estimate of the private value distribution obtained previously using data from the ascending auctions.

Campo et al. (2011) study the identification and estimation of the first-price auction model with risk-averse bidders within the IPV framework. First, the authors show that the model is not identified when either the bidders' utility function only or their private value distribution only is parametrically specified. The authors then show that the model can be identified when both the bidders' utility function and a single conditional quantile of the private values are parametrically specified. The authors then propose a corresponding semiparametric estimation procedure to estimate the risk aversion parameters in the parametrically specified utility function as well as the private value distribution nonparametrically.

In this model, the equilibrium bidding strategy is characterized by the following equation:

$$v_{il} = b_{il} + \lambda^{-1}\left(\frac{1}{I_l-1}\frac{G(b_{il}|I_l,z_l)}{g(b_{il}|I_l,z_l)},\theta_0\right), \tag{3.17}$$

where I_l is the number of bidders in auction l, z_l is the observed heterogeneity for auction l, $\lambda = \frac{U(\cdot)}{U'(\cdot)}$ and θ_0 denotes the parameters in the parametrically specified utility function. Then (3.17) can be rewritten as

$$\frac{G(b_{il}\,|\,I_l,z_l)}{g(b_{il}\,|\,I_l,z_l)} = (I_l - 1)\lambda(v_{il} - b_{il}; \theta_0).$$

Evaluating this equation at the upper bound, we have

$$g(\bar{b}\,|\,I_l,z_l) = \frac{1}{(I_l - 1)}\frac{1}{\lambda(\bar{v} - \bar{b}; \theta_0)}. \tag{3.18}$$

The semiparametric estimation procedure consists of the following steps. In the first step, the upper bound for the bid, $\bar{b}(I_l,z_l)$ and the density of the bids at the upper bound $g(\bar{b}\,|\,I_l,z_l)$ are estimated nonparametrically. To estimate the upper bound, conditional on a particular I, we partition Z into k_N bins and then the estimate of the upper bound in each bin k using $\hat{a}_k + \hat{b}_k(z - \underline{z}_k)$, where $\underline{z}_k$ is the lower bound of bin k and $\hat{a}_k$ and $\hat{b}_k$ are solutions to the following constrained minimization problem:

$$\min_{a_k,b_k} \int_{\underline{z}_k}^{\bar{z}_k} \left[a_k + b_k(z - \underline{z}_k) \right] dz$$

$$\text{s.t. } B_{il} \leq a_k + b_k(Z_l - \underline{z}_k) \text{ where } Z_l \in \left[\underline{z}_k, \bar{z}_k\right].$$

Once the estimate for the upper bound $\hat{\bar{b}}_N(I_l,z_l)$ is obtained using the procedure just described, we can estimate the density of the bids at the upper bound

$$\hat{g}(\bar{b}\,|\,I_l,z_l) = \hat{Y}_{il} = \frac{1}{h_N}\Phi\left(\frac{B_{il} - \hat{\bar{b}}_N(I_l,z_l)}{h_N}\right),$$

where h_N is a bandwidth, N is the sample size and $\Phi(\cdot)$ is a one-sided kernel function with support on $[-1, 0]$.

In the second step, a nonlinear least squares estimator based on (3.18) is used to estimate $\bar{v}$ and θ_0. In particular, the estimates for $\bar{v}$ and θ_0, by solving the following minimization problem,

$$\min_{\theta, \hat{\bar{b}}_N(I_l,z_l) + \frac{\delta}{2} \leq \bar{v} \leq \bar{v}_{\text{sup}}} \sum_{l=1}^{L} \sum_{i=1}^{I_l} w(I_l,z_l) \left[\hat{Y}_{il} - \frac{1}{(I_l - 1)}\frac{1}{\lambda(\bar{v} - \hat{\bar{b}}_N(I_l,z_l); \theta)} \right]^2,$$

where δ and $\bar{v}_{\text{sup}}$ are positive constants to make sure $\bar{v} - \hat{\bar{b}}_N(I_l,z_l)$ is bounded away from 0 and $w(I_l, z_l)$ are strictly positive weights.

In the third step, the method in Guerre et al. (2000) was used to estimate $\frac{\hat{G}(b_{il}|I_l,z_l)}{\hat{g}(b_{il}|I_l,z_l)}$ nonparametrically. Then, with the estimated $\hat{\theta}_0$ from the second step, we can use (3.17) to recover bidders' private values $\hat{V}_{il}$. Then, in the final step, the density of the private values is estimated nonparametrically using the method in Guerre et al. (2000) and the recovered $\hat{V}_{il}$ from the third step.

The authors then prove that this multi-step semiparametric estimator converges at the optimal rate.

Li and Zheng (2009) propose a semiparametric estimation method for estimating model primitives for three competing game-theoretic models of entry and bidding in procurement auctions. As the estimation methods are similar for all three models, here we focus on the first model studied in the paper. Suppose there are N potential bidders for a contract. Each potential bidder is risk neutral with a disutility equal to his private cost c of completing the contract, which is drawn from a distribution $F(\cdot)$ with support $[\underline{c}, c]$. Each potential bidder must incur an entry cost k to learn his private cost for completing the job and hence how to bid for the project. Thus, the auction is modeled as a two-stage game. At the first stage, knowing the number of potential bidders, N, each potential bidder learns the specifications of the project and the entry cost, calculates their expected profit from entering the auction conditioning on his winning and then decides whether to participate in the auction and actually submit a bid. After the first entry stage, the n contractors who decide to enter the auction learn their own costs of completing the job and submit their bids.

In the entry stage, denote $E\pi(b, c|q^*)$ as the payoff for the actual bidder who optimally bids b using a Bayesian–Nash equilibrium strategy given his own cost c, the unique equilibrium entry probability q^* and the belief that there must be at least two bidders (including himself) in the auction, as well as conditioning that he is the winner. Then, q^* is determined from the equilibrium where the ex ante expected payoff is equal to the entry cost k as given in the following equation:

$$\int_{\underline{c}}^{\bar{c}} E\pi(b,c|q^*)f(c)dc = k. \tag{3.19}$$

Following the entry stage and using the mixed strategy described above, each actual bidder learns his private cost c for completing the job. The Bayesian–Nash equilibrium bidding strategy can be written as

$$s(c|q^*) = c + \frac{\sum_{j=2}^{N} [P_{B,q^*}(n=j|n\geq 2)\int_{c}^{\bar{c}}(1-F(x))^{j-1}dx]}{\sum_{j=2}^{N}[P_{B,q^*}(n=j|n\geq 2)(1-F(c))^{j-1}]}, \tag{3.20}$$

with the boundary condition $s(\bar{c}) = \bar{c}$ and where $P_{B,q^*}(n=j|n\geq 2) = \dfrac{\binom{N-1}{j-1}(q^*)^{j-1}(1-q^*)^{N-j}}{1-(1-q^*)^{N-1}}$ is the probability for j actual bidders to enter the auction. As a result, (3.19) can be rewritten as

$$\int_{\underline{c}}^{\bar{c}}\sum_{j=2}^{N}[P_{B,q^*}(n=j|n\geq 2)\int_{c}^{\bar{c}}(1-F(x))^{j-1}dx]f(c)dc = k. \tag{3.21}$$

As for estimation, a semiparametric specification is used. The density of contractors' private costs and entry costs are specified parametrically using the exponential density,

$$f(c|\mathbf{x},u) = \frac{1}{\exp(\alpha+\mathbf{x}\beta+u)}\exp\left[-\frac{1}{\exp(\alpha+\mathbf{x}\beta+u)}c\right],$$

and

$$h(k \mid \mathbf{x}, u) = \frac{1}{\exp(\gamma + \mathbf{x}\delta + u)} \exp\left[-\frac{1}{\exp(\gamma + \mathbf{x}\delta + u)}k\right], \tag{3.22}$$

where $\mathbf{x}$ and u are observed and unobserved auction heterogeneities. On the other hand, the distribution of the unobserved heterogeneity u is left unspecified. With these specifications, the equilibrium bidding strategy (3.20) becomes

$$s(c) = c + \frac{\displaystyle\sum_{j=2}^{N} P_{B,q^*}(n = j \mid n \geq 2)\exp\left[-\frac{j-1}{\exp(\mu_1)}c\right]\frac{\exp(\mu_1)}{j-1}}{\displaystyle\sum_{j=2}^{N} P_{B,q^*}(n = j \mid n \geq 2)\exp\left[-\frac{j-1}{\exp(\mu_1)}c\right]}, \tag{3.23}$$

where $\mu_1 = \alpha + \mathbf{x}\beta + u$. For the entry equilibrium, equation (3.21) can be written as

$$\sum_{j=2}^{N}\left\{\frac{\left(\dbinom{N-1}{j-1}\right)(q^*)^{j-1}(1-q^*)^{N-j}}{1-(1-q^*)^{N-1}}\frac{\exp(\mu_1)}{j(j-1)}\right\} = k.^4. \tag{3.24}$$

Joint estimation of the entry and bidding models is intractable if not impossible using the classical likelihood or moment-based methods because of the complexity of the two models and the presence of latent variables in both models. The Bayesian method, on the other hand, provides a computationally feasible alternative because of the use of the data augmentation and Monte Carlo Markov Chain (MCMC) techniques. To make use of the semiparametric Bayesian estimation and the MCMC algorithm, first some transformations are needed. Let $e_{new} = \alpha + u$ represent the (unnormalized) unobserved heterogeneity term. Then $\mu_1 = \mathbf{x}\beta + e_{new}$. With the private cost distribution specified and equation (3.20) one can obtain the following implied distributions for the equilibrium bids:

$$f(b \mid \mu_1) = \frac{1}{\exp(\mu_1)}\exp\left[-\frac{1}{\exp(\mu_1)}\varphi(b)\right]\left|\frac{\partial\varphi(b)}{\partial b}\right| \tag{3.25}$$

for $b \in \sum_{j=2}^{N} P_{B,q^*}(n = j \mid n \geq 2)\frac{\exp(\mu_1)}{j-1} / \sum_{j=2}^{N} P_{B,q^*}(n = j \mid n \geq 2), \infty)$, where $\varphi(b)$ is the inverse bidding function, and

$$\frac{\partial\varphi(b)}{\partial b} = \frac{\left[\displaystyle\sum_{j=2}^{N} P_{B,q^*}(n = j \mid n \geq 2)\exp(-\frac{j-1}{\exp(\mu_1)}\varphi(b))\right]^2}{\left[\displaystyle\sum_{j=2}^{N} P_{B,q^*}(n = j \mid n \geq 2)\exp(-\frac{j-1}{\exp(\mu_1)}\varphi(b))\frac{1}{j-1}\right]\left[\displaystyle\sum_{j=2}^{N} P_{B,q^*}(n = j \mid n \geq 2)\exp(-\frac{j-1}{\exp(\mu_1)}\varphi(b))(j-1)\right]}. \tag{3.26}$$

Note that the lower support of b expressed here clearly indicates its dependence on the structural parameters, which violates the regularity conditions of the classical maximum likelihood estimation (Donald and Paarsch, 1993, 1996; Chernozhukov and Hong, 2004; Hirano and Porter, 2003). Also note that, although equation (3.20) gives a complicated relationship between b and c, this relationship is monotone increasing. Moreover, it is computationally tractable to compute both $\varphi(b)$ and $\partial\varphi(b)/\partial b$ and hence to evaluate (3.25). Also, define

$$\mu_2 = \mu_1 - x\delta^* - \gamma^*,$$

where $\delta^* = \beta - \delta$, $\gamma^* = \alpha - \gamma$. (3.22) can be rewritten as

$$h(k \mid \mu_1, \delta^*, \gamma^*) = \frac{1}{\exp(\mu_1 - x\delta^* - \gamma^*)} \exp\left[-\frac{1}{\exp(\mu_1 - x\delta^* - \gamma^*)} k\right] \qquad (3.27)$$

for $k \in (0, \infty)$.

Using (3.24) and (3.27), because of the one-to-one (inverse) relationship between q^* and k, as discussed previously, the density for q^* implied by the density of k is

$$p(q^* \mid \mu_1, \delta^*, \gamma^*)$$

$$= h(k \mid \mu_1, \delta^*, \gamma^*) \times \left| \frac{\partial k}{\partial q^*} \right| \times 1(k \le 0.5\exp(\mu_1)),$$

where $1(\cdot)$ is an indicator function and

$$\frac{\partial k}{\partial q^*} = \sum_{j=2}^{N} \left\{ \binom{N-1}{j-1} \frac{\exp(\mu_1)}{j(j-1)} \left[\frac{(j-1)(q^*)^{j-2}(1-q^*)^{N-j}}{1-(1-q^*)^{N-1}} + \frac{(N-j)(q^*)^{j-1}(1-q^*)^{N-j-1}}{1-(1-q^*)^{N-1}} \right. \right.$$
$$\left. \left. - \frac{(N-1)(q^*)^{j-1}(1-q^*)^{2N-j-2}}{\left(1-(1-q^*)^{N-1}\right)^2} \right] \right\}.$$

Since the distributions of u and thus of $e_{new} = \mu_1 - x\beta$ are left unspecified, a nonparametric method is used to approximate the distribution. Specifically, an infinite mixture of normals is used to approximate the unknown distributions. This is justified because Ferguson (1983) notes that any probability density function can be approximated arbitrarily closely in the L_1 norm by a countable mixture of normal densities

$$g(\cdot) = \sum_{j=1}^{\infty} p_j \phi(\cdot \mid d_j, \sigma_j^2), \qquad (3.28)$$

where $p_j \ge 0$, $\sum_{j=1}^{\infty} p_j = 1$ and $\phi(\cdot \mid d_j, \sigma_j^2)$ denotes the probability density function for a normal distribution with mean d_j and variance σ_j^2. Then the joint posterior density of the parameters and unobservables $\mu_{1,\ell}$ and q_ℓ^* given the data and the distribution of the unobserved heterogeneity terms is

$$\pi(\Delta, \{\mu_{1,\ell}, q_\ell^*\}_{\ell=1}^{L} \mid b, n, \{d_\ell, \sigma_\ell^2\}_{\ell=1}^{L})$$

$$\propto prior(\Delta) \times \prod_{\ell=1}^{L} p(b_{1\ell}, \ldots, b_{n_\ell\ell} \mid \mu_{1,\ell}, q_\ell^*) \times p(n_\ell \mid n_\ell \ge 2, q_\ell^*) \times p(q_\ell^* \mid \mu_{1,\ell}, \Delta)$$

$$\times p(\mu_{1,\ell} \mid d_\ell, \sigma_\ell^2) \prod_{i=1}^{n_\ell} 1\left[b_{i\ell} \ge \sum_{j=2}^{N_\ell} P_B, q_\ell^*(n_\ell = j \mid n_\ell \ge 2) \frac{\exp(\mu_{1,\ell})}{(j-1)} \right],$$

where ℓ denotes an auction, L is the total number of auctions and Δ collects all the parameters. An MCMC algorithm is then proposed to obtain the posterior densities for the parameters as well as the nonparametric density for e_{new}.

Gentry et al. (2017) study the identification and inference of the first-price auction model with both risk aversion and selective entry within the IPV framework. First, the authors study under what conditions the model primitives can be set or point identified nonparametrically. Then they study identification and inference of the model when the joint distribution of bidders' private signals prior to entry and private values post entry are specified parametrically using a copula function, while other model primitives are still left unspecified. Denote the copula function specified to be $C(a, s; \theta)$, where C belongs to a known parametric copula family indexed by parameter θ. In this case, the authors show that conditional on θ, other model primitives, that is, the utility function and the distribution for the private values, are nonparametrically identified (the distribution for the private signals prior to entry is normalized to be uniform). θ itself, however, can still be only set identified.

The authors then propose the following semiparametric method for inference on θ. Let δ denote all other parameters indexing the model primitives (such as parameters in Bernstein or Chebyshev polynomials if the sieve method is used to estimate the private value distribution and the utility function) than θ. As MLE for the observed bids suffers from the parameter support-dependent problem well known in the literature, the authors propose a novel regularized maximum likelihood estimation method. In this method, convoluted bids are formed using the original bids through the formula $y_{il} = b_{il} + \eta \varepsilon_{il}$, where b_{il} is the observed bid from bidder I in auction l, $\eta > 0$ is a user-specified smoothing parameter and ε_{il} is a random draw from a known and twice differentiable density $\kappa(\cdot)$. The density based on the convoluted bids y_{il} no longer suffers from the parameter support-dependent problem and MLE can be applied to obtain an estimate for δ. We denote it as $\hat{\delta}_\eta(\theta) = \arg\max_\delta \mathcal{L}_\eta(\delta, \theta)$, where $\mathcal{L}_\eta(\delta, \theta)$ is the likelihood function based on the convoluted bids. We can also obtain the unrestricted conditional MLE estimator of θ as $\hat{\theta}_\eta = \arg\max_\theta \mathcal{L}_\eta(\hat{\delta}_\eta(\theta), \theta)$. Inference on θ can then be conducted using the following profiled sieve likelihood ratio test statistic:

$$LR_\eta(\theta) = 2\left[\mathcal{L}_\eta(\hat{\delta}_\eta(\hat{\theta}_\eta), \hat{\theta}_\eta) - \mathcal{L}_\eta(\hat{\delta}_\eta(\theta), \theta)\right].$$

In the specific application of the current study, the asymptotic distribution of $LR_\eta(\theta)$ simplifies to a chi-squared distribution with degrees of freedom equal to the dimensionality of θ.

Compiani et al. (2020) study the identification and estimation of a first-price auction model with symmetric AVs, unobserved auction heterogeneity and endogenous entry. For each auction t, the observed characteristics are denoted as X_t, the unobserved heterogeneity is denoted as U_t and X_t is assumed to be independent from U_t. The value of U_t is normalized to follow a uniform distribution on $[0,1]$. The number of entrants for each auction is denoted as N_t. The bidders' values $V_t = (V_{1t}, ..., V_{N_t t})$ and signals $S_t = (S_{1t}, ..., S_{N_t t})$ are affiliated. The private value is assumed to have the following structure, $V_{it} = \Gamma(X_t, U_t)V_{it}^0$, where Γ is an index that is bounded and weakly increasing in U_t. Conditional on N_t, V_t^0 and S_t are independent of X_t, U_t. The scale of Γ relative to V_{it}^0 is normalized by setting $\Gamma(x^0, 0) = 1$ for an arbitrary point x^0. With these assumptions, the observed bids can be decomposed into

$$B_{it} = \beta(S_{it}; X_t, U_t, N_t) = \Gamma(X_t, U_t)\beta^0(S_{it}; N_t)$$
$$= \Gamma(X_t, U_t)B_{it}^0,$$

where B_{it}^0 is the homogenized bid and β^0 is the bidding strategy when $\Gamma(X_t, U_t) = \Gamma(x^0, 0) = 1$. One conditional expectation of particular relevance is

$$w\left(s_{it};x_t,u_t,n_t\right) = E\left[V_{it} \mid S_{it} = \max_{j\neq i} S_{jt} = s_{it}, N_t = n_t, X_t = x_t, U_t = u_t\right],$$

which is called "pivotal expected value" in the paper. Finally, the entry stage is modeled as a reduced-form relationship, that is, $N_t = \eta(X_t, Z_t, U_t)$, where Z_t is an exogenous variable that affects entry but is excluded from the bidding equation.

The authors first study the nonparametric identification of the primitives of this auction model, that is, the entry function $\eta(x, z, \cdot)$, the index function $\Gamma(x, u)$ as well as the joint distribution of $w(S_{1t}; x, u, n), \ldots, w(S_{nt}; x, u, n)$, the last of which can be regarded as a partial identification of the joint distribution of V_t and S_t, which in turn is non-identifiable (Laffont and Vuong, 1993).

Then the authors propose a two-stage semiparametric estimation procedure to estimate the model primitives. In the first stage, parameters in the entry model, the index function and the joint distribution of the homogenized bids are estimated. First, since $\eta(X_t, Z_t, U_t)$ is weakly increasing in U_t, given $X_t = x$ and $Z_t = z$, we have $N_t = n$ if and only if $U_t \in (\tau_{n-1}(x, z), \tau_n(x, z))$, where $\tau_{n-1}(x, z) = \inf \{u \in [0,1]: \eta(x, z, u) \geq n\}$. Transform $\tau_n(x, z)$ into $\alpha_n(x, z)$ using $\alpha_n(x, z) = H^{-1}(\tau_n(x, z))$ where H is the standard normal cdf. Then specify $\alpha_n(x, z)$ to be

$$\alpha_n(x,z) = \alpha_n - x\alpha_x - z\alpha_z.$$

With these, the likelihood function for the number of entrants can be written as

$$L_{1t}(n_t;\theta_\tau) = \Pr(N_t = n_t \mid X_t = x_t, Z_t = z_t; \theta_\tau)$$
$$= H(\alpha_n(x_t,z_t;\theta_\tau);\theta_\tau) - H(\alpha_{n-1}(x_t,z_t;\theta_\tau);\theta_\tau),$$

where $\theta_\tau = (\{\alpha_n\}_{n=\underline{n}}^{\bar{n}-1}, \alpha_x, \alpha_z)$. Second, the index function is specified parametrically to be

$$\gamma(x,u;\theta_\gamma) = \ln\Gamma(x,u),$$

where θ_γ is the vector of parameters to be estimated.

As for the joint distribution for the homogenized bids, a semiparametric specification is used. The marginal density of a bidder's log homogenized bid is specified nonparametrically using the Bernstein polynomial sieve, that is,

$$\tilde{g}_{B_i^0}(\tilde{b}^0;\theta_b,n) = \sum_{j=0}^{m}\theta_{b,n}^{(j)}q_{jm}\left(\Phi(\tilde{b}^0)\right)\phi(\tilde{b}^0),$$

where $q_{jm}(v) = \binom{m}{j}v^j(1-v)^{m-j}$ and Φ and ϕ are standard normal cdf and pdf functions. Here, θ_b collects all $\theta_{b,n}^{(j)}$ parameters for $j = 0, \ldots, m$ and $n = \underline{n},\ldots,\bar{n}$. The joint density for all the homogenized bids from one auction is then specified using a Gaussian copula,

$$\tilde{g}_{B_i^0}(\tilde{b}_1^0,\ldots,\tilde{b}_n^0;\theta_{b,n},\rho_n,n) = \chi\left(\tilde{G}_{B_i^0}(\tilde{b}_1^0;\theta_{b,n},n),\ldots,\tilde{G}_{B_i^0}(\tilde{b}_n^0;\theta_{b,n},n);\rho_n\right),$$
$$\tilde{g}_{B_i^0}(\tilde{b}_1^0;\theta_{b,n},n)\ldots\tilde{g}_{B_i^0}(\tilde{b}_n^0;\theta_{b,n},n),$$

where $\chi(\cdot;\rho_n)$ is the Gaussian copula with parameter ρ_n and $\widetilde{G}_{B_i^0}$ is the cdf for B_i^0. Denote ρ as the collection of ρ_n for all n and θ_b the collection of $\theta_{b,n}$ for all n. Then the joint density for all the bids conditional on the number of entrants can be written as

$$L_{2t}(b_t \mid n_t;\theta_b,\rho,\theta_\gamma,\theta_\tau) = \int_{\tau_{n_t-1}(x_t,z_t;\theta_\tau)}^{\tau_{n_t}(x_t,z_t;\theta_\tau)} \frac{\tilde{g}_{B^0}(\tilde{b}_{1t}-\gamma(x_t,u;\theta_\gamma),...,\tilde{b}_{nt}-\gamma(x_t,u;\theta_\gamma);\theta_{b,n_t},\rho_{n_t},n_t)}{\tau_{n_t}(x_t,z_t;\theta_\tau)-\tau_{n_t-1}(x_t,z_t;\theta_\tau)} du.$$

Thus, the first-stage parameters can be estimated by maximizing the following quasi-likelihood function:

$$\pounds(\theta) = \Pi_t L_{1t}(n_t;\theta_\tau)L_{2t}(b_t \mid n_t;\theta_b,\rho,\theta_\gamma,\theta_\tau).$$

The likelihood is called quasi-likelihood function because it ignores the correlation between U_t for different auctions while the model allows for that.

In the second stage, the joint distribution of $w(S_{1t};x,u,n),...,w(S_{nt};x,u,n)$ is estimated. From the first-order condition of the model, we have

$$w(s_{it};x_t,u_t,n_t) = b_{it} + \frac{G_{M|B}(b_{it} \mid b_{it},x_t,u_t,n_t)}{g_{M|B}(b_{it} \mid b_{it},x_t,u_t,n_t)},$$

where $G_{M|B}(b \mid b, x, u, n) = \Pr(\max_{j\neq i} B_{jt} \leq m|B_{it} = b, X_t = x, U_t = u, N_t = n)$ and $g_{M|B}$ is the corresponding density. The authors show that, with the assumptions made, $w(s_{it}; x_t, u_t, n_t)$ can be decomposed into

$$w(s_{it};x_t,u_t,n_t) = w^0(s_{it};n_t)\Gamma(x_t,u_t), \tag{3.29}$$

where $w^0(s_{it};n_t) = E[V_{it}^0 \mid S_{it} = \max_{j\neq i} S_{jt} = s_{it}, N_t = n_t]$ is the homogenized pivotal expected value. With this, the first-order condition can be rewritten as

$$w^0(s_{it};n_t) = b_{it}^0 + \frac{G_{M^0|B^0}(b_{it}^0 \mid b_{it}^0,n_t)}{g_{M^0|B^0}(b_{it}^0 \mid b_{it}^0,n_t)},$$

which in turn can be further written as

$$w^0(s_{it};n_t) = \exp(\tilde{b}_{it}^0)\left[1 + \frac{G_{M^0|B^0}(\tilde{b}_{it}^0 \mid \tilde{b}_{it}^0,n_t)}{g_{M^0|B^0}(\tilde{b}_{it}^0 \mid \tilde{b}_{it}^0,n_t)}\right], \tag{3.30}$$

where $\tilde{b}_{it}^0$ is the log homogenized bid previously defined. With the joint distribution of the log homogenized bids estimated from the first stage, one can use (3.30) to recover pseudo-homogenized pivotal expected values $w^0(s_{it}; n_t)$ and then pseudo-pivotal expected values $w(s_{it}; x_t, u_t, n_t)$ through (3.29). Once the pseudo-pivotal expected values are recovered, the joint distribution of $w(S_{1t}; x, u, n), \ldots, w(S_{nt}; x, u, n)$ can be easily estimated.

4. PARTIAL IDENTIFICATION APPROACHES

This section focuses on the partial identification literature in the structural approach. While it is desirable to have an auction model whose model primitives are nonparametrically identified, in various cases, when the model is more general or with weaker assumptions, point identification is no longer possible. The partial identification approach, on the other hand, can often provide useful information for the model primitives as it yields an identified set (bound) that is usually informative, and inference can be made with the recently developed inference methods in the partial identification literature.

4.1 Bounding the Model Primitives

Haile and Tamer (2003) propose a method to estimate the bounds of the private value distribution for an English auction model with weak assumptions. The first assumption is that bidders do not bid more than they are willing to pay. The second assumption is that bidders do not allow an opponent to win at a price they are willing to beat. These two assumptions are weak and intuitively reasonable. In particular, these two assumptions do not exclude the jump bidding phenomenon we often observe in real-world online auctions.

Suppose we have T identical auctions and each auction has N bidders. We observe the last bid b_i by each of the N bidders during the English auction. With our first assumption, we have

$$b_{i:N} \le v_{i:N},\tag{3.31}$$

where $b_{i:N}$ ($v_{i:N}$) is the i-th order statistic of bids (private values), with $i = 1$ being the smallest and $i = N$ the largest. This means that an order statistic of the observed bids is also less than or equal to the corresponding order statistic of the private values. Let us denote G_B^0 as the true distribution for the observed bids and F_v^0 the true distribution of the private values. Then (3.31) implies that

$$G_{i:N}^0(v) \ge F_{i:N}^0(v) \text{ for any } i, v,\tag{3.32}$$

which means the distribution for $B_{i:N}$ first order dominates the distribution for $V_{i:N}$. On the other hand, using the formula from order statistics, we can express $F_{i:N}^0(v)$ in terms of the underlying distribution F_v^0 as

$$F_{i:N}^0(v) = \frac{N!}{(N-i)!(i-1)!} \int_0^{F_v^0(v)} u^{N-i}(1-u)^{i-1} du.\tag{3.33}$$

It can be easily shown that there is a monotone increasing relationship between $F_{i:N}^0(v)$ and $F_v^0(v)$. Therefore, if we write $F_{i:N}^0(v) = \varphi\left(F_v^0(v), N, i\right)$, we can recover $F_v^0(v)$ as

$$F_v^0(v) = \varphi^{-1}\left(F_{i:N}^0(v), i, N\right)$$

$$\le \varphi^{-1}\left(G_{i:N}^0(v), i, N\right),\tag{3.34}$$

where the inequality follows from (3.32) and the fact that φ^{-1} is a monotone increasing function. Since (3.34) holds for any i, it follows that

$$F_V^0(v) \leq F_U^0(v) \tag{3.35}$$

$$= \min_{i=1,\dots N} \begin{bmatrix} \varphi^{-1}\left(G_{1:N}^0(v),1,N\right) \\ ,\dots \varphi^{-1}\left(G_{N:N}^0(v),N,N\right) \end{bmatrix}.$$

Hence, $F_U^0(v)$ is the upper bound for $F_V^0(v)$. Note that $F_U^0(v)$ can be estimated from the data because we know the functional form for φ^{-1}. Also, $G_{i:N}^0(v)$ is the distribution of order statistics for bids and hence can be estimated from observed bid data.

Recovering the lower bound for $F_V^0(v)$ is a little bit more involved. The English auction under consideration allows for jump bidding and let us denote the smallest bid increment allowed as Δ. Then, assumption 2 implies the following:

$$V_i \leq U_i = \begin{cases} \bar{v} \text{ if } B_i = W \\ W + \Delta \text{ if } B_i < W \end{cases}, \tag{3.36}$$

where W denotes the winning bid of the auction, which further implies that

$$V_{N-1:N} \leq W + \Delta, \tag{3.37}$$

where $V_{N-1:N}$ is the second largest order statistic among the N private values. This is because, by definition, $V_{N-1:N} \leq V_{N:N}$ and the bidder with private value $V_{N-1:N}$ is not the winner of the auction. Here, $V_{N:N}$ is the largest order statistic among the N private values. Further, (3.37) implies that

$$F_{N-1:N}^0(v) \geq G_{W+\Delta}^0(v) \text{ for any } v. \tag{3.38}$$

Using (3.34), we have

$$F_V^0(v) = \varphi^{-1}\left(F_{N-1:N}^0(v), N-1, N\right) \tag{3.39}$$

$$\geq \varphi^{-1}\left(G_{W+\Delta}^0(v), N-1, N\right) = F_L^0(v),$$

where the inequality follows from (3.38) and the fact that φ^{-1} is a monotone increasing function. Hence, $F_L^0(v)$ is the lower bound for $F_V^0(v)$. Similarly, the lower bound $F_L^0(v)$ can also be estimated from the observed data on bids.

To estimate the upper and lower bounds, we first use the standard nonparametric methods to estimate the empirical distribution function of $G_{i:N}$ and $G_{W+\Delta}$ using data on the observed order statistics of bids and the winning bid and the bid increment. Then we can estimate the upper and lower bounds as

$$\widehat{F_U}(v) = \min_{i=1,\dots N} \begin{bmatrix} \varphi^{-1}\left(\widehat{G_{1:N}}(v),1,N\right) \\ ,\dots \varphi^{-1}\left(\widehat{G_{N:N}}(v),N,N\right) \end{bmatrix}$$

$$\hat{F}_L(v) = \varphi^{-1}\left(\hat{G}_{W+\Delta}(v), N-1, N\right). \tag{3.40}$$

Gentry and Li (2014) study the nonparametric identification of auction models with selective entry. Consider a two-stage auction game with N potential bidders. In the first stage, the bidders observe private signals of their private values of the object being auctioned. All potential bidders simultaneously decide whether to enter the auction. Those who choose to enter need to incur an entry cost of c. In the second stage, the n bidders who enter learn their actual values of the object and then decide how to bid based on their values. The joint cdf of the values and signals is denoted as $F(v,s)$ and, without loss of generality, the marginal distribution for the signals is normalized to be uniform on [0,1].

In equilibrium, in the first stage, there exists an entry threshold $\bar{s} \in [0,1]$ such that bidder i chooses to enter if and only if $s_i \geq \bar{s}$. Therefore, the selected distribution of values among entrants at threshold $\bar{s}$ is

$$F^*(v;\bar{s}) = \frac{1}{1-\bar{s}}\int_{\bar{s}}^1 F(v\,|\,t)dt, \tag{3.41}$$

where $F(v|s)$ is the conditional cdf of the private value in the second stage conditional on the private signal in the first stage. For a potential bidder with private signal s_i, his expected profit from entering the auction given the entry threshold is $\bar{s}$ and there are N potential bidders can be written as

$$\Pi(s_i;\bar{s},N) = \int_0^{v_u}\left[1-F(y\,|\,s_i)\right]\left[\bar{s}+(1-\bar{s})F^*(v;\bar{s})\right]^{N-1}dy, \tag{3.42}$$

where v_u is the upper bound for the private value distribution. The equilibrium entry threshold is determined by

$$\Pi(s^*;s^*,N) = c. \tag{3.43}$$

It is clear that the equilibrium threshold $s*$ is a function of N and c, denoted as $s_N^*(c)$. The structural elements of this model are the entry cost c and $F(v|s)$. Once $F(v|s)$ is known and the marginal distribution for s is assumed to be uniform, $F(v,s)$ is obtained as well.

This model is general as it encompasses the commonly used random entry model (Levin and Smith, 1994) and perfectly selective entry model (Samuelson, 1985) as polar cases and has recently gained attention in the literature; see for example, Marmer et al. (2013) for testing the selection effect in first price auctions and Roberts and Sweeting (2013, 2016) for using this model in addressing policy issues in timber auctions. However, the model is nonparametrically not identified using observed bids, number of potential bidders, number of actual bidders as well as each potential bidder's entry behavior because the private signal before entry is not observed by the econometrician. Suppose there exists a set of instruments Z that affects the entry cost c and hence the entry behavior of the bidders, but not the private signals and values. Since c is now a function of z, the equilibrium threshold can be written as $s_N^*(c(z))$, which can be estimated using

$$\hat{s}_N(z) = 1 - \frac{E(n\,|\,N,z)}{N}. \tag{3.44}$$

As a result, the selected distribution of the private values conditional on entry can be estimated using

$$\hat{F}(v \mid N, z) = F^*(v; \hat{s}_N(z)).$$ (3.45)

Also, the set of identified signal thresholds can be written as

$$S = \{s \in [0,1] \mid s = \hat{s}_N(z) \text{ for some } (N, z) \in \mathcal{L}\},$$

where $\mathcal{L}$ is the sample space for (N, z).

The authors first study the identification with the ideal case, the case where at least one continuous instrument z is available that induces the set of signal thresholds S to be non-empty. For any $\hat{s} \in S$, from (3.41) we have

$$F^*(v; \hat{s}) = \frac{1}{1-\hat{s}} \int_{\hat{s}}^1 F(v \mid t) dt,$$

which implies that

$$F(v \mid \hat{s}) = -\frac{\partial}{\partial \hat{s}} \left[(1 - \hat{s}) F^*(v; \hat{s}) \right].$$

The value of $\hat{s}$ is identified from (3.44) while $F^*(v; \hat{s}) = \hat{F}(v \mid N, z)$ is identified from the observed bid distribution, the latter of which is a well-established result in the literature. As a result, $F(v \mid \hat{s})$ is point identified for any $\hat{s} \in S$. Also, from (3.42) and (3.43), we have

$$c(z) = \int_0^v \left[1 - F(y \mid \hat{s}_N(z)) \right] \left[\hat{s}_N(z) + (1 - \hat{s}_N(z)) F^*(v; \hat{s}_N(z)) \right]^{N-1} dy.$$

Since $\hat{s}$, $F^*(v; \hat{s})$ and $F(v \mid \hat{s})$ are all point identified, $c(z)$ is also point identified.

When a continuous instrument Z is not available, the identified set of signal thresholds may not be complete. When it is incomplete, we can only identify bounds on the model fundamentals. More specifically, for any $\hat{s} \in [0,1]$, we have

$$F^+(v \mid \hat{s}) \geq F(v \mid \hat{s}) \geq F^-(v \mid \hat{s}),$$

where

$$F^+(v \mid s) = \begin{cases} \widehat{F}^+(v \mid s) \text{ if } s \in S \\ \widehat{F}^+(v \mid t^-(s)), \text{ if } s \notin S, \end{cases}$$

$$F^-(v \mid s) = \begin{cases} \widehat{F}^-(v \mid s) \text{ if } s \in S \\ \widehat{F}^-(v \mid t^+(s)), \text{ if } s \notin S, \end{cases}$$

$$\widehat{F}^{+}(v\,|\,\hat{s}) = \begin{cases} \lim_{t\uparrow t^{-}(\hat{s})} \left\{ \dfrac{(1-t)F^{*}(v;t)-(1-\hat{s})F^{*}(v;\hat{s})}{\hat{s}-t} \right\} & \text{if } \hat{s} \in S \text{ and } t^{-}(\hat{s}) \in S \\[2ex] 1, \text{ otherwise,} \end{cases}$$

$$\widehat{F}^{-}(v\,|\,\hat{s}) = \begin{cases} \lim_{t\downarrow t^{+}(\hat{s})} \left\{ \dfrac{(1-\hat{s})F^{*}(v;\hat{s})-(1-t)F^{*}(v;t)}{t-\hat{s}} \right\} & \text{if } \hat{s} \in S \\[2ex] 1, \text{ otherwise,} \end{cases}$$

$$t^{+}(\hat{s}) = \begin{cases} \inf\{t \in S\,|\,t > s\} & \text{if } \sup\{S\} > s \\[1ex] 1, \text{ otherwise,} \end{cases}$$

and

$$t^{-}(\hat{s}) = \begin{cases} \sup\{t \in S\,|\,t < s\} & \text{if } \inf\{S\} < s \\[1ex] 0, \text{ otherwise.} \end{cases}$$

Furthermore, we have the bounds on the entry cost as

$$c^{+}(z) \geq c(z) \geq c^{-}(z),$$

where $c^{+}(z) = \min_{N \in \mathbb{N}} c_{N}^{+}(z)$, $c^{-}(z) = \min_{N \in \mathbb{N}} c_{N}^{-}(z)$,

$$c_{N}^{+}(z) = \int_{0}^{v_{u}} \left[1 - F^{-}(y\,|\,\hat{s}_{N}(z))\right]\left[\hat{s}_{N}(z) + (1-\hat{s}_{N}(z))F^{*}(v;\hat{s}_{N}(z))\right]^{N-1} dy$$

and

$$c_{N}^{-}(z) = \int_{0}^{v_{u}} \left[1 - F^{+}(y\,|\,\hat{s}_{N}(z))\right]\left[\hat{s}_{N}(z) + (1-\hat{s}_{N}(z))F^{*}(v;\hat{s}_{N}(z))\right]^{N-1} dy.$$

The authors then extend their analysis to accommodate non-separable unobserved auction-level heterogeneity and potential endogeneity of entry shifters.

4.2   Using Bidding Data from First-Price Auctions to Bound Revenues from a Counterfactual Auction Format

Haile and Tamer (2003) show that the optimal reserve price, one of the counterfactual parameters of interest, can be bounded from their bounds on the underlying private value distribution. However, bounds on primitives do not necessarily translate immediately into bounds on counterfactuals of interest. Sometimes it makes more sense to go directly to the counterfactual as the "parameter" of interest. Shneyerov (2006) provides methods for how to use bidding data from first-price auctions to estimate bounds on expected revenue under the counterfactual English auction format in the Milgrom and Weber (1982) AV framework without making parametric assumptions regarding the model primitives.

Consider a first-price auction with n risk-neutral bidders. Each bidder observes a private signal S_i of the object being auctioned. His value of the object is $V(S_i, U)$, where U is the common value component of the bidders' valuations. Bidder i does not observe S_{-i} and U. All the private signals and U are affiliated; V is increasing in S_i and nondecreasing in U. Define $v(x, y) = E(V|S_i = x, \max_{j \neq 1} S_j = y)$. The equilibrium bidding function in this case is defined as a solution to the following differential equation:

$$B'(s) = (v(s,s) - B(s)) \frac{f(s \mid s)}{F(s \mid s)} \text{ for } s \geq s^*, \tag{3.46}$$

where $B(s^*) = r$, r is the binding reserve price, $F(s|s)$ is the conditional distribution of the maximal rival signal and $f(s|s)$ is its corresponding density. Therefore, the expected revenue is $R_F = EB(S_{(1)})$, where $S_{(1)}$ denotes the highest private signal.

In the same framework, if the auction format used is the sealed-bid second-price auction, then each bidder will bid his own value. In this case, the equilibrium bidding strategy is simply

$$B^*(s) = v(s,s),$$

and the expected revenue in this case is simply $R_S = EB^*(S_{(2)})$, where $S_{(2)}$ denotes the second highest private signal.

If the auction format used is an ascending-bid English auction, then the price is formed at the stage when the last two remaining bidders engage in a second-price auction. In this case, suppose the highest private signal is t and the second highest private signal is s then the bidder with the second highest private signal has the expected value of $w(t, s) = E(V|S_{(1)} = t, S_{(2)} = s)$ and this will be the price the winner pays. Hence, in this case the expected revenue is $R_E = E(w(S_{(1)}, S_{(2)}))$.

Milgrom and Weber (1982) prove that, in this framework, we have $R_E \geq R_S \geq R_F$.

To estimate the bounds for R_E, first notice that R_S is the lower bound for R_E. So once R_S is estimated, we obtain a lower bound for R_E. To proceed, Guerre et al. (2000) and Li et al. (2002) notice that (3.46) can be rewritten as

$$E\left[V \mid B(S_1) = b, \max_{i \neq 1} B(S_i) = b\right] = b + \frac{G(b \mid b)}{g(b \mid b)} = \xi(b). \tag{3.47}$$

Therefore, we have

$$\xi(B(s)) = E(V \mid S_1 = s, \max_{i \neq 1} S_i = s) = v(s,s) = B^*(s).$$

Hence, R_S can be estimated using $E\xi(B_{(2)})$, where $B_{(2)}$ is the observed second highest bid. To obtain an upper bound for R_E, we note that

$$w(t,s) = E(V \mid S_{(1)} = t, S_{(2)} = s)$$
$$\leq E(V \mid S_{(1)} = t, S_{(2)} = t)$$
$$= v(t,t) = B^*(t),$$

where the inequality follows from the fact that $w(t, s)$ is nondecreasing in s due to the affiliation of the private signals and monotonicity of V. Therefore, $R_E \leq E(B^*(t)) = E\xi(B_{(1)})$, where $B_{(1)}$ is the observed highest bid.

Finally, to implement the procedure, $\xi(\cdot)$ is estimated using the nonparametric estimation method proposed by Guerre et al. (2000) and Li et al. (2002).

Tang (2011) provides methods for how to use bidding data from first-price auctions to estimate bounds on revenue distributions under counterfactual reserve prices or in a counterfactual second-price auction format in the Milgrom and Weber (1982) AV framework without making parametric assumptions regarding the model primitives.

Consider a first-price auction with N potential, risk-neutral bidders. Each bidder observes a private signal X_i of the object being auctioned. His value of the object is $V_i = \theta(X_i, X_{-i})$, where X_{-i} are the private signals by other bidders than bidder i. Bidder i does not observe X_{-i} and hence V_i. All the private signals are affiliated and their joint distribution is F. The value of V_i is increasing in X_i and nondecreasing in X_{-i}. Define $v(x, y) = E(V_i|X_i = x, Y_i \leq y)$, where $Y_i = \max_{j \neq i} X_j$; therefore, $v(x, x)$ denotes the winner's expected value conditional on his signal being x. If there is a binding reserve price r, then $x^*(r) = v^{-1}(r)$ is the screening level in the signal such that only bidders with a signal higher than $x^*(r)$ would bid. The equilibrium bid in this case is

$$b_r(x;x^*) = rL(x^*(r)|x) + \int_{x^*(r)}^{x} v_h(s,s)dL(s|x), \tag{3.48}$$

where $L(s|x) = \exp\{-\int_s^x \Lambda(u)du\}$, $\Lambda(x) = \frac{f_{Y|X}(x|x)}{F_{Y|X}(x|x)}$ and $v_h(x, y) = E(V_i|X_i = x, Y_i = y)$.

The main idea of the proposed method is the following. Without making any parametric assumptions regarding the model primitives, bounds on v can be derived, which further implies the bounds on $x^*(r)$, which in turn leads to bounds on b_r and the distributions of revenues with reserve price r. More specifically, note we have the following relationship:

$$v_h(x,y) \geq E[v_h(x,s)|x,s \leq y]$$

$$= \int_{x_L}^{y} E(V_i|X_i = x, Y_i = s)\frac{f_{Y|X}(s|x)}{F_{Y|X}(y|x)}ds$$

$$= \int_{\underline{v}}^{\bar{v}} \frac{V_i}{\Pr(Y_i \leq y|x)}\int_{x_L}^{y} f(V_i, Y_i = s|X_i = x)dsdV_i$$

$$= \int_{\underline{v}}^{\bar{v}} V_i f(V_i|X_i = x, Y_i \leq y)dV_i$$

$$= E(V_i|X_i = x, Y_i \leq y) = v(x,y)$$

$$\geq \int_{x_L}^{y} v_h(s,s)\frac{f_{Y|X}(s|x)}{F_{Y|X}(y|x)}ds = v_l(x,y),$$

where x_L is the lower bound for the signal, the $\geq$ in the first line follows from the assumption that V_i is nondecreasing in X_{-i} and the $\geq$ in the last line follows from the assumption that V_i is increasing in X_i.

Define $x_l^*(r) = v_l^{-1}(r)$ and $x_h^*(r) = v_h^{-1}(r)$, where v_h^{-1} is the inverse function for $v_h(x,x)$ and v_l^{-1} is the inverse function for $v_l(x,x)$. It is then proved that $x_l^*(r)$ and $x_h^*(r)$ form tight bounds on $x^*(r)$, pointwise for all r. The bounds are tight in the sense that (i) there exists some

$\{\theta, F\}$ satisfying the assumptions previously made such that $x_l^*(r) = x^*(r)$ for all r and (ii) for all $\varepsilon > 0$ there exists some structure $\{\theta^\varepsilon, F^\varepsilon\}$ satisfying the assumptions made such that $\sup_r |x_h^*(r) - x^*(r)| \le \varepsilon$. Plugging the bounds $x_l^*(r)$ and $x_h^*(r)$ into (3.48) gives the bounds on the bids, $b_r(x_k^*(r); x_k^*)$ for $k = l, h$. With the bounds on the bids, one can then construct the bounds for the counterfactual distribution of revenues $H(.;r)$ as follows:

$$H^k(t;r) = 0 \text{ for } t < v_0$$

$$H^k(t;r) = \Pr(X^{(1)} < x_k^*(r)) \text{ for } v_0 \le t < r$$

$$H^k(t;r) = \Pr(X^{(1)} < \eta_{k,r}(t;x_k^*)) \text{ for } t > r,$$

where v_0 is the seller's own value of the object being auctioned, $X^{(1)}$ is the highest private signal and $\eta_{k,r}(t;x_k^*)$ is the inverse bid function. These bounds are sharp in the sense that, for any t and r greater than v_0 and for any $H^l(t;r) \le p \le H^h(t;r)$, there exists some structure $\{\theta, F\}$ satisfying the assumptions such that the true counterfactual revenue distribution is $H(t;r) = p$.

To estimate the bounds, v_h and v_l can be estimated nonparametrically using the same method as in Shneyerov (2006) by estimating (3.47) nonparametrically, which then leads to nonparametric estimates of the bounds $x_k^*(r)$, $b_r(x_k^*(r); x_k^*)$ and $H^k(t;r)$ for $k = l, h$.

The bounds for the distribution of revenues for a counterfactual second price auction can also be estimated using a similar methodology.

5. CONCLUSIONS

Empirical analysis of auction data has become a significantly developed area in empirical industrial organization over the past thirty years. In this chapter, we focus on discussing the three topics that have been given less attention and some of the most recent work that has not been discussed in the existing surveys. As previously mentioned, these three topics, namely, testing model implications or informational assumptions, semiparametric approaches and partial identification approaches, are important as they are at the center of integrating theory with empirical analysis, and have also both pushed and benefited from the recent frontier research in econometrics. They also share a common feature in that all are very useful in providing robust and feasible empirical methods to analyze auction data, without making assumptions that are too strong, which should be the direction of future research in econometric analysis of auction data.

NOTES

* We thank Phil Haile for his insightful comments.
1. Hendricks, Porter and Spady (1989) extend Hendricks and Porter (1988) to assume that the reserve price is random and independent of the common value of the tract (V) and the private signal of the informed bidder (X). The model implications and testing strategies are both similar to the *American Economics Review* (AER) paper. This paper is further extended in Hendricks, Porter and Wilson (1994) by assuming the random reserve price, the private signal and the common value are affiliated. The model predicts the following: (1) the percentage rate of increase in the distribution of the highest uninformed bid is never greater than the percentage rate of increase of the distribution of the highest informed bid; (2) the two distributions are identical at bids above the support of the reserve price; and (3) the informed bidder is more likely to submit low bids. They then conduct some informal tests of these predictions using empirical cdfs of the two bid distributions and their associated statistics.

2. de Castro and Paarsch (2010) propose to use discretized bids to test for affiliation.
3. Since our focus here is on testing collusion, we will not discuss the work in using the structural approach to analyzing bidders' collusive behavior (for example Asker (2010), and Bajari and Ye (2003)).
4. Note that the left-hand side of this equation is a function of $q^*_{M_1}$ only given N and μ_1 and it goes to its maximum value $0.5\exp(\mu_1)$ as $q^*_{M_1} \to 0$. Therefore, the entry cost equation implies that, for this model, the entry costs in the observed auctions must satisfy the restriction $k \le 0.5\exp(\mu_1)$, which has to be taken into account in the estimation.

REFERENCES

Asker, J. (2010): "A Study of the Internal Organization of a Bidding Cartel," *American Economic Review*, 100, 724–62.

Athey, S. C. and P. A. Haile (2007): "Nonparametric Approaches to Auctions," in James J. Heckman and Edward E. Leamer, editors, *Handbook of Econometrics*, Volume 6A, pp. 3847–966. Elsevier.

Bajari, P. and L. Ye (2003): "Deciding between Competition and Collusion," *Review of Economics and Statistics*, 85, 971–89.

Baldwin, L. H., R. C. Marshall and J.-F. Richard (1997): "Bidder Collusion at Forest Service Timber Sales," *Journal of Political Economy*, 105, 4, 657–99.

Beggs, S., S. Cardell and J. Hausman (1981): "Assessing the Potential Demand for Electric Cars," *Journal of Econometrics*, 17, 1, 1–19.

Campo, S., E. Guerre, I. Perrigne and Q. Vuong (2011): "Semiparametric Estimation of First-Price Auctions with Risk-Averse Bidders," *Review of Economic Studies*, 78, 112–47.

Chernozhukov, V. and H. Hong (2004): "Likelihood Estimation and Inference in a Class of Nonregular Econometric Models," *Econometrica*, 72, 5, 1445–80.

Compiani, G., P. Haile and M. Sant'Anna (2020): "Common Values, Unobserved Heterogeneity, and Endogenous Entry in U.S. Offshore Oil Lease Auctions," *Journal of Political Economy*, 128, 10, 3872–912.

de Castro, L. I., and H. J. Paarsch (2010): "Testing for Affiliation in Private-Values Models in First-Price Auctions using Grid Distributions," *Annals of Applied Statistics*, 4, 2073–98.

Donald, S. G. and H. J. Paarsch (1993): "Piecewise Pseudo-Maximum Likelihood Estimation in Empirical Models of Auctions," *International Economic Review*, 34, 1, 121–48.

Donald, S. G. and H. J. Paarsch (1996): "Identification, Estimation and Testing in Parametric Empirical Methods of Auctions Within the Independent Private Values Paradigm," *Econometric Theory*, 12, 517–67.

Fang, H. and X. Tang (2014): "Inference of Bidders' Risk Attitudes in Ascending Auctions with Endogenous Entry," *Journal of Econometrics*, 180, 198–216.

Ferguson, T. S. (1983): "Bayesian Density Estimation by Mixtures of Normal Distributions," in H. Rizvi and K. Rustagi, editors, *Recent Advances in Statistics: Papers in Honor of Herman Chernoff on His Sixtieth Birthday*, Academic Press, pp. 287–302.

Gentry, M., T. P. Hubbard, D. Nekipelov and H. J. Paarsch (2018): "Structural Econometrics of Auctions: A Review," *Foundations and Trends in Econometrics*, 9, 2–4, 79–302.

Gentry, M. and T. Li (2014): "Identification in Auctions with Selective Entry," *Econometrica*, 82, 1, 315–44.

Gentry, M., T. Li and J. Lu (2017): "Identification and Inference in First-Price Auctions with Risk Averse Bidders and Selective Entry," Working Paper.

Guerre, E., I. Perrigne, and Q. Vuong (2000): "Optimal Nonparametric Estimation of First-Price Auctions," *Econometrica*, 68, 525–74.

Haile, P. A., H. Hong and M. Shum (2003): "Nonparametric Tests for Common Values in First-Price Sealed-Bid Auctions," NBER Working Paper.

Haile, P. and E. Tamer (2003): "Inference with an Incomplete Model of English Auctions," *Journal of Political Economy*, 111, 1–51.

Hendricks, K., J. Pinkse and R. H. Porter (2003): "Empirical Implications of Equilibrium Bidding in First-Price, Symmetric, Common Value Auctions," *Review of Economic Studies*, 70, 115–45.

Hendricks, K. and R. H. Porter (1988): "An Empirical Study of an Auction with Asymmetric Information," *American Economic Review*, 78, 865–83.

Hendricks, K. and R. H. Porter (2007): "An Empirical Perspective on Auctions," In Mark Armstrong and Robert H. Porter, editors, *Handbook of Industrial Organization*, Volume 3. Elsevier, pp. 2073–2143. Elsevier, New York.

Hendricks, K., R. H. Porter and B. Boudreau (1987): "Information, Returns, and Bidding Behavior in OCS Auctions: 1954–1969," *Journal of Industrial Economics*, 35, 517–42.

Hendricks, K., R. H. Porter and R. H. Spady (1989): "Random Reservation Prices and Bidding Behavior in OCS Drainage Auctions," *Journal of Law and Economics*, 32, S83–S106.

Hendricks, K., R. H. Porter and G. Tan (2008): "Bidding Rings and the Winner's Curse," *RAND Journal of Economics*, 39, 4, 1018–41.

Hendricks, K., R. H. Porter and C. A. Wilson (1994): "Auctions for Oil and Gas Leases with an Informed Bidder and a Random Reservation Price," *Econometrica*, 62, 6, 1415–44.

Hickman, B. R., T. P. Hubbard, and Y. Sağlam (2012): "Structural Econometric Methods in Auctions: A Guide to the Literature," *Journal of Econometric Methods*, 1, 67–106.

Hill, J. B. and A. Shneyerov (2013): "Are There Common Values in First-Price Auctions? A Tail-Index Nonparametric Test," *Journal of Econometrics*, 174, 144–64.

Hirano, K. and J. R. Porter (2003): "Asymptotic Efficiency in Parametric Structural Models with Parameter-Dependent Support," *Econometrica*, 71, 5, 1307–38.

Hubbard, T. P., T. Li and H. J. Paarsch (2012): "Semiparametric Estimation in Models of First-Price, Sealed-Bid Auctions with Affiliation," *Journal of Econometrics*, 168, 4–16.

Jun, S. J., J. Pinkse and Y. Wan (2010): "A Consistent Nonparametric Test of Affiliation in Auction Models," *Journal of Econometrics*, 159, 46–54.

Klemperer, P. D. (2004): *Auctions: Theory and Practice*. Princeton University Press.

Krishna, V. (2010): *Auction Theory, 2nd ed.* Academic Press, San Diego.

Laffont, J. J. and Q. Vuong (1993): "Structural Econometric Analysis of Descending Auctions," *European Economic Review*, 37, 329–41.

Levin, D. and J. L. Smith (1994): "Equilibrium in Auctions with Entry," *American Economic Review*, 84, 3, 585–99.

Li, T., J. Lu and L. Zhao (2015): "Auctions with Selective Entry and Risk Averse Bidders: Theory and Evidence," *RAND Journal of Economics*, 46, 3, 524–45.

Li, T., I. Perrigne and Q. Vuong (2002): "Structural Estimation of the Affiliated Private Value Auction Model," *RAND Journal of Economics*, 33, 171–93.

Li, T., I. Perrigne and Q. Vuong (2003): "Semiparametric Estimation of the Optimal Reserve Price in First-Price Auctions," *Journal of Business and Economic Statistics*, 21, 1, 53–64.

Li, T. and B. Zhang (2010): "Testing for Affiliation in First-Price Auctions Using Entry Behavior," *International Economic Review*, 51, 3, 837–50.

Li, T. and X. Zheng (2009): "Entry and Competition Effects in First-Price Auctions: Theory and Evidence from Procurement Auctions," *Review of Economic Studies*, 76, 1397–429.

Lu, J. and I. Perrigne (2008): "Estimating Risk Aversion from Ascending and Sealed-Bid Auctions: The Case of Timber Auction Data," *Journal of Applied Econometrics*, 23, 871–96.

Marmer, V., A. Shneyerov and P. Xu (2013): "What Model for Entry in First-Price Auctions? A Nonparametric Approach," *Journal of Econometrics*, 176, 1, 46–58.

Milgrom, P. R. (2004): *Putting Auction Theory to Work*. New York: Cambridge University Press.

Milgrom, P. R. and R. J. Weber (1982): "A Theory of Auctions and Competitive Bidding," *Econometrica*, 50, 5, 1089–1122.

Paarsch, H. J. (1992): "Deciding Between the Common and Private Value Paradigms in Empirical Models of Auctions," *Journal of Econometrics*, 51, 191–215.

Paarsch, H. J. and H. Hong (2006): *An Introduction to Structural Econometrics of Auction Data*. MIT Press.

Papke, L. E. and J. M. Wooldridge (1996): "Econometric Methods for Fractional Response Variables with an Application to 401(K) Plan Participation Rates," *Journal of Applied Econometrics*, 11, 619–32.

Perrigne, I. and Vuong, Q. H. (1999): "Structural Econometrics of First-Price Auctions: A Survey of Methods," *Canadian Journal of Agricultural Economics/Revue Canadienne D'agroeconomie*, 47, 203–223.

Pesendorfer, M. (2000): "A Study of Collusion in First-Price Auctions," *Review of Economic Studies*, 67, 381–411.

Pinkse, J. and G. Tan (2005): "The Affiliation Effect in First-Price Auctions," *Econometrica*, 73, 263–77.

Porter, R. H. and J. D. Zona (1993): "Detection of Bid Rigging in Procurement Auctions," *Journal of Political Economy*, 101, 3, 518–38.

Porter, R. H. and J. D. Zona (1999): "Ohio School Milk Markets: An Analysis of Bidding," *RAND Journal of Economics*, 30, 2, 263–88.

Roberts, J. and A. Sweeting (2013): "When Should Sellers Use Auctions?" *American Economic Review*, 103, 5, 1830–61.

Roberts, J. and A. Sweeting (2016): "Bailouts and the Preservation of Competition: The Case of the Federal Timber Contract Payment Modification Act," *American Economic Journal: Microeconomics*, 8, 3, 257–88.

Samuelson, W. F. (1985): "Competitive Bidding with Entry Costs," *Economics Letters*, 17, 1–2, 53–7.

Shneyerov, A. (2006): "An Empirical Study of Auction Revenue Rankings: The Case of Municipal Bonds," *RAND Journal of Economics*, 37, 1005–22.

Tang, X. (2011): "Bounds on Revenue Distributions in Counterfactual Auctions with Reserve Prices," *RAND Journal of Economics*, 42, 1, 175–203.

Wilson, R. (1977): "A Bidding Model of Perfect Competition," *Review of Economic Studies*, 44, 511–18.

Vickrey, W. S. (1961): "Counterspeculation, Auctions, and Competitive Sealed Tenders," *Journal of Finance*, 16, 8–37.

4. An introduction to flexible methods for policy evaluation[*]

Martin Huber

1. INTRODUCTION

The last decades have witnessed important advancements in policy evaluation methods for assessing the causal effect of a treatment on an outcome of interest, which are particularly relevant in the context of data with many observations and/or observed covariates. Such advancements include the development or refinement of quasi-experimental evaluation techniques, estimators for flexible (that is, semi- or nonparametric) treatment effect models and machine learning algorithms for a data-driven control for covariates in order to tackle confounding, learn effect heterogeneities across subgroups and target groups for which the treatment is most effective. Policy evaluation methods aim at assessing causal effects despite the problem that, for any subject in the data, outcomes cannot be observed at the same time in the presence and absence of the treatment. As an illustration of this fundamental problem for causality, consider the treatment effect of a job application training for jobseekers on employment. Identifying this effect at the individual level requires comparing the employment state for a specific subject at a particular point in time with and without training participation. However, at a specific point in time, an individual can be observed to have either participated or not participated in the training, but not both. Therefore, treatment effects remain unidentified on the individual level without strong assumptions.

Formally, denote by D a binary treatment such that $D = 1$ if, for instance, someone participates in a training and $D = 0$ otherwise. Furthermore, denote by Y the observed outcome, for example employment. Following Rubin (1974), let $Y(1)$ and $Y(0)$ denote the potential outcomes a subject would realize if D was set to 1 and 0, respectively, for example the potential employment state with and without training. It is assumed throughout that $Y(1)$ and $Y(0)$ only depend on the subject's own treatment and not on the treatment values of other subjects, which is known at the "Stable Unit Treatment Value Assumption"; see Rubin (1990). Observed employment Y corresponds to either $Y(1)$ if the individual receives the training ($D = 1$) or to $Y(0)$ otherwise. The fact that not both potential outcomes are observed at the same time is formally expressed in the following equation:

$$Y = Y(1) \cdot D + Y(0) \cdot (1 - D). \tag{4.1}$$

It is easy to see that (4.1) is equivalent to $Y = Y(0) + D \cdot [Y(1) - Y(0)]$, where the observed outcome is the sum of the potential outcome without intervention and D times $Y(1) - Y(0)$, that is, the causal effect of D on Y. As either $Y(1)$ or $Y(0)$ is unknown depending on the value of D, the treatment effect can in general not be identified for any subject.

Under specific assumptions, however, aggregate treatment effects are identified based on groups of individuals receiving and not receiving the treatment. Two parameters that have received substantial attention are the average treatment effect (ATE, denoted by Δ) in the population, for example among all jobseekers, and the treatment effect on the treated population (ATET, denoted by $\Delta_{D=1}$), for example among training participants:

$$\Delta = E[Y(1) - Y(0)], \quad \Delta_{D=1} = E[Y(1) - Y(0) \mid D = 1]. \qquad (4.2)$$

One assumption yielding identification is statistical independence of treatment assignment and potential outcomes. Formally,

$$\{Y(1), Y(0)\} \perp D, \qquad (4.3)$$

where "$\perp$" denotes statistical independence. Expression (4.3) implies that there exist no variables jointly affecting the treatment and the potential outcomes. It is satisfied by design in experiments where the treatment is randomized, that is, not a function of any observed or unobserved characteristics such as education, gender or income. The ATE is then identified by the mean difference in observed outcomes across treated and nontreated groups. This follows from the fact that by (4.1) $E[Y|D=1] = E[Y(1)|D=1]$ and $E[Y|D=0] = E[Y(0)|D=0]$, while it follows from (4.3) that $E[Y(1)|D=1] = E[Y(1)]$ and $E[Y(0)|D=0] = E[Y(0)]$. As the average outcomes among treated and nontreated are representative for the respective mean potential outcomes under treatment and nontreatment in the population, $E[Y|D=1] - E[Y|D=0] = \Delta$.

When the treatment is not randomized, however, a mean comparison of treated and nontreated outcomes is generally biased due to selective treatment take up, implying that subjects in the treated and nontreated groups differ in characteristics that also affect the outcome. Jobseekers attending a job application training could, for instance, on average have a different level of labour market experience or education than those not participating. Differences in the observed outcomes of treated and nontreated subjects therefore not only reflect the treatment effect, but also the effects of such characteristics, which are thus confounders of the treatment–outcome relation. Formally, the selection biases for the ATE and ATET are given by

$$E[Y \mid D=1] - E[Y \mid D=0] - \Delta = E[Y \mid D=1] - E[Y(1)] + E[Y(0)] - E[Y \mid D=0], \quad (4.4)$$
$$E[Y \mid D=1] - E[Y \mid D=0] - \Delta_{D=1} = E[Y(0) \mid D=1] - E[Y \mid D=0].$$

Different strategies have been developed for avoiding or tackling selection in treatment in order to identify causal effects. This chapter reviews the most prominent approaches, focusing on methods for flexible model selection and estimation particularly appropriate in big data contexts. Section 2 covers methods relying on selection-on-observables assumptions, implying that observed preselected covariates are sufficient to control for characteristics jointly affecting the treatment and the potential outcomes. Section 3 discusses practical issues to be verified in the data when invoking the selection-on-observables assumption, for example the similarity of treated and nontreated subjects used for estimation in terms of observed characteristics, as well as extensions, for example to multivalued treatments and different treatment parameters. Section 4 covers causal machine learning, where observed covariates are not preselected, but it is assumed that important confounders can be controlled for in a data-driven way by machine learning algorithms. Section 5 outlines the application of machine learning for the data-driven detection of effect heterogeneities across subgroups defined upon observed covariates as well as for learning optimal policy rules to target subgroups in a way that maximizes the treatment effect.

Section 6 considers treatment evaluation based on instrumental variables. Here, treatment selection may be related to unobserved characteristics if a quasi-random instrument exists that affects the treatment but not the outcome directly. Section 7 discusses difference-in-differences methods, where identification hinges on common trends in mean potential outcomes under nontreatment over time across actually treated and nontreated groups. It also presents the changes-in-changes approach, which assumes that, within treatment groups, the distribution of unobserved characteristics that affect the potential outcome under nontreatment remains constant over time. Section 8 introduces the regression discontinuity design, which assumes the treatment probability to discontinuously change and be quasi-randomly assigned at a specific threshold value of an observed index variable. It also discusses the regression kink design, which assumes a kink in the (continuous) association of the treatment and the index variable at a specific threshold. Section 9 concludes.

2.   SELECTION ON OBSERVABLES WITH PRESELECTED COVARIATES

The selection-on-observables assumption, also called conditional independence or exogeneity, postulates that the covariate information in the data is rich enough to control for characteristics jointly affecting the treatment and the outcome. This implies that one either directly observes those characteristics confounding the treatment–outcome relationship or that, conditional on the observed information, the effects of unobserved confounders on either the treatment or the outcome (or both) are blocked. As a further assumption known as common support, it is required that, for any empirically feasible combination of observed covariates, both treated and nontreated subjects can be observed, which rules out that the covariates perfectly predict participation. Finally, the covariates must in general not be affected by the treatment but measured at or prior to treatment assignment.

Denote by X the vector of observed covariates and $X(1)$, $X(0)$ the potential covariate values with and without treatment. Formally, the assumptions can be stated as

$$\{Y(1), Y(0)\} \perp D \,|\, X, \quad 0 < p(X) < 1, \quad X(1) = X(0) = X, \tag{4.5}$$

where $p(X) = \Pr(D = 1 | X)$ is the conditional treatment probability, also known as the propensity score. The first part of (4.5) means that the distributions of the potential outcomes are conditionally independent of the treatment. This implies that D is as good as randomly assigned among subjects with the same values in X. The second part says that the propensity score is larger than zero and smaller than one, such that D is not deterministic in X. The third part states that X is not a function of D and therefore must not contain (post-treatment) characteristics that are affected by the treatment, in order to not condition away part of the treatment effect of interest. This identification approach mimics the experimental context with the help of observed information. After creating groups with and without treatment that are comparable in the covariates, differences in the outcomes are assumed to be exclusively caused by the treatment.

The first part of (4.5) is somewhat stronger than actually required for ATE identification and could be relaxed to conditional independence in the means (rather than all moments) of potential outcomes, $E[Y(d)|D = 1, X] = E[Y(d)|D = 0, X]$ for $d \in \{1, 0\}$. In empirical applications it might, however, be hard to argue that conditional independence holds in means but not in other distributional features, which would for instance rule out mean independence for nonlinear (for example log) transformations of Y. Furthermore, the stronger conditional independence assumption in (4.5) is required for the identification of distributional parameters such as the quantile treatment effect, which corresponds to the effect at a particular rank of the potential outcome distribution. Also note that, for the identification of treatment parameters among the treated (rather than the total) population like the ATET, (4.5) can be relaxed to $Y(1) \perp D|X, p(X) < 1$.

Let $\mu_d(x) = E[Y|D = d, X = x]$ denote the conditional mean outcome given D corresponding to $d \in \{1, 0\}$ and X equalling some value x in its support. Analogous to identification under a random treatment discussed in section 1, $\mu_1(x) - \mu_0(x)$ under (4.5) identifies the conditional average treatment effect (CATE) given X, denoted by Δ_x:

$$\Delta_x = E[Y(1) - Y(0) \mid X = x] = \mu_1(x) - \mu_0(x). \tag{4.6}$$

Averaging CATEs over X in the population or among the treated yields the ATE or ATET, respectively:

$$\Delta = E[\mu_1(X) - \mu_0(X)], \tag{4.7}$$
$$\Delta_{D=1} = E[\mu_1(X) - \mu_0(X) \mid D = 1] = E[Y \mid D = 1] - E[\mu_0(X) \mid D = 1].$$

Noting that the propensity score possesses the so-called balancing property, see Rosenbaum and Rubin (1983), such that conditioning on $p(X)$ equalizes or balances the distribution of X across treatment groups (that is, $X \perp D|p(X)$), the effects are also identified when substituting control variables X by $p(X)$:

$$\Delta = E[\mu_1(p(X)) - \mu_0(p(X))], \tag{4.8}$$
$$\Delta_{D=1} = E[\mu_1(p(X)) - \mu_0(p(X)) \mid D = 1] = E[Y \mid D = 1] - E[\mu_0(p(X)) \mid D = 1].$$

By basic probability theory, implying for example $\mu_1(X) = E[Y \cdot D|X]/p(X)$, and the law of iterated expectations, the ATE and ATET are also identified by inverse probability weighting (IPW), see Horvitz and Thompson (1952), using the propensity score:

$$\Delta = E\left[\frac{Y \cdot D}{p(X)} - \frac{Y \cdot (1 - D)}{1 - p(X)}\right], \tag{4.9}$$

$$\Delta_{D=1} = E\left[\frac{Y \cdot D}{\Pr(D = 1)} - \frac{Y \cdot (1 - D) \cdot p(X)}{(1 - p(X)) \cdot \Pr(D = 1)}\right].$$

Finally, the effects can be obtained from a combination of conditional mean outcomes and propensity scores related to the so-called efficient score function; see Robins et al. (1994), Robins and Rotnitzky (1995) and Hahn (1998):

$$\Delta = E[\phi(X)], \quad \text{with } \phi(X) = \mu_1(X) - \mu_0(X) + \frac{(Y - \mu_1(X)) \cdot D}{p(X)} - \frac{(Y - \mu_0(X)) \cdot (1 - D)}{1 - p(X)},$$

$$\Delta_{D=1} = E\left[\frac{(Y - \mu_0(X)) \cdot D}{\Pr(D=1)} - \frac{(Y - \mu_0(X)) \cdot (1 - D) \cdot p(X)}{(1 - p(X)) \cdot \Pr(D=1)} \right]. \tag{4.10}$$

Note that the identification results in (4.10) coincide with those in (4.9) and (4.7) because

$$E\left[\frac{(Y - \mu_1(X)) \cdot D}{p(X)} - \frac{(Y - \mu_0(X)) \cdot (1 - D)}{1 - p(X)} \right] = 0 \quad and$$

$$E\left[\frac{-\mu_0(X) \cdot D}{\Pr(D=1)} - \frac{-\mu_0(X) \cdot (1 - D) \cdot p(X)}{(1 - p(X)) \cdot \Pr(D=1)} \right] = E\left[\mu_0(X) \cdot \left(\frac{p(X)}{\Pr(D=1)} - \frac{p(X)}{\Pr(D=1)} \right) \right] = 0.$$

Assuming the availability of a randomly drawn sample, treatment effect estimation proceeds using the sample analogues of the identification results and plug-in estimates for $p(X)$, $\mu_1(X)$, $\mu_0(X)$ whenever required. When considering the estimation of $\Delta_{D=1}$ based on (4.7), an estimate of $\mu_0(X)$ for each treated observation is obtained as a weighted average of nontreated outcomes, where the weights depend on the similarity of the treated and nontreated observations in terms of X. One class of methods in this context are matching estimators; see for instance Rosenbaum and Rubin (1983), Rosenbaum and Rubin (1985), Heckman et al. (1998a), Heckman et al. (1998b), Dehejia and Wahba (1999) and Lechner et al. (2011). Pair matching, for instance, assigns a weight of 1 (or 100 per cent) to the most similar nontreated observation and of 0 to all others. There are 1: M matching estimates $\mu_0(X)$ based on the mean outcome of the M most similar nontreated observations, where M is an integer larger than 1. Radius or calliper matching defines a maximum tolerance of dissimilarity in X and relies on the mean outcome of all nontreated observations within the tolerance. Compared to 1: M estimation, this may reduce the variance when many similar nontreated observations are available. Due to the multidimensionality of X, similarity is to be defined by a distance metric. Examples include the square root of the sum of squared differences in elements of X across some treated and nontreated observation, either normalized by the inverse of the sample covariance matrix of X (then called the Mahalanobis distance) or by the diagonal thereof (that is, the variance). See Zhao (2004) for a discussion of alternative distance metrics.

Abadie and Imbens (2006) show that, in contrast to other treatment estimators, pair or 1: M matching does generally not converge with a rate of $n^{-1/2}$ to the true effect (that is, it is not $n^{-1/2}$-consistent) if X contains several continuous elements, with n being the sample size. Second, even under $n^{-1/2}$-consistency, it does not attain the semiparametric efficiency bounds derived in Hahn (1998). Therefore, pair or 1: M matching has a higher large sample variance than the most efficient (or least noisy) treatment effect estimators that rely on the same assumptions. Third, Abadie and Imbens (2008) demonstrate that bootstrapping, a popular inference method based on estimating the standard error based on repeatedly resampling from the data, is inconsistent due to the discontinuous weights in pair and 1: M matching. The authors, however, provide a consistent asymptotic approximation of the estimator's variance based on matching within treatment groups.

To improve upon its properties, matching can be combined with a regression-based correction of the bias that stems from not fully comparable treated and nontreated matches; see Rubin (1979) and Abadie and Imbens (2011). This matching-weighted regression is $n^{-1/2}$-consistent and its weights are smooth, such that bootstrap inference is consistent. Another smooth method is kernel matching, which estimates $\mu_0(X)$ by a kernel function giving more weight to nontreated observations that are more similar to the treated reference observation and can attain the semiparametric efficiency bound. This requires no distance metric, as kernel functions are applied to each element in X and then multiplied. Finally, genetic matching of Diamond and Sekhon (2013) matches treated and nontreated observations in a way that maximizes the balance of covariate distributions across treatment groups according to predefined balance metrics, based on an appropriately weighted distance metric.

In empirical applications, matching on the estimated propensity score is much more common than matching directly on X. The propensity score is typically specified parametrically by logit or probit functions. Collapsing the covariate information into a single parametric function avoids the curse of dimensionality, which implies that in finite samples the probability of similar matches in all elements of X quickly decreases in the dimension of X. At the same time, it allows for effect heterogeneity across X. On the negative side, a misspecification of the propensity score model may entail an inconsistent treatment effect estimator, which is avoided by directly matching on X or using a nonparametric propensity score estimate. Matching on the estimated propensity score has a different variance than matching directly on X, which for the ATET can be either higher or lower; see Heckman et al. (1998b). Abadie and Imbens (2016) provide an asymptotic variance approximation for propensity score matching that appropriately accounts for uncertainty due to propensity score estimation.

Matching estimators typically require the choice of tuning parameters, be it the number of matches M, the bandwidth in kernel or radius matching or the distance metric. However, theoretical guidance is frequently not available; see Frölich (2005) for an exception. Practitioners commonly pick tuning parameters ad hoc or based on data-driven methods that are not necessarily optimal for treatment effect estimation, as for example cross-validation for estimating $\mu_0(X)$. It appears thus advisable to investigate the sensitivity of the effect estimates with respect to varying these parameters.

As an alternative to matching, Hirano et al. (2003) discuss treatment effect estimation based on the IPW sample analogue of (4.9) using series regression to obtain nonparametric plug-in estimates of the propensity score, which attains the semiparametric efficiency bounds. Ichimura and Linton (2005) and Li et al. (2009) consider IPW with kernel-based propensity score estimation. Practitioners mostly rely on logit or probit specifications, which are generally not semiparametrically efficient; see Chen et al. (2008). In any case, it is common and recommended to use normalized sample analogues of the expressions in (4.9), which ensures that the weights of observations within treatment groups sum up to one; see Busso et al. (2014). Compared to matching, IPW has the advantages that it is computationally inexpensive and does not require the user to choose tuning parameters (other than for nonparametric propensity score estimation, if applied). On the negative side, IPW is likely sensitive to propensity scores that are very close to one or zero; see the simulations in Frölich (2004) and Busso et al. (2014) and the theoretical discussion in Khan and Tamer (2010). Furthermore, IPW may be less robust to propensity score misspecification than matching, which merely uses the score to match treated and nontreated observations rather than plugging it directly into the estimator; see Waernbaum (2012).

Variations of IPW are the empirical likelihood methods of Graham et al. (2012) and Imai and Ratkovic (2014). In a spirit comparable to genetic matching, the methods iterate an initial propensity score estimate (for example by changing the coefficients of a logit specification) until prespecified moments of X are maximally balanced across treatment groups. A related approach is entropy balancing, see Hainmueller (2012), which iterates initially provided (for example uniform) weights until balance in the moments of X is maximized, under the constraint that the weights sum to one in either treatment group. In contrast to methods aiming for perfect covariate balance in prespecified moments, Zubizarreta (2015) trades off balance and variance in estimation. The algorithm finds the weights of minimum variance that balance the empirical covariate distribution up to prespecified levels, that is, approximately rather than exactly.

Estimation based on the sample analogue of (4.10) with plug-in estimates for $p(X)$, $\mu_1(X)$, $\mu_0(X)$ is called doubly robust (DR) estimation, as it is consistent if either the conditional mean outcome or the propensity score is correctly specified; see Robins et al. (1992) and Robins et al. (1995). If both are correctly specified, DR is semiparametrically efficient. This is also the case if the plug-in estimates are nonparametrically estimated; see Cattaneo (2010). Furthermore, Rothe and Firpo (2013) show that nonparametric DR has a lower first order bias and second order variance than either IPW using a nonparametric propensity score or nonparametric outcome regression. This latter property is relevant in finite samples and implies that the accuracy of the DR estimator is less dependent on the accuracy of the plug-in estimates, for example the choice of the bandwidth in the kernel-based estimation of propensity scores and conditional mean outcomes. A further method satisfying the DR property is targeted maximum likelihood (TMLE), see van der Laan and Rubin (2006), in which an initial regression estimate is updated (or robustified) based on an IPW parameter.

3.   PRACTICAL ISSUES AND EXTENSIONS

This section discusses practical issues related to propensity score methods as well as extensions of treatment evaluation to nonbinary treatments and different effect parameters. One important question is whether the estimated propensity score successfully balances X across treatment groups, for example in matched samples or after reweighting covariates (rather than outcomes) by IPW. Practitioners frequently consider hypothesis tests, for example two-sample t-tests applied to each element in X or F-tests for jointly testing imbalances in X; see also the joint tests of Sianesi (2004) and Smith and Todd (2005). As an alternative to hypothesis tests, Rosenbaum and Rubin (1985) consider a covariate's absolute mean difference across treated and nontreated matches, divided or standardized by the square root of half the sum of the covariate's variances in either treatment group prior to matching. In contrast to a t-test, which rejects balance under the slightest difference if the sample grows to infinity, this standardized difference is insensitive to the sample size. Rather than judging balance based on a p-value as in hypothesis tests, a standardized difference larger than a specific threshold, say 0.2, may be considered an indication for imbalance. On the negative side, the choice of the threshold appears rather arbitrary and data-driven methods for its determination are currently lacking. Taking the average of standardized differences for each covariate permits constructing a joint statistic for all covariates.

A second practical issue is whether common support in the propensity score distributions across treatment groups is sufficiently decent in the data. For the ATET, this implies that, for each treated observation, nontreated matches with similar propensity scores exist, while for the ATE this also needs to hold vice versa. Strictly speaking, common support is violated whenever, for any reference observation, no observation in the other treatment group with exactly the same propensity score is available. In practice, propensity scores should be sufficiently similar, which requires defining a criterion based on which dissimilar observations may be discarded from the data to enforce common support. However, discarding observations implies that effect estimation might not be (fully) representative of the initial target population and thus sacrifices (some) external validity. On the other hand, it likely reduces estimation bias within the subpopulation satisfying common support, thus enhancing internal validity. For possible common support criteria, see for instance Heckman et al. (1998a), who suggest discarding observations whose propensity scores have a density of or close to zero in (at least) one treatment group. For ATET estimation, Dehejia and Wahba (1999) propose discarding all treated observations with an estimated propensity score higher than the highest value among the nontreated. For the ATE, one additionally discards nontreated observations with a propensity score lower than the lowest value among the treated. Crump et al. (2009) discuss dropping observations with propensity scores close to zero or one in a way that minimizes the variance of ATE estimation in the remaining sample. Huber et al. (2013) discard observations that receive a too large relative weight within their treatment group when estimating the treatment effect. See Lechner and Strittmatter (2019) for an overview of alternative common support criteria and an investigation of their performance in a simulation study.

The discussion so far has focussed on a binary treatment; however, the framework straightforwardly extends to multivalued discrete treatments. The latter may either reflect distinct treatments (such as different types of labour market programs, for example a job search training, a computer course, and so on) or discrete doses of a single treatment (such as one, two or three weeks of training). Under appropriate selection-on-observable assumptions, treatment effects are identified by pairwise comparisons of each treatment value with nontreatment, or of two nonzero treatment values, if the effect of one treatment relative to the other is of interest. More formally, let d' and d'' denote the treatment levels to be compared and $I\{A\}$ the indicator function, which is one if event A holds and zero otherwise. Assume that conditions analogous to (4.5) are satisfied for $D = d'$ and $D = d''$ such that conditional independence assumptions $Y(d') \perp I\{D = d'\}|X$ and $Y(d'') \perp I\{D = d''\}|X$ hold and the so-called generalized propensity scores satisfy the common support restrictions $\Pr(D = d'|X) > 0$ and $\Pr(D = d''|X) > 0$; see Imbens (2000). Then, replacing D by $I\{D = d'\}$ and $1 - D$ by $I\{D = d''\}$ as well as $p(X) = \Pr(D = d'|X)$ by $\Pr(D = d'|X)$ and $1 - p(X)$ by $\Pr(D = d''|X)$ in the identification results (4.7–4.10) yields the ATE when comparing $D = d'$ vs. $D = d''$ as well as the ATET when considering those with $D = d'$ as the treated. As shown in Cattaneo (2010), a range of treatment effect estimators for multivalued discrete treatments are $n^{-1/2}$-consistent and semiparametrically efficient under nonparametric estimation of the plug-in parameters. See also Lechner (2001) for a discussion of matching-based estimation with multivalued discrete treatments.

When D does not have discrete probability masses but is continuously distributed, the generalized propensity score corresponds to a conditional density, denoted by $f(D = d'|X)$, to distinguish it from the previously used probability $\Pr(D = d'|X)$. In the spirit of (4.7) for binary treatments, Flores (2007) proposes kernel regression of Y on D and X for estimating the mean potential outcomes of the continuous treatment. In analogy to (4.8), Hirano and Imbens (2005) regress Y on polynomials of D and estimates of $\Pr(D|X)$ along with interactions, while Imai and van Dyk

(2004) consider subclassification by the generalized propensity score. IPW-based methods as considered in Flores et al. (2012) require replacing indicator functions, for example $I\{D = d'\}$, by continuous weighting functions in the identification results. Consider, for instance, the kernel weight $K((D - d')/h)h$, where K is a symmetric second-order kernel function (for example the standard normal density function) that assigns more weight to values of D the closer they are to d'. Here, h is a bandwidth gauging how quickly the weight decays as values in D become more different to d' and must go to zero as the sample size increases (albeit not too fast) for consistent estimation. Then, IPW-based identification of the ATE, for instance, corresponds to

$$\Delta = \lim_{h \to 0} E\left[\frac{Y \cdot K((D-d')/h)/h}{f(D=d' \mid X)} - \frac{Y \cdot K((D-d'')/h)/h}{f(D=d'' \mid X))} \right], \tag{4.11}$$

where $\lim_{h \to 0}$ means "as h goes to zero". See Galvao and Wang (2015) for a further IPW approach and Kennedy et al. (2017) for kernel-based DR estimation under continuous treatments, including data-driven bandwidth selection.

A further conceptual extension is the dynamic treatment framework; see for instance Robins (1986), Robins et al. (2000) and Lechner (2009). It is concerned with the evaluation of sequences of treatments (like consecutive labour market programs) based on sequential selection-on-observable assumptions with respect to each treatment. Related assumptions are also commonly imposed in causal mediation analysis aimed at disentangling a total treatment effect into various causal mechanisms; see for instance Robins and Greenland (1992), Pearl (2001), Imai et al. (2010), Tchetgen Tchetgen and Shpitser (2012) and Huber (2014), or the survey by Huber (2021). Finally, several contributions consider effect parameters related to distributions rather than means. Firpo (2007) proposes an efficient IPW estimator of quantile treatment effects (QTE) at specific ranks (such as the median) of the potential outcome distribution and derives the semiparametric efficiency bounds. Donald and Hsu (2014) suggest IPW-based estimation of the distribution functions of potential outcomes under treatment and nontreatment; see also DiNardo et al. (1996) and Chernozhukov et al. (2013) for estimators of counterfactual distributions. Imbens (2004) and Imbens and Wooldridge (2009) provide comprehensive reviews on treatment evaluation under selection on observables.

4.   CAUSAL MACHINE LEARNING

The treatment evaluation methods discussed so far consider covariates X as being preselected or fixed. This assumes away uncertainty related to model selection with respect to X and requires substantial or strictly speaking exact contextual knowledge about the confounders that need to be controlled for and in which functional form. In reality, however, practitioners frequently select covariates based on their predictive power for the treatment, typically without appropriately accounting for this model selection step in the causal inference to follow. Fortunately, this issue can be tackled by more recent treatment evaluation methods that incorporate machine learning to control for important confounders in a data-driven way and honestly account for model selection in the estimation process. This is particularly useful in big, and more specifically in wide, data with a vast number of covariates that could potentially serve as control variables, which can render researcher-based covariate selection complicated if not infeasible.

It is important to see that when combining evaluation methods for the ATE or ATET with machine learning, henceforth called causal machine learning (CML), the data must contain sufficiently rich covariate information to satisfy the selection-on-observables assumption, just as discussed in section 2. Therefore, CML is not a magic bullet that can do away with fundamental assumptions required for effect identification. However, it may be fruitfully applied if there exists a subset of covariate information that suffices to by and large tackle confounding but is unknown to the researcher. Under the assumption that a relative to the sample size limited subset of information permits controlling for the most important confounders, CML can be shown to be approximately unbiased, even when confounding is not perfectly controlled for.

Chernozhukov et al. (2018) consider a CML approach called double machine learning that relies on so-called orthogonalized statistics. The latter imply that treatment effect estimation is rather insensitive to approximation errors in the estimation of $p(X)$, $\mu_1(X)$, $\mu_0(X)$. As discussed in section 2, the sample analogue of (4.10) satisfies this (doubly) robustness property along with its desirable finite sample behaviour. In contrast, estimation based on (4.7) is rather sensitive to approximation errors of $\mu_1(X)$, $\mu_0(X)$, while estimation based on (4.9) is sensitive to errors in $p(X)$. However because DR incorporates both propensity score and conditional mean outcome estimation, the approximation errors enter multiplicatively into the estimation problem, which is key for the robustness property; see for instance Farrell (2015).

A further element of many CML approaches, including double machine learning, is the use of independent samples for estimating the specifications of plug-in parameters such as $p(X)$, $\mu_1(X)$ and $\mu_0(X)$ on the one hand, and of the treatment effects Δ, $\Delta_{D=1}$ on the other hand. This is similar in spirit to the idea of training and testing data in conventional machine learning or cross-validation for tuning parameter selection and obtained by randomly splitting the sample. After estimating models for $p(X)$, $\mu_1(X)$, $\mu_0(X)$ in one part of the data, the model parameters (for example coefficients) are used in the other part to predict $p(X)$, $\mu_1(X)$, $\mu_0(X)$ and ultimately estimate the treatment effect. Sample splitting prevents overfitting the models for the plug-in parameters but comes at the cost that only part of the data are used for effect estimation, thus increasing the variance. So-called cross-fitting tackles this issue by swapping the roles of the data parts for estimating the plug-in models and the treatment effect. The treatment effect estimate is obtained as the average of the estimated treatment effects in each part, and in fact more than just two data splits may be used for this procedure. When combining DR with sample splitting, it suffices for $n^{-1/2}$ convergence of treatment effect estimation that the estimates of $p(X)$, $\mu_1(X)$, $\mu_0(X)$ converge to their respective true values at a rate of $n^{-1/4}$ (or faster); see Chernozhukov et al. (2018). Under specific regularity conditions, this convergence rate is attained by many machine learning algorithms and even by deep learning (which is popular in computer science, for example for pattern recognition); see Farrell et al. (2021).

However, it needs to be stressed that CML is conceptually different to standard machine learning, which aims at accurately predicting an outcome by observed predictors based on minimizing the prediction error (for example the mean squared error) through optimally trading off prediction bias and variance. This mere forecasting approach does generally not allow learning of the causal effects of any of the predictors. One reason is that a specific predictor might obtain a smaller weight (for example regression coefficient) than implied by its true causal effect if the predictor is sufficiently correlated with other predictors, such that constraining its weight hardly affects the prediction bias, while reducing the variance. Therefore, predictive machine learning with Y as outcome and D and X as predictors generally gives a biased estimate of the causal effect of D due to correlations between the treatment and the covariates. In CML, however, machine learning is not directly applied to ATE or ATET estimation but merely for predicting the plug-in parameters, for example those of the DR expression (that is, the sample analogue of (4.10)) in the case of double machine learning. To this end, three separate machine learning predictions of D, Y among the treated and Y among the nontreated are conducted with X being the predictors in each step. This is motivated by the fact that covariates X merely serve the purpose of tackling confounding, while their causal effects are (contrarily to the effect of D) not of interest, which makes the estimation of $p(X)$, $\mu_1(X)$ and $\mu_0(X)$ a prediction problem to which machine learning can be applied.

Assume for instance that $\mu_1(X)$ and $\mu_0(X)$ are estimated by a linear lasso regression, see Tibshirani (1996), where X as well as higher order and interaction terms thereof may be included as predictors to allow for flexible model specifications. Including too many terms with low predictive power (as would be the case in an overfitted polynomial regression) likely increases the variance of prediction, with little gain in terms of bias reduction. On the other hand, omitting important predictors implies a large increase in prediction bias relative to the gain in variance reduction due to a parsimonious specification. For this reason, lasso regression aims to optimally balance bias and variance through regularization, that is, by shrinking the absolute coefficients obtained in a standard ordinary least squares (OLS) regression toward or exactly to zero for less important predictors, for example based on cross-validation for determining the optimal amount of shrinkage. Analogously, lasso logit regression may be applied for the prediction of $p(X)$, which is a regularized version of a standard logit regression. Alternatively, lasso-based estimation of $\mu_1(X)$ and $\mu_0(X)$ can be combined with approximate covariate balancing of Zubizarreta (2015) instead of estimating a propensity score model for $p(X)$; see the CML algorithm suggested by Athey et al. (2018).

As discussed in Chernozhukov et al. (2018), lasso regression attains the required convergence rate of $n^{-1/4}$ under so-called approximate sparsity. The latter implies that the number of important covariates or interaction and higher order terms required for obtaining a sufficiently decent (albeit not perfect) approximation of the plug-in parameters is small relative to the sample size n. To see the merits of cross-fitting, note that when disregarding the latter and instead conducting the lasso and treatment estimation steps in the same (total) data, the number of important predictors is required to be small relative to $n^{-1/2}$ rather than n; see Belloni et al. (2014). Importantly, neither cross-fitting nor the estimation of the plug-in parameters by some $n^{-1/4}$-consistent machine learning algorithm affects the asymptotic variance of treatment effect estimation (albeit it may matter in small samples). Therefore, CML is $n^{-1/2}$ consistent and attains the semiparametric efficiency bound as if the covariates to be controlled for in DR estimation had been correctly preselected. In large enough samples, standard errors may thus be estimated by conventional asymptotic approximations without adjustment for the machine learning steps. For a more in-depth review of various machine learning algorithms and CML, see for instance Athey and Imbens (2019).

5.   EFFECT HETEROGENEITY, CONDITIONAL EFFECTS AND POLICY LEARNING

Machine learning can also be fruitfully applied to investigate treatment effect heterogeneity across X, while mitigating inferential multiple testing issues related to snooping for subgroups with significant(ly different) effects that might be spurious. For randomized experiments where (4.3) holds or under the selection-on-observables assumption (4.5) with preselected X, Athey and Imbens (2016) suggest a method that builds on a modification of so-called regression trees; see Breiman et al. (1984). In standard machine learning for outcome prediction, the tree structure emerges by recursively partitioning the sample with respect to the predictor space such that the sum of squared deviations of outcomes and their respective partition means is minimized. This increases outcome homogeneity within and heterogeneity between partitions. Prediction of $E[Y|X = x]$ proceeds by taking the average of Y in the partition that includes the value $X = x$. This is equivalent to an OLS regression with predictors and interaction terms that are discretized according to specific threshold values in the covariate space as implied by the partitions. Cross-validation may be applied to find the optimal depth of partitions, for example with respect to the mean squared error.

The causal tree approach of Athey and Imbens (2016) contains two key modifications when compared to standard regression trees. First, instead of Y the mean difference in Y across treatment groups within partitions serves as an outcome in the experimental context, while under selection on observables with preselected X outcomes are reweighted by the inverse of the propensity score (in analogy to (4.9)) prior to taking mean differences. In either case, recursive partitioning increases the homogeneity in estimated treatment effects within and its heterogeneity between partitions in order to find the largest effect heterogeneities across subgroups defined in terms of X. Secondly, applying sample splitting in order to use different data parts for estimating (a) the tree's model structure and (b) the treatment effects within partitions prevents spuriously large effect heterogeneities due to overfitting.

Wager and Athey (2018) and Athey et al. (2019) provide a further approach for investigating effect heterogeneity that is based on the related concept of random forests, see Breiman (2001), and also applies under selection on observables when control variables are not preselected but to be learnt from the data; see section 4. Random forests consist of randomly drawing many subsamples from the original data and estimating trees in each subsample. Differently to standard trees, only a random subset of predictors (rather than all) is considered at each partitioning step, which safeguards against heavily correlated trees across subsamples. Predictions are obtained by averaging over the predictions of individual trees, which makes the random forest a smooth estimator and also reduces the variance when compared to discrete partitioning of a single tree. Forest-based predictions can therefore be represented by smooth weighting functions that bear some resemblance with kernel regression.

More concisely, the so-called generalized random forest of Athey et al. (2019) proceeds as follows. First, both Y and D are predicted as a function of X using random forests and leave-one-out cross-fitting. The latter implies that the outcome or treatment of each observation is predicted based on all observations in the data but its own in order to prevent overfitting when conditioning on X. Second, the predictions are used for computing residuals of the outcomes and treatments, which is in the spirit of orthogonalized statistics as discussed in the context of DR in section 4. Third, the effect of the residuals of D on the residuals of Y is predicted as a function of X by another random forest that averages over a large number of causal trees with residualized outcomes and treatments that use different parts of the respective subsamples for tree modelling and treatment effect estimation. Bluntly speaking, this method combines the idea of sample splitting and orthogonalization to control for important confounders as discussed in section 4 with the approach of Athey and Imbens (2016) for finding effect heterogeneity.

When comparing a single causal tree and a generalized random forest, an advantage of the former is that it directly yields an easy-to-interpret partitioning based on the most predictive covariates in terms of effect heterogeneity. On the negative side, tree structures frequently have a rather high variance such that a small change in the data may entail quite different partitions. The generalized random forest is more attractive in terms of variance but does not provide a single covariate partitioning due to averaging over many trees. It, however, yields an estimate of the CATE $\Delta_x = E[Y(1) - Y(0)|X = x]$, see (4.6), such that its heterogeneity as a function of X can be investigated. Also note that averaging over the estimates of Δ_x in the total sample or among the treatment provides consistent estimates of the ATE and ATET, respectively. For surveys on further machine learning methods for investigating treatment effect heterogeneity, see for instance Powers et al. (2018) and Knaus et al. (2021).

A concept related to the CATE is optimal policy learning, see for example Manski (2004), Hirano and Porter (2009), Stoye (2009), Qian and Murphy (2011), Bhattacharya and Dupas (2012) and Kitagawa and Tetenov (2018), which typically aims at optimally allocating a costly treatment in some population under budget constraints. This requires analysing which observations in terms of covariate values X should be assigned the constrained treatment to maximize the average outcome. Examples include the optimal selection of jobseekers to be trained to maximize the overall employment probability or the optimal choice of customers to be offered a discount in order to maximize average sales. Formally, let $\pi(X)$ denote a specific treatment policy defined as function of X. To give just one example, $\pi(X)$ could require $D = 1$ for all observations whose first covariate in X is larger than a particular threshold and $D = 0$ otherwise. The average effect of policy $\pi(X)$, denoted by $Q(\pi(X))$, corresponds to the difference in mean potential outcomes under $\pi(X)$ vs. nontreatment of everyone:

$$Q(\pi(X)) = E[Y(\pi(X)) - Y(0)] = E[\pi(X) \cdot \Delta_x]. \tag{4.12}$$

The second equality highlights the close relationship of policy learning and CATE identification. The optimal policy, denoted by $\pi^*(X)$, maximizes the average effect among the set of all feasible policies contained in the set $\prod$:

$$\pi^*(X) = \max_{\pi \in \Pi} Q(\pi(X)). \tag{4.13}$$

Equations (4.12) and (4.13) permit defining the so-called regret function associated with treatment policy $\pi(X)$, which is denoted by $R\pi(X)$ and equals the (undesirable) reduction in the average policy effect due to implementing $\pi(X)$ rather than the optimal policy $\pi^*(X)$:

$$R(\pi(X)) = Q(\pi^*(X)) - Q(\pi(X)). \tag{4.14}$$

Finding the optimal policy among the set of feasible policies $\prod$, which implies that the average policy effect Q is maximized and regret R is equal to zero, amounts to solving the following maximization problem:

$$\pi^*(X) = \max_{\pi \in \Pi} E[(2\pi(X) - 1) \cdot \phi(X)]. \tag{4.15}$$

Note that $\phi(X)$ is the DR statistic of (4.10); see for instance Dudík et al. (2011), Zhang et al. (2012) and Zhou et al. (2017) for DR-based policy learning. The term $(2\pi(X) - 1)$ implies that the CATEs of treated and nontreated subjects enter positively and negatively into the expectation, respectively. Maximizing the expectation therefore requires optimally trading off treated and nontreated subjects in terms of their CATEs when choosing the treatment policy among all feasible policies. Estimation of the optimal policy may be based on the sample analogue of (4.15), where $\phi(X)$ is estimated by cross-fitting and machine learning-based prediction of the plug-in parameters as outlined in section 4. Athey and Wager (2018) demonstrate that, similar to ATE estimation, basing policy learning on DR machine learning has desirable properties under specific conditions, even if the important elements in X driving confounding and/or effect heterogeneity are a priori unknown. The regret of the estimated optimal policy in the data when compared to the true optimal policy $\pi^*(X)$ decays at rate $n^{-1/2}$ under selection on observables if all plug-in parameters are estimated at rate $n^{-1/4}$. Zhou et al. (2018) show how this result extends to policy learning for multivalued discrete treatments, as also considered in Kallus (2017).

6.   INSTRUMENTAL VARIABLES

The selection-on-observables assumption imposed in the previous sections fails if selection into treatment is driven by unobserved factors that affect potential outcomes conditional on X. As an example, consider an experiment with imperfect compliance in which access to a training program is randomly assigned but a subset of jobseekers that are offered the training does not comply and decides to not participate. If compliance behaviour is driven by unobserved factors (for example ability or motivation) that also affect the outcome (for example employment), endogeneity jeopardizes a causal analysis based on a naive comparison of treated and nontreated outcomes even when controlling for observed characteristics. However, if mere treatment assignment satisfies a so-called exclusion restriction such that it does not directly affect the outcome other than through actual treatment participation, it may serve as instrumental variable (IV), denoted by Z, to identify the treatment effect among those complying with the assignment. The intuition of IV-based identification is that the effect of Z of Y, which is identified by the randomization of the instrument, only operates through the effect of Z on D among compliers due to the exclusion restriction. Therefore, scaling (or dividing) the average effect of Z on Y by the average effect of Z on D yields the average effect of D on Y among compliers; see Imbens and Angrist (1994) and Angrist et al. (1996).

However, in many applications it may not appear credible that IV assumptions like random assignment hold unconditionally, that is, without controlling for observed covariates. This is commonly the case in observational data in which the instrument is typically not explicitly randomized like in an experiment. For instance, Card (1995) considers geographic proximity to college as IV for the likely endogenous treatment education when assessing its effect on earnings. While proximity might induce some individuals to go to college who would otherwise not, for example due to housing costs associated with not living at home, it likely reflects selection into neighbourhoods with a specific socioeconomic status that affects labour market performance, implying that the IV is not random. If all confounders of the instrument-outcome relationship are plausibly observed in the data, IV-based estimation can be conducted conditional on observed covariates. For this reason, Card (1995) includes a range of control variables like parents' education, ethnicity, urbanity and geographic region.

To formally state the IV assumptions that permit identifying causal effects conditional on covariates X in the binary instrument and treatment case, denote by $D(1)$ and $D(0)$ the potential treatment decision if instrument Z is set to 1 or 0, respectively. This permits the defining of four compliance types: Individuals satisfying $(D(1) = 1, D(0) = 0)$ are compliers as they only take the treatment when receiving the instrument. Non-compliers may consist of never takers who never take the treatment irrespective of the instrument $(D(1) = D(0) = 0)$, always takers $(D(1) = D(0) = 0)$, and defiers, who counteract instrument assignment $(D(1) = 0, D(0) = 1)$. Furthermore, denote (for the moment) the potential outcome as $Y(z, d)$, that is, as function of both the instrument and the treatment. Then, the local average treatment effect (LATE) among compliers, denoted by $\Delta_{D(1)=1,D(0)=0} = E[Y(1) - Y(0)|D(1) = 1, D(0) = 0]$, is nonparametrically identified under the following assumptions; see Abadie (2003).

$$Z \perp (D(z), Y(z',d)) | X \text{ for } z,z',d \in \{1,0\}, \quad X(1) = X(0) = X, \tag{4.16}$$

$$\Pr(D(1) \geq D(0) | X) = 1, \quad E[D|Z=1,X] - E[D|Z=0,X] \neq 0,$$

$$\Pr(Y(1,d) = Y(0,d) = Y(d) | X) = 1 \text{ for } z,z',d \in \{1,0\}.$$

The first line of (4.16) says that, conditional on X (which must not be affected by D), the IV is as good as random and thus not influenced by unobserved factors affecting the treatment and/or outcome. This is a selection-of-observables assumption similar to (4.5), however now imposed with respect to the instrument rather than the treatment. Therefore, the effects of Z on Y and on D are identified conditional on X, just in analogy to the identification of the effect of D on Y given X in section 2. For this reason, replacing D by Z and the treatment propensity score $p(X) = \Pr(D = 1|X)$ by the instrument propensity score $\Pr(Z = 1|X)$ in the identification results for the ATE in (4.7–4.10) yields the average effect of the instrument on the outcome. The latter is known as intention-to-treat effect (ITT) and henceforth denoted by θ. Additionally, replacing Y by D yields the average effect of the instrument on the treatment (that is, $E[D(1) = 1, D(0))$, the so-called first stage effect, denoted by γ.

The second line of (4.16) rules out the existence of defiers but requires the existence of compliers conditional on X due to the non-zero conditional first stage, while never and always takers might exist too. By the law of total probability, this implies that γ corresponds to the share of compliers, as $D(1) - D(0)$ equals one for compliers and zero for never and always takers. The third line invokes the exclusion restriction such that Z must not have a direct effect on Y other than through D. By the law of total probability, the ITT in this case corresponds to the first stage effect γ times the LATE $\Delta_{D(1)=1,D(0)=0}$. This follows from the nonexistence of defiers and the fact that the effect of Z on Y is necessarily zero for always and never takers, whose D is not affected by Z. Therefore, the LATE is identified by scaling the ITT by the first stage effect. Formally,

$$\theta = \Delta_{D(1)=1,D(0)=0} \cdot \gamma \quad \Leftrightarrow \quad \Delta_{D(1)=1,D(0)=0} = \frac{\theta}{\gamma}. \tag{4.17}$$

If X is preselected, estimation of $\Delta_{D(1)=1,D(0)=0}$ proceeds by estimating both θ and γ based on any of the treatment effect estimators outlined in section 2 and by dividing one by the other, which is $n^{-1/2}$ consistent under specific regularity conditions. Frölich (2007), for instance, considers nonparametric matching- and (local polynomial and series) regression-based estimation. Hong and Nekipelov (2010) derive semiparametric efficiency bounds for LATE estimation and propose efficient estimators. Donald et al. (2014a) and Donald et al. (2014b) propose IPW estimation using series logit and local polynomial regression-based estimation of the instrument propensity score. Tan (2006) and Uysal (2011) discuss DR estimation with parametric plug-in parameters. If IV confounders are not preselected but in analogy to section 4 are to be learnt from possibly high dimensional data, then causal machine learning may be applied to the DR representation of both θ and γ in order to estimate the LATE; see for instance Belloni et al. (2017). Finally, the analysis of effect heterogeneity and optimal policies discussed in section 5 also extends to the IV context by using doubly robust statistics appropriate for LATE estimation; see Athey and Wager (2018) and Athey et al. (2019).

Frölich and Melly (2013) discuss the identification of the local quantile treatment effect on compliers (LQTE) and propose an IPW estimator based on local polynomial regression for IV propensity score estimation. Belloni et al. (2017) consider LQTE estimation based on causal machine learning when X are not preselected and important instrument confounders are to be learned from the data. In contrast to the previously mentioned studies, Abadie et al. (2002) consider estimation of the conditional LQTE given particular values in X by applying the so-called κ-weighting approach of Abadie (2003). The latter permits identifying a broad class of complier-related statistics, based on the following weighting function κ:

$$\kappa = 1 - \frac{D \cdot (1-Z)}{1 - \Pr(Z=1\,|\,X)} - \frac{(1-D) \cdot Z}{\Pr(Z=1\,|\,X)}. \tag{4.18}$$

For instance, $\frac{E(\kappa \cdot X)}{E(\kappa)} = E[X\,|\,D(1)=1, D(0)=0]$ yields the mean of X among compliers, which permits judging the similarity of this subgroup and the total population in terms of observed characteristics.

The LATE assumptions are partly testable by investigating specific moment inequalities with respect to outcomes across complier types that need to hold for valid instruments; see the tests proposed by Kitagawa (2015), Huber and Mellace (2015), Mourifié and Wan (2017), Sharma (2016) and Farbmacher et al. (2020). The latter uses a modified version of the causal tree of Athey and Imbens (2016) to increase asymptotic power by searching for the largest violations in IV validity across values X in a data-driven way. It is also worth noting that, even if monotonicity $\Pr(D(1) \geq D(0)|X) = 1$ is violated and defiers exist, the LATE on a fraction of compliers can still be identified if a subset of compliers is equal to the defiers in terms of the average effect and population size; see de Chaisemartin (2017).

When extending the binary instrument and treatment case to a multivalued instrument Z and a binary D, LATEs are identified with respect to any pair of values (z'', z') satisfying the IV assumptions. Each of them may have a different first stage and thus complier population. The LATE for the largest possible complier population appears particularly interesting. The latter is obtained by defining the treatment propensity score $p(z,x) = \Pr(D = 1|Z = z, X = x)$ as instrument and considering the pair of propensity score values that maximizes compliance given $X = x$; see Frölich (2007). A continuously distributed instrument even permits identifying a continuum of complier effects under appropriately adapted IV assumptions. Specifically, a marginal change in the instrument yields the so-called marginal treatment effect (MTE), see Heckman and Vytlacil (2001) and Heckman and Vytlacil (2005), which can be interpreted as the average effect among individuals who are indifferent between treatment or nontreatment given their values of Z and X. Technically speaking, the MTE is the limit of the LATE when the change in the instrument goes to zero.

In contrast to multivalued instruments, generalizing identification from binary to nonbinary treatments is not straightforward. Assume a binary instrument and an ordered treatment $D \in \{0,1 \ldots,J\}$, with $J + 1$ being the number of possible (discrete) treatment doses. Angrist and

Imbens (1995) show that effects for single compliance types at specific treatment values, for example for those increasing the treatment from 1 to 2 when the increasing the instrument from 0 to 1, are not identified. It is, however, possible to obtain a non-trivially weighted average of effects of unit-level increases in the treatment on heterogeneous complier groups defined by different margins of the potential treatments. Albeit this is a proper causal parameter, its interpretability is compromised by the fact that the various complier groups generally enter with non-uniform weights. Similar issues occur if both instruments and treatments are multivalued.

There has been a controversial debate about the practical relevance of the LATE, as it only refers to the subgroup of compliers; see for example Deaton (2010), Imbens (2010) and Heckman and Urzúa (2010). It is therefore interesting to see under which conditions this effect can be extrapolated to other populations. As discussed in Angrist (2004), the LATE is directly externally valid, that is, corresponds to the ATE when either all mean potential outcomes are homogeneous across compliance types, or at least the average effects. For testing the equality of mean potential outcomes across treated compliers and always takers as well as across nontreated compliers and never takers, see Angrist (2004), de Luna and Johansson (2014), Huber (2013) and Black et al. (2015). See also Donald et al. (2014b) for a related but different testing approach. If equality in all mean potential outcomes holds at least conditional on X, instruments are in fact not required for identification as selection into D is on observables only; see section 2. Angrist and Fernández-Val (2010) and Aronow and Carnegie (2013) do not consider homogeneity in mean potential outcomes but discuss extrapolation of the LATE when assuming homogeneous effects across compliance types. This assumption, which rules out selection into treatment by unobserved gains as assumed in standard Roy (1951) models, is testable if several instruments are available. For a comprehensive survey on methodological advancements in LATE evaluation, see Huber and Wüthrich (2019).

7.   DIFFERENCE-IN-DIFFERENCES

The difference-in-differences (DiD) approach bases identification on the so-called common trend assumption. The latter says that the mean potential outcomes under nontreatment of the actually treated and nontreated groups experience a common change over time when comparing periods before and after the treatment. Assuming that both groups would in the absence of the treatment have experienced the same time trend in potential outcomes, however, permits for differences in the levels of potential outcomes due to selection bias. As an example, assume that of interest is the employment effect of a minimum wage (D), which is introduced in one geographic region but not in another one; see for instance Card and Krueger (1994). While the employment level (Y) may differ in both regions due to differences in the industry structure, DiD-based evaluation requires that employment changes, for example due to business cycles, would be the same in the absence of a minimum wage. In this set-up, a comparison of average employment in the post-treatment period across regions does not give the effect of the minimum wage due to selection bias related to the industry structure. A before-after comparison of employment (that is, before and after treatment introduction) within the treated region is biased, too, as it picks up both the treatment effect and the business cycle–related time trend. Under the common trend assumption, however, the time trend for either region is identified by the before–after comparison in the nontreated region. Subtracting the before–after difference in employment in the nontreated region (time trend) from the before–after difference in the treated region (treatment effect plus time trend) therefore gives the treatment effect on the treated. That is, taking the difference in (before–after) differences across regions yields identification under the common trend assumption.

In many empirical problems, common trends may only appear plausible after controlling for observed covariates X. For instance, it could be argued that the assumption is more likely satisfied for treated and nontreated subjects within the same occupation or industry. Formally, let T denote a time index equal to zero in the pre-treatment period, when neither group received the treatment, and one in the post-treatment period, after one out of the two groups received the treatment. To distinguish the potential outcomes in terms of pre- and post-treatment periods, the subindex $t \in \{1,0\}$ is added such that $Y_0(1)$, $Y_0(0)$ and $Y_1(1)$, $Y_1(0)$ correspond to the pre- and post-treatment potential outcomes, respectively. The following conditions permit identifying the ATET in the post-treatment period, denoted by $\Delta_{D=1,T=1} = E[Y_1(1) - Y_1(0)|D = 1, T = 1]$, see the review of the DiD framework in Lechner (2010):

$$E[Y_1(0) - Y_0(0)\,|\,D=1,X] = E[Y_1(0) - Y_0(0)\,|\,D=0,X], \quad X(1) = X(0) = X, \qquad (4.19)$$

$$E[Y_0(0) - Y_0(0)\,|\,D=1,X] = 0,$$

$$\Pr(D=1,T=1\,|\,X,(D,T) \in \{(d,t),(1,1)\}) < 1 \text{ for all } (d,t) \in \{(1,0),(0,1),(0,0)\}.$$

The first line of (4.19) imposes that X is not affected by D and formalizes the conditional common trend assumption stating that, conditional on X, no unobservables jointly affect the treatment and the trend of mean potential outcomes under nontreatment. This is a selection-on-observables assumption on D, but with respect to the changes in mean potential outcomes over time, rather than their levels as in (4.5) of section 2. The two types of assumptions are not nested such that neither implies the other and they cannot be combined for the sake of a more general model; see the discussion in Chabé-Ferret (2017). The second line in (4.19) rules out (average) anticipation effects among the treated, implying that D must not causally influence pre-treatment outcomes in expectation of the treatment to come. The third line imposes common support: For any value of X appearing in the group with $(D = 1, T = 1)$ subjects with such values of X must also exist in the remaining three groups with $(D = 1, T = 0)$, $(D = 0, T = 1)$ and $(D = 0, T = 0)$.

Given that the identifying assumptions hold, the DiD strategy applies to both panel data with the same subjects in pre- and post-treatment periods as well as to repeated cross-sections with different subjects in either period. Under (4.19), $E[Y|D = 0, T = 1, X] - E[Y|D = 0, T = 0, X] = E[Y_1(0) - Y_0(0)|D = 0, X] = E[Y_1(0) - Y_0(0)|D = 1, X]$. This may be subtracted from $E[Y|D = 1, T = 1, X] - E[Y|D = 1, T = 0, X] = E[Y_1(1) - Y_0(1)|D = 1, X] = E[Y_1(1) - Y_1(0)|D = 1, X] + E[Y_1(0) - Y_0(1)|D = 1, X] = E[Y_1(1) - Y_0(1)|D = 1, X] = E[Y_1(1) - Y_0(0)|D = 1, X] + E[Y_1(0) - Y_0(0)|D = 1, X]$, where the second equality follows from subtracting and adding $Y_1(0)$ and the third from ruling out anticipation effects in order to obtain the conditional ATET $E[Y_1(1) - Y_1(0)|D = 1, X]$. Therefore, averaging over the distribution of X among the treated in the post-treatment period yields the ATET in that period:

$$\Delta_{D=1,T=1} = E[\mu_1(1,X) - \mu_1(0,X) - (\mu_0(1,X) - \mu_0(0,X))\,|\,D=1,T=1] \qquad (4.20)$$

$$= E\left[\left\{\left[\frac{D \cdot T}{\Pi} - \frac{D \cdot (1-T) \cdot \rho_{1,1}(X)}{\rho_{1,0}(X) \cdot \Pi}\right] - \left(\frac{(1-D) \cdot T \cdot \rho_{1,1}(X)}{\rho_{0,1}(X) \cdot \Pi} - \frac{(1-D) \cdot (1-T) \cdot \rho_{1,1}(X)}{\rho_{0,0}(X) \cdot \Pi}\right)\right\} \cdot Y\right],$$

where $\Pi = \Pr(D=1,T=1)$, $\rho_{d,t}(X) = \Pr(D=d,T=t\,|\,X)$, and $\mu_d(t,x) = E[Y\,|\,D=d,T=t, X=x]$.

As pointed out in Hong (2013), many DiD studies at least implicitly make the additional assumption that the joint distributions of treatment D and covariates X remain constant over time T, formalized by $(X,\,D)\perp T$. This rules out that the composition of X changes between periods in either treatment group. Under this additional assumption, $\Delta_{D=1,T=1}$ coincides with the "standard" ATET $\Delta_{D=1}$, which is then identified by the following expressions:

$$\Delta_{D=1} = E[\mu_1(1,X) - \mu_1(0,X) - (\mu_0(1,X) - \mu_0(0,X))\,|\,D=1] \qquad (4.21)$$

$$= E\left[\left\{\left[\frac{D\cdot T}{P\cdot \Lambda} - \frac{D\cdot(1-T)}{P\cdot(1-\Lambda)}\right] - \left(\frac{(1-D)\cdot T\cdot p(X)}{(1-p(X))\cdot P\cdot \Lambda} - \frac{(1-D)\cdot(1-T)\cdot p(X)}{(1-p(X))\cdot P\cdot(1-\Lambda)}\right)\right\}\cdot Y\right]$$

$$= E\left[\left\{\left[\frac{D\cdot T}{P\cdot \Lambda} - \frac{D\cdot(1-T)}{P\cdot(1-\Lambda)}\right] - \left(\frac{(1-D)\cdot T\cdot p(X)}{(1-p(X))\cdot P\cdot \Lambda} - \frac{(1-D)\cdot(1-T)\cdot p(X)}{(1-p(X))\cdot P\cdot(1-\Lambda)}\right)\right\}\cdot (Y-\mu_0(T,X))\right],$$

where $p(X) = \Pr(D=1|X)$, $P = \Pr(D=1)$ and $\Lambda = \Pr(T=1)$. Exploiting the identification results after the first, second and third equalities in (4.21), $n^{-1/2}$-consistent estimation may be based on regression or matching, on IPW as considered in Abadie (2005) or on DR estimation as in Sant'Anna and Zhao (2020). Zimmert (2018) shows that in the presence of high dimensional covariate information, causal machine learning based on the DR representation in (4.21) can be semiparametrically efficient in analogy to the results in section 4.

A general practical issue concerning DiD inference is clustering, due to a correlation in uncertainty over time (for example in panel data due to having the same subjects in either period) or within regions (for example due to being exposed to the same institutional context). In this case, observations are not independently sampled from each other, implying that inference methods not accounting for clustering might perform poorly. See for example Bertrand et al. (2004), Donald and Lang (2007), Cameron et al. (2008), Conley and Taber (2011) and Ferman and Pinto (2019) for discussions of this issue as well as of (corrections of) asymptotic or bootstrap-based inference methods under a large or small number of clusters in the treatment groups. The findings of this literature suggest that cluster- and heteroskedasticity-robust variance estimators might only work satisfactorily if the number of treated and nontreated clusters is large enough, while a small number of clusters requires more sophisticated inference methods.

The subsequent discussion reviews some methodological extensions. de Chaisemartin and D'Haultfeuille (2018) discuss identification when the introduction of the treatment does not induce everyone in the treatment group to be treated but (only) increases the treatment rate more than in the nontreated group in the spirit of an instrument; see section 6. Abraham and Sun (2018), Athey and Imbens (2018), Borusyak et al. (2021), Callaway and Sant'Anna (2020), Goodman-Bacon (2018), Hull (2018), Strezhnev (2018), de Chaisemartin and D'Haultfeuille (2020) and Imai and Kim (2021) discuss DiD identification with multiple time periods and treatment groups that might experience treatment introduction at different points in time. Arkhangelsky et al. (2019) consider unit- and time-weighted DiD estimation.

Athey and Imbens (2006) suggest the so-called changes-in-changes (CiC) approach, which is related to DiD in that it exploits differences in pre- and post-treatment outcomes but based on different (and non-nested) identifying assumptions. While CiC does not invoke any common trend assumption, it imposes that potential outcomes under nontreatment are strictly monotonic in unobserved heterogeneity and that the distribution of the latter remains constant over time within treatment groups. Such a conditional independence between unobserved heterogeneity and time is satisfied if the subjects' ranks in the outcome distributions within treatment groups do not systematically change from pre- to post-treatment periods. In contrast to DiD, CiC allows identifying both the ATET and QTET but generally requires a continuously distributed outcome for point identification. Finally, another approach related to but in terms of identification yet different from DiD is the synthetic control method of Abadie and Gardeazabal (2003) and Abadie et al. (2010), which was originally developed for case study set-ups with only one treated but many nontreated units. It is based on appropriately weighting nontreated units as a function of their pre-treatment outcomes and/or covariates to synthetically impute the treated unit's potential outcome under nontreatment. More concisely, the treated unit's potential outcome under nontreatment is estimated as a weighted average of the observed post-treatment outcomes coming from a "donor pool" of nontreated units. The weight some nontreated unit receives for computing this average depends on how similar it is to the treated unit in terms of pre-treatment outcomes and/or covariates. See for instance Abadie (2021) for a survey on the synthetic control method, including recent methodological advancements.

8.   REGRESSION DISCONTINUITY AND KINK DESIGNS

The regression discontinuity design (RDD), see Thistlethwaite and Campbell (1960), is based on the assumption that at a particular threshold of some observed running variable, the treatment status either changes from zero to one for everyone (sharp design) or for a subpopulation (fuzzy design). As an example, assume that the treatment of interest is extended eligibility to unemployment benefits, to which only individuals aged 50 or older are entitled; see for instance Lalive (2008). The idea is to compare the outcomes (like unemployment duration) of treated and untreated subjects close to the (age) threshold, for example of individuals aged 50 and 49, who are arguably similar in characteristics potentially affecting the outcome, due to their minor difference in age. The RDD therefore aims at imitating the experimental context at the threshold to evaluate the treatment effect locally for the subpopulation at the threshold.

Formally, let R denote the running variable and r_0 the threshold value. If the treatment is deterministic in R such that it is one whenever the threshold is reached or exceeded, that is, $D = I\{R \geq r_0\}$, the RDD is sharp: All individuals change their treatment status exactly at r_0. Identification in the sharp RDD relies on the assumption that mean potential outcomes $E[Y(1)|R]$ and $E[Y(0)|R]$ are continuous and sufficiently smooth around $R = r_0$, see for example Hahn et al. (2001), Porter (2003) and Lee (2008), meaning that any factors other than D that affect the outcome are continuous at the threshold. Continuity implies that if treated and nontreated populations with values of R exactly equal to r_0 existed, the treatment would be as good as randomly assigned with respect to mean potential outcomes. This corresponds to a local selection-on-observables assumption conditional on $R = r_0$. Furthermore, the density of the running variable R must be continuous and bounded away from zero around the threshold such that treated and nontreated observations are observed close to $R = r_0$.

Under these assumptions, the ATE at the threshold, denoted by $\Delta_{R=r_0}$, is identified based on treated and nontreated outcomes in a neighbourhood $\varepsilon > 0$ around the threshold when letting ε go to zero:

$$\lim_{\varepsilon \to 0} E[Y \mid R \in [r_0, r_0 + \varepsilon)] - \lim_{\varepsilon \to 0} E[Y \mid R \in [r_0 - \varepsilon, r_0)] \tag{4.22}$$

$$= \lim_{\varepsilon \to 0} E[Y(1) \mid R \in [r_0, r_0 + \varepsilon)] - \lim_{\varepsilon \to 0} E[Y(0) \mid R \in [r_0 - \varepsilon, r_0)] = E[Y(1) - Y(0) \mid R = r_0] = \Delta_{R=r_0}.$$

In the fuzzy RDD, D is not deterministic in R but may also depend on other factors. It is, however, assumed that the treatment share changes discontinuously at the threshold. Assume for example that admittance to a college (D) depends on passing a particular threshold of the score in a college entrance exam (R). While some students might decide not to attend college even if succeeding in the exam, a discontinuous change in the treatment share occurs if compliers exist that are induced to go to college when passing the threshold. Denote by $D(z)$ the potential treatment state as a function of the binary indicator $Z = I\{R \geq r_0\}$, which serves as an instrument in an analogous way, as discussed in section 6. Similar to Dong (2014), assume that around the threshold defiers do not exist and that the shares of compliers, always takers and never takers as well as their mean potential outcomes under treatment and nontreatment, are continuous. This implies that IV-type assumptions similar to those postulated in (4.16) conditional on X hold conditional on $R = r_0$.

Under these conditions, the first stage effect of Z on D, denoted by $\gamma_{R=r_0}$ is identified by

$$\lim_{\varepsilon \to 0} E[D \mid R \in [r_0, r_0 + \varepsilon)] - \lim_{\varepsilon \to 0} E[D \mid R \in [r_0 - \varepsilon, r_0)] \tag{4.23}$$

$$= \lim_{\varepsilon \to 0} E[D(1) \mid R \in [r_0, r_0 + \varepsilon)] - \lim_{\varepsilon \to 0} E[D(0) \mid R \in [r_0 - \varepsilon, r_0)] = E[D(1) - D(0) \mid R = r_0] = \gamma_{R=r_0}.$$

Furthermore, the first line of (4.22) identifies the ITT effect of Z on Y at the threshold, denoted by $\theta_{R=r_0}$ in the fuzzy RDD (rather than $\Delta_{R=r_0}$ as in the sharp RDD). In analogy to (4.17) in section 6, the LATE on compliers at the threshold, denoted by $\Delta_{D(1)=1,D(0)=0,R=r_0} = E[Y(1) - Y(0) \mid D(1) = 1, D(0) = 0, R = r_0]$, is identified by dividing the ITT by the first stage effect at the threshold:

$$\Delta_{D(1)=1,D(0)=0,R=r_0} = \frac{\theta_{R=r_0}}{\gamma_{R=r_0}}. \tag{4.24}$$

In empirical applications of the RDD, the treatment effect is predominantly estimated by a local regression around the threshold. Practitioners frequently use a linear regression for estimating $E[Y|D = 0, R < r_0]$ and $E[Y|D = 1, R \geq 0]$ within some bandwidth around r_0 in order to estimate $\Delta_{R=r_0}$ by the difference of the regression functions at r_0 in the case of the sharp RDD. A smaller bandwidth decreases estimation bias because observations closer to the threshold are more comparable and effect estimation is more robust to model misspecification, see Gelman and Imbens (2019), but increases the variance due to relying on a lower number of observations. Imbens and Kalyanaraman (2012) propose a method for bandwidth selection that minimizes the squared error of the estimator. However, the optimal bandwidth for point estimation is generally suboptimal (and too large) for conducting inference, for example for computing confidence intervals. For this reason, Calonico et al. (2014) propose inference methods that are more robust to bandwidth choice and yield confidence intervals more closely matching nominal coverage, along with optimal bandwidth selection for inference. Their results imply that when $\Delta_{R=r_0}$ is estimated by linear regression within some bandwidth, then quadratic regression (that is one order higher) with the same bandwidth should be used for the computation of the standard error and confidence intervals. Armstrong and Kolesár (2018) suggest an alternative approach to inference that takes into account the worst case bias that could arise given a particular bandwidth choice. Cattaneo et al. (2015) develop randomization methods for exact finite sample inference in the RDD under somewhat stronger identifying assumptions.

The identifying assumptions of the RDD are partly testable in the data. McCrary (2008) proposes a test for the continuity or the running variable at the threshold, as a discontinuity points to a manipulation of R and selective bunching at a one side of the threshold. In the previous example based on Lalive (2008), certain employees and companies might for instance manipulate age at entry into unemployment by postponing layoffs such that the age requirement for extended unemployment benefits is just satisfied. As a further test, Lee (2008) suggests investigating whether observed pre-treatment covariates X are locally balanced at either side of the threshold. Covariates also permit weakening the RDD assumptions to only hold conditional on X, implying that all variables jointly affecting manipulation at the threshold and the outcome are observed; see Frölich and Huber (2018), who propose a nonparametric kernel estimator in this context. In contrast, Calonico et al. (2019) do not exploit covariates for identification but investigate variance reductions when linearly controlling for X and provide methods for optimal bandwidth selection and robust inference for this case.

Several studies investigate conditions under which the rather local RDD effect can be extrapolated to other populations. Dong and Lewbel (2015) show the identification of the derivative of the RDD treatment effect in both sharp and fuzzy designs, which permits identifying the change in the treatment effect resulting from a marginal change in the threshold. Angrist and Rokkanen (2015) test whether the running variable's association with the outcome vanishes on either side of the threshold conditional on covariates X. For the case of the sharp RDD, this implies that X is sufficient to control for confounding just as under the selection-on-observables framework of section 2, such that effects are also identified away from the threshold. In context of the fuzzy RDD, Bertanha and Imbens (2020) propose a test for the equality in mean outcomes of treated compliers and always takers, as well as of untreated compliers and never takers. This permits an investigation of whether the effect on compliers at the threshold may be extrapolated to all compliance types at and away from the threshold. Cattaneo et al. (2020) demonstrate extrapolation under multiple thresholds, that is, when the threshold may vary for various subjects instead of being equal for everyone, as considered in Cattaneo et al. (2016).

Lee and Card (2008), Dong (2015) and Kolesár and Rothe (2018) discuss identification and inference when the forcing variable is discrete rather than continuous, which is highly relevant for empirical applications. Papay et al. (2011) and Keele and Titiunik (2015) extend the regression-discontinuity approach to multiple running variables. Imbens and Wager (2019) propose an optimization-based inference method for deriving the minimax linear RDD estimator, which can be applied to continuous, discrete and multiple running variables. Frandsen et al. (2012) discuss the identification of quantile treatment effects in the RDD. See also Imbens and Lemieux (2008) and Lee and Lemieux (2010) for surveys on the applied and theoretical RDD literature.

Related to the fuzzy RDD is the regression kink design (RKD), see Card et al.(2015), which is technically speaking a first derivative version of the former. The treatment is assumed to be a continuous function of the running variable R (rather than discontinuous as in the RDD) with a kink at r_0. This implies that the first derivative of D with respect to R (rather than the level of D as in the RDD) is discontinuous at the threshold. In Landais (2015), for instance, unemployment benefits (D) are a kinked function of the previous wage (R): D corresponds to R times a constant percentage up to a maximum previous wage r_0 beyond which D does not increase any further but remains constant. For this piecewise linear function, the derivative of D with respect to R corresponds to the percentage for $R < r_0$ and to zero for $R \geq 0$. As the treatment is deterministic in the running variable, this is known as sharp RKD.

Given appropriate continuity and smoothness conditions with respect to mean potential outcomes and the density of R around r_0, scaling the change in the first derivatives of mean outcomes with respect to R at the threshold by the corresponding change in first derivatives of D identifies a causal effect. The latter corresponds to the average derivative of the potential outcome with respect to D when the latter corresponds to its value at the threshold, denoted by d_0, within the local population at $R = r_0$:

$$\Delta_{R=r_0}(d_0) = \frac{\partial E[Y(d_0)\,|\,R=r_0]}{\partial D} = \frac{\lim\limits_{\varepsilon\to 0}\dfrac{\partial E[Y\,|\,R\in[r_0,r_0+\varepsilon)]}{\partial R} - \lim\limits_{\varepsilon\to 0}\dfrac{\partial E[Y\,|\,R\in[r_0-\varepsilon,r_0)]}{\partial R}}{\lim\limits_{\varepsilon\to 0}\dfrac{\partial D\,|\,R\in[r_0,r_0+\varepsilon)}{\partial R} - \lim\limits_{\varepsilon\to 0}\dfrac{\partial D\,|\,R\in[r_0-\varepsilon,r_0)}{\partial R}}. \quad (4.25)$$

The fuzzy RKD permits deviations from the kinked function characterizing how the running variable affects the treatment such that D is not deterministic in R; see for instance Simonsen et al. (2016) for a study investigating the price sensitivity of product demand. Under specific continuity conditions and the monotonicity-type assumption that the kink of any individual either goes in the same direction or is zero, a causal effect at the threshold is identified among individuals with nonzero kinks. To this end, the derivatives of the treatment in (4.25), namely $\frac{\partial D|R\in[r_0,r_0+\varepsilon)}{\partial R}$ and $\frac{\partial D|R\in[r_0-\varepsilon,r_0)}{\partial R}$, are to be replaced by the derivatives of expectations $\frac{\partial E[D|R\in[r_0,r_0+\varepsilon)]}{\partial R}$ and $\frac{\partial E[D|R\in[r_0-\varepsilon,r_0)]}{\partial R}$. As the expectation of a treatment maybe continuous even if the treatment itself is not, the fuzzy RKD may also be applied to a binary D; see Dong (2014). Calonico et al. (2014) provide robust inference methods for the RKD, while Ganong and Jäger (2018) propose a permutation method for exact finite sample inference.

9. CONCLUSION

This chapter provided an overview of different approaches to policy evaluation for assessing the causal effect of a treatment on an outcome. Starting with an introduction to causality and the experimental evaluation of a randomized treatment, it subsequently discussed identification and flexible estimation under selection on observables, instrumental variables, difference-in-differences, changes-in-changes and regression discontinuities and kinks. Particular attention was devoted to approaches combining policy evaluation with machine learning to provide data-driven procedures for tackling confounding related to observed covariates, investigating effect heterogeneities across subgroups and learning optimal treatment policies. In a world with ever increasing data availability, such causal machine learning methods aimed at optimally exploiting large amounts of information for causal inference will likely leverage the scope of policy evaluation to unprecedented levels. Besides the classic domain of public policies, this concerns not least the private sector, with ever more firms investing in data analytics to assess and optimize the causal impact of their actions like price policies or advertising campaigns.

NOTE

* The author is grateful to Colin Cameron, Selina Gangl, Michael Knaus, Henrika Langen and Michael Lechner for their valuable comments.

REFERENCES

Abadie, A. (2003), 'Semiparametric instrumental variable estimation of treatment response models', *Journal of Econometrics* **113**, 231–63.

Abadie, A. (2005), 'Semiparametric difference-in-differences estimators', *Review of Economic Studies* **72**, 1–19.

Abadie, A. (2021), 'Using synthetic controls: Feasibility, data requirements, and methodological aspects', *Journal of Economic Literature*, **59** (2): 391–425. DOI: 10.1257/jel.20191450.

Abadie, A., Angrist, J. & Imbens, G. W. (2002), 'Instrumental variables estimates of the effect of subsidized training on the quantiles of trainee earnings', *Econometrica* **70**, 91–117.

Abadie, A., Diamond, A. & Hainmueller, J. (2010), 'Synthetic control methods for comparative case studies: Estimating the effect of California's tobacco control program', *Journal of the American Statistical Association* **105**, 493–505.

Abadie, A. & Gardeazabal, J. (2003), 'The economic costs of conflict: A case study of the Basque country', *The American Economic Review* **93**, 113–32.

Abadie, A. & Imbens, G. W. (2006), 'Large sample properties of matching estimators for average treatment effects', *Econometrica* **74**, 235–67.

Abadie, A. & Imbens, G. W. (2008), 'On the failure of the bootstrap for matching estimators', *Econometrica* **76**, 1537–57.

Abadie, A. & Imbens, G. W. (2011), 'Bias-corrected matching estimators for average treatment effects', *Journal of Business & Economic Statistics* **29**, 1–11.

Abadie, A. & Imbens, G. W. (2016), 'Matching on the estimated propensity score', *Econometrica* **84**, 781–807.

Abraham, S. & Sun, L. (2018), 'Estimating dynamic treatment effects in event studies with heterogeneous treatment effects', working paper, *Massachusetts Institute of Technology*.

Angrist, J. & Fernández-Val, I. (2010), 'Extrapolate-ing: External validity and overidentification in the late framework', working paper, *NBER* 16566.

Angrist, J. & Imbens, G. W. (1995), 'Two-stage least squares estimation of average causal effects in models with variable treatment intensity', *Journal of American Statistical Association* **90**, 431–42.

Angrist, J., & Imbens, G. W. & Rubin, D. (1996), 'Identification of causal effects using instrumental variables', *Journal of American Statistical Association* **91**, 444–72 (with discussion).

Angrist, J. D. (2004), 'Treatment effect heterogeneity in theory and practice', *The Economic Journal* **114**, C52–C83.

Angrist, J. D. & Rokkanen, M. (2015), 'Wanna get away? Regression discontinuity estimation of exam school effects away from the cutoff', *Journal of the American Statistical Association* **110**, 1331–44.

Arkhangelsky, D., Athey, S., Hirshberg, D. A. and Wager, G. W. I. S. (2019), 'Synthetic difference in differences', working paper, *Stanford University*.

Armstrong, T. B. & Kolesár, M. (2018), 'Optimal inference in a class of regression models', *Econometrica* **86**(2), 655–83.

Aronow, P. M. & Carnegie, A. (2013), 'Beyond late: Estimation of the average treatment effect with an instrumental variable', *Political Analysis* **21**, 492–506.

Athey, S. & Imbens, G. (2006), 'Identification and inference in nonlinear difference-in-differences models', *Econometrica* **74**, 431–97.

Athey, S. & Imbens, G. (2016), 'Recursive partitioning for heterogeneous causal effects', *Proceedings of the National Academy of Sciences* **113**, 7353–60.

Athey, S. & Imbens, G. (2018), 'Design-based analysis in difference-in-differences settings with staggered adoption', working paper, *Stanford University*.

Athey, S. & Imbens, G. W. (2019), 'Machine learning methods that economists should know about', *Annual Review of Economics* **11**.

Athey, S., Imbens, G. W. & Wager, S. (2018), 'Approximate residual balancing: Debiased inference of average treatment effects in high dimensions', *Journal of the Royal Statistical Society Series B* **80**, 597–623.

Athey, S., Tibshirani, J. & Wager, S. (2019), 'Generalized random forests', *The Annals of Statistics* **47**, 1148–78.

Athey, S. & Wager, S. (2018), 'Efficient policy learning', working paper, *Stanford University*.

Belloni, A., Chernozhukov, V., Fernández-Val, I. & Hansen, C. (2017), 'Program evaluation and causal inference with high-dimensional data', *Econometrica* **85**, 233–98.

Belloni, A., Chernozhukov, V. & Hansen, C. (2014), 'Inference on treatment effects after selection among high-dimensional controls', *The Review of Economic Studies* **81**, 608–50.

Bertanha, M. & Imbens, G. W. (2020), 'External validity in fuzzy regression discontinuity designs', *Journal of Business & Economic Statistics* **3**, 593–612.

Bertrand, M., Duflo, E. & Mullainathan, S. (2004), 'How much should we trust differences-in-differences estimates?', *Quarterly Journal of Economics* **119**, 249–75.

Bhattacharya, D. & Dupas, P. (2012), 'Inferring welfare maximizing treatment assignment under budget constraints', *Journal of Econometrics* **167**, 168–96.

Black, D. A., Joo, J., LaLonde, R. J., Smith, J. A. & Taylor, E. J. (2015), 'Simple tests for selection bias: Learning more from instrumental variables', *IZA Discussion Paper*, no. 9346.

Borusyak, K., Jaravel, X. & Spiess, J. (2021), 'Revisiting event study designs: Robust and efficient estimation', working paper, *University College London*.

Breiman, L. (2001), 'Random forests', *Machine Learning* **45**, 5–32.

Breiman, L., Friedman, J., Olshen, R. & Stone, C. (1984), *Classification and Regression Trees*, Belmont, California: Wadsworth.

Busso, M., DiNardo, J. & McCrary, J. (2014), 'New evidence on the finite sample properties of propensity score matching and reweighting estimators', *Review of Economics and Statistics* **96**, 885–97.

Callaway, B., & Sant'Anna, P. H. (2020). 'Difference-in-differences with multiple time periods,' *Journal of Econometrics*, https://doi.org/10.1016/j.jeconom.2020.12.001.

Calonico, S., Cattaneo, M. D., Farrell, M. H., & Titiunik, R. (2019). 'Regression discontinuity designs using covariates', *Review of Economics and Statistics*, **101**(3), 442–51.

Calonico, S., Cattaneo, M. D. & Titiunik, R. (2014), 'Robust nonparametric confidence intervals for regression-discontinuity designs', *Econometrica* **82**, 2295–326.

Cameron, A. C., Gelbach, J. B. & Miller, D. L. (2008), 'Bootstrap-based improvements for inference with clustered errors', *Review of Economics and Statistics* **90**, 414–27.

Card, D. (1995), 'Using geographic variation in college proximity to estimate the return to schooling,' in L. Christofides, E. Grant R. Swidinsky (eds), *Aspects of Labor Market Behaviour: Essays in Honour of John Vanderkamp*, Toronto: University of Toronto Press, pp. 201–22.

Card, D. & Krueger, A. B. (1994), 'Minimum wages and employment: A case study of the fast-food industry in New Jersey and Pennsylvania', *The American Economic Review* **84**, 772–93.

Card, D., Lee, D. S., Pei, Z. & Weber, A. (2015), 'Inference on causal effects in a generalized regression kink design', *Econometrica* **83**, 2453–83.

Cattaneo, M. D. (2010), 'Efficient semiparametric estimation of multi-valued treatment effects under ignorability', *Journal of Econometrics* **155**, 138–54.

Cattaneo, M. D., Frandsen, B. R. & Titiunik, R. (2015), 'Randomization inference in the regression discontinuity design: An application to party advantages in the U.S. senate', *Journal of Causal Inference* **3**, 1–24.

Cattaneo, M. D., Keele, L., Titiunik, R. & Vazquez-Bare, G. (2016), 'Interpreting regression discontinuity designs with multiple cutoffs', *The Journal of Politics* **78**, 1229–48.

Cattaneo, M. D., Keele, L., Titiunik, R., & Vazquez-Bare, G. (2020), 'Extrapolating treatment effects in multi-cutoff regression discontinuity designs', *Journal of the American Statistical Association*, https://doi.org/10.1080/01621459.2020.1751646.

Chabé-Ferret, S. (2017), 'Should we combine difference in differences with conditioning on pre-treatment outcomes', working paper, *Toulouse School of Economics*.

Chen, X., Hong, H. & Tarozzi, A. (2008), 'Semiparametric efficiency in gmm models with auxiliary data', *The Annals of Statistics* **36**, 808–43.

Chernozhukov, V., Chetverikov, D., Demirer, M., Duflo, E., Hansen, C., Newey, W. & Robins, J. (2018), 'Double/debiased machine learning for treatment and structural parameters', *The Econometrics Journal* **21**, C1–C68.

Chernozhukov, V., Fernández-Val, I. & Melly, B. (2013), 'Inference on counterfactual distributions', *Econometrica* **81**, 2205–68.

Conley, T. & Taber, C. (2011), 'Inference with "difference in differences" with a small number of policy changes', *Review of Economics and Statistics* **93**, 113–25.

Crump, R., Hotz, J., Imbens, G. & Mitnik, O. (2009), 'Dealing with limited overlap in estimation of average treatment effects', *Biometrika* **96**, 187–99.

de Chaisemartin, C. (2017), 'Tolerating defiance? Local average treatment effects without monotonicity', *Quantitative Economics* **8**, 367–96.

de Chaisemartin, C. & D'Haultfeuille, X. (2018), 'Fuzzy differences-in-differences', *Review of Economic Studies* **85**, 999–1028.

De Chaisemartin, C., & d'Haultfoeuille, X. (2020), 'Two-way fixed effects estimators with heterogeneous treatment effects', *American Economic Review*, **110**(9), 2964–96.

de Luna, X. & Johansson, P. (2014), 'Testing for the unconfoundedness assumption using an instrumental assumption', *Journal of Causal Inference* **2**, 187–99.

Deaton, A. S. (2010), 'Instruments, randomization, and learning about development', *Journal of Economic Literature* **48**, 424–55.

Dehejia, R. H. & Wahba, S. (1999), 'Causal effects in non-experimental studies: Reevaluating the evaluation of training programmes', *Journal of American Statistical Association* **94**, 1053–62.

Diamond, A. & Sekhon, J. S. (2013), 'Genetic matching for estimating causal effects: A general multivariate matching method for achieving balance in observational studies', *Review of Economics and Statistics* **95**, 932–45.

DiNardo, J. E., Fortin, N. M. & Lemieux, T. (1996), 'Labor Market Institutions and the Distribution of Wages, 1973–1992: A Semiparametric Approach', *Econometrica* **64**, 1001–44.

Donald, S. G. & Hsu, Y. C. (2014), 'Estimation and inference for distribution functions and quantile functions in treatment effect models', *Journal of Econometrics* **178**, 383–97.

Donald, S. G., Hsu, Y.-C. & Lieli, R. P. (2014a), 'Inverse probability weighted estimation of local average treatment effects: A higher order mse expansion', *Statistics and Probability Letters* **95**, 132–38.

Donald, S. G., Hsu, Y.-C. & Lieli, R. P. (2014b), 'Testing the unconfoundedness assumption via inverse probability weighted estimators of (L)ATT', *Journal of Business & Economic Statistics* **32**, 395–415.

Donald, S. & Lang, K. (2007), 'Inference with difference-in-differences and other panel data', *Review of Economics and Statistics*, **89**, 221–33.

Dong, Y. (2014), 'Jumpy or kinky? Regression discontinuity without the discontinuity', working paper, *University of California Irvine*.

Dong, Y. (2015), 'Regression discontinuity applications with rounding errors in the running variable', *Journal of Applied Econometrics* **30**, 422–46.

Dong, Y. & Lewbel, A. (2015), 'Identifying the effect of changing the policy threshold in regression discontinuity models', *Review of Economics and Statistics* **97**, 1081–92.

Dudík, M., Langford, J. & Li, L. (2011), 'Doubly robust policy evaluation and learning', *Procceedings of the 28th International Conference on Machine Learning*, pp. 1097–1104.

Farbmacher, H., Guber, R., & Klaassen, S. (2020), 'Instrument validity tests with causal forests', *Journal of Business & Economic Statistics*, 1–10.

Farrell, M. H. (2015), 'Robust inference on average treatment effects with possibly more covariates than observations', *Journal of Econometrics* **189**, 1–23.

Farrell, M. H., Liang, T. & Misra, S. (2021), 'Deep neural networks for estimation and inference', *Econometrica*, **89**, 181–213.

Ferman, B. & Pinto, C. (2019), 'Inference in differences-in-differences with few treated groups and heteroskedasticity', *The Review of Economics and Statistics* **101**, 1–16.

Firpo, S. (2007), 'Efficient semiparametric estimation of quantile treatment effects', *Econometrica* **75**, 259–76.

Flores, C. A. (2007), 'Estimation of dose-response functions and optimal doses with a continuous treatment', working paper, *University of California, Berkeley*.

Flores, C. A., Flores-Lagunes, A., Gonzalez, A. & Neumann, T. C. (2012), 'Estimating the effects of length of exposure to instruction in a training program: the case of job corps', *The Review of Economics and Statistics* **94**, 153–71.

Frandsen, B. R., Frölich, M., & Melly, B. (2012). Quantile treatment effects in the regression discontinuity design. *Journal of Econometrics*, **168**(2), 382–395.

Frölich, M. (2004), 'Finite sample properties of propensity-score matching and weighting estimators', *The Review of Economics and Statistics* **86**, 77–90.

Frölich, M. (2005), 'Matching estimators and optimal bandwidth choice', *Statistics and Computing* **15**, 197–215.

Frölich, M. (2007), 'Nonparametric IV estimation of local average treatment effects with covariates', *Journal of Econometrics* **139**, 35–75.

Frölich, M., & Huber, M. (2019). Including covariates in the regression discontinuity design. *Journal of Business & Economic Statistics*, **37**(4), 736–748.

Frölich, M. & Melly, B. (2013), 'Unconditional quantile treatment effects under endogeneity', *Journal of Business & Economic Statistics* **31**, 346–57.

Galvao, A. F. & Wang, L. (2015), 'Uniformly semiparametric efficient estimation of treatment effects with a continuous treatment', *Journal of the American Statistical Association* **110**, 1528–42.

Ganong, P. & Jäger, S. (2018), 'A permutation test for the regression kink design', *Journal of the American Statistical Association* **113**, 494–504.

Gelman, A., & Imbens, G. (2019). 'Why high-order polynomials should not be used in regression discontinuity designs,' Journal of Business & Economic Statistics, 37(3), 447–56.

Goodman-Bacon, A. (2018), 'Difference-in-differences with variation in treatment timing', working paper, *Vanderbilt University*.

Graham, B., Pinto, C. & Egel, D. (2012), 'Inverse probability tilting for moment condition models with missing data', *Review of Economic Studies* **79**, 1053–79.

Hahn, J. (1998), 'On the role of the propensity score in efficient semiparametric estimation of average treatment effects', *Econometrica* **66**, 315–31.

Hahn, J., Todd, P. & van der Klaauw, W. (2001), 'Identification and estimation of treatment effects with a regression-discontinuity design', *Econometrica* **69**, 201–9.

Hainmueller, J. (2012), 'Entropy balancing for causal effects: A multivariate reweighting method to produce balanced samples in observational studies', *Political Analysis* **20**, 25–46.

Heckman, J., Ichimura, H., Smith, J. & Todd, P. (1998a), 'Characterizing selection bias using experimental data', *Econometrica* **66**, 1017–98.

Heckman, J. J., Ichimura, H. & Todd, P. (1998b), 'Matching as an econometric evaluation estimator', *Review of Economic Studies* **65**, 261–94.

Heckman, J. J. & Urzúa, S. (2010), 'Comparing iv with structural models: What simple IV can and cannot identify', *Journal of Econometrics* **156**, 27–37.

Heckman, J. J. & Vytlacil, E. (2001), 'Local instrumental variables,' in C. Hsiao, K. Morimune J. Powell (eds), *Nonlinear Statistical Inference: Essays in Honor of Takeshi Amemiya*, Cambridge: Cambridge University Press.

Heckman, J. J. & Vytlacil, E. (2005), 'Structural equations, treatment effects, and econometric policy evaluation 1', *Econometrica* **73**, 669–738.

Hirano, K. & Imbens, G. W. (2005), *The Propensity Score with Continuous Treatments*, Hoboken, NJ: Wiley-Blackwell, pp. 73–84.

Hirano, K., Imbens, G. W. & Ridder, G. (2003), 'Efficient estimation of average treatment effects using the estimated propensity score', *Econometrica* **71**, 1161–89.

Hirano, K. & Porter, J. (2009), 'Asymptotics for statistical treatment rules', *Econometrica* **77**, 1683–1701.

Hong, H. & Nekipelov, D. (2010), 'Semiparametric efficiency in nonlinear late models', *Quantitative Economics* **1**, 279–304.

Hong, S.-H. (2013), 'Measuring the effect of napster on recorded music sales: difference?in?differences estimates under compositional changes', *Journal of Applied Econometrics* **28**, 297–324.

Horvitz, D. & Thompson, D. (1952), 'A generalization of sampling without replacement from a finite population', *Journal of American Statistical Association* **47**, 663–85.

Huber, M. (2013), 'A simple test for the ignorability of non-compliance in experiments', *Economics Letters* **120**, 389–91.

Huber, M. (2014), 'Identifying causal mechanisms (primarily) based on inverse probability weighting', *Journal of Applied Econometrics* **29**, 920–43.

Huber, M. (2021), 'Mediation Analysis', in Zimmermann K. F. (ed), *Handbook of Labor, Human Resources and Population Economics*. Springer, Cham. see https://link.springer.com/referenceworkentry/10.1007%2F978-3-319 -57365-6_162-2#DOI

Huber, M., Lechner, M. & Wunsch, C. (2013), 'The performance of estimators based on the propensity score', *Journal of Econometrics* **175**, 1–21.

Huber, M. & Mellace, G. (2015), 'Testing instrument validity for late identification based on inequality moment constraints', *Review of Economics and Statistics* **97**, 398–411.

Huber, M. & Wüthrich, K. (2019), 'Local average and quantile treatment effects under endogeneity: A review', *Journal of Econometric Methods* **8**, 1–28.

Hull, P. (2018), 'Estimating treatment effects in mover designs', working paper, *University of Chicago*.

Ichimura, H. & Linton, O. (2005), 'Asymptotic expansions for some semiparametric program evaluation estimators,' in D. Andrews & J. Stock (eds), *Identification and Inference for Econometric Models*, Cambridge: Cambridge University Press, pp. 149–70.

Imai, K., Keele, L. & Yamamoto, T. (2010), 'Identification, inference and sensitivity analysis for causal mediation effects', *Statistical Science* **25**, 51–71.

Imai, K., & Kim, I. S. (2021). On the use of two-way fixed effects regression models for causal inference with panel data. Political Analysis, 29(3), 405–15.

Imai, K. & Ratkovic, M. (2014), 'Covariate balancing propensity score', *Journal of the Royal Statistical Society: Series B (Statistical Methodology)* **76**, 243–63.

Imai, K. & van Dyk, D. A. (2004), 'Causal inference with general treatment regimes', *Journal of the American Statistical Association* **99**, 854–66.

Imbens, G. & Kalyanaraman, K. (2012), 'Optimal bandwidth choice for the regression discontinuity estimator', *The Review of Economic Studies* **79**, 933–59.

Imbens, G. W. (2000), 'The role of the propensity score in estimating dose-response functions', *Biometrika* **87**, 706–10.

Imbens, G. W. (2004), 'Nonparametric estimation of average treatment effects under exogeneity: A review', *The Review of Economics and Statistics* **86**, 4–29.

Imbens, G. W. (2010), 'Better late than nothing: Some comments on Deaton (2009)) and Heckman and Urzua (2009))', *Journal of Economic Literature* **48**, 399–423.

Imbens, G. W. & Angrist, J. (1994), 'Identification and estimation of local average treatment effects', *Econometrica* **62**, 467–75.

Imbens, G. W. & Lemieux, T. (2008), 'Regression discontinuity designs: A guide to practice', *Journal of Econometrics* **142**, 615–35.

Imbens, G. W. & Wager, S. (2019), 'Optimized regression discontinuity designs', *Review of Economics and Statistics* **101**, 264–78.

Imbens, G. W. & Wooldridge, J. M. (2009), 'Recent developments in the econometrics of program evaluation', *Journal of Economic Literature* **47**, 5–86.

Kallus, N. (2017), 'Balanced policy evaluation and learning', working paper, *Cornell University*.

Keele, L. J. & Titiunik, R. (2015), 'Geographic boundaries as regression discontinuities', *Political Analysis* **23**, 127–55.

Kennedy, E. H., Ma, Z., McHugh, M. D. & Small, D. S. (2017), 'Non-parametric methods for doubly robust estimation of continuous treatment effects', *Journal of the Royal Statistical Society Series B* **79**, 1229–45.

Khan, S. & Tamer, E. (2010), 'Irregular identification, support conditions, and inverse weight estimation', *Econometrica* **78**, 2021–42.

Kitagawa, T. (2015), 'A test for instrument validity', *Econometrica* **83**, 2043–63.

Kitagawa, T. & Tetenov, A. (2018), 'Who should be treated? Empirical welfare maximization methods for treatment choice', *Econometrica* **86**, 591–616.

Knaus, M. C., Lechner, M., & Strittmatter, A. (2021), 'Machine learning estimation of heterogeneous causal effects: Empirical Monte Carlo evidence', *The Econometrics Journal*, **24**(1), 134–61.

Kolesár, M. & Rothe, C. (2018), 'Inference in a regression discontinuity design with a discrete running variable', *American Economic Review* **108**, 2277–304.

Lalive, R. (2008), 'How do extended benefits affect unemployment duration? A regression discontinuity approach', *Journal of Econometrics* **142**, 785–806.

Landais, C. (2015), 'Assessing the welfare effects of unemployment benefits using the regression kink design', *American Economic Journal: Economic Policy* **7**, 243–78.

Lechner, M. (2001), 'Identification and estimation of causal effects of multiple treatments under the conditional independence assumption,' in M. Lechner F. Pfeiffer (eds), *Econometric Evaluations of Active Labor Market Policies in Europe*, Heidelberg: Physica.

Lechner, M. (2009), 'Sequential causal models for the evaluation of labor market programs', *Journal of Business and Economic Statistics* **27**, 71–83.

Lechner, M. (2010), 'The estimation of causal effects by difference-in-difference methods', *Foundations and Trends in Econometrics* **4**, 165–224.

Lechner, M., Miquel, R. & Wunsch, C. (2011), 'Long-run effects of public sector sponsored training in West Germany', *Journal of the European Economic Association* **9**, 742–84.

Lechner, M. & Strittmatter, A. (2019), 'Practical procedures to deal with common support problems in matching estimation', *Econometric Reviews* **38**, 193–207.

Lee, D. (2008), 'Randomized experiments from non-random selection in U.S. house elections', *Journal of Econometrics* **142**, 675–97.

Lee, D. & Card, D. (2008), 'Regression discontinuity inference with specification error', *Journal of Econometrics* **142**, 655–74.

Lee, D. & Lemieux, T. (2010), 'Regression discontinuity designs in economics', *Journal of Economic Literature* **48**, 281–355.

Li, Q., Racine, J. & Wooldridge, J. (2009), 'Efficient estimation of average treatment effects with mixed categorical and continuous data', *Journal of Business and Economics Statistics* **27**, 206–23.

Manski, C. F. (2004), 'Statistical treatment rules for heterogeneous populations', *Econometrica* **72**, 1221–46.

McCrary, J. (2008), 'Manipulation of the running variable in the regression discontinuity design: A density test', *Journal of Econometrics* **142**, 698–714.

Mourifié, I. & Wan, Y. (2017), 'Testing late assumptions', *The Review of Economics and Statistics* **99**, 305–13.

Papay, J. P., Willett, J. B. & Murnane, R. J. (2011), 'Extending the regression-discontinuity approach to multiple assignment variables', *Journal of Econometrics* **161**, 203–7.

Pearl, J. (2001), Direct and indirect effects, in M. Kaufman (ed), *Proceedings of the Seventeenth Conference on Uncertainty in Artificial Intelligence*, San Francisco: pp. 411–20.

Porter, J. (2003), *Estimation in the Regression Discontinuity Model*, New York: mimeo.

Powers, S., Qian, J., Jung, K., Schuler, A., Shah, N. H., Hastie, T. & Tibshirani, R. (2018), 'Some methods for heterogeneous treatment effect estimation in high dimensions', *Statistics in Medicine* **37**, 1767–87.

Qian, M. & Murphy, S. A. (2011), 'Performance guarantees for individualized treatment rules', *Annals of Statistics* **39**, 1180–210.

Robins, J. M. (1986), 'A new approach to causal inference in mortality studies with sustained exposure periods – application to control of the healthy worker survivor effect', *Mathematical Modelling* **7**, 1393–512.

Robins, J. M. & Greenland, S. (1992), 'Identifiability and exchangeability for direct and indirect effects', *Epidemiology* **3**, 143–55.

Robins, J. M., Hernan, M. A. & Brumback, B. (2000), 'Marginal structural models and causal inference in epidemiology', *Epidemiology* **11**, 550–60.

Robins, J. M., Mark, S. D. & Newey, W. K. (1992), 'Estimating exposure effects by modelling the expectation of exposure conditional on confounders', *Biometrics* **48**, 479–95.

Robins, J. M. & Rotnitzky, A. (1995), 'Semiparametric efficiency in multivariate regression models with missing data', *Journal of the American Statistical Association* **90**, 122–9.

Robins, J. M., Rotnitzky, A. & Zhao, L. (1994), 'Estimation of regression coefficients when some regressors are not always observed', *Journal of the American Statistical Association* **90**, 846–66.

Robins, J. M., Rotnitzky, A. & Zhao, L. (1995), 'Analysis of semiparametric regression models for repeated outcomes in the presence of missing data', *Journal of the American Statistical Association* **90**, 106–21.

Rosenbaum, P. R. & Rubin, D. B. (1983), 'The central role of the propensity score in observational studies for causal effects', *Biometrika* **70**, 41–55.

Rosenbaum, P. R. & Rubin, D. B. (1985), 'Constructing a control group using multivariate matched sampling methods that incorporate the propensity score.', *The American Statistician* **39**, 33–8.

Rothe, C. & Firpo, S. (2013), 'Semiparametric estimation and inference using doubly robust moment conditions', *IZA*, discussion paper no. 7564.

Roy, A. (1951), 'Some thoughts on the distribution of earnings', *Oxford Economic Papers* **3**, 135–46.

Rubin, D. B. (1974), 'Estimating causal effects of treatments in randomized and nonrandomized studies', *Journal of Educational Psychology* **66**, 688–701.

Rubin, D. B. (1979), 'Using multivariate matched sampling and regression adjustment to control bias in observational studies', *Journal of the American Statistical Association* **74**, 318–28.

Rubin, D. B. (1990), 'Formal mode of statistical inference for causal effects', *Journal of Statistical Planning and Inference* **25**, 279–92.

Sant'Anna, P. H., & Zhao, J. (2020). 'Doubly robust difference-in-differences estimators', *Journal of Econometrics*, **219**(1), 101–22.

Sharma, A. (2016), 'Necessary and probably sufficient test for finding valid instrumental variables', working paper, *Microsoft Research, New York*.

Sianesi, B. (2004), 'An evaluation of the swedish system of active labor market programs in the 1990s', *The Review of Economics and Statistics* **86**, 133–55.

Simonsen, M., Skipper, L. & Skipper, N. (2016), 'Price sensitivity of demand for prescription drugs: Exploiting a regression kink design', *Journal of Applied Econometrics* **31**, 320–37.

Smith, J. & Todd, P. (2005), 'Rejoinder', *Journal of Econometrics* **125**, 365–75.

Stoye, J. (2009), 'Minimax regret treatment choice with finite samples', *Journal of Econometrics* **151**, 70–81.

Strezhnev, A. (2018), 'Semiparametric weighting estimators for multi-period difference-in-differences designs', working paper, *University of Pennsylvania*.

Tan, Z. (2006), 'Regression and weighting methods for causal inference using instrumental variables', *Journal of the American Statistical Association* **101**, 1607–18.

Tchetgen Tchetgen, E. J. & Shpitser, I. (2012), 'Semiparametric theory for causal mediation analysis: Efficiency bounds, multiple robustness, and sensitivity analysis', *The Annals of Statistics* **40**, 1816–45.

Thistlethwaite, D. & Campbell, D. (1960), 'Regression-discontinuity analysis: An alternative to the ex post facto experiment', *Journal of Educational Psychology* **51**, 309–17.

Tibshirani, R. (1996), 'Regresson shrinkage and selection via the lasso', *Journal of the Royal Statistical Society* **58**, 267–88.

Uysal, S. D. (2011), 'Doubly robust IV estimation of the local average treatment effects', *University of Konstanz*.

van der Laan, M. & Rubin, D. (2006), 'Targeted maximum likelihood learning', *The International Journal of Biostatistics* **2**, 1–38.

Waernbaum, I. (2012), 'Model misspecification and robustness in causal inference: Comparing matching with doubly robust estimation', *Statistics in Medicine* **31**, 1572–81.

Wager, S. & Athey, S. (2018), 'Estimation and inference of heterogeneous treatment effects using random forests', *Journal of the American Statistical Association* **113**, 1228–42.

Zhang, B., Tsiatis, A. A., Davidian, M., Zhang, M. & Laber, E. (2012), 'Estimating optimal treatment regimes from a classification perspective', *Stat* **1**, 103–14.

Zhao, Z. (2004), 'Using matching to estimate treatment effects: Data requirements, matching metrics, and Monte Carlo evidence', *Review of Economics and Statistics* **86**, 91–107.

Zhou, X., Mayer-Hamblett, N., Khan, U. & Kosorok, M. R. (2017), 'Residual weighted learning forestimating individualized treatment rules', *Journal of the American Statistical Association* **112**, 169–87.

Zhou, Z., Athey, S. & Wager, S. (2018), 'Offline multi-action policy learning: Generalization and optimization', working paper, *Stanford University*.

Zimmert, M. (2018), 'Efficient difference-in-differences estimation with high-dimensional common trend confounding', working paper, *University of St. Gallen*.

Zubizarreta, J. R. (2015), 'Stable weights that balance covariates for estimation with incomplete outcome data', *Journal of the American Statistical Association* **110**, 910–22.

PART II

HOUSEHOLDS, BUSINESSES AND SOCIETIES

5.   Econometric models of fertility
*Alfonso Miranda and Pravin K. Trivedi**

1.   INTRODUCTION

This chapter reviews some key contributions to econometric analysis of human fertility in the last 20 years, with special focus on the discussion of prevailing econometric modelling strategies. To keep the task manageable and the result useful, we restrict our focus to the strand in the literature that seeks to highlight the role of the key drivers of the birth outcomes, that is, where investigations model outcomes such as the age at entry into motherhood, the number of children and the time between births. Hence, we are mainly concerned with work that views fertility and related variables as the outcome variables of interest and socioeconomic characteristics as key explanatory covariates. Thus we exclude works where the main interest lies in interdependence between and interactions with fertility and other response variables such as infant mortality, labour force participation, labour supply and/ or educational attainment, in which fertility enters as an important predetermined or jointly determined control variable.

Our overall approach is to use single equation reduced form type modelling of fertility. Such an approach suffers from limitations; typically, does not shed much light on detailed causal mechanisms through which exogenous factors such as birth control and infant mortality, and policy variables such as child allowances and tax incentives, impact fertility. Structural models that embed causal mechanisms explicitly are better suited for this objective. Nevertheless the reduced form approach is widely used, especially in the demographic literature. It is useful for studying associations, projecting fertility patterns and trends and related demographic features.

We start with a description of the subject matter, including a brief review of existing theories of fertility behaviour and a detailed discussion of the sources of data that are available to the analyst. At this point, we stress the intrinsic dynamic nature of fertility decisions and how such dynamics create data with empirical features that pose important challenges for modelling.

Once the nature of the problem and the characteristics of the data are spelled out, we proceed to review the different econometric approaches that have been used for modelling fertility outcomes with cross-section and panel data. We shall discuss the properties of a standard ordinary least squares (OLS) estimator before reviewing more popular count and hazard models. Notwithstanding the popularity of this class of models, there are important aspects of the fertility process that can be better handled econometrically using a discrete-time dynamic multi-spell duration model, which we then go on to analyse. A detailed discussion of the main advantages and limitations of each approach is provided. The chapter ends with an illustrative example of an econometric modelling strategy based on panel data.

2. NATURE OF THE SUBJECT MATTER

2.1 Theories of Fertility Behaviour

How do couples decide on the number of children and the timing of arrival of each child? Do they set a plan at the outset for the full fertility cycle that is strictly followed to completion or are the outcomes sequentially determined? Does economics play a role or are traditional and established socioeconomic norms dominant? Why does fertility decline (or transition to a lower level) as economies transition from low average income to high average income? Generations of demographers, sociologists and economists have wrestled with these questions and yet a consensus view has not emerged, even though it is widely acknowledged that the *homo economicus* and *homo sociologicus* positions are not necessarily mutually exclusive. Both components are present in a typical reduced form model.

The remainder of this section will briefly review the main ideas in the field. To keep the scope of the chapter manageable, here we focus on reviewing "micro theories," which are concerned with explaining individual behaviour at the level of family, and for which econometric models are typically based on cross-section or longitudinal data collected over relatively short periods of time, including studies on desired fertility. These studies have a microeconometric flavour. At the other end of the spectrum are "macro theories" concerned with explaining population or society-wide phenomena—such as the epidemiological and fertility transition triggered by the industrial revolution (see, for instance, Landry, 1909; Thompson, 1929; Notestein, 1945). These studies attempt to model long-term movements in population fertility rates—such as the total fertility rate[1]—using country or region level time series or panel data that span many decades and generations. Studies of the so-called "great transition" from a low-income–high-fertility state to a high-income–low-fertility state, especially in Europe, are a leading example of this type of research with macroeconometric flavour (see, for instance, Boldrin et al., 2015; Sánchez-Barricarte, 2017).

Another topic with a similar macro emphasis concerns short run variations in age- or group-specific fertility rates that are observed in wars, famines and humanitarian crises stemming from social and political upheavals. There are numerous examples in the literature. For example, Vandenbroucke (2014) finds that the birth rate decreased dramatically during WWI and then later recovered. Caldwell (2006) shows that European countries, the United States and Japan had their fertility levels reduced due to local armed conflicts. There are also other studies of fertility changes using data from Angola (Agadjanian and Prata, 2002), Rwanda (Jayaraman et al., 2009), Eritrea (Woldemicael, 2008) and so forth, documenting similar significant short-term fluctuations. A different strand in the literature uses data from Columbia (Torres and Urdinola, 2019) and Mexico (Torche and Villarreal, 2014) and explores the connection between within-country violence and its differential impact on adolescent and older women's pregnancies, and, more generally, on changes in age at first pregnancy. A third strand in the literature concerns the impact of humanitarian crises arising from famines, tsunamis and earthquakes on birth rates. An example is the Dutch famine of 1944–45 (Stein and Susser, 1975). We group these three strands in the literature under the heading of short-term variations in fertility. From a microeconometric viewpoint these studies raise several unresolved issues such as How do these shocks fit into the established micro theories? Is the observed behaviour optimal in some sense? Are the observed short-term changes driven by behavioural responses to transitory shocks or are there biological mechanisms at work? Are observed changes purely transitory and mean reverting or do they interact with underlying long-term trends? These issues are important but beyond the scope of this chapter.

2.1.1 Main ideas from economics

We may begin by asking, Why do people have children? There are two main, not necessarily contradictory, views. One theory is based on the idea that people derive utility from having and raising children, so that children are just like any other consumption good c that gives utility to the consumer. We call this the child-in-the-utility-function approach. A major complication is that parents may care not only about the number n but also about the "quality" q of their children. Parents face the following problem:

$$\max_{\{c,qn\}} U(c,qn) = \alpha \, log(c) + (1-\alpha)log(qn) \tag{5.1}$$

$$st. \, c + qn = m,$$

where, without loss of generality, we have set the price of the quantity and quality of children to one and use the price of the consumption good as a numeraire—so that q plays the role of relative price for n and n plays the role of relative price for q. The solution is

$$qn = (1-\alpha)m \tag{5.2}$$

$$c = \alpha m.$$

Notice that the number and quality of children remain indeterminate but the relationship between the quantity and quality of children takes the form of

$$n = \frac{(1-\alpha)m}{q}, \tag{5.3}$$

so that for every level of quality there is an optimal number of children. Hence, a quantity–quality trade-off of children arises because the shadow price of quantity depends on quality—and vice versa. In their seminal work Becker (1960) and Becker and Lewis (1973) introduce these ideas in a general form utility function and show that, if the income elasticity for quality is larger than the income elasticity of quantity, parents will substitute quality for quantity when income increases. This mechanism, they conclude, may explain the fertility transition that was triggered by the industrial revolution: fertility declines when households become wealthier.

To consider the role of technological change we may introduce a quality production function (see, for instance Morand, 1999; Rosenzweig and Wolpin, 1980)

$$q = b(t)n^{-\delta} \tag{5.4}$$

that keeps the inverse relationship between quantity and quality of children but introduces a new multiplicative term $b(t)$ that is a function of time. Then we solve for n and q,

$$n = \left[\frac{(1-\alpha)m}{b(t)}\right]^{\frac{1}{1-\delta}} \tag{5.5}$$

$$q = b(t)^{\frac{1}{1-\delta}} \left[(1-\alpha) m \right]^{\frac{\delta}{1-\delta}},$$
(5.6)

and conclude that technological change plays the role of increasing the quality of children over time, which leads to a reduction in the quantity of children. Think of $b(t)$, for instance, as the effect of the discovery of antibiotics and the improvement of health care on child mortality and life expectancy. Now the fertility transition can be seen not just as the result of an income effect but, more generally, as the result of technological change.

A different theory is based on the idea that people do not enjoy children—and thus do not directly derive utility from them—but use children to transfer consumption over time. This is an overlapping generations model where individuals live for two periods, receive income m_1 only in period one and cannot save for old age (see, for instance, Allais, 1947; Samuelson, 1958; Diamond, 1965). The only way of securing an old-age pension is having children in period one. Hence parents solve the following problem:

$$\max_{\{c_1, c_2\}} U(c_1, c_2) = \alpha \log(c_1) + (1-\alpha) \log(c_2)$$
(5.7)

$$st. c_1 + \frac{c_2}{1 + \pi q n} = m_1,$$
(5.8)

where for an investment of $(m - c_1)$ monetary units in child services qn in period one, parents are paid an old-age pension of $(1 + \pi q n)(m - c_1)$ monetary units from their children in period two. The solution is

$$c_1 = \alpha m_1,$$
(5.9)

$$c_2 = (1-\alpha)(1 + \pi q n) m_1.$$

Here, again, the number and quality of children remain indeterminate. However, if we fix the rate of return of child services to $\bar{\kappa} = \pi q n$, appealing to the existence of a known and binding contract between overlapping generations, the relationship between the quantity and quality of children takes the form of

$$n = \frac{\bar{\kappa}}{\pi q},$$
(5.10)

which describes a quantity–quality trade-off of children that is very similar to the one we had before. Again, for every level of quality there is an optimal quantity of children. We call this the child-in-the-budget-constraint approach, which describes what is known in the literature as the old-age pension motive for fertility (Nugent, 1985; Srinivasan, 1988).

An alternative description of the old-age pension motive argues that children are an insurance device that allow parents to reduce uncertainty about unforeseeable shocks to their health and/or income (Nugent, 1985; Pörtner, 2001). In modern times, however, where well-developed security markets and pension systems exist, the old-age pension motive for fertility is weaker and couples may set fertility to near zero (Neher, 1971).

In this model, we may also introduce a quality production function as the one in (5.4) to investigate the role of technology. Consider the following technology:

$$q = b(t) + n^{-\delta}$$
(5.11)

so that parents solve the problem of

$$max_{\{n\}}Q(n) = m_1\left(1-\alpha\right)\left(1+\pi\left(b(t)n - n^{1-\delta}\right)\right),\qquad(5.12)$$

which has the solution

$$n = \left(\frac{(1-\delta)}{\pi b(t)}\right)^{\frac{1}{\delta}}\qquad(5.13)$$

$$q = b(t) + \left(\frac{\pi b(t)}{(1-\delta)}\right).\qquad(5.14)$$

Here, once again, the quality increases with technological change whereas the quantity decreases with it.

There are many other complementary ideas. For instance, Willis (1973) explores how women's participation in the labour market could affect their fertility decisions. As women enter the labour market, the argument goes, the opportunity cost of children increases because the time women spend in child-rearing activities is time they cannot spend at work. Therefore, it is predicted, couples demand fewer children when female education and wage increase. A similar argument is put forward by Becker et al. (1990) and Galor and Weil (1996) in the context of a growth model with endogenous fertility and by Rosenzweig and Wolpin (1980) and Heckman and Walker (1990a) in a joint model of labour supply and fertility.

Becker and Barro (1986, 1988) and Becker et al. (1990) investigate how introducing altruism into the child-in-the-utility-function framework affects fertility decisions. Parents, they argue, do not care only about their own welfare, but also about the welfare of their children, their grandchildren, and their great grandchildren. So, when deciding about their own fertility, parents act like central planners who take into account how current fertility decisions affect the welfare of their whole "dynasty." Physical and human capital accumulation are allowed. While physical capital is subject to diminishing or constant returns to scale, human capital accumulation exhibits increasing returns to scale. All these features come together in what is known today as a growth model with endogenous fertility in the literature, which in turn is a type of endogenous growth model; see for instance Uzawa (1965), Nelson and Phelps (1966), Arrow (1972) and Romer (1990). Besides the classic quantity–quality trade-off that is present in all child-in-the-utility-function specifications, these models show that the demand of children is a function of all goods and time that are spent on childcare activities.

Moreover, Becker et al. (1990) show that an economy needs a minimum stock of human capital to create enough incentives for individuals to invest in education and be able to reach a steady state with low fertility and high human capital. When this minimum human capital is not present, the economy converges to a steady state with high fertility and no human capital accumulation. Becker et al. (1990) think of this mechanism as an explanation of the fertility transition and the way large economic disparities were created between modern developed and developing countries.

Regarding the timing of children, the main blocks of theory are due to Happel et al. (1984). The authors start with a child-in-the-utility framework and force parents to have only one child within their lifetime, a span known and limited to, say, three "days."[2] Women are young during the first two days and may work and have children in that period of life. On day three women are old, retired and may not have children. So, once the quantity of children issue is gone, which day should parents have their child "delivered"?

If parents like children and no cost is paid for rearing them, then it is dynamically optimal to have their child delivered on day one. However, when parenthood involves some costs, things are no longer clear-cut. For instance, as Happel et al. (1984) put forward, if women leave work for some time after a birth and human capital "depreciates" while away from the workplace, then those who are highly qualified will have incentives to postpone motherhood toward the end of their fertile period—that is, the end of day two—in order to avoid as much as possible the depreciation of their human capital that inevitably motherhood will bring about. Those with low human capital, on the contrary, may find postponement not quite attractive and choose to have their child delivered on day one.

To summarize, consistent with Becker's (1960) human capital theory, Happel et al. (1984) predict that women postpone motherhood as they accumulate human capital.

2.1.2   Alternative ideas from other fields

Demographers and sociologists have put forward ideas that extend and/or depart from the mainstream ideas based on Becker's (1960) human capital theory.

An important idea put forward by demographers and sociologists is that, besides socio-economic factors, fertility is strongly influenced by social norms for family size/composition and uncertainty about the availability and costs of contraception. Effective contraception technology became widely available at the turn of the 20th century. Adoption of contraceptives, however, took decades and varied widely across the globe. Among other things, people of different countries and social backgrounds had, and still have, different levels of access to health services and, as a consequence, face widely different mortality risks let alone different religious beliefs and social/political institutions. In such contexts, some women may find it more difficult than others to get reliable information about the costs and risks of using contraceptives—many get information and opinions about family planning from family members, friends, and social contacts, who are not necessarily well informed themselves (see, for instance, Bongaarts and Watkins, 1996). From this perspective, the demographic transition is seen as a dynamic process of diffusion of knowledge and adoption of new techniques of contraception and fertility "norms"; see for example Montgomery and Casterline (1993), Rosero-Bixby and Casterline (1993), Bongaarts and Watkins (1996) and Kohler (1997, 2000). In such a scenario, women, who are the decision unit, choose either to follow traditional fertility patterns or to adopt modern contraceptives and reduce their lifetime fertility. In this context social-network effects are present so that an individual's costs and/or benefits from innovation are a function of the number and identity of other innovators in their social network. By these means, "contagion" or diffusion of a new fertility standard is generated (Kohler, 1997; Montgomery and Casterline, 1993; Ellison and Fudenberg, 1995; Kapur, 1995; Kirman, 1993; Chwe, 2000). This is, as a whole, an alternative micro-founded mechanism that explains the fertility transition.

Following the idea that norms, or preferences, are the main drivers of actual behaviour, another strand of the literature studies how desired—or planned—fertility is determined and how people react when current fertility is different from desired fertility (see, for instance, Knodel and Prachuabmoh, 1973; Bongaarts, 1990, 1992, 2001; Miranda, 2008). Findings show that people do react by increasing actual family size when current fertility is below target and use contraceptive methods, with different levels of efficiency depending on education as well as female labour market outcomes and female empowerment, once their planned fertility has been achieved (see, for instance, Doepke and Tertilt, 2018; Günther and Harttgen, 2016; Adsera 2006, among others).

2.2   Types and Features of Fertility Data

In this section we illustrate some key features of fertility data that econometric models would be expected to account for. Two broad population categories are low-fertility–high-income and high-fertility–low-income. In 2012, total fertility rate (TFR) was 2.4 for the world, 1.7 for high-income developed countries, 5.2 for sub-Saharan Africa and 5.7 for Nigeria; see Fagbamigbe and Adebowale (2014). In high-income populations, birth counts cluster around a handful of values such as (0,1,2,3) with a very short tail; in low-income populations, both the mean and variance tend to be higher. Long time series (especially) European historical data show a rapid transition from the high- to low-fertility regime as family incomes rise. At the risk of slight oversimplification, one can summarize these features by treating the low TFR case as one involving underdispersed counts and the high TFR case as one of overdispersed counts. Such a distinction takes the Poisson distribution, which has the property of mean-variance equality (equidispersion) as a benchmark.

There are two types, or flavours, of fertility data analyses: (a) using completed fertility data and (b) using fertility history data.

A completed fertility datasets are by far the most widely used. They contain information on a cross-section of women who, at the time of the survey, are at the end of their childbearing life (normally aged 45 and over) and can report their "completed fertility"—that is, the total count of children ever born alive to a woman. Besides the number of children, completed fertility data typically have information on some characteristics of the mother, as measured at the time of interview, including education, income, work status, occupation and offspring sex composition. Measuring the mother's characteristics at the end of the fertile life may provide current or recent information but is less likely to provide information about the conditions (for example, income, employment status, information about contraception) that prevailed at the time of each birth; this, in turn, is likely to lead to specification errors. So, the cross-section nature of the data becomes a serious drawback.

Because completed fertility comes as a count—that is, a non-negative integer variable with values that accept a cardinal interpretation—the use of count data econometric models based on cross-section data is a popular choice. We review those techniques in section 4.

Several features of completed fertility data are important and require careful consideration. We illustrate the relevant points with two examples. Table 5.1 reports data on completed fertility from the British Household Panel Survey (BHPS). This is a low-fertility–high-income setting ($N = 5706$). The sample mean number of children is 1.84 and the standard deviation is 1.5. There is some overdispersion with a sample variance 1.23 times the mean. The distribution is clearly bimodal (see Figure 5.1) with a half-mode at 0 and a more pronounced mode at 2. This latter feature has led Melkersson and Rooth (2000) to describe the distribution as being "inflated at zero and two." Overdispersion and inflation at specific frequencies are features that motivate empirically important extensions of the Poisson regression that we cover in section 4.

Table 5.1   Number of children: Actual frequency distribution British data (N=5706)

Children	0	1	2	3	4	5	6	7	8	9	10	11
Freq.	1524	675	1779	1075	409	153	50	22	12	3	3	1
Per cent	26.7	11.8	31.2	18.8	7.2	2.7	0.9	0.4	0.2	0.1	0.1	0.0

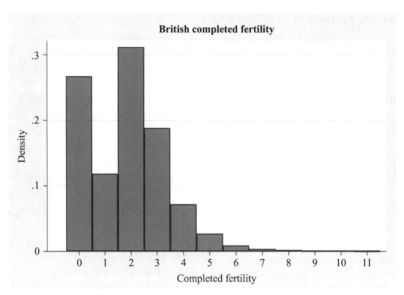

Source: British Household Panel Survey (BHPS).

Figure 5.1 Frequency distribution for British completed data

From this example, it is possible to observe that completed fertility data in a low-fertility–high-income setting is characterized by limited support, in the sense that just a few event counts dominate the frequency distribution. A flexible econometric modelling strategy is required to capture such population differences in regression models.

Data from high-fertility–low-income settings are different. Consider for example the case of the Mexican Family Life Survey (2002) ($N = 3674$); the distribution of completed fertility is reported in table 5.2. In this case, the sample mean is 3.19 and the standard deviation is 1.97, so the sample variance is 1.21 times the mean—a lower mean/variance ratio than what is typically observed in a low-fertility–high-income setting. Overdispersion, however, is not all that is different. Here, there is not so much of a spike at 0 or 2 (see Figure 5.2). In fact, a two-child outcome is almost as popular as a three-child outcome. More importantly, the fertility distribution exhibits a much longer tail in the high-fertility–low-income setting than in the low-fertility–high-income setting. For the Mexican data, outcomes 4 and 5 still carry a non-ignorable portion of the total probability mass. Miranda (2010) analyses Mexican fertility data from the National Survey of Demographic Dynamics (1997) and reports a similar distribution. The author suggests that data from developing countries may show "an excess of large counts" that requires explicit modelling—and understanding of the underlying behavioural drivers.[3]

Table 5.2 Number of children: Actual frequency distribution for Mexican data (N=3674)

Children	0	1	2	3	4	5	6	7	8	9	10	11	12	13	14	15	16
Frequency	137	432	903	968	548	265	175	107	62	38	15	11	6	5	0	1	1
Per cent	3.7	11.8	24.6	26.4	14.9	7.2	4.8	2.9	1.7	1.0	0.4	0.3	0.2	0.1	0	0.0	0.0

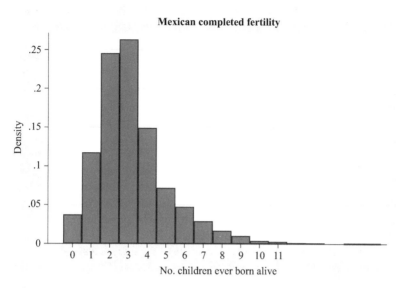

Source: Mexican Family Life Survey W1, 2002.

Figure 5.2 Frequency distribution for Mexican completed fertility data

Regarding the timing of children, data typically come in the form of an event history, where a sample of women, not necessarily at the end of fertile life, provide exact birth dates for each child they have ever given birth to by the time of the survey interview. An event history has a longitudinal design from the onset. However, data may be collected in a retrospective or prospective manner.

Retrospective data are collected in a single point of time—and from this point of view, the data are cross-sectional—but involve asking people to look back and report events that occurred in the past, such as the date they first married or the date they left school. Using this technique, it is possible to "rebuild" a fertility history retrospectively. The downside is that people may suffer substantial problems of "recall bias" or "telescoping." Recall bias arises when people selectively recall better certain (positive) things or experiences than others (negative), while telescoping is present when an individual's perceived elapsed time since the occurrence of an event is different depending on whether the experience was pleasant. In both cases, recall bias and telescoping, retrospective collection of an event history may introduce serious measurement error and bias (see, for instance, Gray, 1955; Mathiowetz and Ouncan, 1988; Bound et al., 2001; Pyy-Martikainen and Rendtel, 2009). Such issues are worse for some variables than for others. For instance, most people can recall the exact birth dates of their children but have serious difficulties recalling their past salary.

In contrast, prospective longitudinal data ("panel data") survey a sample of women over time and pregnancy and childbirth events are carefully recorded along many other individual characteristics. From a theoretical point of view, building an event history using prospective longitudinal data is better than building it retrospectively. It is not only that prospective data are less susceptible to recall bias and telescoping; the real advantage is that a number of important fertility determinants, such as income and employment status, get measured contemporaneously at each follow-up. Hence, besides a fertility history, panel data deliver a detailed history of the factors or/and variables that determine woman's fertility behaviour. From this point of view, analyses based on panel data are more promising. In practice, however, commonly available prospective longitudinal data may have gaps that impede identification.

In cohort studies, for example, children who are born in a given year/date are followed through time. For this type of study researchers may have to wait between 20 and 30 years to get interesting fertility data. Unfortunately, by the time cohort members start marrying and having children, most cohort studies may have to rely on data that are subject to substantial attrition bias due to dropouts; see Cheng and Trivedi (2015) and chapter 19.9 in Wooldridge (2010).

A household panel study based on a random sample of the population also has its own problems. A major issue is that, by design, these studies follow a sample of women of different ages. As a consequence, many panel members enter the study years after they started having children. Discarding individuals who have already entered motherhood by the start of the study is an option. However, in most cases, taking such a step results in small sample sizes that still require time to deliver full-blown fertility histories. Hence, as before, attrition becomes a potentially serious problem unless it is purely random.

What then is the best option to build a fertility history? We suggest that the best option is to use a combination of prospective and retrospective data. The British Household Panel Data (BHPS) took such approach. Indeed, the BHPS follows prospectively all women who are panel members and records contemporaneously any births that occur during the study time. To complement, the BHPS introduced a retrospective fertility module in waves 2, 11 and 12. An example of the layout of a fertility history in the "long form" (ready for analysis) is given in Table 5.3.

Table 5.3   *Example of prospective and retrospective longitudinal fertility history data from the UK (long form)*

pid	Year	occ	resp	Parity	Clock	Age	Girl at P = 1	Twins	Same sex at P = 2	Income	Mother's edu
1	1960	1	0	0	1	18	0	0	0	7.20	GCSE
1	1961	2	0	0	2	19	0	0	0	8.35	GCSE
1	1962	3	0	0	3	20	0	0	0	8.35	GCSE
1	1963	4	0	0	4	21	0	0	0	7.97	GCSE
1	1964	5	0	0	5	22	0	0	0	9.33	GCSE
1	1965	6	1	0	6	23	0	0	0	8.88	GCSE
1	1966	7	0	1	1	24	1	0	0	7.40	GCSE
1	1967	8	0	1	2	25	1	0	0	8.57	GCSE
1	1968	9	1	1	3	26	1	0	0	9.92	GCSE
1	1969	10	0	2	1	27	0	0	1	10.33	GCSE
1	1970	11	1	2	2	28	0	1	1	10.67	GCSE
1	1970	12	1	2	2	28	0	1	1	10.67	GCSE
1	1971	13	0	4	1	29	0	0	0	11.30	GCSE
1	1972	14	0	4	2	30	0	0	0	11.77	GCSE

In the example, the fertility history of a woman is recorded after age 18. Every row constitutes a new measurement occasion (*occ*), which is not necessarily equivalent to the passage of calendar time, and a record of the status of all relevant variables gets included. The main response (*resp*) is a 0/1 binary variable that takes value one if on a given measurement occasion a new birth is registered. The variable *parity* measures the total number of children, or fertility, that the woman has had at each measurement occasion. So, parity increases by one unit every time period $resp = 1$.[4] In our example, the survey follows the woman for 13 years (periods) who has a child at age 23 and at age 26. At age 28 she has twins. The clock indicates, on each occasion, the time elapsed since the woman entered a particular parity and initiated a new duration spell to the next pregnancy/birth. With each new birth the clock gets restarted. Age, calendar time and duration time are three concepts that vary in a different manner for each woman in the sample and, as a consequence, can be identified separately. To complete the picture, the data contain information on a set of control variables (regressors) observed during the fertility history. There are variables that are time varying, such as income and age; variables that are time fixed, such as (our individual) mother's education; and variables that change with parity, such as whether the first born was a girl or whether two children of the same sex occurred at parity two. The example illustrates the richness that a longitudinal fertility history can offer to the analyst. These types of data are typically analysed with discrete hazard models, which are discussed in section 5.

Another form in which fertility histories may come is presented in Table 5.4. We call this "the wide form," and each row contains data for one event (that is, one birth) along with a measure of how long the duration spell or waiting time to event lasted (*dur*). In our context, an event is a new birth. Along with the length of the duration spell, a dummy variable *fail* indicates whether the spell was ended by the occurrence of a birth *fail* = 1, called a "failure" in survival analysis, or ended as a censored observation *fail* = 0. Finally, we have data on various control variables, which may include time-fixed, time-varying and parity-varying variables. Notice that going from the long to the wide form of the fertility history we have "thrown way"

Table 5.4 Example of longitudinal fertility history data from the UK (wide form)

pid	dur	Fail	Parity	Girl at $P = 1$	Age	Income	Same sex at $P = 2$
8	22	1	0	0	33	8.3518252	0
8	27	0	1	1	60	6.8155894	0
9	12	1	0	0	23	4.3997666	0
9	2	1	1	0	25	4.3997666	0
9	2	1	2	0	27	4.3997666	1
9	5	1	3	0	32	4.3997666	0
10	6	1	0	0	17	0	0
10	3	1	1	1	20	0	0
10	2	1	2	0	22	0	1
10	34	0	3	0	55	0	0

a substantive part of the covariate history. From that point of view, and despite the fact that both fertility histories are longitudinal, modelling using data that have a wide form seems less promising. These types of data are typically analysed with continuous hazard models.

2.3   Dynamic Inter-Dependencies

From the discussion in section 2.2 is clear that successful modelling of fertility needs start by recognizing that each pregnancy is a decision in its own right.

Indeed, when deciding whether to become pregnant, women take into account all the information they have at the time (see, for instance, Barmby and Cigno, 1990; Wolpin, 1984). This includes the current number of her offspring (incentives and child benefit systems) (Barmby and Cigno, 1990), their sex composition (due to gender preference) (Williamson, 1976; Angrist and Evans, 1998), the outcome of her last pregnancy (reduced fecundity after a c-section or miscarriage) (Kok et al., 2003; Hassan and Killick, 2005; O'Neill et al., 2014; Sapra et al., 2014), her work status and salary (Bettio and Villa, 1998; Mira and Ahn, 2001) and the available childcare support (see, for instance, Ermisch, 1989; Boca, 2002; Rindfuss et al., 2010). Many such conditions change with time and can influence whether the same woman goes from childless to having had her first child, but not whether she goes from having one child to having had two or three children. That is, in general, factors that affect the transition from parity 0 to parity 1 may not play any role in the transition from parity 1 to parity 2. Dynamics are an essential feature of how a fertility history is generated.

To illustrate this point with the British data we present in Figure 5.3 a smoothed kernel estimate of the probability of observing a birth at any point of time given that the birth has not yet arrived—also known as the hazard function.

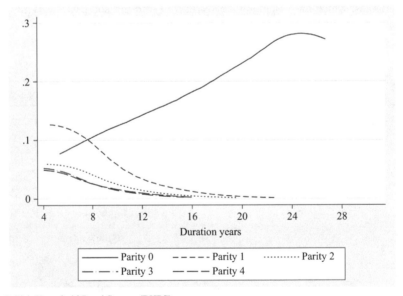

Source: British Household Panel Survey (BHPS).

Figure 5.3   Hazard kernel estimate for British fertility data

From Figure 5.3 we can conclude that the form of the hazard function is very different for each parity. While at parity 0 (no children) the hazard function exhibits a U-inverted form, the hazards at parities 1,2,3,4 are monotonically decreasing. Moreover, although the hazards at parities 1,2,3,4 are a non-increasing monotonic function, the hazard function at parity 2 is clearly not a parallel shift of the hazard function at parity 1, nor is the hazard function of parity 3 a parallel shift of the hazard function at parity 2. These descriptive stylized facts have important implications for econometric modelling as the most popular methods cannot deal with non-monotonic hazard functions, let alone deal, at the same time, with a whole fertility history that implies specifying a model that is flexible enough to accommodate for the special features of the data.

More to the challenge, Figure 5.4 shows that, even after fixing the parity, the hazard function depends on the outcome of the previous pregnancy. In particular, simple inspection shows that having two boys or two girls at $P = 2$ shifts the hazard function outward—increasing the risk of a new pregnancy as well as decreasing the average duration time to it—but there is no descriptive evidence that sex composition plays a role at any other parity. In a similar vein, Figure 5.5 shows descriptive evidence that having twins at any parity shifts the hazard function inward, dramatically decreasing the likelihood of observing any further births. These descriptive data examples illustrate that dynamics, other than duration dependence, play an important role in specifying an econometric model of fertility history.

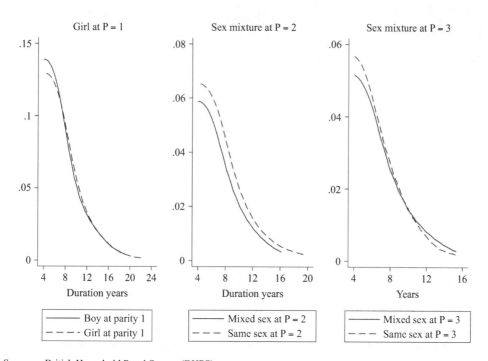

Source: British Household Panel Survey (BHPS).

Figure 5.4 Hazard kernel estimate at selected parities

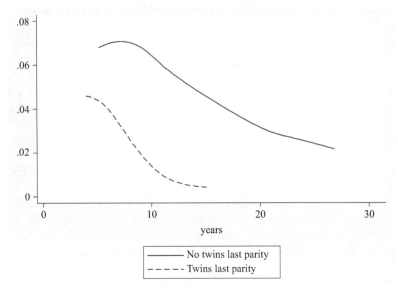

Source: British Household Panel Survey (BHPS).

Figure 5.5 Hazard kernel estimate for twins in last parity

3. REDUCED FORM VS. STRUCTURAL MODELLING

As in many fields of the social sciences, there are many possible modelling approaches available to the applied researcher when dealing with fertility data. Which approach is taken depends, among other things, on the research objectives and questions of interest, the intended use of the empirical findings and the quality and coverage of the available data.

Broadly stated, the research objective is to understand the fertility process in specific populations. More specifically, researchers try and shed light on the long–running debate on the demographic versus economic perspectives on fertility behaviour.

From a purist economic perspective, completed fertility is determined by economic optimizing behaviour of a woman. A full specification of the optimization problem requires specification of the utility function and all relevant constraints facing the woman, which may depend on government interventions such as those in welfare states. Even in a model that ignores dynamic interdependence between a sequence of birth events, the challenge of finding a theoretical optimum is compounded by issues such as whether the utility function reflects purely personal preferences or includes dependence on social norms of individual-specific reference groups. Economists, relative to demographers and sociologists, in the past have emphasized much less the role of social interactions and stress the role of individual preferences and economic constraints and opportunities. If dynamic interdependence is introduced in the model, and the issue of optimal spacing of preferred number of children is also considered, the goal of empirically identifying the parameters of the utility function, the parameters characterizing social interaction and parameters that determine responses to interventions becomes even more complex. If such a goal is achievable, then the estimated parameters have a clear causal interpretation, given the fully specified model structure; for examples, see Hotz and Miller (1988) and Manski and Mayshar (2003). Following standard practice, we will refer to such an approach as structural modelling as the goal is to identify structural or causal parameters.

Arroyo and Zhang (1997) have provided a useful taxonomy for dynamic models of fertility. They distinguish between structural models explicitly based on relationships derived from the solution of a dynamic programming problem (for example Hotz and Miller, 1993) and reduced form models that "may have a basis in some dynamic programming problems but do not rely heavily on that structure for specification of estimating equations," for example, the hazard function approach used in Heckman and Walker (1990a).

Structural modelling requires strong priori behavioural and functional form assumptions and, given typical data constraints, is difficult to implement fully. Many, if not most, empirical studies are of reduced form type, especially in the demographic literature. They focus on regression models of variables such as completed fertility, in which the regressors are socio-economic individual or family-specific factors. Where relevant they may also include incentive variables such as child support. Cross-sectional survey data are widely used and information from retrospective surveys may be incorporated. Within such models the mechanism that connects birth outcomes or (unobserved) individual gender and family size preferences with regressors is at best implicit, which makes unambiguous interpretation of results difficult. Despite this limitation reduced form models are useful descriptive models and can capture associations with predictive potential, fertility trends and intergroup heterogeneity; we provide references in the next section.

4.   SELECTED COUNT REGRESSION MODELS

The raw material of fertility data consists of the count of number of live births to a woman in a specific year-of-birth cohort and during a specific period called *exposure*. The completed fertility data consist of non-negative integers in a range that varies both over time and over socioeconomic groups—a feature we explore further later in this section. A fertility *rate* is derived as a ratio of birth counts to corresponding population exposure. Age- and order-specific fertility rates measure childbearing intensity among women of specific age and parity (the number of previous live births). Such a fertility rate, a continuous variable, can be person-period specific or age or cohort specific.

4.1   Semiparametric Regression

A simple starting point for modelling the total number of births (y), given cross-sectional or panel data, is a linear-in-parameters regression estimated by OLS. In that case one usually ignores the nonnegative integer-valued nature of the outcome variable, treats zeros and positive outcomes as generated by a common (but unspecified) process and treats regressors ($\mathbf{x}$) as exogenous. No specific probability distribution of outcomes is assumed.

Given a count of live births (denoted y) exposure (denoted t) and other information on socioeconomic and demographic information of surveyed households (denoted by $\mathbf{x}$), age- and cohort-specific fertility rates can be constructed as descriptive data, as is standard practice in demography. However, such an exercise will not adequately control for differences in observable characteristics of the individual and the household. Regression analysis based on $(y,t,\mathbf{x})$ provides a more informative framework for estimating fertility rates as well as studying the drivers of fertility. Poisson regression, based on the Poisson distribution and Poisson process, is a well-established benchmark regression model for birth events despite its strong underlying assumption of independence of events.

If one wishes to avoid distributional assumptions and ignore the integer-valued feature of births, a simple solution is to estimate a regression with an exponential mean by nonlinear least squares:

$$y_i = \exp(\mathbf{x}'_i \beta) + u_i. \tag{5.15}$$

Standard Poisson-type regression models use the same functional form for the conditional mean, $E[y|\mathbf{x}] = \mu$, but estimation is the more efficient maximum likelihood method. The marginal impact of a unit change in x_j is $\beta_j \mu$.

4.2   Poisson Regression

When completed fertility is the non-negative outcome variable of interest, either Poisson regression or some extension of it, such as the negative binomial regression, is a popular starting point. Poisson regression and several of its extensions derive from the Poisson process and Poisson distribution, which embody strong assumptions that are easily violated in practice.

Consider the cross-section regression of n independent observations, $(y_i, \mathbf{x}_i)$, where the dependent variable y_i denotes the number of occurrences of birth events and $\mathbf{x}_i$ is the vector of linearly independent regressors. Poisson regression model conditions the distribution of y_i on covariates, $\mathbf{x}'_i = [x_{1i},...,x_{ki}]$ and parameters β through a continuous function $\mu(\mathbf{x}_i, \beta)$, such that $E[y_i|\mathbf{x}_i] = \mu(\mathbf{x}_i, \beta)$. Thus, y_i given $\mathbf{x}_i$ is Poisson distributed with probability mass function

$$f(y_i | \mathbf{x}_i) = \frac{e^{-\mu_i} \mu_i^{y_i}}{y_i!}, \qquad y_i = 0,1,2,... \tag{5.16}$$

This one-parameter distribution embodies the restriction of equality of mean μ and variance, also known as equidispersion, that is, $E[y_i|\mathbf{x}_i] = \mu(\mathbf{x}_i, \beta) = Var[y_i|\mathbf{x}_i]$. The inherent variability of birth events increases with the mean—the average number of births per period. In the standard version of the Poisson regression the mean is parameterized as

$$\mu_i = \exp(\mathbf{x}'_i \beta) \tag{5.17}$$

to ensure $\mu > 0$. Estimation of the parameters β by maximum likelihood is straightforward and feasible using widely available software; see Cameron and Trivedi (2013).

The direct application of this model to birth data assumes that all subjects have the same exposure period and are at equal "risk" of experiencing the event. Often the subjects in the survey have different exposure risk. This feature is handled by introducing an "offset" feature that decomposes the mean μ_i as a product of fertility rate λ_i and the length of exposure t_i, that is, $\mu_i = t_i\lambda_i$, which implies a log-linear mean function with an offset term, that is, $ln(\mu_i) = ln(t_i) + \mathbf{x}'_i\beta$. Most software packages allow inclusion of the offset term.

The use of regression adds flexibility by combining features of descriptive data analysis with regression analysis, and also facilitating statistical inference on estimated parameters. The regression framework allows conditioning on relevant factors that affect the birth event, something that is not possible when a purely descriptive methodology is used in which the fertility rates are computed using cohort- and period-specific ratios. However, because such descriptive features are of interest per se, they can be added in a regression framework. For example, one can do this by adding dummy (indicator) variables for each category of observation of interest and then defining the reference group in analysis. That is the Poisson regression model now has the conditional mean function

$$\ln(\mu_i) = ln(t_i) + \sum \mathbf{x}_i\beta_i + \sum \mathbf{z}_j\gamma_j, \tag{5.18}$$

where $\mathbf{z}_j$ denotes the indicator variable, such as age group or cohort. The estimated coefficient γ_j measures the difference in birth rates of a selected category j relative to the reference category, while controlling for other differences due to observed regressors $\mathbf{x}$; see Schoumaker and Hayford (2004).

If the conditional mean function is correctly specified, but the equidispersion assumption is suspect, then the literature often substitutes pseudo-maximum likelihood (PML) in place of maximum likelihood. The main practical consequence is that a Huber–White-type robust variance estimator is substituted in place of the standard maximum likelihood estimator. Perhaps the most frequent justification for this practice is to appeal to the overdispersion of data which one can test for formally; see Cameron and Trivedi (2013), chapter 3.4. Note, however, that, as previously mentioned, fertility data from high-income–low-fertility economies are likely to display *underdispersion*.

The Poisson regression model works well if the key assumptions underlying it, such as equidispersion, are satisfied. In practice, count models often fail to fit fertility data well for several reasons. First, as was seen in the examples in previous sections, frequency distributions have limited support with most of the mass concentrated on just three or four values. Second, count regression may identify sources of the average difference between high and low outcomes but may not be very informative about the underlying drivers of events, which makes interpretation of results difficult. Third, total birth counts involve aggregation of event information over time; and completed fertility typically span many years—a period over which many individual-specific observed and unobserved time-varying factors could potentially impact the decision to have a child. Fourth, when the event frequency distribution is bimodal, the underlying Poisson distribution assumptions are invalid. Finally the Poisson process assumption that events are independent may be unrealistic in the context of birth outcomes.

4.3 Negative Binomial Extension of the Poisson

A major limitation of the Poisson regression model is its property of equidispersion, which restricts the mean and variance of outcome variable to be equal. Many data sets exhibit overdispersion (variance greater than the mean) or underdispersion (variance less than the mean).

Overdispersion stretches the distribution of outcomes, and underdispersion squeezes it. If, for example, an actual count frequency distribution is trivially different from a binomial, data would show underdispersion. If, on the other hand, the mean outcome is subject to unobserved heterogeneity with some well-defined properties, then the data would be overdispersed. Populations with low fertility often display underdispersion, and those with high fertility the opposite; later we will show data examples with these features. Other non-Poisson features of fertility data and methods for handling them will be discussed later in the chapter.

A well-established alternative to the Poisson regression, and one supported in most software packages, is the negative binomial (NB) regression model, which can be used to model overdispersed data. Overdispersed counts can be generated by replacing the constant mean parameter μ_i by (say) $\mu_i^* \, \varepsilon_i$, where ε denotes an individual-specific heterogeneity term with mean 1 and variance α. While there are at least two widely used variants of the NB regression, the most commonly used is the NB2 model, with mean μ and variance function $\mu + \alpha\mu^2$, with density

$$f(y\,|\,\mu,\alpha) = \frac{\Gamma(y+\alpha^{-1})}{\Gamma(y+1)\Gamma(\alpha^{-1})}\left(\frac{\alpha^{-1}}{\alpha^{-1}+\mu}\right)^{\alpha^{-1}}\left(\frac{\mu}{\alpha^{-1}+\mu}\right)^{y}, \quad \alpha \geq 0,\ y = 0,1,2,\dots \qquad (5.19)$$

The function $\Gamma(\cdot)$ is the gamma function. Excess variance relative to Poisson is $\alpha\mu^2$, which reflects unobserved heterogeneity. NB2 reduces to the Poisson if $\alpha = 0$.

The specification of the conditional mean under NB2 is exactly as in the Poisson case. Estimating the Poisson regression by maximum likelihood when NB2 is the relevant model will still yield consistent estimates of the regression coefficients but their standard errors will be incorrect; see Cameron and Trivedi (2013). Many software packages support maximum likelihood estimation of NB2. A test of the null hypothesis H_0: $\alpha = 0$ can be implemented using one of several different approaches (see Cameron and Trivedi, 2013, chapter 5.5), and this often serves as a selection criterion between NB2 and Poisson. However, this test leaves open the possibility that even the selected model has other misspecification(s). A more precise indicator of model deficiency is a Pearson-type goodness of fit test based on comparison of fitted and observed frequencies of events, which can point to potential misspecification that affects specific frequencies.

4.4   Modelling Underdispersed Counts

Although underdispersion gets less attention in the fertility literature, a number of authors have attempted to extend the parameterization of the Poisson regression to accommodate both over- and underdispersion via an additional parameter. For example, Winkelmann (1995) develops a duration model of events that directly leads to an underdispersed count model; Winkelmann and Zimmermann (1991, 1994) develop a parameterization based on the Katz family of distributions in which the variance function takes the form $\mu + (\sigma^2-1)\mu^{k+1}$ with an additional parameter k. Underdispersion corresponds to $\sigma^2 < 1$, and $\mu^k \leq 1/(1-\sigma^2)$. For additional details see Cameron and Trivedi (2013), chapter 4.11.

4.5   Other Non-Poisson Features of Fertility Counts

Many studies that have used count data regressions to analyse the role of socioeconomic factors and social norms on fertility using cross-section data have pointed out non-Poisson features of fertility data that call for a modelling strategy that goes beyond the standard Poisson and negative binomial regressions. The Poisson distribution is unimodal, displays equidispersion and is based on the assumption of independent events. These features are often at least partly absent in observed data. This is unsurprising because birth outcomes do not simply follow invariant biological stochastic processes but are responsive to social norms (for example popular notions of optimum number of children), heterogeneity of individual preferences (for example gender preferences) and economic constraints (for example absence of social security) and incentives (for example child allowances), as discussed in section 2. These factors affect the trends in fertility, as is evident in the extensive literature of fertility transitions, as populations experience improvement in living standards and governments provide substitutes for family support for ageing populations.

In a previous section we have alluded to differences in the distributional characteristics of births in high-income–low-fertility populations, such as Western industrialized countries, and low-income–high-fertility countries, such as developing countries in Africa and Asia. Birth distributions in the former characteristically show a low mean, underdispersion and departure from unimodality. The last feature appears in the data through a significant bump in frequencies $y = 0$ and $y = 2$ and a dip at $y = 1$, features that could indicate preference for no children and weaker preference for a single child; see, for instance Melkersson and Rooth (2000). Modifications of standard count data models are needed to capture these features of data and to provide a relatively better statistical fit to data, especially in the low-fertility populations.

We next discuss modified Poisson and NB regression models, which attempt to deal with the problem of "zero inflation," which refers to the presence in the data of more zero outcomes than is consistent with the underlying parent distribution. One might also interpret this as a statistical solution of the problem of unobserved or unstated individual preferences for family size and composition. That is, the refinements we next discuss would be superfluous if we had data on such family preferences.

4.5.1 Hurdle or two-part models

Hurdle or two-part models (Mullahy, 1986) specify a process for events that differ between zero and positive outcomes. Specifically, a zero-valued outcome constitutes a hurdle, which, once passed, transits to a different probability law. With probability $f_1(0)$ the threshold is not crossed, in which case we observe a count of 0. If the threshold is crossed, we observe positive counts, with probabilities coming from the truncated density $f_2(y)/(1 - f_2(0))$ (which is multiplied by $(1 - f_2(0))$ to ensure probabilities sum to one). The first part of the model is a binary (usually logit or probit) model, while the second part models the positive outcomes. Here and in the next section we use $f(\cdot)$ generically to denote distribution, which in the current context is most often Poisson or NB, and Pr to denote probability. This model is formally stated as follows:

$$Pr[y = j] = \begin{cases} f_1(0) & \text{if } j = 0 \\ \dfrac{1 - f_1(0)}{1 - f_2(0)} f_2(j) & \text{if } j > 0. \end{cases} \tag{5.20}$$

The standard model is a special case if $f_1(0) = f_2(0)$. If $f_1(0) > f_2(0)$, the model generates excess zeros, though in principle it can also model too few zeros if $f_1(0) < f_2(0)$. The density $f_2(\cdot)$ is a count density such as Poisson or NB2, while $f_1(\cdot)$ could also be a count data density or dichotomous density. The two parts are independent and so can be separately estimated by maximum likelihood.

Miranda (2010, 2013) introduces a double-hurdle model that addresses the spike-at-zero and long tail, or excess-of-large counts, that is present in Mexican completed fertility data. The hypothesis is that Mexico is undergoing a transition from a traditional high-fertility social norm to a modern low-fertility social norm though a process of diffusion of knowledge/influence about contraceptive technologies and innovative behaviour. No everyone adopts the new low-fertility norm at the same time; the population is a mixture of "conservative" and "innovative" women—and the mixture is changing over time. In this context, the long-tailed count data may reflect the fact that in developing countries women often fall, by accident or choice, into social conditions where the opportunity cost of having more children becomes particularly low. For instance, if part-time work is not a widespread option in the local labour market a woman who has certain number of children—say four—is locked out of the labour market; work is incompatible with raising her children. In this model there is a hurdle at zero that determines whether a woman enters motherhood,

$$Pr\left(y_i = j\right) = \begin{cases} \exp(-\mu_{0i}) & \text{for } j = 0 \\ [1 - \exp(-\mu_{0i})]P(y_i \mid y_i > 0) & \text{otherwise,} \end{cases} \tag{5.21}$$

and a second hurdle at three that determines whether a woman adopts a high- or a low-fertility norm,

$$Pr\left(y_i \mid y_i > 0\right) = \begin{cases} \left[1 - \exp\left(-\mu_{1i}\right)\right]^{-1} \dfrac{\exp\left(-\mu_{1i}\right)\mu_{1i}^{j}}{j!} & \text{if } j = 1,2,3 \\[2ex] \left[1 - \sum\limits_{k=1}^{3}\left[1 - \exp\left(-\mu_{1i}\right)\right]\right]^{-1} & \text{if } j = 4,5,6,\ldots \\[2ex] \cdot \dfrac{\exp\left(-\mu_{1i}\right)\mu_{1i}^{k}}{k!} \mathbb{P}(y_i \mid y_i \geq 4), \end{cases} \tag{5.22}$$

with,

$$\mu_{0i} = \exp\left(\mathbf{x}'_{0i}\beta_0\right), \tag{5.23}$$

$$\mu_{1i} = \exp\left(\mathbf{x}'_{1i}\beta_1\right). \tag{5.24}$$

The model is extended to allow for unobserved individual heterogeneity in both μ_{0i} and μ_{1i}, which are potentially correlated. Hence, the double hurdle of Miranda (2010, 2013) makes the choice of high- or low-fertility norm endogenous.

4.5.2 Zero-inflated models

Suppose the base count density is now $f_2(y)$, using the same notation as for the hurdle model, but this underpredicts zeros. We can add a separate component that inflates the probability of a zero by, say, π. Then the *zero-inflated model* specifies

$$Pr\left(y_i = j\right) = \begin{cases} \pi + (1-\pi)f_2(0), & \text{if } j = 0 \\ (1-\pi)f_2(j) & \text{if } j > 0, \end{cases} \tag{5.25}$$

where the proportion of zeros, π, is added to the baseline distribution, and the probabilities from the base model $f_2(y)$ are decreased by the proportion $(1-\pi)$ to ensure that probabilities sum to one. The probability π may be set as a constant or may depend on regressors via a binary outcome model such as logit or probit. Such a specification will improve the statistical fit of the model while leaving open the question as to the interpretation of the inflation component. As mentioned by Melkersson and Rooth (2000), birth data for some European countries also show "excess 2s," a feature that is consistent with a high family preference for two children, indicating a contemporary social norm. This inflation can be modelled analogously to excess zeros. However, using a statistical device to capture the inflation at a particular cell frequency does not constitute an explanation.

4.5.3 Other modelling options

One further limitation of the count data models applied to cross-section birth data is that whereas the range of recorded outcomes can span as many as 10 or 12 values, most of the probability mass is likely concentrated on relatively few values. This implies as many as half or more cells will be thinly populated, making it difficult to achieve a good fit. One way to deal with this problem is to aggregate (combine) the cells into fewer ordered categories and then use a multinomial model. For example, one might choose to aggregate cells with frequencies between six and higher into a single cell, or perhaps two less aggregated cells. As the cells are then ordered into about seven categories one could apply the ordinal probit or ordinal logit model, which accommodates the natural ordering of discrete outcomes. The ordered outcomes model is different from the Poisson process–based models in that it treats the data as generated by a continuous unobserved latent variable which, on crossing a threshold, increases the outcome value by one unit. This framework, though not often used, is an attractive option for modelling data that are distributed over a small number of cells, as in the case of underdispersed samples.

5. EVENT HISTORY MODELS

Count data regressions are static models and hence necessarily uninformative about dynamic aspects of the fertility process that are captured by a complete events history of births. One alternative is to model the elapsed duration between successive transitions (births) conditional on the previous history of the event and on observed covariates. A second alternative is a discrete hazard model, which is typically specified with the objective of modelling the transition between the status quo state $y = 0$ and one additional event state $y = 1$, conditional on the previous history of transitions and on information about (usually) exogenous covariates. In a given time interval, y has a binomial distribution. The conditional hazard of the transition between states can be derived from this property. We label this as the Modified Dynamic Event History (MDEH) model.

5.1   Restructuring Event History Data for MDEH

The building blocks of the MDEH model are implicit in the description given in section 2.2 of how a "long form" panel data set may be constructed using event history data. A more formal description follows. For each sampled individual there is information over a historical period of calendar length T_i, $i = 1, \ldots, N$, which begins at $T_{b,i}$ and ends at $T_{e,i}$, $T_{e,i} > T_{b,i}$. T_i could be number of weeks, months or similar. In a standard event history analysis the irregular interval between events is left as it is. For established econometric methods, the irregular time interval between events poses a challenge. For example, the distribution of errors is difficult to specify. We propose a simple modification that would allow us to use "standard" panel data methods to estimate our models.

Our modified event history analysis takes irregularly spaced data as a starting point and then restructures the data as follows. The period $(T_{e,i} - T_{b,i})$ is divided into discrete periods of fixed-length common to all observations. The full data set spans a total of T observational periods, which are denoted by $\tau_1, \tau_2, \ldots, \tau_T$, respectively. In our data this fixed-length period will be just a calendar year, but this choice in general would be context dependent. Our choice is motivated by the consideration that, for a binary outcome model, we require that within each observational period at most one event/transition would be observed; this condition might be violated in some cases.

In general, the sampled individuals will have event histories spanning overlapping observation periods with different beginnings and ends because individuals will enter or leave the survey at different times. Hence, a given individual will be observed over a subset of these T periods, which then constitutes the length of the observed event history for that individual. Different subsets of individuals may share particular beginnings or endings.

In this setup a transition may occur for an individual from the current state to another state. In case there are S different states, there are $S–1$ different transitions that can occur. The simplest case is $S = 2$, in which case the occurrence of the event signals the change of state. Even when there are more than two states, by appropriate redefinition the setup can be reduced to a simple dichotomy.

5.2   Dichotomous Model

To formulate the standard dichotomous outcome model, we distinguish between the 0/1 observed binary response variable *resp* and an underlying continuous latent variable *resp** that satisfies the single-index model

$$resp^* = \mathbf{x}'\beta + \mathbf{z}'\gamma + u, \tag{5.26}$$

where $\mathbf{x}$ denotes the vector of time-varying covariates, $\mathbf{z}$ the vector of individual-specific time-invariant variables and u is an i.i.d. error. As *resp** is not observed, we specify an observability condition for its observable counterpart *resp*,

$$resp = 1[resp^* > 0], \tag{5.27}$$

where the zero threshold is a normalization. Define $resp_{i\tau}$ as follows:

$$resp_{i\tau} = \begin{cases} 0 \text{ if no transition is observed in period } \tau, \\ 1 \text{ if a transition from the current state is observed in period } \tau. \end{cases}$$

The connection with the count data model results from the fact that $\sum_\tau resp_{i\tau}$ is the number of events observed for i-th individual during the event history, but the length of the event history, also called exposure time in count data models, will in general not be the same for all individuals.

Then the event history data will consist of $(resp_{i\tau}, \mathbf{x}_{i\tau}, \mathbf{z}_i)$, $\tau = \tau_1, \ldots, \tau_P$, and τ refers to a time period of selected length and the subscript P refers to parity, the number of events observed up to a particular point in time. However, once a fixed length of measurement is chosen, it is convenient to index τ as simply $\tau = 1, \ldots, T$. The elements of vector $\mathbf{x}_{i\tau}$ are time-varying regressors, including past outcomes $resp_{i\tau-j}$. Moreover, other observable features of past outcomes may also be included. This setup is more flexible for modelling dynamics than the autocorrelated conditional duration (ACD) model of Bauwens and Giot (2000) because it allows us to bring into our specification dynamic factors that are not satisfactorily reflected as lagged values of outcomes.

The restructured data setup is now analogous to panel/longitudinal data in the "long form" with individual and period-specific subscripts. Because in practice we will have a full event history of different lengths on different individuals, the panel typically will be unbalanced. Notice that we end up with a layout that defines a multi-state recurrent process, as described by Steele and Goldstein (2004), that can be analysed as an instance of the multilevel multistate competing risks model, with the exception that we put emphasis on dynamics and consistent fixed-effects estimation over random effects estimation.

As in the case of panel data, individual specific unobserved effects, denoted c_i, can be added to the model to capture unobserved heterogeneity. Also, as in the standard panel case, different assumptions can be made about c_i; it can be treated as an i.i.d. random variable (random effects assumption), as correlated with $\mathbf{x}_{i\tau}$ (fixed effects assumption), or as a function of observed variables and an i.i.d. random error (conditional correlation assumption). Thus the event history data can be recast as unbalanced panel data model for a binary outcome.

5.3 Discrete Hazards

The dichotomous outcome model is a discrete hazard model for recurrent outcomes, analogous to a linear pooled panel data model in which the panel data are treated as a pooled cross-section. A general formulation of a pooled discrete-time transition model is

$$h_{i\tau} \equiv Pr\left[resp_{i\tau} = 1 \middle| \mathbf{x}_{i\tau}, \mathbf{z}_i, \sum_{j<\tau} resp_{ij} = 0 \right]$$
$$= F\left(\lambda_\tau + \mathbf{x}'_{i\tau}\beta + \mathbf{z}'_i\gamma \right), \quad \tau = 1,\ldots,T, \tag{5.28}$$

where $h_{i\tau}$ represents the discrete hazard for the i-th individual, that is, the probability of an event occurring (that is, $resp = 1$) at time τ given that no event has occurred up to $\tau - 1$, and F denotes the cumulative distribution function (c.d.f.). This specification restricts the coefficients of regressors to be constant over time, while the intercept λ_τ, $\tau = 1, \ldots, T$, can vary over duration time. The only dynamic that allows this model is the one accounted for by λ_τ, which models duration dependence. Dynamics related to state dependence and/or dependence of the hazard on lagged time-varying variables is not accounted for. This is not attractive for the study of fertility behaviour because a fertility history has an additional state dimension: the parity. Taking all three dimensions into account generalises the transition model as follows:

$$
h_{ip\tau} = Pr\left[resp_{ip\tau} = 1 \middle| \mathbf{x}_{ip\tau}, \mathbf{s}_{ip}, \mathbf{z}_i, \sum_{j<\tau} resp_{ipj} = 0 \right]
$$

$$
= F\left(\lambda_{p\tau} + \mathbf{x}'_{ip\tau}\beta + \mathbf{s}'_{ip}\delta + \mathbf{z}'_i\gamma \right), \quad p = 1,...,P_i, \tau = 1,...,T, \tag{5.29}
$$

where explanatory variables may vary across individuals only ($\mathbf{z}$), across individuals and states ($\mathbf{s}$) or across individuals, states and time ($\mathbf{x}$). Duration dependence within each state p is accounted for by a series of coefficients $\lambda_{p\tau} = \lambda_{p,1}, \ldots, \lambda_{p,T}$ that form a step function that flexibly represents the baseline hazard.

For a parametric functional form of F two choices are popular: the standard normal c.d.f., or the logistic c.d.f.; then the parameters $(\lambda, \beta, \delta, \gamma)$ can be estimated by a stacked logit or stacked probit model in which a separate intercept is permitted for each state and for each interval. The resulting likelihood function for a sequence of $\tau{-}1$ zeros and a one at time τ is

$$
L(\lambda, \beta, \delta, \gamma) = \prod_{i=1}^{N} \prod_{p=1}^{P_i} \left[\prod_{g=1}^{\tau-1} \left(1 - F\left(\lambda_{pg} + \mathbf{x}'_{ipg}\beta + \mathbf{s}'_{ip}\delta + \mathbf{z}'_i\gamma \right) \right) \right]
$$

$$
\times F\left(\lambda_{p\tau} + \mathbf{x}'_{ip\tau}\beta + \mathbf{s}'_{ip}\delta + \mathbf{z}'_i\gamma \right). \tag{5.30}
$$

Extending this to allow for unobserved additive individual-specific heterogeneity term c_i leads to the conditional likelihood

$$
L(\lambda, \beta, \delta, \gamma \mid c_i) = \prod_{i=1}^{N} \prod_{p=1}^{P_i} \left[\prod_{g=1}^{\tau-1} \left(1 - F\left(\lambda_{pg} + \mathbf{x}'_{ipg}\beta + \mathbf{s}'_{ip}\delta + \mathbf{z}'_i\gamma + c_i \right) \right) \right]
$$

$$
\times F\left(\lambda_{p\tau} + \mathbf{x}'_{ip\tau}\beta + \mathbf{s}'_{ip}\delta + \mathbf{z}'_i\gamma + c_i \right). \tag{5.31}
$$

Estimation requires the choice of function F. This step causes no major difficulties for the pooled model underlying (5.31).

In the case of the fixed effects (FE) model, the nuisance parameters c_i are not straightforward to eliminate for an arbitrary choice of F. For example, it cannot be eliminated by transformation if we choose F to be the normal c.d.f. For the case of the static logit model, however, it is possible to eliminate the fixed effects by conditioning on the total count $\sum_\tau resp_{i\tau}$ and perform inference on $(\lambda, \beta, \delta, \gamma)$ on the basis of a conditional maximum likelihood strategy using the sample of individuals who experience at least one transition. A major disadvantage of this FE-logit case is that it can only identify the parameters of time-varying regressors, whereas other parameters may also be of interest. Moreover, leaving out individuals who do not experience any transition is unattractive as the study's sample size can suffer importantly because in most samples many women stay childless, especially in low-fertility-high–income settings where nearly 1/4 of women never have children—for instance in our BHPS example 26 per cent of women remain childless by age 45. Beyond loss of efficiency, dropping childless observations is also unattractive because women who never have children may be systematically different from women who eventually enter motherhood. As a consequence, there may be important sample selection issues at play that need explicit modelling (see Heckman, 1979; Heckman and Walker, 1990b).

For the dynamic logit case, that is a model that includes $resp_{i,\tau-1}$ as a covariate, conditioning on a sufficient statistic for (c_i) is more problematic; see Honoré and Kyriazidou (2000). However, Bartolucci and Nigro (2010) have proposed a version of the quadratic exponential model of Cox (1972) and Cox and Wermuth (1994) that closely resembles the dynamic logit model and for which conditioning on a sufficient statistic is feasible as in a static panel logit model. We use the pseudo-conditional maximum likelihood (PCMLE) estimation method of Bartolucci and Nigro (2010, 2012). In this approach, the fixed effects are integrated out by conditioning on a sufficient statistic, which in the case of the binary logit model is the total number of events. This dynamic fixed-effect model is used in our application.

We also estimate our MDEH specification under random effects assumptions. In this case F can be either the probit or the logit as both are computationally manageable; however, both require a parametric assumption about the distribution of c_i, typically followed by numerical integration.

6.   MODELLING DYNAMICS OF TRANSITIONS

There are two important motivations for a dynamic specification. First, in the context of fertility analysis, there is considerable theoretical and empirical work emphasizing the dependence of a new outcome on previous birth outcomes; see Bhalotra and Van Soest (2008) and references there cited. For example, in the Wolpin (1984) dynamic stochastic model of life-cycle fertility, the model generates implications for the number, timing and spacing of children, and there is evidence in the literature that families have preferences over gender composition, which imply that past birth outcomes will affect the desire for additional children (Arnold and Liu, 1986).

A second motivation flows from wanting to distinguish between the effect of individual time-invariant unobserved heterogeneity and state dependence. Individual propensity to remain in the current state may be a consequence mainly of unobserved persistent characteristics of that individual. In such a case controlling for individual-specific effects would account for the state dependence. This is often referred to as spurious state dependence. If, however, simply continuing to remain in one state decreases or increases the probability of transition, no matter what the individual-specific characteristics are, then such dynamic dependence is referred to as true state dependence, or duration dependence. Panel data potentially afford the possibility of distinguishing between the two alternatives, or even simultaneously controlling for the separate contributions of each.

Following Heckman and Borjas (1980), in a discrete hazard model for a binary outcome in which the lagged dependent outcome is a regressor, we may refer to dependence between the current and past outcomes as occurrence dependence; the term *duration dependence* refers to the case when the probability of transition is affected by how long an individual remains in a given state, and state dependence covers both types of dependence. Bhalotra and Van

Soest (2008) consider some approaches for modelling fertility dynamics—from a perspective relevant to fertility studies of less developed economies.

6.1   Autoregressive Dependence

A popular dynamic specification of a binary outcome model simply adds the lagged dichotomous variable $resp_{it-1}$ as an additional control variable; specifically, we modify (5.29) thus:

$$h_{ip\tau} = Pr\left[resp_{ip\tau} = 1 \middle| \mathbf{x}_{ip\tau}, \mathbf{s}_{ip}, \mathbf{z}_i, \sum_{j<\tau} resp_{ipj} = 0, c_i\right]$$

$$= F\left(\lambda_{p\tau} + \mathbf{x}'_{ip\tau}\beta + \mathbf{s}'_{ip}\delta + \mathbf{z}'_i\gamma + \rho resp_{i\tau-1} + c_i\right), \quad \tau = 1,\ldots,P, \tag{5.32}$$

which now includes an individual-specific heterogeneity term c_i and the autoregressive term $resp_{i,\tau-1}$. The parameter ρ reflects occurrence dependence, with $\rho = 0$ indicating zero occurrence dependence. The lagged regressor captures the effect of all unobserved or unmeasured factors that generate state dependence in the outcome. We call this specification Markovian in contrast to other (non-Markovian) specifications we discuss later. As previously indicated, given the presence in the equation of observed variables that capture individual heterogeneity, the lagged variable can potentially capture pure occurrence dependence.

Given this specification, additional assumptions determine whether the random effects (RE), fixed effects (FE) or the flexible FE model, in which the individual-specific parameter is parameterized as a function of exogenous variables plus a random component (often referred to as conditional correlation framework (CCR)), would identify the model. Whether one is in the large-N–small-τ framework common in microeconometric panels, or in the large-N–large-τ framework, is relevant to the choice of framework.

In the RE framework, the model will be augmented with an auxiliary assumption regarding the probability distribution of c_i, subsequent to which these nuisance parameters are (numerically) integrated out of the model—a task analytically more tractable than in the FE specification.

For the FE case, as previously noted, there are several proposed approaches (see Hsiao, 2014) for estimating this FE model, including Honoré and Kyriazidou (2000), Bartolucci and Nigro (2010, 2012) and Al-Sadoon et al. (2017). In a large-N–large-τ setting, controlling for the fixed effects using a comprehensive set of dummy variables is theoretically an option but not much used in practice. In the more common small-τ setting of this paper conditional maximum likelihood has greater appeal. The conditional approach of Bartolucci and Nigro applied to the quadratic exponential specification, which closely mimics the dynamic logit, has been applied to estimate the empirical model in this chapter. The discrete hazard is

$$h_{ip\tau} = Pr\left[resp_{ip\tau} = 1 \middle| \mathbf{x}_{ip\tau}, \mathbf{s}_{ip}, \mathbf{z}_i, \sum_{j<\tau} resp_{ipj} = 0, \sum_{p=1}^{P_i}\sum_{j=1}^{T_{ip}} resp_{ipj} = \kappa, c_i\right], \tag{5.33}$$

which is estimated by conditional maximum likelihood.

The use of the autoregressive form also poses problems of interpretation because it is based on a somewhat narrow view of the nature of dependence. In a *linear* autoregressive model, the lagged dependent variable captures the effect of all past changes in the exogenous drivers as the autoregressive model has a distributed lag representation. This is not so in a nonlinear model. More generally, capturing state dependence via a lagged dependent variable has a black-box character as it is not clear which mechanism is responsible for inertia in the transition from the current state.

6.2 Non-Autoregressive Dynamic Dependence

Autoregressive specifications lead to a loss of observations and in some cases dynamic dependence can be captured without using the autoregressive form, for example through past values of exogenous regressors. Hence, using lagged exogenous variables as predictors of current outcomes instead of lagged outcomes is an appealing way of modelling dynamic dependence, especially because it avoids the complications due to lagged outcomes in fixed effect models.

To model dynamics without autoregression, following the discussion in section 2, we propose to use variables that characterize some observable qualitative features of past events that are potentially related to a woman's preferences and hence have predictive relevance. The dichotomous variable $resp_{it}$ only indicates whether an event occurred. But many events vary in their nature and intensity. In such cases additional auxiliary (synthetic/constructed) regressors based partly on *qualitative features* of several past outcomes, rather than just the previous outcome, can be added because they are potentially useful predictors of future events. The relevance of such predictors may be easier to rationalize than that of the lagged outcome. Moreover, unlike the first-order autoregression, which only takes into consideration the immediately preceding outcome, such constructed variables may reflect the role of a full or partial event history.

The proposed dynamic modelling framework has similarities with Moffit (1984), who has used "panel probit" and "pooled probit" to analyse fertility data from the National Longitudinal Survey of Young Women. The author refers to his key equation as "number-of-children" equation; however, the "panel probit" equation has a binary dependent variable birth/no birth, and the dynamics are captured by including the total number of children as a regressor in the model, which is similar to our use of the *parity* variable. Further, the framework we presented incorporates unobserved heterogeneity by allowing for both random and fixed effects.

7. APPLICATION: A MODIFIED DYNAMIC EVENT HISTORY MODEL FOR BRITISH FERTILITY HISTORIES

In this section we discuss results from a modified dynamic event history (MDEH) model fitted to British longitudinal fertility histories data. We use data from the British Household Panel Survey (BHPS), a nationally representative United Kingdom longitudinal study that began in 1991 and ended in 2008.[5] The 1991 sample is composed by 8167 households and 10 264 individuals. All individuals who belong to the original households were re-interviewed every year from 1991 to 2008.[6] New-born children automatically become panel members, and all children are interviewed individually once they reach age 16. On wave 9 (1999) a refreshment sample of 1500 households and 3395 individuals was taken in Scotland and Wales to allow for country-level comparisons. In wave 11 (2001) a refreshment sample of approximately 2000 new households and 5188 individuals was taken in Northern Ireland.

In section 2.2 we briefly discussed the BHPS and pointed out that this survey takes the strategy of building fertility histories, implementing a prospective fertility follow-up of all panel members, which is complemented by retrospective fertility data collected in wave 2 (1992) for the original sample, and in waves 11 and 12 for the Scotland–Wales and Northern Ireland refresh samples. This approach delivers a detailed fertility history of all panel members along with a complete history of the variables that are suggested by theory to determine the number and timing of children.

The analytical sample contains detailed fertility histories for 14 137 women aged between 18 and 50. The data have a complex hierarchical structure explained at length in section 2.2. Table 5.3 illustrates the layout of the data, and descriptive statistics of the analytical sample are in Table 5.5. The response variable (*resp*) is a 0/1 binary variable that takes value one when a new birth is registered.

We estimate a reduced form model for the fertility history. Two specifications are considered: (a) a model with no autoregressive term and (b) a model that includes an autoregressive term. We implement a number of alternative estimators by either maximum likelihood or conditional maximum likelihood (for FE models): (i) logit, (ii) logit random effects (RE logit), (iii) logit fixed effects (FE) and (iv) quadratic exponential models for binary panel data (cquad).

7.1   Regression results

We now selectively discuss several aspects of the empirical results that are of interest to economists, beginning with findings from non-autoregressive models and then going on to models with some sort of autoregressive inertia. All models include time-varying controls for age (quadratic function) and log-income (000s of 1992 constant pounds) as well as parity-varying controls for the birth of a girl at parity 1, the occurrence of same-sex siblings at parity 2 and 3, and the occurrence of twins in the last parity. For models that implement random effects estimators we add additional time-fixed controls for maximum achieved qualification (GCSE/O level/A level/diploma/1st degree/posgrad/control: no qualification), religion (no religion/Catholic/Muslim/Hindu/other religion/missing religion/control: Anglican), country of birth (born in a EU country/born in a non-EU country/control: born in the UK), age at which the woman left school, work status of the woman's mother when she was 14 and the woman's mother social class (professional and manager/skilled non-manual/skilled manual/partially skilled/social class missing/control: non-skilled).

7.1.1   Non-autoregressive models

Table 5.6 presents empirical results for the logit MDEH models. Here, the dynamic event history is modelled by specifying a hazard function that gives the probability that the count of interest will be increased by one unit at time τ, given the whole history of a set of exogenous variables. The discrete hazard function models $Pr\,[resp_{ip\tau} = 1 | x_{i\tau}, z_i]$ and unobserved individual heterogeneity is explicitly allowed, as discussed in section 5.3.

Because FE logit delivers a consistent estimator of $(\lambda, \beta, \delta, \gamma)$ by conditioning on $\Sigma_\tau resp_{i\tau}$, which eliminates c_i from the conditional likelihood, no estimates for the fixed effects are obtained after fitting the model and, as a consequence, no valid average marginal effects are available. This is rather disappointing because each model has its own parametrization and coefficients may not be directly comparable. To allow comparison, for the each of the

Table 5.5 *Descriptive statistics for longitudinal complemented with retrospective fertility history from BHPS (N = 238 895)*

Variable	Mean	SD	Min.	Max.	Description
resp	0.08	0.27	0	1	Response variable
parity	1.36	1.41	0	15	Parity
clock	7.14	5.78	1	33	Clock
girlat1	0.09	0.28	0	1	girlatparity1
ssex2	0.12	0.32	0	1	Same sex at $P = 2$
ssex3	0.03	0.18	0	1	Same sex at $P = 3$
ltwinpar	0.03	0.16	0	1	Last parity twins
age	32.44	9.20	18	50	Age
agesq	1137	618	324	2500	Age squared
lincome	1.22	1.10	0	6.87	Log-income(000s)
relgion_m	0.25	0.43	0	1	Religion: Missing
norelgion	0.25	0.43	0	1	Religion: None
catholic	0.07	0.26	0	1	Religion: Catholic
othrelgion	0.16	0.37	0	1	Religion: Other
muslim	0.02	0.12	0	1	Religion: Muslim
hindu	0.03	0.16	0	1	Religion: Hindu
noedu	0.43	0.49	0	1	Highest qual: None
olevel	0.23	0.42	0	1	Highest qual: O level
alevel	0.13	0.34	0	1	Highest qual: A level
diploma	0.06	0.23	0	1	Highest qual: Diploma
degree	0.09	0.28	0	1	Highest qual: 1st degree
postgrad	0.02	0.14	0	1	Highest qual: Postgrad
borneu	0.02	0.15	0	1	Born: EU
bornoth	0.03	0.18	0	1	Born: Other
scend	15.11	3.42	0	26	School leaving age
scend_m	0.04	0.20	0	1	School leaving age missing
mnowk14	0.50	0.50	0	1	Mother not working when 14
mscl_m	0.61	0.49	0	1	Mother scl: Missing
msclpromang	0.08	0.27	0	1	Mother scl: Professional/management/technical
msclskllnm	0.10	0.30	0	1	Mother scl: Skilled nonmanual
msclpskll	0.09	0.29	0	1	Mother scl: Partially skilled
Mscluskll	0.07	0.25	0	1	Mother scl: Unskilled

Table 5.6 Modified dynamic event history for BHPS fertility—Average (semi) elasticities of Pr(resp = 1|x,u) from logit discrete hazard

	LOGIT	RELOGIT	FELOGIT
Girl at $P = 1$	−0.012	−0.012	0.462***
	(0.026)	(0.027)	(0.036)
Same sex at $P = 2$	0.144***	0.144***	0.211***
	(0.033)	(0.033)	(0.039)
Same sex at $P = 3$	0.018	0.018	−0.272***
	(0.060)	(0.060)	(0.068)
Last parity twins	−0.209***	−0.209***	−0.769***
	(0.063)	(0.064)	(0.083)
Age	0.316***	0.316***	0.777***
	(0.013)	(0.013)	(0.016)
Age squared	−0.006***	−0.006***	−0.010***
	(0.000)	(0.000)	(0.000)
Log(income)	−0.075***	−0.075***	−0.056
	(0.008)	(0.008)	(0.034)
Max qual: none	−0.006	−0.006	0.000
	(0.036)	(0.036)	(.)
Max qual: O level	−0.083**	−0.083**	0.000
	(0.035)	(0.035)	(.)
Max qual: A level	−0.179***	−0.179***	0.000
	(0.038)	(0.038)	(.)
Max qual: Diploma	−0.202***	−0.202***	0.000
	(0.046)	(0.046)	(.)
Max qual: First degree	−0.201***	−0.201***	0.000
	(0.042)	(0.043)	(.)
Max qual: Postgraduate	−0.228***	−0.228***	0.000
	(0.063)	(0.063)	(.)

Table 5.6   (continued)

	LOGIT	RELOGIT	FELOGIT
ρ		0.0000802	
SE(ρ)		0.0105225	
N. of obs	238 895	238 895	211 639
N. of individuals	14 134	14 134	8009

Note: Average (semi) elasticities of $Pr(resp = 1|x,u)$ reported (see Kitazawa, 2012). Clustered robust standard errors at individual level in parenthesis. *10% significant; **5% significant; ***1% significant. Except for FE logit, regressions include the following time-fixed controls: maximum qualification (6 levels), country of birth (EU vs. non-EU), school leaving age, mother's social class and mother's work status when respondent was 14. For each parity a different baseline hazard is specified so that the form of the hazard function is fully flexible. For parity 0 the baseline hazard has steps at t: $t = 1$–2, $t = 3$–4, $t = 5$–6, $t = 7$, $t = 8$, $t = 9$, $t = 10$, $t = 11$, $t = 12$, $t = 13$, $t = 14$, $t = 16$, $t = 17$, $t = 18$, $t = 19$, $t = 20$, $t = 21$, $t = 22$, $t = 23$, $t = 24$, $t = 25$ and larger (control is $t = 15$). For parity 1 the baseline hazard has steps for t at $t = 1$, $t = 3$, $t = 5$, $t = 6$, $t = 7$, $t = 8$, $t = 9$, $t = 10$, $t = 11$ and larger (control is $t = 2$). For parity 2 the baseline hazard has steps at t: $t = 1$, $t = 2$, $t = 4$, $t = 5$, $t = 6$, $t = 7$ and larger (control is $t = 3$). For parity 3 the baseline hazard has steps at t: $t = 1$, $t = 3$, $t = 4$, $t = 5$, $t = 6$ and larger (control is $t = 2$). Finally, for parities 4 and larger we specify a common baseline hazard with steps at t: $t = 2$, $t = 3$, $t = 4$, $t = 5$, $t = 6$, $t = 7$ and larger (control is $t = 1$).

$j = 1, \ldots, J$ control variables, we define $w_{ipj\tau} = \exp(x_{ipj\tau})$ and calculate the average (semi) elasticity of $x_{ipj\tau}$ as

$$\eta_{ipj\tau}^{w} = \left[\frac{\partial h_{ip\tau}}{\partial w_{ipj\tau}}\right]\left[\frac{w_{ipj\tau}}{h_{ip\tau}}\right],$$

with $h_{ip\tau} = Pr[resp_{ip\tau} = 1 | \mathbf{x}_{ip\tau}, \mathbf{s}_{ip}, \mathbf{z}_i, \Sigma_{j<\tau}\, resp_{ij} = 0]$. Kitazawa (2012) shows that η^w is computable without the fixed effects in the FE logit model and can be calculated without complication for RE logit and logit. Hence, using η^w a meaningful comparison is possible. Table 5.6 reports then average (semi) elasticities.

Logit vs. RE logit. We find little evidence that unobserved individual heterogeneity is present in the RE logit, with an estimated $\rho = 0.001$, which is insignificant at 5 per cent. As a consequence, average (semi) elasticities calculated on the basis of logit and RE logit are essentially the same.

RE logit vs. FE logit. In general, RE estimators give substantially different results from FE estimators. Such a result may arise if age is correlated with the individual heterogeneity term c_i, possibly because the age at which a woman marries and enters motherhood for the first time can be a function of unobserved time-fixed factors such as general attachment to the labour market, taste for family size, fecundity, health frailty, and so on. Such considerations favour the FE estimators and suggest that RE hazard specifications, which are the most popular methods used in the literature, may deliver seriously biased and inconsistent estimators. In fact, our British fertility history example illustrates how even a correlated random effects formulation may not sufficiently control for relevant individual unobserved heterogeneity (see, for instance, Mundlak, 1978; Chamberlain, 1982).

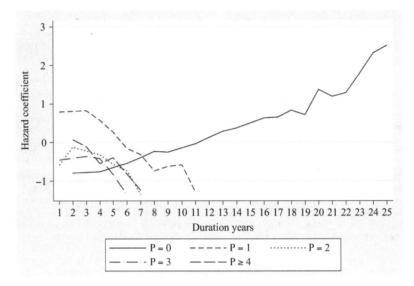

Note: Coefficients on picewise constant time function representing the baseline hazard in a logit MDEH model.

Figure 5.6 *Estimated baseline hazard by parity from a modified dynamic event history model for British (BHPS) longitudinal fertility data*

Baseline hazard and dynamics due to parity. Figure 5.6 presents estimates of the baseline hazard for the logit MDEH, which is similar to the estimates that are obtained from the RE logit and the FE logit. In our descriptive explorations in section 2.2, the kernel estimates of the (unconditional) hazard of entering motherhood (parity 0) showed a U-inverted form whereas the hazard for higher parities was decreasing monotonically. Moreover, descriptive kernel estimates suggested that the hazard for $P = 1$ is always larger than the hazard for $P = 2$, and the hazard of $P = 2$ is always larger than the hazard of $P = 3$ and $P = 4$. Also the hazards for $P = 2$ through $P = 4$ are hardly a parallel shift of the hazard for $P = 1$. Most of these observations still hold when we look at the baseline hazard estimates from the logit MDEH in figure 5.6.

Note that once we condition on covariates, instead of a U-inverted shape the (conditional) hazard of entering motherhood ($P = 0$) increases monotonically with age. A possible reason is that a U-inverted quadratic effect of age, which peaks at 26, accommodates the drop in the probability of entering motherhood (for the first time) as an individual grows older. Another interesting finding is a late peaking of the hazard at parity 1 ($P = 1$), which occurs between 8 and 10 years after the arrival of a woman's first child. This late surge for the second child is consistent with the timing theories of Happel et al. (1984) and the structural models of Rosenzweig and Wolpin (1980) and Heckman and Walker (1990a) that predict that women postpone motherhood as they accumulate human capital. Hence, it is likely that the late surge at $P = 1$ is driven by working mothers with high human capital who wait to the end of their fertile life to have their second child. In fact, our findings suggests that such postponement occurs mainly between the first and the second child. Notice also that for $P = 1$ and $P = 2$ the baseline hazard is increasing only for two or three years, which means that most women who plan to have two and three children schedule their pregnancies quite close once they enter motherhood, which is also predicted by Happel et al. (1984). In summary, the empirical evidence that we obtain suggest that parity is a major determinant of dynamics in the British fertility histories in a way that is consistent with the predictions from the theory of human capital of Becker (1960).

Offspring gender effects. We also find strong support that women prefer a mixed-gender family composition and that they are prepared to increase family size to achieve such a mixture. This is clearly indicated in table 5.6 by the positive, and highly significant, coefficients on the dummy that indicates when a woman reaches parity 2 with all girls or boys. However, a woman who reaches parity 3 with three girls or three boys is likely to stop trying to achieve mixture. Interestingly, we do not find a statistically significant effect of the gender of the first child (girl at $P = 1$) for the logit and RE logit specification, but a positive effect for having a girl at parity 1 is reported by the FE logit specification. This effect is statistically significant at 1 per cent and suggests that, after all, the probability of progressing to the second child increases when couples have a girl as their first child. To put it in other words, there is indeed preference for a boy a $P = 1$.

Note that if we had kept the RE estimator, which is the estimator most used in the literature (see, for instance, Steele and Goldstein, 2004), the inference for *girl at P = 1* would be that couples do not have preference for the gender of their first child. So, using a FE estimator is crucial, maybe because there is a time-fixed unobserved heterogeneity related to offspring sex preference that is correlated with the *girl at P = 1* control. The finding illustrates the relevance of implementing hazard models with fixed effects rather than the popular random effects specification.

These findings are evidence that qualitative features of past outcomes are important and support the hypothesis that fertility is a dynamic sequential decision process. Controlling for such important observable aspects of past outcomes, even within the context of a non-autoregressive hazard model, it is possible to incorporate such dynamics in an easily interpretable way.

Family income. As expected, and suggested by the Beckerian human capital theory and the quantity–quality trade-off of children, the effect of income on the hazard in table 5.6 is negative and statistically significant at 1 per cent in both the RE and the FE specifications. It is important to say, however, that marginal effect calculations for logit and RE logit indicate that the marginal effect is rather small. In fact, an extra 1000 pounds reduces the probability of observing a second birth in less than –0.001 percentage points (p.p. hereafter) at the point of maximum probability of ever observing the arrival of a second child—that is at age 26 and three years after the birth of first child. Moreover, once a FE logit hazard is fitted, the effect of income becomes statistically insignificant. These findings suggest that income incentives, such as the UK child tax credits program (replaced by universal credit in 2012), may have small impact on reproductive behaviour.

Education. Consistent with the Beckerian theory of human capital, women with higher education have a lower hazard of having an additional child at any point of time than those who have compulsory education (the control group). The effect, however, is nonlinear. The stronger protective effect of education is felt when a woman progresses from no education to A levels—a marginal effect of –0.01 p.p. for the logit model. Progressing from A levels to diploma reduces the logit hazard by –0.002 p.p.; and progressing from A levels to first degree reduces the logit hazard by –0.0018 p.p. Given that we already control for family labour income, the nonlinearity in the effect of education may reflect a wealth effect (or permanent income effect) that is not captured by income. That is, part of the smaller effect of education at the higher level may be explained by the fact that wealthier individuals tend to have larger families.

7.1.2   Autoregressive model: CQUAD

These results show that nonautoregressive models can capture important dynamic features of the fertility outcomes. In this section, we consider whether adding lagged outcome variables can further improve the model specification by capturing state dependence. Specifically, we employ the dynamic FE panel model of Bartolucci and Nigro (2010), hereafter referred to as the conditional quadratic exponential (CQUAD) specification.

The substantive difference between models in section 7.1.1 and CQUAD is that, while in the former dynamics of the fertility history are accounted for by changes in explanatory variables, here the dynamics are induced by changes in explanatory variables as well as the autoregressive effect of the lagged dependent variable, which is a genuine shifter of the current transition probability after controlling for individual unobserved heterogeneity in a fixed effects framework—just as in the dynamic logit model of Honoré and Kyriazidou (2000).

Because CQUAD implements a fixed effects approach, the model conditions on total scores $\Sigma_t resp_{it}$ and only uses the subset of observations in the sample for which at least one transition is recorded. Besides, as in any other FE approach, coefficients on time-fixed variables are not identified. However, unlike the dynamic logit of Honoré and Kyriazidou (2000), CQUAD allows for time dummies among the set of control variables because it does not impose conditions on the support of the distribution of regressors. Table 5.7 shows results, reporting coefficients because average marginal effects or average (semi) elasticities are not available for this model. The signpattern of effects is similar to that in the logit fixedeffect hazard shown in table 5.6, so we do not comment further.

Lagged outcome. Of special interest is the negative coefficient on the lagged response variable. This result has to be interpreted with care, following the analysis presented in section 3.1 of Bartolucci and Nigro (2010) who show that the coefficient of lagged outcome variable $resp_{i,\tau-1}$, say γ, can be shown to be

$$\gamma = \log\left\{\frac{Pr(resp_{i\tau} = 1 | c_i, \mathbf{x}_{i\tau}, resp_{i,\tau-1} = 1)}{Pr(resp_{i\tau} = 0 | c_i, \mathbf{x}_{i\tau}, resp_{i,\tau-1} = 1)}\right\} - \log\left\{\frac{Pr(resp_{i\tau} = 1 | c_i, \mathbf{x}_{i\tau}, resp_{i,\tau-1} = 0)}{Pr(resp_{i\tau} = 0 | c_i, \mathbf{x}_{i\tau}, resp_{i,\tau-1} = 0)}\right\}, \quad (5.34)$$

which is the difference between the log-odds (of outcome 1 vs. 0) in τ given $resp_{i,\tau-1} = 1$ and the log-odds in τ given $resp_{i,\tau-1} = 0$. Thus the coefficient does not have an interpretation analogous to the standard linear autoregressive model for continuous outcomes. Clearly, in CQUAD the coefficient on the lagged outcome can be either positive or negative. While the statistical interpretation of the coefficient on the lagged outcome is clear, the economic interpretation is less clear. First, in our fertility application, it is not clear what should be considered the relevant "lagged outcome" as one could focus on $resp_{i,\tau-1}$, as CQUAD does, or on the effect of the outcome of the last pregnancy—live birth vs. still birth, for instance.

Table 5.7   Modified dynamic event history for BHPS fertility from CQUAD discrete hazard

	Coeff.	SE	t-stat	p-value
Girl at $P = 1$	0.558***	0.042	13.3	0.000
Same sex at $P = 2$	0.234***	0.044	5.3	0.000
Same sex at $P = 3$	−0.333***	0.076	−-4.4	0.000
Last parity twins	−1.260***	0.099	−12.7	0.000
Age	0.778***	0.019	41.5	0.000
Age squared	−0.011***	0.000	−37.7	0.000
Log(income)	0.011	0.039	0.28	0.781
Lagged response	−0.394***	0.028	−14.2	0.000
log – likelihood				−36 538.5
N. of obs				211 598
N. of individuals				8007

Notes: Standard errors reported. *10% significant; **5% significant; ***1% significant. Individual level controls: age, age squared, income. For each parity a different baseline hazard is specified so that the form of the hazard function is fully flexible. For parity 0 the baseline hazard has steps at $t = 1$–2, $t = 3$–4, $t = 5$–6, $t = 7$, $t = 8$, $t = 9$, $t = 10$, $t = 11$, $t = 12$, $t = 13$, $t = 14$, $t = 16$, $t = 17$, $t = 18$, $t = 19$, $t = 20$, $t = 21$, $t = 22$, $t = 23$, $t = 24$, $t = 25$ plus (control is $t = 15$). For parity 1 the baseline hazard has steps at $t = 1$, $t = 3$, $t = 5$, $t = 6$, $t = 7$, $t = 8$, $t = 9$, $t = 10$, $t = 11$ plus (control is $t = 2$). For parity 2 the baseline hazard has steps at $t = 1$, $t = 2$, $t = 4$, $t = 5$, $t = 6$, $t = 7$ plus (control is $t = 3$). For parity 3 the baseline hazard has steps at $t = 1$, $t = 3$, $t = 4$, $t = 5$, $t = 6$ plus (control is $t = 2$). Finally, for parities 4 and larger we specify a common baseline hazard with steps at $t = 2$, $t = 3$, $t = 4$, $t = 5$, $t = 6$, $t = 7$ plus (control is $t = 1$).

8.   DISCUSSION AND CONCLUSIONS

Our results support the position that specifying RE hazards, the most popular method used in applied work, may lead to biased and inconsistent estimators when there are control variables that are correlated with individual time-fixed unobserved characteristics. In such cases a FE hazard specification is preferred. The applied researcher should be aware that FE specifications are more robust than RE specifications to misspecification error not only in linear but also in nonlinear models.

Results from our British fertility history data support the position that non-autoregressive models with lagged exogenous variables, such as gender composition and parity indicators, representing qualitative features of past fertility outcomes, can function as proxy variables for dynamic dependence. The role of these variables is easier to interpret than that of lagged dependent variables intended to model duration or occurrence dependence. When the lagged dependent variables are added to the non-autoregressive model, there are interaction effects between them and parity indicators, which add to the difficulty of interpretation. Nevertheless, we detect some evidence of state dependence.

NOTES

*   The usual disclaimers apply. We thank Rainer Winkelmann, whose insightful comments helped to improve this chapter.
1.   A total fertility rate (TFR) is defined as the number of children a woman is expected to have over her lifetime if she behaves according to a current schedule of age-specific fertility rates. Sometimes the TFR is written in terms of expected children per 1000 women. In this definition, an age-specific fertility rate is taken to be the annual number of live births to women of a specified age or age group per 1000 women in that age group.
2.   Limiting the life span to three days and considering that time is measured in discrete units is not the way the dynamic model is set up in Happel et al. (1984). Here we use this simplification to discuss the main results of their model without going into much mathematical detail.
3.   Over time, however, societies may transit from high to low fertility rates as social norms and economic choices favour smaller family units. Planned fertility studies that ask how many children a family would like to have generate samples with just a few realizations even in high-fertility−low-income settings (Miranda, 2008).
4.   In the demographic literature, *parity* refers to the number of children previously born to a woman at a given point of time. Parity increases with the arrival of a newborn.
5.   The BHPS original sample issued in 1991 consisted of 8166 nationally representative addresses randomly drawn from the Postcode Address File (a UK comprehensive list of post codes). A three-stage clustered probability design was implemented, with postcode sectors sampled in the first stage, addresses sampled in the second stage, and households sampled in the third stage. Implicit stratification combined with systematic sampling was used to ensure that the sample is well balanced in key socio-economic characteristics at the sector level. The study design ensures that every household in the population had the same probability of entering the sample.
6.   Panel members are followed when they split from the original household, and all members of the new household are subsequently interviewed as long as they live with the original panel member.
7.   Panel members are followed when they split from the original household, and all members of the new household are subsequently interviewed as long as they live with the original panel member.

REFERENCES

Adsera, A. (2006). An economic analysis of the gap between desired and actual fertility: The case of Spain. *Review of Economics of the Household*, 4(1): 75–95.
Agadjanian, V. and Prata, N. (2002). War, peace, and fertility in Angola. *Demography*, 39(2): 215–31.
Al-Sadoon, M. M., Li, T., and Pesaran, M. H. (2017). Exponential class of dynamic binary choice panel data models with fixed effects. *Econometric Reviews*, 36(6–9): 898–927.
Allais, M. (1947). *Economie et interet*. Imprimerie National.
Angrist, J. D. and Evans, W. N. (1998). Children and their parents' labor supply: Evidence from exogenous variation in family size. *The American Economic Review*, 88(3): 450–77.
Arnold, F. and Liu, Z. (1986). Sex preference, fertility, and family planning in China. *Population and Development Review*, 221–46.
Arrow, K. J. (1972). Economic welfare and the allocation of resources for invention. In *Readings in industrial economics*, 219–36. Springer.
Arroyo, C. and Zhang, J. (1997). Dynamic microeconomic models of fertility choice: A survey. *Journal of Population Economics*, 10(1): 23–65.
Barmby, T. and Cigno, A. (1990). A sequential probability model of fertility patterns. *Journal of Population Economics*, 3(1): 31–51.
Bartolucci, F. and Nigro, V. (2010). A dynamic model for binary panel data with unobserved heterogeneity admitting an-consistent conditional estimator. *Econometrica*, 78(2): 719–33.
Bartolucci, F. and Nigro, V. (2012). Pseudo conditional maximum likelihood estimation of the dynamic logit model for binary panel data. *Journal of Econometrics*, 170: 102–16.
Bauwens, L. and Giot, P. (2000). The logarithmic acd model: an application to the bid-ask quote process of three NYSE stocks. *Annales d'Economie et de Statistique*, (60): 117–49.
Becker, G. (1960). *An economic analysis of fertility and demographic change in developed countries*. Princeton University Press and NBER.
Becker, G. and Barro, R. (1986). Altruism and the economic theory of fertility. *Population and Development Review*, 12: 69–76.
Becker, G. and Barro, R. (1988). A reformulation of the economic theory of fertility. *The Quarterly Journal of Economics*, 103(1): 1–25.

Becker, G. and Lewis, H. (1973). On the interaction between the quantity and quality of children. *The Journal of Political Economy*, 81(2): S279–S288.

Becker, G., Murphy, K., and Tamura, R. (1990). Human capital, fertility, and economic growth. *Journal of Political Economy*, 98(5): S12–S37.

Bettio, F. and Villa, P. (1998). A Mediterranean perspective on the breakdown of the relationship between participation and fertility. *Cambridge Journal of Economics*, 22: 137–71.

Bhalotra, S. and Van Soest, A. (2008). Birth-spacing, fertility and neonatal mortality in India: Dynamics, frailty, and fecundity. *Journal of Econometrics*, 143(2): 274–90.

Boldrin, M., De Nardi, M., and Jones, L. E. (2015). Fertility and social security. *Journal of Demographic Economics*, 81(3): 261–99.

Bongaarts, J. (1990). The measurement of wanted fertility. *Population and Development Review*, 487–506.

Bongaarts, J. (1992). Do reproductive intentions matter? In *International Family Planning Perspectives*, 102–8.

Bongaarts, J. (2001). Fertility and reproductive preferences in post-transitional societies. *Population and Development Review*, 27: 260–81.

Bongaarts, J. and Watkins, S. (1996). Social interactions and contemporary fertility transitions. *Population and Development Review*, 22(4): 639–82.

Bound, J., Brown, C., and Mathiowetz, N. (2001). Measurement error in survey data. In *Handbook of Econometrics*, volume 5, 3705–843. Elsevier.

Caldwell, J. C. (2006). Social upheaval and fertility decline. In *Demographic Transition Theory*, 273–99. Springer.

Cameron, A. C. and Trivedi, P. K. (2013). *Regression Analysis of Count Data*, volume 53. Cambridge University Press.

Chamberlain, G. (1982). Multivariate regression models for panel data. *Journal of Econometrics*, 18(1): 5–46.

Cheng, T. C. and Trivedi, P. K. (2015). Attrition bias in panel data: A sheep in wolf's clothing? A case study based on the Mabel survey. *Health Economics*, 24(9): 1101–17.

Chwe, M. (2000). Communication and coordination in social networks. *Review of Economic Studies*, 67: 1–16.

Cox, D. and Wermuth, N. (1994). A note on the quadratic exponential binary distribution. *Biometrika*, 81(2): 403–8.

Cox, D. R. (1972). The analysis of multivariate binary data. *Applied Statistics*, 113–20.

Del Boca, D. (2002). The effect of child care and part time opportunities on participation and fertility decisions in Italy. *Journal of Population Economics*, 15(3): 549–73.

Diamond, P. (1965). National debt in a neoclassical growth model. *The American Economic Review*, 55(5): 1126–50.

Doepke, M. and Tertilt, M. (2018). Women's empowerment, the gender gap in desired fertility, and fertility outcomes in developing countries. In *AEA Papers and Proceedings*, volume 108, 358–62.

Ellison, G. and Fudenberg, D. (1995). Word-of-mouth communication and social learning. *The Quarterly Journal of Economics*, 110(1): 93–125.

Ermisch, J. (1989). Purchased childcare, optimal family size and mother's employment: Theory and econometric analysis. *Journal of Population Economics*, 2(2): 79–102.

Fagbamigbe, A. F. and Adebowale, A. S. (2014). Current and predicted fertility using Poisson regression model: Evidence from 2008 Nigerian demographic health survey. *African Journal of Reproductive Health*, 18(1): 71–83.

Galor, O. and Weil, D. N. (1996). The gender gap, fertility, and growth. *American Economic Review*, 86(3): 374–87.

Gonzalez, L. (2013). The effect of a universal child benefit on conceptions, abortions, and early maternal labor supply. *American Economic Journal: Economic Policy*, 5(3): 160–88.

Gray, P. G. (1955). The memory factor in social surveys. *Journal of the American Statistical Association*, 50(270): 344–63.

Günther, I. and Harttgen, K. (2016). Desired fertility and number of children born across time and space. *Demography*, 53(1): 55–83.

Happel, S., Hill, J., and Low, S. (1984). An economic analysis of the timing of childbirth. *Population Studies*, 38(2): 299–311.

Hassan, M. and Killick, S. (2005). Is previous aberrant reproductive outcome predictive of subsequently reduced fecundity? *Human Reproduction*, 20(3): 657–64.

Heckman, J. and Walker, J. (1990a). The relationship between wages and income and the timing and spacing of births: Evidence from Swedish longitudinal data. *Econometrica*, 58(6): 1411–41.

Heckman, J. and Walker, J. (1990b). Estimating fecundability from data on waiting times to first conception. *Journal of The American Statistical Association*, 85(410): 283–94.

Heckman, J. J. (1979). Sample selection bias as a specification error. *Econometrica*, 153–61.

Heckman, J. J. and Borjas, G. J. (1980). Does unemployment cause future unemployment? Definitions, questions and answers from a continuous time model of heterogeneity and state dependence. *Economica*, 47(187): 247–83.

Honoré, B. E. and Kyriazidou, E. (2000). Panel data discrete choice models with lagged dependent variables. *Econometrica*, 839–74.

Hotz, V. and Miller, R. (1988). An empirical analysis of life cycle fertility and female labor supply. *Econometrica*, 56(1): 91–118.

Hotz, V. J. and Miller, R. A. (1993). Conditional choice probabilities and the estimation of dynamic models. *The Review of Economic Studies*, 60(3): 497–529.

Hsiao, C. (2014). *Analysis of panel data*. Cambridge University Press.

Jayaraman, A., Gebreselassie, T., and Chandrasekhar, S. (2009). Effect of conflict on age at marriage and age at first birth in Rwanda. *Population Research and Policy Review*, 28(5): 551.

Kapur, S. (1995). Technological diffusion with social learning. *The Journal of Industrial Economics*, 43(2): 173–95.

Kirman, A. (1993). Ants, rationality, and recruitment. *The Quarterly Journal of Economics*, 108(1): 137–56.

Kitazawa, Y. (2012). Hyperbolic transformation and average elasticity in the framework of the fixed effects logit model. *Theoretical Economics Letters*, 2(02): 192–99.

Knodel, J. and Prachuabmoh, V. (1973). Desired family size in Thailand: Are the responses meaningful? *Demography*, 10(4): 619–37.

Kohler, H. (1997). Learning in social networks and contraceptive choice. *Demography*, 34(3): 369–83.

Kohler, H. (2000). Fertility decline as a coordination problem. *Journal of Development Economics*, 63: 231–63.

Kok, H. S., Asselt, K. M., Schouw, Y. T. d., Grobbee, D. E., Velde, E. R., Pearson, P. L., and Peeters, P. H. (2003). Subfertility reflects accelerated ovarian ageing. *Human Reproduction*, 18(3): 644–48.

Landry, A. (1909). *Les trois théories principales de la population*.

Manski, C. and Mayshar, J. (2003). Private incentives and social interactions: Fertility puzzles in Israel. *Journal of the European Economic Association*, 1(1): 181–211.

Mathiowetz, N. A. and Ouncan, G. J. (1988). Out of work, out of mind: Response errors in retrospective reports of unemployment. *Journal of Business & Economic Statistics*, 6(2): 221–29.

Melkersson, M. and Rooth, D. (2000). Modeling female fertility using inflated count data models. *Journal of Population Economics*, 13(2): 189–203.

Mira, P. and Ahn, N. (2001). Job bust, baby bust? Evidence from Spain. *Journal of Population Economics*, 14(3): 505–21.

Miranda, A. (2008). Planned fertility and family background: A quantile regression for counts analysis. *Journal of Population Economics*, 21(1): 67–81.

Miranda, A. (2010). A double-hurdle count model for completed fertility data from the developing world. DoQSS WP No. 10-01, Department of Quantitative Social Science, Institute of Education. https://repec.ucl.ac.uk/REPEc/pdf/qsswp1001.pdf

Miranda, A. (2013). Un modelo de valla doble para datos de conteo y su aplicación en el estudio de la fecundidad en México. In Velázquez, A. M., editor, *Aplicaciones en Economía y Ciencias Sociales con Stata*, Stata Press.

Moffit, R. (1984). Profiles of fertility, labour supply and wages of married women: A complete life-cycle model. *Review of Economic Studies*, 51(2): 263–78.

Montgomery, M. and Casterline, J. (1993). The diffusion of fertility control in Taiwan: Evidence from pooled cross-section time-series models. *Population Studies*, 47(3): 457–79.

Morand, O. (1999). Endogenous fertility, income distribution, and growth. *Journal of Economic Growth*, 4(3): 331–49.

Mullahy, J. (1986). Specification and testing of some modified count data models. *Journal of Econometrics* 33(3): 341–65.

Mundlak, Y. (1978). On the pooling of time series and cross section data. *Econometrica*, 69–85.

Neher, P. (1971). Peasants, procreation, and pensions. *The American Economic Review*, 61(3): 380–89.

Nelson, R. R. and Phelps, E. S. (1966). Investment in humans, technological diffusion, and economic growth. *The American Economic Review*, 56(1/2): 69–75.

Notestein, F. W. (1945). Population: The long view. In T. Schulz, editor, *Food for the World*. University of Chicago Press.

Nugent, J. (1985). The old-age security motive for fertility. *Population and Development Review*, 11(1): 75–97.

O'Neill, S., Khashan, A., Henriksen, T., Kenny, L., Kearney, P., Mortensen, P., Greene, R., and Agerbo, E. (2014). Does a caesarean section increase the time to a second live birth? A register-based cohort study. *Human Reproduction*, 29(11): 2560–68.

Pörtner, C. (2001). Children as insurance. *Journal of Population Economics*, 14(1): 119–36.

Pyy-Martikainen, M. and Rendtel, U. (2009). Measurement errors in retrospective reports of event histories. A validation study with Finnish register data. In *Survey Research Methods*, volume 3, 139–55.

Rindfuss, R. R., Guilkey, D. K., Morgan, S. P., and KRavdal, O. (2010). Child-care availability and fertility in Norway. *Population and Development Review*, 36(4): 725–48.

Romer, P. M. (1990). Endogenous technological change. *The Journal of Political Economy*, 98(5, Part 2): S71–S102.

Rosenzweig, M. and Wolpin, K. (1980). Life-cycle labor supply and fertility: Causal inferences from household models. *The Journal of Political Economy*, 88(2): 328–48.

Rosero-Bixby, L. and Casterline, J. (1993). Modelling diffusion effects in fertility transition. *Population Studies*, 47(1): 147–67.

Samuelson, P. (1958). An exact consumption-loan model of interest with or without the social contrivance of money. *The Journal of Political Economy*, 66(6): 467–82.

Sánchez-Barricarte, J. J. (2017). The long-term determinants of marital fertility in the developed world (19th and 20th centuries): The role of welfare policies. *Demographic Research*, 36: 1255–98.

Sapra, K., McLain, A., Maisog, J., Sundaram, R., and Buck Louis, G. (2014). Successive time to pregnancy among women experiencing pregnancy loss. *Human Reproduction*, 29(11): 2553–59.

Schoumaker, B. and Hayford, S. (2004). A person-period approach to analysing birth histories. *Population*, 59(5): 689–702.

Srinivasan, T. (1988). Fertility and old-age security in an overlapping generations model. *Journal of Quantitative Economics*, 4: 11–17.

Steele, F., Goldstein, H., and Browne, W. (2004). A general multilevel multistate competing risks model for event history data, with an application to a study of contraceptive use dynamics. *Statistical Modelling*, (4): 145–59.

Stein, Z. and Susser, M. (1975). The Dutch famine, 1944–1945, and the reproductive process. i. effects on six indices at birth. *Pediatric Research*, 9(2): 70.

Thompson, W. (1929). Population. *American Journal of Sociology*, 34(6): 959–75.

Torche, F. and Villarreal, A. (2014). Prenatal exposure to violence and birth weight in Mexico: Selectivity, exposure, and behavioral responses. *American Sociological Review*, 79(5): 966–92.

Torres, A. F. C. and Urdinola, B. P. (2019). Armed conflict and fertility in Colombia, 2000–2010. *Population Research and Policy Review*, 38(2): 173–213.

Uzawa, H. (1965). Optimum technical change in an aggregative model of economic growth. *International Economic Review*, 6(1): 18–31.

Vandenbroucke, G. (2014). Fertility and wars: The case of World War I in France. *American Economic Journal: Macroeconomics*, 6(2): 108–36.

Williamson, N. E. (1976). Sex preferences, sex control, and the status of women. *Signs*, 1(4): 847–62.

Willis, R. (1973). A new approach to the economic theory of fertility behavior. *Journal of Political Economy*, 81(2): s14–s63.

Winkelmann, R. (1995). Duration dependence and dispersion in count-data models. *Journal of Business & Economic Statistics*, 13(4): 467–74.

Winkelmann, R. and Zimmermann, K. (1994). Count data models for demographic data. *Mathematical Population Studies*, 4(3): 205–21.

Winkelmann, R. and Zimmermann, K. F. (1991). A new approach for modeling economic count data. *Economics Letters*, 37(2): 139–43.

Woldemicael, G. (2008). Recent fertility decline in Eritrea: Is it a conflict-led transition? *Demographic Research*, 18: 27–58.

Wolpin, K. I. (1984). An estimable dynamic stochastic model of fertility and child mortality. *The Journal of Political Economy*, 92(5): 852–74.

Wooldridge, J. M. (2010). *Econometric analysis of cross section and panel data*. MIT Press.

APPENDIX 5A.1   DATA APPENDIX

We use retrospective fertility data complemented with longitudinal data from the BHPS. The BHPS is a longitudinal study that began in 1991 and ended in 2008; in 2009 a large proportion of the sample of the BHPS became part of the new UK Household Longitudinal Study (UKHLS).

5A.1.1   Coverage

The BHPS original sample issued in 1991 consisted of 8166 nationally representative addresses randomly drawn from the Postcode Address File (a UK comprehensive list of post codes in the country). A three-stage clustered probability design was used, with postcode sectors sampled in the first stage, addresses sampled in the second stage and households sampled in the third stage. In the first stage all postcode delivery points (addresses) listed in the frame were ordered so that an implicit stratification by region and socio-economic status was created using information from the 1981 Census. Such implicit stratification allowed the use of systematic sampling for sample selection, setting a random start and a fixed sampling interval. This procedure ensured that every address in the frame had the same probability of selection and was more convenient than explicit stratification given the large number of existing strata. Postcode sectors were the Primary Sampling Units (PSUs) and have in average of 2500 delivery points.

A total of 250 postcode sectors were selected in the first stage using a selection probability proportional to size, guaranteed by the implicit stratification and the systematic sampling implemented. In the second stage 33 delivery points were selected within each selected postcode sector, using again systematic sampling. Finally, in the third-step non-residential addresses were excluded and all households in the selected delivery point were drawn into the sample unless the delivery point had more than three households, in which case a random sample of three households was taken. Archived response rates were 95 per cent for individuals and 75 per cent for households. The original 1991 sample is composed by 8167 households and 10 264 individuals. All individuals who belong to the original households are the Original Sample Members (OSM) and are re-interviewed every year.[7]

New-born children automatically become panel members and all children are interviewed individually once they reach age 16. Around 13.6 per cent of the original sample was lost due to attrition between wave 1 and wave 2, which amounts approximately to a 86 per cent wave-on-wave response rate. After that, from wave 2 on, wave-on-wave attrition becomes less onerous but still non-negligible, with a loss of around 2 to 3 per cent of the original sample per year. By 2008 the BHPS had a sample of 4411 OSMs, equivalent to 44 per cent of the original sample. On wave 9 (1999) a refreshment sample was taken in Scotland and Wales to complement the survey and alleviate the small sample size (around 500 households in Scotland and 300 households in Wales) taken in each country in the original sample and to allow for country-level comparisons, which became important due to the policy changes that followed the devolution of powers to Scotland and Wales during the 1990s. A total of 1500 extra households and 3395 individuals from Scotland and 1500 households and 3577 individuals from Wales were added to the BHPS sample. In the same vein, in wave 11 (2001) a refreshment sample of approximately 2,000 new households and 5,188 individuals was taken in Northern Ireland.

5A.1.2 Incorporating Retrospective Information

The BHPS is one of the best suited existing surveys to analyse fertility histories in a developed country with a well-established fertility transition. Indeed, the BHPS compiles histories using both retrospective and longitudinal information and carefully records the exact date of birth and gender of every child ever born to a woman even if they do not currently live in the mother's household.

Retrospective fertility data were collected in wave 2 (1992) for the original sample, and in waves 11 and 12 for the Scotland–Wales and Northern Ireland refresh samples. All women aged 16 and over were asked to provide a detailed fertility history, including the number children ever born, the exact date of birth, the gender of the child, and the date of death if the child was no longer alive.

Besides retrospective fertility histories, the BHPS longitudinally logs the exact date of birth and the gender of any child born to an original sample member during the survey study time. Therefore, it is possible to build a detailed and complete fertility history for all adult women in the sample. This is particularly rich fertility data unlike other cross-section or even other longitudinal surveys. (The Swiss Household Panel (SHP), to give an example, only records date of birth and gender of resident children.) The role of some key factors, for example family preference for mixed-gender offspring, cannot be analysed without detailed history of birth outcomes, (see, for instance, Williamson, 1976, Angrist and Evans, 1998). The BHPS allows one to control for such factors.

5A.1.3 The Final Dataset

The analytical sample contains information for 14 134 women aged 15 and over and followed annually during the 1992–2008 period. We have a hierarchical and longitudinal data structure, with newly reported children nested within years, years nested within parity, and parity nested within individuals. There are 87 311 person-year records and, because each woman can report more than one birth per year, a total of 238 895 person-year parity entries are available. A woman can report more than one child in a year either because in that year she gave birth to multiple children (twins, triplets, and so on) or because that year she filled the BHPS retrospective fertility module and reported all children born before the start of the survey. This peculiarity of the data will be fully accounted for in our analysis.

Note that childless women contribute a single row per year and parity is set to zero in all entries. In contrast, women with a positive number of children can contribute one or more rows of data per year. Parity may vary within year. For instance, a woman who had no previous children and gives birth to twins in a particular year will contribute two rows of data that year and parity will have gone from 1 to 2 the same year.

On average there are 1.36 children per woman, with a standard deviation of 1.4, a minimum of 0 and a maximum of 15. The distribution of number of children ever born is given in Figure 5.1. Clearly, 95 per cent of the probability mass is concentrated in the first 5 counts $\{0,1,2,3,4\}$. In fact, 70 per cent of the probability mass falls in the 0,1,2 counts. As a consequence, ignoring outliers in the tail, one could argue that the number of children is a count with limited support. This is typical of fertility data in developed countries and poses a challenge for analysis using count data techniques as standard count models do not fit well counts with limited support. In this context, modelling the whole event history seems to be more attractive.

5A.1.4   Control Variables

Coming back to our fertility history data, the response *resp* is a dichotomous variable that takes on 1 when a birth is reported and zero otherwise. There are a total of 189 999 registered births in our data and various types of controls:

1. Individual-specific and time-fixed variables
2. Individual-specific and time-varying variables
3. Parity-specific and time-invariant variables

Type 1 controls include gender, religion and education. Type 2 controls include age and family income. Finally, type 3 controls include whether the first child was a girl, whether there was a same-gender pair at parity one or whether twins (multiple births) were born in the last pregnancy.

Table 5.5 presents a list of variables and their definition and classifies variables in each control category along presenting some descriptive statistics.

Having type 2 and 3 control variables is critical for modelling and identifying the dynamic and sequential nature of the fertility decisions that women make over their lives. Clearly, each pregnancy is a decision in its own right and when deciding whether to become pregnant women take into account all the information they have at the time (see, for instance, Barmby and Cigno, 1990; Wolpin, 1984). This includes the current number of her offspring (incentives and child benefit systems) (Barmby and Cigno, 1990; Gonzalez 2013), their sex composition (due to gender preference) (Williamson, 1976; Angrist and Evans, 1998), the outcome of her last pregnancy (reduced fecundability after a c-section or miscarriage) (Kok et al., 2003; Hassan and Killick, 2005; O'Neill et al., 2014; Sapra et al., 2014), her work status and salary (Bettio and Villa, 1998; Mira and Ahn 2001), the available childcare support (see, for instance, Ermisch, 1989; Boca, 2002; Rindfuss et al., 2010) and so on. Many such conditions change with time and can influence whether the same woman goes from childless to having her first child, but not whether she goes from having one child to having two or three children. That is, in general, factors that affect the transition from parity 0 to parity 1 may not play any role at all in the transition from parity 1 to parity 2 (a similar argument is put forward in Miranda, 2010, 2013). Here is where using an event history approach to model fertility outcomes becomes attractive, as variation in type 2 and type 3 variables will capture much of the dynamic nature of the counting process.

6.   Measuring discrimination in the labour market
Emmanuel Duguet

Following Heckman (1998), a situation of discrimination against a group is said to arise if an otherwise identical person is treated differently by virtue of that person's group membership, and this group membership by itself has no direct effect on productivity. One important point is that "discrimination is a causal effect defined by a hypothetical ceteris paribus conceptual experiment." In other words, discrimination is defined as an injustice. It should not be confused with inequality, even though the two notions are related. The early theoretical analysis of the economics of discrimination dates back to Becker (1957). The scope of this chapter is more modest. We will simply review the most widespread methodology that the profession uses in order to evaluate discrimination. Discrimination may occur at three main stages in the labour market: hiring, wage setting and promotion. Most empirical studies deal with the first two discrimination types. In the first section, we will present the evaluation in hiring discrimination and, in a second section, the evaluation of wage discrimination.

1.   THE EVALUATION OF HIRING DISCRIMINATION

Hiring discrimination has attracted considerable attention in Europe since the beginning of the 2000s. Baert (2017) surveyed 90 studies conducted in Europe alone between 2005 and 2017, and this number is increasing steadily.[1] Several surveys are available, for Europe and other countries, including Bertrand and Duflo (2017), Neumark (2018) and Rich (2014). In this section, we will present the main tools that have been used in this literature.

The measurement of hiring discrimination needs the collection of specific datasets. Standard databases do not allow for measuring hiring discrimination in a satisfactory manner because of the following problems. First, firm-level datasets only include information about the workers that have been hired. There is no information about the workers whose applications have been rejected. Second, there is a self-selection problem. Workers that feel discriminated against will tend not to apply for the jobs they believe they have no chance of being recruited. Third, the opinion of the workers about whether they have been discriminated against cannot be fully trusted because they generally have no information about their competitors for the job, and they are both judge and jury. Fourth, the information from the recruiters cannot be fully trusted for the same reason and, because discrimination is illegal, they have no incentive to reveal it. Finally, two applications are never identical, so we cannot know for sure whether a candidate was rejected because of discrimination or for an objective, non-observable, difference in the resume.

In order to answer these five questions, researchers perform correspondence tests. A correspondence test is a ground experiment. The researcher replies to the ads instead of real candidates. If we wish to test gender discrimination, we should send two resumes, one for each gender, with comparable productive characteristics. This fixes the five previous problems: first, the data are not limited to the candidates that have been successful but also includes all the applicants that failed to reach an interview. Second, there is no self-selection because the applications are sent by the researcher. Third, we observe an objective answer from the firm, not an opinion from the candidate. Fourth, we observe the true behaviour of the recruiter. Fifth, the applications have been designed to be equivalent.

In a correspondence test, we do not send candidates to the interview in order to avoid personality biases (Riach and Rich, 2002). When called, the candidate replies that they have already found a job. This is the "callback" variable. Here, it is possible to examine in which order the candidates are called. Some workers may be called in priority, but other workers may still be called when the preferred workers are not available.

Several problems have to be fixed. The candidates must be credible, a sufficient number of observations may be collected and some validity test may be provided. Once the data are collected, an adapted statistical analysis should be performed. Experimental data have specificities that should be accounted for. Among them, the researcher sets the values of the candidates' variables.

We will first recall the simplest tests, then we will show how they can be related to the least squares method. Last, we present more advanced methods which can be used to reveal the presence of discriminatory components inside the callback rates. The main point for all these methods is that the answers to all candidates on the same job add are correlated because the recruiter replies to all of them at the same time. This affects the way the standard errors are computed. We indicate how the statistics should be adapted.

1.1　The Correspondence Test

Several fake candidate applications are sent in answer to a job advertisement. The data are collected daily until the end of the experiment, which lasts several months in general. Many precautions must be taken in order to avoid detection. Among them are the following:

- time consistency: the diplomas and the information about tenure must be consistent with the age of the candidates.
- the resumes must be similar but not identical and examined by a professional associated with the correspondence test.
- the postal addresses must exhibit similar transportation times and neighbourhood reputations.
- other causes of discrimination must be avoided. If we test the existence of gender discrimination, we should send candidates from the same origin in order to avoid origin discrimination weakening the identification of gender discrimination.
- resume templates may be rotated among the candidates.
- no photo should be used, since it can influence the answer (Rich, 2018).
- letters must be posted from different post offices.
- emails should be sent from different or undetectable servers.
- each application is followed by one person only.
- the testers must be tested.
- the confidentiality must be complete until all the data are collected.

1.2   Comparisons of Proportions

Let us consider the two-candidate test. We have performed a correspondence test and have collected data about the callback of two candidates, denoted $j \in \mathbf{J} = \{A, B\}$. For each job ad, we have two answers from the recruiter. The candidates, can receive two answers only:[2] yes (coded 1) or no (coded 0). We summarise the situation in Table 6.1:

Table 6.1   Correspondence test

$j = B$ $j = A$	yes (1)	no (0)
yes (1)	$p(1, 1)$, equal treatment	$p(1, 0)$, B discriminated
no (0)	$p(0, 1)$, A discriminated	$p(0, 0)$, equal treatment

where $p(d_A, d_B)$ is the proportion of answers for which candidate A was answered $d_A \in \{0, 1\}$ and candidate B was answered $d_B \in \{0, 1\}$. Equal treatment happens when both candidates have the same answers. The corresponding proportion equals $p(0, 0) + p(1, 1)$. The other proportions indicate an unequal treatment, which is interpreted as a discrimination because the applications have been made equivalent. In practice, the researchers use the *net* discrimination coefficient against candidate B:

$$D(A, B) = \Pr(\text{A called back}) - \Pr(\text{B called back})$$
$$= p(1,1) + p(1,0) - (p(1,1) + p(0,1))$$
$$= p(1,0) - p(0,1),$$

which is the excess probability of discriminatory cases against candidate B.[3] Testing the equality of the callbacks of the two candidates is equivalent to testing $p(1, 0) = p(0, 1)$. If a correspondence test is done on a given occupation, this means that we define discrimination at the job market level rather than at the firm level; $D(A, B) > 0$ means that there is discrimination against candidate B at the job market level and $D(A, B) < 0$ that there is discrimination against candidate A.

Now let us consider the discrimination test globally. What critical value should we use? The null hypothesis is the absence of discrimination $D(A, B) = 0$ against $D(A, B) \neq 0$. Therefore, we may define the type I and II errors as in Table 6.2.

Table 6.2   Error types

Truth Conclusion	$D(A, B) = 0$	$D(A, B) \neq 0$
$D(A, B) = 0$	Correct	Type II error (β)
$D(A, B) \neq 0$	Type I error (α)	Correct

The standard test will take the absence of discrimination as the null hypothesis (H_0: $D(A, B) = 0$). Then, we should distinguish two types of errors. The type I error (α) occurs when we reject the null hypothesis while it is true; in our context, this means that we conclude there is discrimination while there is none. The type II error happens when we accept the null hypothesis while it is wrong; in other words, we conclude that there is no discrimination while there is some (β). The power of the test is $\zeta = 1 - \beta$, which is the probability of concluding that there is discrimination when this is true. Standard test theory fixes α and lets β (and so ζ) be free. Moreover, the lower α, the lower ζ. On small samples, a small type I error can correspond to a very small power. By setting a low value for α, such as 1 per cent, we can end up with a very small probability of finding discrimination when there is some. A first approach keeps the same sample size and argues that α should be taken relatively "high," such as 5 per cent or 10 per cent. A second approach proposes to determine an optimal sample size for a given testing problem. For a given α, we will get a higher ζ if the sample size is larger.

Consider the first approach. Ideally, we would like to measure the cost of each error type and minimise a loss function. What is the cost of a type I error? If we conclude that there is discrimination while there is none, the cost should be close to 0. Indeed, if there is no discrimination, nobody can prove that there is some before a court, and no firm should be condemned for this. There should be no important prejudice. A type II error can also be costly, since it implies that we conclude to no discrimination while there is some. This conclusion could weaken the arguments of the workers discriminated against since discrimination is hard to prove. Moreover, this cost should be multiplied by the size of the population. Considering gender discrimination, even a small discrimination coefficient would imply a very high cost because of the large size of the population. Inconclusive results could even be used to weaken anti-discrimination policies. This gives an incentive not to take a low α.

However, the most satisfactory answer seems to determine an optimal sample size before running the experiment so as to avoid adjusting the α on a qualitative, and somewhat arbitrary, basis. We show how to compute a minimal sample size after presenting the paired Student tests.

Once the data have been collected, we may seek to measure discrimination. However, some caution is to be taken. First, we must keep in mind that the answers to all the candidates on the same job are correlated, since the same recruiter replies to all the candidates. This precludes the use of independent samples tests or standard ordinary least squares (henceforth, OLS) methods. We will use *paired* tests. A common practice consists in using stacked OLS regressions. We show that it provides both a good measurement of discrimination and a bad estimation of the variances. The reason is that standard OLS assume the independence of all observations when computing the standard errors and, for this reason, cannot be used for a valid inference. Instead, one should use either paired OLS regressions or clustered standard errors. We show that the method of Arellano (1987), developed originally for panel data, can be used to compute the standard error used in paired Student statistics. The next section describes how it is possible to extract information from more complicated correspondence tests and reveals the discriminatory component inside the callback rates. This part may also be useful for tests where all the candidates could not reply to all of the job ads. We show how to make optimal use of all the information available.

Proportions tests. Since we have several candidates reply to the same job ad, we can compare them easily with a paired test. The advantage of paired tests is that, on the one hand they use the differences of treatment between two candidates so that their interpretation is straightforward, and, on the other hand, the paired tests do not require us to account explicitly for the correlation among the answers to the candidates, since the statistic includes the right correction.

We consider two candidates selected among the total number of candidates. Consider a job ad $i \in \mathbf{I}$, where $\mathbf{I}$ denotes the index set of all adds and let I denote their number. The set of candidates is denoted $\mathbf{J}$ and their number J. For candidate $j \in \mathbf{J}$ the answer is coded as a dummy variable denoted $d_{ji} \in \{0, 1\}$, where, by convention, $d_{ji} = 0$ represents a "no" and $d_{ji} = 1$ a "yes." The theoretical success probabilities associated with the candidates are denoted p_j. By definition d_{ji} follows a Bernoulli process with probability p_j. Consider two candidates, $\mathbf{J} = \{A, B\}$, we wish to perform the following test:

$$H_0 : p_A - p_B = 0$$

$$H_a : p_A - p_B \neq 0.$$

Paired Student test. The null hypothesis is the absence of discrimination since both candidates are treated equally in responding to the same ads. In the case of rejection, we can have either discrimination against candidate A ($p_A < p_B$) or discrimination against candidate B ($p_A > p_B$). The test can be done with a Student test. However, the reader should keep in mind that we need a *paired* Student test. Indeed, the answers to all the candidates on a given ad are correlated because they are given by the same recruiter. Therefore, we cannot assume that the two candidates come from two independent samples, as is usually done with the two-sample Student test. By convention, we will denote the means with a bar so that the empirical callback rate of candidate j is denoted

$$\bar{d}_j = \frac{1}{I} \sum_{i \in I} d_{ji}, \ j \in J.$$

When we have paired data, we can compute the difference of answers between the two candidates for each ad and take the mean on this difference. Consider two candidates for the job ad i; we observe the couple of answers (d_{Ai}, d_{Bi}), $i \in \mathbf{I}$. The difference between the answers to candidates A and B, denoted $\delta_i = d_{Ai} - d_{Bi}$, can take three values:

$$\delta_i = \begin{cases} 1 & \text{candidate A prefered} \\ 0 & \text{equal treatment} \\ -1 & \text{candidate B prefered} \end{cases}.$$

The paired test is simply the Student test of a zero mean on this difference since

$$E(\delta) = E(d_A - d_B) = p_A - p_B.$$

Since $\bar{\delta} = \bar{d}_A - \bar{d}_B$, testing that this quantity is close to 0 is equivalent to testing for the absence of discrimination. The paired Student statistic, denoted T_p, equals

$$T_p = \frac{|\bar{\delta}|}{\sqrt{\hat{V}(\bar{\delta})}},$$

where $\hat{V}$ denotes the empirical variance. The following unbiased estimator is commonly used:

$$\hat{V}(\bar{\delta}) = \frac{\hat{V}(\delta)}{I} = \frac{1}{I(I-1)}\sum_{i \in I}(\delta_i - \bar{\delta})^2.$$

One can easily show that

$$\hat{V}(\delta) = \hat{V}(d_A) + \hat{V}(d_B) - 2\hat{C}\text{ov}(d_A, d_B),$$

where Côv is the empirical covariance.[4] Notice that the two-sample Student statistic is obtained only when $\hat{C}\text{ov}(d_A, d_B) = 0$. The T_p statistic is used to test the absence of net discrimination. On large samples, we use the normal approximation.[5] For a test at the α level, we will reject the null hypothesis when $T_p \geq z_{1-\alpha/2}$, where z is the quantile of the standard normal distribution.[6] Notice that we measure *net* discrimination since some firms may prefer candidate A and others candidate B. What we measure is whether, at the job market level, comparable candidates are treated equally.

Minimum sample size. The impossibility of controlling the power of the test may be undesirable from a social viewpoint. In this section, we show how to compute the sample size needed for a test with a level α, a power ζ and a minimum detectable value for $\delta = p_A - p_B$. We consider the following test:

$$H_0 : \delta = 0$$

$$H_a : \delta = \delta^*,$$

where $\delta^* > 0$ is a minimum detectable value. It represents the difference threshold from which we consider that there is a relevant amount of discrimination. We wish to reject H_0 with probability α when H_0 is true and to reject H_0 with probability ζ when H_a is true. In order to perform the test, we have a sample of treatment differences, δ_i, and compute their mean $\bar{\delta}$. We assume that δ_i has variance σ^2. Using a normal approximation, $\bar{\delta}$ should be distributed with a variance equal to σ^2 / I, with a 0 mean under the null hypothesis and a δ^* mean under the alternative hypothesis. We should have

$$\Pr\left(\bar{\delta} > \frac{\sigma u_{1-\alpha}}{\sqrt{I}} \Big| H_0\right) = \alpha,$$

where $u_{1-\alpha}$ is the $1 - \alpha$ quantile of the standard normal distribution (1.645 for $\alpha = 0.05$). Under the null hypothesis, $\bar{\delta}$ should converge to zero and this equality should be satisfied. Now consider the power inequality. We should have

$$\Pr\left(\bar{\delta} > \frac{\sigma u_{1-\alpha}}{\sqrt{I}} \Big| H_a\right) \geq \zeta.$$

We have the following equivalence:

$$\bar{\delta} > \frac{\sigma u_{1-\alpha}}{\sqrt{I}} \Leftrightarrow \sqrt{I} \times \frac{\bar{\delta} - \delta^*}{\sigma} > u_{1-\alpha} - \sqrt{I} \times \frac{\delta^*}{\sigma},$$

since the left-hand term follows a standard normal distribution under H_a. We get

$$\Pr\left(\sqrt{I} \times \frac{\bar{\delta} - \delta^*}{\sigma} > u_{1-\alpha} - \sqrt{I} \times \frac{\delta^*}{\sigma} \right) = 1 - \Phi\left(u_{1-\alpha} - \sqrt{I} \times \frac{\delta^*}{\sigma} \right)$$

$$= \Phi\left(\sqrt{I} \times \frac{\delta^*}{\sigma} - u_{1-\alpha} \right),$$

so that

$$\Phi\left(\sqrt{I} \times \frac{\delta^*}{\sigma} - u_{1-\alpha} \right) \geq \zeta \Leftrightarrow I \geq \left(\frac{\sigma}{\delta^*} (\Phi^{-1}(\zeta) + u_{1-\alpha}) \right)^2.$$

Let us take an example. Let $p_A = 0.50$ and $p_A - p_B = \delta^* = 0.10$. We also let $\alpha = \beta = 10$ per cent so that the power is set at 90 per cent ($z_{0.9} = 1.28$). We just need the variance of the statistic. The callback dummies verify $V(d_j) = p_j (1 - p_j)$ and we should compute

$$V(d_A - d_B) = V(d_A) + V(d_A) - 2\text{Cov}(d_A, d_B),$$

and we do not know their covariance. But we can use the following bound on the correlation coefficient:

$$-1 \leq \frac{\text{Cov}(d_A, d_B)}{\sqrt{V(d_A)V(d_B)}} \leq 1,$$

which implies that the variances

$$\sigma^2 = V(d_A - d_B) \leq V(d_A) + V(d_A) + 2\sqrt{V(d_A)V(d_B)} = \tilde{\sigma}^2,$$

and we can use it to get a conservative value for I. In our example, we get

$$V(d_A) = 0.25, \ V(d_B) = 0.24, \tilde{\sigma}^2 = 0.98,$$

so that

$$I \geq \frac{0.98}{0.01} \times (3.29)^2 \simeq 642,$$

which is a relatively high value. A median assumption may ignore the covariance (since it can be negative or positive), and in this case we would have $\sigma^2 = 0.49$ and $I \geq 321$.

Paired OLS regression. It is possible to perform the previous test by running a very simple regression. One should regress the treatment difference variable δ_i on the constant term. The model is: $\delta_i = b_0 \times 1 + u_i$ where b_0 is the intercept and u_i the disturbance. Let e_1 be the column unit vector of size I and δ the column vector of all δ_i. The OLS formula gives

$$\hat{b}_0 = (e_1' e_1)^{-1} e_1' \delta$$

$$= \left(\sum_{i \in I} 1^2 \right)^{-1} \sum_{i \in I} 1 \times \delta_i$$

$$= \frac{1}{I} \sum_{i \in I} \delta_i$$

$$= \bar{\delta} \ .$$

The residual of this regression equals $\hat{u}_i = \delta_i - \hat{b}_0 = \delta_i - \bar{\delta}$. Furthermore, denote $\hat{\sigma}^2$, the empirical variance of the residual, and we have:

$$\hat{V}(\hat{b}_0) = \hat{\sigma}^2 (e_1' e_1)^{-1} = \frac{\hat{\sigma}^2}{I},$$

and standard OLS software will provide:

$$\hat{\sigma}^2 = \frac{1}{I-1} \sum_{i \in I} \hat{u}_i^2 = \frac{1}{I-1} \sum_{i \in I} (\delta_i - \bar{\delta})^2$$

so that we get $\hat{V}(\hat{b}_0) = \hat{V}(\bar{\delta})$. The Student statistic of the paired OLS regression is identical to the paired Student statistic. Unfortunately, this regression is not always used. Instead, stacked regressions are often preferred. We show in the next section that they provide the wrong variance, and we also show how it can be corrected.

Stacked OLS regressions. Stacked regressions are popular in the applied literature. In this setting, one performs a regression of the callback dummy variable on a constant term and a dummy variable for the reference group. Consider our example, we define a dummy variable x_{ji} equal to 1 for belonging to group A (equal to 0 otherwise):

$$\forall i, \ x_{ji} = \begin{cases} 1 & \text{if } j = A \\ 0 & \text{if } j = B \end{cases},$$

where we notice that the definition does not depend on i. This is because, in a field experiment, the explanatory variables are *constructed*: we have the two candidates reply to the same ads. Another interesting point is the number of observations: we stack the I answers of candidates A and B so that the number of observations in the regression in now 2×I. In order to get the probability difference, we write a linear probability model as

$$d_{ji} = c_0 + c_1 x_{ji} + u_{ji},$$

with $E(u_{ji}) = 0$ without loss of generality, provided the model includes a constant term. We easily get:

$$E(d_{Ai}) = c_0 + c_1$$

$$E(d_{Bi}) = c_0$$

so that, using $E(d_{ji}) = p_j$, we get:

$$c_0 = p_B$$

$$c_1 = p_A - p_B.$$

Therefore, the theoretical value of the OLS coefficient c_1 gives the discrimination coefficient. The relationship is also valid for the empirical counterparts. We rewrite the model as:

$$d_{ji} = X_{ji}c + u_{ji},$$

with $X_{ji} = (1, x_{ji})$ and $c' = (c_0, c_1)$. Applying OLS is equivalent to solving the system $X'X\hat{c} = X'd$. The cross-products are specific: $e'_{21}e_{21} = 2I$ since there are $2I$ observations after stacking. For $e'_{21}x = x'e_{21}$, we just need to consider that $x_{Ai} = 1$ and $x_{Bi} = 0$, $\forall i$. This gives

$$e'_{21}x = \sum_{i \in I} \sum_{j \in J} x_{ji}$$

$$= \sum_{i \in I} 1$$

$$= I,$$

and for $x'x$ we only need to remark that $x_{ji} = x_{ji}^2$ since it is a binary variable. Therefore,

$$x'x = \sum_{i \in I} \sum_{j \in J} x_{ji}^2$$

$$= \sum_{i \in I} \sum_{j \in J} x_{ji}$$

$$= I.$$

For the right-hand cross-products, we get:

$$e'_1 d = \sum_{i \in I} \sum_{j \in J} d_{ji}$$

$$= \sum_{i \in I} d_{Ai} + \sum_{i \in I} d_{Bi}$$

$$= I \times (\bar{d}_A + \bar{d}_B),$$

the total number of callbacks, and

$$x'y = \sum_{i \in I} \sum_{j \in J} x_{ji} d_{ji}$$

$$= \sum_{i \in I} d_{Ai}$$

$$= I \times \bar{d}_A,$$

the number of callbacks received by candidate 1. Let $I_j = I \times \bar{d}_j$ be the number of callbacks for the candidate j, we should solve

$$\begin{pmatrix} 2I & I \\ I & I \end{pmatrix} \begin{pmatrix} \hat{c}_0 \\ \hat{c}_1 \end{pmatrix} = \begin{pmatrix} I_A + I_B \\ I_A \end{pmatrix}.$$

Using

$$\begin{pmatrix} 2I & I \\ I & I \end{pmatrix}^{-1} = \frac{1}{I} \begin{pmatrix} 1 & -1 \\ -1 & 2 \end{pmatrix},$$

we get

$$\begin{pmatrix} \hat{c}_0 \\ \hat{c}_1 \end{pmatrix} = \frac{1}{I} \begin{pmatrix} I_B \\ I_A - I_B \end{pmatrix} = \begin{pmatrix} \bar{d}_B \\ \bar{d}_A - \bar{d}_B \end{pmatrix}.$$

The OLS regression coefficient $\hat{c}_1$ of the group dummy variable x_{ij} equals $\bar{\delta}$ and measures discrimination.

The only problem with OLS is that it gives the wrong standard errors. We will first show that it gives the two-sample Student variance and how to fix the problem with a clusterisation of the covariance matrix. For the variance, we need to compute $\hat{\sigma}_u^2 (X'X)^{-1}$. Here, we simply note that $\forall i$:

$$\hat{u}_{Ai} = d_{Ai} - (\hat{c}_0 + \hat{c}_1) = d_{Ai} - \bar{d}_A$$
$$\hat{u}_{Bi} = d_{Bi} - (\hat{c}_0) = d_{Bi} - \bar{d}_B.$$

For the variance we should consider that there are $2I$ observations and 2 parameters, which makes for $2I - 2 = 2(I - 1)$ degrees of freedom:

$$\hat{\sigma}_u^2 = \frac{1}{2(I-1)} \sum_{i \in I} \sum_{j \in J} \hat{u}_{ji}^2$$

$$= \frac{1}{2(I-1)} \sum_{i \in I} (d_{Ai} - \bar{d}_A)^2 + (d_{Bi} - \bar{d}_B)^2$$

$$= \frac{1}{2} (\hat{V}(d_A) + \hat{V}(d_B)),$$

and

$$\hat{V}(\hat{c}) = \frac{1}{2}(\hat{V}(d_A) + \hat{V}(d_B)) \times \frac{1}{I}\begin{pmatrix} 1 & -1 \\ -1 & 2 \end{pmatrix}$$

so that

$$\hat{V}(\hat{c}_1) = \frac{1}{I}(\hat{V}(d_A) + \hat{V}(d_B)),$$

which is the variance used in the two-sample Student statistic. It is not valid in this context because the answers to the same ad are not independent from each other. We show how to correct it in the next section.

Clustered variances. We need to account for the correlation between the callback dummies from the same ad. When the disturbance covariance matrix is $V(u) = \sigma_u^2 \mathrm{Id}_1$, the OLS variance formula is $V(\hat{c}) = \sigma_u^2 (X'X)^{-1}$, but when there are correlations between the observations, we must write $V(u) = \Omega$ and the OLS variance formula becomes $V(\hat{c}) = (X'X)^{-1} X'\Omega X(X'X)^{-1}$. In our case, Ω has a specific shape: it is block diagonal, since the callback decisions are assumed to be correlated on the *same* ad only. Let Ω_i be the 2×2 ad-level covariance matrix, $d_i' = (d_{Ai}, d_{Bi})$ the callback vector of ad i and

$$X_i = \begin{pmatrix} 1 & x_{Ai} \\ 1 & x_{Bi} \end{pmatrix} = \begin{pmatrix} 1 & 1 \\ 1 & 0 \end{pmatrix}, \; U_i = \begin{pmatrix} u_{Ai} \\ u_{Bi} \end{pmatrix},$$

the explanatory variables matrix and the disturbance vector for ad i. Notice that the explanatory variable x is chosen by the econometrician and alternatively takes the values 1 and 0 for each ad. The OLS variance equals

$$V(\hat{c}) = \left(\sum_{i\in I} X_i' X_i\right)^{-1} \sum_{i\in I} X_i' \Omega_i X_i \left(\sum_{i\in I} X_i' X_i\right)^{-1}.$$

The structure of the data is similar to a balanced panel data problem, where the ad i represents the individual, and the candidate j the time dimension. Arellano (1987) proposed the following estimator:

$$\hat{V}_A(\hat{c}) = \left(\sum_{i\in I} X_i' X_i\right)^{-1} \sum_{i\in I} X_i' \hat{U}_i \hat{U}_i' X_i \left(\sum_{i\in I} X_i' X_i\right)^{-1}.$$

In order to get the paired Student test, we just need to add the following correction for the degrees of freedom:

$$\hat{V}(\hat{c}) = \frac{I}{I-1} \hat{V}_A(\hat{c}).$$

Using

$$\hat{U}_i = \begin{pmatrix} d_{Ai} - \bar{d}_A \\ d_{Bi} - \bar{d}_B \end{pmatrix},$$

we get

$$\sum_{i\in I} X_i'\hat{U}_i\hat{U}_i'X_i = (I-1)\times$$

$$\begin{pmatrix} \hat{V}(d_A)+2\hat{C}ov(d_A,d_B)+\hat{V}(d_B) & \hat{V}(d_A)+\hat{C}ov(d_A,d_B) \\ \hat{V}(d_A)+\hat{C}ov(d_A,d_B) & \hat{V}(d_A) \end{pmatrix},$$

and

$$\left(\sum_{i\in I} X_i'X_i\right)^{-1} = I^{-1}\times\begin{pmatrix} 1 & -1 \\ -1 & 2 \end{pmatrix}$$

so that

$$\hat{V}(\hat{c}) = \begin{pmatrix} \hat{V}(\bar{d}_B) & \hat{C}ov(\bar{d}_B,\bar{d}_A-\bar{d}_B) \\ \hat{C}ov(\bar{d}_B,\bar{d}_A-\bar{d}_B) & \hat{V}(\bar{d}_A-\bar{d}_B) \end{pmatrix}$$

$$= \begin{pmatrix} \hat{V}(\bar{d}_B) & \hat{C}ov(\bar{d}_B,\bar{\delta}) \\ \hat{C}ov(\bar{d}_B,\bar{\delta}) & \hat{V}(\bar{\delta}) \end{pmatrix}.$$

Therefore, one just needs to multiply the Arellano Student by $\sqrt{(I-1)/I}$ in order to get the paired t statistic. This correction is negligible on large samples.

1.3   Regression Models

The previous models may be augmented by a list of explanative variables. Indeed, the tester can choose the characteristics of the candidates, but they cannot choose the characteristics of the firm. This opens the possibility of studying conditional discrimination, which is a discrimination that occurs only on some labour contracts. For instance, a worker may be discriminated against on a long-term contract but not on a short-term contract. In order to test for this assumption, we should add the contract term into the model and evaluate its impact on the difference in treatment between the candidates. There are two main ways to extend the comparison tests: paired regressions and stacked regressions. With paired regressions, the relevant variable is the callback difference between two candidates. Any significant variable may reveal conditional discrimination. Let us consider a recruiter that chooses between two candidates, $j = A, B$. We will assume that each candidate generates a utility level and that a candidate will be invited each time a threshold is crossed. The utility of recruiter i for candidate j is denoted

$$v_{ji}^* = X_i b_j + \alpha_i + \varepsilon_{ji}, \tag{6.1}$$

where X_i are the observable firm characteristics and b_j the regression coefficient for the candidate j. The α_i term is the job ad correlated effect (or "fixed effect"), since the same recruiter replies to all the candidates and ε_{ji} is the idiosyncratic error term, typically a white noise. We observe the callback dummy variable:

$$v_{ji} = \begin{cases} 1 & \text{if } v_{ji}^* > 0 \\ 0 & \text{otherwise} \end{cases},$$

where 0 is the normalised reservation utility level without loss of generality provided the model includes a constant term. Note that it may also depend on each recruiter i through the unobservable term α_i. The real assumption here is that all the candidates face the same threshold, a point that may not always be true.[7] Comparing two candidates A and B, we can consider their utility difference for the recruiter:

$$\delta_i^* = v_{Ai}^* - v_{Bi}^*. \tag{6.2}$$

Three outcomes are possible:

$$\delta_i = \begin{cases} 1 & \text{A invited alone, if } \delta_i^* \geq c_A \\ 0 & \text{equal treatment, if } c_B \leq \delta_i^* < c_A, \\ -1 & \text{B invited alone, if } \delta_i^* < c_B \end{cases}$$

where c_A and c_B are unknown thresholds. With our notations, these three events will occur with respective probabilities p_{10}, $p_{00} + p_{11}$ and p_{01}. In other words, candidates with similar utility levels will be treated equally, and discrimination will occur when the recruiter perceives too strong a difference between them. We also notice that the expectation of this variable equals

$$E(\delta) = 1 \times p_{10} + 0 \times (p_{00} + p_{11}) - 1 \times p_{01} = D(A, B),$$

the discrimination coefficient we have already seen. The most straightforward extension to regression is obtained by combining (6.1) and (6.2). We get:

$$\delta_i^* = X_i b_A + \alpha_i + \varepsilon_{Ai} - (X_i b_B + \alpha_i + \varepsilon_{Bi})$$
$$= X_i \beta + \eta_i,$$

with $\beta = b_A - b_B$ and $\eta_i = \varepsilon_{Ai} - \varepsilon_{Bi}$. The specific form of the model will depend on the distributional assumption about η. The simplest case is the difference of two linear probability models, which gives a linear probability model. The δ parameter will measure discrimination since we explain a difference of treatment. In order to simplify the exposition, consider that we run a regression on the centred variables:

$$\delta_i = \beta_0 + (x_i - \bar{x})\beta_1 + \eta_i.$$

Taking the expectation, we get $E(\delta_i) = \beta_0$, the constant term of the model. This is the unconditional discrimination coefficient at the mean point of the sample $(x_i = \bar{x})$. When $\beta_1 = 0$, it is equal to $D(A, B)$. It does not depend on the firms' characteristics or on the characteristics of the labour contract.[8] The other discrimination term β_1, on the contrary, acts in interaction with ad i's characteristics. This is the vector of the conditional discrimination coefficients. A positive coefficient will indicate a discrimination source against candidate B, and a negative coefficient against candidate A. This equation is easily estimated by OLS and does not need a clusterisation of the variances because the left-hand variable is taken in differences.

Ordered models. Although convenient, the linear probability model has the following fault: it could happen that the predictions are outside the $[-1,1]$ range, which is compulsory for δ_i since it is the difference of two binary variables.[9] In this case, one may prefer to make another assumption about the distribution of η_i. Assuming normality, $\eta_i \sim N(0,\sigma^2)$ will give an ordered probit model, with[10]

$$\Pr(d_i = 1) = \Pr[X_i b + \eta_i \geq c_A]$$

$$= 1 - \Phi\left(\frac{c_A - X_i \beta}{\sigma}\right),$$

$$\Pr(d_i = 0) = \Pr[c_B \leq X_i \beta + \eta_i < c_A]$$

$$= \Phi\left(\frac{c_A - X_i \beta}{\sigma}\right) - \Phi\left(\frac{c_B - X_i \beta}{\sigma}\right)$$

$$\Pr(d_i = -1) = \Pr[X_i \beta + \eta_i \leq c_B]$$

$$= \Phi\left(\frac{c_B - X_i \beta}{\sigma}\right).$$

With this type of model, one should be careful that the thresholds will absorb the constant term. For instance, consider the last probability, with $\beta' = (\beta_0, \beta_1')$ and $X_i = (1, x_i - \bar{x})$:

$$\Phi\left(\frac{c_B - X_i \beta}{\sigma}\right) = \Phi\left(\frac{c_B - \beta_0 - \beta_1(x_i - \bar{x})}{\sigma}\right)$$

so that we define a new set of parameters: $\gamma_B = (c_B - \beta_0)/\sigma$ and $\gamma_1 = \beta_1/\sigma$ and get the probability:

$$\Phi\left(\gamma_B - \gamma_1(x_i - \bar{x})\right).$$

Performing a similar operation for the first probability, we define $\gamma_A = (c_A - \beta_0)/\sigma$, so that overall:

$$\Pr(d_i = 1) = 1 - \Phi\left(\gamma_A - \gamma_1(x_i - \bar{x})\right)$$

$$\Pr(d_i = 0) = \Phi\left(\gamma_A - \gamma_1(x_i - \bar{x})\right) - \Phi\left(\gamma_B - \gamma_1(x_i - \bar{x})\right)$$

$$\Pr(d_i = -1) = \Phi\left(\gamma_B - \gamma_1(x_i - \bar{x})\right).$$

The software will typically give an estimate of $(\gamma_A, \gamma_B, \gamma_1)$. When the right-hand variables are centred, the discrimination coefficient at the average point of the sample $(x_i = \bar{x})$ will be given by:

$$\bar{D}(A, B) = \Pr(d_i = 1) - \Pr(d_i = -1)$$

$$= 1 - \Phi(\gamma_A) - \Phi(\gamma_B),$$

and its asymptotic variance can be estimated by the delta method. Letting $g(\gamma) = 1 - \Phi(\gamma_A) - \Phi(\gamma_B)$, we get:

$$\hat{V}(\hat{\gamma}) = \frac{\delta g}{\delta \gamma}(\hat{\gamma})\hat{\Omega}_\gamma \left(\frac{\delta g}{\delta \gamma}(\hat{\gamma}) \right)',$$

where $\hat{\Omega}_\gamma$ is the estimated asymptotic covariance matrix of $\hat{\gamma}$ provided by the software. It is also possible to estimate an effect for each observation of d_i and to compute their average, or to draw their density.

Stacked regressions. When the data are stacked, the estimation raises specific issues. Consider equation (6.1). Considering two candidates for the same ad, we have

$$v_{Ai}^* = X_i b_A + u_{Ai}$$

$$v_{Bi}^* = X_i b_B + u_{Bi},$$

with $u_{ji} = \alpha_i + \varepsilon_{ji}$. Letting $V(\alpha_i) = \sigma_\alpha^2$, $V(\varepsilon_{ji}) = \sigma_j$ and $u_i' = (u_{Ai}, u_{Bi})$ we conclude that there is an ad-level block correlation in the model:

$$V(u_i) = \begin{pmatrix} \sigma_\alpha^2 + \sigma_A^2 & \sigma_\alpha^2 \\ \sigma_\alpha^2 & \sigma_\alpha^2 + \sigma_B^2 \end{pmatrix},$$

so that a clusterisation of the covariance matrix will be needed. Also notice that the model is heteroskedastic between the two candidates, like in Neumark (2012). An additional issue is raised when the ad fixed effect α_i is correlated with the right-hand variables: the estimates may not be consistent anymore.[11]

Furthermore, even in the favourable case where the effect is not correlated, the model should allow for $b_A \neq b_B$. The only solution is adding the cross-products of a group dummy with the X_i variables. In order to develop the argument, let us rewrite the estimation problem. The individual will be indexed by $n = 1,\dots, 2I$ since there are two candidates for the I ads. We introduce a dummy variable, A_n, equal to 1 if the individual n is in the potentially favoured group (A), 0 otherwise. Let us also assume that the data are stacked at the ad level so that all the odd indices refer to the A candidates and all the even indices to the B candidates.[12] The regression equation should be written

$$v_n^* = X_n b_A + A_n X_n (b_A - b_B) + u_n,$$

where $u_n = u_{A,(n+1)/2}$ if n is odd and $u_n = u_{B,n/2}$ if n is even. When $A_n = 1$, we get $X_i b_A + u_{Ai}$ and when $A_n = 0$ we get $X_i b_B + u_{Bi}$. Notice that the X variables include the constant term so that the group dummy is among the regressors. A widespread practice consists in estimating a model with X and A alone. It will be valid as long as $b_A = b_B$ for all variables but the intercept. To make it more sensible, let $X_n = (1, x_n)$ and $b_j' = (b_{0j}, b_{1j})$ for $j \in \{A, B\}$. We get

$$v_n^* = b_{0A} + b_{1A} x_n + A_n (b_{0A} - b_{0B}) + A_n x_n (b_{1A} - b_{1B}),$$

and it is clear that the model with x_n and A_n alone can only be valid if $b_{1A} = b_{1B}$.

Overall, the stacked model raises two problems. First is the fixed effect problem. When there is no significant right-hand variable, ignoring the issue is not problematic (as we saw), because there is no variable in the model that is susceptible to being correlated with the fixed effect. But this result does not extend to models with explanative variables, since a correlation with the fixed effect leads to inconsistent estimates. A second problem happens when the coefficients of the explanative variables differ in the two groups of workers. One should include the cross-products of the explanative variables with the group dummy among the regressors. Forgetting these cross-products will create a missing variable bias because these missing variables are, by definition, correlated with the regressors.

In conclusion, the paired ordered models, based on a difference of treatment between two candidates, seem to be a better tool because they eliminate the fixed effect and allow for a differentiated effect of the explanative variables among the applicants to a job. They are also easier to implement, since they do not require a heteroskedastic Probit estimation.

1.4   Component Models

Some correspondence tests have a more complicated structure than the basic tests we have studied so far. There may be several characteristics studied together (for example gender and age) so that several candidates may be affected by the same type of discrimination. Young women and older women may both be discriminated because they are women. Another example happens when all the candidates do not reply to all the job ads but only some of them, with a rotation. All the paired comparisons cannot be made on all the job ads, but only a number of them. In this case, we need to combine the information from all the possible combinations in a coherent and efficient manner (Duguet et al., 2018). Several types of models can be used: linear or transformed. In the first case, the estimation will proceed from callback rate differences and difference in differences. This may be inconvenient when the callback rates are close to zero and the model leads to prediction outside the unit interval. In the second type of model, the predictions are bounded, and one has to work with concepts such as odds ratios rather than rates. Overall, both models allow us to control for unobserved heterogeneity. These models are also useful in overidentified cases. They allow for testing of some restrictions in the structure of discrimination.

A rationalisation of differences method. The first way to use a component model is to determine the right differences to use in the comparisons and to deal with the case where there are several ways to compute a given coefficient. Consider a situation with two types of discrimination: gender and origin. We send four candidates on each offer:[13] the local origin man ($j = 1$), the foreign origin man ($j = 2$), the local origin woman ($j = 3$) and the foreign origin woman ($j = 4$). Let $\delta_O < 0$ measure discrimination against the foreign origin candidates and $\delta_G < 0$ measure gender discrimination. The first candidate should not be discriminated against and his callback probability should be of the form

$$m_1 = \theta,$$

where θ is labour market tightness. For the local origin woman, we can add a gender discrimination component,

$$m_2 = \theta + \delta_G,$$

and for the foreign origin man, we should add an origin discrimination component:

$$m_3 = \theta + \delta_O.$$

For the last candidate, we could think of adding the two discriminatory components and adding a joint component, known as intersectionality in the literature (Tariq and Syed, 2017). Denote it δ_{OG}. If $\delta_{OG} = 0$, discrimination is additive, and a foreign origin woman will have a discrimination coefficient equal to the sum of the gender discrimination coefficient and of the foreign origin discrimination coefficient. If the coefficient is negative, the discrimination will be stronger, as discrimination is said to be superadditive, and if $\delta_{OG} > 0$ the discrimination of the sum will be less strong that the sum of discriminations and is said to be subadditive

$$m_4 = \theta + \delta_G + \delta_O + \delta_{OG}.$$

The θ parameter does not measure discrimination so that its estimation is not important in this context. We will focus on the δ parameters. Taking the model in differences, we get

$$m_2 - m_1 = \delta_G$$
$$m_3 - m_1 = \delta_O$$
$$m_4 - m_3 - (m_2 - m_1) = \delta_{OG}.$$

We get gender discrimination by comparing the two local candidates since they do not face origin discrimination. The origin discrimination is obtained by comparing the two men since they do not face gender discrimination and the joint discrimination is obtained by comparing gender discrimination among the foreign origin candidates with gender discrimination among the local origin candidates. Writing a components model allows us to determine the right comparisons easily. It also works when there are fewer parameters to estimate than probability differences, as we show later in the chapter.

A discrete choice model. We model the probability of a callback. For any candidate j on job ad i we let v_{ji}^* be the recruiter's gain associated with a callback:

$$v_{ji}^* = m_{ji} + \alpha_i + \varepsilon_{ji}, \tag{6.3}$$

where m_{ji} is the model for candidate j on job i. Its form depends on each experiment and includes the discriminatory components that we wish to estimate. The α_i term is the job ad correlated effect (or "fixed effect"), since the same recruiter replies to all the candidates and ε_{ji} is the idiosyncratic error term, typically a white noise. We observe the callback dummy:

$$v_{ji} = \begin{cases} 1 & \text{if } v_{ji}^* > 0 \\ 0 & \text{otherwise} \end{cases}.$$

It equals 1 when the recruiter calls the candidate back and zero otherwise. We wish to estimate the model from a sample of dummy variables and the characteristics of the candidate, chosen by the researchers who ran the experiment. First, we need to eliminate the unobserved heterogeneity term α_i. Let F_ε be the cumulative distribution function (cdf) of ε. The theoretical callback probability for candidate j on job i can be written as

$$P_{ji} = \Pr(v_{ji} = 1) = \Pr(v_{ji}^* > 0) = 1 - F_\varepsilon\left(-(m_{ji} + \alpha_i)\right).$$

These probabilities have empirical counterparts and, with an assumption on F_ε, we can estimate the model components. Notice that the fit of several distributions can be compared with our method. In order to eliminate the α_i terms, we need to compare the answers to two candidates on the same job ad. Let $j = 1$ be a freely chosen reference candidate, with no loss of generality; we eliminate α_i with the following differencing:

$$D_i(j,1) = F_\varepsilon^{-1}(1 - P_{1i}) - F_\varepsilon^{-1}(1 - P_{ji}) = m_{ji} - m_{1i}.$$

By definition of the callback probabilities, the difference $m_{ji} - m_{1i}$ term contains the discrimination terms that we wish to estimate. Simplification occurs when ε is assumed to have a symmetric distribution. In this case we get[14]

$$P_{ji} = F_\varepsilon\left(m_{ji} + \alpha_i\right),$$

and we can take the difference:

$$\Delta_i(j,1) = F_\varepsilon^{-1}(P_{ji}) - F_\varepsilon^{-1}(P_{1i}) = m_{ji} - m_{1i}.$$

Three well-known cases are worth commenting on. First, the default case of correspondence studies is the linear probability model, which leads to a direct comparison of the callback probabilities. Assuming a uniform distribution, $F_\varepsilon(\varepsilon) = \varepsilon$, we get

$$\Delta_i(j,1) = P_{ji} - P_{1i},$$

and the coefficients can be interpreted as percentage points. Another case encountered is the logit model. It has the advantage of constraining the estimated probabilities in the $[0,1]$ interval. Assuming a logistic distribution, $F_\varepsilon(\varepsilon) = 1/(1 + \exp(-\varepsilon))$, we must take the difference of the log odds ratios of the two candidates:

$$\Delta_i(j,1) = \ln\frac{P_{ji}}{1 - P_{ji}} - \ln\frac{P_{1i}}{1 - P_{1i}},$$

and the coefficients are to be interpreted as log-odds ratios. Finally, with the normit/probit model, we get

$$\Delta_i(j,1) = \Phi^{-1}(P_{ji}) - \Phi^{-1}(P_{1i}),$$

where Φ is the cdf of the standard normal distribution, and the coefficients are more difficult to interpret than in the two previous cases. Now that the unobserved heterogeneity term has been eliminated, we can discuss the identification of the discriminatory components.

Consider the example of gender and origin. We would like to compare the four candidates of our previous example: local origin man ($j = 1$), local origin woman ($j = 2$), foreign origin man ($j = 3$), foreign origin women ($j = 4$). We had

$$m_1 = \theta$$
$$m_2 = \theta + \delta_G$$
$$m_3 = \theta + \delta_O$$
$$m_4 = \theta + \delta_G + \delta_O.$$

For clarity of the exposition, we impose $\delta_{OG} = 0$ in order to get an overidentified case (that is, more probability differences that discrimination parameters). Overidentified cases happen easily when several discrimination items are allowed for. The consequence is that there are now several ways to estimate the discrimination parameters. We get the three following differences:

$$\Delta(2,1) = m_2 - m_1 = \delta_G$$
$$\Delta(3,1) = m_3 - m_1 = \delta_O$$
$$\Delta(4,1) = m_4 - m_1 = \delta_G + \delta_O.$$

Since the left-hand of this system has an empirical counterpart, we should estimate our two parameters from three statistics. Our system is overidentified; there are more statistics than needed. In order to proceed to the estimation, we should use a minimum distance estimation method and test the validity of the restriction: $\Delta(2,1) + \Delta(3,1) = \Delta(4,1)$. It is an additive property. Let us rewrite our constraints:

$$\underbrace{\begin{pmatrix} \Delta(2,1) \\ \Delta(3,1) \\ \Delta(4,1) \end{pmatrix}}_{\pi} = \underbrace{\begin{pmatrix} 1 & 0 \\ 0 & 1 \\ 1 & 1 \end{pmatrix}}_{C} \underbrace{\begin{pmatrix} \delta_G \\ \delta_O \end{pmatrix}}_{\beta}$$

or

$$\pi = C\beta.$$

The auxiliary parameter π is easily estimated from the data; β is the interest parameter, and is not directly observable. In order to estimate β, we need to replace π with an estimate $\hat{\pi}$. Let

$$\hat{\pi} = \pi + \omega,$$

where ω is the estimation error on the auxiliary parameter. Substituting into the identification constraints, we get an equation that can be used for estimation:

$$\hat{\pi} = C\beta + \omega,$$

where $\hat{\pi}$ and C are observable so that a minimum distance estimation is feasible. Let $\Omega = V(\omega)$; its diagonal elements are the variances of the auxiliary parameter estimators, and the off-diagonal term the covariance between the estimators. They are correlated because the answers to all the candidates come from the same recruiter. The optimal estimator of β is the feasible generalised least squares (FGLS) estimator:

$$\hat{\beta} = (C'\hat{\Omega}^{-1}C)^{-1}C'\hat{\Omega}^{-1}\hat{\pi}.$$

It is asymptotically normal and its asymptotic covariance matrix can be estimated by the following statistic:

$$V(\hat{\beta}) = (C'\hat{\Omega}^{-1}C)^{-1},$$

where $\hat{\Omega}$ is a consistent estimate of Ω. The overidentification statistic, denoted S, is simply an estimate of the norm on the identification constraints; we get

$$S = \hat{\omega}'\hat{\Omega}^{-1}\hat{\omega},$$

with $\hat{\omega} = \hat{\pi} - C\hat{\beta}$. Under the null hypothesis (H_0: $\pi = C\beta$), it is asymptotically $\chi^2(1)$ distributed. More generally, for an overidentified system, the degrees of freedom are equal to the difference between the number of auxiliary parameters and the number of structural parameters. This statistic or its p-value can be used as a choice rule for F_ε. Indeed, π depend on the callback probabilities and on the specific functional form F_ε. Taking the distribution with the highest p-value is therefore equivalent to take the distribution that best fits the identification constraints.

Rotating candidates. In order to avoid detection, it is possible to have only some of the candidates respond each time. For simplicity of exposition, suppose that we send the benchmark candidate ($j = 1$) and only one of the other candidates. We could still compute estimates of the Δ_j and apply the method. Notice that we do not even need the number of ads to be the same for all candidates. In fact, we do not even need to send the benchmark candidate all the time, but just two candidates, because what matters is to relate the auxiliary parameters to the structural parameters. With four candidates, there are six possible differences:

$$\Delta(2,1) = m_2 - m_1 = \delta_G$$

$$\Delta(3,1) = m_3 - m_1 = \delta_O$$

$$\Delta(4,1) = m_4 - m_1 = \delta_G + \delta_O$$

$$\Delta(3,2) = m_3 - m_2 = \delta_O - \delta_G$$

$$\Delta(4,2) = m_4 - m_2 = \delta_O$$

$$\Delta(4,3) = m_4 - m_3 = \delta_G,$$

and any combination involving the four candidates will provide an estimate provided that the C matrix is adapted. For instance, if we use $\Delta(2,1)$, $\Delta(3,2)$ and $\Delta(4,3)$, we simply need to write

$$\underbrace{\begin{pmatrix} \Delta(2,1) \\ \Delta(3,2) \\ \Delta(4,3) \end{pmatrix}}_{\pi} = \underbrace{\begin{pmatrix} 1 & 0 \\ -1 & 1 \\ 1 & 0 \end{pmatrix}}_{C} \underbrace{\begin{pmatrix} \delta_G \\ \delta_O \end{pmatrix}}_{\beta}$$

and proceed as before.

Ad-dependent model. In some cases, the model may depend on an ad's characteristics, such as the contract length. The method will be the same, but this time there will be one equation for each candidate, depending on whether they reply to short- or long-term contracts. The same method is applied with more equations.

Backward selection. When a component is not significant, a new estimation should be made in order to reduce the variance of the remaining estimators. The variance is lower because more observations are used to estimate the remaining parameters. In order to illustrate this point, consider the following system:

$$\Delta(2,1) = m_2 - m_1 = \delta_G$$
$$\Delta(4,1) = m_4 - m_1 = \delta_G + \delta_O.$$

If, say, $\delta_O = 0$, the system becomes

$$\Delta(2,1) = m_2 - m_1 = \delta_G \tag{6.4}$$

$$\Delta(4,1) = m_4 - m_1 = \delta_G, \tag{6.5}$$

and, assuming that each candidate replies to all ads, we have twice as many observations to estimate δ_G. Now, we can use both $\Delta(2,1)$ and $\Delta(4,1)$. A standard solution is[15]

$$\frac{1}{2}\Delta(2,1) + \frac{1}{2}\Delta(4,1) = \delta_G, \tag{6.6}$$

and the estimation proceeds as usual, with a change of the left-hand variable. This also shows that the process of backward selection is very different from the standard OLS case. For a more detailed presentation, see Duguet et al. (2018).

Rotation of the candidates. A rotation of the candidate simply reduces the number of observations available for each difference. Therefore, the empirical probabilities are computed as usual, and the method can be applied without any change. This remark is also valid when the rotation is not balanced among the candidates. The only constraint is to have at least two candidates reply to each ad in order to compute a difference of treatment.

1.5 Structural estimation

The previous analyses are often thought of as subject to the Heckman (1998) critique. First, all audit studies adjust as many characteristics as they can. However, there may be other characteristics related to productivity and with a different distribution in the two groups. In this case, the results can be biased. Second, recruiters may apply different rules to different candidates. People from a discriminated group may have applied to them a higher standard for hiring. Neumark (2012) proposes an answer to the first Heckman critique. Consider two groups $j = A$, B, where the group B is subject to discrimination. Let us consider that the productivity of the workers depends on two sets of variables $\tilde{X} = (X, \varepsilon)$, where X is controlled in the experiment and ε is not. Finally, let α be a summary of firm-level characteristics. The productivity of a worker is denoted $y(\tilde{X}, \alpha)$. Let T^* be a function denoting the outcome of the worker in the labour market, such as a callback rate (the "treatment" of the worker). There is discrimination when two identical workers are not treated equally:

$$T^*(y(\tilde{X}, \alpha), A) \neq T^*(y(\tilde{X}, \alpha), B).$$

Assuming a linear model, we can write

$$y(X, \alpha) = Xb + \varepsilon + \alpha,$$

and the treatment

$$T^*(y(X, \alpha), d_B) = y + d \times d_B,$$

$d_B = 1$ or 0 means the worker belongs to group B or group A, respectively. The parameter $d < 0$ measures discrimination since it applies only to the B group, while it is not related to $\tilde{X}$ or α. The expected productivities in the two groups are denoted y_j^*. The experiment sends two candidates $j = A, B$ and records their treatment by the recruiter:

$$T^*(y_B^*, 1) - T^*(y_A^*, 0) = y_B^* - y_A^* + d.$$

The goal of all correspondence tests is to set $y_A^* = y_B^*$ so that the treatment difference reflects discrimination, measured by d. It can be obtained by an OLS regression of T^* on d_B and a constant term. Now consider the detailed list of variables influencing productivity $\tilde{X} = (X, \varepsilon)$. The first variable X is controlled in the experiment, but the second variable ε is not. Let $\tilde{X}_j$ denote their values for the candidate j. A tested pair of candidates (A, B) should verify

$$y_A^* = X_A b + \varepsilon_A + \alpha$$
$$y_B^* = X_B b + \varepsilon_B + \alpha$$

so that the difference of treatment equals

$$T^*(y_B^*, 1) - T^*(y_A^*, 0) = X_B b + \varepsilon_B + \alpha + d - \left(X_A b + \varepsilon_A + \alpha \right)$$

$$= \varepsilon_B - \varepsilon_A + d,$$

when the correspondence test imposes $X_A = X_B$. The hypothesis $E(\varepsilon_A) = E(\varepsilon_B)$ guarantees an unbiased estimation of d. But this is not the end of the argument, since there is also a variance issue.[16]

Let us assume that a callback will be made if the expected productivity (or utility) crosses a given threshold. A recruiter may favour the group with the higher variance because it has a larger probability of crossing the threshold c. More precisely, consider the binary treatment T:

$$T(y(\tilde{X}),d_B) = \begin{cases} 1 & \text{if } T^*(y(\tilde{X}),d_B) > c \\ 0 & \text{otherwise} \end{cases}.$$

Consider a correspondence test with $X = X_A = X_B$; the discriminated group will receive a callback when $Xb + \varepsilon_B + d + \alpha > c$, while the non-discriminated group will receive a callback when $Xb + \varepsilon_A + \alpha > c$. Assuming that $\alpha \sim N(0,s_\alpha^2)$ and $\varepsilon_j \sim N(0,s_j^2)$ are independent, then $u_j = \alpha + \varepsilon_j \sim N(0,\sigma_j^2)$ with $\sigma_j^2 = s_\alpha^2 + s_j^2$. We get the following callback probabilities:

$$p_A = \Pr\left[T^*(y(X,u_j),0) > c\right] \tag{6.7}$$

$$= \Pr\left[Xb + u_A > c\right]$$

$$= \Phi\left(\frac{Xb - c}{\sigma_A}\right),$$

where Φ is the cdf of the standard normal distribution, and similarly

$$p_B = \Pr\left[T^*(y(X,u_j),1) > c\right] \tag{6.8}$$

$$= \Pr\left[Xb + u_B + d > c\right]$$

$$= \Phi\left(\frac{Xb + d - c}{\sigma_B}\right).$$

We get the following callback difference, which is currently used for measuring discrimination:

$$p_A - p_B = \Phi\left(\frac{Xb - c}{\sigma_A}\right) - \Phi\left(\frac{Xb + d - c}{\sigma_B}\right).$$

Therefore, even in the absence of discrimination, $d = 0$, we can have different callback probabilities when $\sigma_A \neq \sigma_B$. Assuming $\sigma_A < \sigma_B$ would imply $p_A > p_B$ in the absence of discrimination. In order to detect discrimination, we would like to estimate the parameter d. If we estimate the callback probability models in the two groups, we get the following:[17]

$$p_A = \Phi\left(c_A + Xb_A\right) \tag{6.9}$$

$$p_B = \Phi\left(c_B + Xb_B\right).$$

The previous parameters $\pi' = (c_A, b_A', c_B, b_B')$ are called the auxiliary parameters because they do not always have a direct interpretation. We simply obtain them directly when we estimate the callback probabilities. Their value is in obtaining the parameters of interest. An obvious example of a parameter of interest is the d parameter, which measures discrimination. Another parameter is the ratio of the standard errors $\psi = \sigma_B / \sigma_A$. We let $\beta' = (\psi, d)$ be the vector of parameters of interest. Since the probit model coefficients are identified up to a positive number, we will set $\sigma_A = 1$ without loss of generality. Using (6.7), (6.8) and (6.9), we get the constraints

$$c_A = \psi c_B - d, \, b_A = \psi b_B,$$

which we can rewrite in the following manner:

$$
\underbrace{\begin{pmatrix} c_A \\ b_A \end{pmatrix}}_{\pi_A} = \underbrace{\begin{pmatrix} c_B & -1 \\ b_B & 0 \end{pmatrix}}_{C(\pi_B)} \underbrace{\begin{pmatrix} \psi \\ d \end{pmatrix}}_{\beta},
$$

and the estimation can proceed with asymptotic least squares (ALS), which was originally developed in Chamberlain (1982, 1984) and Gouriéroux et al. (1985). More precisely, π_A and $C(\pi_B)$ have empirical counterparts so that a consistent and asymptotically normal estimator can be obtained for β. Also note that b_A and b_B may be vectors so that the estimation problem will generally be overidentified. The implicit assumption with this method is that there should be at least one variable in X that has a monotonic effect on the callback rate (positive or negative). Replacing π by an estimate $\hat{\pi}$, we get

$$\hat{\pi}_A = C(\hat{\pi}_B)\beta + \omega,$$

where ω is an error term created by the replacement of π by $\hat{\pi}$. We obtain a first-step estimator by performing OLS on this relationship and get

$$\hat{\beta} = (C(\hat{\pi}_B)' C(\hat{\pi}_B))^{-1} C'(\hat{\pi}_B) \hat{\pi}_A.$$

Letting $\omega = g(\hat{\pi}, \beta) = \hat{\pi}_A - C(\hat{\pi}_B)\beta$, its asymptotic variance equals

$$\Omega(\hat{\pi}, \beta) = V(\omega)$$

$$= \frac{\partial g}{\partial \pi'}(\hat{\pi}, \beta) V(\hat{\pi}) \left(\frac{\partial g}{\partial \pi'}(\hat{\pi}, \beta) \right)',$$

with

$$
\frac{\partial g}{\partial \pi'}(\pi, \beta) = \begin{pmatrix} 1 & 0_{(1,k)} & -\psi & 0_{(1,k)} \\ 0_{(k,1)} & \mathrm{Id}_k & 0_{(k,1)} & -\psi \mathrm{Id}_k \end{pmatrix},
$$

where k is the number of regressors in X (excluding the constant term). Replacing ψ by the $\hat{\psi}$ obtained in the first stage estimation, we get the FGLS estimator,

$$\beta^* = \left(C(\hat{\pi}_B) \Omega(\hat{\beta})^{-1} C(\hat{\pi}_B) \right)^{-1} C(\hat{\pi}_B) \Omega(\hat{\beta})^{-1} \hat{\pi}_A,$$

with the asymptotic covariance matrix:

$$\hat{V}(\beta^*) = \left(C(\hat{\pi}_B) \Omega(\beta^*)^{-1} C(\hat{\pi}_B) \right)^{-1}.$$

1.6 Evaluation with ranks

When the data are collected not only regarding the answers to the candidates but also concerning their order of reception, it is possible to test for the existence of stronger forms of discrimination (Duguet et al., 2015). Consider a recruiter with preferences for the candidates A and B represented by the utilities U_A and U_B. These utilities are specific to each recruiter and result from pre-conceptions about the candidates, because the candidates are equally productive by construction of the correspondence test experiment. Each recruiter has a reservation utility level U_R above which the candidates are invited to an interview. We can define the relative utility levels $v_A = U_A - U_R$ and $v_B = U_B - U_R$. The four potential cases in terms of response can be represented in the following way. If $v_A < 0$ and $v_B < 0$, no candidate is invited to an interview. When $v_A < 0 < v_B$, only candidate B is invited; when $v_B < 0 < v_A$, only candidate A is invited. Finally, when $v_A > 0$ and $v_B > 0$, both candidates are invited. These cases are illustrated in figure 6.1. The standard measure of discrimination against candidate B, used in the literature, considers only cases in which only one of the two candidates is invited. These cases are illustrated by the north–west and the south–east quadrants of figure 6.1. We denote this discrimination coefficient as $D(A, B)$:

$$\begin{aligned} D(A,B) &= \Pr[v_B < 0 < v_A] - \Pr[v_A < 0 < v_B] \\ &= \Pr[\text{A invited, B uninvited}] - \Pr[\text{B invited, A uninvited}]^{\cdot} \end{aligned}$$

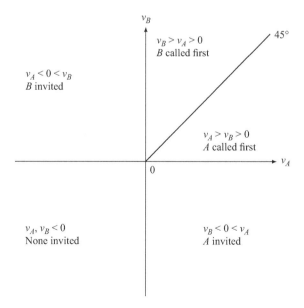

Figure 6.1 Callback decisions

According to this measure, there is no discrimination when both candidates have equal chances of being invited, and a positive number indicates that candidate A is, on average, preferred to candidate B.

It is possible to extend the standard measure of discrimination $D(A, B)$ to the ranking of the candidates when both are invited, which is equivalent to considering all the quadrants in figure 6.1. In order to compare the rankings of the two candidates, we use the concept of first-order stochastic dominance. Suppose that we have J candidates, ranked according to the recruiter's utilities. The candidates who have not been invited satisfy the condition that $v_j = U_j - U_R < 0$. The ranking of the candidates (from 1st to Jth) results from the recruiter's tastes for the candidates. The highest utility corresponds to the candidate ranked first, and negative utilities correspond to the candidates who have not been invited. In order to perform our analysis, we need to separate the candidates who have not been invited from the others by creating a rank $J + 1$. This additional rank is required because the candidates who have not been called cannot be ranked between themselves. We only know that the uninvited candidates' utilities are below the recruiter's reservation utility levels and therefore they are ranked behind the candidates who have been invited. Consider first the case for which all the candidates have been invited. Using the order statistic, denoted (), we obtain the ranking of the utilities of the candidates $\{j_1, j_2, \ldots, j_J\}$, $0 < v_{(j_1)} \leq v_{(j_2)} \leq \ldots \leq v_{(j_J)}$ that corresponds to the ranking $J, J - 1, \ldots, 1$. When only k candidates are invited, we have the ranking $v_{(j_1)} \leq \ldots v_{(j_{J-k})} < 0 < v_{(j_{J-k+1})} \leq \ldots \leq v_{(j_J)}$ that corresponds to the ranking $J + 1, \ldots, J + 1, J, \ldots, 1$. The first stochastic dominance (henceforth, FOSD) of candidate j_1 over candidate j_2 is defined as

$$\Pr[v_{j_1} \geq v] \geq \Pr[v_{j_2} \geq v] \; \forall v,$$

$$\text{and } \exists \, \bar{v} \text{ such that } \Pr[v_{j_1} \geq \bar{v}] > \Pr[v_{j_2} \geq \bar{v}],$$

which means that candidate j_1 has a higher probability of reaching a given utility level than candidate j_2, whatever the utility level is. This relationship is especially easy to interpret when v is set at the reservation utility level of the recruiter, since it means that candidate j_1 has a higher probability of being invited to the interview than candidate j_2. This is the standard discrimination measure. We also see that the FOSD covers more cases than the standard discrimination measure because it makes use of all possible utility thresholds.

For practical reasons we work with the ranks, since they are observable while the utilities are not. We just need to reverse the inequalities inside the probabilities, since the higher the utility the lower the rank (rank 1 for the most preferred candidate with utility $v_{(j_J)}$):

$$\Pr[r_{j_1} \leq r] \geq \Pr[r_{j_2} \leq r] \; \forall r \in \{1, \ldots, J+1\},$$

$$\text{and } \exists \, \bar{r} \text{ such that } \Pr[r_{j_1} \leq \bar{r}] > \Pr[r_{j_2} \geq \bar{r}]. \tag{6.10}$$

Consider the case $r = 1$. Then $\Pr[r_j \leq 1] = \Pr[r_j = 1]$, which gives the probability of being ranked first. If the inequality (6.10) holds, the candidate j_1 has a higher probability of being ranked first than the candidate j_2. Now set $r = 2$. We conclude that candidate j_1 also has a higher probability of being ranked among the two first candidates than candidate j_2. Performing the comparisons up to $r = J$, $\Pr[r_j \leq J]$ is the probability that candidate j is invited to the interview. Therefore, candidate j_1 has a higher probability of being invited to the interview than candidate j_2. In summary, when j_1 FOSD j_2, the candidate j_1 always has a higher probability of being in the preferred group than the candidate j_2, whatever the definition of the preferred group is. This definition is especially relevant for the measurement of discrimination, and this is what motivates the use of the FOSD. Graphically, the FOSD means that the cdf of candidate j_1—defined on ranks—stands above the cdf of candidate j_2.

The implementation of the test is rather straightforward since the correspondence tests provide the empirical cdf directly. Consider the empirical distributions of the ranks for candidate j:

$$\hat{p}' = (\hat{p}_1(j),\ldots,\hat{p}_J(j))$$

and the corresponding empirical covariance matrix $\hat{\Sigma} = \hat{V}(\hat{p})$. The cdf at rank r is given by $\hat{P}_r = M_r\hat{p}$, with

$$M_r = (\underbrace{1,\ldots,1}_{r \text{ times}},\underbrace{0,\ldots,0}_{J-r \text{ times}}) .$$

$$\underset{(1,J)}{}$$

For example, with three ranks,

$$\hat{p} = \begin{pmatrix} \hat{p}_1 \\ \hat{p}_2 \\ \hat{p}_3 \end{pmatrix},$$

the cdf is given by

$$M_1\hat{p} = (1,0,0)\hat{p} = \hat{p}_1$$

$$M_2\hat{p} = (1,1,0)\hat{p} = \hat{p}_1 + \hat{p}_2$$

$$M_3\hat{p} = (1,1,1)\hat{p} = \hat{p}_1 + \hat{p}_2 + \hat{p}_3 = 1,$$

and the covariances are given by $V(M_r\hat{p}) = M_r\hat{\Sigma}M_r'$. Now we consider the distributions of two candidates, j_1 and j_2, and stack them in a $2 \times J$ vector $\hat{p}' = (\hat{p}'_{j_1},\hat{p}'_{j_2})$, where $\hat{\Sigma}$ is the associated joint $2J \times 2J$ covariance matrix, which accounts for the correlation between the ranks. Let $D_r = (M_{r'} - M_r)$; then the difference between the cumulative distribution functions of candidates j_1 and j_2 equals

$$\Delta\hat{P}_r = D_r\hat{p} = (M_r,-M_r)\begin{pmatrix} \hat{p}_{j_1} \\ \hat{p}_{j_2} \end{pmatrix}$$

$$= M_r'\hat{p}_{j_1} - M_r'\hat{p}_{j_2}$$

$$= \hat{P}_{j_1} - \hat{P}_{j_2},$$

and the covariance matrix is obtained by $V(D_r\hat{p}) = D_r\hat{\Sigma}D_r'$. Therefore, we can perform a Wald test at each point r of the cdf. The following statistic is chi-squared distributed, with one degree of freedom under the null hypothesis $P_{j_1} = P_{j_2}$:

$$S_r = D_r\hat{p}(D_r\hat{\Sigma}D_r')^{-1}\hat{p}'D_r'.$$

2.   THE EVALUATION OF WAGE DISCRIMINATION

2.1   The wage regressions

The Mincer equation. Many estimation methods start with the wage equation (Mincer, 1958). Restricted to the people at work, for a sample of size $\mathbf{I}$, it can be written

$$w_i = X_i b_1 + u_i, \, i \in \mathbf{I}, \tag{6.11}$$

where $w_i = \ln W_i$ is the log-wage of worker i, X_i the observable individual data, often called the *endowments*, such as tenure, the years of schooling or the occupation and u_i a zero-mean disturbance, without loss of generality, provided the model includes a constant term. Under standard assumptions, this wage equation can be estimated by OLS. This regression will be used on the data sets where no information is available on the jobless people. This will be the case, for instance, with matched employer–employee data, since workers are sampled inside firms.

The Heckman selection model. Sometimes, more data are available. The labour force surveys generally include information about the workers, the unemployed and the inactive people. In this case, we need a two-part model (Heckman, 1976). First, there is a labour market participation equation. A straightforward motivation is the reservation wage theory. If the offered wage is above the reservation wage, the worker takes the job and we observe the wage; otherwise we do not. This participation equation can be written

$$d_i^* = H_i \gamma + v_i,$$

where d_i^* is a latent, unobservable variable that summarises the labour participation process. One may think of it as the difference between the offered wage and the reservation wage. The right-hand variables H include the determinants of participation. The household composition and the replacement revenues may be important determinants; v_i is a disturbance. We observe the following binary variable, which equals 1 when i participates in the labour market, 0 otherwise:

$$d_i = \begin{cases} 1 & \text{if } d_i^* > 0 \\ 0 & \text{otherwise} \end{cases}.$$

This equation will be estimated with a binary model (probit or other). The important point is that we observe the value of the wage when there is a participation only. Therefore, if there is a correlation between the disturbances (u_i, v_i), OLS will suffer from a selection bias. Several solutions can be proposed to this problem. The first is the joint estimation of the model by maximum likelihood. Assuming the joint normality of the disturbances,

$$\begin{pmatrix} u_i \\ v_i \end{pmatrix} \sim N \left(\begin{pmatrix} 0 \\ 0 \end{pmatrix}, \begin{pmatrix} \sigma^2 & \rho\sigma \\ \rho\sigma & 1 \end{pmatrix} \right),$$

where σ^2 is the variance of the disturbance in the wage equation and ρ is the linear correlation coefficient of the two disturbances. Note that the variance of the participation equation has been normalised to 1, as in a probit model. Under this assumption, we obtain a tobit 2 model in the terminology of Amemiya (1985). SAS and R packages typically allow for the estimation of this two-equation model.[18] The second, more popular method, is the Heckman method (Heckman, 1976). It relies on the following conditional expectation:[19]

$$E\left(w_i \mid X_i, H_i, d_i = 1\right) = X_i b + \sigma \rho \frac{\varphi(H_i \gamma)}{\Phi(H_i \gamma)},$$

where φ and Φ are respectively the probability density function (pdf) and the cdf of the standard normal distribution. Ignoring the sample selection, $d_i = 1$ can be interpreted as a missing regressor problem. The estimation can proceed in two steps. First, one estimates γ with a probit model and computes the estimated inverse of Mills ratio:

$$\hat{\lambda}_i = \frac{\varphi(H_i \hat{\gamma})}{\Phi(H_i \hat{\gamma})},$$

where $\hat{c}$ is the maximum likelihood estimator of the probit model. In a second step, we perform the OLS regression of w_i on the variables $(X_i, \hat{\lambda}_i)$ on the selected sample $(d_i = 1)$. Let $\theta = \sigma \rho$; we get $\hat{b}$ and $\hat{\theta}$ in this second step. The covariance matrix of these estimators should be computed according to Heckman (1979) because one regressor is estimated. In some cases, we need the selection-corrected wage:

$$\tilde{y}_{1i} = y_{1i} - \hat{\theta} \hat{\lambda}_i.$$

In practise, one can combine the two methods and use the tobit 2 maximum likelihood estimate of γ instead of the probit estimate.[20]

2.2 The Oaxaca–Blinder Decomposition

Labour market samples typically exhibit average wage differences between groups (say, men and women). A part of these differences may be justified by objective differences between the workers. In one group, workers may be older or have a longer education. This will create wage differences we can explain. The Oaxaca–Blinder decomposition is a method for separating the average wage differences attributable to the observed characteristics of the workers, from the wage differences attributable to a group membership (Oaxaca, 1973; Blinder, 1973).

Presentation. Let us consider two groups of workers, A and B. Following Becker (Becker, 1971, p. 22), we can define a market discrimination coefficient (MDC) by comparing the observed wage (W_A, W_B) and the theoretical wages without discrimination (W_A^*, W_B^*):

$$\text{MDC} = \frac{W_A}{W_B} - \frac{W_A^*}{W_B^*}.$$

In the previous expression, W_A^* / W_B^* represents the wage difference in the absence of discrimination. This difference comes from the productivity differences of the workers and is therefore justified. The expression W_A / W_B represents the real-world wage difference. It includes both the justified wage difference and the unjustified one, which we refer to as wage discrimination. Since the Mincer equations refer to a wage in logarithm, we will prefer to work with the log wage, denoted $w_j = \ln W_j, j \in \{A, B\}$. We will use the following approximation:[21]

$$\text{MDC} = \frac{W_A - W_B}{W_B} - \frac{W_A^* - W_B^*}{W_B^*}$$

$$\simeq \ln\left(1 + \frac{W_A - W_B}{W_B}\right) - \ln\left(1 + \frac{W_A^* - W_B^*}{W_B^*}\right)$$

$$= \ln W_A - \ln W_B - (\ln W_A^* - \ln W_B^*)$$

$$= w_A - w_B - (w_A^* - w_B^*).$$

Suppose that we have two groups of workers, A and B, with respective wages w_A and w_B. The difference of their wages may reflect any difference between them, including but not restricted to wage discrimination. Suppose that we find a method to compute the non-discriminatory wages; we denote them w_A^* and w_B^*. Then we should measure wage discrimination against group B by the following quantity:[22]

$$\text{MDC} = w_A - w_B - (w_A^* - w_B^*).$$

The justification is the following. Since (w_A^*, w_B^*) are not discriminatory by assumption, the difference $w_A^* - w_B^*$ represents the *justified* wage difference. It comes from the productivity differences between the workers. Since the distribution of the workers' productivity is not the same in the groups A and B, there is an average wage difference. Now consider (w_A, w_B); they are the real-world wage distributions. By definition, they include the effect of all the differences among the two groups of workers, both justified and unjustified. Therefore the difference $D(A, B)$ measures the unjustified wage difference that the workers in group A benefit from (compared to a worker in group B). We obtain this quantity as a "residual," that is as a *difference*. But this is not the definition of the residual that is used in econometrics. It is rather an accounting residual. The methods that we will present in this section simply differ by the definition that they take for (w_A^*, w_B^*). Once a choice is set, a decomposition method follows.

Method. Let b^* be the regression coefficient for the non-discriminatory wage equation; we have the theoretical wage equation

$$w^* = Xb^*,$$

and all the differences of wages between the groups A and B come from differences in productive characteristics X. If the average characteristics of group j is X_j, with $j \in \{A, B\}$, we get

$$w_A^* - w_B^* = (X_A - X_B)b^*.$$

Applying this result at the mean point of the sample, we obtain the average wage difference that we should observe in the absence of discrimination:

$$\bar{w}_A^* - \bar{w}_B^* = (\bar{X}_A - \bar{X}_B)b^*.$$

Now let us consider discrimination. We clearly need the regression coefficient to differ between the two groups. What does this mean? That the same characteristics will not have the same return in the two groups anymore. For instance, one year's worth of experience will be less paid in group B than in group A for discriminatory reasons. This simply states that the average wage difference between two groups of identical workers must originate in a difference of the way their productive characteristics are paid. Now, consider the two real-world regressions, obtained separately from the A and B groups. The observed wage is equal, by definition, to the sum of the predicted wage and the residual. We can write

$$w_j = X_j \hat{b}_j + \hat{u}_j,$$

with $\hat{b}_j = (X_j' X_j)^{-1} X_j' w_j$. Another property is that the mean of the residual is zero provided there is a constant term among the regressors. This allows for writing, with $j = A, B$:

$$\bar{w}_j = \bar{X}_j \hat{b}_j \text{ with } \bar{w}_j = \frac{1}{\mathbf{I}}\sum_{i \in \mathbf{I}} w_{j,i}, \bar{X}_j = \frac{1}{\mathbf{I}}\sum_{i \in \mathbf{I}} X_{j,i}.$$

Therefore, the difference between the groups A and B equals

$$\bar{w}_A - \bar{w}_B = \bar{X}_A \hat{b}_A - \bar{X}_B \hat{b}_B.$$

The discrimination coefficient is defined by

$$\begin{aligned} D(A,B) &= \bar{w}_A - \bar{w}_B - (\bar{w}_A^* - \bar{w}_B^*) \\ &= \bar{X}_A \hat{b}_A - \bar{X}_B \hat{b}_B - (\bar{X}_A - \bar{X}_B)b^* \\ &= \bar{X}_A(\hat{b}_A - b^*) + \bar{X}_B(b^* - \hat{b}_B), \end{aligned}$$

and we get the definition in Oaxaca and Ransom (1994). This is equivalent to using the following decomposition of the average wage:

$$\bar{w}_A - \bar{w}_B = \bar{X}_A(\hat{b}_A - b^*) + \bar{X}_B(b^* - \hat{b}_B) + (\bar{X}_A - \bar{X}_B)b^*. \tag{6.12}$$

Consider the case where B is discriminated against. The first term $\bar{X}_A(\hat{b}_A - b^*)$ measures the nepotism in favour of group A since it is an extra wage compared to the non-discriminatory case. The term $\bar{X}_B(b^* - \hat{b}_B)$ represents, on the contrary, the revenue lost caused by discrimination. The last term represents the wage difference justified by the difference of observable characteristics. There remains to choose b^*; this leads to the "index number problem" (Oaxaca, 1973).

2.3   The index number problem

In the original paper, Oaxaca (1973) makes an application with $b^* = \hat{b}_A$ (the male wage structure, denoted A) and $b^* = \hat{b}_B$ (the female wage structure, denoted B), suggesting that this will give an interval for the non-discriminatory wage structure. Choosing $\hat{b}_A$ is equivalent to assuming that group A, which is not discriminated against, should be a good proxy for the non-discriminatory wage structure. But, theoretically, the situation is more complex since the suppression of discrimination in the labour market may change the whole wage structure, including the wage of the favoured group. The solution may lie somewhere between $\hat{b}_A$ and $\hat{b}_B$. For example, using the (male) A wage structure in equation (6.12), we get the following decomposition:

$$\bar{w}_A - \bar{w}_B = \bar{X}_B(\hat{b}_A - \hat{b}_B) + (\bar{X}_A - \bar{X}_B)\hat{b}_A \tag{6.13}$$

and discrimination is measured by

$$\text{MDC} = \bar{X}_B(\hat{b}_A - \hat{b}_B).$$

At the other end, we could have taken the women wage structure as a reference (B); it would give (with $b^* = \hat{b}_B$)[23]

$$\text{MDC} = \bar{X}_A(\hat{b}_A - \hat{b}_B).$$

The same coefficient difference is used, but they are now weighted according to female characteristics. There are obviously many ways to set b^*, and the index number problem can be interpreted as finding a sensible way of fixing b^*. The solutions adopted in the literature are surveyed in Oaxaca and Ransom (1994).

Weighting. A first way to fix the problem is to weight the two estimators. Reimers (1983) uses the median value; by taking $b^* = \frac{1}{2}(\hat{b}_A + \hat{b}_B)$, we get

$$\text{MDC} = \frac{\bar{X}_A + \bar{X}_B}{2}(\hat{b}_A - \hat{b}_B)$$

so that the average of the mean characteristics in two groups in now used as a benchmark. This clearly leads to the idea of weighting the means according to the size of the populations A and B so as to obtain the sample mean of all workers as the benchmark. This was proposed in Cotton (1988). Let π_A be the share of A workers in the sample (and $\pi_B = 1 - \pi_A$ the share of B workers); we let $b^* = \pi_A \hat{b}_A + \pi_B \hat{b}_B$, so that

$$\text{MDC} = \tilde{X}(\hat{b}_A - \hat{b}_B) \tag{6.14}$$

with

$$\tilde{X} = (1 - \pi_A)\bar{X}_A + \pi_A \bar{X}_B, 0 < f_A < 1.$$

Here, the reader should notice that the weights are inverted: the weight π_A is used to weight the group B average. This is consistent with (6.13).

What weight should we use? Neumark (1988) proposes an elegant solution using the approach of Becker (1971). Let us assume that the employers maximise their utility. This depends on the profits, but not only the profits. The composition of the labour force also matters for them. Let the utility function be

$$U\left(\Pi(L_A, L_B), L_A, L_B\right)$$

with $\Pi(L_A, L_B) = pf(L_A + L_B) - w_A L_A - w_B L_B$,

where p is the output price and f the production function. Notice that the sum of labour inputs only matters for production. This means that the two labour types have an identical productivity and should be considered as equivalent as far as production is concerned. Suppose that the employer likes group A and not group B; we would typically have $\partial U / \partial L_A \geq 0$ and $\partial U / \partial L_B \leq 0$. Utility maximisation implies that

$$\frac{\partial U}{\partial \Pi}\left(pf'(L) - w_j\right) + \frac{\partial U}{\partial L_j} = 0, \; j = A, B, \tag{6.15}$$

which implies the standard result:

$$W_A - W_B = \left(\frac{\partial U}{\partial \Pi}\right)^{-1}\left(\frac{\partial U}{\partial L_A} - \frac{\partial U}{\partial L_B}\right) > 0.$$

The A group will be better paid than the B group when the employers have a taste for the A group ($\partial U / \partial L_A \geq 0$) and a distaste for the B group ($\partial U / \partial L_B \leq 0$). We also see that the discrimination coefficient is decreasing with the taste for profit ($\partial U / \partial \Pi > 0$). These equations can also be used to determine the non-discriminatory wage, provided that we accept an additional assumption.

The identifying assumption is simply that the employer should value the proportion of A workers, not their absolute number. This does not seem unreasonable. Technically, this means that the utility function is homogeneous of degree 0 in (L_A, L_B).[24] Under this assumption, we can apply the Euler theorem:[25]

$$L_A \frac{\partial U}{\partial L_A} + L_B \frac{\partial U}{\partial L_B} = 0.$$

Using this expression with (6.15) gives

$$W^* = \frac{L_A}{L_A + L_B} \times W_A + \frac{L_B}{L_A + L_B} \times W_B,$$

where $W^* = pf'(L)$ is the nominal productivity, which defines the non-discriminatory nominal wage. In order to apply the standard methodology, we need $\ln(W^*)$ rather than W^*. One can use the following shortcut.[26] First, notice that

$$W^* = W_B\left(1 + \pi_A \frac{W_A - W_B}{W_B}\right),$$

with $\pi_A = L_A / (L_A + L_B)$ the share of group A workers. Taking the logarithm, we get[27]

$$\ln W^* \simeq \ln W_B + \pi_A \frac{W_A - W_B}{W_B}.$$

Next, using $(W_A - W_B)/W_B \simeq \ln W_A - \ln W_B$, we obtain

$$\ln W^* \simeq \pi_A \ln W_A + (1 - \pi_A) \ln W_B \simeq \pi_A w_A + (1 - \pi_A) w_B.$$

Inserting the wage equations in this expression, we get (6.14). Here, the reader should notice that one can use either the number of workers or the number of hours worked, the latter being better in a production function. In the case when there is more than one labour qualification, Neumark (1988) also proposes to estimate w^* as the pooled OLS estimator, also proposed in Oaxaca and Ransom (1988). Stacking the wage regressions of groups A and B, we get the following model:

$$\begin{pmatrix} w_A \\ w_B \end{pmatrix} = \begin{pmatrix} X_A \\ X_B \end{pmatrix} b + u,$$

or $w = Xb + u$. Applying OLS, we get[28]

$$\hat{b} = \Omega_A \hat{b}_A + (\mathrm{Id} - \Omega_A) \hat{b}_B,$$

with $\Omega_A = (X'X)^{-1} X'_A X_A$. Notice that this estimator generally differs from Cotton (1988), since the weighting is based on the second-order sample moments of the explanative variables rather than on first-order sample moments.

2.4   Accounting for labour market participation

Wage correction. The previous estimators are applied to the observed wage data. The problem is that these estimates may suffer from a selection bias. This point has been studied in Duncan and Leigh (1980) and Reimers (1983). With this approach, the wage difference is simply corrected for the selection biases (one in each wage equation), according to the Heckman method. Considering the group $j = A, B$, we estimate the probit parts of the two wage equations:[29]

$$d^*_{ji} = H_{ji} \gamma_j + v_{ji}, \, d_{ji} = \begin{cases} 1 & \text{if } d^*_{ji} > 0 \\ 0 & \text{otherwise} \end{cases}$$

and get the coefficients $\hat{\gamma}_j$. This enables us to compute the inverses of the Mills ratios, $\hat{\lambda}_{ji}$ with

$$\hat{\lambda}_{ji} = \frac{\varphi(H_{ji} \hat{\gamma}_j)}{\Phi(H_{ji} \hat{\gamma}_j)}.$$

Then, we run the second-stage regressions on the observed wages only ($d_{ji} = 1$):

$$w_{ji} = X_{ji} b_j + \theta_j \lambda_{ji} + u_{ji}.$$

Replacing λ_{ji} with $\hat{\lambda}_{ji}$ and denoting the mean value as $\overline{\hat{\lambda}}_j = I_j^{-1}\Sigma_{i\in I_j}\hat{\lambda}_{ji}$, we get the regression coefficients $(\hat{b}_j, \hat{\theta}_j)$ and compute the corrected wage difference as

$$\overline{w}_A - \hat{\theta}_A\overline{\hat{\lambda}}_A - \left(\overline{w}_B - \hat{\theta}_B\overline{\hat{\lambda}}_B\right) = \overline{w}_A - \overline{w}_B - \left(\hat{\theta}_A\overline{\hat{\lambda}}_A - \hat{\theta}_B\overline{\hat{\lambda}}_B\right).$$

This difference is then decomposed according to the previous methods. However, the reader should note that this quantity is not equal to the average wage difference, so the next approach may be preferred.

Extended decompositions. In fact, the selection term themselves could be given a discrimination interpretation since they are a part of the average wage decomposition (Neuman and Oaxaca, 2004). We just present one decomposition, which uses the group A wage structure as a reference. An important point to note is that the θ_j coefficients are considered as *not* reflecting discrimination and can, therefore, be kept different in the two groups when defining the non-discriminatory wages. Let use define the function equal to the inverse Mills' ratio:

$$\lambda(x) = \frac{\varphi(x)}{\Phi(x)}.$$

The average observed wages should be

$$\overline{w}_j = \overline{X}_j\hat{b}_j + \hat{\theta}_j\overline{\lambda(H_{ji}\hat{\gamma}_j)},$$

where the bar denotes the sample mean, and the non-discriminatory estimated wages are obtained using $b_j^* = \hat{b}_A$ and $\gamma_j^* = \hat{\gamma}_A$:

$$\overline{w}_j^* = \overline{X}_j\hat{b}_A + \hat{\theta}_j\overline{\lambda(H_{ji}\hat{\gamma}_A)}.$$

Using the definition of the MDC, we get

$$\text{MDC} = \overline{w}_A - \overline{w}_B - \left(\overline{w}_A^* - \overline{w}_B^*\right)$$

$$= \overline{X}_B(\hat{b}_A - \hat{b}_B) + \hat{\theta}_B\left(\overline{\lambda(H_{Bi}\hat{\gamma}_A)} - \overline{\lambda(H_{Bi}\hat{\gamma}_B)}\right).$$

Discrimination has now two components: the classic difference of returns on the endowments and the differences in average wages coming from the difference in participation, assumed to originate from discrimination. Two other components intervene in the wage decomposition: the endowments differences and the selection difference caused by the difference in the θ_j values. The decomposition can be rewritten

$$\overline{w}_A - \overline{w}_B = \text{MDC} + \overline{w}_A^* - \overline{w}_B^*$$

so that we just need to decompose

$$\overline{w}_A^* - \overline{w}_B^* = \underbrace{(\overline{X}_A - \overline{X}_B)\hat{b}_A + \hat{\theta}_A\left(\overline{\lambda(H_{Ai}\hat{\gamma}_A)} - \overline{\lambda(H_{Bi}\hat{\gamma}_A)}\right)}_{\text{endowments}} +$$

$$\underbrace{(\hat{\theta}_A - \hat{\theta}_B)\overline{\lambda(H_{Bi}\hat{\gamma}_A)}}_{\text{selection}}.$$

We get a decomposition in three parts, where the Heckman correction has been allocated to discrimination, endowment differences and selection difference. It relies on the assumption that group A has the non-discriminatory participation and wage structure, and that the θ_j terms do not reflect discrimination. One can easily change the reference wage structure if needed. The issue is different for the θ_j terms since it implies choosing a definition of what is discriminatory.

Neuman and Oaxaca (2004) develop this analysis by considering the cases where the selection term includes some discriminatory components itself. Indeed, $\theta_j = \sigma_j \times \rho_j$, so differences in wage variances or in correlation coefficients could be interpreted as discriminatory. With the maximum likelihood estimation of the tobit 2 model, it is possible to have separate estimates of (b_j, σ_j, ρ_j) and to use them to propose new decompositions. But this relies on sometimes strong assumption about what is discriminatory.[30]

2.5   The productivity approach

The previous approaches rely on the assumptions that the workers have the same productivity. Therefore, one can improve on the evaluations by including independent measures of productivity. This is the contribution of Hellerstein et al. (1999). In this approach, the authors estimate a production function that depends on the workers' demographic characteristics (gender, race and so on) and compare their wages with their productivity.[31] The method requires additional data: one needs plant- (or firm) level data in order to estimate a production function, along with the standard wage data. Consider first the production function. The output Y is a function of capital C, materials M and a labour aggregate $\tilde{L}$, which summarises the effect of all the labour types on production:

$$Y = f(C, M, \tilde{L}).$$

In the previous approach, all the labour types were considered equivalent so that $\tilde{L}$ was the sum of labour hours. Here, we accept that the labour productivity may differ. Let L_j be the labour input of group $j \in \mathbf{J}$, $L = \Sigma_j L_j$ be the total labour input, $\pi_j = L_j / L$ the share of the labour input of group j and ϕ_j be the productivity of group j; the labour aggregate is

$$\tilde{L} = \sum_{j \in \mathbf{J}} \phi_j L_j = L \sum_{j \in \mathbf{J}} \phi_j \pi_j.$$

Restricting ourselves to two groups of workers, $j \in \{A, B\}$, we get

$$\tilde{L} = L\left(\phi_A \pi_A + \phi_B \pi_B\right).$$

Using $\pi_A = 1 - \pi_B$ and using the group A productivity as the benchmark, $\phi_A = 1$, without loss of generality, we get the expression

$$\tilde{L} = L\left(1 + (\phi_B - 1)\pi_B\right)$$

and the production function

$$Y = f\left(C, M, L\left(1 + (\phi_B - 1)\pi_B\right)\right),$$

with which we can estimate ϕ_B the (relative) marginal productivity of group B. Hellerstein et al. (1999) use a translog production function. In order to simplify the exposition, we will retain a Cobb–Douglas function. Let

$$Y = AC^\alpha M^\gamma \tilde{L}^\beta, \qquad (6.16)$$

where A is the total factor productivity. Using (6.16), we can write

$$\ln Y = \ln A + \alpha \ln C + \gamma \ln M + \beta \ln\left(L(1+(\phi_B - 1)\pi_B)\right)$$

$$\simeq \ln A + \alpha \ln C + \gamma \ln M + \beta \ln L + \beta(\phi_B - 1)\pi_B,$$

and the estimation of this equation will provide a consistent estimate of ϕ_B.[32] This productivity differential estimate will be compared to a wage differential obtained in the following way. Consider a plant-level equation. The plants are denoted $k \in \mathbf{K} = \{1, ..., K\}$. Let d_{ijk} be a dummy variable equal to 1 if the worker i belongs to the group j in plant k. The individual-level wage equation is defined as

$$W_{ik} = \sum_{j \in J} d_{ijk} W_j.$$

Summing this equation for all the N_k workers in the plant k gives

$$\sum_{i=1}^{N_k} W_{ik} = \sum_{i=1}^{N_k} \sum_{j \in J} d_{ijk} W_j$$

$$= \sum_{j \in J} W_j \sum_{i=1}^{N_k} d_{ijk}$$

$$= \sum_{j \in J} W_j L_{jk},$$

where $L_{jk} = \sum_{i=1}^{N_k} d_{ijk}$ is the number of group j workers in plant k. This equation is definitional: it says that the total wage bill in plant k is the sum of the wages bills in the J groups of workers. Considering two groups $j \in \{A, B\}$, the total wage bill in plant k is

$$W_k = W_A L_{Ak} + W_B L_{Bk},$$

and the average wage in plant k is obtained by dividing by L_k, the total number of workers in plant k:

$$\frac{W_k}{L_k} = W_A \pi_{Ak} + W_B \pi_{Bk},$$

where $\pi_{jk} = L_{jk} / L_k$. Denoting $\mu_B = W_B / W_A$ the wage ratio, we get

$$\frac{W_k}{L_k} = W_A \pi_{Ak} + W_B \pi_{Bk}$$

$$= W_A\left(1+(\mu_B - 1)\phi_{Bk}\right),$$

Take logarithms

$$w_k = w_A + \ln\left(1 + (\mu_B - 1)\phi_{Bk}\right)$$

$$\simeq w_A + \left(\mu_B - 1\right)\phi_{Bk},$$

with $w_k = \ln(W_k / L_k)$. Since the productivity and wage equations are defined at the plant level, they can be estimated together on consistent employer–employee data. A comparison of ϕ_j and μ_j may provide some evidence of discrimination. Clearly, if $\phi_j > \mu_j$ there is wage discrimination, while the reverse case may indicate nepotism in favour of the group j workers.

NOTES

1.   There have been additional studies in Europe, but not all of them have been published in English.
2.   By a standard convention, the absence of answer is interpreted as a no.
3.   Also notice that $D(A\ B) = -D(B, A)$.
4.   An unbiased estimator is

$$\text{Côv}(d_A, d_B) = \frac{1}{I-1} \sum_{i_1 \in I} \sum_{i_2 \in I} (d_{Ai1} - \bar{d}_A)(d_{Bi2} - \bar{d}_B).$$

5.   The Student distribution with N degrees of freedom converges to the standard normal distribution when $N \to \infty$.
6.   For $\alpha = 1$ per cent, 5 per cent or 10 per cent, we get the respective critical values $Z = 2.58$, 1.96 and 1.645.
7.   Some recruiters may impose a higher standard to discriminated candidates (Heckman, 1998).
8.   Notice that the constant term of this regression does not have the usual interpretation because the left-hand variable is a difference.
9.   One can directly check the predictions of the model.
10.   Ordered logit models have also been used. It is possible to choose the model with a Vuong (1989) test, as in Duguet and Petit (2005).
11.   The issue is similar to the estimation of panel data models. When the individual effect is not correlated, one must account for the covariance matrix between the disturbances. When the effect is correlated, one should difference out the individual effects.
12.   The indices of the A candidates are given by $2i - 1$, for $i = 1, \ldots, I$, and the indices of B candidates by $2i$.
13.   The method can be adapted to any number of candidates, provided that at least two candidates are sent on each offer.
14.   The method can be applied without this assumption.
15.   More generally, the weight of each difference is proportional to its number of observations.
16.   The focus on the two first moments is related to the normal distribution used later, since a normal distribution is fully defined by its two first moments.
17.   It is also possible to estimate a heteroskedastic probit model, as in Neumark (2012). Notice that separate probit estimates insure heteroskedasticity but require additional computations in order to get the joint covariance matrix of both candidates estimates.
18.   SAS with the QLIM procedure and R with the "sampleSelection" package.
19.   Notice that, when the right-hand variables are the same in the two equations, the identification proceeds from a functional form assumption only. It is better to use an exclusion restriction, with at least one variable present in the probit equation and not in the wage equation (see Olsen (1980) for a discussion).
20.   The tobit 2 estimator should reaches the Fréchet–Darmois–Cramer–Rao asymptotic variance lower bound when the distribution is bivariate normal.
21. $\ln(1 + x) \simeq x$, for $x \simeq 0$.
22.   By convention, a positive difference will indicate wage discrimination. We use the logarithm of wages as it is the common practice in the literature.
23.   The reader should notice that the occupations are often gendered, so female wages may reflect the non-discriminatory wage structures in the predominantly female occupations.
24.   A function $U(L_A, L_B)$ is homogeneous of degree k if $U(mL_A, mL_B) = m^k U(L_A, L_B)$. With $k = 0$, we get $U(mL_A, mL_B) = U(L_A, L_B)$. Letting $m = 1/(L_A + L_B)$ and $p_A = L_A/(L_A + L_B)$, we get $U(L_A, L_B) = U(p_A, 1 - p_A)$, so that the utility depends on the proportions of A workers only.

25. If $U(L_A, L_B)$ is homogeneous of degree k, $L_A \partial U / \partial L_A + L_B \partial U / \partial L_B = kU(L_A, L_B)$.
26. For a discussion, see Neumark (1988).
27. We use the approximation $\ln(1+x) \simeq x$, for $x \simeq 0$. In the applications, $0 < \pi_A < 1$ and $(W_A - W_B) / W_B$ is relatively low so that the approximation is good.
28. Here, we assume that A and B workers do not work in the same firms, so that $X_A' X_B = 0$.
29. It is also possible to estimate them from the probit parts of tobit 2 models.
30. With the two-step method, one first obtains an estimate of the product $\sigma \rho_j$, and another step is needed to obtain an estimate of σ_j from the residual variance. Using a tobit 2 software is more convenient than the two-step approach in this case.
31. In the case where the access to specific jobs is discriminatory, productivity differences may come from discrimination itself. Therefore, the method measures wage discrimination in a narrow sense.
32. The use of the delta method is necessary to get a separate estimate of ϕ_B.

REFERENCES

Amemiya, T. (1985): *Advanced econometrics*, Harvard University Press.
Arellano, M. (1987): "Practitioners' corner: Computing robust standard errors for within-groups estimators," *Oxford Bulletin of Economics and Statistics*, 49, 431–34.
Baert, S. (2017): "Hiring discrimination: An overview of (almost) all correspondence experiments since 2005," *GLO discussion paper*.
Becker, G. S. (1957): *The economics of discrimination*, University of Chicago Press.
Becker, G. S. (1971): *The economics of discrimination*, University of Chicago Press, 2nd edition.
Bertrand, M. and E. Duflo (2017): *Field experiments on discrimination*, North Holland, chap. 8.
Blinder, A. S. (1973): "Wage discrimination: Reduced form and structural estimates," *Journal of Human Resources*, 436–55.
Chamberlain, G. (1982): "Multivariate regression models for panel data," *Journal of Econometrics*, 18, 5–46.
Chamberlain, G. (1984): "Panel data," in *Handbook of Econometrics*, ed. by Z. Griliches and M. D. Intriligator, North-Holland, vol. 2, 1247–318.
Cotton, J. (1988): "On the decomposition of wage differentials," *The Review of Economics and Statistics*, 236–43.
Duguet, E., L. Du Parquet, Y. L'Horty, and P. Petit (2015): "New evidence of ethnic and gender discriminations in the French labor market using experimental data: A ranking extension of responses from correspondence tests," *Annals of Economics and Statistics/Annales d'Économie et de Statistique*, 21–39.
Duguet, E., R. Le Gall, Y. L'Horty, and P. Petit (2018): "How does labour market history influence the access to hiring interviews?" *International Journal of Manpower*, 39, 519–33.
Duguet, E. and P. Petit (2005): "Hiring discrimination in the French financial sector: An econometric analysis on field experiment data," *Annals of Economics and Statistics/Annales d'Économie et de Statistique*, 79–102.
Duncan, G. M. and D. E. Leigh (1980): "Wage determination in the union and nonunion sectors: A sample selectivity approach," *ILR Review*, 34, 24–34.
Gouriéroux, C., A. Monfort, and A. Trognon (1985): "Moindres carrés asymptotiques," in *Annales de l'INSEE*, JSTOR, 91–122.
Heckman, J. J. (1976): "The common structure of statistical models of truncation, sample selection and limited dependent variables and a simple estimator for such models," in *Annals of Economic and Social Measurement*, Volume 5, number 4, NBER, 475–92.
Heckman, J. J. (1979): "Sample selection bias as a specification error," *Econometrica: Journal of the Econometric Society*, 153–61.
Heckman, J. J. (1998): "Detecting discrimination," *Journal of Economic Perspectives*, 12, 101–16.
Hellerstein, J. K., D. Neumark, and K. R. Troske (1999): "Wages, productivity, and worker characteristics: Evidence from plant-level production functions and wage equations," *Journal of Labor Economics*, 17, 409–46.
Mincer, J. (1958): "Investment in human capital and personal income distribution," *Journal of Political Economy*, 66, 281–302.
Neuman, S. and R. L. Oaxaca (2004): "Wage decompositions with selectivity-corrected wage equations: A methodological note," *The Journal of Economic Inequality*, 2, 3–10.
Neumark, D. (1988): "Employers' discriminatory behavior and the estimation of wage discrimination," *Journal of Human Resources*, 279–95.
Neumark, D. (2012): "Detecting discrimination in audit and correspondence studies," *Journal of Human Resources*, 47, 1128–57.
Neumark, D. (2018): "Experimental research on labor market discrimination," *Journal of Economic Literature*, 56, 799–866.

Oaxaca, R. (1973): "Male-female wage differentials in urban labor markets," *International Economic Review*, 693–709.

Oaxaca, R. L. and M. R. Ransom (1988): "Searching for the effect of unionism on the wages of union and nonunion workers." *Journal of Labor Research*, 9, 139.

Oaxaca, R. L. and M. R. Ransom (1994): "On discrimination and the decomposition of wage differentials," *Journal of Econometrics*, 61, 5–21.

Olsen, R. J. (1980): "A least squares correction for selectivity bias," *Econometrica*, 1815–20.

Reimers, C. W. (1983): "Labor market discrimination against Hispanic and black men," *The Review of Economics and Statistics*, 570–79.

Riach, P. A. and J. Rich (2002): "Field experiments of discrimination in the market place," *The Economic Journal*, 112, F480–F518.

Rich, J. (2014): "What do field experiments of discrimination in markets tell us? A meta analysis of studies conducted since 2000," *IZA discussion paper*.

Rich, J. (2018): "Do photos help or hinder field experiments of discrimination?," *International Journal of Manpower*, 39, 502–18.

Tariq, M. and J. Syed (2017): "Intersectionality at work: South Asian Muslim women's experiences of employment and leadership in the United Kingdom," *Sex Roles*, 77, 510–22.

Vuong, Q. H. (1989): "Likelihood ratio tests for model selection and non-nested hypotheses," *Econometrica*, 57, 307–33.

7. Microeconomic models for designing and evaluating tax-transfer systems
Ugo Colombino

1. INTRODUCTION

In this chapter, we illustrate microeconomic models for the evaluation and the design of tax-transfer systems. We have made various inclusion/exclusion choices. First, we focus on methods based on economic theory, not just statistical analysis. Therefore, we do not cover the so-called "policy evaluation methods" based solely on statistical identification of the effects of policies. Those methods are not in any way specific to tax-transfer policies: they are identically applied to any kind of policies, or events.[1] Second, the models and the methods illustrated hereafter can, with minor adjustments, be equally applied to households or to firms. However, most of the literature considers households and we will follow this tradition. Third, we only consider income taxes and transfers, although again also capital taxation can be addressed with the same methodology. Fourth, we do not cover the extension to intertemporal decisions, although we mention a useful reference. The surveys by Blundell (2012) and Keane (2011) cover also some of the topics not treated in this chapter.

Evaluation and design, when based on economic modelling, require a representation of the process leading to the results (observed or simulated) of the policy. More specifically, they require a *structural* representation, that is, one in which some parameters are assumed to be invariant with respect to policy changes (Marschak, 1953; Hurwicz, 1962; Lucas, 1976). The basic framework works as follows. Household i faces an opportunity (or feasible) set B_i, whose elements are vectors x that might measure one or more dimensions of choice—that are expected to be affected by the tax-transfer system—for example hours of work, education, sector of occupation, transportation, childcare, training, fertility and so on. The preferences of household i are represented by a utility function $U_i(x; \theta)$, where θ is a vector of invariant parameters. In the simplest case $x = (h, c)$, where h = hours of work and c = net available income. The corresponding representation of B_i is a budget set, that is $B_i = \{(h, c): c \leq f(w_i h, I_i)\}$, where w denotes the hourly gross wage rate and $f(.,.)$ is the tax-benefit rule that transforms gross labour earnings $w_i h$ and unearned income I_i into net available income c_i. More generally, there might be constraints on the feasible values of h, on the way gross earnings are generated depending on labour contracts and so on. In this framework, the policy reforms are represented as changes in the opportunity set B_i. More specifically, tax-transfer reforms are represented as changes in the tax-transfer rule $f(.,.)$.

The decision rule is represented by $x_i = \arg\max_{x \in B_i} U_i(x;\theta)$. If the parameters θ can be estimated, the effects on choices of a new opportunity set B_i^P can be computed as: $x_i^P = \arg\max_{x \in B_i^P} U_i(x;\theta)$.

We use a household-specific index since, when adopting a microeconomic approach, it turns out to be important to account for the heterogeneity of preferences and opportunity sets. This is so both because the effects of a tax-transfer systems are significantly dependent on the different choices of heterogeneous households and because the evaluation of the reforms also depends on how gains and losses are distributed.

Section 2 surveys different approaches to representing and estimating the decision rules while taking tax transfers into account. Section 3 addresses the simulation and the welfare evaluation of the effects of alternative tax-transfer systems. Section 4 is dedicated to the optimal design of tax-transfer systems.

2.   TAKING TAXES INTO ACCOUNT

2.1   Linear Budget Constraints

To begin with, let us consider the case with no taxes and no transfers. Then, the budget constraint is $c \leq wh + I$. With monotonic preferences, the optimal choices h_i, c_i satisfy

$$-\frac{\partial U_i(h_i,c_i;\theta)}{\partial h_i} \Big/ \frac{\partial U_i(h_i,c_i;\theta)}{\partial c_i} = w_i$$

$$c_i = w_i h_i + I_i$$

(7.1)

and the solution h_i in general is a function of w_i, I_i:

$$h_i = h_i(w_i, I_i;\theta).$$

(7.2)

The labour supply function $h_i(.,.; \theta)$ might have been chosen from the very start as a convenient specification or might have been explicitly obtained by choosing a utility function and applying conditions (7.1). Appendix 7A.1 summarizes the relationships between labour supply functions and (direct or indirect) representations of preferences.

In view of empirical applications, a common approach is to allow for a "disturbance" e_i (a random variable) that accounts for the effects of unobserved factors affecting the solution, for example

$$\tilde{h}_i = h_i(w_i, I_i;\theta) + e_i.$$

(7.3)

In this model, the disturbance is usually interpreted as possibly embodying the effects of both unobserved household characteristics and of "optimization errors" (that is involuntary, unforeseen or unrealized displacements from the desired choice). As we will see, in a more complicated model it is important to distinguish the different sources of unobserved heterogeneity. With a sample of observations on $\tilde{h}, w$ and I, it is straightforward to estimate the parameters θ with standard methods such as Ordinary Least Squares, Non-Linear Least Squares or Maximum Likelihood, depending on the shape of $h_i(.,.; \theta)$ and on the distributional assumptions upon e_i.

Let us now introduce taxes in the simplest form. Let $c_i \leq (w_i h_i + I_i)(1 - t)$ be the budget constraint, where t is a constant marginal tax rate. Since the budget constraint reduces to $c_i \leq (1 - t) w_i h_i + (1 - t)I_i$, the solution will have the same form as in (7.3), with the net wage rate

$(1 - t)w_i$ replacing the gross wage rate w_i and the net unearned income $(1 - t)I_i$ replacing the gross unearned income I_i:

$$\tilde{h}_i = h_i((1-t)w_i,(1-t)I_i;\theta)+e_i. \tag{7.4}$$

If the tax-transfer rule preserves the linearity of the gross (or pre-fisc) budget constraint, it does not raise any new estimation problem. Up to the end of the 1960s, empirical studies of labour supply adopted specifications close to expression (7.4), even though the budget constraint is not linear. (for example Kosters, 1969 and Bowen and Finegan, 1969). The assumption that non-linearities are not serious enough or that a linear approximation would work anyway prevails. For example, instead of the gross wage rate w, the analyst would use an average net wage rate $\bar{w}$. But with non-linear taxation (not explicitly represented), $\bar{w}$ would depend on the tax-transfer rule itself: as a consequence, the estimated parameter would not be the policy-independent preference parameters θ, but rather some mixture of the preference parameters θ and of the tax-transfer parameters.[2] Therefore, the estimates could not really be used for policy evaluation. An alternative approximation would consist in replacing the non-linear budget line with a "virtual" linear budget line (Figure 7.1). The "virtual" linear budget line is defined by the observed marginal net wage (computed at the observed value of h_i and by the "virtual" unearned income, that is, the intercept of the line, with slope equal to the marginal wage rate, going through the point of tangency between the indifference curve and the true budget line. This last procedure would then require taking into account the endogeneity of both the marginal net wage rate and the "virtual" income (they both depend on the choice h_i).

Even within the linear budget case, there is a problem that expression (7.2) ignores. We might have a corner solution, that is,

$$-\frac{\partial U_i(0,I_i;\theta)}{\partial h_i} \bigg/ \frac{\partial U_i(0,I_i;\theta)}{\partial c_i} > w_i. \tag{7.5}$$
$$c_i = I_i$$

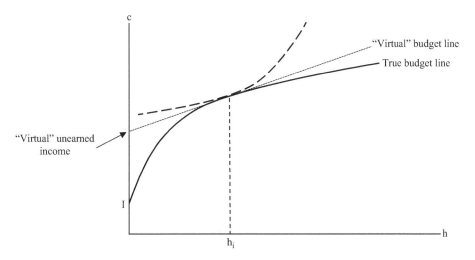

Figure 7.1   Linearization of a non-linear budget line: the "virtual" budget line

Therefore, the general solution is

$$\begin{cases} \begin{cases} h_i = h_i(w_i, I_i; \theta) \\ c_i = w_i h_i + I_i \end{cases} \text{if } -\frac{\partial U_i(0, I_i; \theta)}{\partial h_i} \Big/ \frac{\partial U_i(0, I_i; \theta)}{\partial c_i} \leq w_i \\ \begin{cases} h_i = 0 \\ c_i = I_i \end{cases} \text{if } -\frac{\partial U_i(0, I_i; \theta)}{\partial h_i} \Big/ \frac{\partial U_i(0_i, I_i; \theta)}{\partial c_i} > w_i \end{cases} \tag{7.6}$$

Expression (7.6) leads to a Tobit model; see for example Heckman (1974a).

Corner solutions are also related to taxes and transfers, since the relative desirability of corner solutions vs. interior solutions also depends on the tax-transfer rule.

2.2 Non-linear Budget Constraints and Corner Solutions

The relevance of non-linear budget constraints and of corner solutions started being acknowledged in the second half of the 1960s. There are three main reasons. First, the theory of optimal taxation shows the importance of the incentives induced by the (in general non-linear) design of the tax-transfer rule (Mirrlees, 1971). Second, in the United States, various welfare and "anti-poverty" programs imply complications (non-linearities, non-convexities) in the budget sets. Third, issues related to equality, gender issues, childcare, education and so on bring to the fore the importance of female participation (or not) to the labour market.

2.2.1 The "marginalist" approach
A first approach to modelling non-linear budget constraints and corner solutions goes through the Kuhn–Tucker conditions associated with the constrained maximization of the utility function. The approach is defined as "marginalist" by Aaberge and Colombino (2014, 2018) because it involves comparing "marginal" variations in utility and in the budget constraints. Heckman (1974b) is perhaps the first empirical paper that explicitly uses the conditions characterizing the solution of utility maximization subject to a non-linear budget constraint, with the purpose of addressing a non-standard policy evaluation problem. Burtless and Hausman (1978), Wales and Woodland (1979) and Hausman (1979, 1985) generalize the concept of "virtual" budget constraint and develop a method specifically appropriate for piecewise linear budget constraints.

Most actual or reformed tax-benefit rules belong to the piecewise linear family, that is, they can be represented as a combination of linear segments. A crucial distinction is whether the resulting budget set is convex.

2.2.1.1 *Piecewise linear budget constraint: Convex budget set*
We start with the case in which the budget set is convex. For simplicity, we consider a single-person household, that is, an individual. Let us suppose that, as long as earnings do not exceed a certain amount E, the household is not required to pay taxes. However, for every Euro of earnings above E, taxes must be paid according to a marginal tax rate t. The first segment has slope w_i; the second segment has slope equal to $w_i(1-t)$. It is useful to define

$$H_i = \frac{E}{w_i} = \text{hours of work corresponding to the "kink"},$$

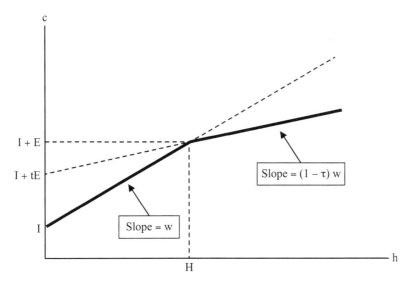

Figure 7.2 Convex budget set: progressive taxation

and $I_i + E - w_i(1 - t)H_i = I_i + Et =$ "virtual" exogenous income associated with the second segment (that is, the intercept of the line that lies on the second segment). Note that the exogenous income associated with the first segment is instead I_i (Figure 7.2). Then the problem is

$$\max_{h,c} U_i(h,c;\theta)$$

s.t.

$$c \leq I_i + w_i h \tag{7.7}$$

$$c \leq I_i + Et + w_i(1-t)h$$

$$h \geq 0.$$

The so-called non-negativity constraint $h \geq 0$ accounts for the possibility of corner solutions. In principle there is a second possible corner solution, that is, $h = T$, where T denotes some maximum amount of work, but we ignore it for simplicity. Working through the Kuhn–Tucker conditions, it turns out that the solution to problem (7.7) can be characterized as follows. Let us define $h_i(n, q; \theta)$ as the "virtual" labour supply given a generic wage rate n and a generic exogenous income q, that is, the value of h that solves the problem

$$\max_{c,h} U_i(h,c;\theta)$$

s.t. $\tag{7.8}$

$$c = q + nh.$$

Then the solution to problem (7.7) is

$$
h_i^* = \begin{cases}
0 \text{ if } h_i(w_i, I_i; \theta) \leq 0 \\
h_i(w_i, I_i; \theta) \text{ if } 0 < h_i(w_i, I_i; \theta) < H_i \\
H_i \text{ if } h_i(w_i, I_i; \theta) \geq H_i \text{ and } h_i(w_i(1-t), I_i + Et; \theta) \leq H_i \\
h_i(w_i(1-t), I_i + Et; \theta) \text{ if } h_i(w_i(1-t), I_i + Et; \theta) > H_i
\end{cases}
\tag{7.9}
$$

Given θ, w_i and I_i the choice of household i is determined. However, due to "optimization errors," the observed value $\tilde{h}_i$ will differ from h_i^*. Given a sample of N households, the parameters θ can be estimated by solving

$$
\min_{\theta} \sum_{i=1}^{N} \left(\tilde{h}_i - h_i^* \right)^2.
\tag{7.10}
$$

In the above model, preferences are fixed and randomness is due to "optimization errors." Alternatively, we can assume randomness due to unobserved components of preferences. A common specification of the labour supply function that embodies this assumption is the following: $h(w_i, I_i; \theta_i)$. Here, the random variable ε_i is not an "optimization error" or a displacement from the desired position. Instead, it measures the effect of preference components that are known by household but not by the analyst. In our presentation it can be interpreted as a (household-specific) random part of one of the parameters θ. Therefore, expression (7.9) can be rewritten as follows:

$$
h_i^* = \begin{cases}
0 \text{ if } h_i(w_i, I_i; \theta) + \varepsilon_i \leq 0 \\
h_i(w_i, I_i; \theta) + \varepsilon_i \text{ if } 0 < h_i(w_i, I_i; \theta) + \varepsilon_i < H_i \\
H_i \text{ if } h_i(w_i, I_i; \theta) + \varepsilon_i \geq H_i \text{ and } h_i(w_i(1-t), I_i + Et; \theta) + \varepsilon_i \leq H_i \\
h_i(w_i(1-t), I_i + Et; \theta) + \varepsilon_i \text{ if } h_i(w_i(1-t), I_i + Et; \theta) + \varepsilon_i > H_i
\end{cases}
\tag{7.11}
$$

Expression (7.11) tells us that the observed $\tilde{h}$ is generated according to four alternative events. Let n_1, n_2, n_3 and n_4 be the sets of indices of the households for which the four events respectively apply. Let us assume $\varepsilon_i \sim \text{Normal}(0, \sigma_\varepsilon^2)$. The parameters θ can be estimated by the maximizing likelihood function:

$$
\Lambda = \prod_{i \in n_1} \Phi\left(\frac{-h_i(w_i, I_i; \theta)}{\sigma_\varepsilon} \right) \times \prod_{i \in n_2} \phi\left(\frac{\tilde{h}_i - h_i(w_i, I_i; \theta)}{\sigma_\varepsilon} \right)
$$
$$
\times \prod_{i \in n_3} \left[\Phi\left(\frac{H_i - h_i(w_i(1-t), I_i + Et; \theta)}{\sigma_\varepsilon} \right) - \Phi\left(\frac{h_i(w_i, I_i; \theta) - H_i}{\sigma_\varepsilon} \right) \right]
\tag{7.12}
$$
$$
\times \prod_{i \in n_4} \phi\left(\frac{\tilde{h}_i - h_i(w_i(1-t), I_i + Et; \theta)}{\sigma_\varepsilon} \right),
$$

where $\theta(.)$ and $\Phi(.)$, respectively, denote the standard normal probability density function and the standard normal distribution function.

Simulations based on the estimates of model (7.11) tend to overestimate the bunching of observations at H. As a response to this problem, a further extension of the model consists of introducing a second random component u_i that accounts for "optimization errors." Therefore,

$$\tilde{h}_i = h_i^* + u_i. \tag{7.13}$$

The probability (density or mass) of observing a particular value $\tilde{h}_i$ will now depend jointly on ε and on u:

$$
\begin{aligned}
\Pr(\tilde{h}_i > 0) = &\Pr\Big((0 < h_i(w_i, I_i; \theta) + \varepsilon_i < H_i) \cap (\tilde{h}_i = h_i(w_i, I_i; \theta) + \varepsilon_i + u_i)\Big) + \\
&\Pr\Big((h_i(w_i(1-t), I_i + Et; \theta) + \varepsilon_i > H_i) \cap (\tilde{h}_i = h_i(w_i(1-t), I_i + Et; \theta) + \varepsilon_i + u_i)\Big) + \\
&+ \Pr\Big((h_i(w_i, I_i; \theta) - H_i \le \varepsilon_{ii} \le H_i - h_i(w_i(1-t), I_i + Et; \theta)) \cap (\tilde{h}_i = H_i + u_i)\Big);
\end{aligned} \tag{7.14}
$$

$$
\begin{aligned}
\Pr(\tilde{h}_i = 0) = &\Pr\Big((0 < h_i(w_i, I_i; \theta) + \varepsilon_i < H_i) \cap (h_i(w_i, I_i; \theta) + \varepsilon_i + u_i \le 0)\Big) + \\
&\Pr\Big((h_i(w_i(1-t), I_i + Et; \theta) + \varepsilon_i > H_i) \cap (h_i(w_i(1-t), I_i + Et; \theta) + \varepsilon_i + u_i \le 0)\Big) + \\
&+ \Pr\Big((h_i(w_i, I_i; \theta) - H_i \le \varepsilon_{ii} \le H_i - h_i(w_i(1-t), I_i + Et; \theta)) \cap (u_i \le -H_i)\Big) + \\
&+ \Pr\Big(h_i(w_i, I_i; \theta) + \varepsilon_i \le 0\Big).
\end{aligned}
$$

The probability of $\tilde{h}_i = 0$ in expression (7.14) allows for involuntary unemployment but not for involuntary employment. By choosing a joint distribution function for ε_i and u_i (usually a bivariate normal), one can write down the likelihood function to be maximized with respect to θ. See for example Moffit (1986), Arrufat and Zabalza (1986) and Colombino and Del Boca (1990) for details.

The same procedure can be used to characterize the solution when the problem involves more than two segments and can be extended (with due modifications) to cases with non-convex budget sets.

2.2.1.2 *Piecewise linear budget constraint: Non-convex budget set*
The treatment of non-convex budget sets is essentially specific to the case at hand. An instructive example is provided by the non-convexity introduced by a minimum income guaranteed (Figures 7.3a and 7.3b). For simplicity, we set $I = 0$. If the pre-fisc income wh is less than G, the household receives a transfer equal to $(G - wh)$. If $wh > G$, the household pays a tax equal to $(wh - G)t$. The household's choice involves the comparison of the utility attained at $h=0$, that is, $U(0, G; \theta)$ and the maximum utility attainable on the virtual budget line $c = tG + (1 - t)wh$, that is, $V(w, tG; \theta)$, where $V()$ is the indirect utility function. Figures 7.3a and 7.3b, respectively, illustrate a corner solution ($h_i = 0$) and an interior solution ($h_i > 0$). As in the convex budget case, one can model the household's choice accounting for "optimization errors" or random preferences or both. A sufficiently general explanation of how to build the likelihood function when the budget set is not convex is provided by Moffit (1986). A useful application (to housing taxation) is presented by Hausman and Wise (1980).

The "marginalist" approach can be extended to cover simultaneous (wife and husband) household decisions and intertemporal decisions. Useful presentations are provided by

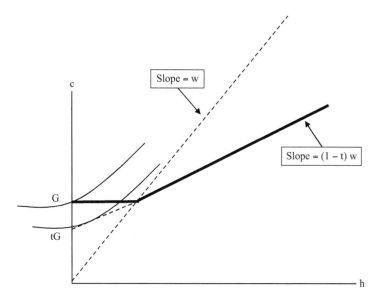

Figure 7.3a   Non-convex budget set: minimum income guaranteed, corner solution

Hausman (1979, 1985), Moffit (1986), Heckman and MaCurdy (1986) and Blundell and MaCurdy (1999). Applications to different countries and different tax-benefit rules and reforms include Burtless and Hausman (1978), Hausman (1985), Blomquist (1983), Zabalza (1983), Arrufat and Zabalza (1986), Blomquist and Hansson-Brusewitz (1990), Bourguignon and Magnac (1990), Colombino and Del Boca (1990), MaCurdy et al. (1990), Triest (1990) and Van Soest et al. (1990). More general surveys also covering contributions that belong to the structural "marginalist" approach include Blundell and MaCurdy (1999), Blundell et al. (2007), Meghir and Phillips (2010) and Keane (2011).

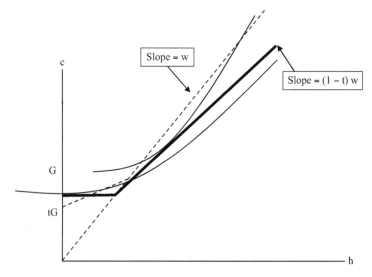

Figure 7.3b   Non-convex budget set: minimum income guaranteed, interior solution

Although the "marginalist" approach can in principle be extended to more complex scenarios, for example simultaneous (wife and husband) household decisions or intertemporal decisions, the methods proposed by Heckman as well as the method proposed by Hausman and co-authors in practice turn out to be not so easily applicable to problems that are more complicated than those for which they were originally exemplified. First, the methods become computationally cumbersome when the decision makers face non-convex budget sets and/ or when more than two goods are the object of choice. Second, in view of the computational problems, this approach essentially forces the researcher to choose relatively simple specifications for the utility function or the labour supply functions. Third, computational and statistical consistency of ML estimation of the model requires imposing a priori the quasi-concavity of the utility function (Keane, 2011).

2.2.2 The random utility maximization approach

The most popular approach to modelling labour supply (and more generally household decisions) is now the random utility model (RUM) developed by McFadden (1974, 1984).

Although McFadden's original formulation adopted a discrete choice version, it is useful to start from a continuous version that is more easily linked and compared to the models illustrated in section 2.2.1. The basic idea is to directly represent utility as random:

$$U_i(h,c) = v_i(h, f(wh, I); \theta) + \varepsilon. \tag{7.15}$$

Clearly the choice (h_i, ε_i) is such that

$$(h_i, \varepsilon_i) = \arg\max_{h,\varepsilon}(v_i(h, f(wh, I); \theta) + \varepsilon), \tag{7.16}$$

where θ represents a vector of non-random preference parameters and $\varepsilon_i(h, c)$ is the contribution of unobserved (by the analyst) random factors.

Since ε is known by the household but not by the analyst, the best the analyst can do is to model the choices in terms of probability. By assuming ε is i.i.d. Type I Extreme value, it can be shown that the probability density function of observing household i choosing h_i turns out to be

$$\Pr_i(h_i) = \frac{\exp\{v_i(h_i, f(w_i h_i, I_i); \theta)\}}{\int_0^T \exp\{v_i(h, f(w_i h, I_i); \theta)\} dh}. \tag{7.17}$$

Expression (7.17) directly gives the contribution of household *i* choosing h_i to the likelihood function.

In the discrete choice version, the denominator of expression (7.17) is replaced by a sum:

$$\Pr_i(h_i) = \frac{\exp\{v_i(h_i, f(w_i h_i, I_i); \theta)\}}{\sum_{h \in D} \exp\{v_i(h, f(w_i h, I_i); \theta)\}}, \tag{7.18}$$

where D is some discrete set of values $h \in [0, T]$.

We can interpret expression (7.18) either as an approximation of expression (7.17) or as a realistic representation of the household's choice that accounts for quantity constraints. For example, it might be the case that few alternative values of h might be available, such as non-working, part-time and full-time: an assumption (and a simplification) that many empirical studies adopt.

In order to improve the fit of model (7.18) some refinements are commonly used. Van Soest (1995) notes that model (7.18) tends to over-predict the number of people working part-time. Besides (h,c) (and besides $\varepsilon(h, c)$) jobs might differ according to a number of systematic factors that are not accounted for by the observed variables contained in $v(.,.)$, for example availability or fixed costs. In order to account for these unobserved systematic factors, the following "dummies refinement" (as defined in Colombino, 2013)) can be adopted. We define subsets $S_0, \ldots, S_L$ of the set of values $[0, T]$. The definition of the subsets reflects some hypothesis upon the different incidence of the unobserved systematic factors upon different ranges of value of h. The choice probability is then specified as follows (Van Soest 1995):

$$\Pr_i(h_i) = \frac{\exp\left\{v_i(h_i, f(w_i h_i, I_i); \theta) + \sum_\ell \gamma_\ell 1(h \in S_\ell)\right\}}{\sum_{h \in D} \exp\left\{v_i(h, f(w_i h, I_i); \theta) + \sum_\ell \gamma_\ell 1(h \in S_\ell)\right\}},\tag{7.19}$$

where $1(.)$ is the indicator function.

An alternative to the "dummy refinement" of model (7.19) consists of imputing a monetary cost (or benefit) K to some ranges of work hours:

$$P(h_i) = \frac{\exp\left\{v(h_i, f(w_i h_i, I_i) + \sum_\ell K_\ell 1(h \in S_\ell)); \theta)\right\}}{\sum_{h \in D} \exp\left\{v(h, f(w_i h, I_i) + \sum_\ell K_\ell 1(h \in S_\ell)); \theta)\right\}}.\tag{7.20}$$

More specifically, expression (7.20) can be interpreted as accounting for fixed costs of working (for example, Duncan and Harris (2002) and the survey by Blundell et al. (2007)).

Aaberge et al. (1995) adopt the continuous approach but develop a more complex model. They assume that the opportunity set contains jobs characterized by $(h, w, \varepsilon(h, w))$. There are many jobs with the same values (h, w) but different values of the random variable $\varepsilon(h, w)$. Among the jobs of same type (h, w), the household will consider only the one with the highest $\varepsilon(h, w)$, say $\varepsilon^*(h, w)$. Therefore, at this point the household choice can be represented as

$$(h_i, w_i) = \arg\max_{h,w}(v_i(h, f(wh, I_i); \theta) + \varepsilon^*(h, w)).$$

If $\varepsilon(h, w)$ has an extreme value distribution, $\varepsilon^*(h, w)$ also does.[3] Let $p_i(h, w; \gamma)$ denote the probability density functions of jobs with the same (h, w), where γ is a vector of parameters to be estimated. Then it turns out (for example Aaberge et al., 1995) that the choice probability can be written as follows:

$$\Pr_i(h_i, w_i) = \frac{\exp\left\{v_i(h_i, f(w_i h_i, I_i); \theta)\right\} p_i(h_i, w_i; \gamma)}{\int_0^\infty \int_0^T \exp\left\{v_i(h, f(wh, I_i); \theta)\right\} p_i(h, w; \gamma) \, dh \, dw}.\tag{7.21}$$

A simplified version with exogenous wage rates is

$$\Pr_i(h_i) = \frac{\exp\{v_i(h_i, f(w_i h_i, I_i); \theta)\} p_i(h_i; \gamma)}{\int_0^T \exp\{v_i(h, f(w_i h, I_i); \theta)\} p_i(h; \gamma) dh}. \tag{7.22}$$

One can specify $p_i(h; \gamma)$ in such a way that model (7.22) can be interpreted as a continuous version of model (7.19). Namely, if $p(h; \gamma)$ is uniform with "peaks" at certain values of h (for example at $h = 0$, part-time, full-time), it reduces to a set of dummy variables as in model (7.19). The same applies to model (7.21). Details can be found in Colombino (2013). However, models (7.21) and (7.22) are more general since they allow—through alternative specifications of the probability density function $p(h; \gamma)$ or $p(h, w; \gamma)$—for a richer representation of the opportunity set. The statistical foundations of (generalized versions of) model (7.21) were developed by Dagsvik (1994). Expressions (7.21) and (7.22) are close to the continuous spatial model developed by Ben-Akiva and Watanatada (1981). They can also be seen as extensions of McFadden's (1974, 1984) conditional logit model where the non-random part of the utility of a "job" of type h or (h,w) is "weighted" by the density of jobs of the same type in the opportunity set. Aaberge and Colombino (2014) define models (7.21) and (7.22) as the RURO (random utility, random opportunities) model, since both the utility function and the opportunity set are random. Among others, Aaberge et al. (1995), Aaberge et al. (1999), Aaberge and Colombino (2006, 2012, 2013), Dagsvik et al. (2009, 2014), Dagsvik and Strøm (2006), Colombino (2013), Islam and Colombino (2018) and Coda Moscarola et al. (2020) have adopted model (7.21)—or variants of it.

When adopting models (7.17)–(7.22), we face the problem of how to represent the opportunity set in practice.

For the discrete models (7.18), (7.19) and (7.20), the opportunity set is just a discrete set of values in the range [0, T]. The number of values varies across applications and authors but in most cases is between 3 and 10 (for a single-person household). A common procedure consists of dividing the range [0, T] into subsets of equal size. Then the opportunity set of each household will contain 0 and the mid-value of the subsets. The mid-value of the subset that contains the observed value of h might be replaced by the observed value. Alternatively, one might replace the observed value with the mid-value of the corresponding subset: this procedure will imply a measurement error, but experiments with different sizes of the subsets show that this is of minor importance.

In the case of the continuous models, the opportunity set in principle contains an infinity of values. The integral at the denominator in general does not have a closed form and must be evaluated numerically. A common approach consists of turning to a discrete approximation. The procedure proposed by McFadden (1978) works as follows. Let us consider model (7.18). First, choose M values $h^1, \ldots, h^M$. One of them is 0, another one is the observed value. The others are sampled from a probability density function $q_i(h)$. Then, it can be shown that one can obtain consistent estimates of the parameters by replacing expression (7.18) with

$$\Pr_i(h_i) = \frac{\exp\{v_i(h_i, f(w_i h_i, I_i); \theta)\} \dfrac{1}{q_i(h_i)}}{\displaystyle\sum_{h=h^1}^{h^M} \exp\{v_i(h, f(w_i h, I_i); \theta)\} \dfrac{1}{q_i(h)}}. \tag{7.23}$$

The same procedure applies also to the implementation of model (7.22). In that case, we choose a probability density function $q_i(h, w)$ and M couples $(h^1, w^1) \ldots, (h^M, w^M)$. Then the RURO analogue of expression (7.23) is

$$\Pr_i(h_i, w_i) = \frac{\exp\{v_i(h_i, f(w_i h_i, I_i); \theta)\} \dfrac{p_i(h_i, w_i; \gamma)}{q_i(h_i, w_i)}}{\displaystyle\sum_{j=1}^{A} \exp\{v_i(h^j, f(w^j h^j, I_i); \theta)\} \dfrac{p_i(h^j, w^j; \gamma)}{q_i(h^j, w^j)}}. \qquad (7.24)$$

Notice that expression (7.18) can be interpreted as the special case of (7.23) when $q_i(h)$ is a constant, that is, $q_i(.)$ is assumed to be uniform. Analogously, expression (7.22) can be interpreted as the (continuous) special case of (7.24) when $q_i(.,.)$ is constant. The choice of the probability density function $q_i(.)$ or $q_i(.,.)$ has implications for the efficiency of the estimates. From this perspective, simulation exercises suggest that using a q_i close to the empirical distribution of the observed values of h or of (h,w) might be a sensible choice (Atherton et al., 1990). Aaberge et al. (2009) discuss various topics related to the empirical representation of the opportunity set.

The crucial advantage of the RUM (or of the RURO variant) is that the (probabilistic) solution of the utility maximization problem is represented in terms of comparisons of levels of utility rather than in terms of marginal variations of utility, and it is not affected by the specification of the utility function, nor of the tax-transfer rule. This approach is very convenient when compared to the previous ones, since it does not require going through complicated Kuhn–Tucker conditions involving derivatives of the utility function and of the budget constraints. Therefore, it is not affected by the complexity of the rule that defines the budget set or by how many goods are contained in the utility function and how many decision makers are present in the household. For example, it is easy to see that modelling couples simply require h, w and I to be vectors with two components; the form of the choice probabilities remains the same. Equally important, the deterministic part of the utility function can be specified in a very flexible way without worrying about the computational problems. Models (7.17)– (7.22) can be extended in many directions. For example, one might want to allow for one of more of the parameters θ to be random, or in general introduce a more complex structure of the stochastic part of the model (for example McFadden and Train, 2000). These extensions usually require simulation-based estimation. A survey is provided by Train (2003).

2.2.3   Unobserved wages

So far, we have assumed that the wage rate w is observed for everyone. As a matter of fact, sample surveys report earnings and hours of work (or, more rarely, wage rates) only for people who are observed working. Presentations of how to address the problem can be found in Bargain and Peichl (2016) and in Aaberge and Colombino (2014, 2018). Within the "marginalist" approach, Heckman (1974a) presents maximum likelihood estimates of a simultaneous model of hours of work and wage rate (with a linear budget constraint), accounting for corner solutions with $h = 0$ and unobserved wage rates, essentially a bivariate version of the tobit model (Tobin, 1958). Alternatively, one can estimate the same model with a two-step procedure, that is, the so-called "Heckit" model (Heckman, 1979). First, a wage rate equation is estimated on the subsample where wage rates are observed, correcting the bias introduced by the truncated sample. Second, the predicted wage rates (based on the estimates obtained at step 1) replace the observed wage rates as well as the missing values in the labour supply equation. Both the simultaneous procedure and the two-step procedure can be used within the "marginalist" approach with non-linear budget constraints. This literature usually allows for a correlation between the random component of the wage rate equation and the random component(s) of the labour supply equation. Bargain and Peichl (2016) provide a useful survey of different methods and results.

Turning to the RUM approach, the basic model (7.18), when accounting for unobserved wages, might be reformulated as follows:

$$
\Pr_i(h_i) = \begin{cases} \dfrac{\exp\{v_i(h_i, f(w_i h_i, I_i); \theta)\}}{\displaystyle\sum_{h=0}^{T}\exp\{v_i(h, f(w_i h, I_i); \theta)\}} & \text{if } h > 0 \\[2em] \displaystyle\int \dfrac{\exp\{v(0, f(0, I_i); \theta)\}}{\displaystyle\sum_{h=0}^{T}\exp\{v(h, f(wh, I); \theta)\}} m(w)\,dw & \text{if } h = 0 \end{cases}, \tag{7.25}
$$

where $m(w)$ is the assumed (typically log-nomal) probability density function of w. The same could be done with models (7.17) and (7.22). Alternatively, with the same models, one could use the two-step procedure and replace the unobserved wage rates with the predictions based on the estimation of the first step (for example, Van Soest 1995). Expression (7.25) assumes that the wage rate w is exogenously given with respect to the household's labour supply choice. In RURO model (7.21), the wage rate is instead an object of choice and the opportunity density $p_i(h, w; \gamma)$ is estimated simultaneously with the utility function.

Both expressions (7.25) and (7.21) assume that the random component of the wage rate is uncorrelated with the random term of the utility function. This does not imply that choice of h is uncorrelated with the random term of the wage rate equation. However, one might want to allow (for example, Gong and Van Soest, 2002; Blundell and Shephard, 2012) for a correlation of the wage rate random component with one or more random parameters—if any—of $v(h, f(wh, I); \theta)$, for example, because the wage rate might also depend on previous decisions and therefore on preferences.

2.2.4 Intertemporal decisions

Both the "marginalist" and the random utility approaches can be extended to modelling intertemporal decisions. This is particularly relevant if one is willing to consider a more general concept of labour supply, including decisions concerning education, occupational choice or retirement. Or if the research interest involves other decisions with intertemporal implications, such as savings or childcare. The tax-transfer system can have important effects on those choices. Keane (2011) provides a survey of themes related to taxes and labour supply with a prominent focus on intertemporal decisions.

3. SIMULATION AND EVALUATION OF TAX-TRANSFER REFORMS

3.1 Producing Simulation Outcomes

Typically, we are interested in predicting (some function of) h and/or c—for example participation rate, poverty index and so on—given a new tax-transfer rule f^P different from the current f.

In view of social welfare evaluations (to be addressed in section 3.3) we also want to simulate the level of utility attained or attainable under a given tax-transfer system.

Within the "marginalist" approaches (as defined in section 2) we estimate a labour supply function and—using one of the approaches illustrated in the Appendix—a direct and/or indirect representation of the preferences. With convex budget sets, the labour supply function is sufficient. With a non-convex budget set, in general we also need the (direct and/or indirect) utility function. It is in general also possible to identify the distribution of the random component capturing unobserved heterogeneity of preferences and/or the distribution of the measurement/optimization error (whichever is present in the model). Given the estimates of the (non-random parameters of) the labour supply function and/or of utility function, those random components are simulated so that their values are compatible with the observed values of h. Arrufat and Zabalza (1986) provide a clear and exhaustive explanation of this procedure.

With random utility models, we can choose between two alternative procedures:

a. Compute the expected chosen value of the variable of interest, based on the estimated choice probabilities, for example Colombino and Narazani (2013), Colombino (2013, 2015) and Islam and Colombino (2018). If the variable of interest is some function of h, say $\varphi_i(h)$, its expected value given the tax-transfer rule f^P is

$$E(\varphi_i(h_i) \setminus f^P) = \int_0^T \mathrm{Pr}_i(h \setminus f^P)\varphi_i(h)\,dh, \qquad (7.26)$$

   where $Pr_i(h \backslash f^P)$ is the probability (or probability density function)—evaluated according to one of the models illustrated—that, given the new tax-transfer rule f^P, the chosen value is h. The integral can be replaced by a sum operator depending on the whether a continuous or a discrete model is adopted.

   If instead the variable of interest is the (expected) maximum attained utility, say U_i^*, then its expected value is (McFadden, 1978; Ben-Akiva and Lerman, 1985)

$$E(U_i^* \setminus f^P) = \ln \int_0^T \exp\big\{v_i(h, f^P(w_i h, I_i);\theta)\big\}\,dh. \qquad (7.27)$$

b. Simulate the value of the systematic utility and of the random component corresponding to each alternative in the opportunity set. Identify the alternative with the highest utility and compute the corresponding value(s) of the variable(s) of interest. Typically, the random components are kept fixed across the different policy regimes that one might want to simulate and compare. As to the current policy regime, one might simulate it as well: its results will not be identical to the observed one but will be reasonably close, at least in large samples. Alternatively, one might adopt the procedure suggested by Creedy and Kalb (2005), that is, generating a vector of random components that, given the estimated parameters of the utility function, are consistent with the observed choices under the current policy regime.

When simulating sample aggregates, such as the total hours worked or total gross income, procedures (a) and (b) should be asymptotically equivalent; however, they might diverge on small samples or sub-samples. See Ben-Akiva and Watanatada (1981), Ben-Akiva and Lerman (1985) and Atherton et al. (1990) for the properties of alternative methods for producing predictions with random utility models.

3.2 Interpretation of the Policy Simulation Results: Short-Run, Long-Run, Comparative Statics

Non-behavioural policy microsimulations—that do not account for new household decisions as a response to policy changes—are usually interpreted as "day after" predictions,
that is, predictions of the very short term, when household and market interactions did not
have time to adjust to the policy changes. The interpretation of behavioural microsimulation results might vary depending on which reactions are taken into account. The typical
tax-transfer reform simulation computes the labour supply effects while leaving the wage
rates unchanged. Creedy and Duncan (2005) interpret this scenario as the "month after"
prediction, with households making new choices but the market mechanisms still late in the
process of adjusting wage rates, labour demand and so on. Alternatively, one might interpret
the typical behavioural simulation exercise as a "very long-run" prediction, with a perfectly
elastic labour demand defined by the current wage rates. Colombino (2013) observes that
comparative statics is the appropriate perspective with behavioural microsimulation models
based on a static representation of agents' choices, that is, we want to compare two different
equilibria induced by two different policies. With the notion of equilibrium, we refer in
general to a scenario in which the economic agents make optimal choices (that is, they choose
the best alternative among those available in the opportunity set) and their choices are mutually consistent or feasible. The comparative statics perspective is relevant both when the new
equilibrium is reached in a short time and might be temporary (as might be the case with an
intervention explicitly designed to have an immediate effect) and when instead we evaluate
reforms of institutions or policies with long-run (and possibly long-standing) effects. In
order to produce simulation results that respect the comparative statics perspective, Creedy
and Duncan (2005) and Peichl and Siegloch (2012) have proposed procedures where random
utility models (as defined in section 2) are complemented by a function of labour demand
and the wage rates are adjusted so that an appropriate or feasible equilibrium criterion is
satisfied. RURO models already include a representation of the density of market jobs of
different types at the time of observation. A notion of equilibrium consistent with the RURO
approach will imply some relationship between the opportunity density and the size and
composition of labour supply: since a reform will induce a change in labour supply, it follows
that in equilibrium also the opportunity density will have to change. Colombino (2013) and
Coda Moscarola et al. (2020) propose and exemplify an iterative simulation procedure that
exploits the structural interpretation of the coefficients of the alternative-specific constants
given in expression of section 2. For example, let us consider the simplified RURO model
(7.22) with fixed individual specific wage rates. If the opportunity density $p(h; \gamma)$ is specified
as uniform with a "peak" at alternatives with $h > 0$, it can be shown that expression (7.22)
reduces to

$$\Pr_i(h) = \frac{\exp\left\{v(h, f(wh, I); \theta) + \gamma \mathbf{1}(h > 0)\right\}}{\sum_{y \in B} \exp\left\{v(y, f(wy, I); \theta) + \gamma \mathbf{1}(y > 0)\right\}}, \qquad (7.28)$$

and it can be shown that

$$\gamma = \ln J + A, \qquad (7.29)$$

where J = number of alternatives with $h > 0$ (that is, the number of "market jobs" in the opportunity set), and A is a constant that can be retrieved from the data. Assuming that the pre-reform economy is in equilibrium, we can set J = number of working people in the pre-reform equilibrium. If a tax-transfer reform is implemented, in general, the number of people willing to work will change. Equilibrium requires [number of people willing to work] = [number of available jobs]. This implies that J and therefore γ_0 will have to change accordingly. In a market economy, this happens through a change in wage rates. The equilibrium simulation iteratively updates wage rates, J and γ until the equilibrium constraint is satisfied.

3.3   Social Evaluation of Policy Reforms

3.3.1   Comparable individual welfare functions
There are three empirical approaches to the interpersonal comparability:

(1) Deaton and Muellbauer (1980) propose using a common utility function as a tool for making interpersonal comparisons of welfare. The household-specific utility functions can be used to simulate household choices under alternative tax-transfer systems, while a common utility function is used for the welfare evaluation, the outcomes of simulation exercises. Let h_i be the solution to $\max_h U_i(h, f(w_i h, I_i); \theta)$. The corresponding maximized level of utility is $U_i(h_i, f(w_i h_i, I_i); \theta)$. The common utility approach consists of evaluating the household welfare, not with $U_i(h_i, f(w_i h_i, I_i); \theta)$ but with $U_R(h_i, f(w_i h_i, I_i); \theta) \equiv u_{iR}$, where UR( ) is the common, or "reference," utility function. We can also use a money-metric representation solving $U_R(h_i, f(w_i h_i, I_i); \theta) \equiv u_{iR}$ to get $\omega_i = \omega(u_{iR}, w_i; \theta \setminus f)$. The choice of the common utility function is essentially arbitrary. Experimenting with alternative functions might be a sensible suggestion. The common utility approach is used by Aaberge and Colombino (2013).
(2) King (1983) proposes an approach whereby different preferences are represented by different characteristics or parameters Z_i within a common parametric utility function. The characteristics account for a different productivity in obtaining utility from the opportunities available in the budget set, that is $U_i(h, f(w_i h, I_i); \theta) = U(h, f(w_i h, I_i); Z_i, \theta)$. The maximum attained utility is $U(h_i, f(w_i h_i, I_i); Z_i, \theta) = V(w_i, I ; Z_i, \theta \setminus f)$. We consider a "reference" household who, given a "reference" tax-transfer rule f^R, attains maximum utility $V(w_R, I_R; Z_R, \theta \setminus f^R)$. Then, the comparable money-metric utility ω_i (called "equivalent income" by King (1983)) is defined by $V(w_i, I; Z_i, \theta \setminus f) = V(w_R, \omega_i; Z_R, \theta \setminus f^R)$. A similar concept is defined by the "indirect money-metric utility" by Varian (1992). Empirical examples of applications of this approach are provided by King (1983), Aaberge et al. (2004) and Islam and Colombino (2018).
(3) While the approaches discussed in points (1) and (2) adopt arbitrary normalization of utilities in order to make them comparable, Fleurbaey (2008) and Fleurbaey and Maniquet (2006) propose a method—based on the "fair allocations" theory—where reference wages and reference endowments (that is, available time and/or exogenous income) can be given an ethical justification. The method is interesting in that it respects household-specific preferences and the way in which reference wages and endowments are computed already reflects social preferences. Empirical applications are provided by Bargain et al. (2013) and Decoster and Haan (2015).

3.3.2 Social welfare functions

Given a sample of N households, let $\omega_1, \ldots \omega_N$ represent their comparable measure of utility or welfare, computed according to one of the methods of section 3.3.1. In order to compare a household's welfare attained under different tax-transfer systems, it is useful to "aggregate" $\omega_1, \ldots \omega_N$ into a scalar measure of "social welfare." A practical basic idea—originally applied to income rather than welfare—goes back to Sen (1973):

$$W = (1-G)\bar{\omega}, \tag{7.30}$$

where $\bar{\omega} = \frac{\Sigma_{i=1}^N \omega_i}{N}$ and G is the Gini coefficient of the distribution of ω. With $\Sigma_{i=1}^N \omega_i$ the total size of the "welfare cake," $\bar{\omega}$ is the average size of the cake's slices allocated to the N households and is commonly referred to as an efficiency index. With G a measure of inequality, $1-G$ is an index of equality. This leads to an interpretation of (7.30) as: Social Welfare (W) equals Efficiency ($\bar{\omega}$) times Equality ($1 - G$).

Let $W^0, G^0, \bar{\omega}^0$ be values under the current tax-transfer system and let $W^1, G^1, \bar{\omega}^1$ be the values (observed or simulated) under a reform. Then the reform is welfare improving if

$$\frac{W^1}{W^0} \equiv \frac{(1-G^1)}{(1-G^0)}\frac{\bar{\omega}^1}{\bar{\omega}^0} > 1, \tag{7.31}$$

where the social welfare effect (on the left-hand side) is multiplicatively decomposed (on the right-hand side) into the equality effect and the efficiency effect.

Alternative definitions of the inequality index produce more sophisticated measures of social welfare. A first approach is based on the rank-dependent measurement of inequality (Weymark, 1981; Yaari, 1988; Aaberge, 2007) and is also related to the special case of the Gini coefficient. Social welfare is computed as follows:

$$W_k = \sum_{i=1}^N p_k(t_i)\omega_i, \tag{7.32}$$

where t_i is the rank position of household i, that is, the relative frequency of households with $\omega \leq \omega_i$. The "weight" $p_k(t_i)$ depends on t_i and on a parameter k that is an index of (decreasing) social aversion to inequality. The corresponding index of inequality is

$$G_k = 1 - \frac{W_k}{\bar{\omega}}, \quad k = 1, 2, \ldots \tag{7.33}$$

The weight $p_k(t)$ can be specified as follows (Aaberge, 2007):

$$p_k(t) = \begin{cases} -\log t, & k = 1 \\ \dfrac{k}{k-1}(1-t^{k-1}), & k = 2,3,\ldots \end{cases} \tag{7.34}$$

It turns out that G_2 = Gini coefficient and G_1 = Bonferroni coefficient. As $k \to \infty$, W_k approaches $\bar{\omega}$ and G_k approaches 0, that is, the distribution of welfare across the households becomes irrelevant.

Clearly, we can also write

$$W_k = (1-G_k)\bar{\omega}. \tag{7.35}$$

Among others, Palme (1996) and Aaberge and Colombino (2012, 2013) follow this method for the evaluation of tax-transfer reforms.

An alternative approach is proposed by Atkinson (1970). In this case, the (money-metric) index of social welfare can be computed as follows:

$$W_\rho = \left(\frac{\sum_{i=1}^{N} \omega_i^{1-\rho}}{N} \right)^{\frac{1}{1-\rho}},$$ (7.36)

where $\rho \geq 0$ is the degree of social inequality aversion. The associated index of inequality is

$$I_\rho = 1 - \frac{W_k}{\bar{\omega}},$$ (7.37)

and therefore

$$W_\rho = (1 - I_\rho)\bar{\omega}.$$ (7.38)

Expression (7.30) reveals that, for $\rho = 0$, we have $W_0 = \sum_{i=1}^{N} \omega_i / N$ and $I_0 = 0$, that is, a purely utilitarian criterion where only the size of the "welfare cake" is considered, irrespective of its distribution across the households. It can be shown that as $\rho \to \infty$ the social welfare index approaches $\min(\omega_1, \ldots, \omega_N)$. Atkinson's method has been widely adopted for tax-transfer reform evaluation, for example King (1983), Fortin et al. (1993), Creedy and Hérault (2012) and Aaberge et al. (2004).

Expressions (7.33) and (7.37) define indices of inequality that are invariant with respect to multiplicative constants. Kolm (1976) instead proposes an index of inequality that is invariant with respect to additive constants:

$$I_\alpha = \frac{1}{\alpha} \ln \left[\frac{\sum_{i=1}^{N} \exp\{\alpha(\bar{\omega} - \omega_i)\}}{N} \right],$$ (7.39)

where $\alpha > 0$ is a parameter that measures the social aversion to inequality. The corresponding index of social welfare is additive instead of multiplicative:

$$W_\alpha = \bar{\omega} - I_\alpha.$$ (7.40)

Here, W_α approaches $\bar{\omega}$ as $\alpha \to 0$ and $\min\{\omega_1, \ldots, \omega_N\}$ as $\alpha \to \infty$.

This method is adopted, among others, by Aronsson and Palme (1998) and Islam and Colombino (2018). A similar index is also used by Blundell and Shephard (2012). In empirical applications, it is often a required or convenient rescaling of the arguments of the social welfare indices; then, depending on the different circumstances, a multiplicative or rather an additive rescaling might turn out as more appropriate.

In applied research, it is common practice to produce results for different values of the inequality aversion parameter (k, ρ or α depending on which method is adopted) as a menu of choice for whoever is responsible for the decision concerning tax-transfer reforms.

4.   EMPIRICAL OPTIMAL TAXATION

Rather than evaluating the social welfare desirability of specific reforms, we might pursue a more ambitious aim, namely identifying an optimal (social welfare-wise) tax-transfer system. This is the problem addressed by Optimal Taxation theory. As far as income taxation is concerned, the basic theoretical framework is defined in a path-breaking contribution by Mirrlees (1971).

4.1   Intensive Labour Supply Responses Only: Mirrlees (1971) and Saez (2001)

Here, we consider a simplified version. Let us consider a population of agents that differ only with respect to skill or productivity n with distribution function $F(n)$ and probability density function $f(n)$. The (common) preferences are represented by a utility function $U(h, c)$, where c = income and h = effort. A level h of effort produces income hn. In principle, n and h are not observed, but of course for the purpose of empirical simulation one could interpret n as the wage rate and h as the labour supply. The Government (that is the "principal") solves

$$\max_{T(.)} \int_0^\infty W\left[U\big(h(n), z(n) - T(z(n))\big)\right] f(n) dn$$

s.t.

$$\int_0^\infty T(z(n)) f(n) dn \geq R$$

$$h(n) = \arg\max{}_h u\big(h, nh - T(nh)\big).$$

(7.41)

The first constraint is the public budget constraint, with R = per-capita required net tax revenue. The second constraint is the so-called incentive-compatibility constraint, which in this simple formulation says that $h(n)$ is effort level that maximizes the utility of the agent with productivity n. We have defined $z(n) = nh(n)$. Only interior solutions are considered. Here, $W(.)$ is a social welfare function, $T(.)$ is a tax-transfer function to be determined optimally and R is the average tax revenue to be collected. As a simple example, by assuming a quasi-linear $U(.,.)$—that is, no income effects—one can obtain

$$\frac{T'(z(n))}{1 - T'(z(n))} = \left(1 + \frac{1}{e}\right)\left(\frac{1 - F(n)}{nf(n)}\right)(1 - S(n)),$$

$$L = \int_0^\infty T(z(n)) f(n) dn - R,$$

(7.42)

where $T'(n)$ is the marginal tax rate applied to agents with productivity n (and earnings $z(n)$, e is the elasticity (assumed to be constant) of h with respect to n, L is a lump-sum paid to agents with no income and

$$S(n) = \frac{1}{1 - F(n)} \int_n^\infty \frac{\partial W}{\partial U\big(h_m, c_m\big)} \frac{\partial U\big(h_m, c_m\big)}{\partial c_m} dF(m) \Bigg/ \int_0^\infty \frac{\partial W}{\partial U\big(h_m, c_m\big)} \frac{\partial U\big(h_m, c_m\big)}{\partial c_m} dF(m) \quad (7.43)$$

is a social weight put on agents with productivity n. In this literature, it is common to label $F(.)$, $f(.)$, e, R and $S(.)$ as the "primitives" (or the basic characteristics of the economy). Therefore, to a given configuration of "primitives" there corresponds an optimal tax-transfer rule. It is possible to allow for income effects, obtaining a more complicated solution. Empirical applications of these results, in order to compute the optimal tax for a given level of income, require making assumptions about the "primitives" and to specify the household decision rule that relates productivity to income. The most direct procedure would be to equate the skill or productivity n to the wage rate, effort h to labour supply and specify a utility function $U(.,.)$. Examples of empirical simulations are survey by Tuomala (1990). Tuomala (2010) shows that the results are very sensible to the assumptions about preferences and productivity distribution.

While Mirrlees (1971) solves problem (7.41) using optimal control theory, Saez (2001) uses a more intuitive "perturbation" argument and obtains the same result as Mirrlees (1971) but expressed in terms of (taxable) income z instead of productivity n,

$$\frac{T'(z)}{1-T'(z)} = \left(\frac{1}{e(z)}\right)\left(\frac{1-F(z)}{zf(z)}\right)(1-\Lambda(z)), \qquad (7.44)$$

where the functions are now redefined as follows: $T'(z)$ is the marginal tax rate applied at (taxable) income z, $e(z)$ is the elasticity of z with respect to $1 - T'(z)$,[4] $F(z)$ and $f(z)$ are the distribution function and the probability density function of z, respectively, and $\Lambda(z)$, analogously to $S(z)$ of expression (7.43), is a relative social weight attached to individuals with income z. The parameter $\Lambda(z)$ summarizes the social preferences and—in view of empirical applications—can be directly specified as a number in the range $[0, 1]$. Since expression (7.44) contains observables such as z, the distribution of z and $e(z)$, it might suggest the conclusion that the optimal marginal tax rates can be directly computed in terms of observables without making assumptions about preferences. This conclusion would be unwarranted since $e(z)$, $f(z)$ and $F(z)$ depend themselves on the tax-transfer rule. In order to compute optimal taxes one has to specify how z, $e(z)$, $f(z)$ and $F(z)$ depend on taxes. In general this requires some assumption (either a structural model or a reduced-form approximation) on how z is obtained given n and the tax-transfer rule; that is, it essentially requires going back to Mirrlees (1971). The procedure used by Saez (2001) and Brewer et al. (2010) in their empirical simulations works as follows, where we refer to Mirrlees' problem (7.41) and solution (7.42).

a) Specify a quasi-linear (that is with no income effects) utility function $U(h,c) = c - h^{1+\frac{1}{e}}$, where e is the elasticity of labour supply with respect to n and $c = nh - T(nh)$. The optimal choice of h is $h(n) = [(1 - T'(z(n))n]^e$, where we have defined $z(n) = nh(n)$.

b) Calibrate $F(n)$ such that, using the actual $T(\cdot)$ and $h(n) = [(1 - T'(z(n))n]^e$, the resulting distribution of z is approximately equal to the actual distribution of earnings. Notice that the method does not use the actual distribution of the wage rate w, since the last might be endogenous with respect to the tax-transfer system.

c) Given an initial guess $T_0'(.)$:
    i.   Compute $h(n) = [(1 - T'(z(n))n]^e$.
    ii. Get L_0 from the public budget constraint.
    iii. Compute $U(h_0(n), c_0(n)) = [z_0(n) - T(z_0(n))] - h_0^{1+\frac{1}{e}}$, with $z_0(n) = nh_0(n)$.
    iv. Use (7.43) to compute $S_0(n)$.
    v.   Use (7.42) to compute $T_1'(.)$.

d) Iterate c) until convergence, that is, $T_{t+1}'(.) \approx T_t'(.)$.

4.2 Intensive and Extensive Labour Supply Responses: Saez (2002)

As we have noted, Mirrlees (1971) and Saez (2001) do not account for corner solutions, that is, they ignore extensive participation decisions. Saez (2002) adopts a discrete choice framework that accounts for both intensive and extensive responses. There are $J + 1$ types of jobs, each paying (in increasing order) $z_0, z_1, \ldots z_J$. Job "0" denotes a non-working condition (non-participation or unemployment). Net available income on job j is $c_j = z_j - T_j$, where T_j is the tax paid at income level z_j. Each agent is characterized by one of the potential incomes z_0, $z_1, \ldots z_J$ and, if she decides to work, she is allocated to the corresponding job. The extensive margin (or participation) elasticity is defined as

$$\eta_j = \frac{c_j - c_0}{\pi_j} \frac{\partial \pi_j}{\partial \left(c_j - c_0 \right)}, \tag{7.45}$$

where π_j is the proportion of agents on job of type j. Working agents can also move to a different job if income opportunities change, but the movements (for reasons implicit in the assumptions of the model) are limited to adjacent jobs (that is, from job j to job $j - 1$ or job $j + 1$). The intensive margin elasticity is defined as

$$\xi_j = \frac{c_j - c_{j-1}}{\pi_j} \frac{\partial \pi_j}{\partial \left(c_j - c_{j-1} \right)}. \tag{7.46}$$

Then, it turns out that the optimal taxes satisfy

$$\frac{T_j - T_{j-1}}{c_j - c_{j-1}} = \frac{1}{\xi_j} \frac{\sum_{k=j}^{J} \pi_k \left[1 - g_k - \eta_k \frac{T_k - T_0}{c_k - c_0} \right]}{\pi_j}, \tag{7.47}$$

where g_k is a social welfare weight assigned to a household for job k. Its structural expression is given in the Appendix to Saez (2002); however, Saez (2002), in his simulation exercise, adopts instead the following empirical specification, to be substituted into expression (7.47):

$$g_k = \frac{1}{p\pi_k} c_k^\gamma, \tag{7.48}$$

where $\gamma = 0.25, 1, 4$, is an index of social inequality aversion and p is the multiplier associated with the public budget constraint.

The model is attractive in view of empirical applications because it seems to fit well to the discrete choice framework illustrated in section 2. Note that expression (7.47) cannot be used directly to compute the optimal taxes, since the proportions π depends on are the optimal taxes. Either we develop a structural specification of how those proportions are determined or we chose some adhoc approximation; see Saez (2002) for details. There are $J + 1$ tax levels $T_0, T_1, \ldots, T_J$ to be determined. We have J equations of type (7.47). Moreover, we have two additional equations. One is the public budget constraint,

$$\sum_{j=0}^{J} T_j \pi_j = R, \tag{7.49}$$

with R = per-capita required net tax revenue. The other one can be shown to be implied by the assumption of no-income effects:

$$\sum_{j=0}^{J} h_j g_j = 1.$$ (7.50)

Altogether we have then $J + 2$ equations that allow us to solve for $T_0, T_1, \ldots, T_J$ and for the multiplier p.

The model is also particularly convenient for the so-called Inverse Optimal Taxation, that is, identifying the social preferences that justify the observed current tax-transfer rule as optimal, for example Blundell et al. (2009).

Another simulation exercise is presented by Immervoll et al. (2007) (evaluation of income maintenance policies in European countries).

4.3   Combining Microeconometric Modelling, Microsimulation and Numerical Optimization

The approach pioneered by Mirrlees (1971) and innovated by Saez (2001, 2002) is a fundamental theoretical framework for addressing the design of optimal tax-transfer mechanisms. However, so far, its empirical applications suffer from four main shortcomings. First, Mirrlees (1971) and Saez (2001), among others, only cover interior solutions, and therefore only intensive labour supply responses are considered. Saez (2002) presents a (discrete choice) model that includes extensive responses but introduces special restrictive assumptions on the intensive responses.[5] Second, so far, the empirical implementations of the analytical approach have considered individuals, not couples. Third, when an explicit utility function is specified, it is typically a quasi-linear one, that is, with no income effects (for example Saez (2001) and Brewer et al. (2010)). An exception is Tuomala (2010), who finds that results are very sensible with respect to the assumptions upon the productivity distribution and the specification of the utility function. Fourth, Saez (2001, 2002) introduces the so-called "sufficient statistics" approach (Chetty, 2009), which essentially consists of expressing optimal tax-transfer rules—as in (7.44) and (7.47)—in terms of observed quantities and non-parametric estimates (notably estimates of elasticities) without appealing to explicit structural assumptions on preferences and behaviour. However, explicit structural assumptions must then be replaced somehow by approximations (which imply non-explicit structural assumptions). These limitations might be overcome in the future. Using more flexible utility functions and/or productivity distributions is just a computational issue. Research is being done to extend the model to couples (for example Kleven et al., 2009). Advances in algorithmic analysis of "big data" might lead to the identification of behavioural relationships (such as those between n and z) that, although not strictly structural, are sufficiently general and robust to provide reliable predictions on policy results. Meanwhile, recent contributions have proposed an alternative (or complementary) microeconometric-computational approach (Fortin et al., 1993; Aaberge and Colombino, 2006, 2012, 2013; Ericson and Flood, 2012; Blundell and Shephard, 2012; Creedy and Hérault, 2012; Colombino and Narazani, 2013; Colombino, 2015; Islam and Colombino, 2018). Modern microeconometric models of labour supply can account for many realistic features such as simultaneous decisions of household partners, non-unitary household decisions, intensive and extensive margin choices, non-standard opportunity sets, heterogeneity of households and jobs, quantity constraints and so on. At least so far, it is simply not feasible to obtain analytical solutions for the optimal tax-transfer systems in such environments. The alternative (or complementary) approach combines microeconometric modelling, microsimulation and numerical optimization. The microeconometric model simulates the agents' choices by utility maximization and replaces the incentive-compatibility constraint of Mirrlees (1971). This microsimulation is embedded in a global maximization algorithm that computationally solves (instead of analytically) the social planner's problem, that is, the maximization of a social welfare function subject to the public budget constraint. A further feature departs from the Mirrlees–Saez "non-parametric" tradition and goes back to the "parametric" tradition of Ramsey (1927). The former does not impose any a priori parametric class of tax-transfer rules. In practice, however, in most cases the results boil down to a system with an income support mechanism (close either to a Minimum Income Guarantee or to Negative Income Tax or to an In-work Benefit policy) combined with a (flat or mildly non-linear) tax. These systems can be easily interpreted as members of parametric classes of tax-transfer rules. Giving up some of the (possibly unnecessary) generality on the side of the tax-transfer rule permits more generality and flexibility on the side of the representation of agents, preferences, constraints and behaviour (for example Heathcote and Tsujiama, 2021).

In order to highlight both the differences and the analogies between the microeconometric-computational approach with respect to the Mirrlees–Saez tradition, we start with a formulation of the former as close as possible to Mirrlees' problem (7.41):

$$\max_{\tau} W\left(U_1\left(h_1, w_1 h_1 + I_1 - T\left(w_1 h_1, I_1; \tau\right); \theta\right), \ldots, U_N\left(h_N, w_N h_N + I_N - T\left(w_N h_N, I_N; \tau\right); \theta\right)\right)$$

s.t.

$$\frac{1}{N}\sum_{i=1}^{N} T\left(w_i h_i, I_i; \tau\right) \ge R \tag{7.51}$$

$$h_i = \arg\max_h U_i\left(h, w_i h + I_i - T\left(w_i h, I_i; \tau\right); \theta\right), i = 1, \ldots, N.$$

We consider a class $T(., \tau)$ of tax-transfer rules, defined up to a vector of parameters τ. For example, any tax-transfer rules that induce a piecewise linear budget constraint can be defined by a vector of marginal tax rates and of income ranges to which the marginal tax rates are applied. A negative income tax + flat tax rule can be defined by a basic income, an exemption level and the flat tax applied above the exemption level. Any generic non-linear rule can be approximated by polynomial.

The social welfare maximization is performed with respect the parameters τ, that is, we look for the best member of the class $T(., \tau)$.

The arguments of the social welfare function W are the maximized utility functions of a sample of N households. The preference parameters θ are (previously) estimated with one of the methods illustrated in section 2.

Each household solves a maximization problem according to the second constraint of expression (7.45). This choice can be represented according to a "marginalist" approach or a random utility (either continuous or discrete). With a RURO model, we model the choice of (w_i, h_i), not just h_i. Moreover, in most of the applications of this approach, h and w are vectors containing hours and wage rates for the two household's partners. The optimal choice and the maximized utilities are computed by microsimulation, that is, by simulating the microeconometric model of household labour supply.[6]

Depending on the different applications, the maximized utilities that enter the social welfare function can be replaced by comparable and/or money-metric transformations according to one of the methods illustrated in section 3.3.1.

The solution process proceeds as follows:

a)   Start with an initial τ^0.

b)   Simulate the households' optimal choices $h_1^0, \ldots, h_N^0$.

c)   Compute $W(U_1(h_1^0, w_1 h_1 + I_1 - T(w_1 h_1^0 I_1; \tau); \theta), \ldots, U_N(h_N^0, w_N h_N^0 + I_N - T(w_N h_N^0, I_N; \tau); \theta))$.

d)   Iterate until W is maximized and $\frac{1}{N} \sum_{i=1}^{N} T(w_i h_i, I_i; \tau) \geq R$ is satisfied.[7]

As opposed to the exercises based on the Mirrlees (1971) or Saez (2001), the microeconometric-computational approach allows for a more flexible and heterogeneous representation of households' preferences and choice opportunities. This can have significant implications on the results. For example, Islam and Colombino (2018), looking for optimal rules within the negative income tax + flat tax class, find a large variety of results across different countries. Islam and Colombino (2018) propose and exemplify a further step. Let $\tau^* = \{\tau_1^*, \ldots, \tau_C^*\}$ be a collection of optimal tax-transfer parameter vectors (in a given class of tax-transfer systems) for a sample of C economies. They could be nations, or aggregates of nations or even artificial economies. Let $\psi = \{\psi_1, \ldots, \psi_C\}$, the collection of respective vectors of "primitives" as in the Mirrlees-Saez tradition: "deep" features of the economies such as productivity, elasticity, public budget constraint and features of optimization exercise (for example index of social inequality aversion). Then the challenge is to identify the mapping $\psi \to \tau^*$. The result might attain a level of generality close to the one attained in the Mirrlees–Saez tradition, but based on more flexible assumptions and more realistic representations of household behaviour.

NOTES

1.   A useful reference for statistical policy analysis is, among others, Josselin and Le Maux (2012).
2.   The problem is analogous to the one raised by Lucas (1976) in macroeconomic policy evaluation.
3.   See for example Ben-Akiva and Lerman (1985).
4.   If $z = (1 - T)wh$, then $e(z)$ is also equal to 1 + elasticity of h with respect to w.
5.   Jacquet et al. (2013) present a different theoretical model with different implications.
6.   Usually the observed (or imputed when missing) wage rates w are used, but in principle one could also adopt a procedure to calibrate a distribution of "latent" productivities as in steps (a) and (b) of the Mirrlees–Saez simulation procedure (section 4.1).
7.   In general, we can expect local maxima; therefore, a global (derivative-free) optimization algorithm or a search for different initial values should be used. Fortin et al. (1993), Colombino and Narazani (2013) and Colombino (2015) directly explore a grid of tax-transfer parameter values and rank (social welfare-wise) the tax-transfer reforms.

REFERENCES

Aaberge, R. (2007) Gini's nuclear family, *Journal of Economic Inequality*, 5(3), 305–22.
Aaberge, R. and U. Colombino (2006) Designing optimal taxes with a microeconometric model of household labour supply. IZA Discussion Papers 2468, Institute for the Study of Labor (IZA).

Aaberge, R. and Colombino, U. (2012) Accounting for family background when designing optimal income taxes: A microeconometric simulation analysis, *Journal of Population Economics*, 25(2), 741–61.

Aaberge, R. and Colombino, U. (2013) Using a microeconometric model of household labour supply to design optimal income taxes, *Scandinavian Journal of Economics*, 115(2), 449–75.

Aaberge, R. and U. Colombino (2014) Labour Supply Models. In Cathal O'Donoghue (Ed.): *Handbook in Microsimulation Modelling – Contributions to Economic Analysis*. Emerald Group Publishing Limited, UK.

Aaberge, R. and Colombino, U. (2018) Structural labour supply models and microsimulation, *International Journal of Microsimulation*, 11(1).

Aaberge, R., U. Colombino and S. Strøm (1999) Labour supply in Italy: An empirical analysis of joint household decisions, with taxes and quantity constraints, *Journal of Applied Econometrics*, 14(4), 403–22.

Aaberge, R., Colombino, U. and Strøm, S. (2004) Do more equal slices shrink the cake? An empirical investigation of tax-transfer reform proposals in Italy, *Journal of Population Economics*, 17(4), 767–85.

Aaberge, R., Colombino, U. and Wennemo, T. (2009) Evaluating alternative representations of the choice set in models of labor supply, *Journal of Economic Surveys*, 23(3), 586–612.

Aaberge, R., Dagsvik, J. K. and Strøm, S. (1995) Labor supply responses and welfare effects of tax reforms, *Scandinavian Journal of Economics*, 97(4), 635–59.

Aronsson, T. and Palme, M. (1998) A decade of tax and benefit reforms in Sweden: Effects on labour supply, Welfare and Inequality, *Economica*, 65(257), 39–67.

Arrufat, J. L. and Zabalza, A. (1986) Female labor supply with taxation, random preferences, and optimization errors, *Econometrica*, 54(1), 47–63.

Atherton, T., Ben-Akiva, M., McFadden, D. and Train, K. E. (1990) Micro-simulation of local residential telephone demand under alternative service options and rate structures. In De Fontenay, A. et al. (Eds.), *Telecommunication demand systems*, North-Holland pp. 137–63.

Atkinson, A. B. (1970) On the measurement of inequality, *Journal of Economic Theory*, 2(3), 244–63.

Bargain, O., Decoster, A., Dolls, M., Neumann, D., Peichl, A. and Siegloch, S. (2013) Welfare, labor supply and heterogeneous preferences: Evidence for Europe and the US, *Social Choice and Welfare*, 41(4), 789–817.

Bargain, O. and Peichl, A. (2016) Own-wage labor supply elasticities: Variation across time and estimation methods, *IZA Journal of Labor Economics*, 5, 1–31.

Ben-Akiva M. and S. Lerman (1985) *Discrete Choice Analysis: Theory and application to travel demand*. MIT Press.

Ben-Akiva, M. and T. Watanatada (1981) Application of a continuous spatial choice logit model. In Manski, C. F. and McFadden D. (Eds.) *Structural Analysis of Discrete Data with Econometric Applications*. MIT Press.

Blomquist, N. S. (1983) The effect of income taxation on the labor supply of married men in Sweden, *Journal of Public Economics*, 22(2), 169–97.

Blomquist N. S. and U. Hansson-Brusewitz (1990) The effect of taxes on male and female labor supply in Sweden, *Journal of Human Resources*, 25(3), 317–57.

Blundell, R. (2012) Tax policy reform: The role of empirical evidence, *Journal of the European Economic Association*, 10(1), 43–77.

Blundell, R., Brewer, M., Haan, P. and Shephard, A. (2009) Optimal income taxation of lone mothers: An empirical comparison of the UK and Germany, *The Economic Journal*, 119(535), F101–F121.

Blundell, R. and MaCurdy, T. (1999) Labor supply: A review of alternative approaches. In Ashenfelter, O and Card, D. (Eds.), *Handbook of labor economics*, volume 3, chapter 27, 1559–695. Elsevier.

Blundell, R., MaCurdy, T. and Meghir, C. (2007) Labor supply models: Unobserved heterogeneity, nonparticipation and dynamics. In Heckman, J. and Leamer, E. (Eds.), *Handbook of Econometrics*, volume 6. Elsevier.

Blundell, R. and Shephard, A. (2012) Employment, hours of work and the optimal taxation of low-income families, *Review of Economic Studies*, 79(2), 481–510.

Bourguignon F. and T. Magnac (1990) Labor supply and taxation in France, *Journal of Human Resources*, 25(3), 358–89.

Bowen, W. and T. Finegan (1969) *The Economics of Labor Force Participation*. Princeton University Press.

Brewer, M., Saez, E. and A. Shephard (2010) Means-testing and tax rates on earnings (Mirrlees Commission Report), Institute for Fiscal Studies, London.

Burtless, G. and Hausman, J. A. (1978) The effect of taxation on labor supply: Evaluating the Gary negative income tax experiment, *Journal of Political Economy*, 86(6), 1103–30.

Chetty, R. (2009) Sufficient statistics for welfare analysis: A bridge between structural and reduced-form methods, *Annual Review of Economics, Annual Reviews*, 1(1), 451–88.

Coda Moscarola, F., Colombino, U., Figari, F. and Locatelli, M. (2020) Shifting taxes away from labour enhances equity and fiscal efficiency, *Journal of Policy Modeling*, 42(2), 367–84.

Colombino, U. (2013) A new equilibrium simulation procedure with discrete choice models, *International Journal of Microsimulation*, 6(3), 25–49.

Colombino, U. (2015) Five crossroads on the way to basic income. An Italian tour, *Italian Economic Journal* 1(3), 353–89.

Colombino, U. and D. Del Boca (1990) The effect of taxes on labor supply in Italy, *Journal of Human Resources*, 25(3), 390−414.

Colombino, U. and Narazani, E. (2013) Designing a universal income support mechanism for Italy: An exploratory tour, *Basic Income Studies*, 8(1), 1–17.

Creedy, J. and Duncan, A. (2005) Aggregating labour supply and feedback effects in microsimulation, *Australian Journal of Labour Economics*, 8(3), 277–90.

Creedy, J. and N. Hérault (2012) Welfare-improving income tax reforms: A microsimulation analysis, *Oxford Economic Papers*, 64(1), 128−50.

Creedy, J. and G. Kalb (2005) Discrete hours labour supply modelling: Specification, estimation and simulation, *Journal of Economic Surveys*, 19(5), 697−734.

Dagsvik, J. K. (1994) Discrete and continuous choice, Max-stable processes, and independence from irrelevant attributes, *Econometrica*, 62(5), 1179−205.

Dagsvik, J. K, Jia, Z, Kornstad, T and T, Thoresen. (2014) Theoretical and practical arguments for modeling labor supply as a choice among latent jobs, *Journal of Economic Surveys*, 28(1), 134−51.

Dagsvik, J. K., Locatelli, M. and Strøm, S. (2009) Tax reform, sector-specific labor supply and welfare effects, *Scandinavian Journal of Economics*, 111(2), 299−321.

Dagsvik, J. K. and Strøm, S. (2006) Sectoral labour supply, choice restrictions and functional form, *Journal of Applied Econometrics*, 21(6), 803–26.

Deaton, A. and Muellbauer, J. (1980) *Economics and Consumer Behavior*. Cambridge University Press.

Decoster, A. and Haan, P. (2015) Empirical welfare analysis with preference heterogeneity, *International Tax and Public Finance,* 22(2), 224−51.

Duncan, A. and Harris, M. (2002) Simulating the behavioural effects of welfare reforms among sole parents in Australia, *The Economic Record*, The Economic Society of Australia, 78(242), 264−76.

Ericson, P. and Flood, L. (2012) A microsimulation approach to an optimal Swedish income tax, *International Journal of Microsimulation*, 2(5), 2–21.

Fleurbaey, M. (2008) *Fairness, Responsibility and Welfare*. Oxford University Press.

Fleurbaey, M. and F. Maniquet (2006) Fair income tax, *Review of Economic Studies*, 73(1), 55−84.

Fortin, B., Truchon, M. and L. Beauséjour (1993) On reforming the welfare system: Workfare meets the negative income tax, *Journal of Public Economics*, 31, 119−51.

Gong, X. and Van Soest, A. (2002) Family structure and female labor supply in Mexico City, *Journal of Human Resources*, 37(1), 163−91.

Hausman, J. A. (1979) The econometrics of labor supply on convex budget sets, *Economics Letters*, 3(2), 171−74.

Hausman, J. A. (1985) Taxes and labor supply. In Auerbach, A. J. and Feldstein, M. (Ed.), *Handbook of Public Economics*, volume 1, chapter 4, 213−63. Elsevier.

Hausman, J. A. and Wise, D. A. (1980) Discontinuous budget constraints and estimation: The demand for housing, *Review of Economic Studies*, 47(1), 75−96.

Heathcote, J. and H. Tsujiyama (2021) Optimal income taxation: Mirrlees meets ramsey, forthcoming in *Journal of Political Economy*. https://doi.org/10.1086/715851.

Heckman, J. J. (1974a) Shadow prices, market wages, and labor supply, *Econometrica*, 42(4), 679−94.

Heckman, J. J. (1974b) Effects of child-care programs on women's work effort, *Journal of Political Economy*, 82(2), S136−S163.

Heckman, J. (1979) Sample selection bias as a specification error, *Econometrica*, 47(1), 153−61.

Heckman. J. and T. MaCurdy (1986) Labor econometrics. In Z. Griliches (Ed.), *Handbook of econometrics*, North-Holland.

Hurwicz, L. (1962). On the structural form of interdependent systems. Nagel, E., Suppes, P. and Tarski, A. (Eds.) *Logic, methodology and philosophy of science*. Stanford University Press, 232−9.

Immervoll, H., Kleven, H. J., Kreiner, C. T., and Saez, E. (2007). Welfare reform in European countries: a microsimulation analysis, *The Economic Journal*, 117(516), 1−44.

Islam, N. and Colombino, U. (2018) The case for negative income tax with flat tax in Europe. An empirical optimal taxation exercise, *Economic Modelling*, 75C, 38−69.

Jacquet, L., Lehmann, E., and Van der Linden, B. (2013). Optimal redistributive taxation with both extensive and intensive responses, *Journal of Economic Theory* 148(5), 1770−805.

Josselin, J. and Le Maux, B. (2012) *Statistical Tools for Program Evaluation*. Springer.

Keane, M. P. (2011) Labor supply and taxes: A survey, *Journal of Economic Literature*, 49(4), 961–1075.

King, M. A. (1983) Welfare analysis of tax reforms using household data, *Journal of Public Economics*, 21(2), 183–214.

Kleven, H., Kreiner, C. and Saez, E. (2009) The optimal income taxation of couples, *Econometrica*, 77(2), 537−60.

Kolm, S. C. (1976) Inequal inequalities I, *Journal of Economic Theory*, 12, 416−42.

Kosters, M. H. (1969) Effects of an income tax on labor supply. In Harberger, A. C. and Bailey, M. J. (Eds.), *The taxation of income from capital*. Studies of Government Finance, Brookings Institution, 301−32.

Lucas, R. (1976) Econometric policy evaluation: A critique, *Carnegie-Rochester Conference Series on Public Policy*, 1(1), 19−46. Elsevier.

MaCurdy, T., Green, D. and H. Paarsch (1990) Assessing empirical approaches for analyzing taxes and labor supply, *Journal of Human Resources* 25(3), 414−90.

Marschak, J. (1953) Economic measurements for policy and prediction. In Hood, W. and Koopmans, T. (Eds.), *Studies in econometric method*. Wiley.

McFadden, D. (1974) The measurement of urban travel demand, *Journal of Public Economics* 3(4), 303−28.

McFadden, D. (1978) Modeling the choice of residential location. In Karlqvist, A., Lundqvist, L., Snickars, F. and Weibull, J. (Ed.), *Spatial Interaction Theory and Planning Models*, North Holland, 75−96.

McFadden, D. (1984) Econometric analysis of qualitative response models. In Griliches, Z. and Intrilligator, M. (Eds.), *Handbook of econometrics*, II. Elsevier.

McFadden, D. and Train, K. (2000) Mixed MNL models for discrete response, *Journal of Applied Econometrics*, 15(5), 447−70.

Meghir, C. and Phillips, D. (2008) Labour supply and taxes, IZA Discussion Paper No. 3405.

Mirrlees, J. A. (1971) An exploration in the theory of optimum income taxation, *Review of Economic Studies*, 38(114), 175−208.

Moffitt, R. (1986) The econometrics of piecewise-linear budget constraints: A survey and exposition of the maximum likelihood method, *Journal of Business & Economic Statistics*, 4(3), 317−28.

Palme, M. (1996) Income distribution effects of the Swedish 1991 tax reform: An analysis of a microsimulation using generalized Kakwani decomposition, *Journal of Policy Modeling*, 18(4), 419−43.

Peichl, A. and Siegloch, S. (2012) Accounting for labor demand effects in structural labor supply models, *Labour Economics*, 19(1), 129−38.

Ramsey, F. (1927) A contribution to the theory of taxation, *The Economic Journal*, 37 (145), 47−61.

Rosen, S. (1974) Effects of child-care programs on women's work effort: Comment, *Journal of Political Economy*, 82(2), S164−S169, Part II.

Saez, E. (2001) Using elasticities to derive optimal income tax rates, *Review of Economic Studies*, 68(1), 205−29.

Saez, E. (2002) Optimal income transfer programs: Intensive versus extensive labor supply responses, *Quarterly Journal of Economics*, 117(3), 1039−73.

Sen, A. (1973) *On Economic Inequality*. Oxford New York: Clarendon Press Oxford University Press.

Tobin, J. (1958) Estimation of Relationships for Limited Dependent Variables, *Econometrica*, 26(1) 24−36.

Train, K. (2003) *Discrete Choice Methods with Simulation*. Cambridge University Press.

Triest, R. (1990) The effect of income taxation on labor supply in the United States, *Journal of Human Resources*, 25(3) 491−516.

Tuomala, M. (1990) *Optimal Income Tax and Redistribution*. Oxford University Press.

Tuomala, M. (2010) On optimal non-linear income taxation: Numerical results revisited, *International Tax and Public Finance*, 17(3), 259−70.

Van Soest, A. (1995) Structural models of family labor supply: A discrete choice approach, *Journal of Human Resources*, 30(1), 63−88.

Van Soest, A., Woittiez, I. and Kapteyn, A. (1990) Labor supply, income taxes, and hours restrictions in the Netherlands, *Journal of Human Resources*, 25(3), 517−58.

Varian, H. (1992) *Microeconomic Analysis*. Norton.

Wales, T. J. and Woodland, A. D. (1979) Labour supply and progressive taxes, *The Review of Economic Studies*, 46(1), 83−95.

Weymark, J. A. (1981) Generalized Gini inequality indices, *Mathematical Social Sciences*, 1(4), 409−30.

Yaari, M. E. (1988) A controversial proposal concerning inequality measurement, *Journal of Economic Theory*, 44(2), 381−97.

Zabalza, A. (1983) The CES utility function, non-linear budget constraints and labour supply: Results on female participation and hours, *The Economic Journal*, 93(37), 312−30.

APPENDIX 7A.1 CONSISTENCY OF LABOUR SUPPLY FUNCTIONS, DIRECT AND INDIRECT REPRESENTATIONS OF PREFERENCES

The overall structural approach adopted in the main text requires us to maintain a mutual consistency between the behavioural function (for example labour supply functions) and the representation of preferences. Typically, one might want to obtain a labour supply function from a direct or indirect utility function, or recover a direct or indirect representation of preferences from an empirically estimated labour supply function. What follows resumes the main paths that can be followed.

(1) Specify a direct utility $U(h, c)$ function and solve

$$\max_{c,h} U(h,c)$$

$$s.t.$$

$$c = wh + I$$

in order to get a labour supply function $h(w, I)$, where
   c = consumption (= income)
   h = hours of work
   w = wage rate
   I = exogenous income.

(2) Specify the indirect utility function $V(w, I)$ and obtain the labour supply function through Roy's theorem: $h(w,I) = -\frac{\partial V(w,I)}{\partial w} \Big/ \frac{\partial V(w,I)}{\partial I}$.

(3) Specify the uncompensated labour supply function $h(w, I)$—for example a linear function—remembering that if we want it to be consistent with the model of constrained utility maximization it will have to satisfy the Slutsky's conditions. In fact, this is the approach followed for example by Burtless and Husman (1978) and Hausman (1985), where a linear labour supply function is specified. The indirect utility function can be retrieved by "integrating" Roy's identity (treated as a differential equation). The dual relationship between the indirect and the direct utility function allows, if needed, to recover the latter from the former (see for example Varian 1992).

(4) Specify the compensated labour supply function $\tilde{h}(w,u)$ and use Shephard's lemma, that is $\frac{\partial e(w,u)}{\partial w} = \tilde{h}(w,u)$, in order to recover (by integration) the expenditure function and, by setting $e(w, u) = I$, obtain (by inversion) the indirect utility function: $u = V(w, I)$). Roy's theorem can also be applied to obtain the uncompensated labour supply function $h(w, I)$. The method used by Heckman (1974b) is in fact a variant of this fourth way of proceeding (Rosen, 1974).

8. Bounds on counterfactuals in semiparametric discrete-choice models[*]

Khai X. Chiong, Yu-Wei Hsieh and Matthew Shum

1. INTRODUCTION

Since the seminal work of McFadden (1978, 1981, 1984), discrete choice modeling based on the random utility framework has been at the core of modern empirical research in many areas of economics, including labor, public finance, industrial organization and health economics. Many applications of discrete choice models utilize strong parametric assumptions (such as probit or logit), and hence are not robust to misspecification. Moreover, the parametric assumptions can lead to unrealistic substitution patterns in the subsequent counterfactual analysis. There is now a growing literature on semiparametric estimation of discrete choice models[1] aiming to resolve the robustness issue in estimation.

Our main contribution is to provide bounds on the counterfactual choice probabilities (or market shares) in semiparametric discrete-choice models. To the best of our knowledge, this is the first study to address the counterfactual evaluations in semiparametric *multinomial* choice models. In the case of semiparametric *binary* choice models, Hausman et al. (1998) propose an approach based on isotonic regression, which can be used to construct counterfactual choice probabilities without the knowledge of the distribution of the random error terms. Khan (2013) considers another approach based on semiparametric sieve probit/logit estimation. These ideas, however, work only for the binary choice case. We provide an approach which works for both multinomial and binary choice settings.[2]

Counterfactual evaluation is often the primary goal in industrial organization and marketing, such as predicting the market shares under the new pricing scheme or conducting merger simulations. Despite the potential pitfall of imposing strong assumptions on substitution patterns, parametric models such as logit or probit remain a dominant approach for practitioners. In addition, mixed logit or probit models allow flexibly for heterogeneity in preferences.[3] In these parametric models, counterfactuals can be easily obtained via simulation. The applicability of semiparametric estimators, by contrast, is largely limited by the absence of methods for counterfactual evaluations.

In this chapter, we propose using *cyclic monotonicity*, a *cross-market* restriction on market-level data derived from discrete-choice theory, to bound the counterfactual market shares in a semiparametric multinomial choice framework. We do not impose a functional form for the probability distribution of the utility shocks, and hence the counterfactual market shares cannot be obtained even via simulations. Since this approach is semiparametric, it accommodates rich substitution patterns among alternatives. Such generality, however, comes at the cost of losing point identification in general. We show that the identified set of the choice probability vector can be expressed in terms of linear moment inequalities. In particular, the marginal bound for the individual choice probability can be solved by linear programming (LP). One can then apply relevant methods in the moment inequality literature to conduct inference on the counterfactual choice probabilities.[4] We therefore omit inference details in this article.

In the next section, we lay out the assumptions and key results on cyclic monotonicity. In section 3 we discuss how to construct bounds for counterfactual market shares, the computational issue as well as the economic meaning of cyclic monotonicity. In section 4 we show that the bound is very informative using a Monte Carlo experiment. In section 5 we show our method can produce very different substitution patterns using actual data.

2. SETUP

There are $\mathcal{M} = \{1,\ldots, M\}$ markets. In each market, there are $\mathcal{J} = \{1,\ldots,J\}$ alternatives or products. The latent indirect utility that a consumer i derives from product j at market m is given by $U_{ij}^m = \mathbf{X}_j^m \beta + \varepsilon_{ij}^m$, where $\mathbf{X}_j^m$ is a $1 \times b$ vector of observed product-specific attributes, β is a $b \times 1$ vector of unknown parameters and $\varepsilon_i^m = (\varepsilon_{i1}^m,\ldots,\varepsilon_{iJ}^m)'$ is a vector of latent utility shocks. Further, let the market share of product J in market m be $s_j^m = \Pr(\mathbf{X}_j^m \beta + \varepsilon_{ij}^m \geq \max_{k \neq j}\{\mathbf{X}_k^m \beta + \varepsilon_{ik}^m\})$. The model is semiparametric as we do not specify the distribution of the utility shocks, ε_i^m. Similar to Berry (1994), we denote the mean utility as $\delta_j^m \equiv \mathbf{X}_j^m \beta$.

The basic idea is that, under the assumption that shocks across individuals and markets are identical and independently distributed (Assumption 1), the mean utilities and the observed market shares must satisfy a set of inequalities (Proposition 1). To conduct a counterfactual exercise, suppose then the counterfactual market is characterized by $\tilde{X}_j, j = 1, \ldots, J$. Its mean utility vector can be obtained by $\tilde{\mathbf{X}}_j \hat{\beta}$. We then use the aforementioned cross-market restrictions to infer the set of counterfactual market shares that are consistent with (i) all the mean utilities and (ii) all the observed market shares.

We now formally state Assumption 1 and Proposition 1, which serve as the backbone of our counterfactual procedure.

Assumption 1 *The vector of utility shocks ε_i^m is distributed identically and independently across individual i and market $m = 1, \ldots, M$, with the joint distribution F. Further, F does not depend on $(\mathbf{X}_j^m)_{j=1,\ldots,J}$, that is, $\mathbf{X}_j^m$ and ε_i^m are independent.*

Our assumption allows the utility shocks to follow an unknown joint distribution that can be arbitrarily correlated among different products j. This accommodates many discrete-choice demand model specifications in the literature, including multinomial logit, nested logit (Goldberg, 1995), cross-nested logit (Bresnahan et al., 1997) and multinomial probit (Goolsbee and Petrin, 2004). However, the framework does not apply to random-coefficient logit models of demand (Berry et al., 1995), as these violate our Assumption 1.

The key restriction we use for constructing counterfactual market shares is the property of *cyclic monotonicity*, which we define next. Let s^m be the vector of market shares evaluated at the mean utilities δ^m. That is, $s_j^m = \Pr(\delta_j^m + \varepsilon_{ij}^m \geq \max_{k \neq j}\{\delta_k^m + \varepsilon_{ik}^m\})$, and $\mathbf{s}^m = (s_1^m,\ldots,s_J^m)$.

Definition 1 (Cyclic Monotonicity): *Define a cycle of length K as a permutation of K distinct elements from $\{1, 2, \ldots, M\}$. Denote a generic cycle of length K by $(l_1, l_2, \ldots, l_K, l_{K+1})$ with*

$l_{K+1} = l_1$. The market shares s^m and mean utilities δ^m satisfy cyclic monotonicity if the following inequality (8.1) holds for all possible cycles of length K and for all $K \geq 2$.

$$\sum_{k=1}^{K} (\delta^{l_{k+1}} - \delta^{l_k}) \cdot s^{l_k} \leq 0 \tag{8.1}$$

Cyclic monotonicity is a defining property of the gradients of vector-valued convex functions, analogous to how monotonicity is a property of the derivatives of scalar-valued convex functions. We exploit cyclic monotonicity to construct counterfactual market shares using the next proposition.

Proposition 1. *Under Assumption 1, the market shares s^m and mean utilities δ^m for all markets $m = 1, \ldots, M$ satisfy cyclic monotonicity.*

Proof. Proposition 1 arises from the convexity properties of the *social surplus function* (or the expected indirect utility) of the discrete choice problem (McFadden, 1978, 1981):[5]

$$\mathcal{G}(\delta) = \mathbb{E}_F \left[\max_{j \in \{1,\ldots,J\}} (\mathbf{X}_j \beta + \varepsilon_{ij}) \mid \mathbf{X}\beta = \delta \right],$$

where $\mathbf{X}_\beta = (\mathbf{X}_1 \beta, \ldots, \mathbf{X}_J \beta)$, and $\delta = (\delta_1, \ldots, \delta_J)$. Under Assumption 1 we have

$$\mathcal{G}(\delta) = \mathbb{E}_F \left[\max_{j \in \{1,\ldots,J\}} (\delta_j + \varepsilon_{ij}) \right],$$

which is a convex function of the vector of mean utilities δ. The social surplus function has an important property. Define the function $s : \mathcal{U} \subset \mathbb{R}^J \to \Delta^J$ as the mapping from mean utilities to market shares, where the j-th component is $s_j(\delta) = \Pr(\delta_j + \varepsilon_{ij}^m \geq \max_{k \neq j} \{\delta_k + \varepsilon_{ik}^m\})$ and $\mathcal{U}$ is a convex super-set of the unknown true mean utilities $\{\delta^1, \ldots, \delta^m\}$. By the Williams−Daly−Zachary Theorem,[6] $s(\delta)$ lies in the subgradient of $\mathcal{G}$ evaluated at δ, for all $\delta \in \mathcal{U}$. That is,

$$s(\delta) \in \partial \mathcal{G}(\delta). \tag{8.2}$$

By a well-known result in convex analysis (Rockafellar, 2015), the subgradient of a convex function satisfies *cyclic monotonicity*. (This is just the multidimensional generalization of the fact that a convex function of one variable has a derivative which is monotonically increasing.) More precisely, because the mapping s is a gradient function of a convex function, it follows that for every cycle $x_0, x_1, \ldots, x_n, x_{n+1} = x_0$ in $\mathcal{U}$, we have $s(x_0) \cdot (x_1 - x_0) + s(x_1) \cdot (x_2 - x_1) + \cdots + s(x_n) \cdot (x_{n+1} - x_n)$.[7] In particular, we can take the cycle in $\mathcal{U}$ consisting of the unknown mean utilities. This proves Proposition 1. □

For binary-choice models, semiparametric estimation using the maximum score or maximum rank correlation approaches (Han, 1987; Manski, 1975) exploits the feature that the (scalar-valued) choice probability function $s(\delta)$ is increasing in the mean utility δ. Cyclic monotonicity is a natural extension of this insight into multinomial-choice models, where cyclic monotonicity formalizes the idea that $s(\delta)$ is monotonic in δ in a vector sense.

3. COUNTERFACTUALS IMPLIED BY CYCLIC MONOTONICITY

In this section, we show how to compute the counterfactual market shares using the cyclic monotonicity restriction (Proposition 1). We assume that the first-step estimation of the parameters β has been carried out by some semiparametric estimator such as Fox (2007) or Shi et al. (2018).[8] The researchers observe $s = (s^1, \ldots, s^M)$ vectors of market shares in markets $m = 1, \ldots, M$, and the corresponding mean utilities $\delta = (\delta^1, \ldots, \delta^M)$ with $\delta_j^m = \mathbf{X}_j^m \beta$. The counterfactual market, indexed by market $M + 1$, is characterized by its mean utility vector δ^{M+1}. The corresponding market share vector is denoted by s^{M+1}. Since δ^{M+1} is known by construction, the remaining problem is to determine s^{M+1}. First, market shares must be non-negative and must add up to one, we have the following constraints:

$$\sum_{j=1}^{J} s_j^{M+1} = 1$$

$$s_j^{M+1} \geq 0 \quad \forall j.$$

Second, the counterfactual market (δ^{M+1}, s^{M+1}) must satisfy the cyclic monotonicity for any cycle containing $M + 1$. That is, given any cycle of length K, $(l_1, l_2, \ldots, l_K, l_1)$, such that $l_K = M + 1$ corresponds to the counterfactual market, cyclic monotonicity implies that

$$\sum_{k=1}^{K} (\delta^{l_{k+1}} - \delta^{l_k}) \cdot \mathbf{s}^{l_k} \leq 0. \tag{8.3}$$

Notice that where the cycle starts and ends is irrelevant to the definition of cyclic monotonicity as only the "sum" matters. For example, the cycle $(1, 2, 3, 1)$ is equivalent to $(2, 3, 1, 2)$ and $(3, 1, 2, 3)$ when computing (8.3). Therefore, without loss of generality one can always put the counterfactual market at the end of the cycle.

3.1 Computing Bounds for Market Shares

Given the constraints in the previous section, the upper bound for the counterfactual market share of the i-th good is given by the LP problem:

$$\max s_i^{M+1} \tag{8.4}$$

$$\text{s.t.} \sum_{j=1}^{J} s_j^{M+1} = 1$$

$$\sum_{k=1}^{K} (\delta^{l_{k+1}} - \delta^{l_k}) \cdot \mathbf{s}^{l_k} \leq 0; l_K = M+1; 2 \leq K \leq M$$

$$s_j^{M+1} \geq 0 \quad \forall j.$$

Similarly, the lower bound can be found by changing maximization to minimization. Several policy-relevant counterfactuals can be computed by choosing a suitable objective function and mean utilities δ^{M+1}. As examples, the elasticity of substitution matrix is often a key input for merger simulations (Nevo, 2000); counterfactual market shares resulting from large price changes are also used to evaluate the welfare benefits of new product introductions (Hausman, 1996; Petrin, 2002). For evaluating the effects of price changes, we proceed by introducing a counterfactual market, which we label $M+1$, which is identical to the benchmark market m, except that the price of product i in market $M+1$ is higher than p_i^m. By solving (8.4) for all $j \in \mathcal{J}$ one is able to bound the effect of the price increase $p_i^{M+1} - p_i^m$ on market shares of product j.

More complicated counterfactuals are possible. For example, a multi-product firm may want to predict the maximum total share $(s_1^{M+1} + s_2^{M+1})$ or revenue $(p_1^{M+1} \cdot s_1^{M+1} + p_2^{M+1} \cdot s_2^{M+1})$ under the new pricing scheme (p_1^{M+1}, p_2^{M+1}), holding other things equal. This can be done by choosing a benchmark market first and changing the objective function.

3.2   LP Formulation

At the first glance the LP problem of (8.4) appears to be computationally intensive, because even considering cycles up to length 3 would result in $M + \binom{M}{2} \times 2!$ constraints, which is proportional to M^2. To better understand the complexity of the LP problem, we first need to express the constraints associated with cyclic monotonicity in terms of

$$\mathbf{A} \cdot (\mathbf{s}^{M+1})' \leq \mathbf{b}. \tag{8.5}$$

A and b will be referred as the constraint matrix and the right-hand side vector, and $(\mathbf{s}^{M+1})'$ are the unknown parameters (the vector of counterfactual market shares) to be determined.[9] The dimension of b, and the number of rows in A, are equal to the number of cyclic monotonicity inequalities, that is, the number of possible cycles. For a given cycle $(l_1, l_2, \ldots, M+1, l_1)$ we will next derive the corresponding row and entry in A and b corresponding to this cycle. Now consider the following $K \times J$ matrices D and S stacked by the relevant utility and market share row vectors:

$$\mathbf{D} = \begin{bmatrix} \delta^{l_2} \\ \delta^{l_3} \\ \vdots \\ \delta^{M+1} \\ \hline \delta^{l_1} \end{bmatrix} - \begin{bmatrix} \delta^{l_1} \\ \delta^{l_3} \\ \vdots \\ \delta^{l_{K-1}} \\ \hline \delta^{M+1} \end{bmatrix} = \begin{bmatrix} \mathbf{D_1} \\ \hline \delta^{l_1} - \delta^{M+1} \end{bmatrix}$$

$$\mathbf{S} = \begin{bmatrix} \mathbf{s}^{l_1} \\ \mathbf{s}^{l_2} \\ \vdots \\ \mathbf{s}^{l_{K-1}} \\ \hline \mathbf{s}^{M+1} \end{bmatrix} = \begin{bmatrix} \mathbf{S_1} \\ \hline \mathbf{s}^{M+1} \end{bmatrix}.$$

The cyclic monotonicity inequality corresponding to this cycle (see equation (8.3)) can be written as

$$(\delta^{l}_{1} - \delta^{M+1}) \cdot (\mathbf{s}^{M+1})' \le -\mathbf{1}'(D_{1} \circ S_{1})\mathbf{1}, \tag{8.6}$$

where $\mathbf{1}$ is a $(K-1) \times 1$ vector of 1s and $\circ$ is the Hadamard product. For this cycle, then, the corresponding row of A and entry in $\boldsymbol{b}$ is given by (8.6).

It turns out that, by rewriting the cyclic monotonicity inequalities for each cycle, we can show that the number of effective constraints in the LP problem is much smaller than the number of cycles. The following Lemma shows that our counterfactual problem can always be formulated as a LP problem with at most M distinct constraint inequalities, where M is the number of markets (the LP problem also includes J non-negativity constraints). That is, the number of effective constraints increases only *linearly* in the number of markets M, rather than exponentially as it might seem at first glance.

Lemma 1. *Expressing the LP constraints imposed by cyclic monotonicity in the form of (8.5), there are at most M distinct rows in A.*

Proof. From (8.6), the constraint coefficient always takes the form $\delta^{i} - \delta^{M+1}$, where i $\in \{1, \ldots, M\}$. Since there are M markets, there are at most M distinct constraint coefficients. $\quad\square$

Lemma 1 implies that our counterfactual procedure is a computationally easy LP problem.[10] Although the number of constraints appears to increase exponentially as the number of markets increases, Lemma 1 implies that most of them are parallel to each other, which are then easily eliminated in a pre-solved step.

3.3   Gross Substitution

In this section, we analytically demonstrate a simple counterfactual using the LP formulation. Suppose we increase the price of product j in market m; our counterfactual framework shows that its market share weakly decreases. In another words, there is at least one product $i \in \mathcal{J} \setminus \{j\}$ such that products i, j are weakly substitute.

Proposition 2. *Suppose the regressors contain price for each product p_{p} and the price coefficient $\beta_{p} < 0$ (normal goods). Consider a counterfactual market $M + 1$, which is identical to the benchmark market m, except that δ^{M+1}_{j} differs from δ^{m}_{j} due to the price change of product j. Cyclic monotonicity implies that $(p^{M+1}_{j} - p^{m}_{j})(s^{M+1}_{j} - s^{m}_{j}) \le 0$. Since the market share of product j weakly decreases when its price increases, there must be some product in $\mathcal{J} \setminus \{j\}$ whose market share weakly increases.*

Proof. Consider the cycle of length 2 containing both the benchmark and counterfactual market $(m, M + 1)$. We have $(\delta^{M+1} - \delta^{m}) \cdot \mathbf{s}^{m} + (\delta^{m} - \delta^{M+1}) \cdot \mathbf{s}^{M+1} \le 0$. $\because (\delta^{M+1} - \delta^{m}) = [0, \ldots, \beta_{p}(p^{M+1}_{j} - p^{m}_{j}), \ldots, 0]$, $\therefore \beta_{p}(p^{M+1}_{j} - p^{m}_{j})s^{m}_{j} - \beta_{p}(p^{M+1}_{j} - p^{m}_{j})s^{M+1}_{j} \le 0$. If $\beta_{p} \le 0$, we have $(p^{M+1}_{j} - p^{m}_{j}) \cdot (s^{M+1}_{j} - s^{m}_{j}) \le 0$.

While our framework asserts that the market share of a product is weakly decreasing in its price, it does not assert gross substitution more broadly. That is, whenever the price of j

increases, the market shares for *all* other products weakly increase. Our framework thus allows for some degree of complementarity.

When desired, we can easily impose gross substitution in our counterfactual framework. Suppose we are interested in the counterfactual of increasing the price of product v in market m. Then the upper bound counterfactual market share for products $i = 1, \ldots, J$ is given by

$$\max s_i^{M+1} \tag{8.7}$$

$$\text{s.t.} \sum_{j=1}^{J} s_j^{M+1} = 1$$

$$\sum_{k=1}^{K} (\delta^{l_{k+1}} - \delta^{l_k}) \cdot \mathbf{s}^{l_k} \le 0; l_K = M+1; 2 \le K \le M$$

$$s_j^{M+1} \ge s_j^{m} \quad \forall j \ne v \quad \text{(gross substitution constraints)} \pm$$

$$s_v^{M+1} \ge 0$$

On the other hand, when we conduct the counterfactual of decreasing the price of v, the gross substitution constraints are $s_j^{M+1} \le s_j^{m}$ for all $j \ne v$. For some problems, it is reasonable to assume that all products are gross substitutes.[11] Imposing gross substitution also narrows down the identified set.

4. MONTE CARLO SIMULATIONS

In this section we conduct a Monte Carlo simulation to study the identified set of counterfactuals. The main finding is that our counterfactual bounds always cover the true logit counterfactual market shares in all 100 runs; therefore, it has a coverage probability of 100 per cent. We also find that the length of the bounds is typically tight, with the worst-case average of around 5 per cent of market shares (see Table 8.1).

We first generate (market-invariant) product-specific regressors $X_j = (x_{j1}, x_{j2}, x_{j3})$ from multivariate normal with

$$\mu - \begin{bmatrix} 0.5 \\ 0.5 \\ 0.5 \end{bmatrix}, \quad \Sigma = \begin{bmatrix} 1 & -0.7 & 0.3 \\ \cdot & 1 & 0.3 \\ \cdot & \cdot & 1 \end{bmatrix}.$$

The price of product j, p_j^m, in market m is generated according to

$$p_j^m = |1.1(x_{j1} + x_{j2} + x_{j3}) + \zeta_j^m|$$
$$\zeta_j^m \sim \mathcal{N}(0, 0.3^2).$$

The mean utility δ_j^m is then computed as $[X_j, p_j^m]\beta$, where $\beta = [1.5, 1.5, 0.8, -2.2]'$. The market shares are computed under the logit model, assuming a Type-I Extreme Value distribution. We set the number of products to be $J = 3$. We first generate one benchmark

Table 8.1   Monte Carlo simulation: (upper bound−lower bound)

	M = 200			M = 500			M = 1000		
	s_1	s_2	s_3	s_1	s_2	s_3	s_1	s_2	s_3
$p_1 +1\%$	0.0417	0.0263	0.0525	0.0297	0.0161	0.0340	0.0233	0.0114	0.0256
	(0.0012)	(0.0007)	(0.0013)	(0.0008)	(0.0004)	(0.0013)	(0.0007)	(0.0004)	(0.0008)
$p_2 +1\%$	0.0566	0.0151	0.0581	0.0355	0.0113	0.0364	0.0263	0.0090	0.0283
	(0.0018)	(0.0005)	(0.0018)	(0.0009)	(0.0003)	(0.0009)	(0.0008)	(0.0002)	(0.0008)
$p_3 +1\%$	0.0474	0.0260	0.0416	0.0334	0.0165	0.0306	0.0240	0.0122	0.0231
	(0.0013)	(0.0007)	(0.0013)	(0.0009)	(0.0005)	(0.0008)	(0.0008)	(0.0003)	(0.0006)

Note: Reported figures are averages across 100 replications. We report the width of the bounds rather than coverage, because our bounds always cover the true (logit) counterfactual, and so the coverage probability is 100 per cent.

market, which is then held fixed across Monte Carlo repetitions. For each Monte Carlo repetition, we generate another $M − 1$ markets from the DGP (Data-Generating Process). We then compute the upper and lower bounds counterfactuals s_i^{M+1} for $i = 1, 2, 3$ under +1 per cent increase in $p_j^{\bar{m}}, j = 1, 2, 3$ of the benchmark market $\bar{m}$. We repeat this procedure 100 times and report the average length of the bounds in Table 8.1. The standard deviations across the 100 repetitions are reported in parentheses.

We also vary the number of markets, that is, $M \in \{200, 500, 1000\}$. The results are summarized in Table 8.1. We use only cycles of length 2, but using cycles up to length 3 does not make much of a difference.

5.   EMPIRICAL ILLUSTRATION: SUPERMARKET SALES OF COFFEE

For our empirical application, we use the IRI Marketing Dataset (Bronnenberg et al., 2008)—which is a retail scanner dataset containing weekly pricing, sales volume and promotion data of participating retail stores. We will focus on the product category of *coffee*, within the time frame of the year 2005.

Each observation in the IRI dataset is at the level of store-product week. We take all stores and aggregate them at the level of six major metropolitan areas: Boston, Chicago, Dallas, Houston, Milwaukee and Washington DC. As such, the unit of observation is (j, t), where j is the product, and t is the market—each market is defined as a week-metro combination. For instance, Houston during Week 3 is one such market. Therefore, there are 318 markets in total.

The consumer's choice set consists of seven brands: *Chock Full O Nuts, Eight O Clock, Folgers, Maxwell House, Private Label, Seattle's Best and Starbucks. Private Label* is the brand of coffee carried by the participating individual stores. We also include an *Outside Option* as a composite good consisting of all other smaller coffee brands. The average market share of a coffee brand is tabulated in Table 8.2.

The dependent variable is *Share*, which is the number of units sold in a market divided by the total number of all units sold in a market. The main covariate is *Price*, which is the average

Table 8.2   Average market share of a brand across 318 markets

Brands	Average Market Share (%)
Chock Full O Nuts	1.86
Eight O Clock	6.10
Folgers	27.38
Maxwell House	15.59
Outside	29.33
Private Label	10.53
Seattle's Best	1.22
Starbucks	7.99

retail price paid per unit of the product in a market. We have three other covariates measuring the degree of product promotions: *PR, Display* and *Feature*. The variable *PR* is a binary variable indicating a temporary price reduction of 5 per cent or more. The variable *display* takes values in {0, 1, 2} and is defined by IRI as the degree to which the product is exhibited prominently in the store. The variable *Feature* takes values in {0, 1, . . ., 4}, which are coded as the degree of advertisement featured by the store retailer. These product-specific variables are aggregated to the level of week-metro by means of weighted average across stores, the weights used are the number of units sold.[12]

5.1   Result

First, we obtain point estimates of the model coefficients using the semiparametric method of Shi et al. (2018). Then, we run a series of counterfactual exercises as follows: for each brand, we increase its price in the median market by 1–20 per cent and then compute the changes in the market shares of all brands in the median market.[13]

The counterfactual market share is partially identified. In fact, our identified set is multidimensional (one dimension for each product). We slice the identified set in the following way to further narrow it down. First, we look at the set of counterfactual market shares that are consistent with Gross Substitution (as discussed in section 3.3). That is, we restrict attention to only those counterfactual market shares such that s_j is weakly increasing for all $j \neq i$ when we increase the price of i. Second, we look at the component-wise midpoints of the identified set.

The main result is given in Figure 8.1. We plot the absolute increases in market shares for different brands as a function of percentage increases in the price of a reference brand. The changes in market shares are relative to the pre-counterfactual benchmark market, which is the median market.

In figure 8.1(c), we increase the price of the reference brand, Folgers, and examine the substitution effects on other brands. (We label the lines in Figures 8.1 and 8.2 such that the

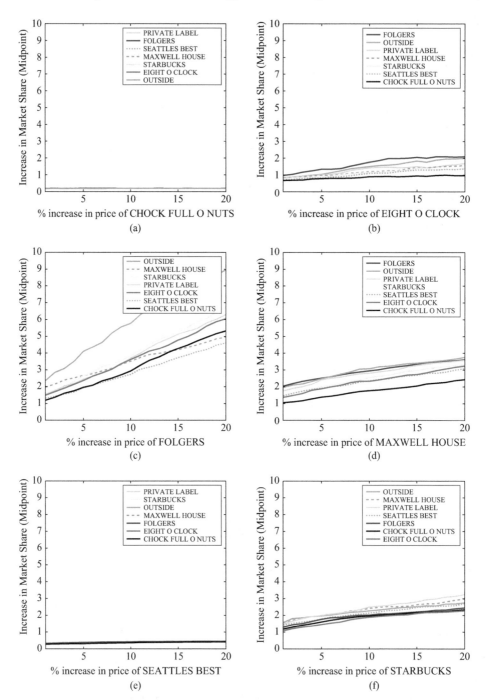

*Figure 8.1   Absolute increases in market shares for different brands as a result of
percentage increases in the price of a reference brand. Each line corresponds
to a brand. The labeling of lines is such that the brand corresponding to the
lowest line (weakest substitution) appears last in the graph legend, and so on*

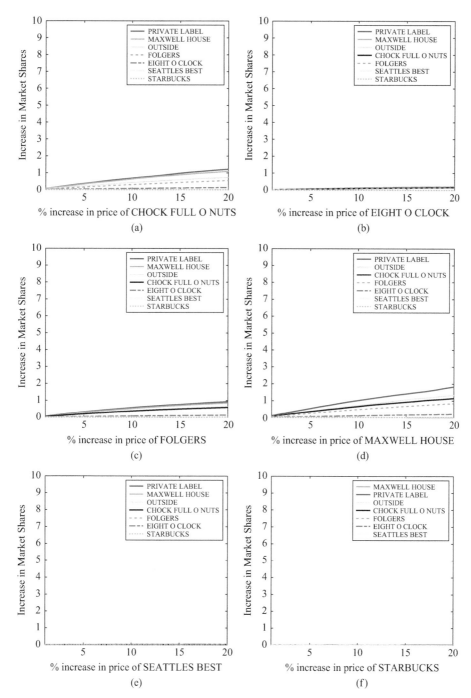

Figure 8.2   Substitution between products assuming the logit model. The labeling of lines is such that the brand corresponding to the lowest line (weakest substitution) appears last in the graph legend, and so on

brand with the highest substitution strength appears first in the graph legend and so on.) We see that Seattle's Best is the coffee brand that benefits the least; its market share increases from 1 per cent to 4.5 per cent as the price of Folgers increases from 1 per cent to 20 per cent. In comparison, Starbucks is a stronger substitute—its market share increases from 1.5 per cent to 7 per cent at the same range.

Crucially, our framework allows for a much richer pattern of substitutions than the logit model. The logit model implies that the elasticity of substitution from product j to i does not depend on the identity of j. This leads to Figure 8.2, where the ordering of brands in terms of substitution strengths is fixed. In contrast, the ordering of how strongly one brand substitutes another brand changes widely depending on the reference brand.

For example, our analysis shows that (i) Starbucks is a very strong substitute to Seattle's Best while being a weak substitute to Eight O Clock. (ii) Folgers is a strong substitute to all other brands except Seattle's Best and Starbucks. Using the logit model, such a remark is not possible; Starbucks is the weakest substitute no matter which reference brand we are considering. We also observe that the substitution lines can cross one another, that is, one brand could be a stronger substitute when price increase is modest, but could be a weaker substitute when price increase is large. In all the figures, there is a noticeable upward jump at the zero per cent price change (corresponding to the observed market shares in the data). This is because we are reporting the *midpoint* of the identified interval for each market share.

6.   CONCLUDING REMARKS

While the literature on semiparametric discrete-choice models is quite large and mature, empirical applications utilizing these methods have been relatively sparse. This may be due in part to the absence of methods for counterfactual evaluation utilizing results from these semiparametric models. Our chapter fills in this gap by providing an approach for evaluating bounds for counterfactual choice probabilities for semiparametric multinomial choice models, in which the systematic components of utility are specified as a single index but the distribution of the error terms are left unspecified. Exploiting the property of *cyclic monotonicity* (a convex-analytic property of the random utility choice model), we derive upper and lower bounds on choice probabilities for hypothetical counterfactual scenarios which may lie outside the range of the observed data. Monte Carlo simulations and an empirical illustration using scanner data show that our method works well in practice.

NOTES

*   We thank Whitney Newey and seminar participants in Ohio State, Texas-Austin, UBC, UCLA, and 39th Marketing Science Conference for helpful comments.
1.   Examples include Manski (1975) and Han (1987), among many others.
2.   Recently, Allen and Rehbeck (2016) have studied the nonparametric identification of counterfactuals in a class of perturbed utility models, which includes random utility multinomial choice models.
3.   See, for instance, McFadden and Train (2000), Train (2009), Ackerberg et al. (2007) and Rossi et al. (2012).
4.   See, for example, Andrews and Barwick (2012), Andrews and Soares (2010), Bontemps et al. (2012), Freyberger and Horowitz (2015), Hsieh et al. (2017), Kaido and Santos (2014), and Pakes et al. (2015).
5.   See Shi et al. (2018), Chiong and Shum (2018) and Fosgerau et al. (2020) for full details.

6. See Rust (1994). Chiong et al. (2016) generalize it to the case when the social surplus function may be non-differentiable, corresponding to cases where the utility shocks ε have bounded support or follow a discrete distribution.
7. See Rockafellar (2015, Theorem 23.5) and Villani (2003). Conversely, any function that satisfies cyclic monotonicity must be a subgradient of some convex function.
8. While Fox's (2007) estimator is based on the *rank-order property*, which involves utility comparisons among all pairs of options in the choice set, it turns out that the bounds on market shares implied by the rank-order property have undesirable properties for the evaluation of counterfactual choice probabilities, which we describe in appendix 8 A.1. Because of that we focus on the implications of cyclic monotonicity in this chapter.
9. For notational convenience, in this section, we will take the vectors of mean utilities and market shares (δ^i and s^i) as $1 \times J$ row vectors.
10. The main computational bottleneck is to find all possible cycles itself (generate constraints) due to its combinatorial nature, not LP.
11. Berry et al. (2013) show that certain forms of gross substitution, in particular connected substitution, are sufficient for the invertibility of demand, which is fundamental for many demand estimation methods such as Berry et al. (1995).
12. For example, PR_{jt} is constructed as the number of units of j sold that had a temporary price reduction in market t divided by the total number of units of j sold in market t.
13. The median market in the data is determined using the algorithm PAM (Partitioning Around Medoid).

REFERENCES

Ackerberg, D., Benkard, C. L., Berry, S., and Pakes, A. (2007). Econometric tools for analyzing market outcomes. *Handbook of econometrics*, 6: 4171–276.

Allen, R. and Rehbeck, J. (2016). Identification of average demand models. Technical report, Working paper.

Andrews, D. W. and Barwick, P. J. (2012). Inference for parameters defined by moment inequalities: A recommended moment selection procedure. *Econometrica*, 80(6): 2805–26.

Andrews, D. W. and Soares, G. (2010). Inference for parameters defined by moment inequalities using generalized moment selection. *Econometrica*, 78(1): 119–57.

Berry, S., Gandhi, A., and Haile, P. (2013). Connected substitutes and invertibility of demand. *Econometrica*, 81(5): 2087–111.

Berry, S., Levinsohn, J., and Pakes, A. (1995). Automobile prices in market equilibrium. *Econometrica*, 841–90.

Berry, S. T. (1994). Estimating discrete-choice models of product differentiation. *RAND Journal of Economics*, 242–62.

Bontemps, C., Magnac, T., and Maurin, E. (2012). Set identified linear models. *Econometrica*, 80(3): 1129–55.

Bresnahan, T. F., Stern, S., and Trajtenberg, M. (1997). Market segmentation and the sources of rents from innovation: Personal computers in the late 1980s. *RAND Journal of Economics*, S17–S44.

Bronnenberg, B. J., Kruger, M. W., and Mela, C. F. (2008). Database paper: The IRI marketing data set. *Marketing Science*, 27(4): 745–8.

Chiong, K. X., Galichon, A., and Shum, M. (2016). Duality in dynamic discrete-choice models. *Quantitative Economics*, 7(1): 83–115.

Chiong, K. X. and Shum, M. (2019). Random projection estimation of discrete-choice models with large choice sets. *Management Science*, 65(1): 256–71.

Fosgerau, M., Melo, E., de Palma, A., and Shum, M. (2020). Discrete choice and rational inattention: A general equivalence result. *International Economic Review*, 61(4): 1569–89.

Fox, J. T. (2007). Semiparametric estimation of multinomial discrete-choice models using a subset of choices. *RAND Journal of Economics*, 38(4): 1002–19.

Freyberger, J. and Horowitz, J. L. (2015). Identification and shape restrictions in nonparametric instrumental variables estimation. *Journal of Econometrics*, 189(1): 41–53.

Goldberg, P. K. (1995). Product differentiation and oligopoly in international markets: The case of the us automobile industry. *Econometrica*, 891–951.

Goolsbee, A. and Petrin, A. (2004). The consumer gains from direct broadcast satellites and the competition with cable tv. *Econometrica*, 72(2): 351–81.

Han, A. K. (1987). Nonparametric analysis of a generalized regression model: the maximum rank correlation estimator. *Journal of Econometrics*, 35(2–3): 303–16.

Hausman, J. A. (1996). Valuation of new goods under perfect and imperfect competition. In *The economics of new goods*, 207–48. University of Chicago Press.

Hausman, J. A., Abrevaya, J., and Scott-Morton, F. M. (1998). Misclassification of the dependent variable in a discrete-response setting. *Journal of Econometrics*, 87(2): 239–69.

Hsieh, Y.-W., Shi, X., and Shum, M. (2021). Inference on estimators defined by mathematical programming. *Journal of Econometrics*, forthcoming.

Kaido, H. and Santos, A. (2014). Asymptotically efficient estimation of models defined by convex moment inequalities. *Econometrica*, 82(1): 387–413.

Khan, S. (2013). Distribution free estimation of heteroskedastic binary response models using probit/logit criterion functions. *Journal of Econometrics*, 172(1): 168–82.

Manski, C. F. (1975). Maximum score estimation of the stochastic utility model of choice. *Journal of Econometrics*, 3(3): 205–28.

McFadden, D. (1978). Modeling the choice of residential location. *Transportation Research Record*, (673).

McFadden, D. (1981). Econometric models of probabilistic choice. In *Structural analysis of discrete data with econometric applications*, 198–272.

McFadden, D. and Train, K. (2000). Mixed mnl models for discrete response. *Journal of Applied Econometrics*, 447–70.

McFadden, D. L. (1984). Econometric analysis of qualitative response models. In *Handbook of econometrics*, 2: 1395–457.

Nevo, A. (2000). Mergers with differentiated products: The case of the ready-to-eat cereal industry. *RAND Journal of Economics*, 395–421.

Pakes, A., Porter, J., Ho, K., and Ishii, J. (2015). Moment inequalities and their application. *Econometrica*, 83(1): 315–34.

Petrin, A. (2002). Quantifying the benefits of new products: The case of the minivan. *Journal of Political Economy*, 110(4): 705–29.

Rockafellar, R. T. (2015). *Convex analysis*. Princeton University Press.

Rossi, P. E., Allenby, G. M., and McCulloch, R. (2012). *Bayesian statistics and marketing*. Wiley.

Rust, J. (1994). Structural estimation of Markov decision processes. In *Handbook of econometrics*, 4: 3081–143.

Shi, X., Shum, M., and Song, W. (2018). Estimating semi-parametric panel multinomial choice models using cyclic monotonicity. *Econometrica*, 86: 737–61.

Train, K. E. (2009). *Discrete choice methods with simulation*. Cambridge University Press.

Villani, C. (2003). *Topics in optimal transportation*, 58. American Mathematical Society.

APPENDIX 8A.1   ADDITIONAL REMARKS: RANK-ORDER PROPERTY

Here, we study the *rank order* condition studied by Fox (2007): $\delta_i > \delta_j \Leftrightarrow s_i > s_j$ and consider its implications for evaluating counterfactual choice probabilities. The rank order condition can be viewed as a generalization of the IIA (Independence of Irrelevant Alternatives) property and is implied by the exchangeable, continuously distributed error terms with full support. This allows for dependence between the random utility errors ε's and X, which is less restrictive than what we require in Assumption 1. Applied to the counterfactual evaluation, the rank order condition states

Assumption 2 (*Rank Order*): *Suppose σ is the permutation on $\{1, 2, \ldots, J\}$ such that $\delta_{\sigma(1)} \geq \delta_{\sigma(2)} \geq \ldots \geq \delta_{\sigma(J)}$. The rank order condition implies that the same permutation also sorts the market shares in decreasing order:* $s_{\sigma(1)} \geq s_{\sigma(2)} \geq \ldots \geq s_{\sigma(J)}$.

By definition, rank order is a *within-market* restriction: it only places restriction directly on (δ^{M+1}, s^{M+1}), regardless of other sample information as well as the magnitude of the price change. To investigate further, we rewrite these inequalities in matrix form. Suppose s^{M+1} is a $J \times 1$ column vector and P is the $J \times J$ permutation matrix representing σ: $P[j, \sigma(j)] = 1$, $j = 1, \ldots, J$ and zero otherwise.

$$D \cdot P \cdot s^{M+1} \leq 0,$$

where D is the $(J-1) \times J$ bi-diagonal matrix with the elements $(-1, 1)$ in the $(j, j+1)$ positions in row j. From this representation, we see that the constraint matrix $D \cdot P$ only contains $(-1, 1, 0)$ and hence does not depend on other market-level data (δ^m, s^m). As a result, its identified set will be *invariant* to the sample size and the magnitude of the price change. Moreover, the rank order condition implies a simple component-wise upper bound for s_j:

Proposition 3. $s_{\sigma(j)}$ *is bounded above by $\frac{1}{j}$, regardless of the number of alternative J.*

Proof: It is trivial to show that the upper bound for the market share $s_{\sigma(1)}$ corresponding to the largest mean utility $\delta_{\sigma(1)}$ is 1, as $s_\sigma = (1, 0, \ldots, 0)$ does not violate the rank order condition. Similarly, max $s_{\sigma(j)}$ is at most $\frac{1}{j}$, otherwise $s_{\sigma(j)} > \delta_{\sigma(1)}$ violating the rank order condition.

9.   Bank performance analysis[*]
Natalya Zelenyuk and Valentin Zelenyuk

1.   INTRODUCTION

Banks play a major role in any economy through money creation, borrowing and lending, which fuels economic activity. Financial intermediation of banks has a direct and indirect impact on all types of firms and their production capacities that can be restricted by or enriched with lending from banks. Banks are studied in the economic literature as special firms because of their connecting role between the financial markets and real economic growth (Sealey and Lindley, 1977; Diamond and Dybvig, 1983; Mester, 1993; Bikker and Bos, 2008). Indeed, liquidity provided by banks to other industries is instrumental for an economy at any time, and especially during times of economic uncertainty. The importance of banks is evidenced by the attention paid to them by central banks or various government agencies. During 2007–09 only, the US Federal authorities allocated trillions of dollars to restore liquidity creation in the economy (Bai et al., 2018; Berger and Bouwman, 2009).

Regulatory and prudential authorities monitor the performance of banks and introduce various regulations aimed at the direct enhancement of the performance of banks and the indirect prevention of any liquidity deficits to develop the productive functioning of firms (Casu et al., 2004). Besides the national levels, banking is monitored and regulated on an international level. Specifically, a key global Accord of banking regulation is documented in the Basel Rules (BIS, 2020a). The Accord was developed by the Basel Committee and directs internationally converging regulatory rules. The Basel Committee was established in 1974, in response to an increased volatility in the currency exchange markets and a failure of key banks (a prominent example is Herstatt in Germany) betting on the direction of currency pricing trends (Goodhart, 2011). The cyclicality of crisis further occurring in 1980s with the Latin American debt crisis, 1990s dot-com bubble and the 2000s Global Financial Crisis reinforced the need for the removal of the sources of competitive inequality and harmonized the regulatory requirements to bank capital, liquidity and transparency (BIS, 2020b). The most recent regulatory accords are identically standardized and implemented in almost every country in the world and are based on the advanced performance methods balancing risk with return.

The goal of this chapter is to present practical tools that have been extensively applied to performance analysis of banks. The toolset in this chapter covers ratio analysis, efficiency techniques of Stochastic Frontier Analysis (SFA) and Data Envelopment Analysis (DEA) as well as outlines other econometric methods, including causal inference, which recently became very popular in the financial literature, comprising of difference-in-differences and regression discontinuity design methods. We believe that our chapter will be valuable for academics, including PhD students, studying banking as well as banking industry experts and professionals engaged in research and consulting, regulation and prudential monitoring and analysis of banks.

1.1 DEA and SFA

DEA has its roots in economic theory models, mainly known as *Activity Analysis Models* (AAM), developed by Koopmans (1951), Debreu (1951) and Shephard (1953), which were in turn influenced by the works of Leontief (1925), Von Neumann (1945), to mention just a few. *Inter alia*, these and other important works led to the seminal paper of Farrell (1957), who tailored the AAMs into the foundation for measuring what he referred to as "productive efficiency". Besides a few papers, his work was largely overlooked for two decades, until two streams of research basically exploded from his work. One stream was largely due to the influential research of Charnes et al. (1978), where Farrell's approach was generalized and empowered with linear programming theory and the practice to implement it, as well as being branded as DEA. The second stream was largely due to the seminal works of Aigner et al. (1977) and Meeusen and van den Broeck (1977), who at about the same time proposed SFA, building on the research of Farrell (1957), among others.

Over the last four decades, both of these streams, DEA and SFA, have developed into very rich streams of literature, with many branches, often interconnected and mutually developing and spanning several fields of research: economics and econometrics, statistics (including data science and business analytics), operations research/management science and so on. A key, and in some respects more important, part of the literature concerns the applications of these methods virtually to any sector of the economy. Among the most popular applications are those to the banking industry, which we briefly overview and give references for further details.

Among the first papers using DEA in banking were Sherman and Gold (1985), English et al. (1993) and Fukuyama (1993), which were followed by many others. Ferrier and Lovell (1990) and Hughes and Mester (1998) were among the first applying SFA in banking, followed by many interesting works thereafter. Now, both literature streams are massive, for example Google Scholar search (in April 2020) yielded about 58 400 results for "DEA and Banking" and 14 000 for "SFA and Banking", while a more general Google search for "DEA" and "SFA" yielded about 6 660 000 and 2 000 000 results, respectively. Obviously, it is practically impossible to review even 10 per cent of the published papers. Our goal is more modest to overview the major methods and to mention a few popular papers that we think represent valuable examples, as well as to refer to previous reviews where more examples could be found.

1.2 Causal Inference Methods

Causal methods are rooted from the randomized experiments of Splawa-Neyman et al. (1990, 1923)[1] and Fisher (1925), where both authors introduced an experimental design around the testing of treatment effects. These seminal works and their later developments into agricultural, biological and medical research lead to an application of the difference (in differences) methods in empirical economics (where fundamental works include Ashenfelter, 1978; Ashenfelter and Card, 1985) and finance (Harris, 1989; Trezevant, 1992).

The recent prominent papers applying difference-in-differences (DD) in banking include Anginer et al. (2018) in an application to corporate governance, Buchak et al. (2018) in an application to "fintech" lending and Duchin and Sosyura (2014) in studies of government bailouts of banks, among many others.

Another popular method that is identifying causality between the two variables is regression discontinuity design. It gained popularity from the seminal work of Thistlethwaite and Campbell (1960) and received attention in the economic and finance literature due to the minimal assumptions involved in modeling. Hahn et al. (2001) and Imbens and Lemieux (2007) provide theoretical and empirical guidelines on regression discontinuity design (RDD). In banking research, RDD applications are relatively new, a few prominent papers include the works by Bonner and Eijffinger (2015) on the impact of regulatory liquidity requirements on the demand for long-term lending, Liberman (2016) on the effects of renegotiations on credit card lending and Berg (2018) on the effects of precautionary savings in the transmission of credit supply shocks.

1.3 Chapter Structure

Our chapter is organized as follows. Section 2 starts with a review of the development of performance analysis in banking from the simple methods based on financial ratios to explaining inefficiency with more advanced methods (data envelopment analysis, stochastic frontier analysis, causal inference). Section 3 presents the basics of the productivity and efficiency theory. Section 4 reviews DEA. Section 5 reviews the SFA. Section 6 presents an overview of other econometric methods based on the recent developments in the causal inference analysis of performance, and section 7 concludes.

2. EVOLUTION OF PERFORMANCE ANALYSIS OF BANKS

In this section we present how the methods of performance analysis of banks developed from very straightforward managerial techniques of financial statements analysis to advanced linear programming methods enabling the explanation of the inefficiency of banks.

2.1 Analysis of Financial Ratios

Traditionally, analysis of bank performance starts with an analysis of financial statements, mostly statements of financial position and a comprehensive income statement (Casu et al., 2006). The simplest measures of performance include the assets of a bank and the income that was generated with these assets during a financial year. The other methods, including very complex methods of performance analysis in banking, often use these measures as building components or generalize over them.

An analysis with financial ratios is based on combining two (absolute) financial measures into a ratio. For example, net income over assets would signal about how much net income a bank has generated per dollar of assets. In the efficiency analysis literature, it is an example of the "return-to-dollar" measure, advocated by Georgescu-Roegen (1951) and advanced further in Färe et al. (2019).

Bank counter-parties, including shareholders and regulators, are often interested in the performance analysis of banks with financial ratios. Financial ratios are arithmetically simple and usually very intuitive. Various management information systems are designed around financial ratios and the breakdown of the key ratios into driving components. One of the methods of ratio decomposition follows the famous DuPont Identity, where the interesting ratio for shareholders, return on equity, is decomposed as a product of the two other ratios—the return on assets and the equity multiplier (Ross et al., 2017). Each of these two ratios could be further decomposed into the component-driving ratios. For example, the return on assets is a product of the profit margin and the total assets turnover. This way, one can describe the drivers of the return on equity (measured by net income/total equity) with operating efficiency (measured by net income/sales), asset use efficiency (sales/assets) and financial leverage (assets/total equity) (Ross et al., 2017). The most detailed management information systems include decision trees that relate the top "all bank performance" return on equity to the sales efficiency of a loan officer in a single branch.

In essence, the key financial performance ratios of interest to any bank and bank stakeholders will include the return on assets (ROA), return on equity (ROE) and the non-performing loan ratios and capital ratios (Casu et al., 2006). Interestingly, after the global financial crisis banks increasingly applied risk-adjusted measures of performance (BIS, 2015), including risk-adjusted return (Bikker and Bos, 2008) on capital (RAROC), defined as

$$RAROC = \frac{\text{Risk-adjusted Net Income}}{\text{Economic Capital}}, \tag{9.1}$$

return on risk-adjusted capital (RORAC), defined as

$$RORAC = \frac{\text{Expected Net Income}}{\text{Allocated Economic Capital}}, \tag{9.2}$$

and risk-adjusted return on risk-adjusted capital (RARORAC), defined as

$$RARORAC = \frac{\text{Economic Value Added}}{\text{Allocated Economic Capital}}. \tag{9.3}$$

Meanwhile, the risk-adjusted return measures the net income a business has earned in relation to a risk in a given time frame. With accounting measures, it could be calculated as

$$\text{Risk-adjusted return} = \text{Revenue} - \text{Expenses} - (\text{Expected Loss}) + (\text{Net Interest Margin of Capital Change}). \tag{9.4}$$

As a result, this formula ensures that a business with a lower risk and a constant level of return will have a higher risk-adjusted return. The denominator of the RAROC ratio, economic capital, attributes bank capital securing the effects of risk taking by business. It is often parametrized to the level of capital a bank needs to handle unexpected losses during a particular time period within a decided confidence interval. For better management, economic capital is calculated at a total bank level and at the level of divisions. Building blocks of economic capital vary by type of risk. For example, credit risk modeling would require an estimation of probability of default, loss given default and exposure at default (Roncalli, 2020).

The economic value added (EVA), in a numerator of the RARORAC, presents a measure of economic profit as an incremental difference between a rate of return and the cost of capital. It is calculated as a net income in a difference to an invested capital times the cost of capital. EVA is presented in absolute measures and is also calculated at the level of a bank and its divisions (BIS, 2015).

Alternatively, risk-adjusted return is measured with the asset pricing approach, where RARORAC is given by

$$RARORAC = \frac{[(r_p - r_f) - \beta_p(r_m - r_f)]\mathcal{I}_0}{\text{Economic Capital}},$$
(9.5)

where r_p is return on a portfolio of assets;
r_f is a return on a risk–free asset, that is, government bond;
r_m is the market return;
β_p is a systematic risk of the portfolio;

$\mathcal{I}_0$ is an investment in a project at time = 0, at the beginning of the project. It is a utilized capital at risk (BIS, 2015).

In the denominator, the economic capital, or allocated capital at risk, is a value at risk (VaR), which is the measure of a loss on a portfolio over a fixed time period (Roncalli, 2020).

The difference in the calculation of the two measures of RARORAC with an EVA and with an excess return is driven by the availability of accounting versus market data applied in the calculations. For example, the value added versus the loss on the loan portfolio is presented with accounting data, whereas the return on a bond portfolio is likely to be measured with the market pricing data.

For regulatory and investment purposes, bank performance ratios are combined into the CAMELS system. The most recent governmental capital support of the banks during the global financial crisis in the United States was grounded on a review of the bank applicants according to the CAMELS rating system (Duchin and Sosyura, 2014; Aparicio et al., 2018). CAMELS stands for capital adequacy, asset quality, management, earnings, liquidity and sensitivity to market ratios (Federal Reserve, 2020). Table 9.1 summarizes the key regulatory requirements corresponding to each of the CAMELS criteria and the ratios applied in research to represent these criteria.

Each of the rating measures in CAMELS is focused on balancing returns with the risks. To start with returns, every bank is aiming at increasing returns to shareholders by maximizing revenues and minimizing cost, that is, by improving the efficiency of a bank (Bikker and Bos, 2008). The key to efficiency is a technology that transfers inputs (cost-related contributors to the production process of a bank) into outputs (revenue-related contributors to the production process of a bank).

In contrast to productivity, which measures the output produced relative to the input, efficiency measures the difference between the actual/observed and optimal/unobserved input–output result. Thus, the challenge of estimating efficiency is in the observability of both technology and optimal efficiency. The roadmap to overcoming these challenges is discussed in the next sections.

2.2   Variables for Modeling Production Process in Banking

A critical step in the analysis of productivity and efficiency of any system is defining the inputs and outputs of the production process of this system. A conceptual framework for the economics of production analysis of banks was proposed in a prominent work by Sealey and Lindley (1977) defining inputs and outputs of banks in their production, installing the

Table 9.1   CAMELS rating system, corresponding regulatory expectations and ratios

Rating Component	Uniform Regulatory Expectation from https://www.fdic.gov	Corresponding Financial Ratio
Capital Adequacy	Level of capital commensurate with the degree of credit, market and other on and off-balance sheet risks.	Tier 1 risk-based capital ratio = (Tier 1 capital)/(risk-weighted assets) (Duchin and Sosyura, 2014). Common equity ratio = (common equity)/ (total assets) (Anginer et al. (2018)).
Asset Quality	The adequacy of allowance for credit risk, including loan and other investment portfolios losses.	Non-performing loans ratio = (loans past due 90 days or more and non-accruals)/ (total loans) (Acharya and Mora, 2015).
Management	Sound management practices to ensure balanced bank performance and risk profile.	Return on assets = (net income)/(total assets) (Martinez-Peria and Schmukler, 2001). Non-interest expense ratio = (non-interest expense)/(income) (Aparicio et al., 2018).
Earnings	Strong developing quantity and quality of earnings adequate to the risks.	Return on equity = (net income)/(total equity capital) (Duchin and Sosyura, 2014).
Liquidity	Adequate liquidity position compared to funding needs, availability of assets convertible to cash, access to money markets and sources of funding.	Loan-deposit ratio = loans/deposits (Aparicio et al., 2018) Cash ratio = cash/(total assets) (Assaf et al., 2019).
Sensitivity to Market Risk	The degree to which changes in interest rates, foreign exchange rates, equity prices or commodity prices can adversely affect the earnings or an economic capital of a bank. The nature and complexity of market risk exposure due to trading and foreign operations.	Sensitivity to interest rate risk = (short term assets – short-term liabilities)/ (earning assets) (Duchin and Sosyura, 2014; Berger and Roman, 2017).

economics foundation for both DEA and SFA. Since then, three major approaches prevailed in the literature for modeling the technological process of banks: production, value-added and intermediation. Many studies, while arriving at similar, or different, conclusions on the same or similar data differ in how they apply inputs and outputs to describe the technological role of banks in modeling with both DEA and SFA. Fruitful reviews on this and other aspects can be found in Berger and Humphrey (1997), Fethi and Pasiouras (2010) and Paradi and Zhu (2013), to mention just a few.

In the production approach, the role of a bank is similar to an industry decision making unit (DMU), that is, labor and capital are needed to produce goods, including customer accounts, loans and securities. This approach is mostly applied in studies at bank-level and branch-level efficiency rather than in the studies about an industry's efficiency. For application examples, see Berger et al. (1997), Camanho and Dyson (2005) and Kenjegalieva et al. (2009a).

In the value-added approach, the role of a bank is to create income with a difference between earnings from outputs and cost from inputs. This approach is particularly relevant for diversified activities, extending to insurance and "bancassurance". Application examples include Eling and Luhnen (2010) and Leverty and Grace (2010). Recently, Humphrey (2020) extended this approach to creating value for bank customers, where outputs are measured with value creation with both assets and liabilities of a bank, that is, loans and securities are redefined into adding value flows that are important for users. In this model, inputs are deposits, labor and capital.

In the most commonly applied intermediation approach, the role of a bank is to transform savings (mostly deposits) into investments (mostly loans). The bank is viewed as a DMU which collects deposits with labor and capital and produces loans and other earning assets (Sealey and Lindley, 1977). Application examples of this approach include analysis at the bank level and can be found in Aly et al. (1990), Isik and Hassan (2002), Casu et al. (2013), Almanidis et al. (2019) and Mamatzakis et al. (2019), to mention a few.

Implementation of inputs and outputs to formally model the banking production process is described in section 3.

2.3   Variables for Explaining Inefficiency in Banking

One of the major aspects of interest in the analysis of productivity and efficiency of banks is modeling the inefficiency on other covariates, or explanatory variables. An established econometric strategy here is based on choosing the explanatory variables grounded on theoretical, or practical, considerations of the relevance of the covariates to the analyzed inefficiency. In a prominent methodological paper, Simar and Wilson (2007) illustrate how the algorithm of their model can work with banking data by including covariates of the size of a bank, product diversity and characteristics of the environment where a bank operates (for example, see Aly et al., 1990; Assaf et al., 2019). While applying a similar conceptual variable selection, the proxies for each of the concepts differ in these studies and, in this section, we briefly overview some of the most typical choices.

Size of a bank. The common explanatory covariate that appears in many (if not all) studies of the performance analysis literature is size, due to the belief that larger banks might utilize scale effects better. Larger banks often have greater diversification capacities (Assaf et al., 2019). The common specifications of size include the natural logarithm of total assets (Simar and Wilson, 2007) and total deposits/loans and number of bank branches (Aly et al., 1990). By a scale effect, a common belief is that size would have a positive impact on bank efficiency. For example, Berger and Mester (1997) found a positive impact of bank size on cost efficiency and a negative impact of bank size on profit efficiency. Separately, Aly et al. (1990) found a positive effect of size on both the technical and allocative efficiency of a bank. In a more recent study, Almanidis et al. (2019) found that two top-tier large banking groups were more efficient than four smaller sized banking groups.

The banks are often differentiated by size because larger banks require more regulatory attention based on their systemic importance. Systemically important banks are considered to be "too big to fail" (Bikker and Bos, 2008). In the event of a stress, the government would need to bail these banks out because the failure of a big bank could pose too big of a risk to the real sector in the economy (Adrian and Brunnermeier, 2016). One of the approaches to studying the impact of the size of a bank on its performance is to assign a dummy variable of one to a larger and systemically important bank (Acharya and Mora, 2015) and zero to all other banks. Most of the regulatory rules link the systemic importance of a bank to the size of a bank. The Dodd–Frank Act in the United States defines a banking organization as systemically important when its total assets exceed $50–$250 billion (Federal Reserve, 2020).

The primary global regulatory standard establisher, the Basel Committee on Banking Supervision, added more criteria to the definition of systemic importance. In particular, the Basel criteria also include complexity, interconnectedness, substitutability and the global significance of a banking organization (BCBS, 2019). The banks that meet the Basel criteria on significance are included in the annual lists of Global Systemically Important Banks published by the Financial Stability Board in the European Union. The list comprises of Bank of China, BNP Paribas, Citigroup, Commerzbank, Erste, Lloyds and Mitsubishi Group, to mention a few (EBA, 2020).

Many countries adopted (sometimes with modifications) the Basel criteria to their environments. For example, in Australia, the Australian Prudential Regulator followed the Basel Guidelines and IMF consultations to apply all four criteria to the definition of domestic systemically important banks and has identified the four biggest banks as systemically important. Total resident assets of the smallest of these four banks, ANZ, exceed AUD 400 billion (APRA, 2013), about the size of the GDP of Singapore.

Product diversity presents the proportion of a firm's revenue generated with the products that a bank offers to its customers. Greater diversification is usually preferred for a bank for risk-reduction purposes. For example, Aly et al. (1990) and Simar and Wilson (2007) apply an index representing zero for single-product lending banks that increases with the number of products added.

Another common approach to presenting diversity is with a dollar value of a particular product in a dollar value of total assets. Isik and Hassan (2002) apply a share of loans to total assets as explanatory variables and find a positive association between the share of loans in assets and efficiency. A similar result was found in a classic study by Berger and Mester (1997), suggesting that a bank loan product could be higher valued than a bank security. More recently, Assaf et al. (2019) applied commercial real estate loans in total assets as a control variable to explain which banks performed better during the crisis and found that the higher this ratio is, the lower the risk of bank failure during the crisis. The proportion of loans in other assets and what types of loans are to be issued by a bank comprise strategic questions for bank management.

Risk, as one of the most important financial concepts (along with return), is applied in numerous studies (Assaf et al., 2019; Berger et al., 2010; Altunbas et al., 2007) to explain bank inefficiency. Risk is usually proxied with the two variables capital ratio and non-performing loans (NPL) ratio. In the simplest form, capital ratio, as the share of equity to total assets, represents a bank's ability to absorb losses for "safety and soundness" of the bank (BIS, 2020a). It is expected that a higher capital ratio signals better bank management (Assaf et al., 2019) and better performance (Berger and Bouwman, 2013).

The impact of capitalization on efficiency is presented with mixed evidence. Conditional on a model specification, Mamatzakis et al. (2019) found both positive and negative associations between capitalization and efficiency for a sample of Japanese banks. In a study of 10 European banking systems, Lozano-Vivas et al. (2002) found that the capital ratio is important for explaining efficiency differences for banks in the United Kingdom and France. In a recent study of 15 European countries, Altunbas et al. (2007) found a positive association between a change in capital and bank inefficiency. Overall, the majority of reviewed papers signaled a positive association between capitalization and efficiency. An explanation for a strength of the capitalization–efficiency link could be an avenue for future research.

NPLs are often presented as a credit risk proxy. Regulators often require banks to hold higher levels of equity capital when the banks have higher than average NPL ratios. The risk arising from NPL has accumulative features. Higher current NPL ratios constrain loan production in the future periods (Fukuyama and Weber, 2015). The association between the level of NPLs and efficiency is found to be positive. Efficient banks take a higher risk (Altunbas et al., 2007). Yet, when the NPL ratio is applied as a measure of management quality (better managed banks have lower NPLs (Berger and DeYoung, 1997), the association between NPLs and efficiency appears to be negative (Koutsomanoli-Filippaki et al., 2009). Although risk proxies have been found to have an association with efficiency, a number of more recent studies model NPLs as an undesirable output that is reducing the value of a desirable net loan output (for example, see related discussion in Pham and Zelenyuk, 2019).

Local economic conditions are an important determinant of inefficiency when banking systems are compared across regions. Aly et al. (1990) find a positive effect of urbanization on the efficiency of US banks. In a European cross-country study, Lozano-Vivas et al. (2002) included income per capita and salary per capita to show a positive association between the higher levels of these environmental variables and bank efficiency. Other common variables applied in international bank performance studies include the level of real GDP growth (Leary, 2009) and inflation.

Ownership represents a major part of the corporate governance puzzle, in particular, a discussion of its combination with management (Shleifer and Vishny, 1997). Ownership is usually differentiated into two categories to explain efficiency: private versus public (Berger et al., 2010; Sturm and Williams, 2004) and foreign versus domestic (Berger et al., 2010; Sturm and Williams, 2004; Berger et al., 2000). These two types of ownership are often included in one study because foreign ownership inflow into a country often follows with a degree of deregulation and could be accompanied by privatizations.

For instance, Berger et al. (2010) document that privatization in China followed by increased foreign ownership had a positive effect on bank efficiency. In an earlier study, Berger et al. (2000) found that domestic banks were more efficient than foreign-owned banks in four countries: Germany, France, Spain and the United Kingdom. In contrast, Sturm and Williams (2004) found that foreign banks were more efficient than domestic banks in Australia, especially after complex de-regulation in the 1980s that included removal of the interest rate controls and loan quality controls.

More recently, Berger et al. (2010) suggest that the effect of ownership on efficiency differs by country due to the stages of development of the country. In particular, they discuss that foreign-owned banks are more efficient in developing countries and domestic banks are more efficient in developed countries. In this vein, Koutsomanoli-Filippaki et al. (2009) find that foreign ownership brought positive efficiency change to all the banks in Central and Eastern Europe, including domestic private and state-owned banks. On the other hand, Zelenyuk and

Zelenyuk (2014) found that the efficiency of foreign-owned banks was insignificantly different from the efficiency of the domestic banks when a foreign bank owns a domestic bank partially. Foreign banks only exceed domestic banks by efficiency when foreign ownership comprises 100 per cent of a bank.

Overall, the conclusions about the effect of ownership on efficiency are mixed, perhaps because ownership status is evolving and the agency problems associated with ownership and management are avenues that are being resolved dynamically, which might be challenging to capture with modeling.

In this section, we overview the most popular "environmental variables" believed to be associated with the efficiency of banks. Any particular variable is research-question specific and is often limited by the data availability. The pool of explanatory variables could be extended with control variables applied in causal inference analysis, which we discuss further in section 2.4.

Implementation of the covariates in the formal efficiency modeling is discussed in sections 4 and 5.

2.4 Variables in Analysis of Causal Effects in Banking

In studies of causal effects, the emphasis is on a small number of parameters, often only one identifying parameter (Cameron and Trivedi, 2010). A distinction is made between an outcome variable and a treatment/forcing variable. For example, the bank interest margin could be the outcome variable, while the regulatory liquidity requirement can be thought of as a treatment variable (for example, see Bonner and Eijffinger, 2015). The other variables in the estimation are often controls.

While a choice of variables for a causal treatment effect is a challenging research task that can be novel, the set of control variables is often standard. Similar to the environmental variables in section 2.3, controls typically include the size of a bank and the managerial ability of balancing risk with return, reflected with the CAMELS ratios presented in Table 9.1.

In particular, column 1 of Table 9.1 names the CAMELS component, column 2 specifies a uniform regulatory expectation about each of the components and column 3 defines the corresponding financial ratios. While interpreting the financial ratios, column 3 also provides examples of how these ratios were applied as controls in banking studies. The most comprehensive approach to controls includes both size and all of the CAMELS variables (Duchin and Sosyura, 2014; Eichler et al., 2011). The proxies for CAMELS may vary.

In a prominent study on market discipline, Martinez-Peria and Schmukler (2001) apply a ROA to control for both management and earnings. ROA presents an amount of net income generated with the bank's assets and reflects the managerial ability of creating the former with the latter. At the same time, from an accounting point of view, income reflects the difference between earnings and cost, thereby, the ROA ratio also signals earnings quantity and quality. To further control for any heterogeneity between the banks, a common practice is to include bank fixed effects that capture all the remaining differences between the banks that are time invariant during the study period (Duchin and Sosyura, 2014). In recent work by Boubakri et al. (2020) about the post-privatization state ownership and bank risk taking, the authors control for bank fixed effects as well as (and similarly to discussed variables in section 2.3) for environmental variables of competition within the banking industry, information sharing with the private/public loan registries and creditor rights.

Due to the recent global convergence of banking regulations to uniform standards, environmental variables that describe legal and competitive local conditions gain particular significance in the cross-sectional studies (Bonner and Eijffinger, 2015).

3. PRODUCTIVITY AND EFFICIENCY THEORY FOR BANKING

Before estimating the efficiency or productivity of banks, it is important to sketch a theoretical model that represents the essence of their production activities. For this, let $x = (x_1,...,x_N)' \in \Re_+^N$ represent the vector of inputs that a bank, its branch or, more generically, its DMU used to produce outputs, denoted by vector $y = (y_1,...,y_M)' \in \Re_+^M$. As discussed in section 2.2, in recent efficiency studies on banking, researchers typically proxy inputs with capital and labor while for the outputs they apply loans and other earning assets, although this may vary depending on the goals of the study.

3.1 Technology Characterization

In reality, each bank, or DMU, may use its own specific technology to produce its outputs from various inputs. A natural starting point is a simple case when technology involves only one output—then the technology (and its frontier) of a bank can be characterized with what economists call a *production function*. In general terms, a production function, call it ψ, is defined as a function yielding the maximal output producible with the knowledge and level of input (x) available at time t and conditions (Z) faced by a bank i at time t. More formally,

$$\psi_{it}(x \mid Z_{it}) \equiv \max_x \{y \ : \ y \text{ is producible from } x \text{ at time } t \text{ with conditions } Z_{it}\}.$$

In practice, of course, banks typically produce more than one output; as a result, a more general characterization is needed. This can be done with what production economists call *technology set*, which we denote as Ψ, and define as

$$\Psi_{it}(Z_{it}) \equiv \{(x, y) \ : \ y \text{ is producible from } x \text{ at time } t \text{ with conditions } Z_{it}\}. \qquad (9.6)$$

To compare different banks in terms of performance, one has to define a common benchmark. Often, researchers take what can be called an egalitarian approach, in the sense that all DMUs are measured, or benchmarked, with respect to the same frontier in a given period, t, sometimes referred to as the observed "grand frontier", or the unconditional frontier, that is,

$$\Psi_\tau = \cup_i \Psi_{it}(Z_{it} \mid t = \tau), \qquad (9.7)$$

where the union is taken over all the possibilities available for all i in a specific time period $t = \tau$. In a sense, this is similar to some athletic competitions; for example, everyone runs the same distance regardless of the actual technologies they used for developing their training skills for running.

In further discussions we will mainly focus on this unconditional frontier Ψ_p, but for simplicity of notation also drop the subscript t unless it is needed.[2] We will also assume that the technology meets the requirements of standard regularity conditions or axioms of production theory (see Sickles and Zelenyuk (2019) for more details).

Upon estimating such an unconditional frontier, a researcher may then try to analyze the association of the resulting efficiency scores (with respect to the unconditional frontier) and Z_{it} and, possibly, t. This would be the so-called two-stage efficiency analysis, popular in the DEA literature for many years and more recently revitalized due to the key work of Simar and Wilson (2007), although also see the caveats discussed in Simar and Wilson (2011) and related discussion in Sickles and Zelenyuk (2019, Chapter 10). Ideally, a one-stage approach, where association of efficiency with other variables is modeled explicitly when estimating the frontier, is preferred whenever it is possible. This is particularly true in the SFA approach, as clarified by Wang and Schmidt (2002), as we will discuss in section 5.

3.2 Relativity

Efficiency is a relative and normative concept—it always depends on the selected criterion that defines the benchmark of comparison and answers the question "Relative to what?" Indeed, it could very well be that a bank is very or even 100 per cent efficient relative to one criterion, while very inefficient relative to another, or perhaps many other criteria. It is therefore imperative to clarify which criterion is selected and motivate why it was selected.

For example, a natural criterion is the frontier of the technology set, yet there are different (and not always equivalent) definitions of the frontier. A popular definition is the efficient frontier according to the Pareto–Koopmans criterion, or optimality principle, that says (x, y) is *Pareto–Koopmans efficient* for technology Ψ if and only if with such technology it is infeasible to increase any outputs without decreasing some other outputs or increasing some of the inputs, and also infeasible to decrease any of the inputs without increasing some other inputs or decreasing some of the outputs in y. Thus, mathematically, the *Pareto–Koopmans efficient subset of the technology frontier* Ψ can be defined as

$$\textit{eff } \partial\Psi \equiv \{(x, y) \,:\, (x, y) \in \Psi, (x^0, y^0) \notin \Psi, \forall (-x^0, y^0) \geq (-x, y)\}. \tag{9.9}$$

Another relevant criterion is the level where the optimal scale of using resources is reached, sometimes referred to as the socially optimal level.

Yet another relevant criterion, and usually the ultimate benchmark for measuring the performance of banks, is the maximal profit feasible for a technology Ψ and some output and input prices, which can be formally stated as

$$\pi := \max_{x,y}\{p(y)y - w(x)x \,:\, (x, y) \in \Psi\}, \tag{9.10}$$

where $p(y)$ is the vector of inverse demand functions for each output and $w(x)$ is the vector of inverse supply functions for each input faced by the bank.

From economic theory we know that full efficiency is reached with perfect competition and this implies a relevant benchmark for comparison. Specifically, perfect competition will imply that the prices are exogenous to any individual firm and so the optimization criterion (9.10) simplifies to

$$\pi(p, w) = \max_{x,y}\{py - wx \,:\, (x, y) \in \Psi\}. \tag{9.11}$$

By accepting this benchmark, various profit efficiency measures can be constructed and, in fact, many were offered in the literature. Most recently, Färe et al. (2019) proposed a very general profit efficiency measure that unified many other efficiency measures in the literature. Färe et al. (2019) also showed that the Farrell measures of technical efficiency, which are the most popular in practice, are components, or special cases, of their general profit efficiency measure. In the next section we briefly discuss some of them, while more can be found in Färe et al. (2019) and Sickles and Zelenyuk (2019).

3.3   Popular Efficiency Measures

By far the most popular efficiency measures in general, and in the context of banking in particular, are the Farrell measures of technical efficiency and, to save space, we will mainly focus on them.

Specifically, the Farrell input-oriented technical efficiency can be defined as

$$ITE(x,y) \equiv \frac{1}{IDF(x,y)}, (x,y) \in \Psi ,$$

where $IDF(x, y)$ is the input oriented Shephard distance function, $IDF : \mathfrak{R}_+^N \times \mathfrak{R}_+^M \to \mathfrak{R}_+ \cup \{+\infty\}$, defined as

$$IDF(x,y) \equiv \sup\{\theta > 0 : (x/\theta, y) \in \Psi\}.$$

Meanwhile, the Farrell output oriented technical efficiency can be defined as

$$OTE(x,y) \equiv \frac{1}{ODF(x,y)}, (x,y) \in \Psi ,$$

where $ODF(x, y)$ is the output-oriented Shephard distance function, $ODF : \mathfrak{R}_+^N \times \mathfrak{R}_+^M \to \mathfrak{R}_+ \cup \{+\infty\}$, defined as

$$ODF(x,y) \equiv \inf\{\lambda > 0 : (x, y/\lambda) \in \Psi\}.$$

These distance functions are multi-output generalizations of the notion of the production function. Indeed, note that for a one-output case, we have

$$ODF(x,y) = \frac{y}{\psi(x)},$$

where $\psi(x)$ is the production function. This special case reveals that the ODF is a natural measure of technical efficiency that relates the actual output to the potential (or maximal) output.

The Farrell technical efficiency measures described are radial measures in the sense that they measure inefficiency in a radial way, that is, along the ray from the origin and through the point of interest all the way to the frontier in either input or output direction while holding, respectively, the output or input vectors fixed. This means that all the inputs (outputs) are contracted (expanded) by the same proportion, while keeping the outputs (inputs) and technology fixed.

Finally, another very general efficiency measure and a complete characterization of technology is based on the *directional distance function, $DDF_d : \mathfrak{R}_+^N \times \mathfrak{R}_+^M \rightarrow \mathfrak{R} \cup \{+\infty\}$*, defined as

$$DDF_d(x,y) \equiv \sup_{\theta} \{\theta \in \mathfrak{R} : (x,y) + \theta d \in \Psi\}, \tag{9.12}$$

where $d = (-d_x, d_y) \in \mathfrak{R}_-^N \times \mathfrak{R}_+^M$ is the direction that defines the orientation of measurement.[3] By choosing different directions, many efficiency measures can be derived from this function.

Under the standard regularity conditions, these distance functions (and hence the Farrell technical efficiency measures) have many desirable mathematical properties and, in particular, provide complete characterizations of technology Ψ, in the sense that

$$1/IDF(x,y) \in (0,1] \Leftrightarrow ODF(x,y) \in (0,1] \Leftrightarrow DDF_d(x,y) \geq 0 \Leftrightarrow (x,y) \in \Psi.$$

From duality theory in economics, we also know that, under certain conditions, the technology set can be characterized by cost, revenue and profit functions, which can be used to define the dual efficiency measures, cost efficiency, revenue efficiency and profit efficiency, which can be then decomposed into the technical efficiency and various allocative efficiencies (see Sickles and Zelenyuk (2019, Chapter 3) for details).

4. ENVELOPMENT ESTIMATORS

For several decades the DEA has been a standard and very popular approach in the toolbox for performance analysis in general and for banks in particular. The literature on DEA is vast and growing. Among the first was the work of Sherman and Gold (1985), who evaluated the operating efficiency of bank branches using early DEA models. This work was followed by three now seminal studies that appeared in top econometric journals: Aly et al. (1990), Charnes et al. (1990) and Ferrier and Lovell (1990). Shortly after there appeared the interesting, and now classic, works of English et al. (1993) and Wheelock and Wilson (2000). While all of these works were focusing on US banking, besides explaining particular research questions, they helped in popularizing the novel methods at that time, and eventually they found applications for many (if not all) other countries globally.

For example, Du et al. (2018) focused on the performance of banks in China, Fukuyama (1993); Fukuyama and Weber (2015) in Japan, Casu et al. (2013) in India, Simper et al. (2017) in Korea, Curi et al. (2013, 2015) in Luxembourg, Camanho and Dyson (2005) in Portugal and so on. Meanwhile, a few studies focused on a set of countries, for example, Casu et al. (2004), Koutsomanoli-Filippaki et al. (2009), Kenjegalieva et al. (2009a) and Lozano-Vivas et al. (2002) analyzed subsets of European countries. Of note, many of these and other studies used both DEA and SFA, and some also made comparisons to other approaches. As mentioned in the introduction, there are thousands of studies on this topic, and these are just a few, while many more examples can be found in Berger and Humphrey (1997), Fethi and Pasiouras (2010) and the recent Liu et al. (2013).

It is also critical to note that, while a myriad of existing works are identified as "DEA in banking" studies, many of them chose a particular variant of the many different variants within the DEA approach, besides also varying the type of efficiency measures, such as those described in the previous section or their alternatives. It is, therefore, useful to understand at least the major variants within the DEA approach. Consequently, the goal of the rest of this section is to give a concise overview of different DEA models for efficiency and productivity analysis in general and for banking in particular. This overview is indeed brief, as covering it more extensively would take a book by itself, and these types of books already exist.[4] Here, we give a primer that we hope will help learning from more detailed and much lengthier sources.

4.1 The Basic DEA Model

In their seminal work, Charnes et al. (1978) formulated a fractional programming problem for measuring efficiency of a DMU with an allocation (x^j, y^j), using data on n observations in a sample, denoted as $\mathcal{S}\mathcal{S}_n \{(x^k, y^k)\}_{k=1}^n$, for similar DMUs that can be considered relevant peers for each other. This formulation (in our notation) was given by

$$\widehat{ITE}_{CCR}(x^j, y^j \mid \mathcal{S}_n) = \max_{\substack{v_1,\dots,v_N; \\ u_1,\dots,u_M}} \frac{\sum_{m=1}^{M} u_m y_m^j}{\sum_{l=1}^{N} v_l x_l^j} \tag{9.13}$$

$$s.t.$$

$$\frac{\sum_{m=1}^{M} u_m y_m^k}{\sum_{l=1}^{N} v_l x_l^k} \leq 1, \; k = 1,\dots,n,$$

$$u_m \geq 0, \; m = 1,\dots, M,$$

$$v_l \geq 0, \; l = 1,\dots, N,$$

where $u' = (u_1, \dots, u_M)$ and $v' = (v_1, \dots, v_N)$ are optimization variables (also called "multipliers").

To explain, the objective function in (9.13) is the ratio of a weighted average of outputs to a weighted average of inputs for the observation (x^j, y^j). That is, intuitively, it is a productivity index for the observation (x^j, y^j): the ratio of its aggregate output to its aggregate input, where the weights are obtained in the optimization problem (9.13), u and v, respectively. Moreover, it can also be seen as the so-called "return to dollar" performance measure, that is, the total revenue of this observation (x^j, y^j) divided by the total cost associated with (x^j, y^j), where the output and input prices are, again, obtained from the optimization problem (9.13), u and v, respectively. Furthermore, note the way these prices are obtained: the model searches for the best prices for the observation (x^j, y^j), in terms of the "return to dollar" performance measure, subject to the constraints that this measure (with the same prices) is within $[0, 1]$ for all the observations in the sample. In this sense, the optimal values of u and v can be intuitively understood as (normalized) shadow prices that show (x^j, y^j) in the best possible light for the considered sample.

After transforming (9.13) to a linear programming (LP) problem, Charnes et al. (1978), obtained its dual formulation, which was the generalization (to multi-output case) AAM proposed by Farrell (1957), given by

$$\widehat{ITE}(x^j, y^j \mid \mathcal{S}_n) \equiv \min_{\theta, z^1, \dots, z^n} \{\theta$$

$$s.t.$$

$$\sum_{k=1}^{n} z^k y_m^k \geq y_m^j, \ m = 1, \dots, M,$$

$$\sum_{k=1}^{n} z^k x_l^k \leq \theta x_l^j, \ l = 1, \dots, N,$$

$$\theta \geq 0, z^k \geq 0, \ k = 1, \dots, n\}, \tag{9.14}$$

which is usually called the "envelopment form of DEA" assuming CRS, additivity and free disposability (see Sickles and Zelenyuk (2019) on how to derive the DEA formulation from these assumptions) and is more common in economics literature. Meanwhile, the formulation (9.13) is more common in the management science/operations research literature and is usually referred to as the "multiplier form of DEA" (also under CRS, additivity and free disposability), or simply the "CCR model" to honor its authors.

Both formulations compute or estimate (from the sample) the input-oriented Farrell technical efficiency measure because, as can be seen from (9.14), it minimizes inputs equiproportionately, while keeping outputs and the estimated technology fixed.

Similarly, the DEA-*estimator of the Farrell output-oriented technical efficiency* for an observation (x^j, y^j), assuming CRS, free disposability of all outputs and all inputs and additivity, is given by

$$\widehat{OTE}(x^j, y^j \mid \bar{\mathcal{S}}_n) \equiv \max_{\lambda, z^1, \dots, z^n} \{\lambda$$

$$s.t.$$

$$\sum_{k=1}^{n} z^k y_m^k \geq \lambda y_m^j, \ m = 1, \dots, M,$$

$$\sum_{k=1}^{n} z^k x_l^k \leq x_l^j, \ l = 1, \dots, N,$$

$$\lambda \geq 0, z^k \geq 0, \ k = 1, \dots, n\}. \tag{9.15}$$

It is worth noting here that $\widehat{ITE}(x, y \mid \mathcal{S}_n) = 1 / \widehat{OTE}(x, y \mid \mathcal{S}_n)$ for any (x, y) when they are obtained from (9.14) and (9.15), due to CRS, which is convenient and removes some ambiguity pertinent to the choice of one of these orientations.

Moreover, the estimates of the Shephard distance functions (Shephard, 1953, 1970), can be obtained by taking the reciprocals of the estimated Farrell efficiency measures.

If one is not willing to keep either inputs or outputs fixed and rather prefers expanding outputs and contracting inputs, simultaneously, then more general measures can be estimated (Sickles and Zelenyuk, 2019, Chapter 8). For example, the directional distance function can also be estimated with DEA. When assuming CRS, free disposability of all outputs and all inputs and additivity, we can use

$$\widehat{DDF}(x^j, y^j \mid d_x, d_y \mid \mathcal{G}_n) \equiv \max_{\beta, z^1, \dots, z^n} \{\beta$$

$$s.t.$$

$$\sum_{k=1}^{n} z^k y_m^k \geq y_m^j + \beta d_{y_m}, \; m = 1, \dots, M,$$

$$\sum_{k=1}^{n} z^k x_l^k \leq x_l^j - \beta d_{x_l}, \; l = 1, \dots, N,$$

$$z^k \geq 0, \; k = 1, \dots, n\}. \tag{9.16}$$

Similarly, DEA is applicable to modeling the cost, revenue and profit functions and related efficiency measures. In particular, in such frameworks researchers estimate the overall (in) efficiency (for example, cost, revenue or profit) and then decompose it into technical and allocative (in)efficiency parts. Sickles and Zelenyuk (2019, Chapters 3 and 8) elaborate on this in more detail.

4.2   Other Variations of DEA

Many other types of DEA models were suggested in the literature, most of which are modifications of the basic models presented. The modifications add various constraints to either the multiplier form of DEA or the envelopment form.

4.2.1   Returns to scale and convexity
The first modifications tried to relax assumptions about CRS and convexity. The most popular among them is the DEA under the assumption of variable returns to scale (VRS) and, a bit less so, under the non-increasing returns to scale, while still assuming free disposability of all inputs and all outputs (and sub-additivity). These models impose additional constraints, $\sum_{k=1}^{n} z^k = 1$ or $\sum_{k=1}^{n} z^k \leq 1$, respectively, to the DEA-CRS formulation (9.14) or (9.15) or (9.16), depending on the chosen orientation or direction and, in general, these may yield different (and potentially very different) estimates. The multiplicative form of the DEA-VRS model is usually referred to as the BCC model due to Banker et al. (1984) (also see Afriat, 1972; Färe et al., 1983). In the context of banking, these types of models were applied by Aly et al. (1990), Charnes et al. (1990), Ferrier and Lovell (1990), English et al. (1993), Wheelock and Wilson (2000), Fukuyama (1993), Fukuyama and Weber (2015), Camanho and Dyson (2005), Du et al. (2018), Casu et al. (2013), Curi et al. (2013, 2015), Simper et al. (2017), Casu et al. (2004), Koutsomanoli-Filippaki et al. (2009) and Kenjegalieva et al. (2009a), to mention a few.

About the same time, the Free Disposal Hull (FDH) approach was developed and advocated by Deprins et al. (1984), where the idea is to relax the convexity (and, therefore, also additivity) and only keep the free disposability of all inputs and all outputs. While having its own name, FDH is a special case of DEA, where the envelopment form of DEA ((9.14) or (9.15) or (9.16), depending on the chosen orientation or direction) is amended into the DEA-VRS, but where the constraints $z^k \geq 0$, $k = 1, \ldots, n$ are replaced with $z^k \in \{0, 1\}$, $k = 1, \ldots, n$. As a result, it is a hybrid of LP and integer programming (IP) problems.

In the context of banking this type of approach was applied by Bauer and Hancock (1993) and Resti (1997). FDH typically has much lower discriminative power (and a slower rate of statistical convergence) and was used substantially less than DEA, although its popularity has increased more recently because of related work on conditional frontiers (for example, see Daraio and Simar, 2007).

4.2.2   Modeling with undesirable outputs or with congesting inputs

All the models assumed free disposability of inputs and outputs. This assumption is violated when there is a congestion phenomenon for inputs. For example, when there are too many bank employees per square meter in an office, adding one more employee while keeping other inputs and technology fixed may even lead to lowering of the total output, implying that inputs are not freely disposable. Similarly, the free disposability of outputs is violated when there is an undesirable (or bad) output produced as a byproduct, along with a good output. In the context of banking, the nonperforming loan (NPL) is often considered a typical example of a bad output. If the NPLs are known, some researchers simply subtract their total value from the total loans. An alternative way to handle them is to apply the DEA models that allow for weak disposability of outputs.

The roots for this type of modeling can be found in Shephard (1974), and more formalized in Färe and Svensson (1980), Färe and Grosskopf (1983), Grosskopf (1986), Tyteca (1996) and Chung et al. (1997) and applied to various industries, with more recent developments in Seiford and Zhu (2002), Färe and Grosskopf (2003, 2004, 2009) and Pham and Zelenyuk (2018, 2019), to mention a few.[5]

4.2.3   Other streams of DEA

A number of streams of DEA modeling considered how to account for the network nature of production, both in static and dynamic contexts, starting from the seminal works of Färe and Grosskopf (1996), Färe et al. (1996) and many papers since then (for example, see Kao (2014) for an excellent review).

Another stream of literature on DEA modeling focused on weight restrictions for the multiplier form of DEA; see Dyson and Thanassoulis (1988), Charnes et al. (1990), Thompson et al. (1990) and more recently Podinovski and Bouzdine-Chameeva (2013) and reviews from Allen et al. (1997) and Podinovski (2015).

Yet another promising stream of literature developed symbioses of DEA with game theory and can be found in Hao et al. (2000), Nakabayashi and Tone (2006), Liang et al. (2008), Lozano (2012) and references therein.

Finally, a very important stream of DEA literature is about its statistical aspects—the wave largely developed by the seminal contributions by Léopold Simar and his co-authors, which we discuss in the next section.

4.3   Statistical Analysis of DEA and FDH

4.3.1   Convergence and limiting distributions

The earliest proof of consistency of the basic DEA estimator, with a single output for specification with output orientation was sketched by Banker (1993), who noticed that it is also a maximum likelihood estimator. Korostelev et al. (1995) advanced these results by proving more rigorous convergence of DEA and FDH estimators and also deriving their speeds of convergence (as orders of dimension of the production model), and proving their optimality properties. Kneip et al. (1998) generalized the theorems about convergence for the multi-input–multi-output case, Gijbels et al. (1999) discovered the limiting distribution of the DEA estimator (for the one-input–output case) and it was then generalized by Park et al. (2000), Jeong and Simar (2006), Kneip et al. (2008), Park et al. (2010).

4.3.2   Analysis of distributions and averages of DEA and FDH estimates

A sub-stream of this literature has focused on analyzing the estimates of the DEA (or FDH) efficiency scores. Indeed, once such estimates are obtained, it is useful, for example, to look at the estimated densities (at least histograms) of such scores, overall, or for some groups within the sample and, in particular, test for the equality of distributions, as was explored in Simar and Zelenyuk (2006). In the context of banking, this type of approach was considered by Kenjegalieva et al. (2009b), Simper et al. (2017) and Du et al. (2018), to mention a few.

One can also analyze the averages of the efficiency scores, including weighted averages, that account for an economic weight of each DMU in the aggregate, as were explored by Simar and Zelenyuk (2007) and more rigorously in Simar and Zelenyuk (2018). The latter work developed several new central limit theorems for aggregate efficiency, building on the recent breakthrough due to Kneip et al. (2015). At about the same time, Kneip et al. (2016) and Daraio et al. (2017) also applied the foundation from Kneip et al. (2015) to develop various statistical tests. Some further finite-sample improvements to these approaches (via improving the variance estimator) were developed by Simar and Zelenyuk (2020).

4.3.3   Regression analysis with DEA and FDH estimates

A very popular approach in DEA literature is the so-called "two-stage DEA". In the first stage, the efficiency scores are estimated and, in the second stage, they are regressed on various explanatory factors that are believed to explain the variation in the efficiency scores. Early models applied OLS and then, to account for the "boundedness" of the dependent variable, Tobit regression was often deployed. Currently, the state of the art here (albeit with its own caveats) is the method of Simar and Wilson (2007), who pointed out that (under certain conditions) truncated regression is more appropriate and the inference can be improved with the help of bootstrap.[6]

For the context of banking, these types of models were considered by Curi et al. (2013, 2015) and Du et al. (2018), to mention a few.

For example, a simple model that tries to explain (in terms of statistical dependencies) the distances between particular observations and the (estimate of the) *unconditional* frontier Ψ, can be stated as

$$\text{Efficiency}_i = f(Z_i) + \varepsilon_i, \quad i = 1, \ldots, n, \tag{9.17}$$

where Z_i is a d-variate row vector of explanatory variables (also called "environmental" variables) for observation i, which are expected to be associated with the (in)efficiency score of this observation, which we denoted as Efficiency$_i$, via some functional form f, and ε_i is a statistical noise.

The type of the score, Efficiency$_{i}$ will determine the nature of the truncation. For example, if output (input)-oriented Farrell-type efficiency is applied, then both sides of (9.17) are bounded from below (above) by 1, implying that the distribution of ε_i is also bounded from below (above). Typically, one also makes parametric assumptions on f (for example, linear in parameters) and the distribution of ε_i (for example, truncated normal) and proceeds with parametric estimation using MLE.[7]

Because the true efficiency scores are unobserved and replaced by their estimates, which are inherently biased, the usual inference may be inaccurate; therefore, Simar and Wilson (2007) proposed two alternative bootstrap algorithms that can (under certain conditions) mitigate these issues to some extent and improve the inference. If a researcher deals with panel data, then the model (9.17) can be modified to exploit the richness of panel data, for example, by estimating annual frontiers or accounting for a fixed or random effect. (For example, see Du et al. (2018) and Sickles and Zelenyuk (2019, Chapter 10).)

Here, it is important to emphasize that the analysis and the interpretation of this two-stage approach should be for the (in)efficiency scores with respect to the unconditional frontier, Ψ, which does not depend on the covariates Z_i by construction. At the same time, one should recognize that each DMU may have their own "conditional" frontiers relative to which they might be even perfectly efficient. Recalling the analogy with an athletics competition: each athlete may have their own capacity (or "technology") to perform at a given moment and the interest is to measure that performance not relative to their own capacity but relative to all other competitors. Alternatively, approaches like those in Daouia and Simar (2007), Bădin et al. (2012), Park et al. (2015), Simar et al. (2017) and related literature can be used if one is interested in measuring efficiency relative to conditional frontiers.

To conclude this section, it is also worth clarifying that, while the models of production, cost, revenue and profit functions are well-defined economic concepts where the researcher must know which variables to include, the selection of the "environmental" variables is somewhat subjective, often varies across studies and therefore needs careful justification (see section 2.3 for the relevant discussion). Moreover, it is worth remembering that, whether it is the conditional frontier approaches that are used or the truncated regression with respect to the unconditional frontier approaches, they are designed to estimate the statistical dependencies in the data under the assumed model and may or may not reveal causal relationships of the reality. Indeed, potential issues of endogeneity, reverse causality and selection bias may be relevant here (as for many other statistical analyses). Hence, integrating the existing methods to address these issues (for example, those we briefly discuss in section 6) and their methods is a promising area for current and future research.

4.3.4 Noisy data

A caveat of DEA and FDH is not explicitly handling noise in the data and hence a sensitivity to the so-called "super-efficient" outliers. Various approaches were recommended to deal with this issue in the literature, from standard outlier-detection techniques to more sophisticated approaches tailored specifically to the DEA context. For example, Simar (2007) and Simar and Zelenyuk (2011) proposed a formulation of stochastic DEA (and stochastic FDH). This approach goes in two stages:

Step 1. Filter the noise from the data with a non-parametric SFA method (discussed in the next section).

Step 2. Apply DEA (or FDH) for the filtered data from step 1.

All in all, DEA proved to be a very useful technique, enabling a meaningful investigation of the bank efficiency in dimensions of types of inefficiencies, inefficiencies by bank divisions and input versus output orientation.

5.   THE SFA FOR BANKING

SFA also gained significant popularity in research in general and on banking performance in particular. In a sense, it was inspired by DEA literature: it was developed as its competitor, its complement and also as its symbiotic partner. Like DEA, the SFA literature is vast and growing. It became a standard approach in the toolbox for the performance analysis of banks.

Among the first studies that applied SFA to banks was Ferrier and Lovell (1990), which we have already mentioned among the first DEA studies on banks, as they applied and compared both approaches in their basic, yet novel (at that time) forms. Being published in top econometrics journals, this work set the tone for many other future papers on SFA for banking and related fields. Among the first followers were Bauer and Hancock (1993), Berger (1993), Mester (1993), Akhavein et al. (1997), Berger and DeYoung (1997), Berger et al. (1997), Berger and Mester (1997), Berger and Hannan (1998), Hughes and Mester (1998) and Adams et al. (1999), to mention a few among those that became classic for this literature.

More recent works include Kumbhakar et al. (2001), Casu et al. (2004), Kumbhakar and Tsionas (2005), Bos and Schmiedel (2007), Delis and Tsionas (2009), Casu et al. (2013) and Malikov et al. (2016), to mention a few.[8] Again, these are just a few examples from thousands of studies that are impossible to mention here, although an interested reader can find many more examples in reviews by Berger and Humphrey (1997) and Fethi and Pasiouras (2010).

Similarly to DEA, while thousands of existing works are identified as "SFA in banking" studies, many of them deployed particular variations out of the many within the SFA approach, as well as variations on the type of efficiency they looked at. Thus, the goal of this section is to provide a concise review of the different methods within the SFA approach. Again, the review is aimed to be brief, because covering it in more detail would take several chapters, or a whole book, which already exists.[9]

5.1   The Basic SFA Model

The first stochastic frontier models were developed at about the same time by Aigner et al. (1977) (hereafter ALS) and Meeusen and van den Broeck (1977). The idea was to add one more term to the standard regression model—the inefficiency term, u, unobserved by researchers and random, with a one-sided asymmetric distribution for it (for example, half-normal or exponential). This term is in addition to the usual error term with a symmetric (for example, normal) distribution. It was first suggested in the single output cross-sectional framework, where the output is modeled as

$$y_i = \psi(x_i)\exp\{\varepsilon_i\}, \quad i = 1,...,n, \tag{9.18}$$

where

$$\psi(x) = \max\{y \; : \; (x,y) \in \Psi\}$$

is the deterministic frontier, or production function (for any fixed x), to be estimated and ε_i is a composed error, defined as a convolution of the usual and unobserved statistical error, or "white noise", v_i, and an unobserved inefficiency term $u_i \geq 0$ that forces the DMU i to produce below the frontier output, that is,

$$\varepsilon_i = v_i - u_i. \tag{9.19}$$

Thus, the efficiency of firm i can be measured by

$$\text{Efficiency}_i = \exp\{-u_i\} \equiv \frac{y_i}{\psi(x_i)\exp\{v_i\}}, \quad i = 1,\ldots,n \tag{9.20}$$

and is often approximated (around 1) as $1 - u_i$, and hence u_i approximates the inefficiency of DMU i.

The model is usually estimated in natural logs, that is,

$$\log y_i = \log \psi(x_i) + v_i - u_i, \quad i = 1,\ldots,n, \tag{9.21}$$

most commonly with some parametric assumptions on $\log \psi(\cdot)$, for example, linear in logs (that is, $\psi(\cdot)$ is assumed to be Cobb–Douglas) or translog, or any other suitable functional form, although more recent developments proposed various semi and non-parametric generalizations (for example, see Sickles and Zelenyuk (2019, Chapter 16) and Parmeter and Zelenyuk (2019) for more detailed comparisons).

While many distributions can be used for u and v, the most common is the original specification from Aigner et al. (1977), where

$$v_i \overset{iid}{\sim} \mathcal{N}(0,\sigma_v^2),$$

and

$$u_i \overset{iid}{\sim} |\mathcal{N}(0,\sigma_u^2)|,$$

and also assuming that v_i and u_i are independent from each other and from x_i. In turn, this implies that ε_i is an i.i.d. random variable, independent from x_i, with a density given by

$$f_\varepsilon(\varepsilon) = \frac{2}{\sigma}\phi\left(\frac{\varepsilon}{\sigma}\right)\left[1 - \Phi\left(\frac{\varepsilon\lambda}{\sigma}\right)\right], \quad -\infty \leq \varepsilon \leq +\infty, \tag{9.22}$$

where $\phi(\cdot)$ and $\Phi(\cdot)$ are the standard normal probability density function and cumulative distribution function, respectively, while $\lambda = \sigma_u/\sigma_v$ is sometimes referred to as the "signal-to-noise" ratio and $\sigma = \sqrt{\sigma_v^2 + \sigma_u^2}$. Then, the (approximate) average inefficiency is given by

$$E(u_i) = \sqrt{\frac{2}{\pi}}\sigma_u = \left(\frac{2}{\pi(1+\lambda^2)}\right)^{1/2}\sigma\lambda. \tag{9.23}$$

The model can then be estimated with a standard maximum likelihood estimator (MLE) or even with a method of moments estimator (MME) due to Olson et al. (1980), which will generate estimates of β, λ and σ, which in turn can be used to obtain estimates of σ_v and σ_u. Plugging the estimate of σ_u or (σ and λ) into (9.23) will give an estimate of the (approximate) average inefficiency. The model can also be re-parametrized to obtain estimates of $E(\exp\{-u_i\})$, although estimation of (9.23) appears to be more common in practice.

The estimates of the individual inefficiencies are usually proxied by the so-called JLMS estimator, due to Jondrow et al. (1982), who estimate $E(u_i|\varepsilon_i)$ for specific distributions of u_i and v_i. Specifically, when u_i and v_i are half-normal and normal, respectively, then Jondrow et al. (1982) showed that

$$E(u_i|\varepsilon_i) = \frac{\sigma_v \sigma_u}{\sigma} \left[-\frac{\varepsilon_i \lambda}{\sigma} + \frac{\phi(\varepsilon_i \lambda / \sigma)}{1 - \Phi(\varepsilon_i \lambda / \sigma)} \right], \tag{9.24}$$

where the unobserved quantities σ_v, σ_u, ε_i, λ, σ can be replaced with their MLE or MM estimates to obtain the estimates of $E(u_i|\varepsilon_i)$ for each observation $i = 1, \ldots, n$. Again, it is also possible to re-parametrize the model to obtain $E(\exp\{-u_i\}|\varepsilon_i)$.[10]

Finally, by convention we outlined SFA for the case of production frontier estimation, and a similar logic (with some modifications) applies to the estimation cost frontier, revenue frontier and profit frontier approaches. In these contexts, researchers try to estimate the overall (in)efficiency (for example, cost, revenue or profit efficiency) and then decompose it into technical and allocative (in)efficiency, which may require estimation of a system of equations.[11]

5.2   Panel Stochastic Production Frontiers

Often researchers have panel data, where each observation i is observed over several periods, $t = 1, \ldots, T$. One can still employ the ALS approach described by pooling the panel and treating it as a cross-section (hence the name "pooled SFA"). While this is a good start, it is usually beneficial to exploit the richness of the panel data by using SFA approaches tailored specifically for panel data, and we briefly describe some of them. More details can be found in Sickles and Zelenyuk (2019, Chapters 11−15) and its brief version in Sickles et al. (2020).

5.2.1   Basic panel data SFA
The first attempts at the SFA for panel data go back to Pitt and Lee (1981) and Schmidt and Sickles (1984). In a nutshell, they modeled the frontier as

$$y_{it} = \alpha + x_{it} \beta + v_{it} - u_i, \quad i = 1, \ldots, n; t = 1, \ldots, T, \tag{9.25}$$

where x_{it} is the row vector of N inputs used by firm i in period t, and then re-parametrized it, by letting $\alpha_i = \alpha - u_i$, as

$$y_{it} = \alpha_i + x_{it}\beta + v_{it}, \quad i = 1, \ldots, n; t = 1, \ldots, T. \tag{9.26}$$

Observing (9.26), one can see it looks exactly like a standard panel data regression model, which can be estimated (and tested) using the pooled OLS approach, the fixed effects (FE) approach or the random effects (RE) approach.

In the case of the FE estimation approach, one can obtain the estimates of the individual fixed effects, α_i, call them $\hat{\alpha}_i$ and then find their maximum value in the sample, $\hat{\alpha} = \max_i\{\hat{\alpha}_i\}$, to serve as the benchmark and then define estimates of inefficiency scores as

$$\hat{u}_i = \hat{\alpha} - \hat{\alpha}_i \geq 0, \quad i = 1,...,n.$$

This means that the most efficient DMU in the sample is assigned zero per cent inefficiency by construction.

All approaches have their own caveats and the main one for this approach is that the estimates of (in)efficiency are assumed to be time-invariant. Moreover, with the nature of the FE approach in general, all the time-invariant heterogeneity pertinent to the individuals is absorbed by the estimates of FEs, which all feed into the estimates of efficiency scores.

5.2.2 Other panel data SFA approaches

Various modifications of SFA for panel data were later suggested in the literature, mainly to account more for the unobserved heterogeneity at various levels, including allowing for time-varying inefficiency. For example, Cornwell et al. (1990), started with the model

$$y_{it} = Z_i\alpha + x_{it}\beta + w_{it}\delta_i + v_{it}, \quad i = 1,..., n; \, t = 1,..., T, \tag{9.27}$$

where Z_i and w_{it} are row vectors of explanatory factors affecting y_{it} via corresponding column vectors of parameters α and δ_i, besides the affects from the inputs x_{it} via the column vector β. They then re-parametrized model, by letting $\delta_i = \delta_0 + u_i$ where $\delta_0 = E[\delta_i]$, as follows:

$$y_{it} = Z_i\alpha + x_{it}\beta + w_{it}\delta_0 + \varepsilon_{it},$$

where ε_{it} is a composed error generalization of (9.19), given by

$$\varepsilon_{it} = v_{it} + w_{it}u_i \tag{9.28}$$

and it is assumed that u_i is i.i.d. random variable with a finite positive-definite covariance matrix Ω while the statistical noise term, v_{it}, is i.i.d. with zero mean and constant variance σ_v^2 and is uncorrelated with Z_i, x_{it}, and u_i. Furthermore, various time-dependency structures can then be assumed, for example, by setting $w_{it} = (1, t, t^2)$. They also discussed various strategies of estimating this model, which were adaptations of the fixed-effects estimator, random-effects estimator and Hausman–Taylor estimator, depending on the assumed correlation structure between the errors and regressors.

Other variations of panel data SFA were also proposed in many other interesting works, most notably in Kumbhakar (1990), Lee (1991) and Lee and Schmidt (1993), Battese and Coelli (1995). More recent elaborations on the panel data SFA can be found in Greene (2005a,b), Ahn et al. (2007) and one of the most general approaches by Kneip et al. (2012) (which is analogous to seminar works of Bai and Ng (2002) and Bai (2009)). Also see Colombi et al. (2011), Colombi et al. (2014), Tsionas and Kumbhakar (2014) and a special issue in *Journal of Econometrics* edited by Kumbhakar and Schmidt (2016) for many interesting discussions.

5.3   Explaining Inefficiency

Special attention has been paid to many SFA models (especially those mentioned in the previous subsection) and how to explain the inefficiency with some of the explanatory variables. The works of Kumbhakar et al. (1991) and Battese and Coelli (1995) seem to be very popular on this, in practical work, probably due to its simplicity and availability of software for it from the early days. The idea of this approach is to model the frontier as

$$y_{it} = X_{it}\beta + v_{it} - u_{it} \quad i=1,...,n\,;\, t=1,..., T, \tag{9.29}$$

with additional assumption that u_{it} is not purely random but has some regularities or deterministic part, for example,

$$u_{it} = Z_{it}\delta + w_{it}, \tag{9.30}$$

where Z_{it} and is a row vector of explanatory factors (also called "environmental" variables) believed to explain u_{it} via the corresponding column vector of parameters δ, up to some noise w_{it}. Because of the requirement that $u_{it} \geq 0$, truncation restriction must be imposed on w_{it}, namely $w_{it} \geq -Z_{it}\delta$ and some distribution assumed to disentangle it from other error terms. They specifically considered

$$w_{it} \sim \mathcal{N}(0, \sigma_w^2), \quad w_{it} \geq - Z_{it}\delta, \quad i=1,..., n;\, t=1,..., T \tag{9.31}$$

which (as they noted) is also is equivalent to stating that

$$u_{it} \sim \mathcal{N}(Z_{it}\delta, \sigma_u^2), \quad s.t. \quad u_{it} \geq 0, \quad i=1,..., n;\, t=1,..., T. \tag{9.32}$$

Since the model is fully parametrized, one likelihood function can be constructed after substituting (9.34) into (9.29) and can be optimized to get the ML estimates of β, σ_w, σ_v and δ and their standard errors (from the Fisher information matrix). The estimate of δ will indicate the association of u_{it} on z_{it} in the sense of (9.34), and significance tests can be done in the usual way in econometrics (for example, using t-tests or LR-tests).

Here it is worth noting that some researchers also tried to analyze SFA efficiency scores in two stages, first estimating JLMS efficiency scores in the ALS framework and then regressing them onto explanatory variables. While this may seem natural, it is incoherent in the ALS framework: if there is a belief that inefficiency scores u_i, $i = 1, \ldots, n$ are not i.i.d. and they depend on some characteristics, then the assumptions of ALS are violated and instead one should incorporate those beliefs into the model and the corresponding likelihood structure, for example, as in Battese and Coelli (1995).[12]

While very intuitive and relatively simple, it is important to realize that such approaches may suffer from computational problems and numerical identification issues in particular. One reason for the problems is because $Z_{it}\delta$, while believed to be part of the inefficiency, is influencing y_{it} in essentially the same way as $X_{it}\beta$ (except for the impact through truncation on w_{it}, which can be minimal). A way to mitigate this problem is to model the inefficiency through the second (rather than the first) moment of u, that is, via σ_u, for example,

$$u_{it} \sim \mathcal{N}(0, \sigma_u^2(Z_{it})), \quad s.t. \quad u_{it} \geq 0, i = 1,...,n; t = 1,..., T$$

with some structure assumed for $\sigma_u^2(Z_{it})$ that makes sure it is non-negative.[13] For example, one can assume

$$\log(\sigma_u^2(Z_{it})) = Z_{it}\delta, \quad i = 1,...,n; t = 1,..., T \tag{9.33}$$

and then estimate this relationship in the MLE framework and obtain fitted values of $\sigma_u^2(Z_{it})$ for particular Z_{it} of interest (for example, observed points), and then, in this (half-normal) case, one can estimate

$$E(u_{it} \mid z_{it}) = \sqrt{\frac{2}{\pi}} \sigma_u(Z_{it}), \quad i = 1,...,n; t = 1,..., T \tag{9.34}$$

which (under certain assumptions) will give estimates of the individual inefficiency scores for any particular Z_{it}.

To conclude this section, it is also worth reiterating the caveats, which are similar to those we already mentioned for the analogous DEA context. Namely, while the models of production, cost, revenue and profit functions are well-defined economic concepts where the researcher must know which variables to include, the selection of the "environmental" variables is more subjective, may vary across studies and thus demands careful justifications (for example, see section 2.3 for some examples). Moreover, these and most of SFA approaches are also designed to estimate the statistical dependencies in the data under the assumed statistical model, which may or may not reveal the causal relationship of the reality. Therefore, adapting various methods for mitigating potential issues of endogeneity, reverse causality and selection bias may be relevant here (for example, such as those we briefly discuss in section 6) to SFA methods and is a promising area for current and future research. Some of the fundamental works on this include Horrace et al. (2016), Kumbhakar and Tsionas (2016), Simar et al. (2016)[14] and more recently Amsler et al. (2017), to mention just a few.

5.4 Other Variations of SFA

All the SFA models were parametric in the sense that parametric assumptions on the functional form for the frontier had to be made (in addition to parametric assumptions on the inefficiency and noise in some cases). More recent literature has tried to avoid such assumptions. Among the first works on this are the papers by Fan et al. (1996) and Kneip and Simar (1996), who suggested kernel-based methods. The latter work was also considered in the panel data context, which was soon complemented by the research of Adams et al. (1999) and Park et al. (2003).

More recent elaborations came due to Park et al. (2007), which employed the local likelihood approach, and a similar approach by Martins-Filho and Yao (2015), and further generalizations by Park et al. (2015). These approaches estimated the frontier non-parametrically, yet required local parametric assumptions on the inefficiency and the statistical noise. A somewhat simpler to compute (and with less assumptions) approach was more recently proposed by Simar et al. (2017). The latter work also developed a novel way of estimating the marginal effects of covariates onto expected inefficiency without imposing any parametric assumptions, exploiting the advantages of the one-parameter distribution family that is natural to assume for the inefficiency term. For more discussions of these methods, see Parmeter and Zelenyuk (2019).

Finally, as in virtually any other field involving statistics, various Bayesian approaches for SFA have been developed. Among the classical works on this are due to Koop et al. (1994, 1995, 1997, 1999) and more recently by Griffin and Steel (2007), Tsionas and Papadakis (2010) and Liu et al. (2017), to mention a few. For the context of banking these types of models were considered by Kumbhakar and Tsionas (2005) and Malikov et al. (2016), to mention examples.

Overall, SFA proves to be an evolving technique enabling both aggregation of data in the focus of analysis and breakdown into identified specifications of cost and profit efficiencies that could be enriched with the conditional variables, specified by researcher.[15]

6.   OTHER ECONOMETRIC APPROACHES

Recent finance literature on banking performance dedicated significant attention to causal inference. The roots of the methods of causal evaluation take their origins from the seminal works of Splawa-Neyman et al. (1990) and Fisher (1925) on statistical tests of treatment effects in randomized experiments. Methods of causal inference currently thrive in microeconometrics, in particular, in labor and health economics (Bertrand et al., 2004) and other areas (Imbens and Wooldridge, 2009).

Recent applications of these methods in banking include Laeven and Levine (2009), Aiyar et al. (2014), Duchin and Sosyura (2014), Nanda and Nicholas (2014), Schepens (2016), Anginer et al. (2018), Buchak et al. (2018), Neuhann and Saidi (2018), Zelenyuk et al. (2019) and Zelenyuk et al. (2020), to mention a few.

The literature on casual inference is fairly large by itself and it seems infeasible to cover it even briefly within the few remaining pages of this chapter. Instead, we recommend the reader get familiar with these methods through already written excellent books, for example, by Manski (2009), Angrist and Pischke (2009), Imbens and Rubin (2015), to mention a few that also provide many references.[16] Our goal here, therefore, is to discuss a few recent examples of how the causal analysis can be applied in the context of performance of banks and to provide references for further details.

6.1   The Importance of Causal Inference in Analysis of Banking Performance

Causal inference has received significant attention in the recent banking literature on the topics of the performance effects that change after the passage of regulatory laws, or rules. Most interesting econometric questions consider the cause and the resulting effect triggered by the new rule. Popular empirical questions here would be of a nature as to whether the new capital requirements introduced by the regulatory rule affect the riskiness of bank loans. The research question is often about the drivers (for example, see Berger and Bouwman (2013), Acharya and Mora (2015)) that could have a causal effect on the performance of banks. For example, Bonner and Eijffinger (2015) find the causal effect of liquidity requirements on bank interest margins. In another study, Hamadi et al. (2016) find that capital increase due to Basel rules increases market valuation of loan loss provisions. Both outputs of interest margins and loan loss provisions are in attention of studies of bank performance because they contribute to the major banking function of lending.

To address these and similar policy-type questions with econometric methods a theoretical model is needed. A model is basically a framework for inter-relationships between parameters. If these parameters can be identified, then the model is estimable (Cameron and Trivedi, 2010). In the presence of economically and statistically significant results, conclusions about the policy effects would be valuable for the literature and for the policy makers. To derive relevant conclusions the most interesting model set-up needs to identify the causal and "effect" parameters and control for any observed confounding variables. If the confounding factors are observed (and controlled for) the conclusions could be derived about causality. In the event, when confounders are unobserved, causal effects could be derived with the instrumental variables techniques (Angrist and Pischke, 2009).

The key three questions in the modeling are about the event (or treatment), the cause–effect relationship and the confounding factors. In application to banking, causal inference is often driven by an exogenous (beyond control of the bank) event. Rarely, this event is entirely random (global crises, pandemics and so on), yet more often it is a policy intervention (regulation of bankers pay gaps and so on). In an empirical framework, any of these events can create an experimental setting, where a relevant question is about the effects that this event brings on the parameters of interest, in particular, effects on the lending of banks, and so on. The literature examples include the effects of bailouts (Duchin and Sosyura, 2014) and capital enhancement (Berger and Bouwman, 2013) policies on bank performance, where the bank performance is presented with loans and market share, respectively.

Investigation of the effects of the policy enhancements with the research methods involves identification of the banks that were impacted by the policy (Zelenyuk et al., 2019), the counterfactual (not impacted) and identification of the impact-related parameters. The impact of an event could vary among banks because of a different assignment to the policy rules and the differential response of banks to the rules. For example, capital-enhancing policies could affect only banks of a certain size in a certain state. The banks of the same size in a similar state could form a control group. And the affected parameter could be bank lending.

Of critical importance for an empirical design is whether the banks are self-selecting by the results of an event, whether they are assigned to comply with the rule (assigned to "treatment"), and whether the assignment is random. If a regulator has selected banks to a mandatory capital adequacy increase, an assignment to treatment is beyond the control of the bank and the effect of the policy can be evaluated with the DD methods. If the change in law is random, causal methods of RDD could be applied. Alternatively, if banks are self-selecting to treatment, for example, banks are deciding on the provision of information about their capital adequacy and they inform the market voluntarily, then DD methods may be inappropriate for causal inference. For these types of problems, the instrumental variable (IV) approach can be more relevant, yielding consistent estimates, if the underlying regularity conditions hold. Fuzzy versus sharp RDD design are applied in similar situations to IV methods.

We now embark on the task to briefly present the essence of each of these methods in their application to studying bank performance.

6.2   The Role of DD in Causal Inference on Bank Performance

DD is one of the working models in modern econometric analysis and its detailed description can be found in many textbooks, for example, in Cameron and Trivedi (2010), Greene (2011), Wooldridge (2013) and Imbens and Rubin (2015), and papers, including by Bertrand et al. (2004), Imbens and Wooldridge (2009), that we follow here. In its idea, DD method is a comparison between the outcomes post and pre an event versus the difference to the outcomes of similar banks that are unaffected by the event. The emphasis is on a "causal parameter" impacting the resulting outcome. The rest of the variables are considered as controls. More specifically, with the assumption that a policy-changing parameter δ measures the impact on the treated sample and X is a conditional variable of the treatment, an outcome variable Y can be formally described via

$$Y_{it} = X_{it}\beta + \delta D_{it} + \varepsilon_{it}. \qquad (9.35)$$

In a simple regression, comparing treated and untreated samples, β_2 measures the difference in average outcomes pre and post intervention for a treated group:

$$Y_{it} = \beta_1 + \beta_2 D_{it} + \varepsilon_{it}, \qquad (9.36)$$

where the average outcome conditional on $D_{it} = 0$, of those who did not receive treatment, is compared to an average outcome conditional on $D_{it} = 1$, of treated.

In a banking example, Duchin and Sosyura (2014) focused on the effect of government aid on risk taking by banks. Specifically, the authors studied the difference between "before" and "after" the government assistance approval for the qualifying banks in the difference to a number of control banks: unapproved, those that did not apply for aid and eligible banks. The range of variables of interest affected with the government capital program included retail mortgages, corporate loans and securities. Interestingly, the authors find no significant effect of the government aid programs on the loan volume, yet they find that the loans originated by the approved banks are riskier than the loans of any of the control groups of banks. The findings are based on a linear probability regression, where an outcome variable is 1/0 for approved/ unapproved loans. The authors found that the approved for aid banks increased their new credit origination by 5.4 percentage points for riskier mortgages, as well as for syndicated loans and riskier securities. To deal with possible selection bias and to demonstrate that the treatment effect is due to a government program rather than due to a selection of approved banks, the authors apply propensity score matching and the IV techniques.

In a further example, the effect is of the capital adequacy increase on lending. Here, lending is an outcome variable and capital adequacy is distinguished between the treated–required to increase the capital adequacy of banks and untreated (control) banks that do not need to increase their capital adequacy. The difference between the capital adequacy of the treated versus the capital adequacy of control banks after the policy intervention would contribute to the determination of the average treatment effect resulting from a policy event. For a more complete analysis of the policy effect the researcher would need to evaluate the difference post versus pre policy intervention. The sample is comprised of four groups: the treatment group before the policy change, the treatment group (the one required to increase capital adequacy) after the policy change, the control group before the policy change and the control group (not required to increase capital adequacy) after the policy change.

Formally, let Y_{it} be the outcome variable of interest, lending for bank i in period t, then the model can be specified, similarly to Zelenyuk et al. (2019), as follows:

$$Y_{it} = \alpha_0 + \beta_1 C_{it} + \beta_2 Post_t + \beta_3 C_{it} Post_t + X_{it}\gamma + \varepsilon_{it}, \tag{9.37}$$

where

$Post_t$ is a variable equal to zero before the capital increasing reform and one after the reform;

C_{it} is a variable that equals 1 if the bank is in the treatment group and is required to increase its capital after the reform milestone and zero otherwise;

X_{it} is a row vector of control variables and γ is the corresponding column vector of parameters. A usual guide for selecting bank-level controls is the CAMELS system (see Table 9.1), where variables are considered to explain bank performance remarkably well (for example, see Eichler et al. (2011) for the related discussion);

β_3 is the DD coefficient that captures the difference between the lending outcomes for the treatment group and the control group post reform. The estimate of β_3 provides the average treatment effect because it measures the effect of the policy of capital increase on the average outcome of lending;

ε_{it} is an error (that is, unexplained) term, assumed to satisfy certain regularity conditions (for example, see Cameron and Trivedi (2010), Wooldridge (2013), Imbens and Rubin (2015) for the formal details and the related discussions of the limitations, as well as Cameron and Trivedi (2010) for implementation in Stata).

Overall, and as with any approach, the causalities identified with the average treatment effects have certain caveats. In particular, for any effect to be causal, the governmental policies need to be unexpectedly assigned to the banks, while the treatment and control groups need to be similar by their key characteristics before the policy-changing event. Some of these challenges in estimation could be dealt with application of RDD methods, others can be approached with the IV techniques. Both of these methods are discussed in sections 6.3 and 6.4, respectively.

6.3   The Role of RDD in Causal Inference on Bank Performance

In cases when randomized assignment to treatment is impossible, yet there is an effect of a policy change that is "as good as random", an alternative to DD strategy is RDD. The foundations of this method go back to at least Thistlethwaite and Campbell (1960) and are further described and elaborated by Angrist and Pischke (2009), with the famous application by Hahn et al. (2001) and a practical guide by Imbens and Lemieux (2007), Cameron and Trivedi (2010) and Greene (2011), which we follow here.

In its essence, the RDD approach allocates observations to a treatment and a control group based on the value of an assignment variable, exogenous to an experiment. Examples of an assignment variable include poverty rate and its effect on educational programs and class size on examination performance Greene (2011). Continuing the example in section 6.2. of the capital increase, suppose the treatment is assigned based on the systemic importance of a bank. In particular, in macroeconomics literature a bank is often considered to be systemically important if its failure might be a trigger to a financial crisis (Adrian and Brunnermeier, 2016), which in turn implies a threshold on certain variables, for example, assets of a bank.

When the assignment to treatment is activated by the crossing of a fixed threshold, that is, the size of a bank, the effects of the treatment can be evaluated with the RDD. Discontinuity stems from different values of the outcome variable depending on whether the bank is above or below the treatment threshold, or a certain cut-off point. It is assumed that the banks closest to the cutoff are similar by their key characteristics. In our example, the lending growth could be different for the increasing capital banks versus the non-increasing capital banks when the assignment to treatment is determined based on crossing the cutoff. The idea here is that the banks cannot manipulate the assignment variable, that is, if the banks cannot change their size, or systemic importance, over a very short period of time, then the treatment occurs with certainty and the policy effects of the capital increase on lending can be evaluated.

This assignment to treatment feature of the RDD allows for matching the banks relatively well. Importantly, the matching is based on the cutoff characteristics rather than on any other complex method of propensity score estimator, or the "nearest neighbor" estimator.[17] RDD presents an alternative to the matching experiment (Thistlethwaite and Campbell, 1960), when there is an equivalency in treatment and control groups prior to a policy event. Alternatively, RDD allocates observations to the treatment and control groups conditional on the value of a predictor to the left and to the right sides of a cutoff (Imbens and Lemieux, 2007). The caveat of RDD is that the predictor might be associated with the outcomes, yet, if the association is functionally continuous (only an outcome variable is discontinuous), any distributional discontinuity of the outcome variable, conditional on the predicting variable at the cut-off point, is subject to a causality interpretation, provided that the regularity conditions on the data-generating process hold (see Imbens and Lemieux (2007) for further details).

Critically, any estimated treatment effect with RDD has "local" properties. It is an assumption that if the banks are well matched around the cutoff, the further an observation is from the cutoff the more different the banks are expected to be. How well the banks are matched is testable. The outcome variable would be continuous without the policy intervention and discontinuity arises as a result of the policy event. Therefore, it is expected that the effect is causal and dominates the effect of the other variables, except for an identified relationship between the outcome (Y) and the forcing (X) variable.

To identify causality, an analysis needs to find the discontinuity (Imbens and Lemieux, 2007). An interesting example is the recent study about liquidity-enhancing policies by Bonner and Eijffinger (2015), who found that the interest rates distribution is discontinuous around the liquidity buffer cutoff.

After the discontinuity is identified, a test is needed to estimate whether the difference of the outcome variable is significant. In the capital increase example, if X_i is a dummy variable for whether a bank needs to increase capital with a new policy and Z_i is a variable representing the systemic importance of the bank based on size, then

$$X_i = 1, \quad \text{if } Z_i \geq Z_0$$
$$= 0, \quad \text{otherwise}$$

where Z_0 is the systemic important threshold.

Here, the RDD implementation is an estimation of two regressions of outcome variable Y_i (lending) on X_i in samples to the left and to the right of the size cutoff. A comparison of the intercepts from these two regressions estimates a change in the lending variable Y_i given treatment X_i. For further flexibility of implementation, the model can be formulated in general terms as

$$Y_i = \alpha(Z_i) + X_i\beta + \varepsilon_i, \tag{9.38}$$

where $\alpha_i = \alpha(Z_i) + \varepsilon_i$ is a function of Z_i and other unobservables ε_i, with the assumptions that $E[\alpha_i|Z_i = Z]$ is continuous in Z at Z_0, while the density of Z_i is positive in the neighborhood of Z_0, along with other regularity conditions that allow identification and consistent estimation and valid inference for this model (see Hahn et al. (2001) for details).

To conclude, in the application of the RDD, as for any other method, researchers need to be aware of its caveats. In particular, the estimated treatment effects are likely to have "local" features due to an analysis of observations that are placed close to a cutoff.

6.4   Performance Analysis in the Presence of Selection Bias

Selection bias presents a significant challenge in research, aiming to conduct causal inference. An impossibility of observing the outcome after the policy change in a difference to the outcome for the same banks should the policy change not occur, creates a fundamental problem of causal inference, described by Holland (1986). Selection bias is essentially the difference between the outcome of the treatment banks should the policy change not occur and the outcome of the control banks. Randomization in the "ideal" experiment resolves the selection bias questions. However, in the presence of selection bias, an estimate of an average treatment effect may be inconsistent. For an extensive review we recommend Holland (1986), Heckman (1990), Heckman et al. (1997), Imbens and Wooldridge (2009), Angrist and Pischke (2009) and Cameron and Trivedi (2010). In the performance of banks literature, Allen et al. (1990), Cantor and Packer (1997) and Maskara and Mullineaux (2011) deal with selection bias by changing the sample, inclusion of the possible determinants of the resulting variable and the IV type estimation, respectively.

To summarize, two types of selection bias are most common (Imbens and Wooldridge, 2009; Cameron and Trivedi, 2010); these are selection on observable and selection on unobservable variables. In selection bias on observables, the treatment variable is correlated with the error in the outcome equation due to an omitted observable variable that determines both the treatment and outcome variable. In selection bias on unobservables, the correlation between the treatment variable and the error in the outcome equation is due to an omitted unobservable variable that partly determines both treatment and outcome variables.

To deal with the selection bias problem, in the first event a common approach is to include all the observable variables (potentially correlated with an error term in the outcome equation) into an outcome equation and then estimate this equation with least squares. In the event of selection on unobservables, a usual approach is to remedy the selection bias problem in a two-stage procedure, parametric or semiparametric estimation.

Recently Zelenyuk et al. (2020) adapted a two-stage approach of Heckman (1976) and Maddala (1983) to deal with the selection bias in a study of the impact of voluntary disclosure of capital adequacy on bank lending in the United States. In a two-stage procedure the model includes an outcome variable, treatment assignment and IV.[18] To be more precise, in their model, when banks self-select to voluntary disclosure, treatment of disclosure on lending can be endogenous and is assumed to follow the process

$$Y_i = X_i\beta + aD_i + \varepsilon_i, \tag{9.39}$$

where Y_i is the lending adjusted for past performance (essentially a growth of lending) for bank i, X_i is a row vector of control variables and β is the corresponding column vector of parameters, while D_i is a treatment participation decision variable that equals 1 or 0. Moreover, the treatment participation indicator depends on the IV Z, via the following specification:

$$D_i^* = \gamma_0 + \gamma_1 Z_i + v_i, \tag{9.40}$$

where D_i^* is a latent variable with an observable counterpart D_i defined as 1 or 0 dummy variable.

Importantly, the variable Z is in the equation of D (9.40), but not in the equation of Y in (9.39). Leveraging on the linear nature of the model, assuming $cov[Z, v] = 0$, $cov[\varepsilon, Z] = 0$, $cov[X, \varepsilon] = 0$, and $cov[D, Z] \neq 0$ and other assumptions on random errors v_i and the data generating process in general, it can be shown that a consistently estimates the average treatment effect (for example, see Cameron and Trivedi (2010) and references therein).

An indicator about treatment participation depends on the IV. Zelenyuk et al. (2020) selected an instrument based on the theory of voluntary disclosure (Diamond and Dybvig, 1983) and corporate governance (Shleifer and Vishny, 1997). In particular, they chose stock-based managerial compensation as an instrument because of the role of the stock-related compensation in dealing with the agency problems. Then, the two-stage algorithm was applied to the model for an estimation of probability of voluntary disclosure and the effect of this disclosure on the lending. Here an estimate of a is an IV-type estimate that has local properties (Gippel et al., 2015). The local average treatment effect depends on Z being applied in the treatment evaluation and on an instrument. With this approach, Zelenyuk et al. (2020) found significant evidence of a positive effect of a voluntary bank capital adequacy disclosure on lending.

Finally, it is important to note that a limitation of the IV application to an inference involving selection bias is that treatment and control groups may not be representative of the whole population; therefore, the results of these types of estimations may not be robustly supporting big policy questions, yet they could still be informative of more local changes, such as policy thresholds.

7.   CONCLUDING REMARKS

In this chapter, we overview major approaches of performance analysis in banking. These approaches include envelopment-type estimators (DEA and FDH, in many variations), stochastic frontier estimators (parametric, semiparametric and nonparametric) and other non-efficiency type econometric methods. We provide a relatively brief overview of each stream and cite many (although, of course, not all) works we believe would be useful for the interested readers to find more details about them.

It might be also worth emphasizing that the inclusion of the last part, briefly describing methods of DD, RDD, IV, is a key difference of our chapter relative to most (if not all) other works on performance analysis in banking and, perhaps, overall that we are aware of to date. The reason for including this interesting area of research in our review, however, is not just to distinguish our work from others. The goal is to bring attention of both audiences, which have so far largely developed on their own. This is because, indeed, we strongly believe a lot of interesting research should result from the synthesis and the synergies of these approaches, both for new theoretical developments and for future interesting practical applications.

Finally, there are also other areas of performance analysis that we have not covered here. One of them, which so far has been largely under-explored and we believe has a fruitful future, is the adaptation of methods in machine learning and artificial intelligence (including the contexts of big data and social networks) for performance analysis in general and for performance of banking in particular.[19] We hope and encourage this to be addressed with future research endeavors.

NOTES

* Both authors have contributed to all sections, and about equally overall, yet with some degree of specialization. Specifically, Natalya Zelenyuk mainly focused on banking aspects and especially on sections 2 and 6, while Valentin Zelenyuk mainly focused on DEA and SFA methodology (especially sections 3, 4, 5). We thank the editors and reviewers of this Handbook, as well as many colleagues, Karligash Glass, Woo-Young Kang, Ana Lozano-Vivas, Dimitris Margaritis, Bao Hoang Nguyen, Evelyn Smart, Tom Smith, Pravin Trivedi and Zhichao Wang, among others, for their fruitful feedback that helped shape this work.

1. This work was translated and edited in 1990 by D. M. Dabrowska and T. P. Speed from the Polish original that appeared in *Roczniki Nauk Rolniczych Tom X* (1923) 1–51 (Annals of Agricultural Sciences).

2. It is also worth noting that when having "too few" observations in a time period, researchers consider pooling over several time periods, that is,

$$\Psi = \cup_{t \in \{1,...,T'\}} \Psi_t = \cup_{t \in \{1,...,T'\}} \cup_i \Psi_{it}(Z_{i\tau} \mid \tau = t), \tag{9.8}$$

where the union is taken over all the possibilities available for all i in a specific time range $\{1, \ldots, T'\}$, which can be all the sample or part of the sample with the moving window approach. A caveat of this approach is that it presumes (or ignores) the technological change that may have happened over that period and, therefore, should be done with caution and relevant justifications.

3. The ideas of this measure go back to as early as 1940s, and were more thoroughly developed by Chambers et al. (1996, 1998).

4. For example, see Färe et al. (1994), Ray (2004) and most recent textbook-style treatment in Sickles and Zelenyuk (2019).

5. Also see Dakpo et al. (2017) for a good review of the research about undesirable outputs and congesting inputs.

6. Also see Simar and Wilson (2011).

7. A nonparametric approach via local likelihood is also available, although with some degree of "curse of dimensionality" and greater computational costs (for example, see Park et al., 2008).

8. Note that some of these and other studies used particular versions of both DEA and SFA.

9. A classic book here is Kumbhakar and Lovell (2000), although many more developments came after it and the most recent summary to date can be found, in Sickles et al. (2020) as a very short practical review, and a more thorough review in Kumbhakar et al. (2021a,b), while a comprehensive textbook style treatment can be found in Chapters 11 through 16 of Sickles and Zelenyuk (2019), which also connects to the economic theory foundations and DEA described in prior chapters.

10. For example, see Sickles and Zelenyuk (2019, Chapter 11).

11. For detailed discussion on this see the classic work of Kumbhakar (1997) and some more recent developments in Kumbhakar (1997), Kumbhakar and Tsionas (2005), Mamatzakis et al. (2015) and Malikov et al. (2016) as well as a textbook-style discussion in Sickles and Zelenyuk (2019).

12. More discussion on this can be found in Wang and Schmidt (2002). Also see Kim and Schmidt (2008) for various statistical testing issues in this context.

13. This approach is in the spirit of Caudill et al. (1995), and is a special case of the nonparametric approach developed by Park et al. (2015) in a local-likelihood framework and Simar et al. (2017) in a local-least squares framework.

14. Also see other articles in the same special issue and the introduction from the editors, Kumbhakar and Schmidt (2016).

15. "For practical implementation of the methods discussed here using Stata, see the Chapter 17 of this Handbook, while for implementation in Matlab and R, see Sickles and Zelenyuk (2019)."
16. Also see the relevant chapters of this Handbook (for example, Chapters 11–13, 16), which focus on different aspects in fair detail and provide many useful references and examples.
17. For more details on propensity score matching and nearest neighbor estimator, see Rubin and Thomas (1996), Rubin (2006), while for practical implementation, see Cameron and Trivedi (2010).
18. For related discussions, also see Cameron and Trivedi (2010).
19. For example, see Mullainathan and Spiess (2017), Athey and Imbens (2019) as well as Chapters 14–16 of this Handbook for general reviews and Zelenyuk (2020) and Chen, Tsionas and Zelenyuk (2021) for some recent examples of such studies for performance analysis.

REFERENCES

Acharya, V. V. and Mora, N. (2015). A crisis of banks as liquidity providers. *The Journal of Finance*, 70(1): 1–43.
Adams, R. M., Berger, A. N., and Sickles, R. C. (1999). Semiparametric approaches to stochastic panel frontiers with applications in the banking industry. *Journal of Business and Economic Statistics*, 17(3): 349–58.
Adrian, T. and Brunnermeier, M. K. (2016). CoVar. *American Economic Review*, 106(7): 1705–41.
Afriat, S. N. (1972). Efficiency estimation of production functions. *International Economic Review*, 13(3): 568–98.
Ahn, S. C., Lee, Y. H., and Schmidt, P. (2007). Stochastic frontier models with multiple time-varying individual effects. *Journal of Productivity Analysis*, 27(1): 1–12.
Aigner, D., Lovell, C., and Schmidt, P. (1977). Formulation and estimation of stochastic frontier production function models. *Journal of Econometrics*, 6(1): 21–37.
Aiyar, S., Calomiris, C. W., Hooley, J., Korniyenko, Y., and Wieladek, T. (2014). The international transmission of bank capital requirements: Evidence from the UK. *Journal of Financial Economics*, 113(3): 368–82.
Akhavein, J. D., Berger, A. N., and Humphrey, D. B. (1997). The effects of megamergers on efficiency and prices: Evidence from a bank profit function. *Finance and Economics Discussion Series 1997-9, Board of Governors of the Federal Reserve System*.
Allen, D. S., Lamy, R. E., and Thomson, G. R. (1990). The shelf registration of debt and self-selection bias. *The Journal of Finance*, 45(1): 275–87.
Allen, R., Athanassopoulos, A., Dyson, R. G., and Thanassoulis, E. (1997). Weights restrictions and value judgements in data envelopment analysis: Evolution, development and future directions. *Annals of Operations Research*, 73: 13–34.
Almanidis, P., Karakaplan, M. U., and Kutlu, L. (2019). A dynamic stochastic frontier model with threshold effects: U.S. bank size and efficiency. *Journal of Productivity Analysis*, 52(2): 69–84.
Altunbas, Y., Carbo, S., Gardener, E. P., and Molyneux, P. (2007). Examining the relationships between capital, risk and efficiency in European banking. *European Financial Management*, 13(1): 49–70.
Aly, H. Y., Grabowski, R., Pasurka, C., and Rangan, N. (1990). Technical, scale, and allocative efficiencies in U.S. banking: An empirical investigation. *The Review of Economics and Statistics*, 72(2): 211–18.
Amsler, C., Prokhorov, A., and Schmidt, P. (2017). Endogenous environmental variables in stochastic frontier models. *Journal of Econometrics*, 199(2): 131–40.
Anginer, D., Demirguc-Kunt, A., Huizinga, H., and Ma, K. (2018). Corporate governance of banks and financial stability. *Journal of Financial Economics*, 130.
Angrist, J. and Pischke, J.-S. (2009). *Mostly Harmless Econometrics: An Empiricist's Companion*. Princeton University Press.
Aparicio, J., Duran, M. A., Lozano-Vivas, A., and Pastor, J. T. (2018). Are charter value and supervision aligned? A segmentation analysis. *Journal of Financial Stability*, 37: 60–73.
APRA. (2013). Domestic systemically important banks in Australia. *Australian Prudential Regulation Authority Information Paper*.
Ashenfelter, O. (1978). Estimating the effect of training programs on earnings. *The Review of Economics and Statistics*, 60(1): 47–57.
Ashenfelter, O. and Card, D. (1985). Using the longitudinal structure of earnings to estimate the effect of training programs. *The Review of Economics and Statistics*, 67(4): 648–60.
Assaf, A. G., Berger, A. N., Roman, R. A., and Tsionas, M. G. (2019). Does efficiency help banks survive and thrive during financial crises? *Journal of Banking and Finance*, 106: 445–70.
Athey, S. and Imbens, G. W. (2019). Machine learning methods that economists should know about. *Annual Review of Economics*, 11(1): 685–725.
Bădin, L., Daraio, C., and Simar, L. (2012). How to measure the impact of environmental factors in a nonparametric production model. *European Journal of Operational Research*, 223(3): 818–33.

Bai, J. (2009). Panel data models with interactive fixed effects. *Econometrica*, 77(4): 1229–79.

Bai, J., Krishnamurthy, A., and Weymuller, C.-H. (2018). Measuring liquidity mismatch in the banking sector. *The Journal of Finance*, 73(1): 51–93.

Bai, J. and Ng, S. (2002). Determining the number of factors in approximate factor models. *Econometrica*, 70(1): 191–221.

Banker, R. D. (1993). Maximum likelihood, consistency and data envelopment analysis: A statistical foundation. *Management Science*, 39(10): 1265–73.

Banker, R. D., Charnes, A., and Cooper, W. W. (1984). Some models for estimating technical and scale inefficiencies in data envelopment analysis. *Management Science*, 30(9): 1078–92.

Battese, G. E. and Coelli, T. J. (1995). A model for technical inefficiency effects in a stochastic frontier production function for panel data. *Empirical Economics*, 20(2): 325–32.

Bauer, P. W. and Hancock, D. (1993). The efficiency of the Federal Reserve in providing check processing services. *Journal of Banking and Finance*, 17(2–3): 287–311.

BCBS. (2019). An examination of initial experience with the global systemically important bank framework. *Banking Commission on Banking Supervision Bank for International Settlements Working Paper 34.*

Berg, T. (2018). Got rejected? Real effects of not getting a loan. *The Review of Financial Studies*, 31(12): 4912–57.

Berger, A., DeYoung, R., Genay, H., and Udell, G. F. (2000). Globalization of financial institutions: Evidence from cross-border banking performance. *Brookings-Wharton Papers on Financial Services*, 28(7): 23–120.

Berger, A. N. (1993). "Distribution-free" estimates of efficiency in the US banking industry and tests of the standard distributional assumptions. *Journal of Productivity Analysis*, 4(3): 261–92.

Berger, A. N. and Bouwman, C. H. (2013). How does capital affect bank performance during financial crises? *Journal of Financial Economics*, 109(1): 146–76.

Berger, A. N. and Bouwman, C. H. S. (2009). Bank liquidity creation. *The Review of Financial Studies*, 22(9): 3779–837.

Berger, A. N. and DeYoung, R. (1997). Problem loans and cost efficiency in commercial banks. *Journal of Banking and Finance*, 21(6): 849–70.

Berger, A. N. and Hannan, T. H. (1998). The efficiency cost of market power in the banking industry: A test of the "quiet life" and related hypotheses. *Review of Economics and Statistics*, 80(3): 454–65.

Berger, A. N., Hasan, I., and Zhou, M. (2010). The effects of focus versus diversification on bank performance: Evidence from Chinese banks. *Journal of Banking and Finance*, 34(7): 1417–35.

Berger, A. N. and Humphrey, D. B. (1997). Efficiency of financial institutions: International survey and directions for future research. *European Journal of Operational Research*, 98(2): 175–212.

Berger, A. N., Leusner, J. H., and Mingo, J. J. (1997). The efficiency of bank branches. *Journal of Monetary Economics*, 40(1): 141–62.

Berger, A. N. and Mester, L. J. (1997). Inside the black box: What explains differences in the efficiencies of financial institutions? *Journal of Banking and Finance*, 21(7): 895–947.

Berger, A. N. and Roman, R. A. (2017). Did saving Wall Street really save Main Street? The real effects of TARP on local economic conditions. *Journal of Financial and Quantitative Analysis*, 52(5): 1827–67.

Bertrand, M., Duflo, E., and Mullainathan, S. (2004). How much should we trust differences-in-differences estimates?*. *The Quarterly Journal of Economics*, 119(1): 249–75.

Bikker, J. and Bos, J. (2008). Bank performance: A theoretical and empirical framework for the analysis of profitability, competition, and efficiency.

BIS. (2015). Making supervisory stress tests more macroprudential: Considering liquidity and solvency interactions and systemic risk. *Bank for International Settlements Working Paper 29*, https: //www.bis.org.

BIS. (2020a). The Basel Framework. Bank for International Settlements, https: //www.bis.org.

BIS. (2020b). History of the Basel Committee. Bank for International Settlements, https: //www.bis.org/bcbs/history .htm.

Bonner, C. and Eijffinger, S. C. W. (2015). The impact of liquidity regulation on bank intermediation. *Review of Finance*, 20(5): 1945–79.

Bos, J. and Schmiedel, H. (2007). Is there a single frontier in a single European banking market? *Journal of Banking and Finance*, 31(7): 2081–102.

Boubakri, N., El Ghoul, S., Guedhami, O., and Hossain, M. (2020). Post-privatization state ownership and bank risk-taking: Cross-country evidence. *Journal of Corporate Finance*, 64: 101625.

Buchak, G., Matvos, G., Piskorski, T., and Seru, A. (2018). Fintech, regulatory arbitrage, and the rise of shadow banks. *Journal of Financial Economics*, 130(3): 453–83.

Camanho, A. S. and Dyson, R. G. (2005). Cost efficiency measurement with price uncertainty: A DEA application to bank branch assessments. *European Journal of Operational Research*, 161(2): 432–46.

Cameron, C. and Trivedi, P. (2010). *Microeconometrics Using Stata: Revised Edition*. Stata Press.

Cantor, R. and Packer, F. (1997). Differences of opinion and selection bias in the credit rating industry. *Journal of Banking Finance*, 21(10): 1395–417.

Casu, B., Ferrari, A., and Zhao, T. (2013). Regulatory reform and productivity change in Indian banking. *The Review of Economics and Statistics*, 95(3): 1066–77.

Casu, B., Girardone, C., and Molyneux, P. (2004). Productivity change in European banking: A comparison of parametric and non-parametric approaches. *Journal of Banking and Finance*, 28(10): 2521–40.

Casu, B., Girardone, C., and Molyneux, P. (2006). *Introduction to Banking*. Prentice Hall Financial Times.

Caudill, S. B., Ford, J. M. and Gropper, D. M. (1995). Frontier estimation and firm-specific inefficiency measures in the presence of heteroscedasticity. *Journal of Business & Economic Statistics*, 13(1): 105–11.

Chambers, R., Chung, Y., and Färe, R. (1998). Profit, directional distance functions, and Nerlovian efficiency. *Journal of Optimization Theory and Applications*, 98(2): 351–64.

Chambers, R. G., Chung, Y., and Färe, R. (1996). Benefit and distance functions. *Journal of Economic Theory*, 70(2): 407–19.

Charnes, A., Cooper, W., and Rhodes, E. (1978). Measuring the efficiency of decision making units. *European Journal of Operational Research*, 2(6): 429–44.

Charnes, A., Cooper, W. W., Huang, Z. M., and Sun, D. B. (1990). Polyhedral cone-ratio DEA models with an illustrative application to large commercial banks. *Journal of Econometrics*, 46(1–2): 73–91.

Chen, Y., Tsionas, M. G., and Zelenyuk, V. (2021). LASSO+DEA for small and big wide data. Omega, 102(C), doi: 10.1016/j.omega.2021.102419.

Chung, Y. H., Färe, R., and Grosskopf, S. (1997). Productivity and undesirable outputs: A directional distance function approach. *Journal of Environmental Management*, 51(3): 229–40.

Colombi, R., Kumbhakar, S. C., Martini, G., and Vittadini, G. (2014). Closed-skew normality in stochastic frontiers with individual effects and long/short-run efficiency. *Journal of Productivity Analysis*, 42(2): 123–36.

Colombi, R., Martini, G., and Vittadini, G. (2011). A stochastic frontier model with short-run and long-run inefficiency random effects. *University of Bergamo Department of Economics and Technology Management Working Paper No. 012011*.

Cornwell, C., Schmidt, P., and Sickles, R. C. (1990). Production frontiers with cross-sectional and time-series variation in efficiency levels. *Journal of Econometrics*, 46(1): 185–200.

Curi, C., Guarda, P., Lozano-Vivas, A., and Zelenyuk, V. (2013). Is foreign-bank efficiency in financial centers driven by home or host country characteristics? *Journal of Productivity Analysis*, 40(3): 367–85.

Curi, C., Lozano-Vivas, A., and Zelenyuk, V. (2015). Foreign bank diversification and efficiency prior to and during the financial crisis: Does one business model fit all? *Journal of Banking and Finance*, 61(S1): S22–S35.

Dakpo, K. H., Jeanneaux, P., and Latruffe, L. (2017). Modelling pollution-generating technologies in performance benchmarking: Recent developments, limits and future prospects in the nonparametric framework. *European Journal of Operational Research*, 250(2): 347–59.

Daouia, A. and Simar, L. (2007). Nonparametric efficiency analysis: A multivariate conditional quantile approach. *Journal of Econometrics*, 140(2): 375–400.

Daraio, C. and Simar, L. (2007). Conditional nonparametric frontier models for convex and nonconvex technologies: A unifying approach. *Journal of Productivity Analysis*, 28(1): 13–32.

Daraio, C., Simar, L., and Wilson, P. W. (2017). Central limit theorems for conditional efficiency measures and tests of the "separability" condition in nonparametric, two-stage models of production. *The Econometrics Journal*.

Debreu, G. (1951). The coefficient of resource utilization. *Econometrica*, 19(3): 273–92.

Delis, M. D. and Tsionas, E. G. (2009). The joint estimation of bank-level market power and efficiency. *Journal of Banking and Finance*, 33(10): 1842–50.

Deprins, D., Simar, L., and Tulkens, H. (1984). Measuring labour efficiency in post offices. In Marchand, M., Pestieau, P., and Tulkens, H., editors, *The Performance of Public Enterprises: Concepts and Measurement*, 243–67. Amsterdam, NL: Springer.

Diamond, D. W. and Dybvig, P. H. (1983). Bank runs, deposit insurance, and liquidity. *Journal of Political Economy*, 91(3): 401–19.

Du, K., Worthington, A. C., and Zelenyuk, V. (2018). Data envelopment analysis, truncated regression and double-bootstrap for panel data with application to Chinese banking. *European Journal of Operational Research*, 265(2): 748–64.

Duchin, R. and Sosyura, D. (2014). Safer ratios, riskier portfolios: Banks' response to government aid. *Journal of Financial Economics*, 113(1): 1–28.

Dyson, R. G. and Thanassoulis, E. (1988). Reducing weight flexibility in data envelopment analysis. *Journal of the Operational Research Society*, 39(6): 563–76.

EBA. (2020). Global systemically important institutions. *European Banking Authority*.

Eichler, S., Karmann, A., and Maltritz, D. (2011). The term structure of banking crisis risk in the United States: A market data based compound option approach. *Journal of Banking and Finance*, 35(4): 876–85. Crete Conference 2010: The Future of Universal Banking.

Eling, M. and Luhnen, M. (2010). Efficiency in the international insurance industry: A cross-country comparison. *Journal of Banking and Finance*, 34(7): 1497–509.

English, M., Grosskopf, S., Hayes, K., and Yaisawarng, S. (1993). Output allocative and technical efficiency of banks. *Journal of Banking and Finance*, 17(2–3): 349–66.

Fan, Y., Li, Q., and Weersink, A. (1996). Semiparametric estimation of stochastic production frontier models. *Journal of Business & Economic Statistics*, 14(4): 460–68.

Färe, R. and Grosskopf, S. (1983). Measuring congestion in production. *Zeitschrift für Nationalökonomie/Journal of Economics*, 43(3): 257–71.

Färe, R. and Grosskopf, S. (1996). *Intertemporal Production Frontiers: With Dynamic DEA*. Norwell, MA: Kluwer Academic Publishers.

Färe, R. and Grosskopf, S. (2003). Nonparametric productivity analysis with undesirable outputs: Comment. *American Journal of Agricultural Economics*, 85(4): 1070–74.

Färe, R. and Grosskopf, S. (2004). Modeling undesirable factors in efficiency evaluation: Comment. *European Journal of Operational Research*, 157(1): 242–5.

Färe, R. and Grosskopf, S. (2009). A comment on weak disposability in nonparametric production analysis. *American Journal of Agricultural Economics*, 91(2): 535–8.

Färe, R., Grosskopf, S., and Logan, J. (1983). The relative efficiency of Illinois electric utilities. *Resources and Energy*, 5(4): 349–67.

Färe, R., Grosskopf, S., and Lovell, C. A. K. (1994). *Production Frontiers*. New York, NY: Cambridge University Press.

Färe, R., Grosskopf, S., and Roos, P. (1996). On two definitions of productivity. *Economics Letters*, 53(3): 269–74.

Färe, R., He, X., Li, S. K., and Zelenyuk, V. (2019). A unifying framework for Farrell efficiency measurement. *Operations Research*, 67(1): 183–97.

Färe, R. and Svensson, L. (1980). Congestion of production factors. *Econometrica: Journal of the Econometric Society*, 48(7): 1745–53.

Farrell, M. J. (1957). The measurement of productive efficiency. *Journal of the Royal Statistical Society. Series A (General)*, 120(3): 253–90.

Federal Reserve. (2020). BHC supervision manual. Board of Governors of the Federal Reserve System, www.federalreserve.gov.

Ferrier, G. and Lovell, C. (1990). Measuring cost efficiency in banking: Econometric and linear programming evidence. *Journal of Econometrics*, 46(1–2): 229–45.

Fethi, M. D. and Pasiouras, F. (2010). Assessing bank efficiency and performance with operational research and artificial intelligence techniques: A survey. *European Journal of Operational Research*, 204(2): 189–98.

Fisher, R. (1925). *Statistical methods for research workers*. Oliver and Boyd.

Fukuyama, H. (1993). Technical and scale efficiency of Japanese commercial banks: A non-parametric approach. *Applied Economics*, 25(8): 1101–12.

Fukuyama, H. and Weber, W. (2015). Measuring Japanese bank performance: a dynamic network DEA approach. *Journal of Productivity Analysis*, 44(3): 249–64.

Georgescu-Roegen, N. (1951). The aggregate linear production function and its applications to von Neumann's economic model. In Koopmans, T., editor, *Activity Analysis of Production and Allocation*. New York, NY: Wiley.

Gijbels, I., Mammen, E., Park, B. U., and Simar, L. (1999). On estimation of monotone and concave frontier functions. *Journal of the American Statistical Association*, 94(445): 220–28.

Gippel, J., Smith, T., and Zhu, Y. (2015). Endogeneity in accounting and finance research: Natural experiments as a state-of-the-art solution. *Abacus*, 51(2): 143–68.

Goodhart, C. (2011). *The Basel Committee on banking supervision: A history of the early Years 1974–1997*. Cambridge University Press.

Greene, W. H. (2005a). Fixed and random effects in stochastic frontier models. *Journal of Productivity Analysis*, 23(1): 7–32.

Greene, W. H. (2005b). Reconsidering heterogeneity in panel data estimators of the stochastic frontier model. *Journal of Econometrics*, 126(2): 269–303.

Greene, W. H. (2011). *Econometric Analysis*. Prentice Hall, 7th edition.

Griffin, J. E. and Steel, M. F. (2007). Bayesian stochastic frontier analysis using winbugs. *Journal of Productivity Analysis*, 27(3): 163–76.

Grosskopf, S. (1986). The role of the reference technology in measuring productive efficiency. *The Economic Journal*, 96(382): 499–513.

Hahn, J., Todd, P., and Van der Klaauw, W. (2001). Identification and estimation of treatment effects with a regression-discontinuity design. *Econometrica*, 69(1): 201–9.

Hamadi, M., Heinen, A., Linder, S., and Porumb, V.-A. (2016). Does Basel II affect the market valuation of discretionary loan loss provisions? *Journal of Banking and Finance*, 70: 177–92.

Hao, G., Wei, Q. L., and Yan, H. (2000). A game theoretical model of DEA efficiency. *The Journal of the Operational Research Society*, 51(11): 1319–29.

Harris, L. (1989). S&P 500 cash stock price volatilities. *The Journal of Finance,* 44(5): 1155–75.

Heckman, J. (1976). The common structure of statistical models of truncation, sample selection and limited dependent variables and a simple estimator for such models. *Annals of Economic and Social Measurement*, 5: 475–92.

Heckman, J. (1990). Varieties of selection bias. *American Economic Review*, 80(2): 313–18.

Heckman, J. J., Ichimura, H., and Todd, P. E. (1997). Matching as an econometric evaluation estimator: Evidence from evaluating a job training program. *The Review of Economic Studies*, 64(4): 605–54.

Holland, P. W. (1986). Statistics and causal inference. *Journal of the American Statistical Association*, 81(396): 945–60.

Horrace, W. C., Liu, X., and Patacchini, E. (2016). Endogenous network production functions with selectivity. *Journal of Econometrics*, 190(2): 222–32.

Hughes, J. and Mester, L. (1998). Bank capitalization and cost: Evidence of scale economies in risk management and signaling. *The Review of Economics and Statistics*, 80(2): 314–25.

Humphrey, D. (2020). Distance functions, bank output, and productivity. *Journal of Productivity Analysis*: 13–26.

Imbens, G. and Lemieux, T. (2007). Regression discontinuity designs: A guide to practice. *NBER Working Papers 13039, National Bureau of Economic Research, Inc.*

Imbens, G. and Rubin, D. (2015). *Causal Inference for Statistics, Social, and Biomedical Sciences*. Cambridge University Press.

Imbens, G. W. and Wooldridge, J. M. (2009). Recent developments in the econometrics of program evaluation. *Journal of Economic Literature*, 47(1): 5–86.

Isik, I. and Hassan, M. (2002). Technical, scale and allocative efficiencies of Turkish banking industry. *Journal of Banking and Finance*, 26(4): 719–66.

Jeong, S.-O. and Simar, L. (2006). Linearly interpolated FDH efficiency score for nonconvex frontiers. *Journal of Multivariate Analysis*, 97(10): 2141–61.

Jondrow, J., Lovell, C. A. K., Materov, I. S., and Schmidt, P. (1982). On the estimation of technical inefficiency in the stochastic frontier production function model. *Journal of Econometrics*, 19(2–3): 233–8.

Kao, C. (2014). Network data envelopment analysis: A review. *European Journal of Operational Research*, 239(1): 1–16.

Kenjegalieva, K., Simper, R., Weyman-Jones, T., and Zelenyuk, V. (2009a). Comparative analysis of banking production frameworks in Eastern European financial markets. *European Journal of Operational Research*, 198(1): 326–40.

Kenjegalieva, K., Simper, R., Weyman-Jones, T., and Zelenyuk, V. (2009b). Comparative analysis of banking production frameworks in Eastern European financial markets. *European Journal of Operational Research*, 198(1): 326–40.

Kim, M. and Schmidt, P. (2008). Valid tests of whether technical inefficiency depends on firm characteristics. *Journal of Econometrics*, 144(2): 409–27.

Kneip, A., Park, B. U., and Simar, L. (1998). A note on the convergence of nonparametric DEA estimators for production efficiency scores. *Econometric Theory*, 14(6): 783–93.

Kneip, A., Sickles, R. C., and Song, W. (2012). A new panel data treatment for heterogeneity in time trends. *Econometric Theory*, 28(3): 590–628.

Kneip, A. and Simar, L. (1996). A general framework for frontier estimation with panel data. *Journal of Productivity Analysis*, 7(2–3): 187–212.

Kneip, A., Simar, L., and Wilson, P. W. (2008). Asymptotics and consistent bootstraps for DEA estimators in nonparametric frontier models. *Econometric Theory*, 24(6): 1663–97.

Kneip, A., Simar, L., and Wilson, P. W. (2015). When bias kills the variance: Central limit theorems for DEA and FDH efficiency scores. *Econometric Theory*, 31(2): 394–422.

Kneip, A., Simar, L., and Wilson, P. W. (2016). Testing hypotheses in nonparametric models of production. *Journal of Business & Economic Statistics*, 34(3): 435–56.

Koop, G., Osiewalski, J., and Steel, M. F. (1994). Bayesian efficiency analysis with a flexible form: The AIM cost function. *Journal of Business & Economic Statistics*, 12(3): 339–46.

Koop, G., Osiewalski, J., and Steel, M. F. (1997). Bayesian efficiency analysis through individual effects: Hospital cost frontiers. *Journal of Econometrics*, 76(1): 77–105.

Koop, G., Osiewalski, J., and Steel, M. F. J. (1999). The components of output growth: A stochastic frontier analysis. *Oxford Bulletin of Economics and Statistics*, 61(4): 455–87.

Koop, G., Steel, M. F., and Osiewalski, J. (1995). Posterior analysis of stochastic frontier models using Gibbs sampling. *Computational Statistics*, 10: 353–73.

Koopmans, T. (1951). *Activity Analysis of Production and Allocation*. New York, NY: Wiley.

Korostelev, A., Simar, L., and Tsybakov, A. B. (1995). Efficient estimation of monotone boundaries. *Annals of Statistics*, 23(2): 476–89.

Koutsomanoli-Filippaki, A., Margaritis, D., and Staikouras, C. (2009). Efficiency and productivity growth in the banking industry of Central and Eastern Europe. *Journal of Banking and Finance*, 33(3): 557–67.

Kumbhakar, S. and Schmidt, P. (2016). *Endogeneity Problems in Econometrics, Special Issue of the Journal of Econometrics*, 190. Amsterdam, Netherlands: Elsevier.

Kumbhakar, S. C. (1990). Production frontiers, panel data, and time-varying technical inefficiency. *Journal of Econometrics*, 46(1): 201–11.

Kumbhakar, S. C. (1997). Modeling allocative inefficiency in a translog cost function and cost share equations: An exact relationship. *Journal of Econometrics*, 76(1): 351–6.

Kumbhakar, S. C., Ghosh, S. and McGuckin, J. T. (1991). A generalized production frontier approach for estimating determinants of inefficiency in U.S. dairy farms. *Journal of Business & Economic Statistics*, 9(3), 279–86.

Kumbhakar, S. C. and Lovell, C. A. K. (2000). *Stochastic Frontier Analysis*. Cambridge University Press.

Kumbhakar, S. C., Lozano-Vivas, A., Lovell, C. A. K., and Hasan, I. (2001). The effects of deregulation on the performance of financial institutions: The case of Spanish savings banks. *Journal of Money, Credit and Banking*, 33(1): 101–20.

Kumbhakar, S. C., Parmeter, C. F., and Zelenyuk, V. (2021a). *Stochastic frontier analysis: Foundations and advances I*. In: Ray, S.C., Chambers, R.G., and Kumbhakar, S.C., editors, *Handbook of Production Economics. Springer*.

Kumbhakar, S. C., Parmeter, C. F., and Zelenyuk, V. (2021b). *Stochastic frontier analysis: Foundations and advances II*. In: Ray, S.C, Chambers, R.G., and Kumbhakar, editors, *Handbook of Production Economics*. Springer.

Kumbhakar, S. C. and Tsionas, E. G. (2005). Measuring technical and allocative inefficiency in the translog cost system: A Bayesian approach. *Journal of Econometrics*, 126(2): 355–84.

Kumbhakar, S. C. and Tsionas, E. G. (2016). The good, the bad and the technology: Endogeneity in environmental production models. *Journal of Econometrics*, 190(2): 315–27.

Laeven, L. and Levine, R. (2009). Bank governance, regulation and risk taking. *Journal of Financial Economics*, 93(2): 259–75.

Leary, M. T. (2009). Bank loan supply, lender choice, and corporate capital structure. *The Journal of Finance*, 64(3): 1143–85.

Lee, Y. H. (1991). *Panel data models with multiplicative individual and time effects: Applications to compensation and frontier production functions*. PhD thesis, Michigan State University, East Lansing, MI, USA.

Lee, Y. H. and Schmidt, P. (1993). A production frontier model with flexible temporal variation in technical efficiency. In Fried, H. O., Lovell, C. A. K., and Schmidt, S. S., editors, *The Measurement of Productive Efficiency: Techniques and Applications*, 237–55. New York, NY: Oxford University Press.

Leontief, W. (1925). Die Bilanz der Russischen Volkswirtschaft – Eine methodologische Untersuchung. *Weltwirtschaftliches Archiv*, 22(2): 338–44.

Leverty, J. T. and Grace, M. F. (2010). The robustness of output measures in property-liability insurance efficiency studies. *Journal of Banking and Finance*, 34(7): 1510–24.

Liang, L., Wu, J., Cook, W. D., and Zhu, J. (2008). The DEA game cross-efficiency model and its Nash equilibrium. *Operations Research*, 56(5): 1278–88.

Liberman, A. (2016). The value of a good credit reputation: Evidence from credit card renegotiations. *Journal of Financial Economics*, 120(3): 644–60.

Liu, J., Sickles, R. C., and Tsionas, E. G. (2013). *Bayesian treatments to panel data models*. Unpublished manuscript, Rice University, Houston, TX.

Liu, J., Sickles, R. C., and Tsionas, E. G. (2017). Bayesian treatments to panel data models with time-varying heterogeneity. *Econometrics*, 5(33): 1–21.

Lozano, S. (2012). Information sharing in DEA: A cooperative game theory approach. *European Journal of Operational Research*, 222(3): 558–65.

Lozano-Vivas, A., Pastor, J. T., and Pastor, J. M. (2002). An efficiency comparison of European banking systems operating under different environmental conditions. *Journal of Productivity Analysis*, 18(1): 59–77.

Maddala, G. (1983). *Limited-Dependent and Qualitative Variables in Econometrics*. Cambridge: Cambridge University Press.

Malikov, E., Kumbhakar, S. C., and Tsionas, M. G. (2016). A cost system approach to the stochastic directional technology distance function with undesirable outputs: The case of US banks in 2001–2010. *Journal of Applied Econometrics*, 31(7): 1407–29.

Mamatzakis, E., Matousek, R., and Vu, A. N. (2019). What is the impact of problem loans on Japanese bank productivity growth? *Financial Markets, Institutions & Instruments*, 28(2): 213–40.

Mamatzakis, E., Tsionas, M. G., Kumbhakar, S. C., and Koutsomanoli-Filippaki, A. (2015). Does labour regulation affect technical and allocative efficiency? Evidence from the banking industry. *Journal of Banking and Finance*, 61: S84–S98.

Manski, C. F. (2009). *Identification for Prediction and Decision*. Princeton University Press.

Martinez-Peria, M. S. and Schmukler, S. (2001). Do depositors punish banks for bad behavior? Market discipline, deposit insurance, and banking crises. *The Journal of Finance*, 56(3): 1029–51.

Martins-Filho, C. and Yao, F. (2015). Semiparametric stochastic frontier estimation via profile likelihood. *Econometric Reviews*, 34(4): 413–51.

Maskara, P. K. and Mullineaux, D. J. (2011). Information asymmetry and self-selection bias in bank loan announcement studies. *Journal of Financial Economics*, 101(3): 684–94.

Meeusen, W. and van den Broeck, J. (1977). Efficiency estimation from Cobb-Douglas production functions with composed error. *International Economic Review*, 18(2): 435–44.

Mester, L. J. (1993). Efficiency in the savings and loan industry. *Journal of Banking and Finance*, 17(2–3): 267–86.

Mullainathan, S. and Spiess, J. (2017). Machine learning: An applied econometric approach. *Journal of Economic Perspectives*, 31(2): 87–106.

Nakabayashi, K. and Tone, K. (2006). Egoist's dilemma: a DEA game. *Omega*, 34(2): 135–48.

Nanda, R. and Nicholas, T. (2014). Did bank distress stifle innovation during the great depression? *Journal of Financial Economics*, 114(2): 273–92.

Neuhann, D. and Saidi, F. (2018). Do universal banks finance riskier but more productive firms? *Journal of Financial Economics*, 128(1): 66–85.

Olson, J. A., Schmidt, P., and Waldman, D. M. (1980). A Monte Carlo study of estimators of the stochastic frontier production function. *Journal of Econometrics*, 13(1): 67–82.

Paradi, J. C. and Zhu, H. (2013). A survey on bank branch efficiency and performance research with data envelopment analysis. *Omega*, 41(1): 61–79.

Park, B. U., Jeong, S.-O., and Simar, L. (2010). Asymptotic distribution of conical-hull estimators of directional edges. *Annals of Statistics*, 38(3): 1320–40.

Park, B. U., Sickles, R. C., and Simar, L. (2003). Semiparametric-efficient estimation of AR(1) panel data models. *Journal of Econometrics*, 117(2): 279–309.

Park, B. U., Sickles, R. C., and Simar, L. (2007). Semiparametric efficient estimation of dynamic panel data models. *Journal of Econometrics*, 136(1): 281–301.

Park, B. U., Simar, L., and Weiner, C. (2000). The FDH estimator for productivity efficiency scores: Asymptotic properties. *Econometric Theory*, 16(6): 855–77.

Park, B. U., Simar, L., and Zelenyuk, V. (2008). Local likelihood estimation of truncated regression and its partial derivatives: Theory and application. *Journal of Econometrics*, 146(1): 185–98.

Park, B. U., Simar, L., and Zelenyuk, V. (2015). Categorical data in local maximum likelihood: Theory and applications to productivity analysis. *Journal of Productivity Analysis*, 43(2): 199–214.

Parmeter, C. F. and Zelenyuk, V. (2019). Combining the virtues of stochastic frontier and data envelopment analysis. *Operations Research*, 67(6): 1628–58.

Pham, M. D. and Zelenyuk, V. (2018). Slack-based directional distance function in the presence of bad outputs: Theory and application to Vietnamese banking. *Empirical Economics*, 54(1): 153–87.

Pham, M. D. and Zelenyuk, V. (2019). Weak disposability in nonparametric production analysis: A new taxonomy of reference technology sets. *European Journal of Operational Research*, 274(1): 186–98.

Pitt, M. M. and Lee, L.-F. (1981). The measurement and sources of technical inefficiency in the Indonesian weaving industry. *Journal of Development Economics*, 9(1): 43–64.

Podinovski, V. V. (2015). DEA models with production trade-offs and weight restrictions. In Zhu, J., editor, *Data Envelopment Analysis: A Handbook of Models and Methods*, 105–44. New York, NY: Springer.

Podinovski, V. V. and Bouzdine-Chameeva, T. (2013). Weight restrictions and free production in data envelopment analysis. *Operations Research*, 61(2): 426–37.

Ray, S. C. (2004). *Data Envelopment Analysis: Theory and Techniques for Economics and Operations Research*. Cambridge University Press.

Resti, A. (1997). Evaluating the cost-efficiency of the Italian banking system: What can be learned from the joint application of parametric and non-parametric techniques. *Journal of Banking and Finance*, 21(2): 221–50.

Roncalli, T. (2020). *Handbook of financial risk management*. Chapman and Hall/CRC.

Ross, T., Van de Venter, B., and Westerfield, J. (2017). *Essentials of corporate finance*. McGraw-Hill Education (Australia).

Rubin, D. (2006). *Matched Sampling for Causal Effects*. Cambridge University Press, Cambridge, UK.

Rubin, D. and Thomas, N. (1996). Matching using estimated propensity scores: Relating theory to practice. *Biometrics*, 52(1): 249–64.

Schepens, G. (2016). Taxes and bank capital structure. *Journal of Financial Economics*, 120(3): 585–600.

Schmidt, P. and Sickles, R. C. (1984). Production frontiers and panel data. *Journal of Business & Economic Statistics*, 2(4): 367–74.

Sealey Jr., C. W. and Lindley, J. T. (1977). Inputs, outputs, and a theory of production and cost at depository financial institutions. *The Journal of Finance*, 32(4): 1251–66.

Seiford, L. M. and Zhu, J. (2002). Modeling undesirable factors in efficiency evaluation. *European Journal of Operational Research*, 142(1): 16–20.

Shephard, R. W. (1953). *Cost and Production Functions*. Princeton University Press.

Shephard, R. W. (1970). *Theory of Cost and Production Functions*. Princeton University Press.

Shephard, R. W. (1974). Indirect production functions. In *Mathematical Systems in Economics*, volume 10. Hain, Meisenheim am Glan.

Sherman, H. D. and Gold, F. (1985). Bank branch operating efficiency: Evaluation with data envelopment analysis. *Journal of Banking and Finance*, 9(2): 297–315.

Shleifer, A. and Vishny, R. W. (1997). A survey of corporate governance. *The Journal of Finance*, 52(2): 737–83.

Sickles, R. and Zelenyuk, V. (2019). *Measurement of Productivity and Efficiency: Theory and Practice*. New York, Cambridge University Press.

Sickles, R. C., Song, W., and Zelenyuk, V. (2020). Econometric analysis of productivity: Theory and implementation in R. In Vinod, H. D. and Rao, C., editors, *Financial, Macro and Micro Econometrics Using R*, volume 42 of *Handbook of Statistics*, 267–97. Elsevier.

Simar, L. (2007). How to improve the performances of DEA/FDH estimators in the presence of noise? *Journal of Productivity Analysis*, 28(3): 183–201.

Simar, L., Van Keilegom, I., and Zelenyuk, V. (2017). Nonparametric least squares methods for stochastic frontier models. *Journal of Productivity Analysis*, 47(3): 189–204.

Simar, L., Vanhems, A., and Van Keilegom, I. (2016). Unobserved heterogeneity and endogeneity in nonparametric frontier estimation. *Journal of Econometrics*, 190(2): 360–73.

Simar, L. and Wilson, P. (2007). Estimation and inference in two-stage, semi-parametric models of production processes. *Journal of Econometrics*, 136(1): 31–64.

Simar, L. and Wilson, P. W. (2011). Two-stage DEA: Caveat emptor. *Journal of Productivity Analysis*, 36(2): 205–18.

Simar, L. and Zelenyuk, V. (2006). On testing equality of distributions of technical efficiency scores. *Econometric Reviews*, 25(4): 497–522.

Simar, L. and Zelenyuk, V. (2007). Statistical inference for aggregates of Farrell-type efficiencies. *Journal of Applied Econometrics*, 22(7): 1367–94.

Simar, L. and Zelenyuk, V. (2011). Stochastic FDH/DEA estimators for frontier analysis. *Journal of Productivity Analysis*, 36(1): 1–20.

Simar, L. and Zelenyuk, V. (2018). Central limit theorems for aggregate efficiency. *Operations Research*, 166(1): 139–49.

Simar, L. and Zelenyuk, V. (2020). Improving finite sample approximation by central limit theorems for estimates from data envelopment analysis. *European Journal of Operational Research*, 284(3): 1002–15.

Simper, R., Hall, M. J. B., Liu, W., Zelenyuk, V., and Zhou, Z. (2017). How relevant is the choice of risk management control variable to non-parametric bank profit efficiency analysis? The case of South Korean banks. *Annals of Operations Research*, 250(1): 105–27.

Splawa-Neyman, J., Dabrowska, D. M., and Speed, T. P. (1990). On the application of probability theory to agricultural experiments. *Statistical Science*, 5(4): 465–72.

Sturm, J.-E. and Williams, B. (2004). Foreign bank entry, deregulation and bank efficiency: Lessons from the Australian experience. *Journal of Banking and Finance*, 28(7): 1775–99.

Thistlethwaite, D. L. and Campbell, D. T. (1960). Regression-discontinuity analysis: An alternative to the ex post facto experiment. *Journal of Educational Psychology*, 51: 309–17.

Thompson, R. G., Langemeier, L. N., Lee, C.-T., Lee, E., and Thrall, R. M. (1990). The role of multiplier bounds in efficiency analysis with application to Kansas farming. *Journal of Econometrics*, 46(1–2): 93–108.

Trezevant, R. (1992). Debt financing and tax status: Tests of the substitution effect and the tax exhaustion hypothesis using firms' responses to the economic recovery tax act of 1981. *The Journal of Finance*, 47(4): 1557–68.

Tsionas, E. G. and Kumbhakar, S. C. (2014). Firm heterogeneity, persistent and transient technical inefficiency: A generalized true random-effects model. *Journal of Applied Econometrics*, 29(1): 110–32.

Tsionas, E. G. and Papadakis, E. N. (2010). A Bayesian approach to statistical inference in stochastic DEA. *Omega*, 38(5): 309–14.

Tyteca, D. (1996). On the measurement of the environmental performance of firms—a literature review and a productive efficiency perspective. *Journal of Environmental Management*, 46(3): 281–308.

Von Neumann, J. (1945). A model of general equilibrium. *Review of Economic Studies*, 13(1): 1–9.

Wang, H.-J. and Schmidt, P. (2002). One-step and two-step estimation of the effects of exogenous variables on technical efficiency levels. *Journal of Productivity Analysis*, 18(2): 129–44.

Wheelock, D. C. and Wilson, P. W. (2000). Why do banks disappear? The determinants of U.S. bank failures and acquisitions. *The Review of Economics and Statistics*, 82(1): 127–38.

Wooldridge, J. (2013). *Introductory Econometrics: A Modern Approach*. Mason, OH: South-Western, 5th edition.

Zelenyuk, N., Faff, R., and Pathan, S. (2019). Size-conditioned mandatory capital adequacy disclosure and bank intermediation. *Accounting & Finance*, https://doi.org/10.1111/acfi.12536.

Zelenyuk, N., Faff, R., and Pathan, S. (2020). The impact of voluntary capital adequacy disclosure on bank lending and liquidity creation. *Accounting & Finance*, forthcoming.

Zelenyuk, N. and Zelenyuk, V. (2014). Regional and ownership drivers of bank efficiency. Working Paper 11, Centre for Efficiency and Productivity Analysis.

Zelenyuk, V. (2020). Aggregation of inputs and outputs prior to data envelopment analysis under big data. *European Journal of Operational Research*, 282(1): 172–87.

10.   Empirical methods in social epidemiology
Christopher F. Baum

1.   INTRODUCTION

This chapter presents research methods commonly used in empirical microeconomics that are becoming increasingly relevant to research in social epidemiology. As many economists may not be familiar with this field, a definition is in order. While epidemiology is "the study of the distribution and determinants of states of health in populations", social epidemiology is "that branch of epidemiology concerned with the way that social structures, institutions, and relationships influence health" (Berkman and Kawachi, 2014, pp. 1–2). Research into the social determinants of health includes "both specific features of and pathways by which societal conditions affect health" (Krieger, 2001, p. 697). Krieger argues that social epidemiology

> is distinguished by its insistence on explicitly investigating social determinants of population distributions of health, disease, and wellbeing, rather than treating such determinants as mere background to biomedical phenomena. (p. 693)

This distinction clarifies why the field should be of interest to many economic researchers, as these social determinants are likely to include a number of socioeconomic factors that are the focus of labor economists and those studying poverty, the economics of discrimination and the economics of gender. Understanding the origins of health disparities and analyzing the policies that have been used to address them involve the same tools employed by economists to study disparities in income, wealth and human capital within and between societies. From a methodological standpoint, multi-level analysis is often employed, in which factors influencing outcomes are measured at different levels: individual, household, neighborhood, city, state or country. Health status may depend not only on an individual's characteristics but also on the characteristics of the area in which they live or work. Aspects of their local environment such as the availability of health care, access to outlets selling nutritious food, enforcement of sanitary housing laws, prevalence of air pollution and access to public transportation may all have important influences on individuals' well-being in terms of both physical and mental health. Given this confluence of research interests, it is not surprising that the empirical methods appropriate for research in social epidemiology overlap those widely applied in empirical microeconomics.

In an invited commentary, Hawkins and Baum (2016) promoted an interdisciplinary approach to policy evaluation. They suggested that social epidemiologists working with observational data should become acquainted with empirical methodologies commonly employed in economics, such as difference-in-difference models, in order to resolve problems of reverse causation and unobserved confounders in those data. In evaluating health policies, they argued

> Researchers need to build networks across disciplines and harvest state-representative data to rigorously test nascent and established policies to determine for whom and in what context are policies working (or not). In particular, the unintended consequences and downstream effects of policies must

be examined and balanced with the intended health, social, or economic benefits. . . . In summary, we want to challenge economists to think more like epidemiologists and consider not just the overall effect of policies but also whom they may be affecting and whether they are increasing disparities. Equally, epidemiologists need to think more like economists and use rigorous methods for policy evaluation. (p. 541)

This chapter presents several of those empirical methods that may be of particular relevance to this argument, with examples of their employment. These include fixed effects models, instrumental variables methods, difference-in-difference models, binary and ordered response models, count data models, generalized linear models and conditional mixed-process models. The discussion of each of these modeling techniques is necessarily brief, with references to more detailed presentations in the literature.

2.   FIXED EFFECTS MODELS

Empirical research in social epidemiology using observational data often raises concerns over unobserved confounders. If the data are longitudinal data or panel data, with repeated observations on each individual or household identified by subscripts i and t, we could represent a linear regression model as

$$y_{i,t} = X_{i,t}\beta + \alpha_i + \epsilon_{i,t},$$ (10.1)

where the X matrix does not contain a units vector, as the coefficient α_i is allowed to differ across individuals, capturing unobserved heterogeneity at the individual level. If there is unobserved heterogeneity, the subset F test $\alpha_i = \alpha^*$, $\forall i$ will reject its null hypothesis.

As there may be hundreds or thousands of individuals or households in the data, we apply the within transformation, producing a fixed effects model. That transformation, $z_{i,t}^* = (z_{i,t} - \bar{z}_i)$, removes individual-specific means from each variable. That implies that any time-invariant factor, such as gender or race, cannot be included in the model. The original data contain both within variation (individuals' measures varying over time) and between variation (some individuals have higher mean values than do others). The fixed effects estimator removes the between variation, and the model will have explanatory power if and only if the movements over time of the demeaned X are correlated with the movements over time of the demeaned y.

By the same logic, fixed time effects can be included in a panel data model such as

$$y_{i,t} = X_{i,t}\beta + \alpha_i + \lambda_t + \epsilon_{i,t},$$ (10.2)

where the λ_t parameters capture time-varying factors. The within transformation is applied to remove the mean value of each variable over all panel units for each time period. This allows all "macro" factors that affect every individual at a point in time to be captured. However, this implies that any factor that does not vary over individuals at a point in time cannot be included in the equation to be estimated. If the number of time periods is not too large, a set of indicator variables for each time period can be included, leaving one out to prevent perfect collinearity. A Wald F test for the joint significance of the estimated λ_t parameters will indicate whether there is unobserved heterogeneity in the time dimension.

The rationale for using fixed individual effects and fixed time effects arises due to unobserved heterogeneity. In a pure cross-sectional dataset, each individual has heterogeneous characteristics affecting their behavior, but their idiosyncratic variation is captured in the equation's error term. The key assumption that permits use of regression techniques states that the distribution of the included factors is statistically independent of the distribution of the error term ϵ; that is, $E[\epsilon \,|X] = 0$: the zero conditional mean assumption. If a relevant explanatory variable is omitted from the equation, this assumption is violated, and standard regression estimates will be biased and inconsistent.

Even if there are no omitted explanatory variables, once we add observations for each individual over time, the set of error terms for that individual are likely to be correlated with included factors in the equation due to idiosyncratic differences between individuals, violating the zero conditional mean assumption. It is likely that any set of quantifiable factors that might be added to the equation will fail to capture some aspects of the unobserved heterogeneity. For instance, an individual's aptitude or intelligence is likely to influence their wage earnings, but we may not be able to reliably measure those factors. Likewise, in the time dimension, we might identify a number of macro-level factors that influence the outcome, but that list is likely to be incomplete. Fixed effects models deal with these issues by subsuming all heterogeneous aspects of the individual (or time period) in the estimated fixed effect.

2.1   Fixed Effects at the Group Level

Fixed effects can also be used in a context where they identify groups of observations rather than individual observations to allow for the fact that the heterogeneity to be captured appears at a higher level of aggregation. For instance, we might include fixed effects (using indicator variables) to group households into census tracts, cities, counties or states. In that context, we could capture differences in the average level of the outcome variable across those geographic units without explicitly specifying the pathways by which geography matters. Do health outcomes across geographic areas differ due to differences in household income, housing costs, pollution levels or the availability of supermarkets? Rather than attempting to assemble a comprehensive list of potential factors, we could include geographic indicator variables to capture all heterogeneous effects.

Although fixed effects are often considered as merely shift factors for the conditional mean of the outcome variable, indicator variables defined at the group level can be interacted with other variables to render those variables' marginal effects dependent on group membership. For instance, in a dataset where individuals are members of one of G groups, we might estimate the model

$$y_{i,t} = (G_g \times X_{i,t})\beta_g + G_g^{*}\gamma_g + \epsilon_{i,t} \tag{10.3}$$

where the G_g are a set of indicator variables denoting group membership. In this specification, each group has its own vector of estimated parameters, β_g, and all but one of the groups (denoted G^{*}) has a parameter γ_g capturing a group-level shift in the conditional mean. Subset F tests can be used to assess the importance of between-group variation in both the slope coefficients of the X variables and the intercepts over groups. As the i individuals are nested within groups, this specification cannot make use of individual fixed effects in the context of panel data, as those effects would be perfectly collinear with group-level fixed effects.

As an example of the employment of fixed effects in an epidemiological context, consider Noelke et al. (2019), who model 149 million US births to evaluate the impact of economic downturns on birth outcomes such as preterm birth. The authors fit linear probability models (as well as logistic regression models) for the probability of adverse birth outcomes, explained by the average unemployment rate in their state from three months prior to conception, during the first trimester and during the second and third trimesters. Their model includes 51 state fixed effects, 470 calendar date monthly fixed effects and 51 interactions between state fixed effects and linear trends. Those interactions allow for state-specific trends, which

> control for time-varying state-level variables that confound the association between economic conditions and birth outcomes. (p. 1095)

Using this empirical strategy, the authors find sizable and statistically significant effects of economic conditions on birth outcomes, which differ considerably across ethnicity and levels of education.

3. INSTRUMENTAL VARIABLES MODELS

Another approach to the problem of unobserved heterogeneity, or unobserved confounders, relies on the method of instrumental variables (IV) estimation. This method is a generalization of ordinary least squares (OLS) regression, $y = X\beta + u$, in that a second set of variables Z is defined: the matrix of instruments. If there are k columns in the regressor matrix, there must be $l \geq k$ columns in the Z matrix. The special case of OLS regression is defined by $X = Z$.

A model may violate the zero conditional mean assumption because the outcome y is jointly determined with one or more of the X variables: the problem of simultaneity, or reverse causation. Variables that are jointly determined with the outcome variable are said to be endogenous in the model, while those that are not are said to be exogenous. In the context of a model fit to data with time subscripts, we can also characterize variables as predetermined; that is, $X_{i,t}$ may be jointly determined with $y_{i,t}$, but $X_{i,t-1}, X_{i,t-2}$ or even $y_{i,t-1}$ are merely past history at time t. In econometric terms, they cannot be strictly exogenous (that is, statistically independent of the error process past, present and future) but they can be weakly exogenous, serving as their own instruments in an IV context. A strictly exogenous variable might be a time trend or seasonal indicator variable, or an environmental factor such as temperature or the level of $PM_{2.5}$ pollutants in the atmosphere.

Simultaneity, or the presence of endogenous explanatory variables, is often given as the textbook example requiring the use of IV techniques. But from a mathematical standpoint, that violation may also arise through the omission of relevant variables, leading to a correlation between regressor and error.[1] To produce consistent estimates, we must define appropriate instruments. The instrument matrix Z can be partitioned into $[Z1|Z2]$, where $Z1$ are the excluded instruments—the variables not included in the model—and $Z2$ are exogenous (and predetermined) variables included in X, serving as their own instruments. The excluded instruments are variables that satisfy three conditions:

1. An element of $Z1$ must not be correlated with u.

2. An element of $Z1$ must have a nontrivial correlation with the elements of X that require instruments.
3. An element of $Z1$ must be properly excluded from X.

The methods of two-stage least squares (TSLS) and IV-GMM (IV using the generalized method of moments) can be used to estimate an IV regression.[2] If $l > k$, the model is said to be overidentified, and condition 1 can be tested by a Sargan–Hansen test. It is always preferable to have $l > k$, as we cannot evaluate condition 1 in an exactly identified model where $l = k$. Thankfully, nonlinear transformations of valid instruments are themselves valid instruments, so that if Z_i is valid, then Z_i^2 will also be valid unless Z_i is an indicator variable. Likewise, if Z_{1i} and Z_{2i} are valid instruments, $(Z_{1i} \times Z_{2i})$ should be as well.

Condition 2 can be tested by examination of the "first stage" models fit by TSLS or IV-GMM. Condition 3 can be tested in the context of an overidentified model by including the instrument in the estimated equation, where it should not have a statistically significant coefficient.

Although a number of epidemiological studies have made use of IV techniques, some have misinterpreted aspects of the method, for instance, referring to IV estimates as being potentially unbiased. Unlike OLS regression estimates, which under appropriate assumptions will be unbiased, IV estimates are innately biased. The rationale for their use lies in their consistency if the conditions are satisfied, leading to a bias that should be smaller than that of OLS estimates. Research into the effect of "weak instruments" suggests that IV methods may not reduce bias if instruments are sufficiently weak: the problem that condition 2 essentially may not be satisfied.[3]

The Durbin–Wu–Hausman test[4] can be used to compare the estimates from OLS and IV of the same model. The underlying concept of the Hausman test is that if both OLS and IV estimators are consistent—honing in on the population parameters as sample size increases—then their point estimates should not systematically differ. In the presence of simultaneity bias, the OLS point estimates will be inconsistent and might be expected to sizably differ from IV point estimates, which will be consistent if the model is correctly specified. The null hypothesis of the Hausman test is that OLS is appropriate and will be unbiased and relatively efficient, exhibiting greater precision. If that hypothesis is rejected, there is clear evidence against reliance on the OLS results, and IV estimates are to be preferred.

One of the challenges of using IV methods is the choice of suitable instruments. Ertefaie et al. (2017, p. 359), in analyzing choice of treatment for diabetes, suggest that calendar time, provider preference, geographic distance to a specialty care provider and characteristics of a health insurance plan might be used as instruments to account for unmeasured confounders.

In Pesko and Baum (2016), the authors investigate whether individuals smoke in times of short-term stress in order to self-medicate that stress. As there could be complex associations between stress and the prevalence of smoking, the authors test for exogeneity in the relationship and find clear evidence of endogeneity, requiring an IV approach. The underlying data represent interviews conducted over a period of time. The temporal distance between the date of interview and 11 September 2001 (the events of 9/11) was used as an instrument for short-term stress, while measures of cigarette price changes and distance to state borders are used as instruments for smoking. When accounting for endogeneity, the authors found no evidence of smoking affecting short-term stress, but a consistent positive effect of short-term stress on smoking.

In Kim et al. (2011), the authors evaluate the associations between area-level social capital and health in a cross-national setting, arguing that estimates from prior research may exhibit bias due to reverse causation. The results of Hausman tests clearly reject the validity of OLS estimates of this relationship. As instruments for country-level trust measures derived from social surveys, they use measures of perceptions of corruption, population density and religious fractionalization. Their findings

> support the presence of beneficial effects of higher country-level trust on self-rated health. Previous findings for contextual social capital using traditional regression may have underestimated the true associations. Given the close linkages between self-rated health and all-cause mortality, the public health gains from raising social capital within and across countries may be large. (p. 1689)

4. DIFFERENCE-IN-DIFFERENCES MODELS

A technique for policy evaluation commonly applied in economics is the difference-in-differences (DiD) model.[5] This model has become more frequently used in social epidemiological studies, as it can yield estimates of causal effects if its underlying assumptions are satisfied. The DiD model can be applied in the context of repeated cross-sections, before and after a policy change, as well as the context of panel, or longitudinal data. In its simplest form, measurements of an outcome variable are available for two groups: a treatment group of those affected by the policy, and a control group unaffected by the policy. OLS regression techniques can be used to estimate the model

$$y_i = \mu + \beta s_i + \gamma t_i + \delta(s_i \cdot t_i) + \epsilon_i, \tag{10.4}$$

where we have data for $i = 1, \ldots, N$ observations, with $s_i = 1$ for those in the treatment group and 0 for those in the control group. Each observation is dated $t_i = 0$ prior to treatment or $t_i = 1$ post-treatment. The conditional means of y_i can be computed as

$$Ey_{00} = \hat{\mu}, s_i = 0, t_i = 0 \tag{10.5}$$

$$Ey_{01} = \hat{\mu} + \hat{\gamma}, s_i = 0, t_i = 1$$

$$Ey_{10} = \hat{\mu} + \hat{\beta}, s_i = 1, t_i = 0$$

$$Ey_{11} = \hat{\mu} + \hat{\beta} + \hat{\gamma} + \hat{\delta}, s_i = 1, t_i = 1.$$

The first two conditional means represent the average of y for observations in the control group, reflecting the fact that they may differ over time. The third conditional mean is that of the treatment group prior to treatment, while the fourth conditional mean is that of the treatment group post-treatment. A key assumption is that of common trends: other things equal, the effect of time should be the same for the two groups, as implied by the parameter γ appearing in both of the post-treatment conditional means.

The concept of difference-in-differences is the comparison of the change, or difference, in the control group's conditional mean to the change, or difference, in the treatment group's conditional mean. If the policy had no effect, then the difference in those differences would be insignificant. If the policy was effective in altering the outcome for the treatment group, the parameter δ on the interaction term $(s_i \cdot t_i)$ is a consistent estimate of the average treatment effect, or ATE.

It has not always been realized that the DiD framework can be applied to much more general settings than that of a single policy change at a point in time, with measurements before and after the change. Difference-in-differences models can be generalized to include more than two time periods as well as multiple treatment and control groups. However, in the context of multiple periods, the validity of an important assumption must be analyzed: that the treatment and control groups followed parallel trends before the treatment was applied. The implications of this assumption and the tests that can be applied to evaluate it are fully described in Cerulli (2015), chapter 3.

In the context of panel data, we might be concerned with the impact of a particular law's adoption in different jurisdictions at different points in time. Many US states have approved the use of medical marijuana over the last decade. The control groups correspond to those states which have not adopted the law at each point in time, while the treatment groups include all states that have adopted the law.

In Coley et al. (2019), the authors analyze data from several waves of the Youth Risk Behavior Survey, conducted every other year in most US states. Associations between the prevalence of adolescent marijuana use, the legalization of medical marijuana and the decriminalization of marijuana possession were evaluated in a DiD framework. A logistic regression model of the use of marijuana by an individual in a particular state and year estimated its relationship to medical marijuana, decriminalization and several individual characteristics as well as other state-level factors. The authors found small, significant decreases in the likelihood of current marijuana use by high school–age adolescents in states following the adoption of medical marijuana laws. These findings are broadly similar to those presented in Cerdá et al. (2018) who used DiD models on a different survey of US adolescents.

5. BINARY AND ORDERED RESPONSE MODELS

A binary response is often the outcome to be modeled in epidemiological studie; for instance, did a woman smoke during her pregnancy? The simplest approach of a linear probability model (LPM) expresses this as an OLS regression equation of a (0,1) variable on the chosen factors. The LPM will often be found wanting as it maps a linear combination of factors and their coefficients into a predicted outcome, ignoring the interpretation of that outcome as a conditional probability. Nothing constrains the predictions to lie between (0,1), and a sufficiently large value of a significant factor can always drive the prediction out of bounds.

The alternatives of the binomial logit model or the binomial probit model avoid this difficulty by evaluating the linear combination of factors and coefficients using the cumulative distribution function (CDF) of the logistic function or the normal distribution, respectively. As the predicted values become arbitrarily close to 0 or 1 in the limit, the predictions of the logit or probit model are properly bounded. The magnitudes of their estimated coefficients are not themselves interpretable beyond sign and statistical significance. However, software estimating these models supports the computation of average marginal effects (AMEs, for example,

Stata's `margins, dydx(*)` command) for the entire sample or for subsets of the sample. By design, the marginal effects $\partial Pr[y_i = 1|X]/\partial X_{ij}$ depend upon all elements of X for individual i.

The proponents of LPMs argue that this is unnecessarily complex, and that the LPM coefficients may be quite similar to those computed as AMEs. This may be so for the entire sample, but they will differ considerably when examining a subsample of individuals, for instance, those of a particular ethnicity living in a certain state.

The choice of estimating with a logit or probit model is largely one of taste, as the CDFs of the underlying distributions are quite similar. In epidemiological studies, logistic regression is often preferred, as the closed form of the logistic distribution supports the computation of odds ratios (in Stata, the option on the `logit` command and the default output from the `logistic` command). If the selected confidence interval for the odds ratio does not contain 1.0, then that factor has a statistically significant effect on the outcome.

The fixed-effect approach discussed in section 2.1 can also be used in a logit model by including one or more sets of indicator variables. In the panel data context, this model becomes the conditional logit (in Stata, the `clogit` command), incorporating fixed effects for each individual. However, in that context, the only individuals entering the model are those who experienced a change in their binary status. The random-effects version of this panel estimator (in Stata, the `xtlogit` command's default) overcomes this limitation.

In Ghiani, Hawkins, and Baum (2019a), the authors analyze nine biennial waves of the Youth Behavioral Risk Survey (YRBS), evaluating US high school students' responses to several questions related to school safety. These included dichotomous measures of being threatened or injured by a weapon on school property; of carrying a weapon on school properly; weapon or gun carrying at any location; and missing school due to feeling unsafe. The study considered associations of these responses with a state-level index of gun control developed by Siegel et al. (2017), incorporating 133 firearms laws over more than two decades. Logistic regression models were used to estimate difference-in-difference models capturing the effects of state-level changes in their firearms laws over the period of study. Both state and year fixed effects were included in the analysis, which was also stratified by age, gender and ethnicity of the respondents where those factors were found to be significant. The authors found

> evidence that stronger gun control was associated with a decreased likelihood of students carrying weapons and being threatened with weapons at school, as well as an improved perception of school safety. (p. 5)

Modeling of binary outcomes with logistic regression or probit models can be generalized to the case of ordered outcomes, using ordered logit or ordered probit models. The outcome variable is considered as an ordinal measurement, rather than a cardinal measurement, so that the model considers whether individual i chose outcome j from the ordered choices $j = 1, \ldots,$ J. This generalizes the binary outcome model, where zero is taken to be the threshold between choosing to act or not (for instance, whether or not to have a child or accept a vaccine). In the ordered model with J choices, there are $J - 1$ threshold values, which also must be estimated. The impact of a policy change on an ordered outcome can be viewed as reallocating the probabilities of choosing each outcome, making it more likely to choose a higher (lower) outcome while making it less likely to choose a lower (higher) outcome, given that the probabilities must always sum to unity.

In evaluating the impact of state tobacco control policies on adolescent smoking frequency, Hawkins et al. (2016a) used an ordered probit regression model. Survey responses were grouped into four categories, defining the number of days per month that adolescents smoked: 0, 1–5, 6–29 and 30 days. Combined with a model of smoking prevalence, the authors found that higher cigarette taxes decreased the overall likelihood of smoking among younger adolescents. The adoption of smoke-free legislation not only decreased the overall likelihood of smoking, but reduced the frequency of smoking per month.

6. COUNT DATA MODELS

Although textbook examples of difference-in-difference models employ linear regression, the DiD methodology can be applied in the context of other estimation techniques. In section 5, I discuss the use of DiD in the context of logistic regression. The method can also be applied to the analysis of count data, in which the outcome variable is expressed as a non-negative integer. The basic technique for count data analysis is Poisson regression, in which the outcome is expressed as a function of a number of explanatory variables. The negative binomial (NB) model, a generalization of the Poisson model, is appropriate where the underlying assumption of Poisson regression—that the mean of the error distribution is also its variance—is rejected. That rejection, known as overdispersion, implies that an additional parameter should be estimated to capture the degree to which the variance exceeds the mean. An extension of the NB model to capture the phenomenon of zero inflation—where a sizable fraction of observations contain zero counts—is known as the zero-inflated negative binomial (ZINB) model, in which one or more additional parameters determine the likelihood that an observation will be nonzero.

A negative binomial model was used by Hawkins and Baum (2014) in a study of maternal smoking behavior. In that analysis of over 17 million US birth certificate records, logistic regression models were used to analyze whether a mother smoked during her pregnancy and how this behavior may have been affected by increases in cigarette taxes. Sizable variations in maternal smoking were found over age groups, ethnicity and the level of education. Those who reported smoking also reported the number of cigarettes smoked daily, which was then modeled in a NB framework. The authors found meaningful associations between tobacco control policies and the number of cigarettes smoked among high school dropouts and those with a high school degree.

Negative binomial regression was employed by Hawkins et al. (2016b) in a study of children's emergency department (ED) visits for several common diagnoses and their association with state smoke-free legislation in three New England states and their municipalities, controlling for cigarette excise taxes. Analysis at the municipality level was required as many cities and towns passed smoke-free legislation prior to statewide laws. Counts of ED visits were computed at the municipality level, varying by age category, gender and calendar month over an 8–10-year period. Evidence of overdispersion recommended use of the NB model rather than Poisson regression. The initiation of smoke-free legislation, as well as health care reform in Massachusetts, the first US state to mandate universal coverage, was associated with reductions in ED visits for selected age groups, as evidenced by estimated adjusted incidence rate ratios (aIRRs).

In a recent study, Ghiani et al. (2019b) applied a DiD approach in a zero-inflated negative binomial model to analyze US data on suicides over 10 years, grouped as count data for each state, year, race/ethnicity, sex and age bracket. These counts are modeled as a function of a state-level index of gun control developed by Siegel et al. (2017), incorporating 133 firearms laws and a number of controls. Although the primary relationship of interest was firearm suicides, the authors also considered non-firearm suicides (which represent almost 50 per cent of total US suicides) as alternatives; in a state where access to firearms is more limited, other means may be more commonly employed. In their analysis of the relationship between firearm suicides and the index of gun control, the authors found that those states that strengthened firearms laws were likely to experience lower rates of firearm suicides. The size of effects differed over sex and ethnicity.

7.   GENERALIZED LINEAR MODELS

Many variables of interest, such as individual health expenditures, are highly skewed. Standard regression techniques are not well suited to dealing with these outcomes and may also be prone to producing negative predicted values. In this case, a generalized linear model, or GLM, might be a more appropriate modeling technique. GLMs, first described by McCullagh and Nelder (1989), are generalizations of the regression framework. They rely on three assumptions: (i) an index function, $x_i'\beta$, specifies the relationship between covariates and the outcome variable. It is linear in x, but may be nonlinear in underlying variables, so that x might include polynomials, interactions, and the like. (ii) A link function $g(\cdot)$ relates the expectation of the outcome variable, μ, to the index function, $g\{E(y_i|x_i)\}$. This implies that the inverse of the link function produces the conditional mean of the outcome variable. For instance, if $g(\cdot)$ is $\log(\cdot)$, the mean of y is $\exp(x_i'\hat{\beta})$. Other links include the identity link (which corresponds to regression via maximum likelihood), the logit link, the probit link and the power link, among others. (iii) The outcome y is generated by a distribution in the linear exponential family, including Gaussian, inverse Gaussian, gamma, Bernoulli, Poisson and negative binomial. Continuous outcomes make use of Gaussian and inverse Gaussian distributions, while Poisson and negative binomial are applied to count data, Bernoulli to binary data, and gamma to duration data.

Researchers often use a log-linear regression model, where the outcome variable is the logarithm of a positive quantity. The resulting coefficients are then semielasticities, or predicted percentage changes, for a unit increase in a covariate. The difficulty with this model is prediction, as a standard regression model will produce predictions of $\log(y)$ rather than y itself. This gives rise to retransformation bias, as applying $\exp(\cdot)$ to the predicted series does not yield unbiased predictions. Although there are several proposed adjustments that mitigate this bias, they cannot eradicate it. In contrast, a GLM with errors of the Gaussian family with a log link will produce predictions of the original outcome variable, without the need for any transformation.

GLMs can also be applied to models in which the outcome is bounded, such as grouped data in which the fraction of individuals who choose to receive an influenza vaccination is recorded. Some researchers would employ a two-limit tobit model to apply the constraints of the outcome lying in the unit interval. Papke and Wooldridge (1996) argued for the use of a "fractional logit" model in this context, which is a GLM with a Bernoulli error and a logit link function, estimated with a robust variance–covariance matrix.[6] A formal test of the adequacy of the fractional logit specification versus the two-limit tobit specification can be performed, as described by Pregibon (1980).[7]

GLM techniques were applied to the analysis of workplace homicide rates in the US over the 2010–17 period by Sabbath et al. (2020). They related changes in state-level firearms laws over the period, expressed by an index with a number of categories, to the strictly positive values of homicides by state–year. The GLM used a log link and gamma-distributed errors, clustered by state. A number of state-level time-varying factors were used as controls, as well as year fixed effects. The authors found that variations in state firearms laws—both strengthening and weakening over this period in various states—had clear effects on the incidence of workplace homicides.

8.   CONDITIONAL MIXED-PROCESS MODELS

In modeling outcome variables, it may be necessary to specify multiple outcomes and their causal linkages. For instance, we might model the probability that a pregnant woman smokes as one equation, and use the predicted probability from that equation as a factor in a second equation that models the baby's birthweight for smoking mothers. In such a model, the potential correlation of the error processes of those two equations should be taken into account, requiring the use of a system estimation approach.

Models of this sort, combining continuous outcomes with binary, censored, ordered, multinomial or fractional outcomes, can be estimated with a community-contributed Stata routine known as cmp (Roodman, 2011). Many of the same capabilities are available in official Stata's gsem command, supporting generalized structural equation modeling. The cmp acronym stands for conditional mixed-process modeling. The conditional aspect is that the data entering each equation may differ: for instance, in the example, we include all pregnant women in the equation predicting smoking behavior, but only include those who smoke in the birthweight outcome equation. The mixed-process label refers to the differing nature of outcomes described.[8] Likewise, the "generalized" aspect of gsem refers to the notion that traditional structural equation models (SEMs) only model continuous outcomes, while the generalized form allows for outcomes that are not assumed to be normally distributed.

In an analysis of state tobacco control policies, Hawkins and Baum (2019) used a conditional mixed-process model to evaluate impacts on the prevalence of maternal smoking during pregnancy and birth outcomes. Their analysis considers over 26 million births in the US over the 2005–15 period. The first equation in their model revealed that higher state-level cigarette taxes served to reduce maternal smoking during pregnancy, with wide variations in effects across race/ethnicity and maternal education. This was linked to a second equation, using the predicted probability of smoking as a covariate, which expressed the outcome in terms of changes in babies' birthweight as well as several birth outcomes, such as low birth weight, preterm birth and small for gestational age.

9.   CONCLUSIONS

Analyses in the field of social epidemiology have been enhanced by the availability of population-level datasets containing detailed information on individuals' characteristics and health-related factors and outcomes. The burgeoning data produced by the COVID-19 pandemic have supported many fruitful investigations into the evolution of this phenomenon. But as in all studies making use of "big data", it is not enough to have access to massive datasets. Researchers also need to employ the appropriate statistical methodologies for their analyses to gain credibility and survive rigorous peer review. As Hawkins and Baum (2016) argued, social epidemiologists, economists and econometricians should cooperate in understanding the milieu of each others' disciplines, taking from each what will best address the research questions at hand. This chapter provides an introduction to some of the methodologies developed in applied microeconometrics, with examples of their application in social epidemiology.

NOTES

1. Violation of the zero conditional mean assumption may also be caused by "errors-in-variables", or measurement error, in the explanatory factors.
2. See Baum et al. (2003, 2007) for more details on IV methods.
3. See section 7.3 of Baum et al. (2007) for details.
4. See section 5.1 of Baum et al. (2003) for details.
5. See Imbens and Wooldridge (2009) for an excellent survey.
6. In Stata, the `fracreg logit` and `fracreg probit` commands provide the appropriate GLM specifications for the fractional logit and fractional probit models.
7. In Stata, see `linktest`.
8. Although we do not discuss it further, both `cmp` and `gsem` have the capability to estimate multi-level models where coefficients and errors may appear at different levels of a hierarchy.

REFERENCES

Baum, C. F., Schaffer, M. E., & Stillman, S. (2003). Instrumental variables and GMM: Estimation and testing. *Stata Journal*, *3*, 1–31.

Baum, C. F., Schaffer, M. E., & Stillman, S. (2007). Enhanced routines for instrumental variables/generalized method of moments estimation and testing. *Stata Journal*, *7* (4), 465–506.

Berkman, L., & Kawachi, I. (2014). A historical framework for social epidemiology: Social determinants of population health. In L. Berkman, I. Kawachi, & M. Glymour (Eds.), *Social epidemiology* (pp. 1–16). Oxford, UK: Oxford University Press.

Cerdá, M., Sarvet, A. L., Wall, M., Feng, T., Keyes, K. M., Galea, S., & Hasin, D. S. (2018). Medical marijuana laws and adolescent use of marijuana and other substances: Alcohol, cigarettes, prescription drugs, and other illicit drugs. *Drug and Alcohol Dependence*, *183*, 62–8.

Cerulli, G. (2015). *Econometric Evaluation of Socio-Economic Programs*. Springer.

Coley, R. L., Hawkins, S. S., Ghiani, M., Kruzik, C., & Baum, C. F. (2019). A quasi-experimental evaluation of marijuana policies and youth marijuana use. *American Journal of Drug and Alcohol Abuse*, *45*, 292–303.

Ertefaie, A., Small, D. S., Flory, J. H., & Hennessy, S. (2017). A tutorial on the use of instrumental variables in pharmacoepidemiology. *Pharmacoepidemiology and Drug Safety*, *26* (4), 357–67.

Ghiani, M., Hawkins, S. S., & Baum, C. F. (2019a). Gun laws and school safety. *Journal of Epidemiology & Community Health*, *73*, 509–15.

Ghiani, M., Hawkins, S. S., & Baum, C. F. (2019b). Associations between gun laws and suicides. *American Journal of Epidemiology*, *188*, 1254–61.

Hawkins, S. S., Bach, N., & Baum, C. F. (2016a). Impact of tobacco control policies on adolescent smoking. *Journal of Adolescent Health*, *58*, 679–85.

Hawkins, S. S., & Baum, C. F. (2014). Impact of state cigarette taxes on disparities in maternal smoking during pregnancy. *American Journal of Public Health*, *104* (8), 1464–70.

Hawkins, S. S., & Baum, C. F. (2016). Invited commentary: An interdisciplinary approach for policy evaluation. *American Journal of Epidemiology*, *183* (6), 539–41.

Hawkins, S. S., & Baum, C. F. (2019). The downstream effects of state tobacco control policies on maternal smoking during pregnancy and birth outcomes. *Drug and Alcohol Dependence*, *205*, 107634. https://doi.org/10.1016/j.drugalcdep.2019.107634.

Hawkins, S. S., Hristakeva, S., Gottlieb, M., & Baum, C. F. (2016b). Reduction in emergency department visits for children's asthma, ear infections, and respiratory infections after the introduction of state smoke-free legislation. *Preventive Medicine*, *89*, 278–85.

Imbens, G. W., & Wooldridge, J. M. (2009, March). Recent developments in the econometrics of program evaluation. *Journal of Economic Literature, 47* (1), 5–86.

Kim, D., Baum, C. F., Ganz, M. L., Subramanian, S., & Kawachi, I. (2011). The contextual effects of social capital on health: A cross-national instrumental variable analysis. *Social Science & Medicine, 73* (12), 1689–97. https://doi.org/10.1016/j.socscimed.2011.

Krieger, N. (2001). A glossary for social epidemiology. *Journal of Epidemiology and Community Health, 55* (10), 693–700.

McCullagh, P., & Nelder, J. A. (1989). *Generalized Linear Models* (2nd ed.). London: Chapman & Hall.

Noelke, C., Chen, Y.-H., Osypuk, T. L., & Acevedo-Garcia, D. (2019). Economic downturns and inequities in birth outcomes: Evidence from 149 million US births. *American Journal of Epidemiology, 188* (6), 1092–100.

Papke, L. E., & Wooldridge, J. M. (1996). Econometric methods for fractional response variables with an application to 401(k) plan participation rates. *Journal of Applied Econometrics, 11* (6), 619–32.

Pesko, M. F., & Baum, C. F. (2016). The self-medication hypothesis: Evidence from terrorism and cigarette accessibility. *Economics & Human Biology, 22,* 94–102.

Pregibon, D. (1980). Goodness of link tests for generalized linear models. *Applied Statistics, 29* (1), 15–24.

Roodman, D. (2011). Fitting fully observed recursive mixed-process models with cmp. *Stata Journal, 11* (2), 159–206.

Sabbath, E., Hawkins, S. S., & Baum, C. F. (2020). State-level changes in firearm laws and workplace homicide rates: United States, 2011 to 2017. *American Journal of Public Health, 110* (2), 230–36.

Siegel, M., Pahn, M., Xuan, Z., Ross, C., Galea, S., Kalesan, B., . . . Goss, K. (2017). Firearm-related laws in all 50 US states, 1991–2016. *American Journal of Public Health, 107,* 1122–9.

PART III

POLICY EVALUATION
AND CAUSALITY

11. Policy evaluation using causal inference methods[*]
Denis Fougère and Nicolas Jacquemet

1. INTRODUCTION

Over the past twenty years, the number of impact evaluation studies, whether experimental or quasi-experimental, has increased exponentially. These methods have been applied in many research fields. For example, in the field of educational policy, the number of randomized controlled trials (RCTs) that have resulted in international publications has increased from just a few in 1980 to more than 80 per year since 2010 (see Figure 11.1). Quasi-experimental evaluations have followed a similar trend and nowadays together constitute what some have called an "empirical revolution" (Angrist and Pischke, 2010). These studies and the quantitative assessments that they contain are resources of prime importance when it comes to choosing, designing and implementing public policies.

The recent publication of several reference articles and books also shows just how developed and diverse econometric evaluation methods have become. These include the books by Imbens and Rubin (2015), Lee (2016) and Sperlich and Frölich (2019), which follow on from the survey papers by Angrist and Krueger (1999), Heckman et al. (1999), Heckman and Vytlacil (2007a,b), Abbring and Heckman (2007) and Imbens and Wooldridge (2009). The *Handbook of Field Experiments* published by Duflo and Banerjee (2017) is the reference book on randomized field experiments. For laboratory experiments, the book by Jacquemet and L'Haridon (2018) is the most recent reference. Finally, the list of papers on causal inference methods published in the best international economic or statistical journals over the past 30 years is too long to be included here. The interested reader will find it in the bibliographies of the mentioned works.

These methods make it possible to identify, using individual survey data, relationships between variables that can be rigorously interpreted as cause-and-effect relationships. They are based on observation and research schemes that ensure that estimated differences in outcomes (for example, in terms of earnings, employability, productivity or educational results) are mainly due to the intervention or the policy implemented, and that selection and self-selection biases that tarnish many empirical studies are significantly reduced or even eliminated. In particular, these methods aim to statistically identify so-called "counterfactual" outcomes, that is, those that would have occurred had the intervention in question not been implemented. The identification of the causal effect of the intervention on the outcome variable (its "impact") is then deduced by comparing the observed outcomes for the statistical units (unemployed people, employees, firms, students and so on) benefiting from that policy. In addition to studies directly applying them with experimental or quasi-experimental data, much work has been devoted in the last ten years to refining these methods, or to coming up with solutions to overcome some of their limitations.[1]

This chapter is devoted to presenting the developments that are particularly promising in the field of impact evaluation methods. Section 2 presents in a non-technical way these methods, both experimental and quasi-experimental, in order to familiarize the

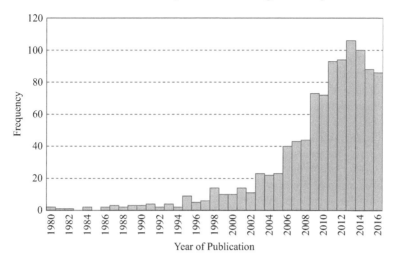

Year of Publication

Note: Number of randomized controlled trials conducted between 1980 and 2016 in the field of educational policy that have been published in international scientific journals, according to Connolly et al. (2018).

Figure 11.1 Publication trends of RCTs

reader with their general principles. Section 3 describes the canonical statistical model of potential outcomes, which is the basis of all these methods. Then it introduces the main causal estimands (that is, parameters) and presents each impact evaluation method more formally. Section 4 discusses the external validity of impact evaluation methods. The synthetic control approach, which overcomes some limitation of the difference-in-differences method, is presented in section 5. Section 6 underlines the role and the choice of explanatory variables (that is, covariates). Beyond the importance of the choice of the parameter to be estimated (which must take precedence over the choice of the identification method) and the choice of relevant covariates to be incorporated into the model, the heterogeneity of the treatment effect constitutes a significant limitation to the ability to generalize the estimated effects of an intervention in the context of a particular empirical study. That is why section 7 is devoted to methods dealing with heterogeneous effects of interventions. In section 8, we focus on the need to pay particular attention to the accuracy of the estimated effects. Section 9 emphasizes the need of replication studies, carried out by experimentation or quasi-experimentation, in order to distinguish false positives from proven effects. Finally, section 10 is devoted to the crucial issue of interference in experimental and quasi-experimental studies.

2. A NON-TECHNICAL REVIEW OF POLICY EVALUATION TECHNIQUES

To achieve this goal, the simplest experimental method, which consists in randomly drawing units that benefit from the policy to be evaluated and comparing their post-intervention situation with that of the units (individuals or firms) that do not benefit from this policy ensures that a causal relationship between the policy and the observed effect is demonstrated, without the analyst having to make overly restrictive assumptions. The other methods, known as quasi-experimental methods, seek to identify situations where, depending on a certain number of factors, the fact of benefiting from the intervention is independent of the characteristics, observable or not, of the units targeted by that intervention. These methods can be grouped into four categories, which are presented next in a non-technical manner.

Instrumental Variables. Let us suppose that we observe the wages of two groups of workers, the first group having recently benefited from an active labor market policy such as a training program, the other group having not benefited from it. Using the linear regression method, it is possible to estimate not only the effects of several variables characterizing the workers, such as age, gender, family situation, level of education, place of residence and so on, but also the effect of the participation in the training program on the post-program wage, that is, the wage received at the time of the survey. However, this simple method may produce biased estimates. The problem is that participation in the training program is not exogenous: it can not only be correlated with the observed characteristics that we have just mentioned, but also with variables not observed by the analyst, such as a desire to change profession, a desire to learn new skills, the employee's productivity as assessed by their employer and so on. Consequently, the fact of having participated in the training program is likely to be correlated with the error term of the regression, the value of that error term generally being dependent on these unobserved characteristics. This correlation is the cause of the so-called "endogeneity" bias. To deal with this problem, econometricians have for a long time used the instrumental variable method. By definition, an instrumental variable must have a very significant impact on access to the program being evaluated – in this case, the training program – without directly affecting the wage level received after participating in that program. The estimation method used in this case is the so-called "two-stage-least-squares" technique. The first step consists in regressing participation in the training program on all exogenous variables (age, gender and so on) but also on the value of the instrumental variable (which can be, for example, the date of a significant amendment made to the conditions governing access to this program). In a second step, individual wages must be regressed on the same exogenous variables and on participation in the training program, not as actually observed, but as predicted by the first regression. The coefficient associated with this "instrumented" value can be interpreted, under certain very restrictive conditions, as "the causal effect" of the training program on trainees' wages.

Matching Methods. The main purpose here is to compare beneficiaries and non-beneficiaries by neutralizing the differences due to the distribution of observable characteristics. These methods are based on two assumptions. The first stipulates that the assignment to the group of beneficiaries depends exclusively on observable exogenous characteristics and not on the anticipated outcomes of the intervention: this assumption is called the "conditional independence assumption". The second assumption is that any individual or firm has a non-zero probability (comprised strictly between 0 and 1) of being a priori a beneficiary of the intervention, whatever the characteristics of that individual or firm, or whether that the individual or the firm is actually (that is, a posteriori) a beneficiary of the intervention: this assumption is called the "overlap assumption". When these two assumptions are valid, the method consists in comparing the outcome for each beneficiary with the average of the outcomes for the non-beneficiaries who are "close" in terms of the observable characteristics (age, gender, level of education and so on), and then averaging all these differences among the group of beneficiaries. Proximity to the beneficiary under consideration, that is the choice of their "closest neighbors", can be made using a distance (such as the Euclidean distance or the Mahalanobis distance), or even more simply using a propensity score, defined as the probability of being a beneficiary of the intervention given the observable variables characterizing the individual; this probability can be estimated in a first step, using for example a logit or a probit model, independently of the value of the observed outcome variables.

Difference-in-Differences Methods. These methods are based on a simple assumption. Suppose that we observe the variations between two dates of an outcome variable such as the wage within two distinct groups. The first of these groups, called the "target group", "treated group" or "treatment group", benefits from a given intervention or an employment policy; the second, called the "control group", does not. The employment policy is implemented between the two dates under consideration. The method relies on the following assumption: in the absence of that policy, the average wage change for individuals in the treated group would have been identical to that observed in the control group (the "parallel trends" assumption). The validity of this assumption, which cannot be verified, can be assessed by the fact that, before the policy was implemented, wages evolved in the same way in both groups (that is, the so-called "common pre-trends" assumption). Unlike the previous assumption, this second one can be tested on the basis of data observed prior to the implementation of the intervention, provided that repeated observations are available during this period. This method thus exploits the longitudinal (or pseudo-longitudinal)[2] dimension of the data.

The Regression Discontinuity Method. This method can be applied when the access to an intervention or a public policy is dependent on an exogenous threshold set by the authorities in charge of that policy. This threshold may be an age condition (for retirement, for example), an employment-level threshold (for example, a tax reduction policy for firms with less than 20 employees) or a level of resources giving access to a scholarship or a tax credit. In its simplest form, regression discontinuity makes it possible to compare the average value of the outcome variable in the group of beneficiaries, for example those whose income or age is just below the eligibility threshold, with the average value of this variable in the comparable control group, composed of those whose income or age is just above that threshold. The underlying assumption is that, for people who otherwise have the same characteristics in terms of employment skills, level of education or gender, those just below and above the threshold are identical. Only sheer chance, for instance a date of birth, distinguishes them. Under these conditions, a simple difference between the means of the outcome variable (for example, the level of wage or education after the policy is implemented) makes it possible to estimate the causal effect of the intervention in question. However, this difference is only a local measure, close to the threshold, and its extrapolation to income levels or ages far from that threshold has no scientific validity. For this reason, it is said that regression discontinuity makes it possible to estimate a local average treatment effect (discussed in detail later).

Each type of method therefore corresponds to very specific assumptions. In practice, particularly when it is not possible to conduct a randomized experiment, it is important to recognize the information available to the analyst and to know which of these assumptions are most likely in order to choose the method best suited to the data available. Since the pioneering article published by LaLonde (1986), several studies have been devoted to the comparison of evaluations carried out using experimental and quasi-experimental methods, and in particular to the estimation biases that may result from using quasi-experimental methods. Due to space constraints, it is not possible to summarize the results of those comparisons here. On this topic, the reader may consult, for example, papers written by Glazerman et al. (2003), Chabé-Ferret (2015), Wong et al. (2017) and Chaplin et al. (2018).

3. THE CANONICAL IMPACT EVALUATION MODEL

From its original formulation by Rubin (1974), the canonical impact evaluation model emphasizes the heterogeneity of the response of economic agents following an intervention (or treatment) $T_i \in \{0,1\}$. In this model, each observation unit is characterized by two "potential outcomes": y_{0_i} is the outcome that would be observed for the unit i in the absence of the intervention, and y_{1_i} is the outcome that would be observed as a result of the intervention. For each unit, only one of these two effects is observed. Rather than a "causal effect", the intervention is therefore associated with a distribution of situational changes in a sample of size N: $\Delta_i = y_{1_i} - y_{0_i}, \forall i = 1, \ldots, N$. The first step of the evaluation process is therefore to choose how this distribution will be approached based on the limited information delivered by the sample. Among the many parameters that could be used to summarize this distribution, the most common are the average treatment effect and the average treatment effect on the treated.

The average treatment effect (ATE), $\Delta^{ATE} = \mathbb{E}(y_{1_i} - y_{0_i})$ measures the average change in outcome for an individual randomly selected from the population. The average treatment effect on the treated (ATT), $\Delta^{ATT} = \mathbb{E}(y_{1_i} - y_{0_i} \mid T_i = 1)$, is specific to the sub-population of individuals who actually benefit from the program. The two parameters are only equal under very restrictive assumptions. For example, they trivially coincide if the intervention is applied to the whole population (for instance, an increase in the minimum age for leaving the school system, a measure that concerns all pupils), or if the treatment is supposed to act in the same way on all the individuals $\Delta_i = \Delta (= \Delta^{ATE} = \Delta^{ATT}), \forall i$. In all other circumstances, these two parameters are distinct. They provide different information on the distribution of the causal effect: the average treatment effect on the treated measures the effectiveness of the program through the change in the beneficiaries' outcome, while the average treatment effect indicates how effective it would be if the program were to be applied to the entire population. The evaluation method chosen strongly influences the parameter that can be measured.

3.1 Causal Effects and Endogenous Participation

The observed outcome y_i is linked to the potential outcomes through the individual's treatment status: $y_i = T_i y_{1_i} + (1 - T_i) y_{0_i}$. This relationship is sufficient to highlight the two issues that evaluation must overcome: a missing data problem and the endogeneity of the treatment. The first issue arises because data only deliver partial information about either y_{1_i} for individuals who received the treatment or y_{0_i} for those who did not. Such data allow to compute the distribution of the treatment in the population, $\ell(T_i)$, as well as the distribution of the outcome resulting from the treatment among beneficiaries, $\ell(y_{1_i} \mid T_i = 1) = \ell(y_i \mid T_i = 1)$, and the distribution of the outcome absent the treatment for non-beneficiaries, $\ell(y_{0_i} \mid T_i = 0) = \ell(y_i \mid T_i = 0)$. But it does not allow to compute any of the relevant policy parameters. Evaluation methods must thus rely on counterfactual observations—information on what would have happened in a state of the world that is not observed.

Finding counterfactuals is even more challenging because of the second issue, that is, the endogenous program participation, which implies that these conditional distributions are different from the conditional ones:

$$\ell\left(y_{1_i} \mid T_i = 1\right) \neq \ell\left(y_{1_i} \mid T_i = 0\right) \neq \ell\left(y_{1_i}\right), \ell\left(y_{0_i} \mid T_i = 0\right) \neq \ell\left(y_{0_i} \mid T_i = 1\right) \neq \ell\left(y_{0_i}\right),$$

in such a way that the distribution of the outcome, both before and after the implementation of the treatment, is correlated with the treatment status. The main consequence is that the distribution of the outcome among untreated cannot be used as a counterfactual for the outcome among treated individuals. The observed sample provides information on the following parameters:

$$\mathbb{E}\left(y_i \mid T_i = 0\right) = \mathbb{E}\left(y_{0_i} \mid T_i = 0\right)$$

$$\mathbb{E}\left(y_i \mid T_i = 1\right) = \mathbb{E}\left(y_{1_i} \mid T_i = 1\right) = \mathbb{E}\left(y_{0_i} \mid T_i = 0\right) + T\left[\mathbb{E}\left(y_{1_i} \mid T_i = 1\right) - \mathbb{E}\left(y_{0_i} \mid T_i = 1\right)\right].$$

The naive (or cross-section) estimator, which relies on this counterfactual, $\hat{\Delta}^C = \bar{y}^{T_i=1} - \bar{y}^{T_i=0}$ is linked to the distribution of the potential outcomes since $\hat{\Delta}^C \xrightarrow{\mathbb{P}} \Delta^C = \mathbb{E}(y_i \mid T_i = 1) - \mathbb{E}(y_i \mid T_i = 0)$, where

$$\Delta^C = \mathbb{E}\left(y_{1_i} \mid T_i = 1\right) - \mathbb{E}\left(y_{0_i} \mid T_i = 1\right) + \mathbb{E}\left(y_{0_i} \mid T_i = 1\right) - \mathbb{E}\left(y_{0_i} \mid T_i = 0\right) = \Delta^{\text{ATT}} + \mathcal{B}^C . \quad (11.1)$$

The estimator thus measures a mix between the ATT and $\mathcal{B}^C = \mathbb{E}(y_{0_i} \mid T_i = 1) - \mathbb{E}(y_{0_i} \mid T_i = 0)$, the selection bias. This bias can be due to either self-selection into the treatment (if individuals who expect to benefit the most from it decide to participate, namely, to be treated) or to the implementation of the treatment itself, if the policy aims to target a specific sub-population. Estimating the ATE is even more demanding, as

$$
\begin{aligned}
\Delta^C \;=\; & \mathbb{E}\left(y_{1_i}\right) - \mathbb{E}\left(y_{0_i}\right) \;+\; \left[1 - \mathbb{P}\left(T_i = 1\right)\right]\left[\mathbb{E}\left(y_{1_i} \mid T_i = 1\right) - \mathbb{E}\left(y_{1_i} \mid T_i = 0\right)\right] \\
& +\quad \mathbb{P}\left(T_i = 1\right)\left[\mathbb{E}\left(y_{0_i} \mid T_i = 1\right) - \mathbb{E}\left(y_{0_i} \mid T_i = 0\right)\right] \\
\;=\; & \Delta^{\text{ATE}} \quad + \quad \mathcal{B}^C_{\text{ATE}}
\end{aligned}
$$

from which another source of bias arises:

$$\mathcal{B}^C_{\text{ATE}} = \mathcal{B}^C + \left[1 - \mathbb{P}\left(T_i = 1\right)\right]\left[\mathbb{E}\left(y_{1_i} - y_{0_i} \mid T_i = 1\right) - \mathbb{E}\left(y_{1_i} - y_{0_i} \mid T_i = 0\right)\right].$$

On top of the selection bias, $\mathcal{B}^C$, the evaluation must now take into account the heterogeneity in the response to the treatment.

3.2 Identification through Randomization

Randomization of individuals into the treatment allows to break the link between the outcome variable and the treatment status giving rise to the selection bias. If the value of T_i, $\forall_i$, is decided randomly, then $\mathbb{E}(y_{0_i} \mid T_i = 1) = \mathbb{E}(y_{0_i} \mid T_i = 0)$, and hence

$$\mathbb{E}(y_{1_i} \mid T_i = 1) - \mathbb{E}(y_{0_i} \mid T_i = 0) = \mathbb{E}(y_{1_i} \mid T_i = 1) - \mathbb{E}(y_{0_i} \mid T_i = 1) = \mathbb{E}(y_{1_i} - y_{0_i} \mid T_i = 1).$$

But randomization also breaks the correlation between the treatment status and the outcome from the treatment, $\mathbb{E}(y_{1_i} - y_{0_i} \mid T_i = 1) = \mathbb{E}(y_{1_i} - y_{0_i} \mid T_i = 0) = \mathbb{E}(y_{1_i} - y_{0_i})$, in a such a way that $\mathbb{E}(y_{1_i} \mid T_i = 1) - \mathbb{E}(y_{0_i} \mid T_i = 0) = \Delta^{ATT} = \Delta^{ATE}$. Randomized experiments thus make it possible to estimate the ATE—provided that the random assignment to experimental groups is made in the entire population and that all individuals selected to take part in the experiment actually do so. They cannot deliver the ATT unless some of the selected individuals refuse to take part in the experiment (in which case the treatment effect is conditional on endogenous refusal, which might select a subpopulation, which is different from the one generated by endogenous participation), or if randomization is performed within a well-chosen sub-population.

3.3 Difference Estimators

Several difference estimators overcome the missing data issue by relying on different counter-factuals. They are typically applied to data produced by the implementation of a policy, which is treated as a "natural experiment". In this context, individuals are observed at different points in time and $T_{it} \in \{0,1\}$ depending on whether i receives or does not receive the treatment in t. Time periods before and after the implementation of the policy in t_0, respectively denoted $\underline{t} = \{t < t_0\}$ and $\overline{t} = \{t > t_0\}$, define the dummy variable $P_{it} = 1_{\{t>t_0\}}$ such that $P_{i\overline{t}} = 1 - P_{i\underline{t}} = 1$. In this context, two pairs of potential outcomes must be considered, depending on the date at which the outcome is observed:

$$y_{it} = \begin{cases} y_{0_{i\underline{t}}} & \text{if} \quad P_{it} = 0, T_{i\overline{t}} = 0 \\ y_{0_{i\overline{t}}} & \text{if} \quad P_{it} = 1, T_{i\overline{t}} = 0 \\ y_{0_{i\underline{t}}} & \text{if} \quad P_{it} = 0, T_{i\overline{t}} = 1 \\ y_{1_{i\overline{t}}} & \text{if} \quad P_{it} = 1, T_{i\overline{t}} = 1 \end{cases}, \quad \forall i,t.$$

3.3.1 The cross-section estimator
The cross-section estimator only makes use of post-implementation data and compares treated individuals to untreated ones. Formally, it is similar to the naive estimator defined (section 3.1) and may be written as:

$$\hat{\Delta}^C = \overline{y}_{it}^{\,T_{-it}=1,P_{it}=1} - \overline{y}_{it}^{\,T_{-it}=0,P_{it}=1} \xrightarrow{P} \Delta^C = \mathbb{E}\left(y_{it}\,\middle|\,T_{-it}=1, P_{it}=1\right) - \mathbb{E}\left(y_{it}\,\middle|\,T_{-it}=0, P_{it}=1\right).$$

The estimator is biased because of selection into the treatment since the resulting outcome can be decomposed as:

$$\Delta^C = \Delta^{ATT} + \mathbb{E}\left(y_{0_{it}}\,\middle|\,T_{-it}=1, P_{it}=1\right) - \mathbb{E}\left(y_{0_{it}}\,\middle|\,T_{-it}=0, P_{it}=1\right) = \Delta^{ATT} + \mathcal{B}^C\left(P_{it}=1\right),$$

but does not depend on selection on the outcome in the absence of the treatment, $\mathcal{B}^C(P_{it}=0)$.

3.3.2   The before−after (BA) estimator

The BA estimator focuses on treated individuals ($\forall i, T_{-it}=1$); it uses their outcome before the implementation of the treatment to define a counterfactual of their post-treatment situation:

$$\hat{\Delta}^{BA} = \overline{y}_{it}^{\,T_{-it}=1,P_{it}=1} - \overline{y}_{it}^{\,T_{-it}=1,P_{it}=0} \xrightarrow{P} \Delta^{BA} = \mathbb{E}\left(y_{it}\,\middle|\,T_{-it}=1, P_{it}=1\right) - \mathbb{E}\left(y_{it}\,\middle|\,T_{-it}=1, P_{it}=0\right).$$

It can be written as the OLS estimator of Δ^{BA} in the linear model:

$$y_{it} = b_0 + \Delta^{BA}P_{it} + u_{it}, \forall t, \forall i : T_{-it} = 1.$$

Given the observation rule that applies to y_{it}, the parameter may be written as:

$$\Delta^{BA} = \Delta^{ATT} + \mathbb{E}\left(y_{0_{it}}\,\middle|\,T_{-it}=1, P_{it}=1\right) - \mathbb{E}\left(y_{0_{it}}\,\middle|\,T_{-it}=1, P_{it}=0\right).$$

It thus measures a combination of the ATT and

$$\mathcal{B}^{BA}\left(T_{-it}=1\right) = \mathbb{E}\left(y_{0_{it}}\,\middle|\,T_{-it}=1, P_{it}=1\right) - \mathbb{E}\left(y_{0_{it}}\,\middle|\,T_{-it}=1, P_{it}=0\right) = \mathbb{E}\left(y_{0_{it}} - y_{0_{i\underline{t}}}\,\middle|\,T_{-it}=1\right),$$

which measures the change in the outcome that would have happened over time even without the implementation of the treatment—this corresponds to a simultaneity bias. It thus relies on the identifying assumption that the outcome only changes as a result of the treatment. It does not depend on whether the same assumption applies to untreated individuals, $\mathcal{B}^{BA}(T_{-it}=0)$.

3.3.3   The difference-in-differences (DD) estimator

The DD estimator makes use of the entire data produced by P_{it} and T_{it}. It is based on the change over time in the untreated individuals' situation as a counterfactual for the change observed in the treated group. It thus amounts to compute the difference between two difference estimators: the BA computed in both groups generated by T_{-it}, or, equivalently, the cross-section estimators at both time periods defined by P_{it}:

$$\hat{\Delta}^{DD} = \left[\overline{y}_{it}^{\,T_{-it}=1,P_{it}=1} - \overline{y}_{it}^{\,T_{-it}=1,P_{it}=0}\right] - \left[\overline{y}_{it}^{\,T_{-it}=0,P_{it}=1} - \overline{y}_{it}^{\,T_{-it}=0,P_{it}=0}\right] = \hat{\Delta}^{BA}_{T_{-it}=1} - \hat{\Delta}^{BA}_{T_{i\underline{t}}=0}$$

$$= \left[\overline{y}_{it}^{\,T_{-it}=1,P_{it}=1} - \overline{y}_{it}^{\,T_{-it}=0,P_{it}=1}\right] - \left[\overline{y}_{it}^{\,T_{-it}=1,P_{it}=0} - \overline{y}_{it}^{\,T_{-it}=0,P_{it}=0}\right] = \hat{\Delta}^C_t - \hat{\Delta}^C_{\underline{t}}.$$

Thanks to this double differentiation, the DD estimator gets rid of the biases affecting each kind of simple-difference estimator provided the bias remains constant in the dimension over which the differencing is performed. The estimator measures:

$$\hat{\Delta}^{DD} \xrightarrow{\mathbb{P}} \Delta^{DD} = \Delta^{ATE} + \left[\mathbb{E}\left(y_{0_{it}} \middle| T_{\tilde{i}} = 1, P_{it} = 1\right) - \mathbb{E}\left(y_{0_{it}} \middle| T_{\tilde{i}} = 1, P_{it} = 0\right)\right]$$

$$- \left[\mathbb{E}\left(y_{0_{it}} \middle| T_{\tilde{i}} = 0, P_{it} = 1\right) - \mathbb{E}\left(y_{0_{it}} \middle| T_{\tilde{i}} = 0, P_{it} = 0\right)\right] = \Delta^{ATE} + \mathcal{B}^{DD},$$

where the bias affecting the DD estimator, $\mathcal{B}^{DD} = \mathbb{E}(y_{0_{\tilde{i}}} - y_{0_{it}} \mid T_{\tilde{i}} = 1) - \mathbb{E}(y_{0_{\tilde{i}}} - y_{0_{it}} \mid T_{\tilde{i}} = 0)$, measures the difference in trends between the control and treatment group, subject to $\mathcal{B}^{BA}(T_{\tilde{i}} = 1) \neq \mathcal{B}^{BA}(T_{\tilde{i}} = 0)$. This bias can be equivalently interpreted as the change over time in the selection bias: $\mathcal{B}^{C}(P_{it} = 1) \neq \mathcal{B}^{C}(P_{it} = 0)$. The identification property of the estimator thus relies on the parallel trends assumption:

$$\left[\mathbb{E}\left(y_{0_{it}} \middle| T_{\tilde{i}} = 0, P_{it} = 1\right) - \mathbb{E}\left(y_{0_{it}} \middle| T_{\tilde{i}} = 0, P_{it} = 0\right)\right]$$

$$= \left[\mathbb{E}\left(y_{0_{it}} \middle| T_{\tilde{i}} = 1, P_{it} = 1\right) - \mathbb{E}\left(y_{0_{it}} \middle| T_{\tilde{i}} = 1, P_{it} = 0\right)\right].$$

It is worth noting that this assumption does not require either the lack of selection into the treatment group $-\mathcal{B}^{C}(P_{it} = 1) \neq 0 -$ or the lack of simultaneity bias $- \mathcal{B}^{BA}(T_{\tilde{i}} = 1) \neq 0$. It only requires that such confounding variations are balanced over time $- \mathcal{B}^{C}(P_{it} = 1) = \mathcal{B}^{C}(P_{it} = 0) -$ or, equivalently, between groups $- \mathcal{B}^{BA}(T_{\tilde{i}} = 1) = \mathcal{B}^{BA}(T_{\tilde{i}} = 0)$.

As such, the DD estimator relies on the trend experienced by individuals from the control group as a counterfactual for the trend that individuals from the treatment group would have experienced without the intervention. Figure 11.2 provides a graphical illustration of this identifying assumption: the two parallel lines show the evolution of $y_{0_{it}}$ over time within each group (the dotted part on the right thus provides the counterfactual evolution of this quantity in the treatment group: it reproduces the trend observed in the control group). Under this assumption, the double difference measures the ATT of the intervention. Although this assumption is less demanding than the identifying assumptions of either the cross-section or the BA estimators, Figure 11.3 describes two typical sources of its failure. Figure 11.3a illustrates the Ashenfelter's (1978) "dip", which refers to a change in the outcome among treated individuals before the policy is implemented (for instance because the expected benefits from the intervention lead treated individuals to reduce the resources devoted to the outcome). In Figure 11.3b, the failure is rather due to the behavior of individuals from the control group: due to an indirect effect of the policy, the average treatment on the untreated (Δ^{ATU}) is non-zero.

3.4   Conditional Independence

Instead of eliminating confounding heterogeneity through differentiation, identification can also be achieved by finding covariates conditional on which the assignment can be assumed to

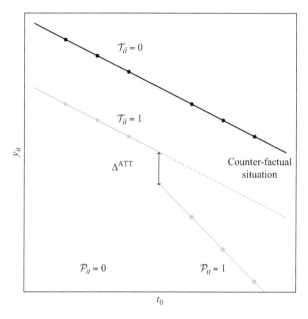

Note: The figure illustrates the assumption that the trends in the treatment ($T_i = 1$) and control ($T_i = 0$) groups would be parallel over time (P_{it}) with no treatment (dashed line). The double difference then estimates the ATT, Δ^{ATT}.

Figure 11.2   The parallel trends assumption

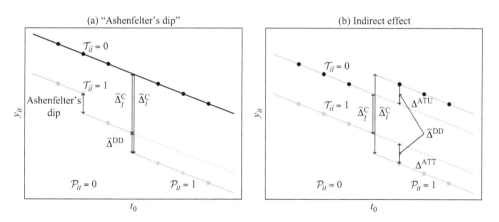

Note: The figure displays two typical failures of the assumption that the trends in the treatment ($T_i = 1$) and control ($T_i = 0$) groups would be parallel over time (P_{it}) with no treatment, resulting in biased difference-in-difference estimates, $\hat{\Delta}^{DD}$.

Figure 11.3   Well-known failures of the parallel trends assumption

be random. To expose this method, we consider a sample of N individuals for whom the pair $\{y_i, T_i\}$ is observed. The model of interest is

$$y_i = b_0 + b_1 T_i + u_i, \forall i,$$

in which unobserved heterogeneity is correlated to the treatment variable due to endogenous participation in the program. Control variables are observed covariates, x, whose aim is to wash out the noise from confounding factors. Denoting $u_i = x_i c + v_i$, the model may now be written as

$$y_i = b_0 + b_1 T_i + x_i c + v_i.$$

Those covariates are sufficient to achieve identification if they lead to the independence between the outcome variable and the treatment variable, conditional on the values of the control variables. Control variables thus achieve a quasi-experiment, with statistically identical individuals in both groups. This independence condition is weak if $\ell(y_{0_i} | T_i, x_i) = \ell(y_{0_i} | x_i)$, in which case the output observed among untreated individuals provides a counterfactual for the situation of treated individuals: $\mathbb{E}(y_{0_i} | T_i, x_i) = (y_{0_i} | x_i)$, which is sufficient to identify Δ^{ATT}. Independence is strong if this property also concerns the output induced by the treatment $\ell(y_{1_i}, y_{0_i} | T_i, x_i) = \ell(y_{1_i}, y_{0_i} | x_i)$, which means that we also impose that $\mathbb{E}(y_{1_i} | T_i, x_i) = (y_{1_i} | x_i)$, and the output comparison between groups thus identifies Δ^{ATE}.

3.4.1   Regression discontinuity

One of the most popular applications of the identification based on conditional independence is regression discontinuity. Denote by $\mathcal{D}_i$ the observed variable for which the threshold rule applies, and $\bar{d}$ the threshold which determines participation in the program, $T_i = 1\{\mathcal{D}_i > \bar{d}\}$. There is a "regression discontinuity" if there exists $\varepsilon > 0$ such that:

$$\ell\left(y_{0_i}, y_{1_i} \middle| \mathcal{D}_i = \bar{d} - \varepsilon\right) = \ell\left(y_{0_i}, y_{1_i} \middle| \mathcal{D}_i = \bar{d} + \varepsilon\right) \Leftrightarrow \ell\left(y_{0_i}, y_{1_i} \middle| T_i, \mathcal{D}_i = \bar{d}\right) = \ell\left(y_{0_i}, y_{1_i} \middle| \mathcal{D}_i = \bar{d}\right).$$

This rule thus produces a quasi-experiment in the neighborhood of the threshold, $\bar{d}$, as individuals can be assumed to be randomly assigned to the treatment conditional on $\mathcal{D}_i \in [\bar{d} - \varepsilon; \bar{d} + \varepsilon]$. Thus, the distance to the threshold $\mathcal{D}_i - \bar{d}$ is a control variable which generates conditional independence.

3.4.2   Matching estimators

In the more general case of a vector of control variables x_i generating conditional independence, the estimation of the causal parameter relies on finding, for each treated individual i, a counterfactual, $\mathbb{E}(y_{0_i} | T_i = 1, x_i)$. The matching estimator (Rubin, 1977) implements this strategy by matching each treated individual, characterized by control variables x_i, with a statistical twin belonging to the control group, namely an untreated individual $j(i)$ whose observed values of the control variables are the same, $j(i) \in \{j | T_j = 0, x_j = x_i\}$. Under such circumstances, the outcome $y_{j(i)}$ fulfills the weak independence condition:

$$\mathbb{E}\left(y_i \middle| T_i = 0, x = x_i\right) = \mathbb{E}\left(y_{0_i} \middle| T_i = 0, x = x_i\right) = \mathbb{E}\left(y_{0_i} \middle| x = x_i\right) = \mathbb{E}\left(y_{0_i} \middle| T_i = 1, x = x_i\right).$$

This allows to measure the individual change in the outcome induced by the treatment as $\hat{\Delta}_i = y_i - y_{j(i)}$, which yields a consistent estimator for the ATT:

$$\hat{\Delta}^{\mathrm{ATT}} = \frac{1}{N_{T_i = 1}} \sum_{i \in T_i = 1} \left(y_i - y_{j(i)}\right) \xrightarrow{\mathbb{P}} \mathbb{E}\left(\Delta_i \middle| T_i = 1\right) = \Delta^{\mathrm{ATT}},$$

where $N_{T_i=1}$ denotes the size of the treatment group. Strong independence allows us to extend the matching strategy to individuals from the control group, $T_i = 0$, with statistical twins $j(i) \in \{j \mid T_j = 1, x_j = x_i\}$; to estimate the ATE we can calculate:

$$\hat{\Delta}^{ATE} = \frac{1}{N} \left[\sum_{i \in T_i=1} \left(y_i - y_{j(i)}\right) + \sum_{i \in T_i=0} \left(y_{j(i)} - y_i\right) \right] \xrightarrow{\mathbb{P}} \mathbb{E}\left(\Delta_i\right) = \Delta^{ATE}.$$

The conditional independence assumption required to apply this strategy only holds if control variables bring enough information to conditionally break the endogeneity of the treatment. This concern very often leads to include many control variables, which makes the perfect matching described more and more challenging as the number of cells increases. An alternative is to define counterfactuals based on the closest neighbors, rather than finding a perfect statistical twin. The increase in the number of control variables also reduces the number of degrees of freedom of the model. This can be addressed by aggregating the control variables, which is the aim of the propensity score.

3.4.3 Aggregating control variables: The propensity score
The propensity score summarizes the information provided by the entire set of control variables through the change in the probability of being treated (Rosenbaum and Rubin, 1983): $s(x_i) = \mathbb{P}(T_i = 1 \mid x_i)$. This score aims to balance the distribution of the control variables across the treatment and control groups.[3] This allows to compute a counterfactual for each treated individual based on $\mathbb{E}[y_{j(i)} \mid s(x_{j(i)}) = s(x_i), T_{j(i)} = 0]$, and then to compute the ATT. By computing a counterfactual for untreated individuals, $\mathbb{E}[y_{j(i)} \mid s(x_{j(i)}) = s(x_i), T_{j(i)} = 1]$, we can obtain an estimator of the ATE.

Such counterfactuals can only be found if it is possible to observe for each individual whose score is $s(x_i)$ a counterfactual individual (untreated if $T_i = 1$, treated otherwise) with a similar score. This possibility depends on the extent to which the support of the two distributions $\ell[s(x_i) \mid T_i = 1]$ and $\ell[s(x_i) \mid T_i = 0]$ overlap: $S_\cap = \ell[s(x_i) \mid T_i = 1] \cap \ell[s(x_i) \mid T_i = 0]$. This common support property has important consequences on the consistency of the estimators derived from this conditional independence assumption (see Heckman et al., 1998). Identification is indeed restricted to the range of values of the score belonging to the common support: $\mathbb{E}[\Delta_i \mid s(x_i), T_i = 1] = \mathbb{E}[\Delta_i \mid s(x_i) \in S_\cap, T_i = 1]$ and $\mathbb{E}[\Delta_i \mid s(x_i)] = \mathbb{E}[\Delta_i \mid s(x_i) \in S_\cap]$. As illustrated in Figure 11.4, this condition is more likely to be restrictive when the explanatory power of the score is higher: on each graph, the score gives more probability to the conditioning outcome, as expected, but the common support is much thinner in Figure 11.4b than in Figure 11.4a due to the improved accuracy of the score.

3.5 Instrumental Variable Estimator

Instruments are exogenous observed variables which achieve identification thanks to their correlation with the treatment variable. Consider the simplest implementation, in which the binary treatment variable, T_i, is instrumented by a binary instrument $z_i^e \in \{0,1\}, \forall i$, in the linear model:

$$y_i = b_0 + b_1 T_i + u_i, \mathbb{E}(T_i u_i) \neq 0, \forall i.$$

(a) Limited common support

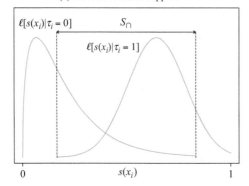

(b) Tiny common support

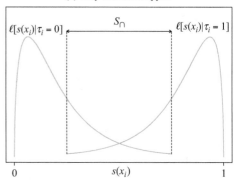

Note: The figure plots the distributions of the score, $s(x_i)$, conditional on the value of the treatment variable, T_i, in two cases with varying size of the common support, $S_\cap$.

Figure 11.4   The common support property of the propensity score

The variable z^e can be used as an instrument if it is exogenous, namely $\mathbb{E}(u_i | z_i^e) = 0$ (the "orthogonality condition"), in such a way that $\mathbb{E}(y_i | z_i^e) = b_0 + b_1 \mathbb{E}(T_i | z_i^e) + \mathbb{E}(u_i | z_i^e)$. Under this assumption, the variations in the outcome resulting from changes in the instrument,

$$\mathbb{E}(y_i | z_i^e = 1) = b_0 + b_1 \mathbb{E}(T_i | z_i^e = 1)$$

$$\mathbb{E}(y_i | z_i^e = 0) = b_0 + b_1 \mathbb{E}(T_i | z_i^e = 0),$$

identify the effect of the treatment:

$$b_1 = \frac{\mathbb{E}(y_i | z_i^e = 1) - \mathbb{E}(y_i | z_i^e = 0)}{\mathbb{E}(T_i | z_i^e = 1) - \mathbb{E}(T_i | z_i^e = 0)}.$$

This relation only defines the parameter if changes in the instrument actually induce changes in the treatment, that is, $\mathbb{E}(T_i | z_i^e = 1) - \mathbb{E}(T_i | z_i^e = 0) \neq 0$ (the "rank condition"). The closer this difference to 0, the weaker the instrument, leading to poor identification of the parameter. This target parameter can be estimated based on the Wald (1940) estimator (denoting $\overline{w}^{z_i^e = 0/1} = \frac{1}{\Sigma_i 1_{\{z_i^e = 0/1\}}} \Sigma_i w_i \times 1_{\{z_i^e = 0/1\}}$, $w \equiv \{y, x\}$):

$$\hat{\Delta}^{\text{WALD}} = \frac{\overline{y}^{z_i^e = 1} - \overline{y}^{z_i^e = 0}}{\overline{x}^{z_i^e = 1} - \overline{x}^{z_i^e = 0}} \frac{\mathbb{E}(y_i | z_i^e = 1) - \mathbb{E}(y_i | z_i^e = 0)}{\mathbb{E}(T_i | z_i^e = 1) - \mathbb{E}(T_i | z_i^e = 0)}. \tag{11.2}$$

3.5.1   The local average treatment effect (LATE)

To clarify the interpretation of the true parameter measured by the Wald estimator presented, let us denote T_{1_i} and T_{0_i} the potential treatment status of individual i depending on the value of the instrument:

$$T_i = \begin{cases} T_{0_i} & \text{if } z_i^e = 0 \\ T_{1_i} & \text{if } z_i^e = 1. \end{cases}$$

As shown in Table 11.1, this relationship between the treatment and the instrument defines four types of individuals. Two among them do not react to the instrument, that is, $T_{0_i} = T_{1_i} = 0$ for *Never takers*, and $T_{0_i} = T_{1_i} = 1$ for *Always takers*, while the two other types do react to the instrument. The response is positive for *Compliers*, $T_{1_i} > T_{0_i}$, and negative for *Defiers*, $T_{1_i} < T_{0_i}$. The rank condition is meant to exclude the possibility that the sample is only made of the first two kinds of individuals. Defiers are often excluded by assumption by imposing monotonicity of the change in the treatment. The monotonicity assumption means that $T_{1i} - T_{0i} \geq 0, \forall i$. Under these assumptions, only compliers contribute to the identification of the effect of the treatment, and the Wald estimator measures the Local Average Treatment Effect (LATE):

$$\hat{\Delta}^{WALD} \xrightarrow{\mathbb{P}} \frac{\mathbb{E}(y_i \mid z_i^e = 1) - \mathbb{E}(y_i \mid z_i^e = 0)}{\mathbb{E}(T_i \mid z_i^e = 1) - \mathbb{E}(T_i \mid z_i^e = 0)} = \mathbb{E}(y_{1_i} - y_{0_i} \mid T_{1_i} - T_{0_i} > 0) = \Delta^{LATE} .$$

Since the work of Imbens and Angrist (1994), who introduced the LATE, the interpretation of the instrumental variable estimator as the "average treatment effect on the treated" has been called into question. It is only valid if the effect of the program is the same for all individuals, regardless of their age, gender, experience, and so on, which is obviously a very unrealistic assumption. Imbens and Angrist (1994), and many econometricians following them, show that if the effect of an intervention or public policy is likely to vary from one group of individuals to another, and more generally to be heterogeneous within a given population, only a local estimator can be produced for those individuals who decide to benefit from the program when it becomes available as a result of a variation of the instrument. Those individuals are called "compliers", that is, they are people who comply or adhere to

Table 11.1   *Response of the treatment status to a change in the (binary) instrumental variable*

	$T_{1_i} = 0$	$T_{1_i} = 1$
$T_{0_i} = 0$	Never taker	Complier
$T_{0_i} = 1$	Defier	Always taker

Note: The table describes the four types of observations resulting from the combination of the potential treatment variables generated by a binary instrument, z^e: $T_{0_i} = T_i \mid_{z_i^e = 0}; T_{1_i} = T_i \mid_{z_i^e = 1}$.

the program when the value of the instrument changes. The group of compliers is probably best defined when confronted with people who systematically refuse the program ("never takers") and those who are always willing to participate in it ("always takers"), regardless of the value of the instrument.

The LATE estimator therefore measures the effect of the intervention only on the group of compliers, which unfortunately cannot always be identified. When it is, for instance when a lottery or a random procedure changes the assignment to the treatment (that is, the proposed intervention or program), the LATE estimator can be obtained using the two-stage least squares procedure. Angrist and Imbens (1995) propose a more general method that takes into account the effect of other exogenous variables (such as age) in the implementation of the LATE. Angrist et al. (2000) apply this approach to the estimation of simultaneous equation models.

4.   THE EXTERNAL VALIDITY OF IMPACT EVALUATION METHODS

Several of the methods cited are characterized by strong internal validity: they provide credible estimators of the average effects of interventions for the samples under consideration. However, the possibility of extrapolating their outcomes to a larger population, that is, their external validity, is often called into question.

In the case of randomized trials, this criticism is based on the fact that the samples are generally quite small and concern particular groups, for example people living in some given environments or with specific characteristics; they are not representative of the population as a whole, or at the very least of all the potentially eligible people. The issue of external validity is fundamentally linked to the heterogeneity of the effects of interventions. Suppose that a trial is conducted in a setting A, which may correspond to a given location, period or sub-population of individuals. How do the estimates of the effects of this particular intervention conducted in this particular setting inform us of what the effects of the same intervention would be in another location, in a different period, for a different group of individuals, that is, in a setting B that is different from setting A? The differences may result from observed and unobserved characteristics of those other locations, periods or individuals, and possibly from changes (no matter how slight they are) in the intervention procedures. To answer these questions, it is useful to have access to the results of multiple trials, carried out in different settings, and if possible, with fairly large samples representative of the eligible population (at least in terms of the main observable characteristics). Microfinance represents a particularly interesting example. For instance, Meager (2019) analyzed the results of seven trials conducted on this topic and found that the estimated effects were remarkably consistent.

Another approach is to explicitly account for the differences between the distributions of the characteristics specific to the groups or periods in question. Hotz et al. (2005) and Imbens (2010) propose a theoretical setting in which the differences in effects observed within a group of several locations stem from the fact that the units established in these locations have different characteristics. By means of an adjustment procedure that consists in reweighting individual units (persons, households, firms and so on), they can compare the effects of the intervention in these different locations. This technique is close to the inverse probability weighting methods recommended by Stuart and co-authors (Imai et al., 2008; Stuart et al., 2011; Stuart et al., 2015).[4]

It should be recalled that the instrumental variable estimator is often interpreted as a local estimator of the average treatment effect, that is, as a LATE estimator that measures the average treatment effect for those members of the population (the compliers) whose assignment to the treatment is modified by a change in the value of the instrument. Under what conditions can this estimator be interpreted as the average treatment effect for the entire population? In other words, what are the conditions that ensure its external validity? There are two groups that are never affected by the instrumental variable: the always takers who always receive the treatment, and the never takers who never receive it. To answer the question, Angrist (2004) suggests testing whether the difference between the average outcomes of the always-takers and the never-takers is equal to the average treatment effect on the outcome of the compliers. Angrist and Fernandez-Val (2013) seek to exploit a conditional effect ignorability assumption stipulating that, conditional on certain exogenous variables, the average effect for compliers is identical to the average effect for always takers and never takers. Bertanha and Imbens (2019) suggest testing the combination of two equalities, namely the equality of the average outcomes of untreated compliers and never takers, and the equality of the average outcomes of treated compliers and always takers.

In the case of regression discontinuity, the lack of external validity is mainly due to the fact that this method produces local estimators, which are only valid around the considered eligibility threshold. If, for example, that threshold is an age condition, regression discontinuity does not make it possible to infer what the average effect of the intervention would be for people whose age differs significantly from the age defining the eligibility threshold. Under what conditions can the estimated effects obtained through regression discontinuity be generalized? Dong and Lewbel (2015) note that in many cases the variable that defines the eligibility threshold (called the "forcing variable") is a continuous variable such as age or income level. These authors point out that, in this case, beyond the extent of the discontinuity of the outcome variable in the vicinity of the threshold, it is also possible to estimate the variation of the first derivative of the regression function, and even of higher order derivatives. This makes it possible to extrapolate the causal effects of the treatment to values of the forcing variable further away from the eligibility threshold. Angrist and Rokkanen (2015) propose to test whether, conditional on additional exogenous variables, the correlation between the forcing variable and the outcome variable disappears. Such a result would mean that the allocation to treatment could be considered independent of the potential outcomes (this is called the unconfoundedness property)[5] conditional on those additional exogenous variables, which would again allow the result to be extrapolated to values of the forcing variable further from the threshold. Bertanha and Imbens (2019) propose an approach based on the fuzzy regression discontinuity design.[6] They suggest testing the continuity of the conditional expectation of the outcome variable, for a given value of the treatment and of the forcing variable at the threshold level, adjusted by variations in exogenous characteristics.

5.   DIFFERENCE-IN-DIFFERENCES AND SYNTHETIC CONTROL

As noted, the implementation of the difference-in-differences method requires a control group whose evolution over time reflects what the treatment group would have experienced in the absence of any intervention. This assumption cannot be tested over the period following the intervention, during which differences in outcome between groups also reflect the effect of the policy. A testable component of this assumption is that the past evolution of the outcome variable (before the policy being evaluated is implemented) is on average similar to that of the same variable in the treatment group. When it is rejected, it is possible to create an artificial control ("synthetic control") unit, based on the observations of the control group, using an appropriate weighting system. This synthetic control is constructed in such a way that the past evolution of the outcome variable within it is identical to that of this variable in the treatment group.

The method was introduced by Abadie and Gardeazabal (2003) in a study aimed at assessing the effect of ETA terrorist activity on the development of the Basque Country's GDP between 1975 and 2000, a period when the Basque separatist terrorist organization was most active, frequently committing extreme acts of violence. The problem is that between 1960 and 1969, the decade preceding the beginning of the period of terrorist activity, the Basque Region's GDP evolved very differently from the average GDP of the other sixteen Spanish regions, leading to the assumption of a common pre-treatment trend being rejected. Abadie and Gardeazabal (2003) then proposed to construct a synthetic control region whose GDP evolution between 1960 and 1969 would be similar to that of the Basque Country's GDP. This can be achieved by minimizing the distance between the annual observations of the Basque Country's GDP between 1960 and 1969 and those of this synthetic region. More formally, the annual GDP values in the Basque Country between 1960 and 1969 are denoted $y_{1,t}, \forall t = 1960, \ldots, 1969$, and grouped together in a vector $\boldsymbol{y}_{1,0} = [y_{1,1960}, \ldots, y_{1,1969}]$. Similarly, the annual observations concerning the GDP of each of the other sixteen Spanish regions are denoted $y_{j,t}, \forall j = 2, \ldots,$ 17, $t = 1960, \ldots, 1969$, and stored in a (10×16) matrix denoted $\boldsymbol{Y}_{0,0}$. The synthetic control region is constructed from a (16×1) weighting vector $\boldsymbol{w} = [w_1, \ldots, w_{16}]'$, which minimizes the following weighted Euclidean norm for a given matrix V:

$$\| \boldsymbol{Y}_{1,0} - \boldsymbol{Y}_{0,0}\boldsymbol{w} \| = \sqrt{\left(\boldsymbol{Y}_{1,0} - \boldsymbol{Y}_{0,0}\boldsymbol{w}\right)' V \left(\boldsymbol{Y}_{1,0} - \boldsymbol{Y}_{0,0}\boldsymbol{w}\right)}.$$

In a first simple application, Abadie and Gardeazabal (2003) choose the identity matrix as the matrix V. This allows them to easily find the weighting system $\boldsymbol{w}^*$ that minimizes this norm.[7] They verify that the ten annual GDPs of that synthetic region, which are calculated as $\boldsymbol{Y}_{0,0}^* = \boldsymbol{Y}_{0,0}\boldsymbol{w}^*$ during the 1960–69 period, are similar to the yearly GDPs of the Basque region observed during the same period. This allows them to then calculate the counterfactual GDPs of the Basque region during the period of terrorist activity (1975–2000). These counterfactual GDPs are denoted $\boldsymbol{y}_{0,1}^*$ and are calculated in the (26×1) vector $\boldsymbol{y}_{0,1}^* = \boldsymbol{Y}_{0,1}\boldsymbol{w}^*$, where $\boldsymbol{Y}_{0,1}$ is the (26×16) matrix which groups together the observations concerning the 26 (=2000–1974) annual GDPs of each of the sixteen Spanish regions other than the Basque Country. The causal effect of terrorism on the Basque GDP is then measured as $\boldsymbol{y}_{1,1} - \boldsymbol{y}_{0,1}^*$ where $\boldsymbol{y}_{1,1}$ is the (26×1) vector, which groups together the 26 annual observations of the Basque GDP from 1975 to 2000.

In general, V is a diagonal matrix with non-negative diagonal elements. In an extended version of this method, Abadie and Gardeazabal (2003) and Abadie et al. (2010, 2015) propose to choose matrices V whose elements are data driven. The number of units treated may be greater than one: in this case, a synthetic control must be calculated for each unit treated. However, when the number of units treated is very large, the synthetic control of a treated unit may not be unique. Abadie and l'Hour (2017) propose a variant that takes this difficulty into account. Their estimator is written

$$\| \boldsymbol{Y}_{1,0} - \boldsymbol{Y}_{0,0}\boldsymbol{w} \|^2 + \lambda \sum_{j=2}^{J+1} w_j \| \boldsymbol{Y}_{j,0} - \boldsymbol{Y}_{1,0} \|^2 \text{, with } \lambda > 0 .$$

In this expression, $Y_{j,0}$ is the vector whose elements are the observed values of the outcome variable for the control unit j, $\forall j = 2, \ldots, J + 1$, during each of the periods preceding the implementation of the intervention. The estimator proposed by Abadie and l'Hour (2017) includes a penalty λ for differences between the values of the outcome variable of a treated unit and those of each control unit in the period before the intervention was implemented. Abadie and l'Hour (2017) show that, under these conditions, and except in a few specific cases, their estimator provides a single synthetic control.

Extended versions of the synthetic control estimator have also been proposed by Amjad et al. (2018) and Athey et al. (2018), who suggest the use of matrix completion techniques, but also by Hahn and Shi (2017), who base their approach on sampling-based inferential methods.

6. THE ROLE AND CHOICE OF EXPLANATORY VARIABLES

Regardless of the type of intervention or evaluation method chosen by the researcher, the individuals, households, firms and so on sampled, whether or not they are beneficiaries of the intervention, whether they are members of the target group (that is the treatment group) or the control group, may still differ in terms of some exogenous characteristics (such as age, gender, number of years of labor market experience and so on, for individuals, or number of employees, date of creation, short-term debt level and so on, for a firm). In the case of a non-stratified RCT or a sharp regression discontinuity design, a simple regression of the observed outcome variable on a constant and a treatment group dummy variable is sufficient to obtain a convergent estimator of the average treatment effect in the sample. The addition of exogenous variables to this regression will mainly improve, in theory, the accuracy of the estimator of the average treatment effect.

However, in cases other than non-stratified randomization or sharp regression discontinuity design, it is necessary to add assumptions about the role of exogenous variables in order to obtain consistent estimators. The most commonly used assumption is that of conditional independence. This assumption states that the assignment to the treatment group, represented by a random variable T, and the potential outcomes of the intervention, denoted y_{i_1} for a treated individual and y_{i_0} for an untreated individual, are independent conditional on all relevant exogenous variables x, that is, all those affecting the probability of benefiting from the intervention. This assumption is crucial for implementing a technique such as matching. Once this hypothesis is accepted, if the sample is large enough and/or the number of exogenous variables is not too high, it is possible to implement an exact matching method: this is based on comparing the outcome of each treated individual with that of an untreated individual having exactly the same observable characteristics. When this method cannot be implemented, particularly when the number of exogenous variables is too high, this exact matching is often replaced by a distance criterion making it possible to associate each treated individual's "closest neighbor" in the sense of the chosen distance, or to implement the technique of the propensity score, as defined: the outcome of each treated individual is compared with that of the untreated individual who has a propensity score whose value is very close to that of the treated individual's propensity score.[8] Exogenous variables that can be used to construct a valid propensity score should be conditionally independent of the assignment to the treatment group for a given value of this score ("balancing score property"). The set of these exogenous variables is potentially extremely large. In addition to these variables, it is possible to include in this set some of their interactions, dichotomous indicators for those with multiple modalities (for example levels of education or socioprofessional categories), some transformations of these variables such as their powers or logarithms, and so on.

Faced with the multiplicity of exogenous variables that can be mobilized, several recent studies have recommended the implementation of model and variable selection methods such as machine learning methods (McCaffrey et al., 2004; Wyss et al., 2014; Athey and Imbens, 2017a; Chernozhukov et al., 2018) and LASSO[9] methods (Belloni et al., 2014, 2017; Farrell, 2015). For example, McCaffrey et al. (2004), like Wyss et al. (2014), combine the method of random forests[10] with the LASSO technique in order to estimate the propensity score. It should be noted that these methods can be applied to evaluation methods other than matching. This is the case, in particular, of the method proposed by Belloni et al. (2017), which consists of a double variable selection procedure. The LASSO regression is used first to select the variables that are correlated with the outcome variable, and then again to select those that are correlated with the treatment dummy variable. After that, ordinary least squares can be applied by combining these two sets of variables, which improves the properties of the usual estimators of the average treatment effect, especially compared to simpler regularized regression techniques such as ridge regression.

7.   THE HETEROGENEITY OF THE EFFECTS OF AN INTERVENTION

Recent work has often focused on the heterogeneity of the effects of an intervention between groups of eligible individuals. Figure 11.5 illustrates this situation using a fictional example drawn from Leamer (1983). To make it easier to depict graphically, the heterogeneity of the treatment effect is assumed to be related to a variable x, the values of which differentiate individuals from each other. Figure 11.5a describes the identification of the causal effect using a sample of individuals for whom the values of the exogenous variable, plotted on the x-axis, are dispersed only to a low extent (denoted x). The variation in the outcome variable between individuals in the control group and those in the treatment group (that is, the heterogeneity of the treatment effect) is measured by the slope of the regression line $\Delta(\mathrm{x})$, but it does not allow us to disentangle between the many possible generalizations of the effect to other ranges of heterogeneity (of which two examples, $\Delta_1(x)$ and $\Delta_2(x)$ are drawn on the figure). Figure 11.5b shows that having access to additional data, corresponding to greater heterogeneity among

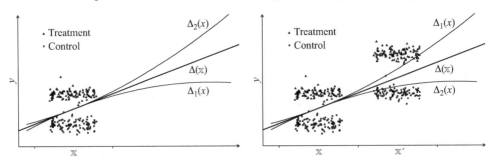

Note: The figure illustrates the empirical identification of the effect of a treatment using an exogenous variable x with low ($x \in \mathrm{x}$, left-hand side) and high ($x \in \{\mathrm{x} \cup \mathrm{x'}\}$, right-hand side) dispersion.

Figure 11.5   Empirical identification and generalizability

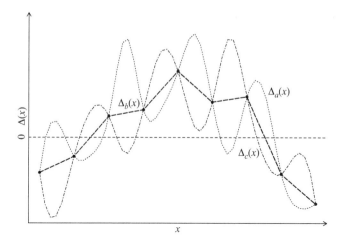

Figure 11.6 *(Non-)Identification of the full distribution of the treatment effect based on (any) estimates*

individuals ($x \in \{\mathrm{x} \cup \mathrm{x}'\}$), allows the analysis to be refined and pins down the distortion of the treatment effect in the population to be measured.

A wider range of observed situations therefore makes it possible to refine the estimation of the causal effect of the treatment, and to characterize its heterogeneity according to the observable characteristics of the individuals. As rich as the available data may be, the identification of the distribution of the treatment effect cannot be solved empirically. As an illustration, Figure 11.6 presents various measurements of the effect of a treatment, estimated for a wide range of values of the exogenous variable x. Nevertheless, these point values of the treatment effect are compatible with an infinite number of underlying distributions, of which Figure 11.6 presents three examples: $\Delta_a(x)$, $\Delta_b(x)$ and $\Delta_c(x)$. No matter how detailed the information provided by the data may be, and however heterogeneous the sample may be, the ability to describe the entire distribution of the treatment effect requires prior modeling to select the form of the relationship between the outcome variable and the treatment.

In the case where the sample is large and contains information on many variables, as is the case with big data, it is possible to estimate heterogeneous treatment effects by combining quasi-experimental causal inference methods with LASSO methods and, more generally, with machine learning techniques (see, for example, Wager and Athey, 2018; Knaus et al., 2017, 2018). This statistical approach can be generalized on a case-by-case basis with several treatments (Lechner, 2019).

Recent empirical work has focused on measuring the heterogeneity of effects, often in conjunction with the question of the external validity of the estimators used. Particularly compelling examples of this approach are given in the work of Bisbee et al. (2017) and Dehejia et al. (2019), who examine, using LATE-type estimators and data from more than 100 international censuses, the causal link between fertility and female labor force participation. Their results are relatively convergent. Another example is provided by Allcott (2015), who assesses the variation in the effect of an energy-reduction policy that has been gradually implemented at 111 sites in the United States; he finds that the effect of this policy has been stronger at the 10 sites where the scheme was initially applied, suggesting that these first sites were selected because of their particular characteristics.

8.　ACCURACY OF THE ESTIMATED EFFECTS: THE QUALITY OF IDENTIFICATION BEYOND UNBIASEDNESS

The attention paid to the estimation of causal effects in the policy evaluation literature has confined thoughts about identification to the unbiasedness of the estimated effects. In this context, the precision of the estimates is mainly addressed on the basis of the statistical significance of the estimated effects – an intervention being considered worthy of interest provided that its estimated effect is significantly different from 0.

A first limitation of statistical significance, which is well known but still largely overlooked in the empirical literature (see McCloskey and Ziliak, 1996; Ziliak and McCloskey, 2004), is that it does not make it possible to assess the quantitative importance of the measured effects. For each of these effects, statistical significance depends only on the precision of their estimation. A very small point estimate can thus be statistically very significant, while a very large effect can be insignificant due to its very low precision. In fact, hypothesis testing is nothing more than an alternative formulation of a confidence interval (provided the confidence level matches the level of the test). In this sense, statistical significance only provides information on whether the value zero belongs to the confidence interval built on the estimated parameter, that is, to all the underlying effects compatible with the point estimate. Relying solely on statistical significance, whether to reject an intervention or to consider it beneficial, is tantamount to giving disproportionate weight to one of the many values within the confidence interval, many of which lead to a decision contrary to that indicated by statistical significance in the strict sense: in other words, a too wide confidence interval (that is, a too imprecise estimation of an effect with a high point estimate) may lead to discarding the intervention if this interval includes zero, or being considered beneficial if this interval, although gathering negligible values, is narrow enough to exclude zero (Amrhein et al., 2019).

The attention paid to statistical precision must be just as close as the attention to the identification of causal effects. Improving precision requires, in particular, minimizing uncontrolled sources of variation. The control over the environment—that is, blocking the sources of variation other than those of the variables of interest, such as the level of a "treatment" or the way it is administered—is an experimental approach that not only achieves identification but also increases the precision of the estimates (see Deaton and Cartwright, 2018). Randomization, often presented in an excessive or even activist manner as the "golden rule" of policy evaluation, achieves identification of the causal effect based on the statistical similarity of the units belonging to the control and the treatment groups. It does not control, however, for all the unobserved factors that can add noise to the estimation.[11]

The importance given to the significance of the estimated effects may also lead to a certain number of deviations in the interpretation of the statistical tests. In particular, the limit value of the test statistic that leads to the rejection of the null hypothesis of no effect does not, in any way, measure the probability that the alternative hypothesis, stipulating the existence of an effect, is true. This probability is measured by the power of the test, the value of which is dependent on the distribution that produces the test statistic when the alternative hypothesis is true, and therefore on the true (unknown) value from which the estimation results. An additional issue is that the p-value does not correspond either to the probability that the null hypothesis (that is, the absence of effect) is true. This probability is indeed conditional on the null hypothesis: the distribution of the test statistic associated with the estimation is deduced from the value of the effect under the null hypothesis. If the calculated value of the test statistic is denoted $\hat{s}$ and the null hypothesis is denoted H_0, the p-value therefore formally measures the quantity $\mathbb{P}(\hat{s} \mid H_0)$. The probability that the null hypothesis is true corresponds to the reverse conditioning, $\mathbb{P}(H_0 \mid \hat{s})$. The confusion between these two probabilities can be illustrated by what the behavioral science literature calls the "prosecutor fallacy", introduced by Thompson and Schumann (1987): although, for example, the probability of winning at roulette without cheating is very low, it is obviously wrong to infer that a winner at roulette must be a cheater. Assessing the probability that the null hypothesis is true entails measuring the unconditional probability of this event, as illustrated in the next section.

9.   THE INCREASING RISK OF "FALSE POSITIVES" AND THE NEED FOR REPLICATION STUDIES

Significance tests are subject to two types of risks of error: "false positives" are situations in which the estimation wrongly leads to thinking that a non-zero effect exists, and "false negatives" relate to the opposite situation, where the absence of an estimated relationship is only apparent. The respective probabilities of these cases correspond to the Type I error (also known as the "level" of the test), which is often denoted α and the most commonly chosen value of which is 5 per cent, and the Type II error, β, which is the opposite of the power, $1 - \beta$. The power measures the probability of detecting the effect of the intervention and depends on the intensity of that effect; it does not correspond to a probability, but to a function that also depends crucially on the sample size.[12]

An estimated effect is "statistically significant at the 5 per cent threshold" if the probability of getting this estimate while the effect is actually zero is less than 5 per cent. This property implies a 5 per cent probability of making a mistake when concluding that the estimated effect of an intervention is statistically significant. This probability is often interpreted as measuring the proportion of statistically significant results that are incorrect. This conclusion is only true in very specific circumstances, and the consequences of Type I errors on the credibility of empirical work are in fact often much more serious than its value suggests.

To illustrate this point, Wacholder et al. (2004) describe the components of the False-Positive Report Probability (hereinafter denoted "FPRP") as a function of the statistical properties of significance tests. The FPRP is the probability that the effect of an intervention is actually zero, even though the estimation produces a statistically significant effect. The calculation of this probability involves an unknown quantity (which is not usually discussed, even though it is fundamental) that corresponds to the proportion, denoted $\bar{y}$, of interventions that have a non-zero effect amongst all the interventions that are being evaluated. Table 11.2 describes the probability of occurrence of the four types of possible situations: the legitimate detection of an absence (true negative) or presence (true positive) of an intervention effect, as well as the occurrence of false positives, or false negatives.

Table 11.2   Components of the probability of occurrence of a false positive

Truth of the alternative hypothesis	Significance of test		Total
	Significant	Not significant	
True association	$(1-\beta)\bar{y}$ [True positive]	$\beta\bar{y}$ [False negative]	$\bar{y}$
No association	$\alpha(1-\bar{y})$ [False positive]	$(1-\alpha)(1-\bar{y})$ [True negative]	$1-\bar{y}$
Total	$(1-\beta)\bar{y}+\alpha(1-\bar{y})$	$\beta\bar{y}+(1-\alpha)(1-\bar{y})$	$\bar{y}$

Note: Subject to the existence or absence of an intervention effect, each of the cells describes the probability that the estimated effect is statistically significant (first column) or statistically insignificant (second column), taking account of the level (α) of the test, its power (β) and the proportion $\bar{y}$ of interventions that have a non-zero effect amongst all those evaluated.

Source: Wacholder et al. (2004, p. 440), Table 1.

Given the probabilities of Type I and Type II errors, the probability of a false positive occurring (the proportion of effects that are only apparent amongst all the interventions having a significant effect) is measured by:

$$FPRP(n) = \frac{[1-(1-\alpha)^n](1-\bar{y})}{[1-(1-\alpha)^n](1-\bar{y})+(1-\beta^n)\bar{y}}.$$

Most of the commonly used statistical tests are consistent, that is, their power tends toward one as the sample size increases. In this very favorable situation (where $\beta = 0$), this probability is lower than the level α of the test only if at least half of all the interventions that are evaluated have a non-zero effect. If this frequency is higher, the probability of occurrence of false positives is lower than the level of the test. It is higher than this level under the opposite (and certainly more credible) hypothesis that, of all the interventions evaluated, less than one in two has a non-zero effect, a situation that is all the more likely to occur as more evaluations are undertaken. It is of course impossible to quantify $\bar{y}$ and very difficult to collect objective information on this proportion. Still, the consequences of low values of $\bar{y}$ on the credibility that results from evaluations deserve may be very serious: under the extreme hypothesis that one intervention out of 1000 has a non-zero effect ($\bar{y} = 0.001$), the probability of reporting false positives is greater than 98 per cent.

This situation may be further aggravated by the conditions under which the results of the evaluation are made public.[13] Ioannidis (2005) focuses in particular on two types of biases that increase the probability of reporting false positives, namely the publication bias and the communication bias. Publication bias refers to the particular appeal of works highlighting a non-zero effect at all stages of the process—from project-funding decisions to the results being communicated to the general public, after having been validated academically by being published in prestigious scientific journals. These publication biases lead to a distorted proportion of positive results. They are reinforced through communication biases, which consist in reporting on an evaluation only if it leads to significant effects, while at the same time not reporting evaluation results that conclude to no effect of other kinds of interventions. As stressed by Roth (1994), this risk is particularly high when an intervention is developed following a trial-and-error process, which leads to changes in the terms and conditions of a "pilot" intervention after it has been found to have no effect, until a final proposal is developed that gives rise to the expected significant effect on the outcome. This process is legitimate because it allows us to design effective public policies; it does not affect the probability of reporting false positives if all trials are made public at the same time as the final evaluation. Conversely, this process leads to a communication bias as soon as only significant effects are made public, while previous unsuccessful attempts are ignored.

Publication biases, like communication biases, lead to an increase in the proportion of false positives. To illustrate this point, the proportion of positive results caused by one of these two types of bias is denoted $\mathcal{B}$. Amongst the $\bar{y}$ interventions that actually have an effect, the analysis will make it possible to accurately conclude that there is a non-zero effect for a proportion $(1 - \beta)$ of cases, while a certain number $(\mathcal{B} \times \beta)$ will appear to have an effect due to one of the types of biases. Similarly, a proportion α of interventions amongst the $(1 - \bar{y})$ actually having zero effect will appear as having no effect, while a certain number $\mathcal{B} \times (1 - \alpha)$ will appear as having a non-zero effect due to bias. In total, the FPRP becomes:

$$FPRP(B) = \frac{(1-\bar{y})[\alpha + \mathcal{B}(1-\alpha)]}{(1-\bar{y})[\alpha + \mathcal{B}(1-\alpha)] + (1-\beta)\bar{y} + \mathcal{B}\beta\bar{y}}.$$

For the "credibility revolution" announced by some authors (Angrist and Pischke, 2010) to fully succeed, public policy evaluation cannot be based solely on convincing identification strategies. The replication of policy evaluation results, making it possible to distinguish false positives from the proven effects of an intervention (Clemens, 2017), remains essential, as is the need to ensure the precision of the estimated effects.

10.   INTERFERENCE BETWEEN UNITS IN EXPERIMENTAL AND OBSERVATIONAL STUDIES

Usually, the post-treatment outcome of one unit (either treated or control) is assumed to be unaffected by the potential outcomes of other units. This assumption of no interference, introduced by Cox (1958), is called the SUTVA assumption (Stable Unit Treatment Value Assumption) by Rubin (1978), or the individualistic treatment response by Manski (2013). In the presence of interference, treatments may have direct effects on the units (individuals, schools, neighborhoods, cities, firms and so on) receiving the treatment as well as indirect effects on units not receiving the treatment. In other terms, each unit may have several potential outcomes depending on the treatment status and the outcomes and the behaviors of other units. During the last fifteen years, a burgeoning academic literature has been devoted to measuring the effects of interference between units in experimental and observational studies. Among this body of research, we may distinguish works relative to partial interference and those concerning general interference. This section gives a brief overview of these developments.

It is useful to introduce some concepts. Following Halloran and Struchiner (1991, 1995), we can define direct, indirect, total and overall effects in the presence of interference in RCTs. To illustrate these definitions, let us consider two clusters, denoted A and B. In cluster A, a certain proportion of randomly chosen units is treated while the rest remains untreated. In cluster B, all units are untreated. The direct effect of the treatment is defined as the difference between the average outcomes of treated units and untreated ones in cluster A. The indirect effect is the difference between the average outcome of untreated units in cluster A and the average outcome of untreated units in cluster B. The total effect is defined as the difference between the average outcome of treated units in cluster A and the average outcome of untreated units in cluster B. In general, the total effect can be decomposed as a function of direct and indirect effects. The overall effect is defined by the contrast in the average outcome in the entire cluster A compared to the average outcome of the entire cluster B.

10.1   Partial Interference

In the presence of interference, Halloran and Struchiner (1995) propose individual-level causal estimands by letting the potential outcomes for any individual depend on the vector of treatment assignments to other individuals. However, with a binary outcome, one treatment and one control, if there are N people in a population, there are 2^N possible treatment vectors and 2^N possible potential outcomes. Causal inference in the presence of so many potential outcomes is difficult, if not impossible, without making additional assumptions.

It is then possible to add some further assumptions which simplify the problem substantially. For instance, units can be partitioned into groups such as there is no interference between groups. This assumption is called partial interference by Sobel (2006), who considers interference in a housing mobility experiment in poor neighborhoods.

10.1.1   Two-stage randomization

Suppose that we consider two different treatment strategies. The first strategy might be to treat 50 per cent of the units in a population, the other strategy might be to treat no one. What are the direct, indirect, total and overall effects of the 50 per cent treatment strategy compared to the no treatment strategy? Assuming partial interference, Hudgens and Halloran (2008) define group- and population-level causal estimands for direct, indirect, total and overall causal effects of treatment under two different treatment allocations. To obtain unbiased estimators of the population-level causal estimands, Hudgens and Halloran (2008) propose a two-stage randomization scheme, the first stage at the group level, the second stage at the unit level within groups. For example, suppose there are 10 groups of units. At the first stage, we could randomize 5 groups to the 50 per pent treatment strategy and the remaining groups to the no treatment strategy. In the second stage, within 5 groups, 50 per cent of units are randomly assigned to the treatment, and in the other 5 groups no unit receives the treatment. Unbiased estimates of the direct, indirect, and total effects can be obtained by contrasts in average outcomes among treated and untreated units under the different strategies. Likewise, contrasts in average outcomes of all units under the two treatment strategies produce unbiased estimates of the overall effect.

Hudgens and Halloran (2008) propose variance estimators under an additional assumption called stratified interference, stipulating that the indirect treatment effects depend only on the proportion of other individuals in the group who receive treatment. More recently, Tchetgen and VanderWeele (2012), Liu and Hudgens (2014) and Rigdon and Hudgens (2015) calculate exact asymptotic confidence intervals.

In order to measure spillover effects in the context of economic experiments, Baird et al. (2018) consider a similar two-stage randomized design. They refer to the level of (treatment) coverage in a cluster as the saturation level and their study design as the randomized saturation design. The intention to treat effect, the spillover on the non-treated effect and the total causal effect, are analogous to the total, indirect, and overall effects defined. Moreover, consider optimal design of two stage randomized trials, particularly choosing the optimal coverage level, to detect the different effects.

10.1.2 Partially randomized and observational studies

In studies which do not utilize two-stage randomization, the estimators described in the previous subsection are generally biased or inconsistent due to potential confounding. In the observational approach where the treatment assignment mechanism is not known (or not random) and there is no interference, the propensity score is one method to adjust for confounding (see section 10.1.1). Propensity score methods have then been extended to the case where interference may be present. For example, Hong and Raudenbush (2006) consider the effect on reading scores of being retained in kindergarten versus being promoted to the first grade. They classify schools by whether they retain a high proportion or a low proportion of children. Interference within a school is summarized by the dichotomous dummy variable representing a high or low retention rate. Their study is observational at two levels: schools are not randomized to have high or low retention, and students at risk to be retained are not randomized to be retained. Assuming partial interference, Hong and Raudenbush (2006) use a multilevel propensity score stratification allowing for interference. The school propensity of adopting a high retention rate is estimated thanks to pre-treatment information. Then the child propensity of repetition in high-retention schools and the child propensity of repetition in low-retention schools are also estimated by using pre-treatment information. Estimation of causal effects is based on stratifications by the estimated school and child propensity scores.

Tchetgen and VanderWeele (2012) also use group-level propensity scores to propose inverse probability weighted (IPW) estimators of the direct, indirect, total and overall causal effects in observational studies in the absence of two-stage randomization. Lundin and Karlsson (2014) develop similar IPW estimators of direct, indirect and total effects under interference where treatment assignment is randomized only at the first stage, while in some groups all units are untreated. Perez-Heydrich et al. (2014) and Liu et al. (2016) consider the asymptotic properties of different IPW estimators in the presence of partial interference.

10.2 General Interference

In the general interference setting, each unit is assumed to have a unique set of other units whose treatment might affect the outcome of this unit. Research assessing treatment effects in the presence of general interference include papers by Rosenbaum and Rubin (1983), Toulis and Kao (2013), Ugander et al. (2013), Eckles et al. (2017), van der Laan (2014), Liu et al. (2016) and Aronow, Samii, et al. (2017). These papers typically assume one finite population of N units. For each unit, there exists a set of other units which may interfere with that unit. This interference set is assumed to be known and fixed. It is also usually assumed that the number of units in these interference sets is smaller than N and that any indirect or spillover effect on a unit sets from this known interference set.

10.2.1 Randomized experiments

For instance, Ugander et al. (2013) and Eckles et al. (2017) consider randomized experiments on networks where treatment of one unit could have indirect/spillover effects on neighboring units. Their causal estimand of interest is the average of the difference in the potential outcomes under two extreme assignments, one where every unit in a network receives treatment and one where no units receive treatment. If units were independently randomized to treatment and control, for units which share many connections with other units, the probability that all their neighbors would (i) all receive treatment or (ii) all receive control would be low. Thus, Ugander et al. (2013) consider a partition of the network into clusters of units and propose randomizing some of the clusters to receive treatment and the remaining clusters to receive control. Then they introduce the notion of network exposure wherein a unit is network exposed to treatment (control) if the unit's response under a specific assignment vector is the same as if every unit in the network had received the treatment (control). They derive an unbiased estimator of the average treatment effect using inverse probability weighting for any randomization design for which the network exposure probabilities can be explicitly computed.

Toulis and Kao (2013) propose causal estimands for peer influence (indirect) effects describing interference in a social network. For each unit, a neighborhood is defined by the other units with whom that unit shares some connections. If at least one neighbor receives treatment, then the unit is considered exposed to peer influence effects. The potential outcome for each unit can depend on its treatment and that of its neighbors. Then Toulis and Kao (2013) define two causal estimands. The causal estimand for the primary effect is the average over the whole population of the difference in outcomes if a unit receives treatment versus receives control when every other unit in the neighborhood receives control. The main causal estimands for peer influence effects are defined by fixing the specific number of neighbors who receive treatment. For example, if k neighbors receive treatment, the k-level causal estimand for peer-influence effects is averaged over units with at least k neighbors. Two estimation procedures are proposed: a frequentist model-based estimator assuming some sequential randomization design and known network, and a Bayesian approach which accounts for uncertainty in the network topology.

10.2.2   Observational studies

In recent contributions, van der Laan (2014) and Sofrygin and van der Laan (2017) have considered statistical inference about causal effects in the presence of general interference in observational studies. They define the population of interest to be a set of (possibly) dependent units and assume that only a single draw from the true data-generating process is observed. Namely, contrary to traditional statistical inference, multiple independent and identically distributed (hereafter, i.i.d.) replicates are not assumed. With partial interference, one may assume that the groups are i.i.d., which allows us to apply existing statistical theory. However, with general interference, the observation of i.i.d. replicates is generally not possible, such that standard large sample frequentist approaches do not apply. Thus, van der Laan (2014) and Sofrygin and van der Laan (2017) derive asymptotic properties of targeted maximum likelihood estimators in this setting, providing a method for statistical inference in the presence of general interference in observation studies.

NOTES

*   This project is supported by the Agence nationale de la recherche (National Research Agency, ANR) and the French government under the LIEPP Labex investment programme for the future (ANR-11-LABX-0091, ANR-11-IDEX-0005-02).
1.   An extensive review of recent developments and future research directions can be found in the papers written by Athey and Imbens (2017a, b), and Abadie and Cattaneo (2018).

2. The repeated observations may not be those concerning the same individuals but may be repetitions of random samples taken from the same population and form a "pseudo panel".
3. This *balancing score* property implies that $x_i \perp T_i | s(x_i)$. Given that $s(x_i) = \ell(T_i | x_i)$, and hence $\ell[T_i | s(x_i)] = \ell[T_i | x_i, s(x_i)]$, conditional independence implies:

$$\ell[x_i, T_i | s(x_i)] = \ell[x_i | T_i, s(x_i)]\ell[T_i | s(x_i)] = \ell[T_i | x_i, s(x_i)]\ell[x_i | s(x_i)].$$

4. Inverse probability weighting is a statistical technique for calculating standardized statistics for a pseudo-population that is different from the one from which the data were collected.
5. "The unconfoundedness assumption states that assignment is free from dependence on the potential outcomes" (Imbens and Rubin, 2015, p. 257).
6. The sharp regression discontinuity design corresponds to the case where nobody can derogate from the constraint of the eligibility threshold. This case is opposite to that of the fuzzy regression discontinuity design, in which treated individuals, or untreated individuals, are observed on both sides of the threshold.
7. The only regions with weights well above zero are Madrid and Catalonia.
8. It is sometimes preferable to compare it with a weighted average of the outcomes of untreated individuals whose propensity scores have similar values. This is the principle that is implemented in the case of kernel matching.
9. LASSO stands for Least Absolute Shrinkage and Selection Operator. This method, introduced by Tibshirani (1996), is a method for shrinking regression coefficients that essentially involves estimating the coefficient vector by minimizing the sum of the squared residual under an additional regularization constraint.
10. To implement this technique, the reader can in particular use the R package randomForest (https://cran.r?project.org/web/packages/ran? domForest/index.html).
11. In a paper that is relatively critical of the mechanical applications of the randomized trial procedure, Deaton (2010) reviews the identification problems that remain despite random assignment to the treatment and control groups.
12. The benchmark power level in applied work is 80 per cent, although Ioannidis et al. (2017) show that in more than half of applied economics work, the median power is 18 per cent or even less.
13. We have deliberately left out the issue of questionable practices that force the significance of results, for example by deliberately choosing the outcome variable from among all the variables on which the intervention may act, a practice that artificially increases the proportion of false positives (see, for example, List et al., 2001). Christensen and Miguel (2018) present an overview of practices that cause the credibility of empirical results in economics to be weakened and list a certain number of possible solutions.

REFERENCES

Abadie, A. (2015): "Comparative Politics and the Synthetic Control Method," *American Journal of Political Science*, 59(2), 495–510.

Abadie, A., A. Diamond, and J. Hainmueller (2010): "Synthetic Control Methods for Comparative Case Studies: Estimating the Effect of California's Tobacco Control Program," *Journal of the American Statistical Association*, 105(490), 493–505.

Abadie, A., and J. Gardeazabal (2003): "The Economic Costs of Conflict: A Case Study of the Basque Country," *American Economic Review*, 93(1), 113–32.

Abadie, A., and J. l'Hour (2017): "A Penalized Synthetic Control Estimator for Disaggregated Data," *MIT Working Paper*.

Abadie, A., and M. D. Cattaneo (2018): "Econometric Methods for Program Evaluation," *Annual Review of Economics*, 10, 465–503.

Abbring, J. H., and J. J. Heckman (2007): "Econometric Evaluation of Social Programs, Part III: Distributional Treatment Effects, Dynamic Treatment Effects, Dynamic Discrete Choice, and General Equilibrium Policy Evaluation," in *Handbook of Econometrics*, ed. by J. J. Heckman, and E. Leamer, vol. 6, Part B, chap. 72, pp. 5145–303. Elsevier.

Allcott, H. (2015): "Site Selection Bias in Program Evaluation," *Quarterly Journal of Economics*, 130(3), 1117–65.

Amjad, M., D. Shah, and D. Shen (2018): "Robust Synthetic Control," *The Journal of Machine Learning Research*, 19(1), 802–52.

Amrhein, V., S. Greenland, and B. McShane (2019): "Scientists Rise up against Statistical Significance," *Nature*, 567, 305–7.

Angrist, J. D. (2004): "Treatment Effect Heterogeneity in Theory and Practice," *Economic Journal*, 114(494), 52–83.

Angrist, J., and G. Imbens (1995): "Two-Stage Least Squares Estimation of Average Causal Effects in Models with Variable Treatment Intensity," *Journal of the American Statistical Association*, 90(140), 431–42.

Angrist, J. D., and A. B. Krueger (1999): "Empirical Strategies in Labor Economics," in *Handbook of Labor Economics*, ed. by O. C. Ashenfelter, and D. Card, vol. 3, Part A, chap. 23, pp. 1277–366. Elsevier.

Angrist, J. D., and I. Fernandez-Val (2013): "Extrapolate-Ing: External Validity and Overidentification in the Late Framework," in *Advances in Economics and Econometrics: Theory and Applications, Tenth World Congress*, ed. by D. Acemoglu, M. Arellano, and E. Dekel, vol. III of *Econometric Society Monographs*. Cambridge University Press/National Bureau of Economic Research.

Angrist, J. D., K. Graddy, and G. W. Imbens (2000): "The Interpretation of Instrumental Variables Estimators in Simultaneous Equations Models with an Application to the Demand for Fish," *Review of Economic Studies*, 67(3), 499–527.

Angrist, J. D., and J.-S. Pischke (2010): "The Credibility Revolution in Empirical Economics: How Better Research Design Is Taking the Con out of Econometrics," *Journal of Economic Perspectives*, 24(2), 3–30.

Angrist, J. D., and M. Rokkanen (2015): "Wanna Get Away? Regression Discontinuity Estimation of Exam School Effects Away from the Cutoff," *Journal of the American Statistical Association*, 110(512), 1331–44.

Aronow, P. M., C. Samii, et al. (2017): "Estimating Average Causal Effects under General Interference, with Application to a Social Network Experiment," *The Annals of Applied Statistics*, 11(4), 1912–47.

Ashenfelter, O. (1978): "Estimating the Effect of Training Programs on Earnings," *Review of Economics and Statistics*, 60(1), 47–57.

Athey, S., and G. W. Imbens (2017a): "The State of Applied Econometrics: Causality and Policy Evaluation," *Journal of Economic Perspectives*, 31(2), 3–32.

Athey, S., and G. W. Imbens (2017b): "The Econometrics of Randomized Experiments," in *Handbook of Economic Field Experiments*, ed. by A. V. Banerjee, and E. Duflo, vol. 1, chap. 3, pp. 73–140. Elsevier.

Athey, S., M. Bayati, N. Doudchenko, G. Imbens, and K. Khosravi (2018): "Matrix Completion Methods for Causal Panel Data Models," *NBER Working Paper*, 25132.

Baird, S., J. A. Bohren, C. McIntosh, and B. Özler (2018): "Optimal Design of Experiments in the Presence of Interference," *Review of Economics and Statistics*, 100(5), 844–60.

Belloni, A., V. Chernozhukov, I. Fernández-Val, and C. Hansen (2017): "Program Evaluation and Causal Inference with High-Dimensional Data," *Econometrica*, 85(1), 233–98.

Belloni, A., V. Chernozhukov, and C. Hansen (2014): "Inference on Treatment Effects after Selection among High-Dimensional Controls," *Review of Economic Studies*, 81(2), 608–50.

Bertanha, M., and G. W. Imbens (2019): "External Validity in Fuzzy Regression Discontinuity Designs," *Journal of Business & Economic Statistics*, Forthcoming.

Bisbee, J., R. Dehejia, C. Pop-Eleches, and C. Samii (2017): "Local Instruments, Global Extrapolation: External Validity of the Labor Supply–Fertility Local Average Treatment Effect," *Journal of Labor Economics*, 35(S1), S99–S147.

Chabé-Ferret, S. (2015): "Analysis of the Bias of Matching and Difference-in-Difference under Alternative Earnings and Selection Processes," *Journal of Econometrics*, 185(1), 110–23.

Chaplin, D. D., T. D. Cook, J. Zurovac, J. S. Coopersmith, M. M. Finucane, L. N. Vollmer, and R. E. Morris (2018): "The Internal and External Validity of the Regression Discontinuity Design: A Meta-Analysis of 15 within-Study Comparisons," *Journal of Policy Analysis and Management*, 37(2), 403–29.

Chernozhukov, V., D. Chetverikov, M. Demirer, E. Duflo, C. Hansen, W. Newey, and J. Robins (2018): "Double/Debiased Machine Learning for Treatment and Structural Parameters," *The Econometrics Journal*, 21(1), C1–C68.

Christensen, G., and E. Miguel (2018): "Transparency, Reproducibility, and the Credibility of Economics Research," *Journal of Economic Literature*, 56(3), 920–80.

Clemens, M. A. (2017): "The Meaning of Failed Replications: A Review and Proposal," *Journal of Economic Surveys*, 31(1), 326–42.

Connolly, P., C. Keenan, and K. Urbanska (2018): "The Trials of Evidence-Based Practice in Education: A Systematic Review of Randomised Controlled Trials in Education Research 1980–2016," *Educational Research*, 60(3), 276–91.

Cox, D. R. (1958): *Planning of Experiments*. Wiley.

Deaton, A. (2010): "Instruments, Randomization, and Learning about Development," *Journal of Economic Literature*, 48(2), 424–55.

Deaton, A., and N. Cartwright (2018): "Understanding and Misunderstanding Randomized Controlled Trials," *Social Science & Medicine*, 210, 2–21.

Dehejia, R., C. Pop-Eleches, and C. Samii (2019): "From Local to Global: External Validity an A Fertility Natural Experiment," *Journal of Business & Economic Statistics*, Forthcoming.

Dong, Y., and A. Lewbel (2015): "Identifying the Effect of Changing the Policy Threshold in Regression Discontinuity Models," *Review of Economics and Statistics*, 97(5), 1081–92.

Duflo, E., and A. Banerjee (2017): *Handbook of Field Experiments*, vol. 1. Elsevier.

Eckles, D., B. Karrer, and J. Ugander (2017): "Design and Analysis of Experiments in Networks: Reducing Bias from Interference," *Journal of Causal Inference*, 5(1).

Farrell, M. H. (2015): "Robust Inference on Average Treatment Effects with Possibly More Covariates Than Observations," *Journal of Econometrics*, 189(1), 1–23.

Glazerman, S., D. M. Levy, and D. Myers (2003): "Nonexperimental versus Experimental Estimates of Earnings Impacts," *The Annals of the American Academy of Political and Social Science*, 589(1), 63–93.

Hahn, J., and R. Shi (2017): "Synthetic Control and Inference," *Econometrics*, 5(4), 52.

Halloran, M. E., and C. J. Struchiner (1991): "Study Designs for Dependent Happenings," *Epidemiology*, 331–38.

Halloran, M. E., and C. J. Struchiner (1995): "Causal Inference in Infectious Diseases," *Epidemiology*, 142–51.

Heckman, J. J., and E. J. Vytlacil (2007a): "Econometric Evaluation of Social Programs, Part I: Causal Models, Structural Models and Econometric Policy Evaluation," in *Handbook of Econometrics*, ed. by J. J. Heckman and E. Leamer, vol. 6, Part B, chap. 70, pp. 4779–874. Elsevier.

Heckman, J. J., and E. J. Vytlacil (2007b): "Econometric Evaluation of Social Programs, Part II: Using the Marginal Treatment Effect to Organize Alternative Econometric Estimators to Evaluate Social Programs, and to Forecast Their Effects in New Environments," in *Handbook of Econometrics*, ed. by J. J. Heckman and E. Leamer, vol. 6, Part B, chap. 71, pp. 4875–5143. Elsevier.

Heckman, J. J., H. Ichimura, and P. E. Todd (1998): "Matching as an Econometric Evaluation Estimator," *Review of Economic Studies*, 65(2), 261–94.

Heckman, J. J., R. Lalonde, and J. Smith (1999): "The Economics and Econometrics of Active Labor Market Programs," in *Handbook of Labor Economics*, ed. by O. C. Ashenfelter and D. Card, vol. 3, Part 1, chap. 31, pp. 1865–2097. Elsevier Science.

Hong, G., and S. W. Raudenbush (2006): "Evaluating Kindergarten Retention Policy: A Case Study of Causal Inference for Multilevel Observational Data," *Journal of the American Statistical Association*, 101(475), 901–10.

Hotz, V. J., G. W. Imbens, and J. H. Mortimer (2005): "Predicting the Efficacy of Future Training Programs Using Past Experiences at Other Locations," *Journal of Econometrics*, 125(1–2), 241–70.

Hudgens, M. G., and M. E. Halloran (2008): "Toward Causal Inference with Interference," *Journal of the American Statistical Association*, 103(482), 832–42.

Imai, K., G. King, and E. A. Stuart (2008): "Misunderstandings between Experimentalists and Observationalists about Causal Inference," *Journal of the Royal Statistical Society: Series A*, 171(2), 481–502.

Imbens, G. W. (2010): "Better LATE Than Nothing: Some Comments on Deaton (2009) and Heckman and Urzua (2009)," *Journal of Economic Literature*, 48(2), 399–423.

Imbens, G. W., and D. B. Rubin (2015): *Causal Inference in Statistics, Social, and Biomedical Sciences*. Cambridge University Press.

Imbens, G. W., and J. D. Angrist (1994): "Identification and Estimation of Local Average Treatment Effects," *Econometrica*, 62(2), 467–75.

Imbens, G. W., and J. M. Wooldridge (2009): "Recent Developments in the Econometrics of Program Evaluation," *Journal of Economic Literature*, 47(1), 5–86.

Ioannidis, J. P. A. (2005): "Why Most Published Research Findings Are False," *PLoS Med*, 2(8), e124.

Ioannidis, J. P. A., T. D. Stanley, and H. Doucouliagos (2017): "The Power of Bias in Economics Research," *Economic Journal*, 127(605), F236–F265.

Jacquemet, N., and O. L'Haridon (2018): *Experimental Economics: Method and Applications*. Cambridge University Press.

Knaus, M. C., M. Lechner, and A. Strittmatter (2017): "Heterogeneous Employment Effects of Job Search Programmes: A Machine Learning Approach," *IZA DP*, 10961.

Knaus, M., M. Lechner, and A. Strittmatter (2018): "Machine Learning Estimation of Heterogeneous Causal Effects: Empirical Monte Carlo Evidence," *CEPR Discussion Paper*, DP13402.

LaLonde, R. J. (1986): "Evaluating the Econometric Evaluations of Training Programs with Experimental Data," *American Economic Review*, 76(4), 604–20.

Leamer, E. E. (1983): "Let's Take the Con Out of Econometrics," *American Economic Review*, 73(1), 31–43.

Lechner, M. (2019): "Modified Causal Forests for Estimating Heterogeneous Causal Effects," *CEPR Discussion Paper*, DP13430.

Lee, M.-J. (2016): *Matching, Regression Discontinuity, Difference in Differences, and Beyond*. Oxford University Press.

List, J. A., C. Bailey, P. Euzent, and T. Martin (2001): "Academic Economists Behaving Badly? A Survey on Three Areas of Unethical Behavior," *Economic Inquiry*, 39(1), 162–70.

Liu, L., and M. G. Hudgens (2014): "Large Sample Randomization Inference of Causal Effects in the Presence of Interference," *Journal of the American Statistical Association*, 109(505), 288–301.

Liu, L., M. G. Hudgens, and S. Becker-Dreps (2016): "On Inverse Probability-Weighted Estimators in the Presence of Interference," *Biometrika*, 103(4), 829–42.

Lundin, M., and M. Karlsson (2014): "Estimation of Causal Effects in Observational Studies with Interference between Units," *Statistical Methods & Applications*, 23(3), 417–33.

Manski, C. F. (2013): "Identification of Treatment Response with Social Interactions," *The Econometrics Journal*, 16(1), S1–S23.

McCaffrey, D. F., G. Ridgeway, and A. R. Morral (2004): "Propensity Score Estimation with Boosted Regression for Evaluating Causal Effects in Observational Studies," *Psychological Methods*, 9(4), 403.

McCloskey, D. N., and S. T. Ziliak (1996): "The Standard Error of Regressions," *Journal of Economic Literature*, 34(1), 97–114.

Meager, R. (2019): "Understanding the Average Impact of Microcredit Expansions: A Bayesian Hierarchical Analysis of Seven Randomized Experiments," *American Economic Journal: Applied Economics*, 11(1), 57–91.

Perez-Heydrich, C., M. G. Hudgens, M. E. Halloran, J. D. Clemens, M. Ali, and M. E. Emch (2014): "Assessing Effects of Cholera Vaccination in the Presence of Interference," *Biometrics*, 70(3), 731–41.

Rigdon, J., and M. G. Hudgens (2015): "Exact Confidence Intervals in the Presence of Interference," *Statistics & Probability Letters*, 105, 130–35.

Rosenbaum, P. R., and D. B. Rubin (1983): "The Central Role of the Propensity Score in Observational Studies for Causal Effects," *Biometrika*, 70(1), 41–55.

Roth, A. E. (1994): "Lets Keep the Con out of Experimental a Methodological Note," *Empirical Economics*, 19(2), 279–89.

Rubin, D. B. (1974): "Estimating Causal Effects of Treatments in Randomized and Nonrandomized Studies," *Journal of Educational Psychology*, 66(5), 688–701.

Rubin, D. B. (1977): "Assignment to Treatment Group on the Basis of a Covariate," *Journal of Educational and Behavioral Statistics*, 2(1), 1–26.

Rubin, D. B. (1978): "Bayesian Inference for Causal Effects: The Role of Randomization," *The Annals of Statistics*, pp. 34–58.

Sobel, M. E. (2006): "What Do Randomized Studies of Housing Mobility Demonstrate? Causal Inference in the Face of Interference," *Journal of the American Statistical Association*, 101(476), 1398–407.

Sofrygin, O., and M. J. van der Laan (2017): "Semi-Parametric Estimation and Inference for the Mean Outcome of the Single Time-Point Intervention in a Causally Connected Population," *Journal of Causal Inference*, 5(1).

Sperlich, S. A., and M. Frölich (2019): *Impact Evaluation: Treatment Effects and Causal Analysis*. Cambridge University Press.

Stuart, E. A., C. P. Bradshaw, and P. J. Leaf (2015): "Assessing the Generalizability of Randomized Trial Results to Target Populations," *Prevention Science*, 16(3), 475–85.

Stuart, E. A., S. R. Cole, C. P. Bradshaw, and P. J. Leaf (2011): "The Use of Propensity Scores to Assess the Generalizability of Results from Randomized Trials," *Journal of the Royal Statistical Society: Series A*, 174(2), 369–86.

Tchetgen, E. J. T., and T. J. VanderWeele (2012): "On Causal Inference in the Presence of Interference," *Statistical Methods in Medical Research*, 21(1), 55–75.

Thompson, W. C., and E. L. Schumann (1987): "Interpretation of Statistical Evidence in Criminal Trials," *Law and Human Behavior*, 11(3), 167–87.

Tibshirani, R. (1996): "Regression Shrinkage and Selection via the Lasso," *Journal of the Royal Statistical Society: Series B*, 58(1), 267–88.

Toulis, P., and E. Kao (2013): "Estimation of Causal Peer Influence Effects," *Proceedings of Machine Learning Research*, 28(3), 1489–97.

Ugander, J., B. Karrer, L. Backstrom, and J. Kleinberg (2013): "Graph Cluster Randomization: Network Exposure to Multiple Universes," *Proceedings of the 19th ACM SIGKDD International Conference on Knowledge Discovery and Data Mining*, pp. 329–37.

van der Laan, M. J. (2014): "Causal Inference for a Population of Causally Connected Units," *Journal of Causal Inference*, 2(1), 13–74.

Wacholder, S., S. Chanock, M. Garcia-Closas, L. El Ghormli, and N. Rothman (2004): "Assessing the Probability That a Positive Report Is False: An Approach for Molecular Epidemiology Studies," *Journal of the National Cancer Institute*, 96(6), 434–42.

Wager, S., and S. Athey (2018): "Estimation and Inference of Heterogeneous Treatment Effects Using Random Forests," *Journal of the American Statistical Association*, 113(523), 1228–42.

Wald, A. (1940): "The Fitting of Straight Lines If Both Variables Are Subject to Error," *Annals of Mathematical Statistics*, 11(3), 284–300.

Wong, V. C., J. C. Valentine, and K. Miller-Bains (2017): "Empirical Performance of Covariates in Education Observational Studies," *Journal of Research on Educational Effectiveness*, 10(1), 207–36.

Wyss, R., A. R. Ellis, M. A. Brookhart, C. J. Girman, M. J. Funk, R. J. LoCasale, and T. Stürmer (2014): "The Role of Prediction Modeling in Propensity Score Estimation: An Evaluation of Logistic Regression, bCART, and the Covariate-Balancing Propensity Score.," *American Journal of Epidemiology*, 180(6), 645–55.

Ziliak, S. T., and D. N. McCloskey (2004): "Size Matters: The Standard Error of Regressions in the American Economic Review," *Journal of Socio-Economics*, 33(5), 527–46.

12. Regression discontinuity designs in policy evaluation

Otávio Bartalotti, Marinho Bertanha and Sebastian Calonico

1. INTRODUCTION

Regression Discontinuity (RD) has become a mainstay of policy evaluation in several fields of social sciences. (Hahn et al., 2001; Imbens and Lemieux, 2008; Lee and Lemieux, 2010; Cattaneo et al., 2020, 2021)

The main appeal of RD comes from a "clean" identification strategy that relies on transparent assumptions. In its simplest form, RD designs exploit an abrupt change in the probability of receiving treatment based on a score or "running variable" crossing a known cutoff. For example, eligibility for medical insurance might be determined by an individual's age reaching 65 years, remedial classes might be mandatory for students scoring below a particular level in tests, additional care might be available for newborns classified as very low birth weight or tax credits might be available in areas where the share of low-income households exceeds a determined level.

The insight of RD designs is that, under some relatively mild conditions, we should not expect a difference in outcomes between observations just above and below the cutoff in the absence of the policy. Thus, differences across the two groups characterize the causal impact of the policy. For example, in many places, the assignment of students to summer-school programs is based on test scores being below a certain threshold. Figure 12.1(a) illustrates the probability of attending summer school conditional on a test score, using administrative data on third graders from public schools in Chicago (Jacob and Lefgren, 2004; Bertanha and Imbens, 2020). Most of the students eligible for summer school do attend it, and the change in the probability of attendance at the cutoff is close to 1. Figure 12.1(b) shows the conditional mean of the math test score after summer school, given the test score prior to summer school. There is a significant discontinuity in outcome at the cutoff for those who are eligible to attend summer school compared to those who are not eligible to attend summer school. The discontinuity provides evidence of a positive causal effect of summer school on students with test scores close to the cutoff.

This chapter is divided into three parts. First, we discuss the parameters of interest that RD can identify and the basic set of assumptions required. The second part considers estimation, inference and overall implementation, focusing on local polynomial estimation, bandwidth choice alternatives and robust inference. Finally, we discuss recent extensions addressing common challenges faced by researchers implementing RD, such as running variable manipulation, multiple cutoffs, measurement error and sample selection.

2. IDENTIFICATION

We adopt the potential outcomes framework (Rubin, 1974; Holland, 1986; Imbens and Rubin, 2015). Let Y_1 represent the potential outcome of interest if an observation receives treatment and Y_0 the potential outcome if it does not. The researcher's interest lies in estimating the

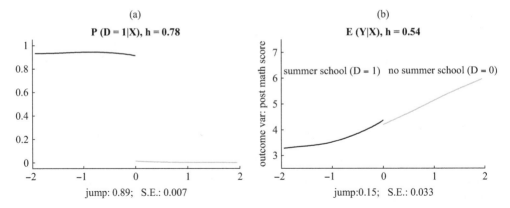

Notes: Outcome variable (*Y*): math score in the year after summer school; forcing variable (*X*): minimum between reading and math score before summer school minus the cutoff; *D*: participation indicator; *h*: the bandwidth choice for the local polynomial estimators (section 3.1).

Source: Plots reproduce Figures 1(a) and 1(b) in Bertanha and Imbens (2020); administrative data for third grade public school students in Chicago from 1997–99 in Jacob and Lefgren (2004).

Figure 12.1   *Visual representation of a Regression Discontinuity design*

average treatment effect (ATE) of a program or policy. Treatment status is denoted $D = \{0,1\}$, which is potentially endogenously determined. Treatment assignment changes discontinuously when the running variable X crosses a known cutoff c. Under a mild set of assumptions, we can exploit the discontinuity on treatment assignment to learn about the causal effect of treatment at the cutoff.

2.1   Sharp RD Design

In the sharp RD design, the treatment assignment is fully determined by crossing the threshold:

$$D = \mathbb{1}[X \geq c]. \tag{12.1}$$

That is, the probability of treatment conditional on X jumps from zero to one at $X = c$. The discontinuous treatment assignment rule yields identification of the ATE at the threshold, $\tau = \mathbb{E}[Y_1 - Y_0 \mid X = c]$, if observable and unobservable factors vary smoothly with X around the cutoff. More formally, we assume that $\mathbb{E}[Y_0 \mid X]$ and $\mathbb{E}[Y_1 \mid X]$ are continuous functions of X in a neighborhood of the threshold, that is, $X \in (c - \varepsilon, c + \varepsilon)$ for ε small. Identification is achieved by comparing the conditional expectation of the observed outcome $Y = DY_1 + (1 - D)Y_0$ on both sides of the cutoff:

$$\lim_{a \downarrow 0} \mathbb{E}[Y \mid X = c + a] - \lim_{a \uparrow 0} \mathbb{E}[Y \mid X = c + a] = \mathbb{E}[Y \mid X = c^+] - \mathbb{E}[Y \mid X = c^-] = \tau. \tag{12.2}$$

Intuitively, the continuity assumption means that the average potential outcome of individuals under treatment or control does not suddenly change at the cutoff, so individuals on both sides are comparable. Therefore, the difference in observed outcomes Y across the threshold identifies the causal effect of the treatment.

2.2 Fuzzy RD Design

In the more general case, the treatment assignment is not fully determined by the running variable, but it also depends on unobserved factors that are potentially endogenous. In this fuzzy RD design, the jump in probability of treatment at the cutoff is smaller than one:

$$\lim_{a \downarrow 0} \mathbb{E}\left[D \mid X = c+a\right] - \lim_{a \uparrow 0} \mathbb{E}\left[D \mid X = c+a\right]$$

$$= \mathbb{P}\left(D = 1 \mid X = c^{+}\right) - \mathbb{P}\left(D = 1 \mid X = c^{-}\right) \neq 0. \tag{12.3}$$

The nonzero change in the conditional probability of treatment implies that some individuals do change treatment status due to the cutoff assignment rule and identification of the treatment effect is possible for those individuals. Using potential outcomes notation, let $D(c)$ denote the potential treatment status of an individual given the policy threshold is set at $X = c$. In the sharp RD design, everyone complies to the policy and $D(c) = \mathbb{1}[X \geq c]$. In the fuzzy RD design, there are four types of compliance types local to the threshold: always takers $D(c) \equiv 1$, never takers $D(c) \equiv 0$, compliers $D(c) = \mathbb{1}[X \geq c]$ and defiers $D(c) = \mathbb{1}[X < c]$. Hahn et al. (1999) demonstrate identification of the ATE on compliers at the cutoff under the assumptions that there are no defiers and that the distribution of $(Y_0, Y_1, D(c))$ conditional on X is continuous:

$$\tau_c = \mathbb{E}\left[Y_1 - Y_0 \mid X = c, D(c^{+}) = 1, D(c^{-}) = 0\right]$$

$$= \frac{\lim_{a \downarrow 0} \mathbb{E}\left[Y \mid X = c+a\right] - \lim_{a \uparrow 0} \mathbb{E}\left[Y \mid X = c+a\right]}{\lim_{a \downarrow 0} \mathbb{E}\left[D \mid X = c+a\right] - \lim_{a \uparrow 0} \mathbb{E}\left[D \mid X = c+a\right]} \tag{12.4}$$

$$= \frac{\mathbb{E}\left[Y \mid X = c^{+}\right] - \mathbb{E}\left[Y \mid X = c^{-}\right]}{\mathbb{P}\left(D = 1 \mid X = c^{+}\right) - \mathbb{P}\left(D = 1 \mid X = c^{-}\right)},$$

where the conditioning event $(D(c^{+}) = 1, D(c^{-}) = 0)$ means complier individuals. The parameter τ_c is often referred to as the local average treatment effect (LATE).[1] Intuitively, the compliers are those whose treatment status follows the assignment rule at the cutoff. This is the subgroup of the population for whom we learn the impact of the policy by looking at the discontinuity. It is important for the researcher to keep this in mind when interpreting empirical results.

Although fuzzy RD is a non-parametric model that differs from the classic linear instrumental variables (IV) model, there is an insightful analogy with the binary instrument and binary treatment setting of Imbens and Angrist (1994). The instrument from the IV setting becomes the indicator variable $\mathbb{1}[X \geq c]$ in the fuzzy RD setting. The IV estimand is the slope from regressing outcomes on the instrument divided by the slope from regressing treatment status on the instrument. The fuzzy RD estimand in equation (12.4) equals the IV estimand, except that regressions control for X being "approximately" equal to c. In fact, it is possible to show that the IV estimator applied to a shrinking neighborhood of $X = c$ is consistent for (12.4). The formal statistical problem of choosing this neighborhood combined with inference implications of doing so are the main reasons fuzzy RD cannot be simply treated as a linear IV model.

2.3   Other Parameters of Interest

The basic RD design described can be generalized to identify treatment effects even if the conditional mean of outcomes does not have a jump discontinuity at the cutoff. The kink RD framework exploits discontinuities in the slope of the conditional mean function to identify causal effects of a policy. In this subsection, we also discuss identification of distributional treatment effects.

Kink RD. We consider two main identification results exploiting different types of kinks.

1. Nielsen et al. (2010) take advantage of policy rules that create a kink in the relationship between the *continuous* treatment variable and the running variable, which is called a regression kink design (RKD). For example, marginal tax rates change discontinuously at specific income thresholds, leading to a kink in the connection between income and taxes paid. Similar to the intuition for the usual RD design, if observations above and below the threshold are comparable, any kink in the outcome at the cutoff would be caused by the change in the policy variable. Nielsen et al. (2010) consider a model in which the treatment effect is constant and the outcome is

$$Y = \tau B + g(X) + U, \qquad (12.5)$$

where B denotes the continuous treatment of interest (taxes paid), which is a function of the running variable (income), that is, $B = b(X)$. If the policy function $b(\cdot)$ has a slope change at the cutoff, we identify τ by

$$\tau = \frac{\lim\limits_{a\downarrow 0} \frac{\partial \mathbb{E}\left[Y \mid X = c + a\right]}{\partial X}\bigg|_{a=0} - \lim\limits_{a\uparrow 0} \frac{\partial \mathbb{E}\left[Y \mid X = c + a\right]}{\partial X}\bigg|_{a=0}}{\lim\limits_{a\downarrow 0} \frac{\partial b(X = c + a)}{\partial X}\bigg|_{a=0} - \lim\limits_{a\uparrow 0} \frac{\partial b(X = c + a)}{\partial X}\bigg|_{a=0}}. \qquad (12.6)$$

In this case, the goal is to estimate the slope change at the threshold, as opposed to the shift in the intercept. The running variable is allowed to affect the outcome, as long as its marginal effect is continuous at the cutoff. Both $g(X)$ and $\mathbb{E}[U \mid X]$ need to be continuously differentiable for the validity of RKD.

Equation (12.6) is the RKD estimand, which measures the change in slope of the expected value of the outcomes at the kink point (cutoff), divided by the difference in the treatment intensity given by the change in slope of the function that determines treatment, $b(\cdot)$, at the kink. For example, it could represent the change in tax rates at the cutoff.

Card et al. (2015, 2017) analyze the more general case in which the outcome model has nonseparable unobserved heterogeneity, U, and the treatment effect is allowed to be heterogeneous across individuals, that is, $Y = y(B, X, U)$. This extension could be important for cases in which we want to allow for heterogeneity in the relationship between the outcome and the endogenous regressor, B. In this case, the authors recover a "treatment-on-the-treated" parameter (Florens et al., 2008), which is a weighted average of the marginal effects for individuals across the population, with weights given by the likelihood that an individual with a particular level of "unobservables" or "type" would be at the cutoff. Formally, under some additional conditions,

$$\mathbb{E}\left[\frac{\partial y(b(c), c, U)}{\partial b}\bigg| X = c\right] = \int_u \frac{\partial y(b(c), c, U)}{\partial b} \frac{f_{X\mid U = u}(c)}{f_X(c)} dF_U(u). \qquad (12.7)$$

We refer the reader to Card et al. (2015, 2017) for more details and extensions.

2. Dong (2018a) analyzes the case of a *binary* treatment when there is a kink in the probability of receiving treatment at the cutoff, a scenario called the regression probability kink (RPK). In this case, we can recover a marginal treatment effect (MTE) (Heckman and Vytlacil, 1999, 2005) under the usual condition that selection into treatment is monotone with respect to the running variable close to the cutoff, also known as the "no defiers condition" (Angrist et al., 1996; Vytlacil, 2002). The endogenous selection into treatment is given by $D = 1\{P(X) - U > 0\}$, where U once again is an unobserved individual heterogeneity and $P(x) = \mathbb{E}[D \mid X = x]$:

$$\frac{\lim_{a\downarrow 0}\frac{\partial\mathbb{E}\big[Y \mid X = c + a\big]}{\partial X}\bigg|_{a=0} - \lim_{a\uparrow 0}\frac{\partial\mathbb{E}\big[Y \mid X = c + a\big]}{\partial X}\bigg|_{a=0}}{\lim_{a\downarrow 0}\frac{\partial\mathbb{E}\big[D \mid X = c + a\big]}{\partial X}\bigg|_{a=0} - \lim_{a\uparrow 0}\frac{\partial\mathbb{E}\big[D \mid X = c + a\big]}{\partial X}\bigg|_{a=0}} = \mathbb{E}[Y_1 - Y_0 \mid U = P(c), X = c]. \tag{12.8}$$

Similar to the RKD case, the first term is the ratio of the change in slope of the expected value of the outcomes at the kink, with the denominator measuring the shift in the slope of the probability of receiving the binary treatment for individuals on different sides of the cutoff. The second term is the MTE, that is, the treatment effect for compliers at the cutoff. As discussed in Dong (2018a) and following the MTE literature, those are the individuals who are indifferent between being treated or not at the kink point. We refer the reader to Dong (2018a) for more details and extensions.

Distributional Effects. It is natural to consider Quantile Treatment Effects (QTE) or, more generally, Distributional Treatment Effects (DTE) when the interest is on the impact of treatment on the distribution of the outcome and its potential heterogeneity. Frandsen et al. (2012) and Shen and Zhang (2016) show identification and propose non-parametric estimators for the local QTE and DTE in the RD design, respectively LQTE and LDTE.

The LDTE is defined as the difference in the potential outcomes marginal cumulative distribution functions (CDFs) for compliers at the cutoff. For simplicity, let the notation $\mathcal{C}$ be the conditioning set representing this subset of the population $\{X = c, D(c^+) = 1, D(c^-) = 0\}$

$$\tau_{LDTE}(y) = F_{Y_1 \mid \mathcal{C}}(y) - F_{Y_0 \mid \mathcal{C}}(y). \tag{12.9}$$

The effect captures how the treatment changes the share of compliers that have an outcome below a certain level, for example, wages below $20,000. Naturally, since this is an RD design, the comparison is valid only for those individuals at the cutoff.

We might prefer to evaluate the impact of treatment on outcome levels instead of population shares. The LQTE is defined as the difference in potential outcomes at the same quantile of their respective distributions. For example, the individual in the 25th quantile of the income distribution if everyone is treated would earn $3,500 more that the individual in the same relative position in the untreated distribution

$$\tau_{LQTE}(q) = Q_{Y_1 \mid \mathcal{C}}(q) - Q_{Y_0 \mid \mathcal{C}}(q), \tag{12.10}$$

where $Q_{Y_j|C}(q)$ is the q quantile of the potential outcome distribution for local compliers. These distributions are identified in the observed data by

$$F_{Y_1|C}(y) = \frac{\lim_{a\downarrow 0}\mathbb{E}\left[1(Y \leq y)D \mid X = c + a\right] - \lim_{a\uparrow 0}\mathbb{E}\left[1(Y \leq y)D \mid X = c + a\right]}{\lim_{a\downarrow 0}\mathbb{E}\left[D \mid X = c + a\right] - \lim_{a\uparrow 0}\mathbb{E}\left[D \mid X = c + a\right]}, \tag{12.11}$$

$$F_{Y_0|C}(y) = \frac{\lim_{a\downarrow 0}\mathbb{E}\left[1(Y \leq y)(1 - D) \mid X = c + a\right] - \lim_{a\uparrow 0}\mathbb{E}\left[1(Y \leq y)(1 - D) \mid X = c + a\right]}{\lim_{a\downarrow 0}\mathbb{E}\left[(1 - D) \mid X = c + a\right] - \lim_{a\uparrow 0}\mathbb{E}\left[(1 - D) \mid X = c + a\right]}. \tag{12.12}$$

Then, $\tau_{LQTE}(q) = \inf\{u : F_{Y_1|C}(u) \geq q\} - \inf\{u : F_{Y_0|C}(u) \geq q\}$. Identification requires smoothness of the potential outcomes conditional CDF and differentiability of the density of the running variable at the cutoff, which are slightly stronger assumptions than those of section 2.1. As noted by Frandsen et al. (2012) it is important to interpret these parameters as treatment effects on the population and not as measures of the impact on specific individuals, who could be at different ranks in the Y_0 and Y_1 distributions.

Recent contributions in RD distributional effects include Shen and Zhang (2016), who propose consistent uniform tests for distributional effects that provide valuable information for policymakers. The tests seek to determine whether a policy intervention unambiguously improves or deteriorates the conditional outcome distribution evaluated at the cutoff. Moreover, Chiang and Sasaki (2019) and Chen et al. (2020) discuss identification and inference of QTE for RKD.

2.4 Identification Away from the Threshold

The RD design focuses on obtaining the ATE for individuals at the cutoff, which might not be representative of the average effect for other groups of interest in the population. In this subsection, we briefly discuss recent advances to identify a broader scope of parameters in RD designs.

Angrist and Rokkanen (2015) explore the role of a conditional independence assumption to extrapolate the RD effect away from the cutoff. The key assumption is that, conditional on a set of covariates (other than the score) that predict the outcome, the conditional expectation of potential outcomes given the running variable is a flat function of the forcing variable. That way, the size of the jump discontinuity is constant regardless of the location of the cutoff. This conditional independence assumption (CIA)–based identification strategy is used to study the effect of Boston exam schools on test scores outcomes. They find that the effects of exam school attendance for 9th grade applicants with running variable values well away from admissions cutoffs differ little from those for applicants on the margin of acceptance given by the cutoff.

Dong and Lewbel (2015) provide inference procedures for the derivative of the ATE as a function of the cutoff. First, they non-parametrically identify the side-limit derivatives at the cutoff of the conditional mean function of outcomes given the running variable. Under a policy invariance assumption, the difference of these side-limit derivatives equals the marginal change in treatment effects with respect to the policy threshold. Intuitively, that is interpreted as how the treatment effect would change if the policymaker were to change the cutoff slightly. They analyze the impacts of being awarded a scholarship in Massachusetts that waives tuition at in-state public colleges. Evidence suggests that the scholarship mainly benefits low-skilled students, while high-skilled students normally attend private and more competitive colleges. In fact, their findings suggest that increasing the admission cutoff for the scholarship negatively affects attendance of public colleges, providing valuable information for public policy regarding the location of thresholds.

Bertanha and Imbens (2020) provide a practical test for external validity in fuzzy RD (see section 3.3.2 for details). Under external validity, potential outcomes are independent of compliance types (always takers, never takers and compliers) conditional on the running variable (and possibly additional covariates). External validity results in two implications for extrapolation of RD effects. First, the average effect on compliers at the cutoff (LATE) equals the average effect of non-compliers at the cutoff. Second, if external validity holds in a neighborhood of the cutoff, one is able to identify $\mathbb{E}[Y_1 - Y_0 \mid X = x]$ for x in that neighborhood by simply comparing treated and untreated outcomes. Under the stronger assumption that external validity holds for every x, we identify the global ATE, that is, $\mathbb{E}[Y_1 - Y_0]$.

A recent branch of the RD literature utilizes data with multiple cutoffs to extrapolate effects. Returning to the scholarship example, suppose the award cutoff changes with the year and the student's city of origin. Bertanha (2020) proposes methods to estimate ATEs over distributions of students that are more general than simply the distribution of students with running variables equal to a single cutoff (see section 4.2 for details). The main assumption is that $\mathbb{E}[Y_1 - Y_0 \mid X]$ does not vary across cities and years. Then, in large samples with sufficient variation of cutoff values, it is possible to non-parametrically identify the global average effect of giving scholarships to all students. Cattaneo et al. (2020) identifies $\mathbb{E}[Y_1 - Y_0 \mid X = x]$ for x values different than the cutoffs under different conditions. Their key assumption is that functions $\mathbb{E}[Y_d \mid X], d \in \{0,1\}$, computed for each city and year, are parallel functions of X. The constant parallel shifts can be identified using those individuals subject to different cutoff values but the same values of X and treatment D.

2.5 Threats to Identification

Several pitfalls could make the use of RD designs inappropriate. For example, if individuals can perfectly manipulate their value of the running variable, there will be selection into treatment, and people *choosing* to be above and below the cutoff might not have comparable potential outcomes. In that case, the RD identification argument fails, and the treatment effect at the cutoff is not identified by the difference in observed outcomes above and below the threshold. Similarly, the argument fails if there is measurement error in the running variable. In that case, without further assumptions, the researcher cannot compare outcomes for observations with similar values of the running variable without measurement error. These failures and other extensions of the usual RD design will be discussed in section 4.

3.   ESTIMATION AND INFERENCE

Recovering the effects of policies with RD designs relies on approximating the discontinuity in the regression functions at the cutoff by extrapolating from observations very close to it. In this section, we describe the most popular estimation choice based on local polynomial methods. We also discuss statistical inference and implementation issues.

3.1   Estimation

The estimation of the RD treatment effect τ relates to standard non-parametric regression with specific features: we are only interested in the regression function at a single point, which is also a boundary point. Standard non-parametric kernel regression does not work very well at boundary points, because they have a slower rate of convergence than they do at interior points. For this reason, local polynomial estimation is a more suitable approach (see Fan and Gijbels (1996) for a general discussion).

Local polynomial methods estimate the RD effect by fitting two polynomial regressions of order p using only observations near the threshold, separately for units above and below the cutoff. Observations close to the threshold are selected using a bandwidth h that determines the size of the neighborhood around the cutoff where the estimation is conducted. Within this bandwidth, it is common to weight observations using a kernel function, $K(\cdot)$.[2]

The researcher chooses a polynomial order p, a kernel function $K(\cdot)$ and a bandwidth $h > 0$. Then, the local polynomial estimator for the sharp RD parameter τ is

$$\hat{\tau} = e_0' \hat{\beta}_+ - e_0' \hat{\beta}_-,$$

where e_0 is a column vector of the same length as beta with zeros everywhere except for the first coordinate; $\hat{\beta}_-$ and $\hat{\beta}_+$ correspond to the weighted least squares coefficients given by

$$\hat{\beta}_- = \arg \min_{\beta \in \mathbb{R}^{p+1}} \sum_{i=1}^{n} \mathbb{I}\{c \geq X_i\} (Y_i - r_p(X_i - c)'b)^2 \, K_h(X_i - c), \qquad (12.13)$$

$$\hat{\beta}_+ = \arg \min_{\beta \in \mathbb{R}^{p+1}} \sum_{i=1}^{n} \mathbb{I}\{c < X_i\} (Y_i - r_p(X_i - c)'b)^2 \, K_h(X_i - c), \qquad (12.14)$$

with $r_p(x) = (1, x, \ldots, x^p)'$ and $K_h(\cdot) = K(\cdot / h) / h$ for a kernel function $K(\cdot)$. The least squares estimators depend on h, p and $K(\cdot)$. We discuss these choices next.

The *polynomial order* is usually set to $p = 1$ (or $p = 2$), meaning that the researcher fits a linear (quadratic) function on the data within the bandwidth in each side of the cutoff. As mentioned, the simple local difference in means ($p = 0$) can be ruled out as a constant fit because of undesirable theoretical properties at boundary points. At the same time, higher-order polynomials tend to overfit the data and also lead to unreliable results at boundary points, as discussed in Gelman and Imbens (2019). Pei et al. (2018) propose a data-driven selector for the polynomial order using the asymptotic mean squared error of the local regression RD estimator as the selection criteria.

The *kernel function* $K(\cdot)$ assigns weights to each observation according to its distance from the cutoff c, with observations closer to the threshold typically receiving higher weights. The triangular kernel function, $K(u) = (1-|u|)1(|u| \leq 1)$, is the most common choice, because it leads to point estimators with optimal properties (Cheng et al., 1997). The triangular kernel function assigns zero weight to all observations with scores outside the range given by the bandwidth and positive weights to all observations within this interval. The weight is maximized at the cutoff and declines symmetrically and linearly as we move away from it. Other common alternatives are the uniform kernel, which provides equal weight to all observations within the interval. It is also a popular choice as it relates directly to standard linear regression. Finally, the Epanechnikov kernel is also commonly used, giving a quadratic decaying weight to observations in the interval.

Finally, the *bandwidth h* is the most crucial tuning parameter in RD implementation as it controls the width of the neighborhood around the cutoff that is used to fit the local regressions. The choice of h directly affects the statistical properties of the estimation and inference procedures. Also, empirical findings are often sensitive to this choice. Bandwidth selection methods typically try to balance some form of bias-variance trade-off. Intuitively, we can expect that choosing a small h will reduce the bias of the local polynomial estimator as we are only using observations very close to the cutoff. In that case, even a linear function should be able to reasonably capture the main features of the conditional mean of the outcome within that small window, thus reducing the misspecification error. At the same time, using only a few observations implies that the variance will increase. On the other hand, a larger h will result in more misspecification error if the unknown function differs considerably from the polynomial model used for approximation, but will reduce the variance because of the larger number of observations in the interval given by the bandwidth.

The most popular approach in practice is to select h to minimize the Mean Squared Error (MSE) of the RD local polynomial estimator, given a choice of polynomial order p and kernel function $K(\cdot)$. Since the MSE of an estimator is the sum of its variance and squared bias, this approach chooses h to optimize a bias-variance trade-off. Using an asymptotic approximation of the RD estimator's MSE, we can optimize it with respect to h and then use a data-driven version to estimate the unknown quantities in the resulting formula of the optimal bandwidth.

Under standard regularity conditions, the asymptotic MSE expansion for the RD treatment effect estimator $\hat{\tau}$ is.

$$\mathbf{MSE}(\hat{\tau}) = \mathbb{E}\left[(\hat{\tau} - \tau)^2 \big| \mathbf{X}\right] \approx h_n^{2(p+1)} \mathbf{B}^2 + \frac{1}{nh_n} \mathbf{V},$$

where $\mathbf{B}$ and $\mathbf{V}$ represent the leading asymptotic bias and asymptotic variance of $\hat{\tau}$, respectively. Their exact form can be found in Calonico et al. (2014). The MSE-optimal bandwidth selection rule is then given by

$$h_{\mathrm{MSE}} = \left(\frac{\mathbf{V}}{2(p+1)\mathbf{B}^2}\right)^{1/(2p+3)} n^{-1/(2p+3)}.$$

Imbens and Kalyanaraman (2012), henceforth IK, provide a data-driven version of this optimal bandwidth:

$$\hat{h}_{\mathrm{MSE}} = \left(\frac{\hat{\mathbf{V}}}{2(p+1)\hat{\mathbf{B}}^2 + \hat{\mathbf{R}}}\right)^{1/(2p+3)} n^{-1/(2p+3)},$$

where the additional term $\hat{\mathbf{R}}$ is a regularization factor introduced to avoid small denominators in samples of moderate size. Calonico et al. (2014), henceforth CCT, propose an alternative plug-in bandwidth selection approach with two distinct features relative to IK. First, the estimators $\hat{\mathbf{V}}$ and $\hat{\mathbf{B}}$ (and $\hat{\mathbf{R}}$) are consistent for their population counterparts, and the preliminary bandwiths used in their constructions are consistent estimators of the population MSE-optimal bandwidths. Second, motivated by finite-sample performance considerations, CCT propose an alternative estimator of $\mathbf{V}$, which does not require an additional choice of bandwidth for its construction but relies instead on a fixed-matches nearest-neighbor estimate of the residuals, following the work of Abadie and Imbens (2006).

As noted by Bartalotti and Brummet (2017), the MSE-optimal bandwidth is affected by dependence in the data, such as clustering, which alters the trade-off between variance and leading bias as the bandwidth changes. Researchers should be cognizant of the dependence structure of the data both when choosing the bandwidth and performing inference.

An alternative approach to bandwidth selection is presented in Calonico et al. (2020), who established valid coverage error (CE) expansions of some of the confidence intervals discussed later, and use these results to develop CE-optimal bandwidth choices. This alternative bandwidth selector is inference optimal, in the sense that the CE (the gap between the test's nominal and actual sizes) is the smallest possible given the choice of point estimator used.

A basic graphical display of the standard RD design model using local polynomial methods is presented in Figure 12.2. Panel (a) graphs the true conditional potential outcomes expectations and the treatment effect at the cutoff. Panel (b) adds the scatter plot for a sample drawn from that population. Panel (c) visually displays the estimation approach described in section 3.1. Observations receiving more (less) weight in estimation have brighter (faded) colors, as determined by the kernel choice and bandwidth. The solid black line within the bandwidth window in each side of the cutoff is the local linear function fitted at the cutoff. Note that even though the conditional means on panel (a) are nonlinear, the local linear fit still provides a reasonable approximation of its behavior, especially close to the cutoff. The difference between the two black lines where they intersect $X = c$ is the estimated ATE at the cutoff.

3.2   Inference

To implement valid confidence intervals and hypothesis testing in practice, we need to carefully consider the role of the leading bias ($\mathbf{B}$) and the variance ($\mathbf{V}$) in the asymptotic distribution of the RD estimator. Under appropriate regularity conditions and restrictions on the rate for the bandwidth sequence $h_n \to 0$, a natural starting point would be to construct confidence intervals based on the distributional approximation,

$$\sqrt{nh_n}\left(\hat{\tau} - \tau - h_n^{p+1}\,\mathbf{B}\right) \to_d \mathcal{N}(0, \mathbf{V}),$$

leading to an asymptotic $100(1-\alpha)$ -per cent confidence interval for τ given by

$$\mathbf{CI}_{1-\alpha}^*(h_n) = \left[\left(\hat{\tau} - h_n^{p+1}\,\mathbf{B}\right) \pm \Phi_{1-\alpha/2}^{-1}\sqrt{\frac{\mathbf{V}}{nh_n}}\right],$$

with Φ_q^{-1} being the q-th quantile of the standard normal distribution.

The variance component $\mathbf{V}$ can be estimated using plug-in estimated residuals or a fixed-matches estimator. Calonico et al. (2014) provide a detailed discussion on these alternatives, including implementations issues.

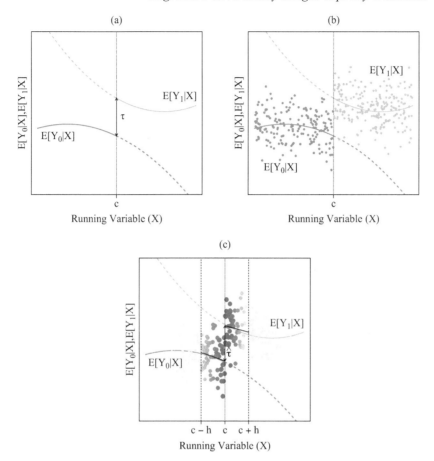

Notes: The figure illustrates the standard RD model and estimation.
Panel (a) graphs the true conditional mean functions of each potential outcome conditional on the forcing variable. The size of the discontinuity at the cutoff corresponds to the average treatment effect. Panel (b) is the scatter plot for a sample drawn from the population model that generates the functions in panel (a). Panel (c) illustrates the estimator discussed in section 3.1.
First, an estimation window is fixed (that is, [c–h, c+h]); second, observations closer to the cutoff receive more weight (darker colors) than observations farther from the cutoff (lighter colors); third, the best fit lines on either side of the cutoff are depicted in black; finally, the RD estimator is the difference between the lines at the cutoff c.

Figure 12.2 Estimation in a Regression Discontinuity design

For the leading bias **B**, we discuss three alternatives: "undersmoothing", "bias correction" and "robust bias correction".

Undersmoothing. This means to choose a bandwidth "small enough" so that the bias is negligible. Theoretically, this approach simply requires selecting a bandwidth sequence $h_n \to 0$ that vanishes fast enough such that the leading bias term approaches zero:

$$\sqrt{nh_n}\left(\hat{\tau} - \tau - h_n^{p+1}\,\mathbf{B}\right) = \sqrt{nh_n}\left(\hat{\tau} - \tau\right) + o_p(1) \to_d \mathcal{N}(0, \mathbf{V}).$$

This procedure proves difficult to implement in practice because most bandwidth selectors, including, h_{MSE}, will not satisfy the conditions required for undersmoothing. A non-negligible leading bias in the distributional approximation will bias the associated confidence intervals, thus invalidating inference.

Bias Correction. The second approach to dealing with the leading bias **B** is to construct an estimator of the bias, $\hat{\textbf{B}}$, which can be subtracted from the RD point estimate. This idea can be easily implemented by using a higher order local polynomial to estimate the unknown derivatives present in the leading bias, since **B** is proportional to the change in the $(p + 1)$ derivatives of the regression function at the cutoff. For example, the $(p + 1)$ derivatives can be estimated at each side of the cutoff by using a q-th-order local polynomial (with $q \geq p+1$) with pilot bandwidth b_n. The resulting bias-corrected estimator is

$$\hat{\tau}^{\text{bc}} = \hat{\tau} - h^{p+1}\,\hat{\textbf{B}}\,.$$

Using this bias-corrected estimator, under appropriate regularity conditions, we obtain

$$\sqrt{nh_n}\left(\hat{\tau}^{\text{bc}} - \tau\right) = \underbrace{\sqrt{nh_n}\left(\hat{\tau} - \tau - h_n^{p+1}\,\textbf{B}\right)}_{\to_d\,\mathcal{N}(0,\textbf{V})} - \underbrace{\sqrt{nh_n}\,h_n^{p+1}(\hat{\textbf{B}} - \textbf{B})}_{\to_p\,0},$$

which is valid if $h_n / b_n \to 0$. This result justifies bias-corrected confidence intervals, where the unknown bias in $\textbf{CI}^*_{1-\alpha}(h_n)$ is replaced by the bias-estimate $\hat{\textbf{B}}$, using a pilot bandwidth b_n, which could be obtained using an asymptotic MSE expansions for the appropriate estimators.

3.2.1   Robust RD inference

Both confidence intervals discussed have some unappealing properties that could seriously affect their performance in empirical work. Undersmoothing could lead to large coverage distortions if the bias is not removed appropriately. Bias correction will usually have poor performance in empirical applications, leading to potentially large coverage distortions, because the bias estimate introduces additional variability in $\hat{\tau}^{bc}$, which is not accounted for when forming the associated confidence intervals.

The main innovation in CCT is to construct robust confidence intervals using alternative asymptotic approximation for $\hat{\tau}^{bc}$, provided that $\frac{h_n}{b_n} \to \rho \in [0,\infty)$ and appropriate regularity conditions hold:

$$\sqrt{nh_n}\left(\hat{\tau}^{\text{bc}} - \tau\right) \to_d \mathcal{N}(0, \textbf{V}^{\text{bc}}),$$

where $\textbf{V}^{\text{bc}}$ is the asymptotic variance for the bias-corrected estimator, which is different from **V** since it is constructed to account for the variability of both the original RD treatment effect estimator ($\hat{\tau}$) and the bias-correction term ($\hat{\textbf{B}}$) in the distributional approximation of the studentized statistic. Further theoretical implications of this alternative approach to non-parametric bias correction are discussed in Calonico et al. (2018, 2021).

Robust bias-corrected (RBC) confidence intervals asymptotically equivalent to the ones described can be obtained by an iterative wild bootstrap procedure as described by Bartalotti et al. (2017), and He and Bartalotti (2020).[3] This bootstrap builds on the RBC literature's insight by resampling from higher order local polynomials to obtain estimates of the leading bias term. To account for the additional variability introduced by the bias correction, an iterated bootstrap procedure is used: generate many bootstrap datasets from local quadratic models, and calculate the bias-corrected estimate for each of them. The resulting empirical distribution of bias-corrected estimators is then used to construct confidence intervals (CIs). The bootstrap implementation does not require extensive derivations and thus complements plug-in implementation methods. This can be useful in situations for which the analytical results or statistical software have not yet been developed or are cumbersome. Some cases include more complex RD designs, with objects of interest involving multiple cutoffs and nonlinear functions of discontinuity parameters.[4] Additionally, the bootstrap has the flexibility to accommodate dependent (clustered) data by adjusting the resampling algorithm accordingly.

Calonico et al. (2021) established valid CE expansions of confidence intervals based on undersmoothing and robust bias correction for the RD treatment effects, showing that RBC confidence intervals never have asymptotically larger CEs and can indeed offer higher order refinements whenever the underlying regression functions are smooth enough, both pointwise and uniformly over standard data-generating classes. They also use these results to develop a CE-optimal bandwidth choice as mentioned in section 3.1.

3.2.2 Randomization inference

A number of recent papers have employed randomization inference techniques to test null hypotheses of zero treatment effects. One of the key insights of RD is that treatment is assigned almost randomly for those individuals with forcing variables close to the cutoff. Building on this insight, Cattaneo et al. (2015) developed a randomization test where the researcher specifies a small window around the cutoff (where treatment assignment is supposedly random) and a distribution for the treatment indicator. The test statistic is re-computed for multiple draws of the treatment indicator for individuals inside the specified window, while keeping the rest of the data intact. This procedure generates a randomization distribution for the test statistic, from which the researcher obtains critical values and compares to the original value of the test statistic. Under the sharp null hypothesis that nobody responds to treatment, the original value of the test statistic should not appear extreme with respect to the randomization distribution. If the window and treatment distribution are correctly specified by the researcher, the test has exact size in finite samples, providing a useful inference alternative to empirical researchers when the number of observations close to the cutoff is small, a problem commonly faced by researchers.

Ganong and Jäger (2018) propose a similar randomization test, except that the test statistic is re-computed for different values of the cutoff that are drawn from a distribution specified by the researcher. Canay and Kamat (2018) present a permutation test for the null hypothesis that the distribution of pre-treatment characteristics conditional on the running variable varies continuously with the running variable at the cutoff. Rejecting that hypothesis indicates manipulation of the running variable around the cutoff, which would invalidate the RD approach (see section 4.1). Although the test always has correct size in large samples, it also has correct size in finite samples if the distribution of pre-treatment characteristics does not depend on the running variable near the cutoff. More recently, Bertanha and Chung (2021) provide permutation tests and confidence sets for RD parameters that have exact size in finite samples under symmetry restrictions and correct asymptotic size without such restrictions. Their methods do not require the researcher to specify the distribution of the treatment indicator or the cutoff as in previous papers.

3.3 Inference Issues with Fuzzy RD

3.3.1 Weak identification

The analogy between fuzzy RD and IV models drawn in section 2.2 immediately raises the question of weak identification in the case of small compliance, that is, when $\mathbb{P}(D=1\,|\,X=c^+)-\mathbb{P}(D=1\,|\,X=c^-)$ is small. Feir et al. (2016) show that, in these cases, the usual t-test for inference on the LATE suffers from similar woes as the standard IV setting, including significant asymptotic size distortion. Furthermore, after examining several applied articles, they conclude that weak identification problems are widespread.

Weak identification occurs when the sampling error noise is of similar magnitude or larger than the signal used in estimating a model's parameters (Feir et al., 2016). In these cases, the usual asymptotic normality approximations used to develop tests is a poor approximation to the actual test distribution, and inference is inadequate. The severity of the weak identification problem and related size distortions of usual tests is related to the concentration parameter d_n^2,

$$d_n = \sqrt{nh}\left(\frac{f_x(c)}{k}\right)^{\frac{1}{2}}\frac{|\mathbb{P}(D=1\,|\,X=c^+)-\mathbb{P}(D=1\,|\,X=c^-)|}{\sigma_D},$$

where k is a known constant that depends on the kernel function used. If $d_n^2 \to \infty$, identification is strong, and the usual tests and critical values provide appropriately sized inference. Intuitively, the strength of identification (measured by the concentration parameter) depends on the size of the discontinuity in treatment assignment, with larger changes in the treatment at the cutoff being more informative. Also, d_n^2 depends on the density of the running variable at the cutoff, reflecting how much information/data are available locally around the cutoff. Smaller values of $f_x(c)$ imply more acute weak identification problems.

As described in Feir et al. (2016), size distortions decrease as the concentration parameter increases, with two-sided asymptotic 5 per cent (1 per cent) testing achieving nearly zero size distortions for $d_n^2 \geq 64(\geq 50^2)$. When analyzing weak IV, Stock and Yogo (2005) propose rule-of-thumb critical values for the F test on the strength of the "first-stage". A similar approach applied to RD requires a concentration parameter of at least 64 to ensure small size distortions for a two-sided 5 per cent test. This implies that we should reject the null hypothesis of weak identification if $F > 93$, a significantly more stringent level than the $F > 10$ usually referred to in the weak IV literature. Intuitively, this is related to the local nature of RD designs, where we concentrate on the information around the cutoff.

Feir et al. (2016) propose asymptotic tests and confidence sets that control size uniformly over fuzzy RD models regardless of the strength of the first stage. The test is based on an Anderson–Rubin type of statistic,

$$T_n^R(\beta_0)=\sqrt{nh}\left(\hat{\beta}-\beta_0\right)\left(\sqrt{\frac{k\hat{\sigma}^2(\beta_0)}{\hat{f}_x(c)\left(\widehat{\Delta D}\right)^2}}\right)^{-1}$$

$$\widehat{\Delta D}=\hat{P}\left(D=1\,|\,X=c^+\right)-\hat{P}\left(D=1\,|\,X=c^-\right).$$

In the statistic, the null value β_0 is used instead of $\hat{\beta}$ when computing the standard error, eliminating size distortions when the usual rejection rule $|T_n^R(\beta_0)| > z_{1-\alpha/2}$ is used. We refer the reader to Feir et al. (2016) for further details, including one-sided testing and alternative approaches. They revisit studies of class size effects and find substantial differences by applying their methods to data previously studied by Urquiola and Verhoogen (2009).

More recently, Noack and Rothe (2021) propose confidence sets that are also based on an Anderson–Rubin-type construction. These confidence sets take into account the worst-case smoothing bias inside a class of conditional mean functions (see discussion in section 3.4).

3.3.2 External validity

While compliance may be big enough to avoid a weak identification problem, it might still be far from being large. A small compliance rate means that there is a large percentage of the population for which the average effect is unknown and generally different than the effect on compliers.

Bertanha and Imbens (2020) study this problem and propose a practical test for external validity over compliance types. They define external validity as independence between potential outcomes and compliance types conditional on the forcing variable X. Under external validity, the causal effect identified for compliers equals the causal effects for always takers and never takers at the cutoff. The test for external validity consists of testing the null hypothesis that $\mathbb{E}[Y \mid X = c^+, D = 1] = \mathbb{E}[Y \mid X = c^-, D = 1]$ and $\mathbb{E}[Y \mid X = c^+, D = 0] = \mathbb{E}[Y \mid X = c^-, D = 0]$.

Bertanha and Imbens show that the difference $\mathbb{E}[Y \mid X = c^+, D = 1] - \mathbb{E}[Y \mid X = c^-, D = 1]$ equals the difference between treated outcomes of always takers and an average of treated outcomes of compliers and always takers. Similarly, $\mathbb{E}[Y \mid X = c^+, D = 0] - \mathbb{E}[Y \mid X = c^-, D = 0]$ captures differences in untreated outcomes between never takers and compliers. Thus, external validity implies that these two equalities hold.

The implementation of the test for external validity is as practical as testing for a discontinuity in sharp RD. The only difference is that you estimate the discontinuities separately for the treated and untreated subsamples and then combine them in a Wald statistic. Figure 12.3 illustrates the estimates separately for each subsample. Bertanha and Imbens revisit the fuzzy RD analyses by Jacob and Lefgren (2004) and Matsudaira (2008) of remedial summer schools in the United States, and they reject the external validity in both studies. Evidence suggests that always takers, who are sent to summer school regardless of their score, have lower potential outcomes than complier students. The same is not true for the Jacob–Lefgren data after conditioning the analysis on math scores before the summer school. This suggests that heterogeneity of compliance groups is well captured by observable characteristics, in which case we say there is external validity conditional on covariates.

3.4 Uniform Inference

An appealing feature of RD is its presumed ability to identify causal effects under minimal functional form restrictions. However, recent studies (Kamat, 2018; Bertanha and Moreira, 2020) highlight that standard RD methods might fail unless the researcher imposes more functional form restrictions than previously thought.

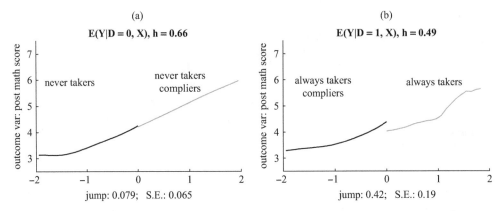

Notes: these plots reproduce Figures 1(c) and 1.1(d) by Bertanha and Imbens (2020) using administrative data from Jacob and Lefgren (2004). These are third grade students from public schools in Chicago during the years of 1997–99. The outcome variable Y is the math score in the year after summer school; the forcing variable X is the minimum between the reading and math score before summer school minus the cutoff; D is the participation indicator; h is the bandwidth choice for the local polynomial estimators.

Figure 12.3   Test for external validity in fuzzy RD

The majority of empirical studies relies on asymptotic approximations assuming that there is **one** possible data-generating process (DGP) with continuously differentiable conditional mean functions $\mathbb{E}[Y_0 \mid X]$ and $\mathbb{E}[Y_1 \mid X]$. However, these approximations are not uniformly valid over the class of all DGPs that satisfy the same differentiability requirement. Intuitively, the issue comes from the fact that a conditional mean function with a jump discontinuity at the threshold is well approximated by a continuous conditional function that is very steep at the threshold. The lack of uniformity implies that the quality of asymptotic approximations for a given sample size highly depends on the shape of the true conditional mean function, which is a priori unknown.

Kamat (2018) demonstrates that it is impossible to find a hypothesis test that controls size and has non-trivial power if we only assume continuous differentiability. Bertanha and Moreira (2020) connect the problem to the literature on impossible inference in econometrics. They further demonstrate that it is impossible to find almost-surely bounded confidence sets that have correct coverage. These findings imply that usual hypothesis tests and confidence intervals based on t-ratios and Gaussian approximations fail to control size. The problem can be avoided if we place a finite bound on a higher order derivative of $\mathbb{E}[Y_0 \mid X]$ and $\mathbb{E}[Y_1 \mid X]$. Imbens and Wager (2019) and Armstrong and Kolesár (2020) derive optimal confidence sets and show that they depend on the value of such bounds.

Lack of uniform validity of standard inference procedures come from the impossibility of approximating the distribution of a test statistic uniformly well over a general class of DGPs. A critical component in this approximation is the bias involved in the non-parametric estimation of the jump discontinuity. The bias of such estimators can be arbitrarily large if the class of DGPs contains any continuously differentiable function. Finite bounds on derivatives imply finite bounds on the bias. Imbens and Wager (2019) and Armstrong and Kolesár (2020) propose inference procedures based on fixed-length confidence intervals as defined in Donoho (1994). These are built by considering the nonrandom *worst-case bias* of the estimator among all possible conditional expectation functions in a restricted class of functions.

For concreteness, consider the following simplified case, most relevant for RD designs. Assume that $\mathbb{E}[Y_d \mid X]$, $d \in \{0,1\}$, can be approximated by a polynomial of order "J" on neighborhoods on both sides of the cutoff:

$$\mathbb{E}[Y_d \mid X] = \sum_{j=0}^{J} X^j \beta_j + R_d(x), \tag{12.15}$$

where $R_d(x)$ is the error of the polynomial approximation. For a given bandwidth, the polynomial function is an imperfect approximation of the true conditional expectation of the outcome, and the estimate of τ is biased. For a finite constant M, assume further that $\mathbb{E}[Y_d \mid X]$ are functions of X in the following Taylor class of functions:

$$\left\{ f : \left| f(x) - \sum_{j=0}^{J} f^{(j)}(0) \frac{x^j}{j!} \right| \le \frac{M}{p!} \mid x^{J+1} \mid, \text{ for every } x \right\}. \tag{12.16}$$

If we were to approximate the true conditional mean by a Taylor polynomial of order J, the misspecification error at each value of X is bounded by the $(J + 1)$-th derivative of the function. Thus, we can construct confidence intervals that adjust for the worst-case scenario bias that would take place among all possible functions for which the $(J + 1)$-th derivative is bounded by M, capturing the level of smoothness assumed in the conditional mean function. This implies that

$$\mid R_d(x) \mid \le \frac{M}{p!} \mid x^{J+1} \mid, \ d \in \{0,1\}, \tag{12.17}$$

and that the worst-case bias for the local polynomial estimator is

$$\overline{bias}_M(\hat{\tau}) = \frac{M}{p!} \sum_{i=1}^{n} \mid w_+^n(x_i) + w_-^n(x_i) \mid \mid x^{J+1_i} \mid, \tag{12.18}$$

where $w_+^n(x_i)$ and $w_-^n(x_i)$ capture the influence of i-th observation in the regression intercept estimates of each treatment group. Equation (12.18) gives the worst possible distortion that would be introduced to the estimate of τ if we incorrectly assume that $R_d(x) = 0$. Armstrong and Kolesár (2020) obtain the CI as

$$\hat{\tau} \pm cv_\alpha \left(\frac{\overline{bias}_M(\hat{\tau})}{\hat{se}_n} \right) \cdot \hat{se}_n, \tag{12.19}$$

where $\hat{se}_n$ is a consistent standard error estimator, $cv_\alpha(t)$ is the $1 - \alpha$ absolute value of a $|N(t,1)|$ distribution and t is the worst bias and standard deviation ratio. Note that the critical values are from a folded normal distribution re-centered around t and will differ from the usual critical values (for example, ± 1.96). These CIs guarantee uniformly valid coverage over all possible conditional expectation functions inside the Taylor class in (12.16).

Using a similar approach, Imbens and Wager (2019) propose a method for estimation and inference in RD designs based on numerical convex optimization to directly obtain the finite-sample-minimax linear estimator for the RD parameter, subject to bounds on the second derivative of the conditional response function. Instead of placing restrictions on second differences relative to the response surface at the threshold, they assume bounded second derivatives away from the threshold.

The main challenge for implementation of these methods is to select M in particular applications. This is because, in order to retain uniformity, the researcher must choose it a priori rather than employing a data-driven method.

3.5 The Role of Covariates

While the standard RD design model only requires knowledge of the outcome and running variables, researchers often like to include pre-determined covariates in their models, for example to account for demographic or socioeconomic characteristics of the agents. Calonico et al. (2019) extend the standard RD model based on local polynomial regression to include covariates in a linear way. Linearity is used as a local linear projection and not as an assumption about the functional form of the underlying regression functions, allowing for the covariates to be continuous, discrete or mixed, without the need to employ additional smoothing methods. This extended model leads to a consistent estimator for the original RD effect under the assumption that the treatment has no effect on the covariates at the cutoff, and that the conditional expectations of potential outcomes and covariates given the score be continuous at the cutoff. These conditions are in line with non-parametric identification results in the RD literature and with standard regression adjustment arguments in the context of randomized experiments. Their framework is best suited for settings where the inclusion of covariates is intended to increase the precision of the estimator, in the same way as covariates are often included in the analysis of randomized experiments.

An alternative motivation for the inclusion of covariates in RD analysis is to increase the plausibility of the design, for example in cases where researchers fear that the potential outcomes are discontinuous at the cutoff; and the inclusion of covariates is intended to restore identification of some RD parameter. This approach generally requires either parametric assumptions on the regression functions to enable extrapolation or other design assumptions that redefine the parameter of interest in a fixed local neighborhood, rather than at the cutoff point. Frölich and Huber (2019) develop a model to account for covariates in the RD design using non-parametric kernel estimation over both the running variable and the covariates. This method allows for discontinuity in the distribution of the covariates at the cutoff, recovering a weighted average of local treatment effects, which coincides with the standard RD effect when the covariates are balanced at the cutoff.

Both Calonico et al. (2019) and Frölich and Huber (2019) discuss conditions under which including covariates in an RD model could reduce the asymptotic variance and thus increase precision of the RD treatment effect estimator.

4. RECENT EXTENSIONS ON EMPIRICAL ISSUES

As discussed in the previous sections, one of the main strengths of RD designs lies in its easy and intuitive nature for identification of the treatment effect under relatively mild assumptions. Nevertheless, researchers need to be cautious as many application-specific aspects might invalidate the RD approach. Those could be linked to individuals' behavior, data quality or inference.

For example, if individuals are able to manipulate their value of the running variable, the treatment assignment might no longer be considered ignorable at the cutoff. The policy or program might be determined based on multiple cutoffs, which requires a careful interpretation of the parameters recovered and opens the door to evaluate treatment effect heterogeneity. Specific models can be employed to account for certain features of the data, for example to deal with categorical outcomes.

Also, if the running variable is mismeasured we are unable to correctly estimate the expected outcomes at the cutoff by the usual approaches. Sample selection might also impact our ability to learn about the ATE at the cutoff, due to differential selection on each side of the cutoff.

We discuss all of these issues next.

4.1 Manipulation of the Running Variable

An important concern to the validity of RD designs is the possibility that individuals might manipulate their value of the running variable, therefore being able to endogenously affect their treatment assignment probabilities. In that case, people who might benefit from treatment could make sure that they are on the "correct side" of the threshold, invalidating comparisons across the cutoff as a reliable measure of the effects of treatment.

Under manipulation, the distribution of potential outcomes no longer vary smoothly at the cutoff. For instance, this could be the case if financial aid is awarded to students based on a known test score and students who came short can bargain with teachers to change their score; or if workers become eligible to unemployment insurance after having been employed by a minimum number of days, in which case they might wait to quit their jobs until after they crossed the threshold.

Based on this intuition, McCrary (2008) proposed a test for a jump of the density of the running variable at the cutoff, since an accumulation of observations in one side would be evidence of sorting on the running variable. Recently, Cattaneo et al. (2019) proposed an alternative test based on local polynomial density estimators, that can be easily implemented using their provided software `rddensity`. While testing for manipulation is a good empirical practice, it is important to keep in mind that a rejection does not necessarily imply that the RD approach is uninformative, while a lack of rejection does not guarantee that there is no manipulation (Gerard et al., 2016). Frandsen (2017) proposes a similarly intuitive alternative test for manipulation that can be used when the running variable is discrete.

More recently, Bugni and Canay (2020) propose an approximate sign test for continuity of a density at a point based on the so-called g-order statistics. The test is based on the intuition that, when the density of the running variable is continuous at the cutoff, the fraction of units under treatment and control local to the cutoff should be roughly the same. This means that the number of treated units out of the q observations closest to the cutoff is approximately distributed as a binomial random variable with sample size q (the number of observations local to the cutoff) and probability 1/2. They show that the test is asymptotically valid in the sense that it has limiting rejection probability under the null hypothesis not exceeding the nominal level, while it also exhibits finite sample validity if the distribution is symmetric. Bertanha and Chung (2021) provide a permutation test for continuity of a density that also has exact size if the distribution is symmetric and correct asymptotic size without symmetry. One of the main differences between the Bugni-Canay and Bertanha-Chung tests is that the first obtains the critical value from maximizing a function of a binomial distribution, while the second computes quantiles from a permutation distribution.

Lee (2008) frames the RD set-up as a randomized experiment, and shows that even if individuals can *imperfectly* manipulate their running variables, comparing outcomes above and below the cutoff still provides some information about the treatment effects. Specifically, it identifies a weighted average of the treatment effect, where the weights will be proportional to the probability that an individual will have the actual running variable $(\tilde{X})$ close to the cutoff given their targeted manipulation value (X), as long as the deviations from their target are continuous at the policy cutoff:

$$\tau^* = \int_{-\infty}^{\infty} (y_1(x) - y_0(x)) \frac{f_{\tilde{X}|X}(c\,|\,x)}{f_{\tilde{X}}(c)} dF_X(x). \tag{12.20}$$

For example, if a scholarship is granted for students who score above a certain known threshold, more driven individuals can affect (manipulate) their target scores (X) by putting more effort in preparing for the exam. However, manipulation is imperfect as they are not able to exactly choose their actual score $(\tilde{X})$, which could be affected by random chance. Then, the usual RD approach identifies a weighted average of the effect with larger weights for those individuals who are more likely to have actual scores equal to the cutoff, conditional on their target.

Gerard et al. (2016) exploit the information in a potential discontinuous jump on the density of the running variable to partially identify the causal effect of treatment when there is one-sided manipulation of the running variable. First, they consider that there are two types of individuals: those who are "potentially assigned" (PA) to treatment for which the usual RD conditions hold and those who are "always assigned" (AA), for which the running variable is manipulated to guarantee it will always be above the cutoff, an assumption referred as one-sided manipulation.

The existence of always assigned individuals invalidates the RD approach if their type is correlated to their response to treatment. Intuitively, if individuals in the AA group benefit more from treatment than those on PA, the comparison of outcomes above and below the cutoff does not adequately reflect the causal effect.

The partial identification approach relies on the one-sided manipulation requirement. In that case, any discontinuity in the density of the running variable (that is, any accumulation of individuals in one side of the threshold) identifies the share of individuals manipulating the running variable close to the cutoff. Specifically, the proportion of AA individuals at the cutoff is given by

$$P_{AA} = P(AA\,|\,X = c^+) = 1 - \frac{f_X(c^-)}{f_X(c^+)}. \tag{12.21}$$

Gerard et al. (2016) focus on using this information to obtain sharp bounds for the ATE for the PA group at the cutoff. For intuition, focus on the sharp RD case, where the observed outcomes for individuals just below the cutoff point identifies the expected value of Y_0 for the PA group. Bounds for the $\mathbb{E}[Y_1\,|\,X = c, PA]$ are obtained by considering that the P_{AA} share of "highest" and "lowest" values for the outcomes are associated with the individuals manipulating their running variables just above the cutoff:

$$\tau_{PA}^L = \mathbb{E}[Y\,|\,X = c^+, Y \le Q_{Y|X=c^+}(1 - P_{AA})] - \mathbb{E}[Y\,|\,X = c^-] \tag{12.22}$$

$$\tau_{PA}^U = \mathbb{E}[Y\,|\,X = c^+, Y \ge Q_{Y|X=c^+}(P_{AA})] - \mathbb{E}[Y\,|\,X = c^-], \tag{12.23}$$

where $Q_{Y|X=c^+}(q)$ is the value of the q-th quantile of the conditional outcome distribution.

Intuitively, the smaller the share of manipulators around the cutoff, the tighter the bounds for the ATE, since the observed outcomes for individuals above the cutoff reflects more information about the PA population. In the fuzzy design, one needs to consider that not all individuals have their treatment status affected by crossing the threshold, but the intuition is similar. We refer the interested reader to Gerard et al. (2016) for the details in estimation, inference and extensions, including quantile treatment effects, discrete outcomes and the role of covariates.

4.2 Multiple Cutoffs

Many empirical applications involve RD designs with multiple cutoffs and treatments (Black et al., 2007; Egger and Koethenbuerger 2010; De La Mata 2012; Pop-Eleches and Urquiola, 2013). Recent theoretical treatments of multi-cutoff RD include Cattaneo et al. (2020), who use cutoff variation to extrapolate local effects, and Abdulkadiroglu et al. (2019), who apply RD to cutoffs generated by matching students to schools.

To gain statistical power, researchers often pool the data from various cutoffs by re-centering the forcing variable of individuals at their nearest cutoff. This pooling procedure estimates an average of local treatment effects weighted by the relative density of individuals near each of the cutoffs (Cattaneo et al., 2016). Such an average effect is a meaningful parameter only in two scenarios: (i) local effects are constant and the weighting scheme does not matter; or (ii) local effects are heterogeneous but interest lies in the average effect over marginal individuals at the existing cutoffs. In practice, researchers would like to utilize data with assumptions weaker than (i) to make inferences on average effects computed over distributions of individuals more general than (ii).

Bertanha (2020) proposes an inference procedure for a class of ATE parameters in the context of RD with multiple cutoffs. The class of ATEs is defined by two features making them more meaningful than the average effect estimated by the pooling procedure described. First, the researcher explicitly chooses the counterfactual distribution for the ATE among a wide range of distributions. Second, the researcher does not need to restrict the heterogeneity of local effects across different cutoffs.

As an example, suppose we are interested in the effect of Medicaid benefits on health care utilization. The eligibility for Medicaid is dictated by income thresholds that vary across states. Current RD methods estimate the average effect on individuals with income equal to a given threshold in the data. Bertanha's method allows for ATEs of giving Medicaid benefits to individuals with any distribution of income ranging between the *smallest and largest* threshold in the data.

Denote local treatment effect at cutoff c as $\beta(c) = \mathbb{E}[Y_1 - Y_0 \mid X = c]$. The data consist of several groups of individuals that face cutoffs $c_j, j = 1, \ldots K$. A pooling assumption guarantees that local effects in these subgroups are represented by the same function $\beta(c)$. Cutoff variation lies in a compact interval C and arises from observing multiple groups at multiple time periods. For a counterfactual distribution with continuous probability density function (PDF) $\omega(c)$, the parameter of interest is

$$\mu = \int_C \beta(c)\omega(c)\, dc.$$

Identification of μ relies on a population with infinitely many cutoff values that cover C. For the Medicaid example, De La Mata (2012) has many income cutoffs that differ by state, age and year, with variations between US \$21 394 and \$36 988. Other examples of rich variation in cutoff values include (i) Agarwal et al. (2017) who have 714 credit-score cutoffs distributed between 620 and 800 (see their Figure II(E)); (ii) Hastings et al. (2013) who have at least 1100 cutoffs on admission scores varying between 529.15 and 695.84 (refer to their online appendix's Table A.I.I); and (iii) Pop-Eleches and Urquiola (2013) who have nearly 2000 cutoffs on admission scores for high schools in Romania with variation between 6.5 and 8.5 (see Figure 2 in Bertanha (2020)).

Estimation of μ proceeds in two stages. In the first stage, the researcher estimates $\beta(c_j)$ for each j using a local polynomial regression of Y on X in a neighborhood of c_j defined by a first-stage bandwidth h_{1j}. These bandwidths define estimation windows $[c_j \pm h_{1j}]$ that may overlap. In the second stage, the researcher estimates μ by integrating $\hat{\beta}(c)\omega(c)$ over $\mathcal{C}$, where $\hat{\beta}(c)$ is non-parametric estimate of $\beta(c)$. This is constructed by a local polynomial regression of $\hat{\beta}(c_j)$ on $c_j, j = 1, \ldots, K$, in a neighborhood of c defined by a second-stage bandwidth h_2. The formula for $\hat{\mu}$ amounts to a weighted average:

$$\hat{\mu} = \sum_{j=1}^{K} \Delta_j \hat{\beta}(c_j) \, ,$$

where $\hat{\beta}(c_j)$ are the first-stage estimates and Δ_j are weights that depend on the values of the cutoffs c_j, the bandwidth h_2, kernel weights and polynomial order in the second stage.

A practical summary of the steps to compute $\hat{\mu}$ and pick the tuning parameters is as follows; the formulas for Δ_j, $\hat{V}(h_2)$ and other details can be found in Bertanha (2020). First, use observations pertaining to each cutoff j, compute the bandwidths $\tilde{h}_{1j}$ as described in section 3.1 (for sharp RD, local-linear regression with the edge kernel) and adjust the rate[5] of the bandwidths so that $h_{1j} = \tilde{h}_{1j} \times n^{-0.3}$ Second, obtain $\hat{\beta}(c_j)$ by local-linear regressions with edge kernel and bandwidth h_{1j}. Third, create a grid of possible values for h_2. For each value on the grid, compute $\hat{\mu}(h_2)$ by averaging $\hat{\beta}(c_j)$s using Δ_j weights. Fourth, compute the variance of $\hat{\mu}(h_2)$, and call it $\hat{V}(h_2)$. Fifth, evaluate the MSE of $\hat{\mu}(h_2)$ for each h_2 on the grid. To do that, repeat steps 2–4 using local-quadratic regressions instead of local-linear regressions and call the new estimates $\hat{\mu}'(h_2)$ and $\hat{V}'(h_2)$. The estimated MSE at h_2 (bias squared plus variance) is equal to $(\hat{\mu}'(h_2) - \hat{\mu}(h_2))^2 + \hat{V}'(h_2)$. Sixth, choose h_2^* on the grid that minimizes the MSE. The bias-corrected estimate is $\hat{\mu}'(h_2^*)$ and its variance estimate is $\hat{V}'(h_2^*)$.

The framework also handles the more general case of non-binary treatment, that is, when $\beta(c, d, d') = \mathbb{E}[Y(d') - Y(d) \mid X = c]$, where $Y(d)$ denotes the potential outcome of a continuous treatment dose d. Bertanha illustrates this setting using data previously studied by Pop-Eleches and Urquiola (2013) on the assignment of high school students in Romania. Different cutoffs give admission to different schools, and school quality (that is, treatment dose d) is credibly measured by average performance of peers in each school. The data feature multiple schools in multiple towns and years and exhibit sufficient variation to identify ATEs of policies that change cutoffs and dose values.

Many applications of RD with multiple cutoffs are fuzzy as opposed to sharp. In the high school assignment example, a student may not simply choose the school with highest d among the feasible schools. Multiple treatments result in multiple compliance behaviors, and non-parametric identification at any given cutoff is impossible. This sheds light on the interpretation of two-stage least squares (2SLS) estimates using fuzzy RD data with multiple cutoffs, a common practice in applied work (for example, Angrist and Lavy, 1999; Chen and

Van der Klaauw, 2008; Hoekstra, 2009). In the single-cutoff case, both the non-parametric RD estimator and 2SLS applied to a neighborhood of the cutoff are consistent for the ATE on compliers. In the multiple-cutoff case, the 2SLS estimator is consistent for a data-driven weighted average of treatment effects on a generalization of compliers called "ever compliers". Unless the researcher specifies a parametric function $\beta(c,d,d')$ for ever compliers, it is not possible to identify averages using different weighting schemes, which severely limits the interpretation of 2SLS.

To properly estimate effects on ever compliers, assume the treatment effect function is parametric, that is, $\beta(c,d,d';\theta) = [W(c,d') - W(c,d)]\theta$, for some unknown parameter $\theta \in \mathbb{R}^q$ and some known vector-valued function $W(c,d)$. Estimation then proceeds in two steps. First, the researcher obtains non-parametric estimates of (a) $\mathbb{E}[Y|X=c_j^+] - \mathbb{E}[Y|X=c_j^-]$ and (b) $\mathbb{E}[W(c_j,D_i)|X=c_j^+] - \mathbb{E}[W(c_j,D_i)|X=c_j^-]$ at each cutoff j, where D_i is the treatment dose that student i receives. Second, regress estimates of (a) on estimates of (b) from all cutoffs to obtain $\hat{\theta}$. Precision in the second step can be greatly improved by re-weighting the regression by the inverse of the covariance matrix of first-step estimates. We direct the readers to Bertanha (2020) for more details.

4.3 Measurement Error in the Running Variable

Measurement error is a common occurrence with potentially serious consequences in RD designs, as the researcher relies both on treatment being assigned based on the running variable and on observations with similar values of X around the cutoff serving as counterfactuals for each other. Measurement error invalidates the standard implementations of RD, as one no longer can reliably match comparable treated and untreated observations based on the running variable. The basic idea of focusing on a small neighborhood around the cutoff becomes untenable. Without assumptions about the measurement error, units that "look" closer to the cutoff based on the mismeasured running variable might actually be further away from each other in terms of the true X.

Relevant examples of measurement error in the running variable include age rounding in the evaluation of Medicare's impact on health insurance coverage (Dong, 2015), imperfect reporting on tenure at last firm to determine eligibility to unemployment insurance (UI) in France (Davezies and Le Barbanchon, 2017), distance to the border in geographic RD when evaluating the impacts of UI duration extensions on employment levels (Dieterle et al., 2020), differential rounding and precision on recorded birth weight and impact of neonatal care on infant mortality (Barreca et al., 2016), among others.

We illustrate how measurement error invalidates the usual RD approach by focusing on the sharp RD case in which the treatment is assigned based on the true running variable, X, but the researcher observes a mismeasured version of it, $\tilde{X} = X + e$, where the measurement error (e) has a continuous conditional distribution.

As described in Bartalotti et al. (2020), ignoring the measurement error and implementing standard RD techniques effectively estimates

$$\tau^* = \int_{X \geq c^*} y_1(x)(f_{x|\tilde{X}}(x\,|\,\tilde{X}=c^+) - f_{x|\tilde{X}}(x\,|\,\tilde{X}=c^-))dx$$

$$+ \int_{X < c^*} y_0(x)(f_{x|\tilde{X}}(x\,|\,\tilde{X}=c^+) - f_{x|\tilde{X}}(x\,|\,\tilde{X}=c^-))dx, \tag{12.24}$$

which equals zero in the absence of a discontinuity in $f_{x|\tilde{X}}(x|\tilde{X}=c)$ (or equivalently $f_{e|\tilde{X}}(e|\tilde{X}=c)$. This is an example of the loss of identification induced by the presence of continuous measurement error in the running variable described in Pei and Shen (2017) and Davezies and Le Barbanchon (2017). Intuitively, the measurement error smooths out the conditional expectation of the outcome close to the observed "cutoff" in $\tilde{X}$. This occurs because the measurement error induces the misclassification of treatment to some observations by the researcher.

Even if the treatment is determined by the mismeasured running variable, using standard RD techniques ignoring measurement error will estimate

$$\tau^* = \int_{-\infty}^{\infty}(y_1(x)-y_0(x))\frac{f_{\tilde{X}|X}(c|x)}{f_{\tilde{X}}(c)}dF_X(x). \tag{12.25}$$

Hence, instead of estimating the ATE at the cutoff, we recover a weighted ATE for the population in the support of X for which $X+e=\tilde{X}=c$. The weights are directly proportional to the *ex ante* likelihood that an individual's value of $\tilde{X}$ will be close to the threshold. This is similar to the effect of running variable manipulation with imperfect control (Lee, 2008; Lee and Lemieux, 2010), discussed in section 4.1.

To recover the parameter of interest, we need additional information about the measurement error and the data-generating process. The solutions available in the literature depend crucially on the type of RD design and assumptions about the measurement error.

For example, Lee and Card (2008) consider a restrictive case where measurement error can be cast as random specification error. Barreca et al. (2016) demonstrate that estimates of the ATE at the cutoff are biased in the presence of non-random "heaping" of the running variable and suggest procedures to address the issue. In particular, they propose to perform estimation on the heaped and non-heaped observations separately. For the case of discrete running variables (and under additional assumptions for continuous running variables) Pei and Shen (2017) recover the ATE at the cutoff by assuming that the measurement error is discrete, bounded and "classical"; that is, the mismeasurement and true value of the running variable are assumed to be independent.

Dong (2015), Davezies and Le Barbanchon (2017) and Bartalotti et al. (2020) allow for non-classical measurement error. Dong (2015) focuses on the rounding case in which the measurement error distribution is homogeneous across individuals and *known* to the researcher, using this knowledge of the measurement error distribution to identify the ATE at the cutoff.

Davezies and Le Barbanchon (2017) use auxiliary data on the treated individuals to recover identification of the effect of interest and propose a non-parametric estimator for the continuous running variable case. Their approach has the benefit of not requiring auxiliary data for the untreated group and does not rely on local parametric assumptions for identification. However, it can only be used in "two-sided fuzzy designs", meaning that there must be both treated and untreated units on both sides of the cutoff.

Bartalotti et al. (2020) allows for sharp and fuzzy designs, with group-specific non-classical measurement errors and both continuous and discrete running variables. That generality comes at the cost of requiring a parametric approximation for the conditional mean of the outcomes around the cutoff and auxiliary information/data on the measurement error for both treated and untreated individuals in each group. This information is used to transform the observed data to recover the polynomial approximation around the cutoff that would have been obtained if the correctly measured running variable was available.

To illustrate the problem and the proposed correction in Bartalotti et al. (2020), consider the simple case where the researcher fits local quadratic regressions around the cutoff for $\mathbb{E}[Y_t \mid X] = f_t(x_i)$ for $t = 0,1$ with parameters $b_{p,t}$ for $p = 2$, the polynomial order used:

$$f_t(x_{ig}) = b_{0,t} + b_{1,t} x_i + b_{2,t} x_i^2$$

$$= b_{0,t} + b_{1,t}(\tilde{x}_i + e_i) + b_{2,t}(\tilde{x}_i + e_i)^2$$

$$= b_{0,t} + b_{1,t}\left(\tilde{x}_i + e_i\right) + b_{2,t}\left[\tilde{x}_i^2 + 2e_i\tilde{x}_i + e_i^2\right].$$

They assume that the measurement error does not provide additional information about the conditional mean of the outcome for both treatment regimes, $\mathbb{E}[Y \mid x,\tilde{x},D = t] = \mathbb{E}[Y \mid x,D = t] = f_t(x)$. Then, by using the mismeasured running variable we obtain,

$$\mathbb{E}[Y \mid \tilde{x}, D = t] = \mathbb{E}\left[f_t(x_i) \mid \tilde{x}\right]$$

$$= \left(b_{0,t} + b_{1,t}\mu^{(1)} + b_{2,t}\mu^{(2)}\right) + \left(b_{1,t} + 2\mu^{(1)}\right)\tilde{x}_i + b_{2,t}\tilde{x}_i^2 \tag{12.26}$$

$$= b_{0,t} + b_{1,t}\left(\tilde{x}_i + \mu^{(1)}\right) + b_{2,t}\left(\tilde{x}_i^2 + 2\mu^{(1)}\tilde{x}_i + \mu^{(2)}\right), \tag{12.27}$$

where $\mu^{(p)} = \mathbb{E}(e^p \mid \tilde{x})$ is the $p-th$ moment of the measurement error distribution. Equation (12.26) highlights the problems with using the mismeasured running variable. Specifically, when regressing the observed Y on the mismeasured $\tilde{x}$, the mean outcomes evaluated at $\tilde{x}_i = c = 0$ will be $b_{0,t} + b_{1,t}\mu^{(1)} + b_{2,t}\mu^{(2)}$, rather than $b_{0,t}$. Intuitively, the same measurement error can generate different biases on each side due to how it interacts with shape of $\mathbb{E}[Y_t \mid X]$.

Equation (12.27) is helpful for understanding the intuition for the correction procedure in Bartalotti et al. (2020). It provides a representation of the mean of the outcome conditional on the variable of interest, the unobserved x, in terms of the observed $\tilde{x}$ and the first p moments of the measurement error distribution. In other words, equation (12.27) says that the coefficients in $f_t(x)$ can be recovered by projecting Y on the "corrected" regressors $x_1^* = \tilde{x}_i + \mu^{(1)}$, $x_2^* = \tilde{x}_i^2 + 2\mu^{(1)}\tilde{x}_i + \mu^{(2)}$ and a constant.

In general, for any polynomial order J, the vector of the mismeasured running variable $\tilde{X}' = [1,\tilde{x},\tilde{x}^2,\ldots,\tilde{x}^J]$, is replaced by the vector of the "corrected" running variable of same dimensions $X^* = [1,x_1^*,x_2^*,\ldots,x_J^*]$, where $x_j^* = \sum_{k=0}^{j} \binom{j}{k}\mu^{(j-k)}\tilde{x}^k$. Naturally, the moments for the measurement error need to be replaced by consistent estimates, which is why this approach requires auxiliary data with information about the measurement error distribution. Since $\mathbb{E}(e^k \mid \tilde{x}) = \mu^{(k)}(\tilde{x})$, it is natural to use a local kernel estimator,

$$\hat{\mu}^{(j)}(\tilde{x}) = N_a^{-1}\sum_{i=1}^{N_a} K_h(\tilde{x})e_i^j, \tag{12.28}$$

where N_a is the size of the auxiliary sample on which we observe the measurement error, h is a bandwidth and $K_h(\tilde{x})$ a bounded kernel (Fan and Gijbels, 1996).

From the applied researcher's perspective, it is useful to keep in mind that this approach requires only information about the measurement error distribution moments. It is not necessary that the auxiliary data match specific observations, nor does it need to be nested within the main sample.

This method easily covers group-specific measurement errors, which can also depend on $\tilde{x}$. Note that, in obtaining equation (12.27), the measurement error moments can be specific to particular groups (denoted by g), $\mathbb{E}(e_g^k \mid \tilde{x}) = \mu_g^{(k)}(\tilde{x})$. Since the "corrected" running variables transform observations individually, the measurement error heterogeneity is incorporated by the appropriate $\mu_g^{(k)}(\tilde{x})$ for each observation, defined based on the source (group) of measurement error. In that case, the auxiliary data must have information about measurement error in each group. We refer the reader to Bartalotti et al. (2020) for the implementation and inference details.

An important example in which group-specific measurement error plays a significant role is the analysis of the effect of additional care received by newborns classified as very low-birth weight (VLBW) on infant mortality (Almond et al., 2010); Barreca et al., 2011, 2016). Bartalotti et al. (2020) revisit that by considering that each "heap" in the birth weight data reflects a separate type of measurement error, induced by different rounding standards by hospital staff or scale precision, say to the nearest ounce, or 5, 10, 25 or 50 grams multiple. Information about the measurement error distribution is obtained by looking at the "non-heaped" data in their analysis.

In another instance, Dieterle et al. (2020) analyze the impact of UI benefits extensions on unemployment duration and wages using household distance to state borders as the running variable. In that case, the main data set reports geographic location at the county level, but the underlying running variable is household distance to the border. Calculating distance to the border based on the geographic center of the county leads to mismeasurement in this context. They implement the correction described using auxiliary data on within-county population distribution relative to a state boundary from the 2010 Census. In that case, each county is a group with a specific measurement error distribution.

Even in light of these recent developments, it is the case that measurement error in the running variable is a very important issue that can invalidate RD analyses, and it needs to be carefully addressed by the researcher on a case-by-case basis. Solutions depend on the type of RD design, nature of the running variable and treatment assignment and the availability of additional information on the nature of the measurement error.

4.4 Sample Selection

Similar to manipulation of the running variable and measurement error, non-ignorable sample selection and missing data are common issues in many empirical applications. Differential selection on each side of the cutoff invalidates the RD identification strategy, as observations above and below the threshold are no longer comparable.

For example, McCrary and Royer (2011) consider the effect of female education on infant health, relying on an RD design based on age-at-school-entry policy differences. However, infant health is only observed for individuals who gave birth. This fertility decision naturally depends, among other factors, on the education level of the potential mother, leading to a selected sample in terms of observed outcomes. Similarly, Martorell and McFarlin (2011) evaluate the impact of a policy on wages, which are only observed if an individual chooses to work at prevalent salaries. Dong (2019) studies the impact of college probation on college completion and final GPA, which are observed only for those students who decide to keep taking courses, leading to sample selection.

The first two papers propose a control function approach, relying on parametric assumptions about the relationship between the sample selection and the outcome. In this context, controlling for the inverse Mills ratio adequately addresses the sample selection bias.

Dong (2019) develops a general framework to partially identify the LATE for subgroups of the population under mild assumptions on the sample selection mechanism. As usual in the LATE set-up, we learn about the effects of treatment on individuals around the threshold that are compliers (denoted by C). As before, compliers are those individuals who have treatment status affected by the side of the cutoff they are. In addition to the usual RD continuity and no defiance assumptions, identification relies on smoothness of the joint distribution of potential outcomes and sample participation (Y_0^*, Y_1^*, S_0, S_1) around the cutoff. This implies no discontinuities at the cutoff for the density of the running variable and pre-determined covariates. This implication can be tested, as described in section 4.1.

Consider the potential outcomes Y_0^* and Y_1^*, and the realized outcome is given by $Y^* = DY_1^* + (1-D)Y_0^*$, just like in the usual RD set-up. Due to sample selection, the researcher might not observe the realized outcome for all individuals. Let S be a binary variable that equals one to indicate participation of an observation in the sample. Similarly define the potential sample participation under each treatment status, S_0, S_1. Then the observed sample selection indicator is given by $S = DS_1 + (1-D)S_0$. The data actually observed by the researcher are described as $Y^*S = Y$.

The endogenous sample selection makes it harder for the researcher to learn about the potential outcomes from observed data. Dong (2019) points out that we can connect the information in our sample to the unobserved potential outcomes by realizing that $Y = Y^*S = Y_t^*$ when $S = 1$ and $D = t$; that is, for the treated individuals in the sample we observe Y_1^* and similarly for the untreated. Then, by exploiting the RD design and its LATE interpretation we can recover:

$$\mathbb{E}[Y_t^* \mid S_t = 1, X = c, C] = \frac{\lim_{a\downarrow 0}\mathbb{E}\left[1(D=t)Y^*S \mid X = c+a\right] - \lim_{a\uparrow 0}\mathbb{E}\left[1(D=t)Y^*S \mid X = c+a\right]}{\lim_{a\downarrow 0}\mathbb{E}\left[1(D=t)S \mid X = c+a\right] - \lim_{a\uparrow 0}\mathbb{E}\left[1(D=t)S \mid X = c+a\right]}, \tag{12.29}$$

$$\mathbb{E}[S_t \mid X = c, C] = \frac{\lim_{a\downarrow 0}\mathbb{E}\left[1(D=t)S \mid X = c+a\right] - \lim_{a\uparrow 0}\mathbb{E}\left[1(D=t)S \mid X = c+a\right]}{\lim_{a\downarrow 0}\mathbb{E}\left[1(D=t) \mid X = c+a\right] - \lim_{a\uparrow 0}\mathbb{E}\left[1(D=t) \mid X = c+a\right]}. \tag{12.30}$$

In this set-up, point identification for the extensive margin effects of treatment is provided, that is, how much the treatment impacts the probability of participation in the sample. Given the equations, this can be simplified to the standard fuzzy RD estimand:

$$\mathbb{E}[S_1 - S_0 \mid X = c, C] = \frac{\lim_{a\downarrow 0}\mathbb{E}\left[S \mid X = c+a\right] - \lim_{a\uparrow 0}\mathbb{E}\left[S \mid X = c+a\right]}{\lim_{a\downarrow 0}\mathbb{E}\left[D \mid X = c+a\right] - \lim_{a\uparrow 0}\mathbb{E}\left[D \mid X = c+a\right]}.$$

This is a parameter of interest for a policymaker learning whether a particular job training program makes people (compliers) more likely to be employed (and hence have $S = 1$), for example. If the probability of sample selection is smooth at the cutoff, the extensive margin effect is zero. In that case, the usual RD estimand on the observed data for the outcome point identifies the aggregate effect of treatment on the *observed* outcomes:

$$\mathbb{E}[Y_1^* \mid S_1 = 1, X = c, C] - \mathbb{E}[Y_0^* \mid S_0 = 1, X = c, C]$$

$$= \frac{\lim_{a\downarrow 0}\mathbb{E}\big[Y \mid X = c + a, S = 1\big] - \lim_{a\uparrow 0}\mathbb{E}\big[Y \mid X = c + a, S = 1\big]}{\lim_{a\downarrow 0}\mathbb{E}\big[D \mid X = c + a, S = 1\big] - \lim_{a\uparrow 0}\mathbb{E}\big[DS \mid X = c + a, S = 1\big]}.$$

This parameter describes how the observed outcome is likely to differ depending on the existence of treatment. This is not a measure of causal effect of the treatment, as it will mix changes in the potential outcomes $Y_1^* - Y_0^*$ with changes in the composition of the observed sample S_1, S_0. For example, this measures the average change in observed wages, which is composed by changes in wages for individuals who were already in the labor force $(S_1 - S_0 = 0)$ and the wages of new entrants into the workforce due to treatment $(S_1 - S_0 = 1)$. While useful, this does not reflect an appropriate counterfactual.

While a proper causal effect for the compliers is not point identified, we can obtain bounds for LATE for a relevant latent subgroup of the population. Define a new set of latent groups based on the potential selection status of individuals:

Table 12.1   Participation status subgroups

Subgroups	S_0	S_1	Designation
AP	1	1	Always Participants
QU	1	0	Quitters
EN	0	1	New Entrants
NP	0	0	Never Participants

We can obtain sharp bounds on the treatment effect for those always participating compliers, reflecting the true causal effect of treatment for that group,

$$\mathbb{E}[Y_1^* - Y_0^* \mid S_0 = 1, S_1 = 1, X = c, C],$$

for example, that measures the impacts of a job training program among workers who have high attachment to the labor force, that is, the ones who would be working regardless of receiving extra training.

The key intuition behind the bounds is to notice that while the two elements composing the LATE $(\mathbb{E}[Y_t^* \mid S_0 = 1, S_1 = 1, X = c, C]$ for $t = 0,1)$ are not point identified, we know from Equation 12.29 that $\mathbb{E}[Y_t^* \mid S_t = 1, X = c, C]$ can be recovered. Furthermore, from the columns on Table 12.1 it is evident that the average outcomes for individuals with $S_1 = 1(S_0 = 1)$ are a weighted average of two types, AP and $EN(QU)$. That is, for the untreated,

$$\mathbb{E}[Y_0^* \mid S_1 = 1, X = c, C]$$

$$= \lambda \mathbb{E}[Y_0^* \mid S_0 = 1, S_1 = 1, X = c, C] + (1 - \lambda)\mathbb{E}[Y_0^* \mid S_0 = 1, S_1 = 0, X = c, C],$$

where $\lambda = \frac{Pr(S_0=1,S_1=1 \mid X=c,C)}{Pr(S_0=1 \mid X=c,C)}$, the share of always participants among the observed untreated individuals. Hence, we can bound $\mathbb{E}[Y_0^* \mid S_0 = 1, S_1 = 1, X = c, C]$ by considering best-case (worst-case) scenarios, in which the bottom (top) share λ of the outcomes among the observed untreated individuals belongs to always participants.

If monotonicity in selection is assumed ($Pr(S_0 \geq S_1) = 1$), treatment can only affect sample participation in one direction, and $\mathbb{E}[Y_1^* \mid S_0 = 1, S_1 = 1, X = c, C]$ is point identified. For example, the researcher might assume that job training can only induce workers to join the labor force, rather than quit. See Dong (2019) for more general results and discussion.

Also, under monotonicity in selection λ is identified as

$$\lambda = \frac{\lim_{a\downarrow 0}\mathbb{E}\big[S \mid X = c + a\big] - \lim_{a\uparrow 0}\mathbb{E}\big[S \mid X = c + a\big]}{\lim_{a\downarrow 0}\mathbb{E}\big[S(1 - D) \mid X = c + a\big] - \lim_{a\uparrow 0}\mathbb{E}\big[S(1 - D) \mid X = c + a\big]}.$$

And the bounds for $\mathbb{E}[Y_0^* \mid S_0 = 1, S_1 = 1, X = c, C]$ can be described as

$$UB_0 = \mathbb{E}[\mathbb{1}(Y_0^* \geq Q(\lambda))Y_0^* \mid S_0 = 1, X = c, C],$$

$$LB_0 = \mathbb{E}[\mathbb{1}(Y_0^* \leq Q(1 - \lambda))Y_0^* \mid S_0 = 1, X = c, C],$$

where $Q(\lambda)$ is the λ-th quantile of the conditional distribution for $Y_0^* \mid S_0 = 1, X = c, C$. Combining these results, the LATE on the always participants ($LATE_{AP}$) is

$$\mathbb{E}[Y_1^* \mid S_1 = 1, X = c, C] - \frac{1}{1 - \lambda}UB_0$$

$$\leq LATE_{AP}$$

$$\leq \mathbb{E}[Y_1^* \mid S_1 = 1, X = c, C] - \frac{1}{1 - \lambda}LB_0.$$

Implementation requires a sequence of different steps, involving fuzzy RD estimands using combinations of S, D, Y as outcomes to obtain all the necessary pieces of the bounds. The procedure is described step by step in section 3.1 in Dong (2019). We refer the reader to that paper for the details and further results.

4.5   RD Designs with Categorical Outcomes

Another recent extension to the standard RD design includes models with *categorical outcomes*, for example, the decision to take paternity leave (binary), graduation from college within a four-year period or longer, or occupational choices (multi-valued). Xu (2017) proposes a non-parametric extension of the multinomial logit model that permits joint inference across outcome categories, as well as optimal bandwidth selection and robust confidence intervals. The methods are illustrated by looking at the effect of very low birth weight (VLBW) on infant morbidity, for both first-day and one day–to–one year mortality, finding that the VLBW status reduces infant mortality more importantly for later-term than first-day deaths in a statistically significant fashion, while combining the categories leads to insignificant results. Furthermore, they reject that the ATE is similar for each type of outcome. In a follow-up paper, Xu (2018) proposes alternative methods to the special case of *discrete duration outcomes*, such as unemployment spells, by exploiting the ordinal structure of the variables of interest.

5.   STATISTICAL SOFTWARE

- rdrobust: RD plots, estimation, robust inference, bandwidth selection and other related features for RD designs employing local polynomial and partitioning methods. It is described in more detail in Calonico et al. (2017). Stata and R packages:
  https://rdpackages.github.io/rdrobust/
- frdboot: iterative bootstrap from Bartalotti et al. (2017) and He and Bartalotti (2020). R package:
  github.com/yhe0802/FRD-bootstrap/
- rdexo: implements external validity tests of Bertanha and Imbens (2020). Stata and Matlab packages:
  https://sites.google.com/site/mbertanha/home/code-bertanha-imbens.
- rdlocrand: statistical inference and graphical procedures for RD designs employing local randomization methods. It provides point estimators, confidence intervals estimators, windows selectors, automatic plots, sensitivity analysis and other related features. Stata and R packages:
  https://rdpackages.github.io/rdlocrand/
- optrdd: optimized inference in RD designs, as proposed by Imbens and Wager (2019). R package:
  https://github.com/swager/optrdd
- rdhonest: honest confidence intervals in fuzzy and sharp RD designs using procedures from Armstrong and Kolesár (2020). R package:
  https://github.com/kolesarm/RDHonest
- rdmulti: RD plots, estimation, inference and extrapolation methods for RD designs with multiple cutoffs and multiple scores. Stata and R packages:
  https://rdpackages.github.io/rdmulti/
- rddensity: manipulation tests employing local polynomial density estimation methods. It provides hypothesis tests and bandwidth selectors for manipulation testing. Stata and R packages:
  https://rdpackages.github.io/rddensity/
- rdcont: continuity test for the density of the running variable based on g-order statistics developed in Bugni and Canay (2020). Stata package:
  https://bitbucket.org/iacanay/rdcont-stata/overview

- `rdperm`: test of continuity of covariates in RD using the permutation tests from Canay and Kamat (2018). `Stata` package:
  `https://bitbucket.org/iacanay/rdperm-stata`
- `rdpower`: power and sample size calculations using robust bias-corrected local polynomial inference methods. `Stata` and `R` packages:
  `https://rdpackages.github.io/rdpower/`

NOTES

1. Identification of τ_c is also possible if one replaces the continuity assumption with the stronger combination of assumptions that the distribution of $(Y_1 - Y_0, D(c))$ conditional on X is independent of D in a neighborhood of $X = c$ and that the distribution of (Y_0, Y_1) conditional on X is continuous. See condition C.3 and Appendix A by Hahn et al. (1999), and discussion by Dong (2018b).
2. This local estimation approach can also be used to obtain LQTE and DMTE estimates described in section 2.3 with relatively straightforward modifications, and careful attention to inference challenges; see Frandsen et al. (2012).
3. Another bootstrap approach uses a multiplier bootstrap based on a Bahadur representation of a general class of Wald estimators which provides uniform inference focusing on the LQTE case; see Chiang et al. (2019).
4. For a practical example, see Bertanha and Imbens (2020), described in section 3.3.
5. The IK and CCT bandwidths do not converge fast enough for the asymptotic experiment with a large number of observations and cutoffs. See discussion by Bertanha (2020), including his Figure 1.

REFERENCES

Abadie, A. and G. W. Imbens (2006). Large sample properties of matching estimators for average treatment effects. *Econometrica 74* (1), 235–67.

Abdulkadiroglu, A., J. D. Angrist, Y. Narita, and P. A. Pathak (2019). Breaking ties: Regression discontinuity design meets market design. *Cowles Foundation Discussion Paper no. 2170.*

Agarwal, S., S. Chomsisengphet, N. Mahoney, and J. Stroebel (2017). Do banks pass through credit expansions to consumers who want to borrow? *Quarterly Journal of Economics 133* (1), 129–90.

Almond, D., J. J. Doyle, A. E. Kowalski, and H. Williams (2010). Estimating marginal returns to medical care: Evidence from at-risk newborns. *Quarterly Journal of Economics 125* (2), 591–634.

Angrist, J. D., G. W. Imbens, and D. B. Rubin (1996). Identification of causal effects using instrumental variables. *Journal of the American Statistical Association 91* (434), 444–55.

Angrist, J. D. and M. Rokkanen (2015). Wanna get away? regression discontinuity estimation of exam school effects away from the cutoff. *Journal of the American Statistical Association 110* (512), 1331–44.

Angrist, J. D. and V. Lavy (1999). Using maimonides' rule to estimate the effect of class size on scholastic achievement. *The Quarterly Journal of Economics 114* (2), 533–75.

Armstrong, T. B. and M. Kolesár (2020). Simple and honest confidence intervals in non-parametric regression. *Quantitative Economics 11* (1), 1–39.

Barreca, A. I., J. M. Lindo, and G. R. Waddell (2016). Heaping-induced bias in regression-discontinuity designs. *Economic Inquiry 54* (1), 268–93.

Barreca, A. I., M. Guldi, J. M. Lindo, and G. R. Waddell (2011). Saving babies? Revisiting the effect of very low birth weight classification. *Quarterly Journal of Economics 126* (4), 2117–23.

Bartalotti, O. and Q. Brummet (2017). Regression discontinuity designs with clustered data. In M. D. Cattaneo and J. C. Escanciano (Eds.), *Regression Discontinuity Designs: Theory and Applications (Advances in Econometrics)*, pp. 383–420.

Bartalotti, O., G. Calhoun, and Y. He (2017). Bootstrap confidence intervals for sharp regression discontinuity designs. In M. D. Cattaneo and J. C. Escanciano (Eds.), *Regression Discontinuity Designs: Theory and Applications (Advances in Econometrics)*, pp. 421–53.

Bartalotti, O., Q. Brummet, and S. Dieterle (2021). A correction for regression discontinuity designs with group-specific mismeasurement of the running variable. *Journal of Business & Economic Statistics 39* (3), 833−48.

Bertanha, M. (2020). Regression discontinuity design with many thresholds. *Journal of Econometrics 218* (1), 216–41.

Bertanha, M. and E. Chung (2021). Permutation tests at nonparametric rates. Working paper, arXiv:2102.13638.

Bertanha, M. and G. W. Imbens (2020). External validity in fuzzy regression discontinuity designs. *Journal of Business and Economic Statistics 38* (3), 593–612.

Bertanha, M. and M. Moreira (2020). Impossible inference in econometrics: Theory and applications. *Journal of Econometrics 218* (2), 247–70.

Black, D. A., J. Galdo, and J. A. Smith (2007). Evaluating the worker profiling and reem- ployment services system using a regression discontinuity approach. *American Economic Review 97* (2), 104–7.

Bugni, F. A. and I. A. Canay (2021). Testing continuity of a density via g-order statistics in the regression discontinuity design. *Journal of Econometrics 221* (1), 138–59.

Calonico, S., M. D. Cattaneo, and M. H. Farrell (2018). On the effect of bias estimation on coverage accuracy in nonparametric inference. *Journal of the American Statistical Association 113* (522), 767–79.

Calonico, S., M. D. Cattaneo, and M. H. Farrell (2020). Optimal bandwidth choice for robust bias-corrected inference in regression discontinuity designs. *The Econometrics Journal 23*, 192–210.

Calonico, S., M. D. Cattaneo, and M. H. Farrell (2021). Coverage error optimal confidence intervals for local polynomial regression. arXiv:1808.01398.

Calonico, S., M. D. Cattaneo, M. H. Farrell, and R. Titiunik (2017). rdrobust: Software for regression-discontinuity designs. *Stata Journal 17* (2), 372–404.

Calonico, S., M. D. Cattaneo, M. H. Farrell, and R. Titiunik (2019). Regression discontinuity designs using covariates. *The Review of Economics and Statistics 101* (3), 442–51.

Calonico, S., M. D. Cattaneo, and R. Titiunik (2014). Robust nonparametric confidence intervals for regression-discontinuity designs. *Econometrica 82* (6), 2295–326.

Canay, I. A. and V. Kamat (2018). Approximate permutation tests and induced order statistics in the regression discontinuity design. *The Review of Economic Studies 85* (3), 1577–608.

Card, D., D. S. Lee, Z. Pei, and A. Weber (2015). Inference on causal effects in a generalized regression kink design. *Econometrica 83* (6), 2453–83.

Card, D., D. S. Lee, Z. Pei, and A. Weber (2017). Regression kink design: Theory and practice. In M. D. Cattaneo and J. C. Escanciano (Eds.), *Regression Discontinuity Designs: Theory and Applications (Advances in Econometrics)*, pp. 341–82.

Cattaneo, M. D., B. R. Frandsen, and R. Titiunik (2015). Randomization inference in the regression discontinuity design: An application to party advantages in the US senate. *Journal of Causal Inference 3* (1), 1–24.

Cattaneo, M. D., L. Keele, R. Titiunik, and G. Vazquez-Bare (2016). Interpreting regression discontinuity designs with multiple cutoffs. *Journal of Politics 78*, 1229–48.

Cattaneo, M. D., L. Keele, R. Titiunik, and G. Vazquez-Bare (2020). Extrapolating treatment effects in multi-cutoff regression discontinuity designs. *Journal of the American Statistical Association* (Forthcoming).

Cattaneo, M. D., M. Jansson, and X. Ma (2019). Simple local polynomial density estimators. *Journal of the American Statistical Association 115* (531), 1449–55.

Cattaneo, M. D., N. Idrobo, and R. Titiunik (2020). *A practical introduction to regression discontinuity designs: Foundations.* Cambridge Elements: Quantitative and Computational Methods for Social Science, Cambridge University Press.

Cattaneo, M. D., N. Idrobo, and R. Titiunik (2021). *A practical introduction to regression discontinuity designs: Extensions.* Cambridge Elements: Quantitative and Computational Methods for Social Science, Cambridge University Press.

Chen, H., H. D. Chiang, and Y. Sasaki (2020). Quantile treatment effects in regression kink designs. *Econometric Theory 36* (6), 1167–91.

Chen, S. and W. Van der Klaauw (2008). The work disincentive effects of the disability insurance program in the 1990s. *Journal of Econometrics 142* (2), 757–84.

Cheng, M.-Y., J. Fan, and J. S. Marron (1997). On automatic boundary corrections. *The Annals of Statistics 25* (4), 1691–708.

Chiang, H. D., Y.-C. Hsu, and Y. Sasaki (2019). Robust uniform inference for quantile treatment effects in regression discontinuity designs. *Journal of Econometrics 211* (2), 589–618.

Chiang, H. D. and Y. Sasaki (2019). Causal inference by quantile regression kink designs. *Journal of Econometrics 210* (2), 405–33.

Davezies, L. and T. Le Barbanchon (2017). Regression discontinuity design with continuous measurement error in the running variable. *Journal of Econometrics 200* (2), 260–81.

De La Mata, D. (2012). The effect of Medicaid eligibility on coverage, utilization, and children's health. *Health Economics 21* (9), 1061–79.

Dieterle, S., O. Bartalotti, and Q. Brummet (2020). Revisiting the effects of unemployment insurance extensions on unemployment: A measurement-error-corrected regression discontinuity approach. *American Economic Journal: Economic Policy 12* (2), 84–114.

Dong, Y. (2015). Regression discontinuity applications with rounding errors in the running variable. *Journal of Applied Econometrics 30* (3), 422–46.

Dong, Y. (2018a). *Jump or kink? Regression probability jump and kink design for treatment effect evaluation.* Unpublished manuscript.

Dong, Y. (2018b). Alternative assumptions to identify late in fuzzy regression discontinuity designs. *Oxford Bulletin of Economics and Statistics 80* (5), 1020–27.

Dong, Y. (2019). Regression discontinuity designs with sample selection. *Journal of Business & Economic Statistics 37* (1), 171–86.

Dong, Y. and A. Lewbel (2015). Identifying the effect of changing the policy threshold in regression discontinuity models. *Review of Economics and Statistics 97* (5), 1081–92.

Donoho, D. L. (1994). Statistical estimation and optimal recovery. *Ann. Statist. 22* (1), 238–70.

Egger, P. and M. Koethenbuerger (2010). Government spending and legislative organization: Quasi-experimental evidence from Germany. *American Economic Journal: Applied Economics 2* (4), 200–212.

Fan, J. and I. Gijbels (1996). *Local polynomial modelling and its applications: Monographs on statistics and applied probability 66*, Volume 66. CRC Press.

Feir, D., T. Lemieux, and V. Marmer (2016). Weak identification in fuzzy regression discontinuity designs. *Journal of Business & Economic Statistics 34* (2), 185–96.

Florens, J. P., J. J. Heckman, C. Meghir, and E. Vytlacil (2008). Identification of treatment effects using control functions in models with continuous, endogenous treatment and heterogeneous effects. *Econometrica 76* (5), 1191–206.

Frandsen, B. (2017). Party bias in union representation elections: Testing for manipulation in the regression discontinuity design when the running variable is discrete. In M. D. Cattaneo and J. C. Escanciano (Eds.), *Regression Discontinuity Designs: Theory and Applications (Advances in Econometrics)*, pp. 281–315.

Frandsen, B. R., M. Frölich, and B. Melly (2012). Quantile treatment effects in the regression discontinuity design. *Journal of Econometrics 168* (2), 382–95.

Frölich, M. and M. Huber (2019). Including covariates in the regression discontinuity design. *Journal of Business & Economic Statistics 37* (4), 736–48.

Ganong, P. and S. Jäger (2018). A permutation test for the regression kink design. *Journal of the American Statistical Association 113* (522), 494–504.

Gelman, A. and G. Imbens (2019). Why high-order polynomials should not be used in regression discontinuity designs. *Journal of Business & Economic Statistics 37* (3), 447–56.

Gerard, F., M. Rokkanen, and C. Rothe (2020). Bounds on treatment effects in regression discontinuity designs with a manipulated running variable. *Quantitative Economics 11* (3), 839–70.

Hahn, J., P. Todd, and W. Van der Klaauw (1999). Evaluating the effect of an anti-discrimination law using a regression-discontinuity design. *National Bureau of Economic Research Working Paper No. 7131.*

Hahn, J., P. Todd, and W. V. der Klaauw (2001). Identification and estimation of treatment effects with a regression-discontinuity design. *Econometrica 69* (1), 201–9.

Hastings, J. S., C. A. Neilson, and S. D. Zimmerman (2013). Are some degrees worth more than others? Evidence from college admission cutoffs in Chile. *NBER Working Paper 19241.*

He, Y. and O. Bartalotti (2020). Wild bootstrap for fuzzy regression discontinuity designs: obtaining robust bias-corrected confidence intervals. *The Econometrics Journal 23* (2), 211–31.

Heckman, J. J. and E. Vytlacil (1999). Local instrumental variable and latent variable models for identifying and bounding treatment effects. *Proceedings of the National Academy of Sciences 96*, 4730–34.

Heckman, J. J. and E. Vytlacil (2005). Structural equations, treatment effects, and econometric policy evaluation 1. *Econometrica 73* (3), 669–738.

Hoekstra, M. (2009). The effect of attending the flagship state university on earnings: A discontinuity-based approach. *Review of Economics and Statistics 91* (4), 717–24.

Holland, P. W. (1986). Statistics and causal inference. *Journal of the American Statistical Association 81* (396), 945–60.

Imbens, G. and K. Kalyanaraman (2012). Optimal bandwidth choice for the regression discontinuity estimator. *The Review of Economic Studies 79* (3), 933–59.

Imbens, G. and S. Wager (2019). Optimized regression discontinuity designs. *The Review of Economics and Statistics 101* (2), 264–78.

Imbens, G. W. and D. B. Rubin (2015). *Causal Inference in Statistics, Social, and Biomedical Sciences.* Cambridge University Press.

Imbens, G. W. and J. D. Angrist (1994). Identification and estimation of local average treatment effects. *Econometrica 62* (2), 467–75.

Imbens, G. W. and T. Lemieux (2008). Regression discontinuity designs: A guide to practice. *Journal of Econometrics 142* (2), 615–35.

Jacob, B. A. and L. Lefgren (2004). Remedial education and student achievement: A regression-discontinuity analysis. *Review of Economics and Statistics 86* (1), 226–44.

Kamat, V. (2018). On nonparametric inference in the regression discontinuity design. *Econometric Theory 34* (3), 694–703.

Kolesár, M. and C. Rothe (2018). Inference in regression discontinuity designs with a discrete running variable. *American Economic Review 108* (8), 2277–304.

Lee, D. S. (2008). Randomized experiments from non-random selection in U.S. house elections. *Journal of Econometrics 142* (2), 675–97.

Lee, D. S. and D. Card (2008). Regression discontinuity inference with specification error. *Journal of Econometrics 142* (2), 655–74.

Lee, D. S. and T. Lemieux (2010). Regression discontinuity designs in economics. *Journal of Economic Literature 48* (2), 281–355.

Martorell, P. and I. McFarlin (2011). Help or hindrance? The effects of college remediation on academic and labor market outcomes. *The Review of Economics and Statistics 93* (2), 436–54.

Matsudaira, J. D. (2008). Mandatory summer school and student achievement. *Journal of Econometrics 142* (2), 829–50.

McCrary, J. (2008). Manipulation of the running variable in the regression discontinuity design: A density test. *Journal of Econometrics 142* (2), 698–714.

McCrary, J. and H. Royer (2011). The effect of female education on fertility and infant health: Evidence from school entry policies using exact date of birth. *American Economic Review 101* (1), 158–95.

Nielsen, H. S., T. Sørensen, and C. Taber (2010). Estimating the effect of student aid on college enrollment: Evidence from a government grant policy reform. *American Economic Journal: Economic Policy 2* (2), 185–215.

Noack, C. and C. Rothe (2021). *Bias-aware inference in fuzzy regression discontinuity designs.* arXiv:1906.04631.

Pei, Z., D. S. Lee, D. Card, and A. Weber (2021). Local Polynomial Order in Regression Discontinuity Designs, *Journal of Business & Economic Statistics 00* (0), 1–9.

Pei, Z. and Y. Shen (2017). The devil is in the tails: Regression discontinuity design with measurement error in the assignment variable. In M. D. Cattaneo and J. C. Escanciano (Eds.), *Regression Discontinuity Designs: Theory and Applications (Advances in Econometrics)*, Volume 38, pp. 455–502.

Pop-Eleches, C. and M. Urquiola (2013). Going to a better school: Effects and behavioral responses. *American Economic Review 103* (4), 1289–324.

Rubin, D. B. (1974). Estimating causal effects of treatments in randomized and nonrandomized studies. *Journal of Educational Psychology 66* (5), 688–701.

Shen, S. and X. Zhang (2016). Distributional tests for regression discontinuity: Theory and empirical examples. *The Review of Economics and Statistics 98* (4), 685–700.

Stock, J. and M. Yogo (2005). Asymptotic distributions of instrumental variables statistics with many instruments. In D. Andrews and J. Stock (Eds.) *Identification and inference for econometric models: Essays in honor of Thomas Rothenberg, 1*, 109–20.

Urquiola, M. and E. Verhoogen (2009). Class-size caps, sorting, and the regression- discontinuity design. *American Economic Review 99* (1), 179–215.

Vytlacil, E. (2002). Independence, monotonicity, and latent index models: An equivalence result. *Econometrica 70* (1), 331–41.

Xu, K.-L. (2017). Regression discontinuity with categorical outcomes. *Journal of Econometrics 201* (1), 1–18.

Xu, K.-L. (2018). A semi-nonparametric estimator of regression discontinuity design with discrete duration outcomes. *Journal of Econometrics 206* (1), 258–78.

13. Measuring the effect of health events in the labour market
Emmanuel Duguet

Human capital fully relies on health (Grossman, 1972). Therefore, it is important to evaluate the consequences of health variations on the labour market performance. For a long period of time, many labour market studies have ignored health issues so that health was the missing variable, a source of "unobservable" individual variations in the labour market variables. Recently, more data have been made available. First, one can rather easily find survey data, with many variables on health and some on labour. Most of them are declarative. Second, more recently, administrative data have been made available to researchers. They are not declarative and thus offer a better measurement of some diseases. They also have a systematic time dimension because they are collected by the administration for its own purpose (for example, reimbursement of health expenditures). This opens the way to panel data analysis. This chapter presents the most common methods used for evaluating the effect of a health event (illness, accident) on outcome variables, like participation in the labour market.

1. THE RUBIN APPROACH

We wish to estimate the effect of a health event on a labour market outcome, using the Rubin (1974) causal model framework. In statistical terms, the health event will in fact be called a "treatment". Since our treatment is dichotomous, the outcome can take on two values $Y(0)$ when no health event happened, and $Y(1)$ when it did. We observe the following value:

$$Y = (1 - W) \times Y(0) + W \times Y(1) = \begin{cases} Y(0) & \text{if} \quad W = 0 \\ Y(1) & \text{if} \quad W = 1 \end{cases}.$$

Therefore, we have an observational problem. We only observe one of the two potential outcomes at a time. From the data, we would like to infer one of the following quantities:

- $E(Y(1) - Y(0))$, the average treatment effect (ATE).
- $E(Y(1) - Y(0)|W = 1)$, the average effect of the treatment on the treated (ATT). It is the treatment effect evaluation, since it refers to the population who was actually treated. It is also the most commonly used.
- $E(Y(1) - Y(0)|W = 0)$, the average effect of the treatment on the not treated (ATN). This effect represents a prospective evaluation, since it tries to evaluate what would have happened to the population who did not get the treatment.

There are many ways to estimate these effects. We will consider the most widespread methods in this chapter.

Originally, the goal was to estimate the effect of a treatment on a given population. Ideally, we would like to have experimental data. The people would be given the treatment at random. The people in the treatment group would be compared to the people in the placebo group or control group. The randomness of the selection here is to ensure that, on a large enough sample, the distribution of both observable and unobservable characteristics are similar in the two samples. There would remain two sources of differences: treatment and outcomes.[1]

Unfortunately, it is not always possible to collect experimental data in the social sciences. Consider health events, such as accidents or chronic illnesses. The social science researcher can obviously not deliberately cause a car accident to someone or inoculate a disease to a given worker. There is no other choice than to work with observational data. Increasingly, health insurance data include decades of information about large samples of individuals. We will observe a health event and labour market outcomes at the same time.

Unfortunately, we cannot compare the people with and without accidents directly, not least because of differences in the *confounding variables*. These variables are related both to the health events and to the labour market outcomes. Consider gender: women and men do not have the same illnesses and do not have the same participation in the labour market when they are not ill. By comparing two data sets with and without health events, the outcome variables may differ because these data sets have different proportions of women, and not only because of differences in health status. Two other typical confounding variables are the age and the education level. Some disease, such as cancers, will occur more often in an older population, and the education level is also associated with different behaviours toward risks. Therefore, when we compare the treated and the control groups, the differences may stem from both the confounding variables and the treatment.

A related issue is unobservable heterogeneity, which is considered when panel data are available. Non-observable characteristics, such as genetics or the childhood living conditions, may be related to the occurrence of some diseases or accidents and, at the same time, influence the outcome in the labour market. If the sample really is random, these characteristics should be balanced in the treated and control groups. Otherwise, bias-reducing techniques should be used.

Consider the following mean difference, which has an observable counterpart:

$$\underbrace{E(Y(1)|W=1) - E(Y(0)|W=0)}_{\text{Average outcome difference}} = \underbrace{E(Y(1)|W=1) - E(Y(0)|W=1)}_{\text{ATT}}$$

$$+ \underbrace{E(Y(0)|W=1) - E(Y(0)|W=0)}_{\text{Selection bias}}.$$

The left hand gives the mean outcome difference in the two groups. The right hand gives the sum of two terms; first, what we are looking for, the ATT, and, second, an additional term, which is the mean outcome difference in the absence of treatment $Y(0)$ between the treated group $W = 1$ and the control group $W = 0$. This term comes from a group selection difference (treated or not) and is termed a selection bias because it calls into question the use of the mean difference as a valid ATT estimator from observational data. With experimental data, we would not have this problem because, by definition, the distribution of the outcomes would be the same in the two groups, so the selection bias cancels. We could use the outcomes of the not treated to estimate what would have happened to the treated if they had not been treated. Statistically, it corresponds to the assumption

$$Y(0) \perp\!\!\!\perp W.$$

This assumption may be too strong for observational data; we need a weaker assumption. When observational data are available, it is still possible to estimate the effect of the treatment on the treated (ATT) with the following conditional independence assumption:

$$\text{CIA-0} : Y(0) \perp\!\!\!\perp W \mid X . \tag{13.1}$$

This assumption means that, given X, the people in the two groups would reach the same outcome in the absence of treatment $Y(0)$. Consider participation in the labour market so that X includes age, gender and the education level. People with the same age, gender and education should reach comparable outcomes on average in the labour market in the absence of treatment (here, in the absence of disease). When this assumption holds, it is possible to use the data about the people in the control group to infer what would have happened to the treated in the absence of treatment. We do this because it is not possible to observe the outcome of the treated when they are not treated. The credibility of the CIA-0 depends on the data available. The basic ingredient of our estimators will be the conditional mean outcome difference:

$$c(x) = E\Big(Y(1)\mid W = 1, X = x\Big) - E\Big(Y(0)\mid W = 0, X = x\Big)$$
$$= E\Big(Y\mid W = 1, X = x\Big) - E\Big(Y\mid W = 0, X = x\Big).$$

The second line in the previous expression states that $c(x)$ has an empirical counterpart, since Y is always observable. Now, consider the estimation of the ATT. We let

$$c_1(x) = E\Big(Y(1) - Y(0)\mid W = 1, X = x\Big),$$

and we can rewrite the ATT,

$$c_1 = E\Big(c_1(X)\Big) = \int E\Big(c_1(x)\Big)dP_{X|W=1}(x),$$

where P denotes the cdf of $X|W = 1$. When X is continuous we get

$$\int c_1(x)p(x\mid W = 1)dx,$$

where p is the density of $X|W = 1$, and when X is discrete, we get

$$\sum_x c_1(x)\Pr(x\mid W = 1),$$

where $\Pr(x|W = 1)$ is the probability that $X = x$ among the treated. This simply means that one can compute the ATT in two steps. First, we compute the average outcome differences $c(x)$ for each group of individuals $X = x$. Second, we average the averages according to the distribution of X in the treated group $W = 1$. We can write

$$c_1 = E\Big(c_1(X)\Big)$$
$$= E\Big(E\Big(Y(1)\mid X, W = 1\Big) - E\Big(Y(0)\mid X, W = 1\Big)\Big),$$

assuming that CIA-0 holds,

$$E\big(Y(0) \mid X,W = 1\big) = E\big(Y(0) \mid X,W = 0\big) \Rightarrow c_1(x) = c(x), \forall x,$$

and we get the following expression, which has an empirical counterpart:

$$c_1 = E\big(c(X)\big).$$

Overall, the CIA-0 assumption opens the possibility of using some outcomes of the control group in order to estimate the average outcome of the treated if they had not been treated. This will justify the following method: set a value of $X = x$, compute the average of $Y(1)$ in the treated group with $X = x$, the average of $Y(0)$ in the control group with the same value $X = x$ and take their difference $c(x)$. Then aggregate these differences according to the distribution of *X in the treatment group* in order to get the ATT.

This method implies the following additional assumption: there must be both treated and controls for *all* the values of $X = x$. This is a common support hypothesis. Notice that it can fail if some people are excluded from the treatment group for specific values of X.

The estimation of the ATN is similar to the ATT. One just needs to define the absence of treatment as the treatment and proceed as before. The ATN is defined by:

$$c_0 = E(c_0(X)),$$

with

$$c_0(x) = E\big(Y(1) - Y(0) \mid W = 0, X = x\big).$$

The identifying assumption becomes:

$$\text{CIA-1}: Y(1) \perp\!\!\!\perp W \mid X. \tag{13.2}$$

Therefore, we will be able to use the data of the treated to estimate the outcome the controls would have had if they had been treated. Under CIA-1, we get the conditional effect $c_0(x) = c(x)$, $\forall x$, so that:

$$c_0 = E\big(c_0(X)\big) = \int c(x) dP_{X|W=0}(x).$$

We also use $c(x)$ but with a different weighting distribution than in the ATT case. Also notice that we implicitly assume that we can find treated individuals with the same values of X as the not treated, all along the distribution of $X|W = 0$. Last, we can estimate the Average Treatment Effect (ATE), c_2, by assuming:

$$\text{CIA-2}: Y(0), Y(1) \perp\!\!\!\perp W \mid X. \tag{13.3}$$

This is the most demanding assumption, and one may well question which of the three effects is the most relevant in order to avoid useless assumptions. The ATE uses the marginal distribution of X:

$$c_2 = E\big(c(X)\big) = \int c(x)dP_X(x).$$

2.   CROSS-SECTION ESTIMATION

2.1   Matching

We will first consider multidimensional matching methods. Health and labour often include categorical variables and few continuous variables, so we will consider exact matching and calliper matching. When these methods are not applicable, propensity score matching may be welcome.

Exact matching. Consider the estimation of the treatment effects. All the individuals in the data set have an identification variable. The levels of this variable allow us to form index sets of the treated and controls; $\mathbf{I}^W$ will denote the index set in the treatment group W, and I^W the number of elements in $\mathbf{I}^W$. By convention, we will let $W = 0$ denote the control group, $W = 1$ denote the treated group and $W = 2$ denote all the individuals in the data set ($W = 0$ and $W = 1$). Therefore, we have $\mathbf{I}^2 = \mathbf{I}^0 \cup \mathbf{I}^1$ and $I^2 = I^0 + I^1$, because an individual cannot be in the treated group and in the control group at the same time. Each index set defines a treatment effect: the ATT relies on the distribution of X in $\mathbf{I}^1$, the ATN in $\mathbf{I}^0$ and the ATE in $\mathbf{I}^2$.

We take the estimation of the ATT as an example. The derivations of the other estimators are similar, and we will only give the associated results. The treated are identified by their index $i \in \mathbf{I}^1$. For each value of i, we have twins in the control group, who share the same value of the matching variables. With exact matching, we can define the twins of the treated i by a matching function directly giving the index set of the twins $\mathbf{M}$. Let X_i be the matching variables for the treated i, the index set of the twins is denoted $\mathbf{M}(X_i)$ or, shortly $\mathbf{M}(i)$:

$$\mathbf{M}(i) = \{ j \in \mathbf{I}^0 : X_j = X_i \}, i \in \mathbf{I}^1.$$

Similarly, we can apply this matching function to a whole set of individuals so that $\mathbf{M}(I^1)$ is the twin set of all the treated. By convention, M will denote the number of elements in $\mathbf{M}$. The estimator of the ATT is defined by:

$$\hat{c}_1 = \frac{1}{I^1} \sum_{i \in \mathbf{I}^1} \left(Y_i - \frac{1}{M(i)} \sum_{j \in \mathbf{M}(i)} Y_j \right).$$

With a perfect matching, the values of X define groups of the treated and controls and we can decompose the previous difference according to the values of X. With categorical data, there will be a finite number of groups. In order to use the CIA-0 condition, we will partition the treated set $\mathbf{I}^1$ according to the values of X, into G^1 groups. Matching is straightforward for categorical data. Each realization of X can be interpreted as a sorting key that defines groups of data. Consider gender (two levels, 1 and 2) and education (three levels, 1, 2 and 3), we can define six groups from these data $G^1 = \{(1, 1), (1, 2), (1, 3), (2, 1), (2, 2), (2, 3)\}$. We can index the groups by $g \in G^1$ and let $G^1 = 6$ denote the number of groups. Inside each group g there are I^1_g treated and $M(I^1_g)$ controls. We let:

$$\mathbf{I}^1 = \bigcup_{g \in G^1} \mathbf{I}^1_g \text{ and } \mathbf{I}^1_g \cap \mathbf{I}^1_{g'} = \varnothing \ \forall g \neq g',$$

so that

$$\hat{c}_1 = \frac{1}{I^1} \sum_{g \in G^1} \sum_{i \in \mathbf{I}^1_g} \left(Y_i - \frac{1}{M(i)} \sum_{j \in M(i)} Y_j \right).$$

The first term of the difference is proportional to the mean of the outcome variable in the treatment group g denoted ($\bar{Y}^1_g$):

$$\sum_{i \in \mathbf{I}^1_g} Y_i = I^1_g \times \frac{1}{I^1_g} \sum_{i \in \mathbf{I}^1_g} Y_i = I^1_g \times \bar{Y}^1_g.$$

For the second term, consider that inside each set $\mathbf{I}^1_g$ the control group $M(i)$ does not depend on i because all the treated i have the same value of X and, therefore, exactly the same twins. We can set $M(i) = M(\mathbf{I}^1_g) \ \forall i \in \mathbf{I}^1_g$ and the second term in the sum is simply the mean of the outcome variable in the control group g, denoted $\bar{Y}^0_g$:

$$\frac{1}{M(i)} \sum_{j \in M(i)} Y_j = \frac{1}{M(\mathbf{I}^1_g)} \sum_{j \in M(\mathbf{I}^1_g)} Y_j = \bar{Y}^0_g,$$

which implies that

$$\sum_{g \in G^1} \frac{1}{M(i)} \sum_{j \in M(i)} Y_j = I^1_g \times \bar{Y}^0_g,$$

and we estimate the ATT by

$$\hat{c}_1 = \sum_{g \in G^1} \frac{I^1_g}{I^1} \left(\bar{Y}^1_g - \bar{Y}^0_g \right)$$
$$= \sum_{g \in G^1} \omega^1_g \left(\bar{Y}^1_g - \bar{Y}^0_g \right),$$

with $\omega^1_g = I^1_g / I^1$. Notice that ω^1_g is simply the proportion of treated that lies in the $\mathbf{I}^1_g$ set, that is, the empirical distribution of $X|W = 1$. It is easily checked that $0 < \omega^1_g < 1$ and $\Sigma_g \omega^1_g = 1$.

This presentation strongly simplifies the computation of the variance for the following reasons (Barnay et al., 2019). First, by construction, there is no individual in common between different $\mathbf{I}^1_g$ sets, and this property extends to the twins because the matching is perfect. Second, by definition, there is no intersection between the treated and the control sets (one individual is treated or not). This implies that

$$V(\hat{c}_1) = \sum_{g \in G^1} V\left(\omega^1_g \left(\bar{Y}^1_g - \bar{Y}^0_g \right) \right)$$
$$= \sum_{g \in G^1} (\omega^1_g)^2 \left(V\left(\bar{Y}^1_g \right) + V\left(\bar{Y}^0_g \right) \right).$$

The same principles can be used for the two other effects. The ATN is identified under the conditional independence assumptions CIA-1 (13.2) and the ATE is identified under CIA-2 (13.3). Notice that the support of X differs for each estimator: $X|W = 1$ for the ATT, $X|W = 0$ for the ATN and X for the ATE. We get the following estimates of the three effects:

$$\hat{c}_W = \sum_{g \in G^W} \omega_g^W \left(\bar{Y}_g^1 - \bar{Y}_g^0 \right), W = 0, 1, 2,$$

with $\omega_g^W = I_g^W / I^W$. The variance equals

$$V\left(\hat{c}_W\right) = \sum_{g \in G^W} (\omega_g^W)^2 \left(V\left(\bar{Y}_g^1\right) + V\left(\bar{Y}_g^0\right) \right),$$

and we use the following unbiased estimators ($W = 0, 1$) for the variances of the means:

$$\hat{V}\left(\bar{Y}_g^W\right) = \frac{1}{(I_g^W - 1)I_g^W} \sum_{i \in I_g^W} \left(Y_i - \bar{Y}_g^W \right)^2.$$

There are two sources of difference between these estimators:

1. The support of the matching variables, which defines the matching rates. Each estimator potentially relies on a different distribution of the confounding variables X. One may directly check the variations in this distribution when comparing the effects. Notice that we must find enough individuals in the counterfactual group for the computation to make sense.
2. The weights ω_g^W used in the computation, for a given support. These weights can vary strongly when X includes determinants of the treatment variable, because the treatment is not allocated at random between the individuals.

Continuous variables. The CIA assumptions may hold for continuous variables too and perfect matching may be impossible because there are too few observations in the data set. This will obviously raise the problem of the matching rate. For the ATT, it is the proportion of treated who *can* be matched. In order to fix this problem, we need to adapt the matching method. Among them, we could use coarsened exact matching, calliper matching, nearest neighbour matching or propensity score matching. In all these cases, we should care about the matching rate because it indicates the fulfilment degree of the common support condition. One important decision to make is whether we use a twin only once or several times (that is, for several treated). Obviously, drawing with replacement will always make more twins available, increase the matching rate and reduce bias. But the variance will be bigger and more difficult to compute. Drawing without replacement makes the computations easier, but if the twins are scarce, some treated cannot be matched, and the ones who are matched may belong to a non-representative set. The trade-off is clearly related to the size of the data set. With a very large reservoir of controls, drawing without replacement will not be a problem because all the treated can be matched with several twins. But if the data set is smaller, drawing with replacement may be the only relevant option. In this case, matching everyone with all the available twins may be the only way to avoid biases. Also notice that the availability of panel data may make matching easier for the following reason: one may match the treated with both the people who are never treated and with those who will be treated at a later date. This increases the number of available matches.

Several adaptations are possible: coarsened exact matching, calliper matching or nearest neighbour matching. Coarsened exact matching simply transforms continuous variables into categorical ones by taking intervals. Exact matching is applied afterward to the new categorical variables. Calliper matching is more interesting because it sets a maximum distance for the matching. The difference between the two methods is important. Consider a matching on age. With a coarsened exact matching we would define intervals such as 16–29, 30–49 and 50+. This implies that someone aged 30 will be matched with someone aged 49, 19 years of age difference, but not with someone age 29 while there is only one year of age difference. With calliper matching, one sets the difference explicitly, such as, say, 3 years. Someone aged 30 will be matched with people in the 27–33 range, which looks much better than with intervals.

Calliper matching. When matching variables include continuous variables, it is not possible to perform exact matching. However, one can set a tolerance margin for the continuous variable. This margin is called a *calliper*. For example, if we study the effect of cancer on employment participation, we may tolerate a difference of, say, three years between the treated and the controls. It could be justified by the fact that, on the one hand, the incidence probability of cancer does not vary much in three years, as well as the participation rate in the labour market, provided that the workers are far enough from the legal retirement age. More generally, explicit methods should be preferred to automatic methods, because they constrain the researcher to justify the distance allowed between the treated and the controls. A good survey of the literature should allow us to determine a reasonable calliper for the main continuous variables. In what follows, we take the example of one continuous variable, although the extension to several variables is straightforward. Let X denote the matching variables. We will separate the discrete variables D from the continuous variables C, so that $X = (D, C)$. Considering the discrete variables first, we get a matching reservoir $\mathbf{M}(i)$:

$$\mathbf{M}(i) \triangleq \left\{ j \in \mathbf{I}^0 : X_j = X_i \right\}, i \in \mathbf{I}^1.$$

The important point is that this reservoir does not depend on i. All the individuals $i \in \mathbf{I}_g$ share the same reservoir $\mathbf{M}(i)$ because they share the same value of the discrete matching variables. Introducing continuous variables will restrict the part of the reservoir that we can use and the matching will become individual. We denote it $\mathbf{R}(i)$:

$$\mathbf{R}(i) \triangleq \mathbf{M}(i) \cap \left\{ j \in \mathbf{I}^0 : |C_j - C_i| \leq r \right\}, i \in \mathbf{I}^1,$$

where $r > 0$ is the calliper. It is simply the largest difference tolerated for a matching on the continuous variable. By convention $R(i)$ denotes the number of twins for the treated i.

The introduction of a calliper creates the following complication, when matching is done with replacement.[2] For the same value of the discrete variables, the twins' sets are no longer disjoint. In other words, if the calliper equals three years, the treated with less than three years difference will have similar twins and this will create a correlation between their performance differences. This must be accounted for both in the mean and in the variance formulas.

In order to simplify the exposition of the ATT, we use the following matching dummies, $r_{ij} = 1$ when j can be matched with i:

$$\forall j \in \mathbf{M}(i), r_{ij} = \begin{cases} 1 & \text{if } j \in \mathbf{R}(i) \\ 0 & \text{otherwise} \end{cases}.$$

With this definition, the number of twins for the treated i equals:

$$R(i) \triangleq \sum_{j \in \mathbf{M}(i)} r_{ij},$$

and their mean outcome variable can be written indifferently:[3]

$$\bar{Y}_i^0 \triangleq \frac{\sum_{j \in \mathbf{R}(i)} Y_j}{R(i)} = \frac{\sum_{j \in \mathbf{M}(i)} r_{ij} Y_j}{\sum_{j \in \mathbf{M}(i)} r_{ij}}.$$

The ATT can be estimated by:

$$\hat{c}_1 = \frac{1}{I^1} \sum_{g \in \mathbf{G}^1} \sum_{i \in I_g^1} \left(Y_i - \bar{Y}_i^0 \right).$$

Here, we should notice that, for $i \in I_g^1$, we have $\mathbf{M}(i) = I_g^0$ so that we can rewrite the ATT in the following way:

$$\hat{c}_1 = \sum_{g \in \mathbf{G}^1} \omega_g^1 \left(\bar{Y}_g^1 - \tilde{Y}_g^0 \right),$$

with:

$$\tilde{Y}_g^0 = \frac{1}{I_g^0} \sum_{j \in I_g^0} \bar{r}_j Y_j,$$

with the counterfactual weights:

$$\bar{r}_j \triangleq \frac{1}{I_g^1} \sum_{i \in I_g^1} \left(\frac{r_{ij}}{\frac{1}{I_g^0} \sum_{j \in I_g^0} r_{ij}} \right).$$

Consider some special cases. When one control j can be matched with all the treated, we get $r_{ij} = 1$ $\forall i$ and $\bar{r}_j = 1$ so that we get the exact matching case $\tilde{Y}_g^0 = \bar{Y}_g^0$. When the control j cannot be matched with any of the treated i, we get $r_{ij} = 0$ and $\bar{r}_j = 0$ so that Y_j is excluded from the computation of the counterfactual. In the standard case, the control j can be matched with a part of the treated, and its contribution to the counterfactual will be increasing with its number of matches (that is, the number of i such that $r_{ij} = 1$).

More generally, the effects can be written

$$\hat{c}_W = \sum_{g \in \mathbf{G}^W} \omega_g^W \left(\bar{Y}_g^1 - \tilde{Y}_g^0 \right), W = 0, 1, 2,$$

and their variance (Duguet and Le Clainche, 2020)

$$V\left(\hat{c}_W\right) = \sum_{g \in G^W} (\omega_g^W)^2 \left(V\left(\bar{Y}_g^1\right) + V\left(\tilde{Y}_g^0\right)\right),$$

but now, the variance of the counterfactual must account for the fact the same controls are used several times. Let us assume that the variance of the matchable twins' outcome inside the group g is $(\sigma_g^0)^2$, we get

$$V\left(\tilde{Y}_g^0\right) = \left(\sigma_g^0\right)^2 \frac{\sum_{j \in I_g^0} \bar{r}_{\cdot j}^2}{\left(r_g^0\right)^2},$$

and one can use the following estimator:[4]

$$(\hat{\sigma}_g^0)^2 = \frac{1}{\sum_{j \in I_g^0} r_{gj}} \sum_{j \in I_g^0} \left(r_{gj} Y_j - \frac{\sum_{j \in I_g^0} r_{gj} Y_j}{\sum_{j \in I_g^0} r_{gj}} \right)^2,$$

where $r_{gj} = 1$ if there exists $i \in I_g^1$ such that $r_{ij} = 1$. In short, we keep the only controls that can be matched with at least once in I_g^1 in order to compute the outcome variance.

Propensity score matching. Exact or even calliper matching may not be possible when there are many continuous variables. In this situation, it is possible to reduce the dimension of the matching problem by using the propensity score method. The propensity score, $e(X)$, is the probability to get the treatment conditional of the observable variables X:

$$e(X) = \Pr(W = 1 \mid X).$$

Rosenbaum and Rubin (1983) showed that the following property holds for evaluating the ATE:

$$(Y_0, Y_1) \perp\!\!\!\perp W \mid X \text{ and } 0 < e(X) < 1, \forall X$$

$$\Rightarrow (Y_0, Y_1) \perp\!\!\!\perp W \mid e(X) \text{ and } 0 < e(X) < 1, \forall X.$$

For the other effects, we use

$$Y_k \perp\!\!\!\perp W \mid X \text{ and } 0 < e(X) < 1, \forall X$$

$$\Rightarrow Y_k \perp\!\!\!\perp W \mid e(X) \text{ and } 0 < e(X) < 1, \forall X,$$

with $k = 0$ for the ATT and $k = 1$ for the ATN.

These results open the possibility of matching on the propensity score $e(X)$, a real number, rather than directly on X. The intuition is the following: if two individuals have the same probability of being treated, and one is treated while the other is not, then the treatment may be allocated at random among them. This reduces the matching to one dimension. Several methods may then be applied in order to estimate the causal effects.[5]

The reader may, however, be conscious that matching on the propensity score is inefficient compared to matching on X (Frölich, 2007) so that this method should be used when direct matching is not feasible.

In practise, we do not observe $e(X)$ but an estimate, $\hat{e}(X)$. It may be obtained by a logit or a probit model. This will have consequences for the regression methods presented later. Let W^* be a latent variable determining the (random) allocation to treatment:[6]

$$W_i^* = X_i\theta + u_i, i \in \mathbf{I}^2,$$

where u is the disturbance of the model with cdf F_u and X includes a constant term.[7] We observe the following treatment variable:

$$W_i = \begin{cases} 1 & \text{if } W_i^* > 0 \\ 0 & \text{otherwise} \end{cases},$$

which is Bernoulli distributed, with probability

$$\begin{aligned} \Pr[W_i = 1 \mid X_i] &= \Pr[W_i^* > 0 \mid X_i] \\ &= \Pr[u_i > - X_i\theta] \\ &= 1 - F_u[- X_i\theta] \\ &= e(X_i; \theta). \end{aligned}$$

In a probit model, this reduces to $e(X_i; \theta) = \Phi(X_i\theta)$, where $F_u(u) = \Phi(u)$ is the cdf of the standard normal distribution; in a logit model, we get $e(X_i; \theta) = \Lambda(X_i\theta)$, where $F_u(u) = 1/(1 + \exp(-u))$ is the cdf of the logistic distribution. The estimation proceeds by maximum likelihood. The log-likelihood for one observation i is:

$$\ell_i(W_i \mid X_i; \theta) = W_i \ln\left(e(X_i; \theta)\right) + (1 - W_i) \ln\left(1 - e(X_i; \theta)\right),$$

and the maximum likelihood estimator is defined as:

$$\hat{\theta} = \arg\max_\theta \sum_{i \in \mathbf{I}^2} \ell_i(W_i \mid X_i; \theta).$$

We get the estimated propensity score by:

$$\hat{e}(X_i) = e(X_i; \hat{\theta}).$$

From there, we can use a calliper matching, a kernel prediction of the counterfactual or a regression including the propensity score.[8]

Common support and balancing. The propensity score should verify $0 < e(X) < 1$. This means that no individual is excluded from the treatment, or has treatment imposed. This implies that, for all values of X, there may be some randomness in the allocation of the treatment among individuals. We have a distribution of the treatment probability in the interval $\mathbf{E}_1 = [e_1^-, e_1^+]$ and, similarly for the not treated $\mathbf{E}_0 = [e_0^-, e_0^+]$. Generally, the distribution of the treated will be shifted to the right because the treated tend to have higher probabilities of being treated. If we wish to estimate the ATT, we will need to find matches for the probabilities in $\mathbf{E}_1$. Ideally, this requires $\mathbf{E}_1 \subseteq \mathbf{E}_0$. When this property fails, we can still compute a matching rate and proceed to the estimation when it remains close to 100 per cent. Obviously, all the effects can be estimated when $\mathbf{E}_0 = \mathbf{E}_1$. However, nothing guarantees that this condition holds, and it should be examined carefully. Notice that taking the common support automatically, $\mathbf{E}_0 \cap \mathbf{E}_1$, may cause a bias when it removes an important part of the data. When the matching possibility is reduced, it is recommended to turn to methods with replacement, so as to use each match several times.

The condition $Y_k \perp\!\!\!\perp W \,|\, e(X)$ does not imply the condition $Y_k \perp\!\!\!\perp W \,|\, X$, which remains the motivation behind the method. For this reason, authors have suggested checking for covariate balancing inside subclasses of the propensity score (Imbens and Rubin, 2015, chapter 14). From a matching perspective, one should focus on the continuous variables. Indeed, with replacement, one can always match the value of a categorical variable if there is a least one individual in the matching reservoir. Since one can match both on the categorical variables and the propensity score at the same time, the only difference should come from the continuous variables.[9] Rosenbaum and Rubin (1985) propose to compute the following *normalized difference* for each stratum defined by the propensity score:[10]

$$\hat{\Delta} = 100 \times \frac{\bar{z}_1 - \bar{z}_0}{\sqrt{(s_1^2 + s_0^2)/2}},$$

where $\bar{z}_W = (1/I^W)\sum_{i\in I^W} z_i$, $s_W^2 = 1/(I^W - 1)\sum_{i\in I^W}(z_i - \bar{z}_W)^2$ and $W = 0, 1$. This statistic is different from the Student statistic, since it measures the deviation of means expressed in standard errors. The Student statistics for testing the equality of the means is

$$\hat{T} = \frac{\bar{z}_1 - \bar{z}_0}{\sqrt{s_1^2/I^1 + s_0^2/I^0}},$$

and it will increase with the sample size when the means are different, while $\hat{\Delta}$ may not. More generally, other differences may be examined, involving variances or a measure of the distributions overlap, as indicated in Imbens and Rubin (2015).

Dehejia and Wahba (2002) propose an algorithm that relates the specification of the propensity score to its capacity to ensure the balancing of the observables X. After estimation, the propensity score intervals are determined and the Student tests are performed. If the tests pass for all the strata, the algorithm stops. Otherwise, if a variable does not pass the test, the authors suggest adding higher order and interaction terms in the specification of the propensity score and running the test again.

Calliper matching on the propensity score. Let $\hat{e}_i = \hat{e}(X_i)$, then the matching set for the individual i on the population $W \in \{0, 1\}$:

$$\mathbf{M}_i^W \triangleq \left\{ j \in \mathbf{I}^W : \left| \hat{e}_j - \hat{e}_i \right| \le r \right\}, \; i \in \mathbf{I}^{1-W},$$

where $r > 0$ is the calliper. The associated counterfactual for an individual i will be

$$\bar{Y}_i^W = \frac{1}{M_i^W} \sum_{j \in \mathbf{M}_i^W} Y_j,$$

where M_i^W denotes the number of observations in $\mathbf{M}_i^W$. The use of a calliper creates an overlap between the matching sets of the individuals. The ATT will be estimated by

$$\hat{c}_1 = \frac{1}{I^1} \sum_{i \in I^1} \left(Y_i - \overline{Y}_i^0 \right),$$

the ATN by

$$\hat{c}_0 = \frac{1}{I^0} \sum_{i \in I^0} \left(\overline{Y}_i^1 - Y_i \right),$$

and the ATE by

$$\hat{c}_2 = \frac{1}{I^2} \sum_{i \in I^2} (1 - W_i) \left(\overline{Y}_i^1 - Y_i \right) + W_i \left(Y_i - \overline{Y}_i^0 \right) = \frac{I^0}{I^2} \hat{c}_0 + \frac{I^1}{I^2} \hat{c}_1. \qquad (13.4)$$

With $I^2 = I^0 + I^1$, the ATE is obtained as the weighted mean of the two other treatment effect estimates. The variances are more complicated to compute, so the bootstrap method may be used (Efron and Tibshirani, 1994).[11] The sampling should be done separately for the treated and the controls. Then, one should run the two estimation steps in order to account for the variability in the estimated propensity scores. Notice, however, that the standard bootstrap method may fail for the nearest neighbour estimators with a fixed number of matches (Abadie and Imbens, 2008).

Kernel estimation. Consider the estimation of the ATT. The main issue is the estimation of the counterfactual:

$$E(Y^0 \mid e, W = 1).$$

Following Heckman et al. (1997), we will treat this issue as a nonparametric prediction problem. More precisely, we will consider that that Y^0 is a function of the propensity score $e(X)$ instead of X:

$$Y^0 = m(e) + u,$$

where m is an unknown function, $u \perp\!\!\!\perp W \mid e$ and $E(u|e) = 0$. We get

$$E(Y^0 \mid e, W = 1) = E(Y^0 \mid e, W = 0).$$

In order to estimate this quantity, we will first restrict ourselves to the not-treated sample ($W = 0$) and perform a nonparametric regression of Y on the estimated propensity score $\hat{e}$. The choice of a nonparametric regression is motivated by the will to avoid restrictions on the function m.

In a second step, we will compute the predictions from the propensity scores in the treated sample ($W = 1$). This is possible when the support condition holds for the estimated propensity scores. For each treated i, we compute the prediction:

$$\hat{Y}_i^0 = \hat{m}(\hat{e}_i),$$

and compute the ATT in the following way:

$$\hat{c}_1 = \frac{1}{I^1} \sum_{i \in I^1} \left(Y_i - \hat{Y}_i^0 \right).$$

In order to compute $\hat{m}$, we use the Nadaraya–Watson estimator (Nadaraya, 1964; Watson, 1964):[12]

$$\hat{m}(e_i) = \sum_{j \in I^0} \omega_j(e_i) Y_j,$$

where $\omega_j(e_i)$ is the weight of the (not-treated) match j in the computation of the local average at e_i. This weight of j should be maximal when the match is perfect, $e_i = e_j$, and decrease with the distance from the match $|e_i - e_j|$. A relevant choice is kernel weighting. It is defined by

$$\omega_j(e_i) = \frac{K(z_{ij})}{\sum_{j \in I^0} K(z_{ij})},$$

where $z_{ij} = (e_i - e_j) / h$, K is the kernel chosen and h the bandwidth parameter. This parameter is a smoothing parameter for the estimation of the m function. In the standard cases, the kernel function is positive, symmetric around 0 and integrates to 1. It reaches its maximum at 0, that is, when $e_i = e_j$. The bandwidth parameter h is determined by cross-validation on the not-treated sample. Let $\hat{h}$ be the estimated bandwidth. It is obtained through cross-validation (Frölich, 2004):[13]

$$\hat{h} = \arg\min_h \sum_{j \in I^0} \left(Y_j - \hat{m}_{-j}(\hat{e}_j) \right)^2,$$

where $\hat{m}_{-j}$ is the kernel estimation obtained by omitting the j-th observation. Finally, the effect of the treatment on the treated is estimated by:

$$\hat{c}_1 = \frac{1}{I^1} \sum_{i \in I^1} \left(Y_i - \sum_{j \in I^0} \hat{\omega}_j(\hat{e}_i) Y_j \right),$$

with

$$\hat{\omega}_j(\hat{e}_i) = \frac{K(\hat{z}_{ij})}{\sum_{j \in I^0} K(\hat{z}_{ij})}, \quad \hat{z}_{ij} = \frac{\hat{e}_i - \hat{e}_j}{\hat{h}}.$$

The main determinant of the weight is the propensity score difference. The weight is strictly decreasing with this difference and may be 0 if the difference is too strong. A widespread kernel that uses all the observations is the Gaussian kernel:

$$K(z) = \frac{1}{h\sqrt{2\pi}} \exp\left(-\frac{z^2}{2} \right), z \in \mathbb{R}.$$

There is always a match with this kernel, but it can be a poor match, far from the desired value. Another interesting special case is the uniform kernel:

$$K(z) = \begin{cases} \dfrac{1}{2h} & \text{if } |z| \leq 1 \\ 0 & \text{otherwise} \end{cases}.$$

With the uniform kernel, the prediction reduces to a local mean of Y_j values for the $\hat{e}_j$ that falls in the interval $[\hat{e}_i - h, \hat{e}_i + h]$. In this case, the bandwidth parameter can be interpreted as a calliper on the propensity score ($h = r$).

The variance of the Nadaraya–Watson estimator may be estimated by the bootstrap. In this situation, we keep the estimate obtained for the original sample, $\hat{c}_1$, and use the bootstrap repetitions in order to estimate the variance. The B draws are done separately in the treated and not-treated samples. The resulting estimation for the bootstrap repetition $b = 1,..., B$ is denoted $\hat{c}_{1b}$ and the variance is estimated by[14]

$$\hat{V}(\hat{c}_1) = \frac{1}{B-1} \sum_{b=1}^{B} (\hat{c}_{1b} - \hat{c}_1)^2.$$

Notice that the standard bootstrap method works well the for the kernel estimators but may fail for other estimators. Abadie and Imbens (2008) showed that the bootstrap may fail for the nearest neighbour estimators with a fixed number of matches.

The extension to the ATN is straightforward since we can define a treatment equal to the absence of treatment. The ATE will clearly require two nonparametric regressions instead of one. A first regression will estimate $E(Y^1|W = 0)$ and another one $E(Y^0|W = 1)$, with different bandwidth parameters. Then we should apply (13.4) in order to get the estimate $\hat{c}_2$, and perform bootstrap repetitions for estimating the variance of the corresponding estimator.

2.2 Regression

Regression on the confounding variables. The first type of regression simply uses the matching variables as regressors (Rubin, 1973; Lee, 2005). Consider the following model:

$$Y^W = \alpha_W + X\beta_W + u_W, W = 0, 1.$$

Two values of W represent the two potential outcomes for the same individual depending on if they are treated ($W = 1$) or not ($W = 0$). We observe:

$$Y = (1 - W) \times Y^0 + W \times Y^1$$
$$= \alpha_0 + X\beta_0 + W(\alpha_1 - \alpha_0) + (WX)(\beta_1 - \beta_0) + u,$$

with $u = (1 - W)u_0 + Wu_1$. We obtain a model with the cross-products WX, which we rewrite

$$Y = \alpha + X\beta + W\gamma + WX\delta + u, \tag{13.5}$$

with $\alpha = \alpha_0$, $\beta = \beta_0$, $\gamma = \alpha_1 - \alpha_0$ and $\delta = \beta_1 - \beta_0$. Several specific cases are of interest:

1. If the treatment is allocated at random and data are collected about Y only, we can write the model without X:

$$Y = \alpha + W\gamma + u,$$

and the ordinary least squares (OLS) estimation of γ will simply give the difference of the outcome means in the treated and control samples: $\hat{\gamma} = \bar{Y}_1 - \bar{Y}_0$. This is also one of the estimators used with experimental data.

2. The variables X have the same effect in the treatment and the control groups, $\beta_0 = \beta_1$. Although the assumption deserves to be tested, this model is often used in applications, without the test. We get

$$Y = \alpha + X\beta + W\gamma + u$$

and obtain a model in which the treatment dummy W is included as a standard additional regressor.

In these two cases, however, we get a constant treatment effect in the following sense. In the first model, we get the following ATT:

$$c_1 = E(y_1 - y_0 \mid W = 1) = \gamma + E(u_1 - u_0 \mid W = 1).$$

Further assuming $E(u_1) = 0$ and a mean independence assumption about u_0, namely $E(u_0 \mid W = 0) = E(u_0 \mid W = 1)$, we get $c_1 = c$. Now consider the ATN:

$$c_0 = E(y_1 - y_0 \mid W = 0) = \gamma + E(u_1 - u_0 \mid W = 0).$$

And, assuming $E(u_0) = 0$ and $E(u_1 \mid W = 0) = E(u_1 \mid W = 1)$, we get $c_0 = c$. The reader can check that we get the same result for the ATE by simply assuming $E(u_1) = E(u_0)$. In the three cases, the OLS will provide an estimate of γ, and this method of estimation does not allow for different values of the average treatment effects in the treated and the control groups. Adding the explanatory variables X does not change this property since their effect is the same whatever W is.

The only way to allow for different estimations of the three treatment effects is to include the cross products WX in the regression. In model (13.5) we get, under the relevant mean independence assumptions:

$$c_0 = \gamma + E(X \mid W = 0)\delta,$$
$$c_1 = \gamma + E(X \mid W = 1)\delta,$$
$$c_2 = \gamma + E(X)\delta.$$

Different conditional distributions for X will give different evaluations. Letting $(\hat{\gamma}, \hat{\delta})$ be the OLS estimator of (γ, δ) and $\bar{X}_w$ be the vector of sample means for the samples defined by $W = 0, 1, 2$, we can use the following estimators:

$$\text{ATN}: \hat{c}_0 = \hat{\gamma} + \bar{X}_0\hat{\delta},$$
$$\text{ATT}: \hat{c}_1 = \hat{\gamma} + \bar{X}_1\hat{\delta},$$
$$\text{ATE}: \hat{c}_2 = \hat{\gamma} + \bar{X}_2\hat{\delta},$$

with

$$\bar{X}_W = \frac{1}{I^W} \sum_{i \in I^W} X_i.$$

However, this way of presenting the problem does not lead to the simplest expression of the variance of these estimators, since $\bar{X}_W$ and $(\hat{\gamma}, \hat{\delta})$ are correlated. To obtain the variances directly from the OLS output, it is better to *centre* the X variables before taking the cross-products. Here, it is important to notice that the mean used in the centring *depends on the effect* we wish to estimate. For the effect $\hat{c}_W$, we use $\bar{X}_W$, with $W = 0, 1, 2$. We rewrite the model (13.5) under the equivalent formulation:

$$y = \alpha + X\beta + W\gamma_W + W(X - \bar{X}_W)\delta + u,$$

with $\gamma_W = \gamma + \bar{X}_W\delta$. Notice that the definition of γ_W changes with the mean used in the centring. The estimates will now be obtained with

$$c_W = \gamma_W + \mathrm{E}(X - \bar{X}_W \mid W)\delta,$$

which can be estimated by

$$\hat{c}_W = \hat{\gamma}_W + \frac{1}{I^W} \sum_{i \in I^W} (X_i - \bar{X}_W) = \hat{\gamma}_W,$$

and we can use the OLS variance of $\hat{c}_W$. Here, one may remark that the structure of the disturbance $u = (1 - W)u_0 + Wu_1$ suggests a heteroskedasticity correction since the error term differs in the treated and control groups (see White, 1980).

Regression on the propensity score. When there are many variables, it may be easier to perform a regression on the propensity score. The implementation is simple: in a first step, one estimates the propensity score $\hat{e}(X)$, and in a second step, one uses $\hat{e}(X)$ instead of X. All the previous methods can be used. The model is (Rosenbaum and Rubin, 1985)

$$Y_W = \alpha_W + \beta_W e(X) + u_W, W = 0, 1,$$

and we would like to estimate

$$y = \alpha + e(X)\beta + W\gamma_W + W(e(X) - \overline{e(X)}_W)\delta + u,$$

in order to get $\hat{c}_W = \hat{\gamma}_W$. Notice that $\overline{e(X)}_W$ is the mean of the propensity scores in group W. Unfortunately, we cannot observe $e(X)$ and we use an estimate of it instead, denoted $\hat{e}(X)$. This is called a *generated regressor* in the literature. The regression becomes.

$$y = d_0 + d_{1W}W + d_2\hat{e}(X) + d_3 W(\hat{e}(X) - \overline{\hat{e}(X)}_W) + v.$$

The OLS estimation $\hat{d}_{1W}$ will still provide a consistent estimator of c_W, but the OLS standard errors are wrong. One important point to notice is that the usual heteroskedasticity corrections are not a good approach to this problem. A specific correction must be made.[15] Our presentation follows the general case of Murphy and Topel (2002). Separating the standard regressors (Z_1) from the generated ones (Z_2), we rewrite the model under the form:

$$y_i = Z_{1i}\delta_1 + Z_{2i}\delta_2 + v, \ i \in \mathbf{I}_2,$$

with

$$Z_{1i} = (1, W_i),$$

$$Z_{2i} = f\left(X_i; \hat{\theta}\right) \triangleq \left(\hat{e}_i, W_i\left(\hat{e}_i - \overline{\hat{e}}_{iW}\right)\right),$$

$$\hat{e}_i = e(X_i; \hat{\theta}),$$

$$\delta_1 = (d_0, d_{1W})', \delta_2 = (d_2, d_3)',$$

$$v_i = u_i + f(X_i; \theta) - f(X_i; \hat{\theta}).$$

Letting:

$$Z = (Z_1, Z_2) \text{ and } \delta = \begin{pmatrix} \delta_1 \\ \delta_2 \end{pmatrix},$$

the OLS estimator is given by:

$$\hat{\delta} = \left(Z'Z\right)^{-1} Z'y,$$

and its asymptotic variance is deduced from:

$$\text{avar}\left(\sqrt{I_2}(\hat{\delta} - \delta)\right) = \sigma^2 Q_0^{-1}$$

$$+ Q_0^{-1}\left(Q_1 J_1^{-1} Q_1' - Q_1 J_1^{-1} Q_2' - Q_2 J_1^{-1} Q_1'\right) Q_0^{-1},$$

with the empirical counterparts:

$$\hat{\sigma}^2 = \frac{1}{I_2} \sum_{i \in \mathbf{I}_2} \hat{v}_i^2,$$

$$\hat{v}_i = y_i - Z_i\hat{\delta},$$

$$\hat{Q}_0 = \frac{1}{I_2} \sum_{i \in \mathbf{I}_2} Z_i'Z_i,$$

$$\hat{Q}_1 = \frac{1}{I_2} \sum_{i \in I_2} Z_i' \frac{\partial f}{\partial \theta} (X_i; \hat{\theta}) \hat{\delta}_2,$$

$$\hat{Q}_2 = \frac{1}{I_2} \sum_{i \in I_2} Z_i' \hat{v}_i \frac{\partial \ell_i}{\partial \theta} (X_i; \hat{\theta}),$$

$$\hat{J}_1 = -\frac{1}{I_2} \sum_{i \in I_2} \frac{\partial^2 \ell_i}{\partial \theta \partial \theta'} (X_i; \hat{\theta}).$$

The first term $\sigma^2 Q_0^{-1}$ corresponds to the usual OLS variance (under homoskedasticity). The other terms represent the bias of the OLS variance. It can have any sign, so the OLS estimation can overestimate or underestimate the true standard errors.

3.   PANEL DATA ESTIMATION

3.1   Data Structure

Treatment group. We consider panel data with a maximum of T years and I_2 individuals. The panel is unbalanced, so the individuals can enter or exit the panel at any time $t = 1,..., T$. We assume that data are missing at random. Compared to the cross-section case, the treatment will now be identified by its date of appearance so that the sample of treated varies over time. In order to simplify the presentation, we assume that each individual i is present over the period $[t_i^-, t_i^+]$ and is treated at date t_i. When the individual is never treated, we use the convention of an infinite treatment date $t_i = \{+\infty\}$ so that the individual cannot be treated in the panel time span.[16]

The time dimension modifies the definition of the treatment and control groups since the status of an individual varies over time. Consider a health event, such as an accident. The control group includes the individuals who have not yet had an accident. After that date, we may consider that the individual has moved into the treatment group. In most studies, we will not allow for individuals to return to the control group after the health event, because it may have long-term effects. An accident can be benign, but it can also cause a permanent disability. A similar definition is used for chronic diseases, since they are long lasting. Interestingly, this convention allows for the measurement of treatment effects after several periods of time. In this approach, we distinguish the effect at the date of the treatment from the effects several periods after. This allows us to see whether the health consequences are on the short-term or on a longer term. Overall, the control group includes the workers who have not had the treatment yet. Notice that this definition is the only one that is compatible with cross-sectional data because we do not observe the future values of the treatment in this case. With a cross-section, there should be a part of the not treated that will be treated at a later date because the future value of the treatment is not available at the time of the sample construction. When the treatment has long-lasting consequences, we may well consider that t_i is the starting date of the treatment rather than the treatment date. In this case, we will use:[17]

$$W_{it} = \begin{cases} 0 & \text{if } t < t_i \\ 1 & \text{if } t \geq t_i \end{cases}. \tag{13.6}$$

This raises the question as to which effects can be estimated. One advantage of panel data is that is allows us to examine how the intensity of the effect varies over time. In this presentation, we will focus on the ATT a periods after the treatment:

$$c_1(a) = \mathrm{E}\left(Y_t(1) - Y_t(0) \,|\, W_{it} = 1, t = t_i + a\right), a \geq 0,$$

where t_i is the treatment date. Here, we insist on the dependence of the effect on the time from treatment a. Notice that, for yearly data, the date of the treatment is not considered as fully informative because the health event can happen at any time between 1 January and 31 December. This is why the first difference often studied is not for $a = 0$ but for $a = 1$. Since we observe $Y_t(1)$ for the treated after the treatment, we will need to estimate a counterfactual representing the outcome the treated would have had if they had not been treated. Matching and regression can be used to fill this purpose.

3.2 Difference in Differences

A popular estimator on panel data is the Difference-in-differences (henceforth, DiD) estimator.[18] We can derive it from the following panel data model:

$$Y_{i,t}(W_{i,t}) = c_0 + c_1(t - t_i)W_{i,t} + \alpha_i + \beta_t + \varepsilon_{i,t}, \tag{13.7}$$

where c_0 is the constant term, α is an individual fixed effect, also called "correlated effect" in the literature, β a time effect representing a flexible time trend and ε the idiosyncratic error term, which is uncorrelated with the other elements of the model. Without loss of generality, we can set $\mathrm{E}(\alpha) = \mathrm{E}(\beta) = \mathrm{E}(\varepsilon) = 0$. The treatment dummy W is defined by (13.6).

In this model, it is readily checked that the ATT after a periods is given by $c_1(a)$, with the convention $c_1(a) = 0, \forall a < 0$:[19]

$$\mathrm{E}\left(Y_t(1) - Y_t(0) \,|\, W_{it} = 1, t = t_i + a\right) = c_1(a), a \geq 0.$$

There are several ways to estimate this model. A popular one is the DiD estimator. This method consists of eliminating (c_0, α, β) by differencing and attenuating ε by averaging. First, consider the treatment date of one treated individual i and compute the outcome variation b periods before and a periods after this date.[20] We get

$$D_i(a,b) = Y_{i,t_i+a} - Y_{i,t_i-b}$$
$$= c_1(a) + \beta_{t_i+a} - \beta_{t_i-b} + \varepsilon_{i,t_i+a} - \varepsilon_{i,t_i-b}.$$

Second, take one not treated who is present on the same dates and compute the before–after outcome difference. Here, we should define what a not treated is in a dynamic context. One can adopt a static definition: anyone who is treated at any date. With this convention, the not-treated belong to the set

$$\mathbf{M}^S(i) = \left\{ j \in I^2 : (t_j = +\infty) \cap (t_j^- \leq t_i - b) \cap (t_j^+ \geq t_i + a) \right\},\tag{13.8}$$

but one can also choose to adopt a *dynamic matching* convention by taking all the individuals in $\mathbf{I}^2$ who did not had a treatment up to $t_i + a$:

$$\mathbf{M}^D(i) = \left\{ j \in I^2 : (t_j > t_i + a) \cap (t_j^- \leq t_i - b) \cap (t_j^+ > t_i + a) \right\}.\tag{13.9}$$

Clearly, we have $M^S(i) \subseteq M^D(i)$ since the condition $(t_j > t_i + a)$ is always fulfilled for $t_j = \{+\infty\}$. Once the set is chosen, we take the difference:

$$D_j(a,b) = Y_{j,t_i+a} - Y_{j,t_i-b}$$

$$= \beta_{t_i+a} - \beta_{t_i-b} + \varepsilon_{j,t_i+a} - \varepsilon_{j,t_i-b}.$$

Therefore, the difference-in-differences equals:

$$D_i(a,b) - D_j(a,b) = c_1(a) + \varepsilon_{i,t_i+a} - \varepsilon_{i,t_i-b} - (\varepsilon_{j,t_i+a} - \varepsilon_{j,t_i-b}),$$

and we get an unbiased estimate of the ATT:

$$E(D_i(a,b) - D_j(a,b)) = c_1(a).$$

In practice, we compute the mean of all the double differences, so that the estimator is

$$\hat{c}_1(a) = \frac{1}{I^1} \sum_{i \in I^1} \left[\left(Y_{i,t_i+a} - Y_{i,t_i-b} \right) - \frac{1}{M(i)} \sum_{j \in M(i)} \left(Y_{j,t_i+a} - Y_{j,t_i-b} \right) \right],\tag{13.10}$$

where $\mathbf{M}(i)$ is either the static (13.8) or the dynamic (13.9) matching set. Even though the previous notations insist on the dependence of the ATT on a, it obviously depends on the reference period b. There are often robustness checks on this parameter. In the context of program evaluations Chabé-Ferret (2015) even recommends the use of symmetric DiD methods (with $a = b$).

The computation of the variance can be made by several methods. When the differences are uncorrelated, one can use the methods adapted to cross-sectional data. This assumption is generally valid for the terms in $Y_{i,t_i+a} - Y_{i,t_i-b}$ when the individuals have independent outcomes. For the terms in $Y_{j,t_i+a} - Y_{j,t_i-b}$ it may also be the case if each twin is used only once. But, in the general case, the computations involve correlated components because the same twins are used at different dates, and we can reasonably expect that their time series are autocorrelated. With the time dimension, belonging to a matching group does not exclude a twin from another matching group. A bootstrap method may fix this issue. In this case, we draw the individuals separately in the treated and the control groups and keep their entire time series each time.

3.3   Matching

If we use the time dimension for differencing and estimate longer run effects, we may well match as before. Consider the evaluation of the ATT. What we need is an estimate of the outcome of the treated if they had not been treated. Indeed, we do observe what the treated did before to be treated thanks to the time dimension of the panel.

Then, one may think that a simple assumption like $Y_{t+a}(0) \perp\!\!\!\perp W \mid X$ may be enough. However, this would miss the possibility of eliminating the fixed effect from the outcome equation. For this reason, we take a before–after difference $Y_{t+a}(0) - Y_{t-b}(0)$ and this explains the form of the conditional independence assumption. Another point relates to the matching variables. In order to avoid some endogeneity issues, we may match on lagged and time-constant variables. The lag used will typically be $t_i - b$, but one may well use a summary of past values for matching.

Exact matching. Considering an additive model, we need to take a difference in order to eliminate the fixed effect. Then, we will look for a similar difference for the not treated in order to compute a DiD estimator.[21] Therefore, in order to estimate the $c_1(a)$, we will assume

$$\text{CIA} - \text{0P} : Y_{t+a}(0) - Y_{t-b}(0) \perp\!\!\!\perp W_t \mid X_{t-b}, \text{ for some } b \geq 1.$$

Under this assumption, we get:

$$\text{E}\left(Y_{t+a}(0) - Y_{t-b}(0) \mid W_t = 1, X_{t-b}\right) = \text{E}\left(Y_{t+a}(0) - Y_{t-b}(0) \mid W_t = 0, X_{t-b}\right),$$

and we can use the outcome variation of the not treated in order to evaluate the outcome variation of the treated if they had not been treated. The matching set now depends on observable variables. They typically include the variables that do not vary over time, such as gender, the period of birth or the education level, denoted X_j^1, and lagged time varying variables $X_{i,t-b}^2$. For the treated i, we get the dynamic matching set:[22]

$$\mathbf{M}^D(i) = \left\{ j \in \mathbf{I}_2 : (t_j > t_i + a) \cap (X_j^1 = X_i^1) \cap (X_{j,t_i-b}^2 = X_{i,t_i-b}^2) \right\},$$

and the estimators are given by (13.10).

Calliper matching. Here, we just need to add constraints to the continuous variables. They may vary over time or not. Let C_i^1 be a continuous variable stable over time, with calliper r_1 and $C_{i,t}^2$ its time-varying equivalent with calliper r_2. The matching set becomes:

$$\mathbf{M}(i)^D = \left\{ j \in \mathbf{I}_2 : (t_j > t_i + a) \cap (X_j^1 = X_i^1) \cap (X_{j,t_i-b}^2 = X_{i,t_i-b}^2) \right.$$

$$\left. \cap (|C_j^1 - C_i^1| \leq r_1) \cap (|C_{j,t_i-b}^2 - C_{i,t_i-b}^2| \leq r_2) \right\},$$

and the same formula as before (13.10) applies for the ATT estimation.

Propensity score matching. The most difficult issue in this case is, in fact, the estimation of the propensity score itself. The use of panel data opens the possibility of accounting for the existence of individual heterogeneity in the probability of getting the treatment. This is relevant when one thinks that the list of explanatory variables does not include all the determinants of the treatment allocation. This will happen if time-constant variables have been used to allocate the treatment and if these variables are not observable by the econometricians. In practice, however, researchers rarely estimate a propensity score with an individual effect. Here are some practices and suggestions:

- Pooled regressions. One runs a regression as in the cross-section case, adding a time-varying constant term.
- Separate regressions. Each treatment year is used to estimate a binary variable model separately. All the regression coefficients vary with each year.
- Panel data estimation. Ideally, one would like to estimate a model such as:[23]

$$e(W_{it};\theta) = P(\theta_t^0 + \theta_i^1 + X_{i,t-b}^2 \theta_2),$$

where θ_t^0 is a time effect and θ_i^1 is an individual fixed effect. After the estimation, we would use

$$e(W_{it};\hat{\theta}) = P(\hat{\theta}_t^0 + \hat{\theta}_i^1 + X_{i,t-b}^2 \hat{\theta}_2).$$

Unfortunately, the estimation of such models is complicated by several problems (Hsiao, 1996). Also notice that we need an estimate of the individual effect $\hat{\theta}_i^1$ in order to estimate the propensity score. Contributions for solving this problem include Chamberlain (1980), Greene (2004), Fernández-Val (2009) and Stammann et al. (2016).[24]

3.4 Regression

Other methods than matching may be used in order to estimate the ATT. Regression methods naturally extend to panel data and allow for control of unobserved heterogeneity. Notice that, when the model is fully saturated, regression may even be equivalent to matching (Angrist and Pischke, 2008).[25]

Data structure. The first thing to do is to select which dates of the treated are to be included in the panel. Indeed, in most situations, all the effects cannot be estimated due to the lack of data. The number of treated available tends to decrease when we get away from the treatment date. Therefore, we set an estimation windows k, which represents the longest tractable period available for the estimation:

$$c_1(a) = E\left(Y_{t+a}(1) - Y_{t+a}(0) \mid W_t = 1\right) \text{with } 0 \le a \le k.$$

Once k is selected, one should drop all the observations of the treated for which $t > t_i + k$, otherwise this case could go in the reference group and bias the estimation. Another possibility is to build an aggregate dummy for all the cases $t > t_i + k$ and compute an average effect over this interval.[26] We will define $k + 1$ treatment dummies, where each dummy corresponds to a lag in the treatment effect:

$$W_{i,t}(a) = \begin{cases} 1 & \text{if } t = t_i + a \\ 0 & \text{otherwise} \end{cases}$$

$$a = 0,\ldots,k.$$

The first dummy is $W_{i,t}(0)$ and should be thought off as an incomplete measurement of the effect, unless the treatment is measured at the beginning of period and the outcome at the end of period. When there are not enough observations to estimate a separate effect per period, one may regroup them into intervals.

Regression on the confounding variables. We include the explanatory variables X_{it}. The model is:

$$Y_{i,t} = \beta_0 + X_{i,t}\beta_1 + \sum_{a=0}^{k} W_{i,t}(a)\left(\gamma_0^r(a) + (X_{i,t} - \bar{X}_r)\gamma_1(a)\right) + u_{i,t}, \tag{13.11}$$

with $\gamma_0^r(a) = \gamma_1(a) = 0, \forall a < 0$. Here, $\bar{X}_r$ is the mean of the reference population (treated, not treated, total) and $u_{i,t}$ the error term with a two-way fixed effects structure. We let

$$u_{i,t} = \alpha_i + \beta_t + \varepsilon_{it}, \ \mathrm{E}(\alpha) = \mathrm{E}(\beta) = \mathrm{E}(\varepsilon) = 0,$$

where α and β are the individual and the time-constant fixed effects, potentially correlated with W and X, and ε is the idiosyncratic error term, uncorrelated with the other components of the model. Notice that the values of the coefficients $\gamma_0^r(a)$ depend on the mean used for the centring of the explanatory variables ($\bar{X}_r$).

For the ATT, we condition the effect on the treated population so that we use the reference mean $\bar{X}_1$. On panel data, this mean must be taken for a specific reference year since the data values vary over time. This condition is fulfilled when the explanatory variables are constant over time. However, even in this case, the unbalanced nature of the panel may alter the mean for different estimation lags a since the set of treated individuals varies over time. By convention, one may take the structure in t_{i-1} since it is the first period before the treatment. This convention can be used when the variables vary over time. We obtain

$$\mathrm{E}\left(Y_{t+a}(1) - Y_{t+a}(0) \mid W_{i,t} = 1, X_{i,t} = \bar{X}_1\right) = \gamma_0^1(a),$$

since $\bar{X}_r = \bar{X}_1$. The model (13.11) is a classic fixed-effect model, so we can use the within estimator.[27] This consists of applying the within transformation to all the time-varying variables and running the OLS method. The within transformation of a variable $Y_{i,t}$, denoted $\tilde{Y}_{i,t}$, is simply its deviation from the individual mean $Y_{i,\bullet}$:

$$\tilde{Y}_{i,t} = Y_{i,t} - Y_{i,\bullet}, \text{with } Y_{i,\bullet} = \frac{1}{T_i}\sum_{t \in T_i} Y_{i,t}, \forall (i,t).$$

Notice that the within transformation of a time-constant variable is zero. In order to account for the time effects, we include time dummies in the regression:[28] Let

$$d_{i,\tau} = \begin{cases} 1 & \text{if } t = \tau \\ 0 & \text{otherwise} \end{cases}$$

$$\tau = 1, \ldots, T$$

We also define the treatment dummies:

$$W_{i,t}^a = \begin{cases} 1 & \text{if } t = t_i + a \\ 0 & \text{otherwise} \end{cases}$$

$$a = 0,\ldots,k$$

so that the regression (13.11) becomes:

$$Y_{i,t} = \beta_0 + X_{i,t}\beta_1 +$$

$$\sum_{a=0}^{k} W_{i,t}^a \gamma_0^r(a) + \sum_{a=0}^{k} W_{i,t}^a \left(X_{i,t} - \bar{X}_r\right)\gamma_1(a)$$

$$+ \sum_{\tau=2}^{T} d_{i,\tau}\beta_\tau + \alpha_i + \varepsilon_{i,t}.$$

Here, we should notice that the time-constant parts of the model will be cancelled by the within transformation. The confounding variables are written:

$$X_{i,t} = (X_i^1, X_{i,t}^2),$$

so that only $X_{i,t}^2$ will remain after the within transformation. The individual effects α_i will also be cancelled but not the cross-products of X_i^1 by the treatment dummies, because the treatment dummies vary over time. Overall, we get the following regression, to which we apply OLS:

$$\tilde{Y}_{i,t} = \tilde{X}_{i,t}^2\beta_1 + \sum_{a=0}^{k} \tilde{W}_{i,t}^a \gamma_0^r(a) + \sum_{a=0}^{k} \tilde{S}_{i,t}^{a,r}\gamma_1(a) + \sum_{\tau=2}^{T} \tilde{d}_{i,\tau}\beta_\tau + \tilde{\varepsilon}_{i,t},$$

with $S_{i,t}^{a,r} = W_{i,t}^a(X_{i,t} - \bar{X}_r)$. The covariance matrix of the within estimator already allows for the autocorrelation involved by the within transformation itself, but we saw that the treatment model suggests that the variance could differ between the treated and the controls. The simplest solution is to account for autocorrelation and heteroskedasticity of an unknown form, following Arellano (1987).[29]

When the variables are adequately centred before taking the cross-products and before taking the within transformations, the effects will be given by the estimations of the $\gamma_0^r(a)$ coefficients. If the centring is performed according to the mean of treated group, we will get the ATTs at different lags. A centring according to the not-treated group $\bar{X}_0$ will give the ATNs and the ATEs will be obtained when the centring is done according to the whole population ($\bar{X}_2$).

Regression on the propensity score. Once the propensity score has been estimated, it is possible to use it instead of the matching variables in a regression similar to the previous one. The model will just include time and fixed effects, compared to the cross-sectional case. The covariance matrix could be obtained like in Murphy and Topel (2002) provided that the propensity score is obtained as an M-estimator with continuous second-order derivatives. It may be more complex to derive than in the cross-sectional case. The use of the bootstrap is possible, but it will be more time consuming on panel data.

NOTES

1. On the method adapted to randomized experiments, see part II of Imbens and Rubin (2015).
2. We favour matching with replacement because it gives the highest matching rates.
3. In the absence of continuous variables, all the dummies $r_{ij} = 1$, and we get $\bar{Y}_0(i) = \bar{Y}_0$, $\forall i$, the mean in the control group.
4. We do not use the correction for the degrees of freedom so that $\hat{\sigma}_g^0 = 0$ when there is only one twin in some subgroups g, as expected.
5. For a presentation of propensity score methods, see Caliendo and Kopeinig (2008) and Austin (2011).
6. This section requires some knowledge of limited dependent variables and maximum likelihood estimation. See Wooldridge (2002), chapter 15.
7. Without loss of generality because matching is always perfect on the constant term.
8. It is possible to match both on the propensity score and other variables. It may be useful for some categorical variables, such as gender.
9. Notice that one can include the categorical variables in the propensity score estimation and match on both the propensity score and the exact value of categorical variables in a later step.
10. In practice, one may choose quantiles of the estimated propensity score to ensure equal size strata. The choice of the quantile should be guided by the number of observations in each stratum. On the use of the normalized differences, see chapters 15 and 16 of Imbens and Rubin (2015).
11. This estimator is similar to kernel matching with a uniform kernel, as shown in the next section.
12. The part that follows requires some notions of nonparametric estimation; see Pagan and Ullah (1999).
13. The method was originally introduced by Clark (1975).
14. On the choice of the number of bootstrap repetitions, see Andrews and Buchinsky (2000).
15. This issue was originally addressed by Pagan (1984). For a more detailed treatment, see the sections 6.1 and 12.4 of Wooldridge (2002).
16. One can allow randomly missing observations in $[t_i^-, t_i^+]$ without altering what follows.
17. With this definition, notice that the convention $t_i = \{+\infty\}$ implies $W_{it} = 0 \ \forall t$.
18. On this estimator, see Lechner (2010).
19. The last condition means that there is no treatment effect before the treatment date. This convention is compatible with the convention $t_i = +\infty$ for the not treated.
20. Standard values are $a = b = 1$.
21. Notice that the not-treated difference is based on the *treated* dates.
22. We favour the dynamic version of the matching set, with replacement, in order to keep the highest number of matches. Otherwise, including many matching variables may make the matching impossible for many treated and bias the estimation.
23. The effect of the time constant variables X_i^1 is included in the θ_i^1 term.
24. The last contribution is associated with the R package "bife", which provides estimation solutions.
25. When X includes only categorical data, this is equivalent to running a regression with all the dummies and their cross-products (including for more than two variables). In practice, we may include a selection of the cross-products to approximate a fully saturated model.
26. This raises the symmetric issue of whether we should keep all the other values of the treated or only $t = t_i - b$. We assume that we keep all the values prior to the treatment when the support of the treatment dates distribution t_i covers all the periods available in the panel. Otherwise, a different convention may be used.
27. For a presentation of panel data models, see Balestra (1996a,b) and chapter 10 in Wooldridge (2002). The within estimator is also known as the "fixed effect" or LSDV (Least-Squares Dummy Variables) estimator in the literature.
28. One of the time dummies must be excluded from the regression in order to avoid a perfect collinearity case. We choose to drop the first one by convention, without loss of generality.
29. The method is implemented under R in the "plm" package, with the vcovHC function, and under SAS, with the hccme=4 option of the "proc panel".

REFERENCES

Abadie, A. and G. W. Imbens (2008): "On the failure of the bootstrap for matching estimators," *Econometrica*, 76, 1537–57.

Andrews, D. W. K. and M. Buchinsky (2000): "A three-step method for choosing the number of bootstrap repetitions," *Econometrica*, 68, 23–51.

Angrist, J. D. and J.-. Pischke (2008): *Mostly Harmless Econometrics: An empiricist's companion*. Princeton University Press.

Arellano, M. (1987): "Computing robust standard errors for within-groups estimators," *Oxford Bulletin of Economics and Statistics*, 49, 431–4.

Austin, P. C. (2011): "An introduction to propensity score methods for reducing the effects of confounding in observational studies," *Multivariate Behavioral Research*, 46, 399–424.

Balestra, P. (1996a): "Fixed effect models and fixed coefficient models," in *The econometrics of panel data*, ed. by L. Mátyás and P. Sevestre, Springer, pp. 34–49.

Balestra, P. (1996b): "Introduction to linear models for panel data," in *The econometrics of panel data*, ed. by L. Mátyás and P. Sevestre, Springer, pp. 25–33.

Barnay, T., E. Duguet, and C. Le Clainche (2019): "The effects of breast cancer on individual labour market outcomes: an evaluation from an administrative panel in France," *Annals of Economics and Statistics*, 136, 103–26.

Caliendo, M. and S. Kopeinig (2008): "Some practical guidance for the implementation of propensity score matching," *Journal of Economic Surveys*, 22, 31–72.

Chabé-Ferret, S. (2015): "Analysis of the bias of matching and difference-in-difference under alternative earnings and selection processes," *Journal of Econometrics*, 185, 110–23.

Chamberlain, G. (1980): "Analysis of covariance with qualitative data," *The Review of Economic Studies*, 47, 225–38.

Clark, R. M. (1975): "A calibration curve for radiocarbon dates," *Antiquity*, 49, 251–66.

Dehejia, R. H. and S. Wahba (2002): "Propensity score-matching methods for nonexperimental causal studies," *Review of Economics and Statistics*, 84, 151–61.

Duguet, E. and C. Le Clainche (2020): "The socioeconomic and gender impacts of health events on employment transitions in France: a panel data study," *Journal of Human Capital,* 14(3), 449−83.

Efron, B. and R. J. Tibshirani (1994): *An introduction to the bootstrap*. CRC Press.

Fernández-Val, I. (2009): "Fixed effects estimation of structural parameters and marginal effects in panel probit models," *Journal of Econometrics*, 150, 71–85.

Frölich, M. (2004): "Finite-sample properties of propensity-score matching and weighting estimators," *Review of Economics and Statistics*, 86, 77–90.

Frölich, M. (2007): "On the inefficiency of propensity score matching," *AStA Advances in Statistical Analysis*, 91, 279–90.

Greene, W. (2004): "The behaviour of the maximum likelihood estimator of limited dependent variable models in the presence of fixed effects," *The Econometrics Journal*, 7, 98–119.

Grossman, M. (1972): "On the concept of health capital and the demand for health," *Journal of Political Economy*, 80, 223–55.

Heckman, J. J., H. Ichimura, and P. E. Todd (1997): "Matching as an econometric evaluation estimator: Evidence from evaluating a job training programme," *The Review of Economic Studies*, 64, 605–54.

Hsiao, C. (1996): "Logit and probit models," in *The econometrics of panel data*, ed. by L. Mátyás and P. Sevestre, Springer, pp. 410–28.

Imbens, G. W. and D. B. Rubin (2015): *Causal inference in statistics, social, and biomedical sciences*. Cambridge University Press.

Lechner, M. (2010): "The estimation of causal effects by difference-in-difference methods," *Foundations and Trends in Econometrics*, 4, 165–224.

Lee, M.-J. (2005): *Micro-econometrics for policy, program, and treatment effects*. Oxford University Press.

Murphy, K. M. and R. H. Topel (2002): "Estimation and inference in two-step econometric models," *Journal of Business & Economic Statistics*, 20, 88–97.

Nadaraya, E. A. (1964): "On estimating regression," *Theory of Probability & Its Applications*, 9, 141–2.

Pagan, A. (1984): "Econometric issues in the analysis of regressions with generated regressors," *International Economic Review*, 25(1), 221–47.

Pagan, A. and A. Ullah (1999): *Nonparametric econometrics*. Cambridge University Press.

Rosenbaum, P. R. and D. B. Rubin (1983): "The central role of the propensity score in observational studies for causal effects," *Biometrika*, 70, 41–55.

Rosenbaum, P. R. and D. B. Rubin (1985): "The bias due to incomplete matching," *Biometrics*, 41, 103–16.

Rubin, D. B. (1973): "The use of matched sampling and regression adjustment to remove bias in observational studies," *Biometrics*, 29, 185–203.

Rubin, D. B. (1974): "Estimating causal effects of treatments in randomized and nonrandomized studies," *Journal of Educational Psychology*, 66, 688–701.

Stammann, A., F. Heiss, and D. McFadden (2016): "Estimating fixed effects logit models with large panel data," *Conference Paper, beiträge zur Jahrestagung des Vereins für Socialpolitik 2016: Demographischer Wandel – Session: Microeconometrics, No. G01-V3*.

Watson, G. S. (1964): "Smooth regression analysis," *Sankhyā: The Indian Journal of Statistics, Series A*, 359–72.

White, H. (1980): "A heteroskedasticity-consistent covariance matrix estimator and a direct test for heteroskedasticity," *Econometrica*, 48, 817–38.

Wooldridge, J. M. (2002): *Econometric analysis of cross section and panel data*. MIT Press.

PART IV

NETWORKS AND BIG DATA
IN MICROECONOMICS

14. Exploring social media: Twitteronomics and beyond
Tho Pham, Piotr Śpiewanowski and Oleksandr Talavera

1. WHAT IS BIG (SOCIAL) DATA?

Social media have dramatically reshaped the way people spend their time, communicate, as well as receive and send information. According to data from an online survey, 49 per cent of the world's population use social media and the average time spent on social media among internet users is nearly 2.5 hours daily.[1] Social distancing measures and lockdowns imposed due to COVID-19 in many countries have led to even more intensive social media consumption for most users.[2] Among the popular social media platforms, Facebook has nearly 2.5 billion monthly active users worldwide. YouTube and WhatsApp have 2 billion users each while Instagram has one billion. Twitter, a microblogging platform that receives the most attention in this chapter, has 386 million users worldwide.[3]

Just like other kinds of big data, social media data are valuable because of their high volume, high velocity and high variety of features. Given the popularity of social media platforms, it is not surprising that a vast amount of information is generated in each platform in a day. In 2012, Facebook announced that 2.5 billion pieces of content, including 300 million photos and more than 500 terabytes of data, were processed and retrieved each day. On average, about 105 terabytes of data were scanned each half hour.[4] Based on these statistics, one could imagine the large size of the historical data accumulated over time. More importantly, these data could be extracted instantly, allowing for real-time analysis.

Moreover, the value of social media data is not only due to their size and instant access, but also the data's complexity. In particular, the generated information could include user-generated content such as a tweet, a YouTube video or a review on Yelp. The information could be also in the form of interactions with content created by other users of the same platforms and interactions with content from other internet sources. An example of such information is comments on a Facebook post or sharing news media links. Other valuable data include information on how people in different parts of the world connect with each other virtually, that is, the users' networks. Furthermore, social media data come in different types, which vary from text, audio and video to images. These data are then stored in different forms, including structured, semi-structured and unstructured data.

Due to these features, social media data have been proven useful for both commercial and non-commercial purposes. For instance, such data are of great value for marketing companies or even the platforms themselves, as they can use the data to profile the preferences of individual users and design advertisements accordingly. Moreover, social media data could be beneficial to the rapid assessment of disaster damage (Kryvasheyeu et al., 2016) or epidemic spread (Broniatowski et al., 2013). There is also an increasing number of studies using social media data for economic research. These studies will be discussed in more detail in the next section of this chapter.

Nonetheless, the benefits of big social data do not come at zero cost. One of the major concerns related to the usage of such data is the users' privacy. The concern has become deeper after the Facebook–Cambridge Analytica scandal in 2018: Cambridge Analytica, a British political consulting firm, had used personal data on millions of Facebook users without consent to build voter profiles for political advertising during the 2016 US presidential election.[5] This scandal has led to the question, to what extent (should) could the personal information of social media users be collected, stored and used? A related concern is about the methods of data collecting. While legal access to data could be implemented through an application programming interface (API) or through the platforms directly, the data types and/or amount that are freely available through these channels are limited. An example is the collection of Twitter data using Twitter APIs: real-time data can be collected at ease and freely whereas collection of historical data is only available at a substantial cost. To overcome these limitations, one could use data-scraping practices, which are not encouraged due to both practical and legal reasons. An introduction of how to legally collect data from Twitter and Google Trends will be presented in sections 3 and 5 of this chapter.

The chapter is organized as follows. In the next section, we present a broad overview of the application of social media data in the economic literature. In section 3, we discuss the technical details of Twitter API and discuss Stata and Python code to download and clean the data. Section 4 presents the basic tools of Twitter data analysis and visualization, including sentiment analysis. Those tools are applied in practice in analyses of exchange rates in response to political uncertainty revealed in Twitter and communication patterns. In section 5, we move to another data source – Google Trends data – and provide Stata code for data collection with application to labour market responses to COVID-19 pandemics. Finally, section 6 concludes.

2. SOCIAL MEDIA IN ECONOMIC RESEARCH

Social media data can tell us a lot about what people say and think, how and with whom this information is shared and what the response of the receivers is. Most frequently, social media data in economics are used to study some aspects of the content of the written communications, especially the sentiment, of social media posts. Modern computers supplied with the right algorithms that identify positive and negative words and phrases and calculate relative frequencies and aggregate millions of posts submitted to social media platforms at any given time to provide a point estimate. Although each individual user post is typically short, for example, on Twitter it is limited to only 140 characters, the aggregate is an accurate representation of the public mood and sentiment. Such aggregate measures providing time series of the public mood are publicly available thanks to services such as Hedonometer, Sina Weibo Index or the now defunct Gross National Happiness Index that use Twitter, Sina Weibo and Facebook data, respectively. A broad range of text mining tools allow us also to identify more nuanced emotions or even the personality of the social media users.

Measures of sentiment or other emotions do not need to be applied, obviously, only to the whole universe of social media messages. Instead, researchers focus on the changes in moods of some specific groups of individuals or topics followed over time to assess the impact of real events or check if changes in sentiment affect real-world behaviour. Such a more customized analysis, however, requires accessing of raw data, which for some social media can be done with relative ease, as described in section 3 of this chapter. Methods that can be used to study sentiment using those data are explained in more detail in section 4.

For the sentiment to be a good explanatory variable, it needs to exhibit reasonable variability and, indeed, this seems to be the case. It has been shown that diurnal and seasonal mood varies with work, sleep and length of day across diverse cultures (Golder and Macy, 2011) and that it varies with air temperature (Baylis, 2020). This line of reasoning has inspired multiple attempts to use sentiment to predict stock markets. In a widely cited study, Bollen et al. (2011) show that moods predict the stock market. Although the authors failed to identify a relationship between a simple measure of sentiment based on a positive vs. negative daily time series of the public mood, they dug deeper and used more sensitive sentiment measures. The authors generated a six-dimensional daily time series to show that only two public mood dimensions, calm and happiness, predict stock market outcomes. The proprietary algorithm used in the study to estimate collective "calm"-ness from Twitter achieved an impressive 86.7 per cent accuracy in predicting the up–down sequence of the Dow Jones Industrial Average, a price-weighted stock market index of 30 large US stocks. It must be noted, however, that attempts at in-sample replication of the study results were not successful (Lachanski and Pav, 2017).[6]

The impact of the public mood on stock markets has been studied using the now defunct Facebook's Global Happiness Index[7] that measures the sentiment of Facebook users. Siganos et al. (2014) find a positive contemporaneous relation between public mood and stock returns. Relatedly, Danbolt et al. (2015) use the same source for sentiment to show a positive relationship between sentiment and bidder announcement returns, which may indicate that the overall mood affects the investor perception of potential merger synergies and risks. Siganos et al. (2017) explore another feature of the Facebook sentiment data and measure divergence of sentiment. Their prediction that higher levels of divergence of sentiment between individuals leads to more diverging views on the value of a stock as revealed by higher trading volumes meets support in the data.

The impact of social media on stock markets goes beyond the ability to aggregate emotions across all social media users. Social media can be also considered an information intermediary – a source of new information and a dissemination tool. Thus, social media, especially Twitter, which is frequently used as a tool for professional communication, are similar to information intermediaries, such as the business press and stock message, studied in most previous stock market–related event-study-type research.

To explore the stock market–related informational content of social media, many researchers focused on emotions shown in social media posts discussing individual stocks. Sprenger et al. (2014a, 2014b) derive good and bad news from a large number of tweets related to the major listed companies to find that the sentiment content of the news has an impact on the returns, and the volume of tweets is related to trading volume while measures of disagreement affect return volatility and the impact of earning announcements on returns (Gianini et al., 2019; Bartov et al., 2018). Behrendt and Schmidt (2018) also discover some statistically significant co-movements of intraday volatility and information from stock-related tweets. However, economically, the impact is of negligible magnitude and does not improve the out-of-sample forecast performance. Zhang et al. (2020) address a similar topic using data from Sina Weibo and find that the variation tendency of the Sina Weibo Index is highly correlated with stock market volatility.

Standard dictionaries used to analyse sentiment may not be structured to capture the vocabulary used by members of specific professions, for example investors. Thus, in studies on sentiment shared among relatively narrow, specialised groups, some refinements may be required to the specific type of lexicon used by those professions. This strategy allowed

Gholampour and van Wincoop (2019) to study Twitter sentiment among Euro–Dollar foreign exchange traders and to show that the sentiment reflects expectations about the future direction of the exchange rate. Furthermore, not all topics are equally important, thus identifying the topic category (for example, posts related to corporate governance, operations or legal issues) from the text messages may increase the accuracy of the predictions (Sprenger et al., 2014a). A case study of the impact of political uncertainty revealed in Twitter posts is presented in section 4.

Impact of numerical measures of Twitter opinions can be studied using time series methodologies, for example, a vector autoregressive (VAR) model which, under some assumptions for example, using sign restrictions, can be used to estimate the impact of belief shocks on macroeconomic variables such as interest rates and exchange rates (Meinusch and Tillman, 2017). In some applications, alternative methods, such as the local projections method (Jordà, 2005) are preferred as they do not constrain the shape of the impulse responses and allow us to test joint hypotheses about the paths of estimated impulse response (Gorodnichenko et al., 2021). The sentiment of the social media discussion has been also shown provide significant information for explaining the spread between the cost of borrowing in the Eurozone's peripheral bond market and Germany during the Greek crisis (Dergiades et al., 2015).

Social media sentiment data have been also shown to successfully predict returns or volatility in some arguably less complete markets such as cryptocurrency markets (Shen et al., 2019) or sports betting (Brown et al., 2018; Feddersen et al., 2017). Outside the financial markets, social media have also been studied for their word-of-mouth effect. Tang (2018) shows that third party–generated product information on Twitter, once aggregated at the firm level, is predictive of firm-level sales. Vujić and Zhang (2018) show that the frequency, sentiment and timing of tweets posted about a film are correlated to a different extent with the movie's box office revenues. However, in both cases, it is difficult to isolate the impact of social media from the inherent quality of the products described.

Social media, especially Twitter, have been also extensively used by listed firms and influential individuals to communicate their corporate plans, or in the case of individuals, more general thoughts with the general audience. Studies on corporate communication show that the information released through social media reduces information asymmetry, especially for firms that receive less coverage in traditional media (Blankespoor et al., 2014). For individuals, a clear outlier in terms of the influence and engagement in social media is the 45th president of the United States, Donald Trump. Unsurprisingly, his short communication via Twitter has received a lot of attention from the scholar community. Numerous studies show how the posts from President Trump that explicitly mentioned publicly traded companies (Ge et al., 2019) or addressed trade issues (Burggraf et al., 2020) or other topics (Klaus and Koser, 2020) had significant impacts on stock markets worldwide. In the different parts of the world, Enikolopov et al. (2018) show that the social media posts of the Russian political activist Alexey Navalny, revealing corruption in Russian state-controlled companies, had a negative causal impact on their market return.

Written communication published on social media or more broadly the entire digital footprint reveals a lot of information about the authors, including hints about the authors' personality traits. Thus, it is not surprising that multiple studies have used social media data to identify individual characteristics and then to evaluate their impact on the actions taken. Indeed, studies using corpora from various types of written communication show that personality measures have strong out-of-sample predictive performance and are stable over time (Gow et al., 2016).

Commercial extensions of the already mentioned LIWC tool also provide "composite" psychological measures, such as the Big Five, which can be applied directly to social media data. This allowed Block et al. (2019) to study Twitter statements of business angels to show that the personality of business angels influences syndication behaviour – extraversion makes syndication more likely, whereas conscientiousness reduces the likelihood of syndication. Similarly, Winkler et al. (2020) investigate whether the personalities of chief marketing officers (CMOs) of technology-based new ventures affect how the increasing maturity of new ventures translates to web traffic. Their findings indicate that a CMO's extraversion positively moderates the relationship between a new venture's maturity and web traffic, while a CMO's conscientiousness is a negative moderator of this relationship.

Social media posts can also be used to analyse the revealed identity of its users. Metzger et al. (2016) study ethnolinguistic identity in Ukraine or which language Twitter users set and which they tweet in in response to Euromaidan and Crimean events.

Social media are also an excellent source to identify salience or the intensity with which certain topics are discussed by the (general) public. This can be measured by a relative frequency of keywords, hashtags (#) or mentions of certain handles (user profiles) in social media posts. Google Trends offers a more representative data on Google Search query intensity based on the population of Google Search queries, also with a geographical dimension. In section 5, we present detailed information on how to access and gather Google Trends data with applications to COVID-19 and the US economy/labour market. Data on the intensity with which topics are discussed in the media can also be obtained from commercial news aggregator sources (for example, Factiva). While all those sources have their pros and cons, only the social media data allow us to also study the dynamic component of information sharing, including the spread of false information (Allcott and Gentzkow, 2017) or how computer algorithms (bots) are used to spread (mis)information (Gorodnichenko et al., 2021).

The use of social media available from Google Trends and Twitter to look for time series spikes in searches and tweets allowed Kearney and Levitt (2015) to identify the impact of an MTV show on interest in contraceptive use and abortion. In section 5, we provide a related example with an application of Google Trends to job searching during the COVID-19 pandemic together with a toolkit to access the data.

Social media are also used to gauge how the salience of climate change is affected by short-run weather deviations and extreme weather events (Sisco et al., 2017), which affects electoral outcomes and congressional voting (Herrnstadt and Muehlegger, 2014). In the context of stock markets, social media data may provide a measure of the significance of otherwise incomparable events affecting for example stock listed firms (Kowalewski and Śpiewanowski, 2020).

The introduction of social media has significantly reshaped how information is spread. Compared to traditional media, social media have much lower entry barriers. Furthermore, its reliance on user-generated content, enhanced by the built-in functionality to repost, reshare and copy content generated by others, strengthens the role of individuals in information transmission. This novelty introduced by the rise of social media clearly requires new research on the information transmission mechanisms and their implications. Multiple studies and news reports indicate that social media have played a pivotal role in determining political outcomes and have been driving coordination enhancing civil unrest.

Acemoglu et al. (2018) show that general discontent expressed on Twitter in Egypt predicted protests in Tahrir Square, suggesting that social media have helped coordinate street mobilizations. In a similar vein, Steinert-Threlkeld et al. (2015), find that increased coordination of messages was associated with increased protests during the Arab Spring in 16 countries in the region. Interestingly, the protests were induced thanks to individuals on the periphery of the social networks rather than the central nodes (Steinert-Threlkeld, 2017). Social media have also ignited successful consumer boycotts. For example, the boycott of cottage cheese organized in Israel on Facebook in 2011 following a steep price increase of that product in previous years reduced the demand by as much as 30 per cent and forced producers to decrease the prices (Hendel et al., 2017).

The diffusion of information on social networks, is, however, driven to a large extent by the network shape, where homophily – a tendency to interact with similar individuals – is crucial. Bakshy et al. (2015) and Halberstam and Knight (2016) study diffusion of political information on social networks and find, perhaps unsurprisingly, that people do encounter less political content aligned with opposing ideologies than with their own ideology. Both studies show that this finding is driven more by individual network decisions than social media algorithms.

The ideological segregation of social media users makes social media platforms particularly conducive to fake news. Literature shows that false news does spread through social media, and it spreads faster, deeper and more broadly than the truth (Vosoughi et al., 2018).[8] False information is, by definition, novel, and novelty is shown to speed up information diffusion. Another contributor is the fact that information from social media is consumed in a different setting than that coming from traditional media, for example on mobile phone screens or news feed windows. Further, the built-in sharing/reposting functionalities mean that information transmission is driven to a greater extent by immediate reactions that are often based on emotions rather than reason. Emotionally charged messages tend to be retweeted more often and more quickly compared to neutral ones (Stieglitz and Dang-Xuan, 2012). False news is typically more emotionally charged than truthful information.

Information is spread not only by real ("human") agents but also social bots – computer algorithms used to produce automated content. Bots can create new bits of information and, through a phenomenon known as "echo chambers", a sense of consensus in society that is favourable for a given candidate/outcome. The first challenge in this strand of literature is to identify bots. Gorodnichenko et al. (2021), compiling findings from various computer science studies, suggest criteria based on Twitter intensity: bots are on average more active than humans, timing of twitter activity; bots are more likely to be active at night, originality of content; bots tend to repeatedly post identical messages, account creation; bot accounts tend to be created and used for particular events, for example elections. The ability of bots to affect humans' tweeting activities is shown, in line with the already mentioned studies on human interaction, to depend on whether the bots' information is consistent with human preferences. This makes bots able to further enhance the polarization mechanism already present on social media. This additional polarization resulting from energizing voters could have marginally contributed to political outcomes such as the Brexit and the 2016 US presidential election.

2.1 Social Connectedness

A separate strand of literature uses social media data to study the effect of social connectedness rather than online communication between social media users described in this chapter so far. Information on a social network together with other self-revealed information, for example about current employment status posted on social media, allows us to study the impact of connectedness on economic outcomes. Such information from de-identified data on 6 million

US users of the social networking website Facebook allowed Gee et al. (2017)[9] to test the importance of social networks and the strength of ties between individuals for finding jobs.

Access to friendship links between social media users can also be used to map the relations between geographical regions. Using data on the universe of the US Facebook users, Bailey et al. (2018a) designed a Social Connectedness Index that shows social connectedness between the US regions and how it may be related to other economic and social interactions between these regions. Although the description is non-causal, the study shows a strong relation between the friendship links and trade flows, patent citations and migration patterns. More research in the field is needed to establish the causal links.

Social media data can also be merged with data from other sources, for example, administrative data such as real estate records. Such data allow us to exploit the plausibly exogenous variation in experiences of geographically distant friends. However, it must be noted that an agreement with a social network provider rather than the methods described in the subsequent sections is required to obtain such data. A merged dataset allows *inter alia* demonstration that friends' experiences shape individual housing market expectations (Bailey et al., 2018b) and consequently determine mortgage leverage choice (Bailey et al., 2019).

The studies mentioned attempt to use social media data to identify the impact of social connections and the information flow between connected individuals. The studies, however, do not tell us much about the role of the social media in the information transmission. There is, however, another, important, albeit limited, due to identification challenges, strand of literature that attempts to estimate the causal effects of social media. Identification requires disentangling content, size (that is, the number of users) and network structure (that is, the connections among the users) aspects of social networks. Thus, as highlighted by Zhuravskaya et al. (2020), to estimate the effect of the content of social media, one needs to hold constant the number of users and the structure of the network connecting them and to find exogenous sources of variation in content. Enikolopov et al. (2020) and Müller and Schwarz (2019) have taken up the challenge and developed identification strategies based on geographical location of early adopters of social media technologies. Those studies, although highly influential for the entire literature on the economics of social media, do not actually use social media other than the geographic distribution of social media users, and thus are only briefly mentioned in this chapter.

Social media, as described, is great for social and economic research. But is it good for the social media users? This question has also been answered by the social media researchers. Allcott et al. (2020) and Mosquera et al. (2020) independently run randomized experiments, reaching similar conclusions that deactivating Facebook for a few weeks leads to an increase in subjective well-being, however at the expense of reducing factual news knowledge.

3.   TWITTERONOMICS: DATA COLLECTING AND PRE-PROCESSING

3.1   Collecting Twitter Data

3.1.1   Twitter credentials

Twitter offers a wide range of data for research including both free data that are publicly available through Twitter standard API endpoints as well as data that are available through paid subscription. To start downloading data using Twitter APIs, one will need a Twitter account and a Twitter developer account and create an application using this link: https://developer.twitter.com/en/apps.

At the registration step, the following fields are required: app name (unique, that is, you cannot use the same name for different apps), application description, website URL, Tell us how this app will be used. After filling in all required fields, you will be able to create your app and see the consumer key and consumer secret key in Application Settings. Next, click on the Key and Access Tokens tab then click on Create my access token button to generate the access token and access the token secret. These credentials will be used to enable the APIs to start the downloading process.

3.1.2   Downloading data using Python

This section will describe the process to obtain tweets through Filter realtime Tweets API and Get Tweet timelines API using Python. The mechanism behind the former API can be understood as an interface between the users and the Twitter system. Through this interface, users can send "requests" filtering keywords, user handles or geo locations to the system and receive back the sample of incoming tweets that match those filters. The latter API is straightforward: it allows for the collection of up to 3200 of a user's most recent (and public) tweets.

For the Filter realtime Tweets API, you need to decide your filters such as tweets sent from specific geo locations, tweets containing certain hashtags/keywords or tweets mentioning certain Twitter users. The example that follows illustrates Python codes used to obtain real-time tweets mentioning "Brexit".

```
# Python 3 code to stream tweets containing 'Brexit' keyword #
import tweepy
access_token = 'YOUR ACCESS TOKEN'
access_token_secret = 'YOUR ACCESS TOKEN SECRET'
consumer_key = 'YOUR CONSUMER KEY'
consumer_secret = 'YOUR CONSUMER SECRET'

auth = tweepy.OAuthHandler(consumer_key, consumer_secret)
auth.set_access_token(access_token, access_token_secret)
api = tweepy.API(auth, wait_on_rate_limit=True,
  wait_on_rate_limit_notify=True)

class Listener(tweepy.StreamListener):
    def on_status(self, status):
        print(status.text)
    def on_error(self, status_code):
        print(status_code)
    return True
keyword_list = ['brexit']
my_stream = tweepy.Stream(auth=api.auth, listener=Listener())
my_stream.filter(track=keyword_list)
```

The streamed data contain tweets, the tweets' metadata and the users' metadata. Depending on your need and capacity, all or specific variables can be stored. Further, while this type of data is often used for research due to its timely nature and large volume, it should be noted that the volume of returned data is capped at 1 per cent of all tweets. If the number of incoming tweets matching the filters is below the 1 per cent threshold, the returned data are complete. Thus, it is highly recommended that the filters are tailored specifically to your research projects to reduce the likelihood of exceeding the threshold.

```
# Python 3 code to obtain the most recent tweets from a user's
  timeline #
import tweepy
access_token = 'YOUR ACCESS TOKEN'
access_token_secret = 'YOUR ACCESS TOKEN SECRET'
consumer_key = 'YOUR CONSUMER KEY'
consumer_secret = 'YOUR CONSUMER SECRET'

auth = tweepy.OAuthHandler(consumer_key, consumer_secret)
auth.set_access_token(access_token, access_token_secret)
api = tweepy.API(auth, wait_on_rate_limit=True,
  wait_on_rate_limit_notify=True)

screen_name = 'realDonaldTrump'
latest_tweets = tweepy.Cursor(api.user_timeline, screen_
  name=screen_name, count=200).items()
```

3.1.3   Downloading data using Stata

Alternatively, if you are not familiar with Python, you can use a user-written Stata command, namely twitter2stata, to obtain Twitter data. This command allows for the downloading of various data types corresponding to different Twitter API types such as search tweets, search users and so on. However, you cannot stream real-time Twitter data, as described in the previous section, using the twitter2stata command.

3.2   Tweet Pre-Processing

Depending on your objectives, pre-processing tweets might be necessary. In what follows, we will discuss how we can make use of regular expression commands in Stata in tweet pre-processing.

Tweets contain html links. In many cases, Twitter users simply share html links without adding any of their own "comments". If such tweets are not considered useful for your analysis, they should be screened and removed from the dataset. Regular expression commands/functions are handy to remove link tokens (starting with "http", "https", "www") from the text.

```
* Stata code
replace tweet = regexr(tweet, "http.*. ", "")
replace tweet = regexr(tweet, "www.*. ", "")
```

Original tweets vs. retweets. One of the drawbacks of real-time Twitter data is that we are not able to observe the "popularity" of the tweets per se, that is, we cannot observe whether a tweet is retweeted. However, the text of retweets has a different structure compared to the text of original tweets. More specifically, the former has the following structure: "RT @username . . .". Thus, screening the tweets' text and using regular expression commands/functions will allow us, at least partially, to differentiate original tweets from retweets and construct the retweeting networks across users.

```
* Stata code
generate retweet_indicator = substr(tweet,1,4) == "RT @"
generate retweet_from = word(tweet,2) if retweet_indicator==1
```

Mentions and hashtags. Regular expressions can also be used to identify users and/or hashtags mentioned in the text through user identifier tokens (starting with "@") and hashtag tokens (starting with "#"). If you are only interested in analysing the content of the tweet, for example, sentiment analysis, then mentions can be removed.

Stopwords. Since stopwords such as "the", "this", "that", and so on yield no information, it is recommended that they should also be removed from the text before any analysis. In Stata, the **txttool** package is useful and easy to implement for this purpose. By default, this package provides a list of frequently used English words. If your tweets are in a different language, you need to compile a list of stopwords of the relevant language yourself.

```
* Stata code
local stopword_file "YOUR CUSTOMIZED STOPWORD LIST"
txttool tweet, replace stopwords(`stopword_file')
```

4.   TWITTERONOMICS: APPLICATIONS

4.1   Text Analysis

4.1.1   Word clouds

A typical Twitter dataset contains thousands of tweets in the form of unstructured text. Gaining insight into the most prominent "topics" in the tweets will help us better understand the data, and thus be able to utilize it for our needs. One of the simplest ways is visualizing the tweets' content in the form of single words, the importance of which is shown by their size and colour, that is, a Word Cloud. The mechanism to create a Word Cloud is straightforward: all tweets in a dataset are considered as a document. Within this "document" frequency counts of all single words will be created and visualized. A word that has a higher frequency is considered more "important", and hence, is presented in a larger font size and/or bolder colour. Following are examples of how to create a Word Cloud using Stata and/or Python. Required input is a text file that contains all tweets in the dataset.

```
* Stata: Install wordfreq and wordcloud packpages
* ssc install wordfreq
* ssc install wordcloud
local tweet_file "YOUR TWEET FILE"
```

```
wordfreq using `tweet_file', clear
* Output: a dataset with two variables word (all single words
  in the tweets) and freq (their frequency)
wordcloud word freq
graph export wordcloud.png, as(png)
```

In Stata16, Python code can be embedded in a do-file, making it easier to call python in the Stata environment.

```
* Stata code
python:
import nltk, matplotlib
import matplotlib.pyplot as plt
from wordcloud import WordCloud
from sfi import Platform

filename = 'YOUR TWEET FILE'
all_text = open(filename, 'r', encoding='utf-8').read()
wordcloud = WordCloud(font_path='arial', max_font_size=75,
max_words=100, background_color='white').generate(all_text)

if Platform.isWindows():
        matplotlib.use('TkAgg')
plt.imshow(wordcloud, interpolation='bilinear')
plt.axis('off')
plt.title('#econtwitter',fontsize=20)
plt.savefig('econtwitter.png')
end
```

Figure 14.1   Econtwitter

4.1.2   Sentiment analysis

Given the growing interest in utilizing text sentiment for research, various techniques to determine the sentiment embedded in text have been developed. Among others, Textblob is the most popular and simplified Python library that is completed in the following steps. First, the text is divided into constituent words and stopwords are removed. Second, part-of-speech tagging is performed. That is, words are classified into categories, that is, noun, verb, adjectives, adverbs and so on. Finally, words are passed into Sentiment Classifier to determine the polarity score for each word and for the whole sentence. The polarity score is within the range [−1.0, 1.0] where negative (positive) value indicates negative (positive) sentiment. Further, since TextBlob is built on Natural Language Toolkit (NLTK), we can make use of the NLTK's Twitter Scopus that contains 10 000 tweets that have been classified into negative and positive sentiment in customizing sentiment classifiers to enhance the accuracy of sentiment analysis on tweets. Following is an example where we use 2000 tweets from the NLTK's Twitter Scopus to train a custom Naïve Bayes Classifier.[10]

```
* Stata code
python:
from textblob import TextBlob
from nltk.corpus import twitter_samples
from textblob.classifiers import NaiveBayesClassifier

positive_tweets = twitter_samples.strings('positive_tweets.json')
negative_tweets = twitter_samples.strings('negative_tweets.json')

positive_tweets_set = []
for tweet in positive_tweets:
      positive_tweets_set.append((tweet, 'positive'))

negative_tweets_set = []
for tweet in negetive_tweets:
      negative_tweets_set.append((tweet, 'negative'))

test_set = positive_tweets_set[:500] + negative_tweets_set[:500]
train_set = positive_tweets_set[1000:2000] + negative_tweets_
  set[1000:2000]

classifier = NaiveBayesClassifier(train_set)
accuracy = classifier.accuracy(test_set)
print(accuracy)
# Output: 0.765: This means that the customized classifier was
  able to correctly classify the sentiment for 76.5% of data in
  the test set.

text = 'We are pleased to announce that @CameliaKuhnen is join-
  ing RCFS as an editor. Camelia is a professor of finance and Sarah
```

```
    Graham Kenan distinguished scholar @kenanflagler and a faculty
    research associate @nberpubs. Please join us in welcoming
    Camelia!'
sentiment = classifier.classify(text)
# Output: positive

# Compare with the default classifier
sentiment = TextBlob(text).sentiment.polarity
# Output: 0.625: The polarity score of 0.625 indicates that the
    text has positive sentiment.
end
```

Another sentiment analysis that is also widely applied to Twitter data is the lexicon-based analysis. With this approach, you need to obtain a list of words with pre-defined sentiment and count the frequency of the negative/positive words in each tweet. Based on the frequencies, one can calculate the sentiment score for the tweets. In the example that follows, we present the Python codes used to measure tweets' sentiment using financial market-related social media lexicon developed by Renault (2017).

```
* Stata code
python:
from nltk.tokenize import word_tokenize
from nltk.tokenize import sent_tokenize

R17_pos = "RENAULT'S POSITIVE WORDS LIST"
R17_neg = "RENAULT'S NEGATIVE WORDS LIST"
pos_list = []
for word in R17_pos:
        pos_list.append(word)
neg_list = []
for word in R17_neg:
        neg_list.append(word)

text = '@viktor89 Nice I got a big big smiling on my face
    hahaha'
pos_words = 0
neg_words = 0
for word in word_tokenize(text):
        if word in pos_tweets: pos_words += 1
        if word in neg_tweets: neg_words += 1
if (pos_words+1)/(neg_words+1) > 0:
        score_renault = math.log((pos_words+1)/(neg_words+1))
# Output: 0.69: The score of 0.69 indicates the dominance of
    positive words over negative words, thus the tweet has positive
    sentiment.
end
```

4.3 Twitter Data for Applied Economics Research

4.3.1 Does echo chamber exist in social media?

With the rapid development of web technology, social media platforms have become an important source of information whose topics vary from social life, entertainment, politics and health to economics. On the one hand, social media users might be able to widen their views and opinions when encountering different worldviews. On the other hand, there is a concern about echo chambers: like-minded people tend to lock themselves into the same groups and ignore opposing views. In this context, it is important to understand the information flows between individuals, that is, whether being exposed to the less preferred opinions/information can get people talking about those views instead of their own. In what follows, an example of how to apply the local projections method developed by Jordà (2005) to Twitter data to answer this question will be illustrated.

A sample of tweets containing the keyword "Brexit" is obtained through the Filter real-time Twitter API. The dataset covers the 24 May 2016–16 August 2016 period. Tweets are pre-processed as described previously. After processing, tweets are classified into two categories, pro-leave vs. pro-remain, based on certain keywords.

Suppose that we are interested in estimating reactions of users supporting campaign X to users advocating campaign Y. The method is equivalent to estimating $h = 0, \ldots, H$ regressions of the following type:

$$\ln X_{t+h,d} = \sum_{k=1}^{K} \alpha_{X,k}^{(h)} \ln X_{t-k,d'} + \sum_{k=0}^{K} \beta_{X,k}^{(h)} \ln Y_{t-k,d'} + \psi_{X,d}^{(h)} + Seasonal_{X,d}^{(h)} + error_{X,d}^{(h)}, \quad (14.1)$$

where t and h represent 10-minute intervals and d represents the day of a campaign. Here, $X_{t+h,d}$ is the volume of new tweets generated by all users supporting campaign X during the $t + h$ 10-minute interval on day d. $Y_{t-k,d'}$ is the volume of new tweets by all users supporting campaign Y during the $t - k$ 10-minute interval on day d' where $d' = d$ if the $t - k$ interval is on the same day with t and $d' = d - 1$ if the $t = k$ interval is on the day proceeding t. $Seasonal_{td}^{(h)}$ is a set of "seasonal" day–hour dummy variables to control for the variations in tweeting activity across days of the week. That is, for each 1-hour interval during a 24-hour day period we have a dummy variable; and that each weekday is allowed to have a potentially different 24-hour profile of intra-day activity. $\psi_d^{(h)}$ is a dummy variable equal to one if the day of campaign is equal to d = {−30, −29, . . . 0, . . ., 29, 30}. Newey–West standard errors are used to account for serial correlation of the error term for $h \geq 1$. In this example, we use $K = 24$, but one can experiment with alternative values of K as robustness checks.

The impulse response of users supporting X to users supporting Y is computed as $\left\{ \hat{\beta}_{X,0}^{(h)} \right\}_{h=0}^{H}$.

This can be understood as the behaviour of the system in response to a structural, serially uncorrelated shock (an increase in the number of tweets supporting campaign Y) when the initial conditions are controlled for. Since log transformation is used, β_0 is elasticity, which can be converted into a multiplier by multiplying β by $\left(Tweets\ supporting\ X\ /\ Tweet\ supporting\ Y \right)$.

Results shown in Figure 14.2 suggest the trivial reactions of users supporting leaving (remain) to an increase in tweets supporting the opposite side. In other words, there is evidence of echo chamber in Brexit-related discussions on Twitter.

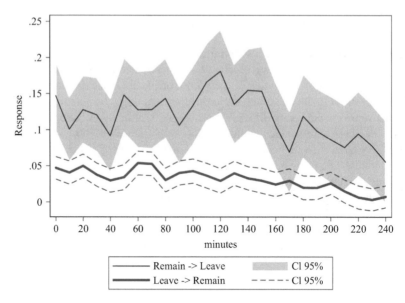

Figure 14.2   Local projections

```
* Stata code
use sample, clear
* ssc install reghdfe

tsset time_10min_interval, delta(10 minutes)
*Create seasonal dummies
generate dow=dow(date_create_tweet)
generate hour=hh(time_10min_interval)
generate campaign_day = date_create_tweet-date("23-06-
  2016","DMY")

*Create variables
generate ln_leave =log(1+pro_leave)
generate ln_remain =log(1+pro_remain)

*Inverse of the ratio
generate L2R=1/((1+pro_remain)/(1+pro_leave))
generate R2L=1/((1+pro_leave)/(1+pro_remain))

*Winsorized the ratios
foreach var in R2L L2R {
      winsor `var', p(0.01) highonly gen(`var'_w)
      summary `var'_w
      scalar ratio_`var'=r(mean)
}
tempname irfs0
postfile `irfs0' horizon ///
```

```
            remain2leave remain2leave_se ///
            leave2remain leave2remain_se ///
            using irfs, replace
*Estimate model (1), obtain residuals to plug in the later esti-
  mations
foreach i in ln_remain ln_leave {
      reghdfe `i' ///
                l(1/`lags0').ln_leave ///
                l(1/`lags0').ln_remain, ///
                absorb(i.hour#i.dow i.campaign_day) ///
                vce(robust(bw(100))) residuals(res_`i')
}

local lags0 = 24
quietly forvalues i=0(1)24 {
      noisily di "horizon `i'"
      reghdfe f`i'.ln_remain res_ln_leave ///
                l(1/`lags0').ln_leave ///
                l(1/`lags0').ln_remain, ///
                absorb(i.hour#i.dow i.campaign_day) ///
                vce(robust(bw(100)))

      local b_remain2leave=_b[res_ln_leave]*ratio_R2L
      local se_remain2leave=_se[res_ln_leave]*ratio_R2L

      reghdfe f`i'.ln_leave res_ln_remain ///
                l(1/`lags0').ln_leave ///
                l(1/`lags0').ln_remain, ///
                absorb(i.hour#i.dow i.campaign_day) ///
                vce(robust(bw(100)))

      local b_leave2remain=_b[res_ln_remain]*ratio_L2R
      local se_leave2remain=_se[res_ln_remain]*ratio_L2R

      post `irfs0' (`i') ///
                (`b_remain2leave') (`se_remain2leave') ///
                (`b_leave2remain') (`se_leave2remain')
}

postclose `irfs0'

*Plot impulse responses
use irfs, clear

foreach var in leave2remain remain2leave {
      generate hi_`var'=`var'+1.96*`var'_se
      generate lo_`var'=`var'-1.96*`var'_se
}

replace horizon=horizon*10
```

```
summary horizon
local mm=r(max)
twoway ///
(rarea hi_leave2remain lo_leave2remain horizon if horizon<=`mm',
  fcolor(gs11) lcolor(white)) ///
(line leave2remain horizon if horizon<=`mm', lpattern(solid)
  lcolor(black)) ///
(line hi_remain2leave horizon if horizon<=`mm', lpattern(dash)
  lcolor(blue)) ///
(line lo_remain2leave horizon if horizon<=`mm', lpattern(dash)
  lcolor(blue)) ///
(line remain2leave horizon if horizon<=`mm', lpattern(solid)
  lcolor(blue) lwidth(thick)), ///
legend(order(2 1 5 3) label(1 "CI 95%") label(2 "Remain ->
  Leave") ///
label(3 "CI 95%") label(5 "Leave -> Remain") rows(2)) ///
ytitle("response") xtitle("minutes") xlabel(0(20)`mm')

graph export LocalProjections.png, as(png)
```

4.3.2   Political uncertainty and exchange rate

A growing number of studies have documented the usefulness of social media content in predicting performance of financial market instruments, for example stock prices, returns or volatility. Following the existing literature, in this section we will describe an example of using Twitter data to measure political uncertainty. The analysis of the link between the Twitter-based uncertainty indicators and exchange rate (fluctuations) will be also illustrated.

A sample of tweets containing the keyword "Brexit" is obtained through the Filter real-time Tweets API. The dataset covers the January 2017–January 2018 period. After the cleaning process, sentiment analysis using TextBlob is performed: each tweet is flagged as either positive, negative or neutral. We also create hard Brexit and soft Brexit indicators based on tweets' content: hard (soft) Brexit equals to one if the keyword "hard (soft) Brexit" appears in the text. These indicators are then aggregated to daily frequency.

We measure the degree of political uncertainty by sentiment-based and opinion-based indicators. Sentiment-based indicators, including *Positiveness* and *Sentiment agreement*, are computed based on the tweets' sentiment:

$$Positiveness_t = \ln\left(\frac{1+ M_t^{positive}}{1+ M_t^{negative}}\right),$$

where $M_t^{positive}$ and $M_t^{negative}$ index the number of positive and negative tweets on day t, respectively. Alternatively, we also measure Positiveness as

$$Positiveness_t = \frac{M_t^{positive} - M_t^{negative}}{M_t^{all}},$$

where M_t^{all} is the total number tweets on day t.

The sentiment agreement measure is given as

$$Sentiment\ agreement_t = 1 - \sqrt{1 - \left(\frac{M_t^{positive} - M_t^{negative}}{M_t^{positive} + M_t^{negative}}\right)^2}.$$

Finally, the degree of agreement across users on hard vs. soft Brexit is calculated as

$$Opinion\ agreement_t = 1 - \sqrt{1 - \left(\frac{M_t^{hard\ Brexit} - M_t^{soft\ brexit}}{M_t^{hard\ Brexit} + M_t^{soft\ Brexit}}\right)^2}.$$

The *Sentiment agreement* variable is equal to one if all tweets are either positive or negative. Similarly, the *Opinion sentiment* variable equals to one if all tweets refer to hard Brexit or all tweets refer to soft Brexit.

We quantify the link between political uncertainty measures and EUR/GBP exchange rate, we employ the following model:

$$FX_t = \alpha + \beta_1 Positiveness_t + \beta_2 Sentiment\ agreement_t + \beta_3 Opinion\ agreement_t \quad (14.2)$$
$$+ \delta_1 M_t^{all} + \delta_2 FEs + \varepsilon_t$$

where FX_t is the EUR/GBP exchange rate on day t. Here, FEs is a vector of various fixed effects, including day of week, month of year and year effects. Other variables were previously described.

Results reported suggest the important role of tweet sentiments in predicting the EUR/GBP exchange rate. Particularly, when the number of positive tweets exceeds the number of negative tweets, an increase in Pound value relative to Euro is observed. Further, the Pound

Table 14.1   Relationship between EUR/GBP and Twitter sentiment

	(1)	(2)	(3)	(4)
FX_{t-1}	0.9395***	0.9393***	0.9400***	0.9396***
	(0.0132)	(0.0134)	(0.0132)	(0.0135)
Positiveness	0.0022**	0.0022*	0.0060**	0.0059*
	(0.0011)	(0.0013)	(0.0029)	(0.0035)
Sentiment agreement	0.0040**	0.0044	0.0085**	0.0089*
	(0.0016)	(0.0051)	(0.0036)	(0.0049)
Opinion agreement	−0.0005	0.0004	−0.0011	0.0001
	(0.0842)	(0.0872)	(0.0845)	(0.0875)
M^{all}		0.0037		0.0055
		(0.0501)		(0.0495)
Observations	690	690	690	690
R-squared	0.9613	0.9613	0.9613	0.9613

Notes: In columns (1)–(2), Positiveness is measured as $\ln\left(\frac{1+M_t^{positive}}{1+M_t^{negative}}\right)$. In columns (3)–(4), Positiveness is measured as $\frac{M_t^{positive} - M_t^{negative}}{M_t^{all}}$.

value also increases if the tweet sentiments are more converged. In contrast, the opinion agreement does not have any significant impacts on exchange rate.

5.   BEYOND TWITTER: GOOGLE TRENDS

In addition to Twitter data, internet search data, for example, Google Trends data, have also widely used for economic research. For examples, search volumes of keywords related to economic conditions and job searches are employed to construct an economic uncertainty index and job search index (for example, Dzielinski, 2012; Baker and Fradkin, 2017; Castelnuovo and Tran, 2017; Pan, 2019). More recently, search intensity for topics "Recession" or "Stock Market Crash" is used to measure the degree of economic anxiety during the global coronavirus pandemic (Fetzer et al., 2020). Such data can be used to forecast various economic variables such as jobless claims, tourism inflows, sales and unemployment rates (Choi and Varian, 2009, 2012; 2017 Fondeur and Karameé, 2013; D'Amuri and Marcucci, 2017). Some other studies use Google Trends data to predict influenza epidemics (Ginsberg et al., 2009) or stock price movements (Da et al., 2011). In this section, we will show an example of utilizing Google Trends data to create various economic indicators.

5.1   Data

There are several ways to obtain Google Trends data. The simplest way is to specify the search query, for example, keywords, location and time period in the Google Trends website (https://trends.google.com/trends/), then download the research results from the website. You can also use the Google Trends API, which requires an application to gain access and to generate the data of interests. Alternatively, one can use various Python libraries such as pytrends to obtain the data. The returned result is the search volume index, which is in the range [0, 100] and shows a proportion of the search interest for the specified keywords/topic relative to all searches on all topics on Google at that time and location. In this sense, 100 indicates the date/time when the searched topic is among the most popular search terms when compared to every other topic within the specified time range, and 0 indicates the lowest search interest relative to the peak.

Following is an example of how to download and visualize Google Trends data using Python code embedded in Stata. The Python library, namely pytrends, is used to collect data on daily search volume of three search terms, that is, COVID-19, Coronavirus and COVID in the United Kingdom during the January 2020–June 2020 period. The search volume by US states for the same period is also collected. The former data are visualized as a timeline plot (Figure 14.3), while the latter data are shown as a map of the US states (Figure 14.4).

```
* Stata code
set scheme s1color
python:
import pandas as pd
from pytrends.request import TrendReq
import matplotlib.pyplot as plt
pytrend = TrendReq()
# Search query for UK, data: search interest over time
pytrend.build_payload(kw_list=['covid19+coronavirus+covid'], geo=
```

```
  'GB', timeframe='2020-01-01 2020-06-01')
data = pytrend.interest_over_time()
data.to_csv('UK.csv')

# Search query for US, data: search interest by states
pytrend.build_payload(kw_list=['covid19+coronavirus+covid'],
  geo= 'US', timeframe='2020-01-01 2020-06-01')
data = pytrend.interest_by_region()
data.to_csv('US.csv')
end

*Create time series figure for COVID19 search interest in the UK
  over time
import delimited UK.csv, clear
g Date=date(date,"YMD")
format Date %td
tsset Date
rename covid* covid
tsline covid
local first_case=date("22-01-2020","DMY")
local lockdown_begin=date("23-03-2020","DMY")
label var covid "Search Volumn Index"
tsline covid, lc(gs0) xline(`first_case' `lockdown_begin') text(40
  `first_case' "First case", orient(vertical) place(se)) text(40
  `lockdown_begin' "Lockdown began", orient(vertical) place(se))
  ti("COVID19")
graph export UK.png, as(png)

*Create heat map for COVID19 search interest by US states
clear
copy "https://www2.census.gov/geo/tiger/GENZ2018/shp/cb_2018_us_
  state_500k.zip" cb_2018_us_state_500k.zip
unzipfile cb_2018_us_state_500k.zip
shp2dta using cb_2018_us_state_500k.shp, database(us_db)
  coordinates(us_coord) replace
use us_db, clear
rename NAME states
replace states=upper(states)
keep _ID states STUSPS
duplicates drop
save us_db, replace

use us_coord, clear
drop if _X==.
collapse (mean) _Xl=_X _Yl=_Y, by(_ID)
merge 1:1 _ID using us_db
drop _merge
```

```
save us_db, replace

import delimited US.csv, clear
rename geoName states
merge 1:1 states using us_db
drop if covid==.|states=="ALASKA"|states=="HAWAII"
spmap covid using us_coord.dta, id(_ID) fcolor(Heat)
  label(l(STUSPS) x(_X1) y(_Y1) si(3)) legend(ring(0) position(8)
  title("COVID19 SVI", size(*.8)) size(medium)) legstyle(2)
graph export US_map.png, as(png)
```

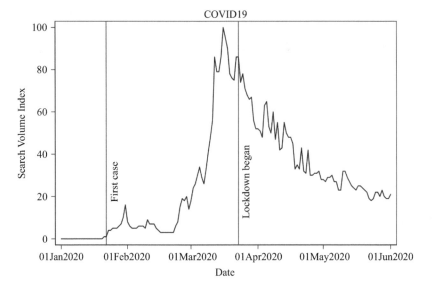

Figure 14.3   UK.png

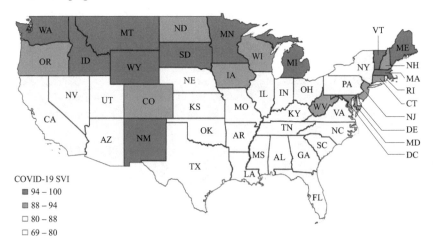

Figure 14.4   US_map.png

5.2   COVID-19 Pandemic and the Economic (Labour Market) Indicators

As suggested in the literature, a search volume index on certain topics, such as jobs, unemployment and recession, can be a good indicator of job searches, labour market conditions and economic anxiety. The example that follows will illustrate how to obtain search data for these topics for each US state and apply the collected data in the analysis of the impacts of the coronavirus pandemic on the search volume indices. In particular, a model with the following form will be estimated:

$$SVI_{s,t} = \alpha + \beta COVID19_{s,t} + FEs + \varepsilon_{s,t}, \qquad (14.3)$$

where $SVI_{s,t}$ is the log of one plus the search intensity in state s in week t for 3 topics: jobs, unemployment and recession. The first indicator can be understood as a job search index. The second one is a proxy for the concern about unemployment. The third index measures the degree of economic unease. $COVID19_{s,t}$ is either the log of one plus the number of new cases or the log of number of deaths in states s in week t. In the model, state fixed effects are included to control for the time-invariant different levels of search volume index across states. The overall trend is captured by the time fixed effects.

As can be seen in Figure 14.5, there are two peaks in search intensity for the topic recession during August 2019 and March 2020. The former peak corresponds to the growing concern about a potential recession due to the increased trade tension between the United States and China. By then, the hashtag #TrumpRecession was trending on Twitter while the US stock markets stumbled (Rushe, 2019). The latter peak reflects individuals' anxiety about the economic stability amid the coronavirus (COVID-19) epidemic. At the same time, the pandemic has also led to an unemployment crisis with a historically large number of job losses, resulting in the high search volume of the topic unemployment. Moreover, the concern about the

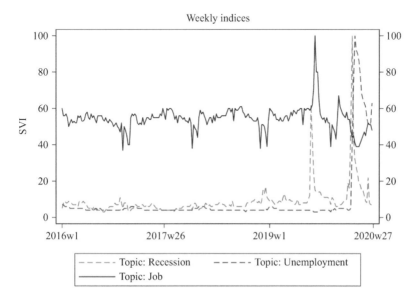

Figure 14.5   SVI_US.png

Table 14.2   Impacts of COVID-19 on search volume index of economic-/labour market–related topics

	(1)	(2)	(3)	(4)	(5)	(6)
	$\ln(SVI^{Job})$		$\ln(SVI^{Unemployment})$		$\ln(SVI^{Recession})$	
ln(new cases)	−0.0023		0.0488***		0.0127	
	(0.0020)		(0.0071)		(0.0257)	
ln(deaths)		−0.0055***		0.0456***		0.0074
		(0.0019)		(0.0067)		(0.0239)
Time FEs	Yes	Yes	Yes	Yes	Yes	Yes
State FEs	Yes	Yes	Yes	Yes	Yes	Yes
Observations	1122	1121	1122	1121	1122	1121
R-squared	0.9297	0.9304	0.9751	0.9751	0.6345	0.6339

likelihood of a recession in 2019 had led to slow hiring (Cox, 2020), which was shown in the spike in job search intensity.

To further examine the impacts of the COVID-19 pandemic on the evolution of these Google-based economic/labour market indicators, model (14.3) is estimated and results are presented in Table 14.2. In the states which have a large number of weekly confirmed COVID-19 cases or a large number of deaths, there is also an increase in the search intensity for the topic of unemployment. This confirms the (unavoidable) significant economic impacts of the pandemic on the economy generally and on the labour market in particular, which have been widely recognized by economists and policymakers (for example, Cerra et al., 2020; Chen et al., 2020; Portes, 2020).

```
* Stata code
python:
import pandas as pd
from pytrends.request import TrendReq
import matplotlib.pyplot as plt
pytrend = TrendReq(timeout=(5,30), retires = 5)

# Required input: A list of US states' abbreviation
abbr_file = 'THE ABBREVIATION LIST'
all_abbr = open(abbr_file, 'r', encoding='utf-8').readlines()
for i in all_abbr:
    geo_code = 'US-'+i.replace('\n', '')
    # Search query for each state, keywords: job
    pytrend.build_payload(kw_list=['job'], geo= geo_code, timeframe
        ='2015-01-01 2020-06-30')
    data = pytrend.interest_over_time()
    data.to_csv(i+'_job.csv')

    # Search query for each state, keywords: unemployment
    pytrend.build_payload(kw_list=['unemployment'], geo= geo_
        code, timeframe='2015-01-01 2020-06-30')
```

```
        data = pytrend.interest_over_time()
        data.to_csv(i+'_unemployment.csv')

        # Search query for each state, keywords: recession
        pytrend.build_payload(kw_list=['recession'], geo= geo_code,
            timeframe='2015-01-01 2020-06-30')
        data = pytrend.interest_over_time()
        data.to_csv(i+'_recession.csv')

end
* Import and clean Google Trends data
* Required input: A list of US states' name and abbreviation
clear
g week =.
g abbr = ""
save ggtrends, replace
local abbr_name "YOUR ABBREVIATION - FULL NAME LIST"

foreach topic in unemployment job recession {
        clear
        g fake=.
        tempfile temp
        save `temp', replace

        local filelist: dir . files "*_`i'.csv"
        foreach i of local filelist {
                import delimited "`i'", clear
                local abbr = substr("`i'",1,2)
                g abbr = "`abbr'"
                g week = wofd(date(date,"YMD"))
                format week %td
                append using `temp'
                save `temp', replace
        }
        cap drop fake
        collapse (max) `topic', by(abbr week)
        merge 1:1 abbr week using ggtrends
        drop _merge
        save ggtrends, replace
}
cap drop fake
drop if week==.
merge m:1 abbr using `abbr_name'
drop _merge
save ggtrends, replace
```

6. CONCLUDING REMARKS

Social media have changed the way we communicate. It has allowed everyone to express feelings and emotions or to share information with the closest friends or the whole world. Researchers can now access large parts of this data. Information that until recently was available only through costly opinion polls and surveys can now be accessed with the few lines of code that we have presented in this chapter. It is thus not surprising that such data have been used in a wide range of applications. Social media data tell us what people think, how they feel and react to news and how these attitudes change over time. This can be used, along with data on internet search activity, as a source of background information or a motivating example fitting almost every research paper. Such data can be used also beyond academia and provide valuable information about perceptions of products, brands or political candidates and has been used, with success in many commercial applications.

The main objective of this chapter is to show how social media are used in economic research and to highlight the ease of accessing and processing such data. The task of identifying research questions and developing appropriate research designs to answer those questions with the support of the social media data we leave to the readers. We have also only touched on the more advanced aspects of social media data, including the network aspects of the information spread or the time dimension of information diffusion. These additional pieces of data are also readily available, but for more detail we refer the readers to the articles mentioned in this chapter.

Obviously, the individuals active on social media may not be representative of the entire population. There is a clear self-selection on social networks in general and on individual platforms. The usage of social media varies greatly between age groups, regions and countries. However, the sheer size of the social media community and the impact it has on the real world make social data a worthy object of analysis, especially as it is difficult to imagine a better source of data on within-network communication and information diffusion.

NOTES

1. https://www.statista.com/statistics/433871/daily-social-media-usage-worldwide/.
2. https://www.businessinsider.com/2020-us-social-media-usage-report?IR=T.
3. https://www.statista.com/statistics/272014/global-social-networks-ranked-by-number-of-users/.
4. https://tinyurl.com/ycbll6n2.
5. https://www.nytimes.com/2018/04/04/us/politics/cambridge-analytica-scandal-fallout.html.
6. Also, the monetization of the research outcomes in the form of a hedge fund (in cooperation with Derwent Capital Markets) was not successful (Mackintosh, 2012). It has to be noted, however, that a similar fate met the authors of the Nobel prize–winning Black–Scholes–Merton asset pricing model involved in the Long-Term Capital Management hedge fund that collapsed in the late 1990s.
7. The procedure is on Text Analysis and Word Count (TAWC) program. The Facebook data team analysed the percentage of "positive" and "negative" terms that are used across all participants using the Linguistic Inquiry and Word Count (LIWC) dictionary.
8. Falsehood can be assessed by comparing the news with information from fact-checking organizations such as snopes.com, politifact.com, factcheck.org, truthorfiction.com, hoax-slayer.com and urbanlegends .about.com.
9. In this study data obtained through an agreement with the social network provider were used.
10. See Brownlee (2016) for more details the Naïve Bayes classifiers.

REFERENCES

Acemoglu, D., Hassan, T.A. and Tahoun, A., 2018. The power of the street: Evidence from Egypt's Arab Spring. *The Review of Financial Studies*, *31*(1), pp. 1–42.

Allcott, H. and Gentzkow, M., 2017. Social media and fake news in the 2016 election. *Journal of Economic Perspectives*, *31*(2), pp. 211–36.

Allcott, H., Braghieri, L., Eichmeyer, S. and Gentzkow, M., 2020. The welfare effects of social media. *American Economic Review*, *110*(3), pp. 629–76.

Antweiler, W. and Frank, M.Z., 2004. Is all that talk just noise? The information content of internet stock message boards. *Journal of Finance*, *59*(3), pp. 1259–94.

Azar, P.D. and Lo, A.W., 2016. The wisdom of Twitter crowds: Predicting stock market reactions to FOMC meetings via Twitter feeds. *The Journal of Portfolio Management*, *42*(5), pp. 123–34.

Bailey, M., Cao, R., Kuchler, T. and Stroebel, J., 2018b. The economic effects of social networks: Evidence from the housing market. *Journal of Political Economy*, *126*(6), pp. 2224–76.

Bailey, M., Cao, R., Kuchler, T., Stroebel, J. and Wong, A., 2018a. Social connectedness: Measurement, determinants, and effects. *Journal of Economic Perspectives*, *32*(3), pp. 259–80.

Bailey, M., Dávila, E., Kuchler, T. and Stroebel, J., 2019. House price beliefs and mortgage leverage choice. *The Review of Economic Studies*, *86*(6), pp. 2403–52.

Baker, S.R. and Fradkin, A., 2017. The impact of unemployment insurance on job search: Evidence from Google search data. *Review of Economics and Statistics*, *99*(5), pp. 756–68.

Bakshy, E., Messing, S. and Adamic, L.A., 2015. Exposure to ideologically diverse news and opinion on Facebook. *Science*, *348*(6239), pp. 1130–32.

Bartov, E., Faurel, L. and Mohanram, P.S., 2018. Can Twitter help predict firm-level earnings and stock returns? *The Accounting Review*, *93*(3), pp. 25–57.

Baylis, P., 2020. Temperature and temperament: Evidence from Twitter. *Journal of Public Economics*, *184*, p. 104161.

Behrendt, S. and Schmidt, A., 2018. The Twitter myth revisited: Intraday investor sentiment, Twitter activity and individual-level stock return volatility. *Journal of Banking & Finance*, *96*, pp. 355–67.

Blankespoor, E., Miller, G.S. and White, H.D., 2014. The role of dissemination in market liquidity: Evidence from firms' use of Twitter. *The Accounting Review*, *89*(1), pp. 79–112.

Block, J.H., Fisch, C.O., Obschonka, M. and Sandner, P.G., 2019. A personality perspective on business angel syndication. *Journal of Banking & Finance*, *100*, pp. 306–27.

Bollen, J., Mao, H. and Zeng, X., 2011. Twitter mood predicts the stock market. *Journal of Computational Science*, *2*(1), pp. 1–8.

Broniatowski, D.A., Paul, M.J. and Dredze, M., 2013. National and local influenza surveillance through Twitter: an analysis of the 2012–2013 influenza epidemic. *PloS one*, *8*(12).

Brown, A., Rambaccussing, D., Reade, J.J. and Rossi, G., 2018. Forecasting with social media: evidence from tweets on soccer matches. *Economic Inquiry*, *56*(3), pp. 1748–63.

Brownlee, J., 2016. Machine learning algorithms from scratch with Python. *Machine Learning Mastery*.

Burggraf, T., Fendel, R. and Huynh, T.L.D., 2020. Political news and stock prices: Evidence from Trump's trade war. *Applied Economics Letters*, *27*(18), pp. 1485–88.

Castelnuovo, E. and Tran, T.D., 2017. Google it up! A Google trends-based uncertainty index for the United States and Australia. *Economics Letters*, *161*, pp. 149–53.

Cerra, V., Fatás, A. and Saxena, S., 2020. The persistence of a COVID-induced global recession, Vox, https://voxeu .org/article/persistence-covid-induced-global-recession>

Chen, S., Igan, D., Pierri, N. and Presbitero, A., 2020. The economic impact of Covid-19 in Europe and the US, Vox, https://voxeu.org/article/economic-impact-covid-19-europe-and-us>

Choi, H. and Varian, H., 2009. Predicting initial claims for unemployment benefits. *Google Inc*, *1*, pp. 1–5.

Choi, H. and Varian, H., 2012. Predicting the present with Google Trends. *Economic Record*, *88*, pp. 2–9.

Cox, J., 2020. Job growth falls short of expectations as August payrolls rise just 130,000. CNBC, https://www.cnbc .com/2019/09/06/us-nonfarm-payrolls-august-2019.html.

D'Amuri, F. and Marcucci, J., 2017. The predictive power of Google searches in forecasting US unemployment. *International Journal of Forecasting*, *33*(4), pp. 801–16.

Da, Z., Engelberg, J. and Gao, P., 2011. In search of attention. *The Journal of Finance*, *66*(5), pp. 1461–99.

Danbolt, J., Siganos, A. and Vagenas-Nanos, E., 2015. Investor sentiment and bidder announcement abnormal returns. *Journal of Corporate Finance*, *33*, pp. 164–79.

Dergiades, T., Milas, C. and Panagiotidis, T., 2015. Tweets, Google trends, and sovereign spreads in the GIIPS. *Oxford Economic Papers*, *67*(2), pp. 406–32.

Dzielinski, M., 2012. Measuring economic uncertainty and its impact on the stock market. *Finance Research Letters*, *9*(3), pp. 167–75.

Enikolopov, R., Makarin, A. and Petrova, M., 2020. Social media and protest participation: Evidence from Russia. *Econometrica*, *88*(4), pp. 1479–514.

Enikolopov, R., Petrova, M. and Sonin, K., 2018. Social media and corruption. *American Economic Journal: Applied Economics*, *10*(1), pp. 150–74.

Feddersen, A., Humphreys, B.R. and Soebbing, B.P., 2017. Sentiment bias and asset prices: Evidence from sports betting markets and social media. *Economic Inquiry*, *55*(2), pp. 1119–29.

Fetzer, T., Hensel, L., Hermle, J. and Roth, C., 2020. Coronavirus perceptions and economic anxiety. *Review of Economics and Statistics*, pp. 1–36.

Fondeur, Y. and Karamé, F., 2013. Can Google data help predict French youth unemployment? *Economic Modelling*, *30*, pp. 117–25.

Fujita, S., 2010. Economic effects of the unemployment insurance benefit. *Federal Reserve Bank of Philadelphia Business Review*, 4.

Ge, Q., Kurov, A. and Wolfe, M.H., 2019. Do investors care about presidential company-specific Tweets? *Journal of Financial Research*, *42*(2), pp. 213–42.

Gee, L.K., Jones, J. and Burke, M., 2017. Social networks and labor markets: How strong ties relate to job finding on Facebook's social network. *Journal of Labor Economics*, *35*(2), pp. 485–518.

Gholampour, V. and van Wincoop, E., 2019. Exchange rate disconnect and private information: What can we learn from Euro-Dollar tweets? *Journal of International Economics*, *119*, pp. 111–32.

Giannini, R., Irvine, P. and Shu, T., 2019. The convergence and divergence of investors' opinions around earnings news: Evidence from a social network. *Journal of Financial Markets*, *42*, pp. 94–120.

Ginsberg, J., Mohebbi, M.H., Patel, R.S., Brammer, L., Smolinski, M.S. and Brilliant, L., 2009. Detecting influenza epidemics using search engine query data. *Nature*, *457*(7232), pp. 1012–14.

Golder, S.A. and Macy, M.W., 2011. Diurnal and seasonal mood vary with work, sleep, and daylength across diverse cultures. *Science*, *333*(6051), pp. 1878–81.

Gorodnichenko, Y., Pham, T. and Talavera, O., 2021. Social media, sentiment and public opinions: Evidence from #Brexit and #US Election. *European Economic Review*, p. 103772.

Gow, I.D., Kaplan, S.N., Larcker, D.F. and Zakolyukina, A.A., 2016. *CEO personality and firm policies* (No. w22435). National Bureau of Economic Research.

Halberstam, Y. and Knight, B., 2016. Homophily, group size, and the diffusion of political information in social networks: Evidence from Twitter. *Journal of Public Economics*, *143*, pp. 73–88.

Hendel, I., Lach, S. and Spiegel, Y., 2017. Consumers' activism: the cottage cheese boycott. *The RAND Journal of Economics*, *48*(4), pp. 972–1003.

Herrnstadt, E. and Muehlegger, E., 2014. Weather, salience of climate change and congressional voting. *Journal of Environmental Economics and Management*, *68*(3), pp. 435–48.

Jordà, Ò., 2005. Estimation and inference of impulse responses by local projections. *American Economic Review*, *95*(1), pp. 161–82.

Kearney, M.S. and Levine, P.B., 2015. Media influences on social outcomes: The impact of MTV's 16 and pregnant on teen childbearing. *American Economic Review*, *105*(12), pp. 3597–632.

Klaus, J. and Koser, C., 2020. Measuring Trump: The Volfefe Index and its impact on European financial markets. *Finance Research Letters*, p. 101447.

Kollanyi, B., Howard, P.N., & Woolley, S.C. (2016). Bots and automation over Twitter during the US election. *Data memo* 2016.4. Oxford, UK: Project on computational propaganda.

Kowalewski, O. and Śpiewanowski, P., 2020. Stock market response to potash mine disasters. *Journal of Commodity Markets*, *20*, p. 100124.

Kryvasheyeu, Y., Chen, H., Obradovich, N., Moro, E., Van Hentenryck, P., Fowler, J. and Cebrian, M., 2016. Rapid assessment of disaster damage using social media activity. *Science Advances*, *2*(3), p. e1500779.

Lachanski, M. and Pav, S., 2017. Shy of the character limit: "Twitter mood predicts the stock market" revisited. *Econ Journal Watch*, *14*(3), p. 302.

Mackintosh, James. 2012. Last tweet for Derwent's absolute return, *Financial Times*, May 24.

Meinusch, A., and Tillmann, P., 2017., Quantitative easing and tapering uncertainty: Evidence from Twitter., *International Journal of Central Banking*, *December 2017* *13*(4), pp. 227–58.

Metzger, M.M., Bonneau, R., Nagler, J. and Tucker, J.A., 2016. Tweeting identity? Ukrainian, Russian, and# Euromaidan. *Journal of Comparative Economics*, *44*(1), pp. 16–40.

Mosquera, R., Odunowo, M., McNamara, T., Guo, X. and Petrie, R., 2020. The economic effects of Facebook. *Experimental Economics*, 23, pp. 575–602.

Müller, K. and Schwarz, C., 2019. From hashtag to hate crime: Twitter and anti-minority sentiment. Available at: https://papers.ssrn.com/sol3/papers.cfm?abstract_id=3149103.

Pan, W.F., 2019. Building sectoral job search indices for the United States. *Economics Letters*, *180*, pp. 89–93.

Portes, J., 2020. The lasting scars of the Covid-19 crisis, Vox, https://voxeu.org/article/lasting-scars-covid-19-crisis.

Renault, T., 2017. Intraday online investor sentiment and return patterns in the US stock market. *Journal of Banking & Finance*, *84*, pp. 25–40.

Rushe, D., 2019. Is a recession coming to the US? Here's what to watch for. The Guardian. https://www.theguardian. com/business/2019/aug/16/us-economy-recession-what-to-watch-for

Shen, D., Urquhart, A. and Wang, P., 2019. Does Twitter predict Bitcoin? *Economics Letters*, *174*, pp. 118–22.

Siganos, A., Vagenas-Nanos, E. and Verwijmeren, P., 2014. Facebook's daily sentiment and international stock markets. *Journal of Economic Behavior & Organization*, *107*, pp. 730–43.

Siganos, A., Vagenas-Nanos, E. and Verwijmeren, P., 2017. Divergence of sentiment and stock market trading. *Journal of Banking & Finance*, *78*, pp. 130–41.

Sisco, M.R., Bosetti, V. and Weber, E.U., 2017. When do extreme weather events generate attention to climate change? *Climatic change*, *143*(1–2), pp. 227–41.

Sprenger, T.O., Sandner, P.G., Tumasjan, A. and Welpe, I.M., 2014a. News or noise? Using Twitter to identify and understand company-specific news flow. *Journal of Business Finance & Accounting*, *41*(7–8), pp. 791–830.

Sprenger, T.O., Tumasjan, A., Sandner, P.G. and Welpe, I.M., 2014b. Tweets and trades: The information content of stock microblogs. *European Financial Management*, *20*(5), pp. 926–57.

Steinert-Threlkeld, Z.C., 2017. Spontaneous collective action: Peripheral mobilization during the Arab Spring. *American Political Science Review*, *111*(2), pp. 379–403.

Steinert-Threlkeld, Z.C., Mocanu, D., Vespignani, A. and Fowler, J., 2015. Online social networks and offline protest. *EPJ Data Science*, *4*(1), pp. 1–9.

Stieglitz, S. and Dang-Xuan, L., 2012. Political communication and influence through microblogging--An empirical analysis of sentiment in Twitter messages and retweet behavior. In 2012 *45th Hawaii International Conference on System Sciences* (pp. 3500−509). IEEE.

Tang, V.W., 2018. Wisdom of crowds: Cross-sectional variation in the informativeness of third-party-generated product information on Twitter. *Journal of Accounting Research*, *56*(3), pp. 989–1034.

Vosoughi, S., Roy, D. and Aral, S., 2018. The spread of true and false news online. *Science*, *359*(6380), pp. 1146–51.

Vujić, S. and Zhang, X., 2018. Does Twitter chatter matter? Online reviews and box office revenues. *Applied Economics*, *50*(34–5), pp. 3702–17.

Winkler, H.J., Rieger, V. and Engelen, A., 2020. Does the CMO's personality matter for web traffic? Evidence from technology-based new ventures. *Journal of the Academy of Marketing Science*, *48*(2), pp. 308–30.

Zhang, T., Yuan, Y. and Wu, X., 2020. Is microblogging data reflected in stock market volatility? Evidence from Sina Weibo. *Finance Research Letters*, *32*, p. 101173.

Zhuravskaya, E., Petrova, M. and Enikolopov, R., 2020. Political effects of the internet and social media. *Annual Review of Economics*, *12*, pp. 415−38.

15. Econometrics of networks with limited access to network data: a literature survey
Pedro C.L. Souza

1. INTRODUCTION

The empirical literature on networks has literally rocketed in the past decade and now spans a number of research fields in economics. The extent to which learning is affected by others was analysed, by Angrist and Lang (2004) and Ammermuller and Pischke (2009). In macroeconomics, Acemoglu et al. (2012) show how a firm's network position amplifies shocks. This is just to name a few examples: see Jackson (2010) and de Paula (2017) for comprehensive reviews of the relevance of questions in which networks play a central role. Yet the pace of growth of the literature – where the interaction between units is a central feature to explain the economic outcomes – is often limited by the availability of network data, which remain scantly available and difficult to collect and elicit from the field.

For a moment, consider the National Longitudinal Study of Adolescent to Adult Health (AddHealth), one of the most well-known and utilized network datasets.[1] The AddHealth is a longitudinal survey within a sample of students who were at the time in grades 7 to 12 in the United States in the 1994–95 school year and follows them through adulthood. The survey contains detailed questions about several aspects of their lives, achievement, behaviour, social and economic well-being, relationships, peer groups and contextual information regarding the participants' family composition and household. It includes several types of network questions, one of which is reproduced here:

Did you talk to {NAME} on the telephone during the past seven days?

where {NAME} is the roster nomination up to the fifth-best female and male friends. Conducting this survey presents several logistical and econometric challenges. To construct the network of telephone conversations, first, the respondent replies to the name of another individual they spoke to in the previous week, who can be in the same school or not, and this name has to be matched back to an identifier. This step usually is time consuming and prone to errors. Typically, in parallel to the network elicitation process, the researcher then obtains a complete census of names, in the expectation that it contains a majority of the network links of those who are surveyed. This process is repeated for every friend nomination. In short, in a group of N individuals, there might be $N(N-1)$ potential links (not considering self-links), and the survey costs rises approximately square-N fast. This is compounded by the potential interest in eliciting different types of links, not just telephone calls. Perhaps this is the reason AddHealth is limited to the five best-friend survey nominations.

Second, there is the issue on how to deal with networks that have both been sampled; unfortunately, as shown by Chandrasekhar and Lewis (2016), non-standard measurement errors are introduced.

These issues are likely to be present in a variety of settings. Moving beyond the interaction between individuals – another prime example is the decision to acquire microfinance in Banerjee et al. (2013) – similar problems arise in network pertaining to applications in macroeconomics and trade. For example, in the so-called gravity equations, the distance between countries is positively associated with the transportation costs and iceberg costs, and consequently trade flows. In this case, the appropriate measure of the distance is unclear: the geodesic distance is likely to be a poor approximation of trade cost – geodesic? travel time? – so even if a proxy could be postulated, it remains unclear what is the functional form and specific measure of distance that should be considered.

In essence, if, on one hand, there has been considerable interest in empirical network questions, on the other hand, the availability (and perhaps suitability) of network data is likely to be, for the foreseeable future, an empirical challenge.

The goal of this chapter is then to conduct a (selective) review on some recent progress on the econometrics and empirical methods suitable for cases where the network is not known, or partially so. For a comprehensive review on the econometrics of network models, the reader is directed to the excellent paper by de Paula (2017). This strand of the literature is new and fast evolving in recent years. Yet, there is a considerable body of papers that could provide a solution to empiricists who are faced with the problems alluded to.

This review is targeted toward researchers and graduate students willing to apply those methods. The focus is not on discussing and developing the methods in all their detail and technical aspects. For that, the reader can consult the papers themselves, which expand on many of the points that I make reference to. The purpose here is to provide an overview of empirical methods that researchers might find useful in their own context and across a range of fields.

I focus on two intertwined strands of the literature. The first strand leverages Aggregate Relational Data (or ARD), which essentially use the answers to aggregated questions and the count of individuals with a certain characteristic to back out either network statistics or the full network itself. This strand of the literature is represented by a sequence of papers, for example Breza et al. (2019a,b), which I review. Since the surveying question does not involve the full elicitation of the links, it has been postulated that this method achieves 70 to 80 per cent cost reduction as compared to the full network elicitation. It still provides for consistent estimation of network descriptive characteristics and the extent to which network spillovers matter in determining the outcomes. I lay out some basic network terminologies in section 2, followed by the review of some recent progress in this literature in section 3.

The second strand of the literature is instead concerned with the estimation of the network links, and it is closely associated with spatial econometric models.[2] It generally specifies that the network links are entirely unknown and fully estimated from within the procedure itself. Situations that these methods can prove useful in are, for example, if no ARD are available, or when units are firms, jurisdictions or countries. The literature here subdivides into two broad approaches. In the first approach, represented by Pinkse et al. (2002) and Sun (2016) and others, the probability that two individuals connect is an unknown function of an observable distance. For example, in the gravity equations, the researcher can speculate that trade is (negatively) associated with geodesic distance but is not willing to pre-specify a functional form. The papers then suggest a semi-parametric approximation based on local polynomials or sieve estimation.

The second approach takes the full network as unknown and basically treats the links as parameters to be estimated, and so it does not require the pre-specification of some measurement of a distance. Since there are $N(N-1)$ links to be estimated, low-dimensional estimation methods, such as Ordinary Least Squares, are unlikely to yield good performance. This literature makes frequent use of high-dimensional techniques – such as the Least Angle Shrinkage and Selection Operator (the LASSO), or the Elastic Net – which in parallel to the literature on network econometrics have enjoyed substantial growth of their own in the past decade (for review articles on high-dimensional methods, see Fan et al. (2011) and Friedman et al. (2016)). It leverages both the time as well as cross-sectional variation, and thus the underlying data are often of a (spatial) panel kind. In a sense, the assumption of a functional form linking the network links to observable distance is replaced by the observation of the same group over a certain number of periods of time. I review those methods in section 4.

I conclude this chapter in section 5, along with a few possible directions for future research. For instance, one could think about explicitly connecting the ARD and the literature on the estimation of networks. It also sheds (some) light on topics that are not explicitly covered in this article: aspects of the micro-foundations of the network models, the empirics of network formation models – and, importantly, cases when networks are themselves endogenous – which are topics of considerable interest and for which the literature is rapidly developing.

2.　(SOME) BASIC NETWORK DEFINITIONS

I start with some common group basic definitions of what a "network" object constitutes. This will be used in much of the work that follows. Describe a network by a graph G, which is a pair of the collection of *nodes* η_G – the individuals, economic agents, firms or countries for our purposes – and *edges* or *links* λ_G between those units. We also refer to the cardinality of those sets as $N \equiv |\eta_G|$ and $|\lambda_G|$, respectively. For example, the circle network among three agents is represented as

$$\eta_G = \{1, 2, 3\}$$

$$\lambda_G = \{(1, 2), (2, 3), (3, 1)\}$$

to symbolize that 1 connects to 2, 2 to 3 and 3 to 1, closing the circle. Networks can be directed or undirected. In the former case, the link from 1 to 2 might or might not be reciprocated, and the elements in set λ_G are ordered. In the undirected case, i connects to j, if and only if j connects to i. Thus the elements of λ_G are not ordered. Moreover, the links can express some notion of intensity, which is captured by a vector ι_G with dimensions $|\lambda_G| \times 1$.

A convenient representation of the graph is through the $N \times N$ network matrix W. We say that the (i, j)-th element of the matrix $W_{ij} = 1$ if $(i, j) \in \lambda_G$, and zero otherwise. Thus, the simple (directed) "circle" network with three units is represented by the 3×3 matrix

$$W = \begin{pmatrix} 0 & 1 & 0 \\ 0 & 0 & 1 \\ 1 & 0 & 0 \end{pmatrix}.$$

Naturally, it is also possible to represent the link intensity, in which case the non-zero elements of W_{ij} would correspond to the entries in ι_G, which may include negative interactions.

Matrix W takes several names, and may be referred to as the neighbouring matrix or the spatial weight matrix. They all allude to the same (perhaps vague) notion that the greater the entries in W_{ij}, the "closer" are the units in some sense – geographically in the case of countries and the gravity equations, or nominations, as in the telephone conversation in the AddHealth survey.[3]

Some descriptive statistics on the graphs (or, equivalently, the networks) are meaningful to describe its local or global properties and so may be of particular interest. I list some of these properties, without any attempt to be comprehensive – for that, the reader may want to see Jackson (2010) – but rather to motivate the discussion that follows.

Degree and degree distribution. The set of nodes that unit i connects to is characterized by $N_i(G) = \{j : (i, j) \in \lambda_G\}$. The number of connections, or the cardinality of N_i, is referred to as the degree of i. I refer to the degree as $d_i \equiv |N_i(G)|$. Since this is a node-level statistic, one can also be interested in the distribution of the degrees across units $i \in \{1, \ldots, N\}$. Note that, in the case of directed networks, one can define in- and out-degrees, respectively, related to the number of units that connect to and from individual i. These are important features of the graph. It is not atypical to observe that some individuals are much more connected than others, it often occurs that the distribution in highly skewed. For example, Costa et al. (2017) use Twitter-level data on posts regarding the Brazilian street protest that occurred in June 2013. They observe the number of followers each user has – which, in the Twitter sphere, is the analogue of the out-degree. The degree distribution is highly skewed, which is reflective of the fact that few have many followers, and many have very few followers. This is shown in Figure 15.1.

Incidentally, I note that we often think of online networks as a diffuse method of communication. The amount of skewness in the degree distribution suggests a different interpretation:

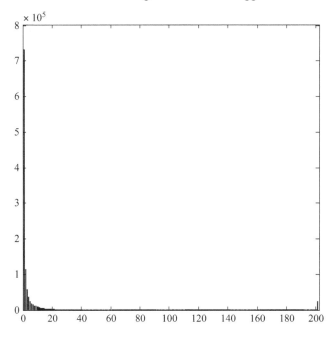

Notes: Out-degree distribution calculated on the network of followers on Twitter, based on the sample of individuals who tweeted using a hashtag associated with the street protests in Brazil in June 2013, from Costa et al. (2017).

Figure 15.1   Out-degree distribution of users in Twitter, based on Costa et al. (2017)

tweets from some individuals are much more "powerful" than from most. Yet, a better description of the network position – relative to others – is given by the centrality measures.

Centrality. A natural question that arises is how "important" an individual is in the network, and the literature offers several definitions of this sort of measurement (see Jackson, 2010). Here, I describe one such measure.

Suppose one were to disseminate one particular type of information – in the case of Banerjee et al. (2013), the availability of microfinance at the community level – and that type of information is given to a single individual in the network. Who should be chosen in order to maximize the spread of information? Clearly, this depends not only on the number of friends individuals have, but also the number of friends of friends, third-order friendships and so on.

To account for this, suppose that there is a probability ρ that the information is passed along, conditional on each individual link, and momentarily suppose that the network is symmetric. Then,

$$(\rho W + \rho^2 W^2 + \rho^3 W^3 + \cdots)\mathbf{1}_N,$$

captures the reach of each individual node, where $\mathbf{1}_N$ is the $N \times 1$ vector of ones. To see this, note that W^2 is the network of friends of friends, and $(W^2)_{ij} \neq 0$, if and only if there is a path of length two between i and j. Because there are two links between i and j, the probability that the information seeded from i reaches j is ρ^2. Then, similarly for the higher-order components $\rho^3 W^3$, and so on. The reach of i – or the number of individuals in expectation that would have received the information from seeding it from i – will be then the sum across the sets of individuals that i directly or indirectly connects to. This is also known as *diffusion centrality*, and, as shown in Banerjee et al. (2013), nests other cases of centrality such as the eigenvector, degree and the Katz-Bonacich centralities.

Clustering. The clustering coefficient is the share friends of i that are also friends themselves. Over the full network, this can be described as the number of connected triples that are also triangles, that is,

$$\text{Clustering} = \frac{\sum\limits_{i,j,k} W_{ij} W_{ik} W_{jk}}{\sum\limits_{i,j,k} W_{ij} W_{ik}},$$

where in the definition it is implicitly assumed that W is binary and undirected. The clustering coefficient is a measure of how closely knit the units are, and it is a stylized fact in a social network that if i relates to both j and k, it is more likely that j and k interact as well.

Average path length and connectedness. Connectedness refers to the property that, starting from every node i, it is possible to reach every other individual in the network, through paths of arbitrary length. If the network is connected, then one can define the average path length across all nodes i and j in the network. If the network is unconnected, the average path length is then not finite.

For brevity, I only discussed a few of the possible network descriptive statistics that the empiricist may be interested in. Microfoundations of those centrality measures can be found in Ballester et al. (2006), Bramoullé et al. (2016) and Banerjee et al. (2013, 2019), among many others. The purpose here is not to give a full account of the network descriptive statistics, but rather to showcase how they can be recovered with partial, aggregated or no network data. One insightful way is to resort to ARD, which I review in the next section.

3.   AGGREGATE RELATIONAL DATA

As mentioned in the introduction, conducting network surveys is challenging, and often very time consuming and expensive. The difficulty in collecting relational data is also inherent to the nature of interactions themselves: individuals are often related to many others (in a group of N units, there are $N(N-1)$ potential interactions); there are several dimensions of interactions and peer friendships; and, even after the data are collected, matching nominations to a unique record in administrative datasets might be problematic, for example, if respondents have partial information about the names of others. To make matters worse, Chandrasekhar and Lewis (2016) show that sampling nodes leads to non-classical measurement errors, so the researchers might need either to implement corrections, as outlined in the paper, or collect the network based on the full census of nodes. This makes the elicitation of networks, at the very least, expensive and inaccessible to many.

ARD, broadly speaking, is a surveying method that greatly reduces the cost of the surveying process. To do so, it instead leverages the network itself to aggregate the information, as opposed to the full elicitation of links. It is based on the collection of the *counts* of network links with a certain characteristic of interest. For a hypothetical example, one could implement an ARD network survey with the following question:

How many friends of your friends are immigrants?

as opposed to

Who are your friends?

and, based on these answers and a separate administrative dataset with the universe of individuals in the network, along with their immigration status, trace ex-post how many of them are from different places of origin. Breza et al. (2019b) argue that collecting ARD leads to between 70 and 80 per cent cost reduction.

In a sense, the surveying mechanisms leverage the network itself as a way to aggregate information – not only about the respondents themselves, but also regarding the information that respondents might have about others. In the past, ARD has been used to estimate the size of hard-to-reach populations. For example, Kadushin et al. (2006) estimate the number of heroin users by asking the following (unsurprising) question: "How many people do you personally know who use heroin?"[4]

Conceptually, one can think about the ARD response as the network interaction with the indicator, which is equal to one if j has a specific trait, for example,

$$y_i = \sum_{j=1}^{N} W_{ij} \cdot \mathbf{1}\left[j \text{ is an immigrant}\right].$$ (15.1)

So, as is clear from the formulation, the ARD response is simply the count of the number of friends who are immigrants.

Breza et al. 's pair of papers (2019a,b) convincingly make the case that ARD may in some cases operate as a substitute for the full elicitation of the network links, especially if one is interested in some aspects of the full network, such as the centrality measures. We generically refer to statistics of a network – such as centrality, clustering or average path length – as $S(W)$.

The literature on the ARD relies on essentially a network formation model driven by latent and unobserved positions in a network space. One can think about these latent positions as some sort of sufficient statistic for how two units interact. More specifically, the latent space representation is given by

$$P(W_{ij} = 1) \propto \exp\{\alpha_i + \alpha_j + \delta \cdot \text{distance}(z_i, z_j)\}, \tag{15.2}$$

where α_i and α_j are fixed effects representing the degree to which units tend to connect and distance(z_i, z_j) is a known measure of distance, for example, distance$(z_i, z_j) = |z_i - z_j|$ along the latent space. The parameters to be estimated are the collection of α_i, z_i, $\forall i \in \{1, \ldots, N\}$ and δ.

The latent space representation of network models is further discussed in Hoff et al. (2002) and McCormick and Zheng (2015) and relates to other models in the literature of statistics regarding the process through which a network forms (we will come back to this topic in section 4.3 and the conclusion). The purpose of this review is not to consider the particular advantages or disadvantages of the latent space formulation. For a review of network formation models, the reader is directed to de Paula (2020).

Breza et al. (2019b) follow a Bayesian framework to estimate the parameters of the model, presumably with large N^*, where N^* is the number of units in the sample, and $N^* < N$, the number of parameters is relatively high.[5] The outcome is the estimates of $\hat{\alpha}_i$, $\hat{z}_i$ and $\hat{\delta}$.

Because not all individuals are in the sample, the researcher has to conduct an auxiliary minimal survey at the census level containing basic information, such as demographics and the ARD characteristics (such as the immigration status). With that, the researcher fits a model to predict α_i and z_i for the units in the census but not in the ARD sample. From there, the researcher can use the estimated probability model to compute $E(S(g))$, given the survey responses. Breza et al. (2019a) show the underpinnings for why this method works, in particular, the conditions under which $E(S(g)) \xrightarrow{p} S(g)$ as the network size grows. They also show through simulations that the statistics are well recovered, and mean-squared prediction errors are generally very small.[6]

Arguably, the researcher could then want to estimate the effect of the properties of the network on economic outcomes. Breza et al. (2019b) showcase how their method can be used to replicate the findings of two other papers, which had previously collected and made use of the full network.

The paper by Breza and Chandrasekhar (2019) shows how social networks can influence savings behaviour. They experiment with the assignment of savings "monitors" – villagers who are frequently informed about the progress of others regarding self-assigned savings targets. The crux of the idea is that progress toward the target is a sign of responsibility and builds reputation with the monitor; this effect, however, should be heterogenous with respect to the social network position of the monitor. The more central they are, the more likely it is that the information is passed along, providing incentives for the monitored to behave responsibly. They are therefore interested in a regression where

$$Y_i = \alpha + \beta \times \text{SignallingValue}_i + \varepsilon_i,$$

where Y_i is the log savings of household i, SignallingValue$_i$ refers to the signalling value of the monitor assigned to household i and ε_i is the error term. The signalling value can be thought as a measure of centrality.[7]

To exemplify the use of the method, they compare the estimates of the coefficient of interest β when the signalling value is computed with access to the full network data, based on the ARD methodology. They find that the estimates from the former method imply that a one unit of standard deviation in the signalling value increases savings by 25.4 per cent, which is a remarkable finding of its own and shows how social networks can influence the behaviour and economic outcomes. Using the ARD methodology, they find a similar number: a one-unit standard deviation jump in the signalling value increases savings by 18.5 per cent.

Another avenue of interest is to understand how the networks themselves might be shaped by a treatment, and here once more the ARD method might prove useful for the empiricist. This second example concerns how the provision of microfinance might change the network itself (previous studies, for example Banerjee et al. (2013), instead focused on the opposite channel, the effect of networks on the adoption and dissemination of microfinance). Here, in principle there are two opposing forces: the expanded supply of credit might create new links through re-lending; on the other hand, previously existing links that provided for risk sharing might no longer be prevalent or useful. The extent to which these potentially counteracting forces compare is then a relevant empirical question, and one that is based on some form of regression of network statistics as a dependent variable, such as

$$E[S(W_g)] = \alpha + \beta \times \text{Treatment}_g + \varepsilon_g,$$

where g indexes different groups, as most often these specifications would leverage across-group variation.

Banerjee et al. (2019) randomize the provision of the treatment for residents of 52 of 104 randomly selected neighbourhoods in Hyderabad, India, look at the social network outcomes six years after the introduction of the experiment and find that clustering decreases by 6.5 per cent in treated neighborhoods.[8] The replication of the ARD methodology instead gives an estimate of a decrease of clustering of 9.0 per cent, which the authors attribute to success in replicating the main findings.

Overall, the use of ARD opens a vast array of applications by substantially lowering the cost of network surveys. This is not a suggestion that full network data should not be collected, but rather that ARD may prove a useful substitute if that is not feasible due to logistical constraints, or any other limitation in the field. It should also be noted that ARD, to some extent, presumes that individual traits are observable to others. Coming back to earlier examples in this section, that others know if their peers are heroin users, as in Kadushin et al. (2006), some of these aspects are conceivably of a private nature, for which the information might not be public or observable to the peers themselves. Another aspect is that the ARD network reconstruction method relies on a structural relation underpinning the network formation process – the latent space representation explored in Hoff et al. (2002) and McCormick and Zheng (2015).

In the next section, I explore a different angle to the reconstruction of the networks. The full network is taken as unknown and does not rely on any network data (ARD or full elicitation of links) at all. Instead, the network is thought of entirely as parameters to be estimated. In a sense, the imposition of a structure concerning the network formation process makes way for other types of assumptions on how individuals might interact; or, if fully non-parametrically estimated, by the observation of the same peer group over several periods of time. I expand on these methods, which are tightly connected to the spatial econometrics literature.

4.   ESTIMATING NETWORKS

The literature with unknown network W in a general sense stipulates a model that links the unobserved network to the outcomes. A functional form is necessary, as, to the contrary, it will be generally unclear how outcomes and covariates relate to each other.

One general formulation is the spatial model with the so-called spatial lags of the endogenous and exogenous variables:[9]

$$y_{jt} = \rho \sum_{j=1}^{N} W_{ij} y_{jt} + x_{jt}\beta + \sum_{j=1}^{N} W_{ij} x_{jt}\gamma + \varepsilon_{it}, \tag{15.3}$$

for $i = 1, \ldots, N$ individuals and $t = 1, \ldots, T$ time periods, and where y_{jt} and ε_{it} are scalars and x_{jt} is $1 \times K$. Note that, in principle, T could be equal to 1, in which case it reduces to a cross-sectional regression. Although the equation is already in the panel data notation, a priori there is no need for the temporal dimension.

The element $\sum_{j=1}^{N} W_{ij} y_{jt}$ captures how endogenous variables of others affects one's own, and unsurprisingly it is referred as the *endogenous effects*. The scalar term ρ captures the strength of those effects. The term $\sum_{j=1}^{N} W_{ij} x_{jt}$ relates to the effect of the exogenous variables of others, and the strength of those effects is captured by γ. To fix ideas, consider a peer effect regression where y_{jt} is achievement (grade scores) and x_{jt} contains contextual effects (such as the parents' education or neighbourhood of living). Finally, the term $x_{jt}\beta$ is one's self-elasticity to the exogenous variables. The endogenous effects capture how achievement of others affects one's own achievement, and the exogenous effects capture the contextual effects – how the overall parents' education in a peer group composition – affects the grade scores of the individuals in that group.

The scalar ρ is of fundamental importance in those models, as it generates feedback effects and the so-called "social multiplier" (Glaeser et al., 2003) There are two immediate implications from the existence of this endogenous channel: stationarity and identification. First, from a technical angle, it suggests that some sort of stationarity is required – not different from the fact that time-series models can be both stationary and non-stationary. For now, it is sufficient to assume that $|\rho| < 1$ and the row sums of W are such that[10]

$$\sum_{j=1}^{N} |W_{ij}| \leq 1,$$

for all $i \in \{1,...,N\}$. This is, in essence, a normalization option, as one could alternatively let $\Sigma_{j=1}^{N} |\rho W_{ij}| \leq 1$. It is customary in the spatial econometrics literature to assume that the rows of W add to exactly 1, that is, $\Sigma_{j=1}^{N} |W_{ij}| = 1$. This is obtained by rescaling each row and defining $W_{ij}^{*} = W_{ij} / \Sigma_{j} |W_{ij}|$. This is known as "row-sum normalization" although, strictly speaking, it involves a loss of generality.

It is also customary to assume that no individual affects themself, so $W_{ii} = 0, \forall i \in 1,...,N$, or else the model has a trivial solution.[11] Second, and importantly, one should pay substantial attention to the issue of the separate identification of the parameters of the models ρ, β and γ. If W is not observed, then the identification argument should include that object as well.

In the stacked notation, defining $y_t \equiv (y_{1t},...,y_{Nt})'$, $x_t \equiv (x_{1t}',...,x_{Nt}')'$ and $\varepsilon_t \equiv (\varepsilon_{1t},...,\varepsilon_{Nt})'$ as vectors with dimensions $N \times 1$, $N \times K$ and $N \times 1$, respectively, we can write model (15.3) in a more concise notation:

$$y_t = \rho W y_t + x_t \beta + W x_t \gamma + \varepsilon_t . \tag{15.4}$$

This type of model has a long tradition in the spatial econometrics literature (Anselin, 1988, 2010), albeit, as per standard, the network (or so-called spatial neighbourhood matrix) is pre-conditioned by the empiricist. In the typical classroom example, one could postulate that every student "connects" to every other student in the classroom, so

$$W = \begin{bmatrix} 0 & \dfrac{1}{N-1} & \cdots & \dfrac{1}{N-1} \\ \dfrac{1}{N-1} & 0 & \cdots & \dfrac{1}{N-1} \\ \vdots & \vdots & \ddots & \vdots \\ \dfrac{1}{N-1} & \dfrac{1}{N-1} & \cdots & 0 \end{bmatrix}, \tag{15.5}$$

or using elicited networks from the field, such as the AddHealth questions on the friendship network. If the units were firms, W could be the input–output network, perhaps obtained from VAT returns. If units are countries, and y_t are the GDPs, the elements of W could be some inverse function of distance. The model in equation (15.4) will form the basis of much of the discussion that follows in the next subsections.

We now return to the issue on identification. For now, we consider that the network is known. We will return in section 4.2 to the issue of identification when W is unknown. In a celebrated article, Manski (1993) showed that if the network is as in equation (15.5), there is no hope that the parameters of the model (ρ, β, γ) may be separately identified (although the presence of a composite social effect can be). That is, there is no single combination of the parameters that yields the same reduced-form observation of the data.[12] This issue came to be known as the "reflection problem".

It took more than a decade to overcome the (non-)identification problem postulated by Manski (1993). In a pair of articles, Bramoullé et al. (2009) and Giorgi et al. (2010) show how one's own variation in the network can be used to identify the parameters of the model. This condition can be summarized in requiring that W is such that

$$c_0 I + c_1 W + c_2 W^2 = 0, \tag{15.6}$$

only with $c_0 = c_1 = c_2 = 0$, that is, I, W and W^2 are linearly independent. Intuitively, this condition means that there is variation and non-overlapping peer groups, in such a way that the set of the peers of the peers of i are not all the direct peers of i. Thus, the peer influence of the non-overlapping set of peers affects only i through the peers, and not directly. In other words, it opens up the avenue to postulate the peers-of-peers variation as an instrumental variable strategy to separately identify the parameters of the model.

Another possibility is to leverage the group size variation, for example, Lee et al. (2010). One could utilize this type of identification strategy if units interact only within the groups, multiple groups are available and there is variation in the group size. This can also be expressed under condition (15.6). To see this, suppose that there are two groups with two and three members, and all individuals relate to each other within the group. W is described by the block-diagonal matrix

$$W = \begin{bmatrix} 0 & 1 & 0 & 0 & 0 \\ 1 & 0 & 0 & 0 & 0 \\ 0 & 0 & 0 & 0.5 & 0.5 \\ 0 & 0 & 0.5 & 0 & 0.5 \\ 0 & 0 & 0.5 & 0.5 & 0 \end{bmatrix} \text{ and thus } W^2 = \begin{bmatrix} 1 & 0 & 0 & 0 & 0 \\ 0 & 1 & 0 & 0 & 0 \\ 0 & 0 & 0.5 & 0.25 & 0.25 \\ 0 & 0 & 0.25 & 0.5 & 0.25 \\ 0 & 0 & 0.25 & 0.25 & 0.5 \end{bmatrix}.$$

Because the main diagonal of W is zero, then it must be that $c_0 = c_2 = 0$, which then implies that $c_1 = 0$, and thus I, W and W^2 are linearly independent. The very same result would not have been achieved if the first group had three members, in which case equation (15.6) would have been satisfied with $c_0 = c_1 = 0.5$ and $c_2 = 1$. In fact, this point is made more generally by Blume et al. (2015), who argue that I, W and W^2 are linearly dependent if, and only if, W is composed of groups of equal size and all units interact with each other within groups. Thus, the Manski (1993) linear-in-means model is a special case with one group. It also highlights how any variation in the peer composition or the group size is sufficient to yield identification of the endogenous effect ρ, the exogenous effect γ and one's own individual elasticity β.

As mentioned, the basic spatial econometric model and identification conditions are established when the network is known. We now return to the main motivation of this review chapter – that of empirical methods for when W is not fully observed or not observed at all.

4.1 Unknown Network, Part 1: Semiparametric Specifications

As suggested, one weakness of the models is the need to pre-specify the spatial neighbour-hood matrix W. This can occur due to a variety of reasons, such as the uncertainty over the correct specification of W (which inverse function?) or data unavailability regarding the interactions. And, indeed, the misspecification of W might have substantial effects on the estimates of ρ, β and γ. In the instrumental variable (IV) parlance, the instrument might not be valid (if the peers of peers were truly one's own friend) or not relevant (if the degree of misspecification is such as to weaken the correlation between the endogenous variables and instruments).

One early contribution was by Pinkse et al. (2002), where they specify that W_{ij} is an unknown function of the distance. Here, there is no asymptotic over time, and thus model (15.4) is taken with $T = 1$. They investigate the case of price competition between firms that produce differentiated products and compete in non-overlapping markets. More specifically, in their case, y_t is a price vector that depends on the price-setting behaviour of others (the endogenous component) and on a vector x_t of observable demand and cost variables that vary at the individual (firm) level. They implicitly assume that $\gamma = 0$ in equation (15.4), that is, the demand and cost components of other firms have no bearings on the price-setting behaviour. In their case, a firm produces a single product, so there is a one-to-one mapping between price setting and firms.

The innovation in Pinkse et al. (2002) is to allow the elements of W_{ij} to depend on an observable distance d_{ij}. They mention that if "products were brands of beer, the measures of distance (or its inverse, closeness) might be alcohol content proximity, market share proximity, and dummy variables that indicate whether brands belong to the same product group (for example, premium, regular, or light)" (p. 1118). Again, distance variables are observable, "it will still be up to the practitioner, however, to select the measures that are included in d_{ij}" (p. 1120). This can be seen as a limitation of the method, and I reiterate this point to differentiate from the more recent literature, which does not presume the availability of any sort of distance measures.[13]

The key is to impose a structure in which

$$W_{ij} \equiv g(d_{ij}) = \sum_{l=1}^{\infty} \alpha_l f_l(d_{ij}), \tag{15.7}$$

where $f_1, f_2, \ldots$ constitute a series expansion of an (unknown) basis function. This could be, for example, a polynomial expansion, and α_l, $l = 1, 2, \ldots$, are parameters to be estimated. To be clear, the function g and thus the basis functions $f_1, f_2, \ldots$ are invariant with respect to i and j. Naturally, there must be some low-dimension truncation of the series expansion, assumed to be at point L_N, so

$$W_{ij} \equiv g(d_{ij}) \approx \sum_{l=1}^{L_N} \alpha_l f_l(d_{ij}), \tag{15.8}$$

where the approximation is due to omitting the higher-order terms. Thus the Pinkse et al. (2002) model can be represented as

$$y_{it} = \sum_{l=1}^{N} \alpha_l \sum_{j=1}^{N} f_l(d_{ij}) y_{ij} + x_{it} \beta + v_{it}.$$

Note that the error v_{it} is different from ε_{it} in equation (15.3) because, here, it incorporates the approximation error due to the truncation. Also note that ρ has been implicitly incorporated into the function $g(\cdot)$, without loss of generality. As is common in the semi- and non-parametric literature, this approach might suffer from the curse of dimensionality, and thus expanding for multiple distance measures might prove especially challenging.

To deal with the endogeneity of having prices on the left- and right-hand sides of the equations, Pinkse et al. (2002) propose an instrumental variable estimator. Since the endogenous variables grow with the sample size, so must the number of instruments. They propose an instrument with $\sum_{j=1}^{N} f_l(d_{ij})x_{jh}$, where x_{jh} is the regressor h for the observation j. This is intuitive as long as the regressors are mean independent, that is, $E[v_{it} \mid X] = 0$. The ability to use the x's of others as instruments also clearly hinges on $\gamma = 0$, as otherwise the exogenous effects constitute part of the error term.

To achieve identification, Pinkse et al. (2002) impose conditions related to the density of the network. In their Assumption (iv) of Theorem 1, they state that, for any bounded set D, $\lim_{N \to \infty} \#\{(i,j): d_{ij} \in D\} / N < \infty$, which basically implies that, as the number of observations increases, the number of areas or markets grow, as opposed to a denser network (which is also related to the linear independence of I, W and W^2). The main theorems in Pinkse et al. (2002) prove the asymptotic convergence and normality of the estimator of the vector $\theta = (\rho, \beta, \alpha_1, \ldots, \alpha_{L_N})$ as N grows. More specifically, the estimator therein is based on the orthogonal projection over the space generated by the instruments. Call the $N \times b_N$ matrix of instruments as Z and the projection as P_Z. Then the proposed estimator is

$$\hat{\theta}_N = (SP_Z S)^{-1} SP_Z Y,$$

where S is the concatenation of the endogenous and exogenous regressors over time, and similarly for Y.

Sun (2016) extends the approach in an important direction: it allows the distance measures d_{ij} to be both endogenous and exogenous with respect to the error term ε_i. Moreover, it relaxes the assumption of linearity of the exogenous effects and uses the local linear and sieve estimation techniques to model the function $g(\cdot)$ that underpins the relation between distance d_{ij} and W_{ij}. More specifically, the paper considers the model

$$y_{it} = \sum_{i=1}^{N} g(d_{ij})y_{jt} + x_{it}\beta(\eta_i) + \varepsilon_{it},$$

where d_{ij} is a measure of distance between i and j and η_i is a continuous and scalar random variable. Again, the paper considers that $\lambda = 0$, and asymptotic derivations presume a growing N and $T = 1$. In addition, both $g(\cdot)$ and $\beta(\cdot)$ are unknown functions. The spatial weight function $g(\cdot)$, similar to Pinkse et al. (2002), is approximated by a series expansion, as in equations (15.7) and (15.8). Function $\beta(\cdot)$ is assumed to be twice continuously differentiable, and estimated via a kernel method. Then, the basis functions are applied both to d_{ij} and η_i, in the same spirit as Pinkse et al. (2002).

One of the new components can be found in the second part of the paper, where the condition about the exogeneity of d_{ij} is partly relaxed. More specifically, it allows

$$g(d_{ij}^1, d_{ij}^2) = g_1(d_{ij}^1) + g_2(d_{ij}^2), \quad d_{ij}^2 = d_i - d_j,$$

where d_{ij}^1 is a non-stochastic spatial distance and d_{ij}^2 is endogenous as ϵ_i correlates with d_i. More specifically, it assumes that $E(\varepsilon_i \mid X_i, \eta_i) = 0$, but conditional independence means that $E(\eta_i \mid X_i, \eta_i, d_i) = E(\eta_i \mid d_i) = \gamma(z_i) \neq 0$. Now, there are three unknown functions: $g_1(\cdot)$, $g_2(\cdot)$ and $\beta(\cdot)$. The paper then shows an adaptation of the estimation method that handles this endogenous component.[14]

4.2 Unknown Network, Part 2: High-Dimensional Methods

This literature departs from the pre-specification of the distance variables and takes the spatial interaction matrix as fully unknown, as parameters to be estimated, and thus is non-parametric in the sense to which it requires no prior information on the distances between the units. Since there are $N(N-1)$ parameters to estimate – the off-diagonal elements of the interaction matrix – this literature employs high-dimensional estimation techniques, which have enjoyed a groundswell of research in the past decade or so (Fan et al., 2011; Friedman et al., 2016). This is feasible as long as W is *sparse*, that is, that most of the elements of W are zero or that there are few connections relative to $N(N-1)$. Luckily, this seems a reasonable assumption in most social network applications, as individuals often tend to connect to a subset of others (Atalay et al., 2011). We will return to the sparsity assumption later. This approach was undertaken by a cluster of papers in a flourishing literature, which includes Ahrens and Bhattacharjee (2015), Manresa (2016), Rose (2019) and de Paula et al. (2019), which I briefly review.

This sequence of papers generally allows for $T \geq 1$, as in some sense it leverages the variation over time to estimate the unknown network matrix. Moreover, even for a brief moment putting aside the issue of the endogeneity, ordinary least squares (OLS) is no longer an appropriate estimation technique. This is due to the high number of parameters to estimate, which implicitly would require a large number of time periods relative to N. This is generally unavailable for most practitioners, or essentially that $N \ll T$.

Ahrens and Bhattacharjee (2015) deal with the estimation of a spatial model of the form

$$y_{it} = \sum_{j=1}^{N} W_{ij} y_{jt} + x_{it} \beta_i + \varepsilon_t, \tag{15.9}$$

where the main differences with respect to equation (15.3) are the absence of an exogenous term, so $\gamma = 0$, but it is generalizes in that β_i is allowed to vary across units $i \in \{1,...,N\}$. The fact that the endogenous scalar parameter ρ is not present in the expression should be treated as a normalization option since ρ is not separately identified from W in this context. They further assume that

$$y_j = \sum_{s=1}^{N} x_s \pi_{j,s} + u_j,$$

where $y_j \equiv (y_{j1},...,y_{jT})'$, and $x_s \equiv (x_{s1}',...,x_{sT}')'$ are the vectors of stacked observations over time of y_{it} and x_{it}, respectively. Moreover, $u_j \equiv (u_{j1},...,u_{jT})'$. This is thus effectively utilizing the spatial lags of x_{it} – the exogenous variables of the peers, which is valid as long as $E[\varepsilon_i | x_t] = 0$ and $\gamma = 0$ – as instruments to identify the elements of W.

The paper stipulates a two-step procedure. The first step chooses the optimal set of instruments, which is then utilized in the second step to estimate the elements of W. For that, define $X \equiv (x_1,...,x_N)$ and $\pi_j' = (\pi_{j,1}',...,\pi_{j,n}')$. They propose to estimate $\hat{\pi}_j$ as the solution to

$$\hat{\pi}_j = \arg\min \| y_i - X\pi_i \|_2^2 + \lambda_1 \| \pi_i \|_1$$

for $\lambda_1 \geq 0$. The estimator is known as the Least Angle Shrinkage and Selection Operator, or the LASSO, and forms the backbone of many high-dimensional estimation methods. It is also central to the literature that follows on the estimation of the networks. The first part, $\| y_i - X\pi_i \|_2^2$ is the L_2 norm of the residuals, or just the mean-squared errors. If $\lambda_1 = 0$, then the LASSO reduces to an OLS regression, which generally requires that the number of parameters is much smaller than the observations. The second part is the main innovation and penalizes for the absolute value of the parameters.[15] Under certain conditions, the LASSO estimator has been shown to perform well.[16]

One can use the fitted values of y_i from the first-stage regression to estimate the elements of W_{ij},

$$\hat{\theta}_i = \arg\min \| y_i - \hat{G}_i \theta_i \|_2^2 + \lambda_2 \| \theta_i \|_1$$

where $\hat{G}_i \equiv (\hat{y}, X_i)$, $\hat{y} \equiv (\hat{y}_1, \ldots, \hat{y}_N)$, $\theta_i' \equiv (W_i, \beta_i')$ and $W_i \equiv (W_{i1}, \ldots, W_{i,i-1}, W_{i,i+1}, \ldots, W_{i,N})$. Ahrens and Bhattacharjee (2015) prove asymptotic convergence of the prediction error and convergence of $\hat{\theta}_i$ to its true value but do not provide the results concerning the asymptotic distribution.

A related contribution is made by Manresa (2016) in her job market paper. She stipulates a spatial model is such that

$$y_t = \alpha_i + x_t \beta_i + W x_t \gamma + \varepsilon_t,$$

where x_{it} could capture either individual-level variables or group-level variables that control for correlated shocks. One feature of the model is that $\rho = 0$, so there are no endogenous channels of interaction, which reduces the problem of identification. She then considers the LASSO and the double-pooled LASSO estimator for W, and provides an application to R&D spillovers.

Finally, Rose (2019) makes an interesting contribution in this line of work: he uses the sparsity of W both for estimation and identification. On the estimation side, some notion of sparsity is required to make high-dimensional methods applicable, as explained. Rose (2019) goes one step further and uses this assumption for identification also, which is essentially equivalent to (unknown) exclusion restrictions. He shows that identification is obtained if certain rank and order conditions are satisfied (see Proposition 4.10 therein), which is related to the existence of a sufficient number of node-independent paths (two paths are node independent if they do not have a common node). The paper derives full conditions for identification using sparsity, which are not necessarily directly testable or observable. Finally, the estimation method in Gautier and Tsybakov (2014) is adapted to the problem of estimating the network, whereby the selection of instruments plays a central role.

The issue of identification is comprehensively characterized by de Paula et al. (2019), without recourse to sparsity conditions. They show identification of the network and parameters (ρ, β, γ) under the assumption that there exists l and k such that $(W^2)_{ll} \neq (W^2)_{kk}$, $l, k \in \{1, \ldots, N\}$, that is, the diagonal of W^2 is not proportional to the vector of ones. It is immediate to see that this implies the linear independence condition of Bramoullé et al. (2009). To see this, note that I, W and W^2 are linearly independent if, and only if, $c_1 = c_2 = c_3 = 0$ in

$$c_1 I + c_2 W + c_3 W^2 = 0.$$

Since the main diagonal of W is empty, and the main diagonal of W^2 is not proportional to the vector of ones, it follows that $c_1 = c_3 = 0$, which implies that $c_2 = 0$. The converse, however, is not true: it is possible that the linear independence of I, W and W^2 is achieved without necessarily implying that the main diagonal of W^2 is not proportional to the vector of ones. In fact, de Paula et al. (2019) provide a counter-example in which the linear independence conditions are satisfied but there are two sets of structural parameters that yield the same reduced form; it follows that linear independence is not sufficient to grant identification when the networks are themselves also unknown. In the estimation side, the paper employs the ideas of Caner and Zhang (2014) in the Adaptive Elastic Net Generalized Method of Moments (GMM). This is based on the solving the problem

$$\hat{\theta} = \arg\min g_{NT}(\theta)' g_{NT}(\theta) + \lambda_1 \sum_{i,j=1}^{N} |W_{ij}| + \lambda_2 \sum_{i,j=1}^{N} W_{ij}^2,$$

where θ is the stacked vector of parameters, that is, $\theta = (\rho, \beta, \gamma, W_{12}, \ldots, W_{1N}, \ldots, W_{N-1N})$. Also, the moment conditions in the first term are defined based on the reduced-form disturbance terms, that is,

$$g_{NT}(\theta) = \sum_{t=1}^{T} \left[x_{1t} e_{\theta}' \cdots x_{Nt} e_t(\theta)' \right]',$$

and $e_t(\theta) = y_t - (I - \rho W)^{-1}(\beta I + \rho W)$ are the reduced-form residuals. Thus the N^2 moment condition is based on the orthogonality between x_{it} and e_{jt} for each $i, j = 1, \ldots, N$. The first penalization term, given by $\lambda_1 \sum_{i,j=1}^{N} |W_{ij}|$, is analogous to the LASSO penalization in equation (15.10). The Elastic Net penalization is composed by the L_2-norm term given by $\lambda_2 \sum_{i,j=1}^{N} W_{ij}^2$ and has been shown to provide better model-selection properties (Zou and Zhang, 2009). It is worth noting that the paper chooses to define the GMM objective function in the reduced form but to penalize in the structural form. This is due to the fact that, even if W is sparse, Π is not necessarily so. To see this, note that model (15.4) has reduced form

$$y_t = \underbrace{(I - \rho W)^{-1}(\beta I + \gamma W)}_{=\Pi} x_t + v_t,$$

where $v_t = (I - \rho W)^{-1} \varepsilon_t$. One can then write

$$\Pi = \beta I + (\rho \beta + \gamma) \sum_{k=1}^{\infty} \rho^{k-1} W^k,$$

which indicates that Π_{ij} is zero if $W_{ij} = (W^2)_{ij} = (W^3)_{ij} = \cdots = 0$. In other words, sparsity in Π is obtained if there is no path between i and j of any length for most (i, j) pairs, which is a much stronger assumption. Indeed, this notion is made more formal in Assumption 3 in Appendix B in their paper. The final estimator is the adaptive version of the Elastic Net GMM estimator, where the L_1-norm is reweighted by the first-stage estimator,

$$\tilde{\theta} = \arg\min g_{NT}(\theta)' g_{NT}(\theta) + \lambda_1 \sum_{i,j=1}^{N} \frac{|W_{ij}|}{|\hat{W}_{ij}|^{\eta}} + \lambda_2 \sum_{i,j=1}^{N} W_{ij}^2,$$

where η is set to 2.5 (see Caner and Zhang (2014) for more details).

Other methods have emerged in the literature dealing with partially observable networks, or situations in which the researcher is interested in some aspect of the network rather than the full elicitation of links. Lam and Souza (2019) deal with the case in which the empiricists might have data on multiple possible dimensions about the extent to which individuals interact but might be unsure about their relevance and accuracy. For example, if the units are countries, the researcher may postulate that GDP spills over according to an inverse measure of geographical distance, trade, financial flows and immigration proximity. They label those observable distances as W_s^{expert} and there may exist $s = 1, \ldots, S$ of them. In addition, they suggest that there might be a sparse deviation A^* from the measured distances. That is, the unobserved W follows

$$W = \sum_{s=1}^{S} \rho_s W_s^{\text{expert}} + A^*,$$

where ρ_s, $s = 1, \ldots, S$ are unknown scalars and A^* is an unobserved $N \times N$ matrix, all to be estimated. If $A^* = 0$, then the model reduces to a standard spatial model with known W. Thus, how close A^* is to zero is also indicative of the misspecification. It is possible that $S = 0$, and, in such a case, it reduces to the full estimation of the linkages as in the papers reviewed.

In many cases, researchers might be interested in identifying or estimating the central individuals in a network, rather than the full network. Peng (2019) offers a solution in this direction. He postulates a model in which

$$y_i = \sum_{j=1}^{N} \rho_j W_{ij} y_j + x_i \beta + \varepsilon_i,$$

where ρ_j is now is the endogenous effect of j is their neighbours; it is perfectly possible that there are individuals who impose no endogenous effects on others; and one can then define the set $\{j : \rho_j \neq 0\}$ as the influentials. Since N can be large, the paper uses again high-dimensional techniques, where now the sparsity is imposed onto the set of $\{\rho_1, \ldots, \rho_N\}$. Identification of (some) centrality measure is also obtained in de Paula et al. (2019): they show that, under minimal conditions, Π and W share a common set of eigenvectors (see their section 2.2). This implies that eigencentralities are immediately observable from the reduced form.

Finally, Lam and Souza (2016) showcase that, even a simple model without exogenous covariates,

$$y_t = W y_t + \varepsilon_t$$

can tell important features of the network. Here, the absence of *any* exogenous features gives no hope that W can be consistently estimated. Rather than doing so, the paper shows that a milder – yet useful – result can be obtained. In a problem akin one of classification, the authors show that a block structure can be detected if individuals interact in a group. That is, the off-block-diagonal zeros are consistently estimated using the Adaptive LASSO technique, and they claim no result for the within-block interactions. The paper uses the voting patterns in the US Congress and finds the network in Figure 15.2.

4.3   Unknown Network, Part 3: Variation Across Groups

The last selection of papers considers using many groups for the estimation for the network effects, in the absence of network data. This leverages the combination of a spatial econometric model with a model for the network formation. I briefly review the approach followed by Souza (2015) and Hsieh and Lee (2016). This approach is particularly useful if T is small and if the research does not care about the identities of the links.[17]

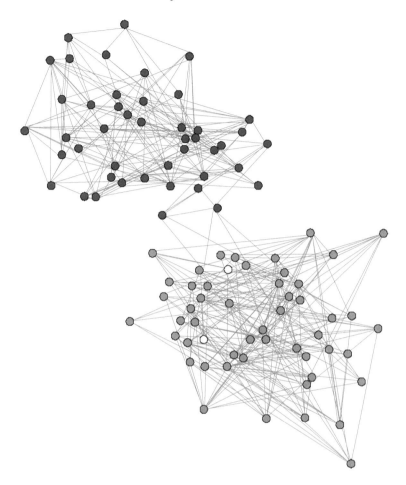

Notes: Network estimated from the voting pattern in the US Senate. Party affiliations are represented by Republicans in dark grey, Democrats in light grey and independents in white. Party affiliations are not used in the estimation procedure. For more information, see Lam and Souza (2016).

Figure 15.2   Network estimated from voting patterns in the US Senate, in 2012, from Lam and Souza (2016)

Denote the likelihood of model (15.4), conditional on W as $\mathcal{L}_{NT}(y\,|\,x;W,\rho,\beta,\gamma)$. The properties of the maximum likelihood estimator in this case have been analysed by Lee (2004).[18] If the network is not known, then the formulation is also not useful as it is conditioned on W. The crux of the idea in Souza (2015) and Hsieh and Lee (2016) is to instead use a profiled likelihood, integrating the observation of the network away,

$$\mathcal{L}_{NT}(y\,|\,x;\rho,\beta,\gamma) = \int \mathcal{L}_{NT}(y\,|\,x;W,\rho,\beta,\gamma) \cdot dP_W(x;\rho,\beta,\gamma),$$

where $dP_W(\rho, \beta, \gamma)$ is a probability distribution over the space of possible candidate networks. Thus, the researcher has to specify a model for the network formation—a much lighter requirement than observing the network itself. Souza (2015) gives a few examples of possible network formation models, and Hsieh and Lee (2016) use the latent space representation—the same underpinnings from Breza et al. (2019a,b). Both papers derive the asymptotic distribution of the maximum likelihood estimates of (ρ, β, γ). In other words, although the network itself is not estimated, nor identified, the strengths of the endogenous and exogenous effects are.

In terms of the estimation, Hsieh and Lee (2016) suggests a Bayesian approach. This is required as the space of possible networks is potentially extremely large: in a group with N individuals, there are potentially $N(N-1)$; in an unweighted and directed network, the network space thus comprehends $2^{N(N-1)}$ possible networks, which is a large number even for low N.

The approach differs in Souza (2015). To avoid the computational challenges, the author suggests to first compute the expected network, $W^e \equiv E[W \,|\, x,\rho,\beta,\gamma] = \int W dP_W(x;\rho,\beta,\gamma)$ and use it in place of the unknown network in the specification of the likelihood, that is, $\mathcal{L}_{NT}(y \,|\, x;W^e,\rho,\beta,\gamma)$. This is inherently a misspecified model, but the author shows that the misspecification is eliminated through the observation of many groups.

5. CONCLUSION

There is nowadays a substantial interest in empirical studies of networks, and the literature has flourished in the past decade or so (see Cai et al., 2015; Beaman et al., 2018; Banerjee et al., 2019; Breza and Chandrasekhar, 2019, among many others). Yet, network data are difficult (and often impossible) to obtain, limiting the amount of empirical research that can be undertaken. This chapter sheds light on a few recent empirical methods that are available. It is not to dig into the particular details of each method – for that, the reader is directed to the original papers themselves – but to serve as an introduction to the various options available today.

As this is a novel area of research, it is very likely that new solutions will be developed in the future. In this sense, this review is likely to be soon outdated, given the speed in which the frontier is currently evolving. Also, a few empirical aspects remain open. For example, the issue of the endogeneity of the network formation process itself merits more attention and research. These are cases where the existence of a network link responds to the outcomes, unobserved error terms or other topological properties of the network, such as coalition behaviour and group formation. In all, networks from the empirical as well as methodological sides are bound to be the object of exciting research well into the foreseeable future.

NOTES

1. For more information, see https://www.cpc.unc.edu/projects/addhealth. The website mentions that "The Add Health bibliography includes more than 8,000 journal articles, presentations, unpublished manuscripts, books, book chapters and dissertations by Add Health researchers".
2. See Anselin (1988) and LeSage and Pace (2009) for introductions to spatial econometric models.
3. In the spatial econometrics literature, it is common to normalize the rows of W to one, that is, to instead use $W_{ij}^* = W_{ij} / \Sigma_{j=1}^{N} W_{ij}$.
4. For other applications of the ARD methodology in estimating hard-to-reach populations, see DiPrete et al. (2011), Scutelniciuc (2012), Jing et al. (2014) and Feehan et al. (2016).
5. Hoff et al. (2002) specify equation (15.2) as a log-odds and arrive at a maximum likelihood expression (see equation 4 therein), which may form the basis for the estimations of the collection of αs, zs and δ.
6. See Figure 1 therein.

7. Breza and Chandrasekhar (2019) implement a different, micro-founded measure which is based on a convex combination of the interaction of monitor and saver centrality and their proximity.
8. More precisely, Banerjee et al. (2019) instead refer to the "support" or the fractions of connected pairs for which a third individual connects to both.
9. For microfoundations of the spatial model, see de Paula (2017).
10. See Anselin (1988) for a broader discussion.
11. In most cases, this is a weak assumption, and also a typical one. Possible violations are the modelling of input-output matrices, which are typically observed at a sector or sub-sector level of aggregation. One can observe that sectors supply to themselves, since firms in the same sector are likely connected. This is suggestive that the level of aggregation is not appropriate, and one should instead consider running the regressions at the firm level.
12. See also the discussion about the reflection problem in de Paula (2017).
13. See also Case (1991, 1992), Pinkse and Slade (1998) and Kelejian and Piras (2011).
14. See also Sun and Malikov (2018) for a model with fixed effects, pre-determined W but with ρ depending on some unknown function of distance.
15. Ahrens and Bhattacharjee (2015) actually allow for element-wise penalization to potentially account for heteroskedasticity. See discussion in page 139 therein.
16. See Tibshirani (1996). Subsequent versions of the LASSO, such as the Adaptive LASSO, are recommended as generally provide large gains in performance under milder conditions (Zou, 2006).
17. Other papers use variation across groups to identify the network effects if the network is able to be observed. See, for example, Graham (2008), Beenstock and Felsenstein (2012) and Bhattacharjee and Jensen-Butler (2013).
18. See also Anselin (1988).

REFERENCES

Acemoglu, D., V. Carvalho, A. Ozdaglar, and A. Tahbaz-Salehi (2012). The network origins of aggregate fluctuations. *Econometrica 80*, 1977–2016.

Ahrens, A. and A. Bhattacharjee (2015). Two-step lasso estimation of the spatial weights matrix. *Econometrics 3*(1), 128–55.

Ammermuller, A. and J.-S. Pischke (2009). Peer effects in European primary schools: Evidence from the progress in international reading literacy study. *Journal of Labor Economics 27*(3), 315–48.

Angrist, J. D. and K. Lang (2004). Does school integration generate peer effects? Evidence from Boston's Metco program. *American Economic Review 94*(5), 1613–34.

Anselin, L. (1988). *Spatial econometrics: Methods and models*. Springer.

Anselin, L. (2010). Thirty years of spatial econometrics. *Papers in Regional Science 89*(1), 3–25.

Atalay, E., A. Hortacsu, J. Roberts, and C. Syverson (2011). Network structure of production. *Proceedings of the American Mathematical Society 108*, 5199–202.

Ballester, C., A. Calvó-Armengol, and Y. Zenou (2006). Who's who in networks. Wanted: The key player. *Econometrica 74*(5), 1403–17.

Banerjee, A., A. G. Chandrasekhar, E. Duflo, and M. O. Jackson (2013). The diffusion of microfinance. *Science 341*(6144), 1236498.

Banerjee, A., A. G. Chandrasekhar, E. Duflo, and M. O. Jackson (2019). Using gossips to spread information: Theory and evidence from two tandomized controlled trials. *The Review of Economic Studies 86*(6), 2453–90.

Banerjee, A., E. Breza, E. Duflo, and C. Kinnan (2019). Can microfinance unlock a poverty trap for some entrepreneurs? Technical report, National Bureau of Economic Research.

Beaman, L., A. BenYishay, J. Magruder, and A. M. Mobarak (2018). Can network theory-based targeting increase technology adoption? *NBER Working Paper 24912*, 62.

Beenstock, M. and D. Felsenstein (2012). Nonparametric estimation of the spatial connectivity matrix using spatial panel data: Estimation of the spatial connectivity matrix. *Geographical Analysis 44*(4), 386–97.

Bhattacharjee, A. and C. Jensen-Butler (2013). Estimation of the spatial weights matrix under structural constraints. *Regional Science and Urban Economics 43*(4), 617–34.

Blume, L. E., W. A. Brock, S. N. Durlauf, and R. Jayaraman (2015). Linear social interactions models. *Journal of Political Economy 123*(2), 444–96.

Bramoullé, Y., A. Galeotti, and B. Rogers (2016). *The Oxford handbook of the economics of networks*. Oxford University Press.

Bramoullé, Y., H. Djebbari, and B. Fortin (2009). Identification of peer effects through social networks. *Journal of Econometrics*, 15.

Breza, E. and A. G. Chandrasekhar (2019). Social networks, reputation, and commitment: Evidence from a savings monitors experiment. *Econometrica 87*(1), 175–216.

Breza, E., A. G. Chandrasekhar, T. H. McCormick, and M. Pan (2019a). Consistently estimating graph statistics using aggregated relational data. *Working Paper*, 34.

Breza, E., A. G. Chandrasekhar, T. H. McCormick, and M. Pan (2019b). Using aggregated relational data to feasibly identify network structure without network data. *American Economic Review*, 28.

Cai, J., A. D. Janvry, and E. Sadoulet (2015). Social networks and the decision to insure. *American Economic Journal: Applied Economics 7*(2), 81–108.

Caner, M. and H. H. Zhang (2014). Adaptive elastic net for generalized method of moments. *Journal of Business and Economic Statistics 32*(1), 30–47.

Case, A. (1991). Spatial patterns in household demand. *Econometrica 59*(4), 953–65.

Case, A. (1992). Neighborhood influence and technological change. *Regional Science and Urban Economics 22*, 491–508.

Chandrasekhar, A. and R. Lewis (2016). Econometrics of sampled networks. *Working Paper.*

Costa, F., H. Helfer, R. Rocha, and P. Souza (2017). The short-run effects of social media activity on street protests: Evidence from Brazil. *Working Paper.*

Crespo Cuaresma, J. and M. Feldkircher (2013). Spatial filtering, model uncertainty and the speed of income convergence in Europe. *Journal of Applied Econometrics 28*(4), 720–41.

de Paula, Á. (2017). Econometrics of Network Models. In B. Honore, A. Pakes, M. Piazzesi, and L. Samuelson (Eds.), *Advances in economics and econometrics*, pp. 268–323. Cambridge: Cambridge University Press.

de Paula, Á. (2020). Econometric models of network formation. *Annual Review of Economics 12*, 775–99.

de Paula, Á., I. Rasul, and P. C. Souza (2019). Identifying network ties from panel data: Theory and an application to tax competition. *Working Paper.*

DiPrete, T. A., A. Gelman, T. McCormick, J. Teitler, and T. Zheng (2011). Segregation in social networks based on acquaintanceship and trust. *American Journal of Sociology 116*(4), 1234–83.

Fan, J., J. Lv, and L. Qi (2011). Sparse high dimensional models in economics. *Annual Review of Economics 3*, 291–317.

Feehan, D. M., A. Umubyeyi, M. Mahy, W. Hladik, and M. J. Salganik (2016). Quantity versus quality: A survey experiment to improve the network scale-up method. *American Journal of Epidemiology 183*(8), 747–57.

Friedman, J., T. Hastie, and R. Tibshirani (2016). *The Elements of Statistical Learning*, Volume 1. Springer.

Gautier, E. and A. Tsybakov (2014). High-dimensional instrumental variables regression and confidence sets. *Working Paper CREST.*

Giorgi, G. D., M. Pellizzari, and S. Redaelli (2010). Identification of social interactions through partially overlapping peer groups. *American Economic Journal: Applied Economics*, 36.

Glaeser, E., B. Sacerdote, and J. A. Scheinkman (2003). The social multiplier. *Journal of the European Economic Association 1*(2–3), 345–53.

Graham, B. S. (2008). Identifying social interactions through conditional variance restrictions. *Econometrica 76*(3), 643–60.

Hoff, P. D., A. E. Raftery, and M. S. Handcock (2002). Latent space approaches to social network analysis. *Journal of the American Statistical Association 97*(460), 1090–98.

Hsieh, C.-S. and L. F. Lee (2016). A social interactions model with endogenous friendship formation and selectivity. *Journal of Applied Econometrics 31*(2), 301–19.

Jackson, M. O. (2010). *Social and economic networks*. Princeton University Press.

Jing, L., C. Qu, H. Yu, T. Wang, and Y. Cui (2014). Estimating the sizes of populations at high risk for HIV: A comparison study. *PloS one 9*(4), e95601.

Kadushin, C., P. D. Killworth, H. R. Bernard, and A. A. Beveridge (2006). Scale-up methods as applied to estimates of heroin use. *Journal of Drug Issues 36*(2), 417–40.

Kelejian, H. H. and G. Piras (2011). An extension of Kelejian's j test for non-nested spatial models. *Regional Science and Urban Economics 41*(3), 281–92.

Lam, C. and P. C. Souza (2019). Estimation and selection of spatial weight matrix in a spatial lag model. *Journal of Business & Economic Statistics*, 1–41.

Lam, C. and P. C. L. Souza (2016). Detection and estimation of block structure in spatial weight matrix. *Econometric Reviews 35*(8–10), 1347–76.

Lee, L.-F. (2004). Asymptotic distributions of quasi-maximum likelihood estimators for spatial autoregressive models. *Econometrica 72*(6), 1899–925.

Lee, L.-F., X. Liu, and X. Lin (2010). Specification and estimation of social interaction models with network structures: Estimation of social network models. *Econometrics Journal 13*(2), 145–76.

LeSage, J. and R. K. Pace (2009). *Introduction to spatial econometrics*. New York: CRC Press.

Manresa, E. (2016). Estimating the structure of social interactions using panel data. *Working Paper*, 63.

Manski, C. F. (1993). Identification of endogenous social effects: The reflection problem. *Review of Economic Studies 60*, 531–42.

McCormick, T. H. and T. Zheng (2015). Latent surface models for networks using aggregated relational data. *Journal of the American Statistical Association 110*(512), 1684–95.

Peng, S. (2019). Heterogeneous endogenous effects in networks. *arXiv:1908.00663 [econ, stat]*.

Pinkse, J. and M. E. Slade (1998). Contracting in space: An application of spatial statistics to discrete-choice models. *Journal of Econometrics 85*(1), 125–54.

Pinkse, J., M. E. Slade, and C. Brett (2002). Spatial price competition: A semiparametric approach. *Econometrica 70*(3), 1111–53.

Rose, C. (2019). Identification of spillover effects using panel data. *Working Paper*.

Scutelniciuc, O. (2012). Network scale-up method experiences: Republic of Kazakhstan. *Consultation on estimating population sizes through household surveys: successes and challenges,* March, 28–30.

Souza, P. (2015). *Essays on the identification and estimation of networks*. PhD thesis.

Stakhovych, S. and T. H. Bijmolt (2009). Specification of spatial models: A simulation study on weights matrices. *Papers in Regional Science 88*(2), 389–408.

Sun, Y. (2016). Functional-coefficient spatial autoregressive models with nonparametric spatial weights. *Journal of Econometrics 195*(1), 134–53.

Sun, Y. and E. Malikov (2018). Estimation and inference in functional-coefficient spatial autoregressive panel data models with fixed effects. *Journal of Econometrics 203*(2), 359–78.

Tibshirani, R. (1996). Regression shrinkage and selection via the lasso. *Journal of the Royal Statistical Society, Series B (Methodological) 58*(1), 267–88.

Zou, H. (2006). The adaptive lasso and its oracle properties. *Journal of the American Statistical Association 101*(476), 1418–29.

Zou, H. and H. H. Zhang (2009). On the adaptive elastic-net with a diverging number of parameters. *Ann. Statist. 37*(4), 1733–51.

16. Machine learning for causal inference: estimating heterogeneous treatment effects

Vishalie Shah, Noemi Kreif and Andrew M. Jones

1. INTRODUCTION

Until recently, most of the causal inference literature has focused on evaluating the average impact of a change in policy, or *treatment*, on a population of interest. The corresponding causal estimand of interest is the average treatment effect (ATE) (Imbens and Rubin, 2015; Imbens and Woolridge, 2009). However, underlying this average effect is substantial variation in how individuals respond to treatment, suggesting that treatment effects are not in fact uniform, but heterogeneous (Athey and Imbens, 2019). Variation in treatment response can be explained by differences in the background characteristics of respondents, as well as differences in the features of treatment. Some members of the population may respond positively to treatment, while others may require a higher *dose* to achieve the same effect. It could also be the case that, although the policy impact on the population as a whole may be limited, certain subgroups of the population may still reap some benefits. For example, in the context of health, the beneficial impact of a national health insurance programme may be greater for vulnerable populations than those who can afford health care. Identifying these subgroups can be extremely informative for personalising treatment regimes, understanding causal mechanisms and guiding policy. It can provide decision makers with important insights into the distributional impacts of policy, including which subpopulations display above- or below-average treatment effects. The estimates of heterogeneous treatment effects, that is, the conditional (on covariates) average treatment effects (CATE), can be used as key inputs into the design of optimal policy rules that give policymakers the tools required to determine which individuals or subpopulations would benefit most from treatment and at what dose (Athey, 2018; Imai and Ratkovic, 2013; Imai and Strauss, 2011).

Variability across units of analysis plays an important role across all empirical social research. In causal inference, heterogeneity can arise in two distinct forms. First, the existence of variation in the response to treatment, either for individual observations or for different strata of the population, based on differences in their observed characteristics. Second, the existence of unobserved or unmeasured differences between units of observation, that are also correlated with the observed and included covariates (also known as *unobserved heterogeneity*). Omitted variables are commonly a feature of causal inference studies, where selection into treatment cannot always be observed. If assignment to treatment is correlated with an omitted variable, it will lead to biased estimates of the treatment effect, as a result of endogeneity. There is a large volume of literature that explores unobserved heterogeneity and selection bias, in particular the role of microeconometric tools, such as instrumental variables analysis and panel data regression methods, that are used to consistently estimate the treatment effect (Heckman, 2001). The focus of this chapter is on the former definition of heterogeneity. That is, we are interested in estimating the variation in treatment effects for population subgroups, based on their observed characteristics.

Methods for estimating heterogeneity in treatment effects have gained popularity across a variety of research disciplines, most notably in clinical research (Foster et al., 2011). Early work on effect heterogeneity focused on detecting quantitative interactions between treatment effects and patient subgroups, often defined by baseline characteristics (Bonetti and Gelber, 2004; Gail and Simon, 1985). This type of subgroup analysis is a popular tool for estimating treatment effects for subpopulations that share similar characteristics. For example, researchers are often interested in how gender plays a role in treatment response. In this scenario, subgroup analysis is fairly straightforward and simply involves separately estimating treatment effects for men and women. Although this type of analysis allows for simple interactions between the treatment and covariates, there are several limitations in using this method for identifying heterogeneity. First, it can lead to *cherry picking*, whereby researchers pre-specify covariates of interest that are favourable to existing results (Assmann et al., 2000; Cook et al., 2004). Second, it can result in reduced sample sizes, invalid *p*-values (due to multiple hypothesis testing) and *false discovery*, especially if statistical inference is not correctly adjusted for (Assmann et al., 2000; Brookes et al., 2001, 2004; List et al., 2016; Wang et al., 2007). Third, it can be impractical to use with high-dimensional data, where more complex covariate-treatment interactions are possible. Given these limitations, finding true heterogeneity through subgroup selection can be a challenging task.

There is a rapidly growing causal inference literature that combines applied econometrics with machine learning for the improved estimation of treatment effects. Machine learning lies at the intersection of computer science and statistics, using learning-based algorithms to make predictions from data. We focus on the branch of machine learning known as *supervised learning*, since its prediction algorithms are particularly useful for solving causal problems (Athey and Imbens, 2017). Supervised learning is based on a predictive model for some outcome Y as a function of covariate vector X. The idea is to select an algorithm (or a combination of algorithms) that produces optimal predictions of Y given new values of X. Although machine learning is primarily geared toward prediction, economists have started to carefully tune and adapt these methods to effectively answer research questions that are causal in nature (Athey, 2017; Athey and Imbens, 2019; Kleinberg et al., 2015; Mullainathan and Spiess, 2017; Varian, 2014). While prediction tools cannot directly assess causality, they can support classical tools for causal inference in producing more accurate estimates of causal effects (Lechner, 2019; Varian, 2014). This is especially helpful when data originate from non-randomised experiments, where selection bias is an issue (Heckman et al., 1998). For example, machine learning is increasingly used in doubly robust estimation; a method that combines outcome and treatment modelling to adjust for selection bias in causal effect estimates (Robins et al., 2007; Van der Laan and Robins, 2003). Incorporating flexible machine learning tools into doubly robust estimation can support the de-biasing of estimators by reducing the risk of model misspecification in the outcome and treatment models (Chernozhukov et al., 2018a; Van der Laan and Rose, 2011).

In recent years, machine learning has been incorporated into methods for exploring heterogeneity in causal effects. It offers a practical solution for situations where the analyst has access to a potentially large number of covariates to form subgroups and limited knowledge on which of these are relevant for heterogeneity (Chernozhukov et al., 2018b). In these high-dimensional settings, correctly specifying a parametric regression for the outcome may prove challenging, particularly if the true model is described by complex interactions. Machine learning algorithms offer a flexible, non-parametric approach to subgroup analysis by selecting covariates of interest in a data-adaptive way, as opposed to *a priori*. These tools can often provide new insights into subpopulations that have not previously been studied (Athey and Imbens, 2015). Further, some algorithms are able to maintain good performance with high-dimensional data and complex covariate-treatment interactions (Knaus et al., 2020; Powers et al., 2018). The most prominent machine learning method for estimating heterogeneous effects is the causal forests estimator developed by Athey et al. (2019b), which uses a tree-like structure to control for observed covariates and estimates the CATE function within each leaf. Other notable advancements in machine learning methods for exploring treatment effect heterogeneity include algorithms based on the least absolute shrinkage and selection operator (LASSO) (Tian et al., 2014), Bayesian causal forests (Hahn et al., 2020), boosting (Powers et al., 2018), neural networks (Shalit et al., 2017) and ensemble methods (Künzel et al., 2019a; Nie and Wager, 2021).

The aim of this chapter is to provide an insight into causal machine learning and to highlight some of the recent developments in the literature, in particular for estimating heterogeneous treatment effects. We focus our attention on three promising algorithms: the X-Learner (Künzel et al., 2019a), the R-learner (Nie and Wager, 2021) and causal forests (Athey et al., 2019b). We select the former algorithm given its flexibility and intuitive design, and the latter two algorithms given their popularity among applied researchers and their doubly robust property. All three algorithms enable statistical inference and construction of valid confidence intervals. Further, each algorithm can easily be implemented through its associated R package. We describe each of these methods in turn, and additionally demonstrate their application to an empirical case study.

The structure of this chapter is as follows. First, we introduce the notation and assumptions required for the identification of the causal estimands of interest, the ATE and CATE, under the potential outcomes framework. Following this, we provide an overview of some key concepts within the area of supervised machine learning. We continue with a review of causal machine learning methods for estimating the ATE and subsequently explore in detail our three selected algorithms for estimating the CATE. Next, we introduce our impact evaluation case study and share our methods and results. We conclude with a brief overview of some empirical applications of the described methods, and recent, notable developments in the literature that extend the methods to other settings. Where possible, we identify the software packages required to implement the methods in R.

2.   METHODS OF CAUSAL INFERENCE AND MACHINE LEARNING

2.1   The Causal Framework

We define our parameters of interest within the potential outcomes framework of causal inference (Imbens and Rubin, 2015; Rubin, 1974). Suppose we have a sample of N units, where $i = 1, \ldots, N$. Let Y be the outcome of interest, X_i be a vector of covariates of size $1 \times K$ and $D_i \in 0,1$ be a binary indicator for treatment, where $D_i = 1$ indicates that unit i received the treatment.[1] Denote by $Y_i(d)$ the potential outcome that would be observed if unit i was assigned to level d of the treatment. The observed outcome Y_i can then be written in terms of potential outcomes as $Y_i = Y_i(1)(D_i) + Y_i(0)(1 - D_i)$. The individual treatment effect (ITE) is defined as the difference in potential outcomes, $\tau_i = Y_i(1) - Y_i(0)$. To measure the average causal effect for the population, we require the ATE:

$$ATE = \tau = E[Y_i(1) - Y_i(0)]. \tag{16.1}$$

For a target population of interest, we can estimate the average treatment effect on the treated (ATT) and controls (ATC).

Since we are interested in how treatment effects vary across individuals or subgroups, based on a specific covariate profile, we estimate CATEs, (Imai and Ratkovic, 2013; Imai and Strauss, 2011). CATEs take the expectations of ATEs conditional on exogeneous pre-treatment covariates:

$$CATE = \tau(x) = E[Y(1) - Y(0) \mid X = x]. \tag{16.2}$$

CATEs can be evaluated at varying levels of aggregation in the population. For example, one might be interested in exploring treatment effects at the individual level (that is, ITEs), in which case the expected potential outcomes will be evaluated using the individual covariate vector X_i. One might also be interested in estimating treatment effects for subpopulations grouped on a set of predefined characteristics (that is, group average treatment effects, or GATEs), and so the expected potential outcomes will be evaluated for a subgroup g that share the same covariate profile $X = x$. CATEs can also be evaluated for different target populations of interest, such as the treated (CATT) and controls (CATC).

The fundamental problem of causal inference is that, for each individual i, we observe either $Y_i(1)$ or $Y_i(0)$, but not both (Holland, 1986). Therefore, $\tau(x)$ cannot be identified without imposing a set of assumptions:

Assumption 1 (Unconfoundedness)

$$(Y_i(0), Y_i(1)) \perp D_i \mid X_i.$$

This assumption, also known as *selection on observables*, states that conditional on the observed covariates, the potential outcomes are independent of treatment status (Rosenbaum and Rubin, 1983). It assumes away the existence of unobserved factors that affect treatment status and are also associated with the outcome. However, the plausibility of this assumption must be carefully assessed through rigorous data collection and expert knowledge about potential confounders. This assumption alone is not sufficient to identify $\tau(x)$.

Assumption 2 (Overlap)

$$0 < P(D_i = 1 \mid X_i = x) = e(x) < 1, \textit{ for all x in the support of } X_i.$$

This assumption states that the propensity score, defined by $e(x) = P(D = 1 \mid X = x)$, must be bounded away from zero and one. This ensures that each unit of observation has a non-zero probability of being selected into treatment and control groups. Individuals who are either ineligible for treatment or automatically selected into either group must be removed from the target population.

The combination of these two assumptions is referred to as *strong ignorability* (Rosenbaum and Rubin, 1983). If these assumptions hold, then $\tau(x)$ can be rewritten as $\tau(x) = E[Y_i \mid D_i = 1, X_i = x] - E[Y_i \mid D_i = 0, X_i = x]$, due to the law of iterated expectations, where $Y_i = Y_i(1)(D_i) + Y_i(0)(1 - D_i)$. This is equivalent to expressing $\tau(x)$ as the difference in conditional mean functions (also known as *response functions*) of the potential outcomes under control μ_0 and treatment μ_1 as $\mu_0(x) = E[Y(0) \mid X = x]$ and $\mu_1(x) = E[Y(1) \mid X = x]$, respectively. This suggests that the estimator of $\tau(x)$ can be constructed using the response functions of the observed outcomes:

$$\hat{\mu}_1(x) = \frac{1}{N_1(x)} \sum_{i:X_i=x}^{D_i=1} Y_i$$

$$\hat{\mu}_0(x) = \frac{1}{N_0(x)} \sum_{i:X_i=x}^{D_i=0} Y_i,$$

where $N_d(x)$ is the number of observations under treatment status $D = d$ with covariate profile $X = x$. The CATE estimator can then be identified as,

$$\hat{\tau}(x) = \hat{\mu}_1(x) - \hat{\mu}_0(x). \tag{16.3}$$

However, this is a crude construction of the CATE estimator. In reality, there will not exist many observations with exactly the same covariate profile. Therefore, although this procedure is not followed in practice, it provides an insight into the intuition behind methods for estimating heterogeneous treatment effects. The notion that the estimator $\hat{\tau}(x)$ is constructed as the difference between the response functions for treated and controls highlights how the causal inference problem can be transformed into a prediction problem. Machine learning tools can provide support in such prediction tasks.

2.2   An Introduction to Supervised Machine Learning

Supervised machine learning focuses primarily on prediction tasks, that is, predictions of Y_i as a function of X_i, or D_i as a function of X_i. For example, given a data set in which the outcomes Y_i and covariates X_i are already labelled (that is, assigned to each unit of observation), the goal of the algorithm is to estimate a model that makes "good" predictions based on the values of Y_i and X_i in the input data (also known as *training* data). The estimated model is then exploited to predict outcomes, given new values of X_i, in the remaining, unseen data (also known as *test* data) (Athey and Imbens, 2017). Data are often divided into a training and test (hold-out) sample; the training data are used to "train" the model, and the test data are used to test the model's predictive power. This idea of splitting a data set into subsamples for the purpose of evaluating model performance, commonly known as *cross-validation*, has been a feature of the statistics literature for many years (Allen, 1974; Stone, 1974). The objective of cross-validation is to gain an insight into how the selected model will generalise to an independent data set, which is crucial for predictive algorithms.

Evaluating model performance is usually defined in terms of a loss function, for example the mean squared error (MSE) or the sum of squared residuals (SSR). The researcher specifies a loss function, for example MSE, as an input and searches for a function that minimises the MSE on new observations of X_i from the test data, not including the observations used to fit the model. A frequently used loss function is the test MSE, defined as the mean squared prediction error among observations in the test data. The ultimate goal of prediction algorithms is to achieve good *out-of-sample* predictions by minimising the test MSE. It is straightforward to build an estimator that works well in-sample, but the difficulty lies in ensuring this same estimator is generalisable to unseen data. At this point, we introduce the concept of the bias-variance trade-off. Suppose we estimate a non-linear model with many higher-order terms and vary the degree of the polynomial M in our estimator of predicted outcome Y. When M is low, the estimator is likely to be "underfitting" the data. The simple model is unable to explain the patterns in the data, resulting in a poor training fit and poor generalisation. In other words, there is high *bias* in the predictive model. As M increases, the model becomes more flexible, thus passing through more data points and subsequently improving the goodness of fit. When M is high, the estimator is likely to be "overfitting" the data. The complex model captures more noise in the data and although there is a near perfect training fit, it will fail to generalise on new data. In this case, there is high *variance* in the predictive model. The solution is to find a balance between bias and variance such that it minimises the total prediction error, that is, the expected test MSE:

$$E[(Y - \hat{Y})^2] = Var(\hat{Y}) + [Bias(\hat{Y})]^2 + Var(\varepsilon), \tag{16.4}$$

where $Var(\varepsilon)$ is the irreducible error resulting from noise in the outcome itself.

There is a two-step process in finding the optimal balance between bias and variance. The first step is *regularisation*, which penalises models for over-complexity. Regularisation techniques reduce the variance of the model so that it captures less noise in the data and improves generalisation. The key question is how to select an appropriate level of regularisation, in other words, how to *tune* the algorithm so that it does not underfit or overfit the data. This leads us to the second step, *empirical tuning*, which uses subsamples of the training data to compare and select the level of regularisation that achieves the best performance (that is, the lowest MSE). This procedure can be made more efficient through a process called *k-fold cross-validation*, which requires the following steps:

1. Select a prediction algorithm.
2. Randomly divide the data set into k mutually exclusive subsets of equal size, $s = 1,...,k$. Start with $s = 1$.
3. Select a value for the tuning parameter, $\gamma \in \{\gamma_1,...,\gamma_m\}$.
4. Fit the model for γ on $k - 1$ subsets of the data.
5. Test the model for γ on subset s and evaluate the associated loss (for example, test MSE).
6. Return to step 4 and iterate this process over all k folds.
7. Compute the average test MSE for γ over all k folds.
8. Go back to step 3, choosing a different value for γ, and repeat this process.

After k-fold cross-validation, there will exist m values of the tuning parameter and the average test MSE. The optimal tuning parameter will correspond to the one with the lowest average test MSE. The most commonly used values of *k* are 5, 10, and the sample size minus 1 (also known as *leave-one-out*). In ideal circumstances, a completely separate subset of the training data, known as the *validation data*, will be used to test the predictive power of the algorithm selected through cross-validation. It is important for the training and validation data to be drawn from the same distribution.

Another important concept in machine learning is ensembling. Ensembling combines several individual machine learning algorithms, called *base learners*, to produce one optimal predictive model, through a reduction in bias and variance. The rationale is that a combination of algorithms can outperform a single algorithm in improving model accuracy and goodness-of-fit (Athey et al., 2019a; Surowiecki, 2005; Varian, 2014). Most ensemble methods use base learners of the same type (that is, homogeneous learners), but there are also some ensembles which use base learners of different types (that is, heterogeneous learners) (Zhou, 2012). A simple example of a homogeneous learner is random forests, which combines predictions across several regression trees (Breiman, 2001). An example of a more complex, heterogeneous learner is the winning entry of the famous Netflix Prize competition, which found that combining predictions from many different algorithms led to the greatest improvement in root mean squared error (RMSE) (Bell et al., 2010).

There are three main types of ensemble algorithms: *bagging*, *boosting* and *stacking*. Bagging (short for bootstrap aggregation) aims to reduce variance by drawing random, repeated samples from the training data with replacement. The prediction of the outcome is obtained by averaging across the predictions in the individual bootstrap samples. Boosting aims to reduce bias and follows a similar process to bagging, except that each base learner is estimated sequentially, using information from previously estimated learners. Each learner in the sequence places more weight on observations with a large prediction error – that is, observations for which the learner incorrectly predicted Y_i from X_i – caused by previous learners in the sequence. The final prediction is obtained by either a vote or a weighted sum of the boosted learners. Boosting and bagging tend to combine homogeneous base learners using deterministic algorithms. Stacking is an alternative type of ensemble method that combines heterogeneous base learners using what is known as a *meta-learner*. The meta-learner takes as inputs the outputs of the base learners and generates an ensemble prediction. Stacking aims to improve predictive power by finding the optimal combination of base learners. The *super learner*, proposed by Van der Laan et al. (2007), is an example of a stacking algorithm that uses *k*-fold cross-validation to train the meta-learner. It involves evaluating the base learners on the same *k*-fold split of the training data and using the out-of-fold predictions to train the meta-learner on how to generate an optimal weighted combination of the predictions. More specifically, the meta-learner selects the combination of predictions that minimises the cross-validated MSE.

2.3   Machine Learning for Estimating Average Treatment Effects

Much of empirical economics is dominated by the study of causal relationships: the effect of treatment *D* on outcome *Y*. Researchers are often interested in the counterfactual impact of a change in policy (or treatment) on a given population. They first define a causal estimand of interest (also known as the *target parameter*), for example the ATE, and carefully consider the assumptions required for identification. The causal estimand is then mapped to an estimator ($\hat{\tau}$) via the identifying assumptions. This converts the causal inference problem into an estimation task. Many estimators, especially in settings with observational data, involve estimating parameters that are not of primary interest but are necessary for estimating the target parameter. Such parameters, often referred to as *nuisance parameters*, enable researchers to obtain unbiased effect estimates by carefully adjusting for confounders under certain causal assumptions. Examples of nuisance parameters include the outcome regression and the propensity score, which are both prediction tasks used to identify causal effects. These parameters are estimated using an objective function, most commonly the SSR or the likelihood function. They are subsequently used as inputs into the estimating model for the target parameter.

The machine learning literature is less concerned with causality and more with developing algorithms for prediction. Although machine learning can also produce familiar outputs such as regression coefficients, the ability to construct valid confidence intervals (for the majority of algorithms) is currently not possible (Athey and Imbens, 2019). Machine learning is more focused on achieving out-of-sample performance, and for many prediction problems, this is more important than being able to conduct inference. If machine learning cannot produce interpretable estimates of the target parameter, then how can it be applied to problems of causal inference? It can be used to improve the prediction component of estimation tasks, such as the nuisance parameters – the outcome regression and the propensity score.

An outcome regression can provide the conditional expectation of the outcome given treatment and confounders, denoted by $E[Y|D,X]$. The ATE can be identified as the difference in conditional expectations under treatment and control, $E[\mu_1(x) - \mu_0(x)]$, where $\mu_d(x) = E[Y|D = d, X = x]$. The propensity score refers to the conditional probability of treatment given observed confounders, denoted by $P(D = 1|X)$. It was introduced by Rosenbaum and Rubin (1983) as a means of reducing confounding bias in treatment effect estimation using observational data by balancing the distribution of observed confounders between treatment and control groups. Weighting or matching individuals based on their propensity score can produce unbiased estimates of the ATE. The literature on estimating $E[Y|D,X]$ and $P(D = 1|X)$ is vast (Angrist and Pischke, 2008; Greene, 2000; Wooldridge, 2010). However, in most cases, these nuisance parameters are estimated using parametric models, making them sensitive to model specification. Parametric models are usually selected based on theory and expert knowledge. They require strong assumptions about the functional form of the model and can lead to biased estimates of the treatment effect, if misspecified. For example, there is sometimes a lack of theory to guide the choice of the covariate vector X_i.

Doubly robust estimation that combines outcome and treatment mechanisms is a popular method for reducing the impact of functional form misspecification. The idea is to exploit propensity score matching or weighting prior to further regression adjustment as a means of fully controlling for confounding bias (Abadie and Imbens, 2006, 2011; Imbens and Wooldridge, 2009). Doubly robust estimators utilise both nuisance parameters and have the special property of being consistent if at least one of the two parameters is correctly specified (Bang and Robins, 2005; Robins and Rotnitzky, 1995). When both models are correctly specified, doubly robust estimators are semi-parametrically efficient and asymptotically normal (Neugebauer and Van der Laan, 2005). Although the nuisance parameters can be estimated using traditional regression models, applying machine learning to nuisance parameter estimation is becoming increasingly popular (Lee et al., 2010; Westreich et al., 2010). These tools enable a more flexible approach to model specification, estimating and comparing many alternative algorithms through cross-validation, to select one that minimises the defined loss function.

The problem with directly applying *off-the-shelf* machine learning methods to estimate τ is that the *ground truth* is never observed, that is, either $Y_i(1)$ and $Y_i(0)$ is observed for each individual. Without the ground truth, validation techniques (such as cross-validation) cannot be used to compare the performance of different prediction algorithms (Künzel et al., 2019b). Therefore, applying off-the-shelf algorithms to causal problems, without any form of adjustment, can produce biased estimates of the treatment effect. There are two sources of bias in the estimator for τ: *regularisation bias* and bias from overfitting. As mentioned previously, machine learning algorithms use regularisation to prevent over-complexity of the model and to reduce overfitting. Although this decreases the variance of the model, it introduces bias and slower convergence. One approach to overcoming regularisation bias is to use *orthogonalisation* by fitting separate treatment and outcome models and then regressing the residual of the outcome model on the residual of the treatment model. The estimated τ is then free of regularisation bias (provided that the unconfoundedness assumption is satisfied) since the associations between X_i and D_i, and Y_i and X_i (conditional on D_i) have been partialled out. The other source of bias in the treatment effect arises from flexible machine learning algorithms overfitting the data. When $\mu_d(x)$ is overfitted, the model may capture some of the noise from the error term. This is an issue if the estimation error from the outcome regression is associated with the error from the propensity model. This means that $\mu_d(x)$ is also associated with the error from the propensity score model, resulting in bias. One approach to tackling bias from overfitting is to use *sample splitting*. This involves partitioning the data into multiple subsamples, fitting the outcome regression and propensity score on the first subsample, and estimating τ on the second subsample. Although this reduces bias, this method of sample splitting can reduce statistical efficiency and power of the estimator. A better approach is to use cross-fitting by estimating the parameters k times (iteratively) across the k subsamples and averaging to obtain the final estimate, $\hat{\tau}$.

The most powerful doubly robust estimators, such as the targeted maximum likelihood estimator (TMLE) (Van der Laan and Rose, 2011; Van der Laan and Rubin, 2006) and the double machine learning (DML) estimator (Chernozhukov et al., 2018a), suggest incorporating machine learning into nuisance parameter estimation. The TMLE uses a two-step approach to de-bias the estimate of the target parameter. The first step involves estimating the nuisance parameters (usually by ensemble machine learning algorithms), which are used to predict the potential outcomes under treatment and control. The second step updates these initial estimates by implementing a substitution targeting step that optimises the bias in the target parameter. It does this by adjusting the parametric fluctuation in the initial estimator until the point at which the fluctuation is zero, thus solving the efficient influence curve-estimating equation (Gruber and Van der Laan, 2010). Van der Laan et al. (2007) further propose the use of the Super Learner to predict the nuisance parameters in the TMLE. The DML estimator combines the doubly robust method with machine learning to obtain accurate estimates of the nuisance parameters in settings with a large number of potential confounders. It does this by combining the residuals of the outcome regression and the propensity score model to form a new regression, based on the partially linear model developed by Robinson (1988). The estimator is constructed using cross-fitting, which splits the sample into k equal folds. The nuisance parameters are estimated on one part of the data, and the predictions used to construct the estimate of the target parameter are obtained using the remaining data. This process is repeated k times, and the average of the predicted values is the DML estimate. The standard errors are based on the influence function from semi-parametric statistical theory (Chernozhukov et al.,

2018a). The TMLE and DML are the only semi-parametric, doubly robust estimators proposed so far that enable free use of machine learning algorithms for parameter estimation (Diaz, 2019). They are examples of how machine learning can successfully complement econometric theory by allowing researchers to produce unbiased treatment effect estimates, while still having favourable statistical properties that enable inference about the causal parameters.

3. MACHINE LEARNING FOR ESTIMATING HETEROGENEOUS TREATMENT EFFECTS

We earlier described that under the assumptions of strong ignorability, the CATE $\tau(x)$ can be identified as the difference in response functions of the observed outcomes under treatment $\hat{\mu}_1(x)$ and control $\hat{\mu}_0(x)$. The literature on methods for estimating CATEs is rapidly expanding, and many recently proposed methods incorporate machine learning tools, including the LASSO (Imai and Ratkovic, 2013; Tian et al., 2014), tree-based algorithms (regression trees (Athey and Imbens, 2016), random forests (Athey et al., 2019b; Foster et al., 2011; Wager and Athey, 2018), and Bayesian additive regression trees (BARTs) (Hahn et al., 2020), neural networks (Shalit et al., 2017), boosting (Nie and Wager, 2021; Powers et al., 2018) and meta-learners (Künzel et al., 2019a; Nie and Wager, 2021). Although we have cited some of the more prominent developments in the literature, this list is not exhaustive and is continually evolving.

The majority of recent work on heterogeneous treatment effects is based on settings with randomised data. This means that when treated and control groups are likely to be *balanced*, the differences in treatment effects attributable to the observed covariates X_i are interpreted as heterogeneous (Ben-Michael et al., 2020). However, in many fields of economics, obtaining randomised data is often unfeasible or ethically impossible, and non-randomised, observational data are more readily available and used. Most studies conducted using observational data often follow a selection on observables identification strategy for estimating causal effects (either ATEs or CATEs), in which the included set of covariates X_i control for all potential confounders, provided that the assumption of strong ignorability holds. Causal effects conditional on covariates can then be estimated via a non-parametric outcome regression (Hahn, 1988; Rosenbaum and Rubin, 1983, 1984). However, this is not a practical approach in high-dimensional settings where the covariate vector X_i is rich and detailed. Although the unconfoundedness assumption becomes more plausible as the number of included covariates increases (Rosenbaum, 2002; Rubin, 2009), the behaviour of non-parametric estimators quickly deteriorates (that is, the convergence rate slows) given the sparsity of data in high-dimensional settings – a sparse statistical model is one in which only a relatively few number of parameters are relevant (Stone, 1980). This poor performance is often referred to as the *curse of dimensionality*. There is a fast growing causal machine learning literature for estimating heterogeneous treatment effects that additionally adjusts for selection bias. These methods employ a selection on observables framework and impose additional measures to control for any residual selection bias arising from the observed covariates.

In the next section, we describe three approaches to heterogeneous treatment effect estimation that have gathered attention in recent years: meta-learners, the R-Learner and causal forests. We explore these methods in detail and identify those which are promising for estimating heterogeneous treatment effects under various settings. For methods that do not adjust for confounding, we propose a pre-processing step to ensure that treatment and control

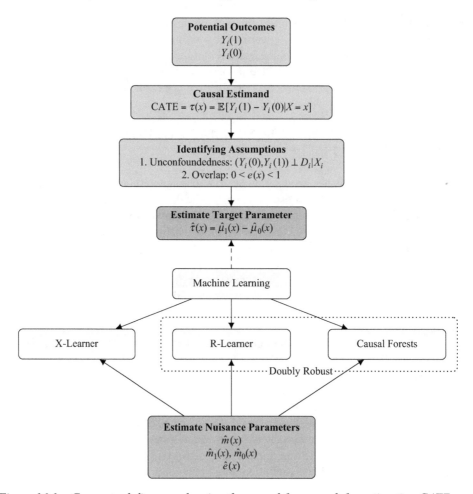

Figure 16.1   Conceptual diagram showing the causal framework for estimating CATEs

groups are balanced prior to estimating treatment effects. See Figure 16.1 for a conceptual diagram showing the causal framework for estimating CATEs using the three selected machine learning methods.

3.1   Meta-Learners

We start by introducing meta-learners for the problem of CATE estimation in the binary treatment case. As described earlier, meta-learners leverage information from several heterogeneous base learners to generate an optimal, ensemble prediction. They can be used to decompose the CATE estimation into multiple regression problems that can be estimated with any regression or supervised machine learning algorithm. The choice of base learner can largely influence predictive performance; therefore, subject knowledge is highly important. For example, BARTs are appropriate for small data sets with a global structure (for example, sparsity or linearity that applies to the entire data set), whereas random forests are more suited to larger data sets with a more local structure (for example, sparsity or linearity that applies to portions of the entire data set). In this section, we describe two commonly used meta-learners for estimating heterogeneous treatment effects, the *T-Learner* and the *S-Learner*, described by Künzel et al. (2019a), and explain some of their strengths and limitations. We then explore a more promising meta-learner that aims to solve some of the challenges encountered by the T- and S-Learners and offers a more favourable approach to CATE estimation in various settings: the *X-Learner* from Künzel et al. (2019a). The T-, S- and X-Learners can be implemented using the `causalToolbox` package in R by Künzel et al. (2019a).

T-Learner

The T-Learner (where "T" means "two") is the most intuitive meta-learner for estimating $\tau(x)$. It involves a two-step process where first, base learners are used to predict $\hat{\mu}_1(x)$ and $\hat{\mu}_0(x)$ on treated and control subsamples respectively, and second, the CATE is estimated by taking the difference between the predicted values:

$$\hat{\tau}_T(x) = \hat{\mu}_1(x) - \hat{\mu}_0(x). \tag{16.5}$$

This approach has been studied with linear regression (Athey and Imbens, 2016) and tree-based algorithms (Foster et al., 2011) as the base learners. When used with trees, this method is often referred to as the *Two Tree* (TT) estimator.

Despite the simplicity of this approach, the T-Learner generally performs poorly in terms of producing unbiased estimates of $\tau(x)$. This is mainly due to the fact that the response functions, $\hat{\mu}_1(x)$ and $\hat{\mu}_0(x)$, are trained separately, not together. In other words, the function does not take into account the controls when predicting potential outcomes for the treated, and vice versa. This is especially problematic in study designs where the number of treated and control observations is unbalanced. In most observational studies using administrative or survey data, the number of control observations exceeds the number of treated observations.[2] This disparity can lead to biased effect estimates, if the fitted response functions for treated and controls vary in terms of complexity. For example, the fitted control function may be more prone to overfitting, while the fitted treated function may be more prone to underfitting. As a result, their difference may not be a good estimator for $\tau(x)$ (Künzel et al., 2019a).

Another issue with the T-Learner is that if the base learners are regularised to solve overfitting, this could unintentionally generate regularisation bias in the CATE estimate. Nie and Wager (2021) demonstrate this point with an example where the LASSO algorithm is used to estimate $\hat{\mu}_1(x)$ and $\hat{\mu}_0(x)$ in the following linear model, $Y_i(d) = X_i \beta_{(d)} + \varepsilon_i(d)$. If the treated and control groups are fitted with two separate LASSO functions,

$$\hat{\beta}_d = argmin_{\beta(w)} \left\{ \sum_{i:D_i=d} (Y_i - X_i\beta_d)^2 + \lambda_d \| \beta_d \|_1 \right\}, \tag{16.6}$$

where $\lambda_{(d)}$ is the tuning parameter that penalises the flexibility of the model. The CATE estimator is then $\hat{\tau}(x) = x(\hat{\beta}_1 - \hat{\beta}_0)$. Since $\hat{\beta}_1$ and $\hat{\beta}_0$ are separately regularised toward zero (that is, the regression shrinks the coefficients towards zero), $\hat{\beta}_1 - \hat{\beta}_0$ is regularised away from zero as a result. This means that $\hat{\tau}(x)$ may display heterogeneity even when the true $\tau(x)$ is near or equal to zero. Therefore, the T-Learner performs well when there exists heterogeneity in treatment effects.

When the treatment effect is simpler, the T-Learner performs less well since it is unable to identify and replicate a common behaviour in the treated and control response functions.

S-Learner

Closely related to the T-Learner is the S-Learner (where "S" means "single"). The key difference is that the treatment D_i is not given any special status and is considered just another covariate in the vector X_i. Therefore, instead of estimating separate response functions for treated and controls, CATE estimation is performed in a single step using a combined response function for all observations:

$$\hat{\tau}_S(x) = \hat{\mu}(x,1) - \hat{\mu}(x,0). \tag{16.7}$$

The estimated CATE $\hat{\tau}(x)$ can be calculated as the difference in expected outcome when treatment status changes from 0 to 1. Any heterogeneity picked up by the S-Learner is therefore driven by the interaction between D_i and X_i. This approach has been studied with regression trees (Athey and Imbens, 2015) and BARTs (Green and Kern, 2012; Hill, 2011) as the base learners. When used with regression trees, this method is referred to as the *Single Tree* (ST) algorithm.

Since treatment is not given any special status, the base learner used to estimate the response function is not obliged to pick up heterogeneity if it does not exist, that is, when $\tau(x) = \tau$. For this reason, base learners that use regularisation techniques to control model complexity (such as the LASSO and tree-based methods) could end up ignoring the treatment variable if it is not a strong predictor of the outcome. This works well when there exists little or no heterogeneity in treatment effects. However, when heterogeneity does exist, and the treatment indicator is not strongly predictive of the outcome, the S-Learner could unintentionally shrink the treatment effects toward zero. In addition, by pooling the data across treated and controls, the S-Learner avoids fitting different functions of X_i for $Y_i(1)$ and $Y_i(0)$. This is particularly problematic when effect heterogeneity is strong, and the respective treated and control response functions of the treated and controls are very different. The S-Learner does not perform so well in such circumstances.

X-Learner

There are challenges associated with both the T-Learner and S-Learner. First, they are unable to adapt to structural properties of the CATE, if known. For example, prior knowledge about the sparseness or smoothness (that is, less "noise") of the underlying treatment effect could determine the choice of regression or adaptive estimator. Second, they do not perform well in unbalanced study designs due to regularisation bias, as described earlier. Künzel et al. (2019a) propose the X-Learner, which builds on the T-Learner and S-Learner, and addresses some of the above concerns. It uses information from the control group to better predict treated outcomes, and vice versa. In particular, it can adapt to the structural nature of the CATE, which is useful given that the treatment effect is often linear or constant. The premise behind the X-Learner is to estimate $\hat{\mu}_1$ and $\hat{\mu}_0$ in such a way that, regardless of any variation in the complexity of the fitted treated and control response functions, the difference remains a good estimator for $\tau(x)$. The X-Learner can be implemented in four stages:

1. Estimate the response functions $\mu_1(x)$ and $\mu_0(x)$ using any non-parametric regression or supervised machine learning algorithm (referred to as base learners of the first stage).

2. Impute the treatment effects based on the response functions from the first stage. The control-outcome estimator (for treated observations) is subtracted from the observed treated outcomes, and the observed control outcomes are subtracted from the treatment-outcome estimator (for control observations) to give the imputed treatment effects:

$$\tilde{\tau}_i^1 = Y_i(1) - \hat{\mu}_0(X_i(1)) \tag{16.8}$$

$$\tilde{\tau}_i^0 = \hat{\mu}_1(X_i(0)) - Y_i(0), \tag{16.9}$$

where $Y_i(0)$ and $Y_i(1)$ are the ith observed control and treated observations and $X_i(0)$ and $X_i(1)$ are the associated covariate vectors.

3. Estimate $\tau(x)$ for treated and controls separately by regressing the imputed treatment effects from the second stage $\tilde{\tau}_i$ on the covariate vector X_i. Use any regression or supervised machine learning algorithm (base learners of the second stage):

$$\hat{\tau}_1(x) = E[\tilde{\tau}_i^1 | X = x] \tag{16.10}$$

$$\hat{\tau}_0(x) = E[\tilde{\tau}_i^0 | X = x]. \tag{16.11}$$

4. Define the X-Learner CATE estimate as the weighted average of $\hat{\tau}_0(x)$ and $\hat{\tau}_1(x)$ from step 3:

$$\hat{\tau}_X(x) = g(x)\hat{\tau}_0(x) + (1 - g(x))\hat{\tau}_1(x), \tag{16.12}$$

where $g \in [0, 1]$ is a weighting function chosen by the analyst to minimise the variance of $\hat{\tau}(x)$. Künzel et al. (2019a) recommend using the estimated propensity score $\hat{e}(x)$ as a potential value for $g(x)$, explaining that in study designs with more control observations than treated, $\hat{\tau}(x)$ will be similar to $\hat{\tau}_1(x)$ since $\hat{e}(x)$ will be small. Alternatively, the value of $g(x)$ can also be set to 1 and 0 to appropriately weight the treated and control observations in unbalanced study designs. The X-Learner produces an estimate of the ITE based on the respondent's covariate profile X_i. The estimated ITEs can be aggregated to the ATE for the entire population, or the GATE for a pre-specified subgroup of interest.

The X-Learner has several advantages compared to the T- and S-Learners. It performs particularly well in unbalanced study designs, or when there is prior knowledge about the structural form of the treatment effect and response functions. It can also reduce any errors inherent in the estimated response functions by including the additional imputation step in the CATE construction. Weighting the CATE estimate by the propensity score can further help to stabilise these errors. See Figure 16.2 for a workflow of the X-Learner.

In general, when the treatment effect is zero or constant, the X-Learner performs better than the T-Learner. The best performing meta-learner in this scenario, however, is the S-Learner, since pooling the treated and control observations is more appropriate when estimating the response function. When there is substantial heterogeneity in treatment effects, and the response functions for treated and controls are very different, the T- and X-Learners will

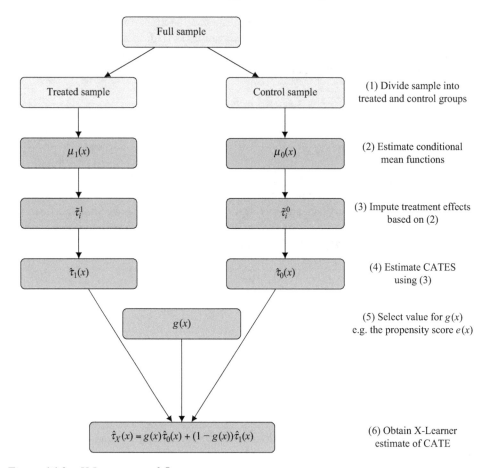

Figure 16.2   X-Learner workflow

perform well since they avoid pooling the data. Although there is no best performing meta-learner given any situation, the X-Learner has the overall best performance according to simulations performed by Künzel et al. 2019a. Further, since the X-Learner does not make any parametric assumptions about the CATE, approximate confidence intervals can be constructed through bootstrapped samples of the training and test data.

The T-, S- and X-Learners are not doubly robust estimators and therefore require an additional pre-processing step to ensure balance between treated and control groups in a selection on observables framework. In their paper, Künzel et al. (2019a) show that under this framework, all three meta-learners are able to handle confounding. Alternatively, there are recent papers that attempt to extend the concept of meta-learners to doubly robust estimation. Kennedy (2020) proposes the *DR-Learner*: a two-stage estimator that constructs estimates of the nuisance parameters in the first stage, followed by a second stage regression that estimates inverse probability-weighted "pseudo-outcomes" on a covariate vector. The estimator relies heavily on sample splitting for each stage and cross-fitting to obtain a final doubly robust estimate of $\tau(x)$. Foster and Syrgkanis (2020) develop an orthogonal learner, where $\tau(x)$ is the minimiser of some expected loss function. Sample splitting is used to estimate the propensity score and the target parameter separately using any two "black-box" algorithms, provided that the nuisance parameter estimation error achieves a guaranteed excess risk bound. This robustness to the estimation error enables the meta-learner to use complex models that achieve the oracle rate. An alternative, more established, doubly robust meta-learner is the *R-Learner* by Nie and Wager (2021).

3.2 R-Learner

Nie and Wager (2021) propose an alternative framework for estimating CATEs using a partially linear model. The latter method was originally formalised by Robinson (1988) to estimate the parametric components in partially linear models but has since become popular in the causal machine learning literature for semiparametric estimation (Athey et al., 2019b; Chernozhukov et al., 2018a). The set-up for the CATE estimator is motivated by the potential outcomes framework. The partially linear model for treatment effect heterogeneity is denoted as

$$Y_i = \mu_0(X_i) + D_i \tau(X_i) + \varepsilon, \tag{16.13}$$

where the shape of $\mu_0(X_i)$ is unspecified. Under the unconfoundedness assumption:

$$E[\varepsilon_i \mid X_i, D_i] = 0, \ where \ \varepsilon_i = Y_i - \mu_0(X_i) - D\tau(X_i). \tag{16.14}$$

Given the conditional mean outcome, $m(X_i) = E[Y_i \mid X_i = x] = \mu_0(X_i) + e(X_i)\tau(X_i)$, where $e(X_i) = E[D_i = 1 \mid X]$, the CATE function $\tau(x)$ can be rewritten in centred form

$$Y_i - m(X_i) = \tau(X_i)(D_i - e(X_i)) + \varepsilon_i. \tag{16.15}$$

This decomposition is referred to as Robinson's transformation and can be used to estimate treatment effect heterogeneity by incorporating modern, machine learning tools.

If there is prior knowledge that $\tau(x)$ is constant for some neighbourhood of X_i, that is, $\tau(x) = \tau$ for all $x \in \mathcal{X}$, the partially linear model can be solved locally over $\mathcal{X}$ in three steps:

1. Predict $\hat{e}(X_i)$ and $\hat{m}(X_i)$ using any supervised machine learning algorithm.
2. Estimate $\hat{V}_i = D_i - \hat{e}(X_i)$ and $\hat{U}_i = Y_i - \hat{m}_i(X_i)$.
3. Regress $\hat{V}_i$ on $\hat{U}_i$ (that is, a residual-on-residual regression) over $\mathcal{X}$ to estimate $\tau(x)$:

$$\hat{\tau}(x) = \frac{\sum\limits_{i: X_i \in \mathcal{N}(x)} (Y_i - \hat{m}^{-i}(X_i))(D_i - \hat{e}^{-i}(X_i))}{\sum\limits_{i: X_i \in \mathcal{N}(x)} D_i - \hat{e}^{-i}(X_i))^2}, \tag{16.16}$$

where $\hat{m}^{-i}(X_i)$ and $\hat{e}^{-i}(X_i)$ are *leave-one-out* predictions, that is, a form of cross-fitting where the training data are split into $k = N$ subsamples and predictions are made on $k - 1$ subsamples. This estimator is semiparametrically efficient for $\tau(x)$ under unconfoundedness (Chernozhukov et al., 2018a; Robinson, 1988). However, it also relies on the strong assumption that $\tau(x)$ is homogeneous within a given neighbourhood of X_i, which is often unknown. There are different approaches to selecting the neighbourhood function, including k-nearest neighbours and kernel averaging. A common approach is to use the random forests algorithm to generate kernel weights by averaging tree-based neighbourhoods. We explore tree-based methods in more detail in the next section.

The CATE estimator in (16.16) is designed for estimating locally constant treatment effects. However, Nie and Wager (2021) show that it can be used in combination with the partially linear model to motivate a loss function $L_n(\tau(x))$ that captures a global estimate of heterogeneous treatment effects:

$$\tau(x) = argmin_{\tau'}\left\{E[(Y_i - m(X_i) - (D_i - e(X_i))(\tau'(X_i))^2]\right\}. \qquad (16.17)$$

The loss function is equivalent to minimising the squared error of the CATE function in (16.15). However, it is dependent on the unknown quantities $m(x)$ and $e(x)$, thus making it unfeasible. The solution is to use a two-step estimator, referred to as the *R-learner* (in recognition of Robinson (1988) and the focus on residualisation):

1. Estimate $\hat{m}(x)$ and $\hat{e}(x)$ using any supervised machine learning algorithm.
2. Estimate $\tau(x)$ via a plug-in version of the loss function,

$$\hat{L}_n(\tau(x)) = \frac{1}{n}\sum_{i=1}^{n}((Y_i - \hat{m}^{-i}(X_i)) - (D_i - \hat{e}^{-i}(X_i))\tau(X_i))^2, \qquad (16.18)$$

where the squared loss $\hat{L}_n(\tau(x))$ is referred to as the *R-loss*.
3. Optimise $\hat{L}(\tau(x))$ using any supervised machine learning algorithm.
4. Tune the algorithm by cross-validation on $\hat{L}(\tau(x))$,

$$\hat{L}_n(\tau(x)) = \frac{1}{n}\{\sum_{i=1}^{n}((Y_i - \hat{m}^{-i}(X_i)) - (D_i - \hat{e}^{-i}(X_i))\tau(X_i))^2 + \alpha_n(\tau(x))\}, \qquad (16.19)$$

where $\alpha_n(\tau(x))$ is a regulariser (or tuning parameter) that controls the complexity of the R-loss. Cross-fitting should be used to address any bias from regularisation.

The R-learner has certain advantages over other methods that estimate $\tau(x)$ in a single estimation step (Powers et al., 2018; Shalit et al., 2017; Wager and Athey, 2018). By separating the estimator into various tasks, the structure of the loss function is able to control for any correlation between $e(x)$ and $m(x)$ prior to estimating $\tau(x)$. This separation of tasks also provides more flexibility in terms of the choice of machine learning algorithm used for optimising the R-loss. The optimisation task is essentially an empirical minimisation problem, which can be solved using various off-the-shelf algorithms, that is, algorithms that do not need to be modified to control for confounding. Therefore, the choice of algorithm will depend solely on its ability to optimise the R-Loss on unseen test data. Since the R-Learner is based on semiparametric efficiency and orthogonality, Nie and Wager (2021) show that if the treatment effect function $\tau(x)$ is simpler than the nuisance parameter functions $m(x)$ and $e(x)$, then $\hat{\tau}(x)$ obtained from equation (16.19) may converge faster than $\hat{m}(x)$ and $\hat{e}(x)$. In other words, if $\hat{m}(x)$ and $\hat{e}(x)$ are $o(n^{-1/4})$ consistent for $m(x)$ and $e(X)$, respectively, in RMSE, then the rate of convergence for $\hat{\tau}(x)$ may be faster and will depend only on the complexity of the treatment effect function.

The R-Learner can be implemented using the `rlearner` package in R by Nie and Wager (2021). Although it can be used in combination with any base learner with optimal predictive performance, its involvement in tree-based causal machine learning has sparked a separate, rapidly growing strand of literature linking tree-based methods, causal inference and orthogonalisation.

4. TREE-BASED METHODS

In this section, we explore the family of tree-based machine learning methods that can be used to estimate $\tau(x)$. The literature on heterogeneous treatment effect estimation using tree-based algorithms is continuously evolving. We provide a few examples of the more notable contributions to the field, starting with the work by Green and Kern (2012), Hill (2011) and Hill and Su (2013) on Bayesian regression trees (BART) (Chipman et al., 2010), an ensemble method that uses the prior to regularise the fitted CATE function. Hahn et al. (2020) further adapt the BART model for problems of causal inference by incorporating the estimated propensity score function into the response model, thus inducing a covariate dependent prior on the estimated CATE function. Foster et al. (2011) apply random forests to estimate effects in treated and control groups separately, taking the differences as predicted values and subsequently running regression or classification trees to find covariates strongly associated with treatment effects. Athey et al. (2019b) and Wager and Athey (2018) develop causal estimators based on classification and regression trees (CARTs), providing the first inferential theory for CATEs using the infinitesimal jackknife – a method of estimating confidence intervals and standard errors using variance estimates from random forests (Efron, 2014; Wager et al., 2014). This contribution moves forest-based methods away from the group of so-called *black box* machine learning estimators toward those established in causal inference methodology for rigorous asymptotic analysis (Wager and Athey, 2018). The popularity of tree-based algorithms stems from their ability to flexibly model covariate treatment interactions, even in high-dimensional settings. They also possess attractive asymptotic properties, which we discuss further later in the section.

We begin with a description of the Classification and Regression Tree (CART); a classic yet powerful decision tree algorithm that provides a foundation for tree-based algorithms. Causal trees are an adaptation of the conventional CART algorithm, developed by economists interested in causal inference as opposed to prediction. We describe the framework for estimating CATEs using causal trees. Next, we move onto ensemble tree-based methods, known as forests, which tend to outperform individual trees. Random forests and causal forests represent ensembles of CARTs and causal trees, respectively. Finally, we show that by combining the adaptive nature of forest-based algorithms with the orthogonalisation of the R-Learner described earlier, causal forests can produce accurate, doubly robust CATE estimates.

4.1 Classification and Regression Trees (CARTs)

CARTs were formalised by Breiman et al. (1984) to aid prediction tasks. The objective is to estimate the conditional expectation $E(Y_i \mid X_i = x)$ based on the covariates and outcomes for observations in a training sample. A covariate profile and threshold are selected that minimise the in-sample loss function, and the CART algorithm splits the sample into two regions in an iterative process. There are two key features of the CART: initial construction of the tree and cross-validation to select a penalty on tree depth.

We use Hastie et al. (2009) to describe the CART framework using the same notation as before, but now introducing p as the number of covariates in the vector X. The CART partitions X into M regions (also known as *terminal nodes* or *leaves*), $R_1, R_2, \ldots, R_M$. The parts of the tree connecting the nodes are referred to as *branches*. Let x_j be a splitting variable, s be a split threshold and $R_1(j,s) = \{X \mid X_j \leq s\}$ and $R_2(j,s) = \{X \mid X_j > s\}$. The algorithm seeks the pair (j,s) that minimises the SSR,

$$\min_{j,s} [\sum_{x_i \in R_1(j,s)} (Y_i - \hat{\delta}_1)^2 + \sum_{x_i \in R_2(j,s)} (Y_i - \hat{\delta}_2)^2], \tag{16.20}$$

where $\hat{\delta}_1$ and $\hat{\delta}_2$ are the estimated conditional means for training observations in R_1 and R_2, respectively. This splitting process is repeated recursively until a tree-like structure is formed. Each region R_m contains either a single observation or a group of observations with similar values of Y. The outcome for unit i in region R_m with covariate profile $X_i = x$ is estimated as the average outcome for all units in the same region. This splitting process, known as *recursive binary partitioning*, is a *top-down*, *greedy* algorithm: top-down meaning that the splitting process begins at the top of the tree; and greedy in that at each split decision, the optimal split is selected at that particular point (as opposed to choosing a split that could produce a better tree in a future split).

Tree depth is a tuning parameter that controls the model's complexity. A larger tree could overfit the data and may not work well out of sample. Alternatively, a smaller tree could underfit the data and may not capture all of the important patterns. The objective is to control the complexity of the model to prevent overfitting while also finding an optimal tree size that maximises predictive performance, that is optimising the bias-variance trade-off. There are two ways to approach this using regularisation. The first approach is to build the tree such that the decrease in SSR at each split exceeds some specified threshold. However, the problem is that a worthless split higher up in the tree could be succeeded by a much better split lower down. The second, more preferred option is to grow a large tree, stopping only when a minimum node size is realised, and then to *prune* it back using a tuning parameter α to create a subtree $T \subset T_0$. T is obtained by collapsing any number of non-terminal tree nodes. For each value of α, there exists a subtree $T \subset T_0$ that minimises the loss function:

$$L_\alpha(T) = \sum_{m=1}^{|T|} \sum_{x_i \in R_m} (Y_i - \hat{\delta}_m)^2 + \alpha |T|, \tag{16.21}$$

where $\hat{\delta}_m = \frac{1}{N_{R_m}} \sum_{x_i \in R_m} Y_i$, $N_{R_m} = \#(x_i \in R_m)$ and $|T|$ is the number of terminal nodes. Adding a penalty term avoids overfitting since we only consider splits where the improvement in goodness of fit is above some threshold. The tuning parameter $\alpha \geq 0$ controls the trade-off between tree size and goodness of fit. Larger values of α lead to smaller trees, and vice versa for smaller values of α. The optimal value is selected through k-fold cross-validation, and the subtree that corresponds with the chosen value of α is subsequently used.

4.2 Causal Trees

Causal trees were developed by Athey and Imbens (2015) as a way of adapting CARTs to problems of causal inference. Conventional machine learning methods, such as CARTs, rely on the *ground truth* being observed to conduct regularisation for tuning the objective function. However, the fundamental problem of causal inference means that the ground truth is unobserved. Causal trees enable machine learning to be used for estimating causal effects and conducting inference. They differ from CARTs in two ways. First, their objective is to estimate heterogeneous treatment effects, as opposed to predicting outcomes. Their resulting leaf estimates R_m represent the difference in conditional means, that is CATEs, rather than just mean outcomes. The treatment effect $\hat{\tau}(x)$ for any $x \in R_m$ can be estimated as

$$\hat{\tau}(x) = \frac{1}{|i:D_i=1, X_i \in R_m|} \sum_{i:D_i=1, X_i \in R_m} Y_i - \frac{1}{|i:D=0, X_i \in R_m|} \sum_{i:D=0, X_i \in R_m} Y_i. \quad (16.22)$$

Second, causal trees are estimated using *honest* methods. This means that the training data used to construct the tree and estimate the leaf-specific effects is partitioned, so that separate training and estimation samples are used for each task respectively (Athey and Imbens, 2016). Honest methods differ from *adaptive* methods, more commonly used in conventional machine learning, where the same sample of data is used for both tasks. We explain in more detail the concepts of adaptive and honest estimation in the following section. Athey and Imbens (2016) propose an honest approach for constructing unbiased estimates of the MSE of the causal effect of the treatment.

4.2.1   Adaptive and honest trees

We start by introducing some new notation. Let $\mathcal{S}^{tr}$ denote the training sample, $\mathcal{S}^{te}$ the testing sample, and $\mathcal{S}^{est}$ the independent estimation sample, where $\mathcal{S}^{est} \subset \mathcal{S}^{tr}$. Let Π represent a partitioning of the covariate vector X_i, π be an algorithm that partitions the full sample N into M regions and $R_m(x, \Pi)$ denote the leaf $R_m \in \Pi$ such that $x \in R_m$.

We define the loss function for minimising the MSE_δ in adaptive CARTs as

$$L^A(\delta, \pi) = E_{\mathcal{S}^{te}, \mathcal{S}^{tr}} \left[\frac{1}{N^{te}} \sum_{i \in \mathcal{S}^{te}} (Y_i - \hat{\delta}(X_i; \mathcal{S}^{tr}, \pi(\mathcal{S}^{tr})))^2 \right], \quad (16.23)$$

where N^{te} is the number of observations in the test sample. Note that the same training sample $\mathcal{S}^{tr}$ is used to partition the tree and estimate the conditional means. The tree is evaluated over $\mathcal{S}^{te}$.

Athey and Imbens (2016) challenge the validity of adaptive methods, highlighting that performing both tasks on the training sample can lead to overfitting. While this is not so much of an issue for CARTs, this can pose certain problems for causal trees since we cannot observe the counterfactual. The estimated CATEs may not reflect true heterogeneity, but noise idiosyncratic to the sample. For example, if there are extreme values of Y_i in the training sample, they could appear in both tree construction and estimation tasks. If these extreme values are placed into the same leaf as other extreme values by the estimation algorithm π, the conditional means in $\mathcal{S}^{tr}$ would be more extreme (that is, higher and lower) than they would on a separate estimation sample. This could result in poor coverage probabilities in confidence intervals. The authors suggest that honest methods can overcome the challenges of adaptive methods in two ways. First, by imposing a separation in data used to grow the tree and predict $\hat{\tau}$. The loss function for minimising MSE in honest causal trees can therefore be defined as

$$L^H(\tau,\pi) = E_{\mathcal{S}^{est},\mathcal{S}^{est},\mathcal{S}^{tr}}\left[\frac{1}{N^{te}}\sum_{i\in\mathcal{S}^{te}}(\tau_i - \hat{\tau}(X_i;\mathcal{S}^{est},\pi(\mathcal{S}^{tr})))^2\right]. \tag{16.24}$$

The tree structure is constructed using $\mathcal{S}^{tr}$, and the predictions $\hat{\tau}$ are obtained using $\mathcal{S}^{est}$. Second, by modifying the splitting function to incorporate the fact that $\mathcal{S}^{est}$ will produce unbiased leaf estimates (thus reducing one aspect of overfitting), and that a larger tree will increase the variance of these estimates. The honest splitting criterion for causal trees aims to minimise the expectation of $\mathrm{MSE}_\tau(\Pi)$, $\mathrm{EMSE}_\tau(\Pi)$, over the test and estimation samples:

$$\widehat{\mathrm{EMSE}}_\tau(\mathcal{S}^{tr},N^{est},\Pi) \equiv -\frac{1}{N^{tr}}\sum_{i\in\mathcal{S}^{tr}}\hat{\tau}^2(X_i;\mathcal{S}^{tr},R) + \left(\frac{1}{N^{tr}} + \frac{1}{N^{est}}\right)\cdot\sum_{\ell\in R}\left(\frac{S^2_{\mathcal{S}^{tr}_{treat}(\ell)}}{p} + \frac{S^2_{\mathcal{S}^{tr}_{control}(\ell)}}{1-p}\right),$$

$$\tag{16.25}$$

where p is the probability of being in the treatment group, and $S^2_{\mathcal{S}^{tr}_{treat}(\ell)}$ and $S^2_{\mathcal{S}^{tr}_{control}(\ell)}$ are the within-leaf variances of the training sample for treated and control observations. The honest criterion is based on the assumption that $\hat{\tau}$ is constant within each leaf and consists of two terms. The first term rewards partitions that find strong heterogeneity. The second term penalises partitions that create variance in the within-leaf estimates. A key difference between the honest criterion for CARTs and causal trees is that in the case of CARTs, both terms select covariates that predict heterogeneity in outcomes, whereas in the case of causal trees, both terms select different types of covariates that maximise heterogeneity in treatment effects. Therefore, the greater the heterogeneity in the leaf estimates, or the lower the within-leaf variance, the greater the improvement in EMSE_τ.

Although the honest splitting criterion is an unbiased estimator for EMSE_τ, repeatedly using the same training sample for constructing the tree can generate some bias. This is because splits higher up in the tree tend to place observations with extreme values into the same leaf. Therefore, after the initial splits, the within-leaf variance of observations in the training sample tends to be lower than the variance would be on an unseen, independent sample. In other words, as the tree is grown deeper, $\widehat{\mathrm{EMSE}}_\tau$ is likely to overstate goodness of fit. Cross-validation can help to reduce this bias by evaluating each partition Π using the cross-validation sample $\mathcal{S}^{tr,cv}$ instead of $\mathcal{S}^{tr,tr}$.

4.3   Forests

A major limitation of CARTs and causal trees is their instability to small changes in the training data. Leaf estimates are therefore susceptible to high variability, or *noise*. Breiman (2001) suggests that instead of searching for a single optimal tree, averaging across a number of unpruned trees can produce better results. Since individual, unpruned trees have low bias and high variance, ensembling helps to reduce the variance of leaf estimates, as well as smoothing decision boundaries (Bühlmann and Yu, 2002).

Random forests, introduced by Breiman (2001), are an ensemble method that make predictions by averaging across B unpruned and *decorrelated* trees. This decorrelation is attained using two approaches: (1) the forest is constructed using bagging, in that for each tree, $b = 1, \ldots, B$, a bootstrap sample S_b is drawn from the training data without replacement; and (2) the tree is grown using recursive partitioning, but at each tree node a random subset m of p covariates is considered for the split decision, where $m \leq p$. This procedure decorrelates trees that would otherwise split on similar covariates that are (most likely) strong predictors of the outcome (Amit and Geman, 1997). The random forest predicts $\hat{\mu}(X)$ as the average of B tree predictions $\hat{\mu}_b(x)$:

$$\hat{\mu}(x) = \frac{1}{B} \sum_{b=1}^{B} \sum_{i=1}^{n} \frac{Y_i \mathbf{1}(X_i \in L_b(x), i \in S_b)}{|i : X_i \in L_b(x), i \in S_b|}, \tag{16.26}$$

where $L_b(x)$ denotes the set of training examples falling into the same leaf as $X_i = x$ (Athey et al., 2019b).

It has been well studied that random forests can be viewed as a type of adaptive neighbourhood with weights (Lin and Jeon, 2006). This idea was first introduced by Hothorn et al. (2004) for survival analysis and Meinshausen (2006) for quantile regression. They show that this adaptive neighbourhood can be used to weight a set of neighbours for a given test point $X_i = x$, which can subsequently be used to solve a local moment equation for a target parameter of interest (Lin and Jeon, 2006). Although neighbourhood weights are usually obtained by kernel functions, this method does not perform well in high dimensions. Athey et al. (2019b) suggest that forest-based algorithms can be used instead, by averaging neighbourhoods generated across B trees:

$$w_{bi}(x) = \frac{1}{B} \sum_{b=1}^{B} \frac{\mathbf{1}(X_i \in \ell_b(x))}{|L_b(x)|}, \quad w_i(x) = \frac{1}{B} \sum_{b=1}^{B} w_{bi}(x), \tag{16.27}$$

where w_i are the weights that sum to 1. The random forest weighting function works by initially giving equal weight to observations in the training sample that fall into the same leaf as the test point $X_i = x$, and zero weight to the remaining observations. The forest then averages the weightings across all B trees and calculates the frequency with which the i-th training example falls into the same leaf as x. The weights $w_i(x)$ are larger for observations where $E[Y_i | X = X_i]$ is similar to $E[Y_i | X = x]$ (Meinshausen, 2006). These weights can be used to solve for $\mu(x)$:

$$\hat{\mu}(x) = \frac{1}{B} \sum_{b=1}^{B} \sum_{i=1}^{n} Y_i \frac{\mathbf{1}(X_i \in \ell_b(x))}{|L_b(x)|} = \sum_{i=1}^{n} Y_i w_{bi}(x). \tag{16.28}$$

Athey et al. (2019b) develop an estimator, which they term *generalised random forests* (GRFs), that can estimate any target parameter of interest $\theta(x)$, identified through local moment conditions:

$$\hat{\theta} \in \operatorname{argmin} \left\{ \sum_{i=1}^{n} w_i(x) \psi_{\theta(x)}(Y_i) \right\}, \tag{16.29}$$

where $\psi(\cdot)$ is some prediction function. They have developed the comprehensive `grf` package in R, which implements the GRF algorithm in a number of steps. The algorithm builds a forest to calculate a weighted set of neighbours for each test point x and then uses these neighbours to solve (16.29). GRFs retain several features of the core random forests algorithm, including greedy recursive partitioning, bagging and decorrelation, but no longer make predictions by averaging estimates across an ensemble of trees. Instead, they make predictions over a weighted average of an ensemble of trees. The forest is also grown using honest methods, in that tree construction and estimation of the various parameters are performed on separate subsamples. The main difference in the tree-building process is that GRFs search for splits that maximise heterogeneity in $\theta(x)$ across the leaves. Once the forest has been grown, the GRF algorithm obtains a prediction in the following steps:

1. Each test point is dropped down each tree to determine which leaf it falls into.
2. The neighbouring training points are weighted by the frequency with which the training point falls into the same leaf as the test point.
3. A prediction $\hat{\theta}$ is obtained using the weighted list of neighbours and the relevant type of forest (selected using the appropriate `grf` function) given the target parameter of interest.

For prediction problems, $\hat{\theta}(x)$ is the average outcome of the neighbours of test point x. For causal problems, $\hat{\theta}(x)$ is the treatment effect, calculated using the outcomes and treatment status of the neighbours of test point x. The GRF estimator is asymptotically normal, therefore confidence intervals for $\hat{\theta}(x)$ can be constructed using plug-in or bootstrap methods.

When applied to causal problems, GRFs can be referred to as *causal forests*. The target parameter of interest is the CATE, where $\theta(x) = \xi \cdot \tau(x)$ for some contrast $\xi \in \mathbb{R}^p$, that can be identified by (16.29) with $\psi_{\tau(x),\mu_0(x)}(Y_i,D_i) = Y_i - \tau(x) - \mu_0(x))(1 \quad D_i^T)^T$, where μ_0 is an intercept term. After the weights have been obtained using (16.29), the estimator $\hat{\tau}(x)$ for $\tau(x)$ is

$$\hat{\tau}(x) = \frac{\sum_{i=1}^{n} w_i(x)(D_i - \bar{D}_w)(Y_i - \bar{Y}_w)}{\sum_{i=1}^{n} w_i(x)(D_i - \bar{D}_w^2)}, \qquad (16.30)$$

where $\bar{D}_w = \Sigma w_i(x)D_i$ and $\bar{Y}_w = \Sigma w_i(x)Y_i$.

Each tree is grown using recursive partitioning so that at each splitting node P (often called the parent node) the aim is to minimise $\text{err}(R_1, R_2)$. However, this minimisation is infeasible as the value of $\theta(\tau, X)$ is unknown and only identified through a moment condition. Athey et al. (2019b) convert this minimisation problem into a maximisation problem:

$$max \; \Delta(R_1, R_2) := \frac{N_{R_1} N_{R_2}}{N_P^2} (\hat{\theta}_{R_1}(\tau) - \hat{\theta}_{R_2}(\tau))^2, \qquad (16.31)$$

where N_{R_1}, N_{R_2} and N_P are the number of observations in the two child nodes (or regions) and the parent node. However, maximising $\Delta(R_1, R_2)$ while also solving for $\hat{\theta}_{R_1}$ and $\hat{\theta}_{R_2}$ in each potential child node using (16.28) is computationally expensive. Instead, the authors suggest maximising an approximate criterion $\tilde{\Delta}(R_1, R_2)$ constructed using gradient-based approximations for $\hat{\theta}_{R_1}$ and $\hat{\theta}_{R_2}$. This requires first computing A_P as the gradient of the expectation of the moment condition: $A_P = \frac{1}{|\{i:X_i \in P\}|}\Sigma_{\{i:X_i \in P\}} \nabla \psi_{\theta(x)}(Y_i)$. When applied to causal forests for estimating $\tau(x)$,

$$A_P = \frac{1}{|\{i:X_i \in P\}|} \sum_{\{i:X_i \in P\}} (D - \bar{D}_P)^{\otimes 2}, \qquad (16.32)$$

where $\bar{D}_p$ is the average of treatment status over the parent P. Given A_p, the pseudo outcomes ρ_i required for the splits can be constructed: $\rho_i = -\xi^T A_P^{-1} \psi_{\hat{\theta}_p(\tau), \hat{v}_p(\tau)}(Y_i)$. When applied to causal forests:

$$\rho_i = \xi^T A_P^{-1}(D_i - \bar{D}_P)(Y_i - \bar{Y}_P) - (D_i - \bar{D}_P)\hat{\tau}_P, \tag{16.33}$$

where $\bar{Y}_p$ is the average outcome over the parent P, and $\hat{\tau}_p$ is the solution of the least-squares regression of Y_i on D_i in the parent. The splitting rule from CARTs can then be performed on the pseudo outcomes ρ_i to maximise the approximate criterion:

$$\tilde{\Delta}(R_1, R_2) = \sum_{m=1}^{2} \frac{1}{|\{i : X_i \in R_m\}|} \left(\sum_{i:X_i \in R_m} \rho_i \right)^2. \tag{16.34}$$

Using this splitting criterion, the tree is grown recursively until the minimum node size is reached.

Although this construction enables asymptotically valid inference for $\tau(x)$, it is not robust to confounding in a selection on observables framework. Athey et al. (2019b) propose an alternative version of the causal forest estimator, motivated by the R-Learner in (16.19), that implements *local centring* to address confounding bias. As previously discussed, the R-Learner can be solved using any machine learning algorithm, and causal forests have become a popular solution. The idea is to orthogonalise the forest by partialling out the effect of X_i on Y_i and D_i using Robinson's transformation (Robinson, 1988). As before, the weights are quasi-automatically obtained from the GRF, and a gradient-based approximation is used to compute the psuedo-outcomes for recursive partitioning. The main difference is that D_i and Y_i in (16.33) are now replaced by $\hat{V}_i = D_i - \hat{e}^{-i}(X_i)$ and $\hat{U}_i = Y_i - \hat{m}^{-i}(X_i)$:

$$\rho_i = (\hat{V}_i - \bar{D}_P)(\hat{U}_i - \bar{Y}_P) - (\hat{V}_i - \bar{D}_P)\hat{\beta}_P) / Var_P(\hat{V}_i). \tag{16.35}$$

The causal forest implements the orthogonalised forest in a few steps. First, two separate regression forests are fitted to obtain estimates of the nuisance parameters $\hat{e}(X_i)$ and $\hat{m}(X_i)$. Second, these first-stage forests are used to make *out-of-bag* predictions for $\hat{e}(X_i)$ and $\hat{m}(X_i)$, where out-of-bag observations are those that have not been included in the bagged training data (Breiman, 1996). Third, the residualised treatment $W_i - \hat{e}(X_i)$ and outcome $Y_i - \hat{m}(X_i)$ are calculated, and the causal forest is then trained on these residuals. There are various tuning parameters in the causal forest that can be chosen by cross-validation on the R-Loss in (16.18) (see Appendix 16A.2 for a description of some of the available tuning parameters). The forests are trained using different values of $\alpha_n(\tau(x))$ for each parameter, and the ones that make out-of-bag estimates of the objective minimised in (16.18) as small as possible are selected. See Figure 16.3 for a workflow of the causal forest algorithm, motivated by the R-Learner.

In recent years, a number of algorithms for estimating $\theta(x)$ have been proposed that build upon the GRF framework and are robust to confounding. In particular, Oprescu et al. (2018) introduce *orthogonal random forests* that combines the causal forest algorithm of GRFs with the orthogonality concept from DML. The objective is to estimate $\theta(x)$ at a rate that is robust to the nuisance parameter estimation error. Unlike previous estimators, this approach enables non-parametric estimation of the target parameter on a low-dimensional set of covariates,

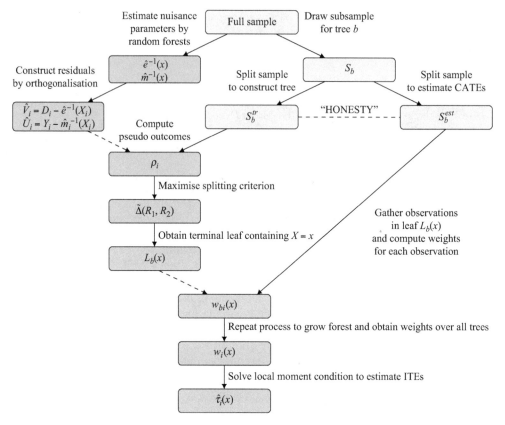

Figure 16.3   Causal forests with R-Learner workflow

while also controlling for a high-dimensional set of confounders. The treatment effect estimates are asymptotically normal and enable valid inference.

5.   CASE STUDY: THE IMPACT OF HEALTH INSURANCE ON HEALTH CARE SERVICE UTILISATION IN INDONESIA

We demonstrate the application of the X-learner, R-learner and causal forests algorithms to a policy impact evaluation of a national health insurance programme in Indonesia, the Jaminan Kesahatan Nasional (JKN). Using cross-sectional, individual-level data from Indonesia's national socioeconomic household survey (the SUSENAS) in 2017, we evaluate the ATE and CATE, where *treatment* corresponds to being covered by the health insurance programme through a subsidised scheme for the poor and disabled. We are interested in the effects of health insurance on health care utilisation, which we measure using a continuous variable for the total length of inpatient stay (in days) at any public or private medical facility in the previous year. We extract 97 variables from the SUSENAS data set to construct the covariate vector X_i, which contains both individual and household characteristics (see Appendix 16A.1 for a full list of included variables). The vector X_i includes two types of variables: *confounders*, that are associated with both the treatment and outcome; and *effect modifiers*, by which the treatment effects vary, as captured in the CATE function. We refer to the existing literature on health insurance and health care utilisation, both in Indonesia and other low- and middle-income countries, to guide our selection of confounders in X_i. As per the impact evaluation of Erlangga et al. (2019a), we control for characteristics that are determinants of health care–seeking behaviour, such as age, gender, marital status, education level and urban/rural place of residence. We additionally control for a number of socioeconomic factors including employment status and type, poverty status (based on the poverty line by province obtained from the Indonesian Central Bureau of Statistics), monthly household consumption expenditure per capita, dwelling characteristics, use of technology and measures of Social Security coverage (Erlangga et al., 2019a; Mulyanto et al., 2019a,b). Finally, we adjust for geographical differences by region (Mulyanto et al., 2019c). We do not include other measures of health status and health care utilisation, such as outpatient visits, that are potential mediators in the causal pathway between the treatment and outcome. An example of a confounder that we include in our model is whether the household is located in an urban or rural area. Urban residents are more likely to seek care compared to rural residents given easier access to health care facilities. They are also more likely to be beneficiaries of health insurance (OECD, 2019).

We anticipate that the impact of health insurance on health care utilisation varies across the population according to various effect modifiers. To motivate our understanding of potential covariates by which treatment effects may vary, we again refer to the existing literature to support our selection of population subgroups for which we will explore heterogeneity. Erlangga et al. (2019a) perform various subgroup analyses in their impact evaluation of JKN on health care utilisation. They explore variation in treatment effects stratified by certain variables: quintiles of the asset index, urban versus rural location and supply-side factors. Their results show that the policy increased the probability of inpatient utilisation among the richer quintiles, those living in rural areas and areas with a high density of health care facilities. Our data set does not include any supply-side variables therefore, we cannot include this in our analysis. However, we can explore CATEs across population subgroups using a measure of socioeconomic status (monthly household consumption expenditure per capita, for example) and a binary indicator for whether the household is located in an urban or rural area.

The final data set contains 912 812 observations, of which 475 930 are in the subsidised, treated group and 436 882 are in the uninsured, control group. Table 16.1 presents some key characteristics of the treated and control populations. Compared to the controls, the treated are more likely to be older, educated, in employment and married. Their home is more likely to be self-owned, in a rural location and without basic facilities. They also tend to have lower monthly consumption expenditure per capita and are defined as poor relative to the provincial poverty line. A key distinction between the two groups is in relation to Social Security, in that the treated are more likely to be beneficiaries than the controls. Geographically, there is some regional variation in where the treated and controls are located. Finally, on comparing the baseline difference in the outcome, the average length of inpatient stay for the treated is more than double that for the controls, even though the absolute values are very small. We include all respondents in our model, regardless of whether they had any inpatient stays to avoid complicating the analysis for our demonstrative purposes.

We provide a step-by-step guide on how to estimate our target parameters with our three selected algorithms using an identification strategy of selection on observables.

Table 16.1   Key descriptive statistics for selected variables included in our model, by health insurance status

	Uninsured (n=436,882)		Insured (n=475,930)		
	Mean	SD	Mean	SD	SMD
Outcome					
Inpatient length of stay (days)	0.116	1.181	0.249	2.132	−0.076
Individual characteristics					
Male	0.504	0.500	0.498	0.500	0.010
Age	28.5	20.5	31.7	20.0	−0.158
Educated	0.802	0.399	0.871	0.335	−0.188
Working	0.429	0.495	0.472	0.499	−0.087
Unemployed/retired	0.028	0.164	0.031	0.174	−0.020
Married	0.440	0.496	0.481	0.500	−0.083
Has used internet in past 3 months	0.209	0.407	0.197	0.397	0.031
Household characteristics					
Urban location	0.381	0.486	0.358	0.479	0.047
No. of people in household	4.556	1.864	4.678	1.894	−0.065
Owns house	0.833	0.373	0.855	0.352	−0.060
Has a private toilet facility	0.849	0.358	0.794	0.404	0.144
Purchases drinking water	0.396	0.489	0.367	0.482	0.061
Has electricity	0.961	0.195	0.933	0.250	0.124
Has experienced a natural disaster in past 1 year	0.132	0.339	0.167	0.373	−0.098
Has received Raskin in past 4 months	0.335	0.472	0.464	0.499	−0.264
Had a Social Security or family welfare card between Aug 16–Mar 17	0.079	0.270	0.296	0.457	−0.579
Did not have enough food to eat in past 1 year	0.258	0.438	0.304	0.460	−0.101
Has a savings account	0.437	0.496	0.405	0.491	0.065
Monthly expenditure per capita (IDR)	881 007	724 248	819 648	648 900	0.089
Poor	0.128	0.334	0.160	0.366	−0.090
Region: Sumatera	0.282	0.450	0.303	0.460	−0.047
Region: Jakarta	0.008	0.089	0.016	0.125	−0.074
Region: Jawa	0.298	0.457	0.253	0.435	0.010
Region: Bali, NTB, NTT	0.083	0.284	0.084	0.277	0.016
Region: Kalimantan	0.120	0.325	0.070	0.254	0.173
Region: Sulawesi	0.131	0.338	0.154	0.361	−0.067
Region: Maluku-Papua	0.073	0.260	0.120	0.325	−0.159

Note: SD = standard deviation, SMD = standardised mean difference.

We compare the resulting treatment effect estimates between the various methods and draw some conclusions about our impact evaluation problem.

Steps:

1. Estimate the nuisance parameters ($\hat{m}(X_i)$, $\hat{m}_1(X_i)$, $\hat{m}_0(X_i)$ and $\hat{e}(X_i)$) using regression and supervised machine learning methods.
2. Assess our assumption of strong ignorability (unconfoundedness and overlap) to confirm that the causal estimands of interest (that is, the ATE and CATE) can be adequately identified. Assess "balance" in the covariate distributions of the treated and controls, and adjust for any imbalances using the estimated propensity score.
3. Perform a simple ordinary least squares (OLS) regression of the outcome (total length of inpatient stay) on treatment (subsidised health insurance) to provide a benchmark for the direction of effects.
4. Estimate the ATE, ATT and ATC using methods that take into account any "imbalance" between treated and controls.
5. Assess heterogeneity in treatment effects by estimating ITEs using our selected machine learning algorithms.
6. Explore heterogeneity in treatment effects across population subgroups by estimating GATEs for specified covariates of interest.
7. Briefly summarise and discuss findings.

Step 1. We estimate the nuisance parameters using honest random forests, which can be implemented using the `regression_forest` function from the `grf` package (v1.2.0). The function includes a range of parameters for training and tuning the forest that can be adjusted by the researcher. We define some of these parameters in Appendix 16A.2 (for a full list of available parameters, see the `grf` help page). All tuneable parameters in our model are tuned by cross-validation using the tuning parameter default settings. The random forest also produces variance estimates by training small groups of trees and comparing the predictions within and across groups (see Appendix 16A.2 for details on variance estimation). The outcome regression (the "Y" model) generates predictions of $\hat{m}(X_i)$, $\hat{m}_1(X_i)$ and $\hat{m}_0(X_i)$, and the propensity score model (the "W" model) generates predictions of $\hat{e}(X_i)$.

Step 2. We now assess our identifying assumption of strong ignorability. Given that we use large-scale survey data, we assume that unconfoundedness is satisfied, conditional on the rich set of observed covariates. To further strengthen this assumption, we referred to the existing literature to guide our selection of covariates in X_i. We test the overlap assumption by reviewing the predicted values from the propensity score model. The range of values is between 0.08 and 0.99, so we are wary that there are a proportion of respondents who had an extremely high probability of being treated given their observed covariates.

Figure 16.4 presents a density plot of the distribution of the propensity score across the treated and controls. There is a substantial mass of treated respondents with a high probability of treatment, which is a potential violation of the overlap assumption. Given this, we focus our attention on the ATC and CATC since we can assume overlap for the control population.

We evaluate any differences in the covariate distributions of treated and control observations using a standardised mean difference threshold of 0.1, finding that out of 97 covariates, 5 are not

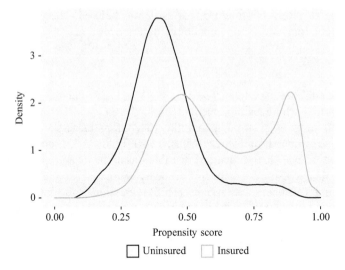

Figure 16.4   Density plot for the distribution of estimated propensity scores for the treated (insured) and controls (uninsured)

balanced. The covariates with the highest imbalance include a binary indicator for whether the respondent had a Social Security or family welfare card between August 2016 and March 2017 and a continuous variable for age, suggesting that the probability of being insured is age dependent.

We use inverse probability of treatment weights, constructed using the inverse of the estimated propensity score, that reweight the data to recreate the covariate distributions for treated and controls. We obtain three sets of inverse probability weights: ATT weights for the target, treated population; ATC weights for the target, control population; and ATE weights for the target, pooled, treated-control population. While we report all three weights, our focus remains on the ATC due to the overlap issue, as discussed before. Figure 16.5 shows the distribution of

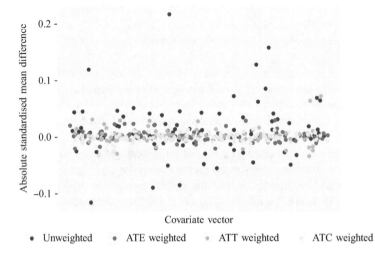

Figure 16.5   Overview of "balance" before and after inverse probability of treatment weighting

Table 16.2   Results from OLS regression of total length of inpatient stay (in days) on insurance status

	OLS1		OLS2	
	Estimate	SE	Estimate	SE
Insured	0.1328*	0.0037	0.1385*	0.0039
N	912 812		912 812	
Covariates	N		Y	

Note: SE = standard error; * p-value < 0.05.

the unweighted and inverse probability of treatment weighted (IPTW) vector of covariates. On reassessment of the weighted data, we find that the covariate distributions for the ATE, ATT and ATC satisfy the balance threshold.

Step 3. We perform a simple OLS regression of the outcome on treatment, with and without controlling for the covariate vector X_i. Table 16.2 presents the results, showing that receiving subsidised insurance increases the total length of inpatient stay by 0.13 days among the population. This estimate is unchanged when controlling for X_i, suggesting that there is little or no confounding bias from the observed covariates. Both estimates are statistically significant at the 5 per cent level.

Our OLS estimates adjust for any "imbalances" between treated and controls, provided that the outcome regression is correctly specified. However, given that this may not be the case, we choose to incorporate methods that are doubly robust into our subsequent analysis.

Step 4. We seek to estimate the effectiveness of subsidised health insurance on the total length of inpatient stay for the controls (ATC). We obtain this estimate using two alternative methods:

1. Weighted linear outcome regression
   We perform a weighted linear regression of Y_i on X_i using the IPTW data, which generates an IPTW-regression estimate for the ATC. We implement this regression using the `survey` package.
2. Causal forests
   We use the `average_treatment_effect` function in the `grf` package to obtain a doubly robust estimate for the ATC in the form of an augmented IPTW estimator (Robins et al., 1994). The algorithm uses the ITEs, generated from the causal forest (described later), as inputs into the estimator.

Figure 16.6 compares the resulting treatment effect estimates. According to the IPTW-regression estimator, the control population would have a statistically significant increase in the total length of inpatient stay (0.14 days) in response to treatment. The causal forest produces a similar, statistically significant estimate (0.14 days). The results from both estimators support those from the OLS estimator in Step 3. For reference, we also report the ATE and ATT estimates.

Step 5. We now explore the variation in treatment effects over the observed covariates using meta-learners (T-, S- and X-Learners) and causal forests motivated by the R-Learner.

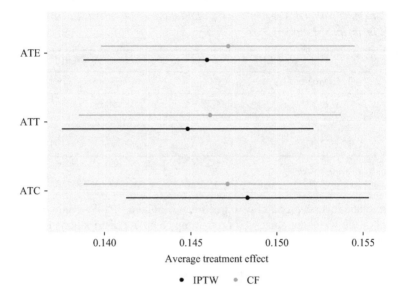

Figure 16.6   *Estimated average treatment effects, ATTs and ATCs (with 95 per cent confidence intervals) using IPTW-regression estimator (IPTW) and causal forests algorithm (CF)*

5.1   Meta-Learners

There are alternative ways of implementing the T-, S- and X-Learners depending on the choice of base learner. We choose to train the meta-learners using honest random forests (from `grf`) as the base learner for two reasons: (1) we are interested in obtaining valid confidence intervals, and (2) we have a large dataset with no apparent global structure. The meta-learners are trained on the training set, using the predicted values from the nuisance parameters as inputs into the model. The T-Learner uses $\hat{m}_1$ and $\hat{m}_0$ from the outcome regression; the S-Learner uses $\hat{m}$ from the outcome regression; and the X-Learner uses both $\hat{m}_1$ and $\hat{m}_0$ from the outcome regression, and $\hat{e}(x)$ from the propensity score model. In Step 1, we estimated the nuisance parameters using `grf`, and we use these estimates as inputs into our meta-learner models. All tuneable parameters are tuned by cross-validation using the tuning parameter default settings. We describe how we construct the functions for each meta-learner:

1.   T-Learner
     We start by calculating the ITEs $\hat{\tau}_i(x)$ using the predictions of $\hat{m}_1$ and $\hat{m}_0$ from the outcome regression; see (16.5). The ITEs also enable us to estimate the ATC using the `weighted.mean` function. We additionally estimate the variance of our causal estimates in order to construct confidence intervals. To describe treatment effect heterogeneity, we regress the ITEs on the covariate vector X_i using the `regression_forest` function. Once the random forest has been grown, the `variable_importance` function ranks the effect modifiers by how often they were split on at each depth in the forest, thus highlighting the most important variables that drive heterogeneity.

2. S-Learner

We incorporate our S-Learner function into our model for estimating the outcome regression, $\hat{m}$. Using `regression_forest`, we regress Y_i on X_i and D_i. We use the trained forest and the predict function, evaluated at $D_i = 1$ and $D_i = 0$, to obtain predictions of $\hat{\mu}(x,1)$ and $\hat{\mu}(x,0)$, respectively, along with their variance estimates. We calculate the ITEs by taking the difference between $\hat{\mu}(x,1)$ and $\hat{\mu}(x,0)$ (see (16.7)) and subsequently estimate the ATC using the `weighted.mean` function. Using `regression_forest` again, we regress the ITEs on X_i to obtain variable importance rankings to identify which variables drive heterogeneity.

3. X-learner

We begin by imputing the treatment effects for the treated and controls using the predictions of $\hat{m}_1$ and $\hat{m}_0$ from the outcome regression. For the treated, we subtract $\hat{m}_0$ from the observed treated outcomes $Y(1)$ to obtain $\tilde{\tau}_i^1$, and for the controls we subtract the observed control outcomes $Y(0)$ from $\hat{m}_0$ to obtain $\tilde{\tau}_i^0$; see (16.8) and (16.9). Then, we separately regress $\tilde{\tau}_i^1$ and $\tilde{\tau}_i^0$ on X_i using `regression_forest`. We use the trained forests and the `predict` function, evaluated at the empirical distribution observed in the sample, to obtain separate CATE estimates for the treated $\hat{\tau}_1(x)$ and the controls $\hat{\tau}_0(x)$; see (16.10) and (16.11). We additionally use the `variable_importance` function to identify the highest-ranked variables in the random forest for both treated and controls. The resulting ITEs (estimates and variance) are obtained using a weighted average of the CATE estimates for treated and controls, with the weights being equal to the estimated propensity score $\hat{e}(x)$; see (16.12). The `weighted.mean` function is used to estimate the ATC.

Figure 16.7 presents histograms of the estimated ITEs from the T-, S- and X-Learners, using honest random forests from `grf` as the base learner. We additionally report the estimated ATC, which for the T- and X-Learners is similar at 0.14 days, and for the S-Learner is slightly lower at 0.10 days. All ATC estimates are statistically significant at the 5 per cent level. The variation in ITEs is quite substantial, with the X-Learner showing the largest range of estimates (−10 days to 23 days), and the S-Learner showing the smallest (−5 days to 8 days). This is expected since the S-Learner produces estimates that may be more biased toward zero, as discussed earlier. Despite this variation in ITEs, the majority of estimates across all meta-learners are concentrated between 0 days and 0.5 days.

Table 16.3 lists the five highest ranked effect modifiers in terms of variable importance, along with their respective percentage of splits, from each of the meta-learners. For the X-Learner, there are separate rankings for treated and controls since two separate random forests are estimated. The most important variable for heterogeneity in the treated group is a binary indicator for whether the respondent is unemployed or retired, which seems plausible since inpatient treatment is likely to be determined by age and scoioeconomic factors. Other important variables include age, a binary indicator for whether the respondent's marital status is single, monthly household consumption expenditure per capita and a binary indicator for whether the respondent is a student. We rely on these variable importance rankings for our subgroup analyses in Step 6.

The T-, S- and X-Learners rely on the flexible outcome regressions capturing the true relationship between the covariates and the outcome to adjust for any residual confounding bias arising from the observed covariates. Given that the correct model specification cannot be guaranteed, it is possible to use additional statistical tools, such as matching for example, that balance treated and control observations prior to running the algorithms.

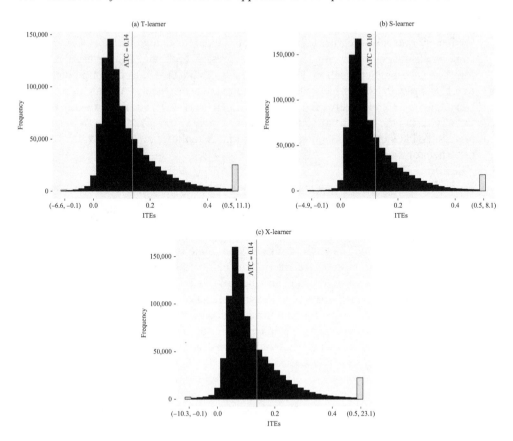

*Figure 16.7   Histograms of ITE estimates from the meta-learners using honest random
forests as the base learner*

5.2   Causal Forests/R-Learner

To implement causal forests, we use the `causal_forest` function in the `grf` package. The
algorithm trains an honest causal forest on the residualised treatments and outcomes using
$\hat{m}(x)$ and $\hat{e}(x)$ as inputs into the model. Similar to the random forest, the causal forest includes
tuning parameters and can produce variance estimates. The main difference is that the parameters for selecting balanced splits in the causal forest are modified slightly for causal splitting
(see appendix 16A.2 for further details).

   We train our `causal_forest` with all tuneable parameters being tuned by cross-validation,
using the tuning parameter default settings. We subsequently use the `predict` function to
obtain out-of-bag predictions of the ITEs (estimates and variance), evaluated at the empirical
distribution of the sample. In addition, we employ the `average_treatment_effect` function
to generate a doubly robust estimate of the ATC. This function implements either augmented
IPTW estimation or targeted maximum likelihood estimation. In Step 3, we obtained these
estimates using the former method. Figure 16.8a plots the distribution of the estimated ITEs and
ATC (0.15 days). The range of ITEs is small (−2 days to 4 days), and similar to the meta-learners,
the majority of estimates are concentrated between 0 days and 0.5 days. We additionally use

Table 16.3   List of the five highest ranked effect modifiers in terms of variable importance

Ranking	Effect modifier	Per cent of splits
T-Learner		
1	Age	27.1
2	Marital status: single	16.1
3	Marital status: widow	10.3
4	Employment status: student	9.1
5	Employment status: working	8.2
S-Learner		
1	Age	24.9
2	Marital status: single	17.2
3	Marital status: widow	11.0
4	Employment status: student	8.0
5	Employment sector: Primary	6.3
X-Learner: Treated		
1	Employment status: unemployed/retired	17.9
2	Age	14.5
3	Marital status: single	9.8
4	Monthly household consumption expenditure per capita	9.8
5	Employment status: student	5.4
X-Learner: Controls		
1	Employment status: unemployed/retired	23.6
2	Age	17.6
3	Marital status: single	11.0
4	Marital status: widow	9.4
5	Employment status: student	5.7
R-Learner		
1	Age	26.4
2	Marital status: single	14.7
3	Monthly household consumption expenditure per capita	10.1
4	Employment status: working	7.0
5	Marital status: widow	5.1

the `variable_importance` function to rank the effect modifiers in our model, as before. Table 16.3 lists the five highest ranked effect modifiers, with age being the most important.

As per the analysis of Athey and Wager (2019) and motivated by the work of Basu et al. (2018), we additionally train a second causal forest, using only those effect modifiers that saw

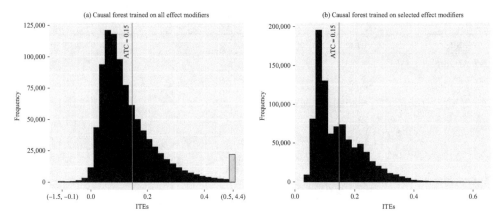

Figure 16.8   Histograms of out-of-bag ITE estimates from the causal forest based on the R-learner

an above-average proportion of splits in the first causal forest, captured by the variable importance measure. The orthogonalisation performed earlier eliminates any residual confounding effects from including only selected effect modifiers. Figure 16.8b plots the distribution of estimated ITEs and ATC (0.15 days) for the second causal forest with selected effect modifiers. Compared to the first causal forest with all effect modifiers, the range of ITEs is even smaller (0 days to 0.6 days).

Although the two causal forests display some form of heterogeneity, these results are not sufficient to confirm that $\hat{\tau}^{-i}(X_i)$ is a better estimate of $\tau(X_i)$ than $\hat{\tau}$. Therefore, we perform two tests to determine whether the heterogeneity in $\hat{\tau}^{-i}(X_i)$ and $\tau(X_i)$ is similar:

1. We estimate separate, doubly robust ATCs for two subpopulations, grouped on whether the out-of-bag ITE estimate for each observation (in terms of its absolute value) is above or below the median estimate. This analysis provides a qualitative assessment of the strength of heterogeneity by separating those with "high" and "low" CATCs. Table 16.4a

Table 16.4   Results from tests for heterogeneity using `grf`

(a) Estimates of "high" and "low" ATCs

	Estimate	SE
High ATC	0.2189	0.0142
Low ATC	0.0784	0.0087
Difference in ATC (high-low)	0.1405*	0.0166

(b) Omnibus test (`test_calibration` function in `grf`)

	Estimate	p-value
mean.forest.prediction	0.9992	0.0000
differential.forest.prediction	1.0587	0.0000

Note: SE = standard error; * p-value < 0.05.

shows that the difference in ATC (high–low) of 0.14 days is statistically significant at the 5 per cent level, suggesting that heterogeneity is present. Using these results, we can also compare the observed characteristics of the control population with high and low CATCs. Table 16.5 presents the results, which shows that respondents with an above median CATC are more likely to be female, older, in work and married. They are also more likely to be of a slightly higher socioeconomic status, according to their household and financial characteristics.

2. Second, we perform an omnibus test of the calibration of the causal forest, using the `test_calibration` function in `grf`. This test for heterogeneity is motivated by the "best linear predictor" method of Chernozhukov et al. (2018a) that aims to find the best linear fit of $\tau(X_i)$ using $\hat{\tau}^{-i}(X_i)$. To do this, the `test_calibration` function regresses $Y_i - \hat{m}^{-i}(X_i)$

Table 16.5   *Comparison of observed characteristics of control population with high and low CATCs*

	Below median CATC		Above median CATC	
	Mean	SD	Mean	SD
Individual characteristics				
Male	0.653	0.476	0.347	0.476
Age	17.7	11.3	45.3	17.1
Educated	0.867	0.340	0.875	0.331
Working	0.319	0.466	0.621	0.485
Unemployed/retired	0.020	0.138	0.043	0.202
Married	0.194	0.395	0.762	0.426
Household characteristics				
Urban location	0.355	0.479	0.361	0.480
No. of people in household	5.05	1.83	4.31	1.88
Owns house	0.843	0.363	0.866	0.340
Has a private toilet facility	0.783	0.412	0.805	0.396
Purchases drinking water	0.366	0.482	0.367	0.482
Has electricity	0.922	0.268	0.943	0.231
Has experienced a natural disaster in past 1 year	0.171	0.376	0.164	0.370
Has received Raskin in past 4 months	0.469	0.499	0.459	0.498
Had a Social Security or family welfare card between Aug 16–Mar 17	0.320	0.466	0.274	0.446
Did not have enough food to eat in past 1 year	0.315	0.465	0.292	0.455
Has a savings account	0.408	0.491	0.403	0.490
Monthly expenditure per capita (IDR)	772 471	585 197	865 671	702 478
Poor	0.181	0.385	0.139	0.346

Note: SD = standard deviation.

on two synthetic predictors, $J_i = \bar{\tau}(W_i - \hat{e}^{-i}(X_i))$ and $K_i = (\hat{\tau}^{-i}(X_i) - \bar{\tau})(W_i - \hat{e}^{-i}(X_i))$, where $\bar{\tau}$ is the average out-of-bag ITE estimate. The coefficient on K_i ("differential.forest. prediction") measures the quality of the CATE estimates, with a coefficient of 1 indicating that the estimates are well calibrated. The coefficient on J_i ("mean.forest.prediction") absorbs the ATE, with a coefficient of 1 indicating that the ATE estimate is valid. Table 16.4b presents the results of the calibration test, confirming a valid ATE estimate and the existence of observable heterogeneity in treatment effects.

Step 6. So far, we have explored heterogeneity in treatment effects at the individual level. However, we are also interested in how treatment effects vary across different populations, stratified by a vector of selected observed covariates, $X = x$. These covariates can be selected pre or post-analysis, according to the research plan. We select our covariates through both methods: a pre-analysis, theory-driven, variable selection process based on previous subgroup analyses in the related literature, and a post-analysis, data-driven, variable selection process based on the highest-ranked variables of importance obtained from `grf` (see Table 16.3). Our chosen covariates of interest consist of continuous variables – age and monthly household expenditure per capita – and binary variables – marital status, employment status and urban/rural location.

First, we construct smooth plots of the ITEs (with 95 per cent confidence intervals) from the T-, S-, X- and R-Learners, as a function of the continuous covariates $X = x$, using the `gam` method in `ggplot2`'s smoothing function. Figure 16.9 presents the results, showing that the policy impact on health care utilisation increases with age and monthly household consumption expenditure, although the marginal increase is greater for the poorest populations.

Second, we estimate GATCs for all of our selected covariates of interest using only the R-Learner. We rely on our second causal forest from Step 5 to construct the GATC estimates.

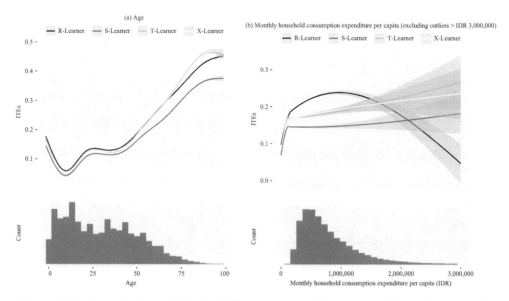

Figure 16.9   *Smooth plots of ITEs (with 95 per cent confidence intervals) as a function of specified covariates of interest, and associated histograms*

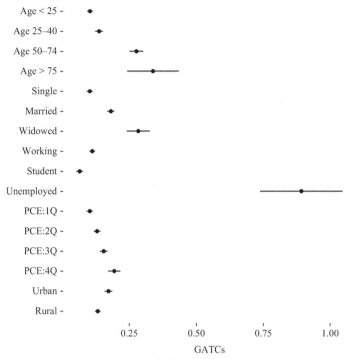

PCE = monthly household per capita expenditure, 1Q = lowest quartile

Figure 16.10   Estimated GATCs (with 95 per cent confidence intervals) using causal forests with selected effect modifiers

We use the `average_treatment_effect` function to aggregate the ITEs to the ATC, as before, only now we restrict the sample to those observations with a given value *x* of a specific covariate *X*. For continuous variables of interest, we group the observations into bins or quartiles. Figure 16.10 presents the results, which confirms our earlier findings that treatment effects increase with age and monthly household expenditure. Treatment effects are particularly large for the unemployed; however, this includes retirees, which could reflect an age effect. We additionally find that effects are larger for married and widowed respondents (again, a likely age effect), and those who live in urban areas.

Step 7. Our results provide additional insights into the average and heterogeneous impacts of subsidised JKN on inpatient, hospital utilisation. We find that overall there is a positive policy effect on the population, in that subsidised health insurance is associated with an increase in health care utilisation, which is supported by the OLS, IPTW-regression and causal forest estimators. These findings are in line with the published literature on Indonesia and other low- and middle-income countries (Erlangga et al., 2019a,b). However, given the demonstrative purpose of this case study, we acknowledge that there are certain limitations in our evaluation approach. In our model, we do not control for respondents' health status. Health status, in this particular context, can serve two purposes: it can be a confounder or a mediator (or both). If health status is a potential confounder, and we do not include it in our model, we are at risk of producing biased treatment effect estimates. A limitation of using cross-sectional data, however, is that we are unable to identify the nature of the health status variable. A more detailed evaluation could also explore the variables in X_i that violate the overlap condition in the treated population and consider whether it may be more appropriate to drop observations contributing to this violation from the sample. Additionally, in the outcome regression, it may also be worth accounting for the substantial mass point at zero (97 per cent of respondents did not report any inpatient utilisation) with a two-part model. We have highlighted a few of the limitations in our simplified analysis; a more rigorous evaluation is required to obtain robust policy impact estimates.

We find that all of the machine learning algorithms produce similar average impact estimates (the S-Learner estimate is more biased toward zero), however the range of ITE estimates varies substantially. Despite this, the majority of estimated ITEs across all algorithms are located in the region of 0 days to 0.5 days. We discover that, in addition to the predefined variables of interest, additional variables – such as age, employment status and marital status – are key drivers of heterogeneity. These data-driven subgroups provide a novel contribution to the evidence base for analysing treatment effect modification, since they have not previously been identified as subgroups of interest in this policy context. By estimating marginal CATEs and GATEs, we are additionally able to identify the levels of the covariates at which treatment effects are highest or lowest. We find that effect modification is largely associated with age, employment status and socioeconomic factors, in that the elderly population, those who are unemployed (including retirees) and households with a high consumption expenditure display the greatest positive response to subsidised health insurance. These findings can provide valuable information for policy makers interested in understanding the variation in treatment effects across the population.

6.   CONCLUSION

In this chapter, we have provided an insight into the current causal machine learning literature, in particular for estimating heterogeneity in treatment effects based on observables. We have defined some of the key concepts behind supervised machine learning and have discussed its recent implementation into methods of causal inference for estimating the ATE and CATE in a selection on observables framework. We have described in detail three causal machine learning algorithms for estimating heterogeneous treatment effects (meta-learners, the R-Learner and causal forests), and have explained their relative strengths and limitations. Meta-learners offer the most intuitive method for estimating CATEs. They are user-friendly, transparent, and compatible with various base learners. The X-Learner, in particular, offers a flexible approach to CATE estimation, and performs particularly well under various settings such as unbalanced study designs, or when the structure of the response functions is known. A limitation of the meta-learners, however, is that if the flexible outcome regressions are misspecified, they are unable to control for residual confounding bias without implementing additional statistical tools. The R-Learner, on the other hand, automatically adjusts for confounding since it is founded on semi-parametric theory and orthogonalisation. This makes the R-Learner particularly suitable for non-randomised settings. A common application of the R-Learner is via causal forests, which combine the double robustness of the R-Learner with the adaptive framework of the random forests algorithm. Through a modified splitting criterion and the introduction of honesty, causal forests offer a flexible, non-parametric approach to CATE estimation, with the ability to construct valid confidence intervals.

We have demonstrated the application of the described methods to a case study of an impact evaluation of a national health insurance programme on health care utilisation in Indonesia. The case study resembles that of a typical, non-randomised, empirical application that uses large-scale, survey data with a binary treatment and a large covariate vector of confounders and effect modifiers. The primary aim of our case study was to show the current scope of analyses using the described methods, most notably that CATEs can be estimated for individuals with the individual covariate vector X_i (ITEs), and for population subgroups that share the same covariate profile $X = x$ (GATEs). However, we highlight that GATEs can only be estimated for population subgroups that have been selected by the researcher in advance, either prior to CATE estimation through some form of pre-specification plan, or after CATE estimation once variables that drive heterogeneity have been identified by the algorithm. In other words, a current limitation of the described methods is their inability to automatically identify GATEs without researcher input.

The causal machine learning literature continues to grow rapidly. In addition to the R-Learner and causal forests already described, alternative, doubly robust methods for estimating heterogeneous treatment effects have been suggested that can be implemented with an identification strategy of selection on observables. We provide some notable examples. Knaus (2020) uses DML to first estimate a doubly robust score for the ATE, which is subsequently used as a pseudo-outcome in a standard regression model to estimate $\tau(x)$. Zimmert and Lechner (2019) use a two-step estimator that performs nuisance parameter estimation (using machine learning) in the first stage, prior to the second stage kernel-based non-parametric regression for estimating CATEs. Other recently developed methods are particularly suited to high-dimensional settings since they use a concept known as *dimensionality reduction*. This reduces the impact of many covariates on convergence rates by including a variable selection step prior to estimating the causal parameter. We highlight some recent methods that incorporate a reduced dimensional function into the estimation process while also adjusting for selection bias. Abrevaya et al. (2015) integrate out the unwanted components of X_i to produce smoothed estimates of the conditional distribution of the inverse probability weighted outcomes given selected covariates. Lee et al. (2017) generate a doubly robust estimator based on parametric regression and propensity score models. Fan et al. (2020) consider a similar approach but use flexible machine learning algorithms to estimate the nuisance parameters.

These developments are particularly welcome for those seeking to employ causal machine learning methods for empirical applications, where observational data and confounding are key features of the study design. The data challenge from the 2018 Atlantic Causal Inference Conference provides a number of examples of how machine learning can be applied to estimate treatment effect modification in a non-randomised study (Carvalho et al., 2019). The eight participants used a diverse set of methods, including semi-parametric estimation and ensemble algorithms, and there was a particular focus on incorporating tools to address confounding. In terms of other applied examples in the broader literature, Appendix 16A.3 displays a selection of economic papers that use machine learning methods to estimate heterogeneous treatment effects. There is a mixture of randomised and non-randomised studies, with causal forests being the most popular algorithm. There is also a large variation in sample size, which highlights the flexibility of these methods.

It is evident that causal machine learning methods are becoming increasingly popular in empirical applications with an identification strategy of selection on observables. However, the development of methods for study designs with an identification strategy of selection on unobservables is still in its infancy. In these designs, confounding cannot be controlled for solely by the observed covariates, given the existence of unobserved heterogeneity. Instrumental variable analysis is a common tool for estimating causal effects when the unconfoundedness assumption is violated. The idea is to identify causal effects by exploiting an exogenous source of random variation via an instrument. There is a growing literature combining causal machine learning and instrumental variables analysis for estimating average and heterogeneous treatment effects. For example, Chen et al. (2021) propose a DML approach to instrumental variable quantile regression (IVQR) for estimating low-dimensional causal parameters in high-dimensional data (Chernozhukov and Hansen, 2005). Athey et al. (2019b) extend the GRF algorithm to instrumental variables regression. As before, the honest random forest estimates heterogeneity in causal effects using local moment conditions but is now identified using the conditional two-stage least squares (2SLS) estimator. Chen and Hsiang (2019) combine these two methods by incorporating IVQR into the GRF algorithm, which produces quantile treatment effects and variable importance measures for heterogeneity. An alternative method of controlling for unobserved heterogeneity is to utilise methods for panel data analysis. The extension of causal machine learning methods from cross-sectional to panel data settings is another area of development in the literature. In terms of effect modification, Semenova et al. (2020) produce an estimation and inference method for high-dimensional panel data settings with a large number of heterogeneous treatment effects using a two-stage method, which they term the *orthogonal lasso*.

Gaining new and important insights into the distributional impacts of treatment can have far-reaching implications for policy. In particular, there is a rich, rapidly evolving literature on optimal policy learning that leverages heterogeneous treatment effects to determine treatment assignment under specific constraints, such as budget and equity (Athey and Wager, 2021; Kallus, 2018, 2020; Kallus and Zhou, 2018; Kitagawa and Tetenov, 2018). For example, in our impact evaluation case study, policy makers may seek to subsidise health care insurance only for those populations who are likely to respond significantly to treatment, in order to maximise some target criterion. As discussed earlier, these population subgroups can be identified according to their observed characteristics. This growing area of policy impact evaluation, that effectively "learns" treatment assignment rules through understanding heterogeneity in treatment effects, further highlights the scope of machine learning in methods of causal inference, and their combined potential for applied economic research.

ACKNOWLEDGEMENTS

We sincerely thank Taufik Hidayat (Center for Health Economics and Policy Studies, Faculty of Public Health, Universitas Indonesia) for helping to prepare and interpret the data, Karla Diaz-Ordaz (Department of Medical Statistics, London School of Hygiene and Tropical Medicine) for providing R code for the T- and X-Learners (see https://github.com/KDiazOrdaz) and Marc Suhrcke (Centre for Health Economics, University of York) for the valuable comments. This work was supported by the Medical Research Council [R22466].

NOTES

1. We include a binary treatment variable in our potential outcomes framework; however, to analyse the distribution of individual or group dose response across the population, a continuous treatment variable would be required instead.
2. In our empirical application, the number of control and treated observations is fairly equal, which is an exception to the norm in non-randomised studies.

REFERENCES

Abadie, A. and Imbens, G. W. (2006). "Large sample properties of matching estimators for average treatment effects". In: *Econometrica* 741, pp. 235–67.

Abadie, A. and Imbens, G. W. (2011). "Bias-corrected matching estimators for average treatment effects". In: *J. Bus. Econ. Stat.* 291, pp. 1–11.

Abrevaya, J., Hsu, Y. -C and Lieli, R. P. (2015) "Estimating conditional average treatment effects". In: *J. Bus. Econ. Stat.* 334, pp. 485–505.

Allen, D. M. (1974). "The relationship between variable selection and data augmentation and a method for prediction". In: *Technometrics* 161, pp. 125–7.

Amit, Y. and Geman, D. (1997). "Shape quantization and recognition with randomized trees". In: *Neural Comput.* 97, pp. 1545–88.

Angrist, J. D. and Pischke, J. (2008). *Mostly harmless econometrics: An empiricist's companion*. Princeton University Press.

Assmann, S. F., Pocock, S. J., Enos, L. E., and Kasten, L. E. (2000). "Subgroup analysis and other (mis) uses of baseline data in clinical trials". In: *The Lancet* 3559209, pp. 1064–9.

Athey, S. (2017). "Beyond prediction: Using big data for policy problems". In: *Science* 3556324, pp. 483–5.

Athey, S. (2018). "The impact of machine learning on economics". In: *The economics of artificial intelligence: An Agenda*. University of Chicago Press, pp. 507–47.

Athey, S., Bayati, M., Imbens, G. W., and Qu, Z. (2019a). "Ensemble methods for causal effects in panel data Settings". In: *AEA Papers and Proceedings* 109, pp. 65–70.

Athey, S. and Imbens, G. W. (2015). "Machine learning for estimating heterogeneous causal effects". Research Papers 3350. Stanford University, Graduate School of Business.

Athey, S. and Imbens, G. W. (2016). "Recursive partitioning for heterogeneous causal effects". In: *Proceedings of the National Academy of Sciences* 11327, pp. 7353–60.

Athey, S. and Imbens, G. W. (2017). "The state of applied econometrics: Causality and policy evaluation". In: *Journal of Economic Perspectives* 312, pp. 3–32.

Athey, S. and Imbens, G. W. (2019). "Machine learning methods that economists should know about". In: *Annual Review of Economics* 11.

Athey, S., Tibshirani, J., and Wager, S. (2019b). "Generalized random forests". In: *The Annals of Statistics* 472, pp. 1148–78.

Athey, S., & Wager, S. (2019). Estimating treatment effects with causal forests: An application. In: *Observational Studies* 5(2), pp. 37−51.

Athey, S., & Wager, S. (2021). Policy learning with observational data. In: *Econometrica* 89(1), pp. 133−61.

Bang, H. and Robins, J. M. (2005). "Doubly robust estimation in missing data and causal inference models". In: *Biometrics* 614, pp. 962–73.

Basu, S., Kumbier, K., Brown, J. B., and Yu, B. (2018). "Iterative random forests to discover predictive and stable high-order interactions". In: *Proceedings of the National Academy of Sciences* 1158, pp. 1943–8.

Bell, R. M., Koren, Y., and Volinsky, C. (2010). "All together now: A perspective on the Netflix Prize". In: *Chance* 231, pp. 24–9.

Ben-Michael, E., Feller, A., and Rothstein, J. (2020). "Varying impacts of letters of recommendation on college admissions: Approximate balancing weights for subgroup effects in observational studies". ArXiv e-prints 2008.04394.

Bonetti, M. and Gelber, R. D. (2004). "Patterns of treatment effects in subsets of patients in clinical trials". In: *Biostatistics* 53, pp. 465–81.

Breiman, L. (1996). "Out-of-bag estimation". Technical report, St Department, University of California Berkeley.

Breiman, L. (2001). "Random forests". In: *Mach. Learn.* 451, pp. 5–32.

Breiman, L., Friedman, J., Olshen, R., and Stone, C. (1984). *Classification and regression trees*. CRC Press.

Brookes, S. T., Whitely, E., Egger, M., Smith, G. D., Mulheran, P. A., and Peters, T. J. (2004). "Subgroup analyses in randomized trials: risks of subgroup-specific analyses; power and sample size for the interaction test". en. In: *J. Clin. Epidemiol.* 573, pp. 229–36.

Brookes, S. T., Whitley, E., Peters, T. J., Mullheran, P. A., Egger, M., and Davey Smith, G. (2001). "Subgroup analyses in randomised controlled trials: quantifying the risks of false-positives and false-negatives". In: *Health Technol. Assess.* 533, pp. 1–56.

Bühlmann, P. and Yu, B. (2002). "Analyzing bagging". In: *Ann. Stat.* 304, pp. 927–61.

Carvalho, C., Feller, A., Murray, J., Woody, S., & Yeager, D. (2019). Assessing treatment effect variation in observational studies: Results from a data challenge. In: *Observational Studies* 5(2), pp. 21–35.

Chen, J.-E. and Hsiang, C.-W. (2019). "Causal random forests model using instrumental variable quantile regression". In: *Econometrics* 74, p. 49.

Chen, J. E., Huang, C. H., & Tien, J. J. (2021). "Debiased/double machine learning for instrumental variable quantile regressions". In: *Econometrics* 9(2), p. 15.

Chernozhukov, V., Demirer, M., Duflo, E., Hansen, C., Newey, W., and Robins, J. M. (2018a). "Double/debiased machine learning for treatment and structural parameters". In: *Econom. J.* 211, pp. C1–C68.

Chernozhukov, V., Demirer, M., Duflo, E., and Fernandez-Val, I. (2018b). "Generic machine learning inference on heterogeneous treatment effects in randomized experiments, with an application to immunization in India" (No. w24678). *National Bureau of Economic Research.*

Chernozhukov, V. and Hansen, C. (2005). "An IV model of quantile treatment effects". In: *Econometrica* 731, pp. 245–61.

Chipman, H. A., George, E. I., and McCulloch, R. E. (2010). "BART: Bayesian additive regression trees". In: *Ann. Appl. Stat.* 41, pp. 266–98.

Cook, D. I., Gebski, V. J., and Keech, A. C. (2004). "Subgroup analysis in clinical trials". In: *Medical Journal of Australia* 1806, p. 289.

Diaz, I. (2019). "Machine learning in the estimation of causal effects: Targeted minimum loss-based estimation and double/debiased machine learning". In: *Biostatistics.*

Efron, B. (2014). "Estimation and accuracy after model selection". In: *Int. Am. Stat. Assoc.* 109507, pp. 991–1007.

Erlangga, D., Ali, S., and Bloor, K. (2019a). "The impact of public health insurance on healthcare utilisation in Indonesia: Evidence from panel data". In: *Int. J. Public Health* 644, pp. 603–613.

Erlangga, D., Suhrcke, M., Ali, S., and Bloor, K. (2019b). "The impact of public health insurance on health care utilisation, financial protection and health status in low- and middle-income countries: A systematic review". In: *PLoS One* 148, e0219731.

Fan, Q., Hsu, Y.-C., Lieli, R. P., and Zhang, Y. (2020). "Estimation of conditional average treatment effects with high-dimensional data". In: *Journal of Business & Economic Statistics,* pp. 1–15.

Foster, D. J. and Syrgkanis, V. (2020). "Orthogonal statistical learning". arXiv: 1901.09036v3 [math.ST].

Foster, J. C., Taylor, J. M. G., and Ruberg, S. J. (2011). "Subgroup identification from randomized clinical trial data". In: *Stat. Med.* 3024, pp. 2867–80.

Gail, M. and Simon, R. (1985). "Testing for qualitative interactions between treatment effects and patient subsets". In: *Biometrics* 412, pp. 361–72.

Green, D. P. and Kern, H. L. (2012). "Modeling heterogeneous treatment effects in survey experiments with Bayesian additive regression trees". In: *Public Opin. Q.* 763, pp. 491–511.

Greene, W. H. (2000). *Econometric analysis,* 4th edition. Prentice Hall, pp. 201–15.

Gruber, S. and Van der Laan, M. J. (2010). "A targeted maximum likelihood estimator of a causal effect on a bound continuous outcome". In: *Int. J. Biostat.* 61, Article 26.

Hahn, J. (1998). "On the role of the propensity score in efficient semiparametric estimation of average treatment effects". In: *Econometrica* 662, pp. 315–31.

Hahn, P. R., Murray, J. S., and Carvalho, C. (2020). "Bayesian regression tree models for causal inference: Regularization, confounding, and heterogeneous effects (with discussion)". In: *Bayesian Anal.* 153, pp. 965–1056.

Hastie, T., Tibshirani, R., and Friedman, J. (2009). *The elements of statistical learning: Data mining, inference, and prediction.* Springer Science & Business Media.

Heckman, J. (2001). "Micro data, heterogeneity, and the evaluation of public policy: Nobel lecture". In: *J. Polit. Econ.* 1094, pp. 673–748.

Heckman, J., Ichimura, H., Smith, J., and Todd, P. (1998). "Characterizing selection bias using experimental data". In: *Econometrica* 665, pp. 1017–98.

Hill, J. and Su, Y.-S. (2013). "Assessing lack of common support in causal inference using Bayesian nonparametrics: Implications for evaluating the effect of breastfeeding on children's cognitive outcomes". In: *The Annals of Applied Statistics* 73, pp. 1386–420.

Hill, J. L. (2011). "Bayesian nonparametric modeling for causal inference". In: *J. Comput. Graph. Stat.* 201, pp. 217–40.

Holland, P. W. (1986). "Statistics and causal inference". In: *Journal of the American statistical Association* 81396, pp. 945–60.

Hothorn, T., Lausen, B., Benner, A., and Radespiel-Tröger, M. (2004). "Bagging survival trees". In: *Stat. Med.* 231, pp. 77–91.

Imai, K. and Ratkovic, M. (2013). "Estimating treatment effect heterogeneity in randomized program evaluation". In: *The Annals of Applied Statistics* 71, pp. 443–70.

Imai, K. and Strauss, A. (2011). "Estimation of heterogeneous treatment effects from randomized experiments, with application to the optimal planning of the get-out-the-vote campaign". In: *Political Analysis* 191, pp. 1–19.

Imbens, G. W. and Rubin, D. B. (2015). *Causal inference in statistics, social, and biomedical sciences.* Cambridge University Press.

Imbens, G. W. and Wooldridge, J. M. (2009). "Recent developments in the econometrics of program evaluation". In: *Journal of Economic Literature* 471, pp. 5–86.

Kallus, N. (2018). "Balanced policy evaluation and learning". In: *Proceedings of the 32nd International Conference on Neural Information Processing Systems.* ACM, pp. 8909–20.

Kallus, N. (2020). "More efficient policy learning via optimal retargeting". In: *Journal of the American Statistical Association,* pp. 1–13.

Kallus, N. and Zhou, A. (2018). "Confounding-robust policy improvement". arXiv: 1805.08593v3 [cs.LG].

Kennedy, E. H. (2020). "Optimal doubly robust estimation of heterogeneous causal effects". arXiv: 2004.14497v2 [math.ST].

Kitagawa, T. and Tetenov, A. (2018). "Who should be treated? Empirical welfare maximization methods for treatment choice". In: *Econometrica* 862, pp. 591–616.

Kleinberg, J., Ludwig, J., Mullainathan, S., and Obermeyer, Z. (2015). "Prediction policy problems". In: *American Economic Review* 1055, pp. 491–95.

Knaus, M. C. (2020). "Double machine learning based program evaluation under unconfoundedness". arXiv: 2003.03191v1 [econ.EM].

Knaus, M. C., Lechner, M., and Strittmatter, A. (2020). "Machine learning estimation of heterogeneous causal effects: Empirical Monte Carlo evidence". In: *Econom. J.* 24, pp. 134–61.

Künzel, S. R., Sekhon, J. S., Bickel, P. J., and Yu, B. (2019a). "Metalearners for estimating heterogeneous treatment effects using machine learning". In: *Proceedings of the National Academy of Sciences* 11610, pp. 4156–65.

Künzel, S. R., Walter, S. J., & Sekhon, J. S. (2019b). "Causaltoolbox—estimator stability for heterogeneous treatment effects". In: *Observational Studies* 5(2), pp. 105−17.

Lechner, M. (2019). "Modified causal forests for estimating heterogeneous causal effects". In: *EEA-ESEM Manchester 2019: 34th Annual Congress of the European Economic Association 72nd European Meeting of the Econometric Society.*

Lee, B. K., Lessler, J., and Stuart, E. A. (2010). "Improving propensity score weighting using machine learning". In: *Stat. Med.* 293, pp. 337–46.

Lee, S., Okui, R., and Whang, Y.-J. (2017). "Doubly robust uniform confidence band for the conditional average treatment effect function". In: *J. Appl. Econ.* 327, pp. 1207–25.

Lin, Y. and Jeon, Y. (2006). "Random forests and adaptive nearest neighbors". In: *J. Am. Stat. Assoc.* 101474, pp. 578–90.

List, J. A., Shaikh, A. M., and Xu, Y. (2016). "Multiple hypothesis testing in experimental economics". In: *Experimental Economics,* pp. 1–21.

Meinshausen, N. (2006). "Quantile regression forests". In: *J. Mach. Learn. Res.* 7, pp. 983–99.

Mullainathan, S. and Spiess, J. (2017). "Machine learning: an applied econometric approach." In: *Journal of Economic Perspectives* 312, pp. 87–106.

Mulyanto, J., Kringos, D. S., and Kunst, A. E. (2019a). "Socioeconomic inequalities in healthcare utilisation in Indonesia: a comprehensive survey-based overview". In: *BMJ Open* 97, e026164.

Mulyanto, J., Kringos, D. S., and Kunst, A. E. (2019b). "The evolution of income-related inequalities in healthcare utilisation in Indonesia, 1993–2014". In: *PLoS One* 146, e0218519.

Mulyanto, J., Kunst, A. E., and Kringos, D. S. (2019c). "Geographical inequalities in healthcare utilisation and the contribution of compositional factors: A multilevel analysis of 497 districts in Indonesia". In: *Health Place* 60, p. 102236.

Neugebauer, R. and Van der Laan, M. J. (2005). "Why prefer double robust estimators in causal inference?" In: *J. Stat. Plan. Inference* 1291, pp. 405–26.

Nie, X., & Wager, S. (2021). Quasi-oracle estimation of heterogeneous treatment effects. In: *Biometrika* 108(2), 299−319.

OECD. (2019). *Social protection system review of indonesia.* OECD Development Pathways, OECD Publishing, Paris.

Oprescu, M., Syrgkanis, V., and Wu, Z. S. (2019). "Orthogonal random forest for causal inference". arXiv: 1806.03467v4 [cs.LG].

Powers, S., Qian, J., Jung, K. Schuler, A., Shah, N. H., Hastie, T., and Tibshirani, R. (2018). "Some methods for heterogeneous treatment effect estimation in high dimensions". In: *Statistics in Medicine* 3711, pp. 1767–87.

Robins, J. M. and Rotnitzky, A. (1995). "Semiparametric efficiency in multivariate regression models with missing data". In: *Journal of the American Statistical Association* 90429, pp. 122–9.

Robins, J. M., Rotnitzky, A., and Zhao, L. P. (1994). "Estimation of regression coefficients when some regressors are not always observed". In: *J. Am. Stat. Assoc.* 89427, pp. 846–66.

Robins, J. M. Sued, M., Lei-Gomez, Q., and Rotnitzky, A. (2007). "Comment: Performance of double-robust estimators when "inverse probability" weights are highly variable". In: *Stat. Sci.* 224, pp. 544–59.

Robinson, P. M. (1988). "Semiparametric econometrics: A survey". In: *J. Appl. Econ.* 31, pp. 35–51.

Rosenbaum, P. R. (2002). *Observational studies, Springer series in statistics.* Springer Science & Business Media, pp. 1–17.

Rosenbaum, P. R. and Rubin, D. B. (1983). "The central role of the propensity score in observational studies for causal effects". In: *Biometrika* 701, pp. 41–55.

Rosenbaum, P. R. and Rubin, D. B. (1984). "Reducing bias in observational studies using subclassification on the propensity score". In: *Journal of the American Statistical Association* 79387, pp. 516–24.

Rubin, D. B. (1974). "Estimating causal effects of treatments in randomized and nonrandomized studies." In: *Journal of Educational Psychology* 665, p. 688.

Rubin, D. B. (2009). "Should observational studies be designed to allow lack of balance in covariate distributions across treatment groups?" In: *Stat. Med.* 289, pp. 1420–23.

Semenova, V., Goldman, M., Chernozhukov, V., and Taddy, M. (2020). "Estimation and inference about heterogeneous treatment effects in high-dimensional dynamic panels". arXiv: 1712.09988v3 [stat.ML].

Shalit, U., Johansson, F. D., and Sontag, D. (2017). "Estimating individual treatment effect: generalization bounds and algorithms". In: *Proceedings of the 34th International Conference on Machine Learning-Volume 70.* JMLR. org, pp. 3076–85.

Stone, C. J. (1980). "Optimal rates of convergence for nonparametric estimators". In: *Ann. Stat.* 86, pp. 1348–60.

Stone, M. (1974). "Cross-validatory choice and assessment of statistical predictions". In: *J. R. Stat. Soc. Series B Stat. Methodol.* 362, pp. 111–47.

Surowiecki, J. (2005). *The wisdom of crowds.* Anchor.

Tian, L., Alizadeh, A. A., Gentles, A. J., and Tibshirani, R. (2014). "A simple method for estimating interactions between a treatment and a large number of covariates". In: *Journal of the American Statistical Association* 109508, pp. 1517–32.

Van der Laan, M. J., Polley, E. C., and Hubbard, A. E. (2007). "Super learner". In: *Stat. Appl. Genet. Mol. Biol.* 6, Article 25.

Van der Laan, M. J. and Robins, J. M. (2003). *Unified methods for censored longitudinal data and causality, Springer series in statistics.* Springer Science & Business Media.

Van der Laan, M. J. and Rose, S. (2011). *Targeted learning: Causal inference for observational and experimental data, Springer series in statistics.* Springer Science & Business Media.

Van der Laan, M. J. and Rubin, D. (2006). "Targeted maximum likelihood learning". In: *Int. J. Biostat.* 21.

Varian, H. R. (2014). "Big data: New tricks for econometrics". In: *Journal of Economic Perspectives* 282, pp. 3–28.

Wager, S. and Athey, S. (2018). "Estimation and inference of heterogeneous treatment effects using random forests". In: *Journal of the American Statistical Association* 113523, pp. 1228–42.

Wager, S., Hastie, T., and Efron, B. (2014). "Confidence intervals for random forests: The jackknife and the infinitesimal jackknife". In: *J. Mach. Learn. Res.* 151, pp. 25–1651.

Wang, R., Lagakos, S. W., Ware, J. H., Hunter, D. J., and Drazen, J. M. (2007). "Statistics in medicine—reporting of subgroup analyses in clinical trials". In: *New England Journal of Medicine* 35721, pp. 2189–94.

Westreich, D., Lessler, J., and Funk, M. J. (2010). "Propensity score estimation: neural networks, support vector machines, decision trees (CART), and meta-classifiers as alternatives to logistic regression". In: *J. Clin. Epidemiol.* 638, pp. 826–33.

Wooldridge, J. M. (2010). *Econometric analysis of cross section and panel data.* MIT Press.

Zhou, Z.-H. (2012). *Ensemble methods: Foundations and algorithms.* Chapman and Hall/CRC.

Zimmert, M. and Lechner, M. (2019). "Nonparametric estimation of causal heterogeneity under high-dimensional confounding". arXiv: 1908.08779v1.

APPENDIX 16A.1

Table 16A.1   List of all confounders and effect modifiers included in our empirical model

Individual covariates (binary)	
Male	Female
Marital status: single	Marital status: married
Marital status: divorced	Marital status: widowed
Has a national identity number	Literacy: Latin letters
Literacy Arabic letters	Literacy: other letters
Education: elementary	Education: junior secondary
Education: senior secondary	Education: university
Education: non-compulsory education	Travelled domestically for tourism in 2016
Victim of crime between March 2016 and February 2017	Had a cell phone in past 3 months
Used a computer in past 3 months	Used internet in past 3 months
Employment: working	Employment status: student
Employment status: housekeeper	Employment status: other activities
Employment status: unemployed/retired	Employment sector: primary
Employment sector: secondary	Employment sector: tertiary
Employment type: self-employed	Employment type: employer assisted by temporary workers
Employment type: employer assisted by permanent workers	Employment type: employee
Employment type: freelance employee	Employment type: unpaid family worker
Smokes electric cigarettes	Smokes tobacco

Individual covariates (continuous)	
Age	Number of cigarettes smoked per week

Household covariates (binary)	
Urban/rural location	Not enough food to eat in past 1 year
Not enough healthy and nutritious food to eat in past 1 year	Little kind of food to eat in past 1 year
Missed eating on a certain day in past 1 year	Ate less than normal quantity in past 1 year
Ran out of food in past 1 year	Felt hungry but there was no food in past 1 year
Unable to eat during the day in past 1 year	Occupancy status: own house
Occupancy status: lease/rent	Occupancy status: rent-free
Occupancy status: company-owned	Occupancy status: other
Has a second house	Roof: concrete
Roof: tile	Roof: asbestos

Table 16A.1　(continued)

Roof: zinc	Roof: bamboo
Roof: wood/shingle	Roof: straw/fibre/leaves/metroxylon sagu
Toilet: private	Toilet: shared
Toilet: none	Drinking water: bottled
Drinking water: tap	Drinking water: pump
Drinking water: protected well	Drinking water: unprotected well
Drinking water: protected spring	Drinking water: unprotected spring
Drinking water: river	Drinking water: rain
Drinking water: other	Purchases drinking water
Has electricity	Has experienced a natural disaster in past 1 year
Has natural tourism in residential area	Has received subsidised rice (Raskin) in past 4 months
Has received Smart Program (PIP) between August 2016 and March 2017	Has had a Social Security card (KPS)/family welfare card (KKS) between August 2016 and March 2017
Has received family of hope program (PKH) between August 2016 and March 2017	Has a savings account
Poverty status: poor	Region: Sumatera
Region: Jakarta	Region: Jawa
Region: Bali, NTB, NTT	Region: Kalimantan
Region: Sulawesi	Region: Maluka-Papua

Individual covariates (continuous)

Number of members in household	Number of children in household
Number of infants in household	Number of households in building/house
Number of families in building/house	Monthly consumption expenditure per capita

APPENDIX 16A.2 LIST OF TRAINING AND TUNING PARAMETERS IN GRF 1.2.0

Training parameters:

- `sample.fraction` controls the proportion of data used to construct each tree (default is 0.5)
- `num.trees` is the number of trees in the forest (default is 2000)
- `honesty` determines whether honest forests are trained (this is the default)
- `honesty.fraction` controls the proportion of training data used in tree splitting (default is 0.5)
- `honesty.prune.leaves` determines whether empty leaves are pruned away after training to ensure each tree can handle all test points (this is the default)
- `mtry` selects the number of variables considered for each split (default is $\sqrt{p} + 20$)
- `min.node.size` is the minimum number of observations in each tree leaf (default is 5)
- `alpha` controls the maximum imbalance of a split (default is 0.05)
- `imbalance.penalty` controls the penalty imposed on imbalanced splits (default is 0).

Tuning parameters:

- `tune.num.trees` selects the number of trees in each "mini forest" (default is 50)
- `tune.num.reps` selects the number of forests (default is 100)
- `tune.num.draws` is the number of random parameter values considered when choosing the optimal parameter values (default is 1000).

The training and tuning parameters listed above represent those available in the `regression_forest` function. The `causal_forest` function uses the same training and tuning parameters, except that the split balancing parameters are modified for causal splitting. This is because in causal settings the number of treated vs control observations (and not just the overall number of observations) in each node is important to obtain a good estimate of the treatment effect. In causal splitting, `min.node.size` reflects the minimum number of treated and control observations in each tree leaf (default is 5), and `alpha` and `imbalance.penalty` measure how much information is captured in each node, given by $\Sigma_{X_i \in P}(W_i - \bar{W})^2$.

All of the above training parameters (apart from `num.trees`) can be tuned via cross-validation using the `tune.parameters="all"` option in `regression_forest`. To use this option, the researcher must only select values for `num.trees` and the tuning parameters (default values can be used). To identify the values of the training parameters selected by cross-validation, the `tunable.params` option can be included in the main function.

Variance estimates can be obtained by providing the `estimate.variance` attribute to the `predict` function. The `ci.group.size` parameter in the `regression_forest` function controls the number of trees in each small group (default is 2). The variance is estimated by training trees in each small group and comparing predictions within and across groups.

See the `grf` help page for more details on all available parameters and features.

APPENDIX 16A.3

Table 16A.2   Examples of applied economic papers that use machine learning methods to estimate heterogeneous treatment effects

Article	Sector	Machine learning algorithm	Type of data	N
Bertrand, Marianne CrÃ©pon, Bruno Marguerie, Alicia Premand, and Patrick. 2017. Contemporaneous and Post-Program Impacts of a Public Works Program. Other Papers. World Bank.	Labour; Development	Causal forests	Randomised	12 188
Davis, Jonathan M. V., and Sara B. Heller. 2017. "Using Causal Forests to Predict Treatment Heterogeneity: An Application to Summer Jobs". *The American Economic Review* 107 (5): 546–50.	Labour	Causal forests	Randomised	6850; 4894
Knaus, Michael, Michael Lechner, and Anthony Strittmatter. n.d. "Heterogeneous Employment Effects of Job Search Programmes: A Machine Learning Approach". *SSRN Electronic Journal*. https://doi.org/10.2139/ssrn.3020462	Labour	LASSO	Observational	85 198
Andini, Monica, Emanuele Ciani, Guido de Blasio, Alessio D'Ignazio, and Viola Salvestrini. 2018. "Targeting with Machine Learning: An Application to a Tax Rebate Program in Italy". *Journal of Economic Behavior & Organization* 156 (December): 86–102.	Labour	Decision trees; k-Nearest Neighbour; Random forests	Observational	3646
Strittmatter, Anthony. 2018. "What Is the Value Added by Using Causal Machine Learning Methods in a Welfare Experiment Evaluation?" arXiv. http://arxiv.org/abs/1812.06533.	Labour	Random forests	Randomised	33 614

Table 16A.2   (continued)

Article	Sector	Machine learning algorithm	Type of data	N
Taddy, Matt, Matt Gardner, Liyun Chen, and David Draper. 2016. "A Nonparametric Bayesian Analysis of Heterogenous Treatment Effects in Digital Experimentation". *Journal of Business & Economic Statistics: A Publication of the American Statistical Association* 34 (4): 661–72.	Business	CARTs; random forests	Randomised	21 000 000
Daoud, Adel, and Fredrik Johansson. 2019. "Estimating Treatment Heterogeneity of International Monetary Fund Programs on Child Poverty with Generalized Random Forest". https://doi.org/10.31235/osf.io/awfjt.	Development	Causal forests	Observational	1 940 734
O'Neill, E., and M. Weeks. 2018. "Causal Tree Estimation of Heterogeneous Household Response to Time-Of-Use Electricity Pricing Schemes". 1865. Faculty of Economics, University of Cambridge. https://ideas.repec.org/p/cam/camdae/1865.html.	Environmental	Causal forests	Randomised	4225
Brand, Jennie E., Jiahui Xu, Bernard Koch, and Pablo Geraldo. 2019. "Uncovering Sociological Effect Heterogeneity Using Machine Learning". arXiv. http://arxiv.org/abs/1909.09138.	Labour	Causal forests	Observational	4584

PART V

STATA AND R IN MICROECONOMETRIC APPLICATIONS

17. Stochastic frontier analysis in Stata: using existing and coding new commands

Oleg Badunenko

1. INTRODUCTION

The Stochastic Frontier (SF thereafter) analysis is an econometric approach to measuring economic efficiency, which is built on an empirical estimation of production and cost functions. SF efficiency analysis gains in popularity and hence many new estimators of technology, efficiency and determinants of efficiency are proposed. If authors offer replication codes, these codes are not necessarily available for the software preferred by the practitioner or indeed installed on computers in research data centers where users have little flexibility. For many researchers Stata remains the software of choice, even though there are free alternatives such as R, Python, Julia and so on are accessible (see for example, Pinzon, 2015). Codes on authors' websites or journal data archives, such as the *Journal of Applied Econometrics* data archive (http://qed. econ.queensu.ca/jae/), are available in Stata, but mostly where practitioners make use of the available commands in Stata. New estimators typically appear in softwares such SAS, R, Gauss, MATLAB and so on, which are considered to be low-level programming languages (see for example, Sickles and Zelenyuk, 2019, chapter 17, and Sickles et al.,2020). However, since version 9, which appeared in April 2005, Stata ships with Mata, which is a full-blown programming language that compiles into a byte code, optimizes it and executes codes fast. In each new release, Stata Corp. not only introduces new estimators but also converts many existing relatively slow ADO.NET programs into codes utilizing the power of Mata.

Why is then Stata not used so frequently by researchers to introduce the new estimators? The existence of two environments Mata and Stata can probably explain the confusion and steepness of the learning curve in programming. The purpose of this chapter is threefold. First, the chapter uses a simple SF model to showcase how straightforward it is to code in software Stata using Mata. Second, two new Stata commands that are programmed using Mata are introduced. Third, the chapter presents an empirical example using the new and existing commands and offers interpretation and explanation of results.

The rest of the chapter is organized as follows. Section 2 describes a basic SF model and logic as well as the steps to produce user-friendly Stata code. Section 3 explained major SF models for panel data. Section 4 introduces Stata commands that estimate the first- and second-generation SF models. An application using these new commands is showcased in section 5. Finally, section 6 concludes and sets out an agenda for the future.

2. FROM FORMULAE TO A STATA CODE

In this section, the logical structure of the coding process will be demonstrated. This is the universal guide, which is applied to coding any estimator in Stata. We will use the simplest SF model to illustrate how to code and compare the results to those obtained from the built-in command.

2.1   The Model

The SF model for the cross-sectional data can be written as

$$\ln q_i = \ln f(X_i;\beta) + v_i - \rho \cdot u_i \qquad (17.1)$$
$$= \ln f(X_i;\beta) + \varepsilon_i,$$

where

$$\rho = \begin{cases} 1 & \text{for a stochastic production frontier model} \\ -1 & \text{for a stochastic cost frontier model,} \end{cases} \qquad (17.2)$$

$\ln q_i$ is logged output for a stochastic production frontier model and logged cost for a stochastic cost frontier model for observation $i = 1, \ldots, N$, X_i is a vector of inputs for a stochastic production frontier and a vector of outputs and input prices for a stochastic cost frontier and β is the set of parameters of the technology once $f(\cdot)$ is specified. If technology is assumed to be Cobb–Douglas (CD), $\ln f(X_i;\beta) = \beta_0 + \Sigma\beta_i \ln x_i$. CD technology is quite restrictive. In section 4, a more flexible translog technology will be used. The random noise term v_i is assumed to be independently and identically distributed (*i.i.d.*) normal with zero mean and variance σ_v^2. $u_i \geq 0$ is the inefficiency term assumed to be *i.i.d.* as half-normal, that is, $u_i = |U_i|$, where is U_i is *i.i.d.* normal with zero mean and variance σ_u^2. The log-likelihood function for the model (17.1) is given by

$$\ln L(\theta) = \sum_{i=1}^{N} \ln\Phi\left(\frac{-\rho\varepsilon_i\lambda}{\sigma}\right) - \frac{\varepsilon_i^2}{2\sigma^2} - \ln\sigma + \frac{1}{2}\ln\frac{2}{\pi'} \qquad (17.3)$$

where $\lambda = \sigma_u/\sigma_v$ and $\sigma = \sqrt{\sigma_u^2 + \sigma_v^2}$, $\Phi(\cdot)$ is the cumulative distribution function of the standard normal distribution and $\theta = [\beta \; \sigma \; \lambda]$. The Maximum Likelihood Estimator (MLE) of θ, $\hat{\theta}$ is obtained by maximizing the likelihood in (17.3). This can be done using the Stata command `frontier`, but for illustration purposes, let's code it using Mata.

2.2   Coding the Estimator Using Mata

To show the logic of coding, we will start from the end and build our way to displaying the estimation results. As the *first* step, we need to identify the elementary operation we need to do to obtain the estimates. For the least squares approach, the estimator is usually obtained using a formula, derived from minimization of the residual sum of squares. In our case, we need to maximize the log-likelihood in (17.3) iteratively. The expression (17.3) can be coded in Mata as a simple one line:

```
1  lnnormal(-cost*ehat*lmd/sig)  -  ehat:^2/2/sig^2:-  log(sig):+
       0.5*log(2/pi())
```

which will return a vector of length N once we provide `cost`, `ehat`, `lmd` and `sig`. The Mata function `sflleval` (any other name can be chosen) to evaluate (17.3) can be coded as follows:

```
 1 void sflleval(real scalar todo, real vector b, ///
 2                real vector y, real matrix X, ///
 3                real scalar cost,
 4                val, grad, hess)
 5 {
 6  real vector ehat
 7  real scalar K, sig, lmd
 8
 9 K      = cols(X)
10 //  b[1..K]
11 ehat  = y - X * (b[1..K])'
12 sig   = b[K+1]
13 lmd   = b[K+2]
14 val   = lnnormal(-cost*ehat*lmd/sig) - ehat:^2/2/sig^2:+
      0.5*log(2/pi()):- log(sig)
15 }
```

In this code b is θ, where the first K elements are β, $(K+1)^{st}$ element is σ and $(K+2)^{nd}$ element is λ. The sflleval function calculates ε_i (ehat) on line 11 based on data for the left- and right-hand sides in (17.1), so y and X are the arguments. cost is also an argument taken by the sflleval. The types of arguments are specified as well to avoid errors and speed up an evaluation. Arguments grad and hess stand for a gradient and Hessian matrix. If they are not provided in the function to be optimized as in the case of sflleval, they will be numerically approximated by Mata. In such a case, the optimization will be slower and sometimes less precise. So, it is advisable to derive both gradient and Hessian, or at least gradient, analytically and code into the evaluator. We will not do this here for simplicity, but the new commands benefit from using both the gradient and Hessian matrix. The speed advantage over the existing command will be discussed later.

The *second* step is the maximization of the sflleval. This can be done using Mata's optimize() function. Our second Mata function is an intermediary (let's also call it so) to get the data from Stata and call sflleval to obtain $\hat{\theta}$.

```
 1 void intermediary(string scalar depvar, string scalar indepvars,
 2                string scalar touse, string scalar constant,
 3                string scalar cost,
 4                string scalar bname, string scalar Vname)
 5 {
 6  real vector y, bh, b0, t0
 7  real matrix X, Vh
 8  real scalar p, n
 9  // get the data from Stata
10  y = st_data(., depvar, touse)
11  n = rows(y)
12  X = st_data(., indepvars, touse)
13  // if noconstant is not specified, add a vector of ones to X
14  if (constant =="") {
```

```
15   X = X, J(n, 1, 1)
16   // obtain
17   p = strtoreal(cost)
18   // get the initial value for 'beta' as OLS
19   b0 = 0.999999 * invsym(quadcross(X,X)) * quadcross(X,y)
20   // suppose initial lambda is 1
21   lmd0 = 1
22   // suppose initial sig is 0.5
23   sig0 = 0.5
24   // vector theta
25   t0 = b0', lmd0, sig0
26   // initialize structure for optimize()
27   S = optimize_init()
28   optimize_init_evaluator(S, &sflleval())
29   optimize_init_evaluatortype(S, "gf0")
30   optimize_init_argument(S, 1, y)
31   optimize_init_argument(S, 2, X)
32   optimize_init_argument(S, 3, p)
33   optimize_init_params(S, t0)
34   bh = optimize(S)
35   Vh = optimize_result_V_oim(S)
36   st_matrix(bname, bh)
37   st_matrix(Vname, Vh)
38 }
```

The `intermediary` function contains five blocks. The first block on lines 6–8 defines all objects (scalars, vectors and matrices) used in the function. Recall that `sflleval` obtains four arguments, three of which are invariant through optimization. We obtain them from Stata on lines 10–18, which are the second block of the `intermediary` function. We obtain data using `st_data` Mata function. The arguments `depvar` is a string that contains the name of the dependent variable and `indepvars` is a string that contains the list of names of the independent variables. Argument `touse` specifies which observations should be used. These three arguments will be discussed when we consider the *third* step.

The third block of the `intermediary` function is the largest. It produces the desired estimates. In the MLE case, it consists of three sub-blocks. The first one defines the initial values for the optimizer. This is done on lines 20–26. Here we can get away with a very naive set of initial values, however, often one would have to do a much more careful job finding clever starting values. We will return to this issue when comparing our function to the built-in command.

The second sub-block of the third block of the `intermediary` function involves setting the optimization problem. The structure `S` is initialized on line 28. On line 29, we tell Mata that we will optimize our function `sflleval`. The type of evaluator is specified on line 30. `gf0` stands for an evaluator that provides only a vector of log-likelihood values for each observation. If the function `sflleval` also evaluates $N \times (K + 2)$ matrix with observation specific gradients, we would use `gf1` type of evaluator. Finally, if the function `sflleval` also evaluated the $(K + 2) \times (K + 2)$ Hessian matrix, we would use `gf2` type of evaluator. The new commands discussed will use `gf2` type of evaluator. On lines 31–33, we specify unchanging arguments to the function `sflleval`. They have running numbers 1, 2 and 3. The first two arguments in `sflleval` must be `todo`, which is defined by the type of evaluator: 0 for `gr0`, 1 for `gr1` and 2 for `gr2`, and vector of parameters, which we call `b` in the function `sflleval`. So, the third argument to `sflleval` is the first that the user can provide. Finally, line 34 specifies the initial values that we feed into the optimizer.

The third sub-block of the third block of the `intermediary` function maximizes the likelihood function `sflleval`. When we call `optimize(S)` on line 35, the optimization starts. The set of optimal parameters are written to `bh`. The variance–covariance matrix `Vh` is obtained on line 36.

The fourth and the last block in the `intermediary` function passes the estimates to Stata. We give the content of Mata matrices `bh` and `Vh` to Stata matrices `bname` and `Vname`, which are the arguments of the `intermediary` function. In this example, we pass only two matrices to Stata. However, many other scalars which include diagnostic such as AIC, R^2, *LR*-statistic and so on or indeed the efficiency scores can be calculated in the `intermediary` function and passed to Stata. So, the fourth block can be extended as needed.

The *third* and final step in the coding involves three universal blocks: (i) obtaining input from the user, (ii) passing the content to the *intermediary* function and getting result from the *intermediary* function and (iii) finally displaying the estimation results.

```
1 program define frontier2, eclass sortpreserve
2  version 16
3  syntax varlist(numeric fv min=2) [if] [in] ///
4     [, COST noCONStant]
5
6  tempname b V p
7
8  marksample touse
9  gettoken depvar indepvars : varlist
10  _fv_check_depvar 'depvar'
11  local p "1"
12  if "'cost'"!= "" {
13   local p "-1"
14  }
15  mata: intermediary("'depvar'", "'indepvars'", "'touse'", ///
16      "'constant'", "'p'", "'b'", "'V'")
17
18  if "'constant'" == "" {
19   local indepvars "'indepvars' _cons"
20  }
21  matrix colnames 'b' = 'indepvars' /:sig /:lmd
22  matrix colnames 'V' = 'indepvars' /:sig /:lmd
23  matrix rownames 'V' = 'indepvars' /:sig /:lmd
24  ereturn post 'b' 'V', esample('touse') buildfvinfo
25  ereturn local cmd "frontier2"
26
```

```
27  display ""
28  display "Stochastic frontier normal/half-normal model"
29  ereturn display
30 end
```

The first block in the `frontier2` function defines what the user can specify. Lines 3 and 4 determine that the user provides at least two variables, the first of which will be a dependent variable. The optional arguments are embraced in squared brackets. For example, the user can indicate subsample by specifying either `if` or `in` or both. The other options are to specify `cost` if the stochastic cost frontier is to be estimated and `noconstant` if intercept β_0 is to be suppressed. If anything else is specified, Stata will return an error. Line 6 is important since it defines names for temporary locals used in the `frontier2`. We will use only three, but typically there will be more depending on the complexity of the command.

Next, the `frontier2` function determines what will be passed to the *intermediary* function. `marksample` takes into account options `if` and `in` as well as possible missing values for any of the variables. `gettoken` defines locals that contain the names of dependent and independent variables. `_fv_check_depvar` just makes sure that the dependent variable is not a factor variable. Lines 11–14 handle the option `cost`. If `cost` is not specified, the `frontier2` will estimate production SF.

The second block in the `frontier2` function is just one call to the *intermediary* function (lines 15 and 16), which (i) takes arguments from Stata, (ii) does the whole estimation work and (iii) passes results to Stata. Recall that the lines 37 and 38 in the `intermediary` function will pass estimated parameters and the variance–covariance matrix to Stata. So, after lines 15 and 16 in the `frontier2` function are completed, locals b and V will contain the estimates.

The third block begins on line 18 by obtaining the names for the parameter vector and the variance–covariance matrix, which are assigned on lines 21–23. They are posted for the possible post-estimation on lines 24 and 25 (and can be viewed by typing `ereturn list` after the execution of `frontier2`). The title of the estimation is displayed on line 28 and, finally, the table with estimation results is displayed on line 29.

2.3   The Universal Coding Guide Using Mata

The previous steps can be summarized as follows:
- The main Stata function
    1. Determine what the user can type and prepare inputs such as dependent and independent variables to be passed to the *intermediary* Mata function.
    2. Call the *intermediary* Mata function, which calculates estimates and other statistics and returns them to Stata.
    3. Prepare results for the post-estimation and display the results.
- The *intermediary* Mata function
    1. Obtain the data from Stata.
    2. Acquire the estimates and all required statistics. This may involve outsourcing computation to another Mata function (for example for the least square estimator) or function evaluator for the MLE.
    3. Pass the results to Stata.

This scheme is universal and any estimator will follow it.

2.4   The Code in Action

Let us use our command `frontier2` and compare the results to those of the shipped command `frontier`. After we have placed the three commands `sflleval`, `intermediary` and `frontier2` and run them in Stata, the code is compiled and can be used.

Consider the data on value added, capital and labor for 25 US states on Transportation Equipment Manufacturing from Zellner and Revankar (1969), which can be accessed at http://pages.stern.nyu.edu/~wgreene/Text/Edition7/tablelist8new.htm and http://www.stern.nyu.edu/~wgreene/Text/Edition7/TableF7-2.txt. Apply first the `frontier` command. Because `cost` is not specified, this is a SF production function:

```
 1  . webuse greene9, clear
 2  . frontier lnv lnk lnl
 3
 4  Iteration 0:   log likelihood =  2.3357572
 5  Iteration 1:   log likelihood =  2.4673009
 6  Iteration 2:   log likelihood =  2.4695125
 7  Iteration 3:   log likelihood =  2.4695222
 8  Iteration 4:   log likelihood =  2.4695222
 9
10  Stoc. frontier normal/           Number of obs    =          25
11      half-normal model            Wald chi2(2)     =      743.71
12  Log likelihood =  2.4695222      Prob > chi2      =      0.0000
13
14  -----------------------------------------------------------------
15      lnv  |    Coef. Std. Err.    z    P>|z|   [95% Conf. Interval]
16  ---------+-------------------------------------------------------
17      lnk  |  .2585478  .098764  2.62  0.009   .0649738   .4521218
18      lnl  |  .7802451 .1199399  6.51  0.000   .5451672   1.015323
19     _cons |  2.081135  .281641  7.39  0.000   1.529128   2.633141
20  ---------+-------------------------------------------------------
21  /lnsig2v |  -3.48401 .6195353 -5.62  0.000  -4.698277  -2.269743
22  /lnsig2u | -3.014599  1.11694 -2.70  0.007  -5.203761  -.8254368
23  ---------+-------------------------------------------------------
24   sigma_v |  .1751688 .0542616                .0954514   .3214633
25   sigma_u |  .2215073 .1237052                 .074134   .6618486
26    sigma2 |  .0797496 .0426989               -.0039388    .163438
27    lambda |  1.264536 .1678684                .9355204   1.593552
28  -----------------------------------------                ------------------------
29  LR test of sigma_u=0: chibar2(01)          Prob >= chibar2 = 0.256
       = 0.43
```

The results of our `frontier2` command are:

```
1 . frontier2 lnv lnk lnl
2 Iteration 0:    f(p) = -23.681441   (not concave)
3 Iteration 1:    f(p) = -2.0572723
4 Iteration 2:    f(p) =  1.4042103
5 Iteration 3:    f(p) =  2.3615845
6 Iteration 4:    f(p) =  2.4387119
7 Iteration 5:    f(p) =  2.4691231
8 Iteration 6:    f(p) =  2.4695035
9 Iteration 7:    f(p) =  2.4695222
10 Iteration 8:    f(p) =  2.4695222
11
12 Stoc. frontier normal/half-normal model
13 ------------------------------------------------------------------
14        |     Coef.    Std. Err.    z     P>|z|   [95% Conf. Interval]
15 ------+-----------------------------------------------------------
16   lnk |   .2585478    .0987643   2.62   0.009    .0649734   .4521222
17   lnl |   .7802451    .1199401   6.51   0.000    .5451668   1.015323
18 _cons |   2.081135    .2816414   7.39   0.000    1.529128   2.633142
19 ------+-----------------------------------------------------------
20  /sig |   .2823997    .0756002   3.74   0.000    .1342261   .4305734
21  /lmd |   1.264536    1.03029    1.23   0.220   -.7547957   3.283869
22 -----------------------------------------------------------------
```

We make two observations. First, the results are the same if we consider the largest value of the loglikelihood, $\hat{\beta}$, and $\hat{\lambda}$ (although the standard error of $\hat{\lambda}$ is different, which may be a result of numerical approximation of the Hessian matrix). Stata uses different parametrization of σ_u and σ_v, namely logged variances $\ln\sigma_u^2$ and $\ln\sigma_v^2$, to avoid the possibility of negative values of either σ_u or σ_v in some intermediate iteration. With our parametrization $\sigma_v = \sigma / \sqrt{\lambda^2 + 1}$ and $\sigma_u = \lambda\sigma_v$. Because we return both parameters and variance–covariance matrix after `frontier2` and `frontier2` is an `eclass`, we can use `nlcom` command to see that $\ln\sigma_v^2$, $\ln\sigma_u^2$, σ_v, σ_u and σ^2 are the same in both `frontier` and `frontier2`:

```
1 . nlcom (lnsig2v: log((_b[/sig] / sqrt(_b[/lmd]^2+1) )^2) ) ///
2 > (lnsig2u: log((_b[/lmd]*_b[/sig] / sqrt(_b[/lmd]^2+1) )^2) )
3   ///
4 > (sigma_v: _b[/sig] / sqrt(_b[/lmd]^2 + 1)) ///
5 > (sigma_u: _b[/lmd]*_b[/sig] / sqrt(_b[/lmd]^2 + 1)) ///
6 > (sigma2: _b[/sig]^2)
7
8      lnsig2v:  log((_b[/sig] / sqrt(_b[/lmd]^2+1) )^2)
9      lnsig2u:  log((_b[/lmd]*_b[/sig] / sqrt(_b[/lmd]^2+1) )^2)
10     sigma_v:  _b[/sig] / sqrt(_b[/lmd]^2 + 1)
11     sigma_u:  _b[/lmd]*_b[/sig] / sqrt(_b[/lmd]^2 + 1)
12      sigma2:  _b[/sig]^2
```

```
13 -------------------------------------------------------------------
14         |     Coef.   Std. Err.     z    P>|z|   [95% Conf. Interval]
15 --------+----------------------------------------------------------
16 lnsig2v |  -3.48401   .6195354   -5.62   0.000   -4.698277   -2.269743
17 lnsig2u | -3.014599   1.11694    -2.70   0.007   -5.203762   -.8254362
18 sigma_v |  .1751688   .0542616    3.23   0.001     .068818    .2815197
19 sigma_u |  .2215073   .1237052    1.79   0.073   -.0209505    .4639652
20  sigma2 |  .0797496   .0426989    1.87   0.062   -.0039388     .163438
21 -------------------------------------------------------------------
```

We can also test if technology is constant returns to scale (CRS):

```
1 . test lnk + lnl = 1
2
3  ( 1)  lnk + lnl = 1
4
5          chi2(  1) =     0.84
6        Prob > chi2 =     0.3580
```

We fail to reject the null hypothesis that the technology is CRS. The estimates for the SF cost function can be obtained by specifying cost option. The estimates from frontier and frontier2 are the same:

```
1 . webuse frontier2, clear
2
3 . frontier lncost lnp_k lnp_l lnout, cost
4
5 Iteration 0:   log likelihood = -2386.9523
6 Iteration 1:   log likelihood = -2386.6923
7 Iteration 2:   log likelihood = -2386.6915
8 Iteration 3:   log likelihood = -2386.6915
9
10 Stoc. frontier normal/          Number of obs    =      1,231
11     half-normal model           Wald chi2(3)     =       9.00
12 Log likelihood = -2386.6915     Prob > chi2      =     0.0293
13
14 -------------------------------------------------------------------
15 lncost |     Coef.   Std. Err.     z    P>|z|   [95% Conf. Interval]
16 -------+-----------------------------------------------------------
17  lnp_k |  .3683036   .2342461    1.57   0.116   -.0908103    .8274175
18  lnp_l |  .6780932   .4950864    1.37   0.171   -.2922584    1.648445
19  lnout |  .7319725   .3463923    2.11   0.035    .0530561    1.410889
20  _cons |  2.890649   1.035186    2.79   0.005    .8617222    4.919576
```

```
21 ---------+------------------------------------------------------------
22 /lnsig2v |    .22894  .1346807    1.70   0.089   -.0350294      .4929094
23 /lnsig2u | 1.517706   .125855    12.06   0.000    1.271035      1.764377
24 -----   --+------------------------------------------------------------
25 sigma_v  | 1.121279 .0755073                      .9826378      1.279481
26 sigma_u  | 2.135825 .1344021                     1.887999      2.416182
27 sigma2   | 5.819015 .4505303                     4.935992      6.702038
28 lambda   | 1.904811 .1999447                     1.512927      2.296696
29 ------------------------------------------------------------------------
30 LR test of sigma_u=0: chibar2(01) = 33.58  Prob >= chibar2 = 0.000
31
32 . frontier2 lncost lnp_k lnp_l lnout, cost
33 Iteration 0:    f(p) = -3186.7233
34 Iteration 1:    f(p) =  -2513.968
35 Iteration 2:    f(p) = -2406.2563
36 Iteration 3:    f(p) = -2406.2417  (not concave)
37 ...
38 Iteration 21:   f(p) = -2402.2301  (not concave)
39 Iteration 22:   f(p) = -2393.2169
40 Iteration 23:   f(p) = -2387.0557
41 Iteration 24:   f(p) = -2386.6937
42 Iteration 25:   f(p) = -2386.6915
43 Iteration 26:   f(p) = -2386.6915
44
45 Stoc. frontier normal/half-normal model
46 ------------------------------------------------------------------------
47        |      Coef.  Std. Err.     z    P>|z|   [95% Conf. Interval]
48 ------+-----------------------------------------------------------------
49 lnp_k |   .3683033  .2342461    1.57   0.116   -.0908106      .8274172
50 lnp_l |   .6780928  .4950878    1.37   0.171   -.2922615      1.648447
51 lnout |   .7319727  .3463926    2.11   0.035    .0530557       1.41089
52 _cons |   2.890648  1.035189    2.79   0.005    .8617151      4.919581
53 ------+-----------------------------------------------------------------
54 /sig  |   2.412264  .0933833   25.83   0.000    2.229236      2.595292
55 /lmd  |   1.904814  .2353377    8.09   0.000     1.44356      2.366067
56 ------------------------------------------------------------------------
```

The second observation that we make is how long it takes for `frontier2` to converge. There could be two explanations. First, as mentioned before, `frontier2` uses very naive starting values for the MLE. Stata uses much smarter ones. Second, `frontier` uses gr2 type of evaluator, that is, both the gradient and the Hessian matrix are analytically derived and coded, while `frontier2` uses gr0, implying that the gradient and the Hessian matrix are numerically approximated. In this simple example, the only cost is time. In other more complicated likelihood functions, the cost may be a lack of convergence as Stata will encounter discontinuous regions because of the precision of the gradient evaluation and will just stop. Hence, it is advisable to derive and code both the gradient and the Hessian matrix, but if the Hessian is very complicated, having an analytical expression for the gradient is an enormous advantage.

3.   THE 1ST AND 2ND GENERATION SF MODELS FOR PANEL DATA

3.1   The Panel Data SF Model

Nowadays, one would hardly use the model (17.1). First, it is very restrictive in terms of what economic questions can be answered and how flexibly it models the efficiency. More specifically, both noise and inefficiency terms are *i.i.d.* and determinants of inefficiency are not allowed. Second, the model (17.1) is for cross-sectional data.

The obvious extension of the model (17.1) when panel data are available is to introduce time dimension and add t to the subscript:

$$\ln q_{it} = \ln f(X_{it};\beta) + \upsilon_{ti} - \rho \cdot u_{it}$$
$$= \ln f(X_{it};\beta) + \varepsilon_{it}. \tag{17.4}$$

The variety of models that are nested within (17.4) are substantial. We start with the simplest one where $u_{it} = u_i$. This class of model is the *first*-generation panel data SF model, in which inefficiency is different across observations but is time invariant (see Pitt and Lee, 1981).

In this model, u_i is half-normal and homoskedastic, $u_i \sim N^+(0,\sigma_u^2)$. This can be generalized along the lines of Stevenson (1980), who suggested using the truncated normal distribution, $u_i \sim N^+(\mu,\sigma_u^2)$. However, the likelihood estimation with the truncated normal distribution can fail to converge (see for example, Ritter and Simar, 1997). Further, the conditional mean of the truncated distribution can be made observation specific $u_i \sim N^+(\mu_i,\sigma_u^2)$. Since estimating $N\mu$ parameters is not feasible, a structure must be imposed. One way to do this is to model determinants of inefficiency and parametrize the pre-truncated inefficiency distribution; that is, the conditional mean of the truncated distribution can be made observation specific by imposing linear structure on it, as in Kumbhakar et al. (1991);

$$\mu_i = E[u_i \mid z_{u_{2i}}] = z_{u_{2i}} \delta_u, \tag{17.5}$$

so that $u_i \sim N^+(z_{u_{2i}} \delta_u, \sigma_u^2)$ and only δ_u parameters are estimated instead of u_i, $i = 1, \ldots, N$. With a half-normal or truncated normal distribution, the inefficiency term is still *i.i.d.*, which can introduce bias. If the heteroskedasticity function is known, bias can be eliminated by making σ_u^2 observation specific (see Caudill et al., 1995):

$$\ln \sigma_{u_i}^2 = z_{u_{1i}} \gamma_u. \tag{17.6}$$

Besides, since $E(u_i) = \sqrt{(2/\pi)} \sigma_{u_i} = \sqrt{(2/\pi)} \exp\left(\tfrac{1}{2} z_{ui} \gamma_u\right)$, the z_{ui} variables can be viewed as determinants of persistent inefficiency. Consider efficiency change due to a change in z_j holding everything else fixed. Since the efficiency is $\exp(-u_i)$, the rate of change in efficiency (CE) due to a change in z_j is given by

$$\text{CE} := \Delta \text{Efficiency}_i = -\frac{\partial u_i}{\partial z_j} \approx -\frac{\partial E(u_i)}{\partial z_j} = -\sqrt{\frac{2}{\pi}} \frac{\partial \sigma_{u_i}}{\partial z_j}. \tag{17.7}$$

Under the assumption $\sigma_{u_i}^2 = \exp(z_{u_{1i}} \gamma_u)$, equation (17.7) becomes

$$-\sqrt{\frac{2}{\pi}} \frac{1}{2} \gamma_{u_j} \exp\left(\frac{1}{2} z_{u_{1i}} \gamma_u\right),$$

where γ_{u_j} is a coefficient of z_j. Variables in $z_{u_{1i}}$ vary across firms, but are time invariant. This means that $\sigma_{u_i}^2$ is explained only by time-invariant covariates. Similar to (17.6), the heteroskedasticity function of noise can be specified:

$$\ln \sigma_{v_{it}}^2 = z_{v_{it}} \gamma_v. \tag{17.8}$$

3.2　The Second-Generation SF Model

The *second*-generation class panel data SF models deal with time-varying inefficiency, that is $u_{it} \neq u_i$. A general specification is of the form $u_{it} = \beta(t) u_i$, where $\beta(t)$ is some function of time. This is a specification that makes use of the scaling property and adds some useful dimensions to the SF model. It allows firm heterogeneity to show up by shrinking or inflating the inefficiency distribution without changing its basic shape. A flexible specification of $\beta(t)$ is offered by Kumbhakar (1990):

$$\beta(t) = (1 + \exp(\gamma t + \delta t^2))^{-1}. \tag{17.9}$$

This specification is such that, depending on the signs of the estimated parameters γ and δ, the function of the inefficiency of time can be upward or downward sloping or be a U-shaped or n-shaped parabola. A modified version of (17.9) is given by

$$\beta(t) = 1 + \gamma(t - T_i) + \delta(t - T_i)^2, \tag{17.10}$$

where T_i is the end period for the observation i. Specification (17.10) also allows a nonlinear development of inefficiency over time. A simplified version of the Kumbhakar (1990) model is that by Battese and Coelli (1992):

$$\beta(t) = \exp(-\gamma(t - T_i)). \tag{17.11}$$

In this model, which also goes by the name "the decay model", the inefficiency can either go up or go down. In some applications, specification (17.11) can be seen to be restrictive in comparison to that of Kumbhakar (1990).

An excellent overview of the first- and second-generation SF models for panel data and collection of formulae required to code the estimators can be found in Kumbhakar and Lovell (2000). Note, in this review, only some of the models are considered. There are other models, that are referred to in this chapter as the first or second-generation models, depending on whether the ineffiency term is time-constant or time-varying. For example, the model of Schmidt and Sickles (1984) or system estimators.

3.3 Next Generations of SF Models

In addition to the first- and second-generation models, two more classes of SF models exist. More specifically, if one more time-constant components ω_i is added to the model (17.4), we obtain the *third*-generation SF model for panel data:

$$\ln q_{it} = \ln f\left(X_{it};\beta\right) + \omega_i + v_{ti} - \rho \cdot u_{it}. \tag{17.12}$$

The parameter ω_i has been treated differently in the literature. For example, Kumbhakar and Hjalmarsson (1993, 1995) and Kumbhakar and Heshmati (1995) have estimated the model in (17.12) assuming that ω_i is the persistent or time-constant inefficiency. Hence the model (17.12) becomes

$$\ln q_{it} = \ln f\left(X_{it};\beta\right) - \rho \cdot u_{0i} + v_{ti} - \rho \cdot u_{it}, \tag{17.13}$$

where observations are assumed to have two types of inefficiencies, namely the transient or short-term inefficiency $u_{0i} > 0$ and persistent or long-term inefficiency $u_{it} > 0$. Park et al. (1998, 2003, 2007) and Greene (2005), on the other hand, assumed that ω_i in (17.12) is an individual effect as we know it from standard panel-data approaches. Hence the model (17.12) becomes

$$\ln q_{it} = \ln f\left(X_{it};\beta\right) + v_{0i} + v_{ti} - \rho \cdot u_{it}. \tag{17.14}$$

While Park et al. (1998, 2003, 2007) considered the time-invariant inefficiency component retrieved similarly to Schmidt and Sickles (1984), Greene (2005) studied time-varying inefficiency. Kneip et al. (2012) is the generalization of the model by Greene (2005), where the intercept in $f()$ is replaced by a general average function and individual effects are nonconstant.

Finally, Colombi et al. (2014), Kumbhakar, Lien and Hardaker (2014) and Tsionas and Kumbhakar (2014) were the first to formulate the *fourth*-generation SF model for panel data, which accounts for both heterogeneity and persistent inefficiency. It is also known as the four-component SF model for panel data:

$$\ln q_{it} = \ln f\left(X_{it};\beta\right) + v_{0i} - \rho \cdot u_{0i} + v_{it} - \rho \cdot u_{it}, \tag{17.15}$$

which later has been extended to allow determinants of both types of inefficiency (see Badunenko and Kumbhakar, 2017).

4. NEW STATA COMMANDS THAT USE MATA TO ESTIMATE THE 1ST AND 2ND GENERATION SF MODELS FOR PANEL DATA

This section introduces two Stata commands that make use of Mata. As mentioned, the commands are limited to the discussed models. The purpose is to enable a suite of options that will encompass a variety of models that were or were not introduced formally. For example, the model by Kumbhakar (1990) did not allow heteroskedasticity, but Stata commands allow us to estimate such a model.

The first Stata command is `xtsf1g`, where `xt` stands for a panel data model, `sf` for SF and `1g` – for the first generation, implying the time-invariant inefficiency model. The command `xtsf1g` has only four modeling options:

1.   `distribution` can be `hnormal` or `tnormal`;
2.   `uilnvariance` specifies the heterskedasticity function in (17.6);
3.   `vitlnvariance` specifies the heterskedasticity function in (17.8);
4.   `uimean` specifies the conditional mean function in (17.5).

Options 2, 3 and 4 require a list of variables. An intercept can be suppressed in each of them by using the `noconstant` option, for example, `uimean(variable1 variable2, noconstant)`. If `uimean` is specified, `distribution` will be set to `tnormal`. If `uilnvariance` is not specified, a homoskedastic inefficiency model will be estimated. If the `vitlnvariance` option is not specified, a homoskedastic noise model will be estimated.

If the `cost` option is specified, the cost SF model is estimated, otherwise, the production SF model is estimated. The intercept can be suppressed in the frontier specification by specifying `noconstant`, but this is not advisable. Finally, the list of variables can involve factor-variable operators such as `#`, which can be useful in postestimation.

The second command is `xtsf2g`. There is only one additional option `model`, which can be `K1990`, `K1990modified` or `K1990modified`, presented in equations (17.9), (17.10) and (17.11), respectively.

4.1   Existing Stata Commands

There are several other possibilities to estimate the first- and second-generation SF models. First, the built-in `xtfrontier` command with the `ti` option corresponds to the time-invariant inefficiency model (the first generation), while the `tvd` option allows estimation of the Battese and Coelli (1992) model (the second generation). The `Xtfrontier`, however, does not allow the flexibility that the (combination of) options `uilnvariance`, `vitlnvariance` and `uimean` offers.

Second, the functionality of `xtsf1g` and `xtsf2g` overlaps with that of `sfpanel` offered by Belotti et al. (2013). While the first- and second-generation models are available in `sfpanel`, they do not offer possibilities provided by `uilnvariance`, `vitlnvariance` and `uimean` in `xtsf1g` and `xtsf2g`. The `sfpanel` code is not open, so it is not possible to extend it. More specifically, the Mata codes are compiled into a Mata dynamic library `mlib`. The third-generation model of Greene (2005) presents more flexibility. On some datasets, the error message "could not calculate numerical derivatives – flat or discontinuous region encountered" is shown implying that `gf0` type of the evaluator program is employed, which can be less precise or be a reason for non-convergence. This is especially true for the simulated maximum likelihood estimator used in true fixed-effects model by Greene (2005).

Third, Kumbhakar et al. (2015) offer codes to estimate a battery of SF models (codes can be found on `https://sites.google.com/site/sfbook2014/`). `sfpan` can be used to estimate the first- and second-generation SF models for panel data with the flexibility offered by `uilnvariance`, `vitlnvariance` and `uimean`. `sfpan` can estimate other panel data models as well. As in the case of `sfpanel`, `sfpan` seems to be using a `d0` type of the evaluator program, which does not specify the analytical expression for the gradient or Hessian matrix.

Table 17.1 Optimization times measured by the `timer` *command, N = 500,* $\sum T_i = 2546$

Command	Evaluator type	# iterations	Time, seconds
`sfpan`	d0	30	102.3070
`sfpanel`	gf0	18	6.8230
`xtfrontier`	d2	17	4.9280
`xtsf2g`	gf2	10	0.6540

While `sfpanel` is implemented using Mata, `sfpan` uses older and relatively slower `ado` programs. Besides, `sfpan` does not allow factor-variable operators.

Table 17.1 indicates the speed of the new commands using the Battese and Coelli (1992) model, where inefficiency is truncated to enable estimation using `sfpanel`. If we compare `xtfrontier` and `xtsf2g`, both commands use analytical expressions for the gradient and Hessian matrix. In this comparison, we see the power of Mata making estimation nearly 7.5 times quicker. `sfpanel` seems to be slower than either `xtfrontier` or `xtsf2g`. The reason may be that `sfpanel` is a gf0 evaluator program type. So, even though both `sfpanel` and `xtsf2g` use Mata, providing analytical expressions for the gradient and Hessian matrix makes a huge difference. Additionally, while the results from `xtsf2g` and `xtfrontier` coincide, the results from `xtpanel` are a bit different, indicating imprecision involving numerical approximation when using the gf0 evaluator program type. Table 17.1 includes also `sfpan`, but the speed performance is wanting. Out of 102 seconds, `sf_srch` used 6 seconds, while `ml max` took 96 seconds, which is quite long. The reason for this is twofold. First, `sfpan` does not use Mata, so it is much slower than `sfpanel`. Second, `sfpan` does not specify an analytical expression for the gradient or Hessian matrix, so it is much slower than the `xtfrontier`.

Even though there are Stata commands that estimate a variety of the first- and second-generation SF models for panel data, there is room for improvement. The purpose of this chapter is not only to introduce a way to estimate a variety of models but also to showcase how other models can be implemented for wider use using Stata software with Mata to make the estimation more efficient and transparent (the Mata codes are on author's website at `https://sites.google.com/view/oleg-badunenko/codes`).

5. APPLICATION AND INTERPRETATION

5.1 Data Management

In this section, we use the commands `xtsf1g` and `xtsf2g` described to estimate the first- and second-generation SF models for panel data using 500 randomly selected banks from data used by Koetter et al. (2012) and accessed at `http://qed.econ.queensu.ca/jae/2014-v29.2/restrepo-tobon-kumbhakar/`. In Chapter 9 of this Handbook Zelenyuk and Zelenyuk provide a more comprehensive performance analysis of banks. The following code is used to obtain a sample of banks between the 25th and 75th percentiles of the size distribution, which are observed at least four times.

```stata
1 import delimited "2b_QLH.txt", varnames(1) clear
2 // rename 'entity' to 'id'
3 rename entity id
4 // keep only banks between 2000 - 2007
5 keep if year >= 2000 & year <= 2007
6 // keep the range
7 summarize ta, detail
8 keep if ta >= r(p25) & ta <= r(p75)
9 // generate required variables
10 // Homogeneity in prices of degree 1
11 generate double lnc    = log(toc/w2)
12 // Gross total equity to gross total assets ratio, ER=Z/TA
13 generate double er     = z / ta
14 // Total loans and leases to gross total assets ratio, LA=Y2/TA
15 generate double la     = y2 / ta
16 generate double lny1   = log(y1)
17 generate double lny2   = log(y2)
18 generate double lnw1   = log(w1/w2)
19 generate double lnta   = log(ta)
20 // keep and order
21 keep id year lnc lny1 lny2 lnw1 lnw2 er la ta llp lnta
22 keep id year lnc lny1 lny2 lnw1 lnw2 er la ta llp lnta
23 xtset id year
24 // complete observations
25 foreach v of var * {
26   drop if missing('v')
27 }
28 // keep only if more than 3 observations
29 bysort id: egen Ti = count(tc)
30 keep if Ti >= 4
31 // random 500 banks
32 set seed 816376586
33 tempname zero2one mysample
34 generate 'zero2one' = uniform()
35 bysort id: replace 'zero2one' = 'zero2one'[1]
36 egen 'mysample' = group('zero2one')
37 keep if 'mysample' <= 500
38 drop 'zero2one' 'mysample'
39 // generate time-constant variables
40 bysort id: egen ta_ave    = mean(ta)
41 bysort id: egen llp_ave   = mean(llp)
42 bysort id: egen er_ave    = mean(er)
43 bysort id: egen la_ave    = mean(la)
44 generate trend   = year - 1999
45 generate half    = 0.5
```

5.2   Translog technology and homogeneity

We will use the full translog specification:

$$\ln(TC) = \beta_0 + \beta_1 \ln y_1 + \beta_2 \ln y_2 + 0.5\beta_{11}(\ln y_1)^2 + 0.5\beta_{22}(\ln y_2)^2 + \beta_{12}\ln y_1 \ln y_2$$

$$+\theta_1 \ln w_1 + 0.5\theta_{11}(\ln w_1)^2 + \theta_2 \ln w_2 + 0.5\theta_{22}(\ln w_2)^2$$

$$+\psi_{11}\ln w_1 \ln y_1 + \psi_{12}\ln w_1 \ln y_2 + \psi_{21}\ln w_2 \ln y_1 + \psi_{22}\ln w_2 \ln y_2$$

$$+\tau_{w_1}t\ln w_1 + \tau_{w_2}t\ln w_2 + \tau_{y_1}t\ln y_1 + \tau_{y_2}t\ln y_2 + \tau_1 t + 0.5\tau_{11}t^2, \tag{17.16}$$

where *TC* is total operating cost, two outputs y_1 and y_2 are securities and gross total loans, two input prices w_1 and w_2 are defined as cost of fixed assets and cost of labor. Because the cost function is homogeneous of degree 1 in input prices, the following set of restrictions is imposed: $\theta_1 + \theta_2 = 1$, $\theta_{11} + \theta_{12} = 0$, $\theta_{22} + \theta_{12} = 0$, $\psi_{11} + \psi_{21} = 0$, $\psi_{12} + \psi_{22} = 0$ and $\tau_{w_1} + \tau_{w_2} = 0$. This is equivalent to scaling total cost and w_1 by w_2. (By the same token, total cost and w_2 could be scaled by w_1.) Thus, (17.16) becomes

$$\ln(TC / w_2) = \beta_0 + \beta_1 \ln y_1 + \beta_2 \ln y_2 + 0.5\beta_{11}(\ln y_1)^2 + 0.5\beta_{22}(\ln y_2)^2$$

$$+\beta_{12}\ln y_1 \ln y_2 + \theta_1 \ln(w_1 / w_2) + 0.5\theta_{11}(\ln(w_1 / w_2))^2$$

$$+\psi_{11}\ln(w_1 / w_2)\ln y_1 + \psi_{12}\ln(w_1 / w_2)\ln y_2$$

$$+\tau_{w_1}t\ln(w_1 / w_2) + \tau_{y_1}t\ln y_1 + \tau_{y_2}t\ln y_2 + \tau_1 t + 0.5\tau_{11}t^2. \tag{17.17}$$

Since we will use the same frontier specification (17.17), it is useful to define global macros:

```
1 global spetech "lny1 lny2 lnw1 trend c.half#(c.lny1#c.lny1
    c.lny2#c.lny2 c.lnw1#c.lnw1) c.lny1#(c.lny2 c.lnw1)
    c.lny2#c.lnw1 c.trend#(c.lny1 c.lny2 c.lnw1 c.trend#c.half)"
2 global year_c = 2001
```

Here, `spetech` is the translog specification. We use the `#` factor operator for better visibility and for commands to create interactions on the fly. In our specification, we will use data when the year is larger than `year_c` to show the functionality of subsetting. `itermax` is defined to make sure that we do not use too few or to many iterations. We add option `iterate($itermax)` to all estimation commands; 1000 would probably be an exaggeration, but allowing at least 250 would be a good idea.

5.3   Half-Normal Distribution of Inefficiency

The models are estimated by using new commands and defined macros:

```
1 xtsf1g lnc $spetech if year > $year_c, cost
2 xtsf2g lnc $spetech if year > $year_c, cost model (K1990)
3 xtsf2g lnc $spetech if year > $year_c, cost model (K1990modified)
4 xtsf2g lnc $spetech if year > $year_c, cost model (BC1992)
```

First, let's look at the result of homoskedastic models where inefficiency is i.i.d. The results are presented in Table 17.2. M1 is the first-generation SF model, so inefficiency is time invariant. M2 uses Kumbhakar (1990) specification of $\beta(t)$. $\beta(t)$ in M3 is given in (17.10) and M4 follows the Battese and Coelli (1992) specification shown in (17.11).

Most of the frontier coefficients are statistically significant. However, it is difficult to interpret these coefficients in isolation. What makes more sense is to report elasticities of cost with respect to both outputs and input prices as well as check the monotonicity of the cost function.

Before we discuss those, let's consider the error components and diagnostics blocks in Table 17.2. Both noise and inefficiency variance are statistically significant and are very similar in magnitude across the four models. M1 is the first-generation model, so $\beta(t)$ is set to 1, and that is why coefficients γ and δ are not reported. γ in M4 is statistically significant, but so is δ in both M2 and M3. So, for these data, the Battese and Coelli (1992) model seems to be misspecified. Both models M2 and M3 allow non-monotonic inefficiency development. Since $\beta(t)$ is not zero, the first-generation model would not be a preferred specification. Of these four specifications, the real choice is between M2 and M3. Hence, we should look at the regression diagnostics, which are shown in the lowest panel. Even though loglikelihood is bigger for M2, residual sum of squares (RSS), $\hat{\sigma}$ as well as information criteria seem to indicate that M3 should be a preferred specification. At this point, however, it would be difficult to say whether M2 or M3 is preferred. One thing is certain, both M2 and M3 are superior to M4.

Table 17.2   Results, homoskedastic models. Standard errors in parentheses

	M1	M2	M3	M4
Frontier				
$\ln y_1$	0.3966***	0.4286***	0.4747***	0.4592***
	(0.1422)	(0.1403)	(0.1418)	(0.1427)
$\ln y_2$	−0.6190	−0.4833	−0.5632	−0.4770
	(0.3989)	(0.3933)	(0.3945)	(0.3985)
$\ln (w_1/w_2)$	0.3852**	0.4970***	0.3933**	0.4166**
	(0.1663)	(0.1625)	(0.1646)	(0.1654)
t	−0.5613***	−0.6561***	−0.5925***	−0.5562***
	(0.0401)	(0.0404)	(0.0405)	(0.0398)
$0.5(\ln y_1)^2$	0.0495***	0.0468***	0.0475***	0.0482***
	(0.0048)	(0.0046)	(0.0047)	(0.0047)
$0.5(\ln y_2)^2$	0.1783***	0.1713***	0.1796***	0.1713***
	(0.0322)	(0.0314)	(0.0316)	(0.0319)
$0.5(\ln (w_1/w_2))^2$	−0.0687***	−0.0616***	−0.0664***	−0.0659***
	(0.0139)	(0.0134)	(0.0138)	(0.0138)
$\ln y_1 \ln y_2$	−0.0669***	−0.0686***	−0.0727***	−0.0718***
	(0.0114)	(0.0112)	(0.0113)	(0.0114)

Table 17.2   (continued)

	M1	M2	M3	M4
Frontier				
$\ln(w_1/w_2)\ln y_1$	−0.0025	0.0001	0.0000	−0.0013
	(0.0055)	(0.0053)	(0.0055)	(0.0055)
$\ln(w_1/w_2)\ln y_2$	−0.0091	−0.0237*	−0.0130	−0.0139
	(0.0134)	(0.0131)	(0.0133)	(0.0133)
$t\ln y_1$	0.0054***	0.0054***	0.0048***	0.0053***
	(0.0017)	(0.0017)	(0.0017)	(0.0017)
$t\ln y_2$	0.0122***	0.0131***	0.0130***	0.0125***
	(0.0031)	(0.0030)	(0.0031)	(0.0031)
$t\ln(w_1/w_2)$	−0.0068***	−0.0058**	−0.0061**	−0.0064**
	(0.0026)	(0.0025)	(0.0026)	(0.0026)
$0.5t^2$	0.0765***	0.0937***	0.0823***	0.0762***
	(0.0018)	(0.0029)	(0.0023)	(0.0018)
Constant	5.3832**	4.4970*	4.7054*	4.1896
	(2.6418)	(2.6172)	(2.6305)	(2.6571)
$\ln\sigma^2_{v_{it}}$				
Constant	−4.4220***	−4.4975***	−4.4352***	−4.4290***
	(0.0320)	(0.0324)	(0.0319)	(0.0320)
$\ln\sigma^2_{u_i}$				
Constant	−2.5216***	−2.3149***	−2.7570***	−2.6381***
	(0.0837)	(0.0889)	(0.0998)	(0.0925)
$\beta(t)$				
γ		−5.0001***	−0.1252***	0.0295***
		(1.8983)	(0.0276)	(0.0093)
δ		0.8193***	−0.0197***	
		(0.3145)	(0.0052)	
AIC	−2.3400	−2.3091	−2.3335	−2.3349
BIC	−2.3033	−2.2724	−2.2968	−2.2982
$\hat{\sigma}$	0.1871	0.1900	0.1877	0.1876
RSS	228.96	250.63	227.45	229.70
Log-likelihood	1430.28	1492.31	1443.69	1435.26
N	500	500	500	500
ΣT_i	2546	2546	2546	2546

Notes: * $p < 0.10$, ** $p < 0.05$, *** $p < 0.01$.

5.4   Monotonicity, Elasticity and Returns to Scale

Returning to reporting the frontier specification result, t of output j is given by

$$\frac{\partial \ln C}{\partial \ln y_j} = \beta_j + \beta_{jj} \ln y_j + \beta_{j,3-j} \ln y_{3-j} + \psi_{1,3-j} \ln(w_1 / w_2) + \tau_{y_j} t, \, j = 1,2. \qquad (17.18)$$

The inverse of the sum of output elasticities is the measure of returns to scale (RTS). The cost function is monotonic if it is not decreasing in input prices and outputs, $\partial C/\partial y_j > 0$ and $\partial C/\partial w_j > 0$. For a monotonic cost function, (17.18) should be positive for all observations. Additionally,

$$\frac{\partial \ln C}{\partial \ln w_1} = \theta_1 + \theta_{11} \ln(w_1 / w_2) + \psi_{11} \ln y_1 + \psi_{12} \ln y_2 + \tau_{w_1} t \qquad (17.19)$$

should be positive. Given the restrictions we impose to ensure homogeneity of the cost function of degree 1, $\partial \ln C/\partial \ln w_2 = 1 - \partial \ln C/\partial \ln w_1$, which holds because we have two input prices. The formula would be different for more than two input prices. We reported coefficients for the frontier only for this model. We will report the monotonicity check and returns to scale for the remaining models instead. Hence, define the following macros:

```
1 global monotonW1 = "_b[lnw1] + _b[c.half#c.lnw1#c.lnw1] *lnw1 +
   _b[c.lny1#c.lnw1] *lny1 + _b[c.lny2#c.lnw1] *lny2 +
   _b[c.trend#c.lnw1] *trend"
2 global elastY1 = "_b[lny1] + _b[c.half#c.lny1#c.lny1] *lny1 +
   _b[c.lny1#c.lny2] *lny2 + _b[c.lny1#c.lnw1] *lnw1 +
   _b[c.trend#c.lny1] *trend"
3 global elastY2 = "_b[lny2] + _b[c.half#c.lny2#c.lny2] *lny2 +
   _b[c.lny1#c.lny2] *lny1 + _b[c.lny2#c.lnw1] *lnw1 +
   _b[c.trend#c.lny2] *trend"
```

To calculate these quantities, we will use the following code in Stata after the estimation command:

```
1 predictnl model_monotonicity_w1 = $monotonW1 if e(sample)
2 predictnl model_monotonicity_w2 = 1 - model_monotonicity_w1 if
   e(sample)
3 predictnl model_elasticity_y1 = $elastY1 if e(sample)
4 predictnl model_elasticity_y2 = $elastY2 if e(sample)
5 generate double model_rts = 1/(model_elasticity_y1 +
   model_elasticity_y2)
```

The results appear in table 17.3, which has four blocks with models M1–M4, shown in Table 17.2. In each block, we see partial derivatives of ln C with respect to the log of input prices and outputs. They all need to be positive for the cost function to be monotonic. The fifth row in each block is reciprocal of the sum of output elasticities.

Table 17.3   Results, homoskedastic models. Standard errors in parentheses

	Min	p25	mean	p75	max	sd
			M1			
$\partial \ln C/\partial \ln w_1$	−0.1766	−0.0165	0.0067	0.0340	0.1234	0.0408
$\partial \ln C/\partial \ln w_2$	0.8766	0.9660	0.9933	1.0165	1.1766	0.0408
$\partial \ln C/\partial \ln y_1$	−0.1627	0.1332	0.1615	0.1942	0.3200	0.0537
$\partial \ln C/\partial \ln y_2$	0.3993	0.6781	0.7475	0.8131	1.2801	0.1074
RTS	0.8636	1.0478	1.1062	1.1583	1.4827	0.0824
			M2			
$\partial \ln C/\partial \ln w_1$	−0.1651	-0.0112	0.0091	0.0336	0.1308	0.0371
$\partial \ln C/\partial \ln w_2$	0.8692	0.9664	0.9909	1.0112	1.1651	0.0371
$\partial \ln C/\partial \ln y_1$	−0.1501	0.1276	0.1561	0.1882	0.3162	0.0525
$\partial \ln C/\partial \ln y_2$	0.4225	0.6782	0.7474	0.8137	1.2823	0.1077
RTS	0.8582	1.0534	1.1129	1.1644	1.4384	0.0834
			M3			
$\partial \ln C/\partial \ln w_1$	−0.1710	-0.0143	0.0076	0.0342	0.1172	0.0391
$\partial \ln C/\partial \ln w_2$	0.8828	0.9658	0.9924	1.0143	1.1710	0.0391
$\partial \ln C/\partial \ln y_1$	−0.1547	0.1307	0.1597	0.1928	0.3257	0.0540
$\partial \ln C/\partial \ln y_2$	0.4048	0.6817	0.7534	0.8209	1.3157	0.1114
RTS	0.8383	1.0432	1.1011	1.1513	1.4546	0.0818
			M4			
$\partial \ln C/\partial \ln w_1$	−0.1709	-0.0141	0.0081	0.0345	0.1207	0.0391
$\partial \ln C/\partial \ln w_2$	0.8793	0.9655	0.9919	1.0141	1.1709	0.0391
$\partial \ln C/\partial \ln y_1$	−0.1587	0.1305	0.1601	0.1932	0.3255	0.0542
$\partial \ln C/\partial \ln y_2$	0.4184	0.6800	0.7494	0.8137	1.2968	0.1077
RTS	0.8521	1.0495	1.1050	1.1541	1.4286	0.0784

Because the assumed technology is translog, the coefficients in the upper panel of Table 17.2 are not very informative. In this case, researchers should avoid reporting them in academic papers or any other reports. That being said, if the Cobb–Douglas technology is assumed, the coefficients are informative (they are elasticities) and should be reported.

One thing we observe in Table 17.3 is that the descriptive statistics are very similar across models, which of course is the result of very marginal changes across model M1 through M4. We notice that the estimate cost function violates monotonicity in input price w_1 for at least 25 per cent of observations. Some of the output y_1 elasticities are negative. Hence, we will try other specifications of error terms to see if these violations can be avoided.

5.5   Truncated Normal Distribution of Inefficiency

The next four models, M5 through M8, are different from M1–M4 in that the inefficiency distribution is truncated normal. M5 is the first-generation model, M6 uses the Kumbhakar (1990) specification of $\beta(t)$, M7 uses the modified version and M8 is that of Battese and Coelli (1992). These models are estimated in Stata by just adding option `distribution(t)` to the commands.

Table 17.4 shows some improvement in comparison to Table 17.3, fewer observations violate monotonicity of the cost function. The mean value of $\partial \ln C / \partial \ln w_1$ is slightly bigger, so it the value of RTS. We see, however, that the results are largely similar.

Table 17.4   Monotonicity, elasticity, and RTS in homoskedastic models

	Min	p25	mean	p75	max	sd
			M5			
$\partial \ln C / \partial \ln w_1$	−0.0684	0.0091	0.0239	0.0410	0.0796	0.0234
$\partial \ln C / \partial \ln w_2$	0.9204	0.9590	0.9761	0.9909	1.0684	0.0234
$\partial \ln C / \partial \ln y_1$	−0.1494	0.1253	0.1482	0.1778	0.2884	0.0481
$\partial \ln C / \partial \ln y_2$	0.2310	0.6525	0.7411	0.8319	1.2766	0.1322
RTS	0.8575	1.0330	1.1409	1.2252	2.1699	0.1430
			M6			
$\partial \ln C / \partial \ln w_1$	−0.0483	0.0119	0.0251	0.0397	0.0729	0.0199
$\partial \ln C / \partial \ln w_2$	0.9271	0.9603	0.9749	0.9881	1.0483	0.0199
$\partial \ln C / \partial \ln y_1$	−0.1466	0.1268	0.1495	0.1792	0.2913	0.0480
$\partial \ln C / \partial \ln y_2$	0.2418	0.6539	0.7411	0.8326	1.2670	0.1315
RTS	0.8629	1.0308	1.1395	1.2245	2.1382	0.1436
			M7			
$\partial \ln C / \partial \ln w_1$	−0.0628	0.0097	0.0241	0.0403	0.0794	0.0228
$\partial \ln C / \partial \ln w_2$	0.9206	0.9597	0.9759	0.9903	1.0628	0.0228
$\partial \ln C / \partial \ln y_1$	−0.1460	0.1235	0.1469	0.1761	0.2888	0.0478
$\partial \ln C / \partial \ln y_2$	0.2248	0.6545	0.7455	0.8388	1.2980	0.1363
RTS	0.8420	1.0278	1.1378	1.2234	2.1940	0.1466
			M8			
$\partial \ln C / \partial \ln w_1$	−0.0618	0.0105	0.0247	0.0409	0.0787	0.0225
$\partial \ln C / \partial \ln w_2$	0.9213	0.9591	0.9753	0.9895	1.0618	0.0225
$\partial \ln C / \partial \ln y_1$	−0.1467	0.1239	0.1472	0.1768	0.2894	0.0480
$\partial \ln C / \partial \ln y_2$	0.2353	0.6552	0.7442	0.8348	1.2883	0.1331
RTS	0.8485	1.0313	1.1380	1.2215	2.1433	0.1417

Table 17.5 Results, homoskedastic models. Standard errors in parentheses

	M5	M6	M7	M8
$\ln \sigma_{v_{it}}^2$				
Constant	−4.5121***	−4.6378***	−4.5188***	−4.5163***
	(0.0314)	(0.0314)	(0.0314)	(0.0314)
$\ln \sigma_{u_i}^2$				
Constant	−3.6457***	−2.7815***	−3.7279***	−3.6967***
	(0.0703)	(0.1211)	(0.0768)	(0.0747)
$E[u_i\|z_i]$				
Constant	0.7969	17.0355*	0.6192***	0.6738***
	(1.8311)	(10.0423)	(0.0839)	(0.1107)
$\beta(t)$				
γ		−0.5946***	-0.0380***	0.0138**
		(0.1284)	(0.0136)	(0.0069)
δ		0.0962***	−0.0048**	
		(0.0204)	(0.0023)	
AIC	−2.3421	1.1370	−2.3338	−2.3343
BIC	−2.3054	1.1737	−2.2971	−2.2976
$\hat{\sigma}$	0.1869	1.0644	0.1877	0.1876
RSS	1710.04	317028.82	1158.39	1317.51
Log-likelihood	1496.47	1623.02	1501.31	1498.55

Notes: * $p < 0.10$, ** $p < 0.05$, *** $p < 0.01$.

Table 17.5 shows the results concerning error components and diagnostics of the regressions. First, the new block $E[u_i|z_i]$ is shown since the distribution of inefficiency is truncated normal. The truncation point is the same for all observations. In the first-generation SF model, it is not statistically significant, so model M5 is effectively not different from M1. In model M6, the truncation point is very large, making inefficiency symmetric. In models M7 and M8, the truncation point is close to 0 but is statistically different from 0. Inefficiency is present in all four models since the constant in $\ln \sigma_{u_i}^2$ specification is significant.

The parameters of $\beta(t)$ are statistically significant, so M5 is inferior to both of the second-generation models. The squared terms in both M6 and M7 are statistically significant, indicating misspecification in the model M8. The choice is again down to M6 or M7. If RSS, $\hat{\sigma}$ or information criteria are considered, M7 seems to be superior.

5.6   Determinants of Inefficiency

The final set of four models that are considered specify the (i) conditional mean, (ii) the heteroskedasticity function of the noise and (iii) the heteroskedasticity function of the inefficiency, to wit:

$$\sigma^2_{v_{it}} = \gamma_{vo} + \gamma_{v1} z_{vit} \tag{17.20}$$

$$\sigma^2_{u_i} = \gamma_{uo} + \gamma_{u1} z_{ui} \tag{17.21}$$

$$\mu_i = E[u_i \mid z_{u_{2i}}] = \delta_1 z_{1i} + \delta_2 z_{2i}, \tag{17.22}$$

where z_{vit} is the size of the bank captured by the log of total assets, z_{ui} is the average ER ratio, defined as gross total equity divided by gross total assets, z_{1i} is the average total loans and leases to gross total assets ratio and z_{2i} is the average loan loss provisions (LLP) for a bank. Specification (17.22) suppresses intercept to show the functionality of new commands.

The model will be estimated by running the following commands:

```
1 xtsf1g lnc $spetech if year > $year_c, cost uimean(llp_ave
    la_ave, noconstant) uilnvariance(er_ave) vitlnvariance(lnta)
2 xtsf2g lnc $spetech if year > $year_c, cost uimean(llp_ave
    la_ave, noconstant) uilnvariance(er_ave) vitlnvariance(lnta)
    model("K1990")
3 xtsf2g lnc $spetech if year > $year_c, cost uimean(llp_ave
    la_ave, noconstant) uilnvariance(er_ave) vitlnvariance(lnta)
    model("K1990modified")
4 xtsf2g lnc $spetech if year > $year_c, cost uimean(llp_ave
    la_ave, noconstant) uilnvariance(er_ave) vitlnvariance(lnta)
    model("BC1992")
```

The results appear in Table 17.6. If one considers noise to be a production shock, the results indicate that banks of different sizes are hit by shocks of different sizes. Since the log of total assets (TA) is negative, the variance of shocks is larger for smaller banks.

The variance of inefficiency is overall different from 0, but it does not depend on the average ER ratio. So, inefficiency is homoskedastic. Note that here the only possibility is checked, and it does not mean that inefficiency is indeed homoskedastic. Some other specifications of the inefficiency heteroskedasticity function can be tried.

Now consider the $E[u_i|z_i]$ block. In comparison to models M5–M8, the results of table 17.6 show that the truncation point of the inefficiency distribution is bank specific and depends on average LLP and the liabilities-to-asset (LA) ratio. This is true for all four models, where regression results differ only marginally. The results imply that both the average LLP and LA ratio increase inefficiency, at the same time being detrimental to the cost efficiency of banks.

As before, the first-generation model is inferior to the second-generation models since parameters of $\beta(t)$ are significant. That δ is significant in M10 and M11 suggests that the Battese and Coelli (1992) model is not appropriate. The choice of the model is again between the original Kumbhakar (1990) specification and its modification. All diagnostics except for the loglikelihood recommend using the modified version of $\beta(t)$ defined in (17.10).

Table 17.6   Results, homoskedastic models. Standard errors in parentheses

	M9	M10	M11	M12
$\ln\sigma^2_{v_{it}}$				
$\ln TA$	0.4298***	0.4538***	0.4123***	0.4228***
	(0.08521)	(0.08462)	(0.08507)	(0.085)
Constant	−9.5016***	−9.8883***	−9.3084***	−9.4288***
	(0.9958)	(0.9883)	(0.9945)	(0.9934)
$\ln\sigma^2_{u_i}$				
$\overline{ER}$	−3.4300	−1.0664	−3.8540	−3.3880
	(2.589)	(2.276)	(2.655)	(2.571)
Constant	−3.3989***	−3.4970***	−3.5403***	−3.5422***
	(0.2815)	(0.2429)	(0.2903)	(0.2805)
$E[u_i|z_i]$				
$\overline{LLP}$	0.0003***	0.0003***	0.0003***	0.0003***
	(0.0000268)	(0.0000278)	(0.0000247)	(0.000025)
$\overline{LA}$	0.4004***	0.5545***	0.3475***	0.3743***
	(0.04805)	(0.04389)	(0.04813)	(0.04547)
$\beta(t)$				
γ		−4.1759***	−0.0784***	0.0319***
		(0.8655)	(0.02055)	(0.008123)
δ		0.6766***	−0.0092**	
		(0.1419)	(0.003806)	
AIC	−2.2954	−2.2110	−2.2876	−2.2825
BIC	−2.2587	−2.1743	−2.2509	−2.2458
$\hat{\sigma}$	0.1913	0.1996	0.1921	0.1926
RSS	428.34	584.25	414.74	434.83
log–likelihood	1524.06	1610.47	1535.34	1531.67

Notes: * $p < 0.10$, ** $p < 0.05$, *** $p < 0.01$.

Table 17.7 shows the results of the monotonicity checks, elasticity and RTS. There are still observations for which monotonicity of the cost function is violated. Even though we have changed how the error components are modeled, it seems that the technology remained virtually the same. There are several ways this could be remedied. First, one can consider a different sample. We have randomly selected 500 banks whose size is between the 25th and 75th percentiles of the distribution. One could consider all banks, for example. Alternatively, one can argue that only banks of the same scale (say larger than the 90th percentile) have the same technology. This is the area that is left for the researcher to investigate. The argumentation

Table 17.7   Monotonicity, elasticity and RTS in homoskedastic models

	Min	p25	mean	p75	max	sd
M9						
$\partial \ln C / \partial \ln w_1$	−0.1121	−0.0075	0.0086	0.0283	0.0838	0.0283
$\partial \ln C / \partial \ln w_2$	0.9162	0.9717	0.9914	1.0075	1.1121	0.0283
$\partial \ln C / \partial \ln y_1$	0.1612	0.1498	0.1768	0.2101	0.3337	0.0545
$\partial \ln C / \partial \ln y_2$	0.2442	0.5997	0.6805	0.7585	1.2298	0.1206
RTS	0.9010	1.0902	1.1781	1.2498	1.9093	0.1206
M10						
$\partial \ln C / \partial \ln w_1$	−0.0946	−0.0001	0.0145	0.0308	0.0862	0.0243
$\partial \ln C / \partial \ln w_2$	0.9138	0.9692	0.9855	1.0001	1.0946	0.0243
$\partial \ln C / \partial \ln y_1$	−0.1534	0.1524	0.1790	0.2114	0.3325	0.0535
$\partial \ln C / \partial \ln y_2$	0.2173	0.5858	0.6704	0.7534	1.2314	0.1268
RTS	0.8962	1.0927	1.1918	1.2716	2.0160	0.1362
M11						
$\partial \ln C / \partial \ln w_1$	−0.1097	−0.0059	0.0096	0.0279	0.0811	0.0271
$\partial \ln C / \partial \ln w_2$	0.9189	0.9721	0.9904	1.0059	1.1097	0.0271
$\partial \ln C / \partial \ln y_1$	−0.1551	0.1460	0.1739	0.2073	0.3327	0.0542
$\partial \ln C / \partial \ln y_2$	0.2430	0.6038	0.6879	0.7688	1.2664	0.1252
RTS	0.8731	1.0845	1.1723	1.2440	1.8977	0.1219
M12						
$\partial \ln C / \partial \ln w_1$	−0.1067	-0.0055	0.0100	0.0280	0.0820	0.0266
$\partial \ln C / \partial \ln w_2$	0.9180	0.9720	0.9900	1.0055	1.1067	0.0266
$\partial \ln C / \partial \ln y_1$	−0.1562	0.1471	0.1749	0.2080	0.3320	0.0541
$\partial \ln C / \partial \ln y_2$	0.2445	0.5997	0.6828	0.7624	1.2529	0.1233
RTS	0.8826	1.0904	1.1778	1.2494	1.8928	0.1211

needs to come from economic rationale rather than from a data-mining consideration. Second, one can try some other technology or varying technologies. Third, one can resort to the system approach, where cost share equations are taken into account.

5.7   Cost Efficiency

Finally, we consider cost efficiency. The inefficiency term u, the efficiency scores based on the mean ($\exp(-E[u_i|\varepsilon_i])$) and the mode ($\exp(-M[u_i|\varepsilon_i])$) of the distribution, as well as $E[\exp(-u_i)|\varepsilon_i])$, are stored after `xtsf1g` and `xtsf2g`. The cost efficiency can be also obtained using the `predict` command. The efficiency from "winners" of the three rounds can be calculated as follows:

```
predict varname, te_jlms_mean
```

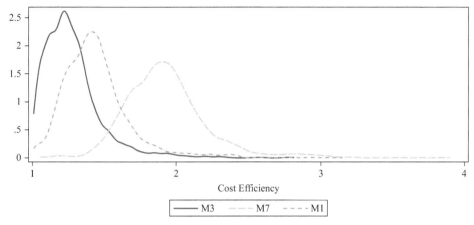

Figure 17.1   The kernel estimated density of cost efficiency from models M3, M7 and M11

where `varname` is for the user to choose. Other options that can be specified are `te_jlms_`
`mode`, `te_bc`, `u_mean`, `u_mode`, the upper and lower bounds for individual efficiency scores
`te_lb` and `te_ub` and also the standard `residuals` and `xb`.

Figure 17.1 presents kernel-estimated densities for the models M3, M7 and M11. Cost
efficiency shows the factor by which costs are larger than the costs of a bank that is on the
frontier. One can obtain the usual cost efficiency score between 0 and 1 by estimating the
model with the `celessthanone` option. Model M7 suggests the most inefficiency among the
three models. And as noted earlier, the distribution is more symmetric. We observe some differences in efficiencies just when we make different assumptions about the error component.
Note that technology is held the same across models. Certainly, one would get other results for
cost efficiency is other things are assumed.

Figure 17.2 shows kernel-estimated densities for the models M9 through M12. If we
consider the same "class" of models, and we only change the assumption about $\beta(t)$, the results
are virtually the same even for the first-generation model.

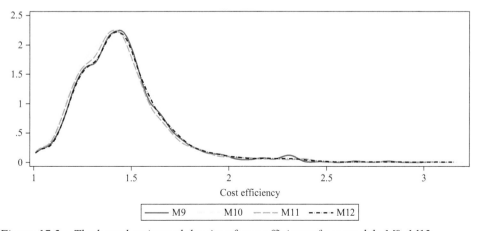

Figure 17.2   The kernel-estimated density of cost efficiency from models M9–M12

The upshot for the practitioner is twofold. First, the single parameter specification of $\beta(t)$ as in Battese and Coelli (1992) seems to be restrictive, and two-parameter specification is preferred. Second, based on economic theory, one should carefully choose the determinants of inefficiency as well as heteroskedasticity function of noise because results will depend on those specifications.

6. CONCLUSION

This chapter deals with the practicability of estimating SF models for panel data in Stata. Section 2 demonstrated that coding in Stata is straightforward and can be made fast when Mata is employed. A cross-software speed comparison is not the purpose of this chapter. Rather, it is advocated that many new estimators need to be coded in Stata. The number of users who prefer Stata for various reasons is large and they will benefit greatly from user-written programs of the modern SF models.

Nowadays, the major first- and second-generation SF models are either available as described in section 4 or are available through new commands `xtsf1g` and `xtsf2g`. The agenda for the future is making the next-generation SF models briefly discussed in section 3 available for a practitioner.

REFERENCES

Badunenko, O. and Kumbhakar, Subal C., "Economics of scale, technical change and persistent and time-varying cost efficiency in Indian banking: Do ownership, regulation and heterogeneity matter?," *European Journal of Operational Research*, 2017, 260(2), pp. 789–803.

Battese, George E. and Coelli, Tim J., "Frontier production functions, technical efficiency and panel data: With application to paddy farmers in India," *Journal of Productivity Analysis*, June 1992, 3(1–2), pp. 153–69.

Belotti, F., Daidone, S., Ilardi, Vincenzo, G., Vincenzo A., "Stochastic frontier analysis using Stata," *Stata Journal*, 2013, 13(4), pp. 719–58.

Caudill, S. B., Ford, J. M. and Gropper, D.M., "Frontier estimation and firm-specific inefficiency measures in the presence of heteroscedasticity," *Journal of Business & Economic Statistics*, 1995, 13(1), pp. 105–11.

Colombi, R., Kumbhakar, Subal C., Martini, G. and Vittadini, G., "Closed-skew normality in stochastic frontiers with individual effects and long/short-run efficiency," *Journal of Productivity Analysis*, 2014, 42(2), pp. 123–36.

Greene, H. W., "Reconsidering heterogeneity in panel data estimators of the stochastic frontier model," *Journal of Econometrics*, 2005, 126(2), pp. 269–303.

Kneip, A., Sickles, R. C. and Song, W., "A new panel data treatment for heterogeneity in time trends," *Econometric Theory*, 2012, 28(3), pp. 590–628.

Koetter, M., Kolari, J. W. and Spierdijk, L., "Enjoying the quiet life under deregulation? Evidence from adjusted Lerner indices for U.S. banks," *The Review of Economics and Statistics*, 2012, 94(2), pp. 462–80.

Kumbhakar, Subal C., "Production frontiers, panel data, and time-varying technical inefficiency," *Journal of Econometrics*, 1990, 46(1–2), pp. 201–11.

Kumbhakar, Subal C., Ghosh, S., McGuckin, J. T., "A generalized production frontier approach for estimating determinants of inefficiency in U.S. dairy farms," *Journal of Business & Economic Statistics*, 1991, 9(3), pp. 279–86.

Kumbhakar, Subal C. and Heshmati, A., "Efficiency measurement in Swedish dairy farms: An application of rotating panel data," *American Journal of Agricultural Economics*, 1995, 77(3), pp. 660–74.

Kumbhakar, Subal C. and Hjalmarsson, L., "Technical efficiency and technical progress in Swedish dairy farms," In *The measurement of productive efficiency. Techniques and applications*, H. O. Fried, C. A. Knox Lovell and S. Schmidt, eds., Oxford: Oxford University Press, 1993, pp. 256–70.

Kumbhakar, Subal C. and Hjalmarsson, L., "Labour-use efficiency in Swedish social insurance offices," *Journal of Applied Econometrics*, 1995, 10(1), pp. 33–47.

Kumbhakar, Subal C., L., Gudbrand and Hardaker, J. B., "Technical efficiency in competing panel data models: A study of Norwegian grain farming," *Journal of Productivity Analysis*, 2014, 41(2), pp. 321–37.

Kumbhakar, Subal C. and Lovell, C. A. Knox, *Stochastic frontier analysis*, Cambridge University Press, 2000.

Kumbhakar, Subal C., Wang, H.-J., Horncastle, A. P., *A practitioner's guide to stochastic frontier analysis using Stata*, Cambridge University Press, 2015.

Park, Byeong U., Sickles, R. C. and Simar, L., "Stochastic panel frontiers: A semiparametric approach," *Journal of Econometrics*, 1998, 84(2), pp. 273–301.

Park, Byeong U., Sickles, R. C. and Simar, L., "Semiparametric-efficient estimation of AR(1) panel data models," *Journal of Econometrics*, 2003, 117(2), pp. 279–309.

Park, Byeong U., Sickles, R. C. and Simar, L., "Semiparametric efficient estimation of dynamic panel data models," *Journal of Econometrics*, 2007, 136(1), pp. 281–301.

Pinzon, Enrique (ed.), *Thirty years with Stata: A retrospective*, College Station, Texas: Stata Press, 2015.

Pitt, M. M. and Lee, L.-F., "The measurement and sources of technical inefficiency in the Indonesian weaving industry," *Journal of Development Economics*, 1981, 9(1), pp. 43–64.

Ritter, C. and Simar, L., "Pitfalls of normal-gamma stochastic frontier models," *Journal of Productivity Analysis*, 1997, 8(2), pp. 167–82.

Schmidt, P. and Sickles, R. C., "Production frontiers and panel data," *Journal of Business & Economic Statistics*, 1984, 2(4), pp. 367–74.

Sickles, R. C., Song, W., and Zelenyuk, V., "Econometric analysis of productivity: Theory and implementation in R," In Vinod, H. D. and Rao, C., Eds., *Financial, macro and micro econometrics using R*, volume 42 of *Handbook of statistics*, North Holland, 2020, pp. 267–97. https://doi.org/10.1016/bs.host.2018.11.007.

Sickles, R. and Zelenyuk, V. *Measurement of productivity and efficiency: Theory and practice*. Cambridge University Press, 2019.

Stevenson, R. E., "Likelihood functions for generalized stochastic frontier estimation," *Journal of Econometrics*, 1980, 13(1), pp. 57–66, ISSN 03044076.

Tsionas, E. G. and Kumbhakar, Subal C., "Firm heterogeneity, persistent and transient technical inefficiency: A generalized true random effects model," *Journal of Applied Econometrics*, 2014, 29(1), pp. 110–32.

Zellner, A. and Revankar, N. S., "Generalized production functions1," *The Review of Economic Studies*, 1969, 36(2), pp. 241–50.

18. Modern R workflow and tools for microeconometric data analysis

Giovanni Baiocchi

1. INTRODUCTION TO THE R SYSTEM

R is the open-source implementation of S, a programming environment for data analysis and graphics conceived in the mid-seventies at Bell Laboratories (Becker et al., 1988; Becker, 1994), and is heavily influenced by the design and minimalist philosophy of the Scheme programming language (Sussman and Steele, 1975). R's source code was initially written by statisticians Ross Ihaka and Robert Gentleman (see, for example, Ihaka and Gentleman, 1996) at the Department of Statistics of the University of Auckland, New Zealand. Since the mid-90s there has been a core group (known as the "R Core Team") who can modify the R source code archive (R Core Team, 2013). After 25 years, R has grown to become a de-facto standard for statistical analysis against which many popular commercial programs may be measured. Several factors contributed to its success, including the concomitant growth in computational power, the increasing data availability, the open-source movement and its original design, based on Scheme, as a functional language with a small set of core primitives and tools to extend the language. Since changing base R code is cumbersome and could affect backward compatibility, most of the innovation in data processing and analysis comes in the form of *packages*. Since their inception, both S and R were designed to be easily extensible allowing users to easily contribute simple or sometimes more ambitious capabilities (Becker and Chambers, 1985; Chambers, 2017).

Another important development in the R system is the integrated support for reproducible research. Independent replication of published findings is at the core of the scientific method. A much less stringent requirement is that the findings be reproducible, that is, that reasonably close results to the ones published can be obtained by independent researchers without excessive cost or effort by using the same data set and computer code. It is well known that research in applied economics does not even pass this minimum standard (see, for example, Vinod, 2001; Dewald et al., 1986). Even though the problem has been acknowledged and solutions were proposed and several implemented since then, the non-replicability issue is still affecting the discipline. Chang and Li (2021) in the paper "Is Economics Research Replicable? Sixty Published Papers from Thirteen Journals Say 'Usually Not'", attempted to replicate 67 economic papers published in 13 high-ranking economics journals using author-provided code and data. They were not able to replicate key qualitative conclusions of most of the papers investigated. Replicability of research findings can be greatly facilitated by using R Markdown, which combines Markdown, a simplified markup language for creating formatted text with images, links, and so on, with embedded R code "chunks" so that their output can be rendered in the final document. All aspects of research done by computer can thus be fully recorded and automated. Several books are useful resources to help organize research to make it more easily reproducible and dynamic. The main references include "Dynamic Documents with R and knitr" by Xie (2017), "R Markdown: The Definitive Guide" by Xie et al. (2018) and "bookdown: Authoring Books and Technical Documents with R Markdown" by Xie (2016). An illustration on how to use of R reproducible tools in econometrics can be found in Racine (2019a).

Econometrics, especially the part that is taught and included in most textbooks on the subject, has been relatively slow at accepting new machine learning methods developed to extract knowledge from larger, less structured and often more complex data, including spatial and network data (Einav and Levin, 2014). In fairness, most of the ongoing machine learning revolution is concerned with processing large data sets and fitting black-box models exhibiting high out-of-sample prediction accuracy rather than with obtaining highly interpretable summarization of the data and with the testing of hypothesis (Varian, 2014). However, as an increasing amount of consumer-level, firm-level and even event-level data are becoming available, they have the potential to offer new insight into an individual's decision. Moreover, machine learning methods have been successfully adapted to address the kind of causal and interpretable problems applied economists tend to focus on (Athey and Imbens, 2019; Molnar, 2019). These developments offer practitioners from both academic and applied domains increasing opportunities to formulate and validate hypotheses that were previously inconceivable. Although applying textbook algorithms to toy data sets remains a useful endeavor to learn the craft's basics in a controlled setting, by itself, it will not equip practitioners with the skills necessary to meet the challenges of doing microeconometrics within this new environment. This chapter introduces modern R as a set of integrated tools for handling data whose design is inspired by principles akin to the economist's principles of job specialization and division of labor. Most of the focus will be on the tidyverse framework to import, transform, model and visualize data. This chapter is also aimed at facilitating the adoption and integration into the analysis of individual-level data of new predictive modeling methods by showcasing a set of tools that can work together seamlessly by standardizing common tasks, such as model fitting, parameter tuning and model selection, that are better suited to developing the skills needed to undertake real-world econometric research by scholars both in academic and corporate environments. The last part will look at how to run traditional microeconometric methods on standard data.

1.1   Setting up the R System

R itself does not have a typical menu driven graphical interface, such as SPSS. The easiest way to interact with R is through graphical platforms that provide extra functionality. A popular choice of graphical frontend to R is **RStudio,** which offers a convenient tool to access our scripts and data, find help, install and update packages and preview plots and outputs all in one place.

- R can be downloaded from CRAN (Comprehensive R Archive Network) repositories where several options for different precompiled binary distributions are available for Linux, Mac and Windows, and source code for all platforms is available.
- After installing R, RStudio, an integrated development environment (IDE) for R, can be downloaded from RStudio where several options for various platforms are available. The RStudio IDE is developed by RStudio, Inc., a commercial enterprise, however, the "Open-Source Edition" is available for free.

Mac users, in addition to R and RStudio, need to install XQuartz. XQuartz is a free X11 server implementation for OS X. X11 is the Unix and Linux graphics drivers.

Extensive help and tutorials on setting up the system and getting started are available on the CRAN and RStudio websites.

1.2 Basic Base R

Once the R environment is set up, it is easy to start the R command prompt and start typing R code. For example,

```
x <- c(23000, 2000, 5000)
mean(x)
```

```
## [1] 10000
```

Note that the operators <- and = assign into the environment in which they are evaluated, so in this case, they are equivalent. The function *c()* (as in concatenate) to make vectors in R. A hash (#) character anywhere on a line will comment out the rest of the line. Data in R are stored as dataframes, a two-dimensional labeled data container that can store potentially different types. To construct one, we can type:

```
df <- data.frame(id = 1:5,
                 inc = runif(5, min = 1000,max=100000),
                 sex = sample(c("female","male"), 5, replace = T))
rownames(df) <- paste("HHID-", 1:5,sep="")
df
```

	id	inc	sex
HHID-1	1	12557.603	female
HHID-2	2	20307.486	male
HHID-3	3	71151.439	male
HHID-4	4	4411.005	female
HHID-5	5	48036.890	male

Elements of the dataframe can be extracted besides the standard integer index, using human readable labels. For example, executing `df["HHID-2", "inc"]`, at the command line or through a script, yields 2.0307486×10^4. A large fraction of data processing functionality in R applies to dataframes. Good introductions to base R can be found in "Advanced R" by Wickham (2015), "Introductory Statistics with R" by Dalgaard (2008) and Venables and Smith (2009).

1.3 Installing R Packages

R can be easily extended through *packages* which can be loosely defined as collections of functions, complied code and sample data, that are conveniently bundled together for a specific purpose. Packages increase the power of R by improving and extending existing base R capabilities. Packages typically contain R code (although C, FORTRAN and other languages are also often used in order to speed up computations), documentation, scripts, tests, data sets and so on.

When starting the R console, only the so-called base packages will already be installed and loaded by default. These include packages such as **base**, **grid**, **splines** and **stats**. *Base* packages are not available on CRAN, or any other repository, but are updated with new releases of R. Other packages, which are already installed, have to be "loaded" explicitly to be used. So-called *recommended* packages are already installed with the basic **R** distribution, but not loaded. These include packages such as **boot**, **cluster**, **kernsmooth**, **rpart** and **survival**. Other specialized packages will have to be installed from a repository and its content made accessible to programs for use.

Traditionally, R packages were made available through CRAN, which is a repository used to store packages using different HTTP and FTP mirrors. CRAN is managed by the R core team and currently stores more than 15 000 packages. To date, CRAN is the official, oldest and largest repository. Packages available on CRAN can go back as far as the oldest available source release in 1997. Sometimes, for compatibility and reproducibility purposes, older versions of packages or R might be required. To install the **ggplot2** package, we can use the following:

```
install.packages("ggplot2")
```

Older versions can be installed the following way:

```
require(devtools)
install_version("ggplot2", version = "0.9.1", repos = "http://
  cran.us.r-project.org")
```

Packages need to be maintained and updated frequently by the developers. Version numbers of the packages keep track of the changes occurring over time and are usually composed of four parts, "major.minor.patch.dev". A "major" version update implies that older code might not run anymore. RStudio provides a menu driven approach to check, install and load packages. There are other R package repositories, including `Bioconductor` (for the analysis and comprehension of high-throughput genomic data), `omegahat.net` (the Omega Project for Statistical Computing) and `R-forge`. GitHub is the most popular development platform that uses the Git version control system for developers of R packages (witness the thousands of R packages hosted on GitHub). CRAN enforces a strict set of policies to ensure that packages and updates distributed through its network meets publication quality standards (https://cran.r-project.org/web/packages/policies.html). Packages need to pass several checks before being accepted for redistribution (http://cran.r-project.org/web/checks/). More experimental or beta testing version of packages can be installed from GitHub. Installing a package from GitHub requires the **devtools** package available from CRAN. In most cases, you just use `install_github("author/package")`. The development version of **ggplot2** from GitHub using the username/packagename combination:

```
# install.packages("devtools")
devtools::install_github("tidyverse/ggplot2")
```

As an example, the **multtest** specializing in computing adjusted *p*-values for simple multiple testing that often arises in economics and finance is available on `Bioconductor` and can be installed with the following commands:

```
if (!requireNamespace("BiocManager", quietly = TRUE))
    install.packages("BiocManager")
BiocManager::available("glm")
BiocManager::install("multtest")
```

GitLab is another development platform that is becoming increasingly popular. Needless to say, options for package repositories can change drastically over time and need to be constantly reviewed.

1.4   Loading Packages with Functions and Data

The simplest way to make a package's content available is by "attaching" the content using a *library()* or a *require()* call. This will work for packages already installed in the file system and stored under a folder called "library" on the computer (whose full path can be found using *.libPaths()*). For example, to load **ggplot2** into memory, we can execute the following command:

```
library("ggplot2").
```

To avoid "polluting" the namespace with potentially conflicting function definitions (often packages will have functions with identical names), and to save memory, functions or data defined in a package can be accessed with the notation `packagename::functionname()`. To remove the content of a package from the *search()* path of available R objects we can run

```
detach("package:ggplot2", unload= TRUE)
```

1.5   Getting Help

`help(package = "packagename")` can be used to get basic help on a package. For help on a specific function or data, we can use `help("function")` or `help(function, package = "package")`. If the package has not been attached, help can be obtained by executing the command below (output not shown):

```
help(package = "AER")
help(Baltagi2002, package = "AER")
```

To determine the authors and maintainers of a package, we can use the *citation()* and *packageDescription()* functions, and run (output not shown):

```
citation("nlme")
packageDescription("nlme")
```

A vignette is a long-form guide to your package. Function documentation is useful but requires knowing the name of the function needed. A vignette is used to show the functions in action through applications in a manner similar to a book chapter or an academic paper. It is available as a PDF file or can be accessed by executing (output not shown):

```
browseVignettes("AER")
```

To obtain a list of datasets supplied by, say, the **AER** package (first 10 lines only), we can execute the following command:

```
data(package = "AER")$results %>%
  head(10) %>%
  select(Package,Item,Title)
```

Item	Title
Affairs	Fair's Extramarital Affairs Data
ArgentinaCPI	Consumer Price Index in Argentina
BankWages	Bank Wages
BenderlyZwick	Benderly and Zwick Data: Inflation, Growth and Stock Returns
BondYield	Bond Yield Data
CASchools	California Test Score Data
CPS1985	Determinants of Wages Data (CPS 1985)
CPS1988	Determinants of Wages Data (CPS 1988)
CPSSW04	Stock and Watson CPS Data Sets
CPSSW3	Stock and Watson CPS Data Sets

If we want to narrow down the search, say, to select data sets that contain "PSID" (Panel Study of Income Dynamics of the University of Michigan) in the title, we can run:

```
data(package = "AER")$results %>%
  filter(str_detect(Title, "PSID")) %>%
  select(-LibPath)
```

Package	Item	Title
AER	PSID1982	PSID Earnings Data 1982
AER	PSID7682	PSID Earnings Panel Data (1976–1982)

The base R function *data()* can be used to list the available data sets in a package or to load a specific one into memory, as follows:

```
data(PSID1982,package = "AER")
PSID1982 %>%
  head()
```

experience	weeks	occupation	industry	south	smsa	married	gender	union	education	ethnicity	wage
9	32	white	yes	yes	no	yes	male	no	9	other	515
36	30	blue	yes	no	no	yes	male	no	11	other	912
12	46	blue	yes	no	no	no	male	yes	12	other	954
37	46	blue	no	no	yes	no	female	no	10	afam	751
16	49	white	no	no	no	yes	male	no	16	other	1474
32	47	blue	yes	no	yes	yes	male	no	12	other	1539

2.   THE TIDYVERSE PACKAGE ECOSYSTEM

Although base R can perform many tasks satisfactorily in most settings, workflows can be made more efficient through the use of packages that implement more consistent arguments, inputs and outputs that can be easily further processed in a data analysis pipeline (using the pipe operator, `%>%`), for example, with functions that consistently use a dataframe as first argument. Another guiding principle that helps transforming raw data into a format that can be further processed is the idea of a tidy data. The development of all packages included in tidyverse follow the principal rules of "The tidy tools manifesto" Hadley (2019). These are:

1.   Reuse existing data structures.
2.   Compose simple functions with the pipe.
3.   Embrace functional programming.
4.   Design for humans.

This approach was inspired by the Unix operating system style of design emphasizing programs that perform specific tasks well and work together connected through pipes that redirect the output of one function to another function as input (see, for example, Raymond, 2003; Salus, 1994) (an economist would probably frame this in terms of *job specialization* and *division of labor* as exemplified by the assembly line manufacturing process). The "ecosystem" of data processing R packages known as the *tidyverse*, which includes **readr**, **tidyr**, **tibble**, **dplyr** and others, was specifically designed with the aim to facilitate research workflows. Figure 18.1 shows how individual *tidyverse* packages could fit into a typical econometric workflow.

The **tibble** package provides a new version of data frames, called *tibbles*, that simplifies working with data in the tidyverse. Tibbles, in the spirit of the approach, tend to do less than base R dataframes. For example, they do not change variable names or types, and do not allow partial matching. They can be created from scratch just like dataframes, just using the *tibble()* instead of the *data.frame* function, or by converting dataframes to tibbles using the *as_tibble* function. So the previously defined dataframe can be converted to a tibble by running:

```
as_tibble(df)
## # A tibble:   5 x 3
##       id      inc sex
##    <int>  <dbl>    <fct>
## 1     1  12558.  female
## 2     2  20307.  male
## 3     3  71151.  male
## 4     4   4411.  female
## 5     5  48037.  male
```

tribble(), short for transposed tibble, is useful for small tables of data that are easy to edit and are both human and machine readable:

Figure 18.1 *Typical econometric workflow with several tidyverse packages associated with the various steps. "Core" tidyverse packages are highlighted in gray fonts*

```
tribble(
  ~firm,          ~cost,
  "a",            10000,
  "b",            20300,
  "c",            33000
)

## # A tibble: 3 x 2
##   firm      cost
##   <chr>     <dbl>
## 1 a         10000
## 2 b         20300
## 3 c         33000
```

Variable names should be formulas, that is, prefixed by the tilde operator.

The **dplyr** package provides functionality that supersedes base R data processing functions like *aggregate()*, *subset()*, *sort()*, *order()*, *merge()* and other data processing functionality supplied earlier packages such as **doBy**, and **plyr** (Wickham and Grolemund, 2017). The **tidyr** package can be used to reshape data from wide to long or from long to wide, providing a tidyverse alternative to the base R function *reshape()* (Wickham and Henry, 2019). **tidyr** also replaced previews packages such as **reshape2**. Note that **tidyr** actually does less than **reshape2**, in the tidy tools spirit of performing fewer tasks well. Another set of tidyverse tools is designed to parse and process many of the data types researchers regularly need to include in their analyses. The **stringr** package provides functions for working with strings and textual information, **forcats** provides tools to handle categorical variables stored as factors, **lubridate** provides simple functions to read and process dates and date–times, **hms** contributes functions for time-of-day values processing and **blob** can be used for storing binary data. All these functions, designed to have an intuitive meaning with consistent interfaces, can be connected to form a pipeline through **magrittr**'s %>% operator (Bache and Wickham, 2014). To install and load the packages in the tidyverse we can run:

```
# install.packages("tidyverse") # only once
library(tidyverse)
```

Table 18.1 shows the research workflow, from importing data to visualization and modeling, and the packages, currently part of the tidyverse, that are associated with each step. Moreover, a more recent addition of the **purrr** package that enhances the functional programming aspect of R can be used inside a pipe workflow and supports the creation of new processing tools.

The main reference for the tidy approach is "R for Data Science: Import, Tidy, Transform, Visualize, and Model Data" by Wickham and Grolemund (2017). In the next sections we look at how modern R can be used in the various steps of the workflows of analyzing microeconomics data.

2.1 The Expanded Tidyverse Ecosystem

There are several other packages, useful to process a variety of more complex data types from different sources and disciplines (many still work in progress), designed to be compatible as much as possible with the tidyverse framework. We can, for example, read spatial data as

Table 18.1   *All packages currently in the tidyverse (including tidymodels) arranged in order of first release according to the CRAN repository*

Package	Released	Updates	Latest	Package description	Downloads
ggplot2	2007-06-01	42	2020-06-19	Create Elegant Data Visualizations Using the Grammar of Graphics	45 948 062
stringr	2009-11-09	16	2019-02-10	Simple, Consistent Wrappers for Common String Operations	32 577 520
lubridate	2010-08-15	27	2020-11-13	Make Dealing with Dates a Little Easier	19 301 250
httr	2012-05-06	19	2020-07-20	Tools for Working with URLs and HTTP	23 285 422
jsonlite	2013-12-03	35	2020-12-09	A Simple and Robust JSON Parser and Generator for R	38 795 928
dplyr	2014-01-16	35	2020-08-18	A Grammar of Data Manipulation	39 301 362
magrittr	2014-02-25	6	2020-11-17	A Forward-Pipe Operator for R	77 645 226
rstudioapi	2014-03-27	15	2020-11-12	Safely Access the RStudio API	18 257 605
tidyr	2014-07-21	27	2020-08-27	Tidy Messy Data	24 270 407
crayon	2014-09-23	10	2017-09-16	Colored Terminal Output	21 874 238
rvest	2014-11-22	11	2020-07-25	Easily Harvest (Scrape) Web Pages	13 201 927
broom	2014-11-23	23	2020-12-16	Convert Statistical Objects into Tidy Tibbles	16 124 631
haven	2015-03-01	16	2020-06-01	Import and Export "SPSS", "Stata" and "SAS" Files	14 363 840
readr	2015-04-09	15	2020-10-05	Read Rectangular Text Data	17 030 579
readxl	2015-04-14	9	2019-03-13	Read Excel Files	15 899 884
xml2	2015-04-20	16	2020-04-23	Parse XML	16 875 876
purr	2015-09-28	15	2020-04-17	Functional Programming Tools	23 293 201
tibble	2016-03-23	22	2020-10-12	Simple Data Frames	36 640 006
hms	2016-05-02	13	2020-01-08	Pretty Time of Day	19 764 994
forcats	2016-08-29	9	2020-03-01	Tools for Working with Categorical Variables (Factors)	11 005 280
modelr	2016-08-31	11	2020-05-19	Modeling Functions that Work with the Pipe	11 998 400
tidyverse	2016-09-09	8	2019-11-21	Easily Install and Load the "Tidyverse"	28 311 192
reprex	2017-01-10	9	2019-05-16	Prepare Reproducible Example Code via the Clipboard	10 122 493
rlang	2017-05-06	27	2020-11-26	Functions for Base Types and Core R and 'Tidyverse' Features	45 633 583

Table 18.1 (continued)

Package	Released	Updates	Latest	Package description	Downloads
dbplyr	2017-06-09	14	2020-11-03	A "dplyr" Back End for Databases	10 182 512
rsample	2017-07-08	10	2020-09-23	General Resampling Infrastructure	786 312
recipes	2017-07-27	18	2020-11-11	Preprocessing Tools to Create Design Matrices	4 430 468
cli	2017-11-05	10	2020-11-20	Helpers for Developing Command Line Interfaces	23 124 925
yardstick	2017-11-12	9	2020-07-13	Tidy Characterizations of Model Performance	338 689
pillar	2017-11-20	19	2020-11-20	Colored Formatting for Columns	28 056 369
infer	2018-01-08	14	2020-07-14	Tidy Statistical Inference	282 159
tidymodels	2018-07-27	8	2020-11-22	Easily Install and Load the "Tidymodels" Packages	254 372
dials	2018-08-13	11	2020-09-16	Tools for Creating Tuning Parameter Values	169 738
parsnip	2018-11-12	14	2020-10-27	A Common API to Modeling and Analysis Functions	249 456
modeldata	2019-12-06	5	2020-10-22	Data Sets Used Useful for Modeling Packages	312 674
workflows	2019-12-30	8	2020-10-08	Modeling Workflows	167 935
tune	2020-02-11	6	2020-11-17	Tidy Tuning Tools	153 509

special dataframes that can be merged with other data and transformed using tidyverse functions (an example of this is shown in a later section to produce a map). This compatibility can simplify the task of expanding the scope of microeconometric research. Complex data types, accessible through specially developed packages with tidyverse functionality, include:

- **Networks and hierarchical trees**. For example, the **tidygraph** and **ggraph** packages allow us to use a powerful network package **igraph** in a manner consistent with the tidyverse workflow to process and integrate network data.
- **Spatial geometries**. **sf** is a recently developed package that combines the power of **sp**, **rgeos** and rgdal to allow spatial vector data to be processed consistently in the tidyverse workflow, for example allowing to filter and merge spatial data with other dataframes using **dplyr** operators. An example of combining economic data with spatial data is shown. Other packages, such as sfraster, bring spatial raster data closer in the tidyverse.
- **Vector fields**. For example, the package **metR** provides data and visualization tools that can work in sync with the tidyverse tools to process vector field data ("vector" in the sense used in physics of quantities that, unlike numerical and categorical data, have both magnitude and direction, such as wind direction and speed or slopes from a digital elevation models), for example interpolation that can be used to match event data with vector field data.

2.2　Importing Data

Doing applied microeconometric research often requires importing data from different sources that are stored in different files and file formats. A good place to get familiar with the tidyverse approach of importing (and exporting) data is chapter 11 of Wickham and Grolemund (2017). The online resources on the package **readr** also provide useful details. Most of **readr's** functions are concerned with turning flat files into tidyverse dataframe, namely tibbles. *read_csv()* reads comma delimited files, *read_csv2()* reads semicolon separated files (if a comma is used as the decimal place), *read_tsv()* reads tab delimited files, *read_fwf()* reads fixed width files and *read_delim()* reads in files with any delimiter, just to name a few. These functions can also be applied to "connections," that is, file-type objects like terminals and URLs. Here is a list of the current functions starting with read_ provided by **readr**:

```
ls("package:readr",pattern="read_")
```

```
##   [1] "read_csv"           "read_csv2"        "read_csv2_chunked"
##   [4] "read_csv            "read_delim"       "read_delim_chunked"
            _chunked"
##   [7] "read_file"          "read_file_raw"    "read_fwf"
##  [10] "read_lines"         "read_lines        "read_lines_raw"
                                _chunked"
##  [13] "read_lines_raw      "read_log"         "read_rds"
            _chunked"
##  [16] "read_table"         "read_table2"      "read_tsv"
##  [19] "read_tsv
            _chunked"
```

Note that tidyverse functions to read file such as *read_csv()* are typically much faster than their analogous base R version, say *read.csv()*. Also, analogous versions ending with _chunked, allow large data files to be processed with **dplyr** while loading only a "chunk" of the data in memory.

We can use wage data from James et al. (2013) to examine a number of factors that relate to wages for a group of males from the Atlantic region of the United States. In particular, we wish to understand the association between an employee's age and education on his wage.

```
Wage = read_csv("https://vincentarelbundock.github.io/Rdatasets/
   csv/ISLR/Wage.csv")
Wage %>%
     select(-c(region,health_ins,logwage)) %>%
     head()
```

X1	year	age	maritl	race	education	jobclass	health	wage
231655	2006	18	1. Never Married	1. White	1. < HS Grad	1. Industrial	1. <=Good	75.04315
86582	2004	24	1. Never Married	1. White	4. College Grad	2. Information	2. >=Very Good	70.47602
161300	2003	45	2. Married	1. White	3. Some College	1. Industrial	1. <=Good	130.98218
155159	2003	43	2. Married	3. Asian	4. College Grad	2. Information	2. >=Very Good	154.68529
11443	2005	50	4. Divorced	1. White	2. HS Grad	2. Information	1. <=Good	75.04315
376662	2008	54	2. Married	1. White	4. College Grad	2. Information	2. >=Very Good	127.11574

read_line() applied to a file or a connection returns lines as a character vector, so it can be used with unstructured data or to check the format of the data before choosing the more appropriate function. For example, to get the first five lines of a data set on choice among four travel modes from Greene (2012) available online, we can run:

```
cat(read_lines('http://people.stern.nyu.edu/wgreene/Lugano2013/
   clogit.csv', n_max=5),
     sep = '\n')

## MODE,TTME,INVC,INVT,GC,CHAIR,HINC,PSIZE,AASC,TASC,BASC,CASC,
   HINCA,PSIZEA
## 0,69,59,100,70,0,35,1,1,0,0,0,35,1
## 0,34,31,372,71,0,35,1,0,1,0,0,0,0
## 0,35,25,417,70,0,35,1,0,0,1,0,0,0
## 1,0,10,180,30,0,35,1,0,0,0,1,0,0
```

With **readr** we can also supply an inline .csv or .tsv file. This is useful for experimenting with **readr** and for creating reproducible examples to share with others:

```
require(tidyverse)
fam.inc <- read_csv("fid,faminc96,faminc97,faminc98,famsize96,fams
   ize97,famsize98
3,75000,76000,77000, 2,3,3
1,40000,40500,41000, 4,3,3
2,45000,45400,45800, 2,2,2")
fam.inc %>% head()
```

```
## # A tibble: 3 x 7
##    fid faminc96 faminc97 faminc98 famsize96 famsize97 famsize98
##    <dbl>  <dbl>    <dbl>    <dbl>    <dbl>    <dbl>     <dbl>
## 1    3   75000    76000    77000      2        3         3
## 2    1   40000    40500    41000      4        3         3
## 3    2   45000    45400    45800      2        2         2
```

Other file formats can be imported as dataframes in R using specific tidyverse packages. The **readxl** package can read spreadsheet saved as Excel files .xls and .xlsx. The **haven** package can read other standard statistical software data formats, including Stata, SPSS and SAS.

```
library(haven)
ls("package:haven", pattern="read_")

## [1] "read_dta"  "read_por"  "read_sas"  "read_sav"  "read_
   spss"  "read_stata"
## [7] "read_xpt"
```

Stata file can be imported with **haven**'s *read_dta()* function.

```
wagepan = read_dta("http://fmwww.bc.edu/ec-p/data/wooldridge/
   wagepan.dta")
```

2.3   Making Data Tidy

Tidy data (Wickham, 2014a; Donoho, 2017) is the unifying principle around a set of tools designed to facilitate the process of transforming raw data into a format that can be processed sequentially in a data analysis pipeline. Tidy data is defined as (Wickham, 2014b):

1. Each variable forms a column.
2. Each observation forms a row.
3. Each type of observational unit forms a table.

This is idea is not new. It is basically a rewording using statistical terms of the Boyce–Codd normal form definition from relational databases and Codd's relational algebra (Codd, (1990), and it is also known as data matrix in multivariate statistics. Tidy data is easier to work with and analyze because the variables are in the same format required by modeling and visualization tools. With tidy data come tidy tools, which have the same input and output: tidy data. This consistency means multiple tools can be composed together in sequence, allowing for rapid, elegant operations. Common problems that make raw data un-tidy include, column headers that contain values instead of only variable names, cells that contain variable names instead of values and data that are split over multiple sources. Typically, data can be made tidy by "reshaping", often by moving between a "wide" and "long" format. **tdyr** provides most of the tools needed to make data tidy. As an example, the family income toy dataset defined above, is not in a tidy form. *fam.inc* has a variable *year* embedded as values in the column headers that contain the *income* and *familysize* variable names. In his case, *pivot_longer()* can be used to accomplish the task. *pivot_longer()*'s improves over *gather()*, a function that is still available but no longer updated. With *pivot_longer()*, we can also specify multiple names for *the names_to* argument. We can also provide a pattern to capture and separate different components of a string. For example:

```
## # A tibble: 9 x 4
##          fid    year   faminc   famsize
##        <dbl>   <chr>    <dbl>     <dbl>
## 1          3   96       75000         2
## 2          3   97       76000         3
## 3          3   98       77000         3
## 4          1   96       40000         4
## 5          1   97       40500         3
## 6          1   98       41000         3
## 7          2   96       45000         2
## 8          2   97       45400         2
## 9          2   98       45800         2

fam.inc %>%
  pivot_longer(cols = starts_with('fam'),
                names_to = c(".value", "year"),
                names_pattern = '([a-z]+)([0-9]+)')

## # A tibble: 9 x 4
##          fid    year   faminc   famsize
##        <dbl>   <chr>    <dbl>     <dbl>
## 1          3   96       75000         2
## 2          3   97       76000         3
## 3          3   98       77000         3
## 4          1   96       40000         4
## 5          1   97       40500         3
## 6          1   98       41000         3
## 7          2   96       45000         2
## 8          2   97       45400         2
## 9          2   98       45800         2
```

Note that the *pivot_longer* function uses *regular expressions*, a small language for describing patterns, to process the strings and automatically separate and extract the variable names and the values implicit in the header strings. Basics on regular expressions can be reviewed, for example, in chapter 14 on strings in Wickham and Grolemund (2017).

2.4 Transforming Data

Many textbooks and examples used in econometrics still use small and heavily sanitized data sets, usually with no missing values, with continuous variables that are already log transformed and categorical variables encoded as dummy variables. This may be good to run examples quickly and follow the material in a textbook, but not to develop the skills needed to apply microeconometrics to new data. The **dplyr** packages takes care of data manipulation needed in applied econometric research, such as producing summaries, applying logarithmic transformations, creating new variables, joining and cleaning data sets, processing regression outputs and so on. *mutate()*, *summarize()*, *select()*, *arrange()*, can accomplish most operations, in conjunction with *group_by()*, that are used to split the data and apply the functions to different subsets. There are also "scoped" versions of these functions, _at, _if, _all, that allow the processing of several variables at the same time and that can be used to automate transformations. Having consistent inputs and outputs, these operations can be chained to achieve complex transformations while keeping the code easily readable. As an example, *mutate()* leaves the number of rows unaltered and can be used to transform variables:

```
fam.inc %>%
  pivot_longer(cols = starts_with('fam'),
               names_to = c(".value", "year"),
               names_pattern = ' ([a-z]+)([0-9]+) ') %>%
    group_by(year) %>%
    mutate(loginc=log(faminc))
## # A tibble: 9 x 5
## # Groups:  year [3]
##       fid   year   faminc   famsize  loginc
##     <dbl>  <chr>   <dbl>    <dbl>     <dbl>
## 1       3   96     75000      2       11.2
## 2       3   97     76000      3       11.2
## 3       3   98     77000      3       11.3
## 4       1   96     40000      4       10.6
## 5       1   97     40500      3       10.6
## 6       1   98     41000      3       10.6
## 7       2   96     45000      2       10.7
## 8       2   97     45400      2       10.7
## 9       2   98     45800      2       10.7
```

summarize() can be used to obtain data summaries:

```
fam.inc %>%
  pivot_longer(cols = starts_with('fam'),
               names_to = c(".value", "year"),
               names_pattern = '([a-z]+)([0-9]+)') %>%
    group_by(year) %>%
    summarize(minc=mean(faminc))

## # A tibble: 3 x 2
##      year      minc
##     <chr>     <dbl>
## 1    96      53333.
## 2    97      53967.
## 3    98      54600
```

2.4.1 Dummy coding and recoding of categorical variables

Qualitative factors often need to be coded as binary information for analysis. In microeconometrics, with focus on individuals, working with dummy variables is of paramount importance. R offers many tools to recode and create dummies.

For this example, we will use a subsample of individuals from the 2014 General Social Survey (GSS), a nationally representative survey of adults in the United States on contemporary American society, made accessible via a Stata for Students web page by UW-Madison. To read the STATA format we can use the *read_dta* function from the tidyverse haven library:

```
gss.dat = read_dta("https://www.ssc.wisc.edu/sscc/pubs/sfs/gss_
   sample.dta")
gss.dat %>%
    select(starts_with("ed")) %>%
    str()

## tibble [254 x 1] (S3: tbl_df/tbl/data.frame)
## $ educ: dbl+lbl [1:254] 16, 16, 12, 16, 13, 10, 14, 13, 12,
   20, 20, 0, 13, 16, 10, 18, . . .
##   ..@ label       : chr "HIGHEST YEAR OF SCHOOL COMPLETED"
##   ..@ format.stata : chr "%8.0g"
##   ..@ labels       : Named num [1:3] NA NA NA
##   .. ..- attr(*, "names")= chr [1:3] "na" "siap" "dk"
```

dplyr's case_when function can be used to recode discrete variables into new categories. Let's turn the educ variable ("HIGHEST YEAR OF SCHOOL COMPLETED") into a categorical variable *edu_cat*, with the categories "Less than High School", "High School", "Some College", "Bachelors" and "Advanced".

```
gss.dat %>%
  select(id,educ) %>%
  mutate(educat = case_when(
    educ<12 ~ "Less than High School",
    educ==12 ~ "High School",
    educ>12 & educ<16 ~ "Some College",
    educ==16 ~ "Bachelors",
    educ>16 ~ "Advanced"
    )) -> edu.dat
edu.dat %>% head()

## # A tibble: 6 x 3
##        id       educ    educat
##      <dbl>    <dbl+lbl>    <chr>
## 1      874         16    Bachelors
## 2      191         16    Bachelors
## 3     1882         12    High School
## 4     1898         16    Bachelors
## 5     1081         13    Some College
## 6     2512         10    Less than High School
```

Since it is basically a form of data reshaping, we can convert the education-level categorical variable into 1/0 multicolumn dummy variables by using **tidyr**'s *pivot_wider()* function:

```
edu.dat %>%
  mutate(unique_row_id = 1:n()) %>% #The rows need to be unique
    for 'spread' to work.
  mutate(dummy = 1) %>%
  pivot_wider(names_from = educat,
              values_from=dummy,
              values_fill= 0,
              names_prefix="Degree: ") -> edu.dum
edu.dum
```

```
## # A tibble: 254 x 8
##        id     educ   unique_row_id 'Degree: Bachel~ 'Degree:
   High S~ 'Degree: Some C~
##     <dbl>  <dbl>        <int>           <dbl>         <dbl>          <dbl>
## 1     874     16           1              1             0              0
## 2     191     16           2              1             0              0
## 3    1882     12           3              0             1              0
## 4    1898     16           4              1             0              0
## 5    1081     13           5              0             0              1
## 6    2512     10           6              0             0              0
## 7    1546     14           7              0             0              1
## 8    2164     13           8              0             0              1
## 9     678     12           9              0             1              0
## 10    75      20          10              0             0              0
## # ... with 244 more rows, and 2 more variables: 'Degree:
   Less than High School' <dbl>,
## # 'Degree: Advanced' <dbl>
```

Note that base R, reading data would have used the function *make.names()* to make syntactically valid names out of character vectors and would have converted the strings such as "Less than High School" into

```
make.names("Less than High School")
```

```
## [1] "Less.than.High.School"
```

The tidyverse, as a default, in the spirit of making code "easy to use by humans", will keep non-syntactic elements. Backticks (also known as acute, back quotes, grave, grave accent, left quote, open quote) will be used to reference the data.

```
edu.dum$'Degree: High School'
## [1] 0 0 1 0 0 0 0 0 1 0 0 0 0 0 0 0 0 0 1 1 1 1 0 0 0 0 1 1 1
   0 0 0 0 0 1 0 0 0 1 0 0 0
```

```
## [43] 1 0 0 1 1 0 0 1 0 0 0 0 0 0 0 0 0 0 0 0 0 0 0 1 0 0 1 0 0
   0 1 1 0 0 0 0 0 1 1 1 0 1
## [85] 0 1 0 0 0 0 1 0 1 0 1 0 0 0 0 0 1 0 0 0 0 0 1 0 0 1 0 1 1
   0 0 0 0 1 0 0 0 0 0 0 0 1
## [127] 0 1 0 0 0 1 0 0 1 1 0 1 0 1 0 0 0 0 0 0 1 1 0 1 0 1 0 0
   0 0 0 0 1 0 0 0 0 1 1 0 0 0
## [169] 0 1 1 0 0 1 0 0 0 0 1 1 0 0 0 1 0 0 0 0 1 0 0 0 1 1 0 1
   0 1 0 0 0 0 0 1 0 0 1 0 1 0
## [211] 0 0 0 1 0 0 0 0 0 0 0 0 1 1 1 0 1 0 0 1 1 0 0 0 0 0 1 1 0
   0 1 0 1 0 0 0 1 0 0 0 1 0 0
## [253] 0 1
```

Using modern R tools from tidymodels (see section on tidy models), that is, the **recipes** package,

```
library('recipes')
dummies <- edu.dat %>% recipe (~.) %>%
   step_dummy(educat,
              one_hot = F) %>%
   prep() %>%
   bake(edu.dat)
dummies
```

```
## # A tibble: 254 x 6
##    id educ educat_Bachelors educat_High.Scho~ educat_Less.than.
  Hi~ educat_Some.Coll~
##    <dbl>  <dbl+l>   <dbl>    <dbl>    <dbl>    <dbl>
## 1    874       16      1        0        0        0
## 2    191       16      1        0        0        0
## 3   1882       12      0        1        0        0
## 4   1898       16      1        0        0        0
## 5   1081       13      0        0        0        1
## 6   2512       10      0        0        1        0
## 7   1546       14      0        0        0        1
## 8   2164       13      0        0        0        1
## 9    678       12      0        1        0        0
## 10    75       20      0        0        0        0
## # . . . with 244 more rows
```

In machine learning, dummy variable coding of categorical variables is known as "one hot encoding". When we apply "one hot encoding" with the one_hot = T option, all the levels of the factors will be present as new variables in the final result. In econometrics, since the general rule for creating dummy variables to avoid falling into the "dummy variable trap" (amounting to perfect multicollinearity) is to have one less variable than the number of starting categories, we need to set one_hot = F.

2.4.2   Factors

R uses *factors*, that is, vectors that store only predefined values, to handle categorical variables; variables that have a fixed and known set of possible values (known as levels). The base R function *read.csv()* will, by default, convert any character variable to a factor. This is often not what wanted, and can be overridden by passing the option `stringsAsFactors = FALSE` to *read.csv()*. Categorical variables are not converted automatically to factors in the tidyverse as this was a common source of frustration with the base R functions. If the variable in the dataframe is character or factor, the regression function *lm()* treats it as categorical and performs dummy codings automatically.

```
lm(wage ~ education + age + I(age^ 2) + year + maritl, data =
   Wage) %>% summary ()
```

```
##
## Call:
## lm(formula = wage ~ education + age + I(age^2) + year +
   maritl,
##      data = Wage)
## Residuals:
##       Min       1Q    Median        3Q       Max
## -112.604  -19.270    -3.227    14.248    216.640
##
## Coefficients:
##
##                      Estimate   Std. Error   t value    Pr(>|t|)
## (Intercept)         -2.395e+03   6.299e+02    -3.801    0.000147 ***
## education2.          1.089e+01   2.404e+00     4.531    6.10e-06 ***
      HS Grad
## education3.          2.362e+01   2.532e+00     9.329    < 2e-16 ***
      Some College
## education4.          3.795e+01   2.518e+00    15.073    < 2e-16 ***
      College Grad
## education5.          6.190e+01   2.736e+00    22.624    < 2e-16 ***
      Advanced Degree
## age                  3.258e+00   3.672e-01     8.872    < 2e-16 ***
## I(age^2)             3.321e-02   4.077e-03    -8.147    5.42e-16 ***
## year                 1.195e+00   3.140e-01     3.804    0.000145 ***
## maritl2.             1.422e+01   1.830e+00     7.772    1.05e-14 ***
      Married
## maritl3.             5.730e-01   8.177e+00     0.070    0.944133
      Widowed
## maritl4.             8.078e-01   2.998e+00     0.269    0.787589
      Divorced
## maritl5.             7.658e+00   4.987e+00     1.536    0.124754
      Separated
## ---
```

```
## Signif. codes:  0 '***' 0.001 '**' 0.01 '*' 0.05 '.' 0.1 ' ' 1
##
## Residual standard error: 34.76 on 2988 degrees of freedom
## Multiple R-squared: 0.3088, Adjusted R-squared: 0.3063
## F-statistic: 121.4 on 11 and 2988 DF, p-value: < 2.2e-16
```

Internally, *lm()* calls **stats'** *model.matrix()* function to generate the matrix of predictor variables used to fit the model:

```
model.matrix(wage ~ education + age, data = Wage)[1: 5, 1: 5]
##   (Intercept)  education2. HS Grad  education3. Some College
## 1           1                    0                        0
## 2           1                    0                        0
## 3           1                    0                        1
## 4           1                    0                        0
## 5           1                    1                        0
##   education4. College Grad   education5. Advanced Degree
## 1                        0                            0
## 2                        1                            0
## 3                        0                            0
## 4                        1                            0
## 5                        0                            0
```

Factors are also helpful for reordering character vectors to improve visualization. The **forcats** package provides a suite of tools that can solve common problems with factors, including changing the order of levels or the values. More details on factors and the modern approach to handle them can be found in chapter 15 of Wickham and Grolemund (2017).

2.5 Visualization with ggplot2

ggplot2 is the oldest and most recognizable package of the tidyverse. It is based on the "Grammar of Graphics" framework developed by Wilkinson (2005), which is a programmatic extension of previous work by Bertin (2010). The underlying principle of the "Grammar" is to define a small set of independent "components" of a graph and a small set of rules that can be used to combine them to produce a large variety of different visualization, highlighting the deeper connections between visualizations (Wilkinson, 2005; Wickham, 2010, 2016a), as opposed to defining a limited set of charts to be used in a menu-driven setting. Building blocks of a graph include:

- data
- aesthetic mapping
- geometric object
- statistical transformations
- scales
- coordinate system
- position adjustments
- faceting

According to this view, choosing a statistical transformation to apply to the data or a coordinates system to represent the data can change the nature of the visual display. For example, a pie chart is nothing but a stacked bar chart in a polar coordinates system, and a histogram also can be viewed as a bar chart of statistically binned data.[1] To create a visualization with **ggplot2**, the first step is to create an empty plot object by calling *ggplot()* by specifying the data and aesthetic mapping to be used and then adding the appropriate geometry as a layer using the + operator, as a minimum to get something displayed. After that, optional statistical transformations, scales, coordinates and so on can be further added as layers, so as to further refine the plot. As there are many defaults in **ggplot**, to get a visualization started, only "data" and the "geometry" need to be specified. The *aes()* aesthetic mapping is used to link variables in the dataframe to features of geometries we can perceive (say, the shape of a point) that will be drawn onto the screen (or any other graphic device). A point geometry (*geom_point*), for example, requires at least two coordinates, *x* and *y*, to be drawn. Figure 18.2 shows the relationship between *age* and *wage* of the north Atlantic wage data. In this case, we connect *age* and *wage* to positions on the *x* and *y* coordinates, respectively. We also connect *education* to the color of the points, and *health* to the shape of the point. Unless directly specified, default breaks, color palette, shapes and so on will be used to create scales that control the appearance of individual guides, axis and legends that allow the viewer to decode the information contained in the plot.

```
Wage %>% filter (year>2007) %>%
  ggplot(mapping=aes(x=age,y=wage)) +
  geom_point(aes(color=education,shape=health),size= 2) +
  geom_smooth(col="skyblue2") +
  scale_y_log10() +
  rcartocolor::scale_color_carto_d(palette = "OrYel", direction
    = 1) +
  labs(title = "Relationship between wage and age of male workers",
       x = "Age of worker (years)",
       y = "Workers wage (in thousands of dollars per year)") ->
          wageplot
wageplot
```

A trellis plot (also called a facet or conditioning plot) is a sequence of similar sub-plots displayed in an array shape that shows different subsets of the same data. This is very much in the spirit of Tufte's (2001) "small multiples." `facet_wrap` can be added to a previous visualization to condition upon a variable. Figure 18.3 shows the result of conditioning the wage-age relationship to *race*.

```
wageplot + geom_point(aes(color=education,shape=health),size= 1) +
  facet_wrap(~race)
```

Useful visualization books using R include ggplot2: Elegant Graphics for Data Analysis by Wickham (2016b), *R Graphics Cookbook* by Chang (2013), *Interactive and Dynamic Graphics for Data Analysis: With R and GGobi* by Cook et al. (2007) and *R Graphics* by Murrell (2018). For an introduction, see the section "Building New Graphical Elements" from the chapter Building Data Visualization Tools of the book *Mastering Software*

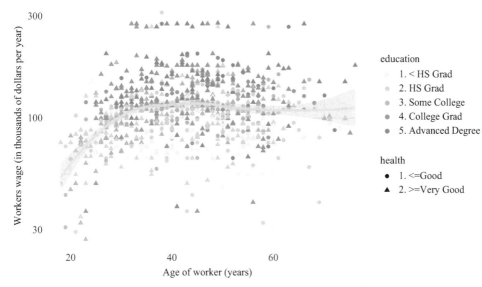

Figure 18.2 *Exploratory scatterplot graphing wages against age of 3000 male workers in the Mid-Atlantic region of the United States. The symbols encode the health status, and the color of the symbols encode the level of education*

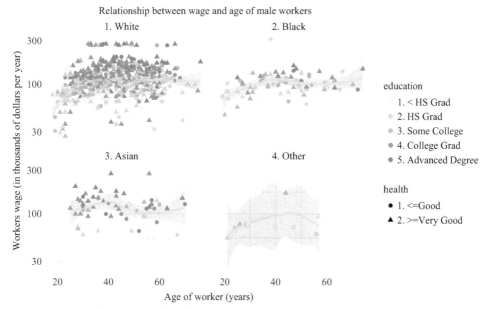

Figure 18.3 *Exploratory trellis plot graphing wages against age of male workers given race in the Mid-Atlantic region of the United States. The symbols encode the health status, and the color of the symbols encode the level of education. Race is used as faceting variable*

Development in R book by Peng et al. (2020). R Graphics focuses on the two core graphics packages in R, **graphics** and **grid**, that you need to have knowledge to program visualization at lower level.

2.5.1   Merging economic data with spatial geometries: Maps

Combining data from different sources enables researchers to expand the scope of their research by enabling novel research designs. In this section, we briefly illustrate how economic data can be merged with spatial geometries to obtain a map visualization using tidyverse and tidyverse-friendly tools. The **sf** package combines the power of **sp**, **rgeos** and **rgdal** to allow spatial vector data describing geographical features to be processed consistently in the tidyverse workflow, for example allowing to filter and merge spatial data with other dataframes using **dplyr** operators.

Data from the Annual Survey of Hours and Earnings can be accessed or downloaded from the UK Office for National Statistics (ONS). We can use the tidyverse package **readr** to read the .csv file into an R tibble:

AREACD	AREANM	earnings
E06000005	Darlington	519.3
E06000001	Hartlepool	557.2
E06000002	Middlesbrough	556.8
E06000003	Redcar and Cleveland	506.2
E06000004	Stockton-on-Tees	537.3
E06000047	County Durham	486.5

```
wwage <- read_csv("datadownload.csv",skip = 5,trim_ws = TRUE,
  na = "x")
wwage
```

GeoJSON, .csv and ESRI Shapefile of vector boundaries for Local Authority Districts in the United Kingdom can be found at data.gov.uk. For the purposes of this exercise, we are going to use the local administrative units (LAUs) Level 1 Boundaries file from https://geoportal.statistics.gov.uk, as this is the administrative level of the earnings data. LAU level 1 represents *districts,* of which there are 417, and level 2 *wards*, of which there are about 10 000. To download the file, follow the link and click on Download > Shapefile and extract the zip file to your working directory. The *st_read()* function from the package **sf** can read many types of geographical formats into a tidyverse tibble, making most of **dplyr**'s functionality available to process and merge the location and shape of the UK geographic features with the earnings data.

```
library(sf)
UK_Boundaries <-st_read("Local_Administrative_Units_Level_1__
  January_2018__Boundaries.shp",
        quiet = TRUE,stringsAsFactors = FALSE, as_tibble = TRUE)
UK_Boundaries
```

```
## Simple feature collection with 400 features and 9 fields
## geometry type: MULTIPOLYGON
## dimension:    XY
## bbox:         xmin: -69.6978 ymin: 5342.7 xmax: 655644.8
                 ymax: 1220302
## epsg (SRID):  NA
## proj4string:  +proj=tmerc +lat_0=49 +lon_0=-2 +k=0.9996012717
                 +x_0=400000 +y_0=-100000 +datum=OSGB36
                 +units=m +no_defs
## # A tibble: 400 x 10
##   objectid lau118cd lau118nm bng_e bng_n long lat st_areasha
        st_lengths
## <int>    <chr>   <chr>      <int>  <int> <dbl> <dbl>   <dbl>       <dbl>
## 1    1 E060000~ Hartlep~ 447157 531476  -1.27 54.7  93597805.  69383.
## 2    2 E060000~ Middles~ 451141 516887  -1.21 54.5  53878997.  42086.
## 3    3 E060000~ Redcar~  464359 519597  -1.01 54.6 244838828.  96190.
## 4    4 E060000~ Stockto~ 444937 518183  -1.31 54.6 204936631. 115439.
## 5    5 E060000~ Darling~ 428029 515649  -1.57 54.5 197482010. 105800.
## 6    6 E060000~ Halton   354246 382146  -2.69 53.3  79111882.  76358.
## 7    7 E060000~ Warring~ 362744 388456  -2.56 53.4 180615806. 111937.
## 8    8 E060000~ Blackbu~ 369490 422806  -2.46 53.7 137057233.  63751.
## 9    9 E060000~ Blackpo~ 332763 436633  -3.02 53.8  34877471.  34573.
## 10 10 E060000~ Kingsto~ 511894 431716 -0.304 53.8  71455773.  63330.
## # . . . with 390 more rows, and 1 more variable: geometry
    <MULTIPOLYGON [m]>
```

We can then join the geographical data with the earning attributes using *left_join()*:

```
UK_Boundaries %>%
   left_join(wwage, c("lau118nm" = "AREANM")) -> map.dat
```

In order to add London as an inset to the main map, we can obtain a subset of the data by using *filter()*. Specifically, the London boroughs have codes beginning with "E09" and can be "filtered" using **stringr**'s *str_detect()* function the following way:

```
map.dat %>%
   filter(str_detect(lau118cd, "E09")) %>% st_simplify() -> london
```

For more information on the coding, please refer to the Code History Database (CHD) from the UK Office for National Statistics page: https://www.ons.gov.uk/. This spatial dataframe can easily be plotted by adding a *geom_sf()* layer in a **ggplot** visualization or through the **tmap** library, also following the Grammar's principles.[2] The plot with inset is shown in Figure 18.4.

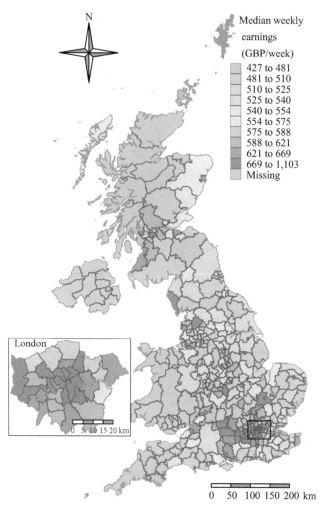

Figure 18.4   Median full-time gross weekly earnings by place of work for Great Britain local authorities, based on the Annual Survey of Hours and Earnings for April 2020 by ONS. The City of London had the highest median gross weekly earnings (GBP 1103), while those living in the Pendle, a borough of Lancashire, had the lowest (GBP 427). This map uses a Transverse Mercator-based national projection for the UK (EPSG:27700)

2.6   Tidy Models

In this section, we look at how tidyverse can facilitate the adoption of new machine learning methods into the analysis of individual-level data by standardizing common tasks such as model fitting, parameter tuning and model comparison and selection. In particular, we will look at packages developed under the *tidymodels* framework. Tidymodels is an ensemble of several different packages, including **rsample**, **recipes**, **parsnip**, and **dials**, for tidy processing of a complete machine learning project. Tidymodels is seen as the successor of the most popular machine learning package **caret** (which stands for Classification and regression Training) developed by Max Kuhn, also in charge of the Tidymodel development, that provides functions aimed at streamlining the model training process for complex regression and classification problems by providing a consistent interface to virtually all third-party machine learning algorithms in R (more than 230 at the moment of writing). At the time of writing, many of these packages are still in an, intensive development phase and thus might take time before the syntax settles down.

The example shown, follows the partial linear model example in the *Applied Econometrics with R* book by Kleiber and Zeileis (2008) using a cross-section dataset originating from the March 1988 Current Population Survey by the US Census Bureau, provided by the **AER** package, estimating the partial relationship between the log of income and experience by splines. We will illustrate how most of the tidymodel packages can be used to accomplish the modeling steps, including splitting the dataset into a training and testing sets, creating a recipe object that defines a model and training the specified model, and selecting the degrees of freedom of the regression splines by tuning. In the code below, we use packagename::functionname() notation to show in which package the functions are defined.

```
library(tidymodels)
library(AER)
data(CPS1988)
CPS1988 %>%
  mutate(wage = log(wage)) -> CPS1988

set.seed(2345, sample.kind="Rounding")
CPS_split <- rsample::initial_split(CPS1988, prop = .7)
CPS_train <- rsample::training(CPS_split)
CPS_test <- rsample::testing(CPS_split)
CPS_cv <- rsample::vfold_cv(CPS_train)
lm_rec <-
    recipes::recipe(wage ~ ., data = CPS_train) %>%
    recipes::step_ns(experience, deg_free = tune("exp df"))

lm_mod <-
    parsnip::linear_reg() %>%
    parsnip::set_engine("lm")

lm_wflow <-
    workflows::workflow() %>%
    workflows::add_recipe(lm_rec) %>%
    workflows::add_model(lm_mod)

lm_param <- lm_rec %>%
    dials::parameters() %>%
    update('exp df' = spline_degree())
```

```
lm_res <-
  lm_wflow %>%
  tune::tune_grid(resamples = CPS_cv,
                  grid = dials::grid_max_entropy(lm_param,
                    size = 10),
                  metrics = yardstick::metric_
                    set(yardstick::rmse))

estimates <- tune::collect_metrics(lm_res)

rmse_vals <-
    estimates %>%
    dplyr::filter(.metric == "rmse") %>%
    arrange(mean)
```

For details on the tidymodel approach please consult the project web page at https://www.tidymodels.org/. Figure 18.5 shows the intermediate and final result of the analysis, plotted with the code.

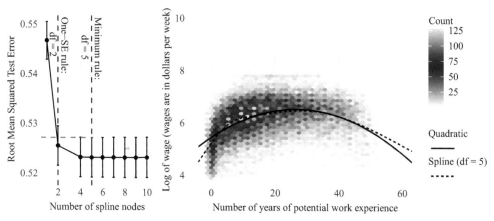

Figure 18.5   *(Left panel) Test Root Mean Square Error (RMSE) estimated by 10-fold cross-validation as a function of the spline's degrees of freedom. The degrees of freedom that minimize the RMSE and the ones consistent with the one standard error rule, both used for model selection in machine learning, are highlighted with dashed vertical lines. The rationale of using the one standard error rule is that if a set of models appear to be more or less equally good, then the simplest model with the smallest number of predictors could be preferable. (Right panel) Hexagon plot between experience and the log of wage with spline nonparametric regression and quadratic polynomial fits superimposed. The bivariate histogram using hexagons bins with count > 0 is plotted by using a color ramp in proportion to the number of individuals falling in the bin. A quadratic curve with a regression spline, with the degree that minimizes the cross-validation RMSE test error are also shown*

The code below shows how we can compare the partial model with splines to a model estimated with random forests. The out-of-sample prediction accuracy of the partial model can be obtained in the following way:

```
best_params <-
    lm_res %>%
    tune::select_best(metric = "rmse")

reg_res <-
  lm_wflow %>%
  tune::finalize_workflow(best_params) %>%
  parsnip::fit(data = CPS_train)

reg_res %>%
  predict(new_data = CPS_test) %>%
  bind_cols(CPS_test, .) %>%
  select(wage, .pred) %>%
  rmse(wage, .pred)

## # A tibble: 1 x 3
##    .metric   .estimator   .estimate
##    <chr>     <chr>            <dbl>
## 1 rmse       standard         0.529
```

Similarly, the out-of-sample prediction accuracy of the random forests model can be obtained in the following way:

```
rf_model <- rand_forest(mtry= 2,trees = 1000) %>%
  set_engine("randomForest") %>%
  set_mode("regression")

rf_wflow <- workflow() %>%
  add_formula(wage ~ .) %>%
  add_model(rf_model)

rf_fit <- rf_wflow %>%
  fit(data = CPS_train)

rf_fit %>%
    predict(new_data = CPS_test) %>%
    bind_cols(CPS_test, .) %>%
    select(wage, .pred) %>%
    rmse(wage, .pred)
```

```
## # A tibble: 1 x 3
##   .metric   .estimator   .estimate
##   <chr>     <chr>            <dbl>
## 1 rmse      standard         0.527
```

3.   R PACKAGES FOR MICROECONOMETRICS

There is an extensive and constantly growing collection of R packages useful for micro-econometrics. A list of such packages is actively maintained by Achim Zeileis at CRAN Task View: Econometrics. Table 18.2 shows relevant information on the main packages identified in the list as microeconometric packages, including the date they were first released, a short description, the number of updates, last package update dates and the total number of CRAN downloads.

Table 18.2   *Packages for microeconometrics, including generalized linear models (GLMs), binary responses, count responses, multinomial responses, ordered responses, censored responses, truncated responses, fraction and proportion responses, high-dimensional fixed effects and miscellaneous tools for Cobb–Douglas, translog, stochastic frontier analysis and so on*

Package	Released	Updates	Latest	Package description	Downloads
effects	2003-04-27	56	2020-08-11	Effect Displays for Linear, Generalized Linear, and Other Models	2 058 853
margins	2017-03-22	6	2018-05-22	Marginal Effects for Model Objects	149 258
mfx	2013-12-13	5	2019-02-06	Marginal Effects, Odds Ratios and Incidence Rate Ratios for GLMs	183 547
LinReg-Interactive	2014-08-18	9	2020-02-08	Interactive Interpretation of Linear Regression Models	36 424
brglm	2008-02-25	13	2020-10-12	Bias Reduction in Binomial-Response Generalized Linear Models	1 033 301
Rchoice	2014-04-02	8	2020-05-27	Discrete Choice (Binary, Poisson and Ordered) Models with Random Parameters	36 085
bife	2016-07-29	10	2020-10-30	Binary Choice Models with Fixed Effects	52 520
glmx	2013-12-10	4	2015-11-19	Generalized Linear Models Extended	46 559

Table 18.2 (continued)

Package	Released	Updates	Latest	Package description	Downloads
MASS	2009-05-08	57	2020-09-09	Support Functions and Datasets for Venables and Ripley's MASS	7 615 050
aod	2005-06-08	30	2019-01-26	Analysis of Overdispersed Data	389 677
pscl	2005-05-31	39	2020-03-07	Political Science Computational Laboratory	854 704
mlogit	2008-05-16	28	2020-10-02	Multinomial Logit Models	506 580
mnlogit	2013-12-07	13	2019-05-28	Multinomial Logit Model	54 319
nnet	2009-05-08	16	2020-04-26	Feed-Forward Neural Networks and Multinomial Log-Linear Models	2 460 516
gmnl	2015-02-23	8	2020-05-27	Multinomial Logit Models with Random Parameters	55 975
apollo	2019-01-16	12	2020-12-05	Tools for Choice Model Estimation and Application	25 709
VGAM	2006-10-24	41	2020-10-23	Vector Generalized Linear and Additive Models	1 345 685
MNP	2004-06-27	42	2020-10-22	Fitting the Multinomial Probit Model	82 783
bayesm	2005-04-15	38	2019-10-15	Bayesian Inference for Marketing/ Micro-Econometrics	618 382
RSGHB	2013-02-14	11	2019-07-03	Functions for Hierarchical Bayesian Estimation: A Flexible Approach	54 613
ordinal	2010-03-07	30	2019-12-15	Regression Models for Ordinal Data	1 007 270
survival	2001-06-22	92	2020-09-28	Survival Analysis	6 832 377
AER	2008-05-05	27	2020-02-06	Applied Econometrics with R	1 605 081
censReg	2010-08-25	15	2020-08-04	Censored Regression (Tobit) Models	114 867
crch	2013-10-22	11	2019-09-03	Censored Regression with Conditional Heteroscedasticity	61 524
mhurdle	2010-08-05	10	2018-09-18	Multiple Hurdle Tobit Models	39 638
sample-Selection	2008-02-27	21	2020-12-15	Sample Selection Models	218 959

Table 18.2   (continued)

Package	Released	Updates	Latest	Package description	Downloads
matching-Markets	2014-11-22	19	2020-01-12	Analysis of Stable Matchings	66 229
SemiPar-SampleSel	2012-04-30	11			33 501
truncreg	2009-02-03	6	2018-08-18	Truncated Gaussian Regression Models	195 921
frm	2014-01-13	5	2015-02-21	Regression Analysis of Fractional Responses	41 378
betareg	2004-04-01	26	2020-02-03	Beta Regression	425 668
gamlss	2012-08-14	32	2020-09-12	Generalized Additive Models for Location Scale and Shape	483 746
durmod	2019-06-28	8	2020-03-30	Mixed Proportional Hazard Competing Risk Model	11 285
lfe	2011-03-10	59			291 093
alpaca	2018-07-31	7	2020-10-30	Fit GLMs with High-Dimensional k-Way Fixed Effects	41 707
micEcon	2005-02-21	32	2017-03-16	Microeconomic Analysis and Modeling	164 654
micEcon-CES	2010-03-15	12	2014-04-23	Analysis with the Constant Elasticity of Substitution (CES) function	44 158
micEcon-Aids	2009-12-28	11	2017-03-16	Demand Analysis with the Almost Ideal Demand System (AIDS)	127 439
micEcon-SNQP	2010-03-15	6	2020-02-11	Symmetric Normalized Quadratic Profit Function	40 227
sfa	2011-01-24	4	2014-01-06	Stochastic Frontier Analysis	42 233
semsfa	2015-02-18	4	2018-04-20	Semiparametric Estimation of Stochastic Frontier Models	29 162
spfrontier	2014-03-23	7	2019-12-18	Spatial Stochastic Frontier Models	32 906
ssfa	2015-05-18	4	2015-06-10	Spatial Stochastic Frontier Analysis	27 521
mvProbit	2011-11-13	6			33 954
reldist	2004-07-20	15	2016-10-09	Relative Distribution Methods	91 198

3.1 R Packages for Panel Data

Table 18.3 shows relevant information on the main packages that are useful for panel data analysis. This table shows how packages such as **plm** for panel data analysis are actively maintained, with dozens of updates, and have hundreds of thousands of downloads.

Table 18.3 *Packages for panel data models, including panel standard errors, linear panel models, generalized estimation equations and GLMs, mixed-effects models, instrumental variables, heterogeneous time trends and miscellaneous tools for autocorrelation and heteroscedasticity correction, tests of nonstationarity, threshold regression and unit root tests and so on*

Package	Released	Updates	Latest	Package description	Downloads
sandwich	2004-02-20	36	2020-10-02	Robust Covariance Matrix Estimators	7 701 671
clusterSEs	2015-03-03	19	2019-09-15	Calculate Cluster-Robust p-Values and Confidence Intervals	143 131
pcse	2007-03-13	14	2018-06-07	Panel-Corrected Standard Error Estimation in R	130 381
club-Sandwich	2016-07-23	18	2020-11-14	Cluster-Robust (Sandwich) Variance Estimators with Small-Sample Corrections	129 095
plm	2006-06-13	41	2020-10-13	Linear Models for Panel Data	1 321 375
geepack	2002-09-19	39	2019-12-13	Generalized Estimating Equation Package	564 821
Ortho-Panels	2015-10-27	7	2019-05-09	Dynamic Panel Models with Orthogonal Reparameterization of Fixed Effects	25 196
feisr	2019-03-01	8	2020-06-17	Estimating Fixed Effects Individual Slope Models	24 953
panelr	2019-05-16	8			24 372
panelvar	2018-04-03	5	2019-01-22	Panel Vector Autoregression	21 351
pglm	2010-07-24	7	2020-01-17	Panel Generalized Linear Models	152 426
phtt	2013-02-25	7			32 252
PANICr	2014-10-24	7			28 987
pdR	2014-09-01	9	2019-07-07	Threshold Model and Unit Root Tests in Cross-Section and Time Series Data	41 684
pampe	2015-02-13	5	2015-11-07	Implementation of the Panel Data Approach Method for Program Evaluation	31 781
collapse	2020-03-19	14	2020-11-10	Advanced and Fast Data Transformation	15 643

3.2 Textbooks Using R and Data Packages

Specific textbooks aimed at econometric practitioners that use R for microeconometric applications include *Panel Data Econometrics with R* by Croissant and Millo (2018), focusing on the **plm** and **pder** packages, *An Introduction to R for Quantitative Economics* by Dayal (2015), *Forecasting: Principles and Practice* by Hyndman and Athanasopoulos (2018), centered around the **forecast** package, *An R and S-Plus Companion to Applied Regression* by Fox and Monette (2002), accompanying the **car** package, and *Applied Econometrics with R* by Kleiber and Zeileis (2008), centered around the **AER** package. The book *Advances in Social Science Research Using R* edited by Vinod (2009) includes several parametric and nonparametric applications of R to economic data analysis. In *An Introduction to the Advanced Theory and Practice of Nonparametric Econometrics: A Replicable Approach Using R* by Racine (2019b), the open-source R platform for statistical computing and graphics is used throughout in conjunction with the R package **np** that also helps readers get up to speed with R, R Markdown, TeX and Git. Other useful books on R application useful for econometrics include *Learning R: A Step-by-Step Function Guide to Data Analysis* by Cotton (2013), *An Introduction to Statistical Learning: With Applications in R* by James et al. (2013), *Introducing Monte Carlo Methods with R* by Robert and Casella (2010), *Bayesian Computation with R* by Albert (2009), *Applied Spatial Data Analysis with R* by Bivand et al. (2008), *Data Analysis Using Regression and Multilevel/Hierarchical Models* by Gelman and Hill (2007) and *Deep Learning with R* by Chollet and Allaire (2018).

Packages such as **AER, Ecdat** and **wooldridge** are particularly worth mentioning as they contain a large selection of data sets from various standard econometric textbooks, including Greene (2012), Stock and Watson (2015), Wooldridge (2013), Baltagi (2008), as well as several data sets from the data archives of the *Journal of Applied Econometrics*, the *Journal of Business & Economic Statistics* and so on. Table 18.4 shows relevant information on packages offering useful microeconometric data. R data sets for *Principles of Econometrics* by Hill et al. (2011) are made available by the **PoEdata** that can be installed from GitHub:

```
install_git("https://github.com/ccolonescu/PoEdata")
```

Table 18.4 Packages containing data useful for microeconometrics

Package	Released	Updates	Latest	Package description	Downloads
AER	2008-05-05	27	2020-02-06	Applied Econometrics with R	1 605 081
Ecdat	2005-03-01	23	2020-11-03	Data Sets for Econometrics	400 803
wooldridge	2017-07-11	7	2018-10-10	111 Data Sets from "Introductory Econometrics: A Modern Approach, 6e" by Jeffrey M. Wooldridge	161 578
pder	2017-09-28	4	2019-09-08	Panel Data Econometrics with R	78 435
erer	2011-02-04	14	2020-05-01	Empirical Research in Economics with R	110 524
psidR	2013-07-22	12	2020-02-26	Build Panel Data Sets from PSID Raw Data	39 979

3.3 Search Packages and Packages for IV

Because of the rapidly changing landscapes, searching for R packages useful for microeconometrics can be difficult even for experienced R users. There are more than 16 000 packages available on CRAN, and the number is constantly increasing. Package names rarely provide the necessary information about their scope, so searching by name can be a frustrating experience. A useful tool to help the search of useful packages is **packagefinder**. The function *findPackage()* searches through the metadata of all CRAN packages. For example, we can search for the "instrumental variable" string in the following way:

```
pt_pkg <- as_tibble(findPackage("instrumental"),limit.results=
  20,silent = TRUE)

## Your are searching packages for the term 'instrumental'
##
## Please wait while index is being searched . . .
##
## Results: 51 out of 17049 CRAN packages found in 6 seconds.
## Top 15 results are shown. Use parameter 'limit.results' to
     increase number of results shown.
pt_downloads <- cran_stats(pt_pkg$NAME)
top_downloads <-  pt_downloads %>% group_by(package) %>%
                  summarize(downloads = sum(downloads)) %>%
                  arrange(desc(downloads))
top_downloads

## # A tibble: 15 x 2
##     package     downloads
##     <fct>           <int>
##  1 ivpack          92340
##  2 LARF            45514
##  3 ivprobit        37263
##  4 ivfixed         35687
##  5 ivpanel         33863
##  6 REndo           29870
##  7 ivmodel         29489
##  8 ImpactIV        27061
##  9 ivtools         16742
## 10 localIV         12504
## 11 naivereg        12043
## 12 iva             10626
## 13 npsr            10002
## 14 ivmte            9880
## 15 ivdesc           6927
```

Table 18.5   Packages for IV models, searched using findPackage() *function from the* `packagefinder` *package*

Package	Released	Updates	Latest	Package description	Downloads
naivereg	2018-02-20	6	2020-03-18	Nonparametric Additive Instrumental Variable Estimator and Related IV Methods	12 043
ivpack	2014-01-14	5	2014-10-25	Instrumental Variable Estimation	92 340
REndo	2015-12-09	14	2020-10-14	Fitting Linear Models with Endogenous Regressors using Latent Instrumental Variables	29 870
ivmodel	2015-05-04	10	2020-02-21	Statistical Inference and Sensitivity Analysis for Instrumental Variables Model	29 489
ivmte	2019-02-08	6	2020-04-18	Instrumental Variables: Extrapolation by Marginal Treatment Effects	9880
ivprobit	2014-09-25	4	2018-02-21	Instrumental Variables Probit Model	37 263
ivtools	2018-04-24	7	2020-02-24	Instrumental Variables	16 742
LARF	2013-04-04	7	2016-07-26	Local Average Response Functions for Instrumental Variable Estimation of Treatment Effects	45 514
localIV	2018-08-05	7	2020-06-26	Estimation of Marginal Treatment Effects using Local Instrumental Variables	12 504

Table 18.5 shows the results of the search in tabular form. Figure 18.6 shows the top five of the most downloaded IV packages. In the next section, we look at some application in microeconometrics using several of those packages.

For packages or developmental versions of packages not on CRAN, searches will have to be tailored on the specific platform. For packages hosted on GitHub there is a package, **install_github**, that provides a function, *gh_search_packages()* that returns a list of R packages with a given keyword in the title. As an example, to get packages with "quantile regression" in the title, we can run:

```
library(githubinstall)
gh_search_packages(regex = "quantile regression", ignore.case = T)

## Error in get(genname, envir = envir): object 'testthat_print'
   not found
```

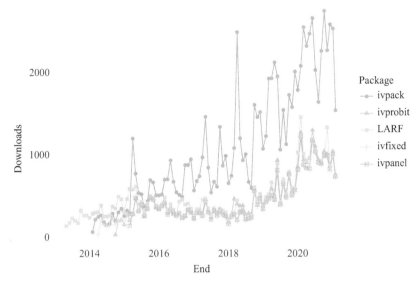

Figure 18.6   Package downloads

The results of this search are shown in Table 18.6. Results for "additive model" and "panel data", as further examples, are shown in Table 18.7 and Table 18.8, respectively. Even more so than with CRAN packages, careful research and testing are needed before using packages of unknown quality for research.

Table 18.6   Packages for "panel data" models on GitHub, searched using gh_search_ packages() function from the **githubinstall** *package*

Username	Package	Package description
CenterFor-Assessment	SGP	Functions to calculate student growth percentiles and percentile growth projections/trajectories for students using large-scale, longitudinal assessment data. Functions use quantile regression to estimate the conditional density associated with each student's achievement history. Percentile growth projections/trajectories are calculated using the coefficient matrices derived from the student growth percentile analyses
KevinSee	qRfish	Estimate carrying capacity with quantile regression forests
MartinRoth	rqIcm	Isotone quantile regression using the iterative convex minorant algorithm
PhilippPro	quantregRanger	Quantile Regression for Ranger
SeoncheolPark	qrandomForest	Quantile regression + random forests
bssherwood	rqpen	Penalized Quantile Regression
lbenitesanchez	ALDqr	EM algorithm for estimation of parameters and other methods in a quantile regression

Table 18.6   (continued)

Username	Package	Package description
lbenitesanchez	lqr	It fits a robust linear quantile regression model using a new family of zero-quantile distributions for the error term. This family of distribution includes skewed versions of the Normal, Student's *t*, Laplace, Slash and Contaminated Normal distribution. It also performs logistic quantile regression for bounded responses as shown in Bottai et al. (2009). It provides estimate and full inference. It also provides envelope plots for assessing the fit and confidences bands when several quantiles are provided simultaneously.
mfasiolo	qgam	Additive quantile regression R package
opardo	GPDP-QuantReg	R Package. Bayesian and non-parametric quantile regression, using Gaussian Processes to model the trend, and Dirichlet Processes, for the error. Author: Carlos Omar Pardo
rjsaito	bpqr	This is a package-in-progress for a statistical technique for Bootstrapped Panel Quantile Regression. Currently, I am hoping to contribute R code of statistical and mathematical procedures in hydrological research.
tnagler	vinereg	D-vine quantile regression
yasui-salmon	CQR	censored quantile regression with three-step estimator
yuchang0321	IVQR	Instrumental Variable Quantile Regression

Table 18.7   Packages for "panel data" models on GitHub, searched using gh_search_packages() *function from the* **githubinstall** *package*

Username	Package	Package description
Japhilko	GPediting	Package for editing Gesis Panel Data
bcallaway11	csabounds	Tight bounds on distributional treatment effect parameters with panel data
bioinf-jku	panelcn.mops	CNV detection tool for targeted NGS panel data
chjackson	msm	The msm R package for continuous-time multi-state modeling of panel data
daroczig	within	R implementation of the most frequently used three-dimensional fixed-effects panel data models the appropriate Within estimators.
floswald	psidR	R package to easily build panel datasets from the PSID
jacob-long	panelr	Regression models and utilities for repeated measures and panel data
joachim-gassen	ExPanDaR	R package for Interactive Panel Data Exploration

Table 18.7   (continued)

Username	Package	Package description
jtilly	cbpR	This R Package downloads and prepares panel data sets from the Census County Business Patterns (CBP)
lrdegeest	panelGMM	General Method of Moments estimators for panel data in R
mbannert	panelaggregation	R Package to aggregate Panel Data
realAkhmed	mixpanelR	R interface for MixPanel data export API
regisely	macrodata	an R package to quickly build cross-country panel data
susanathey	MCPanel	Matrix Completion Methods for Causal Panel Data Models
xinzhou1023	dlmpanel	A package for Dynamic Linear Model on panel data in Marketing-Mix Modeling

Table 18.8   Packages for "additive model' models on GitHub, searched using gh_search_ packages() *function from the* **githubinstall** *package*

Username	Package	Package description
IQSS	ZeligGAM4	General Additive Models for Zelig
SuneelChatla	cmp	R Package for Conway–Maxwell Poisson Regression and Additive Model
asadharis	HierBasis	An R package for nonparametric regression and fitting sparse additive models
boost-R	gamboostLSS	Boosting models for fitting generalized additive models for location, shape and scale (GAMLSS) to potentially high dimensional data. The current release version can be found on CRAN (https://cran.r-project.org/package=gamboostLSS).
dill	msg	Multidimensional Scaling for Generalized additive models. See wiki for examples.
fabian-s	RLRsim	R package for fast and exact (restricted) likelihood ratio tests for mixed and additive models.
hofnerb	gamboostLSS	Boosting models for fitting generalized additive models for location, shape and scale (GAMLSS) to potentially high dimensional data. This is a copy of the r-forge repository hosted at https://r-forge.r-project.org/projects/gamboostlss. The current release version can be found on CRAN (http://cran.r-project.org/package=gamboostLSS).
hofnerb	lethal	Compute lethal doses for count data based on generalized additive models (GAMs) together with parametric bootstrap confidence intervals for the lethal dose.

4. MICROECONOMETRIC APPLICATIONS

Even though many of the methods available for microeconometrics have not yet been integrated in the tidymodel framework, tidyverse tools can still help explore and prepare the data for analysis as well as to process and present the output from an analysis.

4.1 Instrumental Variable Examples

Next, we reproduce the instrumental variable estimation example from Stock and Watson (2015) with Cigarette Consumption Panel Data (*CigarettesSW*) and the instrumental-variable two-stage least squares regression function (*ivreg()*) made available by the **AER** package. We can create the real variables and the additional instrument using tidyverse tools:

```
library(AER)
data("CigarettesSW", package = "AER")
CigarettesSW %>%
  filter(year== 1995) %>%
  mutate(rprice = price/cpi,
         rincome = income/population/cpi,
         tdiff = (taxs - tax)/cpi) -> CigarettesSW.sub
```

We can visualize the variables using the **geofacet** package; multiple panels with spatial data can be arranged on a grid that preserves as much as possible of the geographic location of states as opposed to using the standard matrix arrangement supported by **ggplot2**'s built-in faceting. This approach can display multivariate data using any **ggplot** visualization for each panel as shown in Figure 18.7.

```
library(geofacet)
CigarettesSW.sub %>%
  pivot_longer(cols = c(rprice, rincome, tdiff),
               names_to="variable",
               values_to="value") %>%
  ggplot(aes(variable, value, fill = variable)) +
    geom_col() +
  scale_y_log10() +
  scale_fill_brewer(palette="Accent") +
  coord_flip() +
  facet_geo(~ state, grid = "us_state_grid2") +
  theme_bw(base_size = 8)
```

Next we fit two specifications by two-stage least squares to estimate the elasticity of demand for cigarettes. Diagnostic tests for instrument validity and for model comparisons are available in various methods such as *summary()* and *anova()*.

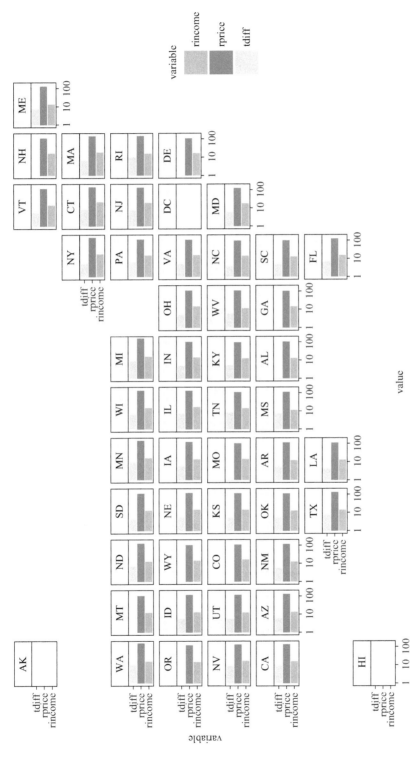

Figure 18.7   Cigarette consumption data plotted by state using **ggplot** *faceting with a US grid mimicking the US map*

```
fm1 <- ivreg(log(packs) ~ log(rprice) | tdiff, data =
  CigarettesSW.sub)
fm2 <- ivreg(log(packs) ~ log(rprice) + log(rincome) |
  log(rincome) + tdiff + I(tax/cpi),
                data = CigarettesSW.sub)
anova(fm1, fm2)

## Analysis of Variance Table
##
## Model 1: log(packs) ~ log(rprice) | tdiff
## Model 2: log(packs) ~ log(rprice) + log(rincome) |
  log(rincome) + tdiff +
##       I(tax/cpi)
##   Res.Df    RSS Df Sum of Sq          F Pr(>F)
## 1     46 1.6668
## 2     45 1.5880  1   0.078748 1.3815    0.246

summary(fm2, vcov = sandwich, df = Inf, diagnostics = TRUE)

##
## Call:
## ivreg(formula = log(packs) ~ log(rprice) + log(rincome) |
##     log(rincome) +
##     tdiff + I(tax/cpi), data = CigarettesSW.sub)
##
## Residuals:
##       Min         1Q      Median         3Q         Max
## -0.6006931  -0.0862222  -0.0009999   0.1164699   0.3734227
##
## Coefficients:
##                Estimate Std. Error z value Pr(>|z|)
## (Intercept)     9.8950     0.9288  10.654   < 2e-16 ***
## log(rprice)    -1.2774     0.2417  -5.286 1.25e-07 ***
## log(rincome)    0.2804     0.2458   1.141    0.254
##
## Diagnostic tests:
##                     df1  df2  statistic  p-value
## Weak instruments      2   44    228.738   <2e-16 ***
## Wu-Hausman            1   44      3.823   0.0569 .
## Sargan                1   NA      0.333   0.5641
## ---
## Signif. codes: 0 '***' 0.001 '**' 0.01 '*' 0.05 '.' 0.1 ' ' 1
##
## Residual standard error: 0.1879 on Inf degrees of freedom
## Multiple R-Squared: 0.4294, Adjusted R-squared: 0.4041
## Wald test: 34.51 on 2 DF, p-value: 3.214e-08
```

4.2 Quantile Regression Example

The package **quantreg** by Koenker (2019) provides the function *rq()* to fit quantile regressions. As an example, we can estimate the wage equation in semi-logarithmic form using the data provided by the **AER** package. The *tidy()* function from the **broom** package can be used to make the output of a regression, usually stored as an R list, "tidy":

```
library("quantreg")
data("CPS1985", package = "AER")
cps <- CPS1985

f <- log(wage) ~ experience + I(experience^ 2) +
               education
ols <- lm(data=cps, formula = f)
ols %>% broom:: tidy (conf.int = TRUE, conf.level = 0.95) -> ols.
  ci
cps_rq <- rq(f, data = cps, tau = seq(0.1, 0.9, by = 0.15))
ols.ci %>% pivot_longer(cols= c(conf.low, conf.high), values_
  to="val") -> ols.ci
```

Figure 18.8 shows the intermediate and final results of the analysis, plotted with the code.

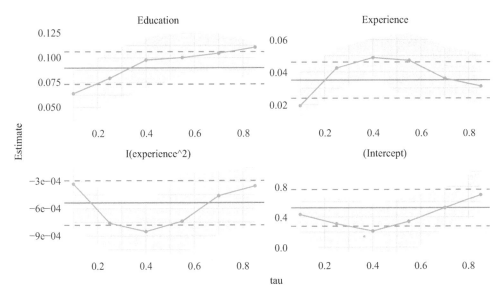

Figure 18.8 *Coefficient estimates of quantile regression and OLS for the wage determinants. The horizontal axis displays the quantiles while the vertical axis shows the coefficients of the conditional quantile regressions. Quantile coefficients and bootstrap-based confidence bands are represented In blue. The solid red lines parallel to the horizontal axis correspond to OLS coefficients with confidence bands dashed*

```
cps_rq %>%
  broom::tidy() %>%
  ggplot(aes(x=tau,y=estimate))+
   geom_hline(data = ols.ci, colour = "tomato", aes(yintercept=
     estimate)) +
   geom_hline(data = ols.ci, colour = "tomato",linetype =
     "dashed", aes(yintercept= val)) +
   geom_ribbon(aes(ymin=conf.low,ymax=conf.high),
             alpha= 0.25, fill="steelblue3") +
   geom_point(color="steelblue3", size = 1)+
   geom_line(color="steelblue3", size = .5)+
   facet_wrap(~term, scales="free", ncol= 2)
```

NOTES

1. Despite the intention of keeping the "ready-made" visualizations to a minimum, because of the popularity, openness and extensibility of the language, many functions that produce specific visualizations such as *geom_histogram()*, that could be produced following the Grammar principles have been created for convenience.
2. The code has been hidden to conserve space but is available in full in the source code of this R markdown document.

REFERENCES

Albert, J. (2009). *Bayesian Computation with R. Use R!* Springer New York.

Athey, S. & Imbens, G. W. (2019). Machine learning methods that economists should know about. *Annual Review of Economics*, *11*(1), 685–725.

Bache, S. M. & Wickham, H. (2014). *magrittr: A Forward-Pipe Operator for R.* R package version 1.5.

Baltagi, B. (2008). *Econometric Analysis of Panel Data*. John Wiley & Sons.

Becker, R. & Chambers, J. (1985). *Extending The S System*. Taylor & Francis.

Becker, R. A. (1994). A brief history of S. *Computational Statistics*, 81–110.

Becker, R. A., Chambers, J. M., & Wilks, A. R. (1988). *The New S Language*. Chapman & Hall.

Bertin, J. (2010). *Semiology of Graphics: Diagrams, Networks, Maps*. Redlands: Esri Press. ISBN: 978-1-589-48261-6.

Bivand, R. S., Pebesma, E. J., & Gómez-Rubio, V. (2008). *Applied Spatial Data Analysis with R*. New York; London: Springer.

Bottai, M., Cai, B. and McKeown, R.E. (2010). Logistic quantile regression for bounded outcomes. *Statist. Med.*, 29, 309–17. https://doi.org/10.1002/sim.3781

Chambers, J. (2017). *Extending R*. Chapman & Hall/CRC The R Series. CRC Press.

Chang, A. C. & Li, P. (2022). Is economics research replicable? Sixty published papers from thirteen journals say "often not". Forthcoming in *Critical Finance Review*, http://dx.doi.org/10.1561/104.00000053.

Chang, W. (2013). *R Graphics Cookbook*. Oreilly and Associate Series. O'Reilly Media, Incorporated.

Chollet, F. & Allaire, J. (2018). *Deep Learning with R*. Manning.

Codd, E. F. (1990). *The Relational Model for Database Management: Version 2*. Addison-Wesley.

Cook, D., Buja, A., Lang, D., Swayne, D., Hofmann, H., Wickham, H., & Lawrence, M. (2007). *Interactive and Dynamic Graphics for Data Analysis: With R and GGobi. Use R!* Springer New York.

Cotton, R. (2013). *Learning R: A Step-by-Step Function Guide to Data Analysis*. O'Reilly Media.

Croissant, Y. & Millo, G. (2018). *Panel Data Econometrics with R*. Wiley.

Dalgaard, P. (2008). *Introductory Statistics with R*. Statistics and Computing. Springer New York.

Dayal, V. (2015). *An Introduction to R for Quantitative Economics: Graphing, Simulating and Computing*. Springer India.

Dewald, W. G., Thursby, J. G., & Anderson, R. G. (1986). Replication in empirical economics: *The Journal of Money, Credit and Banking Project*. *American Economic Review*, *76*(4), 587–603.

Donoho, D. (2017). 50 years of data science. *Journal of Computational and Graphical Statistics*, *26*(4), 745–66.

Einav, L. & Levin, J. (2014). The data revolution and economic analysis. *Innovation Policy and the Economy, 14,* 1–24.

Fox, J. & Monette, G. (2002). *An R and S-Plus Companion to Applied Regression.* SAGE.

Gelman, A. & Hill, J. (2007). *Data Analysis Using Regression and Multilevel/Hierarchical Models.* New York: Cambridge University Press.

Greene, W. (2012). *Econometric Analysis.* Prentice Hall.

Hadley, W. (2019). The tidy tools manifesto. https://cran.r-project.org/web/packages/tidyverse/vignettes/manifesto. html. Accessed: 2021-01-19.

Hill, R.C., Griffiths, W.E., and Lim, G. C. (2011). *Principles of Econometrics,* 4th edition. Wiley.

Hyndman, R. & Athanasopoulos, G. (2018). *Forecasting: Principles and Practice.* OTexts.

Ihaka, R. & Gentleman, R. (1996). R: A language for data analysis and graphics. *Journal of Computational and Graphical Statistics, 5,* 299–314.

James, G., Witten, D., Hastie, T., & Tibshirani, R. (2013). *An Introduction to Statistical Learning: with Applications in R.* Springer New York.

Kleiber, C. & Zeileis, A. (2008). *Applied Econometrics with R. Use R!* Springer.

Koenker, R. (2019). *quantreg: Quantile Regression.* R package version 5.42.1.

Molnar, C. (2019). *Interpretable Machine Learning.* https://christophm.github.io/interpretable-ml-book/.

Murrell, P. (2018). *R Graphics,* 3rd edition. CRC Press.

Peng, R. D., Kross, S. and Anderson, B. (2020). *Mastering Software Development in R.* Victoria, Canada: Leanpub https://bookdown.org/rdpeng/RProgDA/

Racine, J. (2019a). *Reproducible Econometrics Using R.* Oxford University Press.

Racine, J. S. (2019b). *An Introduction to the Advanced Theory and Practice of Nonparametric Econometrics: A Replicable Approach Using R.* Cambridge University Press.

Raymond, E. (2003). *The Art of UNIX Programming.* Pearson Education.

R Core Team. (2013). *R: A Language and Environment for Statistical Computing.* Vienna, Austria: R Foundation for Statistical Computing.

Robert, C. & Casella, G. (2010). *Introducing Monte Carlo Methods with R. Use R!* Springer.

Salus, P. H. (1994). *A Quarter Century of UNIX.* New York: ACM Press/Addison-Wesley.

Stock, J. & Watson, M. (2015). *Introduction to Econometrics.* Pearson Education.

Sussman, G. J. & Steele, G. L. (1975). An interpreter for extended lambda calculus. Technical report, USA.

Tufte, E. (2001). *The Visual Display of Quantitative Informations,* 2nd edition. Cheshire, Conn.: Graphics Press.

Varian, H. R. (2014). Big data: New tricks for econometrics. *Journal of Economic Perspectives, 28*(2), 3–28.

Venables, W. N. & Smith, D. M. (2009). *An Introduction to R,* 2nd ed.. Network Theory Ltd.

Vinod, H. (2009). *Advances in Social Science Research Using R.* Springer New York.

Vinod, H. D. (2001). Care and feeding of reproducible econometrics. *Journal of Econometrics, 100*(1), 87–8.

Wickham, H. (2010). A layered grammar of graphics. *Journal of Computational and Graphical Statistics, 19*(1), 3–28.

Wickham, H. (2014a). Tidy data. *Journal of Statistical Software, Articles, 59*(10), 1–23.

Wickham, H. (2014b). Tidy data. *The Journal of Statistical Software, 59.*

Wickham, H. (2015). *Advanced R.* Chapman & Hall/CRC The R Series. CRC Press.

Wickham, H. (2016a). *ggplot2: Elegant Graphics for Data Analysis.* Springer.

Wickham, H. (2016b). *ggplot2: Elegant Graphics for Data Analysis. Use R!* Springer.

Wickham, H. & Grolemund, G. (2017). *R for Data Science: Import, Tidy, Transform, Visualize, and Model Data.* O'Reilly Media, Inc.

Wickham, H. & Henry, L. (2019). *tidyr: Easily Tidy Data with 'spread()' and 'gather()' Functions.* R package version 0.8.3.

Wilkinson, L. (2005). *The Grammar of Graphics (Statistics and Computing).* Berlin, Heidelberg: Springer-Verlag.

Wooldridge, J. (2013). *Introductory Econometrics: A Modern Approach.* Cengage Learning.

Xie, Y. (2016). *bookdown: Authoring Books and Technical Documents with R Markdown.* Chapman & Hall/CRC The R Series. CRC Press.

Xie, Y. (2017). *Dynamic Documents with R and knitr.* Chapman & Hall/CRC The R Series. CRC Press.

Xie, Y., Allaire, J., & Grolemund, G. (2018). *R Markdown: The Definitive Guide.* Chapman & Hall/CRC The R Series. CRC Press.

19. Robust inference in panel data microeconometrics, using R
Giovanni Millo

1. INTRODUCTION

This chapter is written as a quick companion for the practicing microeconometrician who wants to use R for their analysis. It is concerned with relaxing the restrictive hypotheses of error homoskedasticity and non-correlation, and performing robust inference in the context of panel data. I will systematically reference two textbooks for more formal, technical and thorough treatments: Wooldridge (2010) as a world-leading treatment of the subject and the source for the first worked example I present and the general structure of the first half of the chapter; and Croissant and Millo (2019) for a comprehensive textbook-level treatment of panel data econometrics with the R software.

This chapter has two main parts: the first part introduces the reader to the mechanics of panel data econometrics with R as a necessary step toward the second part, where I expand on the various robust estimators available in the **plm** package (Croissant and Millo, 2008, 2019; Millo, 2017) and how to employ them in a microeconometric context. To this end, first I present the estimators and tests in the order of Wooldridge (2010, chapter 10) with a particular focus on "robustifying" the analysis by employing the *robust*, or *clustered*, covariance matrix, which is likely to be the most appropriate choice in the majority of microeconomic applications. Then, I present alternative sandwich estimators robust to different kinds of dependence in a more data-rich context. Any formality, although minimal, is deferred to this second part in order to make the first as gentle and as practice oriented as possible; therefore, perhaps unusually, the clustering estimator employed in the first part is defined at the beginning of the second.

The main perspective taken is that of fixed number of periods (T), large number of cross-sectional units (N), as in Wooldridge's book and as is most common in microeconometrics; although, in the last part of the chapter, I will consider a second example with a longer time dimension and enlarge the scope of the treatment to a variety of "robust" covariance estimators appropriate for this setting beyond the popular "clustered" covariance employed in the first part.

In particular, I will cover, in this order: estimating the basic specifications (random effects, fixed effects, and first difference) and using the results to test hypotheses of interest; relaxing the typical regularity assumptions on the error covariance to robustify the standard errors of the basic estimators by allowing for unrestricted general heteroskedasticity and within-individual correlation of model errors (so-called "clustered" standard errors); presenting alternative standard error estimators for different kinds of error dependence; applying the latter in combination with different specifications of a model's individual and/or time effects. The increasing level of detail means that the casual reader can refer to the first part of the chapter and have the main methods "just working" in R, while proceeding to the latter sections once they are interested in understanding the many different options available and how they map to the underlying statistical theory.

I stress that reference to Wooldridge (2010) (or another textbook) is a necessary condition for sensible application of the software methods presented here, and that this chapter, unlike Croissant and Millo (2019), cannot be taken as a standalone primer on basic panel methods, its only purpose being to illustrate software operation and to put it into the perspective of the theoretical methods described elsewhere. The reader must be familiar with the subject to properly understand what is going on when a given command is issued.

1.1 Notation

Package names are in **bold**. Commands and parts thereof (like argument names) are in `typewriter` font. Arguments will follow the type: for example, character values will be "quoted", numeric values will not be. Variable (and model) names are in *italics*.

Given that Stata is perhaps the most popular software package in the field of microeconometrics, I will occasionally refer to the equivalent Stata command to help the reader follow what is done in R.

1.2 Software Requirements

Before starting, it is necessary to load some additional software materials into the workspace. In fact, the R system is a large collection of software, of which only the base system and some core packages are loaded by default. Specialized extensions for various statistical tasks are loaded on a by-session basis: either in the structured form of *packages*, large standalone collections of functions, documentation and, often, data sets (such as **plm**); or under form of individual functions or datasets. In the former case, the `library` function will load a complete package; in the latter, individual pieces of code (typically defining a function) can be *sourced* (that is, executed) through the `source` function; individual example datasets can be loaded with `data`. The reader should keep in mind that `data` will only work with built-in example datasets contained in some R package: reading external data into the R session will instead require different statements. An example is presented in section 4.

Next to **plm**, I will employ some other packages of econometric nature, mainly for the purpose of hypothesis testing: **lmtest** (Zeileis and Hothorn, 2002) and **car** (Fox and Weisberg, 2011).

```
> library(plm)
> library(car)
> library(lmtest)
```

Presentation of results and the preparation of documents in general can be made easier by outputting results from **R** directly into LATEX. Two useful packages for this purpose, although not the only options, are **xtable** (Dahl et al., 2019) and **texreg** (Leifeld, 2013).

```
> library(texreg)
> library(xtable)
```

The package **wooldridge** (Shea, 2018) contains the datasets from the "other" manual by Jeffrey Wooldridge, *Introductory Econometrics: a Modern Approach*.

```
> library(wooldridge)
> data(jtrain)
```

Lastly, this chapter has been prepared by dynamically weaving **R** code and LATEX markup through the **Sweave** utility (Leisch, 2002).

1.3 Data Organization and Conventions

Panel data have two dimensions, usually the individual unit of observation (family, firm, state, country . . .) and the time period. Estimators and tests need the indexing information in order to operate correctly. Some widely used econometric programs whose paradigms require us to operate on one dataset at a time require us to organize this dataset at the beginning, once for all, so that the indices are properly specified (like `xtset`-ting the dataset in Stata, or setting the indices of an EViews workfile). R is more flexible, allowing the coexistence of many different datasets in the workspace; therefore, the indices cannot but be an attribute of the (individual) dataset itself.

The convention in **plm** is that `data` can be any regular `data.frame`, provided that the individual index sits in the first column, the time index in the second. Alternatively, a regular `data.frame` with a different ordering of the columns can be used, provided that the `index` argument is specified within every call to estimators and tests (see the examples in the next section). A third possibility is to make and employ a specialized object type, the `pdata.frame`, which will carry over the indexing information. This third way of operating is somewhat more sophisticated and, while it is necessary for operations and tests involving one (or more) panel variable(s), like cross-sectional dependence or panel unit root testing, it goes beyond the scope of this chapter. On `pdata.frames`, see Croissant and Millo (2019).

1.4 The Robustification Framework

R allows us to separate the procedural step of obtaining estimates $\hat{\beta}$ from those of estimating their dispersion $SE(\hat{\beta})$ and presenting the well-known table of significance tests. Some words on the mechanics of the software are in order.

An *estimator* function will create an *estimated model object*; the latter containing $\hat{\beta}$ as well as residuals and other quantities of interest. In turn, another estimator – this time for the estimators' covariance, and hence for $SE(\hat{\beta})$ – can feed on the estimated model for producing the standard errors *according to the chosen method*. Functions in the `summary` and `coeftest` families can draw on these results to compute and present *t*-tests in the familiar tabular format.

The method chosen to compute the SEs can be passed on to the function producing the *t*-statistics and diagnostics table in multiple ways. The "cleanest" way is by supplying a function, like `coeftest(mymodel, vcov=vcovHC)`; otherwise, one can provide a computed matrix, perhaps computing it on the fly inside the same call, along the lines of `coeftest(mymodel, vcov=vcovHC(mymodel))`. See Millo (2017), Croissant and Millo (2019, chapter 5) and the documentation for package **plm** for more detail on the robustification framework in the case of panel data methods; and Zeileis (2004, 2006) for the general approach to flexible covariance specification, of which the one presented here is one special instance.

All operations in the following therefore share the same structure:

- Estimate model of choice.
- Produce coefficient tables or individual statistical tests using either the "standard" (default) or some "special" covariance (for example, clustering by firm).

2.   BASIC PANEL METHODS IN R BY WAY OF EXAMPLE

As a worked introduction to panel methods in R, I go through the examples from Wooldridge (2010, chapter 10), reviewing the practical aspects of estimation. The focus is on applied microeconometrics and on obtaining results; the reader will possibly compare the presented workflow with that of other software packages, for example Stata. For a more structured approach to the software package **plm** for panel data econometrics in R, see Croissant and Millo (2019); for another gentle introduction to panel methods in R, see also Henningsen and Henningsen (2019).

The job training grants example (Example 10.4 in Wooldridge, 2010) regards estimating the effect of job training grants on firm scrap rates. The dataset (*JTRAIN1* in the original source, *jtrain* in package **wooldridge**) contains observations on 54 firms for the years 1987, 1988 and 1989. Grants were not awarded in 1987, then some firms received grants in 1988 and others received grants in 1989; a firm could not receive a grant twice. As per Wooldridge (2010), "Since there are firms in 1989 that received a grant only in 1988, it is important to allow the grant effect to persist one period".

Let us replicate the results in the original source with R. All references to examples and so on are relative to Wooldridge (2010, chapter 10), so I will henceforth omit the citation.

2.1   Random Effects

Here, I produce the estimates in Example 10.4: random effects. The random effects (RE) estimator is obtained from the `plm` function, setting the `model` argument to "random". As observed above, the argument `index=c("fcode","year")` must be set in order to let the program know the correct panel indices, much like Stata's `xtset`. With respect to the latter, however, the `index` will have to be specified with every command, unless the columns of the dataset are ordered in the "standard" way: individual index first, time index second, then the data proper, in which case it is not necessary to specify anything.

```
> ## Example 10.4 (RE Estimation of the Effects of Job Training
     Grants)
> fm <- log(scrap) ~ d88 + d89 + union + grant + grant_1
> ## RE model
> re10.4 <- plm(fm, jtrain, index=c("fcode","year"),
     model="random")
```

The output from the estimating function does, as is usual with R, not appear immediately in the session log. Rather it is stored in a *model* object, which can be inspected with the appropriate functions. To see the overall result of estimation, one can issue a call to `summary`.

```
> summary(re10.4)
Oneway (individual) effect Random Effect Model
(Swamy-Arora's transformation)

Call:
plm(formula = fm, data = jtrain, model = "random", index =
    c("fcode", "year"))

Balanced Panel: n = 54, T = 3, N = 162

Effects:
                  var  std.dev   share
idiosyncratic  0.2477   0.4977   0.114
individual     1.9322   1.3900   0.886
theta: 0.7975

Residuals:
       Min.    1st Qu.     Median    3rd Qu.       Max.
 -2.546798  -0.223892   0.040554   0.255287   1.549791

Coefficients:
              Estimate  Std. Error  t-value  Pr(>|t|)
(Intercept)   0.414833    0.243432   1.7041   0.09035 .
d88          -0.093452    0.109156  -0.8561   0.39324
d89          -0.269834    0.131650  -2.0496   0.04207 *
union         0.547802    0.410625   1.3341   0.18413
grant        -0.214696    0.147784  -1.4528   0.14830
grant_1      -0.377070    0.205352  -1.8362   0.06823 .
---
Signif. codes: 0
```

The statements defining the model formula, performing the estimation and lastly inspecting the results have been kept separate here, for the sake of exposition; and it can be good practice to do so as well. Nevertheless, it is common practice to do everything in one line, such as

```
> summary(plm(log(scrap) ~ d88 + d89 + union + grant + grant_1,
+             jtrain, index=c("fcode","year"), model="random"))
```

The economic result of interest is whether either *grant* or its lagged value, *grant_1*, are significant. A joint significance test – in either χ^2 or F form – is performed in the following way: calling the `waldtest` function and supplying the order numbers (or the names) of the regressors to test. For the sake of illustration, below I supply names in the χ^2 test (default), order numbers in the F test:

```
> ## Wald test for joint significance of grant and grant_1
> wald10.4 <- waldtest(re10.4, c("grant", "grant_1"))
> wald10.4.F <- waldtest(re10.4, 4:5, test="F")
```

As is customary in R, the testing function creates a test object in the workspace but does not automatically produce an output in the log. It is enough to call the object by name (or just some part of it, such as the *p*-value) to display it (here, the test in χ^2 form):

```
> wald10.4


Wald test


Model 1: log(scrap) ~ d88 + d89 + union + grant + grant_1
Model 2: log(scrap) ~ d88 + d89 + union
  Res.Df Df Chisq Pr(>Chisq)
1    156
2    158 -2 3.6645 0.1601
```

However, it is perhaps more common, in practice – and it is what I will do henceforth, for the sake of compactness – to output the result on the fly, without assigning an object (below, the test in *F*-form):

```
> waldtest(re10.4, 4:5, test="F")


Wald test


Model 1: log(scrap) ~ d88 + d89 + union + grant + grant_1
Model 2: log(scrap) ~ d88 + d89 + union
   Res.Df Df      F Pr(>F)
1    156
2    158 -2 1.8323 0.1635
```

2.1.1   Robustifying inference

Wooldridge (2010, p. 262) suggests using a robust covariance matrix for the parameter estimates. The robust covariance estimator is the one described in Wooldridge (2010, chapter 7) and known as the "clustered" or "Arellano" (from Arellano, 1987) covariance. This method is robust to arbitrary heteroskedasticity, both between and within individuals and to arbitrary serial correlation within the same individual; on the contrary, it rules out any correlation between different individuals. Its statistical properties depend on the number of individuals being "large" with respect to that of time periods. For all these reasons, it is usually the estimator of choice in the context of micro panels, all the more so if individuals are sampled independently from a large population. It is implemented as the default in the appropriate panel method vcovHC.plm (Millo, 2017) of the generic function vcovHC (Zeileis, 2006), and as such it will be automatically applied by R to panel models and tests whenever vcovHC is invoked.

I will come back to this more formally in the following; for now, I just show how this is to be done within the framework of **plm** (the results are the same one would obtain using the Stata option robust to the xtreg command). It is enough to specify the vcov argument to vcovHC (for "heteroskedasticity consistent"), thus imposing the use of a robust estimator in place of the standard one:

```
> ## 10.4.2, Ex. 10.4 with robust variance
> summary(re10.4, vcov=vcovHC)

Oneway (individual) effect Random Effect Model
(Swamy-Arora's transformation)

Note: Coefficient variance-covariance matrix supplied: vcovHC

Call:
plm(formula = fm, data = jtrain, model = "random", index =
    c("fcode", "year"))

Balanced Panel: n = 54, T = 3, N = 162

Effects:
                   var  std.dev share
idiosyncratic  0.2477   0.4977 0.114
individual     1.9322   1.3900 0.886
theta: 0.7975

Residuals:
      Min.    1st Qu.     Median    3rd Qu.        Max.
-2.546798  -0.223892   0.040554   0.255287   1.549791

Coefficients:
              Estimate Std. Error  t-value  Pr(>|t|)
(Intercept)   0.414833   0.260766   1.5908   0.11367
d88          -0.093452   0.091489  -1.0215   0.30862
d89          -0.269834   0.183842  -1.4677   0.14419
union    .    0.547802   0.392385   1.3961   0.16467
grant        -0.214696   0.127866  -1.6791   0.09514 .
grant_1      -0.377070   0.260807  -1.4458   0.15024
___

Signif. codes: 0
```

Again, I leave this to intuition for now, but the Wald test (in χ^2 form)[1] can be robustified in the very same way as the *t*-statistics, employing a robust covariance matrix in the calculations:

```
> waldtest(re10.4, 4:5, vcov=vcovHC)

Wald test

Model 1: log(scrap) ~ d88 + d89 + union + grant + grant_1
Model 2: log(scrap) ~ d88 + d89 + union
```

```
      Res.Df Df Chisq Pr(>Chisq)
1      156
2      158 -2 2.8215      0.244
```

2.1.2 Testing for unobserved effects

The unobserved effects test (Wooldridge, 2010, p. 264) is a distribution-free procedure that tests whether the off-diagonal elements in the sub-matrix Σ_i of the overall errors covariance matrix Σ are zero (that is, whether there is any correlation between errors pertaining to the same individual at different times):

```
> ## 10.4.4 Testing for the Presence of an Unobserved Effect
> pwtest(fm, jtrain, index=c("fcode","year"))

        Wooldridge's test for unobserved individual effects

data: formula
z = 4.1451, p-value = 3.396e-05
alternative hypothesis: unobserved effect
```

The test confirms the presence of unobserved effects. It must be stressed that this piece of evidence does not imply that the effects be necessarily of the RE type, as the test also has power against, say, time-decaying serial error correlation. In turn, any of these deviations from error sphericity is consistent with the robust inference methods presented here.

2.2 Fixed Effects

Here, I estimate the model from Example 10.5 (FE Estimation of the Effects of Job Training Grants; Wooldridge, 2010, p. 272) by FE, specifying the `model` argument as `"within"` (another name for the FE estimator, due to the fact that it only uses within-individual variation). Notice that this is the default choice for the `model` argument so that I might have omitted it altogether:

```
> ## Example 10.5 (FE Estimation of the Effects of Job Training
    Grants)
>
> ## FE model
> fe10.5 <- plm(fm, jtrain, index=c("fcode","year"),
  model="within")
```

The Wald test is performed just as before. The model object *fe10.5* contains all the necessary information. This is in a sense similar to what happens with Stata's *post-estimation* commands, only here, the model object will persist in the workspace for later use (again, this is analogous to using `estimates store` in Stata).

```
> ## Wald test for joint significance of grant and grant_1,
```

```
> ## Chi2 or F version
> wald10.5 <- waldtest(fe10.5, 4:5)
> wald10.5.F <- waldtest(fe10.5, 4:5, test="F")
```

2.2.1 Least squares dummy variable

The same estimate as $\hat{\beta}_{FE}$ can be obtained by explicitly augmenting the original regression with individual dummies, which is called the *least squares dummy variable* estimator (LSDV). It is very easy to do this augmentation because R will include any qualitative variable in a linear model under form of a set of dummies; therefore, one just has to include the individual index in the model formula. Notice, in the following syntax, the use of `update` for easily adding the set of dummies to the formula, and the `as.factor` transformation, which makes sure that the individual index is treated as a categorical variable. In fact, if the index were a set of labels, such as country names, there would be no need to do this; but if it is a numeric, as is the *fcode* here, I must specify lest R understands it as just another numerical variable. Moreover, notice that, while I insert a full set of dummies, I specify not to include an intercept in the model (`-1` in the formula); this is cleaner but not strictly necessary, as otherwise one of the dummies would be automatically dropped.

```
> ## Dummy variable regression
> lsdv10.5 <- plm(update(fm, . ~ . + as.factor(fcode) - 1),
+                 jtrain, index=c("fcode","year"), model="pooling")
```

I can now check that the estimates from FE and LSDV are the same:

```
> coef(fe10.5)[c("grant", "grant_1")]

     grant     grant_1
-0.2523149 -0.4215895
```

```
> coef(lsdv10.5)[c("grant", "grant_1")]

     grant     grant_1
-0.2523149 -0.4215895
```

The LSDV estimator automatically provides estimates of the individual effects, for as good as they can be (in a short panel, being *T*-consistent, their estimates are not dependable). In the FE case, Stata produces an average intercept (whose interpretation is not straightforward); `plm` does not. If one wants to recover the estimated individual effects, there is an extractor function `fixef` available so that the "overall intercept", for what it is worth, would simply be `mean(fixef(fe10.5))`. Rather than this, however, as the model postulates a different intercept for each individual, I will look at the population of these.

It can be interesting, in particular, to summarize or plot the distribution of the individual effects "to get some idea of how much heterogeneity is in the population" (Wooldridge, 2010, pp. 273–274). For reasons related to the object orientation of R – which go beyond the

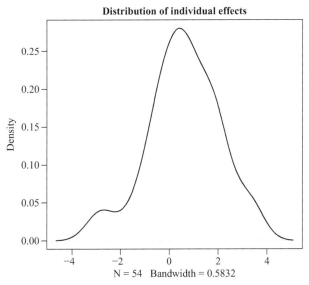

Figure 19.1   Empirical distribution of individual effects obtained by FE estimation

scope of the present chapter but are detailed in Croissant and Millo (2019) – to do so requires transforming the recovered fixed effects to numeric: else, instead of the usual `summary`, producing range, quartiles and the mean, a significance table like that of the coefficients is produced.

```
> ## Recover c_i from FE estimation
> c.i <- fixef(fe10.5)
> summary(as.numeric(c.i))

   Min.   1st Qu.   Median    Mean  3rd Qu.     Max.
-2.9002   -0.2571   0.6103  0.5974   1.7132   3.3144
> ## else summary(c.i) displays a significance table
```

Next, I plot the empirical distribution of the individual effects, smoothed out with a kernel-based smoother:

```
> plot(density(c.i), col="red",
+      main="Distribution of individual effects")
```

2.2.2   Serial correlation in the FE model

In his book, Wooldridge (2010, p.275) proposed a test for serial correlation in FE panel models based on taking into account the serial correlation induced in the model errors by the time-demeaning procedure, so that if the original model's errors are uncorrelated, the transformed errors are correlated with a coefficient of $-\frac{1}{T-1}$, and this is the hypothesis that can be tested on the observed residuals. The procedure he suggests is implemented in the R function `pwartest`:

```
> ## Test for serial error correlation
> pwartest(fm, jtrain, index=c("fcode","year"))

        Wooldridge's test for serial correlation in FE panels

data: plm.model
F = 52.745, df1 = 1, df2 = 106, p-value = 6.667e-11
alternative hypothesis: serial correlation
```

The hypothesis of no serial correlation in the idiosyncratic errors *of the original model* is strongly rejected; therefore, it is appropriate to allow for serial correlation when estimating the standard errors of the estimates. This can be done, as in the RE case, by specifying a robust estimator for the parameters' covariance through the vcov argument to either `summary` or `coeftest`. Here, I extract only the standard errors from the summaries, presenting them just as in the continuation of Example 10.5 in Wooldridge (2010, p. 276):

```
> ## FE 10.5 without or with robust covariance (report only SEs)
> rbind(
+       round(coef(fe10.5), 3),
+       round(summary(fe10.5)$coef[,2], 3),
+       round(summary(fe10.5, vcov=vcovHC)$coef[,2], 3)
+ )

         d88      d89    grant grant_1
[1,] -0.080  -0.247   -0.252   -0.422
[2,]  0.109   0.133    0.151    0.210
[3,]  0.096   0.193    0.140    0.276
```

As observed in the book, the change in the SEs from allowing for robustness is unpredictable: the estimated confidence interval on *grant* becomes narrower, that on *grant_1* wider. The Wald test (in χ^2 form) can be robustified in the same way:

```
> ## Wald test for joint significance of grant and grant_1,
> ## Chisq version (F version would be inappropriate here)
> ## wald10.5.hc <-
> waldtest(fe10.5, 4:5, vcov=vcovHC)

Wald test

Model 1: log(scrap) ~ d88 + d89 + union + grant + grant_1
Model 2: log(scrap) ~ d88 + d89 + union
   Res.Df Df Chisq Pr(>Chisq)
1     104
2     106 -2 3.2585 0.1961
```

2.3   First Difference

The *first difference* (FD) procedure consists in applying ordinary least squares (OLS) to the first-differenced data (Wooldridge, 2010, pp. 279–84). This is another way, next to FE, of eliminating unobserved, correlated heterogeneity. The FD estimator is implemented in the **plm** package as the `model='fd'` argument to the `plm` function, by which the data are automatically transformed, just as happens for FE. Sometimes, however, one does not want to difference some particular variable, such as the time dummies; or in general they want a more flexible specification. In order to replicate Example 10.6 (FD Estimation of the Effects of Job Training Grants; Wooldridge, 2010, pp. 282–83) exactly, instead of differencing at the model level, I do so at the formula level; that is, I specify a formula in differences – model formulae in R, and particularly in **plm**, do support a variety of transformation functions – and apply the pooled OLS estimator to the explicitly transformed data, leaving the 1988 dummy *d88* out (because I lose the first time period in the transformation) and leaving the 1989 dummy *d89* as it is:

```
> ## Example 10.6: First difference estimation
> ## exact formulation as in Wooldridge p.282
> dfm <- diff(log(scrap)) ~ d89 + diff(grant) + diff(grant_1)
> fd10.6 <- plm(dfm, jtrain,
+                  index=c("fcode","year"), model="pooling")
```

The SEs from the FD estimator can be robustified in the usual way. Next, I report the coefficients, the classic and robust SEs as done in Wooldridge:

```
> rbind(
+       round(coef(fd10.6), 3),
+       round(summary(fd10.6)$coef[,2], 3)
+       round(summary(fd10.6, vcov=vcovHC)$coef[,2], 3)
+ )
```

	(Intercept)	d89	diff(grant)	diff(grant_1)
[1,]	-0.091	-0.096	-0.223	-0.351
[2,]	0.091	0.125	0.131	0.235
[3,]	0.088	0.111	0.129	0.265

The R^2 value will be part of the usual model `summary` and will be printed out accordingly, or can recovered specifically with

```
> summary(fd10.6)$r.squared
          rsq          adjrsq
0.036517701  0.008724942
```

The Wald test can be performed as usual (here, in *F* form):
```
> waldtest(fd10.6, 2:3, test="F")
```

```
Wald test

Model 1: diff(log(scrap)) ~ d89 + diff(grant) + diff(grant_1)
Model 2: diff(log(scrap)) ~ d89
    Res.Df Df       F Pr(>F)
1      104
2      106 -2 1.5295 0.2215
```

2.3.1 Serial correlation in the FD specification

The FD transformation, just as happens with FE, will modify the serial correlation properties of the model errors, inducing a serial correlation with coefficient −0.5. In this case (Wooldridge, 2010, p. 282), one could be interested either in testing for non-correlation of the original errors – to test the model specification – or of the differenced errors – to test Assumption FD.3. See section 2.4. Both versions of the Wooldridge first-difference test are implemented in the pwfdtest function, where an argument h0, defaulting to "fd", allows us to test either the original non-correlation hypothesis (on the untransformed model errors) or the derived hypothesis (on the differenced ones). For now, following Example 10.6 (cont.d), I test the differenced errors.

```
> ## Example 10.6 (continued): testing for serial correlation
> pwfdtest(fm, jtrain, index=c("fcode","year"))

        Wooldridge's first-difference test for serial correlation in
    panels

data: plm.model
F = 2.8015, df1 = 1, df2 = 52, p-value = 0.1002
alternative hypothesis: serial correlation in differenced errors
```

As per Wooldridge (2010, p. 283), "a finding of significant serial correlation in the [transformed errors] warrants computing the robust variance matrix for the FD estimator". Although this is not the case here, this can be done the usual way and I report it for the sake of completeness in the same form as before, comparing classical and robust standard errors.

```
> ## FD 10.6 without or with robust covariance (coefs and SEs)
> rbind(
+       round(coef(fd10.6), 3),
+       round(summary(fd10.6)$coef[,2], 3),
+       round(summary(fd10.6, vcov=vcovHC)$coef[,2], 3)
+ )

      (Intercept)      d89 diff(grant) diff(grant_1)
[1,]    -0.091   -0.096      -0.223        -0.351
[2,]     0.091    0.125       0.131         0.235
[3,]     0.088    0.111       0.129         0.265
```

2.4   Comparison between FD and FE

Given that both FE and FD can effectively deal with correlated unobserved heterogeneity, the question arises as to which to prefer in a given setting. Wooldridge (2010, 10.7.1) addresses the subject from the point of view of efficiency: if the original models' errors follow a random walk, then the first-differenced errors will be stationary and FD will be more efficient than FE; if they are instead stationary, then the preferred choice will be FE because it induces less correlation than FD into the transformed errors.

Another possible concern is the lack of strict exogeneity. Correlation between the errors and past values of the regressors can be solved by including (backward) lags of the explanatory variables in a distributed lags specification (Wooldridge, 2010, p. 284); in this respect, remember that **plm** supports panel operators in formulae so that using the `lag` method will work consistently with the panel structure (for example, the initial observation *for each individual* will be NA). An example follows below. Technically, the same is possible with *forward* lags (a forward lag is obtained setting the argument to a negative value, for example $k = -1$); although Wooldridge observes that such a model seldom has a sound economic interpretation.

Testing for strict exogeneity can be done with auxiliary regressions, obtained (in the FD case) augmenting the "explicit FD" formula with the untransformed regressors from the original model, dummies excluded:

```
> ## testing strict exogeneity for FD using a regression-based
    test
> auxmod.h.fd <- plm(update(dfm, .~. + grant + grant_1),
+                      jtrain, model="pooling")
```

and testing for joint significance of the added variables:

```
> waldtest(auxmod.h.fd, 4:5, test="F")

Wald test

Model 1: diff(log(scrap)) ~ d89 + diff(grant) + diff(grant_1) +
    grant + grant_1
Model 2: diff(log(scrap)) ~ d89 + diff(grant) + diff(grant_1)
  Res.Df Df      F Pr(>F)
1     45
2     47 -2 0.5413 0.5857
```

A similar procedure is suggested for testing strict exogeneity in the FE setting. Now the model is augmented by forward lags and estimated by FE:

```
> ## testing strict exogeneity for FE using a regression-based
    test
> auxmod.h.fe <- plm(update(fm, .~. + lag(grant, -1)
+                      + lag(grant_1, -1)),
```

```
+                          jtrain, model="within")
> waldtest(auxmod.h.fe, 4:5, test="F")

Wald test

Model 1: log(scrap) ~ d88 + d89 + union + grant + grant_1 +
    lag(grant, -1) + lag(grant_1, -1)
Model 2: log(scrap) ~ d88 + d89 + union + lag(grant, -1) +
    lag(grant_1, -1)
  Res.Df Df        F Pr(>F)
1    154
2    156 -2 0.7104 0.493
```

2.5   The Relationship between RE and FE

Wooldridge (2010, 10.7.2) shows how the RE estimator can be obtained by applying OLS on *quasi*-time demeaned data, that is, subtracting only a fraction λ of the time mean from each individual's data so that in this framework $\lambda = 1$ yields the FE estimator (and $\lambda = 0$; that is, no demeaning, obviously yields OLS).

Below, I illustrate this point recovering $\hat{\lambda}$ from the estimated RE model, both directly and through the estimates of the two error variance components $\hat{\sigma}_c^2$ and $\hat{\sigma}_u^2$, which demonstrates the calculation in Wooldridge (2010, Eq. 10.77):

```
> ## Example 10.7 (Job Training Grants):
> ## extract the quasi-time demeaning parameter from the RE esti-
  mates
> ## 1) demonstrate calculations in Wooldridge, p. 287
> sigma2.u <- re10.4$ercomp$sigma2[1]
> sigma2.c <- re10.4$ercomp$sigma2[2]
> t. <- length(unique(attr(re10.4$model, "index")[[2]]))
> 1-sqrt(1/(1+t.*(sigma2.c/sigma2.u)))

        id
0.7975426

> ## 2) directly:
> re10.4$ercomp$theta

        id
0.7975426
```

For the sake of illustration, in Table 19.1 I also report a comparison between OLS, RE and FE, which shows how $\hat{\lambda}$ close to 1 produces RE estimates closer to FE than to pooled OLS. To this end, I estimate the pooled OLS specification setting the `model` argument to "pooling".

Table 19.1   Comparison of estimators

	OLS	RE	FE
(Intercept)	0.42	0.41	
	(0.22)	(0.24)	
d88	−0.24	−0.09	−0.08
	(0.31)	(0.11)	(0.11)
d89	−0.47	−0.27*	−0.25
	(0.33)	(0.13)	(0.13)
union	0.54*	0.55	
	(0.25)	(0.41)	
grant	0.21	−0.21	−0.25
	(0.33)	(0.15)	(0.15)
grant_1	−0.02	−0.38	−0.42*
	(0.43)	(0.21)	(0.21)
R^2	0.05	0.15	0.20
Adj. R^2	0.02	0.12	−0.24
Num. obs.	162	162	162
s_idios		0.50	
s_id		1.39	

Notes: *** $p < 0.001$; ** $p < 0.01$; * $p < 0.05$.

```
> ols10 <- plm(fm, jtrain, index=c("fcode","year"),
    model="pooling")
> texreg(list("OLS"=ols10, "RE"=re10.4, "FE"=fe10.5),
+        caption = "Comparison of estimators",
        label="tab:modelcomp")
```

2.5.1   Testing serial correlation in RE errors

As per Wooldridge (2010, p. 288), the random effects hypothesis, by which, after subtracting the random effects, the remainder errors are uncorrelated (RE.3a), can be tested by using the residuals from the regression on partially demeaned data and applying, for example, the

Breusch (1978) and Godfrey (1978) procedure. This is automated in **plm** through the `pbgtest` wrapper function (see also Croissant and Millo, 2008, 2019):

```
> pbgtest(re10.4)

        Breusch-Godfrey/Wooldridge test for serial correlation in
    panel models

data: fm
chisq = 3.5853, df = 3, p-value = 0.3099
alternative hypothesis: serial correlation in idiosyncratic
    errors
```

No evidence of serial correlation is found in the remainder errors.

2.6   Comparison between FE and RE: The Hausman Test

The Hausman test is a popular procedure for testing assumption RE.1b (non-correlation between regressors and individual effects) (Wooldridge, 2010, 10.7.3). Rejection will favour a fixed-effects analysis, while non-rejection is usually interpreted as evidence in favour of the RE specification.[2]

The traditional form of the Hausman test is computed in **plm** by the function `phtest`, which can take as arguments either `formula` and `data` or two estimated model objects. I employ this latter syntax to compare the RE and FE models:

```
> ## "traditional" Hausman test
> phtest(fe10.5, re10.4)

        Hausman Test

data: fm
chisq = 2.8308, df = 4, p-value = 0.5865
alternative hypothesis: one model is inconsistent
```

It is easy to construct the Hausman test statistic from Wooldridge (2010, Eq. 10.78) "by hand" in plain R (remembering to exclude both the intercept and the time-invariant *union* from *re10.4*):

```
> b.re <- coef(re10.4)[-c(1, 4)]
> b.fe <- coef(fe10.5)
> V.re <- vcov(re10.4)[-c(1, 4),-c(1, 4)]
> V.fe <- vcov(fe10.5)
> q <- b.fe - b.re
> Vq <- V.fe - V.re
> H <- crossprod(q, solve(Vq, q))
```

```
> 1 - pchisq(abs(H), df=length(q))
         [,1]
[1,] 0.5865327
```

In this case, the test on one single parameter (or a subset of parameters) can only be performed by restricting q and Vq to the relevant row(s) and column(s). For example, below I do a partial Hausman test of *grant*:

```
> H.part <- crossprod(q[3], solve(Vq[3, 3], q[3]))
> 1 - pchisq(abs(H.part), df=1)


         [,1]
[1,] 0.196689
```

The regression-based version of the Hausman test from Wooldridge (2010, Eq. 10.79) is based on augmenting the regression on quasi-time demeaned data (the one from which the RE estimates were obtained) with the within (that is, time-demeaned) transformations of the variables to test for. The F-test on the added variables is the relevant Hausman statistic.

This procedure can in turn be reproduced easily through the data transformation infrastructure of **plm**. In fact, the time-demeaned and the quasi-time demeaned data needed for Wooldridge (2010, Eq. 10.79) can be retrieved as follows (the reader can check that regressing *y.re* on *X.re - 1* will reproduce model *re10.4*); then the Hausman statistic, under form of an *F* restriction test:

```
> y.re <- pmodel.response(re10.4)
> X.re <- model.matrix(re10.4)
> X.fe <- model.matrix(fe10.5)
> auxmod <- lm(y.re ~ cbind(X.re, X.fe))

> re.ss <- sum(resid(re10.4)^2)
> aux.ss <- sum(resid(auxmod)^2)
> df.auxmod <- fe10.5$df
> m <- dim(X.fe)[[2]]
> aH <- (re.ss-aux.ss)/aux.ss * df.auxmod/m
> pf(aH, df1=m, df2=df.auxmod)

[1] 0.1195879
```

3.   ALTERNATIVE SE ESTIMATORS FOR PANEL DATA

In the previous section I compared inferences obtained using either classical standard errors or their most obvious "robust" counterpart: clustering SEs by individual. This is the safest and most obvious choice in the context of the typical large microeconomic panel, and the default in **plm** for R as well as other software.

The standard clustering estimator presented earlier, although arguably the most widely used of covariance estimators at least in the "large panel" contexts typical of microeconometrics, is not the only possible choice. Different estimators have been put forth that are appropriate in some specific context. Despite the practical orientation of the chapter, a minimum of formality will be unavoidable to give an intuition of the relevant alternatives. While referring the interested reader to textbooks, or to the comprehensive computing-oriented treatment in Millo (2017), I sketch the main ideas here.

Consider a linear model $y = X\beta + u$ and the OLS estimator $\hat{\beta}_{OLS} = (X^\top X)^{-1} X^\top y$. If the error terms u are independent and identically distributed, then the covariance matrix of the OLS estimator takes the following form: $Var(\hat{\beta}) = \sigma^2 (X^\top X)^{-1}$, which can be made operational substituting $\sigma^2 = Var(u)$ by an estimate $\hat{\sigma}^2$ of the error variance. This assumption, which often turns out to be too restrictive, will seldom be appropriate in panel data, where errors – especially those belonging to the same individual – can be expected to be correlated for a variety of reasons. In the following I will address the two main "robust" approaches to standard error estimation – heteroskedasticity-consistent (HC) errors a la White and heteroskedasticity- and autocorrelation-consistent (HAC) errors a la Newey–West – without assuming a panel data structure. Then I will review the specific extensions and combinations of the two methods, which have been proposed in the field of panel data.

3.1   Robust Estimation in General

"Robust" estimation entails relaxing the assumptions of non-correlation and/or homoskedasticity without imposing any particular structure to the errors' variance or interdependence. The first breakthrough in this respect is the so-called *sandwich estimator*, due to Halbert White.

The covariance matrix of the OLS estimator is, in general,

$$V(\hat{\beta}_{OLS}) = (X^\top X)^{-1} (X^\top [\sigma^2 \Omega] X)(X^\top X)^{-1},$$

where $Var(u) = \sigma^2 \Omega$ is the (scaled) error covariance matrix, which is generally unknown. Under homoskedasticity and non-correlation, $\Omega = I_n$ and $Var(u)$ is unknown only up to the variance parameter σ^2, which is easily estimated from the OLS residuals; but relaxing these hypotheses means allowing for an arbitrary structure where the only requirement is that Ω be positive definite and symmetric, so that in principle it may contain up to $n(n + 1)/2$ free parameters.

Yet, as per White (1980), in order to consistently estimate $V_{\hat{\beta}}$ it is not necessary to estimate all the $n(n + 1)/2$ unknown elements in the Ω matrix but only the $K(K + 1)/2$ ones in

$$X^\top [\sigma^2 \Omega] X = \sum_{i=1}^{n} \sum_{j=1}^{n} \sigma_{ij} \mathbf{x}_i \mathbf{x}^\top_j,$$

which is often referred to as the *meat* of the sandwich, the two $(X^\top X)^{-1}$ being the *bread*. *Pointwise consistent* estimates of the unobservable errors u are required, which is satisfied by the OLS residuals $\hat{u}$ by consistency of the estimator $\hat{\beta}_{OLS}$. This structure is still too general but yields feasible estimators in two important special cases.

In the heteroskedasticity case, correlation between different observations is ruled out and the *meat* reduces to

$$S_0 = \sum_{i=1}^{n} \sigma_i^2 \mathbf{x}_i \mathbf{x}_i^{\top},$$

where the n unknown σ_i^2 values can be substituted, for estimation purposes, by the squared residuals $\hat{u}_i^2$ so that $\hat{S}_0 = \sum_{i=1}^{n} \hat{u}_i^2 \mathbf{x}_i \mathbf{x}_i^{\top}$. This is the HC estimator of White, which is appropriate in both cross-sectional and time-series settings:

$$\hat{V}_{White} = (X^{\top}X)^{-1} \hat{S}_0 (X^{\top}X)^{-1}.$$

For the specific case of time series, Newey and West (1987) devise a heteroskedasticity *and autocorrelation* consistent estimator that allows us to relax the hypothesis of error independence and works based on the assumption of correlation dying out "quickly enough" as the distance between observations increases. The Newey–West HAC estimator for the *meat* takes that of White and adds a sum of covariances between the different residuals, smoothed out by a *kernel function* giving weights decreasing with distance:

$$\hat{S}_{Newey-West} = \hat{S}_0 + \sum_{l=1}^{L} \sum_{t=l+1}^{T} w_l \hat{u}_t \hat{u}_{t-l} (\mathbf{x}_t \mathbf{x}_{t-l}^{\top} + \mathbf{x}_{t-l} \mathbf{x}_t^{\top}),$$

with w_l the weight from the kernel smoother, for example, the Bartlett kernel function: $w_l = 1 - \frac{l}{L+1}$ (for a discussion of alternative kernels see Zeileis, 2006)). The lag l is usually truncated well below the sample size, one popular rule of thumb being $L = n^{1/4}$ (see Greene, 2003; Driscoll and Kraay, 1998). The Newey–West HAC estimator is then:

$$\hat{V}_{Newey-West} = (X^{\top}X)^{-1} \hat{S}_{Newey-West} (X^{\top}X)^{-1}.$$

3.2 Clustered SEs

This framework has been extended to a panel data setting where, thanks to added dimensionality, various combinations of the two structures turn out to be able to accommodate very general types of dependence. Besides heteroskedasticity, for example, the added dimensionality allows us to obtain robustness against totally unrestricted timewise *or* cross-sectional correlation, provided this is along the "smaller" dimension. That is, next to heteroskedasticity, wide panels can be robustified against serial correlation, long panels against cross-sectional correlation. In other words, (an appropriate variant of) the HC estimator can become HAC in a panel context.

In the most common case of a wide panel, the *meat* of the clustering estimator of Liang and Zeger (1986) and Arellano (1987) takes the form

$$\hat{S}_{ci} = \sum_{i=1}^{n} X_i^{\top} \hat{\mathbf{u}}_i \hat{\mathbf{u}}_i^{\top} X_i,$$

where X_i is the part of the design matrix, and $\hat{\mathbf{u}}_i$ that of the residuals' vector, pertaining to the i-th individual; so that the full *sandwich* covariance is:

$$\hat{V}_{cluster,i} = (X^T X)^{-1} \hat{S}_{ci} (X^T X)^{-1}.$$

It is symmetric (summing over t) in the case of long panels. In wide panels, the big cross-sectional dimension allows robustness against serial correlation (Arellano, 1987); "long" panels, on the other hand, can be robustified against cross-sectional correlation thanks to the large T. As a general rule, the estimator is asymptotic in the number of clusters. This is the "robust" covariance used in section 2, and what most applied econometricians refer to when they report "robust" or "clustered" standard errors in panel data analysis.

3.2.1   Double clustering
In suitably large datasets, *double clustering* can be performed (Petersen, 2009; Cameron et al., 2011; Thompson, 2011) in order to account for serial and at the same time for cross-sectional or spatial correlation. In fact, this estimator, combining both individual and time clustering, relies on a combination of the asymptotics of each: the minimum number of clusters along the two dimensions must diverge. Any kind of dependence is allowed within each group *or* within each time period, while cross-serial correlations between observations belonging to different groups *and* time periods are ruled out. The double-clustered estimator is calculated by summing up the group-clustering and the time-clustering ones, then subtracting the standard White estimator:

$$\hat{V}_{cluster,it} = \hat{V}_{cluster,i} + \hat{V}_{cluster,t} - \hat{V}_{White}.$$

3.3   Newey−West and SCC

As cited above, in a time series context Newey and West (1987) have proposed an estimator that is robust to serial correlation as well as to heteroskedasticity. This estimator takes into account the covariance between units by weighting it through a kernel smoother function giving less weight to more distant terms.

The Newey−West HAC method can be applied time-wise within each individual in the context of a panel dataset. In this case, the resulting estimator will be robust to general heteroskedasticity and to within-individual serial correlation, provided that the latter is of the time-decaying type and that it dies out "fast enough". The *meat* of the NW estimator for the panel case can be expressed as the sum of the "pure" White estimator (applied to the entire dataset) plus a weighted sum over all lags up to l of weighted time-covariance, by individual terms:

$$\hat{S}_{NW} = \hat{S}_0 + \sum_{l=1}^{L} w_l \left[\sum_{t=1}^{T} \sum_{i=1}^{n} \mathbf{x}_{it} \hat{u}_{it} \hat{u}_{i,t-l}^T \mathbf{x}_{i,t-l}^T + \sum_{t=1}^{T} \sum_{i=1}^{n} [\mathbf{x}_{it} \hat{u}_{it} \hat{u}_{i,t-l}^T \mathbf{x}_{i,t-l}^T]^T \right],$$

so that $\hat{V}_{NW} = (X^T X)^{-1} \hat{S}_{NW} (X^T X)^{-1}$. Notice how – unlike the clustering estimator – it does not make any sense to apply the NW estimator symmetrically, over the cross-section, because the latter does not have a natural ordering.

Driscoll and Kraay (1998) have adapted the Newey–West panel time series estimator to include not only serial correlation between errors of the same individual in different time periods, but also cross-serial correlation between different individuals in different times and, within the same period, cross-sectional correlation (see also Arellano, 2003).

The Driscoll and Kraay estimator (SCC for "spatial correlation consistent") can be calculated as the time clustering plus a sum of lagged cross-serial covariance terms, again weighted by a distance-decreasing kernel function w_l:

$$\hat{S}_{SCC} = \hat{S}_{ct} + \sum_{l=1}^{L} w_l \left[\sum_{t=1}^{T} X_t^\top \hat{\mathbf{u}}_t \hat{\mathbf{u}}_{t-l}^\top X_{t-l} + \sum_{t=1}^{T} [X_t^\top \hat{\mathbf{u}}_t \hat{\mathbf{u}}_{t-l}^\top X_{t-l}]^\top \right] \qquad (19.1)$$

and, as usual, $\hat{V}_{SCC} = (X^\top X)^{-1} \hat{S}_{SCC} (X^\top X)^{-1}$.

Again, the SCC covariance estimator requires the serial and cross-serial dependence to decrease "fast enough" with the T dimension, which is therefore supposed to be fairly large. Driscoll and Kraay (1998), based on Monte Carlo simulation, put the practical minimum at $T > 20 - 25$; the n dimension is irrelevant in this respect and is allowed to grow at any rate relative to T.

3.4   In Practice

Summing up, heteroskedasticity can be taken care of in panel data just as one would in cross-sections or time series; but the panel data econometrician will often be concerned about some kind of dependence as well – and, thanks to the richer structure of panel data, they have a number of weapons at their disposal.

If – next to heteroskedasticity – they are worried about serial correlation within individuals of a panel, if the time dimension T is "small" relative to the cross-sectional n they will want to employ the usual clustering estimator $\hat{V}_{cluster,i}$, which allows for arbitrary serial correlation; on the contrary, $\hat{V}_{NW}$ will be the estimator of choice if T is fairly large and one is willing to make the additional assumption that the time dependence is of the distance-decaying type. Both exclude any cross-sectional correlation of the errors.[3]

Symmetrically to the by-individual clustering case, "long" panels of relatively few time series can be made robust to cross-sectional correlation by employing $\hat{V}_{cluster,t}$, provided that any serial correlation is ruled out.[4] The NW estimator instead has no natural counterpart in this setting because the cross-section does not, in general, have a univariate natural ordering.

Lastly, cross-sectionally dependent panels with potentially large n and a sizeable T (say at least $T > 20 - 25$) can be robustified against heteroskedasticity, unrestricted cross-sectional correlation and time-decaying serial *and cross-serial* correlation by employing $\hat{V}_{SCC}$, at the only cost of assuming that serial and cross-serial correlations fade out after L lags, with L "much shorter" than T.

4.   THE HOUSE PRICING EXAMPLE

In the following, I will apply the described robust standard error estimators in a context where most of the different "flavours" have chances of being meaningful, thanks to the peculiar dimension of the dataset and the fact that the units of observation are sampled in space.

Holly et al. (2010) address the evolution of house prices, showing that state-level real housing prices are driven by economic fundamentals, such as real per capita disposable income, as well as by common shocks, such as changes in interest rates, oil prices and technological change. They employ CCE estimators (Pesaran, 2006) to account for said common factors.

Baltagi and Li (2014) replicate the house pricing model of Holly et al. (2010) over a denser network of spatial units: that is, instead of 49 states over the years 1975 to 2003, as in the original paper, they consider a panel of 381 Metropolitan Statistical Areas (MSAs) observed over the years 1975 to 2011. The model contains three observed regressors: the log of real per capita income, the growth rate of the population and the real cost of borrowing. The log of the real housing price index is the dependent variable.

The original exercises do consider prices and income in levels and assess stationarity and cointegration before proceeding to estimating an error correction specification. Nonstationary data are ill-suited to the standard panel techniques considered here; therefore, I consider a short-term version of their model, relating the changes in housing prices to the changes in income (see also Aquaro et al., 2021). I will estimate the model first by pooled OLS and then account for individual and/or time fixed (or random) effects. In particular, time fixed effects are likely to be necessary to account for common shocks, at least as a first approximation with respect to the more sophisticated and flexible approach predominant in the current literature.[5]

4.1   The Dataset

The dataset can be found in text format in the data archive of the *Journal of Applied Econometrics*, among the materials accompanying the Baltagi and Li (2014) paper, and is easily imported into R as follows:

```
> ## read in data
> msa <- read.table(file="msa_4v.txt", header=TRUE)
```

The dataset contains the following variables: the log of the real house price index (*lhpi_real*), the log of real per capita disposable income (*lpci_real*), the population growth rate (*pgr*) and the real cost of borrowing (*rcb*).

I look at the dataset as a panel so as to perform every analysis with **plm**; non-panel estimators, like OLS, are nested subcases and can be easily obtained.

Notice that the dataset already complies with the simplest conventions of the package, having the firm identifier in the first column and the time identifier in the second, and can be employed as it is.[6] The dataset contains 13 716 observations from 381 units over 36 time periods:

```
> pdim(msa)
Balanced Panel: n = 381, T = 36, N = 13716
```

The model formula is:

```
> blfm <- diff(lhpi_real) ~ diff(lpci_real) + pgr + rcb
```

Notice the seamless treatment of differencing inside the model formula. As already observed, the **plm** package contains a complete data transformation suite of functions performing lagging, differencing and more typical panel data operations such as the *within* or *between* transformations in a consistent way.

4.2 Different SEs for the OLS Estimates

I will first address estimating a model by OLS and, the main focus, obtaining various estimates of the parameter standard errors $SE(\hat{\beta}_{OLS})$ according to the different methods presented above.

Below I estimate the model by OLS and present the results in the typical significance table, using the "classical" standard errors.

```
> ## OLS
> olsmod <- plm(blfm, data = msa, model = "pooling")
> summary(olsmod)

Pooling Model

Call:
plm(formula = blfm, data = msa, model = "pooling")

Balanced Panel: n = 381, T = 35, N = 13335

Residuals:
        Min.      1st Qu.       Median      3rd Qu.         Max.
 -0.13153230  -0.01337601   0.00052791   0.01367578   0.17130641

Coefficients:
                    Estimate   Std. Error    t-value Pr(>|t|)
(Intercept)       0.02210665   0.00034344    64.3675  <2e-16 ***
diff(lpci_real)   0.35639153   0.00767517    46.4343  <2e-16 ***
pgr              -0.02245680   0.01581916    -1.4196  0.1557
rcb              -0.79460176   0.00373741  -212.6075  <2e-16 ***
___

Signif. codes: 0
```

or, equivalently (and not reported), through the `coeftest` function:

```
> olsmod.ols <- coeftest(olsmod)
```

Now I address how to compute *t*-statistics using different kinds of "robust" standard errors. As a first illustration, I present heteroskedasticity-consistent SEs according to White (1980) (without taking into account any panel structure). Notice how the specific covariance estimator used can be passed on either as a user-specified function or as a precalculated matrix; in either case, function definition or matrix calculation can take place within the very same call to `summary` or to `coeftest`:

```
> ## White, no clustering
```

```
> vcovW <- function(x) vcovHC(x, method="white1")
> summary(olsmod, vcov=vcovW)
```

```
Pooling Model
```

```
Note: Coefficient variance-covariance matrix supplied: vcovW
```

```
Call:
plm(formula = blfm, data = msa, model = "pooling")
```

```
Balanced Panel: n = 381, T = 35, N = 13335
```

```
Residuals:
        Min.      1st Qu.      Median      3rd Qu.        Max.
-0.13153230  -0.01337601  0.00052791  0.01367578  0.17130641
```

```
Coefficients:
                  Estimate  Std. Error    t-value Pr(>|t|)
(Intercept)     0.02210665  0.00043337    51.0110  <2e-16 ***
diff(lpci_real) 0.35639153  0.01117625    31.8883  <2e-16 ***
pgr            -0.02245680  0.01992010    -1.1273  0.2596
rcb            -0.79460176  0.00587330  -135.2904  <2e-16 ***
____
```

```
Signif. codes: 0
```

or, equivalently, (and not reported),

```
> coeftest(olsmod, vcovHC(olsmod, method="white1"))
```

In the following, I review computation of all the kinds of *panel-robust* SEs presented in the preceding section, (almost) in the same order.

4.2.1   Clustered (one dimension)

The default behaviour of the vcovHC covariance applied to a panel model is to compute SEs *clustered by individual*:

```
> ## clustered:
> ## by MSA
> olsmod.hci <- coeftest(olsmod, vcovHC)
```

but one can of course specify clustering *by time period*:[7]

```
> ## by time
> olsmod.hct <- coeftest(olsmod, vcovHC(olsmod, cluster="time"))
```

4.2.2   Clustered (two dimensions)

A dedicated function, `vcovDC`, will produce doauble-clustering SEs:

```
> ## double-clustering
> olsmod.dc <- coeftest(olsmod, vcovDC)
```

4.2.3   Newey–West or Driscoll–Kraay

Another "special" covariance function, `vcovNW`, will compute Newey and West (1987) SEs; as usual, see `?vcovNW` for how to set further optional arguments, most importantly the truncation lag.

```
> ## Newey-West
> olsmod.nw <- coeftest(olsmod, vcovNW)
```

In the more general case nesting NW, the SCC estimator of Driscoll and Kraay (1998) will be more appropriate, as spatial correlation between observations and general cross-sectional dependence due to omitted global factors are very likely to be present:

```
> ## Driscoll-Kraay
> olsmod.scc <- coeftest(olsmod, vcovSCC)
```

4.2.4   Comparison of standard errors

In Table 19.2 we compare the SEs from the different estimators (setting the relevant columns from the tables made with `coeftest` side by side).

```
> compare.ols <- cbind(olsmod.ols[,1:2], olsmod.hci[,2],
+                      olsmod.hct[,2], olsmod.dc[,2],
+                      olsmod.nw[,2], olsmod.scc[,2])
> dimnames(compare.ols)[[2]][2:7] <- c("OLS", "Cl. i", "Cl. t",
+                            "Cl. it", "NW", "SCC")
> xtable(compare.ols, digits=3,
+        caption="Comparison of SE estimates, OLS",
+        label="tab:ols.se")
```

Table 19.2   Comparison of SE estimates, OLS

	Estimate	OLS	Cl. i	Cl. t	Cl. it	NW	SCC
(Intercept)	0.022	0.000	0.001	0.003	0.003	0.001	0.004
diff(lpci_real)	0.356	0.008	0.020	0.090	0.091	0.014	0.102
pgr	−0.022	0.016	0.024	0.048	0.049	0.023	0.055
rcb	−0.795	0.004	0.010	0.037	0.038	0.007	0.044

The "fit them all" strategy of computing all different SEs and setting them side by side, perhaps choosing the most conservative ones, has issues from the viewpoint of multiple testing (see Millo, 2017, Section 6) if seen as a formal procedure, but has indeed the merit of highlighting the main sources of correlation. In this case, although qualitative considerations on the significance of regressors are little changed, one can see that the specification of the SEs matters a lot for estimating the precision of $\hat{\beta}$.

Let us focus on the main variable of interest, *lpci_real*. The "classical" errors from the pooled specification are the smallest; they double if allowing for clustering, while the increase of the NW SEs is smaller, hinting at some kind of non-fading correlation (as would be the case for an individual effect. Take heed we are simply pooling the data here); but the real increase occurs if one she allows for cross-sectional correlation, the time-clustering SEs being more than tenfold the OLS ones. Lastly, double-clustering SEs are not far from time-clustering ones, while SCC do increase some more: I take this as evidence that, allowing for both within-individual persistence and cross-serial correlation, the lagged influence of other units of observation is the safest course of action.

This is consistent with the economics of the example, as house prices are very much expected to co-move in the cross-section and also quite likely to correlate cross-serially; moreover, the omission of individual effects of any kind in this pooled specification means that any persistent individual heterogeneity will "contaminate" the errors, inducing serial correlation.

4.3   Fixed Effects with Robust SEs

The previous example employed a pooled specification for the sake of illustration. By contrast, the economic application at hand obviously calls for taking care of unobserved heterogeneity, both along the individual dimension (unobserved, potentially correlated persistent character-istics of individual MSAs, such as being part of an industrial district, or one containing some important amenity or being in the middle of a polluted area) and along time (unobserved common factors driving the behaviour of the whole cross-section of MSAs, period by period, like the national economic cycle or credit conditions).

As already noted in section 2, by its characteristics of robustness in a wide array of situations, the individual FE specification is very popular and hence the default for the `plm` function.

```
> ## individual fixed effects:
> femod <- plm(blfm, data = msa) # model="within" is default
> coeftest(femod)

t test of coefficients:

                   Estimate Std. Error   t value  Pr(>|t|)
diff(lpci_real)   0.3497138  0.0075246   46.4763  < 2e-16 ***
pgr               0.0426255  0.0220757    1.9309  0.05352 .
rcb              -0.8032376  0.0037106 -216.4737  < 2e-16 ***
—
Signif. codes: 0
```

4.3.1   Individual fixed effects with robust SEs

Robust SEs produced by any `vcovXX` function – for example, clustered SEs – can be combined with most of the estimators in **plm**. Next is the obvious pooled OLS case: FE, random effects (RE), first difference (FD) and more. Just like in the OLS case, one specifies the estimated model and the covariance estimation method of choice, for example clustering by individual:

```
> ## with clustering
> coeftest(femod, vcovHC)


t test of coefficients:

                Estimate Std. Error    t value Pr(>|t|)
diff(lpci_real)  0.349714   0.019332    18.0901  <2e-16 ***
pgr              0.042625   0.039552     1.0777  0.2812
rcb             -0.803238   0.007454  -107.7591  <2e-16 ***
____

Signif. codes: 0
```

and any of the above, just substituting *femod* for *olsmod*, for example, SCC with individual fixed effects:

```
> coeftest(femod, vcovSCC)


t test of coefficients:

                Estimate Std. Error    t value  Pr(>|t|)
diff(lpci_real)  0.349714   0.101276    3.4531  0.000556 ***
pgr              0.042625   0.116253    0.3667  0.713877
rcb             -0.803238   0.047750  -16.8217  < 2.2e-16 ***
____

Signif. codes: 0
```

It shall of course be noted, first and foremost, that including (at least) individual FEs in the specification is likely to be necessary for consistency of $\hat{\beta}$. From the point of view of precision, it can be seen that including individual FEs in the specification does very slightly reduce the clustering SE, while the SCC SE remains almost unchanged. In other words, including individual FEs does not "clean away" most of the within-individual error correlation.

4.3.2   Two-way fixed effects with robust SEs: Comparison

As observed, in the example at hand it is crucial to control for time FEs as well, in order to account for unobservable common shocks affecting every cross-sectional unit (the MSA) over time. Therefore, the two-way fixed effects (2FE) – rather than FE – is likely to be the appropriate specification. Combining this with the different SE estimators, as before, yields the Table 19.3.

```
> fe2mod <- plm(blfm, data = msa, effect="twoways")
> ## "classical" SEs
```

```
> fe2mod.ols <- coeftest(fe2mod)
> ## cluster by individual
> fe2mod.hci <- coeftest(fe2mod, vcovHC)
> ## by time
> fe2mod.hct <- coeftest(fe2mod, vcovHC(fe2mod, cluster="time"))
> ## double-clustering
> fe2mod.dc <- coeftest(fe2mod, vcovDC)
> ## Newey-West
> fe2mod.nw <- coeftest(fe2mod, vcovNW)
> ## Driscoll-Kraay > fe2mod.scc <- coeftest(fe2mod, vcovSCC)

> compare.fe2 <- cbind(fe2mod.ols[,1:2], fe2mod.hci[,2],
+                      fe2mod.hct[,2], fe2mod.dc[,2],
+                      fe2mod.nw[,2], fe2mod.scc[,2])
> dimnames(compare.fe2)[[2]][2:7] <- c("OLS", "Cl. i", "Cl. t",
+                                      "Cl. it", "NW", "SCC")
> xtable(compare.fe2, digits=3,
+        caption="Comparison of SE estimates, 2FE",
+        label="tab:fe2.se")
```

Table 19.3   *Comparison of SE estimates, 2FE*

	Estimate	OLS	Cl. i	Cl. t	Cl. it	NW	SCC
diff(lpci_real)	0.160	0.005	0.012	0.021	0.024	0.008	0.030
pgr	−0.018	0.012	0.024	0.026	0.032	0.016	0.030
rcb	−0.927	0.002	0.009	0.009	0.012	0.005	0.012

One can see that, despite the qualitative considerations of section 4.2.4 still being widely applicable, the cross-sectional dependence has been substantially reduced, the double-clustering SEs now being only double the individual clustering ones. Analogously, the SCC SEs are still the largest—at six times the OLS ones—but now are one third of the SCC SEs for the pooling estimates.

4.3.3   Other panel estimators combined with clustering or NW/SCC

As observed, any specification among pooled, FE or RE with individual, time or both kinds of effects, or FD, can be combined with any SE estimator in one (individual or time) or two-way clustering, NW, SCC and some more combinations (see Millo, 2017).

Another potentially meaningful example among the many possible is looking for efficiency combining random effects along the individual dimension (that is, treating the many MSAs as random samples from a larger population) with fixed time effects (RE+TFE). (Notice that the output of `coeftest` is limited to the first four rows to avoid reporting all the estimated year dummies.)

```
> rtfemod <- plm(update(blfm, . ~ . + as.factor(year)), data=msa,
+               model="random")
```

```
> ## for example, RE+TFE with SCC
> coeftest(rtfemod, vcovSCC)[1:4,]

                  Estimate    Std. Error    t value       Pr(>|t|)
(Intercept)     0.004486737  0.000583317   7.6917649  1.553023e-14
diff(lpci_real) 0.161429689  0.032593391   4.9528350  7.403828e-07
pgr            -0.026897148  0.030574309  -0.8797304  3.790213e-01
rcb            -0.924707300  0.011407218 -81.0633489  0.000000e+00
```

The latter specification can be compared with a more standard two-way fixed effects (2FE) by means of the Hausman test. The time FEs, explicitly added to the model formula, are not called into question; the test will instead compare the choice of random vs. fixed for the individual effects:

```
> phtest(update(blfm, .~.+as.factor(year)), data = msa)


  Hausman Test

data: update(blfm, . ~ . + as.factor(year))
chisq = 101.51, df = 37, p-value = 6.391e-08
alternative hypothesis: one model is inconsistent
```

Despite the apparent similarity of the RE+TFE and 2FE estimates, the test rejects the consistency of the former. 2FE is preferred.

5.   CONCLUSIONS

I have reviewed the implementation of the basic panel data estimators and tests in the R language, with a particular focus on estimating the standard errors according to various procedures, each of which is "robust" to general heteroskedasticity *and* to some kind of violation of the non-correlation hypothesis.

The **plm** package provides a comprehensive set of tools that allows syntactical consistency and flexibility in combining estimators for the βs and for the SEs thereof at will, thanks to the feature of R that functions as a data type. The latter, in fact, allows us to pass on a statistical procedure (here, the standard error estimator) to any test.

In particular, one- or two-way fixed effects specifications are especially useful in panel data econometrics because they can take into account unobserved individual or timewise heterogeneity, potentially correlated with the regressors, which would make the estimates inconsistent. A fixed (or a random) effects specification can be easily combined with the most popular "clustering" estimators or with variations of the Newey–West procedure, most notably the "spatial correlation consistent" (SCC) standard errors of Driscoll and Kraay (1998).

In the first part of the chapter I provided a gentle introduction to the subject of panel data econometrics with R by going through the "Basic Panel Methods" chapter of Wooldridge (2010) and replicating all its examples with functionality from **plm**, in particular showing how to perform testing employing clustered standard errors – which are the most obvious choice for the applied econometrician working on the typical micropanel, many individual units observed over a few time periods. The reader needing a basic primer on robust methods in panel data, perhaps as an R companion to Wooldridge (2010, chapter 10), can stop here.

In the second half, I presented a number of different estimators for the standard errors in the light of the two main procedures for heteroskedasticity- and heteroskedasticity and autocorrelation–robust estimation: the HC estimator of White and the HAC estimator of Newey and West, and of their modifications developed for panel data: one- or two-way clustering and adaptations of the kernel-smoothing-based procedure to panel data. I illustrated the different procedures through an example drawing on a dataset with a longer time dimension, whereby a number of different estimators for the standard errors become viable. I combined one- or two-way fixed effects, or combinations of fixed and random effects, with any estimator of the standard errors presented here, showing how the dispersion of estimates can be crucially dependent on the correlation within individuals, within each cross-section or even across different individuals in time, and how making the wrong assumptions can lead to severely overstating the precision of estimates.

NOTES

1. If Assumption RE.3 is violated, the sum of squared residuals form of the F statistic is not valid (Wooldridge, 2010, p. 263).
2. As Wooldridge observes (p. 289), RE.3 is generally assumed as well under the null hypothesis; but while this latter hypothesis (which implies that RE is the efficient estimator) is necessary for the correct distribution of the Hausman statistic in the traditional form, the latter has no power against failures of RE.3.
3. In order to mitigate the cross-sectional correlation problem, the researcher might want to include time dummies in the estimated model so as to control for omitted common time effects. Expanding on this is out of the scope of this chapter; the reader is referred to the literature on panels with common factors and cross-sectional dependence. Neglecting to include time dummies can also induce serial correlation (see Wooldridge, 2010, p. 261).
4. Specifying a distributed lag model is a common solution to residual serial correlation, although the assumptions of the basic panel estimators, in particular FE, can be at odds with dynamic specifications. Again, this is out of the scope of the present chapter; see the literature on dynamic panels.
5. Delving into the possible sources of cross-sectional dependence is out of the scope of the present chapter. In a nutshell, if any common variable drives the outcomes of the entire cross-section, period by period, omitting it will – at a minimum – induce cross-sectional correlation in the errors. Time dummies are often enough to capture the influence of unobserved cross-sectional heterogeneity; but, with respect to the CCE estimator, a time fixed effects specification will constrain all factor loadings measuring the elasticity of every individual observation unit to changes in the common factor(s) to be homogeneous; see for example Pesaran (2006).
6. Otherwise, one would have had to specify the index argument, a character vector of length 2 containing, in this order, the names of the individual and the time index.
7. Strictly speaking, clustering by time would be inappropriate here as N is much larger than T.

REFERENCES

Aquaro M, Bailey N, Pesaran M H (2021). Estimation and inference for spatial models with heterogeneous coefficients: an application to US house prices. *Journal of Applied Econometrics*, 36(1): 18–44.
Arellano M (1987) Computing robust standard errors for within group estimators. *Oxford Bulletin of Economics and Statistics* 49: 431–4.
Arellano M (2003) *Panel Data Econometrics*. Oxford University Press.
Baltagi BH, Li J (2014) Further evidence on the spatio-temporal model of house prices in the United States. *Journal of Applied Econometrics* 29(3): 515–22.
Breusch TS (1978) Testing for autocorrelation in dynamic linear models. *Australian Economic Papers* 17(31): 334–55.
Cameron A, Gelbach J, Miller D (2011) Robust inference with multiway clustering. *Journal of Business and Economic Statistics* 29(2): 238–49.

Croissant Y, Millo G (2008) Panel data econometrics in R: The "plm" package. *Journal of Statistical Software* 27(2), http://www.jstatsoft.org/v27/i02/.

Croissant Y, Millo G (2019) *Panel Data Econometrics with R*. Wiley.

Dahl DB, Scott D, Roosen C, Magnusson A, Swinton J (2019) xtable: Export tables to LaTeX or HTML. https://CRAN.R-project.org/package=xtable, r package version 1.8-4.

Driscoll J, Kraay A (1998) Consistent covariance matrix estimation with spatially dependent panel data. *The Review of Economics and Statistics* 80(4): 549–60.

Fox J, Weisberg S (2011) *An R Companion to Applied Regression*, 2nd ed. SAGE. http://socserv.socsci.mcmaster.ca/jfox/Books/Companion.

Godfrey LG (1978) Testing against general autoregressive and moving average error models when the regressors include lagged dependent variables. *Econometrica: Journal of the Econometric Society*, pp. 1293–301.

Greene W (2003) *Econometric Analysis*, 5th ed. Prentice Hall.

Henningsen A, Henningsen G (2019) Analysis of panel data using R. In: *Panel Data Econometrics*, Elsevier, pp. 345–96.

Holly S, Pesaran MH, Yamagata T (2010) A spatio-temporal model of house prices in the USA. *Journal of Econometrics* 158(1): 160–73.

Leifeld P (2013) Conversion of statistical model output in R to LATEX and HTML tables. *Journal of Statistical Software* 55(8): 1–24, http://dx.doi.org/10.18637/jss.v055.i08.

Leisch F (2002) dynamic generation of statistical reports using literate data analysis. In: *Compstat*, Springer, pp. 575–80.

Liang K, Zeger S (1986) Longitudinal data analysis using generalized linear models. *Biometrika* 73: 13–22.

Millo G (2017) Robust standard error estimators for panel models: A unifying approach. *Journal of Statistical Software* 82(1): 1–27.

Newey W, West K (1987) A simple, positive semi-definite, heteroskedasticity and autocorrelation consistent covariance matrix. *Econometrica* 55(3): 703–8.

Pesaran M (2006) Estimation and inference in large heterogeneous panels with a multifactor error structure. *Econometrica* 74(4): 967–1012.

Petersen MA (2009) Estimating standard errors in finance panel data sets: Comparing approaches. *Review of Financial Studies* 22(1): 435–80.

Shea JM (2018) 111 Data Sets from "Introductory Econometrics: A Modern Approach, 6e" by Jeffrey M. Wooldridge. https://CRAN.R-project.org/package=wooldridge.

Thompson S (2011) Simple formulas for standard errors that cluster by both firm and time. *Journal of Financial Economics* 99(1): 1–10.

White H (1980) *Asymptotic Theory for Econometricians*. Academic Press.

Wooldridge JM (2010) *Econometric Analysis of Cross Section and Panel Data*. MIT Press.

Zeileis A (2004) Econometric computing with HC and HAC covariance matrix estimators. *Journal of Statistical Software* 11(10): 1–17, http://www.jstatsoft.org/v11/i10/.

Zeileis A (2006) Object-oriented computation of sandwich estimators. *Journal of Statistical Software* 16(9): 1–16, http://www.jstatsoft.org/v16/i09/.

Zeileis A, Hothorn T (2002) Diagnostic checking in regression relationships. *R News* 2(3): 7–10, http://CRAN.R-project.org/doc/Rnews/.

20. Econometric estimation of the "Constant Elasticity of Substitution" function in R: the micEconCES package

Arne Henningsen, Géraldine Henningsen and Gergő Literáti[*]

1. INTRODUCTION

The so-called Cobb–Douglas function (Cobb and Douglas, 1928) is the most well-known functional form in economics. However, it imposes strong assumptions on the underlying functional relationship, most notably that all elasticities of substitution[1] are always one. Given these restrictive assumptions, the Stanford group around Arrow et al. (1961) developed the Constant Elasticity of Substitution (CES) function as a generalisation of the Cobb–Douglas function that allows for any (constant) elasticity of substitution. This functional form has become very popular in programming models (for example, general equilibrium models or trade models) but it has been rarely used in econometric analyses. Hence, the parameters of the CES functions used in programming models are often guesstimated and calibrated rather than econometrically estimated. However, in the past one to two decades, the CES function has slowly gained in importance in econometric analyses, particularly in macroeconomics (for example, Amras, 2004; Bentolila and Gilles, 2006; Raurich et al., 2012) and growth theory (for example, Duffy and Walsh, 2000; Caselli, 2005; Caselli and Coleman, 2006; Klump and Papageorgiou, 2008; Chirinko and Mallick, 2016), where it replaces the Cobb–Douglas function.[2] The CES functional form is also frequently used in micro-macro models, that is, a new type of model that links microeconomic models of consumers and producers with an overall macroeconomic model (see for example Davies, 2009). Given the increasing use of the CES function in econometric analysis and the importance of using sound parameters in economic programming models, there is definitely demand for software that facilitates the econometric estimation of the CES function.

The R package **micEconCES** (Henningsen and Henningsen, 2021) provides this functionality. It is developed as part of the **micEcon** project at R-Forge (http://r-forge.r-project.org/projects/micecon/). Stable versions of the **micEconCES** package are available for download from the Comprehensive R Archive Network (CRAN, http://CRAN.R-Project.org/package=micEconCES). Replication studies that further demonstrate the usage of **micEconCES** using data from Sun et al. (2011) and Kemfert (1998) can be found in Henningsen and Henningsen (2011) and Henningsen et al. (2019), respectively. First real-world applications of the **micEconCES** package can be found in Koesler and Schymura (2015), Sethi and Kaur (2015) and Henningsen et al. (2019).

The chapter is structured as follows. In the next section, we describe the classical CES function and the most important generalisations that can account for more than two independent variables. Then we discuss several approaches to estimate these CES functions and show how they can be applied in R. The fourth section describes the implementation of these methods in the R package **micEconCES**. Section 5 provides an empirical illustration. Finally, the last section concludes.

2. SPECIFICATION OF THE CES FUNCTION

The formal specification of a CES production function[3] with two inputs is

$$y = \gamma \left(\delta x_1^{-\rho} + (1-\delta) x_2^{-\rho} \right)^{-\frac{v}{\rho}}, \tag{20.1}$$

where y is the output quantity, x_1 and x_2 are the input quantities and γ, δ, ρ and v are parameters. Parameter $\gamma \varepsilon [0, \infty)$ determines the productivity, $\delta \varepsilon [0, 1]$ determines the optimal distribution of the inputs, $\rho \varepsilon [-1, 0) \cup [0, \infty)$ determines the (constant) elasticity of substitution, which is $\sigma = 1/(1 + \rho)$, and $v \varepsilon [0, \infty)$ is equal to the elasticity of scale.[4]

The CES function includes three special cases: for $\rho \to 0$, σ approaches 1 and the CES turns to the Cobb–Douglas form; for $\rho \to \infty$, σ approaches 0 and the CES turns to the Leontief production function; and for $\rho \to -1$, σ approaches infinity and the CES turns to a linear function if v is equal to 1.

As the CES function is non-linear in parameters and cannot be linearised analytically, it is not possible to estimate it with the usual linear estimation techniques. Therefore, the CES function is often approximated by the so-called "Kmenta approximation" (Kmenta, 1967), which can be estimated by linear estimation techniques. Alternatively, the CES function can be estimated by non-linear least squares using different optimisation algorithms.

To overcome the limitation of two inputs, CES functions for multiple inputs have been proposed. One problem of the elasticity of substitution for models with more than two inputs is that the literature provides three popular but different definitions (see, for example, Chambers, 1988): While the Hicks–McFadden elasticity of substitution (also known as direct elasticity of substitution) describes the input substitutability of two inputs i and j along an isoquant given that all other input quantities are constant, the Allen–Uzawa elasticity of substitution (also known as Allen partial elasticity of substitution) and the Morishima elasticity of substitution describe the input substitutability of two inputs when all other input quantities are allowed to adjust. The only functional form in which all three elasticities of substitution are constant is the plain n-input CES function (Blackorby and Russel, 1989), which has the following specification:

$$y = \gamma \left(\sum_{i=1}^{n} \delta_i x_i^{-\rho} \right)^{-\frac{v}{\rho}} \tag{20.2}$$

$$\text{with} \sum_{i=1}^{n} \delta_i = 1,$$

where n is the number of inputs and $x_1, \ldots, x_n$ are the quantities of the n inputs. Several scholars have tried to extend the Kmenta approximation to the n-input case, but Hoff (2004) showed that a correctly specified extension to the n-input case requires non-linear parameter restrictions on a translog function. Hence, there is little gain in using the Kmenta approximation in the n-input case.

The plain n-input CES function assumes that the elasticities of substitution between any pair of two inputs are the same. As this is highly undesirable for empirical applications, multiple-input CES functions that allow for different (constant) elasticities of substitution between different pairs of inputs have been proposed. For instance, the functional form proposed by Uzawa (1962) has constant Allen–Uzawa elasticities of substitution and the functional form proposed by McFadden (1963) has constant Hicks–McFadden elasticities of substitution.

However, the n-input CES functions proposed by Uzawa (1962) and McFadden (1963) impose rather strict conditions on the values for the elasticities of substitution and thus are less useful for empirical applications (Sato, 1967, p. 202). Therefore, Sato (1967) proposed a family of two-level nested CES functions. The basic idea of nesting CES functions is to have two or more levels of CES functions, where each of the inputs of an upper-level CES function might be replaced by the dependent variable of a lower-level CES function. Particularly, the nested CES functions for three and four inputs based on Sato (1967) have become popular in recent years. These functions increased in popularity, especially in the field of macro-econometrics, where input factors needed further differentiation, for example, issues such as Grilliches' capital-skill complementarity (Griliches, 1969) or wage differentiation between skilled and unskilled labour (for example, Acemoglu, 1998; Krusell et al., 2000; Pandey, 2008).

The nested CES function for four inputs as proposed by Sato (1967) nests two lower-level (two-input) CES functions into an upper-level (two-input) CES function: $y = \gamma[\delta CES_1^{-\rho} + (1-\delta)CES_2^{-\rho}]^{-v/\rho}$, where $CES_1 = \gamma_1(\delta_1 x_1^{-\rho_1} + (1-\delta_1)x_2^{-\rho_1})^{-v_1/\rho_1}$ and $CES_2 = \gamma_2(\delta_2 x_3^{-\rho_2} + (1-\delta_2)x_4^{-\rho_2})^{-v_2/\rho_2}$ indicate the two lower-level CES functions. In these lower-level CES functions, we (arbitrarily) normalise parameters γ_i and v_i to one, because without these normalisations, not all parameters of the (entire) nested CES function can be identified in econometric estimations; an infinite number of vectors of non-normalised parameters exists that all result in the same output quantity, given an arbitrary vector of input quantities (see note 6 for an example). Hence, the final specification of the four-input nested CES function is as follows:

$$y = \gamma\left[\delta\left(\delta_1 x_1^{-\rho_1} + (1-\delta_1)x_2^{-\rho_1}\right)^{\rho/\rho_1} + (1-\delta)\left(\delta_2 x_3^{-\rho_2} + (1-\delta_2)x_4^{-\rho_2}\right)^{\rho/\rho_2}\right]^{-v/\rho}. \tag{20.3}$$

If $\rho_1 = \rho_2 = \rho$, the four-input nested CES function defined in equation (20.3) reduces to the plain four-input CES function defined in equation (20.2).[5]

In the case of the three-input nested CES function, only one input of the upper-level CES function is further differentiated:[6]

$$y = \gamma\left[\delta\left(\delta_1 x_1^{-\rho_1} + (1-\delta_1)x_2^{-\rho_1}\right)^{\rho/\rho_1} + (1-\delta)x_3^{-\rho}\right]^{-v/\rho}. \tag{20.4}$$

For instance, x_1 and x_2 could be skilled and unskilled labour, respectively, and x_3 capital. Alternatively, Kemfert (1998) used this specification for analysing the substitutability between capital, labour, and energy. If $\rho_1 = \rho$, the three-input nested CES function defined in equation (20.4) reduces to the plain three-input CES function defined in equation (20.2).[7]

The nesting of the CES function increases its flexibility and makes it an attractive choice for many applications in economic theory and empirical work. However, nested CES functions are not invariant to the nesting structure and different nesting structures imply different assumptions about the separability between inputs (Sato, 1967). As the nesting structure is theoretically arbitrary, the selection depends on the researcher's choice and should be based on empirical considerations.

The formulas for calculating the Hicks–McFadden and Allen–Uzawa elasticities of substitution for the three-input and four-input nested CES functions are given in appendices B.3 and C.3 of Henningsen and Henningsen (2011), respectively. Anderson and Moroney (1994) showed for *n*-input nested CES functions that the Hicks–McFadden and Allen–Uzawa elasticities of substitution are only identical if the nested technologies are all of the Cobb–Douglas form, that is, $\rho_1 = \rho_2 = \rho = 0$ in the four-input nested CES function and $\rho_1 = \rho = 0$ in the three-input nested CES function.

Like in the plain *n*-input case, nested CES functions cannot be easily linearised. Hence, they have to be estimated by applying non-linear optimisation methods. In the following section, we will present different approaches to estimate the classical two-input CES function as well as three-input and four-input nested CES functions using the R package **micEconCES**.

3. ESTIMATION OF THE CES PRODUCTION FUNCTION

Tools for economic analysis with CES function are available in the R package **micEconCES** (Henningsen and Henningsen, 2021). If this package is installed, it can be loaded with the command:

```
library("micEconCES")
```

We demonstrate the usage of this package by estimating a classical two-input CES function as well as nested CES functions with three and four inputs. For this, we create an artificial data set `cesData`, because this avoids several problems that usually occur with real-world data. The following two commands set the "seed" for the pseudo-random number generator so that these examples can be replicated with exactly the same data set and create a data set with four input variables (called `x1`, `x2`, `x3` and `x4`) that each have 200 observations and are generated from random numbers drawn from a χ^2 distribution with 10 degrees of freedom, respectively:

```
set.seed(123)
cesData <- data.frame(x1 = rchisq(200, 10),
  x2 = rchisq(200, 10), x3 = rchisq(200, 10),
  x4 = rchisq(200, 10))
```

The following three commands use the function `cesCalc`, which is included in the **micEconCES** package, to calculate the "deterministic" output variables for the CES functions with two, three and four inputs (called `y2det`, `y3det` and `y4det`), respectively, given a CES production function. For the two-input CES function, we use the parameters $\gamma = 1$, $\delta = 0.6$, $\rho = 0.5$ and $\nu = 1.1$; for the three-input nested CES function, we use $\gamma = 1$, $\delta_1 = 0.7$, $\delta = 0.6$,

$\rho_1 = 0.3$, $\rho = 0.5$ and $v = 1.1$; and for the four-input nested CES function, we use $\gamma = 1$, $\delta_1 = 0.7$, $\delta_2 = 0.6$, $\delta = 0.5$, $\rho_1 = 0.3$, $\rho_2 = 0.4$, $\rho = 0.5$ and $v = 1.1$:

```
cesData$y2det <- cesCalc(xNames = c("x1", "x2"),
    data = cesData,
    coef = c(gamma = 1, delta = 0.6, rho = 0.5, nu = 1.1))
cesData$y3det <- cesCalc(xNames = c("x1", "x2", "x3"),
    data = cesData,
    coef = c(gamma = 1, delta_1 = 0.7, delta = 0.6, rho_1 = 0.3,
        rho = 0.5, nu = 1.1), nested = TRUE)
cesData$y4det <- cesCalc(xNames = c("x1", "x2", "x3", "x4"),
    data = cesData,
    coef = c(gamma = 1, delta_1 = 0.7, delta_2 = 0.6, delta = 0.5,
        rho_1 = 0.3, rho_2 = 0.4, rho = 0.5, nu = 1.1), nested = TRUE)
```

The following three commands generate the "stochastic" output variables (called y2, y3 and y4) by adding normally distributed random errors to the deterministic output variable and making sure that the stochastic output variables are strictly positive:

```
cesData$y2 <- pmax(cesData$y2det + 1.5 * rnorm(200), 0.1)
cesData$y3 <- pmax(cesData$y3det + 1.5 * rnorm(200), 0.1)
cesData$y4 <- pmax(cesData$y4det + 1.5 * rnorm(200), 0.1)
```

As the CES function is non-linear in its parameters, the most straightforward way to estimate the CES function in R would be to use function nls, which performs non-linear least-squares estimations:

```
cesNls <- nls(y2 ~ gamma * (delta * x1^(-rho) + (1 - delta) *
    x2^(-rho))^(-phi / rho), data = cesData, start = c(gamma = 0.5,
    delta = 0.5, rho = 0.25, phi = 1))
print(cesNls)
## Nonlinear regression model
##    model: y2 ~ gamma * (delta * x1^(-rho) + (1 - delta) *
##                  x2^(-rho))^(-phi/rho)
##    data: cesData
## gamma      delta       rho         phi
## 1.0139    0.6132     0.5259      1.0916
##    residual sum-of-squares: 431
##
## Number of iterations to convergence: 6
## Achieved convergence tolerance: 2.207e-06
```

While the nls routine works well in this ideal artificial example, it does not perform well in many applications with real-world data, either because of non-convergence, convergence to a local minimum or theoretically unreasonable parameter estimates. Therefore, we show alternative ways of estimating the CES function in the following sections.

3.1 Kmenta approximation

Given that non-linear estimation methods are often troublesome—particularly during the 1960s and 1970s when computing power was very limited—Kmenta (1967) derived an approximation of the classical two-input CES production function that could be estimated by ordinary least-squares techniques:

$$\ln y = \ln \gamma + v\, \delta \ln x_1 + v\left(1-\delta\right)\ln x_2 \tag{20.5}$$

$$-\frac{\rho v}{2}\, \delta\left(1-\delta\right)\left(\ln x_1 - \ln x_2\right)^2.$$

While Kmenta (1967) obtained this formula by logarithmising the CES function and applying a second-order Taylor series expansion to $\ln(\delta x_1^{-\rho} + (1-\delta)x_2^{-\rho})$ at the point $\rho = 0$, the same formula can be obtained by applying a first-order Taylor series expansion to the entire logarithmised CES function at the point $\rho = 0$ (Uebe, 2000). As the authors consider the latter approach to be more straightforward, the Kmenta approximation is called—in contrast to Kmenta (1967, p. 180)—first-order Taylor series expansion in the remainder of this chapter.

The Kmenta approximation can also be written as a restricted translog function (Hoff, 2004):

$$\ln y = \alpha_0 + \alpha_1 \ln x_1 + \alpha_2 \ln x_2 \tag{20.6}$$

$$+\frac{1}{2}\beta_{11}\left(\ln x_1\right)^2 + \frac{1}{2}\beta_{22}\left(\ln x_2\right)^2 + \beta_{12}\ln x_1 \ln x_2,$$

where the two restrictions are

$$\beta_{12} = -\beta_{11} = -\beta_{22}. \tag{20.7}$$

If constant returns to scale are to be imposed, a third restriction:

$$\alpha_1 + \alpha_2 = 1, \tag{20.8}$$

must be enforced. These restrictions can be utilised to test whether the linear Kmenta approximation of the CES function (20.5) is an acceptable simplification of the translog functional form.[8] If this is the case, a simple t-test of the hypothesis $\beta_{12} = 0$ (which implies $\beta_{11} = \beta_{22} = 0$) can be used to check if the Cobb–Douglas functional form is an acceptable simplification of the Kmenta approximation.[9]

The parameters of the CES function can be calculated from the coefficients of the restricted translog function by

$$\gamma = \exp(\alpha_0) \tag{20.9}$$

$$v = \alpha_1 + \alpha_2 \tag{20.10}$$

$$\delta = \frac{\alpha_1}{\alpha_1 + \alpha_2} \tag{20.11}$$

$$\rho = \frac{\beta_{12}\left(\alpha_1 + \alpha_2\right)}{\alpha_1 \cdot \alpha_2}. \tag{20.12}$$

The Kmenta approximation of the CES function can be estimated by the function `cesEst`, which is included in the **micEconCES** package. If argument `method` of this function is set to "Kmenta", it (a) estimates an unrestricted translog function (20.6), (b) carries out a Wald test of the restrictions on its coefficients defined in equation (20.7) and eventually also in equation (20.8) using the (finite sample) F-statistic, (c) estimates the restricted translog function defined in (20.6) and (20.7), and finally (d) calculates the parameters of the CES function using equations (20.9) to (20.12) as well as their covariance matrix using the delta method.

The following code estimates a CES function with the dependent variable `y2` (specified in argument `yName`) and the two explanatory variables `x1` and `x2` (argument `xNames`), all taken from the artificial data set `cesData` that we generated above (argument `data`) using the Kmenta approximation (argument `method`) and allowing for variable returns to scale (argument `vrs`):

```
cesKmenta <- cesEst (yName = "y2", xNames = c("x1", "x2"),
   data = cesData, method = "Kmenta", vrs = TRUE)
```

Summary results can be obtained by applying the summary method to the returned object:

```
summary (cesKmenta)
## Estimated CES function with variable returns to scale
##
## Call:
## cesEst (yName = "y2", xNames = c("x1", "x2"), data = cesData,
##    vrs = TRUE, method = "Kmenta")
##
## Estimation by the linear Kmenta approximation
## Test of the null hypothesis that the restrictions of the
## Translog
## function required by the Kmenta approximation are true:
## P-value = 0.4022624
##
## Coefficients:
##          Estimate Std. Error   t value   Pr (>|t|)
## gamma     0.89876    0.07806     1.514   < 2e-16 ***
## delta     0.62255    0.02117    29.409   < 2e-16 ***
## rho       0.58039    0.19969     2.907   0.00365 **
## nu        1.14140    0.03876    29.445   < 2e-16 ***
## -
## Signif. codes:  0 '***' 0.001 '**' 0.01 '*' 0.05 '.' 0.1 ' ' 1
##
## Residual standard error: 1.484319
## Multiple R-squared: 0.899316
##
```

```
## Elasticity of Substitution:
##                 Estimate Std. Error  t value     Pr(>|t|)
## E_1_2 (all)      0.63275    0.07995    7.914     2.49e-15 ***
## -
## Signif. codes:  0 '***' 0.001 '**' 0.01 '*' 0.05 '.' 0.1 ' ' 1
```

The Wald test indicates that the restrictions on the translog function implied by the Kmenta approximation cannot be rejected at any reasonable significance level (P-value: 0.402).

To see whether the underlying technology is of the Cobb–Douglas form, we can check if the coefficient $\beta_{12} = -\beta_{11} = -\beta_{22}$ significantly differs from zero. As the estimation of the Kmenta approximation is stored in component `kmenta` of the object returned by `cesEst`, we can obtain summary information on the estimated coefficients of the Kmenta approximation by

```
coef(summary(cesKmenta$kmenta))
##                     Estimate   Std. Error    t value      Pr(>|t|)
## eq1_(Intercept)   -0.1067436  0.08684947  -1.229065   0.220521035
## eq1_a_1            0.7105785  0.03126399  22.728341   0.000000000
## eq1_a_2            0.4308184  0.03020433  14.263468   0.000000000
## eq1_b_1_1         -0.1556653  0.05217686  -2.983416   0.003212818
## eq1_b_1_2          0.1556653  0.05217686   2.983416   0.003212818
## eq1_b_2_2         -0.1556653  0.05217686  -2.983416   0.003212818
```

Given that $\beta_{12} = -\beta_{11} = -\beta_{22}$ significantly differs from zero (P-value: 0.0032), we can conclude that the underlying technology is not of the Cobb–Douglas form. Alternatively, we can check if the parameter ρ of the CES function, which is calculated from the coefficients of the Kmenta approximation, significantly differs from zero. This should—as in our case—deliver similar results (P-value: 0.0037).

Finally, we plot the fitted output quantities against the actual output quantities (y) to visually check the suitability of the estimated model:

```
library("miscTools")
compPlot(cesData$y2, fitted(cesKmenta), xlab = "actual values",
  ylab = "fitted values")
```

Figure 20.1 shows that the estimated model gives a reasonable "fit" to the data.

However, the Kmenta approximation encounters several problems. First, it is a truncated Taylor series and the remainder term must be seen as an omitted variable. Second, the Kmenta approximation only converges to the underlying CES function in a region of convergence that is dependent on the true parameters of the CES function (Thursby and Lovell, 1978).

Although, Maddala and Kadane (1967) and Thursby and Lovell (1978) find estimates for v and δ with small bias and mean squared error (MSE), results for γ and ρ are estimated with generally considerable bias and MSE (Thursby and Lovell, 1978; Thursby, 1980). More reliable results can only be obtained if $\rho \rightarrow 0$, and thus $\sigma \rightarrow 1$ which increases the convergence region, that is, if the underlying CES function is of the Cobb–Douglas form. This is a major drawback of the Kmenta approximation as its purpose is to facilitate the estimation of functions with non-unitary σ.

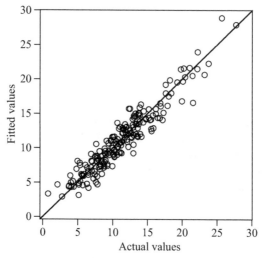

Figure 20.1   *Fitted output quantities from the Kmenta approximation against actual output quantities*

3.2 Gradient-Based Optimisation Algorithms

3.2.1 Levenberg–Marquardt

Initially, the Levenberg–Marquardt algorithm (Marquardt, 1963) was most commonly used for estimating the parameters of the CES function by non-linear least-squares. This iterative algorithm can be seen as a maximum neighbourhood method which performs an optimum interpolation between a first-order Taylor series approximation (Gauss–Newton method) and a steepest-descend method (gradient method) (Marquardt, 1963). The aim of combining these two non-linear optimisation algorithms is to increase the convergence probability by reducing the weaknesses of each of the two methods.

In a Monte Carlo study by Thursby (1980), the Levenberg–Marquardt algorithm outperforms the other methods and gives the best estimates of the CES parameters. However, the Levenberg–Marquardt algorithm performs as poorly as the other methods in estimating the elasticity of substitution (σ), which means that the estimated σ tends to be biased toward infinity, unity or zero.

Although the Levenberg–Marquardt algorithm does not live up to modern standards, we include it for reasons of completeness, as it has proven to be a standard method for estimating CES functions.

To estimate a CES function by non-linear least-squares using the Levenberg–Marquardt algorithm, one can call the `cesEst` function with argument `method` set to `"LM"` or without this argument, as the Levenberg–Marquardt algorithm is the default estimation method used by `cesEst`. The user can modify a few details of this algorithm (for example, different criteria for convergence) by adding argument `control` as described in the documentation of the R function `nls.lm.control`. Argument `start` can be used to specify a vector of starting values, where the order must be γ, δ_1, δ_2, δ, ρ_1, ρ_2, ρ and ν (of course, all parameters that are not in the model must be omitted). If no starting values are provided, they are determined automatically (see section 4.7). The following commands estimate all three (that is, two input, three-input nested and four-input nested) CES functions with the Levenberg–Marquardt algorithm:

```
cesLm2 <- cesEst("y2", c("x1", "x2"), cesData, vrs = TRUE)
cesLm3 <- cesEst("y3", c("x1", "x2", "x3"), cesData, vrs = TRUE)
cesLm4 <- cesEst("y4", c("x1", "x2", "x3", "x4"), cesData, vrs =
  TRUE)
```

In order to reduce space, we present the results of the classical two-input CES function only:

```
summary(cesLm2)
## Estimated CES function with variable returns to scale
##
## Call:
## cesEst(yName = "y2", xNames = c("x1", "x2"), data = cesData,
##     vrs = TRUE)
##
## Estimation by non-linear least-squares using the 'LM'
## optimizer assuming an additive error term
## Convergence achieved after 4 iterations
## Message: Relative error in the sum of squares is at most
## 'ftol'.
##
## Coefficients:
##          Estimate  Std. Error  t value   Pr(>|t|)
## gamma     1.01394     0.06848   14.806   < 2e-16 ***
## delta     0.61319     0.01676   36.587   < 2e-16 ***
## rho       0.52588     0.17162    3.064   0.00218 **
## nu        1.09165     0.02731   39.973   < 2e-16 ***
## −
## Signif. codes: 0 '***' 0.001 '**' 0.01 '*' 0.05 '.' 0.1 ' ' 1
##
## Residual standard error: 1.467952
## Multiple R-squared: 0.9015241
##
## Elasticity of Substitution:
##              Estimate   Std. Error  t value  Pr(>|t|)
## E_1_2 (all)   0.65536      0.07371    8.891   <2e-16 ***
## −
## Signif. codes: 0 '***' 0.001 '**' 0.01 '*' 0.05 '.' 0.1 ' ' 1
```

Finally, we plot the fitted values against the actual output quantities y to assess the suitability of the estimated model. The resulting scatter plots are presented in Figure 20.2.

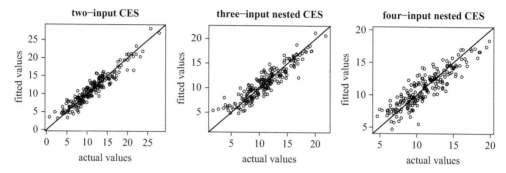

Figure 20.2   Fitted output quantities from the LM algorithm against actual output quantities

```
compPlot (cesData$y2, fitted(cesLm2), xlab = "actual values",
  ylab = "fitted values", main = "two-input CES")
compPlot (cesData$y3, fitted(cesLm3), xlab = "actual values",
  ylab = "fitted values", main = "three-input nested CES")
compPlot (cesData$y4, fitted(cesLm4), xlab = "actual values",
  ylab = "fitted values", main = "four-input nested CES")
```

Several further gradient-based optimisation algorithms that are suitable for non-linear least-squares estimations are implemented in R. Function `cesEst` can use some of them to estimate a CES function by non-linear least squares. As a proper application of these estimation methods requires the user to be familiar with the main characteristics of the different algorithms, we will briefly discuss some practical issues of the algorithms that will be used to estimate the CES function. However, it is not the aim of this chapter to thoroughly discuss these algorithms. A detailed discussion of iterative optimisation algorithms is available, for example, in Kelley (1999) or Mishra (2007). In order to reduce space, we will proceed with examples of the classical two-input CES function only.

3.2.2   Conjugate gradients

One of the gradient-based optimisation algorithms that can be used by `cesEst` is the "Conjugate Gradients" method based on Fletcher and Reeves (1964). This iterative method is mostly applied to optimisation problems with many parameters and a large and possibly sparse Hessian matrix, because this algorithm does not require that the Hessian matrix is stored or inverted. The "Conjugated Gradient" method works best for objective functions that are approximately quadratic and it is sensitive to objective functions that are not well behaved and have a non-positive semi-definite Hessian, that is, convergence within the given number of iterations is less likely the more the level surface of the objective function differs from spherical (Kelley, 1999). Given that the CES function has only few parameters and the objective function is not approximately quadratic and shows a tendency to "flat surfaces" around the minimum, the "Conjugated Gradient" method is probably less suitable than other algorithms for estimating a CES function. Setting argument method of `cesEst` to `"CG"` selects the "Conjugate Gradients" method for estimating the CES function by non-linear least squares:

```
cesCg <- cesEst("y2", c("x1", "x2"), cesData, vrs = TRUE, method
  = "CG")
```

As the "Conjugated Gradient" algorithm generally reaches convergence only slowly, this algorithm will frequently report that it did not converge. In such cases, the user can modify the algorithm (for example, replacing the updated formula of Fletcher and Reeves (1964) by the formula of Polak and Ribière (1969) or the one based on Sorenson (1969) and Beale (1972)) or some other details (for example, convergence tolerance level) by adding a further argument `control` as described in the "Details" section of the documentation of the R function `optim`. Increasing the maximum number of iterations and the tolerance level often leads to convergence:

```
cesCg2 <- cesEst("y2", c("x1", "x2"), cesData, vrs = TRUE, method
  = "CG", control = list(maxit = 1000, reltol = 1e-5))
```

3.2.3   Newton

Another algorithm supported by `cesEst` that is probably more suitable for estimating CES functions than the "Conjugated Gradient" algorithm is an improved Newton-type method. As with the original Newton method, this algorithm uses first and second derivatives of the objective function to determine the direction of the shift vector and searches for a stationary point until the gradients are (almost) zero. However, in contrast to the original Newton method, this algorithm does a line search at each iteration to determine the optimal length of the shift vector (step size) as described in Dennis and Schnabel (1983) and Schnabel et al. (1985). Setting argument `method` of `cesEst` to `"Newton"` selects this improved Newton-type method:

```
cesNewton <- cesEst("y2", c("x1", "x2"), cesData, vrs = TRUE,
  method = "Newton")
```

The user can modify a few details of this algorithm (for example, the maximum step length) by adding further arguments that are described in the documentation of the R function `nlm`.

3.2.4   Broyden–Fletcher–Goldfarb–Shanno

Furthermore, a quasi-Newton method developed independently by Broyden (1970), Fletcher (1970), Goldfarb (1970) and Shanno (1970) can be used by `cesEst`. This so-called BFGS algorithm also uses first and second derivatives and searches for a stationary point of the objective function where the gradients are (almost) zero. In contrast to the original Newton method, the BFGS method does a line search for the best step size and uses a special procedure to approximate and update the Hessian matrix in every iteration. The problem with BFGS can be that although the current parameters are close to the minimum, the algorithm does not converge because the Hessian matrix at the current parameters is not close to the Hessian matrix at the minimum. However, in practice, BFGS proves robust convergence (often superlinear)

(Kelley, 1999). If argument `method` of `cesEst` is `"BFGS"`, the BFGS algorithm is used for the estimation:

```
cesBfgs <- cesEst("y2", c("x1", "x2"), cesData, vrs = TRUE,
  method = "BFGS")
```

The user can modify a few details of the BFGS algorithm (for example, the convergence tolerance level) by adding the further argument `control` as described in the "Details" section of the documentation of the R function `optim`.

3.3   Global Optimisation Algorithms

While the gradient-based (local) optimisation algorithms described above are designed to find local minima, global optimisation algorithms, which are also known as direct search methods, are designed to find the global minimum. These algorithms are more tolerant to objective functions which are not well-behaved, although they usually converge more slowly than the gradient-based methods. However, increasing computing power has made these algorithms suitable for day-to-day use.

3.3.1   Nelder–Mead

One of these global optimisation routines is the so-called Nelder–Mead algorithm (Nelder and Mead, 1965), which is a downhill simplex algorithm. In every iteration, $n + 1$ vertices are defined in the n-dimensional parameter space. The algorithm converges by successively replacing the "worst" point by a new vertex in the multi-dimensional parameter space. The Nelder–Mead algorithm has the advantage of a simple and robust algorithm, and is especially suitable for residual problems with non-differentiable objective functions. However, the heuristic nature of the algorithm causes slow convergence, especially close to the minimum, and can lead to convergence to non-stationary points. As the CES function is easily twice differentiable, the advantage of the Nelder–Mead algorithm simply becomes its robustness. As a consequence of the heuristic optimisation technique, the results should be handled with care. However, the Nelder–Mead algorithm is much faster than the other global optimisation algorithms described below. Function `cesEst` estimates a CES function with the Nelder–Mead algorithm if argument `method` is set to `"NM"`:

```
cesNm <- cesEst("y2", c("x1", "x2"), cesData, vrs = TRUE, method
  = "NM")
```

The user can tweak this algorithm (for example, the reflection factor, contraction factor or expansion factor) or change some other details (for example, convergence tolerance level) by adding a further argument `control` as described in the "Details" section of the documentation of the R function `optim`.

3.3.2   Simulated annealing

The Simulated Annealing algorithm was initially proposed by Kirkpatrick et al. (1983) and Cerny (1985) and is a modification of the Metropolis–Hastings algorithm. Every iteration chooses a random solution close to the current solution, while the probability of the choice is driven by a global parameter T which decreases as the algorithm moves on. Unlike other iterative optimisation algorithms, Simulated Annealing also allows T to increase which makes it possible to leave local minima. Therefore, Simulated Annealing is a robust global optimiser and it can be applied to a large search space, where it provides fast and reliable solutions. Setting argument `method` to `"SANN"` selects a variant of the "Simulated Annealing" algorithm given in Béisle (1992):

```
cesSann <- cesEst("y2", c("x1", "x2"), cesData, vrs = TRUE,
  method = "SANN")
```

The user can modify some details of the "Simulated Annealing" algorithm (for example, the starting temperature T or the number of function evaluations at each temperature) by adding a further argument `control` as described in the "Details" section of the documentation of the R function `optim`. The only criterion for stopping this iterative process is the number of iterations and it does not indicate whether the algorithm converged.

As the Simulated Annealing algorithm makes use of random numbers, the solution generally depends on the initial "state" of R's random number generator. To ensure replicability, `cesEst` "seeds" the random number generator before it starts the "Simulated Annealing" algorithm with the value of argument `random.seed`, which defaults to 123. Hence, the estimation of the same model using this algorithm always returns the same estimates as long as argument `random.seed` is not altered (at least when using the same software and hardware components):

```
cesSann2 <- cesEst("y2", c("x1", "x2"), cesData, vrs = TRUE,
  method = "SANN")
all.equal(cesSann, cesSann2)
## [1] TRUE
```

It is recommended to start this algorithm with different values of argument `random.seed` and to check whether the estimates differ considerably:

```
cesSann3 <- cesEst("y2", c("x1", "x2"), cesData, vrs = TRUE,
  method = "SANN", random.seed = 1234)
cesSann4 <- cesEst("y2", c("x1", "x2"), cesData, vrs = TRUE,
  method = "SANN", random.seed = 12345)
cesSann5 <- cesEst("y2", c("x1", "x2"), cesData, vrs = TRUE,
  method = "SANN", random.seed = 123456)
m <- rbind(cesSann = coef(cesSann), cesSann3 = coef(cesSann3),
  cesSann4 = coef(cesSann4), cesSann5 = coef(cesSann5))
rbind(m, stdDev = apply(m, 2, sd))
##                gamma        delta         rho          nu
## cesSann    0.99603089   0.613607094   0.54166186   1.10054227
## cesSann3   0.97737534   0.609935914   0.43533649   1.10778112
## cesSann4   1.02264519   0.619950361   0.51492172   1.09006996
## cesSann5   1.04939994   0.601735539   0.51252445   1.07951685
## stdDev     0.03143422   0.007604623   0.04579542   0.01234255
```

If the estimates differ remarkably, the user can try increasing the number of iterations, which is 10 000 by default. The following commands re-estimate the model a few times with 100 000 iterations each:

```
cesSannB <- cesEst("y2", c("x1", "x2"), cesData, vrs = TRUE,
   method = "SANN", control = list(maxit = 100000))
cesSannB3 <- cesEst("y2", c("x1", "x2"), cesData, vrs = TRUE,
   method = "SANN", random.seed = 1234,
   control = list(maxit = 100000))
cesSannB4 <- cesEst("y2", c("x1", "x2"), cesData, vrs = TRUE,
   method = "SANN", random.seed = 12345,
   control = list(maxit = 100000))
cesSannB5 <- cesEst("y2", c("x1", "x2"), cesData, vrs = TRUE,
   method = "SANN", random.seed = 123456,
   control = list(maxit = 100000))
m <- rbind(cesSannB = coef(cesSannB), cesSannB3 =
   coef(cesSannB3), cesSannB4 = coef(cesSannB4), cesSannB5 =
   coef(cesSannB5))
rbind(m, stdDev = apply(m, 2, sd))
##                 gamma         delta          rho             nu
## cesSannB     1.01279768   0.608378245   0.49226968   1.091858861
## cesSannB3    1.02598861   0.611394217   0.52008497   1.086818887
## cesSannB4    1.01259706   0.614478149   0.55084522   1.093306428
## cesSannB5    1.01417551   0.616178259   0.51941212   1.091992453
## stdDev       0.00643761   0.003445204   0.02393773   0.002859125
```

Now the estimates are much more similar—only the estimates of ρ still differ somewhat.

3.3.3   Differential evolution

Contrary to the other algorithms described in this chapter, the Differential Evolution algorithm (Storn and Price, 1997; Price et al., 2006) belongs to the class of evolution strategy optimisers and convergence cannot be proven analytically. However, the algorithm has proven to be effective and accurate on a large range of optimisation problems, inter alia the CES function (Mishra, 2007). For some problems, it has proven to be more accurate and more efficient than Simulated Annealing, Quasi-Newton, or other genetic algorithms (Storn and Price, 1997; Ali and Törn, 2004; Mishra, 2007). Function cesEst uses a Differential Evolution optimiser for the non-linear least-squares estimation of the CES function, if argument method is set to "DE":

```
cesDe <- cesEst("y2", c("x1", "x2"), cesData, vrs = TRUE, method
   = "DE", control = list(trace = FALSE))
```

The user can modify the Differential Evolution algorithm (for example, the differential evolution strategy or selection method) or change some details (for example, the number of population members) by adding a further argument control as described in the documentation of the R function DEoptim.control. Contrary to the other optimisation algorithms, the Differential Evolution method requires finite boundaries for the parameters. By default, the bounds are $0 \leq \gamma \leq 10^{10}$; $0 \leq \delta_1, \delta_2, \delta \leq 1$; $-1 \leq \rho_1, \rho_2, \rho \leq 10$; and $0 \leq \nu \leq 10$. The user can specify own lower and upper bounds by setting arguments `lower` and `upper` to numeric vectors.

Like the "Simulated Annealing" algorithm, the Differential Evolution algorithm makes use of random numbers and `cesEst` "seeds" the random number generator with the value of argument `random.seed` before it starts this algorithm to ensure replicability:

```
cesDe2 <- cesEst("y2", c("x1", "x2"), cesData, vrs = TRUE, method
  = "DE", control = list(trace = FALSE))
all.equal(cesDe, cesDe2)
## [1] TRUE
```

When using this algorithm, it is also recommended to check whether different values of the argument `random.seed` result in considerably different estimates:

```
cesDe3 <- cesEst("y2", c("x1", "x2"), cesData, vrs = TRUE,
  method = "DE", random.seed = 1234,
  control = list(trace = FALSE))
cesDe4 <- cesEst("y2", c("x1", "x2"), cesData, vrs = TRUE,
  method = "DE", random.seed = 12345,
  control = list(trace = FALSE))
cesDe5 <- cesEst("y2", c("x1", "x2"), cesData, vrs = TRUE,
  method = "DE", random.seed = 123456,
  control = list(trace = FALSE))
m <- rbind(cesDe = coef(cesDe), cesDe3 = coef(cesDe3),
  cesDe4 = coef(cesDe4), cesDe5 = coef(cesDe5))
rbind(m, stdDev = apply(m, 2, sd))
##               gamma        delta          rho          nu
## cesDe    1.01598491   0.612807112   0.52502981   1.090609166
## cesDe3   1.01279682   0.607906902   0.50378278   1.091996550
## cesDe4   1.02539212   0.614832834   0.57059555   1.086896078
## cesDe5   1.02241444   0.610044836   0.51938122   1.088896692
## stdDev   0.00577354   0.003044257   0.02870793   0.002203611
```

These estimates are rather similar, which generally indicates that all estimates are close to the optimum (minimum of the sum of squared residuals). However, if the user wants to obtain more precise estimates than those derived from the default settings of this algorithm, for example, if the estimates differ considerably, the user can try to increase the maximum number of population generations (iterations) using control parameter `itermax`, which is 200 by default. The following commands re-estimate this model a few times with 1000 population generations each:

```
cesDeB <- cesEst("y2", c("x1", "x2"), cesData, vrs = TRUE,
  method = "DE",
  control = list(trace = FALSE, itermax = 1000))
cesDeB3 <- cesEst("y2", c("x1", "x2"), cesData, vrs = TRUE,
  method = "DE", random.seed = 1234,
```

```
    control = list(trace = FALSE, itermax = 1000))
  cesDeB4 <- cesEst("y2", c("x1", "x2"), cesData, vrs = TRUE,
    method = "DE", random.seed = 12345,
    control = list(trace = FALSE, itermax = 1000))
  cesDeB5 <- cesEst("y2", c("x1", "x2"), cesData, vrs = TRUE,
    method = "DE", random.seed = 123456,
    control = list(trace = FALSE, itermax = 1000))
  rbind(cesDeB = coef(cesDeB), cesDeB3 = coef(cesDeB3),
   cesDeB4 = coef(cesDeB4), cesDeB5 = coef(cesDeB5))
  ##             gamma       delta        rho          nu
  ## cesDeB    1.013942   0.6131871   0.5258763   1.091648
  ## cesDeB3   1.013942   0.6131871   0.5258763   1.091648
  ## cesDeB4   1.013942   0.6131871   0.5258763   1.091648
  ## cesDeB5   1.013942   0.6131871   0.5258763   1.091648
```

The estimates are now virtually identical.

The user can further increase the likelihood of finding the global optimum by increasing the number of population members using control parameter NP, which is 10 times the number of parameters by default and should not have a smaller value than this default value (see documentation of the R function DEoptim.control).

3.4   Constraint Parameters

As a meaningful analysis based on a CES function requires that the function is consistent with economic theory, it is often desirable to constrain the parameter space to the economically meaningful region. This can be done by the Differential Evolution (DE) algorithm as described above. Moreover, function cesEst can use two gradient-based optimisation algorithms for estimating a CES function under parameter constraints.

3.4.1   L-BFGS-B

One of these methods is a modification of the BFGS algorithm suggested by Byrd et al. (1995). In contrast to the ordinary BFGS algorithm summarised above, the so-called L-BFGS-B algorithm allows for box constraints on the parameters and also does not explicitly form or store the Hessian matrix, but instead relies on the past (often less than 10) values of the parameters and the gradient vector. Therefore, the L-BFGS-B algorithm is especially suitable for high dimensional optimisation problems, but—of course—it can also be used for optimisation problems with only a few parameters (as the CES function). Function cesEst estimates a CES function with parameter constraints using the L-BFGS-B algorithm if argument method is set to "L-BFGS-B":

```
  cesLbfgsb <- cesEst("y2", c("x1", "x2"), cesData, vrs = TRUE,
    method = "L-BFGS-B")
```

The user can tweak some details of this algorithm (for example, the number of BFGS updates) by adding a further argument control as described in the "Details" section of the documentation of the R function optim. By default, the restrictions on the parameters are

$0 \le \gamma \le \infty; \; 0 \le \delta_1, \delta_2, \delta \le 1; \; -1 \le \rho_1, \rho_2, \rho \le \infty;$ and $0 \le \nu \le \infty$. The user can specify own `lower` and `upper` bounds by setting arguments lower and upper to numeric vectors.

3.4.2 PORT routines

The so-called PORT routines (Gay, 1990) include a quasi-Newton optimisation algorithm that allows for box constraints on the parameters and has several advantages over traditional Newton routines, for example, trust regions and reverse communication. Setting argument `method` of function `cesEst` to `"PORT"` selects the PORT routines to be used as optimisation algorithm:

```
cesPort <- cesEst("y2", c("x1", "x2"), cesData, vrs = TRUE,
  method = "PORT")
```

The user can modify a few details of the Newton algorithm (for example, the minimum step size) by adding a further argument `control` as described in section "Control parameters" of the documentation of R function `nlminb`. The lower and upper bounds of the parameters have the same default values as for the L-BFGS-B method.

3.5 Technological Change

Estimating the CES function with time series data usually requires an extension of the CES functional form in order to account for technological change (progress). So far, accounting for technological change in CES functions basically boils down to two approaches:

- Hicks-neutral technological change:

$$y = \gamma \, e^{\lambda t} \left(\delta x_1^{-\rho} + (1 - \delta) x_2^{-\rho} \right)^{-\frac{\nu}{\rho}}, \tag{20.13}$$

  where λ is the rate of technological change, t is a time variable and all other parameters and variables are defined as before

- Factor augmenting (non-neutral) technological change:

$$y = \gamma \left(\left(x_1 \, e^{\lambda_1 t} \right)^{-\rho} + \left(x_2 \, e^{\lambda_2 t} \right)^{-\rho} \right)^{-\frac{\nu}{\rho}}, \tag{20.14}$$

  where λ_1 and λ_2 measure input-specific technological change.

There is a lively ongoing discussion about the proper way to estimate CES functions with factor-augmenting technological progress (for example, Klump et al., 2007; Luoma and Luoto, 2010; León-Ledesma et al., 2010a,b). However, so far **micEconCES** only includes Hicks-neutral technological change.

When calculating the output variable of the CES function using `cesCalc` or when estimating the parameters of the CES function using `cesEst`, the name of time variable (t) can be specified by argument `tName`, where the corresponding parameter (λ) is labelled `lambda`.[10]

The following four commands (i) generate an (artificial) time variable t, (ii) calculate the (deterministic) output variable of a CES function with 1 per cent Hicks-neutral technological progress in each time period, (iii) add noise to obtain the stochastic "observed" output variable and (iv) estimate the model, respectively:

```
cesData$t <- c(1:200)
cesData$ytdet <- cesCalc(xNames = c("x1", "x2"),
  data = cesData, tName = "t",
  coef = c(gamma = 1, delta = 0.6, rho = 0.5, nu = 1.1, lambda =
    0.01))
cesData$yt <- pmax(cesData$ytdet + 1.5 * rnorm(200), 0.1)
cesTech <- cesEst("yt", c("x1", "x2"), data = cesData,
  tName = "t", vrs = TRUE, method = "LM")
```

Here, we demonstrated how Hicks-neutral technological change can be modelled in the two-input CES function. In case of more than two inputs—regardless of whether the CES function is "plain" or "nested"—Hicks-neutral technological change can be accounted for in the same way, that is, by multiplying the CES function with $e^{\lambda t}$. Functions cesCalc and cesEst can account for Hicks-neutral technological change in all CES specifications that are generally supported by these functions.

3.6   Grid Search for ρ

The objective function for estimating CES functions by non-linear least-squares often shows a tendency to "flat surfaces" around the minimum—in particular for a wide range of values for the substitution parameters (ρ_1, ρ_2, ρ). Therefore, many optimisation algorithms have problems in finding the minimum of the objective function, particularly in case of n-input nested CES functions (Henningsen and Henningsen, 2012; Henningsen et al., 2019).

However, this problem can be alleviated by performing a grid search, where a grid of values for the substitution parameters (ρ_1, ρ_2, ρ) is pre-selected and the remaining parameters are estimated by non-linear least squares holding the substitution parameters fixed at each combination of the predefined values. As the (nested) CES functions defined above can have up to three substitution parameters, the grid search over the substitution parameters can be either one-, two- or three-dimensional. The estimates with the values of the substitution parameters that result in the smallest sum of squared residuals are chosen as the final estimation result.

The function cesEst carries out this grid search procedure, if argument rho1, rho2 or rho is set to a numeric vector. The values of these vectors are used to specify the grid points for the substitution parameters ρ_1, ρ_2 and ρ, respectively. The estimation of the other parameters during the grid search can be performed by all the non-linear optimisation algorithms described above. Since the "best" values of the substitution parameters (ρ_1, ρ_2, ρ) that are found in the grid search are not known, but estimated (as the other parameters, but with a different estimation method), the covariance matrix of the estimated parameters also includes the substitution parameters and is calculated as if the substitution parameters were estimated as usual. The following command estimates the two-input CES function by a one-dimensional grid search for ρ, where the pre-selected values for ρ are the values from -0.3 to 1.5 with an

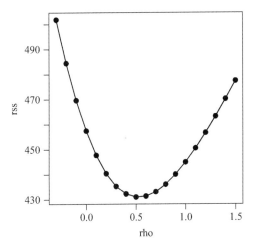

Figure 20.3   Sum of squared residuals depending on ρ

increment of 0.1 and the default optimisation method, the Levenberg–Marquardt algorithm, is used to estimate the remaining parameters:

```
cesGrid <- cesEst("y2", c("x1", "x2"), data = cesData, vrs =
   TRUE, rho = seq(from = -0.3, to = 1.5, by = 0.1))
```

A graphical illustration of the relationship between the pre-selected values of the substitution parameters and the corresponding sums of the squared residuals can be obtained by applying the `plot` method:[11]

```
plot(cesGrid)
```

This graphical illustration is shown in Figure 20.3.

As a further example, we estimate a four-input nested CES function by a three-dimensional grid search for ρ_1, ρ_2 and ρ. Pre-selected values are −0.6 to 0.9 with an increment of 0.3 for ρ_1, −0.4 to 0.8 with an increment of 0.2 for ρ_2 and −0.3 to 1.7 with an increment of 0.2 for ρ. Again, we apply the default optimisation method, the Levenberg–Marquardt algorithm:

```
ces4Grid <- cesEst(yName = "y4",
   xNames = c("x1", "x2", "x3", "x4"),
   data = cesData, method = "LM",
   rho1 = seq(from = -0.6, to = 0.9, by = 0.3),
   rho2 = seq(from = -0.4, to = 0.8, by = 0.2),
   rho = seq(from = -0.3, to = 1.7, by = 0.2))
```

Naturally, for a three-dimensional grid search, plotting the sums of the squared residuals against the corresponding (pre-selected) values of ρ_1, ρ_2 and ρ would require a four-dimensional graph. As it is (currently) not possible to account for more than three dimensions in a graph, the `plot` method generates three three-dimensional graphs, where each of the three substitution parameters (ρ_1, ρ_2, ρ) in turn is kept fixed at its optimal value:

```
plot(ces4Grid, bw = TRUE)
```

The resulting graphs are shown in Figure 20.4.

The results of the grid search algorithm can be used either directly, or as starting values for a new non-linear least-squares estimation. In the latter case, the values of the substitution parameters that are between the grid points can also be estimated. Starting values can be set by argument `start`:

```
cesStartGrid <- cesEst("y2", c("x1", "x2"), data = cesData, vrs =
   TRUE, start = coef(cesGrid))
ces4StartGrid <- cesEst("y4", c("x1", "x2", "x3", "x4"), data =
   cesData, start = coef(ces4Grid))
```

3.7   Additive and Multiplicative Error Terms

So far, we have assumed in the examples (except for the Kmenta approximation) that the error term of the econometric estimations (u) is additive:

$$y = CES + u. \tag{20.15}$$

However, in some empirical applications, the assumption of an additive error term is unsuitable, because this often contradicts the homoscedasticity assumption, particularly if the output quantities in the data set have a wide range of values. In case of an additive homoscedastic error term, measurement errors, unobserved variables and other sources of statistical noise would, for instance, cause that the output quantity of small producers varies between 0 and 20 units of output, while the output quantity of medium-sized producers varies between 90 and 110 units of output and the output quantity of large producers varies between 990 and 1010 units of output. In several empirical applications, the assumption of a multiplicative error term is more appropriate:

$$y = CES \cdot e^u \Leftrightarrow \ln y = \ln CES + u. \tag{20.16}$$

In case of a multiplicative homoscedastic error term, measurement errors, unobserved variables and other sources of statistical noise would, for instance, cause that the output quantity of small producers varies between 9 and 11 units of output, while the output quantity of medium-sized producers varies between 90 and 110 units of output and the output quantity of large producers varies between 900 and 1100 units of output.

The following three commands generate "stochastic" output variables (called `y2m`, `y3m` and `y4m`) by adding multiplicative normally distributed random errors to the deterministic output variables that we calculated in beginning of section 3:

```
cesData$y2m <- cesData$y2det * exp(0.15 * rnorm(200))
cesData$y3m <- cesData$y3det * exp(0.15 * rnorm(200))
cesData$y4m <- cesData$y4det * exp(0.15 * rnorm(200))
```

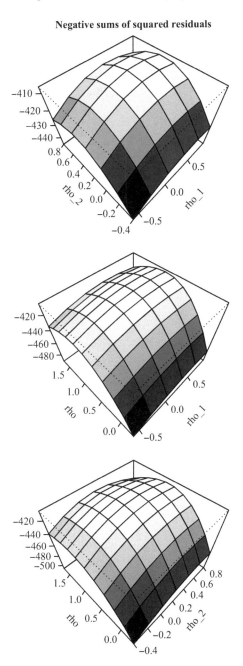

Figure 20.4 Sum of squared residuals depending on ρ_1, ρ_2 and ρ

The following commands estimate all three (that is, two-input, three-input and four-input nested) CES functions with the Levenberg–Marquardt algorithm assuming a multiplicative error term:

```
cesLm2m <- cesEst("y2m", c("x1", "x2"), cesData, vrs = TRUE,
  multErr = TRUE)
cesLm3m <- cesEst("y3m", c("x1", "x2", "x3"), cesData, vrs =
  TRUE, multErr = TRUE)
cesLm4m <- cesEst("y4m", c("x1", "x2", "x3", "x4"), cesData, vrs
  = TRUE, multErr = TRUE)
```

In order to reduce space, we present the results of the classical two-input CES function only:

```
summary(cesLm2m)
## Estimated CES function with variable returns to scale
##
## Call:
## cesEst(yName = "y2m", xNames = c("x1", "x2"), data = cesData,
##     vrs = TRUE, multErr = TRUE)
##
## Estimation by non-linear least-squares using the 'LM'
## optimizer assuming a multiplicative error term
## Convergence achieved after 4 iterations
## Message: Relative error in the sum of squares is at most
## 'ftol'.
##
## Coefficients:
##           Estimate Std. Error   t value  Pr(>|t|)
## gamma      1.07263    0.07393    14.508   <2e-16 ***
## delta      0.62941    0.01828    34.438   <2e-16 ***
## rho        0.34603    0.17317     1.998   0.0457 *
## nu         1.07053    0.03076    34.799   <2e-16 ***
## —
## Signif. codes:  0 '***' 0.001 '**' 0.01 '*' 0.05 '.' 0.1 ' ' 1
##
## Residual standard error: 0.1559523
## Multiple R-squared: 0.8673817
##
## Elasticity of Substitution:
##               Estimate Std. Error  t value   Pr(>|t|)
## E_1_2 (all)    0.74292    0.09558    7.773   7.66e-15 ***
## —
## Signif. codes:  0 '***' 0.001 '**' 0.01 '*' 0.05 '.' 0.1 ' ' 1
```

4.   IMPLEMENTATION

The function `cesEst` is the primary user interface of the **micEconCES** package (Henningsen and Henningsen, 2021). However, the actual estimations are carried out by internal helper functions, or functions from other packages.

4.1   Kmenta Approximation

The estimation of the Kmenta approximation (20.5) is implemented in the internal function `cesEstKmenta`. This function uses `translogEst` from the **micEcon** package (Henningsen, 2021) to estimate the unrestricted translog function (20.6). The test of the parameter restrictions defined in equation (20.7) is performed by the function `linearHypothesis` of the **car** package (Fox and Weisberg, 2011, 2020). The restricted translog model defined in equations (20.6) and (20.7) is estimated with function `systemfit` from the **systemfit** package (Henningsen and Hamann, 2007, 2019).

4.2   Non-Linear Least-Squares Estimation

The non-linear least-squares estimations are carried out by various optimisers from other packages. Estimations with the Levenberg–Marquardt algorithm are performed by function `nls.lm` of the **minpack.lm** package (Elzhov et al., 2016), which is an R interface to the `Fortran` package **MINPACK** (Moré et al., 1980). Estimations with the "Conjugate Gradients" (CG), BFGS, Nelder–Mead (NM), Simulated Annealing (SANN) and L-BFGS-B algorithms use the function `optim` from the **stats** package (R Core Team, 2020). Estimations with the Newton-type algorithm are performed by function `nlm` from the **stats** package (R Core Team, 2020), which uses the `Fortran` library **UNCMIN** (Schnabel et al., 1985) with a line search as the step selection strategy. Estimations with the DE algorithm are performed by function `DEoptim` from the **DEoptim** package (Mullen et al., 2011; Ardia et al., 2020). Estimations with the PORT routines use function `nlminb` from the **stats** package (R Core Team, 2020), which uses the `Fortran` library **PORT** (Gay, 1990).

4.3   Grid Search

If the user calls `cesEst` with at least one of the arguments `rho1`, `rho2` or `rho` being a vector, `cesEst` calls the internal function `cesEstGridRho`, which implements the actual grid search procedure. For each combination (grid point) of the pre-selected values of the substitution parameters (ρ_1, ρ_2, ρ), on which the grid search should be performed, the function `cesEstGridRho` consecutively calls `cesEst`. In each of these internal calls of `cesEst`, the parameters on which no grid search should be performed (and which are not fixed by the user) are estimated given the particular combination of substitution parameters, on which the grid search should be performed. This is done by setting the arguments of `cesEst`, for which the user has specified vectors of pre-selected values of the substitution parameters (`rho1`, `rho2` and/or `rho`) to the particular elements of these vectors. As `cesEst` is called with arguments `rho1`, `rho2` and `rho` being all single scalars (or NULL if the corresponding substitution parameter is neither included in the grid search nor fixed at a predefined value), it estimates the CES function by non-linear least-squares with the corresponding substitution parameters (ρ_1, ρ_2 and/or ρ) fixed at the values specified in the corresponding arguments.

4.4 Calculating Output and the Sum of Squared Residuals

Function cesCalc can be used to calculate the output quantity of the CES function given input quantities and parameters. A few examples of using cesCalc are shown in the beginning of section 3, where this function is applied to generate the output variables of an artificial data set for demonstrating the usage of cesEst. Furthermore, the cesCalc function is called by the internal function cesRss that calculates and returns the sum of squared residuals, which is the objective function in the non-linear least-squares estimations. If at least one substitution parameter (ρ_1, ρ_2, ρ) is equal to zero, the CES functions are not defined. In this case, cesCalc returns the limit of the output quantity for ρ_1, ρ_2 and/or ρ approaching zero.[12] In case of nested CES functions with three or four inputs, function cesCalc calls the internal functions cesCalcN3 or cesCalcN4 for the actual calculations.

Henningsen and Henningsen (2012) show that the calculations of the output quantities using equations (20.1), (20.3) or (20.4) are imprecise if at least one of the substitution parameters (ρ_1, ρ_2, ρ) is close to 0. This is caused by rounding errors that are unavoidable on digital computers, but are usually negligible. However, rounding errors can become large in specific circumstances, for example, in CES functions with very small (in absolute terms) substitution parameters, when first very small (in absolute terms) exponents (for example, $-\rho_1$, $-\rho_2$ or $-\rho$) and then very large (in absolute terms) exponents (for example, $\rho/\rho_1, \rho/\rho_2$ or $-\nu/\rho$) are applied (Henningsen and Henningsen, 2012). Therefore, for non-nested CES functions (20.1) and (20.2), cesCalc uses a first-order Taylor series approximation at the point $\rho = 0$ for calculating the output, if the absolute value of ρ is smaller than, or equal to, argument rhoApprox, which is $5 \cdot 10^{-6}$ by default. In case of nested CES functions (20.3) and (20.4), if at least one substitution parameter (ρ_1, ρ_2, ρ) is close to zero, cesCalc uses linear interpolation in order to avoid rounding errors. In this case, cesCalc calculates the output quantities for two different values of each substitution parameter that is close to zero, that is, zero (using the formula for the limit for this parameter approaching zero) and the positive or negative value of argument rhoApprox (using the same sign as this parameter). Depending on the number of substitution parameters (ρ_1, ρ_2, ρ) that are close to zero, a one-, two- or three-dimensional linear interpolation is applied. These interpolations are performed by the internal functions cesInterN3 and cesInterN4 (see Henningsen and Henningsen (2011) or the documentation of function cesEst for a more detailed description of the procedure).[13]

When estimating a CES function with function cesEst, the user can use argument rhoApprox to modify the threshold for calculating the dependent variable by the Taylor series approximation or linear interpolation. Argument rhoApprox of cesEst must be a numeric vector, where the first element is passed to cesCalc (partly through cesRss). This might not only affect the fitted values and residuals returned by cesEst (if at least one of the estimated substitution parameters is close to zero), but also the estimation results (if one of the substitution parameters was close to zero in one of the steps of the iterative optimisation procedure).

4.5 Partial Derivatives with Respect to Parameters

The internal function `cesDerivCoef` returns the partial derivatives of the CES function with respect to all parameters at all provided data points. For the traditional two-input CES function, these partial derivatives are

$$\frac{\partial y}{\partial \gamma} = e^{\lambda t}\left(\delta x_1^{-\rho} + (1-\delta)x_2^{-\rho}\right)^{-\frac{\nu}{\rho}} \tag{20.17}$$

$$\frac{\partial y}{\partial \lambda} = \gamma\, t\, \frac{\partial y}{\partial \gamma} \tag{20.18}$$

$$\frac{\partial y}{\partial \delta} = -\gamma e^{\lambda t}\frac{\nu}{\rho}\left(x_1^{-\rho} - x_2^{-\rho}\right)\left(\delta x_1^{-\rho} + (1-\delta)x_2^{-\rho}\right)^{-\frac{\nu}{\rho}-1} \tag{20.19}$$

$$\frac{\partial y}{\partial \rho} = \gamma e^{\lambda t}\frac{\nu}{\rho^2}\ln\left(\delta x_1^{-\rho} + (1-\delta)x_2^{-\rho}\right)\left(\delta x_1^{-\rho} + (1-\delta)x_2^{-\rho}\right)^{-\frac{\nu}{\rho}} \tag{20.20}$$

$$+\gamma e^{\lambda t}\frac{\nu}{\rho}\left(\delta \ln(x_1)x_1^{-\rho} + (1-\delta)\ln(x_2)x_2^{-\rho}\right)\left(\delta x_1^{-\rho} + (1-\delta)x_2^{-\rho}\right)^{-\frac{\nu}{\rho}-1}$$

$$\frac{\partial y}{\partial \nu} = -\gamma e^{\lambda t}\frac{1}{\rho}\ln\left(\delta x_1^{-\rho} + (1-\delta)x_2^{-\rho}\right)\left(\delta x_1^{-\rho} + (1-\delta)x_2^{-\rho}\right)^{-\frac{\nu}{\rho}}. \tag{20.21}$$

These derivatives are not defined for $\rho = 0$ and are imprecise if ρ is close to zero (similar to the output variable of the CES function; see section 4.4). Therefore, if ρ is zero or close to zero, we calculate these derivatives by first-order Taylor series approximations at the point $\rho = 0$ using the limits for ρ approaching zero:[14]

$$\frac{\partial y}{\partial \gamma} = e^{\lambda t}x_1^{\nu\delta}\, x_2^{\nu(1-\delta)}\exp\left(-\frac{\rho}{2}\nu\delta(1-\delta)\left(\ln x_1 - \ln x_2\right)^2\right) \tag{20.22}$$

$$\frac{\partial y}{\partial \delta} = \gamma e^{\lambda t}\nu\left(\ln x_1 - \ln x_2\right)x_1^{\nu\delta}\, x_2^{\nu(1-\delta)} \tag{20.23}$$

$$\left(1 - \frac{\rho}{2}[1 - 2\delta + \nu\delta(1-\delta)\left(\ln x_1 - \ln x_2\right)]\left(\ln x_1 - \ln x_2\right)\right)$$

$$\frac{\partial y}{\partial \rho} = \gamma e^{\lambda t}\nu\delta(1-\delta)x_1^{\nu\delta}\, x_2^{\nu(1-\delta)}\left(-\frac{1}{2}\left(\ln x_1 - \ln x_2\right)^2\right. \tag{20.24}$$

$$\left. +\frac{\rho}{3}(1-2\delta)\left(\ln x_1 - \ln x_2\right)^3 + \frac{\rho}{4}\nu\delta(1-\delta)\left(\ln x_1 - \ln x_2\right)^4\right)$$

$$\frac{\partial y}{\partial v} = \gamma e^{\lambda t} x_1^{\nu\delta} x_2^{\nu(1-\delta)} \bigg(\delta \ln x_1 + (1-\delta) \ln x_2 - $$

$$ -\frac{\rho}{2}\delta(1-\delta)\big(\ln x_1 - \ln x_2\big)^2 \big[1 + \nu\big(\delta \ln x_1 + (1-\delta)\ln x_2\big)\big]\bigg). \tag{20.25}$$

If ρ is zero or close to zero, the partial derivatives with respect to λ are calculated also with equation (20.18), but now $\partial y/\partial \gamma$ is calculated with equation (20.22) instead of equation (20.17).

The partial derivatives of the nested CES functions with three and four inputs with respect to the parameters are presented in Appendices B.2 and C.2 of Henningsen and Henningsen (2011), respectively. If at least one substitution parameter (ρ_1, ρ_2, ρ) is exactly zero or close to zero, cesDerivCoef uses the same approach as cesCalc to avoid large rounding errors, that is, using the limit for these parameters approaching zero and potentially a one-, two- or three-dimensional linear interpolation. The limits of the partial derivatives of the nested CES functions for one or more substitution parameters approaching zero are also presented in Appendices B.2 and C.2 of Henningsen and Henningsen (2011). The calculation of the partial derivatives and their limits are performed by several internal functions with names starting with cesDerivCoefN3 and cesDerivCoefN4.[15] The one- or more-dimensional linear interpolations are (again) performed by the internal functions cesInterN3 and cesInterN4.

Function cesDerivCoef has an argument rhoApprox that can be used to specify the threshold levels for defining when ρ_1, ρ_2 and ρ are "close" to zero. This argument must be a numeric vector with exactly four elements: the first element defines the threshold for $\partial y/\partial \gamma$ (default value $5 \cdot 10^{-6}$), the second element defines the threshold for $\partial y/\partial \delta_1$, $\partial y/\partial \delta_2$ and $\partial y/\partial \delta$ (default value $5 \cdot 10^{-6}$), the third element defines the threshold for $\partial y/\partial \rho_1$, $\partial y/\partial \rho_1$ and $\partial y/\partial \rho$ (default value 10^{-3}) and the fourth element defines the threshold for $\partial y/\partial v$ (default value $5 \cdot 10^{-6}$).

Function cesDerivCoef is used to provide argument jac (which should be set to a function that returns the Jacobian of the residuals) to function nls.lm so that the Levenberg–Marquardt algorithm can use analytical derivatives of each residual with respect to all parameters. Furthermore, function cesDerivCoef is used by the internal function cesRssDeriv, which calculates the partial derivatives of the sum of squared residuals (RSS= $\sum_{i=1}^{N} \hat{u}_i^2$) with respect to all parameters by

$$\frac{\partial \text{RSS}}{\partial \theta} = -2 \sum_{i=1}^{N} \bigg(\hat{u}_i \frac{\partial y_i}{\partial \theta} \bigg), \tag{20.26}$$

with $\hat{u}_i = y_i - \hat{y}_i$ for estimations with additive error term and

$$\frac{\partial \text{RSS}}{\partial \theta} = -2 \sum_{i=1}^{N} \bigg(\frac{\hat{u}_i}{\hat{y}_i} \frac{\partial y_i}{\partial \theta} \bigg), \tag{20.27}$$

with $\hat{u}_i = \ln y_i - \ln \hat{y}_i$ for estimations with multiplicative error term, where N is the number of observations, $\hat{u}_i$ is the residual of the ith observation, $\hat{y}_i$ is the "fitted" output quantity of the ith observation, $\theta \in \{\gamma, \delta_1, \delta_2, \delta, \rho_1, \rho_2, \rho, v\}$ is a parameter of the CES function and $\partial y/\partial \theta$ is the partial derivative of the CES function with respect to parameter θ evaluated at the ith observation as returned by function cesDerivCoef. Function cesRssDeriv is used to provide analytical gradients for the other gradient-based optimisation algorithms, that is, conjugate gradients, Newton-type, BFGS, L-BFGS-B and PORT. Finally, function `cesDerivCoef` is used to obtain the gradient matrix for calculating the asymptotic covariance matrix of the non-linear least-squares estimator (see section 4.6).

When estimating a CES function with function `cesEst`, the user can use argument `rhoApprox` to specify the thresholds below which the derivatives with respect to the parameters are approximated by Taylor series approximations or linear interpolations. Argument `rhoApprox` of `cesEst` must be a numeric vector of five elements, where the second to the fifth element of this vector are passed to `cesDerivCoef`. The choice of the threshold might not only affect the covariance matrix of the estimates (if at least one of the estimated substitution parameters is close to zero), but also the estimation results obtained by a gradient-based optimisation algorithm (if one of the substitution parameters is close to zero in one of the steps of the iterative optimisation procedure).

4.6 Covariance Matrix

The asymptotic covariance matrix of the non-linear least-squares estimator obtained by the various iterative optimisation methods is calculated by:

$$\hat{\sigma}^2 \left(\left(\frac{\partial y}{\partial \theta} \right)^{\mathrm{T}} \frac{\partial y}{\partial \theta} \right)^{-1} \tag{20.28}$$

(Greene, 2008, p. 292), where $\partial y / \partial \theta$ denotes the $N \times k$ gradient matrix (defined in equations (20.17) to (20.21) for the traditional two-input CES function and in Appendices B.2 and C.2 of Henningsen and Henningsen (2011) for the nested CES functions), N is the number of observations, k is the number of parameters and $\hat{\sigma}^2$ denotes the estimated variance of the residuals. As equation (20.28) is only valid asymptotically, we calculate the estimated variance of the residuals by:

$$\hat{\sigma}^2 = \frac{1}{N} \sum_{i=1}^{N} \hat{u}_i^2, \tag{20.29}$$

that is, without correcting for degrees of freedom.

4.7 Starting Values

If the user calls `cesEst` with argument `start` set to a vector of starting values, the internal function `cesEstStart` checks if the number of starting values is correct and if the individual starting values are in the appropriate range of the corresponding parameters. If no starting values are provided by the user, function `cesEstStart` determines the starting values automatically. The starting values of δ_1, δ_2 and δ are set to 0.5. If the parameters ρ_1, ρ_2 and ρ are estimated (not fixed as, for example, during grid search), their starting values are set to 0.25, which generally corresponds to an elasticity of substitution of 0.8. The starting value of v is set to 1, which corresponds to constant returns to scale. If the CES function includes a time variable, the starting value of λ is set to 0.015, which corresponds to a technological progress of 1.5 per cent per time period. Finally, the starting value of γ is set to a value so that the mean of the residuals is equal to zero, that is:

$$\gamma = \frac{\sum_{i=1}^{N} y_i}{\sum_{i=1}^{N} CES_i},$$

(20.30)

where CES_i indicates the (nested) CES function evaluated at the input quantities of the ith observation and with parameter γ equal to one, all "fixed" parameters (for example, ρ_1, ρ_2 or ρ) equal to their pre-selected values, and all other parameters equal to the above-described starting values.

4.8   Other Internal Functions

The internal function `cesCoefAddRho` is used to add the values of ρ_1, ρ_2 and ρ to the vector of parameters, if these parameters are fixed (for example, during grid search for ρ) and hence are not included in the vector of estimated parameters.

   If the user selects the optimisation algorithm DE, L-BFGS-B or PORT, but does not specify lower or upper bounds of the parameters, the internal function `cesCoefBounds` creates and returns the default bounds depending on the optimisation algorithm as described in sections 3.3 and 3.4.

   The internal function `cesCoefNames` returns a vector of character strings, which are the names of the parameters of the CES function.

   The internal function `cesCheckRhoApprox` checks argument `rhoApprox` of functions `cesEst`, `cesDerivCoef`, `cesRss` and `cesRssDeriv`.

4.9   Methods

The **micEconCES** package makes use of the "S3" class system of the R language introduced in Chambers and Hastie (1992). Objects returned by function `cesEst` are of class `"cesEst"` and the **micEconCES** package includes several methods for objects of this class. The `print` method prints the call, the estimated parameters and the estimated elasticities of substitution. The `coef`, `vcov`, `fitted` and `residuals` methods extract and return the estimated parameters, their covariance matrix, the fitted values and the residuals, respectively.

   The plot method can only be applied if the model is estimated by grid search (see section 3.6). If the model is estimated by a one-dimensional grid search for ρ_1, ρ_2 or ρ, this method plots a simple scatter plot of the pre-selected values against the corresponding sums of the squared residuals by using the commands `plot.default` and `points` of the graphics package (R Core Team, 2020). In case of a two-dimensional grid search, the plot method draws a perspective plot by using the command `persp` of the graphics package (R Core Team, 2020) and the command `colorRampPalette` of the **grDevices** package (R Core Team, 2020) (for generating a colour gradient). In case of a three-dimensional grid search, the `plot` method plots three perspective plots by holding one of the three parameters ρ_1, ρ_2 and ρ constant in each of the three plots.

The `summary` method calculates the estimated standard error of the residuals ($\hat{\sigma}$), the covariance matrix of the estimated parameters and elasticities of substitution, the R^2 value as well as the standard errors, t-values and marginal significance levels (P-values) of the estimated parameters and elasticities of substitution. The object returned by the `summary` method is of class `"summary.cesEst"`. The `print` method for objects of class `"summary.cesEst"` prints the call, the estimated parameters and elasticities of substitution, their standard errors, t-values and marginal significance levels as well as some information on the estimation procedure (for example, algorithm, convergence). The `coef` method for objects of class `"summary.cesEst"` returns a matrix with four columns containing the estimated parameters, their standard errors, t-values and marginal significance levels, respectively.

5. EMPIRICAL ILLUSTRATION

This section provides an empirical illustration of the use of the **micEconCES** package for estimating a CES production function with a real-world microeconomic data set using various non-linear estimation procedures. To the best of our knowledge, empirical studies that estimate non-linear CES functions have so far only used macroeconomic data sets (for example, Kemfert, 1998; Masanjala and Papageorgiou, 2004; Sun et al., 2011; Fragiadakis et al., 2012; Shen and Whalley, 2013; Koesler and Schymura, 2015; Henningsen et al., 2019). In contrast to these studies, our empirical illustration uses a firm-level panel data set that is a revised version of the data set used in Kumbhakar and Wang (2006). This data set is available at the companion website to Kumbhakar et al. (2015)[16] and also as data set `utility` in the R package **micEcon** (Henningsen, 2021). This data set includes input and output quantities of 72 investor-owned steam electric power generation plants in the United States in the period from 1986 to 1996 with a total of 791 observations. The output of the electric power generation plants is the volume of electricity generated in MWh and the inputs are capital, labour (including maintenance) and fuel. A more detailed description of the data set is available in section 4 of Kumbhakar and Wang (2006).

As the output quantities have a very wide range of values across the various power plants, the assumption of a homoscedastic additive error term is unsuitable. Therefore, we assume a multiplicative error term in our estimations (see section 3.7). Furthermore, in order to reduce rounding errors, we mean scale all input quantities and the output quantity so that their values are centred around one, where rounding errors are supposed to be smallest in relative terms. In order to allow for Hicks-neutral technological change, we use the year as an additional explanatory variable as defined in equation (20.13). Finally, as there are no reasons for assuming that electric power generation plants operate under constant returns to scale, we allow for non-constant returns to scale by estimating the parameter v (instead of setting it *a priori* to one, which would imply constant returns to scale).

We estimate the CES production function with all three possible nesting structures: (capital–labour)–fuel, (capital–fuel)–labour and (labour–fuel)–capital. Each of these three nesting structures we estimate with eleven different estimation procedures. First, we estimate the CES functions with five optimisation algorithms: LM, BFGS, L-BFGS-B, PORT and NM. Then, we apply grid searches for the substitution parameters (ρ_1 and ρ) and use three different optimisation algorithms for estimating the remaining parameters: LM, BFGS and PORT.

Finally, we use again the three optimisation algorithms LM, BFGS and PORT but this time we use the estimates of the corresponding grid-search procedures as starting values. The R code for estimating the three nesting structures with the mentioned estimation procedures is provided in Appendix 20A.1.

Table 20.1 indicates that for the nesting structure (capital–labour)–fuel, estimation results with an economically not meaningful value of $\rho_1 < -1$ give the lowest sum of squared residuals. If the estimation procedure restricts ρ_1 to be in the economically mean-ingful region, its estimate is -1, which indicates perfect substitutability between capital and labour. All eleven estimation procedures result in very similar parameter estimates except for some differences in ρ_1 and ρ between estimation procedures that restrict parameters to be in the economically meaningful region and estimation procedures that do not restrict the parameters.

Table 20.2 presents the estimation results with the nesting structure (capital–fuel)–labour. The Nelder–Mead algorithm does not find the global minimum of the sum of squared residuals and returns estimates that are economically not meaningful. However, the other ten estimation procedures all return economically meaningful estimates and these estimates are very similar for the different estimation procedures.

Table 20.3 indicates that all eleven estimation procedures give very similar—and economically meaningful—parameter estimates for the nesting structure (labour–fuel)–capital.

As all nesting structures use the same dependent variable and have the same number of parameters to be estimated, we can compare the suitability of the three nesting structures by comparing the sums of squared residuals between the three nesting structures. Our results indicate that the nesting structure (capital–fuel)–labour (Table 20.2) generally gives the small-est sum of squared residuals. Hence, it seems that this nesting structure is the most suitable nesting structure for our empirical analysis.

When using this nesting structure, the LM, BFGS and PORT optimisation algorithms—no matter whether used with the default starting values (see section 4.7) or with starting values obtained by a grid search—all give the lowest sum of squared residuals and virtually the same parameter estimates. We use the estimates obtained with the Levenberg–Marquardt optimisa-tion algorithm to present the summary output of one arbitrarily chosen estimation that gives the lowest sum of squared residuals:[17]

```
summary(results[[2]]$LM)
## Estimated CES function with variable returns to scale
##
## Call:
## cesEst(yName = "y", xNames = inputs, data = utility, tName =
## "year",
##    vrs = TRUE, method = "LM", multErr = TRUE)
##
## Estimation by non-linear least-squares using the 'LM'
## optimizer assuming a multiplicative error term
## Convergence achieved after 8 iterations
## Message: Relative error in the sum of squares is at most
## 'ftol'.
##
```

Table 20.1 Estimation results for the nesting structure (capital–labour)–fuel

	γ	λ	δ_1	δ	ρ_1	ρ	ν	c	RSS	R^2
LM	0.2815	0.0141	0.6376	0.4166	−1.3667	1.5300	0.9593	1	52.5869	0.9232
NM	0.2617	0.0150	0.6353	0.4173	−1.2930	1.5758	0.9589	1	52.5929	0.9232
BFGS	0.2815	0.0141	0.6376	0.4166	−1.3668	1.5314	0.9593	1	52.5869	0.9232
L-BFGS-B	**0.2732**	**0.0145**	**0.6242**	**0.4159**	**−1.0000**	**1.6795**	**0.9582**	**1**	**52.6077**	**0.9232**
PORT	**0.2803**	**0.0142**	**0.6219**	**0.4146**	**−1.0000**	**1.6903**	**0.9581**	**1**	**52.6067**	**0.9232**
LM grid	**0.2811**	**0.0142**	**0.6231**	**0.4149**	**−1.0000**	**1.7500**	**0.9578**	**1**	**52.6072**	**0.9232**
LM grid start	0.2815	0.0141	0.6376	0.4166	−1.3664	1.5308	0.9593	1	52.5869	0.9232
BFGS grid	**0.2816**	**0.0142**	**0.6229**	**0.4150**	**−1.0000**	**1.7500**	**0.9579**	**1**	**52.6072**	**0.9232**
BFGS grid start	0.2816	0.0142	0.6229	0.4150	−1.0000	1.7500	0.9579	1	52.6072	0.9232
PORT grid	**0.2811**	**0.0142**	**0.6231**	**0.4149**	**−1.0000**	**1.7500**	**0.9578**	**1**	**52.6072**	**0.9232**
PORT grid start	**0.2811**	**0.0142**	**0.6231**	**0.4149**	**−1.0000**	**1.7500**	**0.9578**	**0**	**52.6072**	**0.9232**

Notes: The first column indicates the optimisation procedure with "LM" = Levenberg–Marquardt, "NM" = Nelder–Mead, "BFGS" = Broyden–Fletcher–Goldfarb–Shanno, "L-BFGS-B" = BFGS with box-constraints and "PORT" = PORT routines, where the addition "grid" indicates a grid search for ρ_1 and ρ and the addition "start grid" indicates that the parameters obtained by the grid search are used as starting values. The seven following columns indicate the estimated parameters. Column "c" indicates whether the optimisation routine reports that the optimisation procedure successfully converged (value "1") or it did not converge (value "0"). Column "RSS" indicates the sum of squared residuals and column "R^2" indicates the R^2-value of the regression. Bold font indicates that the estimation results are economically meaningful; that is, $\gamma \geq 0$, $\delta_1 \in [0, 1]$, $\delta \in [0, 1]$, $\rho_1 \geq -1$, $\rho \geq -1$ and $\nu \geq 0$.

Table 20.2   Estimation results for the nesting structure (capital–fuel)–labour

	γ	λ	δ_1	δ	ρ_1	ρ	ν	c	RSS	R^2
LM	0.2504	0.0155	0.1814	0.8469	3.0534	−0.8753	0.9553	1	52.1889	0.9238
NM	0.1801	0.0190	0.2202	0.8564	1.9521	−1.0197	0.9573	1	52.4229	0.9234
BFGS	0.2504	0.0155	0.1814	0.8470	3.0536	−0.8755	0.9553	1	52.1889	0.9238
L-BFGS-B	0.2496	0.0155	0.1812	0.8445	3.0387	−0.8394	0.9554	1	52.1897	0.9238
PORT	0.2504	0.0155	0.1814	0.8470	3.0534	−0.8755	0.9553	1	52.1889	0.9238
LM grid	0.2526	0.0154	0.1859	0.8560	3.0000	−1.0000	0.9552	1	52.1967	0.9238
LM grid start	0.2504	0.0155	0.1815	0.8470	3.0533	−0.8759	0.9553	1	52.1889	0.9238
BFGS grid	0.2526	0.0154	0.1859	0.8560	3.0000	−1.0000	0.9552	1	52.1967	0.9238
BFGS grid start	0.2504	0.0155	0.1814	0.8470	3.0536	−0.8756	0.9553	1	52.1889	0.9238
PORT grid	0.2526	0.0154	0.1859	0.8560	3.0000	−1.0000	0.9552	1	52.1967	0.9238
PORT grid start	0.2504	0.0155	0.1814	0.8470	3.0534	−0.8755	0.9553	1	52.1889	0.9238

Notes: See notes below Table 20.1.

Table 20.3 Estimation results for the nesting structure (labour–fuel)–capital

	γ	λ	δ_1	δ	ρ_1	ρ	ν	c	RSS	R^2
LM	0.2503	0.0154	0.2000	0.8481	−0.2792	1.6519	0.9564	1	53.5333	0.9218
NM	0.2634	0.0148	0.1903	0.8239	−0.4428	0.7637	0.9597	1	53.7204	0.9216
BFGS	0.2502	0.0154	0.2000	0.8481	−0.2792	1.6524	0.9564	1	53.5333	0.9218
L-BFGS-B	0.2546	0.0152	0.1868	0.8370	−0.5034	1.3175	0.9578	1	53.5866	0.9217
PORT	0.2503	0.0154	0.2000	0.8481	−0.2792	1.6522	0.9564	1	53.5333	0.9218
LM grid	0.2501	0.0155	0.2012	0.8513	−0.2500	1.7500	0.9559	1	53.5355	0.9218
LM grid start	0.2503	0.0154	0.2000	0.8481	−0.2792	1.6520	0.9564	1	53.5333	0.9218
BFGS grid	0.2502	0.0154	0.2012	0.8513	−0.2500	1.7500	0.9559	1	53.5355	0.9218
BFGS grid start	0.2502	0.0154	0.2012	0.8513	−0.2500	1.7500	0.9559	1	53.5355	0.9218
PORT grid	0.2501	0.0155	0.2012	0.8513	−0.2500	1.7500	0.9559	1	53.5355	0.9218
PORT grid start	0.2503	0.0154	0.2000	0.8481	−0.2792	1.6522	0.9564	1	53.5333	0.9218

Notes: See notes below Table 20.1.

```
## Coefficients:
##              Estimate  Std. Error  t value   Pr(>|t|)
## gamma        0.250360    0.067442    3.712   0.000205 ***
## lambda       0.015469    0.002958    5.229   1.71e-07 ***
## delta_1      0.181431    0.050275    3.609   0.000308 ***
## delta        0.846944    0.027809   30.456   < 2e-16  ***
## rho_1        3.053354    1.016342    3.004   0.002662 **
## rho         -0.875347    0.300331   -2.915   0.003561 **
## nu           0.955343    0.010316   92.607   < 2e-16  ***
## -
## Signif. codes:  0 '***' 0.001 '**' 0.01 '*' 0.05 '.' 0.1 ' ' 1
##
## Residual standard error: 0.2568627
## Multiple R-squared: 0.9237908
##
## Elasticities of Substitution:
##                    Estimate Std. Error  t value   Pr(>|t|)
## E_1_2 (HM)          0.24671    0.06186    3.988   6.66e-05 ***
## E_(1,2)_3 (AU)      8.02226   19.32828    0.415     0.678
## -
## Signif. codes:  0 '***' 0.001 '**' 0.01 '*' 0.05 '.' 0.1 ' ' 1
## HM = Hicks-McFadden (direct) elasticity of substitution
## AU = Allen-Uzawa (partial) elasticity of substitution
```

The relatively large estimate of ρ_1, and thus the relatively small value of the Hicks–McFadden (direct) elasticity of substitution between capital and fuel indicates that it is rather difficult for electric power generation plants to substitute capital for fuel, and vice versa. In contrast, the estimate of ρ being close to -1, and thus the rather large Allen–Uzawa (partial) elasticity of substitution between labour and the aggregate of capital and fuel indicates that it is rather easy for electric power generation plants to substitute labour for the aggregate of capital and fuel, and vice versa. However, the relatively large standard errors of ρ and of the Allen–Uzawa (partial) elasticity of substitution between labour and the aggregate of capital and fuel indicate that the estimation of the substitutability between labour and the aggregate of capital and fuel is likely rather imprecise.

The estimate of the parameter λ indicates that there has been a statistically significant Hicks-neutral technological progress in the technology of steam electric power generation with an annual rate of around 1.55 per cent in our sampling period of 1986–96.

The estimate of the parameter ν indicates that the elasticity of scale is around 0.955, that is, the technology of steam electric power generation exhibits decreasing returns scale. As the difference between the estimate of the parameter ν and one (around 0.045) is larger than four times the standard error of this parameter (around 0.0103), we can conclude that a t-test rejects constant returns to scale at any conventional significance level.

The following command creates a 3D-plot that illustrates how the fit of the model (in terms of the sum of squared residuals) depends on the values of the substitution parameters ρ_1 and ρ:

```
plot(results[[2]]$LM_GS, bw = TRUE)
```

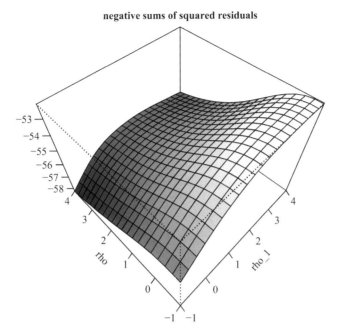

Figure 20.5   Sums of squared residuals for different values of the substitution parameters in the nesting structure (capital–fuel)–labour

The resulting graph is presented in Figure 20.5. It shows that the objective function of the optimisation procedure (that is, the sum of squared residuals) is rather well behaved but that values for the substitution parameter ρ_1 between two and four result in very similar sums of squared residuals.

6.   CONCLUSION

In recent years, the CES function has gained in popularity, particularly in macroeconomics and growth theory, as it is clearly more flexible than the classical Cobb–Douglas function. As the CES function is not easy to estimate, given an objective function that is seldom well behaved, a software solution to estimate the CES function may further increase its popularity.

The **micEconCES** package provides such a solution. Its function cesEst can not only estimate the traditional two-input CES function, but also all major extensions, that is, three-input and four-input nested CES functions as well as these functional forms with Hicks-neutral technological change. Furthermore, the **micEconCES** package provides the user with a multitude of estimation and optimisation procedures, which include the linear approximation suggested by Kmenta (1967), gradient-based and global optimisation algorithms, and a grid-search procedure that returns stable results and alleviates convergence problems. Additionally, the user can impose restrictions on the parameters to enforce economically meaningful parameter estimates.

The function cesEst is constructed in a way that users can easily switch between different estimation and optimisation procedures. This allows users to use several different methods and compare the results. The grid search procedure, in particular, increases the probability of finding a global optimum. Additionally, the grid search allows one to plot the objective function for different values of the substitution parameters (ρ_1, ρ_2, ρ). In doing so, the user can visualise the surface of the objective function to be minimised and, hence, check the extent to which the objective function is well behaved and which parameter ranges of the substitution parameters give the best fit. This option is a further control instrument to ensure that the global optimum has been reached.

The **micEconCES** package is open-source software and modularly programmed, which makes it easy for the user to extend and modify it (for example, including factor-augmented technological change). Moreover, even if some readers choose not to use the **micEconCES** package for estimating a CES function, they will definitely benefit from the insights and practical hints regarding the estimation of CES functions in this chapter.

NOTES

*   The authors thank Frits Møller Andersen for valuable comments on earlier versions of this chapter.

1.   For instance, in production economics, the elasticity of substitution measures the substitutability between inputs. It has non-negative values, where an elasticity of substitution of zero indicates that no substitution is possible (for example, between wheels and frames in the production of bikes) and an elasticity of substitution of infinity indicates that the inputs are perfect substitutes (for example, electricity from two different power plants).

2.   The *Journal of Macroeconomics* published an entire special issue titled "The CES Production Function in the Theory and Empirics of Economic Growth" (Klump and Papageorgiou, 2008).

3.   The CES functional form can be used to model different economic relationships (for example, as production function, cost function or utility function). However, as the CES functional form is mostly used to model production technologies, we name the dependent (left-hand side) variable "output" and the explanatory (right-hand side) variables "inputs" to keep the notation simple.

4.   Originally, the CES function of Arrow et al. (1961) could only model constant returns to scale, but later Kmenta (1967) added the parameter v, which allows for decreasing or increasing returns to scale if $v < 1$ or $v > 1$, respectively.

5.   In this case, the parameters of the four-input nested CES function defined in equation (20.3) (indicated by the superscript n) and the parameters of the plain four-input CES function defined in equation (20.2) (indicated by the superscript p) correspond in the following way:
$\rho^p = \rho_1^n = \rho_2^n = \rho^n$, $\delta_1^p = \delta_1^n \delta^n$, $\delta_2^p = (1-\delta_1^n) \delta^n$, $\delta_3^p = \delta_2^n (1-\delta^n)$, $\delta_4^p = (1-\delta_2^n)(1-\delta^n)$, $\gamma^p = \gamma^n$, $\delta_1^n = \delta_1^p / (\delta_1^p + \delta_2^p)$, $\delta_2^n = \delta_3^p / (\delta_3^p + \delta_4^p)$ and $\delta^n = \delta_1^p + \delta_2^p$.

6.   Papageorgiou and Saam (2005) proposed a specification that includes the additional term $\gamma_1^{-\rho}$:
$$ y = \gamma \left[\delta \gamma_1^{-\rho} \left(\delta_1 x_1^{-\rho_1} + (1-\delta_1)x_2^{-\rho_1} \right)^{\rho/\rho_1} + (1-\delta)x_3^{-\rho} \right]^{-v/\rho} . $$
However, adding the term $\gamma_1^{-\rho}$ does not increase the flexibility of this function as γ_1 can be arbitrarily normalised to one; normalising γ_1 to one changes γ to $\gamma \left(\delta \gamma_1^{-\rho} + (1-\delta) \right)^{-(v/\rho)}$ and changes δ to $\left(\delta \gamma_1^{-\rho} \right) / \left(\delta \gamma_1^{-\rho} + (1-\delta) \right)$, but has no effect on the functional form. Hence, the parameters γ, γ_1 and δ cannot be (jointly) identified in econometric estimations (see also explanation for the four-input nested CES function above equation (20.3)).

7.   In this case, the parameters of the three-input nested CES function defined in equation (20.4) (indicated by the superscript n) and the parameters of the plain three-input CES function defined in equation (20.2) (indicated by the superscript p) correspond in the following way:
$\rho^p = \rho_1^n = \rho^n$, $\delta_1^p = \delta_1^n \delta^n$, $\delta_2^p = (1-\delta_1^n) \delta^n$, $\delta_3^p = 1-\delta^n$, $\gamma^p = \gamma^n$, $\delta_1^n = \delta_1^p / (1-\delta_3^p)$ and $\delta^n = 1-\delta_3^p$.

8.   Note that this test does *not* check whether the *non-linear* CES function (20.1) is an acceptable simplification of the translog functional form, or whether the *non-linear* CES function can be approximated by the Kmenta approximation.

9.   Note that this test does *not* compare the Cobb–Douglas function with the (non-linear) CES function, but only with its linear approximation.

10.   If the DE algorithm is used, parameter λ is by default restricted to the interval $[-0.5, 0.5]$, as this algorithm requires finite lower and upper bounds of all parameters. The user can use arguments `lower` and `upper` to modify these bounds.

11. This `plot` method can only be applied if the model was estimated by grid search.
12. The limit of the traditional two-input CES function (20.1) for ρ approaching zero is equal to the exponential function of the Kmenta approximation (20.5) calculated with $\rho = 0$. The limits of the three-input (20.4) and four-input (20.3) nested CES functions for ρ_1, ρ_2 and/or ρ approaching zero are presented in Appendices B.1 and C.1 of Henningsen and Henningsen (2011), respectively.
13. We use a different approach for the nested CES functions than for the traditional two-input CES function, because calculating Taylor series approximations of nested CES functions (and their derivatives with respect to parameters; see the following section) is very laborious and has no advantage over using linear interpolation.
14. The derivations of these formulas are presented in Appendix A.2 of Henningsen and Henningsen (2011).
15. The partial derivatives of the nested CES function with three inputs are calculated by `cesDerivCoefN3Gamma` ($\partial y/\partial \gamma$), `cesDerivCoefN3Lambda` ($\partial y/\partial \lambda$), `cesDerivCoefN3Delta1` ($\partial y/\partial \delta_1$), `cesDerivCoefN3Delta` ($\partial y/\partial \delta$), `cesDerivCoefN3Rho1` ($\partial y/\partial \rho_1$), `cesDerivCoefN3Rho` ($\partial y/\partial \rho$) and `cesDerivCoefN3Nu` ($\partial y/\partial v$) with helper functions `cesDerivCoefN3B1` (returning $B_1 = \delta_1 x_1^{-\rho_1} + (1-\delta_1) x_2^{-\rho_1}$), `cesDerivCoefN3L1` (returning $L_1 = \delta_1 \ln x_1 + (1 - \delta_1) \ln x_2$) and `cesDerivCoefN3B` (returning $B = \delta B_1^{\rho/\rho_1} + (1-\delta) x_3^{-\rho}$). The partial derivatives of the nested CES function with four inputs are calculated by `cesDerivCoefN4Gamma` ($\partial y/\partial \gamma$), `cesDerivCoefN4Lambda` ($\partial y/\partial \lambda$), `cesDerivCoefN4Delta1` ($\partial y/\partial \delta_1$), `cesDerivCoefN4Delta2` ($\partial y/\partial \delta_2$), `cesDerivCoefN4Delta` ($\partial y/\partial \delta$), `cesDerivCoefN4Rho1` ($\partial y/\partial \rho_1$), `cesDerivCoefN4Rho2` ($\partial y/\partial \rho_2$), `cesDerivCoefN4Rho` ($\partial y/\partial \rho$) and `cesDerivCoefN4Nu` ($\partial y/\partial v$) with helper functions `cesDerivCoefN4B1` (returning $B_1 = \delta_1 x_1^{-\rho_1} + (1-\delta_1) x_2^{-\rho_1}$), `cesDerivCoefN4L1` (returning $L_1 = \delta_1 \ln x_1 + (1-\delta_1) \ln x_2$), `cesDerivCoefN4B2` (returning $B_2 = \delta_2 x_3^{-\rho_2} + (1-\delta_2) x_4^{-\rho_2}$), `cesDerivCoefN4L2` (returning $L_1 = \delta_2 \ln x_3 + (1-\delta_2) \ln x_4$) and `cesDerivCoefN4B` (returning $B = \delta B_1^{\rho/\rho_1} + (1-\delta) B_2^{\rho/\rho_2}$).
16. https://sites.google.com/site/sfbook2014/.
17. The R script presented in Appendix Section 20A.1 must be run before the following command can be used.

REFERENCES

Acemoglu, D. (1998). Why do new technologies complement skills? Directed technical change and wage inequality. *The Quarterly Journal of Economics*, 113(4): 1055–89.

Ali, M. M. and Törn, A. (2004). Population set-based global optimization algorithms: Some modifications and numerical studies. *Computers & Operations Research*, 31(10): 1703–25.

Amras, P. (2004). Is the U.S. aggregate production function Cobb-Douglas? New estimates of the elasticity of substitution. *Contribution in Macroeconomics*, 4(1): Article 4.

Anderson, R. K. and Moroney, J. R. (1994). Substitution and complementarity in C.E.S. models. *Southern Economic Journal*, 60(4): 886–95.

Ardia, D., Mullen, K. M., Peterson, B. G., and Ulrich, J. (2020). *DEoptim: Global Optimization by Differential Evolution*. version 2.2-5.

Arrow, K. J., Chenery, B. H., Minhas, B. S., and Solow, R. M. (1961). Capital-labor substitution and economic efficiency. *The Review of Economics and Statistics*, 43(3): 225–50.

Beale, E. M. L. (1972). A derivation of conjugate gradients. In Lootsma, F. A., editor, *Numerical Methods for Nonlinear Optimization*, pp. 39–43. Academic Press, London.

Bélisle, C. J. P. (1992). Convergence theorems for a class of simulated annealing algorithms on Rd. *Journal of Applied Probability*, 29: 885–95.

Bentolila, S. J. and Gilles, S.-P. (2006). Explaining movements in the labour share. *Contributions to Macroeconomics*, 3(1): Article 9.

Blackorby, C. and Russel, R. R. (1989). Will the real elasticity of substitution please stand up? (a comparison of the Allan/Uzawa and Morishima elasticities). *The American Economic Review*, 79: 882–8.

Broyden, C. G. (1970). The convergence of a class of double-rank minimization algorithms. *Journal of the Institute of Mathematics and Its Applications*, 6: 76–90.

Byrd, R. H., Lu, P., Nocedal, J., and Zhu, C. (1995). A limited memory algorithm for bound constrained optimization. *SIAM Journal for Scientific Computing*, 16: 1190–208.

Caselli, F. (2005). Accounting for cross-country income differences. In Aghion, P. and Durlauf, S. N., editors, *Handbook of Economic Growth*, pp. 679–742. North Holland.

Caselli, F. and Coleman, Wilbur John, I. (2006). The world technology frontier. *The American Economic Review*, 96(3): 499–522.

Cerny, V. (1985). A thermodynamical approach to the travelling salesman problem: an efficient simulation algorithm. *Journal of Optimization Theory and Applications*, 45: 41–51.

Chambers, J. M. and Hastie, T. J. (1992). *Statistical Models in S*. Chapman & Hall, London.

Chambers, R. G. (1988). *Applied Production Analysis. A Dual Approach*. Cambridge University Press, Cambridge.

Chirinko, R. S. and Mallick, D. (2016). The substitution elasticity, factor shares, long-run growth, and the low-frequency panel model. Technical Report 4895, CESIFO Working Paper Series.

Cobb, C. W. and Douglas, P. H. (1928). A theory of production. *The American Economic Review*, 18(1): 139–65.

Davies, J. B. (2009). Combining microsimulation with CGE and macro modelling for distributional analysis in developing and transition countries. *International Journal of Microsimulation*, 49–65.

Dennis, J. E. and Schnabel, R. B. (1983). *Numerical Methods for Unconstrained Optimization and Nonlinear Equations*. Prentice-Hall, Englewood Cliffs (NJ, USA).

Duffy, F. and Walsh, P. P. (2000). A regional analysis of wage determination in Poland. Discussion Paper 87/2000, LICOS Centre for Transition Economics, Katholieke Universiteit Leuven.

Elzhov, T. V., Mullen, K. M., Spiess, A.-N., and Bolker, B. (2016). *minpack.lm: R Interface to the Levenberg-Marquardt Nonlinear Least-Squares Algorithm Found in MINPACK, Plus Support for Bounds*. R package version 1.2-1.

Fletcher, R. (1970). A new approach to variable metric algorithms. *Computer Journal*, 13: 317–22.

Fletcher, R. and Reeves, C. (1964). Function minimization by conjugate gradients. *Computer Journal*, 7: 48–154.

Fox, J. and Weisberg, S. (2011). *An R Companion to Applied Regression*. Sage, Thousand Oaks CA, 2nd edition.

Fox, J. and Weisberg, S. (2020). *car: Companion to Applied Regression*. R package version 3.0-10.

Fragiadakis, K., Paroussos, L., Kouvaritakis, N., and Capros, P. (2012). A multi–country econometric estimation of the constant elasticity of substitution. Technical report, E3M-Lab, Institute of Communication and Computer Systems, National Technical University of Athens, Paper prepared for the WIOD project.

Gay, D. M. (1990). Usage summary for selected optimization routines. Computing Science Technical Report 153, AT&T Bell Laboratories.

Goldfarb, D. (1970). A family of variable metric updates derived by variational means. *Mathematics of Computation*, 24: 23–6.

Greene, W. H. (2008). *Econometric Analysis*. Prentice Hall, 6th edition.

Griliches, Z. (1969). Capital-skill complementarity. *The Review of Economics and Statistics*, 51(4): 465–8.

Henningsen, A. (2021). *micEcon: Microeconomic Analysis and Modelling*. R package version 0.6-16, http://CRAN.R-project.org/package=micEcon.

Henningsen, A. and Hamann, J. D. (2007). systemfit: A package for estimating systems of simultaneous equations in R. *Journal of Statistical Software*, 23(4): 1–40.

Henningsen, A. and Hamann, J. D. (2019). *systemfit: Estimating Systems of Simultaneous Equations*. R package version 1.1-24, http://CRAN.R-project.org/package=systemfit.

Henningsen, A. and Henningsen, G. (2011). Econometric estimation of the "Constant Elasticity of Substitution" function in R: Package micEconCES. FOI Working Paper 2011/9, Institute of Food and Resource Economics, University of Copenhagen.

Henningsen, A. and Henningsen, G. (2012). On estimation of the CES production function—revisited. *Economics Letters*, 115(1): 67–9.

Henningsen, A. and Henningsen, G. (2021). *micEconCES: Analysis with the Constant Elasticity of Scale (CES) Function*. R package version 1.0-0, http://CRAN.R-project.org/package=micEconCES.

Henningsen, A., Henningsen, G., and van der Werf, E. (2019). Capital-labour-energy substitution in a nested CES framework: A replication and update of Kemfert (1998). *Energy Economics*, 82: 16–25.

Hoff, A. (2004). The linear approximation of the CES function with n input variables. *Marine Resource Economics*, 19: 295–306.

Kelley, C. T. (1999). *Iterative Methods of Optimization*. SIAM Society for Industrial and Applied Mathematics, Philadelphia.

Kemfert, C. (1998). Estimated substitution elasticities of a nested CES production function approach for Germany. *Energy Economics*, 20(3): 249–64.

Kirkpatrick, S., Gelatt, C. D., and Vecchi, M. P. (1983). Optimization by simulated annealing. *Science*, 220(4598): 671–80.

Klump, R., McAdam, P., and Willman, A. (2007). Factor substitution and factor-augmenting technical progress in the United States: A normalized supply-side system approach. *The Review of Economics and Statistics*, 89(1): 183–92.

Klump, R. and Papageorgiou, C. (2008). Editorial introduction: The CES production function in the theory and empirics of economic growth. *Journal of Macroeconomics*, 30(2): 599–600.

Kmenta, J. (1967). On estimation of the CES production function. *International Economic Review*, 8: 180–89.

Koesler, S. and Schymura, M. (2015). Substitution elasticities in a constant elasticity of substitution framework—empirical estimates using nonlinear least squares. *Economic Systems Research*, 27(1): 101–21.

Krusell, P., Ohanian, L. E., Ríos-Rull, J.-V., and Violante, G. L. (2000). Capital-skill complementarity and inequality: A macroeconomic analysis. *Econometrica*, 68(5): 1029–53.

Kumbhakar, S. C. and Wang, H.-J. (2006). Estimation of technical and allocative inefficiency: A primal system approach. *Journal of Econometrics*, 134: 419–40.

Kumbhakar, S. C., Wang, H.-J., and Horncastle, A. (2015). *A Practitioner's Guide to Stochastic Frontier Analysis Using Stata*. Cambridge University Press.

León-Ledesma, M. A., McAdam, P., and Willman, A. (2010a). Identifying the elasticity of substitution with biased technical change. *American Economic Review*, 100: 1330–57.

León-Ledesma, M. A., McAdam, P., and Willman, A. (2010b). In dubio pro CES: Supply estimation with mis-specified technical change. Technical Report 1175, ECB Working Paper.

Luoma, A. and Luoto, J. (2010). The aggregate production function of the Finnish economy in the twentieth century. *Southern Economic Journal*, 76(3): 723–37.

Maddala, G. and Kadane, J. (1967). Estimation of returns to scale and the elasticity of substitution. *Econometrica*, 24: 419–23.

Marquardt, D. W. (1963). An algorithm for least-squares estimation of non-linear parameters. *Journal of the Society for Industrial and Applied Mathematics*, 11(2): 431–41.

Masanjala, W. H. and Papageorgiou, C. (2004). The Solow model with CES technology: Nonlinearities and parameter heterogeneity. *Journal of Applied Econometrics*, 19(2): 171–201.

McFadden, D. (1963). Constant elasticity of substitution production function. *The Review of Economic Studies*, 30: 73–83.

Mishra, S. K. (2007). A note on numerical estimation of Sato's two-level CES production function. MPRA Paper 1019, North-Eastern Hill University, Shillong.

Moré, J. J., Garbow, B. S., and Hillstrom, K. E. (1980). *MINPACK*. Argonne National Laboratory.

Mullen, K. M., Ardia, D., Gil, D. L., Windover, D., and Cline, J. (2011). DEoptim: An R package for global optimization by Differential Evolution. *Journal of Statistical Software*, 40(6): 1–26.

Nelder, J. A. and Mead, R. (1965). A simplex algorithm for function minimization. *Computer Journal*, 7: 308–13.

Pandey, M. (2008). Human capital aggregation and relative wages across countries. *Journal of Macroeconomics*, 30(4): 1587–601.

Papageorgiou, C. and Saam, M. (2005). Two-level CES production technology in the Solow and Diamond growth models. Working paper 2005-07, Department of Economics, Louisiana State University.

Polak, E. and Ribière, G. (1969). Note sur la convergence de méthodes de directions conjuguées. *Revue Francaise d'Informatique et de Recherche Opérationnelle*, 16: 35–43.

Price, K. V., Storn, R. M., and Lampinen, J. A. (2006). *Differential Evolution – A Practical Approach to Global Optimization*. Natural Computing. Springer-Verlag.

R Core Team. (2020). *R: A Language and Environment for Statistical Computing*. R Foundation for Statistical Computing, Vienna, Austria.

Raurich, X., Sala, H., and Sorolla, V. (2012). Factor shares, the price markup, and the elasticity of substitution between capital and labor. *Journal of Macroeconomics*, 34: 181–94.

Sato, K. (1967). A two-level constant-elasticity-of-substitution production function. *The Review of Economic Studies*, 43: 201–18.

Schnabel, R. B., Koontz, J. E., and Weiss, B. E. (1985). A modular system of algorithms for unconstrained minimization. *ACM Transactions on Mathematical Software*, 11(4): 419–40.

Sethi, A. S. and Kaur, S. (2015). Productivity performance of Punjab and Haryana vis-à-vis the Indian economy: Production functions analytical approach. *The Journal of Income and Wealth*, 37(1): 36–49.

Shanno, D. F. (1970). Conditioning of quasi-Newton methods for function minimization. *Mathematics of Computation*, 24: 647–56.

Shen, K. and Whalley, J. (2013). Capital-labor-energy substitution in nested CES production functions for China. NBER Working Papers 19104, National Bureau of Economic Research, Inc.

Sorenson, H. W. (1969). Comparison of some conjugate direction procedures for function minimization. *Journal of the Franklin Institute*, 288(6): 421–41.

Storn, R. and Price, K. (1997). Differential Evolution – a simple and efficient heuristic for global optimization over continuous spaces. *Journal of Global Optimization*, 11: 341–59.

Sun, K., Henderson, D. J., and Kumbhakar, S. C. (2011). Biases in approximating log production. *Journal of Applied Econometrics*, 26(4): 708–14.

Thursby, J. G. (1980). CES estimation techniques. *The Review of Economics and Statistics*, 62: 295–9.

Thursby, J. G. and Lovell, C. A. K. (1978). An investigation of the Kmenta approximation to the CES function. *International Economic Review*, 19(2): 363–77.

Uebe, G. (2000). Kmenta approximation of the CES production function. Macromoli: Goetz Uebe's notebook on macroeconometric models and literature, http://www2.hsu-hh.de/uebe/Lexikon/K/Kmenta.pdf [accessed 2010-02-09].

Uzawa, H. (1962). Production functions with constant elasticity of substitution. *The Review of Economic Studies*, 29: 291–9.

APPENDIX 20A.1   R CODE FOR THE EMPIRICAL ILLUSTRATION

20A.1   Estimating the CES Production Function

```
# load the "micEconCES" package
library("micEconCES")

# load the "utility" data set
data("utility", package = "micEcon")

# mean-scale variables
utility$y <- utility$y / mean(utility$y)
utility$k <- utility$k / mean(utility$k)
utility$labor <- utility$labor / mean(utility$labor)
utility$fuel <- utility$fuel / mean(utility$fuel)

# define rho values for the grid searches
rhoVec <- seq(from = -1, to = 4, by = 0.25)

# list object for storing all the estimation
results <- list()

##### loop over all 3 nesting structures ####
for(i in 1:3) {
  # Nesting Structure 1: (k-l)-f #
  if(i == 1) {
    inputs <- c("k", "labor", "fuel")
  # Nesting Structure 2: (k-f)-l #
  } else if(i == 2) {
    inputs <- c("k", "fuel", "labor")
  # Nesting Structure 3: (l-f)-k #
  } else if(i == 3) {
    inputs <- c("labor", "fuel", "k")
  }

  # list object for estimation results of the current nesting
  structure results[[i]] <- list()

  # method: LM
  results[[i]]$LM <- cesEst(
    yName = "y", xNames = inputs, tName = "year",
    data = utility, multErr = TRUE, vrs = TRUE, method = "LM")

  # method: NM
  results[[i]]$NM <- cesEst(
    yName = "y", xNames = inputs, tName = "year",
    data = utility, multErr = TRUE, vrs = TRUE, method = "NM",
    control = list(maxit = 1e4))
```

```
# method: BFGS
results[[i]]$BFGS <- cesEst(
  yName = "y", xNames = inputs, tName = "year",
  data = utility, multErr = TRUE, vrs = TRUE, method = "BFGS")

# method: L-BFGS-B
results[[i]]$LBFGSB <- cesEst(
  yName = "y", xNames = inputs, tName = "year",
  data = utility, multErr = TRUE, vrs = TRUE,
  method = "L-BFGS-B", control = list(maxit = 1e4))

# method: PORT
results[[i]]$PORT <- cesEst(
  yName = "y", xNames = inputs, tName = "year",
  data = utility, multErr = TRUE, vrs = TRUE, method = "PORT",
  control = list(eval.max = 1e4, iter.max = 1e4))

# method: LM + grid search
results[[i]]$LM_GS <- cesEst(
  yName = "y", xNames = inputs, tName = "year",
  data = utility, multErr = TRUE, vrs = TRUE, method = "LM",
  rho1 = rhoVec, rho = rhoVec)

# method: LM + start values from grid search
results[[i]]$LM_Start_GS <- cesEst(
  yName = "y", xNames = inputs, tName = "year",
  data = utility, multErr = TRUE, vrs = TRUE, method = "LM",
  start = coef(results[[i]]$LM_GS))

# method: BFGS + grid search
results[[i]]$BFGS_GS <- cesEst(
  yName = "y", xNames = inputs, tName = "year",
  data = utility, multErr = TRUE, vrs = TRUE, method = "BFGS",
  rho1 = rhoVec, rho = rhoVec)

# method: BFGS + start values from grid search
results[[i]]$BFGS_Start_GS <- cesEst(
  yName = "y", xNames = inputs, tName = "year",
  data = utility, multErr = TRUE, vrs = TRUE, method = "BFGS",
  start = coef(results[[i]]$BFGS_GS))

# method: PORT + grid search
results[[i]]$PORT_GS <- cesEst(
  yName = "y", xNames = inputs, tName = "year",
```

```
    data = utility, multErr = TRUE, vrs = TRUE, method = "PORT",
    rho1 = rhoVec, rho = rhoVec,
    control = list(eval.max = 1e4, iter.max = 1e4))

  # method: PORT + start values from grid search
  results[[i]]$PORT_Start_GS <- cesEst(
    yName = "y", xNames = inputs, tName = "year",
    data = utility, multErr = TRUE, vrs = TRUE, method = "PORT",
    start = coef(results[[i]]$PORT_GS),
    control = list(eval.max = 1e4, iter.max = 1e4))
}

# save the list objects with all estimation results
saveRDS(results, "CES_electricity_estimation.rds")
```

20A.2   Creating Tables that Present the Estimation Results

```
# load R packages
library("micEconCES")
library("xtable")

# load estimation results
results <- readRDS("CES_electricity_estimation.rds")

# define function for extracting the values for a row of a table
makeRow <- function(model) {
  result <- c(
    coef(model),
    ifelse(is.null(model$convergence), NA, model$convergence),
    model$rss,
    summary(model)$r.squared)
  return(result)
}

# list object for the 3 tables for the 3 nesting structures
tables <- list()

# create 3 (empty) matrices that will be exported as a LaTeX
# table
tables[[1]] <- matrix(NA, nrow = 11, ncol = 10)

rownames(tables[[1]]) <- c(
  "LM", "NM", "BFGS", "L-BFGS-B", "PORT",
  "LM grid", "LM grid start",
  "BFGS grid", "BFGS grid start",
  "PORT grid", "PORT grid start")
```

```
colnames(tables[[1]]) <- c(
  paste("$\\", names(coef(results[[1]]$BFGS)), "$", sep = ""),
  "c",
  "RSS",
  "$R^2$")

tables[[3]] <- tables[[2]] <- tables[[1]]

##### loop over all 3 nesting structures ####
for(i in 1:3) {
  tables[[i]]["LM",] <- makeRow(results[[i]]$LM)
  tables[[i]]["NM",] <- makeRow(results[[i]]$NM)
  tables[[i]]["BFGS",] <- makeRow(results[[i]]$BFGS)
  tables[[i]]["L-BFGS-B",] <- makeRow(results[[i]]$LBFGSB)
  tables[[i]]["PORT",] <- makeRow(results[[i]]$PORT)
  tables[[i]]["LM grid",] <- makeRow(results[[i]]$LM_GS)
  tables[[i]]["LM grid start",] <-
    makeRow(results[[i]]$LM_Start_GS)
  tables[[i]]["BFGS grid",] <- makeRow(results[[i]]$BFGS_GS)
  tables[[i]]["BFGS grid start",] <-
    makeRow(results[[i]]$BFGS_Start_GS)
  tables[[i]]["PORT grid",] <- makeRow(results[[i]]$PORT_GS)
  tables[[i]]["PORT grid start",] <-
    makeRow(results[[i]]$PORT_Start_GS)
}


# define function for determining which estimation results (that
# is, rows)
# are economically meaningful and, thus, should be highlighted
# with bold font
markRows <- function(result) {
  rownames(result) <- paste(
    ifelse(!is.na(result[, "$\\delta_1$"]) & (
      result[, "$\\delta_1$"] >= 0 & result[, "$\\delta_1$"] <= 1 &
        result[, "$\\delta$"] >= 0 & result[, "$\\delta$"] <= 1) &
        result[, "$\\rho_1$"] >= -1 & result[, "$\\rho$"] >= -1,
      "MarkThisRow ", ""),
    rownames(result), sep = "")
  return(result)
}


# define a function for creating LaTeX tables and saving them as
# .tex file
printTable <- function(xTab, fileName) {
  tempFile <- file()
  print( xTab, file = tempFile, timestamp = NULL,
```

```
        floating = FALSE, sanitize.text.function = function(x){x})
  latexLines <- readLines(tempFile)
  close(tempFile)
  for(i in grep("MarkThisRow ", latexLines, value = FALSE)) {
    latexLines[i] <- sub("MarkThisRow *([^&]*)",
      "\\\\textbf{\\1}", latexLines[i])
    latexLines[i] <- gsub("&([^&\\]*)", "& \\\\textbf{\\1}",
      latexLines[i])
  }
  writeLines(latexLines, fileName)
  invisible(latexLines)
}


### create LaTeX tables and save them as .tex files
tables[[1]] <- markRows(tables[[1]])
xTabKLF <- xtable(tables[[1]], align = "lrrrrrrrrr",
          digits = c(0, rep(4, 7), 0, 4, 4))
printTable(xTabKLF, fileName = "tables/KLF.tex")

tables[[2]] <- markRows(tables[[2]])
xTabKFL <- xtable(tables[[2]], align = "lrrrrrrrrr",
          digits = c(0, rep(4, 7), 0, 4, 4))
printTable(xTabKFL, fileName = "tables/KFL.tex")

tables[[3]] <- markRows(tables[[3]])
xTabLFK <- xtable(tables[[3]], align = "lrrrrrrrrr",
          digits = c(0, rep(4, 7), 0, 4, 4))
printTable(xTabLFK, fileName = "tables/LFK.tex")
```

Index